GENESIS

GENESIS

A Theological Commentary For Preachers

Abraham Kuruvilla

RESOURCE *Publications* • Eugene, Oregon

GENESIS
A Theological Commentary For Preachers

Resource Publications
An Imprint of Wipf and Stock Publishers
199 W. 8th Ave., Suite 3
Eugene, OR 97401

www.wipfandstock.com

ISBN 13: 978-1-62564-114-4

Manufactured in the U.S.A.

To AK
the בְּכֹר
who gave
the צָעִיר
the eternal בְּרָכָה of Christ

CONTENTS

ACKNOWLEDGMENTS

H AVING TAUGHT THROUGH THE Jacob Story (Gen 25–35) in Dallas Seminary's preaching classes for about a decade, my inordinate fondness for this first book of the Bible has grown to encompass the remainder of its chapters. The stories therein are terrific in and of themselves, but closer attention to the text—*privileging the text*—has yielded a cornucopia of dividends. I have been blessed, challenged, rebuked, and strengthened, as I worked my way through this tome that commences the canon of Christian Scripture. The inspired author's (or authors') *doings* with this marvelous piece of writing are simply mother lodes of riches plentiful—for life, for wisdom, for godliness, and, of course, for preaching. Hopefully, herein, I have succeeded in sharing some of the delight I have experienced and the benefit I have gained from Genesis. And, *Deo volente*, lives will be changed—both that of readers of Genesis, and of those who hear it preached—as mine undoubtedly has and continues to be.

Scattered churches in a variety of lands have heard many of my sermons on Genesis. Thanks are due to all of them for the opportunity afforded me to minister this particular word of God in their midst.

To the many who continue to engage me in discussions esoteric (and animated!) about "worlds in front of texts," "pericopal theology," and what preaching was, is, and should be, and how we can all do it better—and teach it better—I am grateful. They spur me on.

May all of us, God's children, continue to learn what it means to obey the divine demand of God the Father—הִתְהַלֵּךְ לְפָנַי וֶהְיֵה תָמִים, "Walk before Me and be blameless!" (Gen 5:22, 24; 6:9; 17:1; 24:40; 48:15)—as we follow the footsteps of the venerable patriarchs of yore, but even more, as we seek, in the power of God the Spirit, to become conformed to the εἰκών ("image") of God the Son (Rom 8:29).

Abraham Kuruvilla
Dallas, TX
Feast of the Cross 2013

ABBREVIATIONS

ANCIENT TEXTS

1 Clem.	*First Clement*
Ant.	Josephus, *Antiquities*
Apol.	Tertullian, *Apology*
Comm. Gen.	Calvin, *Commentary on Genesis*
Comm. Ps.	Calvin, *Commentary on the Psalms*
Conf.	Augustine, *Confessions*
Doctr. chr.	Augustine, *De doctrina christiana*
Fel.	Augustine, *Contra Felicem*
Giants	Philo, *On Giants*
Haer.	Irenaeus, *Adversus haereses*
Hom. Gen.	*Homiliæ in Genisim*
Inst.	Quintilian, *Institutio oratoria*
J.W.	Josephus, *Jewish Wars*
L. A. B.	Pseudo-Philo, *Liber antiquitatum biblicarum*
Moses	Philo, *On the Life of Moses*
Rhet. Alex.	Anaximenes, *Rhetorica ad Alexandrum*
Serm.	Augustine, *Sermon*
Spec. Laws	Philo, *On the Special Laws*
Summa	Aquinas, *Summa Theologica*

RABBINIC AND TARGUMIC LITERATURE

ʾAbot R. Nat.	*ʾAbot de Rabbi Nathan*
b.	Babylonian Talmud
Exod. Rab.	*Exodus Rabbah*
Gen. Rab.	*Genesis Rabbah*
Ḥag.	*Ḥagigah*

m.	Mishnah
Meg.	*Megillah*
Midr. Ps.	*Midrash on Psalms*
Ned.	*Nedarim*
Num. Rab.	*Numbers Rabbah*
Pesaḥ.	*Pesaḥim*
Pesiq. Rab.	*Pesiqta Rabbati*
Pirqe R. El.	*Pirqe Rabbi Eliezer*
Roš Haš.	*Roš Haššanah*
Sanh.	*Sanhedrin*
Tam.	*Tamid*
Tg. Isa.	*Targum Isaiah*
Tg. Neof.	*Targum Neofiti*
Tg. Onq.	*Targum Onqelos*
Tg. Ps.-J.	*Targum Pseudo-Jonathan*
y.	Jerusalem Talmud

OLD TESTAMENT APOCRYPHA AND PSEUDIEPIGRAPHA

1–2 Macc	1–2 Maccabees
2 Esd	2 Esdras
2 En.	*2 Enoch* (Slavonic Apocalypse)
2 Bar.	*2 Baruch* (Syrian Apocalypse)
Bar	Baruch
Jub.	*Jubilees*
Sir	Sirach/Ecclesiasticus
Wis	Wisdom of Solomon

OTHER ABBREVIATIONS

1Qap Gen[ar]	*Genesis Apocryphon*
AB	Anchor Bible
ACCS	*Ancient Christian Commentary on Scripture: Genesis II* (Sheridan)
AfO	*Archiv für Orientforschung*
ANE	Ancient Near East
ANET	*Ancient Near Eastern Texts Relating to the Old Testament* (Pritchard)
AuOr	*Aula Orientalis*
AUSS	*Andrews University Seminary Studies*
BA	*Biblical Archaeologist*

Abbreviations

BBR	*Bulletin for Biblical Research*
BETL	Bibliotheca ephemeridum theologicarum lovaniensium
Bib	*Biblica*
BibInt	*Biblical Interpretation*
BN	*Biblische Notizen*
BR	*Bible Review*
BSac	*Bibliotheca sacra*
BTB	*Biblical Theology Bulletin*
BZ	*Biblische Zeitschrift*
CBQ	*Catholic Biblical Quarterly*
CBQMS	Catholic Bible Quarterly Monograph Series
CD	Cairo Genizah copy of the *Damascus Document*
COS	*The Context of Scripture* (Hallo)
CTA	*Ras-Shamra Ugarit Tablets* (Herdner)
CTJ	*Concordia Theological Journal*
CTR	*Criswell Theological Review*
DSS	Dead Sea Scrolls
ETL	*Ephemerides theologicae lovaniensis*
EvQ	*Evangelical Quarterly*
ExpTim	*Expository Times*
FOTL	Forms of the Old Testament Literature
GKC	*Gesenius' Hebrew Grammar* (Kautzsch–Cowley)
Greg	*Gregorianum*
HALOT	*Hebrew and Aramaic Lexicon of the Old Testament* (Koehler–Baumgartner–Stamm)
HAR	*Hebrew Annual Review*
HO	Handbuch der Orientalistik
HS	*Hebrew Studies*
HTR	*Harvard Theological Review*
IEJ	*Israel Exploration Journal*
Int	*Interpretation*
JAAR	*Journal of the American Academy of Religion*
JANES	*Journal of the Ancient Near Eastern Society*
JAOS	*Journal of the American Oriental Society*
JASA	*Journal of the American Scientific Affiliation*
JATS	*Journal of the Adventist Theological Society*
JBL	*Journal of Biblical Literature*

JBQ	*Jewish Bible Quarterly*
JETS	*Journal of the Evangelical Theological Society*
JJS	*Journal of Jewish Studies*
JNSL	*Journal of Northwest Semitic Languages*
JPSTC	Jewish Publication Society Torah Commentary
JSJSup	Journal for the Study of Judaism in the Persian, Hellenistic, and Roman Periods: Supplement Series
JSOT	*Journal for the Study of the Old Testament*
JSOTSup	Journal for the Study of the Old Testament: Supplement Series
JTI	*Journal of Theological Interpretation*
JTS	*Journal of Theological Studies*
Jud	*Judaica*
LNTS	Library of New Testament Studies
NAC	New American Commentary
NBD³	*New Bible Dictionary*, third edition (Marshall–Millard–Packer–Wiseman)
Nbp	*Inschriften von Nabopolassar* (Strassmaier)
NICOT	New International Commentary on the Old Testament
Or	*Orientalia*
OTP	*Old Testament Pseudepigrapha* (Charlesworth)
OtSt	Oudtestamentische Studiën
PRSt	*Perspectives in Religious Studies*
RB	*Revue biblique*
ResQ	*Restoration Quarterly*
RRR	*Reformation and Renaissance Review*
SBLDS	Society for Biblical Literature Dissertation Series
Sem	*Semitica*
SNTSMS	Society for New Testament Studies Monograph Series
TDOT	*Theological Dictionary of the Old Testament* (Botterweck–Ringgren)
TJT	*Toronto Journal of Theology*
TOTC	Tyndale Old Testament Commentaries
TrinJ	*Trinity Journal*
TS	*Theological Studies*
TynBul	*Tyndale Bulletin*
USQR	*Union Seminary Quarterly Review*
VE	*Vox Evangelica*
VT	*Vetus Testamentum*

INTRODUCTION

Theology, Assumptions, Goals, Prolegomena, Excursuses

"And God created mankind in His image.
And God blessed them."

Genesis 1:27, 28

THEOLOGY

The crux of the preaching endeavor is to bring to bear divine guidelines for life from the biblical text upon the situations of the congregation, to align the community of God to the will of God for the glory of God. In other words, the ancient text is to be applied to the modern audience. Crucial to this undertaking of homiletics is that such application be both faithful to the textual intention (i.e., authoritative) and fitting for the listening audience (i.e., relevant). This is the preacher's burden—the translation from the *then* of the text to the *now* of listeners, with authority and relevance. This commentary is part of a larger endeavor to help the preacher make this move from text to praxis.

Particularly pertinent is how this translation from text to praxis may be conducted with respect to the "bite-sized" portion or quantum of the Scriptural text that is employed weekly in the corporate gathering of the body of Christ—the pericope.[1] The pericope is the basic textual unit of Scripture handled in such assemblies, and it is the foundational element of the weekly address from the word of God. What in this slice

---

1. While acknowledging its more common connotation of a portion of the Gospels, "pericope" is employed here to demarcate a segment of Scripture, irrespective of genre or length, that forms the textual basis for an individual sermon, i.e., a preaching text.

of Scripture is intended to be carried over into the life of the Christian? What exactly is the author of the text saying that needs to be heard by the listeners of the sermon?[2]

Elsewhere it was proposed that the critical component of the ancient text to be borne into the lives of the modern audience is the *theology of the pericope*. Pericopal theology is the ideological vehicle through which divine precepts, priorities, and practices are propounded for appropriation by readers.[3] A biblical pericope is thus a literary instrument inviting men and women to organize their lives in congruence with the theology revealed in that pericope. The goal of any homiletical transaction, thus, is the gradual alignment of the church, week by week, to the theology of the biblical pericopes preached. Thus it is pericope by pericope that the various aspects of Christian life, individual as well as corporate, are progressively brought into accord with God's design for his creation—the goal of preaching: faith nourished, hope animated, confidence made steadfast, good habits confirmed, dispositions created, character molded, Christlikeness established.[4] All such discrete units of pericopal theology together compose a holistic understanding of God and his relationship to his people, and each individual quantum of pericopal theology forms the weekly ground of life transformation by calling for alignment to the demands of God, resulting in an appropriation and assimilation of Christlikeness—I call this a *christiconic* hermeneutic. Briefly, such an interpretation takes every pericope of Scripture as bearing a gracious divine demand regarding how mankind should conduct itself in God's ideal world—the *world in front of the text*. Since the only one to have perfectly fulfilled such divine demands and perfectly inhabited this ideal world of God is Jesus Christ, the "theologian-homiletician" should consider every pericope as developing for readers/ listeners a facet of Christlikeness. This is at the core of the *theological* hermeneutic followed in this commentary: a hermeneutic specifically geared for preaching. After all, God's goal for his people is that they be "conformed to the image [εἰκών, *eikōn*] of His Son" (Rom 8:29): hence, *christiconic*.[5]

In general, most Bible scholars and theologians have not been coming to the text of Scripture with the eye and heart of a preacher; therefore the pericope has been neglected as a textual unit of theological value, and the goal of life transformation— usually a pastoral concern—has tended to be subjugated to other academic interests. Moreover, looking *through* the text (rather than *at* the text)—using the text merely as a plain-glass window to glimpse those elements *behind* it (rather than as a stained-glass window depicting the author's agenda in itself)—what the author was *doing* with what he was saying has, for the most part, also been given short shrift.[6] In short, the

---

2. For the purposes of this commentary no particular distinction will be made between the divine and human authors of the biblical text.

3. See Kuruvilla, *Privilege the Text!* 89–150; idem, *Text to Praxis*, 142–90; and idem, "Pericopal Theology," 265–83.

4. Adapted from Tertullian, *Apol.* 39.

5. For more details and further development of these ideas, see Kuruvilla, *Privilege the Text!* especially 238–69.

6. For more on this, see ibid., 90–135.

importance of the pericope and its employment in a sermon for the edification of God's people has generally been disregarded. As a consequence, preachers have been left in the lurch.

The intent of this commentary, part of a long-term enterprise to rectify this neglect, is essentially this: to develop the theology of each pericope for preachers so that they may be able to proceed from this crucial intermediary to a sermon that provides valid application, i.e., application that is both authoritative and relevant. Application derived from pericopal theology becomes *authoritative* because of the integral link of the theology to the text: pericopal theology is derived from a close reading of the text and is specific for any given text. Application derived from pericopal theology becomes *relevant* because the homiletician, keenly aware of the circumstances of auditors in his pastoral capacity, seeks to specify application in terms that are pertinent to the situation of these listeners. There is, thus, a twofold aspect to the homiletical transaction: the exposition of the theology of the pericope, and the delineation of how the latter may be applied or appropriated in real life.

The first move, from text to theology, draws meaning *from* the biblical text with authority, the second, from theology to application, directs meaning *to* the situations of listeners with relevance.[7] The advantage of employing pericopal theology as the intermediary between text and applications is that its specificity for (or proximity to) the chosen text makes possible a weekly movement from pericope to pericope, without the tedium of repetition of themes, but with a clear progression and development of theological ideas as one sermonically traverses the length of a book. In sum, the theology of the pericope (a crystallization of which is labeled "Theological Focus" in this commentary) functions as the bridge between text and application, between the circumstances of the text and those of the reading community, enabling the move from the *then* to the *now*, from canonical inscription to sermonic application. The resultant transformation of lives reflects a gradual and increasing alignment to the values of God's kingdom (or a gradual and increasing approximation of Christlikeness), as pericopes are sequentially preached from. Thus, a pericope, as a quantum of the biblical text, is more than *informing*; it is *transforming*, for as the people of God adopt its theological values, they are becoming rightly oriented to God's will, and are more closely reflecting Christlikeness.

7. It should be noted that this commentary expends most of its energy in helping the preacher with the first move, from text to the theology of the pericope. The second move, from theology to sermon and application, will not take up as much space in this work for obvious reasons: beyond a few general guidelines (which the commentary does provide, including two possible sermon outlines for each pericope), it is nigh impossible for a third party to specify application for a particular audience. That task is between the preacher, the Holy Spirit, and the congregation.

ASSUMPTIONS

I come to the book of Genesis, and indeed to all of Scripture, with a reading bias that is Protestant and evangelical. I take it that "a biblical author, including the author of Genesis [i.e., the one(s) who gave the book its final shape], is not simply pasting together a jumbled combination of unrelated sources or random thoughts. Rather, he is writing intelligently with a purpose, and each narrative and each segment of text (whatever the genre) is intentionally chosen to contribute in some way to that purpose."[8] Broad coherence and consistency among the pericopes of Genesis will therefore be assumed, for the book is a unified discourse (just as the canon, as a whole, is construed as unified); "charitable" reading impels readers of any work to assume so as their first reflex.[9]

This commentary also assumes that every pericope in the canonical Scriptures may be employed for application by the church universal.[10] The divine discourse that the canon is, renders it efficacious for the transformation of the individual and community into the will of God, and it asserts the right of every one of its constituent parts to be heard.[11] Thus, no pericope of Genesis may be disregarded for the purposes of sermons and application. Indeed, application of Scripture is the culmination of the move from text to praxis. Augustine wrote that the aim to be pursued by an expositor of the Scriptures was "to be listened to with understanding, with pleasure, and *with obedience*."[12] The employment of the Bible as foundational to the existence, beliefs, and activities of the church assumes that its interpretation *will* culminate in application—life change for the glory of God. Divine discourse always demands a response.[13]

8. Walton, *Genesis,* 21.

9. Understanding involves a starting assumption, an "initative trust, an investment of belief," which is an act of charity towards author and text. To begin with doubt, Booth warned, "is to destroy the datum"—the material and subject of interpretation; a primary act of assent and surrender is the essential first step in approaching a text (*The Company We Keep,* 32).

10. See Kuruvilla, *Privilege the Text!* 65–86, for a set of "Rules for Reading" that respect the unique nature, and the resulting special hermeneutic, of the biblical text.

11. Kelsey, "The Bible and Christian Theology," 395; see Rom 15:4; 2 Tim 3:16–17; etc.

12. *Doctr. chr.* 4.26.56 (italics added). Classical rhetoric knows of three directions of audience responses sought by a rhetor: a *judicial* assessment of past events, a *deliberative* resolve with regard to future actions of the audience, or an *epideictic* appreciation of particular beliefs or values in the present. See Quintilian, *Inst.* 3.7–9; Anaximenes, *Rhet. Alex.* 1421b; also see Black, "Rhetorical Criticism," 261. Sermonic application, in parallel to this three-fold shape of rhetorical purpose, may also be considered broadly as responses culminating in a change of mind (a response of cognition), a change of action (a response of volition), or a change of feeling (a response of emotion). For reasons of clarity and utility, applications in sermons are best conveyed as imperatives (as the examples in the preaching outlines of this commentary depict). Such imperatives may, of course, depending on the preacher, be explicit or implicit in the actual sermon.

13. Along with such an assumption of applicability comes the assumption of universality of the relevance of Scripture. The Bible itself consistently affirms the relevance of its message for future generations: see Deut 6:6–25; 29:14–15; 31:9–13; 2 Kgs 22–23; Neh 7:73b–8:18; Ps 78:5–6; Matt 28:19; Rom 15:4; 1 Cor 9:10; 10:6, 11; 2 Tim 3:16–17; etc.

GOALS

This work does not intend to lead preachers all the way to a fully developed sermon on each pericope; rather, it seeks to take them through the *hermeneutical* aspect of interpretation (i.e., from text to theology). While that is the primary focus of the commentary, it does provide two "Possible Preaching Outlines" for each pericope, to advance homileticians a few more steps closer to a sermon—the *rhetorical* aspect of interpretation (i.e., from theology to application). However, preachers are left to work out this rhetorical aspect on their own, making moves-to-relevance, generating specific application, employing illustrations, etc., all of which can be done only by the shepherd who knows the flock well. Therefore, this is not exactly a *preaching* commentary, in the usual sense. Rather it is a *theology-for-preaching* commentary, i.e., a work that seeks to undertake an extremely focused interpretation of the text, one that moves the preacher from pericope to theology, en route to a sermon. In that sense, this is a *theological* commentary, with theology defined as *pericopal theology* (a distillation of which is the "Theological Focus of the Pericope" in this commentary).

This commentary is primarily geared for those interested in preaching through Genesis, engaging in a multi-part series on the book. While there might be many types of sermons possible from Genesis, this work will help the homiletician preach pericope by pericope, by isolating the theology of the pericope and discerning the momentum and development of the themes of the various sections of Genesis. Larger chunks of text are apportioned as preaching pericopes, in order to break up the entire narrative into a reasonable number of discrete units; thirty-five pericopes are demarcated in this commentary, enough to keep a weekly preaching series going for about eight or nine months, without breaks.[14] While going through all fifty chapters of Genesis is probably the best way to undertake this series, the preacher or teacher may also take breaks between the four major sections of Genesis (see below), coming back to the following section(s) after a detour of a few weeks.

Commentaries were described by Ernest Best as "the backbone of all serious studies of scripture."[15] Therefore, it is hoped that not only preachers, but all interested laypersons, Sunday School teachers, and others who teach Scripture will also find this commentary—a small vertebra in that spinal column—helpful. For that matter, if application is the ultimate goal of Bible study of any kind and at any level, a work such as this promises to be useful even for those working their own way through Genesis devotionally.

---

14. One could, of course, create more than thirty-five sermons from Genesis, splitting up the pericopes that are delineated here. Drawing a line between narrative pericopes is often difficult, in light of the tendency of authors to link adjoining units semantically, literarily, and thematically. Too fine a slicing technique risks the danger of surfacing not-too-different ideas between adjacent, linked passages sharing similar theological foci. Therefore, the decision was made to create the preaching units in Genesis that I felt would have sufficiently discrete theological ideas that are not repeated in adjoining pericopes. In other words, in order to keep the theological foci distinct, I chose to lump some episodes together to constitute single pericopes. The preacher, however, may choose to preach individual episodes in a given pericope separately.

15. "The Reading and Writing of Commentaries," 358.

In an earlier commentary adopting the theological hermeneutic for preaching outlined above, I enjoyed the luxury of including my own translation of the Greek text of Mark's Gospel.[16] Unfortunately, the escalating size of the current work precluded such an extravagance.[17] Yet, the Hebrew text is referred to frequently. While a working knowledge of Hebrew will be handy for the reader, Hebrew terms and phrases, wherever referred to in the commentary, have been transliterated and translated, in order to enable those not as facile with the original languages to work efficiently.[18]

With the goal of maximizing the size-to-benefit ratio, this commentary will not repeat matters discussed extensively in standard works on Genesis—historical criticism, redaction criticism, and textual criticism—unless they are immediately relevant to the theological interpretation of the pericope at hand. Neither will this work dwell upon the authorship, date, and postulated sources of Genesis, abundant information on which may be unearthed from standard commentaries on the book.[19] However, because of the controversies Genesis 1–2 has generated both within and without the church, a few excursuses on concepts of importance to those chapters have been included (see below).

Needless to say, in all sermonic enterprises, quality and depth and intensity of the preaching go only so far towards achieving the spiritual formation of auditors. Augustine (*Doctr. chr.* 4.27.59) noted wisely: "But whatever may be the majesty of the style [of the preaching], the life of the speaker will count for more in securing the hearer's compliance," not to mention the divine work of the Spirit in the hearts of listeners. Therefore, this commentary is submitted with the prayer that preachers, the leaders of God's people, will pay attention to their own lives first and foremost, as they work through Genesis, seeking to align themselves to the divine demand in each pericope, thus becoming, in the power of the Spirit, more Christlike.

PROLEGOMENA

Overall, this book, commencing the Scriptures of God's people, appropriately focuses on divine blessing. Blessing is always divine in origin, for God alone is the source of all that is good, and he alone is the perfect Giver (Jas 1:17). And besides, God's intention has been, and always is, to bless.

---

16. Kuruvilla, *Mark.*

17. I took Kraus's remarks to heart. On the commentator's "problem of too little self-restraint," she notes that such a one tends to "pedantry and prolixity, the vices of the scholar who can't or won't shut up" ("Introduction: Reading Commentaries," 5).

18. The Hebrew text on which this commentary is based is the Masoretic Text (*Biblia Hebraica Stuttgartensia* as encoded in the Michigan-Claremont Hebrew text [1981]). A "general purpose" transliteration is employed throughout for the Hebrew, the goal being to depict wordplays clearly; for that reason the distinctions between the spirantizations of ב, ג, ד, כ, פ, and ת (*b, g, d, k, p,* and *t*) will not be consistently maintained. For clarity, capitalization of pronouns to indicate deity will show up in my English translations of Hebrew verses and phrases.

19. See, for instance, Wenham, *Genesis 1–15*; Hamilton, *Genesis: Chapters 1–17*; and Mathews, *Genesis 1–11:26.*

> Broadly speaking, *a blessing is an offering of God's favor (if coming from God) or a wish for God's favor (if coming from humans).* . . . The resulting theology of blessing goes far beyond Christology or Messianism. It expresses God's love for the people he created and his intention to bless them in spite of rebellion and sin. The picture of love, mercy, and compassion thus portrayed by means of the blessing stands in stark contrast to the self-protection and self-promotion that characterized the gods of the ancient world. It is an essential foundation to the understanding of God's grace. . . .[20]

The concept of blessing, therefore, need not be limited to eternal verities, Christological promises, and eschatological experiences. God's blessing for God's people happens throughout life in a variety of ways, circumstantial and providential, direct and miraculous. Indeed, "every good thing given" is rightly considered divine blessing (Jas 1:17).

Genesis may be broadly conceived of as the inauguration of God's work to bring about blessing to mankind, comprising Primeval History and Patriarchal History, together making up the four major sections of the book; each deals with different facets of that divine blessing.

Text	Section	Overarching Focus
Gen 1:1–11:26	**Primeval History**	*Creating for Blessing*
	Patriarchal History	
Gen 11:27–25:18	Abraham Story	*Moving towards Blessing*
Gen 25:19–36:43	Jacob Story	*Experiencing the Blessing*
Gen 37:1–50:26	Joseph Story	*Being a Blessing*

The Primeval History (1:1–11:26) depicts God *Creating for Blessing.* His creation would be blessed by his presence in the cosmic sanctuary (see on Pericope 1), and everything was geared to maximize the goodness of this divine gift for the acme of God's creation—mankind. Humans were intended to follow divine guidance in order that they may remain in the sphere of God's blessing. That the primeval pair of man and woman proceeded to reject "every good thing given" in favor of their own choices is the sad story of humanity, repeated in every generation. God, however, was not one to give up so easily. He proceeded to choose one individual through whose seed he would bless all of mankind. The Abraham Story (11:27–25:18) describes this patriarch's *Moving towards Blessing,* in fits and starts, with falterings and stumblings, teaching God's people what it means to take God by faith—to have the "fear of Yahweh." God's people are thus taught to have faith in God's timing and his plans to bless. The subsequent sagas continue the family history that began with Abraham. His grandson's story, the Jacob Story (25:19–36:43), tells us how one goes about *Experiencing the Blessing;* this narrative depicts one who is constantly chasing blessing in all the wrong places, and in all the wrong ways, until he comes to the realization that only God can bless—that God alone is the true source of blessing. The Joseph Story (37:1–50:26) carries on the story of Jacob, while prominently figuring one of his sons, Joseph: this section is all about *Being a Blessing,* i.e., being used of God to extend his blessing to those within one's own circle: family, tribe, society—as well as to those without: associates, fellow-citizens,

---

20. Walton, *Genesis,* 53–54.

nations, and the world at large. Thus, the people of God are called to demonstrate integrity and godliness in their lives, that they may be used by God as agents of his blessing to those around them.

In sum, Genesis describes the benevolent intentions of the Creator, and directs his creation as to how to enjoy divine blessing and be agents of its disbursement to others—a fitting start for Scripture. The broad theological thrust of the book of Genesis may therefore be crystallized this way: *The people of God, intended to be blessed by God who created for blessing, move towards blessing in faith, experience God's blessing by recognizing him alone as the source of blessing, and become a blessing to others as they live lives of integrity.*

Despite the marvelous theme of blessing that Genesis introduces, the beginning of the book is fraught with interpretive difficulties and have created no end of divisions among God's people. Therefore, for the remainder of this introduction, I will address, in excursuses, a few specific issues particular to Gen 1–2, the biblical account of creation.[21]

EXCURSUSES[22]

Genre of the Creation Account

The thorny issue of the nature of the creation account has consumed reams of paper, gigajoules of energy, and tons of ill-will. I hold that Gen 1–2 is an integral part of the word of God and as such, it is as much divine discourse as is the rest of the Bible. The question, however, is *how* this particular account is to be read: Is it "a story that explains phenomena and experience, an ideology that explains the cosmos" and "metaphysical concerns that cannot be known by scientific discovery," or is it "history," a scientific or journalistic account of origins?[23] Waltke and Fredricks make helpful dis-

---

21. For more on these matters, here are a couple of very eminently readable tomes: Lennox, *Seven Days*; and Walton, *The Lost World*. For a recent compendium of the debates on Genesis 1–2 among evangelicals, I recommend Charles, ed., *Reading Genesis 1–2*, with contributions from all the major players in the field today.

22. Considering their importance and controversial nature, it will probably be necessary for the preacher to deal with these topics somewhere, though I would not recommend addressing them in sermons. Rather, a Sunday School class, or a Bible Study group, or even a more informal Sunday evening/mid-week service might make a more appropriate venue, with opportunities for questions and answers. Perhaps one could even invite experts on particular issues to conduct church-wide seminars on pertinent issues. As well, reading material could be distributed or recommended (the resources mentioned above, for instance).

23. Waltke and Fredricks, *Genesis*, 74. Neither "story" nor "history" as I use it here indicates Gen 1–2 to be a less-than-inspired account; both descriptions are consistent with a conservative stance on the character of Scripture. Instead of "story," Clifford uses "drama": "In one sense it is no less empirical than the scientific account, but its verisimilitude is measured differently. Drama selects, omits, concentrates; it need not render a complete account" ("The Hebrew Scriptures," 511–12). A scientific theory (or "history"), on the other hand, must be exhaustive and explain all the available data. The biblical account of creation makes no such claim to comprehensiveness; it might actually indicate otherwise, as shown below and in Pericope 1. I, therefore, tend to see the creation account as "story" rather than "history."

tinctions between the Genesis narrative (seen as "story") and science ("history"): they deal with essentially different matters (transcendent God vs. forces of nature); their language is different (every-day and non-theoretical vs. mathematical and technical); one addresses ultimate cause, the other proximal causes; their purposes are discrete: Scripture answers why things are and what ought to be, while science attempts to describe what is and how things are; each is intended for a distinct body of consumers: the community of God on the one hand, and a more general readership on the other; the validation of their assertions differ: the role of the Spirit in the heart (Rom 8:16) is important for one vs. empirical testing for the other.[24]

However one looks at it, there can be no question but that Genesis is a well-crafted narrative that seeks to persuade the reader to move in a certain direction. The discovery of what that direction is, for any given pericope, is the burden of the preacher-interpreter (or "homiletician-theologian"). Like any other biblical narrative, Genesis, too, is decidedly not neutral, dispassionate journalistic reportage. In other words, an authorially determined selectivity operates in the composition of the text, a selectivity dependent on the author's goal. Todorov observed that "[n]o narrative is natural; a choice and a construction will always preside over its appearance; narrative is a discourse, not a series of events."[25] Not everything about each character is portrayed; not everything that was said or done on any particular occasion is described; not everything that happened is revealed. The author's theological agenda determined the choice of what was included in the narrative. It is that theological agenda portrayed in, with, and through the text—and for a small portion of the text this agenda is the *pericopal theology*—that must be discovered by those who would preach the text for life change. Interpreters are therefore called to discern not only what the Author/author is *saying*, but also what He/he was *doing* with what He/he was saying.[26]

Thus, in all likelihood, the Genesis account is not "history," in the sense of a "ball-by-ball commentary" on real events, for the following reasons: a seeming sense of dischronology (e.g., 1:5 vs. 1:14, 18—separations of light and darkness, and of night and day, seemingly occur twice; the seeming existence of an ostensibly solar day before the creation of the sun, 1:5, 16; the premature presence of "Canaanites," 12:16, the tribe of Dan, 14:14, and Israelite kings, 36:31; likely gaps in the Genesis genealogies; etc.), the parallels with similar ancient Near Eastern stories, an incongruence with science

---

Amos Wilder wisely warns readers to be on guard against "the historicist habit of mind" that "may . . . operate unconsciously to handicap a free encounter with a writing in its final form"—story ("Norman Perrin," 95).

24. See Waltke and Fredricks, *Genesis,* 74–75.

25. Todorov, *The Poetics of Prose,* 55.

26. This is the approach taken by the field of pragmatics (see Kuruvilla, *Privilege the Text!* 48–65). Much of the interpretive analysis in this commentary will, therefore, include a close reading of the text and its literary properties. Among those who have espoused this facet of the narrative art of the OT, and whose writings are worth consuming, are: Alter, *The Art of Biblical Narrative*; Bar-Efrat, "Some Observations on the Analysis of Structure"; and idem, *Narrative Art in the Bible*; Berlin, *Poetics*; Sternberg, *The Poetics of Biblical Narrative*; and Fokkelman, *Narrative Art in Genesis.*

as we know it now, and the frequent employment of a poetic style.[27] The ancient narrator had a very different agenda from that of a modern historian—a *theological* agenda. That is to say, the author of Genesis was not writing as a sacred historian but as an inspired theologian. He is not providing "detailed information with quasi-photographic, journalistic accuracy and precision" but rather an organized narratival and rhetorical account that portrays (as does the rest of Scripture) a *world in front of the text* with theological veracity and edifying potential, and that in an infallible manner.[28] In other words, the rehearsal of primeval events in Genesis is not necessarily "history," but "story"—a literary description intended to convey a theological message.

John Colet (1467–1519), the English scholar and theologian, asserted that Moses organized his creation account "after the manner of some popular poet [*modo poetæ alicujus popularis*]."[29] Of course, Gen 1–2 is not a full-blown example of Hebrew poetry, but neither is it purely prose.[30] Signs of poesy include: the strophic structure of this semi-poetic narrative in which several refrains echo: "good," "evening and morning," the employment of ברא (*br'*, "create," Gen 1:1, 21, 27; 2:3; also see Ps 51:12; Ezek 28:13; and see excursus below); אחד (*'khd*, "one") as a cardinal number (Gen 1:5; see excursus below), מרחפת (*mrhpt*, "hover," Gen 1:2; also see Deut 32:11), תהו וָבהו (*tohu wabohu*, "formless and empty," Gen 1:2; also see Isa 34:11; Jer 4:23), and רָקִיעַ (*raqia'*, "expanse/firmament," Gen 1:6; also see Ps 19:2; Isa 42:5)[31]; not to mention anthropomorphisms for God (who exhibits divine speech and sight, and who works and rests), parallelisms (1:27; 2:2), alliteration (1:1), and paronomasia (1:22).[32]

27. Some of these elements are dealt with below; for the rest, see the appropriate section of the commentary.

28. Young, "Scripture in the Hands of Geologists (Part Two)," 294. See Kuruvilla, *Privilege the Text!* 39–65; and idem, *Text to Praxis*, 24–35, 157–64, for a description of this *world in front of the text*, a concept adapted from Paul Ricoeur.

29. Colet, "Second Letter of Colet to Radulphus," 9 (English), 170 (Latin).

30. Collins labels it "exalted prose": "[T]he apparent quasi-liturgical purpose of Gen 1 (to celebrate the creation as an achievement, and thereby to honor the Creator) drives the exalted prose form of the pericope." See "Reading Genesis 1–2," 82.

31. That the "firmament" is not necessarily a solid dome in ancient conception seems to be clear from the fact that the lights (sun, moon, and stars) placed "in the רקיע" (1:14–15, 17) were obviously seen to move across the sky, a movement somewhat akin to that of the birds "upon/on the face of" the firmament (1:20). It appears, then, that the רקיע served as a kind of backdrop for all these atmospheric goings on, with clouds (the water bearers, as Ps 104:2–4 sees them; also see Gen 7:11–12) sometimes even blotting out the lights in the sky. Thus the "waters" above and below, with the "firmament" in between, is likely to be more a poetic depiction than a precise architectonic description, referring respectively to atmospheric and terrestrial vapor/water.

32. See Polak, "Poetic Structure and Parallelism," 6–11. He notes the relative absence of the definite article in the "refrains," e.g., in Gen 1:8, suggesting a "poetic register" (ibid., 7). Notice, also, the variety of other "poetic" verbiage in Gen 1, more than is customary in prose texts: "beasts of the earth" (Gen 1:24; Ps 79:2; 104:11, 20); "creeping things" (Gen 1:24, 25, 26; Hab 1:14; Ps 104:25); "vegetation" (Gen 1:11, 12; Deut 32:2; 2 Kgs 19:26; Prov 27:25); "winged bird" (Gen 1:21; Ps 78:27; Ezek 17:23; Gen 7:14); "rule" (Gen 1:26; Ps 72:8; Isa 14:6; Ps 110:2); "birds of the sky" and "fish of the sea" (Gen 1:26; Hos 4:3; Zeph 1:3) (ibid., 11–15). Moreover, "only a few verses fail to yield an acceptable division into balanced cola" (ibid., 23).

Moreover, the frequencies of key words and phrases are, quite unusually, in multiples of seven: אֱלֹהִים (*'elohim*, ×35); "earth" (×21); "heavens" (×21); "and it was so/light" (×7); "it was (very) good" (×7); "and God made" (×7); days numbered (×7)—all in 1:1–2:3; "light" and "day" together in 1:2–5 (paragraph 1; ×7); "light" in 1:14–19 (paragraph 4; ×7); "water" in 1:6–13 (paragraphs 2 and 3; ×7); חָיָה, *khayah*, "creatures"/"beasts" in 1:20–31 (paragraphs 5 and 6; ×7); etc.. And 1:1 has seven words, 1:2 has fourteen, while the last (seventh) paragraph, 2:1–3, has 35 words—and it deals with the *seventh* day.[33]

The overall structure of the account, with its six days of creation is also formulaic, organized into a double triad.

First triad (Days 1–3):
"Thus the heavens and the earth were completed ..." (Gen 2:1a)

DAYS 1–3	Day 1 light–darkness	Day 2 waters–heaven	Day 3 dry land / plants
Number of creative acts	one	one	two: "and God said" (×2) "it was good" (×2)

Second triad (Days 4–6):
"... and all their hosts" (Gen 2:1b)

DAYS 4–6	Day 4 sun / moon	Day 5 fish / birds	Day 6 land creatures / man
Number of creative acts	one	one	two: "and God said" (×2) "it was good" (×2)

There is parallelism between each of the members in the first triad (Days 1–3) and their corresponding members in the second triad (Days 4–6). The creation of light (Day 1) parallels the creation of luminaries that produce light (Day 4); the creation of sea and heaven (Day 2) parallels that of fauna that inhabit those spaces (Day 5), as also does the creation of dry land (Day 3), paralleling that of land creatures (Day 6). The creation of plants (seed-bearers and fruit-bearers, 1:12; Day 3) parallels the permission for mankind to use them as food (explicitly noted to be plants—seed-bearers and fruit-bearers, 1:29; Day 6). Marking the first triad off from the second, Days 1–3 contain all the naming ("calling") that God does: of day and night, of heavens, of dry land and seas (1:5, 8, 10; the next time anyone "calls" will be when man does so: 2:19, 20, 23).

This formation of the earth and the filling of its "compartments" with appropriate occupants is reflected in the void state of the earth before God began his creative work: תֹהוּ וָבֹהוּ (*tohu wabohu*, 1:2), a hendiadys meaning "formless and empty," the state of the earth not yet having attained the form or gained the occupants with which the original audience was familiar.[34] And this *formless* earth would become *formed*

33. See Cassuto, *Genesis*, 14–15; and Wenham, *Genesis 1–15*, 5, 7. The paragraphs of Gen 1:1–2:3 are 1:2–5; 1:6–8; 1:9–13; 1:14–19; 1:20–23; 1:24–31; and 2:1–3.

34. Alter, *Genesis*, x, translates it "welter and waste." The pair is used only twice more in the OT, in Isa 34:11 and Jer 4:23, and none of these texts "gives any linguistic or exegetical evidence to support the existence of a situation of mythic chaos in the earth." Ouro therefore prefers to call the initial situation "abiotic" rather than "chaotic," for God "did not create it a waste place, but formed it to be inhabited" (Isa 45:18) ("The Earth of Genesis 1:2: Abiotic or Chaotic? Part I," 275, 276). Neither is there any indica-

when God spoke light, heavens, earth, seas, and vegetation into existence on Days 1–3 (the first triad; 1:3–13), and this *empty* earth would become *filled* when God spoke the luminaries and living creatures, including man, into being on Days 4–6 (the second triad; 1:14–31).[35] God's fiat renders what was "formless and empty" into something productive and inhabited (i.e., with form and fullness). The "occupiers," i.e., the luminaries, sea and heavenly creatures, and land creatures and man, rule over the respective "forms"—sun-moon over light-darkness; creatures of the sea and heaven over their respective domains; and land creatures and man over land, consuming its produce. Indeed, the summary on Day 7 (2:1) is bipartite, the two parts corresponding to the two triads: 2:1a reflecting the first triad with the completion of "the heavens and the earth"; and 2:1b reflecting the second triad with the completion of their "hosts."[36] Activity also escalates in each triad. In the first, a simple increase in movement (from immobile light/darkness and sea/heaven to reproducing plants, that exhibit only "growth-mobility"); in the second, "an eruption of kinetic energy" (from moving luminaries with fixed-orbit mobility, to flying, swimming, and roving creatures with instinctive mobility, to humans with the greatest degree of volitional mobility).[37]

The symmetrical presentation of *two* works of creation on each of Days 3 and 6 is also remarkable; the two acts are emphasized by two instances of "and God said" and two instances of "it was good" (1:9, 11, 24, 26; and 1:10, 12, 25, 31). The second work on each day moves the narrative forward: vegetation, on Day 3, though part of the first triad of relatively immobile creations, is, at the same time, animate and bears reproductive potential, anticipating the second triad. Similarly, mankind in Day 6, though part of the second triad of more mobile creations, is, nonetheless, the image of God and therefore will celebrate the sabbatical rest, pointing forward to Day 7.

All this indicates that the structure of this "hymn-narrative" is quite carefully designed. Nothing is random, not God's creation, nor the account thereof. Needless

---

tion in Gen 1 of a judgment of some sort that resulted in the primeval תהו וָבהוּ. The "darkness" in 1:2 is not necessarily anti-God: God "created" it (Isa 45:7), and darkness is often associated with him and controlled by him (Exod 10:21–23; Deut 4:11; 5:23; Ps 18:11, 28; Isa 42:16; Jer 13:16). See Tsumura, *The Earth and the Waters*, 310–29. Thus the account is not portraying "a negative picture but rather a neutral, sterile landscape created by God and subject to his protection" (Mathews, *Genesis 1–11:26*, 143).

35. Vegetation, generally considered inanimate in biblical times, is seen as part of the "form" of the earth.

36. This unique description of the inhabitants of God's world as צְבָא (*tsaba'*) is used often of the "hosts/armies" of heaven, the stars, the angels—organized and differentiated companies functioning by divinely established mandate and within divinely established bounds. Its deployment in 2:1 to refer to the "hosts" of the earth is likely to indicate that at creation, "earth's living creatures followed as perfect an order as the order of the heavens" (Blocher, *In the Beginning*, 71). This army "does not fight, it parades" (*ne combat pas, elle défile*), in perfect sync with its Maker. In other words, this is what creation, particularly mankind, was intended to be—part of the divinely established order (Beauchamp, *Création et séparation*, 377). Aquinas, *Summa* 1.65a, distinguished between God's work of separation (*opus distinctionis*) on Days 1–3, and his work of adornment (*opus ornatus*) on Days 4–6. The medieval tradition that this Dominican Doctor followed was probably the result of the misreading by the LXX and Vulgate of צְבָא in 2:1 as צְבִי (*tsbi*, "adornment"; LXX, κόσμος [*kosmos*]; Vulgate, *ornatus*). Nonetheless, Aquinas's observation distinguishing the two triads remains valid.

37. Waltke and Fredricks, *Genesis*, 57–58.

to say, that is because the Creator of the world and the ultimate Author of the account is not whimsical or capricious, but deliberate and purposeful. He produces an orderly and dependable world and inspires a text that is also orderly and dependable. The scheme of creation in six days, the repetitive formulas that outline divine utterance, the coming into existence of creation, the announcement of goodness, etc., demonstrate that one of the intentions of one of the intentions of Gen 1 is to point to God is to point to God and his creation as orderly and harmonious. Again the meticulous design of the narrative indicates that it is likely to be more poetic ("story") than a literal rendition of scientific information ("history").

In sum, "[t]he theological treasures of the framework of the Genesis days come most clearly to light by means of the 'literary' interpretation. The writer has given us a masterly elaboration of a fitting, restrained anthropomorphic vision, in order to convey a whole complex of deeply meditated ideas."[38] Literarily, the text is God's invitation to his people to live in a world that runs by his precepts, that is geared for his priorities, and that engages his practices. Even in these early chapters of Scripture, theology is taught, a divine demand is made, an ideal world is projected. All God's children, even those living far away in time and space from the originary account are invited to learn the theology, acquiesce to divine demand, and inhabit God's ideal world. The long story that follows Gen 1, from Gen 2:4 through Rev 22:21, can only be comprehended, and its projected world inhabited, if Gen 1, the overture to that story, is rightly heard and understood, rightly read and heeded.

Science and Scripture

How does the creation account of Gen 1–2 comport with science? In the late nineteenth century, Warfield declared: "I am free to say, for myself, that I do not think that there is any general statement in the Bible or any part of the account of creation, either as given in Genesis 1and 2 or elsewhere alluded to, that need be opposed to evolution."[39] Over the last two centuries, there has been a general tendency among evangelicals to jettison any science that appears to contradict how the Bible has been read traditionally—perhaps there has been historical justification for such a stance, provoked by scientists overtly antagonistic to any form of theistic interest. However, a note of caution must be introduced: though the proclamations of science should be carefully examined, the bulk of information gleaned over millennia of scientific research has not contravened any doctrine of Christendom. Therefore, before one suspects that evolutionary hypotheses are necessarily anti-Christian, a thoughtful and reflective analysis must be undertaken.

Take the Copernican revolution as an example. Nicolaus Copernicus's thesis of the earth revolving around the sun was strongly resisted by the religious functionaries of the sixteenth century, often adducing 1 Sam 2:8; 1 Chr 16:30; Job 26:7; Pss 93:1; 104:5; Prov

---

38. Blocher, *In the Beginning*, 59.

39. Warfield, "Evolution or Development," 130 (a lecture delivered at Princeton Theological Seminary on Dec 12, 1888).

30:3; and Eccles 1:5 as evidence for the fixity of the earth. Of course, since then, we have learnt how better to read those texts in the light of indubitable scientific fact. These passages, all along, were never inconsistent with the concept that the earth moved around the sun; it was simply the case that after 1543, with the publication of *De revolutionibus orbium coelestium* by Copernicus (*On the Revolutions of the Celestial Spheres*), those texts of Scripture were *read* differently—as phenomenological reports from earth-bound observers to whom this planet appears quite stationary.[40] In other words, it was not the *text* of Scripture that was shown by Copernicus to be in error, but the *readings* thereof. In the seventeenth century, to his ecclesiastical opponents, Galileo would make the same argument, as he substantiated the theory of Copernicus more rigorously:

> I agree as you most prudently proposed, conceded, and established, that it is not possible for Sacred Scripture ever to deceive or to err; rather its decrees have absolute and inviolable truth. Only I would have added that, although Scripture itself cannot err, nevertheless some of its interpreters and expositors can sometimes err, and in various ways. The most serious and most frequent of these errors occurs when they wish to maintain always the direct meaning of the words, because from this there results not only various contradictions but even grave and blasphemous heresies.[41]

When common sense and science—what is science but glorified common sense?—tell us that a human being cannot be a literal door or an actual loaf of bread, we seek a better reading of Jesus' words in John 6:48 and 10:9. Perhaps the same interpretive operation is valid for Genesis: Is there a better reading of Gen 1–2 in light of science? Of course, one must admit the prospect of current scientific knowledge ("common sense") being preempted and improved by later data that render earlier conclusions moot (nonsense). Nonetheless, interpreters of the Bible must always be open to the possibility that their readings of Scripture are as fallible as they themselves are, and that it is possible that these readings may be better informed by science, as they were after the Copernican Revolution.

I come to Scripture with a background in biology and medicine, having engaged in both bench-top basic science research for a decade, and in hands-on patient care for few more. Yet I am not prepared to argue for the privileging of science over theology. However, I do make the claim that the text of Scripture (properly read) will *never* conflict with science (accurately ascertained): all truth is, after all, God's truth. The question must then be asked: If—and it is a reasonable assumption—if the science of origins is substantially correct, then is it possible to have a reading of Scripture that is *consistent with* such science? I would argue that, yes, such a reading is possible. That does not mean that Scripture affirms the truth of science as we know it now. It simply means that Scripture *can* be read in a way that does not generate conflict with science,

---

40. While the rotation of the earth is a given, even most moderns would be hard-pressed for a quick answer to the question: In which direction does the diurnal rotation of the earth occur? That it occurs from west to east, takes a bit of thought to figure out, grounded as we are upon the phenomenology of the sun "moving" from east to west during the day.

41. Galilei, "Letter to Castelli," 196 (dated Dec 21, 1613).

just as the passages dealing with the fixity of the earth were read in a way that obviated the locking of horns with astronomical discoveries.[42] The reading of Scripture that I adopt as being consistent with origins science is based upon the theological hermeneutic that strives to ascertain what authors were *doing* with what they were saying.

Ultimately, for preaching purposes, attention must be given to the text and what it (or its authors, divine and human) affirm, i.e., what they *do* with what they say. "The Bible speaks truly in all that it literally affirms. It is an egregious mistake, however, to identify the literal with the literalistic sense of Scripture, that is, with the empirical object or state of affairs to which it refers."[43] In other words, with regard to Gen 1–2, what the author is affirming is not necessarily the mechanics of God's creative activity, but a theological thrust (for which see Pericope 1). Or as Augustine put it: "[W]e do not read in the Gospel that the Lord said: I am sending you the Paraclete to teach you about the course of the sun and the moon. After all, he wanted to make Christians, not astronomers" (*Fel.* 10).

Warfield's words are wise:

> The upshot of the whole matter is that there is no *necessary* antagonism of Christianity to evolution, *provided that* we do not hold to too extreme a form of evolution. . . . But if we condition the theory by allowing the constant oversight of God in the whole process, and his occasional supernatural interference for the production of *new* beginnings by an actual output of creative force, producing something *new*, i.e., something not included even *in posse* [potentially] in preceding conditions, we may hold to the modified theory of evolution and be Christians in the ordinary orthodox sense.[44]

I assent to Warfield's sentiments regarding the inclusion of divine and providential activity within the scheme of evolution. Of a totally naturalistic system of origins, the Bible knows nothing. Every step of the way, the involvement of God in human origins and in the continuity of human life—indeed, even in the very existence and ongoing sustenance of the universe—is integral to divine sovereignty, and is part and parcel of biblical truth (see Neh 9:6; Job 9:4–10; 38:1–41; Pss 104:1–35; 148:1–14; Amos 4:13; Matt 6:26–30; Acts 17:24–28; Col 1:16–17; Heb 1:3; etc.). However the world may have come into existence, God's direct involvement is biblically affirmed, a truth that science—at least as we know it on this side of eternity—is incapable of falsifying.

"In the Beginning"

In the beginning," בְּרֵאשִׁית (*bre'shith*, 1:1), could either be in a construct form ("In the beginning *when* God created . . .") or in an absolute form with 1:1 as an independent main clause—"In the beginning, God created. . . ." Linguistic and literary reasons per-

---

42. "[T]here is a way of understanding Genesis 1 that does not compromise the authority and primacy of Scripture and that, at the same time, takes into account our increased knowledge of the universe, as Scripture itself suggests we should (Rom 1:19–20)" (Lennox, *Seven Days,* 62).

43. Vanhoozer, "Lost in Interpretation?" 108. He asserts that the literal sense is actually the literary sense (ibid.), what the authors actually affirm, or—as I would put it—what authors are *doing* with what they are saying.

44. "Evolution or Development," 130–31 (emphases original).

suade me to accept the use of בְּרֵאשִׁית in the absolute form. The LXX, Aquila, Theodotion, Symmachus, the Vulgate, and *Tg. Onq.* construe the form as absolute, and they see 1:1 as an independent clause. And בְּרֵאשִׁית in Jer 26:1; 27:1; 28:1; 49:34 (the only other occurrences of this preposition + noun combination in the Bible) is always followed by another noun—thus בְּרֵאשִׁית is in the construct there ("in the beginning *of* [noun]")—whereas it is a verb, "he-created," that follows בְּרֵאשִׁית in 1:1 (in Hebrew).[45] Also, the disjunctive clause that begins 1:2 (*waw* + subject + verb, "and the earth was formless") renders 1:2 non-sequential to 1:1; and 1:2 thus provides background information for the main clause in 1:3—it denotes the circumstances in which "God said . . ." (1:3). This disjunction in 1:2 would rule out a separate first act of creation in 1:1. Moreover, creation is conducted in the rest of Gen 1 by divine utterance (also see Ps 33:6, 9; Heb 11:3); the absence of such speech in Gen 1:1 points to this first verse being more of a summary than any specific event. Besides, such a discrete act of creation in 1:1 would disrupt the carefully organized seven-day structure described in the rest of the pericope (see excursus below). Additionally, the "heavens" are explicitly said to have been created in Gen 1:6–8, and the earth in 1:9–10, precluding the creation of the same pair in a prior act in 1:1.[46] Such a view of 1:1 as a summary "reflects normal Semitic thought which first states the general proposition and then specifies the particulars."[47] Indeed, this syntax in 1:1–3 is parallel to that of the commencement of the next pericope, 2:4–6: each has a summary, a disjunctive clause explaining the circumstances, and a main clause denoting divine action.

1:1	*summary*	
	"In-the-beginning created God the-heavens and the-earth."	
	1:2	*disjunctive clause:* waw + subject (noun) + verb
		"Now-the-earth was …."
		1:3 *main clause:* waw consecutive + prefixed verb + subject]
		"Then-He-said God …."
2:4	*summary*	
	"This [is] the-account [of] the-heavens and the-earth …."	
	2:5–6	*disjunctive clause:* waw + subject (noun) + verb
		"Now-every shrub [of] the-field not-yet was …."
		2:7 *main clause:* waw consecutive + prefixed verb + subject
		"Then-He-formed Yahweh God ….."

Genesis 1:1 is also shown to be a summary when one compares 1:1 with 1:2: the summary mentions *God, heavens,* and *earth,* while the following verse, 1:2, notes that *God*

45. Waltke notes that while Moses could not have used any other construction to denote this word in the absolute, he did have a number of options to indicate the construct. See "The Creation Account in Genesis 1:1–3: Part III," 224. The absence of the article on רֵאשִׁית (*re'shith*) is not an argument against its absolute form; Isa 46:10 has the word without an article (מֵרֵאשִׁית, *mere'shith*) and it is clearly in the absolute.

46. Another reason to consider 1:1 more as a title/summary is that the phrase "heavens and earth" usually indicates a completely-ordered cosmos, the finished product, so to speak (2:1, 4; 14:19, 22; Joel 4:16; Pss 124:8; 148:13; etc.).

47. Waltke, "The Creation Account in Genesis 1:1–3: Part III," 227.

was not yet active, and the *heavens* and *earth* not yet distinct. The remainder of the pericope, of course, details the creative activity of God and how the heavens and earth and all they contained became "distinct."[48]

1:1	In the beginning, **God** created the **heavens** and the **earth**.

1:2   The **earth** was not-yet distinct
           [it was "formless and empty"].
       The **heavens** were not-yet distinct
           [the "deep/waters" had to be separated to create the heavens, 1:6–8].
       God [the Spirit] was not-yet creating
           [he was "moving/hovering" over the waters].

And, as was noted, the "beginning" of the "heavens and the earth" in 1:1 is echoed in 2:1 with the completion of the "heavens and earth," substantiating the roles of 1:1 and 2:1 as epilogue and prologue respectively, to the main account of 1:2–31. In sum, the first verse of the Bible is best considered a summary or caption of what follows in the rest of the chapter.[49] It indicates that God alone was responsible for the "heavens and the earth" and that he was its cause, for it was he who acted to bring the cosmos into being "in the beginning." By this assertion, the transcendence of God, and his separateness from what he created, is emphasized.

"Create" and God's Creative Activity

Reading 1:1 as a summary, of course, leaves open the question of whether God created *ex nihilo* or out of preexisting matter of some sort; there is no indication in 1:2 one way or another. The verb בָּרָא (*bara'*, "create"; 1:1) is only used in the OT with God as subject. But the substrate of God's creation, i.e., the raw material, is never described. The products of creation include sea monsters (1:21), man (1:27; 5:1, 2; 6:7), heavens and the earth (1:1; 2:3, 4), and also "new things" (Num 11:30), "pure heart" (Ps 51:10), "a people" (Ps 102:18), "a cloud" (Isa 4:5), Israel (Isa 43:1), "the blacksmith" (Isa 54:16), mountains (Amos 4:13), etc.—some of these are obviously not creations *ex nihilo*. Moreover, there is quite a bit of flexibility in the use of verbs for creation: Exod 20:11, for instance, uses עָשָׂה (*'asah*, "made," used of both divine and human activity) instead of בָּרָא for the six days of creation. In Isa 41:20; 43:7; 45:7, 12, 18; and Amos 4:13, both עשה and ברא are used in parallel lines, as also in Gen 2:4; indeed, עָשָׂה is used in the creation account itself, in 1:7, 16, 25.

The Semitic origins of the Bible are not particularly concerned with the creation of matter, unlike the Greco-Roman interest in distinguishing between form and matter. In the ancient Near East, creation involved ordering and organizing the "precosmic condition" into the "cosmos" (κόσμος, *kosmos*, also means "order")—the establishment

48. Van Wolde, "The Text as an Eloquent Guide," 138–39.

49. "[I]t is much more than a mere heading . . . the first sentence itself is really a cry of praise" (Westermann, *Genesis 1–11*, 94). Here in Gen 1:1, "beginning" is also likely to be a summarizing period of time than an instant thereof, as in Job 8:7 ("beginning" = early part of Job's life) or Jer 28:1 ("beginning" = the commencement period/accession year of Zedekiah's reign).

of identity and diversity, functions and roles, jurisdictions and domains, and the fixing, ordering, and regulating of destinies.[50] Thus, in Scripture, the focus is on the actual creation of things: seas, luminaries, flora, fauna, man, etc. The material status and the substrates of God's activity (what he worked on, and its shape and structure prior to his "creative" activity) was of minimal interest to the ancients—"something was created when it was given a function." In other words, the "hardware" and its manufacture was incidental; it was the "software"—the functioning of what had been given order—that was important.[51] It makes sense, then, for a creation account to commence with a state in which identities, functions, domains, and destines are *not* fixed—a seeming state of "chaos" (1:1).

Rather than creation from pre-existing matter or *ex nihilo*, the key operation of Gen 1 is *separation*, "not absolute existence, as against nonexistence, but separation into ordered relations and categories" (distinct kinds of plants, animals, trees; distinct functions of luminaries; the distinct and special place of mankind, including the distinction between man and woman; etc.; בדל, *bdl*, "separate": 1:4, 6, 7, 14, 18)—i.e., an establishment of divine order.[52] "Yahweh is not overcoming enemy forces of chaos, but rather he is resolving nonfunctionality (= nonexistence) into a functional, ordered system"—creation by separation. Creation apparently is a process by which, progressively, distinctions are made and maintained.[53]

---

50. Walton, *Genesis 1*, 27–28, 34.

51. Ibid., 43, 44; also see 127–38. With this focus on function rather than material origin of components of the cosmos, one may concede the literary order of light before luminaries. Indeed, Walton (*Genesis*, 124–25) suggests that עשׂה used in 1:16 need not indicate their manufacture from scratch, but rather their functional creation or arranging (as in Job 9:9; Isa 41:17–20; 45:7; 1 Kgs 12:32, 33; etc.). Another way to explain this narrative "anomaly" would be to see God as creating time on Day 1: he called light "day," and darkness "night" (1:5), separating and defining *time periods*: thus "day" = [period of] light; "night" = [period of] darkness. In other words, *time* was created, a fundamental constituent and function of life as we know it. See Arnold, *Genesis*, 39; and Walton, *Genesis*, 78–79. Or did the ancients think of God himself as the "light" before the "lights"? Calvin argues this way: "[T]he Lord, by the very order of the creation, bears witness that he holds in his hand the light, which he is able to impart to us without the sun and moon" (*Comm. Gen.* on 1:3). In fact, in Ps 104:1–2, God is praised as the creator who is covered with light (also see Jas 1:17, "Father of [shadowless] lights"). Worthington points to the priority of light in the Bible: it is important in Jewish history (Exod 10:23; Esth 8:16; 2 Macc 1:32), cultic praxis (Exod 27:20; 35:14; 39:16; Lev 24:2; Num 4:16; 2 Chr 4:20; Ezek 42:7; 1 Macc 1:21; 2 Macc 1:32), and piety (Ps 119:105; Prov 4:18; 6:23; Isa 26:9; 58:8; Sir 24:23, 27, 32; Wis 18:4; Bar 4:1–2; 1 John 1:7; 2:9–10). In fact, God is frequently associated with light (Num 6:25; 2 Sam 23:4; Job 37:3, 11, 21–22; Pss 4:6; 31:16; 36:9; 67:1; 80:3, 7, 19; 89:15; 104:2; 119:135; Isa 2:5; 51:5; 60:1–3, 19–20; Dan 2:22; Hos 6:5; Hab 3:4, 11; Sir 50:29; Bar 5:9; Jam 1:17; 1 Tim 6:16; 1 John 1:5) (*Creation in Paul and Philo*, 81–82).

52. Barr, "Was Everything that God Created Really Good," 59–60.

53. Walton, "Creation in Genesis 1:1–2:3," 59–60; Barr, "Was Everything that God Created Really Good," 59–60. The schema below is derived from Kass, *The Beginning of Wisdom*, 34.

All creations/creatures:
    lack visible place (darkness)
      → have visible place (in light);
        lack definite place (formlessness)
          → have definite place (in the formed heavens, sea, earth);
            lack local motion (plants)
              → have local motion (luminaries);
                lack life (luminaries)
                  → have life (fish, birds);
                    lack terrestrial basis (fish, birds)
                      → have terrestrial basis (animals);
                        lack God's image (animals)
                        → have God's image (man).

All of this was reinforced by the refrain, "after its/their kind" (1:11, 12 [×2], 21 [×2], 24 [×2], 25 [×3]), the separation of plants and animals into distinct species, which "manage, by themselves . . ., to maintain their own distinctness through species-preserving reproduction, each after its kind."[54] Everything was properly placed and specifically stationed, to function according to divine demand. The Creator God is unquestionably a God of order, as the Bible is not hesitant to declare (Job 38–41; Pss 19, 65, 104, 148; Isa 40; 1 Cor 14:33; etc.). Later on, "separation" becomes the key to divine election as well (Lev 20:24 and 1 Kgs 8:53 of the nation; Num 8:14 and Deut 10:8 of the Levites; all בדל). And throughout Scripture, God's elected people are called to be as discriminating as he is, distinguishing ("separating") clean and unclean, holy and profane (Lev 10:10; 20:25). Divine order is thus a key motif of Gen 1.

The variety of ways in which creation is described in the Bible also leads the interpreter to suspect there is more to that event than might be observed from Gen 1[55]: by divine word or command (Gen 1:3, 6, 9, 11, 14, 20, 22, 26, 28; Ps 148:5)[56]; by divine breath (Ps 33:6–9; Job 26:13); by divine hand/arm (Pss 8:3; 102:25; Isa 48:13; Jer 27:5;

---

54. Ibid., 32.

55. Creation is described in poetry (Job 9:8–10; 26:7–14; 38–41; Pss 8; 19:1–6; 24:1–2; 33:6–9; 74:12–17; 89:5–12; 95:5; 102:25–27; 104; 119:90–91; 136:5–9; 148:1–12; Prov 3:19–20; 8:22–31), in narrative (Gen 5:1–2; 6:7; Exod 20:11; 31:17; 2 Kgs 19:15; Neh 9:6), and in prophecy (Isa 40:12–28; 42:5; 44:24; 45:7–18; Jer 5:22; 10:12; 27:5; 32:17; 51:15–16; Amos 9:6; Zech 12:1). For these categories and ideas, I am grateful to my colleague Gordon H. Johnston (personal communication).

56. Auld notes that no less than 40% of the verbs for divine action in Gen 1:1–2:3 are explicitly verbs of speech: "and God said" and "and it was so" echo throughout the chapter (1:3, 6, 7, 9, 11, 14, 15, 20, 24, 26, 30), not to mention God "calls" (×5) and God "blesses" (×3). "In Genesis 1, God is a God who speaks, and who acts by speaking" ("*Imago Dei*," 261). Genesis 1 simply portrays "the expression of an effortless, omnipotent, unchallengeable word of a God who transcends the world" (Hasel, "The Significance of the Cosmology," 11; also see Johnston, "Genesis 1," 187–88). No randomness or hocus-pocus here. Instead there is deliberation, planning, and purposefulness. One also must note that "and God said" occurs ten times in Gen 1 (1:3, 6, 9, 11, 14, 20, 24, 26, 28, 29). Sailhamer speculates that this formulaic construction of divine speech (also found in the Flood story: 6:7a, 13a; 7:1a; 8:15 [×2], 21a; 9:1a, 8a, 12a, 17) may foreshadow the other famous "ten words" in the history of God's people (the Ten Commandments, "the words of the covenant," Exod 34:28); see "Genesis," 131. Essentially, "[w]hat the writer wants most to show in this narrative is not that on each day God 'made' something, but that on each day God 'said' something. The predominant view of God in this chapter is that He is a God who speaks. His word is powerful" (idem, *Genesis Unbound*, 132–33). Of course, in Pericope 2 this powerful word is violated by a created being!

32:17); and by divine victory (Pss 74:14; 89:10; Job 26:12–13; Isa 51:9). God is said to have begotten the cosmos (Deut 32:18; Ps 90:2; Prov 8:24–25), built heaven and earth (Ps 78:69; Amos 9:6), laid its foundations (Job 38:4; Pss 24:2; 78:69; 89:11; 102:25; 104:5, 8; Prov 3:19; Isa 48:13; 51:13; Amos 9:6; Zech 12:1), established them (Pss 8:3; 24:2; 65:6; 74:16; 93:1; 96:10; 103:19; Prov 3:19; 8:27; Isa 45:18; 51:13; Jer 10:12; 51:15), stretched out the heavens (Job 9:8; 26:7; Ps 104:2; Isa 40:22; 42:5; 44:24; 45:12; 51:13; Jer 10:12; 51:15; Zech 12:1), measured before creating (Job 28:25; 38:5; Isa 40:12), and fashioned heaven and earth (Pss 74:17; 95:5; 104:26; Isa 29:16; 45:7, 9; 64:8; Jer 10:16; 51:19; Amos 4:13). The creation of mankind, itself, is accounted for in diverse fashion: the first humans by creative word (Gen 1:26–27); Adam from the dust of the ground and divine breath (2:7; 3:19); Eve from a rib (2:21, 23); all humans from dust (Pss 103:14; 104:29; Eccl 3:20; 12:7); and/or from clay (Job 10:9; 33:6); and formed in the womb by God (Job 31:15; Ps 139:13; Jer 1:5). There is also variation in the order of creation in different biblical texts.

Text	Creation Sequence
Gen 1:1–2:3	light → sky → land/vegetation → luminaries → birds/fish → animals/humans → rest
Ps 104:2–23	spreading out heavens → upper chambers in waters → clouds → earth on foundations → earth covered with water → water separated → animals, birds → vegetation → sun and moon
Prov 8:22–24	primordial waters → mountains → land → heavens → horizons → clouds/springs of the deep → boundaries for seas → humanity

In any case, Gen 1 clearly makes the point that the totality of the cosmos ("heavens and the earth," 1:1) is a creation of God. And, while Genesis does not explicitly take a stance on the matter, it seems to fit the rest of the biblical evidence that God actually created *ex nihilo* (John 1:3, 10; Rom 11:36; 1 Cor 8:6; Col 1:16; Heb 1:2; 11:3; Rev 4:11; also see 2 Macc 7:28; Wis 11:17).[57] Without question, then, this God who created "in the beginning" is supreme and sovereign. The first subject of the Bible is "God"—the second most frequent noun in the OT. The theological thrust of the first pericope of Scripture (see on Pericope 1) also explains the appearance of אֱלֹהִים (*'elohim*) rather than יהוה (*yhwh*) in 1:1–2:3. "Creation extols God's transcendence and the power of his spoken word; thus *Elohim* is preferred, whereas *Yahweh* commonly is associated with the particular covenant agreement between God and Israel (Exod 3:15; 6:2–3)."[58] In short, "the whole of Gen 1 is permeated with the idea of the absolute transcendence of God and of the utter dependence of all being on God for its existence."[59]

---

57. Nachmanides, *Commentary on the Torah: Genesis,* 23, declared that God "created all things from absolute non-existence."

58. Mathews, *Genesis 1–11:26,* 127–28.

59. Arbez and Weisengoff, "Exegetical Notes," 144.

"Day"

McBride remarks on the schematic, rather than a fulsome, description of the days of creation: "[T]he account is succinct, even abbreviated. It resembles an itemized list more than a true narrative. . . . the language seems to be intentionally cryptic, not in an effort to conceal antecedents deemed problematic but rather to entice interest in particular themes, suggesting that their significance is yet to be unveiled"—that is to say, its significance is understood when the interpreter grasps what the author is *doing* with what he is *saying*.[60]

Creation commences with two words from God on Day 1: יְהִי אוֹר (*yhi 'or*, "let there be light"; 1:3). To modern ears, the creative work of God in 1:3–4 immediately creates a problem. The difficulty is not so much that God created light before the sun (Rev 22:5, and perhaps Zech 14:7, remind one of a situation with sun-less light; see 18n51), but how "evening" and "morning" could constitute one "day" in the absence of the sun. Evening and morning before the creation of the sun is also implied in the *Enuma elish,* the Babylonian creation myth: Apsu, one of the gods in the epic, at one point *before* the creation of the luminaries, states: "By day I find no relief, nor repose by night" (Tablet I.38; *ANET* 61). One suspects, again, the non-literal nature of the Genesis account, seeing that this element, among others, appears to have been borrowed from contemporaneous culture, at least for polemic purposes.

That a "day" comprises an "evening" and a "morning" (1:5) seems to indicate a 24-hour period. Steinmann argues that the author is actually defining "day" here: a cycle of light (daytime) and darkness (nighttime), akin to a solar day.[61] Moreover, in the singular, "day" with a number or in a series always indicates a solar day in the OT, never an undefined period of time.[62] However, the syntax of "day" in Gen 1:1–2:3 has some unique characteristics.

	article	number	article	noun
1:5		one		day
1:8		second		day
1:13		third		day
1:19		fourth		day
1:23		fifth		day
1:31	the	sixth		day
2:2,3	the	seventh	the	day

Instead of the ordinal number ("first"), the cardinal, "one," is used in 1:5, and only for Day 1 in the creation account—thus "one day" (or "a single day," as also in Gen 27:45; 33:13). Steinman notes that the cardinal אֶחָד (*'ekhad*) can be employed in place of the ordinal רִאשׁוֹן (*ri'shon*) when enumerating the day of a month (e.g., Gen 8:5, 13), the year of a king's reign (e.g., 2 Chr 36:22; Ezra 1:1), or the first of a small series of count-

---

60. McBride, "Divine Protocol," 6–7.

61. Therefore "day" (יום, *yom*) is used in two senses in 1:5, for the time of light (daytime), and for a period that encompasses both daytime and nighttime to yield a solar day (Steinmann, "אחד as an Ordinal Number," 577–82).

62. Mathews, *Genesis 1–11:26*, 149.

ables with articles on both the number and the noun (e.g., Exod 26:4, 5; 1 Kgs 6:24): in all these cases, אֶחָד would be read as "first." But, of course, none of these paradigms operate in Gen 1:5—it is not the day of the month or the year of a king's reign, and articles are absent. Thus the sentence is deliberately crafted to keep the reader from understanding יוֹם אֶחָד (*yom 'ekhad*) as "the first day." What is intended is simply "one/a single day," a day that is unique.[63] The remainder of the days, also without articles, each comprising an evening and a morning, are likewise single "day" units, though ordinals are used; i.e., "[a] second/third/fourth/fifth day." No sequence is necessarily implied in the text to render these periods of time successive or as making up consecutive solar days. The days that have articles attached—*the* sixth day, and *the* seventh day—simply emphasize the importance of those particular days, when the creation of man and God's rest occurred. In fact, Day 7, is described literally as "*the* seventh *the* day," with articles on both the number and the noun (in 2:2 [×2]); in 2:3, instead of the article, an object marker אֵת, *'et*, precedes "day")—obviously an extra-special slice of time (see on Pericope 1).[64]

All this to say, Gen 1 describes "*one/a* single day" (emphasizing the beginning of creation), "a second day," "a third day," "a fourth day," "a fifth day," "*the* sixth day" (emphasizing the creation of man), and "**the** seventh day" (strongly emphasizing the rest of God). There is no textual constraint that necessitates the interpretation of a chronological sequence of seven days, one after the other.[65] By that token, one also cannot pinpoint how long it took overall for God to finish creating. Were there other activities that went on between the non-sequential days? Also, if God brought light instantaneously into existence on Day 1 (and likewise for each of the other created entities, each on their respective days), did he rest for the remainder of that particular day (making it almost like Day 7), or did he use up the 24 hours of each day, so that the creating enterprise took $6 \times 24 = 144$ hours?

Hummel's analogy is apt. Imagine a historian writing about the conclusion of World War II: "President Harry Truman ordered the use of the atomic bomb on Hiroshima and Nagasaki [in 1945] to end the war with Japan. Those *two days* changed the entire character of modern warfare." Such an account glosses over an incredible amount of detail, from President Roosevelt's decision to build the bomb, to the years of its actual conception and manufacture in the "Manhattan Project" that began in

---

63. The indefinite use of יוֹם אֶחָד is also found in Zech 14:7, which, too, mentions "light," "daytime," and "nighttime" ("day" is used in its two senses here, as well—"daytime" and "daytime + nighttime = solar day").

64. It must be noted that it is the pointing of the word בַּיּוֹם (*bayyom*) in 2:2 that indicates that there is an article on the noun, "day."

65. Sterchi, "Does Genesis 1 Provide a Chronological Sequence?" 533. The assertion in Exod 20:11 and 31:17 that Yahweh created in six days and rested on the seventh does not necessarily make it six (or seven) *sequential* days. Young considers the creation account as the minutes or transactions of the royal edicts and their execution ("let there be . . ."). Thus, for him, the days of creation are not any particular fixed period of time but days of divine action viewed from God's royal and heavenly realm ("Scripture in the Hands of Geologists (Part Two)," 303–4). Bavinck rightly called the creation days "God's workdays" (*In the Beginning*, 126).

1939, involved over 130,000 people, and cost the U.S. almost $2 billion (then), not to mention the extensive planning and execution of the bombing of the two Japanese cities. "The exact details of how and when the commands were implemented over years or weeks are unimportant to the main concern of who and why, and what resulted."[66] Likewise, the thrust of the Genesis writer is the portrayal of a *theological* account of creation. Preoccupation with details not intended to be affirmed by the text—for instance, *how long* God took to create, or even *how* exactly he did so—distracts from the theological thrust and affirmation of Gen 1 and its author. Calvin, as did Augustine before him, declared, "The Holy Spirit had no intention to teach astronomy" (*Comm. Ps.* on Ps 136:7). One might well add that he had no intention to teach biology or geology either. What, then, was the intent of the formulaic use of "day" in this Gen 1? Why the need for a 24–7 framework for the creation account, if God could/did create instantaneously? Why could he not be said to have created everything *statim*? In other words, what is the author *doing* with what he is saying in this fashion in Gen 1:1—2:3?

The poetic and literary nature of the account was noted earlier; right away, those characteristics of Gen 1 hint at a reading that was not meant to be literal, as journalistic, reportorial history. Also, the parallels between the creation orders of Gen 1 and *Enuma elish* indicate a purpose beyond that of merely informing; the comparable sequences include: primeval darkness, light, heavens, dry land, luminaries, and man, followed by the rest of the gods.[67] Moreover, the "6 + 1" pattern, particularly pertaining to days, was common in ancient Near Eastern texts[68]:

> Six days and [six] nights
> Blows the flood wind, as the south-storm sweeps the land.
> When the seventh day arrived,
> The flood(-carrying) south-storm subsided in the battle,
> Which it had fought like an army.
> (*Gilgamesh Epic,* Tablet XI.127–130; *ANET* 94)

> Thou shalt have luminous horns to signify six days,
> On the seventh day reaching a [half]-crown.
> (*Enuma elish,* Tablet V.16–17; *ANET* 68)

> March a day and a second;
>   A third, a fourth day;
>   A fifth, a sixth day—
> Lo! At the sun on the seventh:
>   Thou arrivest at Udum the Great,
>   Even at Udum the Grand.
> (*Keret* A.iii.115–110, also see 111–120; *ANET* 144)

66. Hummel, "Interpreting Genesis One," 182. His account of the atomic bomb's reportage has been modified here.

67. See Heidel's comparison between Gen 1 creation and that in the *Enuma elish* (*The Babylonian Genesis,* 129).

68. See Young, "Scripture in the Hands of Geologists (Part Two)," 145–47, for other examples.

This reuse of a common pattern—both of creation sequence and of the "6+1" motif—moves one away from a literal reading of the Genesis account. "The more it appears that the biblical writer used a stereotype from his cultural milieu in presenting creation in the form of a week, the less likely is it that he limited himself to transcribing a chronological sequence."[69] Instead, one begins to see that Genesis 1 emphasizes the order and perfection of creation, proceeding from an orderly and perfect God (1 Cor 14:33; Matt 5:48), as opposed to the rather *ad hoc* creation enterprises of the gods of pagan myths.[70] While retaining some obvious similarities for polemic purposes, the layout here is clear and simple: God is in charge and he does things in a systematic and orderly fashion, creating forms and then filling them. The six-day schema, along with the account's poetic formulas, refrains, numerical organization, double triadic structure, chiasms and *inclusios*, etc. (see above), underscores the orderliness and perfection of all things God created.[71] The thrust of the narrative, in other words, is topical, not chronological. While the days could have been immediately sequential, the text does not *necessarily* affirm that.[72] Both the genre and style of the writing provide strong evidence for a literary interpretation that could conceivably involve dischronology; such a non-sequential operation on time is the narrator's prerogative—the prerogative of any narrator anywhere, not just biblical ones—intended not to deceive, but merely to further his theological agenda: what he is *doing* with what he was *saying*.[73]

As will be detailed in Pericope 1, the pattern of sevens and the culminating "rest" on Day 7, points to a conception of the cosmos as a divine temple that is constructed and dedicated on its seventh day, when its presiding deity enters the shrine. In any case, however God proceeded to create, instantaneously or in extended fashion, in this particular sequence or some other, the time-marked account of Gen 1:1—2:3 reminds

---

69. Blocher, *In the Beginning*, 53.

70. The declaration of his creation as "good" (1:4, 10, 12, 18, 21, 25, 31) also reflects the perfections of a Creator who is, himself, "good" (Pss 34:8; 100:5; Jer 33:11; Lam 3:25; Nah 1:7; Mark 10:18/Luke 18:19).

71. Wenham, *Genesis 1–15*, 39.

72. See ibid., 40. It is, of course, possible that the topical and chronological coincide. However, the dischronologies noted, including the flourishing of vegetation before the luminaries were created, incline one to consider the account more topical than chronological. Special pleading could, of course, account for all the dischronologies—God could have been working miraculously. But Kline, in an incisive article written over half a century ago, showed that Gen 2:5 (the absence of shrub and plant "because it had not rained" until then) presupposed the normal activity of the laws of nature for the generation and growth of vegetation. See "'Because It Had Not Rained,'" 146–57. As Blocher notes, "If the dry land did not emerge until Tuesday and if vegetation has existed only from that day, an explanation is not going to be given the following Friday [the day of man's creation, 2:7] that there is no vegetation because there is no rain!" (*In the Beginning*, 56). This seeming incompatibility furthers the conclusion that the account of this pericope is more literary and agenda-driven than chronological and historical. A literary interpretation, as we will see, yields sufficient explanation for the text as we have it, without compounding hypotheses with superfluous assumptions; a judicious use of Occam's razor, the principle of parsimony, is always appropriate.

73. Examples abound in the Bible. Mark, for instance, structures his Gospel around Jesus' single journey from Galilee to Jerusalem, whereas John has Jesus going back and forth at least thrice. John's account is likely to be what actually happened; Mark's dischronology serves his agenda to show what it means for disciples to follow Jesus on the single "trip of discipleship" to the cross.

readers that God also created time and the fundamental rhythms of life in his creation: evening + morning = day. The powerful significance of this is that this transcendental God was immanently involved in his creation—he entered into his work.[74] This is a God who is deeply involved with his creation. And the thrust of the account of God's first work is to move his people to a better understanding of the relationship between this Creator God and his creation, and how their lives may be (ought to be) changed thereby.

CONCLUSION

Yahweh, simply put, creates, and he does so in an orderly manner, deliberate and purposeful, that culminates in the creation of man as his image. All of this "suggests that Genesis 1 was originally composed, not as a scientific treatise, but as a theological polemic against the ancient Egyptian models of creation which competed against Yahwism for the loyalty of the ancient Israelites."[75] Stek outlines the contrasts well:

> In them (i.e., the false religions) the first generations of gods came forth from the primordial watery mass; in his word God is before all, and the primeval waters are his creation. In them the fundamental cosmic entities are gods, and their emergence involved divine procreation; in his word the cosmos is composed of an ordered set of created structures fashioned by God's creative word. In them there are gods of the celestial realm, gods of the earth (land), gods of the seas, and gods of the world below; in his word there is one God, who is Creator and Lord of all. In them (especially the Mesopotamian and Canaanite religions) the present ordered world was established only after its creator had conquered the chaos deity or deities, and it remained under the threat of the resurgence of those chaos powers; in his word God sovereignly shaped the plastic medium he had created into the world that now is, and there are no cosmic powers that can threaten to undo it. In them fierce monsters of the deep lurk in the chaos waters (the seas) that surge along the outer bounds of humanity's fragile world; in his word these are mere creatures to be catalogued with the fish of the seas, mere playful denizens of the ocean depths . . . In them the Sun, Moon, and stars are deities that powerfully affect events on earth (the roots of astrology); in his word the heavenly bodies are but the greater and lesser lights that together with the stars give light on the earth and govern day and night and the seasons—nothing more. In them the mysterious powers of life and its generation involve participation in and manifestation of the divine, since procreation belongs primordially to the gods; in his word creaturely life is not an extension of God's life, and procreation is by God's blessing of living creatures. . . . In them humans are but abject slaves and pawns in a metropolis of the gods . . .; in his word humanity is the crown of creation and all humans alike are, while of earth, fashioned in God's image. . . .[76]

74. Yet from the definite statement (twice in Gen 2:2) of the completion of his creative work, we learn that God is not absorbed into his creation. "He remains sovereignly free, holding his creation before him and delighting in it with the joy of the seventh day" (Blocher, *In the Beginning*, 59).

75. Johnston, "Genesis 1," 192, 194.

76. Stek, "What Says the Scripture?" 230–31.

Introduction

The God that created the heavens and the earth is unlike any other god. His powerful and ineffable word marked the beginning; that same mighty word will surely govern the unfolding of the remainder of time-bound history. If the creative word is that powerful, it stands to reason that man is therefore also responsible for abiding by this authoritative God's authoritative word in order to be blessed by his benevolence. The rest of Scripture unfolds man's failure to do so and God's plan to remedy that failure and accomplish his original and ultimate intent to bless mankind, through his Son, Jesus Christ.

PRIMEVAL HISTORY
Creating for Blessing

Genesis 1:1–11:26

PERICOPE 1

The Creation Story

Genesis 1:1–2:3

[Creation; Establishment of the Sabbath]

SUMMARY, PREVIEW[1]

Summary of Pericope 1: The biblical story of creation points unwaveringly to the absolute sovereignty of God; this sovereignty is further reinforced as one compares the text to contemporary ancient Near Eastern accounts of creation. The narrative also describes the role of man, created in God's image, to represent this sovereign Creator to the rest of the cosmos. In the structuring of this pericope and its allusions to temple-dedication, the cosmos becomes a Temple, and the "rest" of God designates his reign in that Temple. It is up to the inhabitants of that cosmos, particularly man, to abide by the divine precepts, priorities, and practices that govern this divine domain.

---

1. In a "deductive" fashion, the Summary of the current pericope will state what the author is *doing* with what he is saying. What is asserted in these summaries will be elucidated in an "inductive" process from the text in the Notes that follow. How this pericope connects with pericopes that precede and follow will also be stated briefly (the Review and Preview, respectively; of course, there is no Review in this chapter).

Preview of Pericope 2: The next pericope (2:4–3:24) shows man and woman in the Garden, wherein is provided everything for their needs. Unfortunately, the first humans choose independence, opting to decide for themselves what is good for them, and sin enters the arena of human history.

1   Genesis 1:1–2:3

THEOLOGICAL FOCUS OF PERICOPE 1[A]

1   **The unchallengeable sovereign status and illimitable creative power of God is exercised over the cosmic Temple, in which he rests and reigns, by deputizing humans, who bear his image, to represent this Creator to the rest of the cosmos (1:1–2:3).**

1.1   The sovereign status of the Creator God is unchallengeable, and the scope of his creative power all-encompassing, negating all other speculations of godhood and notions of creation.

1.2   The creation of mankind in the image of God mandates its responsibility to represent the Creator and his sovereignty to the rest of the cosmos.

1.3   The arena in which mankind, in the image of God, authoritatively represents its sovereign Creator is the cosmos, the Temple of God.

1.4   The "rest" of God within his Temple, the cosmos, following its "dedication," concludes God's creative enterprise and commences his reign over his creation.

A. The Theological Focus of the particular pericope (the essence of the "pericopal theology") is, in effect, what the author is *doing* with what he is saying in his text. The "Focus" is intended to be exactly that: a statement that focusses the theology of the pericope. Such a focus—a North Star, if you will—keeps the one preparing a sermon from straying from the theological thrust of the text. With the intent to be as comprehensive as possible, so as to deal with every major element of the text, each Theological Focus is necessarily long and pedantic. An abridged version, more useful when one begins to craft the sermon, is located towards the end of each chapter, under "Sermon Focus and Outlines." That version of the Theological Focus is a condensed one labeled "Theological Focus of Pericope X for Preaching."

OVERVIEW

The account of creation is an appropriate beginning for the word of God, the Scripture of the church. The narrative establishes the arena in which life is enacted; it sets the stage for everything in the Bible that follows it; and it expresses the parameters by which creation is to function in the presence of an almighty, Creator God. Divine demand is manifest in the detailing of the relationships between the Creator and the products of his creative endeavor. And inhabiting a divine domain calls for alignment with divine demand.

Elsewhere in Genesis, in 6:9; 10:1; 11:10; 11:27; 25:12, 19; 36:1, 9; and 37:2, וְאֵלֶּה תּוֹלְדֹת (*welleh toldot,* "these are the records of"; or a variant in 5:1, "this is the book of the records of") introduces a new section. Thus 2:4, that begins the same way (אֵלֶּה תוֹלְדוֹת, *'elleh toldot*), must also mark the commencement of a new pericope. The chiastic structure of 1:1 with 2:1–3 strengthens the conclusion that 1:1–2:3 forms an integral unit (also note the precision of word numbers—multiples of seven, creating a heptadic structure; moreover, Gen 2:2 has 14 words).

he created (1:1)		
God (1:1)		**21 words**
heavens and the earth (1:1)		
Creation Account (1:2–31)		
heavens and the earth (2:1)		
God (2:2)		**35 words**
he created (2:3)		

And 1:1 and 2:4a, each beginning a new pericope, show correspondences: both deal with time, creation, and heavens and earth (see below). But, in differentiating 1:1–2:3 from what follows, one observes that God is named אֱלֹהִים (*'elohim*) in 1:1–2:3, and יְהוָה אֱלֹהִים (*yhwh 'elohim*) from 2:4 onwards.

NOTES 1[2]

1.1   The sovereign status of the Creator God is unchallengeable, and the scope of his creative power all-encompassing, negating all other speculations of godhood and notions of creation.

The first chapters of Genesis contain a *theology* of creation that asserts the bankruptcy of the contemporary pagan creation epics of the cultures surrounding Israel; it implicitly reproaches the resulting theological inadequacies of such stories—the mistaken notions of the nature of deity; the idolatry of astronomical bodies, natural entities, and animal life; and misconstrual of the position and role of humanity. The biblical account of creation is an artistic and tactical polemic against these constant threats to Israel's ongoing faithfulness to the true and living God, Yahweh.[3] Theirs was the one and only God, who created the heavens and the earth according to his preeminent purpose and prevailing will, an orderly creation that submits to divine demand.[4] Thus the author "was not grappling with issues arising out of modern scientific attempts to understand the structure, forces, processes, and dimensions (temporal and spatial)

---

2. The Notes are essentially interpretive comments geared to deriving the Theological Focus of that section of the pericope. *Caveat*: There will be far more information presented in the Notes than is necessary for, or can be delivered in, a sermon. This excess results from an attempt to demonstrate how every major textual element contributes to the Theological Focus of the respective unit and to the larger, comprehensive Theological Focus of the particular pericope. The preacher should decide on what needs to be presented to the congregation in order to validate the derivation of the Theological Focus. A good deal of preacherly discretion must therefore be employed in deciding what will be (and what needs to be) heard by the audience. Suggestions along those lines are provided with the outlines.

3. Young, "Scripture in the Hands of Geologists (Part Two)," 303. Also see Introduction in this commentary.

4. "The language [of the Genesis account], however, is tranquil . . .; the controversial note is heard indirectly, as it were, through the deliberate, quiet utterances of Scripture, which sets the opposing views at nought by silence or by subtle hint" (Cassuto, *Genesis*, 7).

of the physical universe. He was not interested in the issues involved in the modern debate over cosmic and biological evolution. His concerns were *exclusively religious.*"[5]

Around Israel floated an assortment of theories of theogony (the generation and genealogy of gods) and of cosmogony (the genesis of the cosmos). Here, for instance, is the begetting of the gods in the opening lines of the *Enuma elish,* the Babylonian creation myth, accomplished by the admixture of male and female waters (freshwater and seawater, respectively, perhaps at the mouths of the Tigris and Euphrates)[6]:

> When the skies above were not yet named
> Nor earth below pronounced by name,
> Apsu [male waters], the first one, their begetter,
> And maker Tiamat [female waters], who bore them all,
> Had mixed their waters together, . . .
> Then gods were born within them (1.1–9).

Then follows a genealogy of the gods: Tiamat begets a pair of twins, Lahmu and Lahamu, and Anshar and Kishar. The latter pair bear Anu who is, in turn, the ancestor of Nuddimmud. And "inside" Apsu, Marduk was "created" (1.10–20, 80–90).[7] And so on. Subsequently, there are gory accounts that describe the extensive intramural conflicts between the various hierarchies and assortments of gods, all battling for supremacy (theomachy = strife amongst the gods).[8]

"Then came the Torah and soared aloft, as on eagles' wings, above all these notions. Not many gods but One God; not theogony, for a god has no family tree; not wars nor strife nor the clash of wills, but only One Will, which rules over everything, without the slightest let or hindrance; not a deity associated with nature and identified with it wholly or in part, but a God who stands absolutely above nature, and outside of it."[9] This God is present "in the beginning" (Gen 1:1), uncreated and self-existent and eternal. And all of creation comes from his hand, to do his will. And so begins Scripture, introducing the Creator God, and his creature, man, setting the scene for the rest of the biblical text that recounts the relationship between these two protagonists. The role of Gen 1 must be considered against this backdrop—a communiqué from God to his people surrounded by pagan polytheism and mythology. It is, therefore, clear that the creation account has a polemic tone to it that is consciously and deliberately antimythical.[10] Hurowitz notes that "[t]he ancient Near East was full of conflicting claims to supremacy of this or that god or city over all others. The Bible is part of this polemic. The biblical authors borrowed from foreign Creation stories in order to make the best case possible for YHWH, God of Israel. They were participating in a contemporary international debate on the basis of data considered basic and

5. Stek, "What Says the Scripture?" 230.

6. See Dalley, *Myths From Mesopotamia*, 233.

7. See ibid., 235.

8. See Walton, *Genesis 1*, 68–74.

9. Cassuto, *Genesis*, 8.

10. Hasel, "The Polemic Nature of the Genesis Cosmology," 85. "Much in Gen 1 is patently antipagan" (Hamilton, *Genesis: Chapters 1–17*, 55).

agreed upon by all."[11] Yahweh was the God of power, able to create and control those entities considered by then-prevalent myth as hostile and threatening. The polemic nature of the text will be briefly considered as it concerns the "deep," the luminaries, and the "sea monsters." Rather than autonomous authorities, all of these are seen to be merely celestial or terrestrial instruments in the hands of God, serving his purposes for his creation.[12]

"Deep"

The act of "separation" is a common motif in Genesis 1.[13] In 1:1–10, without any struggle or hint of conflict, but by simple divine fiat, Yahweh separated the waters (or the "deep," תְהוֹם, *thom,* 1:2) to create the heavens and the earth, unlike the struggles of the god, Marduk, who had to create heaven and earth from the upper and lower halves, respectively, of the slain goddess Tiamat (the primeval sea).[14] In Genesis, however, there is no sense that the "deep" is anything but an inanimate force of nature; it is "depersonalized, undifferentiated, unorganized, and passive," and God controls it totally.[15] "Instead of cosmic deities locked in mortal combat, God the Creator works calmly as a craftsman in his shop. There is no more danger that He will fall before the monster of chaos than there is that the chair will devour the carpenter."[16]

Luminaries

The description of the activities of Day 4 (1:14–19) is unusually long, because of an extended and repeated concern with the functions of the sun and moon. Such concern probably arose because of the dominance of these two entities (and that of the stars) in the pantheon of Israel's neighbors, and their purported control of human destiny. For the biblical author, however, these are only creatures in the hands of their Creator—he makes them, he places them, he regulates them (1:16, 17)—creatures with a finite beginning to their existence and a defined function as their *raison d'être.*[17] Strikingly,

---

11. "The Genesis of Genesis," 52.

12. Hamilton, *Genesis: Chapter 1–17,* 150–51.

13. Also see Introduction for the divine act of separation in creation.

14. *Enuma elish* 4.125–140 (Dalley, *Myths from Mesopotamia,* 254–255).

15. Hasel, "The Significance of the Cosmology in Genesis 1," 7. One also remembers that the historical experiences of Israel with "deep" and "waters" had been uniformly victorious (Exod 14:21–22; 15:5, 8; Josh 3:14–17; Ps 106:9; Isa 63:13).

16. Waltke, "The Creation Account," 334.

17. Westermann, *Genesis 1–11,* 127. In the *Enuma elish,* the creation of these bodies is not recorded; rather they are simply stationed in their cosmic loci (the stars) or instructed by Marduk to be located there (the sun and the moon) (5.1–2) (Dalley, *Myths from Mesopotamia,* 255). Johnston observes that the Egyptian creation myth of Hermopolis details the self-generation of the creator-god of light, Rê/Rê-Atum, from the darkness of the primeval waters. In Genesis, on the other hand, Yahweh (ungenerated) creates light from darkness—"a case of the Hebrew author indulging in a bit of one-upmanship" over every other deity. He creates the luminaries, thus laying claim to all their domains and declaring himself to be the God of power, one who is over all—over creation and over creature. See Johnston, "Genesis 1," 187; Mathews, *Genesis 1–11:26,* 154; Clendenen, "Religious Background," 277–90.

"light" created on Day 1 was turned over to the sun and moon that they may regulate day and night; i.e., these celestial bodies were reduced to being managers ("to govern," 1:16) and intrinsically impotent cosmic clocks, serving the interests of the earth.[18] The functions of the luminaries, "to separate" (1:14a, 18b), "to rule" (1:16, 18a), and "to give light" (1:15, 17), are each mentioned twice, underscoring their serving status. The luminaries are created to function under God, for God, according to God. "The utter creatureliness of the heavenly bodies has never before been expressed in such revolutionary terms."[19] And, remarkably, these "managers" are anonymous: the common labels "sun" and "moon" (שֶׁמֶשׁ and יָרֵחַ, *yareakh* and *shemesh*) are not used at all in the Genesis account; perhaps this was a conscious avoidance of names that were also given to the respective deities in the pantheon of Israel's neighbors (as in the Ugaritic sun and moon gods, Shamash and Yarih, respectively).[20] Incidentally, the mention of "stars" in 1:16 occurs almost as an afterthought, clearly denying any metaphysical role for these astronomical actors. And that is all that is said about stars in this chapter, an unusual de-emphasis of entities that were being worshiped in Israel's contemporary culture.[21]

The Hebrews, who knew of their ancestor Abraham's idolatrous inclinations in Ur (Josh 24:2), and who had sojourned in Egypt and were aware of the similar tendencies of their captors, could clearly appreciate the thrust of the polemic in Gen 1. The severest penalty was attached to the worship of the "sun or the moon or any of the heavenly host" (Deut 17:2–5; also see 4:15–20). In sum, Gen 1:14–19 is "a deliberate attempt to reject out of hand any apotheosizing of the luminaries."[22] God alone is all-powerful!

"Sea Monsters"

In Genesis, the "sea monsters" (1:21) are mere creatures lacking any paranormal power, unlike similar beings referred to by cognate terms in contemporary Ugaritic

---

18. Milgrom, "The Alleged 'Hidden Light,'" 42–43. The luminaries are called "lights" (מְאֹרֹת, *m'orot*); the word is otherwise used in the Pentateuch only to refer to items involved in the lighting fixtures of the tabernacle (Exod 25:6; 27:20; 35:8, 14 [×2], 28; 39:37; Lev 24:2; Num 4:9, 16)—a clue that the account of creation is integrally linked to the building of a sanctuary (see below). Milgrom surmises that just as in these cases, where the מְאוֹר (*m'or*) is not the source or power of light (rather it is the oil in the lamps that is), so also, in the case of the cosmic entities, these heavenly מְאֹרֹת are depicted as agents manifesting the light God had created separately. One is reminded of the exchange between Eustace and Ramandu in Lewis's *The Voyage of the* Dawn Treader, 227: When the former points out that "[i]n our world . . . a star is a huge ball of flaming gas," the latter replies sagely: "Even in your world, my son, that is not what is star is but only what it is made of." While such lights may be explained by theories of astrophysics, questions of primary cause and ontology (what they are, and why and how they came to be) cannot be answered in declarations of existential essence (what they are made of). Also see Introduction for further details on the creation of light.

19. Westermann, *Creation*, 44.

20. These names of these luminaries are also possibly echoed in the names of Canaanite cities, Beth-shemesh (בֵּית-שֶׁמֶשׁ, *bet-shemesh,* "house/shrine of the sun") and Jericho (יְרִיחוֹ, *yrikho,* related to יָרֵחַ, "moon").

21. Hasel, "The Significance of the Cosmology," 13–15.

22. Hamilton, *Genesis: Chapters 1–17*, 128.

creation texts. There, a personified dragon, Tunnanu, likely predecessor of the biblical
תַּנִּין (*tannin*, "sea monster"), has to be overcome by Anat, the creator god.[23] Nor are
these creatures in Genesis deified rivals like the oceanic beasts of pagan creation mythology—the Akkadian Tiamat, the Sumerian Enki, or the Egyptian Nu/Nun; rather,
they are but mortal creatures, created for the glory of God (Ps 148:7). And, opposed to
all these mythical hostile interactions between monsters and their ilk, those animals
in Gen 1:21 are said to be brought into being by "creation" (ברא, *br'*); moreover, God
calls them "good"! Outside of the creation of the heavens and the earth (1:1) and the
creation of man (1:27), ברא is used only of the creation of these "great sea monsters."
Besides, they are also blessed—the first blessing in the Bible upon living beings (1:22;
the only other divine blessing in Gen 1 is upon mankind, in 1:28). Of interest is that
land animals are not said to be blessed as are these sea creatures that include "great sea
monsters" (1:21). All of this seems to be emphasizing the absolute power of God even
over fearsome beasts; even they are products of his facile and unopposed creative act,
and they can never jeopardize his sovereign status. In all likelihood, the addition of
swarming water creatures following the mention of these "great" monsters (1:21) was
to distinguish water fauna into large (these monsters) and small (those "swarming"
ones; see Ps 104:25).[24] The "great" beasts are numbered with all other beings in the
sea—they are just another kind of fish! And they are all blessed by their Maker, for
they do the will of God. In sum the Creator God is sovereign, negating every other
speculation of gods and notions of creation.

1.2   *The creation of mankind in the image of God mandates its responsibility to*
       represent the Creator and his sovereignty to the rest of the cosmos.

The longest description of a day of creation is that of Day 6 (1:24–31), in which creation reaches its zenith: man is formed in the image of God. And, unlike the creations
of days past of which God says "it was good," here he affirms emphatically: "behold,
it was very good" (1:31).[25] On this day, moreover, there are no less than four divine
utterances ("and God said," 1:24, 26, 28, 29); the other days had only one or two such
utterances each. In all the other creative enterprises in Gen 1, divine speeches introduce the new formed entity referred to; here, however, God's intention and purpose
for his final creation is stated first (1:26), in a first-person soliloquy, *before* he proceeds
to create (1:27). This final event of Day 6 was the only one to have such a prelude,
implying that it was an occasion of seriousness and moment, one that called for God's
direct and immediate involvement. Three times the first-person plural is employed:
"let us make," "in our image," and "according to our likeness." And humanity, directly
dependent upon God, is not dependent on its habitat for its source of life or its identity,
as are vegetation, sea creatures, and land animals, that are brought forth by the earth
or the waters: "let the earth sprout . . ."; "let the waters teem . . ."; "let the earth bring

23. Lowenstamm, "Anat's Victory," 22.

24. Hasel, "The Polemic Nature of the Genesis Cosmology," 87.

25. Strikingly, on Day 2, God's approval of his work is absent. Waltke and Fredricks remark that
"[e]ven God did not say that Mondays are good!"(*Genesis*, 62n31).

forth . . ." (1:11; 20, 24). Man alone is in an exalted position, created by God without mediation by other agents.[26] The text emphasizes this in other ways as well. While בָּרָא (*bara'*) has already shown up in 1:1 and 1:21, in 1:27 with the creation of mankind, here in 1:27 it is used three times. And, besides, after creating man, God, for the first time, speaks *to* someone—he addresses man and woman with a blessing (1:28): the first time in Scripture that God's communication occurs to one capable of receiving it.[27] Something momentous has happened on Day 6: the image of God has been placed upon one of God's created beings with whom he can commune!

The significance of the *imago Dei* in which man was made has been the source of much debate. From the prepositions employed with "image" and "likeness," to the actual meaning of these two terms, scholarly opinion scatters itself all across the spectrum. Frequently one finds the interpretation that "image" in 1:26, 27 refers to the *mental/spiritual* faculties shared by man with God—his reason, free-will, self-consciousness, etc., facets of humanity not particularly distinguished in ancient Semitic thought. "In every case there is the suspicion that the commentator may be reading his own values into the text as to what is most significant about man."[28] That it refers to some *physical* resemblance between God and man is also unlikely, seeing that God is spirit; Deut 4:15–16 expressly warns against such a comparison. Perhaps it is to preclude such an association between humanity and deity that there is, for the first time in creation, an explicit separation of genders (1:27), a facet of his creation that God obviously does not share.

> "In his image, God created him" (1:27b).
> "Male and female, He created them" (1:27c).

While the first line indicates man's similarity with God ("him," singular; humans created in God's image), the second line indicates man's similarity with creation, especially the animal world ("them," plural; humans created male and female), ensuring the distinction between God and man.[29] If anything, the parallelism is antithetic: *Man*

---

26. Bird, "'Male and Female,'" 145.

27. The blessing of the sea creatures ("God blessed them, saying . . ."; 1:22) was, of course, also divine speech, but it was not explicitly said to be directed *to* those beings, as was his blessing of man (וַיֹּאמֶר לָהֶם, *wayyōmer lahem*, "and he said *to them*," 1:28). Perhaps not surprisingly, then, the first described act of the human in the garden is that he "calls" (2:19), following which he proceeds to "say" (2:23).

28. Wenham, *Genesis 1–15*, 30. Barth calls this "pure invention in accordance with the requirements of contemporary anthropology" (*Church Dogmatics, III/I*, 193). Also, would not these attributes be true of angelic beings, too?

29. The plural form of the noun, "God" (אֱלֹהִים, *'elohim*), need not necessarily be a covert reference to the Trinity. Nor does the plural verb (Let *us* make . . ."; 1:26) have to be a "plural of majesty/power" or a "plural of self-deliberation" (as, for e.g., in Songs 1:11 or 2 Sam 24:14). The plural form of the verb ("let us make") and the other plural nouns ("in our image," and "according to our likeness") in Gen 1:26, simply correspond אֱלֹהִים, the ordinary word for "God"—plural in form, but singular in meaning. It is possible, however, that the plural may indicate God's address to a heavenly court; but how angels may then be included in God's image ("our" image and likeness, 1:26) is unclear. See Wenham, *Genesis 1–15*, 14, 28; Mathews, *Genesis 1–11:26*, 161n171. The abruptness of the introduction of a celestial congress without any prelude also militates against that interpretation. On the other hand, the plural may indicate inclusion of the Spirit (1:2), God's partner in creation, as in Job 33:4; Ps 104:30; Ezek 37 (also see below).

is in the image of God, but *man—in male and female genders—is nonetheless a creation, and unlike the Creator.*[30] What then, exactly, is the image of God in man all about?

The prepositions, בְּ (*b*, "in") and כְּ (*k*, "according to"), used with "image" and "likeness," respectively (1:26) appear to be interchangeable: 1:26 has "in . . . image" and "according to . . . likeness," but 5:1, 3 inverts the prepositions with "in . . . likeness" and "according to . . . image." In 1:26, the LXX employs the same preposition κατά (*kata*) with both "image" and "likeness." This seeming equivalence of prepositions suggests that there is no significant distinction between the two nouns either. Moreover, while in 1:26, 27, the LXX uses εἰκών (*eikōn*) only for צֶלֶם (*tselem*, "image"), in 5:1, εἰκών is also used for דְּמוּת (*dmut*, "likeness"), again indicating the synonymity of the Hebrew terms. Historical evidence appears to agree. A mid-ninth-century BCE statue of a ruler found in Tell Fakhariyeh (close to the Syrian-Turkish border) is referred to by two Aramaic words in its inscription: *dmwt'* and *ṣlm*, corresponding to the biblical דמות and צלם. The Assyrian version of the writing on the statue does not make this lexical distinction, but uniformly refers to the object as *ṣalmu*. It is reasonable, then, to conclude that the Aramaic terms (and therefore the biblical terms also) are coreferential and interchangeable.[31]

Clines takes the preposition בְּ (*b*) before צלם in 1:26 as a *beth essentiae*, meaning "as"—thus, "as God's image" (Exod 6:3 has a similar construction: בְּאֵל שַׁדָּי [*bʾel shadday*], "as El Shaddai"). Thus, man does not *possess* the image of God, neither is he made *in* the image of God; rather he *is* the image of God—"the visible corporeal representative of the invisible, bodiless God." Man is thus the representation of God "who is imaged in a place where he is not." And, it must be noted, this human representation of the divine is not focused solely upon the physical or spiritual or psychological; indeed, it is corporeal man in his entirety, both material and immaterial constituents thereof, that becomes the *imago Dei*.[32] Thus, while Gen 1 powerfully establishes the transcendence of God outside and above the created order, in the doctrine of the *imago Dei* we find the immanence of God in the world through his image, man. Pericope 1 therefore describes a potent collocation of divine transcendence with divine immanence.[33] The role of mankind was to represent God to every other part of God's creation, to make God tangible, if you will, to the world.[34] "As words are composed in a text to be the icons of the newly presented meanings, human beings are created in the world to be icons of God."[35]

---

30. Bird, "Male and Female," 149–50.

31. Millard and Bordreuil, "A Statue from Syria," 135–41; Garr, "'Image' and 'Likeness,'" 227–28.

32. Clines, "The Image of God," 75–80, 87, 101.

33. Ibid., 88. Clines notes how in the ancient Near East, the primary function of the image was to be the dwelling-place of the spirit of the being of whom the image was made (ibid., 81). If this concept was in the mind of the biblical writer, then the divine first-person plural cohortative in 1:26 ("Let *us* make") might well be a summons to the Spirit (introduced in 1:2) to cooperate in the creation of the image, man, who becomes so by virtue of an infusion of divine breath/spirit (2:7) (ibid., 89–90).

34. Dealing with the Assyrian *ṣalmu*, Bahrani echoes the idea that "image" indicates "substitute through representation"—a "mode of presence" (*The Graven Image*, 144).

35. Van Wolde, "The Text as an Eloquent Guide," 151.

Wenham agrees that the "strongest case" is for the view that the divine image of God upon man makes the latter God's *representative* or vice-regent on earth.[36] In the primary and initial use of צלם, its content or implications are spelled out as וְיִרְדּוּ (*wyirddu,* "and let them rule," 1:26).[37] The "image of God" in Gen 1 is therefore "a royal designation, the precondition or requisite for rule"—see use of רדה (*rdh*) in 1 Kgs 4:24; Pss 72:8; 110:2; etc. As the image of the sovereign Creator of the universe who rules over all by virtue of his creatorship, man rules in place of God as God's "*locum tenens* vizier."[38] Bird notes that the idea of the king as an "image" of the god was a common one in ancient Egypt (and, to a more limited extent, in Mesopotamia). And, of course, in God's eyes every human is related to himself, not just royalty. Psalm 8 appropriately links all mankind with dominion and confers upon all individuals the status of rulership. Such identity between God and man is, therefore, not one of substance or essence, but rather of representative character and role. Thus it appears that צלם and its cognates are used figuratively, assigning man to be a representative of God, with a divine mandate to reflect his reign over his creation.[39] In light of divine transcendence and sovereignty emphasized constantly in Gen 1:1—2:3, it is remarkable that God assigns such representative status to one of his creations. "It was this feature of creation that so astonished the psalmist; for him the Infinite One crowned human infancy with the glory of his rule [Ps 8:6–9]."[40]

This concept of man in Gen 1 is completely antithetical to what is found in contemporary ancient Near Eastern accounts of the creation; there "[t]he world is created not for human beings but for the 'cult,' the housing and feeding of gods."[41] The Akkadian *Atrahasis* creation epic opens with a rebellion of junior gods (the Igigi) against the senior gods (the Anunnaki) because the latter made them undertake arduous physical labor. As a result of this protest, the senior gods capitulated, and humans were created to take over the toil of the gods.[42]

> Let him [man] bear the yoke, . . .
> Let man carry the load of the gods (1.iv.196–197).

36. Wenham, *Genesis 1–15*, 31–32. "It is now generally agreed that the image of God reflected in human persons is after the manner of a king who establishes statues of himself to assert his sovereign rule where the king himself cannot be present" (Brueggemann, *Genesis*, 32). "Just as powerful kings [in the ancient Near East], to indicate their claim to dominion, erect an image of themselves in the provinces of their empire where they do not personally appear, so man is placed upon earth in God's image as God's sovereign emblem" (Von Rad, *Genesis*, 58).

37. So also Hart, "Genesis 1:1–2:3," 318–20, who translates וְיִרְדּוּ as "*so that* they may rule" (1:26).

38. Clines, "The Image of God," 98. This is further substantiated by the use of נוח, *nuakh*, "place/set," for Adam's positioning in Eden (2:15); the same word describes deity's own "rest" in Ps 132:14. Thus man is the vice-regent of God.

39. Bird, "Male and Female," 140, 140n27, 143.

40. Mathews, *Genesis 1–11:26*, 169–70. Needless to say, the image is not effaced after the fall; it is mentioned again in Gen 9:6, and the same commandment of 1:28 is reissued in 9:1, 7. Also see 1 Cor 11:7; Jas 3:9; etc.

41. Clifford, *Creation Accounts*, 65.

42. Dalley, *Myths from Mesopotamia*, 15.

So also in the *Enuma elish.* Manual labor was wearisome and beneath the dignity of the gods. In response to their pleas, and in return for building a house for him, Marduk, the chief god, acquiesced to their demand to create surrogate laborers. Henceforth, man would be assigned to undertake toil for the gods, freeing them from that burden. Marduk declared[43]:

> Let me create a primeval man.
> The work of the gods shall be imposed (on him),
> and so they shall be at leisure (6.6–9).

Unlike these accounts, Genesis presents man as the culmination of God's creative activity, created for a specific purpose. Rather than the result of a contingency plan for cheap labor or to provide relief from toilsome drudgery, man is deliberately created, blessed, and provided for by God (1:27–29). The prevailing Mesopotamian view of man's role included their providing food for the gods—"to feed people and sustain the gods" (*Atrahasis* 1.vii.339). But in Genesis, it is the other way around—God instructs man: "every plant . . . it shall be food for you" (1:29).[44]

In sum, the *imago Dei* indicates the royal office of humans as God's representatives and agents, authorized to actualize and manifest the rule of God over his creation. Gen 1 exhorts all of God's people, without exception or distinction, to acknowledge their royal vocation as God's representatives within his creation. Of course the ultimate consummation of the image of God is accomplished only in Christ, the perfection of the divine image, an image mankind will share fully at the eschaton (1 John 3:2). In the present age, however, one becomes conformed more and more to the image of God insofar as one becomes more and more like Christ (Rom 8:29), thus behooving mankind to live worthy of the Son of God, meeting divine demand by the power of the Spirit of God. "The image is fully realized [in this life] only through obedience to Christ; this is how man, the image of God, . . . can become fully man, fully the image of God."[45]

1.3   *The arena in which mankind, in the image of God, authoritatively represents its sovereign Creator is the cosmos, the Temple of God.*

According to Walton, ancient ontology considered the cosmos as a business that related to clients (with a proprietor, I might add), rather than as a relationship-less machine run by Someone (or, in modernist conception, running on its own).[46] However, the best analogy is what the Bible itself employs: the cosmos is a "Temple," with a deity (Yahweh) and devotees (mankind). This potent analogy between temple and cosmos in the creation account of Gen 1 is not merely a possibility; in a number of places in

---

43. Tablets 4–6; see ibid., 249–61.

44. Ibid., 18.

45. Clines, "The Image of God," 103. Also see Kuruvilla, *Privilege the Text!* 238–68.

46. See Walton, *Genesis 1,* 45. Also see Walton, "Reading Genesis 1," 157–62. Walton observes how, in ancient Near Eastern literature, even the names of temples depicted them in cosmic terms: e.g., Edimgalanna = "House of the great bond of heaven," and Etemenanki = "House, foundation platform of heaven and underworld" (ibid., 160).

the OT, this comparison is explicitly brought forth. For instance, in Isa 66:1–2, one sees a "cosmos-sized temple" linked to creation.[47]

> Thus says Yahweh,
> "The heavens are My throne and the earth My footstool.
> Where then is a house you will build for Me?
> And where is a place for My rest?
> For My hand made all these things,
> And all these things came into being," declares Yahweh.

The idea of cosmos being modeled on the temple of the deity was also widely prevalent in the ancient Near East. The Egyptian temple was "a microcosm of the world, the realm of the god"—blue ceilings represented the sky studded with golden stars; the floor represented the earth with lotus and papyrus depicted as growing on columns; the holy of holies was regarded as the primeval hillock from which the god Rê appeared out of the chaos, with two towers representing the horizons between which the sun-god moves; etc.[48] Even in Palestine-Syria, the temple was "a symbolic microcosm of the deity's world."[49] Rabbinic thought attested to this connection between the creation of the cosmos and the temple in Mt. Zion.[50] For Josephus also (*J.W.* 5.5.4–5), the temple was a microcosm with the tapestry of the veil bearing "a panorama/design of the heavens [τὴν οὐράνιον θεορίαν, *tēn ouranion theorian*]" and its colors and material reflecting fire (scarlet), air (blue), sea (purple), and earth (fine linen). On the tabernacle, Josephus noted that "every one of these objects is intended to recall and represent the universe" (*Ant.* 3.7.7). The courts and the holy place, where the priests were allowed access, represented the earth and the sea; and the Holy of Holies, where God dwelt and the high priest could enter once a year, represented heaven (*Ant.* 3.6.4)—"the throne room of God" (Ps 11:4).[51] Likewise, Philo declared: "We ought to look upon the universal world as the highest and truest temple of God, having for its most holy place that most sacred part of the essence of all existing things, namely, the heaven; and for ornaments, the stars; and for priests, the subordinate ministers of his power, namely, the angels.[52] In other words, the primordial character of the world was captured in the temple, and the temple served as the "visible, tangible token of the act

---

47. Ibid., 179. Reflecting Isa 66:1, Solomon exclaims in 1 Kgs 8:27 how even "heaven and the highest heaven" could never contain God, not to mention the temple he had just built.

48. Nelson, "The Significance of the Temple in the Ancient Near East: I," 47–48.

49. Wright, "The Significance of the Temple in the Ancient Near East: III," 67.

50. In fact, it was asserted that the world was created *from* Zion. "[R. Eliezer the Great:] 'But the sages say, both [heavens and earth] were created from Zion . . . as the Bible says, "From Zion, perfect in beauty, God shone forth" (Ps 50:2). This means, from it the beauty of the world was perfected'" (*b. Yoma* 54b). In the same vein is *Tanḥuma, Kedoshim* 10: "And the Temple is in the center [navel] of Jerusalem . . . and beginning with it the world was put on its foundation."

51. Levenson, *Sinai and Zion*, 122.

52. *Spec. Laws* 1.12.66; also see his *Moses* 2.16.80; 2.18.88.

of creation."[53] So much so, "it is axiomatic that every sanctuary is constituted as an *imago mundi* [image of the world], with the cosmos as paradigmatic model."[54]

> And He [Yahweh] built His sanctuary like the heights,
> Like the earth that He founded forever.
> (Psalm 78:69)

Perhaps it is in light of God's creative action that he is the one who is considered in this psalm as the temple-builder, not Solomon. In fact, the building of the temple by Yahweh (Ps 78:69) is said to *precede* even the selection of David as God's regent (78:70). Both history and time are really of less importance than the "deeper meaning" of the temple in its relation to creation—its "protological character."[55] In such a sense then, Yahweh had built his Temple, the "heavens and the earth," and therefore the Solomonic temple simply reflected what Yahweh had already created. This extension of the Temple precincts to the rest of the cosmos "is anything but the desacralization of sacred space. It is, instead, the infinite extension of sacred space, the elimination of the 'profane,' that which stands *pro fano*, 'in front of the temple.' The world in its fullness is the Temple."[56] All of cosmos is God's Temple; and all of cosmos is therefore a sanctified station, and it is in this cosmic arena that man is to represent the sovereign Creator. This is an important thrust of the account of Genesis 1:1–2:3. What man's role might be, as implied in 1:1–2:3, will involve an understanding of 2:1–3 and the concept of the cosmos as the Temple of God.

1.4   The "rest" of God within his Temple, the cosmos, following its "dedication," concludes God's creative enterprise and commences his reign over his creation.

If the cosmos is equivalent to the Temple, the seven-day creation of the cosmos must be, in effect, the dedication of that universal sanctuary. In fact, such seven-day dedications appear to have been the norm in temple- and tabernacle-building elsewhere in the Bible. The inauguration of Solomon's temple was not only seven days long, it also took seven years to build the edifice (1 Kgs 6:38); it was dedicated in the seventh month (8:2) during the Feast of Booths, a seven-day festival (Deut 16:13–15); and, to top it off, this dedicatory event also had a couple of seven-day banquets to go with it (2 Chr 7:9; 1 Kgs 8:65). The play on sevens goes further: Solomon's prayer of dedication of the temple is itself structured with seven petitions.[57] The seventh one (1 Kgs 8:46–48) is, in turn, made up of a seven-fold play on the roots שָׁבָה (*shavah*, "deport/

---

53. Levenson, "The Temple," 283.

54. Meyers, *The Tabernacle Menorah,* 171. See Walton, *Genesis 1,* 101–19.

55. Levenson, *Sinai and Zion,* 106. "Protological," i.e., having the nature of the beginning of things, as opposed to "eschatological" (ibid., 103).

56. Levenson, "The Temple," 296. Thus the physical temple was thus only a local microcosm of the universal macrocosm (Levenson, *Sinai and Zion,* 138).

57. Levenson, "The Temple," 288. Thomas Mann opined wryly: "Partisans of the decimal system might prefer a round number, though seven is a good handy figure in its way, picturesque, with a savour of the mythical; one might even say that it is more filling to the spirit than a dull academic half-' (*The Magic Mountain,* 697).

carry off" into the "land" of captivity) and שׁוּב (*shuv*, "to return"): there are four statements of *deportation to enemy land* alternating with three statements of *return*, for a total of seven.[58]

8:46b	Deportation (שׁבה) to enemy land
8:47aα	Return (שׁוּב)
8:47aβ	Deportation to enemy land
8:47bα	Return
8:47bβ	Deportation to enemy land
8:48aα	Return
8:48aβ	Deportation to enemy land

This multiplex repetition of sevens in the sanctuary narratives leads Levenson to conclude that the temple-dedication account is modeled on the seven days of creation. Walton rightly thinks it is the other way round: the seven days of creation are modeled on the pattern of the seven-day temple dedication, a common-enough motif in the cognitive environment of the ancient Near East.[59] He calls the underlying concept of Genesis 1 a temple *homology*. In distinction to a metaphor that generally goes in one direction (e.g., love is a river, a rock, or a rainbow; but none of these is, itself, love), a homology goes both ways: the cosmos is a Temple and the temple is a cosmos.[60] Therefore, it is not surprising that there are some striking verbal similarities between the account of the construction of the tabernacle (Exod 39–40) and that of the creation of the world (Gen 1–2)[61]:

---

58. Levenson, "Paronomasia," 135–38. *Pesiq. Rab.* 6.6 also connects the Genesis account of creation with the temple construction project. Kearney shows how each of the seven divine speeches of Exod 25–31 (on the institution of the tabernacle) respectively alludes to the corresponding day of creation in Gen 1:1–2:3. Speech 1 (Exod 25:1–30:10): light (in 27:20–21); speech 2 (30:11–16): a division of all Israel into upper and lower, rich and poor (= division of the waters above and below the firmament); speech 3 (in 30:17–21): bronze laver (= sea, 1 Kgs 7:23); speech 4 (Exod 30:22–33): holy anointing oil (= luminaries, to which the Davidic reign was likened, Ps 89: 20, 37–38); speech 5 (Exod 30:34–38): incense from "onycha," a product of marine mollusks (= sea creatures); speech 6 (31:1–11): Spirit-filled manufacturers with wisdom, understanding, and skill (= man, with the breath of God; see 1 Kgs 5:16; 7:14); speech 7 (Exod 31:12–17): Sabbath ("Creation and Liturgy," 375–78). Regarding the construction of the tabernacle, it is notable that God spoke to Moses on the seventh day after the latter went up Mt. Sinai (Exod 24:15–16). And in *Tg. Ps.-J.* to Exod 39:37, the tabernacle's candelabrum is said to have been "ordained to correspond to the seven stars, that rule in their prescribed places in the firmament by day and by night."

59. Levenson, "The Temple," 288–89; Walton, *Genesis 1*, 182. "[T]he 'building account' may safely be added to the list of traditional literary types or forms recognizable as common to Israelite and neighboring literatures of the ancient Near East in general and in Mesopotamia in particular" (Hurowitz, *I Have Built You an Exalted House*, 312).

60. Walton, *Genesis 1*, 187; see also 109n327.

61. Weinfeld, "Sabbath," 503. Also, *Num. Rabb.* 12:13 sees the tabernacle and temple as microcosmic representations of God's creation.

Genesis 1:31	Exodus 39:43
"*all* that He had *done*,	"*all* the work,
and behold, it was good"	*and behold*, they had *done* it"
Genesis 2:1	**Exodus 39:32**
"And they were *completed* … and *all*"	"and it was *completed*, *all*"
Genesis 2:2	**Exodus 40:33**
"And God *completed* …	"Moses *completed*
His *work* which He had done"	the *work*"
Genesis 2:3	**Exodus 39:43**
"and He *blessed*"	"and he *blessed*"
Genesis 2:3	**Exodus 40:9**
"and He *sanctified* it"	"and he shall *sanctify*"

With this correspondence between creation of the world and construction of the sanctuaries, the consequences of both fabrications also turn out to be similar. Both programs culminate in "rest" (נוּחַ, *nuakh*): with regard to the tabernacle, rest is announced in Exod 20:11 (of God); 23:12; and Deut 5:14 (of his people). With regard to the temple, it becomes the place of God's rest (מְנוּחָה, *mnukhah*, from נוּחַ, *nuakh*, Ps 132:13–14; and especially Isa 66:1–2).[62]

The idea in Gen 2 of deity resting in the newly-constructed sanctuary appears to have been extant in contemporary Egypt and Assyria.[63] *Enuma elish* explicitly connected the temple of the deity with rest[64]:

> Let us found a shrine, a sanctuary there.
> Whenever we arrive, let us rest in in it (6.41).

Both the creation of the world and the construction of the tabernacle also conclude with the concept of the Sabbath (שבת, *shbt*, in Gen 2:2 and Exod 31:12–17; 35:13).[65] "Sabbath" and "sanctuary" are considered in parallel in Lev 19:30 and 26:2; in Isa 56:4–7, it is the temple that is juxtaposed with the Sabbath. From the monarchy period on, Israelite practice associated the dedication of a temple with the establishment of a resting place for deity during Sukkoth (Feast of Tabernacles, 1 Kgs 8:2; and see Ezra 3:4, also in the context of "evening" and "morning" sacrifices), which was observed over a seven-day period, after which Yahweh would take up his residence. There is likewise a seven-day connection in Ezekiel's temple (Ezek 43:25–26). In other words, the seven-day Sabbath structure was not a separate motif that had been tacked on to the creation narrative with independent literary or theological intentions. Rather,

---

62. Levenson, *Sinai and Zion*, 144–45. Incidentally, Solomon was chosen to build the temple because he, himself, was a "man of rest" (אִישׁ מְנוּחָה, *'ish mnukhah*, 1 Chr 22:9).

63. Weinfeld, "Sabbath," 502.

64. Also see *Enuma elish* 1.71–77 (Dalley, *Myths from Mesopotamia*, 235, 262).

65. The injunction regarding the Sabbath is also the seventh in a series of commands regarding the construction of the tabernacle; each of these begins with "And Yahweh said to Moses" (Exod 25:1; 30:11, 17, 22, 34; 31:1; and 31:12).

it was reflective of the fact that seven days of furbishing the sanctuary preceded its habitation by deity.[66]

"Seven days" in period literature shows up in the construction of the other contemporary sanctuaries in the ancient Near East: Baal takes that many days to build his abode (*Epic of Baal* 6.16–38[67]). It shows up as well, in the installation of deity in its proper abode: in the á-ki-ti festival, on the seventh day, each city reenacted "the mythologized, original, glorious entry of its own chief god into his city" and "his assumption of suzerainty."[68] Thus the liturgical significance of "seven days" is apparent. Weinfeld declared that "the Israelite priesthood dramatized the conclusion of the creation by means of the Sabbath, just as the peoples of the Ancient Near East dramatized their creation epics in cultic dramas," leading him to conclude that "the *Sitz im Leben* of Gen 1:1–2:3 is indeed cultic-liturgic."[69]

In the Sumerian temple-building account described on the two cylinders of Gudea is yet another seven-day dedication ceremony that concludes with the human ruler (Gudea) entering the throne room to meet with the head deity of the pantheon, Ningirsu, "who has taken up his rest on the dais in order to begin ruling from the temple."[70] The account proclaimed the functions of the temple and installation of the functionaries, enabling the entry of the deity on the seventh day to take up his rest, at which point the temple became functional. Averbeck makes a detailed comparison between the Gudea texts and biblical temple accounts, concluding that there were indeed parallels between the temple dedications in each.[71] He includes, among the parallels: fertility (Gen 1:22); the divine call for building (1:1, 3, 6, 9, 11: "let there be"); construction according to divine plan (1:3, 6, 9, 11, 14–15, 20, 24, 26: "and it was so"); laudatory description of the temple (1, 4, 10, 12, 18, 25, 31: "and it was good"); blessings on the temple (2:3); seven-day temple dedication (1:1–2:3); and the temple's association with kingship including the commissioning of a ruler (1:26–28). In other words, like the seven-day ceremony of the Gudea Cylinders, Gen 1 is performing the preliminaries—establishing functions and functionaries: light/darkness, heavens/waters, dry land/vegetation, luminaries, fish/birds, animals, mankind—prior to Yahweh's "rest."[72] With functions of the temple identified and assigned, with functionaries installed and directed, the deity's entrance into his "rest" in the sanctuary marks the commencement of its proper function. "Only then is the temple functional; only then

---

66. Walton, *Genesis*, 155. God's residence with his people in the tabernacle and temple is well attested in the OT: Exod 40:34–Lev 1:1; Lev 9:23; 16:2; Num 9:15–23; 1 Kgs 8:10–11; 2 Chr 5:13–14; 7:1–2.

67. *Epic of Baal*, CTA 4 VI.22–33; *ANET* 134; also see CTA 6 III.18; *ANET* 140.

68. Cohen, *The Cultic Calendars*, 393, 395, 405.

69. Weinfeld, "Sabbath," 501, 510.

70. Walton, *Genesis 1*, 118. These cylinders, dating back to the third millennium BCE, narrate a Sumerian myth in cuneiform, about the building of a temple for the god Ningirsu. Like the creation story, the temple built by Gudea arises out of the primeval waters. For a translation, see *COS* 2.155 and *ANET* 268–69.

71. See Averbeck, "Sumer," 119–21.

72. Walton, *Genesis 1*, 182–83.

is it real; only then is it a temple. It is at this point that the deity is able to settle into his/her new home and is able to begin the job of ruling the cosmos and maintaining order."[73]

All this to say, the structuring of the creation account of Gen 1:1–2:3 may be less dependent on the historical events behind the text, than with the theological intent in front of it—to portray the cosmos as a Temple for Yahweh, and to mark its preparation and dedication for full functionality, parallel to other temple-dedication schemes, both within and without the Bible. When the cosmos-Temple is dedicated, it becomes functional, for it is then that God enters to "rest." "On the seventh day there is something of a bond, or union, between Creator and creation, as God enters his world, the king enthroned in his temple, vivifying and sanctifying it with his Presence."[74]

What exactly is this "rest"? The question of whether God actually worked on Day 7 has vexed many. After all, God did bless and sanctify on that day (Gen 2:3)—was that work? Or did he only cease from his creative enterprises? But God's creation, employing ברא, *brʾ*, is also found in Exod 34:10; Num 16:30; Ps 51:12; Isa 4:5; 41:20; 43:1, 7, 15; 45:8; 65:17, 18; etc. Thus it seems that God's "rest" was not really a cessation of activity. As early as the second-century BCE, the Hellenistic Jewish writer Aristobulus declared: "[T]hat God rested [from ἀποπαύω, *apopauō*; the LXX of Gen 2:2, 3 uses καταπαύω, *katapauō*, for the same idea] on the seventh day . . . does not mean, as some interpret, that God no longer does anything. . . . [H]aving set all things in order, he maintains and alters them so. . . ."[75] R. Akiba, in reply to a query about whether God was working when he sent wind and rain on the Sabbath, argued that such an action undertaken by God fell within boundaries of the permission for a person to carry objects four cubits on the Sabbath in his own house; the whole world is God's "own, private domain," and thus his actions are entirely admissible (*Gen. Rab.* 11.5; also see *Exod. Rab.* 30.9). Such an understanding may conceivably be the basis of Jesus' declaration that his Father was working and so must he (John 5:17). Dodd observes that John 5 mentions "two aspects of divine activity which are indubitably perpetual, ζωοποιεῖν [*zōopoiein*, giving life, 5:21] and κρίνειν [*krinein*, judging, 5:22]"; these are "but an inevitable accompaniment or consequence of His work for the salvation of men."[76] Thus the "rest" of God is not exactly an abstention from work.[77] So also Chrysostom (*Hom. Gen.* 10.18):

> You see, in saying at this point that God rested from his works, Scripture teaches us that he ceased creating and bringing from non-being into being on the seventh day, whereas Christ, in saying that "my Father is at work up until now and I am at work," reveals his unceasing care for us: he calls "work" the maintenance

---

73. Ibid., 116, 117. "This day of silent divine rest is a consummation of all that has gone before because it inaugurates God's residence within the cosmic temple" (McBride, "Divine Protocol," 14).

74. Morales, *The Tabernacle Pre-figured*, 93.

75. *OTP* 2: 841–42; this is from Fragment 5, 11–12, "On the Sabbath," as cited by Eusebius, *Hist. eccl.* 13:12:9–16.

76. Dodd, *Interpretation*, 322.

77. However, that may be what is mandated for man in the Mosaic Law.

of created things, bestowal of permanence on them, and governance of them through all time.

"Rest" (שָׁבַת and נוּחַ, *shabat* and *nuakh*, both verbs), with Yahweh as the one resting, is rare in the OT.[78] Instead, he is usually the one portrayed as providing or withholding rest from his people. Walton notes that שׁבת in the Qal with God as the subject only occurs in Gen 2:2–3, and נוח in a similar construction only in Exod 20:11. The only other notations of divine rest employ the related noun מְנוּחָה, *mnukhah*, with reference to the temple in Jerusalem, as, for instance, in Ps 132:8, 14[79]:

> Let us go to His tabernacle;
> Let us worship at His footstool.
> Arise, Yahweh, to Your resting place [מְנֻחָתוֹ, *mnukhato*],
> You and the ark of Your strength.
> For Yahweh has chosen Zion;
> He desired it for His dwelling place.
> This is My resting place [מְנֻחָתִי] forever;
> Here I will dwell, for I have desired it.
> (Ps 132:7–8, 13–14)

Psalm 29 describes the mighty Yahweh who controls the waters, fires, hills, the wilderness, forests and animals; and he is seated in his temple as "king forever," from where he strengthens and blesses his people (29:9–11). Psalm 93 is even more explicit about linking creation and enthronement: Yahweh establishes the world firmly and immovably. Indeed, after noting that the *world* is "established" (93:1), the psalmist asserts that Yahweh's *throne* is "established" (93:2), clearly endorsing a link between the two. In fact, this psalm is commonly recited on the day before the Sabbath (*b. Tam.* 7.4; the LXX superscription of this psalm reads "For the day before the Sabbath"). Concurring with the seating of Yahweh as king after his creative endeavors, *b. Roš Haš.* 31a declares: "It has been taught: 'R. Judah said in the name of R. Akiba . . . "On the sixth day they [the Levites] said, 'The Lord reigneth, He is clothed in majesty, because He completed His work and reigned over His creatures.'"'"[80]

Thus, Yahweh's enthronement in the Temple is, essentially, his "rest." In other words, for this deity, "rest" is not disengagement, unlike the portrayal in contemporary polytheistic accounts of divine "rest" as social activity among the gods, conceiving of those gods as human-like, with a need for sleep and sex. "Rest" for Yahweh is, rather, engagement of the divine in "the control room of the cosmos from which order in the

---

78. A third word, נפשׁ, *nfs*, does connote God's "refreshment" (Exod 31:17, the only instance), "but the occurrences are too few to locate the nuance precisely" (Walton, *Genesis*, 147).

79. Also see Isa 66:1 (cited earlier); and Ps 95:11 which, with 95:1–7, suggests a temple location for this royal psalm. See Walton, *Genesis 1*, 180–81n162. A "rest" for the ark in the tabernacle/temple is also found in Num 10:33–35; 1 Chr 6:31; 28:2; 2 Chr 6:41.

80. So also *'Abot R. Nat.* 17b: "Which [psalm] did he [Adam] recite on the sixth day? 'The Lord reigneth; . . .' because He then completed all His works, was exalted and sat enthroned in the heights of the universe."

cosmos is maintained."[81] "'[R]est' does not imply relaxation but more like achieving equilibrium and stability. . . . Inhabiting his resting place is the equivalent to being enthroned—it is connected to taking up his role as sovereign ruler of the cosmos."[82]

In Isa 66:1 (noted earlier) also, Yahweh's "rest" encompasses not only Mt. Zion, but the whole earth; this is similar to 11:9–10 where the "rest" of the root of Jesse, though focused on Zion, influences and brings into its compass a state of rest for the whole earth.[83]

> They will not do evil or destroy in all My holy mountain,
> For the earth will be full of the knowledge of Yahweh
> As the waters cover the sea.
> Then it will come to pass in that day
> The root of Jesse will stand as a signal for the peoples,
> The nations will seek [Him],
> And His resting place [מְנֻחָתוֹ] will become glorious.
> (Isa 11:9–10)

Thus, the "rest" of God and his regent issues in "rest" for the entire world—peoples and nations.[84] In his dedicatory address for the "resting place" for Yahweh (2 Chr 6:41), Solomon refers back to 1 Chr 22:6–10 (see 2 Chr 6:4–11); in that original word of Yahweh to David, God had promised that during Solomon's days, "peace and quiet" would be given to Israel. This implicit linkage of the "rest" of Yahweh with his granting of "peace and quiet" to his people suggests that "YHWH's 'rest' entails not only his permanent residence among the people, but also the *effect* of his presence." The concept of "rest" is thus not only protological, but thoroughly eschatological—the anticipated "total condition of the society under this king," his will being done in all the cosmos. This close connection between Yahweh's rest in the Temple and the occupation of his throne makes it clear that the two notions are equivalent: he rests = he rules.[85] Indeed, following right after the creation of man, it is clear why God can "rest/reign" in his Temple: a surrogate is now doing his work, representing him tangibly to his creation.

In light of this Temple framework (and also because the next pericope contains a description of the Garden of Eden, the archetypal sanctuary and/or the paradisiacal garden in the Temple), "we can conclude that the cosmology of Genesis 1 is built on the platform of temple theology: both of these ideas—rest and the garden—are integral to the temple theology of the ancient world."[86] In sum, in the ancient Near Eastern cognitive environment, "rest" was blended with "rule," akin to an incumbent entering

---

81. Walton, *Genesis 1*, 105, 180.

82. Idem, *Genesis*, 148.

83. Both Isa 11:10 and 66:1, with announcements of rest, are immediately preceded by the assurance that "They will not do evil or destroy in all My holy mountain" (11:9 and 65:25; the phrases are exactly identical).

84. Laansma, *'I Will Give You Rest,'* 51–52.

85. Ibid., 40, 48.

86. Walton, *Genesis 1*, 187. The notion of the Garden of Eden as an archetypal sanctuary will be considered in the next pericope.

into the governor's mansion or the White House, residing and resting, hosting and presiding, engaging in all the prerogatives, enjoying all the perquisites, and exercising all the responsibilities of rulership.[87]

> The entire cosmos is viewed as a temple designed to function on behalf of humanity; and when God takes up his rest in this cosmic temple, it "comes into (functional) existence" . . . by virtue of his presence. The rest that God thereby achieves and enjoys facilitates his rule of the cosmos by providing the means by which he engages in the control of the cosmos that he has set in order (which is what is meant, in modern terms, by "he created").[88]

Thus it makes perfect sense that life inside the temple, this microcosm of the cosmic Temple, is one that is deeply yearned for, especially by the psalmist (23:6; 27:4–6; 42:1–2; 63:1–2; 84:1–2—the "beatific vision"), for this was the original goal of creation.[89] Indeed, Day 7 is the only day that is blessed; and the very first sanctification to occur in the Bible is that of this day of rest (Gen 2:3).[90] In this section is another piece of evidence pointing to the literary form of the account—the absence of the "evening + morning" formula on Day 7, a refrain invariably present for the descriptions of Days 1–6. In light of the meticulous composition of 1:1–2:3, this absence must be recognized as intentional: Day 7 is never concluded.[91] The theology of the Sabbath is thereby established: God's resting and reigning never ends. Day 7 is, as Walton notes, "far from a postscript."[92] It is rather a prologue (or the conclusion of a prologue) to an ongoing saga that is yet to be consummated. It is probably not coincidental that the Hebrew Bible begins with an account of God's creation of heaven and earth (Gen 1:1) and ends with a command from God to build a temple in Jerusalem (2 Chr 36:23; 2 Chronicles is the last book of the Hebrew Bible in Jewish reckoning): in twenty-four books, biblical history goes from creation (Temple) to Temple (creation). "The world which the Temple incarnates in a tangible way is not the world of history but the world of creation, the world not as it is but as it was meant to be and as it was on the first Sabbath. . . . It is the higher world in which the worshiper characteristically wishes he could dwell forever."[93]

87. Walton, *Genesis 1*, 116. "Texts describing the creation of the world and those describing the construction of a shrine are parallel. The Temple and the world stand in an intimate and intrinsic connection. The two projects cannot ultimately be distinguished or disengaged" (Levenson, "The Temple," 288).

88. Walton, *Genesis 1*, 190.

89. Levenson, *Sinai and Zion*, 176.

90. Day 7 is also literarily separated (sanctified?). The prologue of Gen 1:1 has: "In the beginning *God created* the **heavens and earth**." Following the creation account (1:3–31), the epilogue, 2:1–3, separates the emphasized elements with three notices of Day 7 in between: "Thus were completed the **heavens and the earth** . . . ["seventh day" (×3)] . . . which *God created* and made." Thus Day 7 stands apart both theologically and artistically.

91. "[T]he seventh day hath no evening, nor hath it setting; because Thou hast sanctified it to an everlasting continuance" (Augustine, *Conf.* 13.36.51).

92. Walton, *Genesis 1*, 190.

93. Levenson, "The Temple," 295, 297–98.

Thus at the very beginning of Scripture, a relationship with God is established: God is found to be absolutely sovereign; man is created in/as God's image to rule over God's creation in the arena of the cosmos—God's Temple, in which he rests to reign. The "hows" of the relationship between Creator and creation, and the keeping of divine demand, consume the remainder of Scripture.[94] A theology is presented that is indeed alien to that of Israel's neighbors, "so thorough and fundamental in the reorientation it demanded, that one needed, as it were, to be born into another world to understand it."[95] Literally, the text is God's invitation to his people to live in a world that runs by his precepts, that is is geared for his priorities, and that engages his practices. Even in these early chapters of Scripture, theology is taught, a divine demand is made, an ideal world is projected. All God's children, even those living far away in time and space are invited to learn the theology, acquiesce to divine demand, and inhabit God's ideal world. The long story that follows the creation account, detailed in Gen 2:4–Rev 22:21, can only be comprehended, and its world inhabited, if this first pericope, the overture to that story, is rightly heard, understood, and heeded.

SERMON FOCUS AND OUTLINES

THEOLOGICAL FOCUS OF PERICOPE 1 FOR PREACHING[A]

1 God exercises his sovereignty over the cosmic Temple in which he rests and reigns, by deputizing humans bearing his image, to represent him to the rest of the cosmos (1:1–2:3).

A. In the view of preaching espoused in this commentary, the exposition of the theology of the pericope (crystallized in the "Theological Focus"), with all the power and potency of the text, is the critical task of the homiletician. Needless to say, the preacher must also provide the congregation with specifics on how the theological concept of each pericope may be put into practice so that lives are changed for the glory of God.

The preacher must remember that this is the first pericope of the Bible. As such, it sets the stage for everything that follows—the interaction between God and man, God's demands and how man fails to keep them, and God's gracious response to such failure. This first preaching unit thus focusses on preparing for this interaction: God is sovereign and he reigns, with man in his image representing God as his deputy to the rest of God's creation.

A considerable portion of the Notes was given to substantiating this theological focus, the biblical author's *doing* with what he was *saying*. Of course, most of that validation need not (should not!) show up in the sermon, but only what the preacher deems necessary for a particular audience. The role of man is probably what should be focused on in the sermon: created by God, to be like God, to rule for God. As the opening pericope of Scripture, it might be a good occasion to establish some of the foundation that undergirds what application involves, here and in the rest of the Bible. The concept of a world, an ideal realm, as conceived by and created by God, in which

---

94. Blocher, *In the Beginning*, 57–58.
95. Stek, "What Says the Scripture?" 230.

man was made to dwell in alignment with the demands of God, has been discussed briefly in the Introduction and may be worth laying out for the congregation. This ideal world is where God's precepts (how things should go) are paradigmatic, where God's priorities (what things are important) are supreme, and where God's practices (way things are done) are followed. To align with divine precepts, priorities, and practices is to conform to the will of the Creator for his creation. It is the duty of the preacher to employ each pericope in the Bible to call God's people to conform to his will as expressed in that pericope—an alignment with the King—*Represent the Ruler!* i.e., our response is to live as our Ruler would have us, tangibly depicting him to the rest of his creation.

Possible Preaching Outlines for Pericope 1[96]

I. GOD: Sovereign of the Cosmos
      God's creative work: 1:1–25; contemporary ANE accounts
      God's reigning "rest": 2:1–3; cosmos as Temple, and rest as reign

II. MAN: Representative of the Sovereign
      Man as the *imago Dei*: 1:26–31
      Man's representational role in Genesis vs. role in contemporary ANE accounts
      What this representation involves: a tangible depiction of God/godliness to the world
      The concept of living in God's world, abiding by his precepts, priorities, and practices

III. US: *Represent the Ruler!*[97]
      Failure of man to represent the divine Sovereign
      How this representation of the Ruler may be concretely actualized in listeners' lives

Another option is given below, one that might be more textual in sequence[98]:

96. One must see the points in these outlines as "moves," rather than static chunks of information dumped on the unwary listener. Preachers would do well to familiarize themselves—discriminatingly—with the "new homiletic" as espoused by Fred B. Craddock (*Preaching* [Nashville: Abingdon, 1985]; *As One Without Authority* [St. Louis, Mo.: Chalice, 2001]), Eugene L. Lowry (*The Homiletical Plot: The Sermon as Narrative Art Form* [rev. ed.; Louisville: Westminster John Knox, 2001]), and David Buttrick (*Homiletic: Moves and Structures* [Philadelphia: Fortress, 1987]). A helpful summary can be found in Richard Eslinger, *The Web of Preaching: New Options in Homiletical Method* (Nashville: Abingdon, 2002). The outlines provided in every case are deliberately skimpy; they are intended merely to be suggestions for further thought—rough-hewn stones to be polished by the preacher. It is nigh impossible to prescribe an outline without knowing the particular audience it is to be used for, and therefore this commentary will refrain from micromanaging homiletics for the preacher. Some equally abbreviated suggestions for development are provided below each main point.

97. Outlines in this commentary will have an imperative of some sort as a major sermonic point—the application (shown in italics). The specificity and direction of that imperative is between the Holy Spirit, the text, the preacher, and the audience.

98. There is nothing magical about having a sermonic outline that parallels the structure of the text. Spoken sermons are a different form of media than scripted biblical texts. The former do not necessarily have to follow the sequence of argument or parallel the narration of the latter. What kind of outline is appropriate for the audience in the pew, in a sermon uttered by the preacher in the pulpit, must be decided upon preaching event by preaching event. On the other hand, there is something to be said for ease of following along (from a congregant's point of view) with a sermon whose structure closely parallels the structure of the biblical text that lies open in the hearer's lap. Parallelism of structure between text and sermon means fewer ungainly leaps around the text by the preacher. The fewer these leaps, the greater

I. God Creates the World
>   God's creative work: 1:1–25; contemporary ANE accounts

II. [and then . . .] God Creates Mankind
>   Man as the *imago Dei*: 1:26–31

III. [and then . . .] God Rests to Reign
>   God's reigning "rest": 2:1–3; cosmos as Temple, and rest as reign

IV. [because . . .] Man Represents God
>   Man's representational role in Genesis vs. role in contemporary ANE accounts
>   What this representation involves: a tangible depiction of God/godliness to the world
>   The concept of living in God's world, abiding by his precepts, priorities, and practices

V. [so . . .] *Represent the Ruler!*
>   Failure of man to represent the divine Sovereign
>   How this representation of the Ruler may be concretely actualized in listeners' lives

---

the clarity, and thus, hopefully, the firmer the assimilation of truth in the hearts, minds, and lives of listeners.

PERICOPE 2

The Fall

Genesis 2:4–3:24

[Man and Woman Established in the Garden; The Fall and Judgment]

REVIEW, SUMMARY, PREVIEW

Review of Pericope 1: In Gen 1:1–2:3, the cosmos is depicted as a Temple, and the "rest" of God is designated as his reign therein. The role of man, created in God's image, is to represent this sovereign Creator to the rest of the cosmos by abiding by the precepts, priorities, and practices that govern the divine domain of the cosmos-Temple.

Summary of Pericope 2: In this pericope, man and woman are settled in the Garden of Eden, wherein is provided everything for their needs, including that of human relationship, and guidance as to how to conduct their lives within that "sanctuary," in the presence of God, in dependence upon him. Unfortunately, man and woman choose independence, opting to decide for themselves what is good for them, and sin enters the arena of human history. The consequences are grave and ongoing, for themselves, their posterity, and the rest of creation.

Preview of Pericope 3: The next pericope (4:1–26) describes the first human death—murder—and God's discipline visited upon the criminal, Cain. Throughout, he is proud, disdainful, and unrepentant, though God extends much grace. The line of Cain continues this trend of its ancestor, until a new line, that of Seth, is established.

52

2. *Genesis 2:4–3:24*

THEOLOGICAL FOCUS OF PERICOPE 2

2 **Man, created to serve God in the Temple of the cosmos, is to live in dependence upon the Creator, who provides him with whatever is good, but the arrogation of divine prerogatives and the assertion of human independence—the root cause of sin—alienates individuals, society, and creation at large, from each other and from God himself (even as divine grace is offered to sinners) (2:4–3:24).**

2.1 Man, created to serve God in the Temple of the cosmos, is to live in dependence upon the Creator, who provides him with whatever is good, as reflected in the God-ordained human relationship between husband and wife (2:4–25).

   2.1.1 *Man, created to serve God in the Temple of the cosmos, is to live in dependence upon the Creator in his presence.*

   2.1.2 *God-ordained human relationships, particularly between husband and wife, reflect the dependence of man upon the Creator to provide him with whatever is good.*

2.2 The arrogation of divine prerogatives and the assertion of human independence from God—the root cause of sin—has grave, ongoing consequences: individuals, society, and creation at large, are alienated from each other and from God himself (even as divine grace is offered to sinners) (3:1–24).

   2.2.1 *The deliberate choice to know good and evil—the arrogation of divine prerogatives and the assertion of human independence from God—is the root cause of mankind's sin.*

   2.2.2 *The consequence of mankind's sin is alienation—between individuals, and between individuals and God himself.*

   2.2.3 *The ongoing consequences of disobedience—failure to keep divine demand in dependence upon the Creator—are grave, affecting individuals, society, and creation at large, reminding mankind constantly of the enormity and deformity of sin (even as divine grace is offered to sinners).*

OVERVIEW

The phrase וְאֵלֶּה תּוֹלְדֹת (*wĕlleh toldot*, "these are the records of") introduces new sections in Genesis (see 6:9; 10:1; 11:10; 11:27; 25:12, 19; 36:1, 9; and 37:2). Usually, this denotes the "records" of a person; here, in 2:4, with the first instance of תּוֹלְדֹת, it is the "records" of "the heavens and the earth." The construction is similar to that in 5:1 and Num 3:1, a statement of the "records of *X*" followed by a temporal clause beginning בְּיוֹם (*byom*, "in the day" or "when"). In these last two instances, the temporal clause points to an existing prior situation in which the succeeding events ("records") occur. Likewise, in Gen 2:4, the temporal clause refers to the prior situation of Gen 1:1–2:3, making it a fair assumption that what follows is set in that antecedent state of affairs. The בְּיוֹם, in a sense, condenses the six days of creation in Gen 1 into a "day" in 2:4—a flashback with a zoom-in, slow-motion expansion of the events of Days 3 and 6, the creation of vegetation and the creation of man.[1]

---

1. Mathews, *Genesis 1–11:2*, 189. From 2:4 through 3:24, יְהוָה אֱלֹהִים (*yhwh ʾelohim*) is consistently used for God (except in 3:1b–7), also signaling that this is a fresh pericope. Moreover, the *petuḥa* (פ, *p*)

There are comparable doublet accounts in contemporary literature of the creation of man, wherein a general and abstract retelling (as in Gen 1:1–2:3) is followed by a more specific narration (as in 2:4–25). Among the evidence collected by Kikawada are the Sumerian story, *Enki and Ninmah*, and the Akkadian epic, *Atrahasis,* both of which provide a two-phase description of the creation of man.[2] Thus Pericope 2 provides a focus upon particular events that relate directly to mankind—an emphasis that reflects "a conscious literary purpose," a rather different emphasis from that of Pericope 1.[3] In fact the chiastic arrangement in 2:4 may hint at this shift of focus:

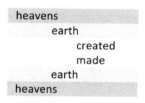

```
heavens
      earth
             created
             made
      earth
heavens
```

The order of creation, "heavens and earth" (1:1; 2:1), is inverted in 2:4 to focus upon subsequent events occurring on earth and involving its inhabitants, particularly man. While Gen 1 has a topical arrangement of creation with an ascending line from lesser to greater creatures, Gen 2 follows a narrative hierarchy, with animals (at least some of them) coming after the creation of man, but before that of the woman. The account thus establishes the woman's suitability for her mate, in contrast to other non-human creatures.[4]

The entire pericope is itself carefully constructed as a chiasm with several literary and linguistic parallels, as well as a neatly structured arrangement of narrative and dialogue. The account begins with the introduction of man into the Garden (*A*) and ends with his expulsion (*A'*), with the infamy of sin in the middle (*D*).[5]

---

after 2:3 points to a new paragraph that is to follow, as recognized by the Masoretes.

2. "The Double Creation," 43–45. A similar movement may be reflected in the pairing of genealogies in Gen 4:16–26 with 5:1–32, and that in and 10:1–32 with 11:10–26. The second genealogy in each pair (that of Seth and Shem in Gen 5 and 10, respectively) is the more significant one for the narrative that follows, and is therefore the one that is focused upon (see Hess, "Genesis 1–2," 144–51, who sees Gen 1:1–2:3 as a genealogy of sorts). Also see Middleton, *The Liberating Image*, 154–56.

3. Hess, "Genesis 1–2," 143.

4. Mathews, *Genesis 1–11:26*, 190.

5. From Ouro, "The Garden of Eden," 224–42; Wenham, *Genesis 1–15*, 50–51; Cotter, *Genesis*, 28; and Walsh, "Genesis 2:4b–3:24," 161.

Narrative introduction/transition (2:4)	

A — **Introduction of man into the Garden (2:5–17)**
Narrative—God as sole actor; man present but passive
"work," 2:5, 15; "ground," 2:5, 7; "garden," "Eden," "east," 2:8; "tree of life," 2:9; "knowledge of good and evil," 2:9; "keep" (שׁמר, *shmr*), 2:15

B — **Organization of human life (2:18–25)**
Narrative—God as main actor; man with minor role; woman and animals passive
man "calls" woman (2:23); harmonious relationships—man, woman, animals; wife/mother (2:24); clothing (2:25)

C — **Temptation (3:1–5)**
Dialogue—Serpent and woman; serpent dominating
eating from tree (3:1, 2); three utterances (3:1, 2–3, 4–5)

D — **Disobedience (3:6–7)**
Narrative—Man and woman

C' — **Judgment (3:8–13)**
Dialogue—God, man, and woman; God dominating
eating from tree (3:11); three sets of questions/answers (3:9–10, 11–12, 13)

B' — **Reorganization of human life (3:14–21)**
Narrative—God as main actor; man with minor role; woman and serpent passive
man "calls" woman (3:20); disharmonious relationships—man, woman, animals; wife/mother (3:20); clothing (3:21)

A' — **Expulsion of man from the Garden (3:22–24)**
Narrative—God as sole actor; man present but passive
"knowing good and evil," 3:22; "work," 3:23; "ground," 3:23; "garden," "Eden," "east," 3:24; "tree of life," 3:24, "guard" (שׁמר, *shmr*), 3:24

Narrative conclusion/transition (3:25)	

"The whole narrative is therefore a masterpiece of palistrophic writing. . . . Not only does the literary structure move in and out in this fashion, but so does the action: it commences outside the garden, the dialogues are conducted within the garden, and the decisive act of disobedience takes place at its very center."[6] Genesis 3:6b is the midpoint of the account with: "and she ate . . . and he ate." And in that centerpiece (*D*, 3:6–7), the humans are alone—no God, no snake: they eat, and the rest is sordid history.

In effect, Pericope 2 informs readers of what happened to God's "good" creation: the introduction of evil. The overturning of the "good" creation is depicted in a series of contrasts between the creation account of Gen 1:1–2:3 (positive) and this second pericope, 2:4–3:24 (negative).[7]

Genesis 1:1–2:3 (positive)	Genesis 2:4–3:24 (negative)
"God said"/"it was so" (1:3, 6, 7, 9, 11, 14, 15, 20, 24, 26, 30)	God's speech disobeyed (3:1–7)
Food permitted, including fruit of trees (1:29–30)	Food prohibited, fruit of a tree (2:16–17)
God blesses (1:22, 28; 2:3)	God curses (3:14, 17)
Creation of animals—"good" (1:25)	One animal crafty/cursed (3:1, 14)
"Land" (feminine singular) is "good" (1:10)	"Ground" (feminine singular) "cursed" (3:17)
Earth produces vegetation—"good" (1:12)	Ground produces products of the curse (3:18)
God's blessing to "multiply" species (1:28)	God's curse to "multiply" sorrow (3:16)

6. Wenham, *Genesis 1–15*, 51.

7. Ouro, "Linguistic and Thematic Parallels," 44–54.

2.1 Genesis 2:4–25

> **THEOLOGICAL FOCUS 2.1**
>
> 2.1 Man, created to serve God in the Temple of the cosmos, is to live in dependence upon the Creator, who provides him with whatever is good, as reflected in the God-ordained human relationship between husband and wife (2:4–25).
>
> > 2.1.1 *Man, created to serve God in the Temple of the cosmos, is to live in dependence upon the Creator in his presence.*
> >
> > 2.1.2 *God-ordained human relationships, particularly between husband and wife, reflect the dependence of man upon the Creator to provide him with whatever is good.*

NOTES 2.1

2.1.1 *Man, created to serve God in the Temple of the cosmos, is to live in dependence upon the Creator in his presence.*

Dependence on God, as if it were not obvious from Pericope 1, is further emphasized as Pericope 2 commences. That the very existence of mankind depends on God is clear from both the reiteration of the creation of man and woman by Yahweh, and the generation of plant life on earth, the source of food for humans. In the OT, the word "shrub" is used only here in Gen 2:5, and in 21:15 and Job 30:4, 7. In the last, it seems to be referring to uncultivated, desert vegetation that grows spontaneously in the wild as a result of rain. The other piece of flora in Gen 2:5, "plant," appears to be a cultivated grain (Exod 9:31, 32; etc.), like barley and wheat.[8] The description of this absence of wild shrub and cultivated grain is followed by two reasons for this lack: there was no rain (for the spontaneously growing wild shrubs to sprout) and there was no cultivator (for the cultivated grains—"plants"—to grow). Thus in 2:5 there is a two-fold problem and a two-fold reason for that problem. Genesis 2:6 proceeds to remedy the first one—rain (via rain-clouds) is provided by God (he had not sent it earlier, 2:5).[9] Subsequently 2:7–8 tackles the second—the creation of man and his placement in the garden as cultivator, expanded in 2:9–25.

---

8. Futato, "Because it had Rained," 3–4.

9. In Gen 2:6, אֵד, *'ed*, is most likely to mean rain clouds (metonymy for rain) for the following reasons: 1) the absence of rain as the reason for the lack of shrubs would be meaningless if there were a non-rainfall type of "mist" or an "underwater spring" (the other possibilities for אֵד) to water the ground; 2) Job 36:27 indicates that "rain" comes from אֵד, suggesting its translation as "rain cloud," making a neat parallelism with 36:28—notice that Gen 2:5 also collocates "rain" and אֵד; 3) rain clouds are seen in the Bible as "rising" from the earth, and Gen 2:6 describes אד also as "rising" from the earth (also see Ps 135:7; Jer 10:13; 51:16); 4) the Targums consistently render אֵד with the Aramaic עֲנַן (*'nn*, "rain cloud"), and *Gen. Rab.* 13.12 notes that clouds are called by five names, one of them being אד. In short, it appears that אד refers to a rain cloud. See Rogland, "Interpreting אֵד," 386, and the discussion on 383–85; also see Futato, "Because it had Rained," 5–10; and Dahood, "Eblaite *i-du*," 534–38. Psalm 104:2–4 and Gen 7:11–12 demarcate clouds as water bearers.

Problem 1: No wild shrub (2:5a)
    Problem 2: No cultivated grain (2:5b)
Reason for Problem 1: No rain (2:5c)
    Reason for Problem 2: No cultivator (man) (2:5d)
Remedy for Problem 1: Rain via rain-clouds (2:6)
    Remedy for Problem 2: Man created and placed in Garden (2:7–8)
        Expansion of Remedy for Problem 2: Garden (2:9–14); man (2:15–25)

All this points to the total dependence of man on his Creator, for his existence and for his sustenance (in an agrarian economy, rain and cultivated grain were the means of subsistence). Needless to say, these events of Days 3 and 6 were already given that significance in Pericope 1 with the assertion in 1:12 that earth's vegetation included seed-bearers and fruit-bearers, the same species mentioned in 1:29 as food for mankind.[10]

It is not only the Bible that depicts man being created from dust (Job 10:9; Pss 90:3; 104:29; Isa 29:16; etc.); the *Gilgamesh Epic* has the goddess Aruru producing Enkidu from clay; the ram-headed Egyptian god Khmun has also been depicted as creating man from clay. A number of Greek writers credit Prometheus, the Titan, with having done the same.[11] "It is evident then that Genesis is here taking up a very ancient tradition of the creation of man and is giving these old ideas its own distinctive flavor."[12] Man is described as a "living being" (2:7); the same phrase is used of sea creatures, land animals, and birds (1:20, 24; 2:19; 9:10, 12, 15, 16; animals, too, have the "breath of life," 7:22). The difference—the "distinctive flavor"—is the direct act of creation of man by God and the image of the latter that man bears.[13] As was observed in Pericope 1, the *imago Dei* is the royal office of humans as divine agents, called to

10. This also indicates that Gen 2:4–25 is not the narrative of a second creation, but rather a zooming-in on certain selected events from Gen 1:1–2:3 (particularly the creative events of the second half of Days 3 and 6), and their narrative expansion with detail. See Futato, "Because it had Rained," 12. He argues that "Gen 2:4–25 provides an example of the Hebrew stylistic technique of synoptic/resumption-expansion. A Hebrew author will at times tell the whole story in brief form (synopsis), then repeat the story (resumption), adding greater detail (expansion)" (ibid.).

11. See *Gilgamesh Epic* 1.34–36 (Dalley, *Myths From Mesopotamia*, 52–53); for Khmun, see Hoffmeier, "Some Thoughts on Genesis 1 and 2," 39–49; for Prometheus, see Plato, *Protagoras* 320c–322a; Ovid, *Metamorphoses* 1.82; Juvenal, *Satires* 4.130–140; etc.

12. Wenham, *Genesis 1–15*, 60.

13. In this connection, one notes that a consensus of scientists holds to a gradual evolution of the human being through a variety of humanoid predecessors. Debates aside, Gen 2 clearly indicates personal divine superintendence over the generation of the first pair of humans. Evolution or no, the first male and first female had to arrive on the scene fairly synchronously, and Gen 2 simply declares that God's hand was in the generation of these two individuals—this is something science cannot rule out (or in). Thus for the purposes of this commentary, the evolutionary question is quite irrelevant. In any case, biblical genealogies trace the line back to Adam in Gen 5:3; 1 Chr 1:1; and Luke 3:38; Jesus himself appears to have accepted this lineage (Matt 19:4–6), as also did Paul (Acts 17:26). In fact, the theological construct of the analogy between Adam and Christ appears to be contingent upon the historicity of both individuals (Rom 5:12–19; 1 Cor 15:21, 45), irrespective of the natural science explanations of the origin of first human. In sum, Adam and Eve were created by God, however one conceives of that act. See Berry, "This Cursed Earth," 35.

align themselves to the divine order, to abide by divine demand. Now the creation of man, and the insufflation of the "spirit" (רוח, 2:7) emphasizes, in no uncertain terms, the dependence of man upon God, his Creator.

The Garden in Genesis 2 is a "special, localized place that is spatially separated from its outside world," with the presence of God within it, and cherubim later preventing entry thereinto (3:24)—all demarcating this verdant locus as the divine sanctuary of the cosmic Temple (Exod 25:18–22; 26:31; 1 Kgs 6:23–29).[14] The "stationing" of the cherubim is described with the verb שׁכן (*shkn*, "to dwell"), also used of God's presence in his sanctuary (Exod 24:16; 25:8; 29:45, 46; etc.).[15] Cherubim, themselves, signify the presence of God: 1 Sam 4:4; 2 Sam 22:11 ; 2 Kgs 19:15; Ps 18:10; etc. Images of these beings are found both in the tabernacle and the temple (Exod 26:31; 1 Kgs 6:29), and on the ark (Exod 25:18–22); large sculptures of these entities also guarded the inner sanctuary of the temple (1 Kgs 6:23–28), just as live ones did the Garden of Eden.[16] So also fire (Gen 3:24)—frequently a theophanic accompaniment, particularly in judgment (Exod 19:18; Ps 104:4). Moreover, Ezek 28:13–14 identifies the Eden as the archetypal holy mountain of God; its elevation is evident in its being the source of the primal stream that issues into four branches, ostensibly to the four quarters of the world (Gen 2:10–14)—Eden is thus the *axis mundi*. "The placement of humankind in the garden as God's image furthers the analogy to the temple, with its image of the deity, drawing together the motifs of kingship and the temple at the beginning of the Bible."[17] Man is thus placed in the very "sanctuary" of the cosmos-Temple, the place of God's dwelling, and in his presence. Again, this special privilege afforded to man reinforces his dependence upon his Creator, with whom he was to abide in close relationship and intimacy.

All of this furthers the cultic imagery of the Garden of Eden. "The garden of Eden is not viewed by the author of Genesis simply as a piece of Mesopotamian farmland, but as an archetypal sanctuary, that is a place where God dwells and where man should worship him." In addition to the parallels between the creation account of Gen 1:1–2:3 and the accounts of the construction of the tabernacle/temple discussed in Pericope 1, there are several elements that link the Garden and future sanctuaries of Israel's history.[18]

14. Dumbrell, "Genesis 2:1–17," 56.

15. The word "tabernacle" (מִשְׁכָּן, *mishkan*) is derived from the verb שׁכן.

16. The Akkadian *karibi* (related to the Hebrew, כְּרֻבִים, *krubim*, "cherubim") were guardians of temples and holy places in the ancient Near East (see Wenham, "Sanctuary Symbolism," 401).

17. Dumbrell, "Genesis 2:1–17," 58–59.

18. Wenham, "Sanctuary Symbolism," 399, 400–404. "Just as Eden is the divine dwelling where a human may encounter God unmediated, so also is the temple the divine dwelling where it is possible for a human to encounter the divine unmediated" (Callender, *Adam in Myth*, 50). *Jubilees* 8:19 notes that "[Noah] knew that Eden was the holy of holies and the dwelling of Yahweh" (also see *Jub* 3:12; 4:26; 8:19). The paradisiacal garden and the temple mount are also equated in Ps 36:7–9, where the temple is a place of refuge, and where God shares his victuals with his people; there is also a river of life wherein is found "your delights" (עֲדָנֶיךָ, *'adaneka* ; the plural construct of עֵדֶן, *'eden*, "Eden," here a homonym meaning "delight"; 36:9). Divine presence is linked with life-giving waters in Ezek 47:1–12; Ps 46:4; Jer

Parallels	Genesis 2–3	Tabernacle/Temple Accounts
God "walks" in the sanctuary	Gen 3:8	Lev 26:12; Deut 23:14; 2 Sam 7:6–7
Sanctuary's east entrance	Gen 2:8; 3:24	Exod 27:9–18; Ezek 8:16; 11:1; 47:1–2
Cherubim	Gen 3:24	Exod 25:18–22; 1 Kgs 6:23–29
Tree of life (stylized as a menorah)	Gen 2:9; 3:22, 24	Exod 25:31–35; 1 Chr 28:15
Garden features/emblems	Gen 2:8–9	Exod 25:31–35; 1 Kgs 6:29, 32, 35
"Cultivate" and "keep" (עָבַד, 'bd, and שָׁמַר, shmr)	Gen 2:15	Num 3:7–8; 8:26; 18:5–6, 8
God/Moses clothing Adam/priests	Gen 3:21	Exod 28:41; 29:8; 40:14; Lev 8:13
Rivers from Eden	Gen 2:10–14	Ps 46:4; Ezek 47:1–12; Joel 3:18
Gold	Gen 2:11–12	Exod 25:3, 11–39; 1 Kgs 6:20–35
Bdellium	Gen 2:12	Num 11:7 (= manna, Exod 16:33)
Onyx	Gen 2:12	Exod 25:7; 28:9, 20; 1 Chr 29:2

With the stylized creation account of Pericope 1 paralleling a temple dedication, as well as the subsequent "rest" (reign) of the deity, Walton concludes that "the cosmology of Genesis 1 is built on the platform of temple theology." There is an intimate and intrinsic connection between Temple and cosmos, with the Garden of Eden being the chamber of divine residence.[19] Genesis to Revelation thus outlines a trajectory of human history that begins in a verdant garden containing the tree of life (Gen 2:8–17), and ends in a glorious city that also contains a tree of life (Rev 22:1–2). The garden at the commencement of the story served as the place where man engaged in "cultivation" (עָבַד, *'abad*, "cultivate," Gen 2:5, 15). עָבַד is commonly used of agricultural tasks (also in 3:23; 4:2, 12; 9:25, 26, 27; etc.); it later acquired strong liturgical connotations and came to be used regularly for the service of God and his worship (as in Exod 3:12; Num 3:7–8; 4:23, 24, 26; 8:25–26; 18:5–6; Deut 4:19; etc.).[20] Likewise, שָׁמַר, *shamar*, "to keep/guard/watch" (2:15), is employed in a non-sacred sense (also in 3:24; 4:9; etc.), as well as for the fulfilling of covenantal responsibilities towards God (Gen 17:9–10; 18:19; 26:5; Lev 18:5; Deut 4:6; 7:12; 29:9). But it, too, connotes the priestly duties with regard to the sanctuary (Num 1:53; 3:7, 8, 10, 28, 32, 38; 28:2; etc.). All of this hints at the kind of activity Adam had symbolically been engaged in, in that primeval agricultural paradise that served as the Temple/sanctuary.[21] It is no coincidence, then, that the δοῦλοι, *douloi*, of the Lamb, in the restored garden that is the heavenly city, will also be "serving" (Rev 22:3; from λατρεύω, *latreuō*, also used frequently of worship as, for example, in Heb 10:2; 13:10; Rev 7:15; etc.). Eden was the garden of God, with God's presence its central and dominating feature (see Isa 51:3 and Ezek 28:13); quite appro-

---

17:12–13; Joel 3:18; Zech 14:8; Rev 22:1–2. Psalm 36:8–10 mentions "delight" (again, עדן), of feasting of the abundance of the divine "house," "river," and "fountain of life." Besides, temple complexes often featured gardens to symbolize the blessings of fertility from the deity (Walton, *Genesis 1*, 185). Fertility is a prominent motif of the Edenic location: Isa 51:3; Ezek 36:35.

19. Walton, *Genesis 1*, 185, 187; Levenson, "The Temple," 288.

20. The noun form of the verb, עֲבֹדָה, *'abodah*, "service," also describes Levitical duties in the tabernacle and Temple (Exod 38:21; Num 3:10; 18:6; 1 Chr 24:3, 19; 2 Chr 8:14).

21. Indeed, on the basis of Exod 3:12 and Num 28:2, *Gen. Rab.* 16.5 (on Gen 2:15) sees the human activity of cultivating and keeping as referring to the temple offerings.

priately, the canon ends with another divine sanctuary, the New Jerusalem wherein is stationed "the throne of God and of the Lamb" (Rev 22:3).[22] In sum, man was created for a grand vocation—to serve God in his Temple, in his perfectly ordered creation, fulfilling covenantal responsibilities, "caring for sacred space."[23] That is to say, man was created to align himself fully with the divine order and to meet divine demand.

Pericope 1 introduced the concept of the responsibility of man to align himself with God's ideal world. Suffice it to say here that at the commencement of the canon, this notion of human responsibility towards a God with whom humans have a relationship is firmly established, a relationship of dependence upon the Creator, in his presence. Of course, this responsibility, as we shall see in this very pericope, was soon abdicated.

2.1.2 *God-ordained human relationships, particularly between husband and wife, reflect the dependence of man upon the Creator to provide him with whatever is good.*

That the account of the creation of man and woman in Gen 2 is an expansion of the creation of mankind on Day 6 (Gen 1:26–27) seems to be further substantiated by God's deliberation on both occasions: he reflects in Gen 1:26 prior to creating man in his own image; he does so again in 2:18, this time before creating woman, to remedy a "not good" situation. As was noted in Pericope 1, "good" signifies optimal function; thus the "not good" (the first such state in Scripture) indicates less than optimal function.[24] Optimal function within the divine order, an alignment with the demand of God, mandates the complementary functioning of male and female units; community is thus an essential requirement, established very early in the history of mankind. In other words, mankind is dependent upon God to provide it with whatever is good, including appropriate relationships.

Needless to say, to be someone's "help" (עֵזֶר, 'ezer, 2:18), as the woman was for man, does not necessarily mean that the helper is weaker than the one helped: the descriptor is used of God himself, Ps 30:11; 54:4. Neither does it necessarily mean that the helper is superior or stronger. The phrase "suitable for him" (כְּנֶגְדּוֹ, knegdo) is found only here in the OT, and indicates complementarity, rather than identity or hierarchy (see Eccl 4:9–10; Prov 31:10–31).[25] Woman was "not made out of his head to top him, not out of his feet to be trampled upon by him, but out of his side to be equal with him, under his arm to be protected, and near his heart to be beloved."[26] That woman is linked to man as "bone of my bones, and flesh of my flesh" (Gen 2:23), the traditional kinship formula, underscores their equality. But there is more to that

---

22. Dumbrell, "Genesis 2:1–17," 53–65.

23. Walton, *Genesis 1*, 173.

24. "Whoever has no wife, lives without good, without help, without joy, without blessing, without atonement" (*Gen. Rab.* 17.2). This author, a confirmed celibate, would beg to disagree with the venerable rabbis!

25. See Wenham, *Genesis 1–15*, 68.

26. Henry, *An Exposition of the Old and New Testament*, 36.

phrase. Brueggemann shows that in all cases when these terms, bones and flesh, are used together in this fashion (here, and in Gen 29:14; Jdg 9:2; 2 Sam 5:1/1 Chr 11:1; 2 Sam 19:13), the phrase indicates more a covenant relationship between the protagonists, rather than an assertion of genetic connection. It is essentially "an oath of abiding loyalty," a mutual commitment of partners who oblige themselves to each other for every circumstance of life.[27] This covenant relationship is hinted at in the "cleaving" mentioned in 2:24, frequently a formal term denoting loyalty of covenant partners (Deut 4:4; 10:20; 11:22; 13:5; etc.). On the other hand, the "leaving" in the same verse is employed to describe the forsaking of covenant commitments (Jer 1:16: 2:13, 17, 19; 5:7; Hos 4:10; etc.).[28] While this is the first time "woman" (אִשָּׁה, 'ishshah) occurs, it is often forgotten that this is also the first time "man" (אִישׁ, 'ish) occurs in the Bible (2:23); till now he had always been referred to as אָדָם, 'adam. Man has not only labeled woman "woman" (perhaps better "wife"), he has thereby labeled himself "man" (better, "husband").[29] Truly, something new has happened here, with two people united in a covenant relationship, unique and separate from every other relationship. And besides, they are to be one flesh—solidarity is being emphasized. "Whereas the appearance of the animals elicited names, the appearance of the woman elicits poetry."[30] In fact, the first time man speaks is after meeting woman! The "not good" situation had become "good," as a result of divine provision, upon which man was utterly dependent.

2.2 Genesis 3:1–24

THEOLOGICAL FOCUS 2.2

2.2 The arrogation of divine prerogatives and the assertion of human independence from God—the root cause of sin—has grave, ongoing consequences: individuals, society, and creation at large, are alienated from each other and from God himself (even as divine grace is offered to sinners) (3:1–24).

    2.2.1 *The deliberate choice to know good and evil—the arrogation of divine prerogatives and the assertion of human independence from God—is the root cause of mankind's sin.*

    2.2.2 *The consequence of mankind's sin is alienation: between individuals, and between individuals and God himself.*

    2.2.3 *The ongoing consequences of disobedience—failure to keep divine demand in dependence upon the Creator—are grave, affecting individuals, society, and creation at large, reminding mankind constantly of the enormity and deformity of sin (even as divine grace is offered to sinners).*

---

27. Brueggemann, "Of the Same Flesh," 535, 537.

28. Ibid., 540.

29. Though, of course, by translating "husband" and "wife" (rather than "man" and "woman"), the wordplay of אישׁ and אשׁה is lost.

30. Kass, *The Beginning of Wisdom*, 78.

*2.2.1 The deliberate choice to know good and evil—the arrogation of divine
    prerogatives and the assertion of human independence from God—is the root
    cause of mankind's sin.*

The fact that the trees God planted in the Garden of Eden were "pleasing to the sight
and good for food" (2:9), suggests that Eve's evaluation of the tree of the knowledge of
good and evil as "good for food" and "a delight to the eyes" (3:6) was neither erroneous
nor illegitimate. Rather, the problem lay with her focus upon the tree being "desirable
to make one wise," perhaps making that characteristic equivalent to "knowing good
and evil," the peculiar feature of *this* tree.[31] What exactly did this knowledge entail?

If eating the fruit tree of the tree life would have led to immortality (3:22), it is
reasonable to assume that consuming the fruit of the tree of the knowledge of good
and evil would have led to a knowledge of good and evil. Wenham makes the case
for "knowledge of good and evil" being divine wisdom, "a wisdom that is God's sole
preserve" (Job 15:7–9; Prov 30:1–4).[32] The emphasis of the author of Genesis is not on
the substance or content of knowledge (what specifically was good or bad), but rather
on man's moral autonomy and his seeking to make moral judgments *without privileging divine revelation*. Indeed, the attributes of the fruit of the tree of the knowledge of
good and evil that the woman extols ("good for food," "delight to the eyes," "desirable
to make one wise," Gen 3:6) are also shared by divine revelation, as Ps 19 makes clear
("sure, making wise the simple," "pure, enlightening the eyes," and "sweeter also than
honey," 19:7–10), substantiating the thesis that such wisdom as was sought here by
mankind was being pursued *apart* from God and his revelation.

Genesis 3:8 has man hearing (שָׁמַע, *shm'*, also a synonym for obeying) the voice
of Yahweh, and when questioned, he responds in 3:10: "I heard [שָׁמַע] Your voice in
the garden, and I was afraid." The irony is palpable: man had *not* heard/obeyed what
he should have, and man had *not* feared the way he should have. Instead, lacking the
fear of God, he refuses to hear the voice of God. "Voice" shows up again in 3:17, when
Yahweh accuses the man of having listened, rather, to his wife's voice. One remembers
that all this comes after the powerful voice of God created the entire cosmos with no
opposition whatsoever! "And God said" and "and it was so" resounds throughout Gen
1. Now in Gen 3, apparently God's speaking *fails* to achieve what was intended. With
the arrival of humans on the scene, God's voice is negated, rendered fruitless, nullified.
Literarily, this is the "failure" of God's word to achieve its intended end.

In the accusatory and judgmental phase of the narrative, notice that the tree of
interest mentioned by Yahweh is not designated as the "tree of the knowledge of good
and evil"; instead, he labels it "the tree of which I commanded you not to eat," a description that is repeated (3:11, 17). The focus is upon the command of God, the voice

31. The similarity between the Latin word for "evil" (*malus*) and that for "apple" (*malum*) may have
generated the legend of that particular fruit being incriminated in the fall.

32. Wenham, *Genesis 1–15*, 63–64.

of God, the demand of God, that had been repudiated. For man had decided *he* would be the arbiter of what to eat and what not to, what to do and what not to, what to abide by and what not to. God's words were not going to preclude him from making a decision of his own, even if it were contrary to divine order. Thus this account is about man taking upon himself the responsibility to determine whether something was good for himself or not. "It is not that man had no knowledge before and gained knowledge afterwards, or that to know good and evil meant to experience evil in addition to good. Rather, he takes upon himself the authority to make the declaration of what is good. He does what is good in his own eyes rather than what is good in the eyes of God."[33] Ultimately, such a grasp of "the knowledge of good and evil" is to neglect the fear of the Lord which is the beginning of knowledge (Prov 1:7).[34] This is ultimately a question of dependence upon God vs. independence from God.

Jonathan Edwards said it well, when he asserted that "the predominacy of self-love is the foundation of all sin"[35]; and if only self-love rules in the individual, "it will be contented with nothing short of the throne of God." In the thrall of this self-love, man's choice was antithetical to God's revealed will, and he proceeded to do what he decided was good for him.[36] Or, as Hamilton notes: "Deification is a fantasy difficult to repress and a temptation hard to reject. . . . Whenever one makes his own will crucial and God's revealed will irrelevant, whenever autonomy displaces submission and obedience in a person, that finite individual attempts to rise above the limitations imposed on him by his creator."[37]

"Like every truly great story, it seeks to show us not what happened (once) but what always happens, what is always the case," and it is this transcending force, its inspired nature, that renders it powerful for life-transformation.[38] The theology of the pericope therefore denotes its lasting value that transcends time and space. The thrust of the text is that humans are to depend on God, completely, totally, utterly. Man is carefully formed from the ground; God's breath animates him; woman is subtly fashioned from him; companionship and community is formed for him; the garden is created for him; his sustenance and enjoyment are guaranteed by God; and man's limits in the universe are ordained by God. As Brueggemann notes, humans are

---

33. Clark, "A Legal Background," 276–77.

34. Wenham, *Genesis 1–15*, 63–64. While such wisdom is properly the goal of humanity (Prov 3:13; 8:10–11), it must be achieved only through the fear of Yahweh, not by any other independent or autonomous means (Prov 2:1–6; 3:5–6; 9:10; 11:7, 29; 15:33). See Mathews, *Genesis 1–11:26*, 205–6. Ezekiel 28 lends credence to such an assessment: according to the prophet, the king of Tyre/the anointed cherub (28:1, 12, 14, 16) was ejected from Eden/holy mountain of God (28:13, 14) because of his pride and desire to be like God (28:6).

35. Edwards, "Miscellany: No. 1010," 342.

36. Idem, "Miscellany: No. 534," 78. See Beck, "The Fall of Man," 225.

37. Hamilton, *Genesis: Chapters 1–17*, 190. "Man had taken to himself a right which is God's. God had delegated to man his realm of dominion, the created world. Man broke the confines of his realm to enter the dominion of God" (Kuyper, "'To Know Good and Evil,'" 492).

38. Kass, *The Beginning of Wisdom*, 54.

dependable, vulnerable, and precarious, relying in each moment on the gracious gift of breath which makes human life possible. Moreover, this precarious condition is definitional for human existence, marking the human person from the very first moment of existence.... This is what it means to be human. This rather elemental and straightforward physiology marks the human person as a creature who lives by the daily, moment by moment generosity of God. The narrative of Gen 2–3 concerns the risk of trying to escape or transcend the modest status of creatureliness, the dangerous venture of "being like God" (3:4).[39]

And with that attempt to be like God, the sinning pair brought about the tragedy of the fall.

2.2.2 *The consequence of mankind's sin is alienation: between individuals, and between individuals and God himself.*

While there is no explicit assertion in Gen 3 that the serpent is operating from evil motives, there are plenty of implicit pointers that the whole affair is quite nefarious.

> Serpent's questioning of God's communiqué to man and woman (3:1)
> Serpent's conversion of God's commanding (צוה, *tswh*, 2:16) to God's *saying* (אמר, *'amr*, 3:3)
> Serpent's use of אֱלֹהִים in 3:1–7 ('*elohoim*),
>   in a pericope otherwise punctuated by יְהוָה אֱלֹהִים (*yhwh 'elohim*)
> Serpent's "not eat of any tree" expressing
>   an absolute prohibition and negating God's liberality (3:1)
> Woman's identification of the forbidden tree by its location, avoiding its significance (3:2)
> Woman's acquiescence to the serpent's use of אֱלֹהִים (3:3)
> Woman's acquiescence to the serpent's interpretation:
>   God's *saying* (3:3) vs. God's *commanding*
> Woman's alterations of God's permission/command:
>   "we may eat" (3:2) vs. God's "you may freely eat" (2:16)
>   omission of God's provision to partake from *any* tree of the garden" (2:16)
>   "lest you die" (3:3) vs. God's "you shall surely die" (2:17)
>   "not eat from eat *or touch it*" (3:3), Eve's addendum to God's words in 2:16–17
> Serpent's outright negation of God's warning:
>   "you shall surely die" (2:17) vs. "you shall surely not die" (3:4)
> Serpent's attribution of a base motive for God's prohibition (3:5a)
> Serpent's conversion of God's statement of negative consequences
>   to one of positive outcomes (3:5b)

In addition, the parallelisms in Isa 27:1 seem to suggest an equivalence between Leviathan, the serpent (נָחָשׁ, *nakhash*), and the sea monsters (תַּנִּין, *tannin*, that were already encountered in 1:21); in Exod 7:9–10, תַּנִּין actually refers to "serpent." Likewise, Job 26:12–13 has "Rahab" (the mythical sea monster representing chaos in ancient Near Eastern literature) in parallel with serpent (נָחָשׁ). In fact, a suspicious link may also potentially made between the noun נָחָשׁ ("serpent"), the verb נָחַשׁ ("to practice divination," Gen 30:27; 44:5, 15; etc.), and the cognate noun of the latter, נַחַשׁ ("omen/ spell"). Divination formulas in the ancient Near East were frequently associated with serpents. Moreover, עָרוֹם (*'arom*, "naked," 2:24) is immediately followed by a wordplay with the description of the serpent as עָרוּם (*'arum*, "crafty," 3:1). "Crafty" is an ambigu-

---

39. Brueggemann, "Remember, You are Dust," 4.

ous term that may be a virtue (Prov 12:16; 13:16) or a vice (Job 5:12; 15:5), but the introduction of the assonant word in 3:1 suggests that something negative is in store.[40] All of this makes the serpent of Gen 3:1 a rather vile character, who turns out to be a foe of mankind (3:15) and an embodiment of Satan/the devil (Rev 12:9; 20:2; also see Rom 16:20 and Wis 2:23–24). It appears to be a being (or possessed by one) that has intellect (is crafty, reasons, speaks, deceives) and is anti-God (alters God's words, tempts, battles with man's seed). "The tempter thus initiates a new cult that has the serpent as a competing lawmaker and so ultimately a rival god."[41]

Rather than being godlike and knowing good and evil after eating they fruit, all man and woman end up knowing is that they are naked (see the parallel structure below)—a surprising twist, not at all what they bargained for! The actual consequences of the sin "are so comic as to be hilarious, were it not for the seriousness of the subject."[42]

3:5a	For God knows that
	in the day you eat from it
	3:5b your eyes will be opened,
	3:5c and you will be like God, knowing good and evil.

3:6cde	She took from its fruit and she ate;
	and she gave also to her husband with her, and he ate.
	3:7a Then the eyes of both of them were opened,
	3:7b and they knew that they were naked.

The nakedness and lack of shame prior to sin (2:25) underscored the "one-fleshedness" of the couple. This same nakedness, post-fall, now becomes a negative characterization and a source of shame which necessitates covering (3:7). The unity (even in the plurality of gender) that was established at their creation has been lost: "[S]hame results from one's perception of individuality. Nakedness is not the problem; rather, the problem comes from the realization of self as distinct and separate from others."[43] This nakedness provokes not only shame, but also fear (3:7–8, 10), which it had not done prior to the disobedience (2:25). After partaking of the fruit of the tree of the knowledge of good and evil, the humans' eyes are opened (3:7); ironically, they then proceed to hide, that no eyes might see *them*. They wanted to be "like God" (3:5); now they do not even want to be in his presence (3:8).[44]

---

40. See Ouro, "The Garden of Eden," 239n47; Hamilton, *Genesis: Chapters 1–17*, 187. Wenham reproduces the wordplay with "shrewd" and "nude" (*Genesis 1–15*, 72).

41. Emmrich, "The Temptation Narrative," 16. This speech by an animal is clearly being thought of as supernatural; the only other utterance by an animal in the OT is explicitly noted to be so (by Balaam's donkey, in Num 22:28).

42. Wenham, *Genesis 1–15*, 75. The first four words of the disobedience have a unique phonic color: וַתִּקַּח, מִפִּרְיוֹ, וַתֹּאכַל, and וַתִּתֵּן (*wattiqqakh, mippiryo, watto'kal*, and *wattitten*, respectively; "she took," "from its fruit," "and she ate," "and she gave," 3:6) The "extremely difficult pronunciation (six doubled consonants in the four words, all of them voiceless plosives) forces a merciless concentration on each word." See Walsh, "Genesis 2:4b–3:24," 166.

43. Keiser, "Genesis 1–11," 108.

44. The coupled name, "Yahweh God" (יְהוָה אֱלֹהִים), is used nineteen times in Pericope 2 (and elsewhere in the Pentateuch only in Exod 9:30). But, not surprisingly, in 3:1–7, the personal and ethical

Throughout the serpent's dialogue with Eve, it consistently addresses her in second person plural verbal forms and suffixes (3:1, 4–5). Indeed, somewhat redundantly, it is noted that her husband was "with her" (עִמָּהּ, *'immah*, 3:6).[45] They were, indeed, one, and they had been created to be one—"bone of my bones, and flesh of my flesh" (2:23) and "for this cause a man shall leave . . . and cleave to his wife; and they shall become one flesh" (2:24). But their status was no longer to be as innocent as it once was, for in 3:9–13, the plural forms disappear: it is everyone for himself/herself. And, as proof of the alienation that had occurred between the couple, their eating in 3:7 is their last act together in the account. From now on, they are addressed separately by God (with the singular pronoun "you": 3:9, 11, 13); and they accordingly respond separately to God. In fact, man expressly confesses his own actions: he ate (3:12), he heard, he was afraid, he was naked, he hid (3:10)—all in the singular. And then man blames "the woman" (3:12), the one he had earlier waxed poetic about (2:23). Thus far when she had been mentioned in relationship to him, it had always been as "*his* wife/ woman" (2:24, 25; 3:8). Here it is "*the* woman" and "she" (3:12): "the woman You gave me—she gave me . . ."! They are no longer one; sin has broken them apart—from God before whom they hide, and from each other. The alienation is complete.[46] Preferring independence to dependence, opting for autonomy rather than trust, humans found only separation from God, pain, and death—life *unabundant*!

The relationship between man and woman is further detailed in the judgment upon the woman (3:16). The sentence on the desire of the woman for her husband and on the latter's rule over the woman commences the battle between the sexes, the breakdown of marital harmony. Sin had corrupted the relationship between man and woman, with each one desiring control over the other.[47] What began, in this Pericope, as a unique covenantal and congenial relationship between man and woman—two discrete individuals becoming "one flesh" (2:24), for it was "not good for the man to be alone" (2:18)—had now ended in the destruction of this conjoint life. "Mutual complementarity is replaced by mutual domination, intimacy is replaced by alienation, mutuality and equality become control and distortion. What kills the relationship is the desire to possess, to keep, to hold, to dominate, or to crush the other."[48] In this light, one notes that the pattern of divine judgments are similar, each pointing to a

---

name is absent, when disobedience is contemplated and accomplished. See Mathews, *Genesis 1–11:26*, 192–93; Cassuto, *Genesis*, 87. The sinners have moved away from the personal, dependent relationship with their Creator, a relationship now gravely undermined.

45. And the man concurs with this assessment; later, when he is accused by God, he throws it right back at the Creator: "The woman whom You gave to be *with me* [עִמָּדִי, *'immadi*] . . ." (3:12). "God has moved from beneficent provider to cruel oppressor" (Hamilton, *Genesis: Chapters 1–17*, 189).

46. See Craig, "Misspeaking in Eden," 243–44; and Hauser, "Genesis 2–3," 26–30. It might be noted here that woman is tempted; but man is not. She gives; but he takes, without question or challenge. "Hers is a sin of initiative. His is a sin of acquiescence" (Hamilton, *Genesis: Chapters 1–17*, 191). That there was no excuse for the male partner in the malfeasance is implied in 1 Tim 2:14, as well as 4 Ezra 3:21; 7:118.

47. Foh, "What is the Woman's Desire," 382.

48. Vogels, "The Power Struggle," 209.

struggle between two entities: serpent vs. seed (3:15), woman vs. man (3:16), and man vs. ground (3:17–19).

2.2.3 *The ongoing consequences of disobedience—failure to keep divine demand in dependence upon the Creator—are grave, affecting individuals, society, and creation at large, reminding mankind constantly of the enormity and deformity of sin (even as divine grace is offered to sinners).*

There are three explicit blessings on the "day" of creation (1:22, 28; 2:3, on sea creatures and birds, on man, and on the seventh day), and there are three curses uttered in the two pericopes following: 3:14, 17; 4:11, on the serpent, of the ground, and on Cain, respectively. Literarily, it is the undoing of creation! The consequences of that unraveling are pronounced by Yahweh as a series of sentences upon the protagonists, aspects of which are treated briefly below.

Serpent

Appropriately enough, the one that was more "crafty" (עָרוּם, *'arum*) than any living being of the field (3:1), is "cursed" (אָרוּר, *'arur*) more than any living being of the field, as well (3:14). The curse that the serpent will forever move on its belly may not necessarily indicate that the animal once had legs (as surmised in *Gen. Rab.* 20.5 and *b. Soṭah* 9b); it might simply designate an unclean animal (Lev 11:42). Likewise the eating of dust reflects its abject humiliation and defeat (Ps 72:9; Isa 49:23; 65:25; Micah 7:17). Both the method of locomotion and the item of diet are thus more symbolic than literal. The reptile responsible for the ultimate return of man to dust (Gen 3:19), will consume dust as a perpetual reminder of the evil that had been perpetrated.[49]

Eating

The act of willful independence—eating—echoes throughout Gen 3 (in 3:1, 2, 3, 5, 6, 11, 12, 13, 14, 17, 18, 19). Having tempted the woman to *eat* (3:1–6), the serpent is cursed to *eat* (3:14), too—dust. Man ate of the forbidden tree and his judgment relates to eating as well: henceforth his eating will come only at the expense of hard labor. "The toil that now lies behind the preparation of every meal is a reminder of the fall and is made the more painful by the memory of the ready supply of food within the garden (2:9)."[50]

Keep

The story had begun with no man present to "keep" (שָׁמַר, *shamar*) the ground (2:5); later he was placed in the Garden to "keep" it (שָׁמַר, 2:15). As a result of the fall, man was expelled from the Garden and delegated to "keep" (שָׁמַר) the ground (3:23), while the cherubim "kept" (שָׁמַר) the tree of life from man (3:24). "This depicts the reversal that came about from the expulsion: no longer working the ground of the Garden, he

---

49. Mathews, *Genesis 1–11:26*, 245.

50. Wenham, *Genesis 1–15*, 82.

[man] must work the ground from which he was taken, outside the Garden; and now that no man is there to keep the Garden, angelic beings must keep it—particularly, to keep the humans out!"[51]

Seed

Collins argues that when זֶרַע, *zera'*, indicates "posterity," the associated pronouns are always plural (15:3; 17:7–10; 48:11–12; etc.); however, the pronouns are singular when זֶרַע indicates a specific descendant (4:25; 21:13; 38:9; etc.).[52] Thus it is quite likely that a single "seed" of the woman is in view in 3:15, particularly since the pronoun "he" (הוּא, *hu'*) is somewhat redundant in 3:15—the masculine singular is clearly understood from the inflection of the verb, יְשׁוּפְךָ, *yshufka*, "*he* shall bruise you."[53] The Targums explicitly assign this ultimate victory of the "seed" to the days of the King Messiah (מַלְכָּא מְשִׁיחָא, *mlk' mshykh'*; *Tg. Ps.-J.* and *Tg. Neof.* on Gen 3:15). Of course, the NT also gives this passage messianic significance (Rom 16:20: Heb 2:14; 1 John 3:8; Rev 12:1–6, 13–17).[54] Thus both judgment and promise are revealed here. While God judges humans for their independence, grace extended to them renders them, again, dependent upon God for redemption.

Woman and Man

The woman would experience עֶצֶב (*etsev*, "pain," 3:16) because she ate of the tree (עֵץ, *'ets*)—the wordplay is pungent; Wenham tries to bring it out with "the *tree* brought *trauma*."[55] Sin always results in pain! What is usually translated as "pain in childbirth" is literally "your pain and your conception" (עִצְּבוֹנֵךְ וְהֵרֹנֵךְ, *itsvonek wheronek*). Of course, conception is not a painful process, but labor and delivery is. "Conception" may therefore refer to labor and delivery or even the entire pregnancy; this is also signaled by the parallelism between 3:16a (multiplied pain in conception) and 3:16b (promised pain in childbirth).[56] In this connection, van Ruiten points out the parallels between Gen 3:16 and Isa 65:23: the Isaianic text deals with a vision of the

---

51. Collins, "What Happened to Adam and Eve?" 26.

52. Collins, "A Syntactical Note," 143–44.

53. Indeed, the masculine singular in 3:15 may be employed precisely to indicate an individual.

54. So also Irenaeus, *Haer.* 3.23.7; 5.21.1, among other Fathers, for whom, see Lewis, "The Woman's Seed," 308–18. Notably, in the Hebrew, both "seed" (זֶרַע) and "he" (הוּא) are masculine (3:15); in the LXX, "he" (αὐτός, *autos*) remains masculine, but does not agree with "seed" (σπέρμα) which is neuter. Of the 103 occurrences of הוּא in Genesis, only once in the LXX's translation—here in 3:15—does the gender *not* fit idiomatic Greek: one would have expected the neuter αὐτό, *auto*, in order to match the neuter σπέρμα, *sperma*. "In none of the instances where the translator has translated literally does he do violence to agreement in Greek between the pronoun and its antecedent, except here in Gen 3:15." This is unlikely to have been a result of oversight; the most plausible explanation is that the translator was reading the verse in a messianic fashion (see Martin, "The Earliest Messianic Interpretation," 427).

55. *Genesis 1–15*, 81.

56. The parallelism between "birth" and "conception" in Job 3:3 also suggests their equivalence, at least in poetic terms. Also note 1 Chr 4:17 where the verb "to conceive" is used as a metonym for "to give birth/to deliver."

eschatological kingdom and the lengthy lifespans of its inhabitants (65:20), in contrast to the toil, labor, and death promised in Gen 3:17–20; the vision in Isa 65 involves the creation of new heavens and earth, an obvious link to the Genesis account of creation; Isa 65:25 mentions a serpent and "holy mountain," a point of comparison with the Garden of Eden; both Gen 3:16 and Isa 65:23 have the verb "beget/bring forth"; the LXX and *Tg. Isa.* have "tree of life" in 65:22; the LXX has "they shall not bear children for the curse" in 65:23, while *Tg. Isa.* has "they bring up children for death" (MT has "children of calamity"). All of this leads one to posit that the accounts are deliberately parallel and, what is significant for our purposes, that "conception" and "childbirth" of Gen 3:16 have not just to do with parturition but as childbirth and even further—the turmoil and travail of childrearing in a broken world.[57]

In any case the promise to multiply (רָבָה, *rabah*) children (1:28) is turned on its head and is now the promise to multiply (רְבָה) *pain* through childbirth (3:15). Man shares the same "pain/toil" (עִצָּבוֹן) in 3:17 (see 3:16 for the woman's "pain/toil"), as he struggles with the cursed ground in his attempt to seek sustenance. Before the fall, God caused to grow (צָמַח, *tsamakh*) "every tree that is pleasing to the sight and good for food" (2:9); after the fall the ground "grows" (צָמַח) thorns and thistles (3:18). Work itself was not a punishment for disobedience: man had his responsibilities in the garden prior to the fall (2:15). But the labor and toil, and the frustration and futility, of finding sustenance from the ground was decidedly punitive. In short, woman suffers pain as mother and wife; man shares the pain as father and farmer. "Both divine messages are directed to a point of highest fulfillment in the life of the female and the male. For the female that is, among other areas, her capacity of mother and wife. For the male that is, among other areas, his capacity of breadwinner and family provider."[58] Human creatureliness in conception/gestation/parturition and in the finding of sustenance for life is emphasized in the sentence upon woman and man. They are never to forget their finite nature and their dependence upon God.

Death

Adam actually goes on to live for a total of 930 years. Was the serpent right when it asserted "You surely shall not die" (3:4)? The threat of death was certainly not carried out immediately upon the perpetration of sin. This should actually not be surprising, for God's prohibition only underscored the certainty, not the chronology, of death (see for e.g., 1 Kgs 2:37, 42–46).[59]

There is another way to understand the promise of death. Cassuto suggests that the warning of death indicates that mankind will not be permitted to partake of the tree of life—"you will be unable to achieve eternal life and you will be compelled one

---

57. Van Ruiten, "Eve's Pain," 10–11.

58. Hamilton, *Genesis: Chapters 1–17*, 203.

59. Ibid., 173. The declaration in Gen 2:7 was not a death sentence in a legal sense, which invariably uses the verb "to die" in the Hophal (Exod 21:15–17; Lev 20:9–13, 15–16; etc.). Here, the verb is in the Qal, simply signifying the consequence of the transgression.

day to succumb to death; *you shall die,* in actual fact."[60] In light of the significant cultic parallels that virtually constitute the Garden of Eden as a sanctuary (see above), Wenham also suggests that the promised punishment of death for eating of the fruit of the knowledge of good and evil, as well as the subsequent expulsion from the Garden (2:17; 3:24), are both congruent with punitive exclusion from the camp of Israel (as in Lev 13:45–46; Num 5:2–4; etc.). This discharged a person into the sphere of death, away from the sanctuary where God was present, alienation from the source and center and fullness of life, a fate even more catastrophic than physical death (Ps 36:8–9; Jer 2:13).

> [In Eden] God was present. There he gave life. But to be expelled from the camp, as lepers were, was to enter the realm of death. Those unfortunates had to behave like mourners, with their clothes torn and their hair disheveled (Lev 13:45). If to be expelled from the camp of Israel was to "die," expulsion from the garden was an even more drastic kind of death. In this sense they did die on the day they ate of the tree: they were no longer able to have daily conversation with God, enjoy his bounteous provision, and eat of the tree of life; instead they had to toil for food, suffer, and eventually return to the dust from which they were taken.[61]

In other words, the threatened death in 2:17 was fulfilled in the expulsion of 3:24, as the humans were driven away from God, away from the tree of life, away from deathlessness. Now the only way expelled mankind could live was in sin, the only subjection they would know would be to sin's dominion, and the only sphere in which they could exist would be in sin's realm.[62] With the permission to eat of the tree of life in the original state, it seems that man, in that pre-fall condition of innocence, could have attained immortality by consumption of its fruit. Upon disobedience, however, Yahweh removed that possibility by expelling him from the Garden of Eden. One could view this as an act of mercy; in a *sinful* immortal state (if man had consumed the fruit of the tree of life) there would have been no possibility for redemption and regeneration. In other words, death is, paradoxically, both a bane and a blessing.

Though "death" is not explicitly mentioned in the sentencing phase, it is clearly implied: man formed from the "dust" (2:7) returns to "dust" (3:19; also Job 10:9; 34:15; Ps 103:14; Eccl 12:7). The God-complex of man is struck a severe blow—man's depen-

---

60. Cassuto, *Genesis,* 125.

61. Wenham, *Genesis 1–15,* 74.

62. Idem, "Sanctuary Symbolism," 404; and idem, *Genesis 1–15,* 90. The physical aspect of human death appears to have been introduced as a consequence of the fall. The biological death of other forms of life *prior* to the fall cannot be easily ruled out (without pleading miraculous providence): surely, the production of fruit and seed involved death of cells, not to mention the divine permission granted to man to eat plants. As a practicing dermatologist, I am only too well aware that the topmost layer of the skin, the epidermis, is partly composed of *dead* cells—the stratum corneum, made up of anucleated forms of the keratinocyte. The stratum corneum plays a critical role in normal skin function, primarily the prevention of transepidermal water loss, and these dead cells are integral to this role. Thus if Adam had normal skin, keratinocyte death likely occurred prior to the fall. If one accepts death before the fall, one could well argue that the death that came post-fall, concerned only the death of humans who, unlike other forms of life, possessed a special kind of life, spirituality, and morality. This death was therefore certainly of a different dimension, not like the death of any other living being, tissue, organ, or cell.

dence is powerfully reinforced—and the reality check is emphasized in the neat structuring of 3:19b.[63]

A	you *return*		
	B	to the ground	
		C	*because* (כִּי, *ki*) from it you were taken
		C'	*for* (כִּי) you are dust
	B'	and to dust	
A'	you shall *return*		

The narrator thus avoids explicit mention of death because it was clear to him that only life within the Garden, in the presence of God was true life, life abundant, life indeed. Lest man "stretch out" (שׁלח, *shlkh*) his hand (3:22), God "sends" (שׁלח) him out of the Garden (3:23): "God forestalls man's next step towards self-divinization by his own preemptive first strike."[64] And thus the doom of the first man and all of his descendants was sealed.[65]

Garments

The language of 3:21 is also cultic: "garments" and "clothed" are used of Aaron and the priests (Exod 28:4, 39–41; 29:5, 8; 39:27; 40:14; etc.). In addition, the sacrifice image is also apparent in the implied death of the animal(s) from which skins were procured by God. Of note, Lev 7:8 mandated that the skin of a burnt offering be reserved for the priest. With the Garden of Eden as the sanctuary and the cosmos as the Temple, this image of priestly garb and sacrifice is apropos. Surprisingly, the absence of clothing was not an issue prior to the fall (2:25; 3:11). Perhaps Wenham is right: "In this context God's provision of clothes appears not so much an act of grace, as often asserted, but as a reminder of their sinfulness," and the resulting shame.[66] Thus they bore on their bodies the sign of a "sacrificed" animal. Calvin appeared to agree: "God therefore designed that our first parents should, in such a dress, behold their own vileness—just as they had before seen it in their nudity—and should thus be reminded of their sin" (*Comm. Gen.* on 3:20).

Elements of the story clearly indicate that the drastic effects of the fall are ongoing; even the crawling of snakes that persists to date points to the persistent ramifications of sin, not to mention the turmoil of childbirth, the toil of human labor, the ever-present specter of death, and the irreversible banishment from the Garden—the inheritance of mankind from Adam and Eve. True, the situation of origin in the Garden and removal from it is not the direct experience of any human after Adam: every descendant of the primeval pair begins life *outside* the Garden. But, the condition of sin remains the

63. Mathews, *Genesis 1–11:26*, 253.

64. Wenham, *Genesis 1–15*, 85.

65. The account of the fall ends with the recycling of terms used in the first scene: "knowing good and evil," "work," "ground," "garden," "Eden," "east," "tree of life," and "guard." Introduction of man into the garden that began the scene is now paralleled with the expulsion of man from the garden at the close.

66. Wenham, *Genesis 1–15*, 85.

same for every human post-fall, as structural and lexical parallels between Gen 3 and 4 show (see Pericope 3). Moreover, the judgment pronounced in 3:14–19 goes beyond the timeframe of the original duo of sinners.[67]

God's "good/very good" creation had now been corrupted; and to this day, it remains so. The OT is quite clear about the universality of sin and the "experience of brokenness at every level of existence" (see 1 Kgs 8:46; Psalm 14:1–3; 51; 53; etc.).[68] And all of this the consequence of a yearning for autonomy and independence, control and egoism. This pericope, Gen 2:4–3:24, is therefore a picture of the breakdown of God's created order, brought about by the sin of mankind, the attempt of humanity to usurp the place of God and rid itself of the seeming shackles of dependence upon deity. In sum, the momentum of the drama of Pericope 2 is played out in three phases[69]:

Dependence upon God (2:4–25) →

Independence from God (3:1–13, being like God) →

Re-dependence upon God (3:14–24)

The circle is closed; man is involuntarily returned to the original state of dependence, for there can be no existence absolutely independent of God. The creatureliness of mankind allows for no other state but one of dependence upon the Creator. This narrative is, therefore, "a call to *definitional creatureliness,* which in the middle of our life, as in the middle of the narrative, we tend to forget and seek to override"—"a shared propensity to amnesia that besets us all."

> It is this forgetting, I submit, that lies behind the greed, selfishness, anxiety, and brutality that drives our common life. We imagine that we are free to take whatever we want and can get. We imagine that we are required to take whatever we can get, because there is no one to give us what we need. We imagine that fending off death, which we can do for ourselves and which we must do for ourselves, gives us rights of usurpation and privileges of confiscation from our brothers and sisters, and from the creation all around us.[70]

Theologically, this account points to man's responsibility for the sinfulness of the human condition and its dreadful consequences, not only for themselves and the rest of mankind, but for the entire cosmos, God's Temple: divine creation order was radically upset.[71] All because of man's seeking for independence from God.

---

67. Mathews, *Genesis 1–11:26,* 231.

68. Fretheim, "Is Genesis 3 a Fall Story?" 145. While it is accurate to say that the fall in Gen 3 is not referred to elsewhere in the OT, it must be borne in mind that that corpus does not commonly refer to *any* Genesis text, even one as foundational as Gen 22. Indeed, "one must wait until Rom 5 and 1 Cor 15 for an extensive discussion of Adam" (Hamilton, *Genesis: Chapters 1–17,* 210–11). Also see Wis 2:23–24; Sir 25:24; 2 Esd 3:4–11, 21–22; etc., for other early Jewish appropriations of the concept of an Adamic fall.

69. From Brueggemann, "You Are Dust," 4.

70. Ibid., 5, 7, 8.

71. Walsh, "Genesis 2:4b–3:24," 177.

SERMON FOCUS AND OUTLINES

THEOLOGICAL FOCUS OF PERICOPE 2 FOR PREACHING

2   Man is to live in dependence upon the Creator, but the assertion of human independence from God—the root cause of sin—alienates individuals, society, and creation at large, from each other and from God himself (2:4–3:24).

There may be some overlap in the theological sub-focuses of Pericopes 1 and 2. A brief repeat of those elements in this second sermon of the series is not altogether a bad idea, seeing how foundational the concept of man's responsibility to align himself to God's order is, for understanding and applying the rest of Scripture. In fact, the repetition might help highlight the failure of man to discharge that responsibility, which is the thrust of this pericope.

The dependence upon God is given much emphasis here: the creation of Eden, with the placement of man and the sustenance of man therein, in the "sanctuary," in the presence of God; and the careful creation of woman and the righting of a "not-good" situation. God provides all that is good; God establishes human relationships; God locates man close to him. Yet, man seeks independence, and in his seeking it, severs his dependent relationship with God, as he decides for himself what is "good" for him (i.e., sin). The result of sin is painfully portrayed in Pericope 2: disastrous alienation amongst mankind, between mankind and creation, and, most importantly, between mankind and its Creator. Yet even the ugliness of the scene cannot bar the grace of God that enters it: the death decreed, in one way, creates the gracious possibility for mankind's redemption from a life of sin.

The next pericope (Pericope 3) considers the effects of ongoing sin; therefore, it is advisable that the sermon on the current pericope keep its focus on dependence upon God to keep sin at bay, rather than addressing issues of repentance or return to God (which Pericope 3 will address).

Possible Preaching Outlines for Pericope 2

I.   PROVIDENCE: God's provision for man's every need
      Man created to serve God in the cosmic Temple, representing God (2:4; recap of Pericope 1)
      Man placed in the "sanctuary" (Garden of Eden) with every provision from God (2:5–15)
      Man's "not-good" situation corrected by God (2:18–25)
      Man's explicit guidance from God (2:16–17)
      Man created to be dependent on God
II.   INDEPENDENCE: Man seeks independence from God
      Sin, an act of independence from God and his demands and directives, enters the world (3:1–7)
      Move-to-Relevance: How we, today, sinfully seek independence from God[72]

---

72. The "Move-to-Relevance" here (and in other outlines) is intended to keep the sermon from becoming a lecture; it serves to connect with the audience, answering their implicit question "Why are we listening to this?" Unless such moves are frequently made and such questions constantly answered, the sermon remains a detached endeavor for the most part, unrelated to the audience, adrift in a sea of words.

The consequence of sin—alienation between humans, humans and creation, and humans and God (3:7–24)

III. DEPENDENCE: *Live in dependence!*

God's actions of grace restore man to a state of dependence on him (3:15, 20–21, 22–24)

What we can do to cultivate an attitude of constant dependence upon God

Another option is given below:

I. The Demand of God: Alignment to Divine Order (Obedience)

God's explicit guidance to man (2:16–17)

II. The Intention of God: Dependence upon Divine Creator

Man created to serve God in the cosmic Temple, representing God (2:4; recap of Pericope 1)

Man placed in the "sanctuary" (Garden of Eden) with every provision from God (2:5–15)

Man's "not-good" situation corrected by God (2:18–25)

III. The Response of Man: Misalignment to Divine Order (Disobedience)

Sin, an act of independence from God and his demands and directives, enters the world (3:1–7)

IV. The Intention of Man: Independence from Divine Creator

Move-to-Relevance: How we, today, sinfully seek independence from God

The consequence of sin—alienation between humans, humans and creation, and humans and God (3:7–24)

V. *Live in dependence!*

God's actions of grace restore man to a state of dependence on him (3:15, 20–21, 22–24)

What we can do to cultivate an attitude of constant dependence upon God

PERICOPE 3

Fratricide

Genesis 4:1–26

[Cain and Abel; Evil Generation; Birth of Seth]

REVIEW, SUMMARY, PREVIEW

Review of Pericope 2: Genesis 2:4–3:24 shows man and woman in the Garden of Eden, with everything provided for them, in dependence upon God. Unfortunately, they choose independence, opting to decide for themselves what was good for them, and sin enters the arena of human history.

Summary of Pericope 3: This pericope intertwines human pride and divine grace. Cain's offering to God is rejected, reflecting the former's prideful lack of submission to the demand of God. Upon being cautioned and warned, Cain's response is to murder. For this, God's discipline is visited upon him. Again, Cain's pride rears its head; he is unwilling to accept what comes from God's hand, nor does he evidence any repentance whatsoever for the evil he had perpetrated. God, however, is gracious in planning for Cain's protection from potential avengers. Nonetheless, evil continues to grow and Cain's line culminates in the notorious and savage Lamech. Yet, once again, God's grace is evident: a new line, in Seth, is established, and humanity turns back to God.

Preview of Pericope 4: In the next pericope (5:1–6:8), the spread of evil is described. Ungodliness escalates until God takes action. All humanity is culpable and pays the price, evidenced in the dirge-like refrain of the genealogy of Gen 5: "and he died." But the life of Enoch, who walked

75

with God and did not die, teaches one how to overcome the epidemic of sin and to experience intimacy with God.

3.   Genesis 4:1–26

> **THEOLOGICAL FOCUS OF PERICOPE 3**
>
> 3.   **Man's attitude of pride causes his sinfulness to propagate and perpetuate itself in worsening rebellion against God, manifest in egregious sin that invites God's discipline, yet the operation of God's grace promises respite from the effects of sin (4:1–26).**
>
> > 3.1   Man's attitude of pride (with his unteachable and unrepentant spirit), rendering worship unacceptable and preventing mastery over sin, may culminate in egregious sin that invites God's discipline (though tempered with grace) (4:1–16).
> >
> > > 3.1.1   *Man's attitude of pride is a source of evil, rendering worship unacceptable and preventing mastery over sin.*
> > >
> > > 3.1.2   *Man's attitude of pride, marked by an unteachable and unrepentant spirit, may culminate in egregious sin that invites God's discipline (which is, however, tempered with grace).*
> >
> > 3.2   The sinfulness of man propagates and perpetuates itself in worsening rebellion against God, but the operation of God's grace promises respite from the effects of sin (4:17–26).
> >
> > > 3.2.1   *The sinfulness of man propagates and perpetuates itself in rebellion against God, going from bad to worse.*
> > >
> > > 3.2.2   *The operation of God's grace promises respite from the effects of sin.*

OVERVIEW

It is a fact that if the bulk of this pericope, Gen 4:1–24, the story of Cain (and Abel), were omitted, 3:24 would transition very nicely into 4:25. However, there is a purpose for this "interpolation." While Pericope 2 (2:4–3:24) dealt with the breakdown primarily of the relationship between man and God, Pericope 3 concerns itself with the fragmentation of inter-human relationships.

In the next pericope (Pericope 4 [5:1–6:8]), the genealogical lineage is introduced with the תּוֹלְדֹת (*toldot*)-formula in 5:1. But in Gen 2:3–4:26, Pericopes 2 and 3, it is the תּלדות of the heavens and earth (2:4) that forms the prologue to the account of the fall that destroyed the relationships between man and God (Pericope 2) and between man and man (Pericope 3). And from these we learn truths valid for all of God's people in every generation.

Three sections make up this pericope: 4:1–16 (man's descendants); 4:17–24 (Cain's descendants); and 4:25–26 (Adam's descendants), each of which begins with "*X* knew his wife [and she conceived] and gave birth" (4:1, 17, 25). The pericope is bounded by a double *inclusio*; a birth and the worship of Yahweh occur at both ends[1]:

---

1. From Greidanus, *Preaching Christ from Genesis*, 86.

> **A** "Now the man knew his wife Eve" (4:1)
> **B** Cain and Abel bring offerings to Yahweh (4:3–4)
>
> **A'** "Adam knew his wife again" (4:25)
> **B'** People begin to invoke the name of Yahweh (4:26)

Several elements of the text affirm its unity and integrity: echoes of the concept of "seven" (4:15, 24); and the fact that within 2:4–4:26, אדמה, *'dmh* ("ground"), occurs fourteen times, and "Yahweh" thirty-five times (matching the thirty-five occurrences of אלהים, *'elohim*, in 1:1–2:3). Thus, the last verse of this pericope, 4:26, bears the seventieth mention of deity in Genesis, as well as the fourteenth occurrence of קרא (*qr'*, "call").[2] In 4:1–16, "brother" echoes seven times, as also does "Abel"; and "Cain" occurs fourteen times. Moreover, in all of Gen 4 (4:1–26), "name" occurs seven times. Participial phrases consistently describe the careers of the characters in this pericope: Abel, keeper of flocks (4:2); Cain, tiller of ground (4:2); Enoch, builder of city (4:17); Jabal, dweller in tents (4:20); Jubal, player of instruments (4:21), and Tubal-cain, forger of implements (4:22). The discourse of this pericope matches the style of the others in Genesis: genealogies are interrupted with narrative digressions (Adam to Lamech, 4:1–18, is interrupted by the account of Cain's murder, 4:3–15; Adam to Noah, 5:3–9:29, is interrupted by the account of the flood, 6:1–9:19), bifurcations mark the genealogies of Genesis (Adam, Abraham, Isaac, and Noah, each have two or three sons, with the younger/youngest receiving God's favor), and a list of the descendants of the unfavored sons precedes that of the favored one (Cain's sons before Seth's, 4:17–5:32; Japheth's and Ham's sons before Shem's, Gen 10; Ishmael's sons before Isaac's, 25:12–34; and Esau's sons before Jacob's, Gen 36–37). As was Gen 3, Gen 4:1–16 is also structured with narrative alternating with dialogue.[3]

> **Narrative introduction/transition (4:1–2a)**
> **A** Sacrifices (4:2b–5): *Narrative—Cain and Abel main actors; Yahweh passive*
> **B** Interrogation (4:6–7): *Dialogue—Yahweh [and Cain]*
> Two questions, each with two parts (4:6, 7); sin as a devouring animal (4:7)
> **C** Murder (4:8): *Narrative—Cain and Abel*
> **B'** Judgment (4:9–15a): *Dialogue—Yahweh and Cain*
> Two questions (4:9, 10); land opening mouth to drink blood (4:11)
> **A'** Sign (4:15b): *Narrative—Yahweh main actor; Cain passive*
> **Narrative conclusion/transition (4:16)**

There are also remarkable similarities with the account in Gen 2 and 3: principal characters—two in each case—introduced by function (2:5, 15, 18; 4:2; etc.); prohibition and warning before disobedience (2:17; 4:7); central scene of disobedience (3:6–7; 4:8); divine questioning (3:9–13; 4:9–10); judgment (3:14–19; 4:11–12); post-sin, Adam and Eve are clothed by God (3:21), and Cain is marked by him (4:15b);

---

2. Wenham, *Genesis 1–15*, 96. Lamech (4:23–24), incidentally, is the seventh in line from Adam, an example of the "definite predilection" of biblical genealogists to give prominence to certain individuals. See Sasson, "A Genealogical 'Convention,'" 176 and further, for other examples of this idiosyncrasy.

3. Wenham, *Genesis 1–15*, 96–97, 99–100.

the transgressors are "driven" (3:24; 4:16) from the presence of God; and they move east of Eden (3:24; 4:16).[4] The primary protagonists (Adam and Cain) have the same occupation, "cultivator of the ground" (2:5, 15; 3:23; 4:2, 12), their sins are linked with "fruit" (3:1–6; 4:3), their alienation from God results from their "knowing" (3:5, 7–13, 22; 4:9), and their examination and sentencing follow the same pattern.[5]

> Yet the differences between the two stories [Pericopes 2 and 3] must not be overlooked either. Whereas in [Gen] chap. 2 there is no sense of alienation between man and God to start with, in chap. 4 this is present from the outset because the Lord does not accept Cain's sacrifice. If the two temptation scenes are compared, differences spring readily to the eye. Eve has to be persuaded to disregard the creator's advice by the serpent (3:1–5), but Cain is not dissuaded from his murderous intention by his creator's appeal (4:6–7). Finally, when God pronounces sentence on Adam, Eve, and the serpent, they accept it without demur (3:14–20), but Cain protests that he is being treated too harshly (4:14). Clearly, then, though the writer of Genesis wants to highlight the parallels between the two stories, he does not regard the murder of Abel simply as a rerun of the fall. There is development: sin is more firmly entrenched and humanity is further alienated from God.[6]

In Genesis 2–3, the intimacy of man with woman with God degenerates into alienation; in Gen 4:1–16, intimacy between brothers deteriorates into fratricide (and results in even more alienation from God). Cain is not just a chip off the old block; his sins are greater in magnitude than those of his parents. Not only does he appear to have performed an offering without the requisite internal attitude that pleases God, he responds petulantly and negatively to God's chiding and encouragement to correct himself. He then commits the first murder—the first ever death of a human described in the Bible, perpetrated by the first man born in the Bible—lies to Yahweh, refuses to acknowledge responsibility for his heinous deed, fails to show any repentance when confronted with incontrovertible evidence, and makes protestations against the sentence meted out upon him by Yahweh. Fratricide—"the archetype of all violence"—is not merely between humans, it has to do with the Creator, the one who gives life.[7] As a result of Cain's act, more killings become a possibility (4:14), and indeed that possibility is realized in the iniquitous exploits of Cain's descendent, Lamech (4:23–24).

---

4. Also see 13:10–12 and 25:6 for the same directional advance to the east by those out of favor with God: "In the Genesis narratives, when man goes 'east,' he leaves the land of blessing (Eden and the Promised Land) and goes to a land where the greatest of his hopes will turn to ruin (Babylon and Sodom)" (Sailhamer, "Genesis," 104). Other verbal similarities between Pericopes 2 and 3 include: "conceive" (3:16; 4:1); "keep" (2:15; 3:24; 4:9); "voice" (3:8, 10; 4:10); "face/presence" (3:8; 4:5–6, 14, 16); "desire" and "rule" (3:16; 4:7); "curse" (3:14, 17; 4:11; the latter two references have "curse" and "ground" together); "hiding from face" (3:8; 4:14). See Hauser, "Linguistic and Thematic Links," 297–305.

5. Mathews, *Genesis 1–11:26*, 263.

6. Wenham, *Genesis 1–15*, 100.

7. Peels, "The World's First Murder," 34.

"His [Cain's] aggression against Heaven's dictate is surpassed by the vitriolic voice of Lamech, who imitates his ancestor through murdering the vulnerable."[8]

Adam and Eve do not have to wait for each other's death to see God's judgment of death come to pass—the catastrophic consequence of their rebellion. Before the end of their own lives, they are witness to the slaying of their second son, and the exile of their first away from the presence of God.[9]

3.1   Genesis 4:1–16

> **THEOLOGICAL FOCUS 3.1**
>
> 3.1   Man's attitude of pride (with his unteachable and unrepentant spirit), rendering worship unacceptable and preventing mastery over sin, may culminate in egregious sin that invites God's discipline (though tempered with grace) (4:1–16).
>
> > 3.1.1   *Man's attitude of pride is a source of evil, rendering worship unacceptable and preventing mastery over sin.*
> >
> > 3.1.2   *Man's attitude of pride, marked by an unteachable and unrepentant spirit, may culminate in egregious sin that invites God's discipline (which is, however, tempered with grace).*

NOTES 3.1

3.1.1 *Man's attitude of pride is a source of evil, rendering worship unacceptable and preventing mastery over sin.*

Eve's statement at the birth of her firstborn (4:1), the first human to be born in Scripture—and that outside the Garden—is odd. אִישׁ, *'ish* ("man") is never used to describe a male baby. Perhaps she sees in this child the future man, the beginning of a race. Or, more likely, the woman is hinting that as the אֲדָמָה, *'adamah* ("ground"), brought forth an אָדָם, *'adam* ("man"), so now the אִשָּׁה, *'ishah* ("woman") generates the אִישׁ, *'ish* ("man"). The verb translated "gotten," קנה, *qnh*, is also used of God's creative activity (Deut 32:6–7; Gen 14:19, 22; Ps 139:13; Prov 8:22), as well as in the sense of "get/acquire/buy." Here, too, wordplay may have taken precedence over precision in meaning: the use of קנה echoes the name of Cain (קַיִן, *qyn*). Eve's אֶת־יְהוָה (*'et-yhwh*) is also cryptic—does it mean "with Yahweh['s help]," or "[equally] with Yahweh"?[10] Cassuto sees Eve's utterance in a negative light: "the first woman, in her joy at giving birth to her first son, boasts of her generative power, which approximates in her estimation to the Divine creative power. 'The Lord formed the first man (2:7), and I have formed the second man.' . . . literally, 'I have created a man with the Lord . . . I

---

8. Mathews, *Genesis 1–11:26*, 263.

9. Ibid., 273.

10. The LXX has διὰ τοῦ Θεοῦ, *dia tou theou*, "through God"; the Vulgate, likewise, *per Dominum*; the Peshitta has "unto the Lord."

stand together [i.e., equally] with Him in the rank of creators.'"[11] Eve sees herself as a quasi-creator—she conceived, carried, labored, and bore. Named by her husband as "mother of all living" (3:20), she glories in her generative powers.[12] It is likely that Eve's hubris is being seen as inherited by the entire Cainite line: the account of their deeds commences with a murder (that of Abel) and concludes with another (that by Lamech, 4:23–24).[13]

A disjunctive clause in 4:2c (conjunction + subject + verb) draws a sharp contrast between Eve's children—Abel, the shepherd, *but* Cain, the farmer (literally: "And-was Abel a-keeper of-flocks, *but-Cain was* a-cultivator of-the-ground"). This is the first hint of a tension that is going to be developed to a lethal extreme in the narrative. Yet another disjunctive clause in 4:4 accentuates, again, the contrast between Cain and Abel ("And brought Cain . . ." vs. "But Abel brought . . .")—this time specifically relating to their actions in the sacrifice event. As if the syntactical contrast were not enough, the author throws in גַם־הוּא (*gam-hu'*, "also he"), greatly highlighting the distinction between the two brothers' offerings: "But Abel brought, also he,. . . ." "Brought" (בּוֹא, *bo'*, 4:3, 4) is often a cultic word for the act of offering of sacrifice (e.g., Lev 2:2, 8); "offering" (מִנְחָה, *minkhh*, 4:3) is frequently used of grain offerings (Lev 2:1, 4, 14, 15), though animal offerings are also referred to by the same term (1 Sam 2:17, 29)—Abel's is referred to as מִנחה as well, in Gen 4:4.[14] The difference in the offerings of the two sons of Adam is significant (4:3–4): Abel brings firstlings (that were reserved for God: Exod 13:2, 15; Lev 27:26; etc.) and, particularly mentioned, he brought their choicest portions—the fat (which always has a positive connotation with regard to sacrifices: Exod 29:13, 18; 34:19; Lev 3:3–5, 9–11, 14–16; 4:8–10, 26, 31; etc.). Cain does not bring *first*fruits (Exod 23:19; 34:26; Lev 2:14: Num 15:17–21; etc.); his is merely "of the fruit of the ground" (Gen 4:3). Thus far fruit had come off trees and from the "earth" (1:11, 12, 29; 3:2, 3, 6). For the first time, here in 4:3, fruit is associated with "ground," a linkage that implicitly points to the curse (3:17). In sum, Abel appears to have taken pains to give the best; Cain, on the other hand, appears to have been rather indifferent, simply discharging a duty.[15] One engages in "acceptable, heartfelt worship"; the other merely conducts an "unacceptable tokenism." "By offering the firstborn Abel signified that he recognized God as the Author and Owner of Life. In common with the rest of the ancient Near East, the Hebrews believed that the deity, as lord of the manor, was entitled to the *first share* of all produce. The *first*fruits of plant and the *first*born of animals and man were his. . . . Abel's offering conformed with this theology; Cain's did

---

11. Cassuto, *Genesis*, 201 (italics removed).

12. Kass, *The Beginning of Wisdom*, 126.

13. Eslinger, "A Contextual Identification," 68–69. Like his mother (3:6), Cain also questions God's dictate. And just as his mother was warned after the sin, he is warned, but *before* his sin—both warnings use similar words (3:16; 4:7); see below.

14. The LXX, however, labels Cain's sacrifices θυσία (*thusia*, 4:3, 5), and Abel's δῶρον (*dōron*, 4:4; though Heb 11:4 calls Abel's θυσία).

15. Cassuto, *Genesis*, 205.

not."[16] As a result God has "regard" for the offering of one, but not for that of the other; the chiastic structure of 4:4b–5a emphasizes this differential.

> And Yahweh had regard
>> for Abel and his offering;
>> but for Cain and his offering
> he had no regard.

As the rebuke from God (4:6–7) indicates, what Cain should have done was corrected his wrong attitude (and action) so as to be acceptable to God. Instead, he becomes "very angry" (4:5; literally, "it burned Cain exceedingly"). The pastoral and parental counsel offered by Yahweh to Cain (4:6–7) portrays divine grace. Genesis 4:7, however, has its technical difficulties: "sin" is feminine, but "crouching" is a masculine participle; "*its* desire" has a masculine pronominal suffix—literally, "his desire"; and "you must master *it*" is literally "you must master *him*." It might simply be explained, as Hamilton notes, that Hebrew nouns that are feminine morphologically are sometimes treated as masculine.[17] Moreover, the word רבץ (*rbts*, "crouch") may well have been related to the Akkadian *rābiṣum*, apparently some sort of demonic entity that stood guard at entrances to buildings.[18] Therefore, another option would be to read the phrase as a predicate nominative—"sin is a crouching [demon]."[19] The subtle shift from feminine to masculine may reflect this demonic involvement. In any case, Cain has a choice as well as the ability to "master" sin; succumbing to it is not inevitable. Personal responsibility is emphasized by the redundant use of the pronoun: "you, you-must-master-it." He, tragically, does not. Cain's pride becomes a source of evil, rendering worship unacceptable.

3.1.2 *Man's attitude of pride, marked by an unteachable and unrepentant spirit, may culminate in egregious sin that invites God's discipline (which is, however, tempered with grace).*

It is significant that Cain does not reply to Yahweh's questioning and rebuke, but instead he speaks to Abel (4:8), and in a cluster of *wayyiqtols*, kills him: he spoke,[20] he

---

16. Waltke, "Cain and His Offering," 368, 369. That the issue is not whether a sacrifice was bloody or bloodless is clear from the same term מנחה used to describe both Cain's and Abel's offerings (4:3, 4), as noted earlier. The NT agrees that Abel's sacrifice was a better one: Heb 11:4.

17. *Genesis: Chapters 1–17*, 227. A good example of this would be the title of the author of Ecclesiastes—a male figure with the epithet, קֹהֶלֶת, *qohelet*, a feminine noun; but קֹהֶלֶת is always coupled with the masculine form of the verb.

18. Speiser, *Genesis*, 33. Morales speculates that the "door" at which sin crouched was the entrance to the Garden of Eden, the eastward portal to which sacrifices were brought (see Exod 40:29; Lev 1:3; 4:7, 18, for parallels with the tabernacle cultus). See *The Tabernacle Pre-figured*, 111.

19. While the concept has already been amply pictured in the fall, now for the first time, the word "sin" appears in the Bible!

20. We are not told what Cain told his brother (4:8). The LXX, Vulgate, Samaritan Pentateuch, Peshitta, *Tg. Neof.*, and *Tg. Ps.-J.* attempt to fill in the blanks with a direct quote from Cain to Abel: "Let us go out into the field." The silence, by itself, intensifies the starkness of the killing. Reis notes the double use of the preposition אֶל ('*el*) with הבל (*hbl*) in 4:8; in the second instance, it is translated "against"

rose, he killed. That this is a heinous deed that Cain commits is patently obvious. The account is structured deliberately, going back and forth between the siblings, Cain to Abel, Abel to Cain, and so on.[21]

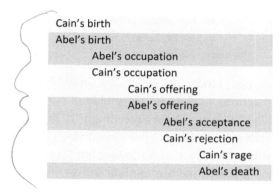

Cain's birth
Abel's birth
Abel's occupation
Cain's occupation
Cain's offering
Abel's offering
Abel's acceptance
Cain's rejection
Cain's rage
Abel's death

We are never allowed to forget that these were brothers and that this was fratricide. In fact, Cain is never called Abel's brother; rather, it is the other way around: Abel is always Cain's brother. Thus, in literary fashion we are being told that Cain does *not* act as Abel's brother. Twice in 4:8 and twice in 4:9 it is noted: "Abel, his brother." And God repeats "your brother" in 4:10 and 11. The horrific nature of Cain's nefarious act is underscored by the use of "kill" five times in Gen 4:1–16 (4:8, 14, 15, 23, 25). Cain's crime, it appears, was premeditated, for any such action "in the field," out of range of cries for help, is proof of a planned misdeed according to the law (Deut 22:25–27). The poignancy of Abel's helplessness is brought out by the use of צָעַק (*tsa'aq*, "cry," 4:10): the desperate cry of the starving (41:55), the persecuted (Exod 14:10), the raped (Deut 22:24, 27), the afflicted (2 Kgs 4:1), the oppressed (Isa 19:20), and the destroyed (Lam 2:18)—cries that reach the ears of Yahweh (Pss 34:17; 77:1; 107:6, 28). Incidentally, this cry comes from the "ground," the very locus that was cursed because of Adam's fall (Gen 3:17), and which is now polluted by Cain's sin. The one who does not utter a word (at least in this narrative) when he is alive, cries out when he is dead.[22] The egregious nature of the slaying is thus foregrounded in this narrative.

Even after the killing, God seeks out the killer with grace, inviting a confession (4:6–7), just as he did with Adam and Eve after their fall in the Garden. But unlike his parents, Cain replies with a brazen lie and an impudent *non sequitur* that throws God's question back into his face: "Am I my brother's keeper?" (שׁמר, *shmr*, 4:10). To "keep" is the prerogative of God and characteristic of his relationship to his people (Ps 121:4–8, where שׁמר occurs five times to describe Yahweh's "keeping" of Israel; also see

(Cain rose up *against* Abel). Perhaps the first one has the same sense: Cain spoke *against* Abel (to his parents? to himself?). See "What Cain Said," 112–13. Considering this a "scenic narrative," McEntire thinks "the narrator may wish for the reader to see Cain speak to Abel without hearing him. The actual words of Cain are left to the reader's imagination" ("Being Seen and Not Heard," 12).

21. From Ross, *Creation and Blessing*, 154.

22. Mathews, *Genesis 1–11:26*, 275. And Abel's "faith still speaks" (Heb 11:4). In Gen 4:10–11, it is Abel's innocent blood that cries out: literally it is "bloods" that cry out (4:10); the plural is always used in the OT of blood that is shed (Exod 4:26; 1 Chr 22:8; Ps 5:7; Isa 1:15).

Num 6:24; Ps 12:7).[23] It appears that Cain is blaming God: "*You* are the keeper—that's *your* job, not mine." This reminds the reader of Adam's attempt to inculpate God: "The woman *you* gave me" (Gen 3:12).

The consequence of his wickedness is that Cain is cursed "from the ground" (4:11), which most likely indicates the source of cursing: the ground which opened its mouth to receive Abel's blood has opened its mouth to deliver a curse (the same sense is found in 4:10, where Abel's blood cries to Yahweh, also "from the ground"). The ground, cursed in 3:17, now curses Cain. Cain tilled the land; Cain offered the fruit of the land; Cain gave the land his brother's blood; and now the land opens its mouth to curse Cain, refusing its fruit, and banishing him from it (4:11–12).[24] What had been rendered difficult after the fall (obtaining yield from the ground, 3:17–18), is now infinitely harder for Cain. In distinction from the curse in Genesis 3, where humans were not cursed (only the snake and the ground were), here, for the first time in the history of mankind, a human being is cursed! The result is Cain's being driven away from the land—loss of community, loss of belonging, and, indeed, loss of identity, a fate perhaps worse than death.[25] Excommunication from among the people often called for quarantine (Lev 13:46; 15:31) or, in some cases, even death (Exod 31:14; Lev 20:2–3; 18:28–29). Cain's cutting off resulted in his banishment to the land of Nod, east of Eden, further away from the garden than were Adam and Eve (3:24 and 4:16). The one destined to be a נוד (*nud*, "wanderer," 4:12, 14) ends up in the land of נוד (*nod*, "Nod," 4:16), forever reminding him of his grave sin.

And Cain's reaction to this discipline? He complains about the unfairness of it all! He is dissatisfied with the yield of the ground promised, the removal from God's presence, his status as a nomad, and with the potential for being killed himself—quite ironic, coming from one who has just slain his brother.[26] All throughout the account, Cain's attitude has been one of pride displayed in choleric irritability. He worships half-heartedly. He sulks when called to account. His petulant outbursts reflect his angry and envious disposition. He ends up a fratricide. And in all of this, there is no remorse or repentance displayed. Neither is there any gratitude for God's grace in protecting him from potential avengers (4:15). Only self-pity marks Cain. That he

---

23. Riemann observes that in all the 450 instances of the participial form of שמר (שׁוֹמֵר, *shomer*), there is not a single instance where it describes one human "keeping" another ("Am I My Brother's Keeper?" 483).

24. Gunkel, *Genesis*, 45.

25. Hamilton, *Genesis: Chapters 1–17*, 232. See Lev 18:24–28; 26:33–35; Num 14:22–24; Deut 28:64. One wonders why capital punishment was not executed on the murderer as the Torah would later mandate (e.g., Num 35:32). Such a measure would have not only purged the world of the evildoer, but also served as a deterrent. In Cain's situation, there might not have been many around who needed such a deterrent. Also, who would have exacted that penalty and how, particularly in the absence of a formal judicial system? See Cassuto, *Genesis*, 221–22. Perhaps the best answer is that God is asserting his prerogative over life and death, an authority he does not deign to share except by divine sanction and under strict guidelines (Mathews, *Genesis 1–11:26*, 278).

26. Who the potential avengers of Abel might be is not the concern of the biblical author. Likely, these are other descendants of Adam and Eve, from whom Cain's wife, also, must have come.

does not once ask for or receive forgiveness is telling. He is finally removed from the divine presence (4:14, 16).[27]

What exactly the "sign" was that God gave Cain is unclear; *Gen. Rab.* 22:12 suggests, rather incredibly, that God gave Cain a dog that would accompany him in his wanderings, scaring off potential assailants! Moberly, working off the preposition "for" (ל, *l*, "sign *for* Cain"), rather than the expected "on" (עַל, *'l*, as in Exod 13:16; Deut 6:8; 11:18, where signs are placed "on" bodies), thinks that the proverb-like saying "Whoever kills Cain is in danger of being avenged sevenfold" (4:15) is, itself, the sign—a sign "for" Cain's protection, rather than a sign "on" Cain's person.[28] In any case, just as the clothing given by God to Adam and Eve after the fall (3:21) reminded them of their sin *and* God's mercy, so also the sign on Cain indicated his sin/guilt; but it also served as a token of God's mercy upon the sinner—Cain was not to be killed in vengeance by anyone. Cain is banned, but he is still blessed: "[h]e leaves God's presence, but not God's protection."[29] Peels notes the irony that "Yahweh wants to be the keeper of the man who did not want to be his brother's keeper."[30]

What began as a narrative of two brothers coming to Yahweh through sacrifice concludes with one murdered and the other excommunicated from God's presence. Thus both Pericopes 2 and 3 end with distance (and even more distance) being put between deity and humanity, the end result of an unteachable and unrepentant spirit that produces egregious sin. However, God's discipline that follows, is also tempered with grace.

3.2 *Genesis 4:17–26*

THEOLOGICAL FOCUS 3.2

3.2 The sinfulness of man propagates and perpetuates itself in worsening rebellion against God, but the operation of God's grace promises respite from the effects of sin (4:17–26).

   3.2.1 *The sinfulness of man propagates and perpetuates itself in rebellion against God, going from bad to worse.*

   3.2.2 *The operation of God's grace promises respite from the effects of sin.*

27. עָוֹן (*'on*, "punishment," 4:13) can also mean "guilt." Early versions (the LXX, *Tg. Onq.*, Vulgate) have, "My guilt is too great to forgive/bear," implying that Cain was expressing remorse for his sin and circuitously asking for forgiveness. However, the combination "guilt + forgive/bear" yields forgiveness only when God is dispensing it (Exod 34:6–7), and never when man is asking for it (also see Lev 7:18; 20:17; and Ezek 44:12, where the sense of punishment is uppermost with this combination).

28. Moberly, "The Mark of Cain," 14–16. The LXX seems to agree; its construction lacks a preposition, and has an indirect object in the dative, "for Cain" (τῷ Κάιν, *tō Kain*).

29. Hamilton, *Genesis 1–17*, 235.

30. Peels, "The World's First Murder," 30.

NOTES 3.2

3.2.1 The sinfulness of man propagates and perpetuates itself in rebellion against God, going from bad to worse.

The remainder of the pericope (4:17–26) is a genealogy broken only by a digression about Enoch and Lamech (4:17–18, 23–24), perhaps to ensure that these two are not confused with the Enoch and Lamech in the genealogy of Seth that is to follow in the next pericope (5:23–24, 28–31). What is clear in this section of Pericope 3, however, is that despite advances in culture and urbanization introduced by Cain's descendants, one thing remained constant—the black mark of Cain's sin: "By virtue of being Cain's descendants, the people named in the genealogy all inherit his curse. Thus the Cainite genealogy becomes part of the Yahwist's account of man's increasing sin."[31] References to killing are scattered throughout the pericope (4:8, 14, 15, 23, 25)—the grim reality of the epidemic of violence unleashed by Cain infecting the human race.

Immediately after a life of wandering and vagrancy is decreed for him, Cain builds a city (4:17). The only other building of a city in Gen 1–11 is the enterprise at Babel—entirely negative in tone. It is likely that that is the tone of Cain's endeavors as well, quite in keeping with his truculent and recalcitrant nature. It is an act of defiance by one who repudiates the nomadic life God had decreed; no living by God's terms for Cain. It is perhaps even a taking charge of his own security on his own terms, refusing to trust God's "sign" and promise of protection.[32] After all, a city in antiquity was not actually determined by size and population but by the degree of protection its walls and gates afforded: it was not so much a populated settlement as it was a place of protection.[33] "For God's Eden he [Cain] substitutes his own, for the goal given to his life by God, he substitutes a goal chosen by himself—just as he substituted his own security for God's. . . . And thus Cain, with everything he does, digs a little deeper the abyss between himself and God."[34]

In a way, Cain's genealogy is a futile and abortive one; his descendants would all die in the flood and so, unlike other genealogies, it does not depict the origin of nations or peoples contemporaneous with the ancient Israelites who would read this account (as would be the case with the lineages in 10:13–19; 19:37–38; 25:12–18; and 36:9–19). Moreover, foregoing the standard form, this genealogy dispenses with years of life and time of death, etc. The intent is obviously not chronology, but theology, and 4:17–24 is essential for the thrust of what the author is *doing* with what he is saying in the pericope as a whole.

> Without this section, the reader would go from the first murder directly to the line of Seth. The impression that would be conveyed is that after Cain is cursed and sent away, everything continues as usual. A substitute for Abel is born, hu-

31. Wilson, *Genealogy and History*, 155.

32. Hamilton, *Genesis: Chapters 1–17*, 238.

33. Lohr, "'So YHWH Established a Sign,'" 102.

34. Ellul, *The Meaning of the City*, 5–6.

manity bears sons and daughters, and everyone lives happily ever after. In fact, nothing could be further from the truth, and this is why these verses about Cain's descendants are so crucial for the flow of the narrative. The verses inform the reader that from the first murderer originated a part of the population which is in dire contrast to the one presented in ch. 5. The descendants of Cain and the descendants of Adam form two sides of humanity. Cain does not leave the stage of world history—he continues to be active and his legacy of rebellion is perpetuated in his descendants.[35]

Civilization is certainly advanced by Cain's line. Enoch has a city named for him (4:17), and Irad's name actually means "city" (4:18). Abel shepherded "flocks" (i.e., sheep and goats), but Jabal had "livestock" (4:20; i.e., all herded animals: sheep, goats, cattle, donkeys, camels; see 47:16–17; Exod 9:3), enabling him to trade with those beasts of burden.[36] Jubal was the father of the humanities, so to speak, being the musician he was (Gen 4:21); and Tubal-cain made strides in metallurgy (and possibly weaponry; 4:22). Interestingly, the names of the brothers and their cousin (Jabal and Jubal, and Tubal-cain) echo "Abel" and "Cain." Mathews observes that these sonic allusions may anticipate 4:25–26 where the Sethite line takes the place of the murdered Abel. "The point is that the progeny of Cain cannot take the place of fallen Abel; it is left to Seth to perpetuate the best of the Adamic line."[37]

But the focus and terminus of this seemingly progressive line is Lamech (4:19, 23–24). If Cain was a brazen murderer, Lamech was even more perverted and depraved than his ancestor, willing even to kill a child/young man and consider it a badge of honor as he boasts about his violent deed. While there is no indication of a weapon employed by Lamech, Tubal-Cain's enterprise of forging metal suggests that Lamech may have possessed instruments of warfare. Vindictive and impious, he seems to have been capable of the most abysmal evil as he protected himself, but without recourse to the divine assistance that Cain, his ancestor, had sought (4:14). The closure of the Cainite line with this malefactor indicates how sin had permeated those who descended from Cain (the first murderer)—clearly, "material progress did not go hand in hand with moral advancement. Not only did violence prevail in the world, but it was precisely in deeds of violence that those generations gloried. The very qualities that are ethically reprehensible, and are hateful in the sight of the Lord, were esteemed in the eyes of men."[38] Surely judgment was coming upon mankind. The progression of evil from Adam to Cain to Lamech is vividly portrayed: one eats a forbidden fruit, the second kills his brother and remains unrepentant, and the third murders a child and arrogantly threatens more wickedness.

---

35. Fockner, "Reopening the Discussion," 446–47.

36. Wenham, *Genesis 1–15*, 113.

37. *Genesis 1–11:26*, 288.

38. Cassuto, *Genesis*, 244. Another Lamech would conclude the parallel line of Seth (5:25–32). That one, unlike his namesake, frets about the curse and hopes for relief through a son, Noah, who, the Bible records, found favor in the eyes of Yahweh (6:8).

3.2.2 *The operation of God's grace promises respite from the effects of sin.*

The conclusion of the pericope with 4:25–26 is deliberate, to draw a contrast between the line of Cain and that of Seth. The former is remembered for its humanistic advances; the latter for its godliness. Parade examples in each line certify this contrast: a Lamech on one side (#7 in that line), bigamist and vicious murderer, and an Enoch on the other (#7 in this line), one who walked with God (5:22).[39] "Genealogies are designed to celebrate life and accomplishment by tracing the continuation of family from one ancestor to the next, but Cain's record involves the cessation of life, as represented by the murderers Cain and Lamech," the first and last in their described lines—one murderer to another.[40] This unusual genealogy, rather than record the continuation of life, commences and concludes with individuals who actually bring life to an end: in other words, "human sin stands in profound contradiction to the created order of God." The disruption of God's order by Cain's line is offset by the genealogy of Seth that has the last word: the reassertion of God's created order.[41]

Thus, despite Cain and his ignominious line culminating in the notorious Lamech, there would be hope for mankind in the new line that commenced with the third son of Adam and Eve (4:25–26). The two earlier conceptions and births in Gen 4—man having relations with Eve who delivered Cain (4:1), and Cain having relations with his wife who delivered Enoch (4:17)—culminated in disaster (4:1–16 and 4:17–24). The third time around—Adam having relations with Eve who delivered Seth (4:23)—promises to be very different in outcome. The contrast between Eve's exclamation at the birth of Cain (4:1), and here at the end of the chapter at the birth of Seth (4:25), is also striking.[42]

	Subject	Verb	Object	Dative/Indirect Object
Cain (4:1)	I [Eve]	have gotten/created	a man	with Yahweh
Seth (4:25)	God	appointed	another seed	to me

It is likely that Eve has had a change of heart here. Her firstborn, she referred to as "man" (4:1); this one she calls "seed." In the first case, her explanation was self-centered: "I have gotten" (4:1); here it is God-focused: "God has appointed" (4:25). "This time Eve does not give voice to feelings of joy and pride such as she expressed when her eldest son was born. Her mood is one of mourning and sorry for the family calamity, and her words are uttered meekly, with humility and modesty. On the first occasion, she gloried in her creative power and her collaboration with the Lord; this son she now regards purely as a gift vouchsafed to her by Heaven."[43] With the first child, she utters the name "Yahweh," her hubris associating herself almost as an equal with this

39. While there is no explicit statement to the effect, the ideal relationship of one man–one woman in the Garden of Eden suggests that Lamech's bigamy was a deviation from the divinely intended pattern for mankind.

40. Mathews, *Genesis 1–11:26*, 279.

41. Robinson, "Literary Functions," 600n8.

42. Eslinger, "A Contextual Identification," 68.

43. Cassuto, *Genesis*, 245–46.

personal God; with her third child, she yields to "God," the Creator, the only one who can give and sustain life, from whom comes, and to whom belongs, all things, living and non-living. And, surprisingly, 4:25 records the first instance of a human uttering the name of Abel. And where Cain refused all along to confess, his mother does so for him, declaring him a killer of his brother, Abel.

> Right into the face of the triumphant victor a woman, carrying her newborn baby, starts to say the name of a victim: *another seed in place of Abel, for Cain has killed him.* Right into the space occupied by the glorious myth of strength, growth, forceful success she talks about one who got lost, who didn't make it—a *desaparecido* [= "disappeared"], her second son, Abel. And she simply calls Lemekh's great grand hero Cain, her first son, a killer. . . . With this one statement about Abel and Cain and God, Eve turns the whole history of ideology of victory upside down and just shows what is there: Abel murdered and Cain a murderer, and a God, who out of mercy beyond understanding grants another son.[44]

Ironically, after a triumphant commencement of the cycle of human birth with Cain, Eve, following the narrative order of 4:1–16, is condemned to watch seven Cainite generations pass by, a line of murderers from beginning to end, even as human civilization developed.[45] Everything that God had seen to be good since creation had turned to evil. With the third "seed" perhaps things would change, Eve must have hoped. Therefore, according to Kahl, she is the "first theologian, teacher, prophetess, and—critical thinker of human history." "Seven generations since Adam have passed and the power-driven male has become God-like. With human life multiplying death seventy-sevenfold, history rushes into disaster before it has really started. But then, just at the point of no return, there *is* another voice. A disruptive and disturbing tune infiltrates Lemekh's song with dissonance"—Eve's exclamation![46] In the description of his name, Seth brings hope because, according to Eve, "God has appointed me another seed [זרע, *zrʾ*]" (4:24), clearly alluding to the nearest antecedent occurrences of זרע in 3:15 (×2), where God had promised victory over evil. Moreover, it is with the line of Seth that "people began to call upon the name of Yahweh" (4:26).[47] A new line had begun and people were calling upon the name of Yahweh.[48] Hope was being kindled afresh.

Despite all the violence and evil perpetrated, Yahweh is shown to be still in control of the cosmos he had created. As if to emphasize that fact, Pericope 3 begins and

44. Kahl, "And She Called His Name Seth." 23.

45. Mathews catches the irony: "Cain's firstborn and successors pioneer cities and the civilized arts, but Seth's firstborn and successors pioneer worship" (*Genesis 1–11:26*, 291–92).

46. Kahl, "And She Called His Name Seth," 22, 26, 27.

47. There is no subject for the sentence in 4:26b: literally, "then to call was begun," best translated as "then *people* began to call." Other instances of "calling upon the name of Yahweh" in Genesis indicate, broadly, the concept of worship (12:8; 13:4; 21:33; 26:25).

48. That the line is new is obvious in more ways than one. Not only is Adam and Eve restarting the process, but the name of their grandson, "Enosh," a proper name (4:26; 5:5–7, 9–11; 1 Chr 1:1), also means an individual "man" (Ps 55:13), or collective mankind (Ps 8:4). He is thus the new Adam, the new man, a replacement line.

ends with a focus on this personal, sovereign Creator: the first generation was raised up "with Yahweh" (4:1), but the next generation calls upon his name (4:26). Peels notes how, in response to Cain's fallen countenance, Yahweh acts *pastorally*: he knows man's heart, he recognizes the dangers, he warns the potential offender, and he offers corrective advice. After the crime, Yahweh acts *judicially*: he calls the perpetrator to question and proceeds to sentence Cain. Subsequently, in grace, Yahweh acts *protectively*: he guards even the criminal from further acts of violence; his last words in the narrative are not an utterance of curse but a mark of protection.[49] In all of his words and deeds, God demonstrates grace for, ultimately, only grace can rescue man from sin and its injurious effects.

SERMON FOCUS AND OUTLINES

THEOLOGICAL FOCUS OF PERICOPE 3 FOR PREACHING

3 **Man's pride propagates and perpetuates his sinful rebellion against God, inviting God's discipline, while God's grace promises respite from the effects of sin (4:1–26).**

The previous pericope (Pericope 2) focused upon the need for an attitude of dependence upon God to keep sin at bay. In this pericope, the focus shifts to issues of prideful sin, rooted in unteachability and unrepentance, that only exacerbate the damaging consequences of sin. God's grace, too, must be emphasized; without his merciful intervention there would be no release for humanity from sin. God's help must be accepted.

This sermon might be a good opportunity to lead into a congregation-wide response of confession and repentance, since that is the thrust of this pericope (what Cain failed to do and what Lamech, apparently, had no intention of doing). As much as possible, the preacher should attempt to coordinate each sermon with the rest of the worship service in the corporate gathering; this particular sermon would be a relatively easy way to accomplish that goal, through responsive readings, corporate confession, Lord's Supper, etc.

Possible Preaching Outlines for Pericope 3

I.   Symptoms of Prideful Sin
        Cain's deficient offering vs. Abel's acceptable one (4:1–5)
        Cain's lack of response to God's gracious recommendation (4:6–7), and his murder of Abel (4:8)
        Cain's protest (4:13–14) against divine discipline (4:9–12)
        God's gracious accommodation of Cain's protest (4:15)
        Move-to-Relevance: Our own unteachable and unrepentant attitudes

II. Contagion of Prideful Sin
        Building of a city (4:16–18)
        Lamech, his bigamy and his brutality (4:19–24)
        Move-to-Relevance: How sin can become an epidemic; things go from bad to worse, if untreated

---

49. Peels, "The World's First Murder," 35.

III.   Therapy for Prideful Sin
God's grace in a fresh start, recognized by Eve (4:25–26; grace is also depicted in 4:6–7 and 4:15)

IV.   Healing from Prideful Sin: *Accept grace and start again!*
To accept God's grace is to demonstrate the attitude God wanted Cain to have: teachability and repentance
Specifics on being healed from pride and sin; how to be teachable and repentant

The contrast between man's pride and God's grace may also be effectively used to outline a sermon.

I.   Pride vs. Grace 1
Cain's deficient offering vs. Abel's acceptable one (4:1–5)
Cain's lack of response to God's gracious recommendation (4:6–7), and his murder of Abel (4:8)
Move-to-Relevance: Our own unteachable attitudes

II.   Pride vs. Grace 2
Cain's protest (4:13–14) against divine discipline (4:9–12)
God's gracious accommodation of Cain's protest (4:15)
Move-to-Relevance: Our own unrepentant attitudes

III.   Pride vs. Grace 3
Building of a city (4:16–18), and Lamech—his bigamy and his brutality (4:19–24)
God's grace in a fresh start, recognized by Eve (4:25–26; grace is also depicted in 4:6–7 and 4:15)
Move-to-Relevance: God's grace (mercy and forgiveness) in our lives

IV.   *Accept grace and start again!*
To accept God's grace is to demonstrate the attitude God wanted Cain to have: teachability and repentance
Specifics on being healed from pride and sin; how to be teachable and repentant

PERICOPE 4

Continued Corruption

Genesis 5:1–6:8

[Genealogy of the Sethites; Evil Increases]

REVIEW, SUMMARY, PREVIEW

Review of Pericope 3: Genesis 4:1–26 describes the first human death—murder—and God's discipline visited upon the criminal, Cain, throughout proud and unrepentant, even though God extends grace. The line of Cain continues this trend of its ancestor until a new line, that of Seth, is established.

Summary of Pericope 4: Here, the spread of evil is described. Ungodliness escalates until God can stand it no more; he regrets having made man. But it is not only the vile evildoers who are culpable; all humanity is, evidenced in the dirge-like refrain of the genealogy of Gen 5: "and he died." All of them did, even hopeful ones like Lamech, even long-lived ones like Methuselah. But there is a bright note that stands out amidst the elegiac lament: Enoch, the one who walked with God, did not die. Pericope 4 therefore explains how to overcome the epidemic of sin and to experience intimacy with God.

Preview of Pericope 5: The next pericope (6:9–5:29) deals with the flood, God's discipline for mankind's gross sin. But quite subtly, with three subsidiary stories, the pericope notes three ways to avoid such disciplinary action: righteousness, intercession, and mankind's authority to deal with sin. However, ongoing sin is not stemmed.

4.   *Genesis 5:1–6:8*

> **THEOLOGICAL FOCUS OF PERICOPE 4**
>
> **4.   The result of the transmission of sin to every human is that death occurs inevitably and ultimately to all, and uncontrolled sin leads to loss of godliness, inviting divine retribution; yet the reward of intimacy with God forever is promised to those who "walk with him," hinting at a respite from the bane of sin provided by God who, himself, grieves over sin (5:1–6:8).**
>
> > 4.1   The result of transmission of sin to every human is that death occurs inevitably and ultimately to every human being, yet the reward of intimacy with God forever is promised to those who "walk with him," hinting at a respite from the bane of sin provided by God who, himself, grieves over sin (5:1–32).
> >
> > > 4.1.1   *The result of transmission of sin to every human, no matter who their progenitors were or how righteous their ancestors had been, is that death occurs inevitably and ultimately to all.*
> > >
> > > 4.2.2   *Those who live a life "walking with God" can expect to attain the reward of intimacy with God forever; death is never an end for the righteous.*
> > >
> > > 4.1.3   *Hope for respite from the bane of sin comes only from God.*
> >
> > 4.2   Sin uncontrolled, with one doing whatever one decides is good for oneself, leads to loss of godliness and gain of worldliness, inviting retribution from a grieving God (6:1–8).

OVERVIEW

A new section begins in 5:1 with the formulaic introduction, "This is the book of the generations [תּוֹלְדֹת, *toldot*] of Adam," as do the other sections of Genesis (2:4; 6:9; 10:1; 11:10, 27; 25:12, 19; 36:1, 9; 37:2). The next one after 5:1 is in 6:9; thus 5:1–6:8 forms an integral pericope. A number of deliberate repetitions reinforce this conclusion: "Adam" occurs fourteen times (seven with, and seven without, the article); אֱלֹהִים (*'elohim*) occurs seven times; "create" and "make" (ברא, *br'*, and עשׂה, *'sh*), seven times; "sons" and "daughters" each occur twelve times (excluding the figurative use in 5:30); and the root "to bear" occurs thirty times. The beginning (5:1–3) and the end (6:5–8) of Pericope 4 connect with what preceded and what follows.[1] For instance, 5:1–2 summarizes 1:1–2:3 employing the key words, "make," "create," "in the day," "likeness of God," "blessed." The commencement of the pericope also looks back at 2:4–4:26: "make," "create," and "in the day" (5:1) are also found in 2:4; also, Enoch's "walking" with God (5:22, 24) echoes Yahweh's "walking" in the garden (3:8), as well as anticipates Noah's identical action (6:9); and Lamech's optimistic comment about his son (5:29) refers back to Yahweh's curse on the ground (3:17), as well as forwards, with the hope of relief in Noah.[2] At the conclusion of the pericope, 6:1–8 harks back to the themes of marriage and procreation sounded in Pericopes 2 and 3, as well as looking

---

1. Wenham, *Genesis 1–15*, 121.

2. Enoch and Lamech, incidentally, are the only two in the Sethite line who have corresponding personages with similar names in the Cainite line (4:17–18, 19–24).

forward to the flood (6:9–9:29, Pericope 5) by providing the grounds for that divine punitive action.

Thus far, in Pericopes 2 and 3, sin had been on the increase. But Pericope 4 points out that sin did not negate the divine blessing of mankind's fruitfulness and multiplication (1:28): sons and daughters are born in every generation and the image of God apparently continues to be transmitted to all mankind (5:3). The Sethite line, in contrast to the Cainite one, appears to have returned to God, or at least focused upon God: 4:26; 5:22–24, 28–29; 6:8. "The long period of peace and apparent prosperity described in this chapter [Gen 4] serves to make the sequel in 6:1–8 the more surprising and shocking"—the growth of sin and evil does not abate, culminating in the divine intent to destroy all mankind, except for Noah and his family. Thus the genealogy of Gen 5:1–32 begins with the first founder of humanity (Adam) and ends with the refounder of humanity (Noah).[3]

Pericope 4 (5:1–6:8) has three broad divisions:

> 5:1–32, the genealogy from Adam through Noah
> 6:1–4, the increase of evil
> 6:5–8, the divine decision to destroy all mankind, save Noah

And the ten paragraphs dealing with ten patriarchs in 5:1–32 follow a formulaic structure:

> A lived *x* years.
> A fathered B.
> A then lived *y* years after he fathered B, and had sons and daughters.
> All the days of A were *z* (= *x+y*) years, and he died.

There are, however, four deviations from this form, alterations of the pattern that are, therefore, theologically significant—the listings of Adam (5:1–2), Enoch (5:21–24), Lamech (5:29), and Noah (5:32).[4] Each of these variations has an intentionality to it, as will be addressed below.[5]

Debates about the dates and years of the patriarchs have been long and extended. I take it as a given that however the events are depicted (and this includes dates and years) there is no deception going on, but there is narrative and literary freedom being exercised by the writer(s). For preaching purposes at least, the interpreter must focus upon the text and attempt to figure out what the author was *doing* with what he was saying, and refrain from dissecting out events *behind* the text and trying to explain how the text corresponds with "reality" in mathematical precision.

Genealogies of Gen 5 and Gen 11 have ten members each; these are linear—vertical, with genealogical "depth"—whereas the genealogy of Gen 10 is segmented—horizontal, with genealogical "breadth"— as it comments more extensively upon multiple

---

3. Wenham, *Genesis 1–15*, 125.

4. Ibid., 122.

5. There is also a variation in the commencement of the account: it is not simply a record of the "generations of Adam," but "*the book of* the generations of Adam" (5:1), the only time a literary source is mentioned in these formulas.

members at the same level in the hierarchy.[6] The former, vertical genealogies "stem from archetypes current among West Semitic tribes from the Old Babylonian period (and possibly earlier), antedating those of the Bible by hundreds of years." In any case, ten-member capsules have been noted in the Assyrian King List, the Sumerian King List, and the genealogy of the Hammurabi dynasty; David's lineage in Ruth 4:18–22 is yet another example.[7] Perhaps this feature, *ten-member* genealogies, found both in Gen 5 and Gen 10, and their occurrence also in contemporary lists, may be an indication that Gen 5 is not to be taken literally. It may not be a valid operation to add up the years of these patriarchs and find the precise date of Adam and his creation. The statement "A fathered B" (from the verb ילד, *yld*) is consistent with "A fathered *a descendant B*."[8] In Gen 5, taking the times literally and the personages without gaps would call for Adam to have been alive until the birth of Noah's father, and all the patriarchs from Adam to Methuselah would have been contemporaries for some length of time. Moreover, post-flood, Shem would almost (and Eber actually would) outlive Abraham. It appears, all things considered, that Gen 5 is "a selective genealogy by its highly structured conventions of language and its schematic ten-generation depth."[9]

6. Wilson, "The Old Testament Genealogies," 179. Genealogies, particularly those that were originally oral, are also characterized by "fluidity"—the addition or loss of names from a list, whether functional in purpose or accidental (ibid., 180).

7. Malamat, "King Lists," 164 (see 163–73); Hartman, "Some Thoughts," 25–32. However, variations in divergent traditions of ancient lists should caution the interpreter from reading too much into the numbers of members in them (Mathews, *Genesis 1–11:26*, 297n4). For that matter, there are significant differences in numbers between the versions of Gen 5 in the MT, the Samaritan Pentateuch, and the LXX.

8. Hamilton, *Genesis: Chapters 1–17*, 254. One remembers, also, that the the genealogy of Matt 1 is structured in three parts, each with fourteen generations (with 14 as the numerical value of the name of David, דוד, *dvd*); some actual ancestors are omitted from this list: Joram is followed by Uzziah (aka Azariah) bypassing 3 generations (1:8; 1 Chr 3:11–12); and Josiah was not the parent of Jeconiah, but the latter's grandfather, and the father of Jehoiakim (Matt 1:11; 1 Chr 3:15–16). The genealogy in Luke 3:36 has Cainan, as the son of Arphaxad (aka Arpachshad); he is missing in Gen 10:24 and 11:12, though he shows up in the LXX in both places. In addition, Ezra's priestly genealogy in 7:1–5 has seven fewer names than its parallel in 1 Chr 6. It is of interest that Kitchen noted the subtle omission of three groups of kings in the Egyptian Abydos King List at three points in an otherwise continuous record (*Ancient Orient and Old Testament*, 38).

9. Mathews, *Genesis 1–11:26*, 303. In the contemporary genealogy of the Sumerian King List (*ANET* 265), ca. 2000 BCE, are antediluvian kings, a flood, and postdiluvian kings; the kings are semi-divine. Of course, there is no such apotheosis of humans in Genesis (Hamilton, *Genesis: Chapters 1–17*, 253). Moreover, the numbers in this King List (they are reigns, not lifespans) are enormous in comparison with those in Gen 5. Methuselah's nine and a half centuries are dwarfed by that of Sumerian List's Enmenluanna who reigned over 43,000 years! It might well be that this distinct difference between biblical and extra-biblical genealogies is evidence of an anti-Mesopotamian polemic against the divinization of the ancients (Cassuto, *Genesis*, 262–63). While the patriarchs lived long, no one attained to the lifespan of a millennium (a "day" in the sight of God, Ps 90:4). The years of the kings in the Sumerian List do diminish with time, as do lifespans in Genesis after the flood, though there is an overall optimism in the former about the progress of mankind, unlike the moral deterioration described in Genesis. See Hasel, "The Genealogies," 361–74; and Freeman, "A New Look," 259–86. Also see "Excursus: The Ages of the Antediluvians" in Wenham, *Genesis 1–15*, 130–34. According to the Lagash King List, not only did the rulers have long lives, but they also lived very "slowly" being in diapers for 100 years (Jacobsen, "The Eridu Genesis," 520–21).

In sum, in Gen 4 and 5, there are two lines being contrasted, one ungodly (the Cainite line) and the other godly (the Sethite line). Longevity confirms divine grace, something that the OT is not reticent to affirm (Deut 4:25; 5:16, 33; 6:2; 11:9; 22:7; 30:20; etc.). And "[t]he fact that life spans diminish radically after the flood may be the Bible's way of saying that history is regressing rather than advancing."[10]

4.1 Genesis 5:1–32

THEOLOGICAL FOCUS 4.1

4.1   The result of transmission of sin to every human is that death occurs inevitably and ultimately to every human being, yet the reward of intimacy with God forever is promised to those who "walk with him," hinting at a respite from the bane of sin provided by God who, himself, grieves over sin (5:1–32).

    4.1.1   *The result of transmission of sin to every human, no matter who their progenitors were or how righteous their ancestors had been, is that death occurs inevitably and ultimately to all.*

    4.2.2   *Those who live a life "walking with God" can expect to attain the reward of intimacy with God forever; death is never an end for the righteous.*

    4.1.3   *Hope for respite from the bane of sin comes only from God.*

NOTES 4.1

The striking feature of this genealogy is the recurrent observation "and he died" (×8), "which baldly and emphatically concludes the entry for each of these antediluvians."[11] Whereas others had died violent deaths (at the hands of Cain and Lamech), only in Genesis 5 do we see that someone simply "dies." The entire thrust of the lives of these patriarchs is clearly moving towards death: death had been promised, and death does occur. Despite urbanization and the accomplishments of civilization in the Cainite line, the ultimate earthly end of every human was (and is) death. While there is some renewed hope in the acknowledgement of divine image and blessing being passed on from generation to generation (5:2), the grim chorus of every age remains the same— death. This refrain of dying in Gen 5 seems rather redundant, especially given that in each case there is also a statement of the total number of the individual's years. Indeed, even the total number of years is superfluous, since both their age at the birth of their children and their years after those births are provided. But there is a purpose for all the repetition of the inexorable conclusion of earthly human life: "This single word in the Hebrew text (וַיָּמֹת [*wayyamot,* "and he died"]) at the close of each patriarch's career becomes a resounding testimony to the inevitable human end. It is literally the last word of each refrain."[12] Thus the genealogy is functioning as a theological commentary. "Theological truth about life and death (under the curse) is being taught by

10. Hamilton, *Genesis: Chapters 1–17*, 256.

11. Clines, *The Theme of the Pentateuch*, 66.

12. Mathews, *Genesis 1–11:26*, 311.

means of this recurring literary pattern and the subsequent break from it [in the life of Enoch]."[13] In other words, people are born, they marry, and they become parents, but in the end they all die![14]

4.1.1 The result of transmission of sin to every human, no matter who their progenitors were or how righteous their ancestors had been, is that death occurs inevitably and ultimately to all.

The deviations from the normal formula of the genealogy are noted below:

Deviations from Formula: Adam

> Adam's story is preceded by a summary of Gen 1 (5:1–2).
> Rather than *A fathered B*, 5:3b has "he fathered a son in his own likeness, according to his image, and he called his name Seth."
> The conclusion reads "all the days of Adam *which he lived*" (5:5)—
> an expansion on the usual formula (also in 25:7).
> The total years of Adam also mentions the hundreds first (900), followed by the tens (30), unlike the other totals.

Genesis 5:1–2 resembles 2:4 not only in the summary of the preceding events, but also in its chiastic structure (see Pericope 2). Both have "created" and "made" in the center of the scheme.[15]

> on the day ... created
>   Adam
>   made
>   created (blessed, called)
>   Adam
> on the day ... created

Thus 1:27–28 is subtly revisited with "man," "created," "likeness," "male and female," and "blessed." After the brief, but horrific interruption in Gen 4, God's blessing continues to rest upon humanity. Genesis 5:1–3 completely eliminates any mention of Cain in the royal line: he has been disowned. His line had commenced with one murderer and concluded with another (an "antigenealogy"[16]). Bridging the creation account with Seth's genealogy, it is as if the human line is being restarted again. God creates in his likeness and names his creation, Man; Adam fathers a son in his likeness and names his son, Seth. Cain, it seems to say, has not even existed.

But with 5:3, this first paragraph creates a contrast: God *creates* and names (5:1–2) vs. Adam *fathers* and names (5:3). While the first humans were originally in the

13. Cole, "Enoch," 290.

14. Vogels, "Enoch Walked with God," 294.

15. These are the only two passages with "on the day they were created," and they are unique in their employment of the verb, ברא, *br'*, in the Niphal infinitive construct with a 3rd person masculine plural suffix.

16. Robinson, "Literary Functions," 600n8.

likeness of God (5:1), subsequent procreation produces children in Adam's own likeness and in his image (5:3). Though it cannot be disputed that the *imago Dei* has been passed on (see 9:6), here the emphasis is on Seth's resemblance to Adam, rather than to God—a hint that it is the sinfulness of mankind that is being transmitted. Irrespective of the quality and characteristic of the progenitor (even Seth, who is much unlike Cain—4:25–26), sin is passed on. The uniqueness of the statement of Adam's lifespan underscores the fact that by the MT chronology, he would have lived to see Lamech, the father of Noah. In other words, he would see the result of his procreation and perhaps even more poignantly, the result of his sins and the sinfulness he had transmitted. And, as was noted earlier, the repeated, and somewhat redundant refrain, "and he died," emphasizes that death is inevitably and ultimately the lot of mankind lost in sin.

4.1.2 *Those who live a life "walking with God" can expect to attain the reward of intimacy with God forever; death is never an end for the righteous.*

Deviations from Formula: Enoch

> Enoch (5:21–24) is described as having "walked with God" (5:22).
> He does not die, but "he was not, for God took him" (5:24).

Leviticus Rabbah 29.11 cites a number of lists wherein the seventh member is considered the most significant (Gen 5:22; Exod 19:3; 1 Chr 2:15; 2 Chr 14:10). One also remembers Lamech in Gen 4:19 as the seventh in that set; Eber as the fourteenth in Gen 11:16 ("Eber" is the eponym of the Hebrews); Abraham the seventh after Eber (11:26); Boaz the seventh in the list of Ruth 4:18–22; etc.[17] Here it is Enoch, the seventh, the one who walked with God and who was taken by God.[18]

"Walking with God" is twice used to describe Enoch (Gen 5:22, 24) and later is employed of Noah (6:9). Other patriarchs are known to have "walked before God" (Abram, 17:1 and 24:40; Abraham and Isaac [and suggestively, Joseph, himself], 48:15; also Hezekiah, 2 Kgs 20:3/Isa 38:3; and see 1 Sam 2:30, 35); the psalmist hoped to walk before God (Ps 56:14; 116:9); and God's priests were expected to do so (Mal 2:6), as was all Israel (Mic 6:8). The phrase indicates "a special intimacy with God and a life of piety."[19] To describe Enoch twice in this fashion was a mark of his great spirituality. God was known to walk with man (Gen 3:8; Lev 26:12; Deut 23:14), but for man to walk with/before God was a special privilege: and instead of the expected formula "Enoch lived" we have "Enoch walked with God."[20]

17. See Sasson, "A Genealogical 'Convention,'" 171–85.

18. Enmeduranki/Enmenduranna, the seventh in the Sumerian King List (*ANET* 265), apparently entered the heavenly realm to learn the secret of the gods. Utuabzu, the seventh of the sages and a contemporary of Enmeduranki, was also thought to have ascended temporarily into heaven. See Wright, "Whither Elijah?" 128.

19. Wenham, *Genesis 1–15*, 127.

20. Hamilton, *Genesis: Chapters 1–17*, 258. He thinks that walking *with* indicates more intimacy than walking *before*, the former capturing and emphasizing communion and fellowship, and the latter more

> To walk "before" God, before his face, suggests that God is a spectator. God sees the person walk before him, the person is, as it were, parading before God [*sic.*]. Walking "with," however, suggests something different; it implies that God too is walking. Enoch is walking "with" God. They are walking together. When two people do so, one can expect that the superior one takes the initiative, while the other accompanies him. Consequently, wherever God decides to go, Enoch goes. The expression denotes, therefore, not only a moral ethical tone (Enoch is a good, perfect, righteous person), but also a more mystical meaning. It implies companionship, closeness, proximity. . . . Enoch is closely united with God, he is God's very intimate friend, and they are always together.[21]

The form of the verb "to walk" is the Hithpael. The intensive aspect of the verb underscores its repetitiveness; Enoch's walking with God was habitual and continuous. He had maintained this submission to the will of God and intimacy with the person of God for all his 365 years, it would seem. No wonder the statement is repeated in that brief cameo. God's "walking" in the Garden (Gen 3:8) also uses the same Hithpael form (as a participle), denoting a habitual action of this deity, perhaps along "with" his human creation. But the banishment of man and woman rendered such companionship impossible. Subsequent generations only compounded the distance between God and man with their sin, violence, and murders. But here is one who was reversing the trend—Enoch: he walked with God.[22] Whereas Adam was ejected from the Garden from before God, and Cain was driven out of the presence of God, Enoch "walks" in the company of God, with God. It makes a striking contrast: when "and he died" punctuates the end of the lives of all the antediluvians, of the end of Enoch's earthly existence the narrator notes that "he was not, for God took him." In fact this "walking with God" is likely the contrary of falling into sin, and being taken by God the contrary of dying. This was what was intended by God for *all* mankind—to dwell in his presence, "with" him.

While the phrase "God took him" (5:24) can refer idiomatically to death (42:13, 32, 36; 37:30; etc.), its unusual deployment instead of "and he died" in this chapter is remarkable.[23] Incidentally, Enoch's lifespan of 365 years was also the shortest of the antediluvians, perhaps an indication that longevity is not what is most laudable; neither is a long life the greatest blessing from the hand of God; it is not necessarily the *summum bonum*.[24] The brevity of Enoch's life, in the context of his loyalty to Yahweh, and in the light of his successor's comment on the painfulness of life (5:29), is therefore being clearly seen as a blessing by the narrator.[25] Perhaps the most perfect of all the

---

a sense of obedience and subordination (1 Kgs 2:4; 3:6; 8:23, 25; 9:4).

21. Vogels, "Enoch Walked with God," 296.

22. Ibid., 297.

23. The only other person "taken" by God was Elijah, in a translation to heaven on a fiery chariot in a whirlwind (2 Kgs 2:1, 5, 9, 11). In contrast, the simplicity of the recounting of Enoch's taking, amidst all the dying around him, makes it stark and bare, without any accompanying pyrotechnics.

24. So, here in Gen 5 is a rather unusual situation indeed: a person who does not die and who has the shortest life (Enoch) fathers the one who lives the longest on earth (Methuselah).

25. Wenham, *Genesis 1–15*, 146.

lives lived on earth thus far, Enoch lives the least number of years, 365. Vogels also notes that there are 365 words in all of Gen 5, of which 65 words make the passage on Enoch (5:22–24); there are 200 words before it, and 100 after. He considers this to be an indication of the fullness of Enoch's life. Limited, but full . . . and "pleasing" to God: the LXX likewise has "Enoch was pleasing [εὐαρεστέω, *euaresteō*] to God" (5:22, 24; also Sir 44:16, and reflected in Heb 11:5 using the same verb) instead of "Enoch walked with God" (likewise for Noah in Gen 6:9 LXX, as well as for the other patriarchs: 17:1; 24:40; 48:15 LXX).[26] And for the one who walked with God, God makes an exception: he does not die. Adumbrated here is, perhaps, the power of divine grace over sin and its deleterious effects.

> [I]ndeed, to take a person refers often to a new profound intimate relationship. When a man "takes" a woman, it means that they get married. In the preceding chapter it is said that Lamech "took" two women (4:19), and in the next chapter we read that the sons of God "took" as many of the daughters of man as they liked (6:2). That God takes Enoch suggests thus a new relationship. Enoch, who walked with God his whole life long, cannot be separated from God; God took him to himself as his own. They have always been together, so they are and remain together.[27]

Vogels makes the intriguing suggestion that Enoch may have been "taken" (לקח, *lqkh*) to paradise, for the same word is used of God "taking" (לקח) and settling man in the Garden of Eden (2:15). The structure of both 2:15 and 5:24 are the same: God is the subject of the verb לקח, and man the object. In the Garden was the tree of life, that could have prevented death (3:22); in fact the expulsion of humanity from the Garden was precisely to prevent their access to its fruit and their living forever. Instead, man is promised that he will return to the ground from which he had been "taken" (again לקח, 3:19). What he did once, God seems to have done again: "God took Enoch with him into a 'place' of life"—"not a descent into Sheol, but an ascent towards God."[28] Thus, not only is death never an end for the righteous, "walking with God" yields the blessed reward of intimacy with him.

4.1.3 Hope for respite from the bane of sin comes only from God.

Deviations from Formula: Lamech

> Lamech's fathering of Noah has an expansion beyond the norm:
> "he fathered a son, and he called his name Noah" (5:28–29).
> Lamech's story recounts the patriarch's hopes about his son Noah,
> including the mention of Yahweh and his curse on the ground (5:29).

That even the "patron saint of geriatrics," Methuselah does not reach the magical number of 1000 years renders humans utterly ungodlike.[29] His son's 777 years, and his

---

26. Vogels, "Enoch Walked with God," 300–301.

27. Ibid., 298.

28. Ibid., 299, 302.

29. Hamilton, *Genesis: Chapters 1–17*, 258.

name, Lamech, reminds one of the other Lamech, in the Cainite line, who promised to be avenged 77-fold (4:24). One Lamech hoped for rest; the other boasted of revenge. This Sethite Lamech's life is centered on that of his son: even the fathering of the latter is given prominence, an expansion from the usual style (5:28–29; see below). But it is the voice of Lamech's hope regarding his son, Noah, that marks his story: יְנַחֲמֵנוּ (ynakhamenu, "he will give us comfort) echoes נֹחַ (noakh, "Noah") and rhymes with מִמַּעֲשֵׂנוּ (mimma'asenu, "from our work").[30] The word נֹחַ alludes to a collection of words with similar consonants (besides יְנַחֲמֵנוּ) in this pericope and the next: וַיִּנָּחֶם (wayyinnakhem, Yahweh "grieved," 6:6)[31]; נִחַמְתִּי (nikhamti, "I am sorry," 6:7); חֵן (khen, Noah found "favor," 6:8); וַתָּנַח (wattanakh, the ark "came to rest," 8:4); מָנוֹחַ (manoakh, no "resting-place," 8:9); יוֹנָה (yonah, "dove," 8:9); and רֵיחַ הַנִּיחֹחַ (reakh hannikhoakh, Yahweh smelled the "soothing aroma," 8:21).[32] This man, Lamech, was obviously anguished by the disaster that had befallen mankind in the Garden, and with the after-effects of sin upon the rest of humankind; he explicitly points to the curse of Yahweh upon the ground (5:29; 3:17)—the reuse of עִצָּבוֹן ('itsabon, "toil/pain," 5:29) from 3:16, 17 is obvious.[33] Noah's naming is set firmly on this background, corresponding to the birth and naming of Seth upon the dark and morbid background of Cain's line. Thus Lamech's longing looks backwards (to the root cause of man's pain, grief, and labor), as well as forwards (to Noah, who, he hopes, will bring rest). Ultimately, his confidence is in God who alone can provide the release.

However, this hope is not realized until after a catastrophic flood, in which Lamech's generation perishes. When the flood abates, Noah's offering of sacrifice is accepted by Yahweh as a רֵיחַ הַנִּיחֹחַ ("soothing aroma," 8:21, assonant with נֹחַ). Lamech's hoped-for "rest" (נַחַם, nakham, 5:29) arrives with "righteous Noah's role in initiating a new era as the 'new Adam' who perpetuates the family blessing."[34] But the realities of the curse of Gen 3:16–19 persist, and sin continues to plague mankind, even though Yahweh reiterates his blessing and his promises of fruitfulness (9:1), and vows to remember his covenant with mankind to keep them from another watery disaster (9:14–16).

That Yahweh "grieves" (from נחם, nkhm) over human sin (6:5–6) is poignant; he too, apparently like Lamech (5:29), experiences a lack of "rest" (also from נחם). Lamech suffers pain (עִצָּבוֹן, 5:29), and God is sorry (from עצב, 'tsb, 6:6)—the turmoil of both are the result of human sin. The suffering of one leads to a yearning for rest; the suffering of the other to a determination of destruction.

---

30. "Comfort" (נָחַם" nakham) and "rest" (נוּחַ, nuakh) are quite similar in meaning; Ezek 5:13 employs them together in a parallelism.

31. נחם ("comfort") is also a homonym meaning "grieve."

32. Mathews, *Genesis 1–11:26*, 317.

33. These are the only occurrences of the word in the OT. The related verb, עָצַב ('atsav, "to grieve"), is found in 6:6, along with נָחַם (nakham, "to be sorry"): both are found together also in 5:29.

34. Mathews, *Genesis 1–11:26*, 318–19.

Deviations from Formula: Noah

> Rather than the expected "Noah lived 500 years" (the stylized version),
>> the text reads literally "Noah was son-of-500 years" (5:32).
> Noah's story is also marked by the naming of three sons,
>> than the expected attention upon a single one.
> The formula of Noah's life, bisected by the flood story, is only completed in 9:29
>> with "All the days of Noah were 950 years, and he died."

Noah is, like Enoch, a special person. His age is described with a unique formula and, unlike most of his predecessors, his three sons are listed (Adam and Terah also have three sons): the linear genealogy thus becomes segmented at this point, preparing for the detailed segmental genealogy of Gen 10. Indeed, the story of Noah is incomplete in Gen 5 and the genealogical description concludes only at 9:28–29, with the matter of a flood interrupting the recital of pedigree and years. The deviation from form in the mention of Noah is likely signaling a change in the narrative, a pause button so to speak, announcing the commencement of a new section—the flood story.

In sum, while the list of Seth's line kept the flame of hope burning for mankind, the repeated refrain "and he died" painfully reminds readers of the extinguishing power of sin. Yet, in the account of Enoch, and in Lamech's wistful longings, hope remains bright.

4.2   Genesis 6:1–8

THEOLOGICAL FOCUS 4.2

4.2   Sin uncontrolled, with one doing whatever one decides is good for oneself, leads to loss of godliness and gain of worldliness, inviting retribution from a grieving God (6:1–8).

NOTES 4.2

4.2   *Sin uncontrolled, with one doing whatever one decides is good for oneself, leads to loss of godliness and gain of worldliness, inviting retribution from a grieving God.*

Divine action in the discrete episodes of 6:1–13 (6:1–4, 5–8, and 9–13) are all launched by statements regarding an entity's "seeing": the sons of God "saw" the daughters of men (6:2); Yahweh "saw" the great wickedness of men (6:5); and God "saw" the corruption of all flesh on the earth (6:12). Besides, in three instances, parallel to the three "seeings," Yahweh/God "speaks" to announce his decision (6:3, 7, 13): delimitation of time is decreed in the first case by Yahweh; destruction of the earth is decreed in the other two.[35]

With regard to 6:1–8, the terminus of Pericope 4, this mini-narrative begins with humans acting after "seeing" (6:1–4) and ends with Yahweh acting, also after "seeing" (6:5–8; see below). One had evil in his "heart" (6:5); the other was, therefore, grieved

---

35. Wallace, "The Toledot of Adam," 30.

in his "heart" (6:6). In both instances there is judgment in the form of divine speech, followed by background information.[36]

> Action of humans after seeing: a two-verse description (6:1–2)
> Declaration of divine judgment: Yahweh "said" (6:3)
> Background information (6:4)
> Action of Yahweh after seeing: a two-verse description (6:5–6)
> Declaration of divine judgment: Yahweh "said" (6:7)
> Background information (6:8)

"Yahweh/God saw" often introduces a definitive intervention in human affairs on the part of God (6:12; 29:31; Exod 2:25; 3:4; 4:31; etc.). What he had seen as "good" in Gen 1, he now sees as "evil" (6:5). The twice repeated כֹּל (*kl*, "*every* intent" and "*all* the time") underscores the depravity of mankind. God sees (6:5); God feels (6:6); God decides to act (6:7).

The key words of the larger pericope are also repeated in the smaller unit, 6:1–8: "man" (×7 in 6:1–7; and 5:2); "ground" (6:1, 7; and 5:29); "born" (6:1, 4; and ×28 in 5:3–32); "name" (6:4; and 5:3, 29); "Yahweh" (6:3, 5, 6, 7, 8; and 5:29); "God" (6:2, 4; and 5:1, 22, 24); "sons"/"daughters" (6:1, 2, 4; and ×10 in 5:3–32); "make" (6:6, 7; and 5:1); "create" (6:7; and 5:1, 2); "Noah" (6:8; and 5:32); etc.[37] These attest to the integrity of this section with the remainder of the pericope. And, in 6:1–8, those "daughters" mentioned in passing in the genealogy of Gen 5 become prominent. As well, the commencement of Gen 6 with its statement about the multiplication of men surely refers to the previous chapter and its list of patriarchs and their progeny. The conclusion of this section, 6:8, however, points forwards to the next pericope that deals with the flood (6:9–9:29): thus 6:1–8 may rightly be called "a trailer to the flood story."[38] Without this crucial section, 6:1–8, one would be hard-pressed to comprehend the exclusive survival of Noah and his family in and through the flood.[39]

> The "sons of God" pericope presents itself as a carefully structured, unified text, one which leads the reader from the multiplication of humanity to the decree of its extermination. By doing so, it serves as an introduction to the flood, which would have been anticipated by its position in the narrative. Because of the way the narrative is designed from Genesis 4 to Genesis 10, the reader expects the passage to deal with the two lines of humanity and the vanishing of one of them.[40]

The closing of this pericope, 6:5–8, is in stark contrast to the hopefulness expressed by Lamech in the last verses of Gen 5: here, the regret of God at the evil of mankind leads him to decide to wipe out mankind and animals and creeping things

36. Fockner, "Reopening the Discussion," 445.

37. Likewise, 6:1–4 is linked to 6:5–8: "face of the land" in 6:1 and 6:7; sons of God "see" (6:2) and God "sees" (6:5).

38. Wenham, *Genesis 1–15*, 136.

39. Fockner estimates that with three sons and three daughters per couple for ten generations, the population around the time of the flood would have been 310 = 59,049 individuals ("Reopening the Discussion," 447).

40. Ibid., 455.

and birds (6:7). In the previous misdemeanors of man, the connection between man (אָדָם) and the land (אֲדָמָה) had been severed: the ground had been cursed (3:17), and Cain had been driven from the "face of the ground" (4:14). But here, man is decreed to be "blotted out from the face of the ground" (6:7), from the very arena on which they had been multiplying (6:1).[41]

There is no question that the account of 6:1–4 is "surely the strangest of all the Genesis narratives."[42] Who exactly are those "sons of God" and "daughters of men"? Rather than postulate that "sons of God" indicate some sort of superhuman beings or the angelic host, this commentary holds the view that both the "sons" and "daughters" are human—the former belonging to the line of Seth (the godly line, 4:26; hence "sons of God"), and the latter to the line of Cain. This interpretation might raise the problem of reading "men" differently in 6:1 and 6:2—in the first case generically of mankind, and in the second as referring to those of Cain's lineage, which in itself, is not a problem, for they too are part of generic mankind.[43] In Jdg 20:3, the sons of Benjamin are contrasted with the sons of Israel, but the former are part of Israel; in Jer 32:20, the Israelites are contrasted with the rest of humankind, but, of course, the former are humans, too; and, likewise, in Ps 73:5, the wicked are contrasted with the remainder of mankind. Thus the "sons of God" are human followers of God, distinct from the rest of mankind who are non-God followers.[44] There is no necessity to see "sons of God" as being non-human; they are labeled differently simply to distinguish them from the other, presumably ungodly, folks.[45] The attribute "of God" (in בְּנֵי־הָאֱלֹהִים, *bne-haʾelohim*) is thus, essentially, a genitive of quality (= "godly sons"). These individuals are godly/covenant offspring (as in Exod 4:22, 23; Deut 14:1; 32:5, 6, 18, 19; Ps 73:15; 82:6; Isa 1:2; 11:1; 43:6; 45:11; Jer 3:14, 19; 31:9, 20; Hosea 1:10; 11:1; Mal 1:6; John

---

41. Marriage and procreation is a recurrent theme in 6:1–4: there is multiplication (6:1), birth (6:1), the taking of wives (6:2), sexual activity (6:4), and bearing of children (6:4).

42. Sarna, *Genesis*, 45.

43. Kline, "Divine Kingship," 189.

44. However, one could see both occurrences of "men" in 6:1–2 as equally having the generic sense, with the Sethite "sons of God" simply failing to show covenantal discrimination in their choice of spouses (as in Gen 24:3–4; 26:34, 35; 27:46; 28:1–3, 6–8; 34). Rather, they made their selection based on their own whims and fancies—"whomever they chose" (6:2). Or it could also be argued that "men," both in 6:1 and 6:2, is similarly restrictive, indicating, in both cases, Cainites: they multiplied, and had daughters who married the "sons of God."

45. That "sons of God" are a nonhuman, godlike/angelic/demonic species is an ancient view and a common one at that: the LXX (Vaticanus contains ἄγγελοι τοῦ θεοῦ, *angeloi tou theou*; the Alexandrinus corrects υἱοί, *huioi*, to ἄγγελοι; the LXX also has ἄγγελοι θεοῦ for "sons of God" [בְּנֵי הָאֱלֹהִים] in Job 1:6; 2:1; 38:7; and Dan 3:25. Philo (*Giants* 2.6), Josephus (*Ant.* 1.31; 1.73), 2 *En.* 18.3–8; 2 *Bar.* 56.11–14; and the DSS (1Qap Genᵃʳ 2:1, 16; CD 2:17–19) also hold to this interpretation, as well as Justin (*Second Apology* 5), Irenaeus (*Haer.* 4.36), Clement of Alexandria (*The Instructor* 3.2), and Tertullian (*On the Veiling of Virgins* 7), among others. "Sons of god" in the OT may stand for heavenly beings (Job 1:6; 2:1; 38:7; Ps 29:1; 82:6; 89:6–7; Dan 3:25; etc.) (see Wenham, *Genesis 1–15*, 139). However, there has been no mention of any angels in Scripture up to this point; moreover, angels do not marry (Matt 22:29–30/ Mark 12:24–25/Luke 20:34–36). Also, the phrase "they took wives for themselves" is a fairly standard expression for normal marriage in the OT (Gen 11:29; Jdg 3:6; 2 Sam 5:13; 1 Chr 14:3; 23:22; etc.); no bizarre super-human conjugal relationship is implied by in the phrase.

1:12–13).[46] The striking contrast between the pietistic elements in Seth's family on the one hand (the result of Seth's birth and his taking the place of Abel, 4:25–26; the pointed mention of Seth's "image" and "likeness," 5:3; his descendants: Enoch, 5:23–24; Lamech, 5:28–31; Noah, 6:8; and even the placement of Gen 6 after the introduction of the Sethites and Noah in Gen 5), and the humanistic characters in Cain's line, on the other hand, leads one to see godliness as the key distinction between the "sons of God" and "daughters of men" in 6:1. Historically, this is the interpretation that has been followed by Julius Africanus (*Chronicles* 2), Chrysostom (*Hom. Gen.* 22.2), Augustine (*City of God* 15.23), Luther (*Lectures on Genesis Chapter 6–14*[47]), and Calvin (*Comm. Gen.* 1.237–238). "There is no reason why some division of the human race, or certain persons by reason of religious privilege or political authority, should not be given this designation ["sons of God"] in order to distinguish them from others."[48]

Further substantiating this interpretation is the fact that the "sons of God" are the ones held culpable: "they saw" and "they took," "whomever they chose" (6:2). However, divine judgment falls only upon mankind in 6:3, and explicitly because "he also is flesh." If angels and other non-/semi-human entities were involved, it seems strange that there should be no hint of divine condemnation upon them.

> We must conclude therefore that there is no biblical support for the view that "the sons of God" were angelic or preternatural beings. The biblical evidence militates against this interpretation and decisively supports the view that the marriages concerned were those between one classification of mankind that could be designated "son of God" and another classification that could not be thus designated. The narrative itself points to this discrimination as that between the Sethites and the Cainites, between those who feared the Lord and those who were worldly.[49]

The corruption of sin progressed without remittance from Gen 3 onwards, culminating in Gen 6. Even though the Sethite line was a godly one, the persistence of sin is clear: "and he died" cannot fail to remind one of the consequences of sin and its transmission to all. With the unholy alliance between the two lines—Cainite and Sethite—godliness was all but eliminated as any distinctive between the two groups was obliterated.

46. See Mathews, *Genesis 1–11:26*, 330n107.

47. *Luther's Works Vol. 2*, 10–13.

48. Murray, *Principles of Conduct*, 246. The supposition that the Nephilim of 6:4 were the products of some abnormal union between divine and human beings is unwarranted. Genesis 6:4 begins with a disjunctive clause indicating that this notation about the Nephilim is parenthetical. This verse only states in a circumstantial way that these "giants" were around when the "sons of God" cohabited with the "daughters of men." These nefarious characters also show up in Num 13:33, so tall (LXX has γίγαντες, *gigantes*, and the Vulgate, *gigantes*) that the Israelites felt like grasshoppers. Mathews considers the Nephilim in Num 13:33 as part of a scare tactic by the frightened spies who were attempting to dissuade the Israelites from proceeding on to Canaan by drawing on the reputation of these ancient (and violent?) peoples (*Genesis 1–11:26*, 338–39). Or it could be that "Nephilim" is simply a generic term for giant-like people and that those in Num 13 are not connected with those in Gen 6; if they were, they would have had to survive the flood, separate from Noah and his clan. The introduction of the "giants" here may simply be to emphasize that even these mighty ones were doomed in the flood (Bar 3:26–28; Sir 16:7; Wis 14:6).

49. Murray, *Principles of Conduct*, 247.

In such a circumstance, sin could only abound and, apparently, it did, incurring the wrath of God.[50] "The flood account . . . is actually embedded within Sethite geneal-ogy, which is not completed until the notice of Noah's death (9:29). This provides the appropriate interpretive key for understanding 6:1–8. During the period of amazing Sethite expansion ([Genesis] chap. 5), the Sethite family marries outside its godly heritage, which results in moral decline. . . . Their unrestricted license accelerated the degeneracy of the whole human family."[51] The text is not explicit about what exactly that moral decline entailed, but the similarities between Eve's sin and that of these "sons of God" are striking: both "saw"; both declared their choices "good"/"beautiful" (טוֹב, *tov*); both "took" (3:6; 6:2). Like the sin of Eve, the sin of the sons of God was their deciding for themselves what was good and what they could do for themselves, and on their own initiative. In any case, the culmination of generations of sin was that "the wickedness of man was great" and "every intent of the thoughts of his heart was only evil all the time" (6:5).

The juxtaposition of the Cainite lineage with the Sethite lineage followed by the narrative transition to Noah is an essential movement of the entire story. Humanity is divided into those who follow God and those who do not (the two lines). But when mingling between the divisions occur, evil abounds, and hope is lost. The godly line disappears, amalgamated into the mass of an ungodly humanity. In the end, the pri-mary reason for divine judgment is the "fleshiness" of man (6:3)—i.e., weak, mortal, and morally flawed as described in 6:2, 12, 13. And *all* were guilty, Cainite and Sethite and everyone else, with the exception of a small remnant described in the next peri-cope, 6:9–9:29 (Pericope 5).

Of course, there were more people on earth than the descendants of Cain and Seth; Adam and Eve did have more sons and daughters (5:4). But they had to be on one side or another, for neutrality was—and never is—an option. It might be that some Sethites were ungodly and some Cainites were godly—some might have switched al-legiances. But that is not the concern of the author; the narrator simply tells the reader about the dangers of compromise and blending.[52] Nonetheless, it was not the mixed marriages per se that resulted in God's condemnation; the text is clear that the bone of contention was that "the evil of man was great on the earth, and that every intent of the thoughts of his heart was only evil all the time" (6:5; also 6:12). This degree of wickedness was, according to the storyline, the result of apostasy.

In light of the parallelism between 6:1–4 and 6:5–8 ("face of the land" in 6:1 and 6:7; sons of God "see" [6:2] and God "sees" [6:5]), the two condemnations in 6:3 and

---

50. The patriarchal leadership structure of families likely is being reflected in the assumption that the union of "sons of God" with "daughters of men" led to greater sinfulness. The cohabitation of "daughters of God" with "sons of men"—which also likely occurred—may not have led to a level of apostasy that disrupted the balance between godliness and wickedness. See Fockner, "Reopening the Discussion," 450–51.

51. Mathews, *Genesis 1–11:26*, 330–31.

52. Fockner, "Reopening the Discussion," 447. The motif of men compromising their religious be-liefs because of unbelieving wives is a common one in the OT: Gen 24:3; 28:6; Exod 34:16; Deut 17:17; Jdg 14:3; 1 Kgs 11:3–4; Ezra 9:11–14; Neh 13:25–26 (see ibid., 450–51).

6:7 are likely to be same, both introduced by "and Yahweh said." Thus the 120 years in 6:3 must have something to do with the wiping out of mankind from the face of the earth in 6:7, rather than being an independent judgment of a contraction of lifespan for every individual henceforth. Moreover, all beings that had "the breath of the *spirit of life*" are said to have died in the judgment of the flood (7:22), linking this with the assertion of Yahweh in 6:3 that his *spirit* would not strive with man. Thus it is more likely that the time period in 6:3 has more to do with a deadline than with a limitation of length of individual human lives. Such a deadline before divine punishment is ushered in is also seen in Jonah's warning to Nineveh (Jonah 3:4), where a forty-day ultimatum was issued. Besides, a lifespan interpretation would call for אדם, *'dm*, in 6:3 to refer to an individual human; in the rest of this section, however, the word refers to humanity in general.[53] Moreover, Noah and many after him live far more than 120 years (see Gen 11; also Abraham lived to be 175 [25:7]; Isaac, 180 [35:28]; and Jacob, 147 [47:28]). Also, the declaration that God's spirit would not remain in man "forever" with regard to human years would be inexplicable as a constraint on lifespan since man had been mortal (i.e., not living "forever") even before the events of Gen 6. In sum, "[b]y withdrawing the *ruah* God withdraws a principle of order and allows the waters of chaos to destroy the chaos of man become בשר [*bshr*, "flesh"]"—a "de-creation" (see below and in Pericope 5).[54]

As was noted earlier, Yahweh's "regret" (נחם, *nkhm*) and "grief" (עצב, *tsv*) that he had "made" (עשה, *'sh*; 6:5) man matches Lamech's hope that Noah would bring "rest" (נחם) from "labor" (מעשה, *m'sh*) and "toil" (עצבון, *tsvn*, from עצב; 5:29). One hoped for relief; the other is regretful. The irony is pungent: Yahweh is grieved in his "heart" (6:6) because of what was in man's "heart" (6:5).[55] After the fall, Eve (3:16) and Adam (3:17) were designated to bear "pain" (עצבון); now it is the Creator who has to, and his anguish is great, as he determines to blot out all living beings from the face of the land (6:7–8)—in essence, a reversal of creation, that reflects the terminology of 1:20, 24–30.[56] While the future is definitely bleak for the earth, Yahweh's expressed regret (נחם, 6:6), and the verb for "blot out" (מחה, *makhah*, 6:7)—that sounds like "Noah" (נח, *noakh*) the one who found "favor" (חן, *khen*, the consonants of Noah's name reversed) in Yahweh's eyes (6:8)—hints at grace, redemption, and hope. Nonetheless, the thrust here is that uncontrolled sin and ungodliness invite divine retribution.

SERMON FOCUS AND OUTLINES

THEOLOGICAL FOCUS OF PERICOPE 4 FOR PREACHING

---

53. Ibid., 451–52.

54. Eslinger, "A Contextual Identification," 72.

55. Also see 8:21, where Yahweh declared *in his heart* his decision never to curse the ground, because of what was *in man's heart*. As Mathews observes, "[t]he making of 'man' is no error; it is what 'man' has made of himself" that was the cause of all this turmoil and the resulting catastrophe (*Genesis 1–11:26*, 343).

56. Hamilton, *Genesis: Chapters 1–17*, 274.

4 Loss of godliness is an ever-present danger that has negative consequences, yet for those who "walk with God" there is the reward of intimacy with him (5:1–6:8).

In contrast to Pericope 3, that emphasized sin and rebelliousness, and the corresponding imperative to be open to God's correction, Pericope 4 focuses upon the dangers of sin, providing an example of one who escaped that danger—Enoch. While there is mention of divine intention to take action because of man's sin, I would save the concept of retribution for the sermon on Pericope 5 where the flood takes a large volume of the narrative space. Here, I would keep the spotlight on Enoch, as the outlines below demonstrate.

I do not normally advocate seeking recourse in other texts when preaching a given pericope, but in this case, to emphasize the LXX's concept of God being pleased with Enoch (Gen 5:22, 24), one might briefly touch on Heb 11:5 that employs the same verb as the LXX (see Notes). And, in the application, this pericope may lend itself to the presentation of the saving news of Jesus Christ's atoning work, the only way man can escape eternal death. However, the preacher must not fail to provide specific application for believers, the ones for whom worship services are geared and for whom sermons are primarily addressed.

Possible Preaching Outlines for Pericope 4

I.   Refrain of Death
> The consequences of sin affect everyone (5:1–20, 27, 31)
> The escalation of ungodliness (6:1–4)
> God's retribution sure (6:5–7)
> Move-to-Relevance: Examples of the universality of sin and its increase

II. Note of Life
> Lamech (not the *other* Lamech), the one who hoped; but he died, too (5:28–31)
> Noah, the one on whom hope rested (6:8); but in his time came a devastating flood
> Methuselah, the one who lived the longest; but he died, too (5:25–26)
> Enoch, the one who walked with God; and he did not die (5:21–24)

III. Song of Pleasure
> Walking with God is to please God (Heb 11:5)
> Finding favor with God (6:8)

IV. Motif of Fellowship: *Walk with God!*
> Please God—walk with him—and enjoy his grace and his presence
> How we can begin to walk with him
> Presentation of the Gospel

A slightly modified version of the above:

I.   Disfavor with God
> The escalation of ungodliness (6:1–4)
> God's retribution sure (6:5–7)
> But it is not only these horribly wicked ones who are guilty—sin affects everyone: all die (5:1–20, 27, 31)

II. Favor with God
> Enoch walked with God and did not die (5:21–24)
> Walking with God is to please God (Heb 11:5)

Finding favor with God (6:8)

III.   *Walk with God!*

Please God—walk with him—and enjoy his grace and his presence
How we can begin to walk with him
Presentation of the Gospel

PERICOPE 5

The Flood and Its Aftermath

Genesis 6:9–9:29

[The Flood; Noah's Rescue; Ham's Sin]

REVIEW, SUMMARY, PREVIEW

Review of Pericope 4: Genesis 5:1–6:8 shows the spread of evil that escalates until God takes action. All humanity is culpable, and all die. But the life of Enoch, who walked with God and did not die, portrays how to overcome the epidemic of sin and experience intimacy with God.

Summary of Pericope 5: This pericope deals with the flood, perhaps the most devastating of God's judgments of sin thus far. In a rather clever fashion, by employing three subsidiary stories, the pericope notes three ways to avoid such disciplinary action: Noah's righteousness would enable his escape; Noah's intercession (sacrifice) would move God to future restraint; and mankind's own empowerment would deal authoritatively with sin. The sad fact is that none of these stem ongoing sin, as portrayed in Ham's actions and curse.

Preview of Pericope 6: The next pericope (10:1–11:26), the last in the Primeval History, describes God's blessing fulfilled in the multiplication and fruitfulness of humankind. Yet its return to its old ways of hubris and rebellion against God is poignantly described in the story of the Babelites. God punishes, but even his disciplinary action is a means to bring about his blessing.

109

5. Genesis 6:9–9:29

> **THEOLOGICAL FOCUS OF PERICOPE 5**
>
> **5** **The intercession of the righteous, who themselves escape God's disciplinary judgment for sin, precludes further judgment on the world, while the empowerment of mankind to act on God's behalf keeps ongoing sin under check (6:9–9:29).**
>
> > 5.1 The holiness of God prompts his disciplinary judgment for sin, judgment that only the righteous will escape (6:9–8:19).
> >
> > > 5.1.1 *The holiness of God prompts his disciplinary judgment of sin.*
> > >
> > > 5.1.2 *Only the righteous escape God's disciplinary judgment of sin.*
> >
> > 5.2 God's further disciplinary judgment on the world is precluded by the intercession of the righteous, and the empowerment of mankind to act on God's behalf keeps ongoing sin under check (8:20–9:29).
> >
> > > 5.2.1 *God's further disciplinary judgment may be precluded by the intercession of the righteous.*
> > >
> > > 5.2.2 *Mankind is empowered to keep sin under check, acting on God's behalf.*
> > >
> > > 5.2.3 *Notwithstanding the means set in place by God to control evil, ongoing sin continues to plague the human situation.*

OVERVIEW

"This is the family history [תּוֹלְדֹת, *toldot*] of Noah" in 6:9a begins a new section (as in 2:4; 5:1 [a variant]; 10:1; 11:10; 11:27; 25:12, 19; 36:1, 9; and 37:2), one that is divided between 6:9b–9:17 (Noah, "the saved saint") and 9:18–29 (Noah, "the drunkard").[1] The final section, as with most of the pericopes in Genesis, is a prelude to the following one; it deals with the multiplication of the families of Noah's sons and naturally leads into the genealogy of Gen 10. The תּוֹלְדֹת of Noah takes the most space in Gen 1–11: it begins at 6:9a, but formally concludes only at 9:28–29, with the story of the flood embedded in between the genealogical details of this last protagonist in the Sethite line.

Thus far, while God's reaction to sin had been somewhat muted, here sin is punished and retribution visited upon all sinners with full intensity—for the first time in Scripture. This narrative also, for the first time, depicts divine choice and the salvation of a few amidst the many who perish—a recurrent theme in God's redemptive economy.

There is no question but that the pericope is carefully structured, and that around four divine speeches, outlining, in essence, two movements: destruction (6:1–7:20) and restoration (8:1b–9:17), linked by the centerpiece, 7:21–8:1a, with the only occurrence of "death" in the account (the verb in 9:29 is simply part of an epilogue).[2]

---

1. Wenham, *Genesis 1–15*, 156.

2. Details from Mulzac, "Genesis 9:1–7," 66; and Cotter, *Genesis*, 51–52. Wenham notes the palistrophic nature of the time stamps in the account, some of which function solely to achieve symmetry of structure (*Genesis 1–15*, 156–57; also see idem, "The Coherence of the Flood Narrative," 339):

Introduction (6:9–10): Genealogical note; Noah's three sons; Noah's righteousness	

A 6:11–22
First Divine Speech: Threat to destroy the earth
God "sees" "corruption" (שָׁחַת, *shakhat*) (6:11–12); "earth filled" (6:13); resolution to "destroy" (שָׁחַת) the earth (6:13, 17); "all flesh" (6:12); "food" (6:21) and "eat" (6:21); establishing covenant (6:18)

B 7:1–9
Second Divine Speech: "Come into the ark" (7:1)
Noah's response: clean animals and birds taken (7:8–9)

C 7:10–16
Flood begins; ark closed (7:16);
after 7 days, and 40 days (7:10, 12);
dating by Noah's age (7:6, 11)

D 7:17–20
Prevailing waters; mountains covered (7:19–20);
ark floats (7:18)

E 7:21–8:1a All life dies, but God remembers Noah

D' 8:1b–5
Receding waters; mountains uncovered (8:4–5);
ark rests (8:4)

C' 8:6–14
Flood ends; ark's window opened (8:6);
after 7 days, and 40 days (8:6, 10, 12);
dating by Noah's age (8:13–14)

B' 8:15–20
Third Divine Speech: "Go out of the ark" (8:16)
Noah's response: clean animals and birds offered (8:20)

A' 8:21–9:17
Fourth Divine Speech: Promise not to destroy the earth
God "sees" rainbow (9:16); "earth to be filled" (9:1); resolution not to "destroy" (שָׁחַת) the earth (9:11, 15); "all flesh" (9:11); "food" (9:3) and "eat" (9:4); establishing covenant (9:9, 11, 17)

Conclusion (9:18–29): Noah shamed; Noah's three sons; genealogical note (9:18–29)	

Ancient Near Eastern Accounts of the Flood

Both Semitic and non-Semitic cultures have deluge stories in their ethnographic material, many of which share a number of elements with the Genesis account of the flood: divine decision to destroy mankind, warning to flood hero, command to build the ark, hero's obedience, command to enter, entry, closing of door, description of flood, destruction of life, end of rain, ark grounding on mountain, hero opening window, birds' reconnaissance, exit, sacrifice, divine smelling of sacrifice, and blessing on flood hero.[3] Nonetheless, the differences are significant: the Genesis account is strictly monotheistic; the Mesopotamian accounts attribute the flood to the annoyance of the gods because of the noisiness of humans (*Atrahasis* 1.354–356[4]); the weakness of the gods is

7 days' wait for flood (7:4)
7 days' wait for flood (7:10)
40 days of flood (7:12, 17)
150 days of water prevailing (7:24)
150 days of water waning (8:3)
40 days' wait (8:6)
7 days' wait for dry land (8:10)
7 days' wait for dry land (8:12)

3. From Wenham, *Genesis 1–15*, 163–64. Also see *Epic of Gilgamesh* Tablet 11 (*ANET* 93–95; Dalley, *Myths from Mesopotamia*, 109–20); Lambert and Millard, *Atrahasis*; Jacobsen, "The Eridu Genesis," 513–29; Lang, "Non-Semitic Deluge Stories," 605–16.

4. Dalley, *Myths from Mesopotamia*, 18. Also incriminated is the overpopulation of humankind

also on display, for they were unable to control the flood once it arrived and they "cower like dogs" (*Gilgamesh Epic* 11:103–106[5]); etc. In stark contrast, the God of Genesis is in complete control of the flood, which he unleashes on account of evil on the earth, rescuing Noah because of the latter's righteousness. In fact, he explicitly asserts his sovereign control over the flood: "And behold, I, even I, am bring the flood of water upon the earth" (Gen 6:17; also see Ps 29:10). A comparison of the Genesis account with that in the *Gilgamesh Epic*, Tablet 11, shows the following parallels; the significant differences are highlighted:

Genesis	Gilgamesh Epic
Flood precipitated by mankind's sin	Flood precipitated by mankind's sin
Noah commanded by God	Utnapishtim commanded by Ea (god)
Ark dimensions provided	Boat dimensions provided
Noah collects animals	Utnapishtim collects "living things"
Ark covered with pitch	Ark covered with pitch
Ark with 3 decks	Ark with 7 decks
No construction information detailed	Construction information detailed
No supplies listed	Supplies, including silver and gold, listed
No sacrifices during construction	Sacrifices made during construction
God shuts the door	Utnapishtim shuts the door
No emotions or words of Noah recorded	Words/emotions of Utnapishtim recorded
God sends the flood	Ellil (god) sends the flood
40 days of rain	7 days of the tempest
Waters from above and below	Waters from above
God in control of the flood	Gods afraid of the flood
Flood is global	Flood is global
Ark comes to rest on Mt. Ararat	Boat comes to rest on Mt. Nimush
Noah opens window post-flood	Utnapishtim opens porthole post-flood
Birds (raven, dove [×2]) sent thrice	Birds (dove, swallow, and raven) sent thrice
Noah sacrifices after the flood	Utnapishtim sacrifices after the flood
God smells fragrance of sacrifice	Gods smell fragrance of sacrifice
God is pleased with the sacrifice	Gods are hungry for the sacrifice
God promises never to repeat the flood	Mistress of the gods promises never to forget
God deliberately saves Noah and family	Ellil surprised by Utnapishtim's salvation
Noah remains mortal and fallible	Utnapishtim becomes immortal and deified

5.1 Genesis 6:9–8:19

THEOLOGICAL FOCUS 5.1

5.1 The holiness of God prompts his disciplinary judgment for sin, judgment that only the righteous will escape (6:9–8:19).

    5.1.1 *The holiness of God prompts his disciplinary judgment of sin.*

    5.1.2 *Only the righteous escape God's disciplinary judgment of sin.*

---

that needed curbing (2.2–8), unlike in Genesis where the emphasis is entirely on mankind's depravity. "Viewed in this light, Gn. 9,1 ff. looks like a conscious rejection of the Atrahasis Epic" (Hamilton, *Genesis: Chapters 1–17*, 313).

5. Dalley, *Myths from Mesopotamia*, 109–16.

NOTES 5.1

5.1.1 *The holiness of God prompts his disciplinary judgment of sin.*

The scope of the disaster is not left to one's imagination: *every* living creature/*all* flesh (כֹּל, *kl*, in both cases) is to be blotted out (7:4, 21 [×3], 22 [×2], 23), for "every" (כֹּל) intent of the thoughts of man's heart was continually evil (כָּל־הַיּוֹם, *kal-hayyom*, "*all* the day," 6:5). "Only Noah" (7:23) and those with him were left.[6] The "blotting out" of every living thing and the "leaving" of Noah alone are both passive verbs, pointing to the divine agent behind them. "Noah does not survive this catastrophe by his own cunning or strength. He is saved because he is left behind . . . by Yahweh."[7] The threefold mention of "enter" in 7:15–16 emphasizes that redemption will happen only via the ark. The solemnity is emphasized in the chiastic structure of 7:21–22:

> **A**   They perished—
> all flesh, all swarming things, and all mankind, and all
> **B**   that was on the dry land, and all in whose nostrils was
> the breath of the spirit of life
> **A'**   died.

6. From the description of the extent of the flood one would assume it was universal: covering the "face of (all) the land": 6:7; 7:3, 4, 23; 8:9. But that phrase need not necessarily indicate a global reach: Gen 4:14 (Cain driven off the "face of the land" = known land; Cain was not removed from the planet); Gen 41:56 ("face of the ground" points to a widespread *local* famine); Num 11:31 (two-cubit depth of quails cover the "face of the ground"—likely local); 1 Sam 20:15 (David's enemies on the "face of the land" could obviously only be local); 2 Sam 18:8 (a battle spread over the "face of the whole land" has to be a local one). Likewise, "all the high mountains under all the heavens," in Gen 7:19, need not indicate every range from the Himalayas to the Andes. If the flood was local, rather than global, then the extent of life lost would also be limited—widespread and vast, no doubt, but not global. Hyperbole employing "all" is, after all, quite common in the Bible, as it is in normal use of language (see Exod 10:15; Josh 11:23; 2 Sam 18:8; 2 Chr 36:23; Jer 34:1; Zech 5:6; Luke 2:1; Acts 2:5; 11:28; etc.). Thus even the phrases "all flesh" (Gen 6:12, 13, 17, 19; 7:15, 16, 21; 9:11, 15), "all in whose nostrils was the breath of the spirit of life" (7:22), "all that was on the dry land" (7:22), and "all mankind" (7:21) could indicate a less-than-universal loss of life (also see Gen 41:57; Deut 2:25). The serious logistical problems with a large-scale, universal flood include the requirement of an extra 630 million cubic miles of water weighing 3 quintillion tons (3,000,000,000,000,000,000) to cover Mt. Ararat (17,000 feet)—the tripling of ocean volume—and, later, a disappearance of all this extra liquid. The rate of rise of flood waters (17,000 feet in 150 days) would be more than 100 feet/day; the magnitude of currents so created would likely render the floating of an ark impossible. See Walton, *Genesis*, 322–24. As has been noted in connection with the creation account (see Introduction), one should also be cautious before jettisoning scientific opinion out of the window. In any case, the thrust of the story is not affected by the extent of the flood, provided one accepts that it was widespread, devastating, and ruinous. And, as far as this author is aware, no expressly stated element of systematic theology is affected one way or another, and no important piece of Christian doctrine is contingent upon the flood being local or global (of course a geographically local flood may conceivably be anthropologically global, if humankind were not present on every continent at the time of the deluge). In sum, let me assert that the text is consistent with either option; I do give some weightage to scientific consensus and therefore lean towards a local flood. Not that it particularly matters for the preaching of this pericope. A flood did happen and it was divine punishment; a vast number of humans and animals did perish; Noah and his family did escape, because "he found favor with God" (6:8). The theological lessons are derivable without needing to establish with certainty the extent of the flood.

7. Hamilton, *Genesis: Chapters 1–17*, 297.

Waters from above ("floodgates of the sky") and from below ("fountains of the great deep") were unloosed (7:11; and they were closed in 8:2).[8] The allusion to the creation waters above and below the firmament is unmistakable, seeming to indicate a return of the earth to a pre-creation state— a "de-creation." Instead of the living beings multiplying as God had promised at creation (רבה, *rbh*, 1:22, 28), here in 7:17 and 18, the waters "multiply" (i.e., "increase," also רבה) decimating the population of living beings, both animal and human, in response to human sin that was "great" (רבה, 6:5). "The waters do not merely multiply greatly; they triumph," or "prevail" (גבר, *gbr*, 7:18, 19, 20, 24), a military term for success in battle (Exod 17:11; Jdg 3:10; 6:2; etc.), and thereby all the mountains under the heavens are covered (Gen 7:19, 20).[9]

The word "died" (מות, *mut*, 7:22) is a new occurrence in the flood story ("perish" and "blot out" have already been encountered in 6:7, 17; etc.); one remembers that this verb first showed up in the account of the fall of man (2:17; 3:3–4), and then in a constant refrain in the Sethite genealogy (5:5, 8, 11, 14, 17, 20, 27, 31) as a stark reminder of the baleful effects of sin. It shows up again here, as a consequence of the punitive action of God against sin. "The narrator's camera lingers longest over the destruction of life by the flood. Elsewhere in Genesis 'expire and die' [גוע, *gawa*', and מות] are used in quick succession to describe the process of dying (25:8, 17; 35:29). . . . Here [in 7:21–22] the members of this standard word pair are spaced out, standing at opposite ends of sentences in chiastic opposition"[10]: "all flesh . . . *perished* [גוע] . . . and cattle and beasts and every swarming thing . . . and all mankind, and all that was on the dry land, all in whose nostrils was the breath of the spirit of life, *died* [מות]." This was a devastating and catastrophic occurrence.[11]

The word שחת (*shkht*, "corrupt" or "destroy") echoes in 6:11–13: the earth is "corrupt" (6:11a, 12a, 12b) and God decides to "destroy" it (6:13b). So "God's decision is to destroy what is virtually self-destroyed or self-destroying already. . . . In a sense vv. 11–12 are a condensation of the narratives extending from Gen 3:1 to 6:4"—a downward spiral of mankind's sinfulness and corruption.[12] That the earth was "filled with violence" is also noted twice (6:11b, 13a). Rather than animals and mankind filling the earth, as was God's original intention (1:22, 28), it is violence that has done so. The last use of "and God saw" was in 1:31 where God recognized all he had created as good; but here, "God sees" (6:12) that the earth was corrupt. In the first instance, he was delighted; now he is disgusted. The consequence would be a spewing out of man from the land that had been desecrated and defiled (Lev 18:25–28). "Blot out," occurs thrice

8. Interestingly, in 7:11 (and in 8:2), the presentation is chiastic: opened (closed) // fountains :: floodgates // opened (closed).

9. Wenham, *Genesis 1–15*, 182.

10. Ibid., 183.

11. The mention of "all . . . in whose nostrils [אף, *'p*]was the breath of the spirit of life" (7:22) harks back to the divine insufflation of the "breath of life" at the creation of man (2:7), as well as to the "sweat of your brow [אף]" (3:9), a consequence of the fall.

12. Hamilton, *Genesis: Chapters 1–17*, 278. He renders שחת with "ruin," to retain the play of words: "*gone to ruin* was the earth . . . indeed, it had *gone to ruin* . . . all flesh had *ruined* its way . . . I will *ruin* them" (ibid.).

in the narrative: 6:7 (resolution concerning the flood), 7:4 (notification regarding the flood), and 7:23 (consummation of the flood).

Genesis 6:7	Genesis 7:4	Genesis 7:23
I will blot out man whom I have created from the face of the land from man to animals to creeping things and to birds of the sky ….	I will blot out every living thing that I have made from the face of the land	He blotted out every living thing upon the face of the land from man to animals to creeping things and to birds of the sky ….

In short, God's perfect holiness leads him to judge sin and discipline sinners.

5.1.2 *Only the righteous escape God's disciplinary judgment of sin.*

Utnapishtim (the Noahic character in the *Gilgamesh Epic*) is an exalted figure, a king (as also is the Sumerian flood hero, Ziusudra, and Atrahasis himself). He is busy with preparations for the flood, lying to his fellowmen as to why he is engaging in this activity, loading his floating "palace" with kith and kin, silver and gold (*Gilgamesh Epic* 11.2[13]). In Genesis, however, the flood hero, Noah, is of <u>humbler</u> dimensions. All through his ark-building endeavor and throughout the subsequent flood, Noah is silent. It is God who does the speaking; Noah simply obeys (in faith). While the Mesopotamian hero declares, "I went aboard the boat and closed the door" (*Gilgamesh Epic* 11.93[14]), in Genesis, Yahweh is the one who shuts Noah in (7:16). Mankind's turning to clay in the flood reduces Utnapishtim to tears (*Gilgamesh Epic* 11.3[15]), but in Genesis there is no disclosure of Noah's feelings. Instead, God's actions are highlighted, and Noah's obedience underscored. No more, no less.

Literally, the Hebrew of Gen 6:9b reads "Noah, a man *righteous, blameless* was he among his contemporaries," employing the significant terms צַדִּיק, *tsaddiq*, and תָּמִים, *tamim*. In addition, 6:9c has: "With God, walked Noah," a pronounced inversion emphasizing Noah's character that also makes the single Hebrew sentence of 6:9 begin and end with this patriarch's name (see below).[16] This was one who was very different from his contemporaries, one whose righteousness is also noted in 6:22–7:1. The structure of 6:8–9 is tailored to highlight the patriarch's character, with each element in the pairs *B* and *B'*, *C* and *C'*, *D* and *D'*, and *E* and *E'*, employing different words for the single idea that each pair shares.[17]

---

13. Dalley, *Myths from Mesopotamia*, 111–12.

14. Ibid., 112.

15. Ibid., 113.

16. Noort, "The Stories of the Great Flood," 27–28.

17. See Wenham, "The Coherence of the Flood Narrative," 341. Interestingly, the sentence that talks about Noah walking with God ends with the three consonants of "Enoch" (חֲנוֹךְ; another one who walked with God, 5:22, 24) spelled backwards (הִתְהַלֶּךְ־נֹחַ, *hithhallek noakh*, "he-walked Noah"). Besides Enoch and Noah, the patriarchs walked with God (17:1; 24:40; 48:15), and presumably Adam did, too (3:8) (see Pericope 4).

A	But Noah						
	B	found favor					
		C	in the eyes of the LORD.				
			D	These are the generations (תּוֹלְדֹת) of Noah.			
				E	Noah was a righteous man;		
				E'	blameless he was		
			D'	in his generations (דֹרֹת, *dorot*);		
		C'	with God,				
	B'	walked					
A'	Noah.						

The blamelessness (תָּמִים) of Noah indicates his lack of guilt in the matters of evil afflicting his generation, about which God was sorely displeased (6:5–7).[18] The word "righteous" (צַדִּיק), always used of persons/God, also stands in contrast with those who are wicked; such a one abides by God's moral standards (Deut 32:4; both תָּמִים and צַדִּיק show up here), i.e., his law (Pss 19:10; 119:1; Ezek 18:5–9). There is no indication of how or why Noah was blameless or righteous; he is simply introduced as being so. But one notes that he is said to have found "favor" with God (חֵן, *khen*, "grace," Gen 6:8) *before* he is said to be blameless and righteous (6:9). Perhaps this reflects the sentiments of Ps 18:31–32; it is the grace of God that enables one to be blameless and righteous. In any case, like Enoch, Noah was one who walked with God.[19]

The instructions for the construction of the ark, as we have it in the text, are quite insufficient for ship-building; nor is there any detail about where exactly this endeavor took place, or if Noah had any help, and how long the project took.[20] Obviously, the bare form simply helps complete the story. But perhaps more than anything else, it highlights the obedience of Noah. Noah's obedience is total, "according to all that God had commanded him" (6:22). The sentence begins and ends with עָשָׂה, *'asah*: "He-did Noah . . . thus he-did," emphasizing the patriarch's compliance with the demands of God—a recurrent theme (6:22; 7:5, 9, 16; see Heb 11:7). The same indication of obedience is used of Moses's work in the construction of the tabernacle: Exod 39:32, 42; 40:16; also see Num 1:54; 2:34; 9:5. Indeed, the tabernacle and Noah's ark—sanctuaries for the righteous—are the only two structures whose building is stipulated and described in the Law.[21] The word for "ark," תֵּבָת, *tebat*, is found only in the flood story

18. For a similar usage of תָּמִים, contrasting righteous and wicked behavior, see: Deut 18:12–13; Pss 15:2–3; 37:17–18; 101:2–6; Prov 2:21–22; 11:5; 28:10. The word is employed in Gen 17:1, also in connection with Abram's "walking with God."

19. It is likely that Noah's sons (and their families) are also considered righteous: for one, they are named in 6:10 before the world is finally declared corrupt in 6:11–12. Also, Ezek 14:14, 16 assert that the righteousness of Noah, Daniel, and Job could not deliver their children, but only themselves. Considering that Noah's sons (and their families) were, in fact, delivered—and Ezekiel must have been aware of that—it must be that they, too, were righteous. See Wenham, *Genesis 1–15*, 170.

20. The dimensions of the ark have been estimated to be 440 feet long × 73 feet wide × 44 feet high, yielding a displacement of about 43,000 tons, and a total deck area of about 96,000 square feet (Hamilton, *Genesis: Chapters 1–17*, 282).

21. Wenham, *Genesis 1–15*, 172.

and in Exod 2:3, 5, where it indicates the basket in which Moses was hidden by his mother—another hero saved from the waters in an "ark." In the first, humanity is saved through one man; in the second a chosen people is saved through another man; "here [in Genesis] it is the macrocosm that has to be preserved, there [in Exodus] it is the microcosm."[22]

The scene preceding the flood (Gen 7:5–16) is marked by a threefold assertion that Noah did all that God/Yahweh commanded him (7:5, 9, 16). On further examination, the account breaks down precisely into two parallel panels (with the second providing more detail for each description); each panel ends with "as God commanded Noah/him."[23]

Description	Panel 1	Panel 2
Date and commencement of the flood	7:6a	7:10–12
Noah and his family enter the ark	7:7	7:13
Animals enter the ark	7:8	7:14
Animals in pairs, male and female	7:9a	7:15–16a
"As God commanded Noah/him"	7:9b	7:16b

While the building of the ark, no doubt an arduous enterprise, takes up only a single verse (7:22), the twin description of the arrival of the flood and the embarkation of Noah and his family consumes eleven verses (7:6–16). The repetition in two panels, as well as the careful numbering of days and years, adds to the emphasis on Noah's actions. Later at the end of the flood, God's command in 8:17 and Noah's studious obedience to it (8:18–19), designated by the repetition of the parade of people and animals, once again underscores the patriarch's righteousness.[24]

> The divine commands are given at a moment when there is as yet no sign of the Flood. In such a situation only a man who regards God as his absolute Lord can accept the wisdom of the command. He trusts in God because he is aware that the ruler of the world alone knows the reasons for his own way of acting and demands. A single instance of obedience cannot be a complete test of righteousness, but when a man survives many trials of his righteousness or faith in his most critical moments, we can safely assume that he has a habit of righteousness. The Lord's statement "for I have seen that you are righteous before me in this generation" (7:1) is evidently based on Noah's righteousness in the past and the present; consequently, God can rely on him in the future.[25]

The centerpiece of the chiastic structure of this pericope (*E*; see above in Overview) details the perishing of all life, "but God remembered Noah" (8:1a). This becomes the turning-point of the story, introducing the next scene where the flood

---

22. Cassuto, *Genesis*, 59.

23. The closing of the door of the ark, though, is stated only once (7:16c).

24. Genesis 7:2 has the first distinction made in the Bible between animals clean and unclean. The seven pairs called for in 7:2–3 do not contradict 6:19 where "pairs of every kind" are called for: in the former, *seven* pairs (literally, "seven sevens") of *clean* animals are specified, obviously in addition to the other set, and presumably for the purposes of sacrifice.

25. Krašovec, "Punishment and Mercy," 17.

abates (8:1b–14). In the previous scene, 7:10–20, "the impersonal waters of destruction triumphing everywhere dominate the whole picture; here 'God remembered Noah' sets the narrative in a new, optimistic, personal direction. There the waters triumph; here they retreat. There the ark floats over the earth; here it lands on the mountains. There the high mountains are covered; here they reappear above the waves."[26] This is the first time God is said to have remembered a person; when God remembers, he acts (also see 19:29, the saving of Lot; 30:22, the conception of Rachel; 1 Sam 1:19, the conception of Hannah; Ps 115:2, the blessing of Israel; etc.); God's remembering is depicted over seventy times in the OT: indeed, the righteous are remembered and saved.

5.2 Genesis 8:20–9:29

THEOLOGICAL FOCUS 5.2

5.2   God's further disciplinary judgment on the world is precluded by the intercession of the righteous, and the empowerment of mankind to act on God's behalf keeps ongoing sin under check (8:20–9:29).

　　5.2.1   *God's further disciplinary judgment may be precluded by the intercession of the righteous.*

　　5.2.2   *Mankind is empowered to keep sin under check, acting on God's behalf.*

　　5.2.3   *Notwithstanding the means set in place by God to control evil, ongoing sin continues to plague the human situation.*

NOTES 5.2

5.2.1 *God's further disciplinary judgment may be precluded by the intercession of the righteous.*

The wind passing over the earth, the receding of the waters, the appearance of dry land (8:1–2, 5–11), all describe the reversal of the deluge; the similarities with the creation account of Gen 1 make this a "re-creation," even with a post-re-creation blessing (1:26–30; 9:1–8).[27] The dryness of the land is mentioned thrice in the space of two verses, 8:13–14, signaling a fresh start to a re-created world born anew from the "watery grave of the old."[28] "Just as God's *ruah* was hovering over the face of the waters at the beginning of the world's creation, when the waters of the deep covered the earth, so now that the waters again submerged the earth, God made a *ruah* pass over them. . . . and in the same way as in the earlier passage God's *ruah* represents the principle and source of life, so here the *ruah* that God causes to blow over the earth indicates the beginning of new life."[29] Similarities between the original creation account and that of the current (re)creation are shown below[30]:

26. Wenham, *Genesis 1–15*, 183–84.

27. Mathews, *Genesis 1–11:26*, 383.

28. Wenham, *Genesis 1–15*, 187.

29. Cassuto, *Genesis*, 101.

30. Table shown is modified from Mathews, *Genesis 1–11:26*, 383. Other parallels between the cre-

Creation Day	Texts	Shared Elements
First Day	1:2	"earth," "deep," "Spirit" (רוּחַ, *ruakh*), "waters"
	8:1b–2a	"wind (רוח), "earth," "waters," "deep"
Second Day	1:7–8	"waters," "sky"
	8:2b	"sky"
Third Day	1:9	"water," "dry ground" (יַבָּשָׁה, *ybshh*) "appear"
	8:3–5, 7, 14	"water," "dried" (יבש, *ybsh*), "appear"
Fourth Day	(no need for re-creation of the luminaries after the flood)	
Fifth Day	1:20	"birds," "above (עַל־פְּנֵי, *'al-pne*) the earth," "across the expanse"
	8:7–8	"raven," "from the earth," "from the face (עַל־פְּנֵי) of the ground"
Sixth Day	1:24, 26	"creatures," "that move along the ground," "wild animals", "man," "image"
	8:17; 9:6	"creature," "animals," "that move along the ground," "image," "man"
Seventh Day	2:1–3	"rest," "blessed"
	8:21–9:2	"restful/soothing," "not rest/cease," "blessed"

And subsequently, the ark "rested"— נוּחַ (*nuakh*, 8:4), an allusion to Noah's name (נֹחַ, *noakh*). Later, the dove sent out by Noah hunts for a "resting place" (מָנוֹחַ, *manoakh*, 8:9), but finds none: "She looked for another Noah outside the ark, but finding none, she returned to the Noah she knew."[31] The ark, where נח is, is the place of נוח!

In the closing scene of the flood narrative, 8:20–9:17, the reader is once again reminded of the newness of the era: whereas the earth had been "filled" with violence pre-flood (6:11, 13), now Noah is commanded to "fill" the earth by being fruitful and multiplying (9:1). What was chaotic violence before, is now going to be controlled, as God introduces measures of restraint in the relationships between man and animals, along with warnings with regard to the shedding of blood (9:2–7). The contrast between then and now is furthered in the declaration of Yahweh: "Now behold, I *Myself*

---

ation and flood accounts include: the divine command to be fruitful and to multiply (1:20–22, 24–25, 28–30 and 8:17; 9:1), and the repeated use of sevens (2:2, 3 and 8:4, 10, 12). The ark's coming to rest in Tishri, the seventh month of the Hebrew religious calendar, is significant, for it is the month that includes the Day of Atonement, the Feasts of Trumpets, and of Tabernacles. "It was appropriate, therefore, that the ark should find refuge in the cultic month celebrating atonement and God's provision" (ibid., 385). Echoes of the creation account are also found later in the poetic epilogue of 8:22: "day" and "night" (1:5, 8, 13, 14, 16, 18, 19, 23, 31; 2:1, 3), "seed" (1:11–12, 29), and "cease/rest" (2:2–3; thus the "Sabbath" shows up at the end of both creation and flood stories). Subsequently, terms from the pre-flood state show up post-flood: blessing (1:28 and 9:1); beasts of the earth (1:25, 30, and 9:2, 10); birds of the sky (1:21, 26, 28, 30; 2:19, and 9:2); creeping (1:24, 25, 26, and 9:3); "given to you" (1:29, and 9:3); "shall be food for you" (1:29, and 9:3); living creature (1:20, 21, 24; 2:7, 19, and 9:10, 12, 15, 16); image of God (1:27 and 9:6); "populate" (1:20, 21, and 9:7). As well, several terms from the antediluvian scene appear in 9:12–17: "covenant" (6:18; and 9:12, 13, 5, 16, 17), "generations" (6:9; and 9:12), "see" (6:12; and 9:14, 16), "confirm" (6:18; and 9:17), "a flood to ruin all flesh" (6:17; and 9:15). See Wenham, *Genesis 1–15*, 195. Moreover, with the later post-flood scene of Noah's drunkenness, there is, in common with the post-creation account, a "fall" in both narratives linked to a plant (2:9; 9:20); nakedness and lack of awareness (2:25; 9:21); opening of eyes and knowing (3:7; 9:24); and pronouncements of punishment (3:14–19; 9:25–27). See Walton, *Genesis*, 344–45.

31. Wenham, *Genesis 1–15*, 186; and Morales, *The Tabernacle Pre-figured*, 138–39.

do establish My covenant . . ." (9:9); earlier he had asserted: "Now behold, I *Myself* am bringing the flood . . . (6:17). Once he had "seen" the corruption of the earth (6:12) and that had prompted the flood; now he "sees" the rainbow (9:16) which will prompt him *not* to destroy all flesh with a flood. The reason for Yahweh's restraint is not clearly spelled out apart from the cryptic comment of 8:21. Paradoxically, the reason for a future non-destruction ("the intent of man's heart is evil from his youth," 8:21) is precisely the reason for the earlier resolution to destroy (6:5). In other words, "[i]n spite of a justifiable motivation for continued judgment, God chooses not to exercise that option. . . . Thus this verse functions as a ringing testimony to the mercy of God, who henceforth will not give man his just deserts. The punishable will not be punished."[32] The verse is asserting that God will refrain from punishment *even though* man is sinful through and through. But why does God extend this grace? Since 9:1–17 does not proceed to explicate this decision to keep future floods at bay, one must attend closely to 8:20–22 to locate the reason for God's gracious withholding of judgment—Noah's sacrifice.

Thus far, we are not shown Noah doing anything on his own initiative, except sending out the birds on a reconnaissance trip—that was, of course, bound by necessity, to see whether the waters had subsided. But in 8:20, Noah does something not demanded by God, or demanded by the exigencies of survival: he builds an altar and performs a sacrifice. The theme of sacrifice by the flood-survivor is common to ancient Near Eastern flood stories. Utnapishtim's sacrifices are appreciated by the gods; in fact, "[t]he gods like flies gathered over the sacrifice" (*Gilgamesh Epic* 11.3[33]). This instance of Noah building an altar is, however, the first of its kind in the Bible (8:20), though one may assume that Abel and Cain performed their respective sacrifices on altars as well (4:3–4). In accordance with what was later codified in the Mosaic Law, Noah sacrifices "clean" animals and birds (Lev 20:25) as burnt offerings on an altar ("altar of burnt offerings," is found in Exod 30:28; 31:9; 35:16; 38:1; 40:6, 10, 29).[34] Noah thus becomes a prototype of Moses, and the former's first act after his disembarkation from the ark, becomes one of faith and gratitude in a God who saved him. "Since this offering was wholly burned, it indicated the person's complete devotion to the Lord. Thus for the Mosaic community it would be viewed as the appropriate sacrifice for Noah, who presented it freely out of thanksgiving to God for sparing his life."[35] Noah, à la Moses, is thus a priest for the postdiluvian world. (Theologically, this would be an intercessory role, as Moses often undertook, a mediation between God and fellowmen. Hence, "intercession," is used in the Theological Focus.)

Genesis 8:22 records the only time Yahweh actually "smells" a sacrifice. In other places, he *refuses* to smell the aroma offered by his disobedient people, in Lev 26:31

---

32. Hamilton, *Genesis: Chapters 1–17*, 310. One might conceivably interpret the כִּי (*ki*, "for," 8:21) as concessional: "*even though* the intent of man's heart is evil."

33. Dalley, *Myths from Mesopotamia*, 114–15.

34. And עָלָה עֹלֹת, *'alah 'olot*, "offer burnt offerings" (Gen 8:20), occurs in Exod 24:5; 32:6; Lev 17:8; Deut 12:13–14.

35. Mathews, *Genesis 1–11:26*, 391, 392.

and Amos 5:21; and David prays that God would smell the former's offering (1 Sam 26:19). For Yahweh to smell the sacrifices, then, is a picture of his acceptance of the sacrifices and of those offering them, an appeasement of his anger regarding sin and evil. "Soothing aroma" was regularly employed for sacrifices: Exod 29:18, 25, 41; Lev 1:9; 2:2, 9; 3:5, 16; etc. Indeed, "soothing" (נִיחוֹחַ or נִיחֹחַ, *nikhoakh*) is related to "rest" (נוּחַ) and "Noah" (נֹחַ); thus, "soothing aroma" is literally a "rest-inducing odor." Lamech's wish for his son had become reality; he hoped Noah would bring rest (5:29), and Noah did: his sacrifice "rested" ("soothed") God, because it reflected the total dedication of this righteous man to God. This would explain the reason for God's resolution never again to send floods to destroy the earth, despite the sinfulness of mankind.

Noah found favor with God, walked with God, and was found righteous before God (6:8, 9; 7:1); now his sacrifice was pleasing to God and affected God's attitude to mankind and its failings—thus, Noah's "priestly" work was, in effect, intercessory.[36] In the Garden of Eden, God pronounced a curse on the ground "because of you [Adam]" (בַּעֲבוּרֶךָ, *ba'avureka*, 3:17); here, after the flood, God promises *not to curse* the ground again "because of man" (בַּעֲבוּר הָאָדָם, *ba'avur ha'adam*, 8:21). Before the flood, Yahweh was grieved "in his heart" (אֶל־לִבּוֹ, *'el libo*) about the state of the world and that "every intent of the thoughts of [man's] heart" was evil (6:5–6); after the flood he says "in his heart" (אֶל־לִבּוֹ, i.e., "to Himself") that "the intent of the man's heart" is evil (8:21).[37] Nothing had substantially changed. The only possible reason for Yahweh's change of heart (!) was Noah's sacrifice and the resultant smelling of the soothing aroma by Yahweh.

> Ultimately, of course, the acceptance of every sacrifice depends on God's antecedent gracious purpose, whereby he appointed the sacrificial system as a means of atonement for reconciliation between God and man [Lev 17:11; etc.]. . . . Looked at in this light, we can view Noah's offering of sacrifice as a prototype of the work of later priests, who made atonement for Israel, or of Job, who offered burnt offerings for his sons and for his "friends" (Job 1:5; 42:8). Here, however, Noah's sacrifice is effective for all mankind.[38]

The reason for the efficacy of Noah's sacrifice is because of the pleasure it brought to God; Noah's sacrifice was symbolic of his offering himself to God, and with Noah's life, God was pleased, as this narrative declared. And, satisfied ("comforted/rested") by the righteous one's offering of himself, God resolved not to curse the ground any further (8:21a), just as he would never again destroy living creatures in a flood (8:21b).[39] In

---

36. Ibid., 393. It was noted earlier how Noah and Moses were similarly rescued from death by means of an "ark" (also see below for similarities between the Noachic and Sinaitic covenants). All along in Gen 1–8, there has been a "very clear interest in cultic and priestly concerns": Sabbath (2:1–3), Garden of Eden as sanctuary (Gen 2–3; see Pericope 1), acceptable sacrifices (4:1–8), clean vs. unclean (Gen 6–8). See Wenham, *Genesis 1–15*, 189–90. Moreover, the "cover" (מִכְסֶה, *mikseh*) of the ark (8:13) is also used of a part of the tabernacle (Exod 26:14; 36:19; Num 3:25).

37. The parallels between 6:5–7 and 8:21 are revealing: both have "man," "imagination," "heart," "evil," and "repent/rest."

38. Wenham, *Genesis 1–15*, 190.

39. Notice also "repent [נֹחַם] . . . Noah [נֹחַ]" (6:7c–8a) chiastically paralleling "Noah [נֹחַ] . . . rest

sum, carrying the thrust of the text to the theological level, one might say that the intercession of the righteous helps influence God in his exercise of disciplinary judgment upon the world.

5.2.2 *Mankind is empowered to keep sin under check, acting on God's behalf.*

The fourth divine speech of Yahweh (9:1–17), can be divided into a section on divine blessing (9:1–7, with 9:1 and 7 forming an *inclusio*), and a section on the divine covenant (9:8–17, with 9:8–9 and 17 forming another *inclusio*). Genesis 9:1–7 begins and ends with the command to be fruitful and to multiply, as mankind was charged in 1:28. "The 'blessing' of procreation and dominion conferred upon the postdiluvian world is a restatement of God's creation promise for the human family and the creatures (1:22–25, 28–30), but now its provisions are modified in light of encroaching societal wickedness." For if a catastrophic flood will not be allowed to happen again, then there must be other means to counter and curb the sinful tendencies of mankind that proved to be ruinous to society, as well to guarantee the continuation of the earth until the day of final redemption.[40] In any case, this reminds the reader that "re-creation" has not yet overcome sin *in toto*.

There is significant similarity between the event of the Sinai covenant with Moses and the postdiluvian covenant with Noah: act of divine salvation (8:1–9 and Exod 19:1–2); altars (Gen 8:20 and Exod 24:4); covenant (Gen 9:9 and Exod 24:7–8); blessing (Gen 9:1 and Exod 23:25); beasts/wild animals/enemies (Gen 9:5–6 and Exod 23:22, 29); the earth preserved (Gen 9:11 and Exod 23:29); and clouds (Gen 9:13–17 and Exod 24:15).[41] Moreover, the stipulations and prohibitions of Gen 9:1–7 have the markings of a covenant: there is a clear definition of the roles of the participants in it—9:7 has "Now, you . . .," balanced in 9:9 by "Now, I. . . ." This also means that the Noahic covenant is conditional, 9:1–7 depicting man's part, and 9:8–17 God's.[42] Nonetheless, it is God who "initiates, sustains, and completes the covenant": "I [am about to] establish" (מֵקִים, *meqim*, 9:9; Hiphil participle, imminent future); "I establish" (וַהֲקִמֹתִי, *wahaqimoti*, 9:11; Hiphil *waw* consecutive perfect); and "I have established" (הֲקִמֹתִי, *haqimoti*, 9:17; Hiphil perfect).[43] The variety of ways in which the partners of the covenant with God are described emphasizes its importance[44]:

> "between Men and you and every living creature that is with you" (9:12)
> "between Me and the earth" (9:13)

[חָם] (5:29a).

40. Mathews, *Genesis 1–11:26*, 398.

41. Sailhamer, *Genesis*, 93.

42. Such an allocation of responsibilities is also found in other covenantal passages: Gen 17:4, 9; Exod 14:16, 17; 31:6, 13; Num 18:6, 7, 8; Jer 1:17, 18; 40:10; and Ezek 37:5, 12, 19, 21 with 36:8; 27:16; 39:1, 17.

43. Mathews, *Genesis 1–11:26*, 408. "*My* covenant," occurs in 6:18; 9:9, 11, 15; and "*my* bow" in 9:13. "I establish My covenant" (6:18; 9:9, 11, 17) also occurs in the covenant with Abraham (17:7, 19) and with Moses and the Israelites at Sinai (Exod 6:4).

44. Wenham, *Genesis 1–15*, 195.

"between Me and you and every living creature of all flesh" (9:15)
"between God and every living creature of all flesh that is on the earth" (9:16)
"between Me and all flesh that is on the earth" (9:17)

What exactly was mankind's responsibility in this covenant? In 9:1–7, one finds stipulations regarding killing; in 9:8–17, it is all about life: "every living creature" (9:10, 12), "every beast of the earth" (9:10 [×2]); "all flesh" (9:11, 17), "every living creature of all flesh (9:15, 16); as well as divine promises not to destroy all flesh (9:11, 15).[45] "According to Genesis 9, in order for humankind properly to dwell on the earth, harmony must exist between humans and any threat to being fruitful and multiplying. This can only take place by implementing a proper authority structure."[46] Mason suspects that the "animals" in 9:2, by extension, stand for the human enemies of Israel evidenced by the language of holy war—"fear" and "terror"; "into your hand they are given"; "I give all to you"; etc.[47] Wild animals are frequently connected with Israel's enemies: Isa 5:29; Ezek 14:21; 33:27; 34:25, 28; 39:4–6; Hos 2:18; etc. Covenantal statements in Lev 26 (בְּרִית, *brit*, "covenant," in 26:9, 15, 25, 42 [×3], 44, 45) are linked with protection from wild animals and enemies (Lev 26:6, 7, 8, 16, 17, 22, 25, 32, 34, 36, 37, 38, 39, 41, 44). "The obvious implication of the curses in Leviticus 26 is that if Israel is obedient to God, then Israel will rule over their enemies and their enemies will be handed over to them. This language represents the 'subdue' ideas of the human–animal relationship in Genesis 9."[48] While it may be going too far to say that "wild animals" in Gen 9 actually represents human enemies, the fact that there were no human enemies immediately after the flood may have moved the narrator to co-opt "wild animals" to indicate general threats to the proliferation of humankind (which, later on, included human enemies of the people of God, of course).

> The point offered here is twofold. First, the human to animal relationship in Genesis 9 characterizes and prefigures Israel's dominion over other nations. Thus, the animals in Genesis 9 serve double-duty. They represent the real relationship between human beings and animals within the world, and they represent in anticipatory fashion the relationship between Israel and its enemies in the promised land. Second, the images and ideas of fruitfulness and multiplication, and subduing threats to this mandate as expressed in Gen 9:1–7, Leviticus 26, and other Old Testament covenant texts . . ., demonstrate that these elements of Gen 9:1–7 are intrinsically covenant ideas.[49]

Violence was clearly a problem in antediluvian world (6:11, 13).[50] Here in 9:5–6, this is addressed decisively; indiscriminate shedding of blood is forbidden, with both man and beast held to account, and the former being called to enforce the stipulation by

45. The word "destroy" (שׁחת, 9:11, 15) was precisely the one used to warn of the flood (6:13, 17).

46. Mason, "Another Flood?" 187.

47. These are martial terms; see Deut 1:21; 2:24, 30; 3:2; 31:8; Josh 8:1; 10:25; etc.

48. Mason, "Another Flood?" 190 (emphases removed).

49. Ibid., 191.

50. "Under the Noahic covenant, in contrast to the original creation, conflict and hostility form part of the fabric of the natural and social orders" (VanDrunen, "Natural Law," 139).

means of the death penalty. While God promised never to destroy the earth with a flood (8:21; 9:8–17)—which once was his response to human violence—now he lays the responsibility of keeping violence under check upon the shoulders of man, emphasized poetically in the chiastic structure of 9:6ab—punishment commensurate with the crime[51]:

> Whoever *sheds*
>> the *blood*
>>> of *man,*
>>>> by *man*
>>> his *blood*
>> shall be *shed.*

According to Mason, the thrust of 9:6c, regarding the image of God in man, is not simply a reassertion of man's bearing the *imago Dei*.

> [T]hese views miss the primary point of v. 6c. Verse 6 sanctions a human being to take the life of another *in the place of God*. In the light of v. 6ab, it is humankind, as bearers of God's image, *who will represent God* in the reckoning of indiscriminate bloodshed. This maintains the idea of rulership and authority inherent in this section and within the image of God idea. This is what is new in light of God's post-flood promise. God relinquishes his own responsibility of just blood punishment. Now humankind . . . holds that (new) position of responsibility since God will restrain himself from destroying all life. This contrast can only be understood when one understands that the eternal covenant of Noah has two sides, vv. 1–7 and 8–17.[52]

Mankind becomes God's appointed instrument as "society's enforcement agency, a restraint on threatening behavior."[53] In other words, such punishment is an indication of the high value God places upon human life, life that bears his image. "Life is to be *respected,* even in the taking of it."[54]

A covenant is in place: God promises never to take punitive action by means of a flood in response to human violence, for he has put in place another plan to keep wanton and indiscriminate bloodshed under check.[55] For its part, mankind, in the image of God, has been deputized to execute blood punishment for such displays of violence. In sum, this was man's responsibility; he had been empowered by God to act

---

51. Three words, each repeated once, compose the entire line, but with every repetition in a different grammatical form.

52. Mason, "Another Flood?" 193.

53. Mathews, *Genesis 1–11:26*, 405. See Rom 12:19; 13:1–5; 1 Pet 2:13–14.

54. Kass, *The Beginning of Wisdom*, 178.

55. The employment of the bow as the covenantal sign likely indicates that this was a guarantee that the waters above the firmament (Gen 1:6–7) would remain in place without disruption and a resulting deluge. Thus, rather than a bow of war (as קֶשֶׁת, *qsht*, frequently means), the rainbow signifies the firmament and its fixity. See Turner, "The Rainbow," 121. God's remembering of the covenant (9:15) is only the second time God remembers something—the first was his remembrance of Noah (8:1). Deity, of course, needs no reminding; 9:15, therefore, is simply a strong rhetorical affirmation of divine intent.

on his behalf to keep societal sin under check. Only then, with this ongoing sin under control, can mankind be fruitful and multiply and fulfill God's design for it.[56]

In any case, the pattern of the charge in 9:2–3 follows that of 2:16–17: an ample permission ("every tree" / "every moving thing"), but a single prohibition ("tree of the knowledge of good and evil" / "flesh with its life, blood"). The prohibition of consumption of blood expressly indicates its symbolic value in representing life and in being given for atonement (see Lev 17:11; also Lev 3:17; 7:26–27; 19:26; etc.). That animals may be eaten means that animal blood may be shed, though not consumed.[57] However, human blood may not even be shed in violence: three times in Gen 9:5, God warns that he will demand a reckoning if that happens, from both culpable man and beast (see Exod 20:13; 21:12–14, 22–25; 21:28–32; Lev 24:17; Num 35:22–25, 31–34). Notably, Gen 9:5 has "from every man's *brother* I will require . . ."; this is the first time "brother" is employed since the narrative of Cain and Abel: there the wickedness of the latter's murder was underscored by the repeated use of "brother" (see Pericope 3). No doubt, the use of the word here alludes to that nefarious incident.[58] In short, man represents God on earth, to maintain order and prevent violence.

5.2.3 *Notwithstanding the means set in place by God to control evil, ongoing sin continues to plague the human situation.*

After "all [antediluvian] flesh had corrupted their way upon the earth" (6:12), one wonders if the postdiluvian humans would fare any better. The answer seems clear: they do not!

Noah as the second Adam is presented in 9:1–7; the two patriarchs are also shown to be similar in 9:18–29: they farm the ground (2:15; 9:20; as also does Cain, 4:2), a fruit plays a role in their story (2:17; 9:20–21; as also in the life of Cain, 4:3), "knowledge" (from ידע, *yd'*) is a shared motif (2:17; 3:1–7; 9:24; as it is in Cain's narrative, 4:1, 9, 17), they are involved with a curse (3:14, 17; 9:25; as also is Cain 4:11) and with a blessing (1:28; 5:2; 9:26), they are naked (3:7; 9:22, 23), and their descendants engage in intramural strife (4:1–15; 9:25–26). "Indeed, Noah is the second Adam both as a

---

56. Mason, "Another Flood," 194–95. Mason notes that in this bipartite agreement, God may renege from his part, if mankind does not keep its end, as Isa 24 appears to indicate.

57. Hamilton, *Genesis: Chapters 1–17*, 314. Presumably, shedding blood in war was permissible, though regrettable (1 Chr 28:3).Why the divinely mandated change in diet from herbivorous (1:29–30) to carnivorous (9:3) at this point in the history of mankind? Was there some restriction in the availability of plant food after the flood? And, therefore, was this an amelioration of the difficulties man would face in finding appropriate food in a new world? The text is silent about these questions.

58. Wenham, *Genesis 1–15*, 193. That animals may be culpable too is an interesting fact. Not to be forgotten is that God's covenant is made with Noah *and with all the animals* (9:9–10, 12, 15, 17). It is also repeated thrice that the animals were "with you [Noah]" (9:10 [×2], 12). The *inclusios* of 9:8–17 are also pointed: the opening one (9:8–10) lists "you," "your descendants," and all the animals, but the concluding one (9:17) is without distinction—"all flesh." "There is no separation or hierarchy; rather, there is a bonding together" (Olley, "Mixed Blessings," 136). Animals are here held responsible for brutality, and God also enters into covenants with them. "Animals have an honorable role in the biblical economy"— the tenth plague judgment is directed not only against the Egyptians but their cattle as well (Exod 11:5); animals are capable of repentance (Jonah 3:7–8); and they are even part of the eschaton (Isa 11:6–9; 65:25; etc.). See Hamilton, *Genesis: Chapters 1–17*, 316.

recipient of divine blessing and as father of a corrupt seed." These similarities between Noah and Adam (and Cain) indicate that while there were "new relationships, new assurances, and a new order to things in the world . . . there remained the same old human heart."[59] That "same old human heart" is depicted in quite an unusual way in 9:18–29.

The rather perplexing account of 9:18–29 is made all the more so because of its cryptic nature: After Noah's drunken disrobing which Ham observed, "he told his two brothers" (9:22), but what he said is left to the imagination. Did he tell his siblings what he *saw* . . . or did he tell them what he *did*? It might very well be the latter, for Noah, awoken from his drunken stupor "knew what his youngest son had *done* to him" (9:24). What had he done? Obviously, whatever it was, it was an act that merited a drastic curse upon the descendants of Ham (9:25–27); such a curse was unlikely to have been invoked simply by the accidental sight of a naked parent. The word for "nakedness," עֶרְוָה ('*erwah*, Gen 9:22–23), different from עָרוֹם, '*arom*, in Gen 2:25; 3:7, 10, 11, "does have an erotic and sexual connotation and is, therefore, best rendered as 'genitals.'"[60] Of course, disrobing and uncovering oneself is not a necessary epiphenomenon of inebriation. On the other hand, "uncovering" often signifies a sexual act in the Pentateuch (Lev 18:6–19 [×17]; 20:11–21 [×7]; Deut 23:1; 27:20), as also does the mention of "nakedness" in these same verses ("seeing nakedness" is found in Lev 20:17). Of interest is that Lev 18:1–5 commences the section by warning Israelites about imitating the debauched practices of Canaanites—the descendants of Ham (9:22; 10:6)—and Egyptians. Of the multiple sexual violations listed in Lev 18, the first is incest committed with one's mother (18:7–8 has "nakedness" of a father, as does Gen 9:22).[61] Drawing from these Leviticus passages, Bassett concludes that "it is possible that the statement that Ham saw the nakedness of his father originally meant that he had sexual intercourse with his father's wife. If so, this would explain the seriousness of the offense which led to the curse. It would also explain why Noah cursed only one of Ham's several sons, if it is further assumed that Canaan was the fruit of such a case of incest."[62] That might also explain why Ham is rather redundantly described as being

---

59. Mathews, *Genesis 1–11:26*, 414–15. Besides, each of these three—Adam, Cain, and Noah—represent three worlds: the world in the Garden of Eden, the world outside the Garden, and the world after the flood. Their individual stories each terminate in a sin: Adam and Eve eat of the forbidden fruit; Cain murders his brother; Noah is violated (Ham's illicit intercourse with Noah's wife; see below). See Steinmetz, "Vineyard, Farm, and Garden," 194.

60. Vervenne, "What Shall We Do with the Drunken Sailor?" 49.

61. Bergsma and Hahn, "Noah's Nakedness," 31–32. The immorality of the Canaanites causes them to be expelled from the land (Lev 18:25); this again parallels the fate of Adam/Eve and of Cain (3:22–24; 4:12–14).

62. Bassett, "Noah's Nakedness," 235. In somewhat similar fashion, Reuben's sexual dalliance with his father's concubine, Bilhah, led to the loss of the preeminence of the Reubenites among the tribes of Israel (35:22; 49:3–4). In such an interpretation, the passivity of the mother/wife is certainly a problem, which the text does not deign to address, just as Bilhah's reaction does not find mention later in Genesis.

"the father of Canaan" (9:18, 22), followed immediately by the account, presumably, of how Ham became the father of Canaan.[63]

In Gen 9:1–17, Noah and his sons are twice commanded to be fruitful and to multiply (9:1, 7). Genesis 9:19 suggests fulfillment of this command. "It is not unreasonable, therefore, to interpret Noah's and Ham's actions in 9:20–22 in the context of procreative activity, however imperfect or distorted. Noah drank and disrobed in an effort to procreate; Ham intervened and succeeded."[64] It is also interesting that preceding the flood story is an account of illicit unions (6:1–4); now, after the flood story, here is another. Thus both the epilogue and the prologue to the deluge may be related in content.[65] Sin is always with mankind.

It might be argued that Ham's brothers' subsequent refusal to "see their father's nakedness" (9:23) has nothing to do with a sexual act (or the avoidance thereof). But it is not unwarranted that a clever writer would utilize a phrase in a *double entendre*—in a figurative sense (seeing nakedness = sexual act), as well as in a literal sense (seeing nakedness = seeing nakedness), both in the same episode. In putting it this way, the author was simply emphasizing that Shem and Japheth, unlike Ham, refused even to *see* their father's (literal) nakedness, thus adding to their righteousness.

> In contrast to the terse brevity with which Ham's deed is described, the description of Shem and Japheth's response is distinctly repetitious and long-winded. The narrative is slowed down so that the listener can appreciate their meritorious deeds and their utter propriety. Notice how it is twice said that they went "backwards," and that they covered and did not see "their father's nakedness" [9:23].[66]

In thus covering the nakedness of their father, they may be being compared with God himself, who covered the first pair of sinners in the Garden of Eden (3:21).

While the reason for Ham's wicked act is not explicitly stated, Bergsma is probably right in declaring that Ham's act was not one of "lust or capricious malevolence";

---

63. Bergsma and Hahn note that the cursing in 9:24–25 may have occurred some time after the despicable event, perhaps at the birth of Canaan ("Noah's Nakedness," 39). Another way to explain the curse on Canaan would be to postulate that Ham's felony of rebellion against his father would be visited on Ham, himself, with Canaan's rebelliousness against him.

64. Ibid., 35. Notable is the fact that in 9:21, it is said that Noah uncovered himself in *"her* tent" (אָהֳלֹה, *'ahaloh*)—his wife's? Whether this is intentionally feminine, or if it is simply an archaic form of the masculine, is unclear (ibid., 38n55).

65. There is no indication that Noah was being censured for consuming wine and becoming drunk. Of course, to be literally uncovered was shameful (2 Sam 6:16) and unacceptable to God (Exod 20:26; Deut 23:13–15) (Wenham, *Genesis 1–15*, 199). Incidentally, the only other incident of intoxication in Genesis (19:31–36) also led to sexual sins. The parallels between the account in this pericope and in the narrative of Lot also leans one towards interpreting this story as dealing with some sexual malfeasance. In the latter, there is catastrophe wrought upon a sinful land because of its sexual wickedness (19:5–7 and the subsequent rain of brimstone and fire; paralleled in 6:1–4 and the subsequent flood); there is drunkenness (19:32–35; see 9:20–21); there is incest, and the generation of the enemies of Israel (19:37–38—Moabites and Ammonites; see 9:22, 25–27; 10:6—Canaanites); and God remembers Noah *et al.* (8:1, after the flood), just as God remembered Abraham (19:29, after the destruction of Sodom and Gomorrah).

66. Wenham, *Genesis 1–15*, 200.

rather, "[b]y humiliating his father, Ham hoped to usurp his father's authority and displace his older brothers in the familial hierarchy"—a power-grab—and so he immediately informs his siblings about his feat![67] In any case, the sin of Ham must have been something quite egregious—"[i]n this last tragicomic scene, the truth that the 'ideas of man's mind are evil from his youth' [8:21] is starkly exhibited for all to see."[68] And, for the first time, a human being utters a curse (9:25): indeed, these are Noah's first and only words recorded in Scripture!

> They are in effect his last will and testament, for the subsequent verses report his death, bringing an end to the ancient Sethite lineage (5:3–32) with the same fateful refrain, "Then he died" (9:28–29). Conversely, in the flood narrative the Lord forewarns, instructs, assures, blesses, and makes covenant with Noah; but in the final episode we do not hear a divine word. Although the passage does not condemn Noah's intoxication, the abrupt silence of God suggests that all is not well [again!] between heaven and earth.[69]

Noah also proceeds to utter words of blessing to his other two sons. Actually, the blessing is directly of Yahweh, and indirectly of Shem whose God is Yahweh. Thus we have the first indication that the chosen line of God's people will come through Shem; "Yahweh, the God of Shem" is similar to the linkage of God with other patriarchs and with the nation of Israel (Gen 24:27; Exod 3:15; 32:27; 34:23). The assonance between אֱלֹהֵי שֵׁם, *ʾelohe shem*, and אָהֳלֵי־שֵׁם, *ʾahale-shem* ("God of Shem," and "tents of Shem," 9:26, 27) hints that Japheth, who would dwell in the tents of Shem, would own the God of Shem as well. On the other hand Ham is cursed, and the slavery of Canaan, his descendant, is mentioned three times (9:25, 26, 27).

Clearly, the account at the tail of Pericope 5 of Ham's dreadful act is intended to move the reader to an immediate conclusion: not the threat and reality of a flood, not the God-pleasing work of the righteous, not the sin-suppressing efforts of mankind— nothing would succeed in keeping sin at bay.

SERMON FOCUS AND OUTLINES

THEOLOGICAL FOCUS OF PERICOPE 5 FOR PREACHING

5   The intercession of the righteous, who themselves escape God's judgment for sin, precludes further judgment on the world, and the empowerment of mankind to act on God's behalf keeps ongoing sin under check (6:9–9:29).

The flood is the most devastating and catastrophic judgment God has executed against sin thus far in the history of mankind. While the extent of the flood may be debated,

67. Bergsma and Hahn, "Noah's Nakedness," 32–33, 38. Also see Kikawada and Quinn, *Before Abraham Was*, 102–3. Waltke and Fredricks, *Genesis*, 149, think Ham's sin was "prurient voyeurism." Rabbinic texts hint at Ham's castration of his father (*b. Sanh.* 70a, *Gen. Rabb.* 36:7; *Pirqe R. El.* 23; etc.). Others consider implications of a sexual violation of Noah by his son (*b. Sanh.* 70a; Steinmetz, "Vineyard, Farm, and Garden," 199n14).

68. Wenham, *Genesis 1–15*, 206.

69. Mathews, *Genesis 1–11:26*, 415.

there is no question that it was a drastic disciplinary action by God. It is not one that is easy to explain, but then again, Christians may also be hard-pressed to explain eternal judgment which will be worse in extent, degree, and consequence. In the sermon on this pericope, it is probably best not to get into the issue of whether God was justified in permitting a flood or not; the text does not seem interested in the matter and neither must the preacher. Perhaps a statement that God's holiness was at stake, and about one's confidence in the perfect justice of God will suffice. Formal or informal conversations from outside the pulpit can, of course, address those issues that this text does not answer. What the text does highlight are three ways of avoiding divine judgment, on oneself and on others: be righteous, intercede for others, exercise divine empowerment to keep ongoing sin under check. (In the interests of time, it might be better to focus on one or two of these three ways.)

This pericope spotlights not only God's act of judgment but how one person and his family escaped it. Noah's righteousness takes center stage throughout the narrative. Clearly, this is one way to avoid divine disciplinary action for sin.

Noah's sacrifice after the flood, and God's "comfort/rest" upon smelling it, point to the satisfaction Noah's life gave to God; Noah's sacrifice was, after all, an offering of himself (so to speak) to God. Evidently the righteousness of one person can influence how God deals with others. That alone should call Christians to diligent intercession for their fellowmen—another way to avoid God's discipline against sin.

The pericope also details how sin is held in check in society. Mankind is empowered to act authoritatively on God's behalf—a third way to avoid divine discipline. The text is specific about the degree of control that human authorities should exercise; by picturing an extreme case, that of homicide, readers are told that even for such a heinous act, mankind would have to police itself. God was seemingly going to be hands-off henceforth. For the purposes of the sermon, this may be applied to all who are in authority in the body of Christ—pastors, elders, parents, teachers,. . . . Certainly, the issue of church discipline may be considered in this context.

Possible Preaching Outlines for Pericope 5

I. Avoid God's Discipline: *Be irreproachable!*
       God's disciplinary judgment of sin (7:10–24)
       Noah's righteousness and his escape (6:9–7:9; 8:1–19)
       Specifics on how we can be irreproachable in a dark world

II. Avoid God's Discipline: *Be interceding!*
       Noah's sacrifice and God's pleasure (8:20–22)
       How we can be interceding for others (neighbors, acquaintances, nations, leaders . . .)

III. Avoid God's Discipline: *Be influential!*
       Ongoing sin—despite God's discipline, despite Noah's example, and despite Noah's intercession (9:18–29)
       God's covenant with all flesh and his empowerment of man to keep sin under check (9:1–17)
       How we can exercise our divine empowerment, influencing those we are responsible for

A simpler version that omits 9:18–29:

PRIMEVAL HISTORY: *Creating for Blessing*

I. How to Expect God's Discipline
   Mankind's sin (6:11–12) and God's disciplinary judgment (6:13; 7:10–24)

II. How to Escape God's Discipline
   Noah's righteousness (6:9–10, 22; 7:5, 9) and God's favor (6:18; 8:1–19)
   Be irreproachable!
   Noah's sacrifice (8:20) and God's pleasure (8:21–22)
   Be interceding!
   Mankind's empowerment to discipline (9:1–17)[70]
   Be influential!

---

70. This last third of the point (dealing with 9:1–17) may also be omitted, if time constrains.

PERICOPE 6

Genealogies and the Tower of Babel

Genesis 10:1–11:26

[Genealogies of the Sons of Noah; The Tower of Babel]

REVIEW, SUMMARY, PREVIEW

Review of Pericope 5: Genesis 6:9–9:29 deals with the flood, God's discipline for mankind's gross sin. With three subsidiary stories, the pericope notes three ways to avoid such disciplinary action: righteousness, intercession, and mankind's authority to deal with sin. However, ongoing sin is not stemmed.

Summary of Pericope 6: This pericope describes what appears to be a genealogy sandwiching a narrative. In reality, however, it is a description of God's blessing fulfilled in the multiplication and fruitfulness of humankind. Yet its return to its old ways of hubris and rebellion is poignantly described in the story of the Babelites (and, indirectly, in that of Nimrod). God punishes, but even his disciplinary action is a means to bring about his blessing.

Preview of Pericope 7: The next pericope (Gen 11:27–12:20) commences the Abraham Story (and the Patriarchal History). After the depressing end of the Primeval History, a new turn is taken: Abram is called, and blessings are promised. However there are hints that the patriarch is not completely obedient or faithful. Nevertheless, God's promise of blessing remains sure.

6. Genesis 10:1–11:26

> **THEOLOGICAL FOCUS OF PERICOPE 6**
>
> **6**   **Mankind's continual hubris and arrogant independence invite divine punishment that, though punitive, is nonetheless gracious, enabling God's promised blessings for all to be fulfilled (10:1–11:26).**
>
> 6.1   Despite the sins of mankind, God's promise of blessing for all is fulfilled (10:1–32).
>
> 6.2   Mankind's actions of hubris and arrogant independence invite appropriate divine punishment that, though punitive, is nonetheless gracious, enabling God's promised blessings to be fulfilled (11:1–26).
>
> 6.2.1   *Mankind's postdiluvian actions of hubris and arrogant independence—similar to its antediluvian pretensions—invite appropriate divine punishment.*
>
> 6.2.2   *The punitive action of God, keeping man in his rightful place, is nonetheless gracious, for it enables his promised blessings to be fulfilled.*

OVERVIEW

This pericope (Pericope 6) and portions of the previous ones (Pericopes 4 and 5) are characterized by narrative blocks bookended by genealogies[1]:

Genealogy	5:32	Noah's sons
Narrative	*6:1–8*	*Sons of God*
Genealogy	6:9–10	Noah's sons
Genealogy	6:9–10	Noah's sons
Narrative	*6:11–9:17*	*The flood*
Genealogy	9:18–19	Noah's sons
Genealogy	10:21–31	Sons of Shem
Narrative	*11:1–9*	*Tower of Babel*
Genealogy	11:10–32	Sons of Shem

Notably, the two genealogies surrounding the Tower of Babel narrative are distinct in nature: 10:21–31 is segmented (or horizontal) with more than one person's descendants being traced; 11:10–32 is linear (or vertical), with the line of one person (Shem) being followed down to Abraham. While the first five in the series of the sons of Shem are paralleled in both genealogies (Shem, Arpachshad, Shelah, Eber, and Peleg), 10:25 breaks away after the mention of Peleg (פֶּלֶג, *peleg*) and a hint of "division" (פָּלַג, *palag*; reflected in his name). The resumption of the genealogy of Shem through Peleg and onwards occurs at 11:10, after an exposition of the division and how it came about— the Tower of Babel account in 11:1–9. This is a deliberate placement of that narrative

---

1. Hamilton, *Genesis: Chapters 1–17*, 350. The usual pattern of the genealogies in Genesis is to attend to the non-elect lines first, before focusing on the elect individuals and their descendants: Cain first (Gen 4), then Seth (Gen 5); Ishmael first (25:1–18), then Isaac (25:19–34). Likewise, here, Japheth (10:2–5) and Ham (10:6–20) are disposed of first, before the chosen line of Shem (10:21–31). Within this line of Shem, Jotkan is considered (10:26–30, leading up to the crowd at Babel) before Peleg, the elect (11:18–26, leading up to the patriarch Abraham). See Mathews, *Genesis 1–11:26*, 428.

between two genealogies.[2] Hamilton, who calls this effect-before-cause location of Gen 10 and 11 (the statement of division in Gen 10 coming before the account of such division in Gen 11) a "dischronologization," observes that had Gen 10 followed Gen 11, the dispersed nations would have been viewed only negatively. In its current sequence, the pericope serves as a reminder that the divine mandate of 9:1, God's command to man to be fruitful and multiply, has been fulfilled.[3] God's sovereignty in accomplishing his purposes is thereby emphasized. In sum, Gen 11:1–9, following upon a list of many nations of the world ("spread out" [10:5, 18, 32] in a "divided" world [10:25], with their various languages [10:5, 20, 31]), explains how this division and spread and variegation of languages occurred.[4] Rather than this human disunion being merely adventitious, the reader learns that it was the consequence of divine judgment upon man. The description in 10:32 of nations "separated on the earth after the flood" was the direct result of God's scattering (11:9). "Though not as catastrophic a sentence as that announced in 6:1–8, after the somewhat similar description of antediluvian man's fertility [10:1–32; see 6:1], the tower of Babel again puts man's intentions in question. He is not master of his own destiny. Indeed, in rebellion he must suffer God's displeasure curtailing his grandiose dreams."[5] The god-complex of man, thus, had not changed; a similar attitude had resulted in the disobedience of the first human pair in the Garden of Eden.

6.1 Genesis 10:1–32

THEOLOGICAL FOCUS 6.1

6.1 Despite the sins of mankind, God's promise of blessing for all is fulfilled (10:1–32).

NOTES 6.1

6.1 Despite the sins of mankind, God's promise of blessing for all is fulfilled.

The pericope begins with the standardized formula that commences a new section of Genesis: "These are the generations [תּוֹלְדֹת, *toldot*] of . . ." (as in 2:4; 5:1 [a variant]; 6:9; 11:10; 11:27; 25:12, 19; 36:1, 9; and 37:2). "After the flood" in 10:1 connects with what has preceded—9:28 has the same phrase.

2. Penley, "A Historical Reading of Genesis 11:1–9," 703.

3. Hamilton, *Genesis: Chapters 1–17*, 347. Moreover, "languages" is found in 10:5, 25, 31, *before* the narration of the division and generation of language diversity in 11:1–9—another dischronology. One also notices that Peleg only lived 239 years, whereas his grandfather, Shelah, lived for 433, and his father, Eber, for 464 (11:14–19). Did the sins of the people in his time, particularly the rebellion of the Babelites, impact their longevity? (Mathews, *Genesis 1–11:26*, 497).

4. In fact, "whole earth" in 11:1 is a précis of Gen 10; and both chapters share motifs: "scatter" (10:18 and 11:4, 8, 9), "land of Shinar" (10:10 and 11:2), "build" (10:11 and 11:4, 5, 8), "earth" (10:5, 8, 10, 11, 20, 25, 31, 32 and 11:1, 2, 4, 8, 9 [×2]), and "east" (10:30 and 11:2).

5. Wenham, *Genesis 1–15*, 209.

The genealogy of Gen 10 forms an integral unit bounded by an *inclusio*: 10:1 has תּוֹלְדֹת, "sons of Noah," "these," and "flood"; and 10:32 has תּוֹלְדֹתָם, *toldotam*, "sons of Noah," "these," and "flood."[6] Genesis 10 begins with Noah's sons listed in the order Shem-Ham-Japheth, but then proceeds to deal with these three in reverse order Japheth (10:2–5)-Ham (10:6–20)-Shem (10:21–31). The lineage of each commences with "the sons of *X* were . . ." (10:2, 6, 21), and ends with a formula that refers to families, languages, lands, and nations (10:5, 20, 31).

Of Gen 10, Cassuto wisely declares: "This chapter does not come to teach us ethnology, just as the first section of Genesis does not purport to instruct us in geology or paleontology or any other sciences."[7] There is more than just information that is provided here. The descendants of the sons of Noah are exactly seventy, not counting the Philistines parenthetically noted in 10:14. Seventy is a traditional figure for the number of one's descendants: the goddess Asherah is said to have had seventy sons (II AB.vi, *ANET* 134); so also Jacob (Gen 46:27[8]), Gideon (Jdg 8:30), and Ahab (2 Kgs 10:1).[9] There is thus an effort to portray Noah's children as a perfect number—"an ideal creation." There is clearly deliberate shaping of this list.[10] "The Torah was concerned only to complete the number of seventy names, and to incorporate therein the names of the principal nations that were near to Israel, or were in some way connected with the Israelites, or were in some manner known to them."[11] Notice that there is no mention of "Israel" in Gen 10; neither is there a hint of the covenant "people" (עַם, *'am*) of God; rather "nations" (גּוֹי, *goy*) echoes here. In a sense, this chapter is anticipating divine blessing upon *all*, as is explicitly noted in 12:3.

Wenham warns the interpreter not to assume that all the names refer to particular individuals: no ages are noted (as they are in the genealogies of Gen 5 and 11:10–32); some names are clearly places (Sidon, Sheba) or peoples (Ludim, Amorites); the formula for fathers begetting sons is quite flexible in Gen 10 ("sons of *X* were . . ."

---

6. As will be seen later, Gen 11 resounds with consonants related to "Babel" (בָּבֶל, *babel*); 10:1 and 10:32 have another anticipatory example: "flood," מַבּוּל, *mabbul*. Wenham suggests this section be called "From Flood to Babel" (*Genesis 1–15*, 209); a more assonant label would be "From *mabbul* to *babel*."

7. Cassuto, *Genesis*, 174.

8. Also see Exod 1:5 and Deut 10:22, though all these texts show differences in specific details and names.

9. Moreover, Israel was governed by seventy elders during their wilderness wanderings (Exod 24:9; Num 11:24). Jesus also sent out seventy disciples (Luke 10:1–17).

10. Other evidence of this purposeful shaping include the following: Japheth has seven sons and seven grandsons (10:2–4); Cush (a son of Ham) has seven sons and grandsons (10:7); and Mizraim (another son of Ham) has seven sons (10:13–14). "Sons" occurs fourteen times, seven times in 10:1–7 and another seven times in 10:20–32.

11. Cassuto, *Genesis*, 180. See, for instance, 10:5, dealing with the line of Japheth; it mentions only the "coastlands of the nations," assuming that there might have been other nations born of Japheth. Deuteronomy 32:8—with terms similar to those in Gen 10, such as "nations," "sons," and "separate" (see Gen 10:5, 32)—identifies the number of Gentile nations as seventy ("according to the number of the sons of Israel"), just as was the total of the children of Israel, evincing narrators' inclination towards uniformity and parallelism, not to mention their penchant for "seventy."

alternates with "*X* fathered . . ."); moreover, "sonship" and "brotherhood" could well designate a relationship by treaty or other design, and not necessarily by blood.[12]

The cameo of Nimrod (10:8–12), a son of Cush, is rather unusual in that he appears after five other sons of Cush *and* two grandsons have been mentioned—Nimrod is almost an afterthought. The first occurrence of "kingdom" in the OT is found in 10:10; Nimrod is thus the "first noted potentate" and a "champion hunter," founding cities, spawning proverbs.[13] His name might be linked to the root מרד, *mrd*, "to rebel," perhaps foreshadowing in Shinar (10:10) what would later happen in that same location—rebellion (11:2). In fact, rabbinic commentary explicitly labels him so: "the wicked Nimrod, who incited the whole world to rebel against Me [Yahweh] during his reign" (*m. Pesaḥ.* 94b).[14] His description in 10:9 as a mighty hunter "before Yahweh" is probably a superlative (as in 30:8; 35:5; Jonah 3:3; etc., which also have "before God"), not necessarily expressing God's approval of the man's enterprises.[15] Hom notes that the description of Nimrod as a hunter-king reflects the portrayal of Assyrian rulers; the description of Nimrod's establishment of four cities (twice, in 10:10 and in 10:11–12), suggests "imperialist notions along the lines of the 'four corners of the earth.'" The vocabulary of 10:8–12 is uniformly negative: the Hiphil of הלל (*hll*, "begin/become") in 11:6 is clearly deprecatory, therefore it is likely to have the same connotation in 10:8 (as also in 6:1; 34:27; 49:4); "Babel" in 11:9 is negative and presumably so also in 10:10; Shinar is often a place of false religion (11:12 and 10:10; also Josh 7:21; Zech 5:11; Dan 1:2); "city" and its "building" in Gen 11:4, 5, 8 meet with God's disapproval, and those words are found also in 10:11; as well, the assonance of the pretentious and vainglorious program of the Babelites (עִיר וּמִגְדָּל, *'ir umigdal*, "city and tower," 11:4) with the last phrase of the Nimrod story (הָעִיר הַגְּדֹלָה, *ha'ir haggdolah*, "the great city," 10:12). Cain, too, like Nimrod, was a "builder" of cities (4:17; found also in 10:11). All of this makes Nimrod's exploits "retroactively reinforced as rebellious."[16]

The many shared items of vocabulary between Gen 10 and 11 thus hint at a less than benign assessment of the lives and activities of those listed in the former; for instance "scatter" shows up innocently in 10:18 (and 9:19), but retrospectively, from the gaze of 11:4, 8, 9 where the word is used to picture divine judgment upon human hubris, Gen 10 may be viewed as pejorative. Also, "the earth" is found in both 11:1, 4, 8, 9 and in 10:8, 10, 11, tending to equate two negative accounts.

While there is, of necessity, some overlap between Shem's genealogy in Gen 10 and that in Gen 11, the main difference is that in the former, a number of dead ends are

---

12. *Genesis 1–15*, 215. See also Num 21:25; Josh 17:11; 2 Sam 7:14; 2 Kgs 16:7; etc., that employ "son" in an almost metaphorical fashion.

13. Mathews, *Genesis 1–11:26*, 450.

14. Likewise, *Tg. Ps.-J.* on Gen 10:8; and *m. Ḥag.* 13a.

15. "Therefore it is said" (Gen 10:9) indicates a proverbial saying (as also in 1 Sam 19:24), suggesting that "before Yahweh" was more idiomatic than literal (Westermann, *Genesis 1–11*, 516).

16. Hom, "'. . . A Mighty Hunter,'" 67–68. Mathews observes that the righteous patriarchs, in contrast, were known for "building" *altars* for the worship of Yahweh, not cities (8:20; 12:7–8) (*Genesis 1–11:26*, 451).

noted (a segmented genealogy); in the latter, the focus is upon a linear configuration leading from Shem to Abram (likewise, the genealogy of Gen 4 is segmented, while that of Gen 5 is linear). As was noted, Shem's line comes after Japheth's and Ham's, since it is the most pertinent to the narrative: it becomes the line of Abram. The importance of this lineage is noted right in its introduction that has an extra statement (10:21: "And also to Shem . . . children were born") that is absent in the introductions to the lineages of Japheth and Ham. Within Shem's descendants, Eber is notably mentioned in the introduction (10:21), as well as in his proper place as the son of Shela and the father of Peleg and Joktan (10:24–25). Therefore, while the Shemites are important, the Eberites are particularly important. "Eber," supposedly, is also the name from which "Hebrew" is derived (14:13; 39:12; 40:15; 41:12; 43:32; etc.).

In Gen 10, Peleg is noted, and then forgotten, after the comment about the division of the earth in his days (10:25); subsequently, in Gen 11, Peleg's line is traced all the way down to Abram. His name comes from the root פלג (*plg*) that means "to divide"; thus the wordplay: in the days of פלג, the earth was נִפְלְגָה (*niplgah*, "divided," 10:25). Though not employed in Gen 11 to describe the division of the nations, Ps 55:10 does use the same word for the division of languages, hinting that what happened in Gen 11 was the cause of the earth's division.

In all of this, the promise of divine blessing in the form of fruitfulness and multiplication is being fulfilled to all peoples. While it appeared that Ham had not obtained Noah's blessing (9:25–27), in the genealogy of Gen 10, Ham is second only to Joktan in reproductive potential: Ham has 11 sons and grandsons; Joktan, 13 sons. God *does* bless, despite sin—whether of Ham, or of his descendant Nimrod, or of that permeating all of mankind. And God's blessings of fruitfulness and multiplication are fulfilled.

6.2 Genesis 11:1–26

THEOLOGICAL FOCUS 6.2

6.2   Mankind's actions of hubris and arrogant independence invite appropriate divine punishment that, though punitive, is nonetheless gracious, enabling God's promised blessings to be fulfilled (11:1–26).

   6.2.1   *Mankind's postdiluvian actions of hubris and arrogant independence—similar to its antediluvian pretensions—invite appropriate divine punishment.*

   6.2.2   *The punitive action of God, keeping man in his rightful place, is nonetheless gracious, for it enables his promised blessings to be fulfilled.*

NOTES 6.2

The *Enuma elish* has echoes of a Babel-like structure in "Babylon"/"Babili"—the Esagila, a "high" shrine to Marduk, complete with descriptions of brick-making, and with a "high ziggurat," all constructed by lesser gods, the Anunnaki (6.47–67[17];

17. Dalley, *Myths from Mesopotamia*, 262–63.

"ziggurat" comes from the Akkadian *zaqaru* = "to raise up/elevate"). The "head" of the Esagila was said to have been raised—Esagila itself means "structure which raises the head." This is parallel to the Babel tower whose "top" (רֹאשׁ, *r'osh*, 11:4, which can also mean "head") was intended to reach into the heavens.[18] The ziggurat was likely to have been the Etemenanki (= "House of the Foundation of Heaven and Earth"), of which, in the seventh century BCE, Nabopolassar records a repair being undertaken "to make its top vie with the heavens" (Nbp 1 i.30–40; iii.34–37).[19] This historical and architectural parallel gives credence to the biblical account of Gen 11:1–9. Moreover, it is known that the Sumerians also believed that, at one point, all of mankind spoke the same language; apparently the gods subsequently confounded man's speech. However, in the Sumerian version the rivalry that led to the confusion of tongues was between god and god (jealousy of one about the universal sway over mankind of the other); in Gen 11:1–9, the confounding and scattering was a result of a conflict between God and man.[20]

6.2.1 Mankind's postdiluvian actions of hubris and arrogant independence—similar to its antediluvian pretensions—invite appropriate divine punishment.

Gen 11:1–9 is structured carefully, paralleling the actions of man in the first half with the actions of God in the second.[21] The turning point, and the midpoint of the narrative (G below), is the scene of divine inspection ("Yahweh came down to see," 11:5), after which the actions of God meticulously dismantle the actions of man. Thus we have "men against God, God against the men: construction followed by destruction, construction may even be said to have invited destruction."[22]

---

18. Mathews, *Genesis 1–11:26*, 471–72; Speiser, "Wordplays," 317–23.

19. George, "The Tower of Babel," 83–84. Herodotus, *Histories* 1.181–182, describes the Etemenanki as series of eight concentric towers, one on top of the other. Kass suggests that astronomy was carried out in these towers, primarily for the prediction of rain. "The Babylonian priests ruled the city on the basis of their knowledge—and divination—regarding heaven. The House of the Foundation of Heaven and Earth thus sought to link the city with the cosmos, and to bring the city into line with the heavenly powers that be, or—perhaps, conversely [and perversely?]—to bring the power that be into line with the goals of the city" (*The Beginning of Wisdom*, 229–30).

20. Kramer, "The 'Babel of Tongues,'" 111.

21. The layout of the narrative also alternates between indirect and direct discourse: indirect (11:1–2); direct (11:3–4); indirect (11:5); direct (11:6–7); indirect (11:8–9). See Baden, "The Tower of Babel," 214.

22. Fokkelman, *Narrative Art in Genesis*, 28. The table is modified from Cotter, *Genesis*, 70, and Wenham, *Genesis 1–15*, 235. Words mirrored in the various units are italicized.

A 11:1	the *whole earth* was of one *language*			
B 11:2	Shinar ... *there*			
	C 11:3a	and *the men* said to *one another*		
		D 11:3b	"Come, let us make bricks" [נִלְבְּנָה, *nilbnah*]	
		E 11:4a	"let us *build* for ourselves"	
			F 11:4b	a *city* and a *tower*
				G 11:5a Yahweh came down to see
			F' 11:5b	the *city* and the *tower*
		E' 11:5c	which the sons of men had *built*	
		D' 11:6–7a	and God said "... *Come*, ... and *let us confuse*" [וְנָבְלָה, *wnablah*]	
	C' 11:7b	"so that *the men* will not understand the speech of *one another*"		
B' 11:8–9a	from *there* ... Babel ... *there*			
A' 11:9b	the *language* of the *whole earth* ... *whole earth*			

Assonances abound. The Shinar gang seem particularly prone to use the consonants *b* and *l* (consonants that make up בָּבֶל, *babel*, "Babel") or others close related, such as *m*, *n*, and *p* (highlighted below)—"a constantly recurring melody," "a kind of *leit-motif*, which accompanies the narrative almost from beginning to end, and reaches its climax in the explanation of the name *Babel*."[23]

(11:3) ... הָבָה נִלְבְּנָה לְבֵנִים וְנִשְׂרְפָה לִשְׂרֵפָה ...
habah nilbnah lbenim wnisrpah lisrepah
"Come, let us make bricks and burn them thoroughly."

(11:4) ... הָבָה נִבְנֶה־לָּנוּ עִיר וּמִגְדָּל
וְרֹאשׁוֹ בַשָּׁמַיִם וְנַעֲשֶׂה־לָּנוּ שֵׁם פֶּן־נָפוּץ עַל־פְּנֵי כָל־הָאָרֶץ׃
hahah nibneh-lanu 'ir umigdal
wro'sho bashamayim wna'aseh-lanu shem pen-naputs 'al-pne kal-ha'arets
"Come, let us build ourselves a city and tower,
and its top to the heavens, and let us make ourselves a name,
lest we be scattered on the face of the whole earth."

Fokkelman observes that 11:3 "simply crackles with pairs"—cognate words used together for emphasis (highlighted).

(11:3) ... הָבָה נִלְבְּנָה לְבֵנִים וְנִשְׂרְפָה לִשְׂרֵפָה
וַתְּהִי לָהֶם הַלְּבֵנָה לְאָבֶן וְהַחֵמָר הָיָה לָהֶם לַחֹמֶר׃
habah nilbnah lbenim wnisrpah lisrepah
watthi lahem hallbenah l'aben whakhemar hayah lahem lakhomer
"Come, let us make bricks and burn them thoroughly."
And they had brick for stone, and tar they had for mortar.

23. Cassuto, *Genesis*, 232–33. Indeed, these consonants appear later as well:, בָּנוּ בְּנֵי (*banu bne*, 11:5); וְנָבְלָה (*wnavlah*, 11:7); וַיַּחְדְּלוּ לִבְנֹת (*wayykhdlu livnot*, 11:8); and בָּבֶל ... בָּלַל (*babel ... balal*, 11:9). Also see ibid., for alliterations of the letters שׁ and ל in this narrative. Moreover, as indicated in the table above, "let us confuse" (נָבְלָה, *nablah*, 11:7) sounds remarkably like נִבְלָה (*nibalah*, "disgrace"), "the folly of the impious" (Gen 34:7; Deut 22:21; Josh 7:15; Job 42:8; Isa 9:16; Isa 32:6; Jer 29:23), which, indeed, it was in Babel. "The name 'Babel' thus stands forever as a reminder of the failure of godless folly" (Wenham, *Genesis 1–15*, 234–35).

He thinks this is deliberate: "The atmosphere in the human community is electrified by the intensive communication which leads to energetic plans: come on, let us do this! come on, let us do that! Standing in the unity of language . . . people exchange ideas. Like sparks they dart to and fro."[24] Their plotting and scheming here is literarily depicted!

And sonic contrasts between their words and those of God are also apparent (see above: *C* and *C'*; *D* and *D'*; *E* and *E'*). Mankind goes east to build "there" (שָׁם, *shm*, 11:2) a tower whose top reaches the "heavens" (שָׁמַיִם, *shmym*), to make a "name" (שֵׁם, *shm*) for themselves (11:4). This was a concerted action by "all the earth" (11:1) to prevent scattering, in contradistinction to the command of God to fill the earth (1:28; 9:1, 7). So, in response, God confuses their language "there" (שָׁם, 11:7, 9), their "name" (שֵׁם, 11:9) is called Babel, and they are scattered "from there" (מִשָּׁם, *mshm*, 11:8, 9) over "all the earth" (11:8, 9 [×2]), an appropriate fate meet for the felony.[25] And notably, "face of the earth" (פְּנֵי כָל־הָאָרֶץ, *pne kal-ha'arets*, 11:4, 8, 9) begins and ends with the consonants that make up פּוּץ (*puts*, "scatter," in the same verses, 11:4, 8, 9).[26] All of this shows how divine action will be apposite for the human action—punishment equal to sin.

At the very beginning of the account, a negative note is struck. The eastward travel of the people in 11:2 is usually negative in Genesis: that was the direction of banishment of Adam and Eve (3:24) and Cain (4:16).[27] And this people settle in a valley (בִּקְעָה, *bq'h*, also "plain," 11:2). Generally, valleys/plains were viewed negatively in ancient Israel (Num 14:25; 22:1; Ps 23:4; Jer 7:31; Ezek 37:1; etc.). God's preferred locations for theophanies were mountains (Exod 17:6; 19:11; Deut 34:1; Ps 2:6); Jesus, himself, opted for mountains to engage in important activities (Mark 3:13; 6:46; 9:2; etc.). And, frequently, in the OT, God seems to have been against towers, perhaps because they were symbols of human hubris and megalomaniacal self-sufficiency: 2 Kgs 17:9; Isa 2:15; 30:25; 33:18; Ezek 26:4, 9. There is also the "ludicrous paradox," in our Babel story, of constructing, in a valley, a tower reaching to the heavens![28]

Shinar, itself, does not appear in a good light, as was noted: it is associated with the sinister Nimrod (Gen 10:10), the grandson of Ham (10:6–8). In the two shameful acts that are noted after the flood, Ham is thus involved in some way (9:20–27 and 11:1–9). Moreover, the king of Shinar was an enemy of Abraham (Gen 14:1, 9); a mantle of Shinar was part of Achan's loot (Josh 7:21); Shinar was where the epitome of wickedness, the woman sitting inside the basket, dwelt (Zech 5:7–11); and it was the center of

---

24. Fokkelman, *Narrative Art*, 27.

25. "'All the world' assembles and the only result is that they are scattered 'all over the world'; precisely what 'all the world' seeks to avoid happens, dispersion 'all over the world'—another flash of the narrator's dialectic irony" (ibid., 16).

26. Wenham, *Genesis 1–15*, 235.

27. East would also be the ill-fated direction in which Lot moves (Gen 13:11); Abraham sends his sons by Keturah to the east "away from his son Isaac" (25:6); Jacob moves to the east, chased away from home, hounded by his brother Esau (29:1). In contrast, an acceptable migration was that of Abraham—westward (12:4–6). On the other hand, if מִקֶּדֶם, *miqqedem* (11:2), indicates "*from* the east," it is still ominous: these folks are coming from the place of exile and quarantine.

28. LaCocque, "Whatever Happened," 36.

idolatry (Dan 1:2).[29] In fact, Sodom and Babylon/Shinar are connected, respectively, through the two descendants of Ham, Canaan (10:19) and Nimrod (10:8–10); also, in the stories of both towns, God comes down to see what was going on (11:7; 18:21), and disaster strikes soon thereafter. Isaiah 13:19 explicitly links Sodom and Babylon:

> And Babylon, the beauty of kingdoms, the glory of the Chaldeans' pride,
> Will be as when God overthrew Sodom and Gomorrah.

The NT, of course, pictures Babylon, in Rev 18, as a wicked city. "City," thus far, has shown up in reference to Cain's establishment of a place to settle in (Gen 4:17), and in referring to Nineveh and its cluster of satellites (10:11–12); later it refers to Sodom (13:12; 18:24, 26, 28, and in Gen 19). All in all, cities are not looked upon favorably in the OT. "Whatever the city means, it seems to be linked, at least in these other cases, with violence, lewdness, and corruption."[30] It stands for independence, control, power, and mastery over one's destiny; "city" is the epitome of self-sufficiency.

Until Gen 11:4, "make" (עשׂה, *ʿsh*) had been used only of God; and thus far, "name" (שׁם, *shm*) had only been used of proper names. Now "name" is used in a different sense, and humans are "making" it for themselves. King David is said to have "made a name" (2 Sam 8:13), but in that case there was no question that he had divine aid in that endeavor (8:14; and 7:9 where God promises to "make his name" great; also see 2 Sam 7:26, where David states his goal that *God's* name would be "magnified forever"). And in the beginning of the Abraham cycle, *God* promises to make the patriarch's name great.[31] The Babelites intention, on the other hand, was the self-manufacture of a great name, by their own resources, for their own glory, apart from God.

> To make a new name for oneself is to remake the meaning of one's life so that it deserves a new name. . . . At once makers and made, the founders of Babel aspire to nothing less than self-*re*-creation—through the arts and crafts, customs and mores of their city. The mental construction of a second world through language and the practical reconstruction of the first world through technology together accomplish man's reconstruction of his own being. The children of man . . . remake themselves and, thus, their name, in every respect taking the place of God.[32]

"[W]hereas human speech has previously been used for a variety of other purposes— naming, self-naming, questioning authority, shifting blame, denying guilt, expressing fear, boasting in song, spreading shame and ridicule, and blessing and cursing—speech is here used by human beings to exhort to action and enunciate a project of *making*, for the first time in Genesis," enabling man to play Creator.[33] Indeed, the stress in

---

29. Ibid., 32.

30. Kass, "The Humanist Dream," 642.

31. Yahweh intended, in Abraham's line, to give what the Babelites had attempted to secure arbitrarily (Von Rad, *Genesis*, 155).

32. Kass, *The Beginning of Wisdom*, 231.

33. Kass, "The Humanist Dream," 642. Strong explains that "when humans state that their motive for building the city and the tall tower is 'to make a name for ourselves' [Gen 11:3] . . ., it would be clear

11:3 on the utterly human creation of a "mountain" to reach the heavens—the making and burning of bricks, and the use for stone and tar for mortar—indicates that this is a flawed enterprise that will only fail.[34] Four first-person plural cohortatives ("let us make bricks"; "let us burn"; "let us build"; "let us make"; Gen 11:3–4) and the two reflexive expressions "for ourselves" (11:4) make the Babelites' self-interest and conceit very clear.[35] First-person cohortatives were first used by God (1:26); now humans are using it, an usurpation, once again, of the divine language of creation.[36]

Such an action on the part of men was an attempt to achieve god-like status, essentially the same engine that powered the sin of mankind in the Garden of Eden (3:5–6). Mathews notes the number of verbal similarities between that account in Gen 2–3 and this in Gen 11: "find" (2:20 and 11:2); "east" (2:8; 3:24 and 11:2); "see" (3:6 and 11:5); "head"/"top" (3:15 and 11:4); "build" (2:22 and 11:4–5); "make" (2:18; 3:1, 7, 13, 14, 21 and 11:4, 6 [×2]); "call" and "name" (2:19; 3:20 and 11:9); and divine plurality and self-reflection before punitive action (3:22–24 and 11:6–8). In fact, even the geographical setting for these two incidents may have coincided: the Garden's proximity to the Tigris and Euphrates (2:14) is likely to have been in the same area as the "plain in the land of Shinar" (11:2). "Genesis 1–11 then has come full circle from 'Eden' to 'Babel.'"[37] And these actions of human hubris invite divine punishment.

6.2.2 *The punitive action of God, keeping man in his rightful place, is nonetheless gracious, for it enables his promised blessings to be fulfilled.*

As was noted, divine inspection ("And Yahweh came down to see the city and the tower," 11:5) reverses the flow of the narrative, just as "And God remembered Noah" (8:1) reversed the literal flow of the flood (see Pericope 5). There, however, God's move initiated rescue; here it announced judgment. In *D* and *D'* above, לְבֵן (*lbn*, "make bricks," 11:3) in the mouth of the people becomes נִבְל (*nbl*, "confuse," 11:7) in the mouth of God: the consonants are literally reversed—*lbn* to *nbl*. "The reversal of the order of the sounds reveals the basic idea of the passage: The construction on earth is answered by the destruction from heaven; men build but God pulls down. The fact

---

to an ancient reader that humans were defacing the image of God and were, in essence, scratching off the name of God and replacing it with their own name. . . . [I]t was an act of hybris" ("Shattering the Image," 632).

34. LaCocque, "Whatever Happened," 35–36.

35. Penley, "A Historical Reading," 711n48.

36. Gnuse, "The Tale of Babel," 237. Kass notes that in the (relatively recent) context of the flood, a high place would have appeared safer than any other; hence, the tower alongside the city: "it is even imaginable that it might be intended as a pillar to hold up heaven, lest it crack open another time" ("The Humanist Dream," 644). It was, if you can believe it, a bolstering of defenses against any future act of God. In fact, *b. Sanh.* 109a describes the enterprise of the Babelites as idolatry.

37. *Genesis 1–11:26*, 467 and 467n134. There are also a number of parallels with Cain's story: sin, punishment and dispersion, urban life (4:17; 11:5); eastward migration (4:16; 11:2); "find" (4:14–15; 11:2); "dwell" (4:16; 11:2); "in the land of Nod" (4:16) and "in the land of Shinar" (11:2); fear of wandering (4:14; 11:4); and wanderings as punishment that resulted in protection and propagation (4:17–24; 11:1–9/9:1).

that God's words are also in the form of man's words (as cohortative ["let us go down and confuse," 11:7]) adds a corroding irony to the passage."[38]

That these builders' conceited efforts were absolutely puny is emphasized by the statement that Yahweh had to "come down" (11:5) to see the heights of their enterprise! In the eyes of God, the inhabitants of the earth "are like grasshoppers," and their works are paltry, indeed (Isa 40:22)—"a tiny tower, conceived by a puny plan and attempted by a pint-sized people." The laughable endeavor is emphasized in the description of its engineers: mere "sons of men" (Gen 11:5).[39] The Babelites goal was to reach the heavens, the habitation of God and, in Genesis, the place from where he speaks (19:24; 21:17; 22:11, 15); obviously, mankind's tower did not arrive anywhere near those lofty heights.

> Here, as in the Garden of Eden, men act in disobedience to definite commands, Adam to the specific prohibition about the tree of knowledge, the builders of the tower to the post-diluvian command to be fruitful and multiply and to fill the earth. . . . in Adam's individual case, autonomy—choosing for yourself—is the opposite of obedience; in the builders' case, independent self-re-creation—making yourself—is the opposite of obedient dependence, in relation to God or anything else. The road from Adam to the builders of the city is straight and true.[40]

But all the efforts of mankind were in vain; the very things they sought, centralization and security and a name, were lost in the divine scattering. Those who sought a "name" for themselves (11:4) did get one, but not what they expected; it was the "name" Babel (11:9), commemorating the failure, not success, of their "antitheocratical program."[41]

God's actions in the latter half of the narrative (11:5–9) ensure that these humans do not make plans (זָמַם, *zamam*) that "are beyond them"—בצר (*btsr*, 11:6). In the Niphal, this verb is used elsewhere only in Job 42:2, where it asserts that no plan (מְזִמָּה, *mzimmah*, from זמם) of Yahweh "is beyond" (בצר) him.[42] The similarity of these unique constructions suggest that there is only One who may plan without limits. In other words, the Babelites' transaction was arrogant, defiant, and rebellious.[43] For the first time in the Bible, the word "people" (עַם, *'am*) occurs, in 11:6, in God's concern about their prideful ambitions; in Gen 10, the crowds had been labeled "nations" (גּוֹי, *goy*, 10:5, 20, 31, 32). In other words, God is here concerned about the amplification of sin in a mob environment. Not only is sin personal after the flood, amply proven

---

38. Ross, "The Dispersion of the Nations," 122.

39. Or mere "earthlings" (ibid., 131). Not that this is only comedy. While man might try, as the Babelites did, to ascend towards the divine, it is always God who has to come down to rescue man—a fundamental phenomenon of biblical theology (Gen 11:5, 7; Exod 19:11, 18, 20; 34:5; Mark 1:10; John 3:16–17; Gal 4:4; 1 Thess 4:16).

40. Kass, "The Humanist Dream," 647.

41. The derision is even more pointed, for the Akkadian name for Babylon, *babili/babilani*, meant "gate of the god(s)." Mathews, *Genesis 1–11:26*, 469; Ross, "The Dispersion of the Nations," 126.

42. These are the only two verses where these concepts occur together in the OT.

43. Wenham, *Genesis 1–15*, 240–41. In fact, according to Wenham, the verb "to plan" (זמם) is exclusively used of God (Jer 4:28; 51:12; Zech 8:15) and of "nefarious human scheming" (Deut 19:19; Ps 31:13; 37:12).

by the misdeeds of Ham, it is augmented and intensified corporately when individuals act as "people."

They had resolved "to make . . ." (עשׂה, *'sh*, 11:4); God acknowledges that the egregiousness of their "doings" (עשׂה, 11:6 [×2]) will only get worse, and so he interrupts the proceedings, just as he did in 3:22. "[I]t can hardly be that the heavens trembled because the 'advancement' of mankind in any way threatened celestial rule. But, on the contrary, God was troubled over the injurious consequences that would fall upon the human family if left unchecked."[44]

> The desire to displace God from heaven, to make a name for oneself rather than allow God to do this, and to scheme without reference to his declared will, prompts one final judgment that will hobble man's attempts at cooperation once and for all. . . . Far from being the last word in human culture, it [Babylon/Babel] is the ultimate symbol of man's failure when he attempts to go it alone in defiance of his creator.[45]

The postdiluvian humans had decided that their security and their growth in power and reputation depended on their homogeneity and concentration in one place; thus, the making of city and tower, symbolic of their vain affectations and their presumptuous defiance of God who had commanded them to fill the earth (1:28; 9:1, 7). Indeed, it would take God's active intervention, the confounding of their languages and the scattering of these peoples, to fulfill his creation and post-flood mandate. That this is the thrust of the Babel story is evident in that the scattering of humanity is mentioned twice in the last two verses of the narrative (11:8, 9). The Babelites' disobedience to the divine mandate to fill the earth (1:28; 9:1, 7) resulted in the scattering that ultimately—and ironically—fulfilled God's command. Genesis 10:5, 18, 20, 30–32 show that the scattered nations did, in fact, fill the earth. Thus, even the dispersion was an act of grace, ensuring that mankind would attain the blessings earlier promised.[46]

> [T]he story of the scattering of the nations is actually the turning point of the book from primeval history to the history of the blessing. From this very confused and dispersed situation nations would develop in utter futility until God would make a great nation through one man who himself would be "scattered" from this alluvial plain to the land of Canaan. The blessings of final redemption and unification would come through his seed.[47]

Pericope 6 closes with the list of the descendants, the תּוֹלְדֹת, *toldot*, of "Shem" (11:10). But, unlike the Babelites, as Kass notes, Shem was one who had "gained a name for himself, not by pursuing it proudly but rather for his leadership in the pious

---

44. Mathews, *Genesis 1–11:26*, 484.

45. Wenham, *Genesis 1–15*, 245.

46. Mathews, *Genesis 1–11:26*, 474. This act of "punitive grace" resembles the driving out of the first pair of humans from the Garden of Eden. Had they consumed of the tree of life, they, and the rest of humanity, would have been consigned to an eternal life distant from God, with sin ever-present, and no hope of redemption.

47. Ross, "The Dispersion of the Nations," 127.

covering of his father Noah's nakedness."[48] A positive outcome of this genealogy is therefore to be expected. There are similarities between this Shemite line in Gen 11 and that of Adam in Gen 5: both are hopeful, following a negative account of mankind's sin (Cain's murder and his dodgy descendants in Gen 4; the sons of Noah and the prideful endeavors of his Babelite posterity in Gen 10–11). Each genealogy has ten links; each provides the age of the individual upon the birth of a son, and the remainder of his years; each ends with a father who had three sons (5:32; 11:26). However, in Gen 11, the total number of years of each member is omitted, as also the recurring refrain "and he died"; instead there is "and he had sons and daughters" (11:11, 13, 15, 17, 19, 21, 23, 25). And in Gen 11, there are no extrapolations, as there were in Gen 5 about Enoch (5:22–24) and Noah (5:29), the emphasis of this pericope being the fruitfulness and multiplication of the line, in accordance with the promise and plan of God—a gracious and providential intervention on his part.

Later, Terah and his family move from Ur to Canaan, a westward migration (11:31). It is indeed possible, that this note is an intentional contrast to the eastward movement of the Babelites in 11:1. Calculating from Terah's age when he fathered Abram (70; 11:26), and his age at his death (205; 11:32), when the 75-year-old Abram left Haran (12:4) he actually left his father there—another deliberate move by Abram further westward, putting this patriarch in far better light than the tower-builders.[49]

It is remarkable that Gen 11 begins and ends with a focus on "settling": both 11:2 and 11:31 employ the verb יֵשֶׁב, *yshb*. But the Babelites were settling in disobedience to the divine mandate and received, as a result, divine punishment; the Terahites (including Abram), on the other hand, were obedient to God in their settling, and are promised divine blessing. The contrast is stark, again pointing to the negative hue of the entire account of the Tower of Babel. In fact, it is through obedient Abram that the peoples of the earth would find blessing (12:3); this is further reinforced as one notes that "lands," "families," and "nations" in 10:5, 20, 31–32, reappear in 12:1–3, in God's call and promise to the patriarch. And God's promise to Abram is a magnificent one, in Gen 12, the chapter following the narrative of the Tower of Babel: "I will *make you a great nation, and I will bless you, and make your name great*" (12:2). After the Babelites attempting to make a name for themselves (11:1–4), God's blessing upon "Shem" (aka the "name") (11:10–26), and his promise of a "great name" for Shem's descendant, Abram (12:2), could not be more stark in contrast: human endeavor vs. divine endeavor.

The purpose of the Tower of Babel story is not to depict the etiology of the diversity of languages. Rather, following the account in the latter part of Gen 9 about the sin of the remnant that survived the flood, readers are made aware that Ham's transgressions were not an isolated case. The Tower of Babel narrative reinforces the sinfulness of post-flood humanity; they are as sinful as the pre-flood species. All of

48. "The Humanist Dream," 655.

49. Also the recurrent use of יָלַד (*yld*, "fathered"/"born") in 10:8, 13, 15, 21, 24, 25, 26, is reflected in מוֹלֶדֶת (*moledet*, "relatives") in 12:1. Abram's move constituted, for the most part, a significant sacrifice on his part.

mankind were sinners, with god-complexes, and afflicted by hubris and egocentricity. Divine judgment is inevitable for such conduct, yet, God's grace is also evident, and his promised blessings are beginning to be fulfilled.

SERMON FOCUS AND OUTLINES

THEOLOGICAL FOCUS OF PERICOPE 6 FOR PREACHING

6   Mankind's hubris—the making of a name for itself—prevents its experiencing God's blessings (10:1–11:26).

In this pericope, the last in the first major section of Genesis (Gen 1–11), mankind seems to have come full circle, i.e., back to the same problems that caused the fall of Adam and Eve in the Garden of Eden—hubris.

It is also an appropriate prologue to the next major section of Genesis, the Abraham Story (Gen 11:27–25:18), that begins to focus upon a particular people, the children of Abraham, later to be the nation of Israel. Pericope 6 deals with nations at large and God's blessing upon them, even though they were consumed with conceit and were generally moving with an anti-God, anti-theocratic trajectory. So henceforth, God's attention would shift to a select group of people, through whom he would, in the future, bless *all* nations.

For the purposes of the sermon, it would be best to focus upon the events at Babel. The activities of the protagonists in that city, arrantly foolish in their aspirations, are actually intended to counter the mandate and blessing of God to be fruitful, multiply, and fill the earth. Thus, unwittingly, their anti-God endeavors only injure themselves. God's punitive action of confounding their language and scattering them, while appropriate as retribution, ultimately serves to actualize his blessing for the nations of mankind.

Possible Preaching Outlines for Pericope 6

I.   God Endows Blessing
     The fruitfulness and multiplication of mankind (10:1–5, 11–32)
     Move-to-Relevance: God's desire is always to bless mankind

II. Man Eschews Blessing
     The sinister Nimrod and his rebellious enterprises: "mighty," "kingdom," "before Yahweh" (10:6–10)
     The arrogant Babelites and their vain overreaching: making themselves a name (11:1–4)
     Move-to-Relevance: How our hubris and independence actually diminish our experience of divine blessing

III. *Be blessed: Let God give you a name!*
     The blessing of mankind in the line of "Shem" (aka "name") (11:10–26)
     How we can "allow" God to make us a name—humility, submission, etc.[50]

50. Of course, this sermon (and every other) will need to provide specifics—concrete application, i.e., ways to begin achieving this goal. To a great extent, this is an exercise of pastoral wisdom and godly sensitivity, for it requires the preacher not only to understand the text and the ways of God's working, but also the listeners and where they may be lacking with regard to the theological thrust of the text.

With a tweak or two, here is another possibility:

I. God Blesses; Man Boasts

    The fruitfulness and multiplication of mankind (10:1–5)

    The sinister Nimrod and his rebellious enterprises: "mighty," "kingdom," "before Yahweh" (10:6–10)

II. God Still Blesses; Man Still Boasts

    The fruitfulness and multiplication of mankind (10:11–32)

    The arrogant Babelites and their vain overreaching: making themselves a name (11:1–4)

    Move-to-Relevance: How our tendencies are in this direction

III. God Punishes; God Still Blesses

    The consequences of hubris (11:5–9)

    The blessing of mankind in the line of "Shem" (11:10–26)

    Move-to-Relevance: God's desire is always to bless mankind

IV. *Let yourself be blessed!*

    How we can be blessed by God—by avoiding boasting, being humble, submitting to God, etc.

Application essentially is direction as to how God's people may take the first step(s) to align themselves to the demand of God in a given pericope. Thus, pericope by pericope, sermon by sermon, the people of God are gradually being aligned more and more to the will of God—they are becoming more Christlike.

PATRIARCHAL HISTORY
Moving Towards Blessing

Genesis 11:27–25:18

(Abraham Story)

PERICOPE 7

Abram's Call and Response

Genesis 11:27–12:20

[Genealogy of Terah; Abram's Call; Abram's Response]

REVIEW, SUMMARY, PREVIEW

Review of Pericope 6: Genesis 10:1–11:26, the final pericope in the Primeval History, is narrative sandwiched by genealogy. God's blessing is fulfilled in the multiplication and fruitfulness of mankind, yet there is a return to rebellion, resulting in divine punishment.

Summary of Pericope 7: With this pericope, the Abraham Story commences. After the depressing end of the primeval era, with the failure of the Babelites, one hopes for something better here. Abram is called, and blessings are promised. However there are hints that the patriarch is not completely obedient: his taking of Lot; his decampment to Egypt during a famine; and his passing off of Sarai, his wife, as his sister. Despite these stumbles on Abram's part, God's promise of blessing is sure.

Preview of Pericope 8: In the next pericope (Gen 13:1–14:24) Abram returns to the Promised Land, where God is, and where his blessing will be experienced—correction of his earlier failures, that includes separation from Lot. This demonstration of Abram's faithfulness is followed by an affirmation (and even an intensification) of the divine promises to the patriarch. Aligning oneself with God's demands yields blessing.

7.   Genesis 11:27–12:20

> **THEOLOGICAL FOCUS OF PERICOPE 7**
>
> **7   God's promise to bless mankind is fulfilled through individuals who obey in faith, despite overwhelming odds and great cost, relinquishing human contrivances in favor of an unshakeable trust in God (11:27–12:20).**
>
> 7.1   God's promise to bless mankind, despite the sins of the past, is fulfilled through individuals who obey in faith, even in the face of overwhelming odds and great cost (11:27–12:3).
>
> 7.1.1   *God's intent to bless mankind remains unchanged despite the sins of the past.*
>
> 7.1.2   *Obedience in faith, to God's promise of blessing, is to be undertaken despite overwhelming odds and great cost.*
>
> 7.1.3   *God's promise to bless mankind is fulfilled through individuals who obey in faith.*
>
> 7.2   Faithful obedience that is to result in divine blessing involves considerable sacrifice and a relinquishing of human contrivances in favor of an unshakeable trust in God (12:4–20).

OVERVIEW

Primeval History (Gen 1–11) leads to Patriarchal History (Gen 12–50). The latter is made up of three separate cycles that deal with Abraham (11:27–25:18), Jacob (25:19–36:43), and Joseph (37:1–50:26), respectively. Each patriarchal story begins with a תּוֹלְדֹת (*toldot*, 11:27; 25:19; 37:2), and ends with the demise of the one whose תלדות was recorded (25:7–10; 35:28–29; 49:33–50:26). Wenham notes a number of parallels between these three protagonists: Departure from homeland (12:1–28:2; 37:28); quarrels with relatives (13:7; 27:41; 37:4); moves towards Egypt (12:10; 37:28; 46:6); patriarch/wife being seduced/abducted (12:14–16; 20:1–14; 26:1–11; 39:1–23); barren patriarchal wives quarrelling (16:1–6; 29:31–30:8); divine favoring of younger sons (17:18–19; 25:23; 48:14; 49:8–12, 22–26); brides meeting grooms/agents at wells (24:15; 29:9); promises of land, seed, and blessing (12:1–3; 26:2–5; 28:13–14; etc.); acknowledgement of God's blessings by Gentiles (21:21–22; 26:28–29; 41:39–40); and burials in the cave of Machpelah (23:1–20; 25:9; 35:27–29; 49:29–32).[1]

The section on Primeval History ends on a rather depressing note (see Pericope 6). Mankind seems prone to sin, and sin only seems to have worsened with each generation. After the fall, one wondered if there was any hope of a fruitful divine-human relationship and the consummation of divine blessings promised in 1:18. The promise of the Sethite line fizzled out and the evil of mankind was punished by the flood. With Noah, God reiterated the blessing of fruitfulness again in 9:1, but Noah's progeny seemed to have gone back to humanity's sinful ways. And after the Tower of Babel episode, it all seemed to have gone irremediably awry.

1. From Wenham, *Genesis 1–15*, 256–57.

According to the text, God more than shares the reader's dismay as well as the reader's hopes, and He decides to take a more direct role in the matter, beginning with Abraham. God Himself, as it were, will take Abraham by the hand, will serve as his tutor, and will educate him to be a new human being, one who will stand in right relation to his household, to other peoples, and to God—one who will set an example for countless generations, who, inspired by his story, will cleave to these righteous ways.[2]

So again God offers a fresh start with the story of Abram, the one who would be the instrument of worldwide blessing. The patriarch is in a privileged position in the genealogy: Abram is the seventh from Eber (11:16–17) who is the eponymous ancestor of the Hebrews (himself the fourteenth from Adam). Both in the Sethite line to Noah (5:1–32) and in the Shemite line to Abraham (11:10–26) one finds the recurring echo of "sons and daughters"—the promise of fruitfulness—and each one ends with a forebear having three children (Noah, 5:32, and Terah, 11:26); in each trio, the chosen one is listed first (Shem and Abram, respectively).[3]

One remembers the irony of the sound of Shem's name (שׁם, *shm*; see previous pericope). It echoed over and over: mankind wanted to build "there" (שׁם, *shm*, 11:2) a tower that reached to the "heavens" (שׁמים, *shmym*), in order that they might make a "name" (שׁם, *shm*) for themselves (11:4). And then begins the genealogy of Shem in 11:10, the most prominent member of which would be *given* a great "name" (שׁם) by God himself (12:2). "Yahweh now intends to give what men attempted to secure arbitrarily."[4] It is as if God is setting things right after they had gone horribly wrong by human initiative and design.

Unlike the self-motivated and self-glorifying endeavors of the tower builders in Gen 11, Yahweh has "an international mission that rivals humanity's self-absorption," as he makes the patriarch the agent of his blessing to all.[5] Thus, even at the outset of his story, Abram is promised blessing and, in some fashion, his blessings will redound to all families of the earth. This blessing of God is, no doubt, linked to the blessings thus far and henceforth in Genesis intended for all mankind (in the past: 1:28; 9:1; 12:1–3; and in the future: 13:15–16; 15:5, 18; 17:6–8; 22:17–18; 25:11; 26:2–4; 27:27–29; 49:28). At long last, the initial creation blessing was now going to be channeled to all peoples through this one man, Abram, and his line. In the sequence of the eleven generations (תולדות, *toldot*) in Genesis, the one listing Abraham (11:27 through 25:11) is the sixth; thus, the Abraham Story conceivably forms the center of the book.[6] Appropriately, the Abrahamic cycle is bounded at its beginning and towards its end with God's first and

---

2. Kass, *The Beginning of Wisdom*, 252.

3. Mathews, *Genesis 1–11:26*, 488–89. However, unlike the list in Gen 5, in Gen 11 the years of members' lives are not noted, neither is the "and he died" refrain. Obviously in the first, as was noted earlier, the thrust was on the deleterious effect of sin. In Gen 11, hope is being proffered.

4. Von Rad, *Genesis*, 160.

5. Awabdy, "Babel, Suspense," 17–18.

6. Mathews, *Genesis 11:27–50:26*, 85.

final recorded revelations to Abraham, respectively, announcing blessings upon all the earth through the patriarch.

"And in you all the families of the earth will be blessed" (12:3).
"In your seed all the nations of the earth shall be blessed" (22:18).

The plot of the Abraham narratives "is tied to the progression of Abraham's faith in the promise of an heir."[7] Yet there is a deep tension between the barrenness of Sarah (11:30) and the promise of seed (12:3, 7). This tension is carefully and artfully maintained throughout the Abrahamic saga, as the patriarch undergoes a series of crises, culminating in the most crucial test of all, in Gen 22. While the promise of land, seed, and blessing is extended to Abram at the commencement of the Patriarchal History (12:1–3, 7), neither land nor blessing is achieved in Abram's life; seed alone is the promise that is actualized in his day, but the arrival of that offspring is increasingly delayed—a delay that drives the entire Abraham cycle and becomes the primary motif of the patriarch's life.

The divine initiative to bless Abram called for a response of faith. "In this regard, the narrator wants to impress upon the reader the necessity and example of Abraham's faith"—the theological thrust of the saga. "The narrator evidently believed that good theology ought to be expounded by means of a good story. He has succeeded in writing both."[8] Events are specifically chosen that relate to this theological theme and to the spiritual development of the patriarch: for e.g., the eleven years from his call to the birth of Ishmael occupy Gen 12–16, but in the next pericope, Gen 17, there is a fast-forward and Ishmael is suddenly thirteen years old (17:1, 24). In other words, it is the character of narrative—*any* narrative—to reveal only selected portions of history: not everything about Abraham is told, not every event is described, not every undertaking is detailed. While the bulk of the account consumes 65 years of his life—between his call by God when he was 75 and up to his finding a bride for his son, Isaac, when he was 140—only some incidents are described: "the text recounts only certain selected episodes in Abraham's life and strings them together in a tight and carefully crafted order that best serves the Bible's overall moral-political and pedagogical [I would say 'theological'] purposes."[9] In fact, it is not only Abraham's education that is being attempted, but ours, as well. All of God's people are to learn from the patriarch, by both positive and negative examples, what it means to have faith in God as he calls—how to move towards divine blessing. In short, a selectivity is operating here, based on the author's theological agenda, as visible in the structure of Gen 11–22.[10]

7. Ibid., 89.

8. Helyer, "The Separation," 86

9. Kass, *The Beginning of Wisdom*, 252. The symmetry of Abraham's life span is remarkable: 75 years with father; then 25 years without father or son; finally, another 75 years with son.

10. From Mathews, *Genesis 11:27–50:26*, 89; Dorsey, *The Literary Structure of the Old Testament*, 56; Greidanus, *Preaching Christ from Genesis*, 140; and Rendsburg, *The Redaction of Genesis*, 28–29.

A   Genealogy of Terah (11:27–32)
     B   Start of Abram's spiritual odyssey; divine promise (12:1–9)
        C   Abram lies; Sarai abducted; God protects;
           Abram and Lot part; promise of descendant (12:10–13:18)
          D   Abram rescues Sodom and Lot (14:1–24)
            E   Divine promise of a son; the child from Abram himself (15:1–21)
              F   Ishmael's birth;
                 divine promise re: Ishmael (16:1–16)
                G   Yahweh's covenant; names changed;
                   Sarah to be mother; circumcision (17:1–21)
             F'   Ishmael and Abraham circumcised;
                divine promise re: Ishmael (17:22–27; 17:18, 20)
           E'   Divine promise of a son; the child from Sarah herself (18:1–15)
         D'   Abraham rescues Sodom and Lot (18:16–19:38)
        C'   Abraham lies; Sarah abducted; God protects;
           Abraham and Ishmael part; birth of descendant (20:1–21:34)
     B'   Climax of Abraham's spiritual odyssey; divine promise (22:1–19)
A'   Genealogy of Nahor (22:20–24)

The incidents in the Abraham cycle have oft been called "trials"; essentially they include: the divine call to leave all, famine, threat of wife abduction, quarrel with Lot, war to save Lot, Sarah's quarrel with Hagar, divine call to circumcise, Abraham's hospitality, his negotiation with God to save Lot, another threat of wife-abduction, separation from his son Ishmael, and the divine call to sacrifice Isaac. For the most part, these are all linked to the immediate issue of the production of seed (less to the fulfillment of the promises of land and blessing)—even circumcision is a rite that leaves a mark on the organ of procreation! In one way or another, these "trials" test Abraham's faith and his relationship to God—"his whole life seemed to be one long series of divinely instituted challenges."[11] The Mishna declares that these trials were documented "to make known how great was the love of Abraham, our father [for God, Isa 41:8; 2 Chr 20:7: both texts use אהב, *'hb*, 'to love']" (*m. Abot.* 5.4).[12]

There are also significant conceptual and linguistic parallels between the account of Noah in Gen 8:15–20 and that of Abraham in 12:1–7. However, in light of the latter's education program, it is interesting to note that Noah is *already* righteous and "blameless" (תָּמִים, *tamim*) when God first addresses him (6:9). Abraham, who was addressed by God without any information provided about his character, is required to *become* "blameless" (17:1; also תָּמִים). Noah's character appears to have been fully formed as he appeared on the scene; Abraham's is a work in progress, as he moves in faith towards blessing.[13]

---

11. Kugel, *Traditions of the Bible*, 296.

12. Nevertheless, the only text explicitly labeled as a trial was the divine call to sacrifice Isaac (22:1).

13. Table derived from Hong, "An Exegetical Reading," 137–38.

Genesis 8:15–20	Genesis 12:1–7
"And God spoke to Noah" (8:15)	"And Yahweh said to Abram" (12:1a)
"Go out of the ark" (8:16)	"Go forth from your country" (12:1b)
"And Noah went out" (8:18)	"And Abram went forth" (12:4)

"And Noah built
    an altar for the Lord" (8:20)
	"And he [Abram] built
	    an altar for the Lord" (12:7)

"And God *blessed* Noah" (9:1)	"And I [God] will *bless* you" (12:2)
"Be fruitful and multiply" (9:1)	"And I will make you a great nation" (12:2)

Covenant with Noah
    and his "descendants" (9:9)
	Promise (covenant) to Abram
	    and his "descendants" (12:7)

New era of the world,
    with one man following the flood
	New era of a people,
	    with one man following a dispersion

In a sense, the events of Gen 12 may also be considered a type of the exodus: famine causes Abraham's migration from Canaan (12:10); he and Sarah "sojourn" (גּוּר, *gur*) in Egypt (12:10; a term used to describe the Israelites' four centuries in Egypt: Lev 19:33–34; Deut 10:19; etc.); conflict with Pharaoh (12:18–19); Egyptians struck with plagues by God (12:17); Abraham commanded to "take and go" (12:19; Exod 12:32); "servants of Pharaoh" (Gen 12:15; Exod 9:20; 10:7; etc.); Pharaoh's house (Gen 12:15; Exod 8:24); Pharaoh "sends" Abraham (Gen 12:20; Exod 5:1, 2; 6:1, 11; 7:2; etc.); Abraham is enriched by the Egyptians (Gen 12:16; Exod 12:35–36); Abraham "went up" (עָלָה, *'lh*) from Egypt (Gen 13:1; Exod 13:18; 17:3; 32:1; etc.); he leaves "very rich in livestock" (Gen 13:2; Exod 12:38); Canaanites in the land (Gen 13:7; Exod 3:8, 17; etc.).[14]

Pericope 7 is essentially a travelogue: from Ur of the Chaldeans (Gen 11:28) to Haran (11:31; 12:4) to Canaan (12:5), traversing Shechem (in the north, 12:6), Bethel (in the center, 12:8), and the Negev (in the south, 12:9), and onward to Egypt (12:10)— and in reverse order in Pericope 8 (Gen 13), as Abram returns to Canaan.

> Shechem, Oak of Moreh (12:6)
>   Bethel (12:8)
>   Negev (12:9)
>   "went down" to Egypt (12:10)
>   "came up" from Egypt (13:1)
>   Negev (13:1)
>   Bethel (13:3)
> Hebron, Oaks of Mamre (13:18)

The three specific sites mentioned during the journey are significant, in that Jacob visits those same sites on his return to Canaan from his uncle's house in Haran (Shechem, 33:18–20 and 35:4; Bethel, 35:14–15; and Hebron, 35:27; for Jacob's stops, see below).[15] In effect, as will be noted, the land promised by Yahweh is being mapped out and spiritually appropriated, with altars and all. Incidental details, but important ones, provided with the description of Abram's journeys in this pericope include: introduction of Lot (11:27, 31: 12:4–5), the barrenness of the matriarch Sarai (11:29–31; 12:5),

14. Lunn, "The Last Words of Jacob," 176n48.

15. Sailhamer, *The Pentateuch as Narrative*, 140. Table from Brodie, *Genesis as Dialogue*, 210.

God's promises to the patriarch of land, seed, and blessing (12:1–3, 7), and Abram's first responses to those promises (12:4, 7–8, 10–20). All of these characters and elements play significant parts in the subsequent story.[16]

7.1 Genesis 11:27–12:3

THEOLOGICAL FOCUS 7.1

7.1 God's promise to bless mankind, despite the sins of the past, is fulfilled through individuals who obey in faith, even in the face of overwhelming odds and great cost (11:27–12:3).

    7.1.1 *God's intent to bless mankind remains unchanged despite the sins of the past.*

    7.1.2 *Obedience in faith, to God's promise of blessing, is to be undertaken despite overwhelming odds and great cost.*

    7.1.3 *God's promise to bless mankind is fulfilled through individuals who obey in faith.*

NOTES 7.1

7.1.1 God's intent to bless mankind remains unchanged despite the sins of the past.

Genesis 11:27–32 and 25:1–11 form bookends for Abraham's story; in both cases there is a genealogy followed by geography ("seed" followed by "land": 11:27–30 and 11:31–32; 25:1–6a and 25:6b–11). The first "land" section deals with a journey *to* Canaan; the second with a burial *in* Canaan. Both bookends report the deaths of the protagonists, Terah and Abraham, respectively; the first dies short of the Promised Land, the second dies in it. And both conclude with an account of a "settling": in 11:31, of Terah and his household; in 25:11, of Isaac.[17]

    This pericope begins with the formulaic structure that introduces new sections of Genesis: "And these are the generations [תּוֹלְדֹת] of . . ." (as in 2:4; 5:1 [a variant]; 6:9; 10:1; 11:10; 25:12, 19; 36:1, 9; and 37:2). Terah died at the age of 205 (11:32), when Abraham was 135 (11:26, 32). Thus it appears Terah was living for most of the span of the Abraham Story (Abraham would die at 175; 25:7). At least in theory, he remained the head of the clan, perhaps explaining the title: the תּוֹלְדֹת of Terah (11:27). Wenham thinks this premature mention of Terah's death is consonant with the practice of biblical history to handle the less important persons first: Japheth and Ham are dealt with before Shem's line is described (10:21–31); Haran and Nahor are accounted for before Abraham's saga is begun (11:26–29); Ishmael's history precedes Isaac's, as does Esau's, preceding Jacob's (25:12, 19; 36:1; 37:2).[18] While Terah's death therefore actually occurs much later in the chronology of the Abraham narratives, the narrator chooses to mention it at 11:32, in order to create a fresh start, the new era of Abram, akin to that

---

16. Wenham, *Genesis 1–15*, 267–68.

17. Campbell, "Refusing God's Blessing," 273.

18. Wenham, *Genesis 1–15*, 269. Stephen, in Acts 7:4, asserts that Abraham left Haran only upon the death of his father Terah. It might be that the martyr had another source for the story; the Samaritan Pentateuch records Terah dying at 145, not at 205 (as does the MT, LXX, Vulgate, Peshitta, and Targums).

of the post-diluvian Noah. Primeval History has concluded; Patriarchal History has begun. God's intent to bless mankind is being rechanneled through one individual and his family.

Since Abram was born in Ur of the Chaldeans (11:27–32), the call to leave "your country" (12:1), must have come to him in Ur, a fact confirmed in 15:7 and accepted as such in Neh 9:7 and Acts 7:2–4. However, that does not preclude a second call in Haran that could have precipitated his departure thence (Gen 12:4). In any case, the journey of the clan, begun in 11:31 ("to go to the land of Canaan"), is disrupted; it finds its terminus only in Abram's life, in 12:5 ("they set out for the land of Canaan; thus they came to the land of Canaan"), and that after the call of God: "Go, yourself . . ." (12:2). Terah's decision to "settle there" (11:31) in Haran is an echo of what happened at Babel (that hubristic mob also "settled there," 11:2), a seeming violation of the divine mandate to fill the earth (1:28:9:1). Both "the whole earth" (11:2) and Terah's household (11:31) appear to have gotten it wrong, the first for reasons of rebellion, and the second because the travelers aborted their journey before their ultimate destination. The earlier migration ends in frustration; the later one is uneventful, and nothing happens in Haran, except that Terah is said to have died there. It would not be until Abram's migration that the will of God is accomplished. Clearly the author is contrasting this doubtful choice on Terah's part with the initiative and obedience of Abram.

There are more parallels here with Gen 11:1–9. Both that section and this begin with an initial movement and a second relocation (11:1–2, and 11:8–9; 11:31 and 12:4–5), separated by a divine interruption (11:6–8; 12:1–4). It seems divine action in both cases is remedying a faulty response: in the one of rebellion, in the other of dereliction.[19] And it might well be that rather than the chiastic patterning of 11:1–9 (see Pericope 6), we find a parallel pattern in 11:31–12:5 (shown below), indicating that in the latter instance, God was not overruling (or reversing), but extending, the movement begun by Terah.[20]

A	Terah *took* his household (11:31a)	
	B	Terah's household *set out to go to the land of Canaan* (11:31b)
	C	Terah's household *came* to Haran (11:31c)
	D	Terah's household settles there (11:31d)
	E	Terah's dies in Haran (11:32)
God's Call (12:1–3) *and Abram's Response* (12:4)		
A′	Abram *took* his household (12:5a)	
	B′	Abram's household *set out to go to the land of Canaan* (12:5b)
	C′	Abram's household *came* to Canaan (12:5c)

God's actions and Abram's response counter the fear of the reader that in the place where Terah settled (Haran, 11:31), his children would repeat the same rebellion of the Babelites when they settled in Shinar (11:2). Thankfully, that does not happen. "Abram's obedient response (12:4–5, 7–8), and Abram's initial entry into Canaan

---

19. Awabdy, "Babel, Suspense," 21.

20. Table modified from ibid., 20–21.

(12:4b–5) conserve, for characters and readers alike, a vestige of optimism for the future divine–human relationship."[21] God's plan to bless mankind is being put in place.

7.1.2 *Obedience in faith, to God's promise of blessing, is to be undertaken despite overwhelming odds and great cost.*

Genesis 11:27–32 raises fears about the whole project: there is early death, there is barrenness, and there is a migration that stops short of its goal. Besides, the preceding genealogy in 11:10–32 is the only section in Genesis 1–11 where the name of God does *not* appear—an ominous omission. "Terah, lacking the vision, lost the will to persist. . . . So the chapter brings the primeval history to a doubly appropriate close, with man's self-effort issuing in confusion at Babel and in compromise here. On his own, man will get no further than this," a fact underscored by the "absence" of God here.[22]

Unlike the prior generations in the genealogy of Gen 11 that named only the firstborn, in 11:27, the names of all three children of Terah are noted. While Abram remains the main actor, descendants from the others become part of the patriarch's family (as his children's wives). But despite this multi-children listing, there is an unusual and unique narrator's "aside" in 11:27–32: it declares Sarai's barrenness, a theme which is the dynamo for the story of Abraham in the remainder of its chapters.[23]

A   Introduction: Terah and his children (11:27)

B   The family lives in *Ur of the Chaldeans;*
Haran (הָרָן, *haran*) dies (11:28)

C   Abraham *takes* Sarai as his *wife;*
Nahor marries Milcah, *daughter of Haran* (11:29)

D   Sarai is barren; she has no children (11:30)

C'   Terah *takes* Abraham,
along with Abraham's *wife Sarai* and Lot, *son of Haran* (11:31a)

B'   The family leaves *Ur of the Chaldeans*
and settles in Haran (חָרָן, *kharan*) (11:31b)

A'   Conclusion: Summary of Terah's life; his death (11:32)

Sarai's antecedents are unknown (20:12 informs us that she was a half-sister to Abram); neither is her future certain—she is barren.[24] The redundant mention of her childlessness in 11:30—"barren," and "had no child"—is unique for Sarai; other similarly afflicted matriarchs are simply described as being "barren" (Rebekah, 25:21; Rachel, 29:31). It is this barrenness of Sarai that is the propulsive thrust of a story in which, ironically, God promises Abram a host of descendants (12:2; 15:4–5; 17:1–23; 18:10), a promise that sets both husband and wife laughing (17:17; 18:11–12). "Nothing like this has happened in Genesis before. Indeed, the book is structured by fecundity, by

---

21. Ibid., 23.

22. Kidner, *Genesis*, 111–12.

23. Waltke and Fredricks, *Genesis*, 200. Table from ibid., 199. "Haran" the person and "Haran" the place are spelled differently in Hebrew; nonetheless, the parallelism is striking (*B* and *B'*, in the table).

24. *Šarratu* was the wife of *Sin* the moon god, perhaps the origin of "Sarai." Ur and Haran were centers of moon worship; it is likely Terah and his family participated in pagan worship (Josh 24:2, 15). See Wenham, *Genesis 1–15*, 273.

the fertility and (re)productivity of humanity as a result of God's blessing 'be fruitful and multiply' (1:28 and 9:1). . . . But here stands Sarai, an exception to the cosmic rule."[25] All those promises of seed to Abram/Abraham notwithstanding, the delay in their fulfillment and the resulting attempts by the patriarch and his wife to "help" God along, taking matters into their own hands, are what give the whole narrative coherence.

In fact, on the whole, 11:27–32 shows that Terah's seed, the entire line, appears to be dead: Abram's wife is barren; Haran dies an early death; and Nahor, though married, is not recorded as having progeny (neither is Lot).

> It is simply reported that this family (and with the whole family of Gen 1–11) has played out its future and has nowhere else to go. Barrenness is the way of human history. It is an effective metaphor for hopelessness. There is no foreseeable future. There is no human power to invent a future. . . . A proper hearing of the Abraham-Sarah texts depends upon the vitality of the metaphor of barrenness. It announces that this family begins its life in a situation of irreparable hopelessness [as does all of mankind].[26]

Then, for the first time since God's utterance of judgment and sentence at the Tower of Babel episode, he speaks. The command from God is made especially stark in the use of rhyming words in 12:2–3 that end in "ךָ" (*ka*; second person masculine singular suffix): וְאֶעֶשְׂךָ (*we'eska*, "I will make you"), וַאֲבָרֶכְךָ (*wa'abarekka*, "I will bless you"), שְׁמֶךָ וַאֲגַדְּלָה (*wa'agaddlah shmeka*, "I will make your name great"), מְבָרְכֶיךָ (*mbarkeka*, "those who bless you"), וּמְקַלֶּלְךָ (*umqallelka*, "and the one who curses you"). The increasing specification of what Abram must leave—country, relatives, father's house—must have had an immediate impact: this obedience was going to be costly.[27] Relational and socioeconomic ties were all to be severed. "In the ancient social order, as for most humans who have ever lived, family and territory were an individual's primary hold on life-sustaining resources and a bulwark against adversarial encroachments. This is what God asks Abram to renounce, no less."[28] God was asking for "faith-full" obedience from Abram, at great cost to himself and to all his. Yet, the benefits also would be considerable, both to the patriarch and to his descendants, and even to the rest of the world.

7.1.3 God's promise to bless mankind is fulfilled through individuals who obey in faith.

The promises to Abram in 12:2–3 are in seven clauses, as also are those to Isaac (26:3–4) and to Jacob (27:28–29). Grammatically, 12:1–3 contains two imperatives ("go forth" and "you shall be a blessing"), each followed by three promises:

25. Arnold, *Genesis*, 128.

26. Brueggemann, *Genesis*, 116–17.

27. Wenham, *Genesis 1–15*, 274.

28. Eslinger, "Prehistory in the Call," 196.

Go forth

I will make you a great nation

I will *bless* you

I will make your name great

You shall be a *blessing*

I will *bless* those who *bless* you

I will curse the one who curses you

All the families of the earth shall be *blessed* in you

The five-fold occurrence of בָּרַךְ (*brk*, "bless," italicized above) may reflect the five-fold mention of curses thus far in Genesis: 3:14, 17, 4:11; 5:29; 9:25; or perhaps the five blessings heretofore (1:22, 28; 2:3; 5:2; 9:1) are being echoed. No doubt, the word-plays with the double consonant *br*, as in אַבְרָם, *'abram* ("Abram"), "bless," "blessed," "blessing" (from בָּרַךְ, 12:2 [×2], 3 [×3]), and in "passed through" (עָבַר, *'br*, 12:6), are all meant to evoke blessing, not to mention the echo of *br* in the patriarch's full title, Abram the Hebrew (אַבְרָם הָעִבְרִי, *'abram ha'ibri*, 14:13). The root בָּרַךְ occurs 88 times in Genesis (310 times elsewhere). "Blessing not only connects the patriarchal narratives with each other (cf. 24:1; 26:3; 35:9; 39:5), it also links them with the primeval history (cf. 1:28; 5:2; 9:1). The promises of blessings to the patriarchs are thus a reassertion of God's original intentions for man," that he will carry out through Abram and his descendants. This original purpose of God, to bless humanity, was not going to be thwarted by human sin (Gen 2–3), murder (Gen 4), gross evil (Gen 6), persistence of sin (Gen 9), or rebellion (Gen 10).[29]

Essentially, the promise to Abram is threefold: land, seed, and blessing to the patriarch and to the nations through him. Thus there seems to be a progression of thought in Yahweh's speech.

12:2b   Abram is blessed

12:2c   Abram is to be a blessing, himself

12:3c   Abram is the means of blessing, to all families of the earth

"As the two parts of an hourglass are joined by a slender neck, the role of this one man connects the universal setting of chaps. 1–11 and the worldwide vista of the promissory call." In the Table of Nations in Gen 10, are the terms "land," "families," and "nations" (10:5, 20, 31–32)—terms which reappear in 12:1–3. So also, the refrain יָלַד (*yalad*, "became the father," 10:8, 13, 15, 21, 24, 25, 26), shows up in the related word, מוֹלֶדֶת (*moledet*, "relatives," 12:1).[30] It is through this one man, Abram, that God's intended blessing for the nations would be accomplished.[31] Abraham is called to be a

---

29. Wenham, *Genesis 1–15*, 275.

30. Mathews, *Genesis 11:27–50:26*, 105.

31. The question of the nuance of וְנִבְרְכוּ (*wnibrku*, Niphal *waw*-consecutive perfect 3rd person plural of בָּרַךְ, *brk*) in 12:3c has long perplexed scholars: "וְנִבְרְכוּ in you all families of the earth." Since the divine promise to Abraham is found in both Niphal and Hithpael forms of בָּרַךְ in Genesis (12:3; 18:18; 28:14; and 22:18; 26:14, respectively), the issue is the sense in our text of interest, 12:3. Possible readings of the Niphal include senses that are passive ("be blessed") or middle ("gain/receive/find blessings"), and rarely reflexive ("bless themselves"). Lee argues that the middle may be ruled out since the verb in this sense is not "bless" but "gain/receive/find," and that in the active voice. Reflexive Niphals are rare in

blessing (12:2c): while his acquisition of blessing is passive, his response is not; he is mandated to transmit, actively, the blessing that he has received. Unlike its parallels (in 27:29 and Num 24:9), Gen 12:3 is a personal statement: "I will . . ., I will . . ."—Yahweh will involve himself personally to see to Abram's blessing and welfare.

> And I will bless
>   those who bless you,
>   And the one who disdains [קלל, *qll*] you
> I will curse [ארר, *'rr*].

Even the one who merely disdains Abram is in danger of being cursed by God. Thus even "illegitimate verbal assaults" would be paid back by a firm judicial malediction.[32] Again, this shows how serious God is about Abram's prosperity. And surprisingly, the second clause deals with the singular person who might disdain Abram, while the first clause dealt with the plural "those" who would bless him. Wenham thinks this implies that "those who disdain Abram will be far fewer than those who bless him. He will flourish to such an extent that few will fail to recognize that God is indeed on his side."[33]

It appears then that God makes a conditional promise to Abram, requiring an obedient response (12:1–3). At the point of obedience (the meeting of God's condition), the promise was reiterated by God (12:7). Later, this promise was transformed into a covenant (covenant inauguration; 15:1–21), the conditions for which were subsequently enumerated (covenant confirmation; 17:1–2, 9–14; 18:18–19), confirming it. Upon Abraham's passing the final test of his faith and obedience, the covenant becomes ratified by God with an oath (covenant ratification; 22:15–18; 26:5). Thus one spies a development from conditional promise to covenant inaugurated, confirmed, and, finally, ratified by an oath.[34]

---

the OT. In the other instances of the Niphal of ברך, Gen 18:18 and 28:14, the passive sense seems to be quite clear. Thus, on grammatical and contextual evidence, Niphal appears to bear a passive meaning in this usage. God is the divine agent of blessing (12:3a), and the preposition ב in 12:3b indicates, most likely, the *means* of blessing (Abraham), rather than the agent or name by which blessing is invoked. In addition, both the LXX and other versions (Vulgate, Targums), as well as Sir 44.21, and the NT (Acts 3:25; Gal 3:8), follow a passive meaning for this verb. See Lee, "Once Again," 286–88.

32. The parallels, Gen 27:29 and Num 24:9, are more balanced: a curse for a curse.

33. *Genesis 1–15*, 277.

34. I am grateful to my colleague, Gordon H. Johnston, for his perspicuous observations on these matters (personal communication, 2012).

	Promise Given 12:1–3, 7; 13:14–17	Covenant Inaugurated 15:1–21	Covenant Confirmed 17:1–27; 18:18–19	Covenant Ratified 22:1–2, 15–18; 26:5
Yahweh	Promise expressed (12:1–3)	Promise re-expressed (15:1–5)	Covenant confirmed (17:1–21)	Covenantal test (22:1–2)
Abraham	Condition met: faithful obedience (12:4–6; Heb 11:8)	Condition met: faith (15:6; Heb 11:9–12)	Condition met: faithful obedience (17:22–27)	Condition met: faithful obedience (22:3–14; Heb 11:17–18)
Yahweh	Promise reiterated (Gen 12:7; 13:14–17)	Covenant inaugurated (Gen 15:7–21)	Covenant reconfirmed (Gen 18:18–19)	Covenant ratified (Gen 22:15–18; 26:5)

Surprising is the divine promise of descendants and a great nation (12:1–3) following soon after the observation about Sarai's barrenness (11:30). The promise, of course, leaves open other non-Sarai-related options for generating progeny, all of which Abram seems keen on exploring in the next several pericopes. "The central impetus for the action in Abraham's life story is to correct the imbalance between the promise of offspring and its fulfillment."[35] In light of history thus far, this tactic of God seems odd. After the growth of the human race and the corresponding culmination of human evil the first time, God sent a flood, but saved one man and his family. Now after the second phase of increase and the rebellion at Babel, God picks a *childless* couple to further his schemes, and moreover, he asks them to divest themselves of every human connection possible—country, relatives, father's house. God's plans are carried out only when one fully—*fully!*—trusts him. The problem, of course, was the man and woman here chosen were *not* particularly inclined in that direction, at least not totally. In fact, it is this recalcitrance that drives the rest of the Abraham Story, including its culmination with the final test of Gen 22.

7.2   Genesis 12:4–20

THEOLOGICAL FOCUS 7.2

7.2   Faithful obedience that is to result in divine blessing involves considerable sacrifice and a relinquishing of human contrivances in favor of an unshakeable trust in God (12:4–20).

---

35. Eslinger, "Prehistory in the Call," 198.

7.2 Faithful obedience that is to result in divine blessing involves considerable sacrifice and a relinquishing of human contrivance in favor of an unshakeable trust in God.

Quite strikingly, after the tripartite promise—regarding land, seed, and blessing—Abraham proceeds to give lie to all three facets of the divine word. He takes Lot, assuming his nephew will be his heir (the seed promise disbelieved), he decamps from Canaan to Egypt (the land promise dismissed) and, by his deception of Pharaoh, brings about plagues upon Egypt (the blessing promise disregarded).

Yahweh's first and last words to Abram begin the same way: לֶךְ־לְךָ, (*lek-lka*, "go forth/go yourself," 12:1; 22:1). The use of the preposition לְ, *l*, with the pronominal suffix ךָ, *ka*, has the "effect of creating a self-contained little cosmos around the subject, detached from the surrounding world, an effect of focusing on the subject"; "the subject establishes his own identity . . . by determinedly dissociating himself from his familiar surroundings. Notions of isolation, loneliness, parting, seclusion, or withdrawal are often recognizable.[36] Terah "took" Abram and others to commence his journey (11:31); now it is Abram's turn to "take" Sarai and others (11:5) to start another—this is a fresh beginning, under his own leadership, with his own household. It is ironic that the first imperative from God employs הלך (*hlk*, 12:2; the first word from Yahweh), and though Abraham did indeed "go" (הלך) "as the Lord had spoken to him" (12:4; the first response of Abram), it is expressly noted that "Lot went [also הלך] with him" (12:4), in contravention of God's demand that Abram leave his relatives (12:1). Strange obedience, indeed, "a hedging pragmatism," asserts Eslinger, "not blind faith."[37] While Abram's obedience is, nonetheless, endorsed in that he goes "as Yahweh had spoken to him" (12:4; also see 17:23), and while there is no question but that Abram performed a creditable action in going (as Heb 11:8 attests), the fact that he did not leave all behind is significant. Immediately after recounting Abram's obedience in going "as Yahweh had spoken to him," we are told "and Lot went with him" (12:4). In fact, it might be better to translate the conjunction ו (*w*) as "but" not "and"—*but* Lot went with him." Rickett thinks this phrase is the "first instance of disobedience on the part of Abraham."[38] "Overall, therefore, Abram's departure is ambiguous. He is following God's word, but the baggage he carries—his years and people

---

36. Muraoka, "On the So-called *dativus ethicus*," 497.

37. "Prehistory in the Call," 197.

38. "Rethinking the Place," 43n24, 44. A wife, however, is an integral part of the household, and therefore no questions are raised about Sarai's accompanying her husband. Another reason to consider Lot's being taken as an act of disobedience is the comparison of this call in 12:1 (Abram's first) with the call in 22:2 (Abram's last): both begin with לֶךְ־לְךָ, *lek-lka*, the only times this phrase shows up in Genesis (see later on that pericope); both have three-fold levels of abandonment: "country/relatives/father's house" in 12:1, and "son/only son/one you love" in 22:2. It makes good sense, in light of the progress of the narrative, to see the first instance leading to a partial obedience and the second to an absolutely total one (ibid., 47n37).

and places and possessions—is not light."[39] The taking along of Lot comes as a surprise; Lot's grandfather, Terah, was still living and could have taken responsibility for the grandson's welfare; there was no call for Abram to adopt him. Besides, Lot's chattel is apparently distinct from Abram's—"their" possessions (12:5); thus there appears to be two discrete households making the move. And later, Abram's nephew is said to have his own "flocks and herds and tents" (13:5). Most likely, Lot was an insurance policy, as good as Abram's own son—just in case God was unable to keep his word and produce progeny for Abram and Sarai! The patriarch must not have thought much of his own seed-producing capacities—an understandable diagnosis, seeing that he was 75 years old. In any case, Abram disbelieves the seed promise given by Yahweh. This lack of total reliance on God is not a good omen; it adumbrates the tense situations that transpire: strife (Gen 13), harm (Gen 14), disaster (Gen 18–19), incest (Gen 19), enmity (Gen 19).

The first time Yahweh "appears" to Abram (12:7) is Yahweh's first expressly recorded "appearance" in Scripture (also see 17:1; 18:1; 26:2, 24; 35:[1], 9; 48:3). Abram had already experienced Yahweh's voice (12:1), but now he sees him. This was a powerful theophany, an event of great moment. In response, the patriarch builds an altar at Shechem/oak of Moreh, the northern boundary of the Promised Land (12:6). And, following this first altar, Abram moves and builds a second one, at the same time calling upon the name of Yahweh (12:8)—another first for a human being in the Bible. The location of this latter altar is significant, with Ai and Bethel on the east and west, respectively. Abram then continues his journey into the Negev (12:9), the southern border of Canaan. (He returns to the first locus in 13:3–4, from where Yahweh asks him to survey the land north, south, east, and west. Thus, roughly, this spot is the middle of the Promised Land, where, in 13:18, a southern altar is built at Hebron/oaks of Mamre.) In other words, Abram's journey in 12:5–9 has taken him from the north to the south of the Promised Land. And he builds altars in the north (12:7), in the middle (12:8), and later, in the south (13:18). This is a virtual possession of the land.

But right after this incident of sacral solemnity in 12:8, readers are told about a famine that causes Abram and his caravan to relocate to Egypt (12:9–10). One wonders where the patriarch's faith was? It is unlikely that his escape into Egypt was sanctioned by God. That Abram intended to "sojourn" (גּור, *gur*, 12:10) in Egypt—with implications of a long-term stay—does not abound to his credit at all, especially as it follows immediately after the divine promise to give him and his descendants "this land"—Canaan (12:7). No doubt the famine was "severe" (12:10), but one would have expected the patriarch to have as much faith in God as he did when he boldly set out from Haran for parts unknown.

The verbs describing his entrance into ("went down," 12:10) and exit from ("went up," 13:1) Egypt form bookends for that scene. "Though the verbs 'went down' and 'went up' are normal vocabulary for this movement, they also symbolically depict his

---

39. Brodie, *Genesis*, 216.

spiritual and physical pilgrimage out of God's blessing and back into it."[40] This appears to have been a pointless journey into Egypt. In fact, later, out of Pharaoh's mouth comes the command to "go" (הלך, 12:19), employing the same word in God's command (12:1): Abram is seemingly being ordered to get back on track with God and his purposes—a reminder from an Egyptian![41] In other words, while Abram is keen on possessing the land (his surveying of its breadth and length, and his altar-building and worship in strategic loci), he does not appear to be *that* keen; at the first instance of a threat to his existence, he takes flight. Thus, Abram dismisses the land promise made by Yahweh.

The next scene is the story of Abram's deceptive endeavor, all in the service of saving his own skin. The wife/sister-abduction stories in Gen 12, 20, and 26 have similar structures[42]:

	Genesis 12:10–20	Genesis 20:1–18	Genesis 26:1–17
Migration	To Egypt (12:10)	To Gerar (20:1)	To Gerar (26:1)
Situation	Famine (12:10)		Famine (26:1)
Description	"beautiful" (12:11)		"beautiful" (26:7)
Deception	Sarai, "sister" (12:13)	Sarah, "sister" (20:2a)	Rebekah, "sister (26:7)
Reason	Fear of death (12:13)	Fear of death (20:11)	Fear of death (26:7)
Ruler	Pharaoh	Abimelech	Abimelech
Abduction	Pharaoh takes Sarai (12:14–16)	Abimelech takes Sarah (20:2b)	
Deliverance	Lord afflicts Pharaoh (12:17)	Lord rebukes Abimelech (20:3–8)	
Confrontation	Patriarch rebuked (12:18–19)	Patriarch rebuked (20:9–13)	Patriarch rebuked (26:9–16)
Conclusion	Abram given wealth (12:16)	Abraham given wealth (20:14–16)	

There is a method to this pattern. The individual details in each structural element are consistently shared in two of the three episodes: Gen 12 and 26 have famines; Gen 12 and 20 have the same couple involved; Gen 20 and 26 are located in Gerar; Gen 12 and 26 mention the beauty of the wife; Gen 12 and 20 report her abduction; Gen 12 and 20 show the direct involvement of Yahweh in delivering the wife; Gen 12 and 20 have the ruler making the patriarch wealthy (in Gen 26 it is Yahweh who does so); Gen 12 and 26 show the patriarch departing the land. The only elements consistently seen across the three episodes is the patriarchs' fear—a lack of trust in God—the resulting "sister" deception, and their rebuke by the ruler involved, emphasizing the irony of God's men being instructed by pagans (see highlighted rows in the table above).[43]

In Egypt, we have Abram's first utterance recorded in the Bible: unfortunately it is one of deception and self-preservation. While Egypt held its dangers for a man

40. Waltke and Fredricks, *Genesis*, 212.

41. Mathews, *Genesis 11:27—50:26*, 122.

42. Modified from Garrett, *Rethinking Genesis*, 132.

43. See Waltke and Fredricks, *Genesis*, 211.

with a beautiful wife, if God had promised him descendants (12:2–3, 7), how could Abram possibly have been in danger of being killed before he had those promised descendants? In this episode and the one about the famine, one observes the recurring motif—the threat to the heir of the divine promise: either by a famine that could kill the patriarch or by the action of Pharaoh that could have him executed for his wife, not to mention the taking of Sarai into an Egyptian harem, potentially jeopardizing the generation of seed through the matriarch. Abram must have thought that either God was incapable of ensuring his promise, or his promises were empty: either he was powerless, or he was a liar. So the patriarch takes matters into his own hands.

Pointedly, the structure of this scene has as its center the abduction of Sarai and the intervention of Yahweh for her deliverance. Abram is nowhere to be seen in the center of the story: he is *not* the hero.[44]

> **A**   Descent of Abram and Sarai (12:10)
>   **B**   Abram instructs Sarai (12:11–13)
>   **C**   Pharaoh abducts Sarai; Yahweh intervenes (12:14–17)
>   **B'**   Pharaoh instructs Abram and his men (12:18–20)
> **A'**   Ascent of Abram (13:1)

That these wife/"sister" stories are negative depictions of the particular patriarch involved is also implied in the parallels with the story of the fall in Gen 2–3: food forms the backdrop (either plenty in Gen 2–3, or famine in Gen 12 and 26); the wife plays an important role; there is the subsequent questioning of the parties involved, admissions of guilt, and expulsion. Between Gen 2–3 and Gen 12, there are also several shared lexical parallels: "tell" (3:11, 13; 12:18); "know" (3:5; 12:11); "live" (3:20; 12:12); "good"/"well" (3:5, 6; 12:13, 16); "for . . . sake" (עֲבוּר, *'abur*, 3:17; 12:13, 16); "saw" and "took" (3:6; 12:15); and "sent" (3:23; 12:20). At the end of both these accounts, an aggrieved party utters the same words: "What is this you have done?" (3:13; 12:18).[45]

A number of parallels between the encounter of patriarch and Pharaoh and the encounter of Moses and Pharaoh further show Abram in a bad light: in one case Pharaoh is the good guy and Abram the bad; in the other Moses is the good guy and Pharaoh the bad.[46]

Similarities	Abram and Pharaoh	Moses/Children of Israel and Pharaoh
Famine	12:10	43:1; 47:4
Sojourn in Egypt	12:10	47:4
Killing of males	12:11–13	Exod 1:16
Bondage	12:14–15	Exod 1:11–14
Wealth	12:16	Exod 12:36
Plagues	12:17	Exod 7–11 (see 11:1)
"Take … go"	12:19	Exod 12:32
"Sent"	12:20	Exod 5:1; 7:16; 8:1, 2, 20, 21; 9:1, 13; 10:3, 4; 12:33

44. Table from Mathews, *Genesis 11:27–50:26*, 126.

45. Ibid., 123.

46. Table from Ross, *Creation and Blessing*, 173. With regard to "wealth" (see table), the narrator mentions that the famine was "severe" (כָּבֵד, *kaber*, 12:10), when Abram departed *for* Egypt. But when he departs *from* Egypt, he is very "rich" (also כָּבֵד, 13:2), ostensibly made so by the Pharaoh (12:16).

While most rabbinic commentators do their best to absolve Abram of blame in the deplorable situation with Sarai, Nachmanides is blunt:

> Know that Abraham our father unintentionally committed a great sin by bringing his righteous wife to a stumbling-block of sin on account of his fear for his life. He should have trusted that G-d would save him and his wife and all his belongings, for G-d surely has the power to help and to save. His leaving the Land, concerning which he had been commanded from the beginning, on account of the famine, was also a sin he committed, for in famine G-d would redeem him from death.[47]

Modern commentators are not particularly reticent either: Abram "practically throws his wife into another man's harem in order to save his skin."[48] Von Rad suggests that one can "recognize in the bearer of the promise himself the greatest enemy of the promise."[49] Indeed! It is quite likely that had Abram told the truth, the seemingly righteous Pharaoh would have left Sarai alone. But because he lied, the abduction occurred, and so did the violation of the matriarch.[50] Unlike in Gen 20 where it is expressly stated that Abimelech was not guilty of sexual congress with the matriarch (he did not "come near" [קרב, *qrb*] Sarai, 20:4), here, in Gen 12, the text is silent about what (might have) happened. It, however, is quite suggestive in the use of the same verb for Abram: 12:11 has Abram "coming near" (קרב) to enter Egypt, while the account, at the same time, makes no statement about Pharaoh's innocence. Indeed, the text may even be suggesting that "ultimately, Abram, and not the Pharaoh, is responsible for his wife's illicit sexual experience."[51]

Thus Abram's meretricious utterance was a grave error that could have had tragic consequences for the genetic line of the patriarch. But God intervened and set things right at the end. Abram had played the deceiver in the hope that "it may go well [יטב, *ytv*]" with him (12:13). It did, but not as he thought it would: in an ironic twist, after

47. *Commentary on the Torah: Genesis*, 173–74.

48. Exum, "Who's Afraid of 'The Endangered Ancestress'?" 95.

49. Von Rad, *Genesis*, 169.

50. The verb that commences 12:17 is נגע (*ng'*, "plague"), and the noun that describes what Yahweh brought down upon Pharaoh's household is also נגע: thus we read: "And Yahweh *plagued* Pharaoh and his house with great *plagues*." But the verb נגע can also mean "touch," and while there is no description of Pharaoh's sin, the utilization of this ambiguous verb in this account hints at what the Egyptian actually did. The ruler's confession in 12:19 that he "took" (לקח, *lqkh*) Sarai for his wife, after she had been "taken" (לקח) to his house (12:15), seems to support some violation of the matriarch. The combination "took her for/as wife" (12:19) suggests a sexual relationship: 11:29; 16:3; 25:1, 20; 30:9; Exod 6:20–25; and most of these texts proceed to discuss offspring, or lack thereof. In Gen 20:6, God observes that he had averted a sin by not permitting Abimelech to touch (נגע, *ng'*) Sarah (20:6). That God is *not* said to prevent Pharaoh from doing so here, but instead afflicts this ruler with נגע, suggests that the Egyptian did, indeed, "touch" Sarai in Gen 12. Interestingly, punishments are often "word for word" in Scripture: Jer 26:3 ("evil" for "evil"); 2 Sam 12:9–10 ("sword" for "sword"); Gen 3:6, 19 ("eat" for "eat"). Thus, when Pharaoh is punished with נגע (12:17), it could likely indicate his crime as being נגע, too. The delicate situation of the gross violation of a matriarch likely prompted the narrator to be suggestive rather than explicit. See Peleg, "Was the Ancestress of Israel in Danger?" 202, 205.

51. Gordis, "Lies, Wives and Sisters," 355.

God took unilateral action, Pharaoh "treated Abram well" (יטב, 12:16).[52] No credit to Abram, though.

The questioning by the indignant Pharaoh is sharp and to the point: "What is this you have done . . .? Why did you not tell . . .? Why did you say . . .?" This is a scandalized ruler questioning his deceiver; in fact, the former has the upper moral card and the last word in this discourse, to which Abram gives no answer and no excuse, tacitly admitting his guilt. The brusque accusatory questions are followed by five words, literally: "Now, here, your-wife, take, go" (12:19). The divine promise-laden command to "go" (12:1) had now become a shameful expulsion at the hands of a pagan ruler (also with "go," 12:19). In silence and disrepute, Abram slinks away.

While the seed promise is in danger here because of Abram's duplicity, what is even more striking is the fact that Pharaoh and his house were afflicted with "great plagues" (12:17). Rather ironic, considering that Abram was supposed to be the agent of blessing for the nations. Instead, Egypt (as represented by its ruler and his house) is plagued! The one who was called to be a blessing and who, God promised, would be a blessing to all the families of the earth (12:2–3) seemed to have proved God wrong by being an agent (howbeit unwittingly) of the plaguing of a nation (12:17). His lack of faith in God's ability to provide and his exertions to take charge of his own security were entirely misplaced. Without relying upon God totally, he would neither be blessed, nor would he become a blessing to others. Thus, Abram disregards the promise of blessing.

In sum, we see here the divine promise of land, seed, and blessing given to Abram. And as soon as the promise is offered, Abram proceeds to act without faith in it. He takes Lot along, disbelieving the promise of seed. He absconds from Canaan to Egypt, dismissing the promise of land. And he manages to get the royal house of Egypt afflicted with plagues, disregarding the promise that he would be a blessing to the nations. All because of his lack of faith. On the other hand, faithful obedience involves sacrifice, and a relinquishing of human stratagems in favor of an unshakeable trust in God's workings.

SERMON FOCUS AND OUTLINES

THEOLOGICAL FOCUS OF PERICOPE 7 FOR PREACHING

7   God's blessings are fulfilled through obedience that sacrifices and that relinquishes human contrivances in favor of an unshakeable trust in God (11:27–12:20).

The corollary of this theological focus is that lack of faith-filled obedience can stand in the way of God's purposes, promises, and blessings. Of course, in the long scheme of things, God's sovereign plan to bless can never be thwarted. But promised blessings

---

52. There is a strange ordering of Pharaoh's gifts to Abram, with male and female servants between "sheep and oxen and donkeys" and "female donkeys and camels" (12:16). One wonders if the servants were deliberately inserted in this odd place to draw attention to that item; especially considering that a female Egyptian servant turns to be yet another threat to the heir of Abram and Sarai, this is entirely possible.

may take another pathway, avoiding the faithless and disobedient. So the question is: Do we want to be participants in God's program, experiencing for ourselves his blessings, and being agents of that blessing to others? God will certainly bless mankind, his creation, but he could as certainly bypass those who refuse to trust in his plans and purposes, who instead seek human recourse to bring about "blessings" for themselves, as Abram did in this pericope.

Without a doubt, there is a *biblical* theology thread that may be followed, tracing the Israelites' appropriation of land, seed, and blessing, the latter extending to all humanity, through Abraham's greatest descendant, the Lord Jesus Christ. But for preaching purposes, considering *pericopal* theology, it is best to stick with the concept of blessing of this one man, the imperative for him to be a blessing, with the consequence of others being blessed.[53] In other words, what the narrator is *doing* with what he is saying is calling upon readers to identify themselves with the patriarch. It is not only Abram who may be blessed or who might be the agent of blessing, but every child of God (though it is granted that the specific blessings to Abram are different as are blessings to each believer; these differential blessings are the sovereign acts of God). The conditions of such blessing, and of its mediation to others, are enumerated in this pericope.[54]

Possible Preaching Outlines for Pericope 7

I. Faithful Obedience Promotes God's Blessings
    God's focus upon blessing humanity resumes after the sin of Babel (11:27–12:3)
    Divine blessing is conditioned upon faithful obedience (12:1–3)
    Abram's obedience in his "going," and scoping out the land (12:4–9)
    Move-to-Relevance: God's desire is always to bless mankind

II. Faithless Disobedience Prevents God's Blessings
    Abram takes Lot, disbelieving the promise of seed (12:5)
    Abram escapes to Egypt, disregarding the promise of land (12:10)
    Abram deceives Pharaoh, bringing plagues upon his house (12:11–20)
    Move-to-Relevance: How our disobedience and lack of trust can stand in the way of experiencing divine blessing

III. *Be blessed by faithful obedience!*
    How we can specifically demonstrate faithful obedience, thus experiencing and being an agent of divine blessing Specifically, our sacrifice and/or the restraint of our manipulative

53. For this entity of pericopal theology, as opposed to biblical and systematic theology, see Introduction to this work, and also Kuruvilla, *Privilege the Text!* 101–18.

54. I want to emphasize that pericopal theology as I am suggesting here is valid primarily for preaching purposes. The use of Scripture for other ecclesial enterprises may, and should, engage biblical and systematic theology. May I also add briefly a word on how I see preaching? It is an activity in the context of the worship of the children of God, i.e., preaching is for the benefit of those who have *already* placed their trust in the Lord Jesus Christ as their only God and Savior from sin. Preaching is thus essentially an instrument of the Holy Spirit for sanctification. So what is being discussed in this pericope is not the blessing of salvation (justification) that is entirely free and unconditioned, given graciously to all who believe the Good News of Jesus Christ and his atoning work. But as Jude exhorted (Jude 20), the reception and experience of subsequent blessings from the hand of God *are* conditioned—"keep yourselves in the love of God." For more on this aspect of the homiletical endeavor, see Kuruvilla, *Privilege the Text!* 252–58.

tendencies

Without changing many of the sub-points, a different emphasis may be generated with the image of a race that is half-run by Abram (and Terah who decided to settle in Haran, 11:31). God calls us, on the other hand, to see it through, to finish well.

I.   Starting well

      God's focus upon blessing humanity resumes after the sin of Babel (11:27–12:3)

      Divine blessing is conditioned upon faithful obedience (12:1–3)

      Abram's obedience in his "going" and scoping out the land (12:4–9)

II. Stopping short

      Abram takes Lot, disbelieving the promise of seed (12:5)

      Abram escapes to Egypt, disregarding the promise of land (12:10)

      Abram deceives Pharaoh, bringing plagues upon his house (12:11–20)

      Move-to-Relevance: How disobedience and lack of trust can stand in the way of experiencing divine blessing

III. Seeing through

      Unlike Abram's incomplete trust/obedience (and unlike Terah, 11:31), God calls us to finish strongly

      How we can specifically demonstrate faithful obedience, thus experiencing and being an agent of divine blessing

      Specifically, our sacrifice and/or the restraint of our manipulative tendencies

PERICOPE 8

Waiting for God to Work

Genesis 13:1–14:24

[Separation of Abram and Lot; Abram's Military Victory and Rescue of Lot]

REVIEW, SUMMARY, PREVIEW

Review of Pericope 7: Genesis 11:27–12:20 commences the Abraham Story. After the depressing end of the Primeval History, a new turn is taken: Abram is called, and blessings are promised. While there are hints that the patriarch is not completely obedient or faithful, God's promise of blessing remains sure.

Summary of Pericope 8: Abram returns to the Promised Land from Egypt, to where God is, and where his blessing will be experienced—a correction of the patriarch's earlier failures, that includes separation from Lot. The latter makes a self-gratifying and God-denying choice of location for dwelling, while Abram relies on God to provide for his needs. This faithfulness is followed by an affirmation (and even an intensification) of the divine promises to Abram. In the military encounter that follows, Abram again trusts God's provision without taking matters into his own hands, and he is blessed further. Aligning oneself with God's demands yields blessing.

Preview of Pericope 9: In the next pericope (Gen 15:1–16:16), Abram's faith is rewarded with an extended revelation from God, further expanding his earlier promises. Despite the patriarch's doubt as he demonstrates a less-than-mature faith, Abram is credited for his trust. Sarai's manipulation, another expression of immature faith, creates domestic chaos.

8. *Genesis 13:1–14:24*

THEOLOGICAL FOCUS OF PERICOPE 8

8   Correction of faithless behavior, and exercise of faithful obedience to God's demands, without taking matters into one's own hands, but rather trusting in God's sovereign timing to keep his promises, results in divine blessing (13:1–14:24).

8.1   Correction of faithless behavior, and exercise of faithful obedience to God's demand, relying upon him without choosing for oneself, returns one to the sphere of divine blessing (13:1–18).

    8.1.1   *Correction of faithless behavior is necessary for one's return to the sphere of divine blessing.*

    8.1.2   *Relying upon God and trusting his sovereignty without choosing for oneself, keeps one in the sphere of blessing.*

    8.1.3   *Full, faithful obedience to the demand of God restores one to God's blessing.*

8.2   Choosing according to the will of God, without taking matters into one's own hands but rather trusting God's sovereign timing to keep his promises, is a mark of faith, and results in divine blessing (14:1–24).

    8.2.1   *Choosing according to the will of God, without taking matters into one's own hands, is a mark of faith.*

    8.2.2   *Trusting God's sovereign timing to keep his promises, results in divine blessing.*

OVERVIEW

Issues regarding land show up frequently in Gen 13 and 14: "went up from Egypt to the Negev" (13:1); "he journeyed from place to place from the Negev as far as Bethel, to the place . . . between Bethel and Ai, to the place of the altar" (13:3–4); "and the land could not support them" (13:6); "the Canaanite and the Perizzite were dwelling in the land" (13:7); "'Is not the whole land before you?'" (13:9); "And Lot . . . saw all the valley of the Jordan . . . like the garden of Yahweh, like the land of Egypt" (13:10); "And Lot chose for himself all the valley of the Jordan" (13:11); "Abram settled in the land of Canaan" (13:12); "'Now lift up your eyes and look from the place where you are . . . for all the land which you see, I will give to you'" (13:14–15); "Arise, walk in the land'" (13:17); and "Abram moved his tent and came and dwelt by the oaks of Mamre, which are in Hebron" (13:18).[1] Then there are the long drawn out descriptions of kings and their parcels of land in 14:1–9, their battles, and Abram's recovery of looted property and people in the rest of Gen 14. It would not be amiss to say that Abram and the land form a central theme of Gen 13–14.

But there are tensions: For one, the Canaanites and Perizzites were dwelling in the Promised Land (1:7); for another, Abram is having to go far away from where Lot chose to dwell, without selfishly seeking the best for himself (13:9). Yet, at the conclusion of a war in Gen 14, quite remarkably, Abram, the undisputed victor of the battle,

---

1. Rickett, "Rethinking the Place," 33–34. The two episodes of this pericope, Gen 13 and Gen 14, are connected with the presence of Lot in each, and with the "oaks of Mamre" showing up in both (13:18; 14:13; 14:24 also has "Mamre").

again refuses anything for himself (14:22–24), when he could quite possibly have appropriated some territory. How is he going to get what God has promised, and when?

All these tensions notwithstanding, God's sovereign actions appear to be moving Abram in the right direction: he "settles" in the land of Canaan (13:12), God reaffirms his promise regarding the land (13:14–17), and Abram, in his movements in the land, seems to have ceremonially claimed it through his symbolic walking (13:17–18; see below). Moreover, Abram himself appears to be trusting in God's sovereign movements, unwilling as he is in both episodes of this pericope to exercise his own power to gain land for himself.

8.1 Genesis 13:1–18

THEOLOGICAL FOCUS 8.1

8.1 Correction of faithless behavior and exercise of faithful obedience to God's demand, relying upon him without choosing for oneself, returns one to the sphere of divine blessing (13:1–18).

  8.1.1 *Correction of faithless behavior is necessary for one's return to the sphere of divine blessing.*

  8.1.2 *Relying upon God and trusting his sovereignty, without choosing for oneself, keeps one in the sphere of blessing.*

  8.1.3 *Full, faithful obedience to the demand of God restores one to God's blessing.*

NOTES 8.1

8.1.1 Correction of faithless behavior is necessary for one's return to the sphere of divine blessing.

There is a clear sense in which Abram's departure from Egypt is a positive event, his return to the sphere of divine blessing, for there are allusions to the exodus of the Israelites from that land—an altogether positive event: Abram "goes up from Egypt" (13:1; and Exod 17:3; Num 20:5; 32:11; etc.); he is enriched in Egypt with silver and gold (Gen 13:2; and Exod 3:22; 11:2–3; 12:35–36); the patriarch moves in stages as he departs Egypt (Gen 13:3; and Exod 17:1[2]); the land to which he goes is occupied by Canaanites and Perizzites (Gen 13:7 and Exod 3:8, 17; 33:2; 34:11); Abram "settles" in Canaan (Gen 13:12 and Num 33:53; 35:34); and he builds an altar there (Gen 13:18 and Exod 17:15).[3]

There was irony in the squabbles for land between Abram's and Lot's people (13:5–7)—who was the true owner of the land? Were the Canaanites and Perizzites who dwelt in that land (13:7) the true owners? As a matter of fact, it is Yahweh who is the true owner, and in whose power it is to dispose of that land to whomever he

---

2. The verb-noun combinations in both give the sense of staged travel: Gen 13:3—הלך, *hlk*, and מסע, *mss'* ("went on his journeys"); Exod 17:1—נסע, *ns'*, and מסע ("they journeyed in stages").

3. Rickett, "Rethinking the Place," 38.

chooses (13:15). Indeed, the land that Abram returns to is not only the Promised Land but, as asserted in Num 35:34, it is also the land in which Yahweh himself dwells. Quite in agreement with that fact, Abram's altar-building enterprises occur only in Canaan (12:6, 7; 13:18). Thus "Abraham's move may be said to have more to do with theology than geography. He is to move to where God is and where God can make him a blessing. God's promise to Abraham, then, hinges on whether or not Abraham will get to where God is."[4]

Abram's return to the land of promise is marked by what appears to be a change of heart, after his deceptive and dangerous transactions in Egypt. He treks to the altar he had built (12:8) and calls upon Yahweh (13:3–4). Genesis 13 thereby commences and concludes with an altar-based communion between deity and patriarch (13:3–4, 14–17), just as it both begins and ends with a statement of travel (13:1–4 and 13:18). Thus, the theology of land is prominent in Gen 12–13, along with an emphasis on altars and the Abram's devotion to God.[5]

> A   Abraham building an altar at Bethel with Lot (13:1–7)
>   B   Abraham's speech: offer of the land (13:8–9)
>   C   Lot's choice of Sodom (13:10–13)
>   B'   Yahweh's speech: offer of the land (13:14–17)
> A'   Abraham building an altar at Hebron alone (13:18)

Thus, as noted, Gen 13 begins and ends with a reference to an "altar," both built by Abram unto Yahweh. "In Egypt, when Abraham feared for his life and doubted God's promises, there were no altars. In this scene, the altars signify Abraham's return to faith and his proclamation of claiming the land in the name of God. The narrator underscores Abraham's return to the place of faith and worship"; this was a correction, a return to God, and a rejection of his faithless behavior exhibited earlier in Gen 12, in the decamping to Egypt and in the deception of Pharaoh.[6] Twice readers are told that Abraham is retracing his steps—"the *place, there* where he pitched his tent at the beginning" and "the *place* of the altar *there*, which he had made formerly" (13:3–4). This was meant to be seen as a return to the spot where he should have been all along. Abram's return to the locus of blessing is a metaphor for the believer's return to the sphere of divine blessing by a correction of faithless behavior.

With regard to Lot, as well, some "corrections" needed to be made by Abram. One notices that in 12:5, the caravan had departed Haran with "*their* possessions that *they* had acquired"; it is also "they" who set out and "they" who come to the land of Canaan). However, in 13:1, it is *Abram* who "goes up" from Egypt with "all that belonged to *him*." While Abram and Lot were a unified force in Gen 12, it might be that after the incidents of Gen 12, Abram was coming to realize that Lot was not the one God had intended to be his heir. Perhaps this was a case of Abram starting over, separating from his relatives as he had originally been called by God to do (12:1). The epi-

---

4. Ibid., 39.

5. Table from Waltke and Fredricks, *Genesis*, 218.

6. Ibid., 219.

sode of Gen 13 certainly ends with Abram realizing the necessity of full obedience to God's demand, without which one keeps oneself outside the sphere of divine blessing. A reversal of sorts is thus depicted in the account.[7]

Lot and Canaanites (12:5–6)
Altar to Yahweh (12:7)
tent between Bethel and Ai (+ altar) (12:8)
toward the Negev (12:9)

went up from Egypt to the Negev (13:1)
tent between Bethel and Ai (13:3)
Altar to Yahweh (13:4)
Lot and Canaanites (13:5–7)

Genesis 13, for Abram, was both historically and literarily a reversal of direction, a correction of faithless behavior, a return to square one, back into the land. And there, in the Promised Land, one more problem needed to be taken care of—Lot.

8.1.2 *Relying upon God and trusting his sovereignty, without choosing for oneself, keeps one in the sphere of blessing.*

Unlike Abram who "settles" in the land of Canaan, Lot chooses to "settle" in the place of wicked men and sinners (13:12–13). The first builds an altar "before/to Yahweh" (13:18), the second dwells with those who are wicked and sinners "before/to Yahweh" (13:13). Lot did not choose the ארץ, *'rts*—the unique descriptor of the Promised Land—but opted to go with the "valley" (ככר, *kkr*, 13:9–10).[8] When Abram suggested that "all the land" (כָּל־הָאָרֶץ, *kal-ha'arets*) was before him, Lot lifted up his eyes but saw only "all the valley" (כָּל־כִּכַּר, *kal-kikkar*) that was "well-watered."[9] Lot walked by sight: he lifted up his eyes and saw. One was told to lift up his eyes (13:14); the other did it himself. One waited for God to give it; the other took it for himself.

Lot is making some significantly bad choices here. He sees the valley of the Jordan as the "garden of Yahweh"—not a good perspective on his part, to "reenter" a place from which mankind had been expelled.[10] Moreover, he travels eastward (13:10): thus far in Genesis, east has not been an auspicious direction in which to move—the route of banishment of Adam and Eve (3:24) and Cain (4:16).[11] And Lot settles in the "valley" (ככר, 13:11, 12), as do a people doomed for disaster in Gen 11:2 (there, "valley" was בקעה, *bq'h*). The account of Lot's choice also has several allusions to two earlier

---

7. Rickett, "Rethinking the Place," 46, 49. Table below from McEvenue, "Reading Genesis," 138.

8. Lot is never noted as settling in the "land," though he chooses a place that is *like* the "land" of Egypt (13:10).

9. Ironically, while Lot *saw* "all the valley" as idyllic (13:10), later Abraham would *see* "all the land of the valley" burning (19:28).

10. In the eyes of the narrator, the "valley of Jordan" is outside the boundaries of the land of Canaan. See Larry R. Helyer, "The Separation of Abram and Lot," 77–80.

11. Later, Abraham dispatches his sons by Keturah to the east "away from his son Isaac" (25:6); and Jacob escapes to the east after deceiving his father and brother (29:1).

(and fatefully wrong) choices in Genesis—that of Eve (Gen 2–3) and that of the "sons of God" (Gen 6): "eyes" (13:10 and 3:6–7); "saw" (13:10 and 3:6; 6:2); "water" (13:10 and 2:6, 10); "destroy" (13:10 and 6:13, 17); "garden" (13:10 and 2:8–10; 3:1–3; etc.); "go in" (13:10 and 6:4); "choose" (13:11 and 6:2); "all" (13:11 and 6:2).[12] Lot sees as far as Zoar (13:10). And that's where he'll end up—in disaster (19:22, 23, 30). What you see, you want. Where you look, you go. In this case, where he looked and what he saw were outside God's will.

Each time Lot is said to be enthused with the fertile areas of the valley of Jordan—so much so, that he settles there (13:10a, 11–12)—the narrator makes a cutting comment about the wickedness and fate of Sodom and Gomorrah (13:10b, 13). "Wicked/evil" (13:13) also described the deeds of those who were blotted out in the flood (6:5; 8:21), but "great sinners" (13:13) is unique for this text and, needless to say, ominous in tone. With that proleptic note, the narrator reminds us that Sodom and Gomorrah were (to be) destroyed by Yahweh, hinting at the poor choice being made by Lot. Thus Abram and Lot are spatially separated (13:11), but even more, morally separated: one settles in the land Yahweh owns and in which Yahweh dwells; the other settles in the land of the wicked and sinful.[13] The silence of Lot in this pericope (and in the previous one) also hints at what the narrator thinks of Lot and his presence in Abram's company.

This was a self-gratifying, God-denying choice on the part of Lot. If he had been paying attention to the divine word that came to his uncle in Gen 12, he might have thought twice about expatriating himself from the latter's company. For, wherever Lot appears in this saga, there is always a threat or a struggle and a subsequent deliverance by Abram (and Yahweh).

	Genesis 13:1–18	Genesis 14:1–24	Genesis 18:1–19:38
Threat to Lot	Strife (13:1–7)	War (14:1–11)	Annihilation (18:17–21)
Deliverance of Lot	By Abram (13:8–13)	By Abram/Yahweh (14:13–16, 20)	By Abraham/Yahweh (18:22–19:29)

On either side of the key chapters instituting the Abrahamic covenant (Gen 15–17) are episodes with Lot stuck in rather unsavory situations: strife and separation from his uncle (Gen 13); taken as a prisoner-of-war (Gen 14); and fleeing from his burning hometown, losing his wife, and fathering children by his daughters (Gen 18–19).[14] In consonance with Gen 12:3, Lot, who leaves the protective fold of the blessed patriarch, will lose the blessing that was his by virtue of his proximity and relationship with

---

12. Mathews, *Genesis 11:27–50:26*, 136.

13. That the rejection of Lot as a potential heir is implied in these topological displacements is substantiated by the similar removal of Ishmael and of Abraham's children by Keturah from consideration for the same status, when they are expelled from the household of the patriarch (21:10, 20–21; 25:6, 18) (see ibid., 131). So also the contrasts between the locations of Isaac and Ishmael (25:11, 18 and 21:21), and between those of Jacob and Esau (37:1 and 36:8–9, 40).

14. Hamilton, *Genesis: Chapters 1–17*, 398.

Abram, as will be evident in Gen 14 and later, in Gen 18–19. This was effectively Lot's self-removal from the sphere of divine blessing by his poorly conceived choices.

There are considerable conceptual parallels between 13:14–18 and 13:9–13, between the actions of nephew and those of uncle.

	13:9–13	13:14–18
Separation	13:9, 11	13:14
Directions (right/left, north/east/south/west and length/breadth)	13:9	13:14, 17
Lifting up eyes	13:10	13:14
Looking	13:10	13:14
All the valley/land	13:10–11	13:15
Moving tents	13:12	13:18

Both Abram and Lot lift up their eyes, both look, both see the whole land, both are offered the land of their choice, and both move. But the contrast is between the one's faithfulness as he chose by faith what God wanted (see below on Gen 14 for the underscoring of Abram's faith-filled choice), and the other's foolishness as he chose by sight and what *he* wanted. One chooses a land fated to be destroyed by Yahweh; the other is assured that the land God gives him would belong perpetually to him and his descendants. It is only a reliance upon God and his sovereignty (as exercised by Abram), without choosing for oneself (as Lot did), that keeps one in the sphere of blessing.

8.1.3 Full, faithful obedience to the demand of God restores one to God's blessing.

Abram's intervention in the conflict between his and Lot's herdsmen concludes with the plea, "Men, brothers [are] we" (13:8). While the fraternity may evidence a desire to be conciliatory, it rather unwittingly makes Lot an equal to Abram. The patriarch's subsequent offer proves this amicable attitude of his—he offers Lot any portion of all the land that he might choose: he wants to share the Promised Land with Lot! Quite magnanimous on his part, he seems to be considering Lot the seed of choice. Abram knows that the land of Canaan will go to his descendants (12:1–3, 7); that he offers this promised parcel to Lot implies that he was priming his nephew to be his descendant. Thus it appears that Gen 13 is not entirely about land, but also about Abram's misperception of seed: Lot, whom he probably thought would be the chosen descendant, turns out to act unlike one worthy to be in that position. In fact, by Lot's self-gratifying choice to dwell *outside* Canaan, he thereby removes himself from the reckoning as Abram's seed and potential heir.[15]

The account notes the moving of Lot's tents and the moving of Abram's tents (both אהל, *'hl*, 13:12, 18). The only time God speaks to Abram in this pericope is *after*

---

15. Abram's interest in prospering and saving Lot in Gen 14, besides the family ties, may also be related to his continued misconception of his nephew as the descendant of promise. There, in Gen 14, Lot has a second chance to get back into the household of his uncle after he is rescued from his captors, but the king of Sodom exerts his "ownership rights" over the people, and Lot apparently returns to Sodom, for that is where we see him next in Gen 18–19. Clearly, Lot is not the "seed" of Abram God had in mind.

Lot and Abram have parted ways. In a sense, then, 13:14 fulfills 12:1, the call for Abram's separation from his relatives. And for the first time, God affirms that "*all* the land" would be Abram's and his descendants' forever. This is significant: only full, faithful obedience (or return thereunto) will retain the blessings of God's promises.

| **12:7** | this land | I will give | | to your descendants |
| **13:15** | *all* the land that you see | I will give | *to you* and | to your descendants *forever* |

Clearly, the promises have increased in their scope—and narrowed through this particular man, Abram. The boundaries of the land are a bit more defined, the land will certainly be given to Abram (not Lot), and to his descendants (implying direct "seed" of Abram), and that forever. Furthermore, the cluster of descendants will be as innumerable "as the dust of the earth" (13:16). That this is asserted after the departure of Lot is telling. "Abram's last link with his father's house is now severed, and a fresh stage in his life begins."[16] What should have happened in Gen 12 is finally happening in Gen 13 as Abram moves further towards full obedience and alignment to the will of God. God's reaffirmation of his promise happens only at that particular juncture. In fact, the final affirmation of the divine promise to Abraham would be provided only after yet another drastic separation, that from his only son, Isaac (22:15–18).

God's reaffirmation of the land promise to Abram and his descendants is prefixed with the particle נא (*nʾ*, 13:14). Though it occurs 60 times in Genesis, only four times in the OT does it come from God as he addresses a human: 13:14; 15:5; 22:2; and Exod 11:2. "In each of these four passages God asks somebody to do something that transcends human comprehension."[17] Coming immediately after Lot's withdrawal, and deliberately using words in 13:14 that were employed in the previous scene ("separate," "lift up your eyes," "look"—all used in 13:9–11; not to mention God's employing the four points of the compass in parallel to Abraham's invitation to Lot to go right or left, 13:9), it seems as if God is issuing a corrective, pointedly stressing that the promise was for the patriarch and his descendants, and not through the one who had broken away and separated himself.

And then, Abram is commanded to take symbolic possession of the land by traversing its length and breadth (13:17).[18] His faith in Yahweh as he returns to full obedience was restoring him to the sphere of divine blessing.

---

16. Sarna, *Genesis*, 100.

17. Hamilton, *Genesis: Chapters 1–17*, 394.

18. So *Tg. Ps.-J.* has for Gen 13:17: "Arise, journey in the land, and make occupation of it in length and breadth; for to thee will I give it." Also see Deut 11:24; Josh 1:3.

8.2 *Genesis 14:1–24*

> **THEOLOGICAL FOCUS 8.2**
>
> 8.2   Choosing according to the will of God, without taking matters into one's own hands but rather trusting God's sovereign timing to keep his promises, is a mark of faith, and results in divine blessing (14:1–24).
>
> > 8.2.1   *Choosing according to the will of God, without taking matters into one's own hands, is a mark of faith.*
> >
> > 8.2.2   *Trusting God's sovereign timing to keep his promises, results in divine blessing.*

NOTES 8.2

Chapter 14 is unique in that it is the only account in Genesis of a military campaign with a named array of kings involved; indeed 14:2 has the first instance of "battle" in the Bible. The narrative takes its own time to unfold, listing the opponents in a chiastic manner.[19]

Chedorlaomer and allies (14:1)

Sodom and allies (14:2)

Sodom and allies (14:8)

Chedorlaomer and allies (14:9)

In fact, Abram and Lot appear only halfway through the story (14:12). Neither is there any mention of God until the "priest of the God Most High" appears on the scene (14:18). Even then, there are only a few references to God in the blessing of Melchizedek and in Abram's acknowledgement of divine providence (14:19–20, 22). In fact this is the only chapter in the Abraham Story from Gen 12 through Gen 22 that contains no divine announcement. Despite the absence of a divine voice, Abram seems to be hearing Yahweh quite clearly.

8.2.1 *Choosing according to the will of God, without taking matters into one's own hands, is a mark of faith.*

The word "king" (מלך, *mlk*) echoes twenty-eight times in Genesis 14 (including the instances of its occurrences in the name "Melchizedek").

> A host of royal players make up this scene: five kings of Canaan, four kings of Mesopotamia, Abraham, Melchizedek the priest-king, and implicitly the Lord. Israel's God, Yahweh, however stands above all as King of kings. . . . . . By repeating *king*, precisely naming the kings and their countries from all over the Fertile Crescent and beyond, and by spreading the battles of this war all over Transjordan and south Palestine, the narrator magnifies the greatness of his

---

19. Wenham, *Genesis 1–15*, 304. There is even comedy in this text with the ridiculous picture of the escaping kings of Sodom and Gomorrah falling into holes, and then climbing up hills in their desperation (14:10)!

hero, Abraham. On earth, God's faithful warrior, though lacking the title *king,* is in fact a greater king.[20]

The two battles won by Chedorlaomer (and his allies, the Northern kings), against the kings of Transjordan and the South (14:5–7, among whom were the Rephaim, Zumim, and Emim, people of gigantic stature: Deut 2:10–12, 20–23), and against the eastern kings (14:1–4, 8–12), underscore the might of Chedorlaomer's coalition and, thereby, emphasize the magnitude of Abram's victory over them, making it all the more impressive (14:13–16). The surprising turn of events is the mustering of an army by a nomadic shepherd (his 318 trained men plus the men with Aner, Eshcol, and Mamre, 14:14, 24[21]), and their defeat of this coalition of four kings under Chedorlaomer (14:1, 9) which had itself made short shrift of that other alliance of five kings (14:2, 8), as well as trounced an assortment of oversized peoples (14:5–7). Abram's triumph is thus quite remarkable, to say the least. He completely reverses the state of loss inflicted by Chedorlaomer and his party: theirs was a taking, but Abram's was a retrieving of what had been taken.

	14:11	14:12
Chedorlaomer & company	"took" "all goods"	"took" Lot + "goods"

	14:16a	14:16b
Abram & company	"retrieved" "all goods"	"retrieved" Lot + "goods"

But even beyond the patriarch's military might, the emphasis on the domains of these regents returns the focus upon land and on how Abram would inherit it. Would it be by the might of an army? Though Chedorlaomer and his allies "took" (14:11, 12), and though the king of Sodom later advises Abram to "take" (14:21), Abram absolutely refuses, except to "take" what he needed as provisions and wages for his own military allies (14:24). The recommendation to appropriate "goods" (14:21) is met with rebuke: not a thread nor a sandal thong or anything would Abram take, he swears, invoking Yahweh, lest he be considered to have been enriched by man (14:21–23). After the defeat of the powerful alliance of Chedorlaomer, it would have been easy enough for Abram to declare himself ruler and establish a kingdom for himself. As the liberator and hero of the peoples, he could surely have won their allegiance and become, at least, the leader of an oligarchy of Canaanite city-states. He, however, pointedly refuses the temptation. After all, none of the kings' domains were part of Canaan, and Canaan was what God had promised him. Genesis 10:19 mentions the lands of four of the five kings in 14:2, but 13:12 establishes those areas as being outside Canaan. One would suppose that the members of the other alliance of the Transjordan (14:1) were also from beyond Canaan. It is explicitly noted in 14:14 that Abram chases these armies as

---

20. Waltke and Fredricks, *Genesis,* 226.

21. Wenham suggests that if Abram had 318 men "born in his house" (14:14), the total number of his household must have been well over a thousand (*Genesis 1–15,* 314). How many did he bring with him when he was asked, in Gen 12, to leave everyone (and everything)?

far as Dan, i.e., out of Canaan. For Canaan, he would wait; and in God he would trust, to give him that land. This, then, was a test: Would Abram fudge on the promises of God, assuming that any land was as good as Canaan? Would he jump at the chance to help God along and become the liege of the areas and peoples he had delivered from captivity? Would he assume that Yahweh's help in his military victory was an indication that he ought to grab with gusto what he can when he can?

Abram's refusal to take land when he easily could have, seems to suggest he had learnt something from the previous episode of this pericope, Gen 13. It appears that the patriarch's faith in God's promise is in a crescendo, a mezzo forte here, a forte in 15:6, and a fortissimo in 22:12. In fact, in his counter to the king of Sodom, Abram explicitly references Melchizedek's speech: "God Most High, Creator [from קָנָה, *qnh*] of heaven and earth" (14:22; from 14:19).[22] While he would not take anything, Abram willingly gave—first a tenth to Melchizedek and then deserved portions to his allies (14:20, 24).

> Melchizedek is primarily an example of a non-Jew who recognizes God's hand at work in Israel: like Abimelech (21:22), Rahab (Josh 2:11), Ruth (1:16), or Naaman (2 Kgs 5:15). Similarly, he may be seen as a forerunner of the Magi (Matt 2:1–12), centurions (Matt 8:5–13; Mark 15:39; Acts 10), or the Syro-Phoenician woman (Mark 7:26–30), let alone the multitude of Gentile converts mentioned in Acts. They are those who have discovered that in Abram all the families of the earth find blessing.[23]

Melchizedek thus becomes the first foreigner to be blessed by Abram, fulfilling 12:3. Instead of seeking to extend his holdings outside Canaan, Abram thsu pointedly aligns himself with Salem, by accepting the offer of its king, Melchizedek, by giving him a tithe, and by echoing his words.[24] Indeed, it might well be that what Abram does here is construed as a sacrifice. "I have sworn" in 14:22 is literally "I have raised" (רוּם, *rum*). The combination of this word with "tithe" shows up again in Num 18:24 (רוּם = "offer/sacrifice"). That a "sacrifice" is made before a priest is quite appropriate, of course![25] In all this, the patriarch demonstrates his faith in God, as he refuses to take matters into his own hands.

8.2.2 Trusting God's sovereign timing to keep his promises, results in divine blessing.

The aftermath of the battle deals with kings who have symbolic names ("Salem," and "Sodom," 14:18, 21), refers to Abram's victory (14:20, 21), and implicitly acknowledges his prowess (14:18–20, 21). Key words/phrases, "God Most High," and derivatives of

---

22. While קָנָה may mean "to possess," Ugaritic roots indicate that this is only one of its root meanings, the other being "to create" (see Gen 4:1 and, perhaps, Deut 32:6). Juxtaposed to "heavens and earth," "Creator" is a better translation than "possessor" (see Ps 115:15; 121:2; 124:8; 134:3). Moreover, the LXX has ὃς ἔκτισεν, *hos ektisen*, "Creator."

23. Wenham, *Genesis 1–15*, 322.

24. However, while Melchizedek identifies "God Most High," only Abram further specifies this deity as "Yahweh" (14:19–20, 22).

25. Hepner, "The Sacrifices in the Covenant," 46.

"bless" and "take," each occur thrice in 14:17–24. "Salem" is likely to be identical to Jebusite old Jerusalem. In Josh 10:1, its king is named Adonizedek (אֲדֹנִי־צֶ֫דֶק, *'adonitsedeq*), and one of David's priests was Zadok (צָדוֹק, *tsadoq*, 2 Sam 8:17)—both names related to Melchizedek (מַלְכִּי־צֶ֫דֶק, *malki-tsedeq*, Gen 14:18). Psalm 110 equates the king of Zion with Melchizedek, king of Salem (Ps 76:2 has Zion and Salem in an equivalent parallelism), and Jerusalem/Zion is frequently linked with צדק (*tsdq*, "righteousness"): Isa 1:21, 26; 33:5; 46:13; 61:3; Jer 33:16; etc.[26] All this to say that Melchizedek, the king of Salem, was the agent of divine action in this pericope, the one who names "God Most High," an appropriate foil for the king of Sodom, the one whose name bore the syllables of evil.[27]

Melchizedek's role as a foil for the king of Sodom perhaps explains the abruptness of the entry of the former into the story: one is associated with deity ("priest of God Most High) and the other is the regent of a wicked and sinful nation (13:13); one "brings out" (יצא, *yts'*, 14:18) bread and wine in a gesture of peace, the other "goes out" (יצא, 14:8) to make war—perhaps his "going out" later (יצא), in 14:17, was not all that peaceful either; one is generous, the other is grudging—he comes empty handed and has no words of gratitude for his deliverance; one brings food for the patriarch, the other asks for spoils from him; the first word of one is "blessed" (14:18), the first word of the other is "give" (14:21). In fact, the king of Sodom can only utter six words (in the Hebrew), rather rudely: "Give to-me people; but-goods take for-yourself" (14:21). Brusque and audacious, he designs to take before he offers, in a command rather than a request, rather unusual for one who had been on the losing side of a battle. "The victor, not a defeated king, has the right to stipulate the disposition of the spoils of war."[28] McConville argues convincingly that the meetings with the two kings carry a deeper contrast of philosophies (theologies?). The ruler of Sodom believes one can hold by right whatever one can gain by might: the one who subdues supposedly retains the privilege of subjugation and possession. And, recognizing Abram's right and privilege by this philosophy, he tries to appease him or perhaps enlist him as an ally. The patriarch, of course, repudiates this advance. On the other hand, the ruler of Salem correctly recognizes God as the source of Abram's victory and strength, and Abram, in turn, acknowledges that truth by tithing to Melchizedek. That is precisely the antithesis painted by the wordplay: Abram's comment about being "made rich" (עשׁר, *'shr*,

---

26. Wenham, *Genesis 1–15*, 316. Moreover, *Gen. Rab.* 43:6, 1Qap Gen^ar 22:13, and Josephus (*Ant.* 1.10.2, 7.3.2; *J.W.* 6.10.1) identify Salem as Jerusalem; all the Targums have Melchizedek as דירושלם מלכא (*mlk' dyrshlm*, "king of Jerusalem). Melchizedek is the first priest to show up in the Bible, and his blessing of Abram is the only priestly blessing in Genesis. However, his precise identity is a mystery. The psalmist (Ps 110) and the writer of Hebrews (Heb 5–7) exploit this priestly regent's cryptic description and absent antecedents to make an analogy to a divine/heavenly priest and the preincarnate Christ.

27. Strikingly, the names in 14:2 of the king of Sodom (Bera, בֶּרַע, *bera'*) and the king of Gomorrah (Birsha, בִּרְשַׁע, *birsha'*) incorporate, respectively, רע (*r'*, "evil") and רשׁע (*rsh'*, "wickedness")!

28. Waltke and Fredricks, *Genesis*, 235. It appears that the king of Sodom, initially silent, demands his due when he sees Abram offering a tenth to the king of Salem.

14:23) by man is in stark contrast to his being enriched by God, alluded to in the tithe (מַעֲשֵׂר, *ma'aser*, 14:20, from עָשַׂר, *'sr*, "take a tithe") offered to Melchizedek.[29]

Melchizedek's generosity (or gratitude?) is remarkable—rather than bread and water, the staple diet, he provides bread and wine, royal fare (1 Sam 16:20).[30] In any case, this king's actions recognize the patriarch's political significance after his campaign and attest to the settlement of Abram in Canaan. "This encounter also denotes an additional stage in the establishment of Abram's right to the Land."[31] In a sense, as the agent of Yahweh, the king of Salem is reaffirming divine promise to the patriarch. He would, like royalty, subdue his enemies in the Promised Land (14:20–21; see Gen 17 for more overtones on the royal status of Abram's line).

Abram is clear about how he will possess the land—it will be as a divine gift given to an outsider. It is perhaps with this idea in mind that the patriarch is described in this episode as "the Hebrew" (14:13).[32] Indeed, Yahweh claims the land is his (Lev 25:23), and therefore it is his prerogative to give it to whom he pleases. "This then is the rationale underlying Melchizedek's sudden appearance on the scene in this drama. Its very suddenness contributes to its power, representing, as it were, the breaking in of God on human affairs and human thought. Melchizedek needs no other justification for accosting Abram than that he represents God. . . . This 'interruption' bespeaks an irruption, and is well suited to its purpose."[33] Melchizedek expressly asserts that it was God Most High who had delivered Abram's enemies into his hand (Gen 14:20). In response, Abram's giving to this "priest of God Most High" (14:18), and his claim that it was not man who made him rich, are indicators of Abram's faith in that same God, Yahweh, the one who had blessed him.[34] The patriarch, in sum, trusts God to work out his land promise in his own time and in his own way.

Again, there is a contrast between uncle and nephew. Lot lives in Sodom (14:12), earlier noted to be wicked and sinful (13:13); but Abram dwelt by the oaks of Mamre (14:13), the place of the altar (13:18). Lot's goods, once the root of the strife with his uncle (13:5–6), are now spoils for a preying army (14:12). Noting Lot's progressive identification with Sodom—choosing it (13:11), settling close (13:12), dwelling therein (14:12)—and his later deplorable activities (19:30–38), Waltke and Fredricks label him a "fool."[35] And, curiously enough, after Lot has been rescued, the king of Sodom

29. McConville, "Abraham and Melchizedek," 114–15.

30. Wenham, *Genesis 1–15*, 316.

31. Elgavish, "The Encounter of Abram," 504.

32. This is the first occurrence of "Hebrew" in the Bible, though "Eber" has already shown up in 10:21, 25; 11:16. "Hebrew" is frequently used to distinguish an Israelite from a non-Israelite (Gen 39:14, 17; 40:15; 41:12; 43:32; Exod 1:15, 16; 2:6, 11, 13). Essentially, it is an ethnic nomen designating an "outsider" (see Hamilton, *Genesis: Chapters 1–17*, 405). Correspondingly, the LXX has περάτης (*peratēs*, "wanderer/migrant," from πέραν, *peran*, "across," that, in Josh 24:3, translates עבר, *'br*, "to pass/cross"). See ibid., 405n4.

33. McConville, "Abraham and Melchizedek," 116.

34. Yahweh's "deliverance," מָגֵן (*magan*, 14:20), leads naturally—and phonetically—to his claim that he was Abram's "shield," מָגֵן (*magen*, 15:1).

35. *Genesis*, 231.

demands from Abram the "people" (14:21), likely including Lot, and indicating the claim of a sovereign over his vassals. "There is an issue here; where and to whom does this man belong? And significantly, Abram does not demur when the King of Sodom makes his claim. Lot who has chosen to live outside the land of promise is claimed in turn by the power that has the authority there."[36] Unlike Lot who was claimed by the king of Sodom, Abram was "claimed" by the king of Salem, the agent of Yahweh. His trust was in God and in that trust he would rest patiently, awaiting the fulfillment of the divine word in God's own sovereign timetable.

SERMON FOCUS AND OUTLINES

THEOLOGICAL FOCUS OF PERICOPE 8 FOR PREACHING

8   Correction of faithless behavior and return to faithful obedience to God's demand, trusting in God's sovereign timing to keep his word, results in divine blessing (13:1–14:24).

Wenham declares that "[t]his episode does not . . . add many new elements to the picture of Abram already painted.[37] That may be true . . . if one looks *through* the text at the events: Abram is powerful, God is blessing him, he blesses others. But if one is looking *at* the text, rather than *through* it, one discerns what the author is *doing* with what he is saying. The two episodes of this pericope, Genesis 13 and 14, deal essentially with the same topic: the issue of returning to the fold of divine blessing. And that happens as one corrects one's faithless behavior and moves towards faithful obedience that involves patiently waiting for God to work out his promises in his own way, in his own time. One does not take matters into one's own hands, as this pericope (and several others ahead) demonstrate.

The following pericope (Pericope 9) shares some facets of this Theological Focus; thus when preaching Pericope 8, it might be appropriate to focus upon the need for correction of faithless behavior and the need to practice waiting.

Possible Preaching Outlines for Pericope 8

I.   Amending Faithless Behavior: Returning to Divine Blessing
     Recap: Abram's faithlessness in his escape to Egypt and in the deception of Pharaoh (12:10–20)
     Abram's return to the land of promise (13:1–4)
     Abram's separation from Lot (13:5–13)
     The consequence of correction: divine blessing (13:14–18)
     Move-to-Relevance: Our faithless behavior, our failure to be blessed

II. Awaiting God's Work: Retaining Divine Blessing
     Abram's military victory and his refusal to touch the property of the vanquished (14:1–16, 21–24)
     Abram blessed by Yahweh's agent (14:17–20a)
     Abram's tithe, a token of trust in God (14:20b)

---

36. McConville, "Abraham and Melchizedek," 114.

37. *Genesis 1–15*, 321.

   III. *Amend and await!*

        How we can demonstrate our faith in our refusal to take matters into our own hands[38]

Another way to structure the sermon is to base it upon the characters in the pericope, with minor tweaks of emphases in each point:

   I. Abram vs. Lot: Return vs. Removal

        Abram's return to the land of promise (13:1–4)

        Lot's poor choices and his removal from the sphere of blessing (13:5–13)

        The consequence of correction: divine blessing (13:14–18)

   II. King of Sodom vs. King of Salem: Ransacking vs. Receiving

        The king of Sodom's recommendation: ransack the property of the vanquished (14:1–16, 21–24)

        The king of Salem's demonstration: receive only what God gives (14:17–20a)

        Abram's tithe, a token of trust in Yahweh who gives (14:20b)

   III. *Return and receive!*

        How we can correct our faithless behavior

        How we can demonstrate our faith in our refusal to take matters into our own hands

---

38. Since tithing is part of the actual story, it might not be a bad idea to focus the specific application on the giving to God of a tangible token of our trust in him and of our reliance upon him, as we wait for divine blessings in our own lives.

PERICOPE 9

The Chaos of Faithlessness

Genesis 15:1–16:16

[Covenant with Abram; Birth of Ishmael]

REVIEW, SUMMARY, PREVIEW

Review of Pericope 8: In Gen 13:1–14:24 Abram returns to the Promised Land, where God is, and where his blessing will be experienced—a correction of his earlier failures, that includes separation from Lot. This demonstration of faithfulness is followed by an affirmation (and even an intensification) of the divine promises to Abram. Aligning oneself with God's demands yields blessing.

Summary of Pericope 9: Abram's faith depicted in the previous pericope is rewarded here with an extended revelation from God, further expanding his earlier promises. Yet the patriarch seems to be doubtful about all of this, even suggesting that Eliezer, his steward, be his heir, a recommendation God rejects. Nonetheless, even a less-than-mature faith as Abram exhibits here is credited to him as righteousness. In the next section, the manipulation of Sarai betokens, once again, immature faith, resulting in domestic chaos. Mature faith patiently waits for God's sovereign provision.[1]

Preview of Pericope 10: The next pericope (Gen 17:1–18:15) has God setting an explicit condition for Abram's blessing: he would need

---

1. As will become clear, by "mature" faith, I intend a faith that is whole, fully developed, complete—a trust in God that is integral, sound, and stable (unlike what the patriarch Abram has demonstrated thus far). Of course, no faith is perfect, and therefore a certain degree of flexibility must be adopted in these designations.

to walk with God and be blameless. Though Ishmael is not part of the Abrahamic covenant, he too is blessed by his association with the patriarch. The human-side commitment to divine promise is actualized in the ritual of circumcision. Walking with God brings divine blessings to pass.

9.   Genesis 15:1–16:16

THEOLOGICAL FOCUS OF PERICOPE 9

9 **Mature faith waits for God even in unfavorable circumstances, refraining from manipulation, thereby enabling the believer to experience divine blessing and to be a channel for such blessing to others (15:1–16:16).**

9.1   While a mighty God who works marvelous things invites a mature faith, even a less-than-mature faith avails for one to be a channel for divine blessing to others (15:1–21).

9.1.1   *A mighty God who works marvelous things invites a mature faith.*

9.1.2   *Even a less-than-mature faith avails for one to to be a channel for divine blessing to others.*

9.2   Mature faith waits for God even in unfavorable circumstances, refraining from manipulation, thereby enabling the believer to experience divine blessing (16:1–16).

9.2.1   *Immature faith that refuses to wait on God for his blessings, but seeks to manipulate events, only results in chaos.*

9.2.2   *Mature faith waits for God even in unfavorable circumstances, thereby keeping the believer in the sphere of divine blessing.*

OVERVIEW

This chapter has a rather narrow national focus, as against the international dimension of the promises in Genesis 12 and 17. What is dealt with here are local particulars: Abram's seed, their fate in a foreign land, their return to the land promised to Abram, and the extent of that land's boundaries.[2]

In response to Abram's faith, reflected in his dependence upon Yahweh to give him the Promised Land and in his not taking matters into his own hands, the patriarch receives an extended revelation from God in Gen 15. This revelation expands on the earlier promises of seed and land: Abram's descendants would be innumerable (15:1–6) and he would possess the land of Canaan (15:7). The vision was followed by a ritual slaughter of animals (15:8–11) and a covenantal rite (15:17) that formally inaugurates the divine-human compact. And these ceremonies are accompanied by amplifications of earlier details regarding the land promise (15:12–16, 18–21). Despite all these solemnities, the tension of the issue of seed still remains: Abram wonders if the "seed" will be a household retainer (15:2) and, later, he suspects his descendant will be through a concubine (16:1–16). Both times, he is proven wrong.

---

2. Nevertheless, Gen 15 shares much with Gen 17 (see Pericope 10).

The two scenes of Genesis 15 (15:1–6 and 15:7–21) are constructed in parallel, with Yahweh making three statements in each panel (15:1b, 4, 5 and 15:7, 13–16, 18b–21) and his name occurring symmetrically; Abram, in turn, raises an objection to the divine promise in each panel (15:2–3 and 15:8). While the first panel deals primarily with seed and the second with land, they are connected, for the promise of innumerable seed requires much land; thus the two promises run together.[3]

	Genesis 15:1–6 (seed)	Genesis 15:7–21 (land)
Introduction	"I am your shield" (15:1a)	"I am Yahweh" (15:7a)
	"Yahweh" (15:1a)	"Yahweh" (15:7a)
Yahweh's promise	Reward (seed) for Abram (15:1b)	Land for Abram (15:7b)
Abram's reaction	"What will You give me?" (15:2–3)	"How will I know?" (15:8)
	"Adonai Yahweh" (15:2)	"Adonai Yahweh" (15:8)
Yahweh's reaction	Error corrected (15:4)	Rite performed (15:9–11)
Yahweh's promise	Innumerable descendants (15:5)	Land for descendants (15:12–16)
	Signs at night: stars (15:5)	Signs at night: oven/torch (15:17)
Conclusion	Abram's faith (15:6)	Yahweh's covenant (15:18–21)
	"Yahweh" (15:6)	"Yahweh" (15:18)

It is surprising that on either side of the remarkable proverbial statement of Gen 15:6 that emphasizes Abram's faith, we see his doubts—in fact, all Abram can muster in this chapter are questions: "What will You give me . . .?" and "How will I know . . .?" (15:2–3, 8). Those are his first recorded words to Yahweh in the entire patriarchal story, and these form his only words in this particular episode.[4] The bulk of the patriarch's speeches to God in the Abrahamic saga concern his doubt (15:2–3, 8; 17:18; 18:23–33). It is his silences that indicate his faith!

All of the talk about his descendants obtaining the land in Gen 15 has stimulated, once again, Abram's deep concern about his childlessness; apparently, his wife, Sarai, too is equally worried about the situation. Together, they take action (16:1–16), demonstrating their inadequate faith in the power of Yahweh and the trustworthiness of his word.

9.1 Genesis 15:1–21

THEOLOGICAL FOCUS 9.1

9.1 While a mighty God who works marvelous things invites a mature faith, even a less-than-mature faith avails for one to be a channel of divine blessing to others (15:1–21).

---

3. The table below is modified from Wenham, *Genesis 16–50*, 325. Other words common to both panels include: "descendants/seed" (15:3, 5 and 15:13, 18); "to inherit/possess" (15:4 [×2] and 15:7, 8), and "bring/go out" (15:5 and 15:7). In 15:1, Yahweh identifies himself to Abraham by the Tetragrammaton—the first such self-identification by God in Scripture.

4. Abram's address of God, "Adonai Yahweh," is found only in this chapter of Genesis (15:2, 8; and in the Pentateuch, also in Deut 3:34 and 9:26).

> 9.1.1   A mighty God who works marvelous things invites a mature faith.
>
> 9.1.2   Even a less-than-mature faith avails for one to be a channel of divine blessing to others.

NOTES 9.1

9.1.1 A mighty God who works marvelous things invites a mature faith.

Abraham is being depicted in Gen 15:1 as being a prophet, justifying the label in Gen 20:7 (and perhaps the one in Luke 13:28): "the word of Yahweh came," found in Gen 15:1 and 15:4, is, in the OT, almost always used to describe a revelation to a prophet, a prefatory formula for prophecy (1 Sam 15:10; 2 Sam 7:4; 24:11; 1 Kgs 13:20; 16:1; 17:2; Jer 34:12; etc.). Moreover "vision" is found only here (Gen 15:1) and in Num 24:4, 16 in the Pentateuch. And this coming of the word of Yahweh constitutes one of the three instances of the name of the patriarch being used by God in direct address to the patriarch (the others are Gen 22:1, 11). This was a special revelation, indeed.

There are several allusions to Gen 14 in this chapter: "deliver/shield" (14:20 and 15:1), "bring/go out" (14:8, 17, 18 and 15:4, 5, 7, 14), "possessions" (14:11–12, 16, 21 and 15:14), "Salem/complete" (שׁלם, *shlm*, 14:18 and 15:16); and "righteousness" (14:18 and 15:6). The connections may explain why God reassures Abram about divine protection ("shield") in 15:1 "after these things": all the bellicose activity in Gen 14 has made the patriarch's stay in the land quite tenuous, making him vulnerable to counterattacks from the powerful kings he had just defeated. No doubt, this apprehension was also linked to a lack of seed, upon which an extended stay in the land would be contingent. Without seed, without progeny, without the innumerable descendants that were promised him in 13:16, how would Abram be expected to remain much longer in the land of promise? Perhaps this is why Yahweh begins with an exhortation to Abram to be unafraid and that he would be a shield (מָגֵן, *magen*) to the patriarch, an allusion to God's deliverance in the previous chapter (מִגֵּן, *magan*, 14:20)—Yahweh is himself emphatically corroborating Melchizedek's declaration.[5] As the LXX has it, in 15:1, God declares that he would cover Abram with a shield (ἐγὼ ὑπερασπίζω σου, *egō huperaspizō sou*, "I will 'over-shield' you").

Yet there is another reason for this current revelation. Abram had acquitted himself well in Gen 14, particularly in the exhibition of his trust in Yahweh's deliverance and timing for the fulfillment of his land promises. The war victor, in complete trust in God, refused to take anything for himself, lest it be alleged that man had made Abram rich (14:22–23; see Pericope 8). Thus God promises him a "reward" in 15:1. He had refused the conqueror's prerogative of retaining the booty (14:22–24), but Yahweh would recompense him for the faith he had thereby demonstrated ("reward" and "recompense" are used in parallel in Isa 40:10; 62:11).

Upon the promise of a reward, Abram immediately questions God about it, seeing that "I go [literally, "walk," הלך, *hlk*] childless." His life journey—his walk as a

---

5. "Shield" is used metaphorically of divine protection in Pss 3:4; 7:11; 18:2, 30, 35; 28:7; 33:20; etc.

nomadic wanderer—would not be fulfilled without a child, even though he had set out "walking" (הלך, 12:4) in faith in accordance with God's command to "go" (also הלך, 12:1). And that plaint was not surprising, seeing that he had been promised descendants at least thrice thus far (12:2, 7; 13:15–16). It is curious that "childless" (15:2) occurs elsewhere in the OT only in Lev 20:20, 21 and Jer 22:30; in these instances, childlessness is a divine affliction for disobedience. Is that a hint that Abram sees his childlessness as some sort of punitive action on the part of God, in the light of which the idea of a promised reward sounded strange to the patriarch? In any case, Abram points to Eliezer of Damascus, probably a steward in his household, as his heir (15:2). There is a clever wordplay here. Literally, it reads: "The son of my acquisition [בֶּן־מֶשֶׁק, *ben-mesheq* = heir] of my house is Eliezer of Damascus [דַּמֶּשֶׂק, *dameseq*]." Besides, "Eliezer" (אֱלִיעֶזֶר, *'eli'ezer*) may itself be a pun on the word זרע (*zr'*, "seed," 15:3): since God has not provided זרע, Abram suggests Eliezer as זרע.[6] All that to say, Abram still did not take God fully at his word; he was still doubtful about his own ability to produce descendants. His faith, it seems, is still to reach maturity, for it keeps waxing and waning every step of the way.

There is an interesting split in Abram's response to God in 15:2–3. With what seems to be some redundancy, Abram's response here is divided into two, each prefixed with "And Abram said." It appears that after his first comment, a question, God did not deign to reply—an indication, likely, of disapproval of Abram's rather uncomprehending faithlessness. So Abram began again, "And Abram said," with a word of excuse for his question—"since I am childless"—as if to say, "Look, I know I'm being skeptical, but you still haven't kept your word. Well, how about my taking as heir one who is born in my household?" But God emphatically rejects Abram's recommendation: "Not your heir—*this one*—but the one coming from your own body—*he* . . ." (15:4). In response to Abram's "behold" (הן, *hn*, 15:3), the narrator adds his own "behold" (הנה, *hnh*, 15:4), reinforcing the divine corrective. Taking the patriarch outside to view the night sky, Yahweh unambiguously asserts that Abram would have innumerable seed.[7] Yahweh who "brought out" (יצא, *yts'*) Abram from Ur (15:7), could surely "bring forth" (יצא) a heir from Abram's body (15:4), as he illustrated by "bringing out" (יצא) Abram to view the night sky (15:5). To this astronomy lesson, Abram's reaction was, finally, belief (15:6). Yet in 15:2–3, Abram has just questioned God, and in 15:8, right after the momentous declaration of 15:6, he doubts again! Whither the faith? The structure of the passage, with Gen 15:6 inserted between two demonstrations of Abram's incredulity, demonstrates a less-than-stellar (no pun intended!) performance by the patriarch, rather than the mature faith invited by a mighty God who works marvelous things.[8]

---

6. Mathews, *Genesis 11:27–50:26*, 164.

7. In light of his response in 15:2–3, the "reward" that God promised Abram in 15:1 must have concerned descendants. To which, Abram objects twice, bemoaning his childlessness (15:2, 3). Yahweh then makes two promises, countering Abram's two objections: Abram's own son will be the heir, and he will have innumerable descendants (15:4, 5). The object lesson of the "stars in the heavens" to indicate innumerable descendants is found here in 15:5, and also in 22:17; 26:4; Exod 32:13; Deut 1:10; 10:22; 28:62; Neh 9:23; 1 Chr 27:23.

8. In fact, considering the subsequent revelation from Yahweh, *b. Ned.* 32a asserts that the Egyptian

9.1.2 Even a less-than-mature faith avails for one to be a channel of divine blessing to others.

Genesis 15:6 begins with וְהֶאֱמִן, *whe'emin* (*waw* conjunctive + Hiphil perfect: the *weqatal* form)—an unusual pattern for a past tense narrative where one would expect *waw* consecutive + imperfect: the *wayyiqtol* form. Longacre asserts that such isolated *weqatal* forms in a narrative framework mark "pivotal/climactic/finalizing events."[9] Thus, the unique structure likely highlights Abram's noteworthy attitude of faith in what God had just promised him. As Moberly notes, 15:6 is a unique assessment in the patriarchal narratives, a third-person description of an attitude towards God, as opposed to a first-person assessment by Yahweh himself.[10] "Righteous" describes the moral conduct of one who keeps the law (Ezek 18:5–9) and who is approved by God (Gen 18:19; 30:3; 38:26). God himself is often referred to as "righteous" (Deut 32:4; Ezra 9:15; Pss 7:9; 116:5; Isa 45:21; Dan 9:14). Thus righteousness is "God-like, or at least God-pleasing, action."[11] However, there is no action on the part of Abram that brings him credit in Gen 15:6; instead it is his faith that is "counted" as righteousness.

This is the first occurrence of the verb אמן, *'mn*, in Scripture, though it is certainly not the first instance of Abram demonstrating faith: "[t]he action of faith preceded the vocabulary of faith."[12] Though the faith exhibited thus far had not been of a flawless kind, it still was faith: his leaving for places unknown in Gen 12:1–3, his return to the Promised Land and his settling there (13:1, 12), his altar-building response (13:18)

---

slavery was decreed on Abraham's house because of his questioning of God in Gen 15:8. Indeed, there is a hint that Yahweh was not too pleased with Abram's frequent doubts. God was clear in 15:7 that *Abram* would possess the land; but in 15:18, it appears that is the *descendants* who would obtain the land. Was this a change, in light of Abram's disbelief, something like Moses' failure to enter the Promised Land? Numbers 20:12 gives the reason for that rebuke as Moses' disbelief, a lack of אמן, *'mn*, the word used in Gen 15:6 of Abram; the consequence of Moses' sin was that he would die before entry into the land, Num 27:14 (he would be "gathered to his people"). Abram, too, would die before acquisition of the land, Gen 15:15—and 25:8 describes his demise also as being "gathered to his people." And was Abram's vision in the darkness parallel to Moses' private vision of the Promised Land, after God had declared he would not see it (Num 27:12–14)? On the other hand, if the promise to give the land to *Abram* still held good, it would necessitate a resurrection on a future day when the patriarch would himself come into possession of Canaan. With regard to the extent of the land (Gen 15:18; its boundaries are more clearly defined in Num 34:1–12), even in Solomon's day, the borders did not seem to have reached as far west as the Nile (1 Kgs 4:21). Thus a future fulfillment of this promise is a valid consideration (as the prophet Isaiah seems to have envisaged: 27:12). The ten-nation list in Gen 15:19–20 (the only such list of Canaanites numbered as ten nations) is likely to be symbolically inclusive of the entire mass of Canaan's occupiers, rather than a historically precise designation of the state of affairs at any given time. See other similar lists that vary in number and order: Exod 3:8, 17; 13:5; 23:23; 33:2; 34:11; Deut 7:1; 20:17; Josh 9:1; 11:3; 12:8; 24:11; etc. All of this might hint at a fulfillment that is future, even from our own present day.

9. Longacre, "*Weqatal* Forms," 95.

10. Moberly, "Abraham's Righteousness," 103–4. The LXX converts the verb into a passive (as also does *Tg. Neof.*): "and it [faith] was reckoned to him" (καὶ ἐλογίσθη αὐτῷ, *kai elogisthē autō*). One also notes that in Gen 15:6 (as in the parallel in Ps 106:31), the person of concern appears as לוֹ (*lo*, "to him"—also in the LXX: αὐτῷ, *autō*). Thus it is not that Abram (or Phinehas) was considered righteous, but that righteousness was counted *to him*.

11. Wenham, *Genesis 1–15*, 330.

12. Hamilton, *Genesis: Chapters 1–17*, 423.

to a promise even greater than the one in 15:1 (13:14–17 promised him not only innumerable descendants, but also land), and his giving tribute to an "agent" of Yahweh (14:20).

But here, the narrator brings it all to a momentous declaration: Abram considered God, the one who had promised, as reliable, capable of fulfilling his promise. Or, in other words, "[t]he human partner counts on God to give him offspring, and the divine partner credits [counts!] that faith as righteousness."[13] The patriarch was trusting his future into the hands of a reliable God. This was an outstanding expression of trust by a human in his God, with consequences that would last for eternity. In fact, what 15:6 accomplishes is to link Israel's existence in the land (the primary concern of Gen 15) with this great faith of the patriarch in Yahweh. "It was not only the promise of Yahweh that gave existence to Israel, primary and fundamental though that was, but also the faithful response of Abraham. It was because Abraham put his faith in Yahweh, and Yahweh reckoned this to him as [צְדָקָה, *tsdaqah*], that Yahweh entered into the ritual that constituted his covenant with Israel."[14] There appears to be a consistent understanding in the OT that צְדָקָה results in the blessing of God—"an enhanced quality of life for both individual and community" (for self: Ps 72; Isa 11:1–9; 32:1–8, 15–20; Jer 23:5–6; 33:15–16; and for others: Gen 6:9; 7:1; 18:16–33).[15]

In this, Gen 15:6 seems to correspond to Ps 106:31. Phinehas' zealous operation resulted "for him and his descendants after him, a covenant of a perpetual priesthood" (Num 25:13)—the lasting legacy of the priest's action, with repercussions for the nation because God "reckoned" it (the same verb used in Gen 15:6) to Phinehas as "righteousness" (also used in 15:6). Just as the priesthood owed its covenant status to Phinehas' stand and Yahweh's response to it, so Israel owed its covenant status to Abram's stand and Yahweh's response to that. "As Phinehas stands to the priesthood, so Abraham stands to Israel." Thus, "in two archetypal and paradigmatic traditions, those of Abraham and Phinehas, the enhanced relationship with God led to a kind of overflow such that enduring blessing was bestowed on Israel also."[16]

The timing of these events is itself interesting: in 15:5, it is obviously the night sky that Abram is pointed to; and in 15:12, a whole day seems to have passed with Abram doing nothing except keeping watch over the divided body parts involved in the ritual, and chasing away the birds of prey (one may assume that 15:17 refers to this same evening and not to a subsequent one[17]). As Ronning puts it:

13. Waltke and Fredricks, *Genesis*, 239.

14. Moberly, "Abraham's Righteousness," 119.

15. Ibid., 123. "Reckoning iniquity/guilt" was a recognized idiom in biblical literature (2 Sam 19:19; Ps 32:2). Since עָוֹן (*'awon*, "iniquity/guilt") and צְדָקָה are contrasting terms (Ps 69:27, 28; 2 Sam 22:24, 25 = Ps 18:23, 24; Isa 53:11), "reckoning iniquity/guilt" is likely antonymous with "reckoning righteousness."

16. Moberly, "Abraham's Righteousness," 117–18, 120, 126.

17. Genesis 15:17 likely continues the narrative of 15:12 on the same evening/night; the two verses are structurally similar: each has a double temporal clause before "behold."

What has happened, then, seems to be that in the early morning darkness Abraham is given the promise, then told to bring the animals. When he does so, nothing happens. He waits around all day, and nothing happens except that some vultures try to get the animals. Finally, the sun sets and he falls into a deep sleep. Then comes the covenant ceremony and a revelation of the future. The rest of Abraham's life will be spent just as this day has been; he will wait, and nothing will happen as far as inheriting the land. Then he will fall asleep (die; v. 15). After 400 years of exile and oppression of his descendants, they will return and inherit the land.[18]

At any rate, even Abram's less-than-mature faith was credited by God for righteousness that would bring about divine blessing for many.

EXCURSUS ON COVENANT AND CONDITIONALITY

Most scholars link the ritual elements of Gen 15:9–10, 17 with Jer 34:18–19 which has a covenant rite wherein a calf is cut in two and the ones with whom the covenant is made pass between the halves of the animal.[19] Unlike in that prophetic text, it is unclear who exactly passes between the divisions of the animals in Gen 15:17 and what the torch and oven/censer represent.

The torch and oven/censer appear together in incantation rituals in ancient Mesopotamia: for instance, to liberate sufferers from sources of evil (the *Maqlu* ritual), or from their personal problems/sins (the *Šurpu* ritual).[20] In the *Maqlu* ritual, the fiery items represented two separate deities, and the incantation sought to release a sufferer from evil powers, including the childlessness. This could be relevant in the context of Abram's own situation.[21] The *Šurpu* ritual was undertaken primarily to obtain a sign regarding how individuals may be liberated from a variety of calamities ("to heal the sick" [4.16]; "to change a bad fate" [4.19]; and also "to give an heir" [4.25]). Thus, in Gen 15, the torch and oven may be a divine oracular sign/confirmation in answer to Abram's doubt (Gen 15:13): "By what [sign] can I know [ידע, *yd'*] . . .?" (15:9), to which God explicitly answers, "Know for certain [יָדֹעַ תֵּדַע, *yadoa' teda'*]. . . ." And it is quite conceivable that deity is being represented by both those fiery elements and that humanity is not at all depicted in the scene. Thus, unlike Jer 34:18–19, the human partner of the covenant, Abram, is depicted as entirely passive through the ceremony—in fact, asleep (15:12, at least during the auditory revelations from Yahweh[22]). The meaning

18. Ronning, "The Naming of Isaac," 16. "Enslaved" and "oppressed" (Gen 15:13) are the exact words used to describe the state of the Israelites in Exod 1:11–14.

19. In terms of parallels in the two texts, some of the vocabulary is shared: עבר (*'br*, "pass through," 15:17), כרת (*krt*, "make/establish," 15:18), בתר (*btr*, "part," 15:10), and "covenant" (15:18) occur in both; also, Jer 34:13 echoes Gen 15:7, and Jer 34:20 echoes Gen 15:11. Besides Jer 34:18–19, there are other examples of second-millennium texts from Alalakh that involve oaths confirmed by the slaying of animals. See Hasel, "The Meaning of the Animal Rite," 61; and Hess, "The Slaughter of the Animals," 55.

20. Johnston, "The Smoking Brazier," 5; Michalowski, "The Torch and the Censer," 152–62; and Abusch, "An Early Form of the Witchcraft Ritual," 1–58.

21. Johnston, "The Smoking Brazier," 5.

22. See Job 4:13; 33:15; Isa 29:10 for "deep sleep" being the occasion for prophetic revelation. The

of the *disjecta membra* in Jer 34 is that breaking of covenantal promises threatens such dismembering of human parties to the covenant—an "acted-out curse rite." But it is quite difficult to see in Gen 15 Yahweh invoking such dramatic sanctions upon himself—a divine self-imprecatory variation of "Cross my heart and hope to die!"[23] All this to say Jer 34 is not the best parallel for Gen 15.

Perhaps the most fruitful analysis for parallels to the enigmatic ritual of Gen 15 has been the examination of the *Ritual of Anniwiyanis*, an ancient Hittite ceremony dating from ca. 1650–1500 BCE[24] This rite has birds (of clay and dough, *Anniwiyanis* 2, 3, 5, 6, 11), sleep (*Anniwiyanis* 4), *disjecta membra* (a dog divided into two, and a goat in multiple pieces but separated into two heaps, *Anniwiyanis* 7, 10), a fireplace and a stove (*Anniwiyanis* 23, 24), and an overnight event (extending multiple days, *Anniwiyanis* 28)—all of which seem to have remarkably parallel elements in Genesis 15.[25] At least part of the ritual was "celebrated for the purpose of driving out the female-producing god of manhood and bringing in the male-producing god of manhood, that is, to secure the birth of sons."[26] This ancient ritual appears to be the closest in its constituent elements and ceremonies to the goings on in Gen 15. Despite these significant parallels, one cannot determine with precision the implications of Gen 15:10–12 and 17. Nonetheless, one might surmise that that "the biblical rite has demythologized the magical elements of the Hittite ritual" (*Maqlu*, *Šurpu*, and the *Ritual of Anniwiyanis*), while yet retaining enough similarity so that Abram will "know for certain" (15:13), by means of a symbolic oracular vision and sign, that Yahweh would keep his word to give the patriarch a male heir.[27]

With Yahweh's declaration of covenant in 15:18, there is no reason to suspect that Abram's expectation was anything but a bilateral and mutually obligatory covenant. In fact, such obligations of faithful obedience pertain to Abram through the entirety of his saga, including: his leaving the land of his fathers (12:1–4; Heb 11:8); the call to be a blessing (Gen 12:2); Abram's building of an altar indicating his resolve to serve Yahweh (Gen 12:7); the return to the land that led to a reaffirmation of the divine promise (13:14–18); his swearing to God presupposing his commitment to obedience (14:22–23); the divine promise in Gen 15 that follows the patriarch's exhibiting his confidence in Yahweh in Gen 14; his obedience in bringing the appropriate animals

---

"terror" of Abram in Gen 15:12, with the great darkness and deep sleep, is appropriate for one unwittingly involved in something numinous, with divine revelation and a sign also involved (see Isa 33:18).

23. Hasel, "The Meaning of the Animal Rite," 68.

24. Johnston, "The Smoking Brazier," 14.

25. Sturtevant and Bechtel, *A Hittite Chrestomathy*, 107–17.

26. Ibid., 118. This interpretation is debated, though scholars concede that the ritual had something to do with reinforcing or restoring the virility of the client, which would still be germane to our patriarch's primary problem. See Hoffner, "Paškuwatti's Ritual," 282. Also see Hutter, "Aspects of Luwian Religion," 229, 255, who claims these rituals were intended "to help restore sexuality and strength" and "to provide fertility."

27. Johnston, "The Smoking Brazier," 15.

for the ritual (15:10[28]); the obvious mutual conditions in 17:1–4, 9[29]; the patriarch's adherence to the condition of circumcision (17:9–14, 23–27); the purpose of God's relationship to Abram (18:18–19); his obedience to God's command in 22:2; the consequences of Abram's obedience spelled out by God in 22:16–18; and even the explicit statement of Yahweh to Isaac regarding the patriarch's adherence to divine demand (26:4–5).[30] If the covenant promise to return Abram's descendants to Canaan from Egypt in the fourth generation were unconditional, it is rather surprising that God did not keep his word: his rescue was of the fourth generation (Exod 6:14–25), but that "evil generation" did not get to see the Promised Land (Deut 1:35). Obviously, then, the promise was conditional, as Moses explained in Deut 4:1; 6:3; 8:1.[31] In fact, "the relationship which grows out of the nature of the *berith* could very well include the obligation also of the receiver, without its being expressly mentioned, if it were simply presumed as well known."[32] Relationship calls for responsibility: "They who will have God to be to them a God, must consent to be to him a people."[33] Genesis 15:7 resembles, in wording, Exod 20:2 and Deut 5:6, the preamble to the Decalogue (the command to obey deity follows the establishment of a relationship with him). And Abram is the prototype of the nation of Israel that Yahweh redeemed. In other words, a relationship with Yahweh demands responsibility for obedience (Deut 6:25; the connection with the exodus is, of course, expressly noted in Gen 15:13–16).[34] Therefore I would agree with Allis:

> The claim which is often made that the Abrahamic covenant was unconditional while the Mosaic was conditioned on obedience, finds no support in Scripture. God's first word to Abram was a command: "Get thee out of thy country . . . into a land that I will show thee" (Gen. xii.1). Abram obeyed this command. The performance of the rite of circumcision was made an indispensable condition to covenant blessing (Gen. xvii). Abram performed it at once. The claim that the Abrahamic covenant was "unconditional" has dangerous implications;

28. Calvin observes: "Therefore by obeying the command of God, of which, however, no advantage was apparent, he hence proves the obedience of his faith" (*Comm. Gen.* 15:9).

29. Wesley, *Notes on the First Book of Moses*, 17:1, calls that covenant mutual: "[U]pright walking with God is the condition of our interest in his all-sufficiency. If we neglect him, or dissemble with him, we forfeit the benefit of our relation to him."

30. Youngblood, "The Abrahamic Covenant," 36–41.

31. Gordon H. Johnston (personal communication).

32. Eichrodt, "Covenant and Law," 305.

33. Wesley, *Notes on the First Book of Moses*, 17:10. The symmetry of command/obedience is found in 12:1–3/12:4–5; 17:9–14/17:23–27; and 22:2/22:3–10 (Youngblood, "The Abrahamic Covenant," 39). "[T]he command-obedience language of 17:9; 22:18; and 26:5 ['obey/keep the covenant,/ and 'obey/hear the voice'] is echoed *verbatim* in the undeniably conditional language of Exod 19:5 ['And now, if you will indeed obey/hear My voice and obey/keep My covenant, then you will be my possession among all the peoples']" (ibid. 40). "Abraham had to 'keep the way of the Lord,' which is defined as 'to do justice and judgment'—that is, to walk obediently, in subjection to God's revealed will—if he was to receive the fulfillment of the divine promises" (Pink, *The Divine Covenants*, 10).

34. So also Ps 81:11 that is parallel to Gen 15:17; and Ps 81:12 declares: "But my people did not obey My voice, And Israel did not submit to Me." The conditionality is clear here, as well.

for it suggests an antithesis between *faith* and *obedience* which is not warranted in Scripture. Paul joins the two together, when he speaks of the "obedience of faith" (Rom. i.5, xvi.26). . . . God's requirement has always been perfect obedience (Gen. iii.11). And the law which so stresses this requirement also contains and unfolds that system of expiations by sacrifice by means of which the penitent sinner may find forgiveness and acceptance with his God.[35]

The traditional understanding is that that covenants, akin to royal grants bestowed upon loyal servants, were unconditional, a construal based primarily on the work of Moshe Weinfeld who identified the Abrahamic covenant as an example of a royal land grant. Johnston posits that this traditional understanding of unconditionality is inaccurate.[36] Weinfeld himself acknowledged that not *all* grants were unconditional; in fact, such a grant was the exception: "The unconditional promise is therefore a special privilege and apparently given for extraordinary loyal service."[37] Form ("royal grant") is thus not predictive of conditionality; that judgment must be based on content. Indeed, Johnston goes on to show that the examples offered by Weinfeld of unconditional grants, in the larger contexts of those analyzed texts, are actually conditional.[38] Knoppers notes that ancient covenantal arrangements may be symmetrical or asymmetrical, the latter sort emphasizing the responsibilities of one party more than those of the other: "[I]t is not particularly helpful to turn these dissimilarities into a typology of two diametrically opposed kinds of covenant [conditional and unconditional]. Even in the case of asymmetrical covenants, a sense of mutuality characterizes the accord. The very composition of a treaty assumes a degree of mutuality between the relevant parties."[39] Formal ratification does not alter this mutuality; it only ensures that the previously covenanted relationship will continue into the future. Even the oath of God that ratifies the covenant (Gen 22:15–18; Heb 6:18: the "two immutable things" = the original divine promise and the subsequent divine oath) is balanced by Abram's oath(s) toward Yahweh: 12:8; 13:4; 13:18 (that have him building altars and calling on the name of Yahweh); and 14:21–23 (his actual swearing of an oath and his commitment

---

35. Allis, *God Spake By Moses*, 72. Also Murray: "The necessity of keeping the covenant is the expression of the spirituality involved. Keeping is the condition of continuance in this grace and of its consummating fruition; it is the reciprocal response apart from which communion with God is impossible" ("Covenant," 265) See Kuruvilla, *Privilege the Text!* 195–209, 252–58, for a discussion of "obedience of faith" and the rewards that accrue therefrom.

36. Johnston, "A Critical Evaluation," 1–20.

37. Weinfeld, "The Covenant of Grant," 193.

38. So also Knoppers: "[C]lose study of the historical and literary setting of royal grants indicates that most are actually conditional" ("Ancient Near Eastern Royal Grants," 670; also see 686, 692). And see Hess, "The Book of Joshua," 493–94. Roberts declares that "the unconditionality of the land grants has been vastly overstated. In administering grants, monarchs do not characteristically swear a self-imprecatory oath, and it is clear that in most cases, whether explicitly stated or not, the crown preserved the right to redistribute the land, depending on the continuing loyalty of the vassal and his descendants" ("Davidic Covenant," 209). "[A]ll covenants are both promissory and obligatory by definition, although either component may be left entirely implicit in the language describing the covenant" (Arnold, *Genesis*, 101).

39. Knoppers, "Ancient Near Eastern Royal Grants," 696.

to Yahweh). Indeed, as was mentioned, Abram's obligations are explicitly spelled out in 12:1–2; 17:1, 9; and 22:1. As was noted in Pericope 7, I would prefer to call this ritual in Gen 15 a ceremonial *inauguration* of the covenant.[40] It is *confirmed* in Gen 17, but *ratified* by an explicit oath of Yahweh only in Gen 22.

	Promise Given 12:1–3, 7; 13:14–17	Covenant Inaugurated 15:1–21	Covenant Confirmed 17:1–27; 18:18–19	Covenant Ratified 22:1–2, 15–18; 26:5
Yahweh	Promise expressed (12:1–3)	Promise re-expressed (15:1–5)	Covenant confirmed (17:1–21)	Covenantal test (22:1–2)
Abraham	Condition met: faithful obedience (12:4–6; Heb 11:8)	Condition met: faith (15:6; Heb 11:9–12)	Condition met: faithful obedience (17:22–27)	Condition met: faithful obedience (22:3–14; Heb 11:17–18)
Yahweh	Promise reiterated (Gen 12:7; 13:14–17)	Covenant inaugurated (Gen 15:7–21)	Covenant reconfirmed (Gen 18:18–19)	Covenant ratified (Gen 22:15–18; 26:5)

9.2 Genesis 16:1–16

THEOLOGICAL FOCUS 9.2

9.2 Mature faith waits for God even in unfavorable circumstances, refraining from manipulation, thereby enabling the believer to experience divine blessing (16:1–16).

   9.2.1 *Immature faith that refuses to wait on God for his blessings, but seeks to manipulate events, only results in chaos.*

   9.2.2 *Mature faith waits for God even in unfavorable circumstances, thereby remaining within the sphere of divine blessing.*

NOTES 9.2

This episode is about two women, one agonized over her barrenness, the other expelled because of her fertility; one is an old, but free, Israelite wife, the other a young, but enslaved, Egyptian maid; one symbolizes authority and domination, the other subservience and subordination.[41] In fact, 16:1 begins with the name "Sarai" and ends with the name "Hagar" (in Hebrew), with Abram caught in the middle, literarily (in a genitive clause: "[wife] of Abram"), as well as literally (he is passive throughout the

---

40. It is likely that Paul's take on this episode, utilized in Rom 4, stems from the concept of covenant *inauguration* that is contingent solely upon the condition of faith, and not works/obedience of any sort on part of Abram. For Paul, covenant inauguration serves as a convenient analogy for justification, the commencement (inauguration) of a right relationship with God, a status entered into solely by faith on part of the believer. (Of course, Abram was in a faith relationship with Yahweh even before Gen 15, at least from Gen 11–12, if not before.)

41. Drey, "The Role of Hagar," 181. "Power belongs to Sarai, the subject of action; powerlessness marks Hagar, the object" (Trible, "The Other Woman," 222).

episode). The episode begins on a negative note: no child was born to Abram; but it ends on a positive note: Ishmael was born to Abram.[42] But he was not the chosen descendant; despite all their artifices and contrivances, for Abram and Sarai it would be another fourteen years before the promise of the chosen son is fulfilled (16:16; 21:5). Trusting in God and his sovereign accomplishment of his plans is always the best way to operate in life.

9.2.1 *Immature faith that refuses to wait on God for his blessings, but seeks to manipulate events, only results in chaos.*

While Gen 12–15 deals primarily with issues relating to the promise of land, Gen 16–22 concerns itself with issues of the promise of seed. This latter focus is particularly appropriate here in Gen 16: "Forced by God directly to contemplate his own death [15:15], Abram now more than ever longs for a son. It is in this frame of mind that, in the immediate sequel, he receives and eagerly accepts Sarai's offer to try to have a child of his own by Hagar the Egyptian."[43] After the divine promise and the astronomy lesson and the ceremonies of cut animals and rituals with fiery objects, one expects that the next scene will have seed being born to Abram. That expectation turns out to be accurate: *a* seed is born to Abram, but not *the* seed. It appears that it is not only the reader who expects the arrival of seed at this point in the story; the very actors of the saga do so, too. And they take action to make sure that their expectations are realized. For, right after the promise of descendants in Gen 15, chapter 16 begins with a reassertion of the barrenness of the matriarch! "Ten years they have stood by (16:3), allowing things to take their course. But when nothing has happened the natural way, they have recourse to a social institution of wide acceptance," concubinage.[44]

> **A**   Introduction: Sarai bears Abram no children (16:1–2)
> > **B**   Indication of time (16:3a)
> > > **C**   Hagar, Abram's wife (16:3b)
> > > > **D**   Hagar's conception, expulsion, return (16:4–14)
> > > **C'**   Hagar, mother of Abram's child (16:15)
> > **B'**   Indication of time (16:16a)
> **A'**   Conclusion: Hagar bears Abram Ishmael (16:16b)

Unlike in Gen 14, Abram and Sarai seem unwilling to wait on God, particularly when the wait seems unfruitful.[45] The two indications of time in Gen 16 reinforce the agony of barrenness throughout the narrative (also see 17:1, 17, 24; 18:12; 21:5). *A*, *B*, *C* and *A'*, *B'*, *C'* are set in Abram's camp; the middle section, *D*, begins in Abram's camp, moves into the wilderness, and returns to home base (see above). Throughout, women

---

42. Ibid., 229–30.

43. Kass, *The Beginning of Wisdom*, 277.

44. Tsevat, *The Meaning of the Book of Job*, 53–54.

45. Does the delay of a decade between intention of plot (16:2) and execution of plot (16:3–4) hint at the couple's hesitation to go through with this machination? Had they waited and waited for Yahweh to work and finally, after ten years, decided they need to shove deity out of the way to get something accomplished?

are the protagonists. While Sarai might be the official wife and the appointed matriarch, in this episode, Hagar is the clear winner. She becomes a "wife" (16:3) and
conceives (16:4), thus usurping the status of the official wife, Sarai.

Sarai and Abram do not come out well in this episode: in the parallel structuring
(below), Sarai is instrumental in the raising of tension, the passing of blame, and, with
her husband, in the exploitation and, later, the expulsion of the maid.[46]

> **A**   Tension: Sarai barren (16:1)
>   **B**   Speech: Sarai blames (16:2a)
>   **C**   Reaction: Abram acquiesces (16:2b)
>   **D**   Result: Hagar given and taken (16:3)
>   *Conception (16:4a)*
> **A'**   Tension: Sarai despised (16:4b)
>   **B'**   Speech: Sarai blames (16:5)
>   **C'**   Reaction: Abram acquiesces (16:6a)
>   **D'**   Result: Hagar harassed and expelled (16:6b)

Sarai's first words seem to be throwing blame at Yahweh for her barrenness. While
there is an element of truth to this in God's sovereign working, the subsequent ploy by
the matriarch reveals her attempt to counteract divine action with human initiative.
Therein lies the irony: can human workings ever resist or refine divine movement? Sarai
is seeking an end run around the designs of Yahweh, and in so doing, Hagar is reduced
to an instrument, a surrogate womb: Sarai "takes" her, and Sarai "gives" her (16:3).
And then she commands her husband: "Go in [בֹּא־נָא, *bo'-na'*] to my maid [אֶל־שִׁפְחָתִי,
'el-shifkhati]" (16:2). Abram acquiesces precisely: "And he went in [וַיָּבֹא, *wayyabo'*] to
Hagar [אֶל־הָגָר, *'el-hagar*]" (16:4).[47]

Of note is that Sarai's interest in this enterprise is all about "building up herself"
(16:2)[48]; it is not about providing a heir for Abram—and in the end, Ishmael is never
claimed by Sarai as her son. Her's is an entirely self-centered view, "God has kept *me*
from bearing" (16:2). She is bent on meeting her own needs without God. All in all,
the matriarch does not seem particularly interested in seed for Abram, in the interests
of Yahweh in this whole matter, or even in the fate of a pregnant maidservant. Sarai's
desire to exclude all competition (here in Gen 16 against herself, and later, in Gen 21,
against her son, Isaac) betokens a fundamental lack of trust in Yahweh's promises. She
is attempting to manipulate the situation for her own ends.

Though God neither negates nor approves Sarai's stratagem, the text clearly announces the problem: twice Sarai is described as Abram's wife (16:1, 3), but Hagar
is also labeled "wife" (16:3). "We are forewarned: should Hagar become pregnant,
the lineage will be confounded and marital harmony challenged. And there is more:
Abram's child will have an Egyptian mother—just as Sarai in Pharaoh's house might

---

46. From Campbell, "Rushing Ahead," 277–78.

47. Trible, "The Other Woman," 222–23. The Code of Hammurabi §146 permitted such an exchange
for child-bearing purposes.

48. Sarai's goal was to be "built up" (בנה, *bnh*, 16:2) through Hagar having a "son" (בֵּן, *bn*, an obvious
pun on the verb בנה).

have borne a son to an Egyptian father."[49] This episode mirrors the earlier wife-sister substitution in Genesis 12—both exhibit a lack of faith in Yahweh.

> In Egypt, Abram asked Sarai to disown the marriage and accept another partner, for his sake . . ., and she obliged. Here, Sarai asks Abram to take another partner and in a sense disown the marriage, for her sake . . ., and he obliges. . . . For whether she knows it or not, Sarai's proposal amounts to measure-for-measure payback for the near-adulterous liaison in Egypt. Just as Abram had pushed Sarai into adultery with Pharaoh, so Sarai pushes Abram into quasi-adultery (actually, polygamy) with Hagar, this time casting herself, as it were, in the role of "sister."[50]

There are a number of parallels between Abram's acquiescence to his wife and Adam's to his in Gen 3, indicating, not so subtly, that Abram's giving in to his wife's demands was not laudatory. Both 3:2 and 16:2 have "[woman/Sarai] said to"; 3:6 and 16:3 have "she took"; 3:6 and 16:3 have "she gave to her husband"; 3:17 and 16:2 have "listened to the voice"; "seed" shows up in both (3:15 and 16:10); "good" (16:6) and "in her/your eyes" (16:5, 6) are allusions to 3:6, where Eve assesses the fruit to be "good" and a delight "to the eyes"[51]; and when God arrives on the scene after the tragic transactions, he asks "Where . . .?" on both occasions (3:9 and 16:8). These allusions make it clear that Sarai's scheming and Abram's compliance are remarkably similar to the sin of Eve and Adam, a lack of faith in God's word and an attempt to operate according to their own wisdom, outside of the will of God. The repetitions of the words "wife" (16:1, 3 [×2]) and "maidservant" (16:1, 2, 3, 5, 6, 8) underscores the rivalry between Sarai and Hagar, made especially poignant when Hagar is called Abram's "wife" (16:3). Prominent also in this verse is the rather redundant statement of the relationship between Abram and Sarai: "Abram's wife" and "her husband Abram." No doubt, this is the narrator's disapproval in evidence, in a verse where Hagar is being given to Abram as his wife! The tragic result was "a runaway slave who carried in her womb the only child of the patriarch."[52]

> Hagar . . . seems to hold no intrinsic interest for anyone. For Sarah, she is strictly a means to acquire children [a womb!], to achieve the full status of a wife. Abraham, while consenting to Sarah's plan, remains passive. He does not seek out Hagar; she is brought to him. No emotional reactions are described. He "consorts with her," and she conceives. When the surrogate startles everyone by taking pride in her pregnancy and Sarah's attitude turns swiftly to jealous resentment, Abraham remains utterly detached. Confronted by his vindictive spouse, who complains that the mouse has roared, he does not refer to Hagar as a wife, concubine, mother of his child, or in any terms referring to his own involvement. He says only, "Your maidservant is in your hand; deal with her as you see fit"(16:6). Years later, Hagar remains a nonperson in Abraham's ethical

---

49. Kass, *The Beginning of Wisdom*, 278.

50. Ibid., 278. Kass adds: "It is worth noting that the Bible's first two episodes of adultery or near adultery arise not from lust but from calculation" (ibid., 279).

51. Abram's subsequent relinquishing of Hagar to Sarai with the words, "Do to her what is good *in your eyes*," is payback for Hagar's disdaining of Sarai: "[Sarai] was despised/slighted *in her eyes*" (16:4).

52. Mathews, *Genesis 11:27–50:26*, 182.

and emotional life. [21:11] . . . His subsequent behavior towards Hagar shows a decent concern for her survival needs, but only her son is personally significant [21:11].[53]

Hagar is being passed around her: in 16:5, Sarai says she had given Hagar to Abram's bosom; in 16:6, Abram counters that Hagar is now in Sarai's hands. She is just an object! While Sarai's anger toward Hagar may have been justified by the latter's disdaining of her (16:4), Sarai's ongoing mistreatment and expulsion of her maid is inexcusable. That this is also the narrator's opinion is evident in the use of ענה (*'nh*, "afflict") to describe Sarai's abuse of Hagar (16:6), a verb that first showed up in 15:13 and that reappears in Exodus and Deuteronomy to refer to the oppression of the Israelites by the Egyptians.[54] And Abram's rather cavalier attitude is equally reprehensible; after all, the woman he was disposing of was his "wife" and the mother of his child. Thus we have yet another woman who is expendable to the patriarch (as was Sarai in Gen 12:10–20). In any case, the familial chaos is total: Hagar, expelled, has lost her home while pregnant; Sarai has lost her maid; and Abram has lost a wife and a child, to say nothing of the loss of marital and domestic peace![55] All of this conniving and manipulation and exploitation marks a lack of faith. And such a failure of faith results in disunity within family, potential loss of a son and, in the long term, generation of a tribe of enemies that are a threat to the descendants of Abram.[56] "Already in Genesis there is a long line of schemes to get blessing apart from God that failed (3:6–8; 4:3–7; 11:1–9; 12:10–20; 13:1–12; 14:21–24), and this one failed too. It did give Abram a son, but not *the* son God intended, and in the end it caused far more problems than it solved, as 16:12 intimates, and as subsequent history demonstrates."[57] This was pure and simple "faithless engineering" and the chaotic consequences thereof.[58]

9.2.2 *Mature faith waits for God even in unfavorable circumstances, thereby keeping the believer in the sphere of divine blessing.*

Hagar is quite the sensation. She is the only woman to be addressed directly by God/ angel of Yahweh and to receive a theophany in Genesis (16:7–12; in fact *two* theophanies—the second in 21:17–18), she is the only woman to call upon Yahweh in this book (16:13), she receives divine promises, and she bears for Abram his first seed—a fact stressed three times in 16:15–16.[59] Moreover, only God is shown as speaking to

---

53. Gordon, "Hagar," 274.

54. Reis, "Hagar Requited," 87–88. See Exod 1:12; 3:7, 17; 4:31; Deut 16:3; etc.

55. Wenham, *Genesis 16–50*, 9.

56. For the Ishmaelites and their interactions with Israelites, see 16:12; 21:9–10; 37:25–28; Jdg 8:24; Ps 83:6.

57. Campbell, "Rushing Ahead," 283.

58. Waltke and Fredricks, *Genesis*, 248.

59. See Wenham, *Genesis 16–50*, 4. This is the first reference to the angel of Yahweh in Scripture (he appears six times in Genesis: 16:7, 9, 10, 11; 22:11, 15). This personage appears to be part of the godhead as 16:10, 13 and 22:1, 15 indicate. The possibility of the angel pardoning sin (Exod 23:20–23) and his absence in the NT have led to the speculation that the angel of Yahweh was the preincarnate Christ.

this woman in Scripture (and God alone addresses her by name, 16:8), and she never speaks to anyone else but God, in the text![60] It is striking that Hagar does not call *upon* the name of Yahweh; rather, she calls the name of Yahweh—it is an identification, not an invocation. And she identifies him as the one who sees.[61] "Hagar actually confers on deity a name. No other character in the OT, male or female, does that. It is not unusual for mortals to give names to family members, to animals, to sacred sites, but never to one's God, with the exception of Hagar."[62]

Yet, Hagar is an unlikely heroine. Her presence in Abram's caravan is probably explained by the possessions the patriarch had acquired in Egypt in Gen 12 (especially note the unusual inclusion of "male and female servants" in the midst of a list of animals, 12:16). Moreover, the mention of the exodus in the prior chapter (15:13–16) has also primed the reader to react negatively to anything Egyptian. There is an irony in this story: Sarai (and Abram, ostensibly) harass the Egyptian and her child; Egyptians enslave and harass Abram and Sarai's descendants.[63] As was noted, Sarai's mistreatment of her maid, described with the verb עָנָה, is precisely echoed in the description of the Egyptians mistreatment of Israel, employing the same verb in Exod 1:12. The consequence of one was that Hagar "fled" (Gen 16:6, 8); the consequence of the other was that the Israelites "fled" (Exod 14:5). And both maid and nation flee to the "wilderness" (Gen 16:7; Exod 15:22; etc.).

Strikingly, in this episode, when asked to return to the (harassing) authority of her mistress (Gen 16:9), Hagar does so without demur. In the structuring of 16:7–14, the second and third speeches of the angel of Yahweh are significant.[64]

A	Angel finds Hagar by a spring of water; location (16:7)
B	First speech of angel; Hagar's response (16:8)
C	Second speech of angel (16:9): condition
C'	Third speech of angel (16:10): consequence
B'	Fourth speech of angel; Hagar's response (16:11–13)
A'	Well named; location (16:14)

In the second utterance of the angel, Hagar was asked to return to Abram's house and to submit to Sarai's authority—the condition (16:9). In the third utterance, the result of meeting that condition is stated: the divine blessing of innumerable descendants (16:10). It was exactly this lesson that had skipped the minds of Abram and Sarai—they were to wait and submit, *if divine blessing were to be fulfilled*. Hagar does so: she returns and submits. She would wait for Yahweh to work out his promises and blessings for her son. Her immediate response was to call upon the name of Yahweh and ex-

---

60. Hagar also becomes the first woman to receive promises directly from Yahweh, not to mention a birth announcement from him as well.

61. Trible, "The Other Woman," 229. "Hagar is a theologian. Her naming unites the divine and human encounter: the God who sees and the God who is seen" (ibid.).

62. Hamilton, *Genesis: Chapters 1–17*, 455.

63. Mathews, *Genesis 11:27–50:26*, 179.

64. From Wenham, *Genesis 16–50*, 3–4.

claim about how she had been seen by the ineffable one (16:13).[65] "Hagar's confident, even joyful response suggests her realization of an all-seeing moral order in which the suffering of the helpless and insignificant do not go unnoticed."[66] The declaration of this Egyptian that this was a God who sees (ראה, *r'h*, 16:13) is echoed in Yahweh's self-assertion that he had surely "seen" (ראה) the "affliction" (ענה, *'nh*) of his people in Egypt (Exod 3:7; also Neh 9:9).[67] The angel of Yahweh, in addition, avers that Yahweh had "heard" (שמע, *shm'*, 16:11) her affliction; that, too, is reflected in Exod 3:7. Hagar is convinced that the Lord "sees" and "hears," as the names "El Roi" (אֵל רְאִי, *el ra'i*) and "Ishmael" (יִשְׁמָעֵאל, *yishma'e'l*) indicate (16:13; 21:9; 16:11; 21:17).[68] Yahweh is a God who sees and hears the ones who trust in him. Coming from an Egyptian, a bond-woman and an alien in a foreign land[69], with no voice in her destiny, such a realization of the sovereignty of God and the exhibition of an unshakeable trust in his plans and purposes—incomprehensible though they surely were, especially when they involved suffering—is quite remarkable. In Gen 16, Hagar is a foil for the untrusting patriarch and the unscrupulous matriarch, both of whom decide to take matters into their own hands to "help" God with this seed-production business.

While the instruction of the angel of Yahweh to Hagar to return to Sarai's oppression (literally, "humble yourself [also from ענה] under her hand," 16:9) sounds unduly harsh in itself, one must remember that true blessing from Yahweh would come only insofar as Hagar was within the sphere of Abram's household and under the patriarch's patronage. There might be no letup in the oppression, but Hagar was at least assured that God had "seen" and "heard" her "affliction" (ענה, 16:11, 13). Hagar and Ishmael are blessed indirectly as they remain with the patriarch, Abram, fulfilling 12:3: they are blessed because of their relationship to him (16:10; 21:13, 18), and by their being part of the covenant when Ishmael, the firstborn, is circumcised (17:23)—in fact, he is the

---

65. Incidentally, Hagar's use of הלם (*hlm*, "here") in 16:13 is the only other use of the word in the Pentateuch; in Exod 3:5 it designates the place of a theophany; that is also likely to have been the thrust of Hagar's use of that word (Reis, "Hagar Requited," 103).

66. Gordon, "Hagar," 276.

67. Hagar's amazement is likely due to the future-sightedness of her divine correspondent: "You are a God who sees" (16:13). Her subsequent exclamation is literally, "Also here I have seen one who after-me [i.e., future generations coming after Hagar, as in Eccles 2:18] sees," or, dynamically, "I have indeed seen the one who sees my future." That would explain the name of the well, "Beer-lahai-roi," i.e., "Well of Living-Seeing," where "living" indicates, again, future generations, as in 3:20, where Eve is the mother of all "living." See Reis, "Hagar Requited," 91–92. Surely Hagar (or the editor) could have used the word "seed" instead of these circumlocutions to indicate future generations. Reis speculates that the reason for not doing so is to keep the pattern of seven uses of "seed" before Hagar's conversation with the angel, and seven uses after, restricted to God's conversations with Abram (before: Gen 12:7; 13:15, 16; 15:3, 5, 13, 18; and after: 17:7 [×2], 8, 9, 10, 12, 19) (ibid., 92–93).

68. From Mathews, *Genesis 11:27–50:26*, 179. Hagar, like Abram, is assured of a descendant at a most critical time, and when the survival of her child is least expected. Her son, like Abram's, was saved from near death: just as Abram "lifted up his *eyes* and saw" a ram, a substitute that would save his son (22:13), so also Hagar's *eyes* were opened and she saw a well, that would save another son of the patriarch (21:19).

69. Even her name is pun on her alien status: הָגָר (*hagar*, Hagar) is a הַגֵּר (*hagger*, "sojourner").

first one to undergo the ritual.[70] In other words, a submissive and waiting faith, i.e., a mature faith, is necessary to keep one in the sphere of divine blessing.

The angel's words to Hagar (16:10) echo the covenant promise of Yahweh to Abram in 15:5.[71] Thus, ironically, what Sarai had been fighting for all along for herself, in the process even exploiting Hagar's womb, the maidservant acquires—*her* descendants would be greatly multiplied and innumerable. In other words, God seems to be taking his covenant promise to the patriarch quite seriously. "No matter that he did not instigate Hagar's conception (Sarai did). No matter that Hagar is not even Hebrew (but Egyptian). A son of Abram is, nevertheless, a son of Abram, and, therefore, part of the covenant. The biblical writer is illustrating that by the covenant of Gen 15 God is willing to bless *any* descendant of Abram."[72] And, even more, God's willingness to bless any human is contingent upon their trust in him—faith is thus *the* sphere of blessing.

On the other hand, those who even "disdain" Abram are threatened divine retribution (12:3). And in this episode, we see one who does—Hagar: she "disdains" Sarai (16:4, 5). The cause of Hagar's disdain is not told us; perhaps it was because her status had now improved—she was Abram's "wife" (16:3). Or perhaps it was because she realized, upon conception, that her child now would potentially have a share of Abram's property.

> If one should agree that everything following 12,1–3 stands under the influence of the thematic question "how does the blessing come in Abraham to the peoples?," then the opposite side of the coin should also apply. "How does the curse (*'rr*) come in Abraham to the people?" The answer must be: "When the people hold Abraham and his family in disdain (*qll*)." . . . To penetrate the kerygma advanced by Gen 12,1–4a, must we not examine texts that describe the curse as well as the blessing? . . . In the following narratives only one story meets the standards of parallel construction with the formulation in 12,3b. That narrative is the Sarah-Hagar story in Gen 16. The point of connection comes explicitly through the verb *qll*.[73]

According to Coats, this episode is less about the seed issue than about the consequences of contempt against Abram and his family, the result of which would be separation from the patriarch, the source of blessing for all families of the earth.[74] This episode, thus, works both ways, showing the blessing of remaining within the sphere of the divine promise and the dangers of not abiding in that realm, either by disdaining Abram's family (Hagar), or by faithlessness (Sarai). Sarai is absent from the final scene

---

70. Hagar fled "from the face" (מִפְּנֵי, *mipne*, "from the presence," 16:6, 8) of her mistress; her son, in turn, would live "away from the face" (עַל־פְּנֵי, *'al-pne*, "against," 16:12) everyone. The "wild donkey" that Ishmael is labeled as, symbolizes one with "an individualistic lifestyle untrammeled by social convention" (Job 24:5–8; 39:5–8; Jer 2:24; Hos 8:9). See Wenham, *Genesis 16–50*, 10–11. That Ishmael will be "against everyone" reinforces this sense of his idiosyncratic, belligerent temperament (see Gen 25:18). Ishmael is also an east-dweller (see Pericope 6 for the significance of an eastern location in Genesis).

71. Also Gen 13:16; 17:2; 22:17; 26:4, 24; 28:3; 35:11; and 48:4.

72. Drey, "The Role of Hagar," 193.

73. Coats, "The Curse in God's Blessing," 33.

74. Ibid., 35.

of Hagar's delivery and the naming of the child; instead, "Hagar bore" appears thrice (16:15 [×2], 16); and "Abram" shows up four times in the two final verses, too. Sarai's goal of being "built up" by Hagar would remain unrealized, for the child is Abram's and Hagar's. While the first word of this episode was "Sarai" (16:1), the last is "Abram" (16:16; in Hebrew). Only those who choose, by faith, to remain within the realm of God's work will be blessed.

SERMON FOCUS AND OUTLINES

THEOLOGICAL FOCUS OF PERICOPE 9 FOR PREACHING

9   Mature faith even in unfavorable circumstances enables the believer experience blessing and bring blessing to others (15:1–16:16).

The previous pericope (Pericope 8) shares a facet of its Theological Focus with that of this pericope: divine blessing as a consequence of a believer's faith. Therefore a sermon on Pericope 9 is best distinguished either by the aspect of blessing that falls upon others as a result of the believer's faith or, even better, by an emphasis on the chaos that immature faith can produce, a removal from the sphere of divine blessing. In fact, one could include both elements, as shown in the outlines below.

Possible Preaching Outlines for Pericope 9

I.   Faith in God's Sovereign Work Brings Blessing to Believers
      Impatient conniving by Abram and Sarai and the resulting chaos (16:1–6)
      Hagar's submission to Yahweh, her return and its consequences (16:7–17)
      Move-to-Relevance: Our impatience and the chaos that results vs. our trust and the blessing it brings

II.   Faith in God's Sovereign Work Brings Blessing to Others
      Abram's faith, though less than perfect (15:1–8)
      The consequences of Abram's faith for his descendants (15:9–21)
      Move-to-Relevance: The person of mature faith as an agent of divine blessing to others

III. *Look up! Look around!*
      Look Up! How we can secure our trust in the God who sees (and hears), amidst unfavorable circumstances
      Look Around! How a mature faith can be exercised so that we may be a source of divine blessing to others

This might also work as a two-movement sermon, with *Look Up!* in the first move and *Look Around!* in the second.

I.   *Look up!* God Works to Bring Blessing to Believers
      Impatient conniving by Abram and Sarai and the resulting chaos (16:1–6)
      Hagar's submission to Yahweh, her return and its consequences (16:7–17)
      Move-to-Relevance: Our impatience and the chaos that results vs. our trust and the blessing it brings
      Look Up! How we can secure our trust in the God who sees (and hears), amidst unfavorable circumstances

II.   *Look around!* Faith in God's Work Brings Blessing to Others
      Abram's faith, though less than perfect (15:1–8)

The consequences of Abram's faith for his descendants (15:9–21)
Move-to-Relevance: The person of mature faith as a agent of divine blessing to others
Look Around! How a mature faith can be exercised so that we may be a source of divine blessing to others

PERICOPE 10

Remembering the Blessing

Genesis 17:1–18:15

[Covenant Confirmed; Conditions Established; Sign Performed; Couple Doubts]

REVIEW, SUMMARY, PREVIEW

Review of Pericope 9: Genesis 15:1–16:16 shows Abram's faith being rewarded with an extended revelation from God, further expanding his earlier promises. Despite the patriarch's doubt, demonstrating a less-than-mature faith, Abram is credited for his trust. But Sarai's manipulation, another expression of immature faith, creates domestic chaos.

Summary of Pericope 10: In this pericope, for the first time God sets an explicit condition for Abram's blessing: he would need to walk with God and be blameless. With his name changed to "Abraham," his identity is now intertwined with divine promise. Though Ishmael is not part of the Abrahamic covenant, he too is blessed by his association with the patriarch. The human-side commitment to divine promise is actualized in the ritual of circumcision. Though Abraham and Sarah laugh in the face of God's assertion that they would have a son, walking with God ultimately brings divine blessings to pass.

Preview of Pericope 11: In Gen 18:16–19:38, the wickedness of the Cities of the Plain results in catastrophic divine judgment—almost a second "deluge." Yet, as the prayer of Abraham sought to achieve, the family of the one associated with the Abrahamic blessing (Lot and his relatives) survives the disaster—just as Noah did during his flood. Both the value of intercessory prayer and of keeping the way of God are emphasized.

10. *Genesis 17:1–18:15*

THEOLOGICAL FOCUS OF PERICOPE 10

10   Divine blessing upon oneself and one's associates is conditioned upon a commitment to walk before God with faith, which commitment may be remembered by a formal, outward act of dedication (17:1–18:15).

10.1   Divine blessing upon oneself and one's associates is conditioned upon a walk before God, a commitment to his way.

10.2   Remembrance of one's commitment to walk before God with faith may be ensured by a formal, outward act of dedication.

OVERVIEW

The narrative of Abraham, as a whole, moves from promise of heir to fulfillment of that promise; within this narrative, there is also the development from statement of Yahweh's promise to the inauguration, (re)confirmation, and ratification of a divine covenant with the patriarch.

This pericope, the first portion of which describes the events of a single day ("the same day," 17:23, 26), comes at the center of the Abraham Story (excluding the "epilogue" of Genesis 23–25).[1]

A   Genealogy of Terah (11:27–32)
  B   Start of Abram's spiritual odyssey; divine promise (12:1–9)
    C   Abram lies; Sarai abducted; God protects;
      Abram and Lot part; promise of descendant (12:10–13:18)
      D   Abram rescues Sodom and Lot (14:1–24)
        E   Divine promise of a son; the child from Abram himself (15:1–21)
          F   Ishmael's birth;
            divine promise re: Ishmael (16:1–16)
            G   Yahweh's covenant; names changed;
              Sarah to be mother; circumcision (17:1–21)
          F'   Ishmael and Abraham circumcised;
            divine promise re: Ishmael (17:22–27; 17:18, 20)
        E'   Divine promise of a son; the child from Sarah herself (18:1–15)
      D'   Abraham rescues Sodom and Lot (18:16–19:38)
    C'   Abraham lies; Sarah abducted; God protects;
      Abraham and Ishmael part; birth of descendant (20:1–21:34)
  B'   Climax of Abraham's spiritual odyssey; divine promise (22:1–19)
A'   Genealogy of Nahor (22:20–24)

The centrality of this pericope is explained by its recording of the confirmation of Yahweh's covenant with Abraham, a statement of its conditions, and the establishment

1. Table below from Dorsey, *The Literary Structure of the Old Testament*, 56; Greidanus, *Preaching Christ from Genesis*, 140; and Rendsburg, *The Redaction of Genesis*, 28–29.

of circumcision, the covenantal sign in the flesh. The covenant, earlier inaugurated in Genesis 15, is now enlarged and confirmed with the sign; the formal ratification with an oath from Yahweh will wait until the patriarch passes his final test in Genesis 22.[2]

	Promise Given 12:1–3, 7; 13:14–17	Covenant Inaugurated 15:1–21	Covenant Confirmed 17:1–27; 18:18–19	Covenant Ratified 22:1–2, 15–18; 26:5
Yahweh	Promise expressed (12:1–3)	Promise re-expressed (15:1–5)	Covenant confirmed (17:1–21)	Covenantal test (22:1–2)
Abraham	Condition met: faithful obedience (12:4–6; Heb 11:8)	Condition met: faith (15:6; Heb 11:9–12)	Condition met: faithful obedience (17:22–27)	Condition met: faithful obedience (22:3–14; Heb 11:17–18)
Yahweh	Promise reiterated (Gen 12:7; 13:14–17)	Covenant inaugurated (Gen 15:7–21)	Covenant reconfirmed (Gen 18:18–19)	Covenant ratified (Gen 22:15–18; 26:5)

In short, the entire saga of the patriarch may be viewed as the giving of a single covenant—initially as a promise (12:1–3, 7; 13:14–17), later as a covenant inaugurated (15:1–21), then confirmed (17:1–27; 18:18–19), and finally ratified (22:1–2, 15–18; 26:5). In every case there appears to be an initial declaration by Yahweh, Abram's response (almost a test?), and, following that, a re-expression or reaffirmation of the promise, which often includes an expansion of the earlier revelation(s). As this tension and progress is maintained throughout the narrative of Abraham, we see the development of his faith, and learn what it means to have mature faith, an unshakeable trust in the person of God, and his provision and his purposes—a movement towards the blessing of God.

Besides the covenantal declarations in Gen 17, there is also the assertion by Yahweh in this pericope that Sarah would be the mother of Abraham's child (17:19). The patriarch needed this unambiguous affirmation, particularly since he and his wife

---

2. Common to Gen 15 and 17 are: the promise of multitudinous offspring (15:5; 17:2, 4, 5, 16, 20), incredulity and the suggestion of surrogate heirs by Abram/Abraham (15:2–3; 17:17–18), "coming forth from your body/you" (15:4; 17:6), the promise of land (15:7, 18; 17:8), ceremonial rituals (15:9–11, 17; 17:10–14, 23–27), and multiple divine communications (15:1, 4, 5, 7, 9, 13, 18; 17:1, 3, 9, 15, 19). See Williamson, *Abraham, Israel and the Nations*, 117. Unlike Williamson, who distinguishes between the covenants in Genesis 15 and 17 primarily on the basis of conditionality, I think the simplest reading, as noted earlier, is to see the entire Abraham Story as developing a single covenant: from promise to covenant inaugurated to covenant confirmed to covenant ratified (ibid., 103–13). The differences between the descriptions in the various chapters of Genesis, I view as progress and enlargement of prior revelation, not as new and discrete covenantal entities. The withdrawal of deity *before* the performance of the rite of circumcision (Yahweh departs in 17:22, before the patriarch begins to undertake the operation in 17:23), as well as the recurring nature of that ceremony, points to circumcision portraying the subject's incorporation into the covenant community rather than it acting as a formal ratification of the covenant, which would have required the presence of both parties at the event (Derouchie, "Circumcision in the Hebrew Bible," 186).

had been prone to doing things their own way, outside of the will of God, in order to generate descendants. Yet, despite the affirmation, the couple's doubts still linger. Genesis 17 recounts events that occur thirteen years after those of Gen 16 and the birth of Ishmael (16:16; 17:1, 24). Abram must surely have been wondering when the promise of Yahweh would be fulfilled. The statement of the man's age, ninety-nine, begins and ends this section (17:1, 24), adding to the tension of the story. More than a decade had passed since Ishmael was born, and over two decades since the patriarch had left his homeland, relatives, and father's house. When would he finally see the descendant promised? "Our text [Gen 17] is situated in that long, uncertain season before fulfillment, where faith in the promise wrestles with loss of confidence in the promise." Perhaps that is why the text of Gen 17 is almost entirely divine speech, "the unfettered decree of the sovereign God whose decree will not be denied by the recalcitrance of circumstance," or, I might add, by the incredulity of man, clearly exhibited by the patriarch all through Gen 12–16.[3] The divine revelation in this chapter therefore reiterates the previous promises of seed and land (12:1–3, 7; 13:14–17; 15:1–5, 18–21), addressing the skepticism voiced by Abram (who had earlier proposed Eliezer as the seed, 15:3) and by Sarai (who had sought to engineer a surrogate womb, 16:2): the divine word was clear—the expected son would be born of Sarah.[4]

Genesis 18:1–15 is related to Gen 17: both begin with Yahweh's appearance (17:1; 18:1); and both have an annunciation of Isaac's birth drawing attention to the "set time next year" (17:19, 21; 18:10, 14).[5]

Genesis 17	Genesis 18
"And Yahweh appeared" (17:1)	"And Yahweh appeared" (18:1)
He speaks to Abraham, not Sarah; and promises son in a year (17:15–16)	He speaks to Abraham, not Sarah, and promises son in a year (18:9–10)
Abraham laughs; secretly reflects on age (17:17)	Sarah laughs secretly; reflects on age (18:12)
Yahweh affirms promise (17:19)	Yahweh challenges (18:13, 15)
"Laugh" motif (יִצְחָק, *yitskhaq*) (17:17, 19, 21)	Sarah denies "laughing" (צָחַק, *tsakhaq*) (18:15)
Yahweh reaffirms promise; "set time" (17:21)	Yahweh reaffirms promise; "set time" (18:14)

These similarities, particularly the issue of Sarah's doubt and laughter (Gen 18) that link with the identical response of Abraham in Gen 17, justify the inclusion of 18:1–15 within Pericope 10.

3. Brueggemann, "Genesis 17:1–22," 55.

4. Mathews, *Genesis 11:27–50:26*, 192.

5. From McEvenue, *The Narrative Style*, 153.

10   Genesis 17:1–18:15

THEOLOGICAL FOCUS 10[A]

10   Divine blessing upon oneself and one's associates is conditioned upon a commitment to walk before God with faith, which commitment may be remembered by a formal, outward act of dedication (17:1–18:15).

> 10.1   *Divine blessing upon oneself and one's associates is conditioned upon a walk before God, a commitment to his way.*
>
> 10.2   *Remembrance of one's commitment to walk before God with faith may be ensured by a formal, outward act of dedication.*

A. Having only one section in this pericope, the "Theological Focus 10" is identical to the "Theological Focus of Pericope 10."

NOTES 10

10.1   Divine blessing upon oneself and one's associates is conditioned upon a walk before God, a commitment to his way.

This is the first time a condition for Abram to be blessed is explicitly stated: "Walk before Me, and be blameless. And I will establish My covenant between Me and you, And I will greatly multiply you" (17:1–2; implicit conditions have, of course, been discerned from the beginning of the Abraham Story). The cohortative (וְאֶתְּנָה, *wĕttnah*, "and I will give/establish," 17:2) following the imperatives demarcates it as the consequence/result of Abram's divinely recommended behavior. Kass observes that while God had promised to be a "shield" to Abram, ostensibly in *front* of the patriarch (15:1), here Abram is to walk in *front* of God! "In sum: go as my champion and emissary before My observing, protecting, guiding, and judging presence."[6] And as Abram is asked to walk "before" (literally, "before the face") of God, he responds by "falling on his face" (17:3). This demand of Yahweh in 17:1, that Abram walk before him and be blameless, may indicate that for the prior quarter century, the patriarch's loyalty and allegiance to the ways of God had not been flawless. That, of course, has been quite clear from the development of the narrative thus far.

The two imperatives that commenced Yahweh's first directive to Abram in Gen 12:1 ("Go [הֵלֵךְ, *hlk*]" and "be a blessing [וֶהְיֵה בְּרָכָה, *wehyeh brakah*]") were structured similarly to the two in 17:1: "Walk [הֵלֵךְ]" and "be blameless [וֶהְיֵה תָמִים, *wehyeh tamim*]." These same demands also characterized the life of Noah who was "blameless" and "walked with God" (6:9). For him, however, it was an already achieved target—Noah's status is declared as being blameless from the outset; Abram would have to learn how

---

6. Kass, *The Beginning of Wisdom*, 310, 310n16. The patriarchs walked "before" God, as God called them to do (17:1; 24:40; 48:15). This is likely to be equivalent to walking "with" God, as Enoch and Noah did (5:22, 24; 6:9). Quite frequently, הֵלֵךְ (*hlk*, "go/walk") shows up as a divine command to Abraham: 12:1; 13:17; 17:1; 22:2 (and describes Abraham's actions in 11:31; 12:4, 5, 9, 19; 22:3, 5, 6, 8, 13, 19). Indeed, the very first word God speaks to Abraham is "go/walk" (12:1).

to be so.[7] To be תָּמִים was to be "undivided, simple, complete, perfect, wholehearted, blameless." Considering the two imperatives as a parallelism, one could reckon that "walk before Me" was being equated to "be blameless." Abram was to be "in his heart and soul, wholly oriented with the Lord and wholly committed to His way," with no subsidiary loyalties adulterating his commitment.[8]

All this to say, the experience of divine blessing was contingent upon meeting the conditions set forth by God. In initiative, however, the covenant is entirely unilateral; Abram had no instigating role in its inauguration or confirmation (or later in its ratification). In fact, in 17:3, the first mention of the establishment of the covenant in Gen 17 is as a verbless clause: "I, behold, my covenant with you." The patriarch does not voice an opinion; he does not exercise a vote; he does not argue. He is simply said to be in covenant with the promoter, Yahweh.[9] The tone is set with the first word of Yahweh's utterances to Abraham (אֲנִי, *'ani*, "I") in 17:1 and 17:4: it is God taking the initiative.

With the formal confirmation of this critical covenant, Abram also undergoes a name change, the first one in the Bible (17:4–5). While "Abraham" is only a dialectical variation of "Abram" it creates a wordplay with אַב־הֲמוֹן, *'ab-hamon*, "father of a multitude."[10] Now Abraham's identity is intertwined with Yahweh's promise: the change of his name (and that of his wife, 17:15–16) signified a break with the past; it was also an adumbration of the multitude of nations that would come from him in the future. From now on, Abram/Abraham could never ignore God's promise of descendants for him. "Abraham's very identity is now inextricable from God's promise of abundant offspring. His *being* depends on God's speech. If God breaks his promise, Abraham ceases to be Abraham."[11] It was a destiny-defining new name; he had left country, relatives, and father's house (12:1), setting out alone, and now he was to become the father of a multitude of nations—a more than adequate return on his costly investment. It is also a name that "universalizes Abraham's experience with God." While his circumcision made him father of the Israelites, his new name designated him as "the father of many *goyim*, not many *yehudim*."[12] The blessing of God through this one man would ripple worldwide.

The command to be fruitful and to multiply was the first one given to mankind (1:28); it was also repeated to Noah, after a fresh start for humanity post-flood (8:17;

---

7. "Walking before" signifies faithful service and devotion to a superior, be that human (1 Kgs 1:2; 10:8; Jer 52:2) or divine (Gen 5:22, 24, 6:9; 17:1; 24:40; 48:15; Deut 10:8; 18:7; Jdg 20:28; Ezek 44:15) (Hamilton, *Genesis: Chapters 1–17*, 461).

8. Kass, *The Beginning of Wisdom*, 310.

9. Brueggemann, "Genesis 17:1–22," 56.

10. The change of his wife's name from "Sarai" to "Sarah" is also a dialectical variation; both mean "princess/queen." These yield "a flexible 'literary' etymology, which takes no account of linguistic differences between the name and the proposed explanation" (Fleishman, "On the Significance of a Name Change," 21). Curiously, הרבה ... במאר (*'rbh . . . bm'r*, "multiply . . . exceedingly," 17:2b), is almost an exact anagram of אברהם (*'brhm*, "Abraham").

11. Kass, *The Beginning of Wisdom*, 312.

12. Hamilton, *Genesis: Chapters 1–17*, 464.

9:1, 7). Now, another new era is being inaugurated and the command is reiterated to Abram (17:2, 6, 20; also see 28:3; 35:11; 47:27; 48:4), but with a slight twist.

> Abraham, . . . like Adam and Noah, stands at the beginning of an epoch in human history. God's original purpose for mankind, thwarted by the fall and faltering again in the post-Noah period, is eventually to be achieved by Abraham's descendants. It may be noted that whereas Adam and Noah were simply commanded "be fruitful" (qal imperative), God makes Abraham a promise, "I shall make you fruitful" (hiphil). This change of conjugation suggests that Abraham will be given divine power to achieve this fertility [Gen 17:6], whereas his predecessors, left simply to themselves, failed.[13]

While the covenant was conditional, ultimately it would be on Yahweh's initiative and benevolence that Abraham would become fruitful and his seed would multiply "exceedingly" (17:2, 6, 20). Incidentally, Sarah is said to be blessed (17:16), and so also is Ishmael (17:20), but for Abraham, there is no explicit statement of divine blessing in this chapter. Instead, in Gen 17, it is the covenant that indirectly describes the abundance, nature, and mode of divine blessing upon the patriarch. Thus the theme of covenant is key in Gen 17; בְּרִית, *brit*, occurs thirteen times (in 17:2, 4, 7 [×2], 9, 10, 11, 13 [×2], 14, 19 [×2], 21). And regarding the covenant, this chapter makes significant enlargements in the divine plan from what had been stated in Gen 15. In Gen 17, we are told for the first time that it would be a perpetual covenant: "everlasting" (17:7, 8, 13), and "throughout their generations" (17:9).[14] And here, the covenant is subsequently confirmed by a sign—circumcision (17:11). Moreover, this covenant would not just be between Yahweh and Abraham, but between Yahweh and Abraham's descendants—an everlasting covenant relationship of Yahweh with the children of Abraham.[15]

All the elements of God's earlier promises—regarding land, seed, and divine blessing/relationship—are found in this chapter and are intimately related to the covenant. Wenham traces the progress of each of these elements through the narrative up to this point.[16] The land was "this land" in 12:7; "all the land which you see" promised "to you and your descendants forever" in 13:15; and "this land, from the river of Egypt as far as the great river, the river Euphrates" in 15:18. However, in 17:8, for the first time the land is identified by Yahweh as "the land of your sojourns, all the land of Canaan."[17] In 12:2, Abraham is promised that he will become a "great nation"; in 13:16,

---

13. Wenham, *Genesis 16–50*, 21–22.

14. Neither the Hebrew עֹלָם, *'lm*, or the Greek αἰώνιον, *aiōnion*, projects the idea of endlessness; they can refer to events or conditions in the past as well (Gen 6:4; Deut 32:7; 1 Sam 27:8; Job 22:15; Prov 22:28; Isa 58:12; Jer 6:16; Ezek 36:2; Micah 7:14; Mal 3:4; etc.). "Thus, while it may be wrong to press the time-period encompassed . . . into the unlimited dimensions of endlessness, the idea of perpetuity is undeniably present"—at the very least, it indicates endurance for a long time. Williamson, *Abraham, Israel and the Nations*, 186; See Macrae, "עֹלָם," 672–73. The land was also described with the motif of perpetuity—it would be an "everlasting" possession (17:8).

15. Those who would "keep" the covenant included both the patriarch ("keep" in 17:9 is singular) and his descendants ("keep" in 17:10 is plural).

16. *Genesis 16–50*, 16–17.

17. The narrator had already implied that the "land of Canaan" would be the patriarch's possession

he is told his descendants will be as innumerable as the "dust of the earth"; in 15:5, they are promised to be as countless as the stars in the sky. But in 17:5–6, 16, Abraham and Sarah would be the progenitors of a "multitude of nations" as well as of "kings" (17:6, 16).[18] Moreover, the mother of the chosen descendant is finally specified as being Sarah (17:19, 21). As for the relationship between God and Abram and his descendants, 12:3 asserted that the patriarch would be blessed, that he himself would be a blessing, and that, in turn, others would be blessed through him. In Gen 13–14, the one who removed himself from Abram's presence (Lot) ended up in trouble as a POW, suggesting that divine blessing was experienced only by association with Abram. In Gen 15, the covenant of blessing between Abram and Yahweh is inaugurated with a ceremony (15:9–17). In Gen 16, again, the one who remains in relationship with Abram is blessed (Hagar). However, it is in 17:1–2, 9–14 that conditions are explicitly stated for the formalizing of the relationship between deity and patriarch: the one to be blessed would have to walk with God and be blameless. The resulting blessing would be the greatest and the most magnificent of its kind conferred upon the patriarch and his seed: Yahweh would be the God of Abram and his descendants—"I will be to you God" and "I will be to them God" (17:7, 8), a personal relationship of deity to humanity. "This latter phrase, used twice here and not again till 28:21, expresses the heart of the covenant, that God has chosen Abraham and his descendants, so that they are in a unique relationship: he is their God, and they are his people" (Exod 4:16; 6:7; 29:45; Lev 11:45; 26:12, 45; Deut 29:13; etc.).[19] The structuring of 17:7–8 reinforces this idea with repetition.[20]

> **A** Yahweh's promise to Abraham and his descendants (17:7a)
>   **B** of an everlasting covenant (17:7b)
>   **C** and to be God to him and to them (17:7c)
> **A'** Yahweh's promise to Abraham and his descendants (17:8a)
>   **B'** of an everlasting possession (17:8b)
>   **C'** and to be God to them (17:8c)

On the other hand, though he was not a beneficiary of the covenant proper (17:21), the blessings upon Ishmael, the firstborn of the patriarch, are considerable (17:20): he is blessed, he will be fruitful (fulfilling 1:22, 28; 9:1, 7; 17:2, 6), he will father twelve princes (25:16; also true of Jacob, 35:22; 49:28), and he will be made a great nation (21:13, 18; also true of Abraham, 12:2; 18:18; also of Jacob, 46:3; Deut 26:5)—all by virtue of his association with Abraham, by his remaining within the realm of

---

in 11:31; 12:5 (×2); 13:12; and 16:3.

18. The promise of descendants who would be kings indicates the creation of autonomous nations (17:6, 16; and 35:11). Abraham himself is not a regent (though he is labeled "prince" in 23:6), but he would be the progenitor of royalty: Ishmael gives rise to tribal rulers, including "kings" and "princes" (17:16; 25:12–17); Edom has kings (36:9–43); and it is expected, from the mention of Judah's scepter (49:10) that the latter's descendants would raise up a royal house (Mathews, *Genesis 11:27–50:26*, 202). The Pentateuch anticipates Israelite kingship outside Genesis as well, in Num 24:17; Deut 17:14–20; 28:36.

19. Wenham, *Genesis 16–50*, 22.

20. Table from Williamson, *Abraham, Israel and the Nations*, 172.

divine blessing (12:3).[21] Indeed, Ishmael seems to have been the first to be circumcised (17:23). But the covenant proper is with Isaac (17:19, 21), and its perpetuity and the permanent inheritance of land are only for the descendants of Abraham through him (17:7, 8, 9). That might explain the redundant employment of "descendants after you" (17:7 [×2], 8, 9, 10, 19) and "throughout their generations" (17:7, 9, 12), pointing, in Gen 17, to Abraham's *subsequent* descendants through Isaac as the specific beneficiaries of the primary articles of the covenant. "Whereas Ishmael, as part of Abraham's family, was himself included within the covenant community, this covenantal status was not explicitly extended to his progeny, as was clearly the case for the line of Isaac (Gen 17:19)."[22]

The scene of divine revelation in Gen 17 begins with Yahweh's "appearance" (17:1) and ends with Yahweh's finished speech (וַיְכַל לְדַבֵּר, *waykal ldabber*, "and when he finished speaking," 17:22), with even Ishmael being blessed by virtue of association with Abram. Interestingly, Gen 18 also commences with a divine "appearance" (18:1) and concludes with a "finished speech" (כִּלָּה לְדַבֵּר, *kilah ldabber*, 18:33). Here, Lot is the recipient of blessing (protection) accruing from his affiliation with his uncle (see Pericope 11). The careful structuring of the beginnings and endings of these chapters reinforces the truth that those who opt to be associated with Abraham will experience divine blessing themselves. Thus "seed," though physiological, also has a symbolic dimension, including all who choose to be related to Abraham and thus to remain within the sphere of divine blessing, even one "bought with money from any foreigner who is not one of your descendants" (17:12, 13, 27). Yet, some of those who are physiologically descendants of Abraham—Ishmael and his progeny, for instance—are excluded (see Gen 21:12).

"In summary, therefore, the central promise in Genesis 17 closely relates to Abraham's phenomenal expansion in a multinational sphere. Abraham will be a 'father' to this international company, not in the sense of being their progenitor, but rather through his special status and the particular responsibilities that he will discharge on their behalf."[23] The fatherhood of Abraham over a multitude of nations likely signifies his status as a mediator of divine blessing to many *outside* Israel (note the distinction in 35:11 between "nation," i.e., Israel, and "company of nations"). Such a non-biological use of "father" is used of humans in Gen 45:8; Jdg 17:10; 18:19; Job 29:16; Isa 22:21; it is similarly used of God in Deut 32:6; 2 Sam 7:14; 1 Chr 7:13; 22:10; 28:6; Pss 68:5; 89:26; Isa 9:6; 63:16; Jer 3:4, 19; 31:9; Mal 2:10. Williamson notes that whenever the preposition לְ, *l*, is linked with אָב ('*b*, "father"), as in 17:4 and in many of these other texts, "a metaphorical concept of fatherhood is undeniably in view." In

---

21. In Gen 17:20, with Ishmael's name (יִשְׁמָעֵאל, *yishma'e'l*) comes a divine assertion, "I have heard you"—שְׁמַעְתִּיךָ, *shma'ttika*, an obvious wordplay. The grace of God operates to bless even those who are simply associated with the primary recipient of divine blessing, a theme that has been encountered in the prior chapters of the Abraham Story.

22. Williamson, *Abraham, Israel and the Nations*, 161–62. Of course, there would be exclusions even within Isaac's line—Esau, for instance (Gen 28:3–4, 13–15; 35:9–12).

23. Ibid., 166.

most of these instances, "[a]s an אב, each has special status and each has particular responsibilities to discharge." Perhaps that is the significance of the conditions attached to the beginning of this pericope: "Walk before Me, and be blameless" (17:1).[24] The one who wishes to be a blessing to others has some special responsibilities to fulfill. Calvin's words are appropriate (*Comm. Gen.* 17:1):

> In making the covenant, God stipulates for obedience, on the part of his servant. . . . Now, from these words, we learn for what end God gathers together for himself a church; namely, that they whom he has called, may be holy. The foundation, indeed, of the divine calling, is a gratuitous promise; but it follows immediately after, that they whom he has chosen as a peculiar people to himself, should devote themselves to the righteousness of God. . . . Wherefore, let us know, that God manifests himself to the faithful, in order that they may live as in his sight.

God's blessings attend those who walk before him, committed to his ways.

10.2 Remembrance of one's commitment to walk before God with faith may be ensured by a formal, outward act of dedication.

This section, 17:1–27, is unique for the five speeches Yahweh makes, each demarcated with the verb "he said" (17:1b, 3b, 9, 15, 19; see highlighted sections below, with the divine utterances numbered 1–5). The first and second (*C, E*) deal with the promise of innumerable descendants; the fourth and fifth (*E', C'*), with the specific descendant that is promised; the third speech (*F*), in the center, instructs the patriarch about the covenantal sign of circumcision. The account concludes with the obedience of Abraham and his household in performing the sign, an outward manifestation of an inward commitment to God.[25]

```
A    Abram is 99 (17:1aα)
  B    Yahweh appears (17:1aβ)
    C    Yahweh 1: self-identification, multiplication, conditions (17:1b–2)
      D    Abram: falls on face (17:3a)
        E    Yahweh 2: name change, nations/kings by Abraham (17:3b–8)
          F    Yahweh 3: covenant sign, circumcision (17:9–14)
        E'    Yahweh 4: name change, nations/kings by Sarah (17:15–16)
      D'    Abraham: falls on face, laughs, offers Ishmael (17:17–18)
    C'    Yahweh 5: specification of seed, future for Isaac and Ishmael (17:19–21)
  B'    Yahweh goes up (17:22)
A'    Abraham is 99; sign of covenant obeyed (17:24–27)
```

Circumcision, itself, was not a new rite being introduced; Egyptians and certain West Semitic peoples were known to have practiced it (see Jer 9:25–26). It appears, though,

---

24. Ibid., 158, 159; Alexander, "Abraham Reassessed," 17. Moreover, the vocalization of אב is unusual in 17:4, the only place in the MT where it is vocalized אַב, *'ab*; the construct form is otherwise always אֲבִי, *'abi*. Williamson suspects it may indicate the unusual connotation of "fatherhood" here: "it is clearly quite legitimate to look for Abraham's multitudinous and international progeny beyond the parameters of his physical descendants" (*Abraham, Israel and the Nations*, 159–60). Also, 17:6 is literally, "I will give you *for/to* nations"—presumably to benefit them as an agent of divine blessing.

25. Table from Mathews, *Genesis 11:27–50:26*, 200.

that during the days of biblical Israel, only this nation completely amputated the fore-skin.[26] The only other signs linked to covenants are that of the rainbow (Gen 9:13–17) and of the Sabbath (Exod 31:13–17). All are "given" by God, and are qualified as being set up "between Me and you" (9:12, 13; 17:2, 10, 11; Ezek 20:12 with Exod 16:29). Since the rainbow and the Sabbath reminded the parties of the covenant about their obligations, it is fair to assume that that was the function of circumcision as well. It was performed "in the flesh" of males, and the consequence of non-conformity to that mandate was their being "cut off" from the community (17:11, 13–14). Thus the sign was essentially for the benefit of Abraham and his descendants, rather than for God (which was the case for the sign of the rainbow, 9:14–16).[27] Therefore, while the exact function of circumcision is not made explicit in Gen 17, apart from its employment as a sign of the covenant, it appears that the rite was primarily a "mnemonic cognition sign" that reminded those who underwent it of Yahweh's covenant and their own responsibilities in that relationship ("walk before Me and be blameless," 17:1), as well as the benefits of obedience (the guarantee of posterity—e.g., Gen 12:2: 15:5; 17:4–5, 19; 18:10—and Yahweh's being God to them), and the consequences of disobedience (being "cut off").[28] It must, however, be remembered that circumcision was only a *sign* of the covenant, and "not the essence of the covenant; the covenant depended ultimately on the spiritual allegiance of the parties" (Lev 26:41; Deut 10:16; 30:6; Jer 4:4; Rom 2:29; Col 2:11).[29]

26. Sasson, "Circumcision in the Ancient Near East," 473–76; Derouchie, "Circumcision in the Hebrew Bible," 187, 187–88n24.

27. While it is imaginative, I do not particularly see Hamilton's point that "God will see the circumcised penis of the Israelite before and during sexual congress, and will then 'remember' his promise to Abraham and to all his descendants to make them very fertile" (*Genesis: Chapters 1–17*, 470). In any case, the "breaking" (17:14) of the covenant was a serious matter; the same verb describes Israel's later apostasy in Isa 24:5; Jer 11:10; 33:21. While ostracism from the community is certainly involved in the resulting punitive "cutting off" of the uncircumcised person, it is unclear whether the death penalty was exacted on such offenders, despite verses that imply this terminal sentence: Exod 31:14; Lev 20:2–5; Josh 11:21; 1 Sam 28:9; 1 Kgs 11:16; Ps 101:8. Incidentally, an entire tractate of the Mishnah is given to this discussion of the meaning of "cutting off" (כרת, *krt*; the discourse is appropriately named *Keritot*).

28. Derouchie, "Circumcision in the Hebrew Bible," "Mnemonic cognition sign" is drawn from Fox, "The Sign of the Covenant," 563: "Mnemonic signs bring to consciousness something already known."

29. Mathews, *Genesis 11:27–50:26*, 203. While Gen 17:10 does seem to equate circumcision with the covenant, it is obvious that the rite is only a synecdoche, a part (the ceremony) for the whole (the covenant). Martin demonstrates how the sign of the covenant generates the three antitheses of Gal 3:28, based upon status of circumcision: between Jew and Greek (i.e., Gentile = uncircumcised), slave and free (the latter did not need to be circumcised; the former did), and male and female (also distinguished by circumcision; this explains the use of terms ἄρσεν/θῆλυ (*arsen/thēly*) for "male/female"—including children and adults of both genders—rather than ἀνήρ/γυνή (*anēr/gynē*), which indicates *adult* "male/female"). The "Greek" and the "free" person in the first two antitheses could choose to become circumcised though they were not obliged to do so; the "female" in the third antithesis obviously could not, even if she wanted to (female circumcision was never practiced by the Jews). This would also explain the variation of syntax between the first two pairs in Gal 3:28 (οὐκ ... οὐδε, *ouk . . . oude*) and the third (οὐκ ... καί, *ouk . . . kai*). Thus, "[w]hen Gal 3:28 proclaims that in Christ there is neither Jew nor Greek, slave nor free, and that in Christ there is no male and female, the proclamation only pertains to the absence of these distinctions as requirements for baptism [entry into the community of faith] in contrast to the requirements in the covenant of circumcision." In the current dispensation, in Christ, the Abrahamic

Such a formal confirmation of the covenant by Yahweh in his five speeches unfortunately did not produce instantaneous mature faith on the part of the Abraham. Right after the details of the rite of circumcision were provided by Yahweh, and immediately following the promise of Sarah's conception and delivery (17:9–16), Abraham falls on his face and laughs (17:17)! Falling on one's face before the Creator and laughing is almost oxymoronic. Clearly, when Abram is reported as falling on his face in 17:3, he was demonstrating his submission to Yahweh, but when he repeats this prostration (17:17–18), he has not yet relinquished his incredulity at God's promise of a child for him through Sarah. Of note, the first time ever that "Abraham" is used as the subject of a verb, it is to denote the man falling on his face and laughing (17:17): he is pessimistic about the very promise that his name was intended to signify—father of a multitude of nations (17:5).[30] And all he can do as he responds in speech is to scoff and offer God a more credible alternative, a counter proposal: Ishmael (17:17–18). First he had thought the chosen descendant would be Lot (Gen 12–14); then he had proposed Eliezer (Gen 15); now he recommends Ishmael. And Isaac? Abraham laughs at the thought. While this chapter is the central pericope of the Abraham story, and epochal in nature with the covenant being confirmed, conditions being laid out, and consequences being offered, the faith of Abraham does not seem to have matured much in thirteen years. All of this is surprising when one considers that in his preamble in this pericope, Yahweh identified himself for the first time in Scripture as El-Shaddai ("God Almighty," 17:1), a phenomenal self-description of deity as ruler of all the cosmos. In the context of God's promise of descendants, and in the light of the other uses of the label in Genesis (which always deal with fruitfulness and multiplication), "Shaddai evokes the idea that God is able to make the barren fertile and to fulfill his promises," for nothing is impossible for a God who is Almighty.[31] But Abraham, he was still skeptical.

The resulting rebuke by Yahweh of Abraham's proposal of Ishmael as his heir (17:17–18) is unequivocal: it commences with "indeed" for emphasis; the patriarch's chosen seed would be Isaac, and he would come from Sarah (17:19). Without waiting for an answer from the dithering patriarch, God departs (17:22). To his credit, Abraham's subsequent response, despite his earlier unbelief, is obedience—"the same

---

blessing is upon *all* marked by the sign of baptism, with no racial, gender, or social distinction. This emphasizes, in no uncertain terms, that salvation in Christ is universally offered without any discrimination of recipients whatsoever. See Martin, "The Covenant of Circumcision," 117, 118, 121, 122. Why there is a masculine mandate for the exhibition of the sign of circumcision cannot be satisfactorily explained, though, clearly, only one in a spousal pair needs the ritual for "they shall be one flesh" (Gen 2:24). Perhaps simplicity of operation and relative safety of the procedure in males may explain the logic of circumcision being instituted for that particular gender, not to mention the relative ease of subsequent identification of those who have undergone the rite.

30. Sailhamer, *The Pentateuch as Narrative*," 159.

31. Wenham, *Genesis 16–50*, 20. "El Shaddai" occurs only in Genesis (in 17:1; 28:3; 35:11; 43:14; 48:3; also see 49:25), and all of these instances deal in some way with the blessings of fertility and/or the restoration of children to a father (48:3). Thus far, in Genesis, we have only seen Melchizedek's El-Elyon ("God Most High," 14:19–20) and Hagar's El-Roi ("God who Sees," 16:13); this was a new revelation of God's person and activity.

day" (mentioned twice: 17:23, 26), and exactly as God had told him.[32] There is no land, no seed, and no obvious outcome of a relationship with Yahweh, but Abraham obeys, cuts flesh, and the covenant is made visible and tangible . . . by faith!

The progression from Gen 17 (with the focus on Abraham, including the covenantal rite) to Gen 18:1–15 (with the focus on Sarah) parallels the similar progress from Gen 15 (Abram's perspective, including covenantal rite) to Gen 16 (Sarai's perspective).[33] Genesis 18:1–15 forms an archetypal annunciation scene. Alter observes that in all other such instances, the first two elements of the standard sequence—the barrenness of the protagonist and the annunciation of conception—are immediately followed in the account by the third element: the birth of the child (25:19–25; Jdg 13; 1 Sam 1; 2 Kgs 4:8–17).[34] However, in the case of Sarah, the annunciation and delivery are interrupted for a couple of chapters: the annunciation is noted in 18:10, 14 (and in 17:19, 21), but Isaac is said to be born only in 21:2 (with conception *and* birth in that same verse!). It may well be that Sarah's doubt further prolongs the suspense: When would their child be born?

Theophany links Gen 17 and 18:1–15.[35] The response of Abraham in 18:2, he "looked up and saw," often marks significant occurrences in the OT: 22:4; 24:63; 43:29; Josh 5:13; Jdg 19:17. The patriarch's response to this theophany is entirely submissive and deferential: he sees, runs, bows (18:2), requests (18:3–5, using "please"—the particle נא, *n'*, twice: 18:3, 4), hurries (18:6 [×2]), runs again (18:7), hurries again (18:8), makes (thrice, 18:6, 7, 8), takes and gives (twice, 18:7, 8), and stands, solicitously watching his guests eat (18:8)—the perfect host![36] Wenham reminds us that elsewhere in the Pentateuch, סלת (*slt*, "fine flour," 18:6) is used only "for cereal offerings and for making the bread of the presence (Lev 24:5), and the regulations about the sacrifice constantly insist on the necessity of offering only top-quality animals (cf. Abraham's

---

32. Other important biblical events are marked by "same day": see Gen 7:13; Exod 12:17, 41, 51; Lev 23:21, 28–30; Deut 32:48; Josh 5:11; Ezek 24:2; 40:1. This, then, was a momentous event in history!

33. Mathews, *Genesis 11:27–50:26*, 208n379.

34. Alter, "Sodom as Nexus," 149.

35. In 18:1, Yahweh is the one who appears to Abraham, but the patriarch sees three men (18:2). In parallel to this sequence, Abraham first uses the singular "your" in 18:3, but the plural form in 18:4–9. And immediately after "they said" (18:9), it again becomes singular: "he said" (18:10). The three are said to rise up, prepare (18:16), and depart (18:22). But only two angels show up in Sodom (19:1). Likewise, in 19:18, Lot seems to be addressing "lords" (plural), but in 19:19 the singular verbs and pronouns depict Lot speaking to one person, who apparently was Yahweh (19:24). This alteration and switching back and forth between singular and plural may emphasize that "though God himself did not appear to Abraham [or, later, to Lot] in physical form, the three men represent his presence" (Sailhamer, *The Pentateuch as Narrative*, 164). "Passing by" (עבר, *'br*, 18:3) is also frequently associated with theophanies (Exod 33:18–23; 34:4–11; 1 Kgs 19:9–21; 2 Kgs 3:8–17; Ezek 16:1–14; Hos 10:11–13). The "return" of Yahweh that is promised to Abraham with surety ("I will surely return," Gen 18:10) likely indicates not a re-visit, but a gracious intervention of Yahweh on behalf of his children in need (see Zech 1:3; Ps 80:14); this "return" is affirmed with a "behold" (Gen 18:10). Such a striking promise proves the visitor is divine; moreover he is omnipotent: though the three strangers have never met Sarah, their spokesman knows her name (18:9), and can discern her reaction to his promise without seeing her (18:13).

36. No wonder he found favor with Yahweh (18:3), the only other to have done so thus far, after Noah (6:8)!

'fine tender bull'). The narrative may be hinting that he is behaving more wisely than he realized."[37] In fact, the word "bowing" (the Hishtaphel of שָׁחַה, *shakhah*) is elsewhere translated "worship" when performed before deity (Gen 24:26; Exod 20:5). Abraham is evidently treating God the way he should. Moreover, his generosity to his divine guest(s) is remarkable. His "fragment of bread" (18:5) turns out to be a quite a feast involving about 22 quarts (six gallons) of wheat and a whole bull, and that for just three guests (18:6).

On the other hand, quite unlike her husband's most recent response to God, upon hearing the divine promise of a son for her, Sarah remarks, quite cynically, about her age and that of her husband (18:12, 13; the narrator has already told us the matriarch was menopausal, 18:10). Yet, in light of this theophany, and her husband's own obsequious response to deity, Sarah should have had no reason to be doubtful, and certainly not for laughing (in derision?). Isaac's birth had already been put on Yahweh's calendar: it would take place at the "set time" (18:14). Nothing would be too difficult for him (18:14; Jer 32:17, 27).[38]

In sum, the formal act of dedication reminds the believer to walk before God with mature faith—hopefully with a faith more firm than that exhibited by Abraham and Sarah in this pericope.

SERMON FOCUS AND OUTLINES

THEOLOGICAL FOCUS OF PERICOPE 10 FOR PREACHING

10 **God's blessing upon oneself and one's associates is conditioned upon a faithful walk before God, a commitment remembered by a formal act of dedication (17:1–18:15).**

This pericope shares aspects of this Theological Focus with that of the previous pericope (Pericope 9), particularly the idea of divine blessing of one overflowing to one's associates (even across generations). Therefore the preacher may do well to focus here upon the facet of conditionality—the walk with God—and upon formalizing such a commitment to do so with a public act of dedication. While there is no specific act that is suggested, wise leaders will choose an endeavor that has long-lasting effects *and* long-lasting visibility, for the goal is that those who take part in it may remember God's promise to bless, for days and decades to come—a "mnemonic cognitive sign." An event of this sort may be planned as a church-wide undertaking that will necessarily need to be coordinated with a number of ministry partners. Obviously a part of such a dedicatory event may be the celebration of Communion together.[39]

---

37. *Genesis 16–50*, 47.

38. Interestingly, the future rivalry between siblings is adumbrated in Sarah's responses: she was "listening" (שמע, *shm'*, related to יִשְׁמָעֵאל, *yishmae'l*, "Ishmael," 18:10), and she "laughed" (צחק, *tskhq*, related to יִצְחָק, *yitskhaq*, "Isaac," 18:12, 13, 15).

39. There is no reason why the act of dedication may not be separated from the actual worship event where the sermon is delivered. Depending upon the size of the church, the commitment may also be entered into in smaller groups in an informal setting. One will also have to tread carefully, for there might certainly be those who are not ready for such a commitment.

Possible Preaching Outlines for Pericope 10

I. Condition for God's Blessing: A Walk Before God
    Blessings are conditioned upon a walk before God (17:1–2)
    This walk before God involves faith, that neither Abraham nor Sarah exhibited (17:17–18; 18:1–15)
    Blessings accrue not only to oneself, but also to one's associates (17:3–8)
    Likewise, removal from the community of faith may lead to loss of blessing: Ishmael (17:15–22)
    Move-to-Relevance: God is interested in abundantly blessing his children and, through them, others

II. Commitment to God's Blessing: An Act of Dedication
    God calls for a sign of the covenant to be enacted (17:9–14)
    Abraham obeys immediately (17:23–27)

III. *Resolve and remember!*
    What we can do individually, but in a corporate setting, to formalize our resolution to walk before God
    How this act may serve to remind us of our resolution and God's promise

A slightly different outline results in a "chain-linked" structure with three imperatives: walk, resolve, remember. Obviously, the "resolve" imperative is the one that is being asked for immediately in this sermon. The "walk" and "remember" are future aspects of what the believer, who has made a resolution before God, should be engaged in.

I. *Walk to be blessed!*
    Blessings are conditioned upon a walk before God (17:1–2)
    This walk before God involves faith, that neither Abraham nor Sarah exhibited (17:17–18; 18:1–15)
    Blessings accrue not only to oneself, but also to one's associates (17:3–8)
    Likewise, removal from the community of faith may lead to loss of blessing: Ishmael (17:15–22)
    Move-to-Relevance: God is interested in abundantly blessing his children and, through them, others

II. *Resolve to Walk!*
    God calls for a sign of the covenant to be enacted (17:9–14)
    Abraham obeys immediately (17:23–27)
    What we can do individually, but in a corporate setting, to formalize our resolution to walk before God

III. *Remember the Resolve!*
    How this act may serve to remind us of our resolution and God's promise

PERICOPE 11

Prayer and Punishment

Genesis 18:16–19:38

[Abraham Negotiates; Yahweh Destroys; Lot Escapes; Daughters Cohabit]

REVIEW, SUMMARY, PREVIEW

Review of Pericope 10: Genesis 17:1–18:15 has God setting an explicit condition for Abraham's blessing: he would need to walk with God and be blameless. Though Ishmael is not part of the Abrahamic covenant, he too would be blessed by his association with the patriarch. The human-side commitment to divine promise is actualized in the ritual of circumcision, and walking with God brings divine blessings to pass.

Summary of Pericope 11: The wickedness of the Cities of the Plain result in catastrophic divine judgment—almost a second "deluge." Yet, as the prayer of Abraham sought to achieve, the family of the one associated with the Abrahamic blessing (Lot and his relatives) survives the disaster—just as Noah did during his flood. All of this points to the poor decision Lot had made, severing relations with the man of promise (his uncle) and taking up with doers of evil (Sodom and Gomorrah), and the consequences thereof. Both the value of intercessory prayer and of keeping the way of God are emphasized.

Preview of Pericope 12: In Gen 20:1–21:34, there is another depiction of faithlessness, Abraham's passing his wife off as his sister—for the second time! Yet God remains faithful, rescuing him from the predicament and keeping Abimelech, a God-fearer, from sinning. Finally, the promised seed, Isaac, arrives, with a resounding endorsement by God

221

of how he had carried out his word. Through the subsequent messiness of the excommunication of the older son, Ishmael, God proves himself faithful again.

11. Genesis 18:16–19:38

THEOLOGICAL FOCUS OF PERICOPE 11

11 **Failure to keep the way of Yahweh results in judgment, whereas the intercession (and life) of one keeping that way brings divine blessing to all those around (18:16–19:38).**

  11.1 Failure to keep the way of Yahweh in righteousness and justice can result in catastrophic judgment.

  11.2 The intercession (and life) of one who walks in Yahweh's way avails for divine blessing to those associated with that one.

OVERVIEW

Genesis 18:16 introduces a new topic, the fate of Lot and Sodom and Gomorrah, justifying the commencement of the new pericope at 18:16. The story has moved from covenant and circumcision (Pericopes 9 and 10) to catastrophe (Pericope 11). The bulk of the action in this pericope occurs within the space of a 24-hour day (18:16–19:29), with the conception and delivery of Lot's daughters occupying the remainder of the pericope (19:30–38).

Divine justice is a distinct theme in 18:16–19:38, later to echo in the mouth of Abimelech (20:4). What characterizes Yahweh must mark his people as well, and therefore Abraham's household is to keep Yahweh's way in righteousness and justice, in contrast to the depravity and turpitude characterizing the locale where Lot is situated—described as wicked and evil (רָעַע *ra'a'*, 19:7, 9). Such an alignment to the demand of God results in life abundant, a life blessed by God. The criterion for this prospering is variously described as "walking before Me" (17:1), "keeping the way of the Lord," and "doing righteousness and justice" (18:19). Failure to so align oneself and to walk in God's way demonstrating such qualities only results in loss of blessing and, potentially, divine punitive justice.

The narrative of Pericope 11 is carefully structured, with the pivot of the story being the announcement of divine action against wickedness, with cause and effect spelled out (19:12–13, *F'* below). The rest of the pericope describes that judgment taking place.[1]

---

1. Table from Wenham, *Genesis 16–50*, 41–42.

Prologue: Birth of Isaac announced (**18:1–15**)
   A   Abraham's visitors "look down" toward Sodom (**18:16**)
     B   Divine reflections; Sodom's destruction (**18:17–21**)
       C   Sodom pled for; "slay," מות, *mot*, 18:25;
            promise to "spare," נשא, *nsh'*, 18:26; "do," 18:17, 25, 29, 30 (**18:22–33**)
         D   "Angels" arrive in Sodom; pressed to stay (**19:1–3**)
           E   Assault on Lot and his visitors; "Lot goes out," 19:6;
               Lot rebuffed, 19:9 (**19:4–11**)
             F   Destruction of Sodom announced (**19:12–13**)
           E'   Lots's sons-in-law reject appeal; "Lot goes out," 19:14;
               Lot rebuffed, 19:14 (**19:14**)
         D'   Departure from Sodom ("angels"); pressed to leave (**19:15–16**)
       C'   Zoar pled for; "death," מות, 19:19;
            request "granted," נשא, 19:21; "do," 19:22 (**19:17–22**)
     B'   Sodom and Gomorrah destroyed (**19:23–26**)
   A'   Abraham "looks down" toward Sodom (**19:27–29**)
Epilogue: Birth of Lot's sons (**19:30–38**)

The location of the action also shows design; it moves from environs of Mamre, to the gate of Sodom, to outside Lot's house, to inside Lot's house, and then—reversing the emplacements palistrophically—back to the outside of Lot's house, to the outside of the city, and finally to the region of Mamre. Again the center of the geographical hierarchy is the location of the announcement of the Sodom's destruction—inside Lot's house (19:12–13).

    Mamre (18:16–33)
       Gate of Sodom (19:1–3)
          Outside Lot's house (19:4–11)
             Inside Lot's house (19:12–13)
          Outside of Lot's house (19:14)
       Outside the city (19:15–26)
    Mamre (19:27–29)

Alter notes that the motif of sight and blindness structures the pericope thematically. Abraham's visitors "look down" upon Sodom (שקף, *shqf*, 18:16). At the conclusion of the pericope, after the destruction of the cities, Abraham "looks down" (19:28) upon Sodom and Gomorrah. Elsewhere, the term when used of Yahweh indicates a gaze upon morally questionable situations (Exod 14:24; Deut 26:15; Ps 14:2; 53:3; 102:20; Lam 3:50). When the men of Sodom threatened evil against Lot and his house, his angelic guests smote the attackers with *blindness*, rendering them unable to locate the doorway (Gen 19:11). Before the catastrophe that engulfed the cities, the angels urged Lot and his family not to *look* back (19:17); of course, his wife did so with devastating results (19:26).[2] It might well be the theme of this pericope that what one looks at, one will become; and what one looks for, one will get: in this case, evil and its dreadful consequences.

Mathews observes four stages in the episode of the destruction of Sodom and Gomorrah, each stage commencing with a reference to time: 19:1–14, 15–22, 23–26,

2. "Sodom as Nexus," 152.

and 27–29. Each succeeding stage is briefer than the preceding one; the second one contains less dialogue than the first (and the third and fourth none at all). The pace of the story, thus, picks up in stages, to culminate in the account of the destruction of Sodom and Gomorrah and, particularly, the conclusion regarding the remembrance of Abraham by Yahweh and the reason for Lot's salvation.[3]

11   Genesis 18:16–19:38

THEOLOGICAL FOCUS 11[A]

11   Failure to keep the way of Yahweh results in judgment, whereas the intercession (and life) of one keeping that way brings divine blessing to all those around (18:16–19:38).

11.1   *Failure to keep the way of Yahweh in righteousness and justice can result in cata-strophic judgment.*

11.2   *The intercession (and life) of one who walks in Yahweh's way avails for divine bless-ing to those associated with that one.*

A. Having only one section in this pericope, the "Theological Focus 11" is identical to the "Theological Focus of Pericope 11."

NOTES 11

11.1   Failure to keep the way of Yahweh in righteousness and justice can result in catastrophic judgment.

Alter describes the destruction of the Cities of the Plain as a "second deluge." Sodom's outcry, described as great (18:20), reflects the magnitude of the sin in the time of the flood (also "great," 6:5). Lot, as was Noah (6:13–21), is warned of coming judgment and advised to conduct his family to safety (19:12–13).[4] As in Noah's case, "saving lives" shows up in Lot's story (19:19, 20; see 6:19, 20). One disaster was an extinction by water; the other, by fire. In fact, Yahweh is said to "rain down" brimstone and fire from the heavens on Sodom and Gomorrah ("rained," 19:24; also in 7:4, of the Flood; and see 7:11, 19; 8:2).[5] Another parallel to the Noahic flood is that post-deluge, the protagonist, Noah, is involved in a shameful episode while in a state of intoxication (his

---

3. Matthews, *Genesis 11:27–50:26*, 230–31.

4. Alter, "Sodom as Nexus," 153. Strikingly, in both situations, "destroy" (שחת, *shkht*) occurs twice, first in the Hiphil, then in the Piel (6:13, 17 and 19:13). The word also shows up in 9:11, 15; and 19:14, 29, as well as in Abraham's parley with Yahweh (18:28 [×2], 31, 32). Other similar elements include: the angels "reaching out their hands" to bring Lot into safety (19:10) and Noah "reaching out his hand" to bring the dove into the ark (8:9); the angels "shutting" the door of Lot's house (19:10) and Yahweh "shutting" Noah and his family in the ark (7:16). Warning also precedes actual destruction in both catastrophes (Wenham, *Genesis 16–50*, 43).

5. "Fire and brimstone" (19:24) are a frequent accompaniment of divine punitive action in Scripture: Ps 11:6; Isa 30:33; Ezek 38:22; Rev 9:17, 18; 14:10; 19:20; 20:10; 21:8. And the redundant use of "Yahweh" in Gen 19:24 ("Yahweh rained . . . brimstone and fire from Yahweh") emphasizes the divine initiative that led to Sodom's affliction.

son Ham "sees his nakedness"; in Pericope 5, this was suggested to be an incestuous relationship). Post-fire, in this pericope, the one rescued from the cataclysm, Lot, also in a state of inebriation, is involved in a reprehensible sexual dalliance (also incest).[6] The statement that Yahweh "remembered" Abraham in the midst of the pyrogenous calamity (19:29) is exactly parallel to his "remembering" Noah during the flood (8:1). This divine memory marks the abatement of the flood in one case and the rescue of Lot in the other. Noah found "favor in the eyes" of Yahweh (6:8), and Lot pleads with the angels on the basis of his finding "favor in their eyes" (19:19). Abraham's "walking" with Yahweh (and his companions; 18:16) evokes Noah's "walking" with Yahweh (6:9; 7:1); both are called (to be) "righteous" (6:9; 7:1; and 18:19). And the divine soliloquy of 18:17–21 is paralleled in 6:5–8.

> Clearly, Genesis sees the two events [the flood and the fiery destruction of Sodom and Gomorrah] as parallel: two cataclysmic acts of divine judgment on outrageously sinful communities, with the only righteous man and his family spared. The flood involved the destruction of the whole human race except Noah and his family; here the destruction involves a group of cities and the saving of one man and his family. Noah is seen as a second Adam from whom all humanity descended; the destruction of Sodom, though not as awesome as the flood, speaks once again of the terrible depravity to which human society can descend and of the need for redemption. So if Noah is seen as a second Adam, Abraham is probably viewed as a third Adam, the new hope of mankind. It was Noah's sacrifice that mollified God's anger after the flood and spared the world another annihilation. Now the narrator suggests that it is Abraham's prayer that saved righteous Lot and that in Abraham all the nations of the earth may hope to find blessing.[7]

After the disaster of the flood (and the debacle at Babel), Abram is selected as the father of a new line. In an act belying his faith, he fathers Ishmael, resulting in the generation of future enemies for the descendants of the patriarch. On the other side of the fire, Lot propagates two other lines in an evil way, and more enemies for Abraham's descendants are produced.

Clearly, Lot and Abraham are being showcased side-by-side in Gen 18 and 19. In both chapters, the same characters show up together—Yahweh and the men with him (identified as angels in 19:1, 15), Abraham (who has a cameo role in 19:27–29), and Lot (who is bargained for in 18:16–33). The episode of Abraham's hospitality, 18:1–15 (included with Pericope 10), is also paralleled by Lot's hospitality to the two angels who appear at his door (19:1–3). Thus there is a comparison between the righteous companion of God, Abraham, and the incestuous Lot who keeps company with the wicked (the distinctions between the two are highlighted in the table below).[8]

---

6. Alter, "Sodom as Nexus," 153. "Interestingly, Ham's two brothers then cover their naked father with a cloak by walking backwards with it into the tent, taking care never to look behind them, in symmetrical contrast to the unfortunate Mrs. Lot" who chose to look back (ibid.).

7. Wenham, *Genesis 16–50*, 64.

8. Table from ibid., 43–44; and Letellier, *Day in Mamre*, 40–41.

Genesis 18	Genesis 19
Abraham "sitting" at tent "door," פתח (*ptkh*, 18:1)	Lot "sitting" (19:1); "doorway" (פתח, 19:6)
Setting: daytime (18:1)	Setting: nighttime (19:2)
"Seeing" visitors, he runs to them (18:2)	"Seeing" visitors, he stood to greet them (19:1)
Abraham "bowed" (18:2)	Lot "bowed" (19:1)
"He said, 'My Lord …'" (18:3)	"He said, '… my lords'" (19:2)
Abraham requests "favor" of guests (18:3)	Lot requests "favor" only for his own escape (19:19)
Refers to himself as "servant" (18:3)	Refers to himself as "servant" (19:2)
Requests that visitors wash feet (18:4)	Requests that visitors wash feet (19:2)
Guests show no hesitation to accept Abraham's offer	Guests initially refuse Lot's offer (19:2–3)
Feast prepared and served and "eaten" (18:6–8)	Feast prepared and served and "eaten" (19:3)
Abraham prepares a royal feast (18:6–8)	Lot prepares a regular meal (19:3)
"Where is your wife?" (18:9)	"Where are the men?" (19:5)
Yahweh promises a son (18:10)	Lot offers daughters (19:8)
Abraham cooperates with God; others doubt (18:12–15)	Lot cooperates with angels; others doubt (19:14, 26)
Sarah questions Yahweh's words (18:12)	Sodomites question Lot's words (19:9)
Sarah "laughed" (צחק, *tskhq*, 18:12, 13, 15)	Lot's sons-in-law thought he was "joking" (צחק, 19:14)
Doubting wife humbled (18:12–15)	Disobedient wife petrified (19:17, 26)
Great "outcry" (18:20, 21)	Great "outcry" (19:13)
Abraham heads household (18:19)	Lot rejected as head of household (19:14)
Warning before destruction (18:10)	Warning before destruction (19:13)
Pleading for Sodom, remnant (18:22–33)	Pleading for Zoar, for himself (19:18–22)
Abraham pleads with Yahweh: he uses אַל־נָא and הִנֵּה־נָא (*hinneh-na* and *'al-na'*) (18:27, 30, 31, 32)	Lot pleads with the Sodomites: he uses אַל־נָא and הִנֵּה־נָא (19:7, 8)
"Sweep away" (18:23, 24)	"Sweep away" (19:15, 17)
"Slay" (מות, *mut*, 18:25)	"Die" (מות, 19:19)
"Destroy" (18:28 [×2])	"Destroy" (19:13 [×2])
Promise to "spare" (נשא, *nsh'*, 18:26)	Request "granted" (נשא, 19:21)
"Do" (= destroy, 18:17, 25, 29, 30)	"Do" (= destroy, 19:22)
Abraham will be a nation (18:18)	Lot fathers two nations (19:37–38)

Notice that while Abraham runs to greet his guests (18:2), Lot merely rises (19:1); the patriarch requests that he "find favor in their eyes" (18:3), while Lot does nothing of the sort (later, in 19:19, he does request their favor, but only to further his own escape from the calamity); the angels initially refuse (and it is a firm refusal, 19:2) to spend the night at Lot's[9]; Abraham provides a royal feast for his guests, hurrying and scurrying to prepare the dishes (18:6–8), while Lot provides a regular meal (19:3, though, perhaps in irony, Lot's meager provision is labeled a "feast"). In sum, Lot does not come off as

---

9. Even Lot's urging of his guests to stay appears tainted: the verb in 19:3 is פצר (*ptsr*, "press"), which is reused in 19:9 to describe the Sodomites pressing Lot to hand over his guests for sexual exploitation. Lot pressures the angels, and the Sodomites pressure Lot. See Hamilton, *Genesis: Chapters 18–50*, 32n21.

stellar as his uncle. The latter also pled for Sodom and Gomorrah to save the lives of others (18:20–33); the former plead for Zoar, entirely on self-interest (19:19–20). It is also obvious here that Lot's pleading with Sodom for his guests is contrasted with Abraham's pleading with Yahweh for Sodom. In the extended "negotiation" by the latter, the deferential terms הִנֵּה־נָא ("behold, please") and אַל־נָא ("surely not") are each employed twice—18:27, 31, and 18:30, 32. In Lot's bargaining, each of the terms is used once (19:8 and 19:7, respectively).[10]

Abraham, as God's "friend" (2 Chr 20:7; Jas 2:23), becomes Yahweh's confidant (Gen 18:17–21; also see Amos 3:7). As a result, God "chooses" (יד׳, *yd'*, also "to know"; Gen 18:19) the patriarch and spells out his purpose—the creation of a godly community that keeps "the way of Yahweh by doing righteousness and justice."[11] This is to abide by divine demand, and to be aligned to the will of God. The fulfillment of the divine promise, thus, was conditional (also see 22:15–18; 26:5). Wenham notes the ubiquity of this promise-obedience-fulfillment pattern in Scripture as being integral to OT theology: following the way of God brings about promised blessing (e.g., Exod 19:4–5).[12] This pericope clearly demarcates the two possibilities: keeping the way of Yahweh, or deviating from it.

Lot is the one who chose land by sight and dwelt with sinners (13:10–13); as for seed, he generated descendants by incest. Abraham, on the other hand, though exhibiting a spotty faith, waited on God for the allotment of land and, despite some false starts, waited on him for seed, too. "[Lot] fails as a host, as a citizen, as a husband, as a father. He wants to protect his guests but needs to be protected by them; he tries to save his family, and they think he is joking; afraid to journey to the mountains, he pleads for a little town, but afraid of the town, he flees to the mountains. His salvation depends on God's mercy (19:16) and Abraham's blessing (19:29)."[13] In sum, in Gen 13, Abraham is the generous uncle to a foolish nephew; in Gen 14, he is the intrepid warrior who rescues a hapless

10. While Lot's desire to protect his guests is commendable, the offer of his daughters to the madding crowd is shocking. Lot permits the townsfolk to "do" whatever they wanted to his engaged daughters, as long as they "did" nothing to his guests (19:8). "Lot's attempt to defend his guests presents him positively, but his sanctioning of the rape of his daughters sounds more 'Sodomite' than 'Israelite'" (Mathews, *Genesis 11:27–50:26*, 232). Rape of a betrothed woman was a capital crime in the Mosaic Law (Deut 22:23–27), as also was homosexuality (Lev 18:22; 20:13). Thus no matter what Lot offered, the Sodomites were preparing for some abominable acts. The wickedness of the Sodomites mentioned in Gen 18:23, 25 is echoed in 19:7, 9 (all use רעע, *r'*); in fact, when Lot beseeches them not to act "wickedly," their response is that they would treat him "more wickedly" than they would treat his guests (19:7, 9). Later, there is "proper" intercourse between man and woman, but with the breaking of other boundaries—incest. That, too, is deprecated in this pericope. Not only was Lot complicit in a capital crime, he also "jeopardized the lives of his daughters, even any hope for a heritage—all for the sake of strangers. By a bizarre twist, however, it is his daughters who finally take advantage of Lot, sexually abusing their father by which he gains male heirs after all" (19:36–38) (ibid., 236–37).

11. The way of Yahweh usually involves the keeping of Torah: see Deut 5:33; 8:6; 9:12; 10:12; 11:22; 19:9; 26:16–19; 28:9; 30:16; Jdg 2:22; 1 Kgs 11:38; 2 Kgs 21:22; Jer 7:23. The way of the righteous is contrasted with the way of the wicked in Deut 11:26–28; 30:15–19; Pss 1; 119; 139:24; Prov 4:18–19; 12:28; 14:2; 15:9; Jer 21:8.

12. *Genesis 16–50*, 50.

13. Waltke and Fredricks, *Genesis*, 274.

prisoner-of-war. In Gen 18, the patriarch is the gracious host, a consultant of Yahweh, and a solicitous pleader, unlike his kinsman in Gen 19, who is less than bountiful, who is rejected as head of his household and as a citizen, and who is focused only on his own survival. Later, in shameful circumstances, Lot is inebriated and abysmally ignorant about his own misdeeds.[14]

Lot, when he made his ill-advised choice to move to Sodom, had seen as far as Zoar (13:10). And that was where he ended up (19:18–23), embedded in a place of evil. Lot's collegiality with the Sodomites is also seen in his address of his fellow citizens as "my brothers" (19:7). This is quite a revelation: earlier Abram had attempted to make peace with Lot in the strife between their herdsmen, by recalling that they were all "brothers" (13:8). The text here seems to be indicating that Lot had, in effect, sacrificed his relationship with his uncle, and relocated to Sodom to forge another fraternity with evildoers. Besides, Lot seemed to be a possession of the King of Sodom who claimed Lot as his own (14:21).

Lot's final disposition, as far as we are told, is in a cave (19:30). "Caves in the OT are used either as graves (25:9) or by refugees (Josh 10:16; 1 Sam 13:6). Lot, the rich rancher who had so many flocks and herds that he had to separate from Abraham (Gen 13:8–11), chose to live in the fertile Dead Sea valley, which has been destroyed and with it all his other relations and property. He and all he has can be accommodated in a cave. His ruin can hardly be more complete."[15]

The disobedience of Lot's wife was costly; it led to her petrification as a pillar of salt (19:26). Her yearning for what she was leaving behind led to her downfall, and she ends up a parable: "Remember Lot's wife" (Luke 17:32). Wenham adds that the daughters were not very different from their mother. The children "had few scruples about their behavior. Like their mother, they too had imbibed a love of Sodom and its attitudes."[16] The subsequent story of their incestuous relations is also carefully described in two parallel panels.[17]

	Panel 1 Genesis 19:31–33	Panel 2 Genesis 19:34–35
Plotting of daughters	19:31a	19:34a
Problem of heritage	19:31b	
Plan to intoxicate	19:32a	19:34b
Plan for intercourse	19:32b	19:34c
Plan for line	19:32c	19:34d
Production of plan	19:33a	19:35a
Portrayal of father	19:33b	19:35b

14. From Mathews, *Genesis 11:27–50:26*, 213. In Isa 5:7, Yahweh looks for "righteousness" (צדקה, tsdqh), "but, behold, a cry of distress" (צעקה, tsʿqh). The same wordplay shows up in Gen 18:19, 21—Abraham is to do צדק, but Yahweh hears צעקה from Sodom (also see 19:13). There is righteousness on one hand, but only the outcry of evil on the other. Genesis 18:20 also has זעקה, zʿqh, a variant of צעקה; that they are synonyms is seen in the employment of both together in the same psalm: Ps 107:6, 28 has צעקה, and 107:13, 19 has זעקה.

15. Wenham, *Genesis 16–50*, 60. Unlike Abraham who died blessed, at a ripe old age, after a full life (24:1; 25:8), we are told nothing about the demise of Lot—a disparaging silence.

16. Ibid., 59.

17. From Mathews, *Genesis 11:27–50:26*, 244.

In solving the problem of heritage, the oldest daughter observed that it was impossible to get married "in the way of the whole world" (19:31). Strikingly the "way of Yahweh" had just been mentioned in 18:19. Abraham took the latter road; Lot (and his family) the former. Lot's ignorance ("he did not *know*," 19:33, 35) of what went on with his daughters, is quite reprehensible; even Noah, after the shameful episode of his violation (of some sort)—and he was inebriated, too—is said to have "known" (ידע, 9:24) what his son had done to him. Lot, though, is blissfully unaware.[18] Irony abounds in the use of ידע in Gen 19: the Sodomites demanded Lot's guests in order that they might "know" them (19:5, i.e., commit sexual indiscretions)[19]; in turn, Lot offered them his daughters who had not "known" a man (19:8). In the end, we are told that Lot did not "know" (19:33, 35) that he had committed incest with his daughters.

The whole tragic episode closes with Abraham going to where he had "stood" before Yahweh, interceding for Sodom and Gomorrah, "looking down" at the devastated plain (19:27–28). This "standing" and "looking down" also marked the patriarch's first introduction to the cities' potential destruction (18:16, 22). Genesis 19, by the way, is the only chapter in the Abraham Story in which the patriarch does not utter a word. He is a silent spectator of the consequences of wickedness and great evil.

> No other twenty-four hour period in Abraham's life is related more fully than that described in Gen 18–19: a midday lunch with three angels that ended with the destruction of Sodom and Gomorrah early next morning. This gives a hint of the importance of this story for the writer of Genesis, a hint that is certainly noted in the rest of Scripture, for the fate of Sodom and Gomorrah becomes a byword in the prophets and the NT and still lingers in popular religious consciousness.[20]

The OT brings up the destruction of Sodom often, as "a paradigm of divine judgment," and a warning against sin—to the Canaanites (Lev 18:3–30; 20:22–23), to the neighbors of Israel (Isa 13:9; Jer 49:18; Zeph 2:9), and to the Israelites themselves (Isa 1:9; 3:9; Jer 23:14; Amos 4:11; Deut 29:23; 32:32). In fact, the sins of this last group were, at times, worse than those of Sodom (Ezek 16:46–47) and their punishment commensurately greater (Lam 4:6).[21] All this reinforces the theological thrust that failure to keep the way of God results in judgment.

11.2 *The intercession (and life) of one who walks in Yahweh's way avails for divine blessing to those associated with that one.*

In the divine soliloquy in 18:17–19, Abraham's reward for righteousness was declared—God recognized the faithfulness of the patriarch. And on this "judicial" principle of recompense for probity, Abraham argues his case for a few other righteous ones that may have remained in Sodom. While the patriarch is to teach his children and household "justice" (משפט, *mshpt*, 18:19), here he is concerned whether Yahweh

---

18. Noah made his own, but one does wonder where Lot's daughters obtained their alcohol.

19. The desire of the men of Sodom to "know" (19:5) is also in contrast with Yahweh coming down to Sodom and Gomorrah to "know" (18:21) the state of their wickedness.

20. Wenham, *Genesis 16–50*, 62.

21. Ibid., 64–65. For such a comparison in the NT, see Matt 10:15; 11:23; Luke 10:12; 17:26–32.

himself will deal "justly" (מִשְׁפָּט, 18:25)—this is also the only scriptural occurrence of "Judge of all the earth." (18:25).

The depth of evil in Sodom is pointed out unequivocally by the narrator—"men of the city, the men of Sodom . . . from youths to old, all the people from every end [quarter]" sought to participate in the coarse and gross endeavor of sexually abusing Lot's guests (19:4). The Sodomites, in a note of irony, accuse the outsider Lot of acting like a judge (19:9), "an eerie echo of the erstwhile appellative, 'Judge of all the earth,'" used by Abraham while negotiating with Yahweh (18:25).[22] They would ultimately be judged, not by Lot, but by *the* Judge.

Abraham pleads six times for the city and each negotiation is accepted by Yahweh. While threefold repeats are common in biblical narrative, "the doubling of the pattern here is significant and gives Abraham's intercession solemnity and weight."[23] Abraham's posture before Yahweh ("standing," 18:22) is used of disputants appearing before deity, judge, or royalty (Exod 9:10 Lev 9:5; Deut 44:10; 19:17; 1 Kgs 3:16; Jer 15:1, 19). This is also the first instance in the Bible of a human initiating a conversation with God, and quite a remarkable conversation at that![24]

MacDonald shows that this back-and-forth between Abraham and God was clearly not haggling, for God does not bid in this price war. All the bids come from the human, and deity agrees to each proposition—there is no bargaining here. Moreover, Abraham lowers his price with each round (one might also see it as an *increase* of price); he starts at fifty and ends at ten. The patriarch also provides some of the vocabulary of the exchange, which Yahweh deigns to reflect ("spare," Gen 18:24, 26, and "destroy," 18:28 [×2], 31, 32, are introduced by Abraham and echoed by Yahweh).[25] The dialogue is more like a child testing parental boundaries than like buyers negotiating with sellers in an oriental bazaar; in 18:32–33, that it is Abraham who concludes the conversation. Yahweh departs only after the patriarch has made his final offer. On God's part, it was always a "yes," never a "no."[26] In any case the graciousness of God and his desire to save rather than to destroy is evident. So also is the philanthropic and altruistic attitude of the patriarch; even if he had been focused on the safety of his kinsmen, their salvation out of a city marked for destruction was not what he had

---

22. Mathews, *Genesis 11:27–50:26*, 233.

23. Wenham, *Genesis 16–50*, 51.

24. In connection with God's appointment of Abraham as the one to "command" his children and household to follow Yahweh and do righteousness and justice (18:19), this depiction of Abraham as intercessor is clearly an illustration of his portfolio as a seeker of righteousness and justice himself. He modeled those attributes for his descendants, unlike Lot who associated with evildoers and committed egregious acts while drunk.

25. The idea of "sparing" (נשא, *nsh'*, 18:24, 26) is employed by Moses in his intercession before Yahweh as a synonym for "forgive" (Exod 32:32). Indeed, Yahweh's character is itself described as the one who "spares/forgives" iniquity (34:6–7).

26. MacDonald, "Listening to Abraham," 35. Why Abraham ceased his bargaining with Yahweh at the figure of ten righteous people present in Sodom (18:32–33) is inexplicable. Was ten the smallest number constituting a social entity? Or was it because of Abraham's acknowledgement that numbers were no longer important, for God was just and could be trusted to act justly all the time? See Mathews, *Genesis 11:27–50:26*, 230.

primarily appealed for. Rather, he would have Yahweh save the *entire* city just because of the presence of his (righteous) relatives there. As it happened, Yahweh orchestrated the escape of six, but it was appropriated only by three; two sons-in-law repudiated the offer and one wife disobeyed instructions. In any case, Abraham's dialogical petitions were heard by Yahweh on the basis of the former's faithfulness. Lot and his daughters were saved because "God remembered Abraham," referring to his negotiations with Yahweh for the life of the righteous (19:29). Thus the ones saved were saved because of Abraham's pleas. Rather than "God remembered Lot," we have, in 19:29, "God remembered Abraham"—another instance of the faith of one bringing blessing to many. While the compassion of Yahweh was upon Lot (19:16), the ground of the divine saving grace was Abraham and his intercession. This remembering by deity is essentially a covenantal concept, indicating God's loyalty to his people (Exod 2:24; 6:5; Pss 105:8; 106:45). It had nothing to do with Lot's righteousness.[27] In a final jab at Lot's poor choices, in the backdrop of God's positive view of Abraham, the narrator notes that the destroyed cities were "where Lot lived" (יָשַׁב, *yshv*, 19:29), which is followed immediately by Lot's "staying" in a mountain, afraid to "stay" in Zoar, and his "staying" in a cave with his daughters (all יָשַׁב, 19:30 [3]).[28] The story had begun with Lot "sitting" (יָשַׁב, 19:1) in the city's gateway, and the verb recollects with regret Lot's earlier choice to "dwell" (again יָשַׁב) in the land of the "exceedingly wicked and sinners against Yahweh" (13:6 [×2], 12 [×2]).[29]

Moreover, Lot is clearly skeptical about God's ability to rescue him and his family: he is certain the disaster will overtake him (19:19). And so he pleads with the angels that he and his family be permitted to go to Zoar, a request based entirely on his own comfort and convenience, for his own survival (19:19–20), as opposed to Abraham who pled with Yahweh for Sodom, on the grounds of divine justice (18:20–33). Nephew is selfish; uncle is altruistic. Lot's plea comes between urgings of the angels that he escape (19:17, 22). Wenham notes that "escape" (מָלַט, *mlt*) occurs five times in this scene (19:17 [×2], 19, 20, 22), an obvious wordplay on "Lot" (לוֹט, *lot*), as if to say "'Lot was *let* out of Sodom." Lot, by his own words, proves to be "fearful, selfish, and faithless."[30] On the other hand, this escape of Zoar from destruction ironically fulfilled Abraham's desire far beyond his imagination or his negotiation: that entire city was saved because of the presence of just *one* "righteous" person—Lot (or three, counting his daughters).

The remarkable power of a faithful person's intercession is subtly hinted at in the account. When Lot pleads in fear to the angels, "*I am not able* to escape" (לֹא אוּכַל, *lo' 'ukal*, 19:19); his words are echoed by the angel: "*I am not able* to do anything"

---

27. However, relatively speaking, in comparison to his fellow citizens in Sodom, Lot was righteous; the man is recorded as being "righteous" in Wis 10:6; 19:17; 2 Pet 2:5–8; *1 Clem.* 11:1.

28. Mathews, *Genesis 11:27–50:26*, 242–43.

29. In 19:15, the angels' recommendation regarding family members "who are here" is literally "who are found"; the verb links with Abraham's pleading with Yahweh about "finding" a number of righteous in Sodom (18:26, 28, 29, 30 [×2], 31, 32).

30. Wenham, *Genesis 16–50*, 58.

(לֹא אוּכַל, 19:22). Indeed! The angel is incapacitated and the hand of God stayed until Lot is saved—the efficacy of Abraham's intercession (19:29)! Even whole nations are blessed by this one man's faith, validated by the fact that land was divinely granted to the nations Lot founded (the Moabites and Ammonites; Deut 2:9, 19), as well as to those founded by Ishmael and Esau (the Ishmaelites and Edomites, respectively; Deut 2:5)—those in the line of Abraham, but not in the chosen line of Isaac.[31] Lot's father-hood is the result of his drunken passivity; Abrahams's fatherhood is the result of his faith in Yahweh. Thus Lot is depicted throughout as a "passive foil" for Abraham, the father of the nation, through whom many are blessed.[32] The intercession of a righteous man surely availeth much (Jas 5:16).

SERMON FOCUS AND OUTLINES

> **THEOLOGICAL FOCUS OF PERICOPE 11 FOR PREACHING**
>
> **11 Failure to keep the way of God can result in punishment, but the prayers (and life) of one keeping that way precludes it (18:16–19:38).**[A]

A. Here, "punishment" also includes loss of divine blessing, and not just punitive action on the part of God. For instance, Lot's subsequent drunken travails are a consequence of his removal from the sphere of God's work.

The theme of faithfulness to Yahweh bringing blessing to others around has been encountered before in previous pericopes. Therefore the focus here is best kept upon the potential risks of divine judgment and punitive action for failing to keep the way of Yahweh, and upon the benefits of prayerful intercession to preclude such action and to bring about blessing to associates.

Possible Preaching Outlines for Pericope 11

I. PUNISHMENT: Judgment for Those Failing to Walk with Yahweh
    Failure to walk with God raises the potential of punishment (19:1–29)
    Lot's reprehensible actions while intoxicated indicate his loss of divine blessing (19:30–38)
    Move-to-Relevance: The dangers of not walking with Yahweh and removing ourselves from the sphere of blessing

II. PRAYER: Intercession by Those Faithfully Walking with Yahweh
    Abraham's intercession for Sodom and Gomorrah was heard by God (18:16–33)
    Lot's salvation came about when God remembered Abraham (19:29)
    Abraham's godly life, keeping the way of God, availed for divine blessing to others (18:16–21)

---

31. Mathews, *Genesis 11:27–50:26*, 214–15.

32. Coats, "Lot a Foil in the Abraham Saga," 126. While this episode clearly points to the loss of blessing when one removes oneself from the way of God and the channels of God's blessings, as Lot did, "one wonders if this would be so had Abraham not brought Lot with him on the journey. Thus both Abraham's obedience in going, which ultimately culminates in the birth of Isaac, and his disobedience in bringing Lot on the journey have drastic effects on his future people" (Rickett, "Rethinking the Place," 50–51n52). It works both ways: one's faithfulness can bring blessing to many; one's faithlessness can be a bane to many.

III.   *Pray to preclude punishment!*
How to engage in intercession for those not keeping the way of God

A more expanded version, seeking to compare Genesis 18 and 19, Abraham's life and actions with Lot's, could look like this:

I.   Abraham's Life
The patriarch's keeping the way of God in righteousness and justice (18:16–21)
Move-to-Relevance: God's recognition and regard for those keeping his way

II.   Lot's Life
Lot's association with Sodom and his less-than-stellar godliness (19:1–38)
Move-to-Relevance: The dangers of not walking in God's way

III.   Abraham's Supplication
Abraham's intercession for Sodom and Gomorrah was heard by God (18:16–33)
Move-to-Relevance: The urgency of intercessory prayer for those not keeping God's way

IV.   Lot's Supplication
Lot's salvation came about when God remembered Abraham (19:29)
Move-to-Relevance: The importance and benefits of intercessory prayer

V.   *Partner with God to save!*
How to engage in intercession for those not keeping the way of God

PERICOPE 12

God Works Despite Sin

Genesis 20:1–21:34

[Wife/Sister Episode; Isaac Born; Ishmael Expelled; Well Obtained]

REVIEW, SUMMARY, PREVIEW

Review of Pericope 11: Genesis 18:16–19:38 shows the wickedness of the Cities of the Plain resulting in catastrophic divine judgment—almost a second "deluge." Yet, as the prayer of Abraham sought to achieve, the family of the one associated with the Abrahamic blessing (Lot and his relatives) survives the disaster—just as Noah did during his flood. Both the value of intercessory prayer and of keeping the way of God are emphasized.

Summary of Pericope 12: Another depiction of faithlessness, Abraham's passing his wife off as his sister—for the second time!—commences this pericope. Yet God remains faithful, rescuing him from the predicament and keeping Abimelech, a God-fearer, from sinning. The promised seed, Isaac, arrives, with an endorsement by God of how he had carried out his word. Through the subsequent messiness of the excommunication of the older son, Ishmael—past sins raising their heads again—God proves himself trustworthy once more. Faithfulness to God brings reward, despite failures of the past.

Preview of Pericope 13: The next pericope (Gen 22:1–19) deals with the sacrifice of Isaac—Abraham's greatest test, which he passes with flying colors, exhibiting the fear of God in holding back *nothing* from God. Believers are called to do likewise.

12. *Genesis 20:1–21:34*

THEOLOGICAL FOCUS OF PERICOPE 12

12 **Faithlessness and the complications of past sin do not preclude God's accomplishment of his purposes and his promised blessings, though sin may incur divine discipline, while faithfulness (fear of God) brings reward (20:1–21:34).**

12.1 Faithlessness does not preclude the faithfulness of God to his word, but faithfulness—fear of God and trust in his word and working—is rewarded (20:1–18).

12.1.1 *Faithlessness does not preclude the faithfulness of God to his word.*

12.1.2 *Fear of God, involving trust in his word and faith in his working, is rewarded.*

12.2 Despite, and through, the messiness and complications of past sin, a trustworthy God accomplishes his purposes and brings about his promised blessing, though the sin might incur divine discipline (21:1–34).

12.2.1 *Despite the twists and turns of life, God can be trusted to keep his word.*

12.2.2 *Through the messiness of life caused by sin all around, God works to accomplish his purposes and to bring about his promised blessings.*

12.2.3 *Human sin does not preclude promised divine blessing, but might incur divine discipline.*

12.2.4 *God's promised blessings will be accomplished, even through the complications of past sins.*

OVERVIEW

A number of stories are found in this pericope, requiring careful negotiation. Genesis 20 deals with a wife/sister episode redux, with Abraham's faithlessness on display. Yet God works through it all, resolving the issue and teaching the patriarch a lesson, through the pagan ruler, Abimelech. Isaac is born in Gen 21, setting off another series of faithless actions, as Hagar and Ishmael are banished. God works through the messiness of that episode as well. Though Ishmael, who was not the chosen seed of Abraham, would not inherit from his father, God would bless him by virtue of his relationship to Abraham. Again, in the removal of Ishmael from the scene, God is carrying out his purposes and fulfilling his promises to the patriarch and his descendants. Abimelech then returns to the stage and a covenant is struck between this ruler and Abraham, guaranteeing the latter a well and some water. Thus through the imbroglio of the wife/sister episode comes divinely wrought good, that helps place Abraham securely in the Promised Land. Indeed, Abraham's "sojourning" (גור, *gur*, 21:34) forms an inclusio with 20:1, not only emphasizing Abraham's rooting in Canaan, but also making 20:1–21:34 an integral unit.

12.1 Genesis 20:1–18

> **THEOLOGICAL FOCUS 12.1**
>
> 12.1 Faithlessness does not preclude the faithfulness of God to his word, but faithfulness—fear of God and trust in his word and working—is rewarded (20:1–18).
>
> > 12.1.1 *Faithlessness does not preclude the faithfulness of God to his word.*
> >
> > 12.1.2 *Fear of God, involving trust in his word and faith in his working, is rewarded.*

NOTES 12.1

12.1.1   Faithlessness does not preclude the faithfulness of God to his word.

This wife/sister episode with which Gen 20 begins is similar to the incident in Gen 12. Both are introduced by the verbs "to journey" and "to sojourn" (in 12:9–10 and 20:1, respectively). But there is no mention here of Sarah's beauty (as there was in 12:14–16, a quarter-century ago); she is now 90 years old (17:17) and is, in her own words, "worn out" (18:12). But Abraham seeks recourse in deception—again!—to save his own skin (20:11). Astonishingly, after the two-fold promise that Isaac would be born to Abraham and Sarah (17:16; 18:10–14), Sarah is taken away—nay, *given* away—into the harem of a local ruler. "Given the announcement of Sarah's impending pregnancy [18:10, 14], Abraham's conduct here is especially hard to fathom. . . . But whatever his motive, in passing Sarah off as his sister Abraham displays a certain recklessness with the promise. . . . Could it be that he is still banking on the ascendancy of Ishmael, his firstborn?"[1] One wonders if the patriarch will ever learn! But even in this story of Abraham's faithlessness and lack of trust, one finds evidence that God's word does in fact come to pass. "That an elderly woman, long past the menopause (18:11–12), should have been thought attractive enough for intercourse with a king is intriguing," and substantiates the possibility that she might actually conceive. God— surprise, surprise!—may actually have been right.[2] That being said, it is obvious God takes Abimelech's action seriously. Adultery was deserving of terminal punishment in most of the ancient Near East, as it was in the biblical world (Lev 20:10; Deut 22:22). The main action of Yahweh's intervention to prevent anything untoward (20:3–7) is recounted in a chiastic panel.[3]

---

1. Kass, *The Beginning of Wisdom*, 283.

2. Wenham, *Genesis 16–50*, 75.

3. From Mathews, *Genesis 11:27–50:26*, 250. It was quite unusual for a non-Israelite to receive a message dream (as opposed to a symbolic dream). See Petersen, "A Thrice-Told Tale," 41.

> **A** "'You are as a *dead* man'" (20:3a)
>> **B** "'the woman [אִשָּׁה, *ishshah*) you have taken'" (20:3b)
>>> **C** "Abimelech had not come near her" (20:4)
>>>> **D** "'Will you also slaughter an innocent nation?'" (20:4)
>>>>> **E** "' in the integrity of my heart'" (20:5)
>>>>>> **F** "God said to him in the dream" (20:6a)
>>>>> **E'** "'in the integrity of your heart'" (20:6b)
>>>> **D'** "'I have kept you from sinning against Me'" (20:6c)
>>> **C'** "'I did not let you touch her'" (20:6d)
>> **B'** "'return the man's wife [אִשָּׁה]'" (20:7a)
> **A'** "'you will live …; if you do not …, you will surely *die*, and all yours'" (20:7b)

The divine threat of 20:3, 7, we learn later, concerns the closure of wombs in Abimelech's household (20:18); yet there may have been some sort of physical affliction upon the man himself, for he is said to have been healed when Abraham prays for him (20:17). In other words, God's faithfulness to his word is manifest: there will be no possibility that Sarah is violated; in fact, there would be no issue at all from the wombs in Abimelech's harem, and there would be no doubt that Sarah's child was Abraham's when she finally conceives.[4] Though Abraham is faithless, God remains faithful, keeping his word.

12.1.2   Fear of God, involving trust in his word and faith in his working, is rewarded.[5]

The narrative of Gen 20 is carefully structured, with narrative alternating with dialogue throughout.[6]

Narrative	**Introduction:** Abraham settles in Gerar (20:1)	
Dialogue	**A**	Abraham speaks (to Abimelech?) about Sarah (20:2a)
Narrative	**B**	Abimelech takes Sarah (20:2b)
Dialogue	**C**	God sues against Abimelech (20:3–7)
Narrative	**D**	Abimelech warns his servants; they are "very afraid" (20:8)
Dialogue	**C'**	Abimelech sues against Abraham (20:9–13)
Narrative	**B'**	Abimelech returns Sarah with compensation (20:14)
Dialogue	**A'**	Abimelech speaks to Abraham and Sarah (20:15–16)
Narrative	**Conclusion:** Abraham prays for Abimelech and household (20:17–18)	

The center of the account recollects the exceeding fear of Abimelech's household (*D* in the table; 20:8), because of the potential of "great sin" that their chieftain may have committed (20:9).[7] In 20:9 and 20:10, after the truth of the wife/sister swap is made public, we have twice "And Abimelech . . . said," without any intervening response

---

4. For Abimelech to realize there was a problem with his wives' conceiving implies that Sarah had been part of the harem for several months in 20:1, before the dream in 20:2.

5. This is, of course, a positive statement of a negative lesson from the life of the patriarch who did *not* fear God; on the other hand, and ironically, this statement was true of the God-fearing ruler, Abimelech.

6. From Wenham, *Genesis 16–50*, 68, and Waltke and Fredricks, *Genesis,* 283.

7. It is possible that "Abimelech" is a generic term for the ruler of Gerar, like "Pharaoh" in Egypt, and thus need not necessitate identity between this individual and the Abimelech in Gen 26 decades later.

from Abraham. Perhaps the patriarch had nothing to say to Abimelech's charge. When he finally responds, Abraham's reply to Abimelech is completely mistaken. How could he not have seen the "fear of God [יִרְאַת אֱלֹהִים, *yir'at 'elohim*] in this place" (20:11)? This is the first instance of "fear of God" in Scripture, and it seems quite clear that it was not Abimelech and his men who did not have this fear of God. In fact, it is expressly noted at the center of the chiastic structure (*D*) that they were "very afraid" (וַיִּירְאוּ . . . מְאֹד, *wayyir'u . . . m'od*, 20:8). One is forced to conclude that it was Abraham, the patriarch, who did not have enough fear of God to trust him to take care of this dangerous situation. "Divine blessing and success have accompanied him ever since Gen 12:1–3; he has been shown to be capable of defeating kings (Gen 14) and to be on intimate terms with the Almighty (cf. Gen 17; 18). It is surprising that he should now take fright, the more so since he had escaped unharmed from Egypt in quite similar circumstances."[8] But that is how Abraham has been operating all along, as we have oft seen. His was a faith adulterated by fear of the wrong things. His was not a faith marked by a fear of God.[9]

Abraham's accusation that there was no fear of God in that place (20:11) assumes that Gerar was as bad as Sodom; Abimelech's probity proves that the patriarch was totally in the wrong. The ruler is rightly indignant about the disservice done to him by Abraham and, when confronted by Yahweh, he phrases his concern with a moral question that tests the justice of God: "Will You slaughter a nation, even an innocent [צַדִּיק, *tsaddiq*] one?" (20:4). This expostulation of innocence by Abimelech is reminiscent of Abraham's own question to God about his justice. The word used by Abimelech, צדיק, is the same one employed by Abraham as he negotiated with God: "Far be it from You to do such a thing—to slay the righteous [צדיק] with the wicked" (18:25). Abimelech's excuse was answered by Yahweh: "I also know . . .; and I also kept . . .; therefore I did not let you touch . . ." (20:6). Thus Abimelech's "integrity of heart" was safeguarded by an act of God.[10] The one who fears God is protected by God.

Interestingly, Pharaoh's concern at the possibility of sinning focused entirely on himself (12:18–19); Abimelech is clearly more enlightened: he is concerned not only about his own status, but also for his kingdom (20:9). In his defense, Pharaoh merely addressed Abraham's lie; Abimelech questions God, underscoring his own decency and guilelessness. Unlike the earlier iteration of the similar situation, where it is quite likely that Pharaoh had violated Sarai (on this, see Pericope 7), for which he and his household were "greatly plagued" (12:17), here, in Gen 21, Abimelech is kept from sin

---

8. Wenham, *Genesis 16–50*, 72.

9. For a conclusive assessment of Abraham's "fear of God," one has to wait till Gen 22. In Abraham's defense of himself, there is an oddity in the grammar of the verb, "wander" (תעה, *t'h*) in 20:13—it is a Hiphil perfect 3rd person *plural*: "they [Elohim] caused me to wander." After having referred to "Elohim," the use of the plural verb might be a rare concession to the plural form of the noun (also in 35:7). Perhaps more likely, it may be a nod to Abimelech's polytheism. "If this is not a simple grammatical accommodation, Abraham reaches an all-time religious low by granting such a concession to the pagan king"—"when the gods caused me to wander." See Mathews, *Genesis 11:27–50:26*, 258; *y. Meg.* 1.11, 71d sees 20:13 as referring to secular gods.

10. "Integrity of heart" was expected of kings (1 Kgs 9:4; 1 Chr 29:17; Pss 15:2; 78:72; 101:2).

by Yahweh. The ruler is burdened by even the possibility of having sinned and, though he was the wronged person, he proceeds to gift Abraham splendidly as if to atone for a potential wrong (20:14–16).[11] Fifty shekels of silver was the going rate for a bride (Deut 22:29), and average monthly wage was about half a shekel.[12] Thus Abimelech's thousand pieces of silver donated to Abraham was an extravagant compensation (20:16), not to mention the livestock and land he also presented (20:14–15). "This royal groveling [gifts + apology + vindication, 20:14–16] must have left a profound impact on its witnesses, elevating the international stature of Abraham in the presence of both parties."[13] The ruler did, however, get in a final thrust against the patriarch as he informs Sarah: "I have given your *brother* a thousand pieces of silver" (20:16), not "your husband."

How ironic that the pagan chief is exceedingly solicitous—God-fearing—when the supposedly godly patriarch does not even care about his wife! Thus one suspects that there is a subtle reason for Abimelech's reproach of Abraham. "One cannot help but think, however, that the rebuke has a divine cast to it; just as God choreographed Abimelech's repentance, does the king speak unwittingly the words of divine correction to Abraham?"[14] It was a rebuke to the patriarch from a God-fearing pagan! All said and done, the pagan looked far more righteous than did the patriarch. After the wickedness of Sodom and the gross unchastity of Lot's daughters, it is surprising that Gerar had a God-fearer for a ruler (this after not even ten righteous people could be located in Sodom): obviously not all foreigners were godless; and, of course, not all Israelites were saints, either!

Abraham's intercession is the first instance of such an utterance being labeled as "prayer" (פלל, *pll*); other appeals are indicated as "calling upon" Yahweh (4:26; 12:8; 26:25). Abraham as a prophet (20:7) had already interceded for many (18:23–32) and he does so again (20:17). That privileged status, however, does not absolve the patriarch of blame in this account. In any case, Abraham successfully prays for the opening of wombs of the women in Abimelech's household; rather ironically, it is never said that he prayed for the pregnancy of his own wife, Sarah. While Abraham's prophetic status is esteemed in this act, the focus is on the rewarding of Abimelech. The one who failed (by being faithless) is compelled to pray for the one who succeeded (by being faithful and God-fearing), and it is the latter who is rewarded.[15]

---

11. The patriarch was also quite well recompensed in Gen 12 by Pharaoh, though there it is a "payment" for a woman he had incorporated into his harem. Moreover, unlike in Gen 20, Abraham and his caravan are summarily expelled by Pharaoh after that earlier event unravels (12:16, 19–20).

12. In Gen 23:15–16, the cave of Machpelah put Abraham back four hundred shekels, a parcel of land in Shechem cost a hundred shekels (33:19), and a slave, twenty shekels (37:28) (see Mathews, *Genesis 11:27–50:26*, 258).

13. Ibid., 259.

14. Ibid., 256.

15. Needless to say, with Abraham being permitted by Abimelech to dwell wherever he saw fit in his eyes (20:15), the patriarch moves another step closer to possessing the land, though he is still a stranger who "sojourns" (20:1; also 21:23, 34).

12.2 Genesis 21:1–34

> **THEOLOGICAL FOCUS 12.2**
>
> 12.2 Despite, and through, the messiness and complications of past sin, a trustworthy God accomplishes his purposes and brings about his promised blessing, though the sin might incur divine discipline (21:1–34).
>
> 12.2.1 *Despite the twists and turns of life, God can be trusted to keep his word.*
>
> 12.2.2 *Through the messiness of life caused by sin all around, God works to accomplish his purposes and to bring about his promised blessings.*
>
> 12.2.3 *Human sin does not preclude promised divine blessing, but might incur divine discipline.*
>
> 12.2.4 *God's promised blessings will be accomplished, even through the complications of past sins.*

NOTES 12.2

12.2.1 *Despite the twists and turns of life, God can be trusted to keep his word.*

After the statement that Yahweh opened the wombs of Abimelech's wives and maids, upon Abraham praying for them (20:17–18), the next words are that Yahweh "visited" Sarah as he had promised and did for her as he had said (21:1). Alter observes that the disjunctive clause (beginning with the subject, Yahweh) and the utilization of the perfect verb ("visited") denote an antithesis: Yahweh had closed the wombs of Abimelech's household but, in contrast, he visited Sarah and opened hers.[16] These events of Gen 21 occur when Abraham is hundred (21:5), i.e., twenty-five years after entering Canaan (12:4). And God's promises are fulfilled exactly as he had declared; that Isaac's birth occurs "at the appointed time" stresses the truth that God knows what he is doing. Besides, the threefold declaration of God having kept his word regarding the birth of Isaac is significant. Earlier this son had been promised (in 17:16–21; 18:10–15); but here, after the fact, the stress is on God being trustworthy: he did "as He had said," and "as He had promised," at the specific time "of which God had spoken" (21:1–2). It is almost as if God, exasperated with Abraham after all of his misadventures and lack of mature faith, is trying to catch the patriarch's attention once and for all: "I am faithful to my word; you *can* trust me." A threefold mention of Abraham's age adds to this thrust—"old age" (21:2, 7) and "one hundred years old" (21:5, literally "son of a hundred years")—as also does the six-fold (twice three) recurrence of ילד (*yld*, "bear"), to refer to Sarah's delivery of her son (21:2, 3 [×2], 5, 7, 8). The name "Isaac" also echoes three times (21:3, 4, 5). God is clearly making a point about his own faithfulness!

The usual naming formula at the birth of a son is: *X* called the name of his son *Y*. But here it is: *Abraham* called the name of his son—the one born to him whom Sarah

---

16. "Sodom as Nexus," 156–57. The verb פקד (*pqd*, "visit," 21:1) is a special intervention of Yahweh on behalf of his people (to save from slavery, 50:24–25; Exod 4:31; to respond to sin, Exod 20:5; to end a famine, Ruth 1:6; to restore exiles, Jer 29:10; and, as in Gen 21:1, to cause the conception of a barren woman, 1 Sam 2:21).

bore to him—*Isaac* (21:3). The expansion underscores that this was a 100-year-old man's son and, even more poignantly, that this was the son *Sarah* bore to him . . . as God had promised. It was not an adopted Lot, or the steward Eliezer, or Hagar's Ishmael. It was Sarah's son with Abraham: Isaac.[17] The pun on the word "Isaac" is expressed by Sarah in 21:6; God had made צְחֹק (*tskhoq*, "laughter") for her, and all who heard (שֹׁמֵעַ, *shmʿ*, a play on "Ishmael," יִשְׁמָעֵאל, *yishmaʿeʾl*—a subtle jab?) would יִצְחַק (*yitskhaq*, "laugh"—the exact replica of Isaac's name, יִצְחָק) with her! And unlike the norm, where the person naming the child provides the reason for the name (4:24; 5:29; etc.), here, one parent gives the name and the other gives the explanation, and that not immediately after the naming, but after the narrative of circumcision and a restatement of the age of the father: 21:3 has the naming, 21:4 has Isaac's circumcision, 21:5 notes Abraham's age, and *then* 21:6–7 details the rationale for the child's name. All those who laughed at God's promise in doubt (17:17; 18:12–15) are now laughing again—this time in joy! Every part of the account points to the incredible nature of this miraculous birth! Again, God's trustworthiness is being emphasized.

12.2.2   *Through the messiness of life caused by sin all around, God works to accomplish his purposes and to bring about his promised blessings.*

There is certainly a strangeness in dealing with Ishmael's history soon after Isaac has been introduced into the story. But this is a common biblical practice: subsidiary characters are dealt with before resuming the main character's storyline: sons of Cain (4:17–24) before those of Seth (4:25); Japheth's and Ham's lines (10:1–20) before Shem's (10:21–31); histories of Terah (11:27–32) and of Lot (Gen 13–14, 19) are completed, before those of Abraham and Isaac continue.

What exactly was Ishmael's "mocking" all about (21:9)? What did he do to his brother, Isaac? The LXX has παίζω (*paizō*) and the Vulgate *ludo* (both mean "to play"); צחק, *tskhq*, may even have sexual overtones, as in 26:8; 39:14, 17. In any event, at the sensitive time of a celebration for the younger son, some kind of public ridicule seems to have occurred, perhaps disdain on the part of Ishmael for Isaac, akin to Hagar's despising of Sarai (16:4). The wordplay of "Isaac" and "mocking" (יִצְחָק, *yitskhaq*, and מְצַחֵק, *mtsakheq*) suggests that what Ishmael was doing was "isaacing." Was this a case of Ishamel trying to be like Isaac—an effort to take over the prerogatives of the heir, a displacement, if you will (*Jub.* 17:2–4 seems to think that was a possibility)? Coming right after the wife-sister episode of Gen 20, Ishmael might well have been taunting Isaac, ascribing the latter's parentage to Abimelech. This, of course, would not only be offensive, it would deny Isaac's legitimacy as the heir. Perhaps the punishment imposed on Ishmael (and Hagar) was appropriate to the offense. Such a scenario would also explain the rather redundant assertion in 21:2–5 that Isaac was, indeed, Abraham's son (four times).[18]

Thus Ishmael (and perhaps his mother as well, as in 16:4) is culpable. Sarah, too, is culpable with her harshness: "her [Hagar's] son" is juxtaposed to "my [Sarah's] son"

---

17. Mathews, *Genesis 11:27–50:26*, 267.

18. Ronning, "The Naming of Isaac," 18–19.

(21:10), even though the boy ("her son") is Abraham's son as well. Abraham, by Sarah's diktat, is to "banish" (גרש, *grsh*, 21:10) Hagar and her son. Elsewhere גרש is a severe action: it is employed in the evictions of Adam and Cain (3:24; 4:14), the expulsion of Moses by Pharaoh (Exod 6:1; 10:11; 11:1; 12:39), and the dispossession of the Canaanites (Exod 23:29–30; Josh 24:18). It is also used to describe a divorcee (Lev 21:7, 14; 22:13; Num 30:9; Ezek 44:22)—perhaps a fitting description of the expulsion of harassed Hagar.[19]

Hagar's son's name, Ishmael, does not show up anywhere in the entire account, implying his loss of status in the patriarch's household as heir: he is merely "son" (Gen 21:9, 10, 11, 13), "child/boy" (21:14, 15, 16), "lad" (21:12, 17 [×2], 18, 19, 20), and "descendant/seed" (21:13). Echoes of his name ("Ishmael," יִשְׁמָעֵאל), however, occur with the consonants of the word "hear" (שמע, 21:6, 12, 17 [×2]). For the rightful, divinely appointed heir, his name, "Isaac," resounds six times (21:3, 4, 5, 8, 10, 12), not to mention its resonance in "laughter/laugh/mocking" (צחק, 21:6 [×2], 9). These contrasts between the son of Sarah and the son of Hagar suggest that something like a usurpation might have transpired with the "mocking" of 21:9. The parallels between the careers of Ishmael and Isaac—particularly between their trips with a parent to the wilderness and to Moriah, respectively (see below; highlighted elements distinguish the two journeys)—lay emphasis on the fundamental issue: Who will be Abraham's heir?[20]

Parallels: Ishmael's trip to the wilderness / Isaac's trip to Moriah (Gen 22:1–19)
Journey by divine command into parts unknown (21:12–14; 22:1–6)
Ishmael's eviction orchestrated by human design (21:10); Isaac's, by divine design
Sarah is the instigator in the first case (21:10); Sarah is absent in the second
Abraham shows reluctance in the first case (21:11); no reluctance in the second
"Abraham rose early in the morning" (21:14; 22:3)
Abraham is resigned and stoic (no pleading with God as he did for the Sodomites, 18:23)
Preparations made, provisions carried (21:14; 22:3)
Sons close to death (21:15–17; 22:6–10)
Both sons are "lads" (Ishmael: 21:12, 17 [×2], 18, 19, 20; Isaac: 22:3, 5 [×2], 12)
Ishmael is "your descendant" (21:13); Isaac is "your son" (22:2, 12, 16)
Abraham assured by God of the future of both sons (21:12, 13)
Angel of God/Yahweh intervenes, calling out from heaven (21:17; 22:11)
Hagar told not to "fear" (21:17); Abraham's "fear" of God acknowledged (22:12)
Yahweh "heard" (21:17 [×2]) Ishmael's voice; Abraham "heard" God (22:18)
Way of salvation (well/ram) is seen by parent whose eyes are "opened" (21:19; 22:13)
Future blessings are promised (21:13,18; 22:16–18)
Ishmael will not "inherit" (21:10); Isaac (seed) will "inherit" (22:17)
Place where Ishmael and, presumably, Isaac lived is noted (21:21; 22:19)
Beersheba mentioned (21:14; 22:19)

19. Wenham, *Genesis 16–50*, 82.

20. From Waltke and Fredricks, *Genesis*, 292. There are other parallels between the life histories of the two sons of Abraham. In an earlier rescue of the pregnant Hagar, it is said that God "saw" (16:13–14); he "sees" as he rescues Isaac, too (22:14); moreover a place is named by both Hagar and Abraham, each appellation recalling the "sight" of Yahweh (בְּאֵר לַחַי רֹאִי, *b'er lakhay ro'i*, 16:14; and יהוה יִרְאֶה, *yhwh yir'eh*, 22:14, "Yahweh will see to it/provide"). Other parallels include Abraham's naming and circumcising both of his children at a certain age (16:15; 17:25 and 21:2,3), parents of both "taking" wives for each son (21:21; 24:3–4), both having twelve sons (17:20; 25:13–16; 35:23), and both finally dying and being "gathered to their people" (25:17; 35:29). See Leviant, "Parallel Lives," 20–25, 47. The interventions of deity in these two accounts are the only OT instances of the angel of God/Yahweh calling out from heaven.

Incidentally, both 21:14 and 22:3 have a clausal structure that is somewhat unusual:

	Verb	Dual direct object	Prepositional phrase	Direct object
21:14	*Placing*	*[bread / skin of water]*	*on her shoulder*	*and the boy*
22:3	*He took*	*his two servants*	*with him*	*and Isaac his son*

The last direct object with אֵת in each case is one of Abraham's sons. The delay before mentioning "and the boy" in 21:14 suggests that "the transference of the child from father to mother's shoulder is undertaken at the last possible moment"—a "syntax of delay."[21] Likewise, again in 22:3—the last "item" Abraham takes with him is his beloved son. In both cases, Abraham nearly loses the two sons he has had so far. Thus the question driving the narrative is no longer *who* the heir will be; rather, it is whether Abraham will have *any*.[22] Does Abraham have faith in God who promised futures to both of his children? Will he comply with God's directives in both instances to send them both to their deaths (as it must have appeared to him)?

While for Sarah, Ishmael is "the son of this slave," for Abraham he is "his son" (21:11). "This brief sentence gives a glimpse of Abraham's strong paternal affection and particularly his deep love for Ishmael. If he cannot contemplate sending Ishmael away, how much harder will he find the command in 22:2?"[23] Yet, his discharge of mother and child with meager provisions, despite divine assurance, is reprehensible. In fact, the poor woman "wandered about" (21:14) lost.

> One glaring difference is that when Abraham takes Isaac to be sacrificed, he also takes an ass. Here in ch. 21, rich man though he is, Abraham does not even spare his first-born son and the woman who has served his household for so many years an ass upon which to carry their personal belongings. Hagar seems to leave Abraham's house with nothing but her son and the bread and water she can carry on her shoulder. This meager disbursement is greatly to Abraham's discredit. Sarah is not alone in iniquity toward Hagar and her offspring.[24]

This, of course, is not the first time Abraham has allowed Hagar to be mistreated; in 16:6 he permitted Sarai to "treat her harshly" causing her to flee her mistress while pregnant. Nachmanides confesses that "our mother [Sarah] did transgress by this affliction [of Hagar], and Abraham also by his permitting her to do so."[25] Thus Abraham learns that often "divine purpose at times can be an unpleasant task," particularly when he is himself culpable.[26] In another example of his dereliction, in 21:21, with our last

---

21. Mathews, *Genesis 11:27–50:26*, 272.

22. Lyke, "Where Does 'the Boy' Belong?" 646–647. Lyke also notes that the Masoretes marked each of these phrases as occurring only once in the OT. Presumably, they caught the connection and linkage between 21:14 and 22:3 (ibid., 647n21).

23. Wenham, *Genesis 16–50*, 83.

24. Reis, "Hagar Requited," 99.

25. *Commentary on the Torah: Genesis*, 213.

26. Mathews, *Genesis 11:27–50:26*, 273. Yet, Abraham's gesture of putting water and child on her shoulder bespeaks his compassion on them; he certainly was "greatly distressed" (21:11, 12). "At one

glimpse of Hagar, she is shown "manfully shouldering full responsibility for her son's future welfare," finding a spouse for her son (normally a father's responsibility), and that with considerable success, as the list of Ishmael's sons later proves (25:13–16).[27] What is conspicuous here in Gen 21, however, is the absence of the father who should have undertaken this duty: Abraham has failed! God's faithfulness, nonetheless, is obvious: Isaac "grew" (21:8) and now Ishmael "grows" (21:20), with God's presence with him.

But despite the uncharitable treatment of Hagar by patriarch and matriarch, Sarah was right: Ishmael would "not inherit with my son Isaac" (21:10), "not because of Sarah's pettiness, or jealousy, or skullduggery," but because of a divine decree. Yahweh endorses Sarah's demand, not that the specifics of her demand are morally validated. What is accepted by God is that one facet of Sarah's fierce desire to protect Isaac's interest coincides with one facet of the divine plan of history—that "through Isaac your descendants shall be named" (21:12).[28] Thus one truth remains: Despite the messiness of life and sin all around—Ishamel (and perhaps Hagar, too) is culpable, Sarah is culpable, and Abraham is culpable—God is working out his purposes inexorably. He can surely be trusted.

That both Ishmael and Isaac are "seed" testifies to God's faithfulness to the patriarchal promise; but it is Isaac through whom the descendants of Abraham will be named (21:12) and it will be he who receives the parental inheritance (see also Pericope 10 where the blessings of the two children of Abraham are distinguished). Nonetheless, Ishmael is blessed, too: he experiences "God's promise (21:13, 18), provision (21:19), and presence (21:20)," and he generates twelve tribes (25:12–18), all of which again testifies to the efficacy of the divine word.[29]

In short, despite the failures of all the protagonists in this story, God continues to accomplish his purposes through these sinful and faithless people, as he continues to do so in our lives today.

12.2.3 *Human sin does not preclude promised divine blessing, but might incur divine discipline.*

Yahweh's promise to make Ishmael also a great nation (21:13) resonates with theme of 17:20 and the promised blessing to many others through Abraham (12:3 and throughout the preceding narrative if Gen 12–20). And as in the previous predicament of Hagar in Gen 16, God demonstrates his gracious salvation of his oppressed and suf-

---

time Abraham hoped that Ishmael would be his heir (17:18); he is surely not indifferent to the plight of the mother and son any more than he is at offering his son Isaac at Moriah. In both cases the author depicts the father as dutifully carrying out the Lord's directions, relying on God to fulfill his promises" (ibid., 271). But Abraham is still culpable: were it not for his conspiracy to generate seed with Hagar, this would not have happened (and later we shall see again that it was Abraham's less than mature faith that necessitated his grueling test in Gen 22).

27. Wenham, *Genesis 16–50*, 86. Finally, Hagar, for the first and only time, is labeled "mother" (21:21), in this last snapshot of the Egyptian.

28. Hamilton, *Genesis: Chapters 18–50*, 81.

29. Waltke and Fredricks, *Genesis*, 292.

fering children, even if they themselves are part of the reason for their own distress. We are told twice that "God heard the lad" (21:17). Surprising, since it was his mother who was calling upon God and weeping (21:16). In any case, God's "hearing" (שמע, *shm'*) again echoes the name Ishmael (יִשְׁמָעֵאל, *yishma'e'l*). "Hagar is out of range of her son's voice, but God is not."[30] And God hears him "where he is" (21:17); there is no place one can be to be out of range of God's hearing. Subsequent events show God being "with the lad" (21:20); he is certainly blessed by virtue of his being the son of the patriarch Abraham. The divine promise of blessing is given to Ishmael (21:13) as the angel of Yahweh addresses Hagar by name (21:17). Thus, Hagar is comforted, and her son's destiny is settled for greatness (21:18). Divine blessing cannot be thwarted by human sin and the by turbulence and turmoil it causes.

Reis notes the parallels between the story of Ishmael in Gen 21 and that of the Israelites in Egypt: both Ishmael and Moses/Israelites flee their homes (Exod 2:15); both encounter God in the desert who bids them return (Exod 3:2; 4:12); both are "banished" (Exod 6:1; 10:11; 11:1; 12:39); both are "sent" (Exod 11:1–2; Deut 15:13); both are provided water (Deut 15:25); both are rescued by a "strong hand" (Deut 3:24; Neh 1:10; Ps 136:12; in Gen 21:18, God commands Hagar to lift her son "strongly by the hand"). Reis propounds an intriguing thesis. She argues that the conditions set forth in Gen 15 for the fulfillment of the land and seed promises are: "strangerhood" (from the root גֵּר, *ger*), "slavery" (עבד, *'bd*), "affliction" (ענה, *'nh*), and the completion of the iniquity of the Amorites (15:13–16). Exodus 1 fulfills the "slavery" (1:13 [×2], 14 [×4]) and "affliction" (1:11, 12) conditions; that of "strangerhood" is not met: "The Israelites have become so alienated from the Lord and so assimilated to Egyptian customs and values that they do not perceive themselves to be strangers in Egypt. Indeed, once free, this generation of Israelites continues to clamor for Egypt, and it is only the next generation that can advance to the Promised Land." That requisite condition of "strangerhood" is achieved only in Exod 2:22 when Moses names his son Gershom (גֵּרְשֹׁם, *gershom*), "for he said, 'I have been a stranger [גֵּר].'" "In the next few verses we are told that God heard, God remembered, God saw and God knew" (2:24–25), and the process of liberation of the children of Israel commences.[31]

In parallel, Hagar (הָגָר, *hgr*, also means "the stranger") has achieved "strangerhood" by virtue of her name and foreignness; she is "afflicted" in Gen 16:6, 9, but not yet called a "slave." Upon her eviction, God asks Hagar to return in Gen 16, "because the iniquity of the patriarch and the matriarch is not yet complete. Just as God does not unjustly exile the Amorites but reserves sentence until they thoroughly deserve their punishment, so too does he permit Abraham and Sarah the full exercise of their free will before he wreaks judgment upon them." With them Hagar remains for another decade, till she is mistreated further and finally labeled a "slave" (אמה, *'mh*, the female counterpart of עבד, *'bd*; 21:10 [×2], 12, 13). *Now* God works her freedom, all the "conditions" having been met. The parallels are unmistakable; Abraham's and Sarah's

---

30. Reis, "Hagar Requited," 101.

31. Ibid., 103–105.

treatment of the Egyptian results in like treatment by Egypt of Abraham's and Sarah's descendants. "Through the narrative of Israelite history, readers learn that afflicting the disadvantaged is an abomination to God, whoever the victims."[32] But the justice of God always, and ultimately, prevails.

Perhaps that is the reason בֶּן־הָאָמָה, *ben-ha'amah*, which is found in Gen 21:10, 13, occurs elsewhere in the Pentateuch only in Exod 23:12 that commands proper treatment of the "son of the female slave." "The observance of the Sabbath is Israel's manner of acknowledging the tragic misalignments of its history, and making restitution for the innocent victims whose collective identity is given its figuration in Hagar."[33] Thus her story is one that is centered upon human injustice corrected by divine justice. In sum, while human sin cannot preclude promised divine blessing, human sin may incur divine punishment, for the God that one deals with is a just deity. In this case, of course, the divine punishment may be viewed as repercussions of sin that may continue to afflict those around and those yet to come in the future.

12.2.4 God's promised blessings will be accomplished, even through the complications of past sins.

The reappearance of Abimelech in a cameo (21:22–34) is somewhat odd at first glance. But closing out a pericope that began with Abraham's faithlessness (lack of fear of God), and that proceeded to the birth of the heir (and the dispossession of another potential, but unelect, heir), this episode makes sense. Sarna considers this section "artfully composed": "Abraham" and "Abimelech" occur seven times each and Abraham takes seven (שֶׁבַע, *shb'*) ewe-lambs (21:28, 29, 30); "oath" (שָׁבַע, *shb'*, 21:23, 24, 31) occurs thrice, and "Beersheba," with שֶׁבַע, *shb'*, embedded, also occurs thrice (21:31, 32, 33). "The account of the stolen well, Abimelech's plea of blamelessness, and the restoration of the property to the patriarch parallels the monarch's kidnapping of Sarah, his protestations of innocence, and her return to Abraham."[34] Moreover, Abimelech's earlier gift to Abraham (sheep and oxen, 20:14) is reciprocated (21:27); both "took and gave."[35] This balanced account making patriarch and ruler look like equals, suggests that Abraham, once faithless before Abimelech, has now, after the birth of the promised son (which was strong evidence of God keeping his word), learnt a lesson about faith in God. (Of course, such a change of heart and life is only implied here; for the

---

32. Ibid., 105, 106.

33. Rosenstock, "Inner-Biblical Exegesis," 49. Quite interestingly, in Exod 23:12, the sequence of laborers is "*your* ox," "*your* donkey," "*your* son-of-female-slave," and—markedly—"*the* stranger" (הגר, *hgr*). This last word would not have echoed the name of Hagar (הגר, *hgr*) had there been a 2nd person possessive suffix ("your") added, in parallel to the others in the series (ibid., 49n13). Reis also notes that "[b]eyond the Sabbath law, the legislation aimed at the relief of the stranger, juridically, economically and socially, is recapitulated over and over [Exod 12:49; Lev 19:10; Exod 22:20; 23:9; Lev 19:33–34]. . . . With few exceptions the word stranger is expressed in the singular (גר [*gr*]). I believe that this is because the plural (גרים [*grym*]) is not so immediately evocative of the name Hagar (הגר)" (Reis, "Hagar Requited," 108).

34. Wenham, *Genesis 16–50*, 91.

35. Sarna, *Genesis*, 145.

paradigmatic and tangible expression of Abraham's faith/fear of God, one must examine Gen 22, the next pericope). The careful structuring of this narrative also reinforces that interpretation of what the narrator is *doing* with what he is saying[36]:

Introduction: Time period (21:22a)
    A   Abimelech and Phicol;
        God who is with Abraham (21:22b)
        B   Oath (שׁבע, *shb'*, ×2) (21:23–24)
            C   Abraham complains about "well";
                 Abimelech's ignorance (21:25–26)
                D   Abraham and Abimelech make a covenant
                        with sheep/oxen (21:27)
            C' Abraham's seven (שׁבע, ×3) ewe lambs for the "well";
                 Abimelech's ignorance (21:28–30)
        B' Beersheba (באר־שׁבע, *b'r-shb'*, ×2), oath (שׁבע), covenant (21:31–32a)
    A' Abimelech and Phicol; Beersheba (באר־שׁבע);
        Yahweh who is God everlasting (21:32b–33)
Conclusion: Time period (21:34)

Abimelech recognizes the blessing of God upon Abraham as he confesses that God was with Abraham (21:22).[37] Wenham thinks this is essentially Abimelech blessing the patriarch: "He seems to take for granted the continuing success and strength of Abraham's family. His attitude expresses an implicit faith in the promises addressed to Abraham."[38] The account thus highlights Abimelech's faith as he acknowledges Abraham's future blessings—he is an outsider, and he believes in Abraham's descendants. Through his mouth, that of a non-Hebrew, God's promises to Abraham are reiterated. There is more: Abimelech wants Abraham to swear he will not deal falsely with the former (21:23)—no doubt, a warning to one who had dealt falsely with Abimelech once before. And, as a result of the covenant between the two, Abraham finally comes into possession of a well in Canaan. With the birth of Isaac, this forms the beginning of fulfillment of the divine promise to the patriarch. What had been a fiasco in Gen 20— the second wife/sister episode—was being used by God to engender a relationship between ruler and patriarch that would be the basis for Abraham's occupation of the Promised Land: he now owned a well and some water, no insignificant achievement, and one orchestrated by God. Abraham's planting of a tamarisk tree at Beersheba, and his calling on Yahweh, the Everlasting God (21:33), recognizes the momentous nature of the event and reflects what was likely the patriarch's change of heart after the birth of Isaac (and God's declaration of his faithfulness). Abimelech's recognition of divine blessing upon Abraham and his acknowledgement of the latter's right to stay in the land also must have provoked powerful feelings of faith in God whose promises were coming true. The patriarch must have thought back upon all the events that had led up to this day and realized the abundance of God's grace and his unremitting faithful-

36. Table from Mathews, *Genesis 11:27–50:26*, 278.

37. As well, God was "with" other patriarchs (26:3; 28:15; 31:3; 39:3; 46:4), "with" Moses (Exod 3:12), Joshua (Josh 1:5, 17; 3:7), and David (2 Sam 7:3). See Wenham, *Genesis 16–50*, 92.

38. Ibid.

ness to his promise and to his chosen man—this despite Abraham's rather insipid and jejune faith thus far. God, Abraham finally realized, had been right after all! And so he dwells in the land of the Philistines "for many days."[39] Promises had come true; seed had arrived; land had been obtained; enemies were at peace. God's promises are fulfilled, even despite past sins.

SERMON FOCUS AND OUTLINES

> **THEOLOGICAL FOCUS OF PERICOPE 12 FOR PREACHING**
>
> **12 The complications of past sin do not preclude God's work and his blessing, though sin may incur discipline (20:1–21:34).**

While the number of episodes in this single pericope may appear daunting to the preacher, the fact that they are connected calls for an integrated treatment of all of them together.[40] The somewhat far-reaching and expansive Theological Focus is therefore trimmed here for preaching purposes. It is be best to focus upon the implicit paradox: man might be faithless through sin (and incur punishment), but a trustworthy God's purposes are never precluded even by sin and its complications, messiness, and trauma. Notice that the positive concept of faithfulness (fear of God) yielding reward has been omitted; Pericope 13 (Genesis 22) will provide another opportunity—and a better one, in my opinion—for the preacher to surface this issue.

Possible Preaching Outlines for Pericope 12

I. Man's Faithlessness and God's Faithfulness
    Abraham's faithless and shameful repetition of the wife/sister episode (20:1–2)
    God's faithful and loyal care of his chosen one, Abraham (20:3–18; perhaps of Abimelech, too, 20:3–7, 17)
    God's trustworthiness in bringing his promises to pass (21:1–7; 22–34)
    Move-to-Relevance: Our past sins need not bog us down

II. Man's Sinfulness and God's Justice
    Abraham and Sarah vs. Hagar = Israelites vs. Egypt (21:8–10; 15–21)
    Patriarch's sin leading to pain and separation (21:11–14)

III. *Rest, but also repent!*
    How to rest in God's faithfulness without being destabilized by past sins
    How to repent of past sins

Without too many manipulations, this sermon may be refocused upon the "fear of God" that Abimelech displayed and that Abraham did not. In this pericope, then, "fear of God" meaning both to rest in God's faithfulness without capsizing from the burden

---

39. Though the term "Philistines" is anachronistic, those peoples not having arrived in Canaan till later (ca. 1200 BCE), its usage is likely reflecting the viewpoint of the author/editor from later in time (see also the mention of "Dan" in Gen 14:14, and Ur of the "Chaldeans" in 15:7; Wenham, *Genesis 16–50*, 94). Or perhaps, this is a different ethnic group altogether, unrelated to the later Philistines.

40. Otherwise, when preaching each episode individually, there is the risk of preaching not very significantly discrete theological ideas in sequence. The chunking of episodes is therefore a pragmatic homiletical stratagem.

of past sins, and also to repent of those past sins in light of divine justice and the possibility of incurring punishment.

I.   Fear of God: *Rest in his faithfulness!*
     Abraham's faithless and shameful repetition of the wife/sister episode (20:1–2)
     God's faithful and loyal care of his chosen one, Abraham (20:3–18; perhaps of Abimelech, too, 20:3–7, 17)
     God's trustworthiness in bringing about his promises (21:1–7; 22–34)
     How to rest in God's faithfulness without being destabilized by past sins

II. Fear of God: *Repent of past sins!*
     Abraham and Sarah vs. Hagar = Israelites vs. Egypt (21:8–10; 15–21)
     Patriarch's sin leading to pain and separation (21:11–14)
     How to repent of past sins

PERICOPE 13

Acing the Test

Genesis 22:1–19

[The Sacrifice of Isaac]

REVIEW, SUMMARY, PREVIEW

Review of Pericope 12: Genesis 20:1–21:34 has another depiction of faithlessness, Abraham's passing his wife off as his sister—for the second time! But God remains faithful, rescuing him from that predicament and keeping Abimelech, a God-fearer, from sinning. Finally, the promised seed, Isaac, arrives, with an endorsement by God of how he had carried out his word. And even through the subsequent messiness of the expulsion of the older son, Ishmael, God proves himself faithful.

Summary of Pericope 13: This pericope deals with the sacrifice of Isaac—Abraham's greatest test, which he passes with flying colors, exhibiting the fear of God in holding back *nothing* from God. Believers are called to do likewise.

Preview of Pericope 14: The next pericope (Gen 22:20–23:20) sees Abraham established further in Canaan: he now owns a burial plot, ironic in light of the extensive land promises God made to him and his descendants. Faith involves continued trust, even when one can see no sign of divine promises being fulfilled or of divine blessings being brought about.

13. *Genesis 22:1–19*

THEOLOGICAL FOCUS OF PERICOPE 13

13 Faith in God's promises and his word—a faith liable to be tested—is a supreme love/fear of God that trumps every other allegiance and that manifests in self-sacrificial obedience (22:1–19).

13.1 Faith in God's promises and his word is required from the child of God, and such a faith is liable to be tested.

13.2 The fear of God is to be demonstrated by God's children, involving self-sacrificial trust in God's promises and wholehearted obedience to his word.

13.3 The love of God's people for God brooks no rival claim for their love, whatever its object.

13.4 The love of God/the fear of God trumps every other allegiance.

13.5 Demonstration of faith in God's promises and his word results in divine blessing/reward.

OVERVIEW

For millennia, Bible scholars, both Jewish and Christian, have exerted themselves at the task of interpreting Genesis 22, the *aqedah*.[1] The perplexities of this narrative are many. How could God test/tempt someone in so gruesome a fashion, seemingly contradicting his own promises? How could Abraham agree to this gory transaction? And, of course, the question of how Christ fits into the scheme has kept Christian interpreters busy, as they sought typological links between the substitutionary sacrifice of Jesus Christ, the Son of God, and the *aqedah*. The concepts of "sacrifice" and "son" and "substitute" in Gen 22 have obvious similarities with the theology of the atonement, and the resulting enterprise of finding typological elements in Gen 22 has been unparalleled in the history of biblical interpretation. The identification of Abraham with God the Father and Isaac with God the Son was articulated by numerous patristic and medieval interpreters.[2] And according to one modern interpreter, "[c]learly, the theme of God providing a lamb leads directly to Jesus Christ and the sacrifice he makes so that his people may live."[3] Despite these Christocentric assertions, ancient and modern, Moberly makes it clear that שֶׂה (*seh*), translated "lamb" in Gen 22:7, is "a generic term for an animal from a flock." Indeed even the LXX of Gen 22:7 has πρόβατον (*probaton*, and not the christological "lamb [ἀμνὸς, *amnos*]" of John 1:29 that one might expect). The precise Hebrew word for lamb is כֶּבֶשׂ (*kebes*, as in the "lamb"

---

1. *Aqedah* comes from עקד, *'qd*, "bind" (Gen 22:9)—a *hapax legomenon*. Portions of this section were published in Kuruvilla, "The *Aqedah*," 489–508.

2. See Balserak, "Luther, Calvin and Musculus," 364–65, for an extensive list and bibliography. See Kuruvilla, *Privilege the Text!* 211–69, for an analysis and critique of this tendency to find Christ in every pericope of Scripture; instead I propose a "christiconic" interpretation.

3. Greidanus, *Preaching Christ from the Old Testament*, 311. He does admit that "there is no agreement" as to which character of the story is a type of Christ—Abraham, Isaac, or the ram (Greidanus, *Preaching Christ from Genesis*, 202, 203).

of the "continuous" offering, Exod 29:38), and not שֶׂה. Thus there appears to be little basis for drawing out any ovine typology from Gen 22.[4] Calvin is honest about these conjectures: "I am not ignorant that more subtle allegories may be elicited; but I do not see on what foundation they rest" (*Comm. Gen.* on 22:13). So rather than immediately flinging out a lifeline from the NT to accomplish a christocentric rescue of the *aqedah*, I suggest that the interpreter privilege the text and its immediate context to figure out what the A/author was *doing* with what he was saying (the theology of *this* pericope). For there is the "strong danger of ultimate superficiality" when the ancient text is not allowed to speak for itself and express its primary message. "If the Old Testament no longer says something to the Christian in its own right, to which the Christian still needs to attend and on which Christian faith necessarily builds, its actual role within Christian faith will tend to become marginal and optional, no matter what rhetoric is used to urge its importance."[5] A sound warning, indeed, and one that I have tried to heed throughout this commentary. It is certainly not universally accepted that Isaac and the ram represent God the Son, and Abraham, God the Father. In fact, the NT does not specifically refer to the *aqedah* at all.[6] Even in the late first-century interpretation of Genesis 22 by Clement of Rome (*1 Clem.* 10:7), there is no indication of typology: "By obedience he [Abraham] offered him a sacrifice unto God on one of the mountains which He showed him."[7] Clement instead pronounces on Abraham's righteousness and faith as aspects of the narrative that ought to be exemplary for the Christian.

13   Genesis 22:1–19

THEOLOGICAL FOCUS 13[A]

13   Faith in God's promises and his word—a faith liable to be tested—is a supreme love/fear of God that trumps every other allegiance and that manifests in self-sacrificial obedience (22:1–19).

4. Moberly, *The Bible, Theology, and Faith*, 107n52.

5. Ibid., 140.

6. Davies and Chilton, "The Aqedah," 532. That Paul makes "little theological capital" of the *aqedah* in his epistles is obvious; Rom 8:32 neither has any explicit mention of Isaac (as in Gal 4:28), nor does it employ the LXX's ἀγαπητοῦ (*agapētou*, "beloved," Gen 22:2, 12, 16). Hebrews 11:17 also refuses to use this potent adjective, preferring μονογενής (*monogenēs*, "only") instead. Kessler, *Bound by the Bible*, 60–61, 121. And, rather than being a definitive statement of the meaning of the *aqedah*, Heb 11:19 simply underscores Abraham's incredible faith in a trustworthy God, as a result of which, "*in a sense/so to speak* [ἐν παραβολῇ, *en parabolē*, "symbolically/figuratively"], he received him [Isaac] back from the dead."

7. Where the patriarch was commanded to make his burnt offering apparently was the same location where the children of Abraham were later called to do so themselves—at the Temple mount (see the use of "Moriah" in Gen 22:2 and 2 Chr 3:1; also note the use of הַר יְהוָה (*har yhwh,* "mountain of Yahweh") in Gen 22:14 and in Ps 24:3; Isa 2:3; etc.). This does not necessitate a connection with the atonement; rather the nexus is with faith. The faith of Abraham (or "fear of God," see below) in the *aqedah* was the attitude God's people were to have as they approached him, in the Temple or elsewhere. Any approach to God, any relationship with God, is to be undergirded with faith; hence the subtle link between the Temple (the place where God was encountered) and the *aqedah* (the paradigmatic biblical demonstration of faith/fear of God).

13.1	*Faith in God's promises and his word is required from the child of God, and such a faith is liable to be tested.*
13.2	*The fear of God is to be demonstrated by God's children, involving self-sacrificial trust in God's promises and wholehearted obedience to his word.*
13.3	*The love of God's people for God brooks no rival claim for their love, whatever its object.*
13.4	*The love of God/the fear of God trumps every other allegiance.*
13.5	*Demonstration of faith in God's promises and his word results in divine blessing/ reward.*

A. Having only one section in this pericope, the "Theological Focus 13" is identical to the "Theological Focus of Pericope 13."

NOTES 13

13.1   Faith in God's promises and his word is required from the child of God, and such a faith is liable to be tested.

The account begins with a time-stamp: "Now it came about *after these things*, that God tested Abraham" (22:1). What exactly were "these things"? A review of the Abrahamic saga is helpful for arriving at what the author was *doing* with what he was saying.

Bergen observes that "[t]his most prominent theme—that of Abraham's search for a proper heir—ties the diverse stories of the Abram cycle together more securely than any other."[8] Indeed! In Gen 12 we have God commanding Abram to leave his relatives and father's house in order to secure a blessing that would, in great part, come through an heir (12:1–3). And, yes, Abram showed faith in stepping out as commanded, but one notices that he took Lot his nephew, even though the divine word called for a separation from relatives and father's house. Was Abram thinking of Lot as the likely heir, seeing that he himself was already 75 years old, and his wife 65 (12:4)? That certainly was not an attitude of faith in God's promise. Later, perhaps still holding on to the hope that his nephew Lot would be the chosen heir, Abram gives him the choicest portion of the land (13:10–11). God appears to Abram soon thereafter, renewing the promise to his descendants (13:16) as if to assert that he, Abraham, had been mistaken in his reckoning of Lot as his heir. The patriarch *was* wrong, for the descendants of Lot would become enemies of the descendants of Abram (19:38).

Soon after he left his father's household and homeland, as Abram stepped into the Negev, his caravan was hit by a famine (12:9–10). He promptly decamped to Egypt. Of course, one knows what happened in that land of refuge—Abraham was willing to pass off his wife, Sarah, as his sister, lest he got killed by Pharaoh for that "very beautiful" woman (12:12–14). Would not God keep his promise about the seed? How would his life be endangered *before* the arrival of that seed? Did he need to worry about his own life, and even put his wife's well-being in jeopardy?

---

8. Bergen, "The Role of Genesis 22:1–19," 323.

In Gen 15, Yahweh's promise to Abram was renewed (15:1). But the patriarch was still childless, and so the heir, he figured, had to be Eliezer, his steward (15:2–3). God completely negated that suggestion: Abram's heir would be "one who shall come forth from your own body" (15:4), a promise set forth in covenant form (15:5–21). Yet Sarai continued to remain barren (16:1). Abram then resorted to a compromise: perhaps the chosen heir, "from your own body," was to come through the maternal agency of a concubine (16:2). Acting on this misconception, Abram fathers Ishmael through Hagar, the Egyptian. God reappeared to Abraham in Gen 17 and once again spelled out his promise to the patriarch. The divine word was crystal clear: *Sarah* would be the mother of the heir (this was iterated thrice this time: 17:16, 19, 21), not the maid, Hagar. Again, faithlessness characterized Abraham's response to God.

Then, to make matters worse, in Gen 20, Abraham palmed his wife off as his sister . . . again! This time to Abimelech (20:2), but for the same reason that he had conducted his subterfuge in Gen 12—out of fear for his own life (20:11), despite the extended account of Yahweh's appearance and re-promise to Abraham and his wife that an heir would be born to them (Gen 19). As in Gen 12, God had to intervene to set things straight (20:6–7).

Thus, all along, Abraham is seen rather clumsily stumbling along in his faith. All of his attempts to help God out with the production of an heir had come to naught. None of his schemes had worked; in fact, they had only created more trouble for himself and, in the future, for his descendants. Genesis 12–20, then, is not the account of a pristine faith on part of the patriarch.

Finally, in Gen 21, the heir is born, and the account makes it very clear that God had done what he had promised to do all along. Three times in two verses, Yahweh's faithfulness is established: "Yahweh took note of Sarah *as He had said*" (21:1a); "Yahweh did for Sarah *as He had promised* (21:1b); "Sarah conceived and bore a son . . . at the appointed time *of which God had spoken to him*" (21:2). This threefold iteration was almost a rebuke to Abraham's faithlessness thus far. God had been faithful; and he had done as he had promised: Abraham could surely trust him! The thorny issue of "seed," a problem that Abraham had been trying to solve on his own (or at least "help" God solve it), had now been settled, as God had promised.

And then, in the very next chapter, Gen 22, Abraham is tested.[9] It was almost as if this test was a necessary one. Had Abraham learnt his lessons? Would he now acknowledge that even against all odds and despite all unfavorable circumstances God's promises *would* come to pass? A test was necessary—not for God's benefit, of course, but for Abraham's, and for the benefit of all succeeding generations of readers of the text, to demonstrate what it meant to trust God fully, to take him at his word.[10]

---

9. That this account of Gen 22 was being closely connected to Gen 21:1 seems obvious in that the first time "Yahweh" appears after Gen 21:1 is in 22:11.

10. "Testing" as an act of God for the good of his people is found in Deut 8:2, 16; Exod 15:25; 16:4; Jdg 2:22; 2 Chr 32:31; Ps 26:2. Both "fear of God" and "test" show up in Exod 20:20, where Moses reassures his people: "Do not fear, for God has come in order to test you, and in order that the fear of Him may be before you, so that you might not sin."

The test in Gen 22 commenced with a divine word. Both in structure and concept, this test was strikingly similar to the "test" in Gen 12:1–7.[11]

Similarities: Genesis 12:1–3 and Genesis 22
Both commands begin identically: לֶךְ-לְךָ (*lek-lka*, "go forth," 12:1; 22:2)
No destination specified
Weighty demand: cut off past (12:1); cut off future (22:1)
Threefold description of sacrifice, each with a מ (*m*) prefix (12:1), or with אֵת (*'t*) marker (22:2)
Abraham leaves father forever; Abraham "leaves" son forever
Building of an altar concludes episode (12:8; 22:9)
Divine blessings promised (12:2–3, 7; 22:16–18)
Traveling together: with Lot (12:4); with Isaac (22:6–8)
Abraham "took" (12:5; 22:3)
Accompanied by people acquired in Haran (12:5) or by servants (22:3)
"Land" and "Moreh" (12:6); "land" and "Moriah" (22:2)
Theophany (12:7; 22:14, all using ראה, *r'h*, "see/appear")
Ends with travel to Negev (12:9; 22:19—Beersheba, in the Negev)

In Gen 12, God spoke to the patriarch for the first time; in Gen 22, for the last time. Both speeches contained the same command, found nowhere else in the Bible (לֶךְ-לְךָ, "Go forth/out," Gen 12:1; 22:2). Both stressed a journey, an altar, and promised blessings. Thus Gen 12 and 22 form the appropriate commencement and conclusion, respectively, of the Abraham Story. But this was his big test, in Gen 22: "Will you, Abraham, walk reverently and wholeheartedly before God even if it means sacrificing all benefits promised for such conduct? Do you, Abraham, fear-and-revere God more than you love your son—and through him, your great nation, great name, and great prosperity—and more even than you desire the covenant with God?"[12] Faith in God is called for from all of his children, and he frequently tests such faith. Would Abraham pass his test?

13.2   *The fear of God is to be demonstrated by God's children, involving self-sacrificial trust in God's promises and wholehearted obedience to his word.*

Notice the key phrase in the acclamation of the angel of Yahweh in Gen 22:12: "Now I know that you *fear God*." Abraham's fear of God had, through this test, been proven. This "fearing of God" is a critical element in the account. The last time fear of God was mentioned in the Abrahamic saga was in 20:11 (in fact these are the first two occurrences of "fear of God" in Bible). When Abimelech confronted Abraham with his wife/sister deception, Abraham's excuse was: "Surely there is no fear [יִרְאַת, *yir'at*] of God in this place; and they will kill me on account of my wife" (20:11). The reader immediately catches the irony. Abimelech was terror-stricken at the possibility of having run up against God; the text explicitly tells us so: "And the men were greatly frightened [וַיִּירְאוּ . . . מְאֹד, *wayyir'u . . . m'od*]" (20:8). On the other hand, it was *Abraham* who did not fear God enough to trust him to take care of him when God had promised him descendants. Surely his life would not be in danger before he produced progeny.

11. From Hong, "An Exegetical Reading," 134–36.

12. Kass, *The Beginning of Wisdom*, 337.

But in Gen 22, Abraham appeared to have learnt his lesson in trusting God. Earlier he had countered God's proposals, attempting to substitute Lot (Gen 12–13), and Eliezer (15:2), and Ishmael (17:18) in place of Isaac. Here he is totally silent, a silence that is deafening: "his only words are absolute compliance and a confidence in the Lord's final provision."[13] From the way the story is discoursed, it seems clear that Gen 21, with the birth of Isaac and Yahweh's triple assertion of his faithfulness (21:1–2), had something to do with that change of heart (see Pericope 12). Apparently, after many blunders and fumbles, Abraham had finally come around to trusting God. And in Gen 22, the divine declaration "Now I know that you fear God" (22:12), gave proof to the fact that Abraham now feared God, trusting him enough to obey him without question. Surely a God who could give him an heir from a dead womb could bring that one back from a charred altar. No wonder God could affirm Abraham's fear of God after this momentous test. "Now I know," the assertion that prefaces God's announcement in 22:12, was often used in the OT to describe solemn declarations (Exod 18:11; Jdg 17:13; 1 Sam 24:20; 1 Kgs 17:24; Ps 20:6).[14] Targumic interpretation put it this way in the mouth of God: "I credit the merit to you for this action as though I had said to you, 'Offer me yourself,' and you did not hold back" (*Gen. Rab.* 56:7).[15] Indeed, this was a sacrifice not of Isaac, but of Abraham himself—all he hoped for, his future, his life, his seed.[16]

Ironically, when Abraham understood that "*God* sees/provides" (אֱלֹהִים יִרְאֶה, *'elohim yir'eh*, Gen 22:8), God in turn acknowledged that *Abraham* "fears God" (אֱלֹהִים יְרֵא, *yre' 'elohim*, 22:12); the paronomasia is obvious.[17] Here, in Gen 22:12, the verb יָרֵא *yare'*, is used substantively to denote Abraham as a "fearer" of God—a (now-proven) characteristic of this patriarch. "Fear of God" is the fundamental OT term for depicting the appropriate human response to God—the Hebrew equivalent to the Christian "faith" (see Deut 10:12; Eccl 12:13, in addition to Pss 103:11, 13, 17; 112:1; 128:1; Prov 31:30; Luke 1:50). Moberly asserts that "Genesis 22 may appropriately be read as a, arguably the, primary canonical exposition of the meaning of 'one who fears God,'"

13. Mathews, *Genesis 11:27–50:26*, 291.

14. Chisholm, "Anatomy of an Anthropomorphism," 13. This phrase, of course, is not to deny an omniscient God the knowledge of Abraham's character even before the test (Pss 44:21; 94:11; 139:1–4; Jer 17:10; 20:12).

15. So also *Jub.* 18.16 (and 4Q225), quoting God: "'I [God] have made know to all that you [Abraham] are faithful to me in everything which I say to you.'"

16. So also Ross: "the real point of the act was Abraham's sacrifice of himself, that is, of his will and his wisdom with regard to his son Isaac" (*Creation and Blessing*, 393). Appropriately enough, Gerhard von Rad's booklet on Gen 22 is titled *Das Opfer des Abraham* ("The Sacrifice of Abraham")—not that of Isaac.

17. The verb רָאָה (*ra'ah*, "to see/provide") echoes through the account: Gen 22:8, 13, 14 (×2). In fact, "Moriah" (מֹרִיָּה, *moriyyah*, 22:2) may also be related to this root: thus, the "place of seeing." Moreover, one could also read בְּהַר יְהוָה יֵרָאֶה (*bhar yhwh yera'eh*, 22:14b) as "in the mount, Yahweh will be seen" (or "in the mount of Yahweh, he will be seen"), thus providing an etiology for what might have been the site of the Temple. The various uses of רָאָה in the story form a chiastic structure, centered about Abraham's faith in God's provision of a substitute for his son, and his discovery of that provision.

entailing "obedience of the most demanding kind" grounded in a deep trust in God.[18] In other words, the *aqedah* defines the meaning of יְרְאַת אֱלֹהִים, *yr'at 'elohim*, "fear of God"—"obedience which does not hold back even what is most precious, when God demands it, and commits to God even that future which he himself has promised."[19] Abraham's sacrifice thus becomes "a paradigm for his successors," in his "wholehearted devotion to God" expressed in his obedience.[20] Maimonides would have agreed with this assessment; according to Rambam (*Guide for the Perplexed* 24):

> The angel, therefore, says to [Abraham], 'For now I know,' etc. [Gen 22:12], that is, 'from this action, for which you deserve to be truly called a God-fearing man, all people shall learn how far we must go in the fear of God.' This idea is confirmed in Scripture; it is distinctly stated that one sole thing, fear of God, is the object of the whole Law with its affirmative and negative precepts, its promises and its historical examples.

And faith is an integral part of that "fear." Abraham's faith in God is underscored in 22:5, where in a series of first person plural verbs, the final outcome of the incident that Abraham expected is described: "I and the lad—we shall go . . ., and we shall worship, and we shall return.[21] The *aqedah*, thus, is an account that teaches God's people what fearing God is all about—the willing sacrifice of *everything!* Two instances of unusual word ordering for Hebrew (subject–verb–object) throw light on the focus of the narrative: "God, he tested Abraham!" (22:1) finds a perfect response in the similarly arranged words from the patriarch: "Yahweh, he will provide!" (22:8).[22] Indeed the structuring of the account seems to reinforce that point—Abraham's faith is being significantly showcased in this account[23]:

A   God announces the name of the "mountain": land of "the place of *seeing*" ("Moriah," 22:2)
   B   Abraham *"sees"* the "place" of sacrifice (22:4)
      C   Abraham asserts God will *"see"*/provide" (22:8)
      C'   Abraham *"sees"* God's provision (22:13)
   B'   Abraham names the "place" "God *sees*/provides" (22:14a)
A'   Narrator announces maxim about the "mountain": where "God will be *seen*" (22:14b)

Rather than an Atonement analogy, this play of words and structure strongly emphasizes Abraham's faith in a faithful God: he sees (with the eyes of faith)—and God in turn sees (to it, meeting Abraham's need).

18. Moberly, *The Bible, Theology, and Faith*, 79, 96. Also see idem, "What is Theological Interpretation?" 176.

19. Wolff, "The Elohistic Fragments," 163–64. As Chisholm put it, "[f]earing God is a metonymy for reverence that results in obedience" ("Anatomy of an Anthropomorphism," 13).

20. Wenham, "The Aqedah," 102.

21. The "faith" of Abraham (אמן, *'mn*, and, in the LXX, πιστός, *pistos*) is specifically noted in Neh 9:7–8.

22. After "and he said," and "and he said," and "and he said"—in the dialogue between father and son in 22:7—we suddenly have "and Abraham said" in 22:8, signifying that what he was going to say was of great importance: Yahweh was being recognized as the Provider.

23. From Kass, *The Beginning of Wisdom*, 341–42n48; and Walters, "Wood, Sand and Stars," 314.

> **A** Divine call to Abraham (22:1a)
>> **B** Abraham's response: "Here I am [הִנֵּנִי, *hinneni*]" (22:1b)
>>> **C** Divine command (22:2)
>>>> **D** Abraham's response (22:3–4): "raised his eyes and saw"
>>>>> **E** Worship (22:5)
>
> Preparation for sacrifice (22:6)
> Isaac's query (הִנֵּנִי, 22:7)/Abraham's response (הִנֵּנִי, 22:7): "Yahweh will provide" (22:8)
> Preparation for sacrifice (22:9–10)
>
> **A'** Divine call to Abraham (22:11a)
>> **B'** Abraham's response: "Here I am [הִנֵּנִי]" (22:11b)
>>> **C'** Divine command (22:12)
>>>> **D'** Abraham's response (22:13–14): "raised his eyes and saw"
>>>>> **E'** Worship implied (22:14)

A cascade of six imperfect verbs marked Abraham's obedience at the outset of the narrative: he rose, he saddled, he took, he split, he arose, he went (22:3). Approaching the place of sacrifice, another six imperfect verbs again point to his obedience: he built, he arranged, he bound, he placed, he stretched, he took (22:9–10). This was faithful obedience *par excellence*: Abraham displayed the "fear of God"—self-sacrificial trust in, and wholehearted obedience to, God.

13.3 The love of God's people for God brooks no rival claim for their love, whatever its object.

The extent of Abraham's willingness to sacrifice "everything" and the depth of his wholehearted obedience is indicated in Gen 22 by its emphasis on the father-son relationship: "father" and/or "son" is mentioned fifteen times in Gen 22:1–20 (in 22:2 [×2], 3, 6, 7 [×3], 8, 9, 10, 12 [×2], 13, 16 [×2]). The readers are never to forget the relationship. In the only conversation recorded in the Bible between Abraham and Isaac, the latter's words begin with "my father" and the former's words end with "my son" (22:7–8)—this is also Abraham's last word before he prepares to slay Isaac (בְּנִי, *bni*, "my son," is a single word in the Hebrew). No matter what the typological lens with which this account is viewed, one thing is clear: a father is called to slay the son he loves. The structural parallels between Gen 21:3 and 22:2 make this paternal-filial attachment even more clear:

Genesis 21:3

Son	who was born to him	whom Sarah bore to him	Isaac
אֵת ... בְּנוֹ	הַנּוֹלַד־לוֹ	אֲשֶׁר־יָלְדָה־לּוֹ שָׂרָה	יִצְחָק
'et ... beno	*hannolad-lo*	*'asher-yaldah-lo sarah*	*yitskhaq*

Genesis 22:2

your son	your only son	whom you love	Isaac
אֶת־בִּנְךָ	אֶת־יְחִידְךָ	אֲשֶׁר־אָהַבְתָּ	אֶת־יִצְחָק
'et-binka	*'et-ykhidka*	*'asher-'ahavta*	*'et-yitskhaq*

The sentiments expressed in *Jubilees* were right on the money: "And the prince Mastema [a demonic being] came and said before God, 'Behold, Abraham loves Isaac his son, and he delights in him above all things else; bid him offer him as a burnt-offering on the altar, and Thou wilt see if he will do this command, and Thou wilt know if he is faithful in everything wherein Thou dost try him'" (*Jub.* 17:16). It is therefore highly significant that the first time the word "love" (אהב, *'hv*) occurs in the Bible is in this account, in 22:2. With the entry of this new word into Scripture came an implicit question: Was Abraham's love for Isaac so strong that his allegiance to God had diminished? It appears then, that this love of Abraham for God was the crucial element in the test—it was this love that was being tested. Would Abraham be loyal to God, or would love for the human overpower trust in the divine?

Without even perusing the details of Abraham's test, one can find the answer to that question of the patriarch's loyalties when one compares the unique descriptors of Isaac. There are three heavenly announcements to Abraham (22:1–2, 11–12, 14–16) with three corresponding descriptors of the (proposed/putative) sacrifice, Isaac. These three descriptors contain the only three instances of בֵּן (*ben*, "son") in the account that are inflected with the second person singular possessive pronoun (בִּנְךָ, *binka*, "your son") and fitted into a patterned construction. However, there is a significant alteration, before and after the test, in how God/angel of Yahweh described Isaac.

Pre-test:
    22:2   "your son, your only son, *the one you love*"
Post-test:
    22:12 "your son, your only son"
    22:16 "your son, your only son"

The trifold description of Isaac in Gen 22:2 was to emphasize that this son, this particular one, was the one Abraham *loved,* with a love that potentially stood in the way of his allegiance to, and faith in, God. The subsequent, post-test deletion of the phrase, "the one you love," was clear indication that Abraham had passed the examination. The three-part description of Isaac *before* the test ("son/only son/one you love") becomes, *after* the test, two-part ("son/only son"). The *aqedah* was, therefore, in reality, a demonstration of Abraham's love for God over and against anything that advanced a rival claim to that love. As Trible observes, "the story has to do with idolatry—the idolatry of the son. Once God had given the gift of Isaac to Abraham, does Abraham focus on Isaac and forget the Giver? The climactic line is 'Now I know that you worship God,' with the implied 'and that you do not worship your son.'"[24]

The author of 4 Maccabees (13:12), Josephus (*Ant.* 1.13.1), and Philo (*On Abraham,* 32.117; 35.195) agree with this reading of Abraham's shift in loyalties from Isaac to God: all see the *aqedah* as pointing the Abraham's "devotion," "piety," or "love" for God. Therefore, Ambrose exhorts, "Let us then set God before all those whom we love, father, brother, mother. . . . Let us, then, imitate the devotion of Abraham" (*On the Decease of His Brother Satyrus,* 2.97, 99).[25] Origen expressed it this way: "For

24. Trible, "The Test," 227.

25. Ambrose also declared that Abraham did not "put love for his son before the commands of his Creator," thus demonstrating his "devotion to God" (*On the Duties of the Clergy,* 1.25.119). Calvin,

Abraham loved Isaac his son, the text says, but he placed the love of God before love of the flesh."[26] In sum, the test "proved" the patriarch's absolute allegiance to God—his unadulterated love for, and loyalty to, deity. Nothing would stand between Abraham and God and, in a circumspect way, the text actually tells us that (see below).

13.4 *The love of God/the fear of God trumps every other allegiance.*

One element of the account that has perplexed interpreters throughout the ages is the apparent disappearance of Isaac from the Abraham Story after the mention of "son" in Gen 22:16. Indeed, father and son are never shown speaking to each other again after this episode; Isaac does not even show up in the account of Sarah's death and burial (Gen 23). The only mentioned "contact" between father and son after the stunning incident of the *aqedah* is at Abraham's funeral (25:9).[27] In fact, in the Gen 22 account itself, it appears that Isaac, after the aborted sacrifice, has vanished. Abraham, we are told, returned from his test, apparently *without* Isaac: "So Abraham returned to his young men, and they arose and they went together to Beersheba; and Abraham lived in Beersheba" (22:19). The use of the same phrase, "walked together," that was used earlier to describe the trip of father and son (22:6, 8), is now used of the return journey of master and servants, making it all the more strange that Isaac is nowhere visible.

So what happened to the lad after the sacrifice of the ram and the reissuing of God's promises? As was noted earlier, there is one significant difference in the description of Isaac in the pre-test and post-test accounts (22:2 vs. 22:12, 16)—the "love" motif, missing after the abandoned sacrifice (see above). Quite interestingly, in parallel, while there are three assertions of Abraham being accompanied by one or more companions (22:6, 8, 19), the last such statement—the post-test version— is significantly different from the other two: in 22:6 and 8, "them" indicates Abraham and Isaac; in 22:19, Isaac is missing, and "they" indicates Abraham and his two young men.

Pre-test:

22:6	"the two of them [Abraham and Isaac] walked together"
22:8	"the two of them [Abraham and Isaac] walked together"

Post-test:

22:19	"they [Abraham and his young men] ... walked together"

---

while agreeing with Abraham's agonies, thought it was directed elsewhere and not primarily a paternal anguish. "For the great source of grief to him was not his own bereavement . . . but that, in the person of this son, the whole salvation of the world seemed to be extinguished and to perish" (Calvin, *Comm. Gen.* on 22:1). It is a little hard to imagine a father with a knife poised to strike his beloved son being more worried about his posterity than about his bound child lying helpless before him on the altar. Kierkegaard depicts the pathos well: "There was many a father who lost his child; but then it was God, . . . it was His hand took the child. Not so with Abraham. For him was reserved a harder trial, and Isaac's fate was laid along with the knife in Abraham's hand" (Kierkegaard, *Fear and Trembling*, 36).

26. Origen, *Hom. Gen.* 8.7. And likewise, "[U]nless you are obedient to all the commands, even the more difficult ones, unless you offer sacrifice and show that you place neither father nor mother nor sons before God [Matt 10:37], you will not know that you fear God. Nor will it be said of you, 'Now I know that you fear God'" (ibid., 8.8).

27. Moreover, "[a]fter the *Aqedah*, there is no more direct divine revelation to Abraham and *vice versa*, no contact of Abraham with God in the rest of Abraham's stories in the book of Genesis" (Kalimi, "'Go, I Beg You,'" 16). All this despite Abraham's endeavors to find a bride for Isaac (24:1–9, 62–67), and his giving his all to Isaac (25:6)—but there is no interpersonal contact between father and son expressed in the text.

After the test, it is as if Isaac has altogether vanished; the narrator apparently took an eraser and wiped out any mention of Isaac after the "sacrifice." But there was a purpose behind this: the author was *doing* something with what he was saying (in this case, with what he *failed* to say, creating a striking gap in the narrative—but that, too, is to "say" something). No more would the account portray father and son speaking to each other or even being in one another's presence until the older one dies (25:8–9). When one remembers that the test was actually an examination of Abraham's loyalties—to God or to son, "the one you love"—one understands what it was the author was *doing* in Gen 22:19: he was describing, in yet another way, Abraham's success in this critical test. A line had been drawn; the relationship between father and son had been clarified, the tension between fear of God and love of son had been resolved. One might almost say: *For Abraham so loved God that he gave his only begotten son.* . . . This test had shown that Abraham loved God more than anyone else.[28] And to bring that home to readers, father and son are separated for the rest of their days—*literally* separated, that is, for the purpose of achieving the narrator's theological agenda.[29] He was *doing* something with what he was saying: the love/fear of God trumps every other allegiance!

13.5 *Demonstration of faith in God's promises and his word results in divine blessing/ reward.*

The consequences of Abraham's action, as depicted in the narrative of Gen 22, also give credence to the interpretation of the story as teaching what it means to fear God. That Abraham successfully passes this test is not only expressly depicted, but it is also strongly implied: the narrative is both the zenith of the Abraham Story and the climax of Abraham's worship. Of the three altars in the patriarch's story (12:8; 13:18; and 22:9), the one in Gen 22 is the only one with a sacrifice; with the others, Abraham only calls on the name of Yahweh (12:8; 13:4).

Scholars have generally held that the Abrahamic promises (in Gen 12, 15, 17, 18, and 22) are unconditional.[30] Yet, upon examination of the promise made to the patriarch at the conclusion of the momentous events of Gen 22, one cannot but notice contingency: the clauses "because you have done this thing and have not withheld your son, your only son" and "because you have obeyed my voice" (*A* and *A'* below) bookend the promised blessing (Gen 22:16c–18).

---

28. The equation of "fear of God" and "love for God" is not illegitimate: Deut 6:2, 13 command fear, while the *Shema* calls for love (6:5); Deut 10:12 and 13:3–4—each has both elements; also see Deut 10:20 with 11:1; as well as Pss 31:19, 23; 145:19–20. There is considerable overlap between these two concepts, fear and love of God, as is evident in the *aqedah* itself.

29. As to whether they were *actually* separated, that is an issue *behind* the text that need not concern the interpreter.

30. However, for recent doubts about that assumption, see Knoppers, "Ancient Near Eastern Royal Grants," 670–97; Hess, "The Book of Joshua," 493–506; and McKenzie, "The Typology of the Davidic Covenant," 152–78. And see Pericope 9 (Gen 15:1–16:16).

> **A**   "Because you have done this thing and have not withheld your son, your only son,
>   **B**   indeed I will greatly *bless* you,
>   **C**   and I will greatly multiply your *seed*
>   **D**   as the stars of the heavens and as the sand which is on the seashore;
>   **C'**   and your *seed* shall possess the gate of their enemies.
>   **B'**   In your seed all the nations of the earth shall be *blessed*
> **A'**   because you have obeyed My voice."

This reiterated promise is quite different from the earlier promises in several ways: Gen 22:17a has "greatly bless" (B above; בָּרֵךְ אֲבָרֶכְךָ, *barek 'abarekka*, emphatic and in the infinitive absolute, unique in Genesis[31]); likewise, "greatly multiply" (C; וְהַרְבָּה אַרְבֶּה, *wharbah 'arbeh*, is also found in 16:10, but 22:17b is the only instance of this promise to the Abraham-Isaac-Jacob lineage). Moreover, 22:17c employs two similes—stars of the heavens, and sand of the seashore (D)—used elsewhere in Genesis singly, but never together (15:5; 26:4; 32:12; also Exod 32:13); and the possession by Abraham's seed of "the gate of their enemies" (C'; Gen 22:17d) is unusual for the promises in Genesis.[32] The nations being blessed "in your descendants" (B'; 22:18a and 26:4; 28:14) is also new—thus far the blessing of the nations had been explicitly "in Abraham" (12:3; 18:18). This focus on descendants is appropriate given that the *aqedah* deals with the "saving" of a descendant.[33] Thus, there are significant differences—*contingent enhancements*—to the promises already given to Abraham in Gen 12, 15, 17, and 18. While the essence of the blessing remains the same in its various iterations, the attachment of the contingency of obedience, along with the enhancements, is certainly striking (though there was already a hint of this in Gen 17:1–2 and 18:19).[34] But Calvin asserts: "Certainly, before Isaac was born, this same promise had been already given; and now it receives nothing more than confirmation" (*Comm. Gen.* on 22:15). However, this is not what one infers from the divine (re)promise in this account (22:16–18). Every element of the original promise is fortified here, ratcheted up a notch, *because of obedience*. It is an enhancement of the earlier promise, especially solidified in Yahweh's unique swearing by himself ("By Myself I have sworn," 22:16)—the first and only such divine oath being made in the patriarchal stories, though that oath is frequently referred to elsewhere (24:7; 26:3; 50:24; Exod 13:5; Num 14:16; Deut 1:8; etc.).[35] The oath is validated further by the addition of "declares Yahweh," which echoes often in the prophetic corpus (Isa 45:23; Jer 22:5; 49:13) but, in the Pentateuch, is only found in Gen 22:14 and Num 19:28. Thus this promise in Gen 22 is made far more definitive than all the preceding ones, and carries added solemnity and gravitas. Abraham's possession of the land was promised earlier in Gen 12:7; 13:14–17; 15:7–21; and 17:8; but here in 22:17, we find the most militant and triumphant version of that promise ("your

---

31. This construct is also found in Num 23:11, 25; Josh 24:10; Deut 15:4; 1 Chr 4:10; Ps 132:15.

32. This phrase also occurs in Gen 24:60, with the blessing of Rebekah by her family.

33. Moberly, "The Earliest Commentary," 316–17.

34. This "enhancement" of the promise is more like an unexpected bonus, which, of course, is what grace is all about.

35. Wenham, *Genesis 16–50*, 111. The phrase, "by Myself," is also unique in Genesis, but is found in Jer 22:5; 49:13; Amos 4:2; 6:8; and in the NT in Heb 6:13–18.

seed shall possess the gate of your enemies" = "conquer your enemies' cities"). And, correspondingly, the blessing is focused upon all the *nations* of the earth, not just the *families* as in 12:3. Contingent upon his obedience, every aspect of the earlier promises to Abraham is now "augmented and guaranteed by the Lord unreservedly."[36]

In sum, there *are* actual changes in the elements of the promised blessing—significant changes in degree of their fulfillment. Thus human obedience has greater value than merely being incorporated into divine plan, and the resulting blessing is more than just a confirmation of what God has already promised. There is, indeed, a *contingent* divine response to human obedience—in a sense, a gracious divine reward for the latter. So Wenham concludes: "God's test had put Abraham on the rack. Yet torn between his love for his son and his devotion to God, he had emerged victorious with his son intact and his faithful obedience rewarded beyond all expectation."[37] It is exactly this divine reward that is emphasized in the promise to Isaac in Gen 26:2–5, where the blessing is expressly based upon the obedience of Abraham ("because Abraham obeyed My voice and kept My charge, My commandments, My statutes, and My laws," 26:5). This contingency of faithful obedience heightens the *degree of blessing*, not that the blessing itself is changed in character, but that, in some sense, the quantum of blessing is supplemented and its quality intensified. Obedience *does* result in reward/blessing, an act of divine grace.

SERMON FOCUS AND OUTLINES

THEOLOGICAL FOCUS OF PERICOPE 13 FOR PREACHING

13   Fear of God trumps every other allegiance and manifests in self-sacrificial obedience (22:1–19).

"What, then, does Abraham teach us? To put it briefly, he teaches us not to prefer the gifts of God to God. . . . Therefore, put not even a real gift of God before the Giver of that gift" (Augustine, *Serm.* 2). Thus the intent of the author was to call for an identification of the readers with the protagonist of this story—Abraham, the paragon of faith. God's people everywhere are to exercise the kind of faith in God that Abraham had, the kind of love for God that Abraham demonstrated, the kind of fear of God that Abraham exhibited: nothing is to come between God and the believer—*nothing!* This is the lesson the preacher must proclaim; this is what the reader must do. That is no less a christological understanding of Gen 22 than any other interpretive option: part of what it means to be Christlike is to exercise the kind of faith, demonstrate the kind of love, and exhibit the kind of fear that Abraham did.[38]

---

36. Ibid., 116.

37. Ibid. Also see idem, "The Aqedah," 101. This, then, is God's gracious reward upon seeing his child's "fear of the Lord" (obedience): notice the use of שָׂכָר (*sakar,* "reward") in the promise of God to Abraham in 15:1.

38. See Kuruvilla, *Privilege the Text!* 238–69, for the development of this concept of *imitatio Christi,* and for details of such a reading that I label a "christiconic" interpretation of Scripture—a theological hermeneutic for preaching.

Possible Preaching Outlines for Pericope 13

I. *Expect a test!*

Abraham's rather clumsy faith-pilgrimage this far (recap Genesis 12–21)

Abraham's test (22:1–2)

Move-to-Relevance: Tests of our faith

What we can do to expect such tests

II. *Experience God's faithfulness!*

Abraham's experience of God's faithfulness thus far (recap Genesis 12–21, particularly 21:1–3)

Abraham's response of faith in his test enabled by his past experience of God's faithfulness (22:3–10)

Move-to-Relevance: Our experiences of God's faithfulness in the past

How we can experience (remember, recollect) God's faithfulness to us constantly

III. *Exhibit God's fear!*[39]

Abraham's exhibition of the fear of God (22:11–16)

Blessings, a consequence of Abraham's fear of God (22:17–18)

Nothing comes between God and Abraham (22:19)

Move-to-Relevance: Things/people that come between us and God

How we can exhibit the fear of God[40]

Focusing more on the fear of God, one might employ a simpler outline.

I. What Fear of God is Not

Abraham's rather clumsy faith-pilgrimage this far (recap Genesis 12–21)

Abraham's testing by God to strengthen faith/fear of God (22:1–2)

Move-to-Relevance: Things that stand between us and God, keeping us from fearing him

II. What Fear of God is

Abraham's experience of God's faithfulness thus far (recap Genesis 12–21, particularly 21:1–3)

Abraham's exhibition of the fear of God, with nothing between him and God (22:3–19)

Move-to-Relevance: Remembering God's faithfulness to us constantly, increases our fear of God

III. *Exhibit the fear of God!*

Blessings, a consequence of Abraham's fear of God (22:17–18)

How we can exhibit the fear of God and thereby be blessed

---

39. By this, I mean "Exhibit the Fear of God."

40. The spiritual disciplines of abstinence (celibacy, fasting, silence, solitude, frugality, simplicity, etc.) may be a good way to begin exhibiting the fear of God, by practicing the sacrifices of abstention.

PERICOPE 14

Will He Come Through?

Genesis 22:20–23:20

[Death of Sarah; Purchase of Property; Burial of Sarah]

REVIEW, SUMMARY, PREVIEW

Review of Pericope 13: Genesis 22:1–19 deals with the sacrifice of Isaac—Abraham's greatest test, which he passes with flying colors, exhibiting the fear of God in holding back nothing from him. Believers are called to do likewise.

Summary of Pericope 14: This pericope sees Abraham established further in Canaan: despite opposition and exploitation, he now owns a humble burial plot, ironic in light of the extensive land promises God had made to him and his descendants. Faith involves continued trust, even when one can see no sign of divine promises being fulfilled or divine blessings being brought about.

Preview of Pericope 15: The next pericope (Gen 24:1–25:18) describes the search for a bride for Isaac. All the protagonists—Abraham, his retainer, and Rebekah—demonstrate a firm trust in God to fulfill his purposes. God sovereignly works things out favorably for the parties involved, but in tandem with human action that is conducted in faith.

14. Genesis 22:20–23:20

THEOLOGICAL FOCUS OF PERICOPE 14

265

> **14** A mature faith in God's promises persists even in the seeming absence of God and the non-fulfillment of his promises, and even when such faith is costly, encountering opposition, suffering exploitation, and experiencing little reward in the present (22:20–23:20).
>
> *14.1 God's promises will be fulfilled in his time.*
>
> *14.2 The seeming absence of God and the non-fulfillment of God's promises do not preclude his working, nor do they stand in the way of faithful commitment to him.*
>
> *14.3 Persistence in the direction of divine promise marks mature faith in God.*
>
> *14.4 A mature faith in God may be costly, encountering opposition, suffering exploitation, and experiencing little reward in the present.*

OVERVIEW

Genesis 22:20–25:18 forms the epilogue of the Abrahamic saga, beginning and ending with genealogies (22:22–24 and 25:1–18; the latter includes the brief תּוֹלְדֹת, *toldot*, of Ishmael, 25:12–18). Following this comes the תּוֹלְדֹת of Isaac (25:19–20), which becomes the introduction to the story of Jacob.

After the mention of her name in 21:12, when she is about 91 years old, Sarah faded out of the Abraham story. Now she shows up again at her death, at the age of 127 (17:17, 21; 21:1–7; 23:1), becoming the only patriarchal wife whose age at demise is noted. Abraham was now 137 (62 years after entering Canaan, 12:4), and Isaac around 37.

"Now it came about after these things," introduces both the *aqedah* (22:1) and the genealogy in 22:20–24. By its use in 22:20, the transition implies the concluding nature of the sacrifice episode and the commencement of a new one. Abraham had passed his final test in Gen 22:1–19; no more would there be recorded an appearance or revelation of God to the patriarch. Old order was changing, yielding place to new. Yet the statement that "Milcah *also* had borne sons" (22:20) connects this genealogy with 21:1–7, where Sarah's bearing a son had been announced. It is not surprising then that Milcah's granddaughter ends up marrying Sarah's son.

14   *Genesis 22:20–23:20*

THEOLOGICAL FOCUS 14[A]

14 A mature faith in God's promises persists even in the seeming absence of God and the non-fulfillment of his promises, and even when such faith is costly, encountering opposition, suffering exploitation, and experiencing little reward in the present (22:20–23:20).

14.1 God's promises will be fulfilled in his time.

14.2 The seeming absence of God and the non-fulfillment of God's promises do not preclude his working, nor do they stand in the way of faithful commitment to him.

14.3 Persistence in the direction of divine promise marks mature faith in God.

14.4 A mature faith in God may be costly, encountering opposition, suffering exploitation, and experiencing little reward in the present.

A. Having only one section in this pericope, the "Theological Focus 14" is identical to the "Theological Focus of Pericope 14."

NOTES 14

14.1 God's promises will be fulfilled in his time.

Through the narrative of Abraham, one has noticed the *curricula vitae* of the two sons of Abraham running parallel to each other: birth, rescue from sure death, promises of nationhood, etc. (see Pericope 12). However, while Ishmael has married, finding a spouse from his mother's people group in Egypt (21:21), in this aspect, Isaac's career has not matched his brother's: a marital account was long overdue. "The reader expects something at this point, but the editor tantalizes him with a mere genealogy. But buried within it is the mention of one grandchild, who is also a girl. This surely raises expectations."[1] The promises of 22:16–18 promised descendants for Abraham, implying the marriage of his son Isaac; Ishmael's getting married made it all the more imperative for Isaac. This four-verse genealogy, 22:21–24, thus points in the direction in which God's word would be fulfilled: there would be descendants for Abraham and future generations, and that through Rebekah (22:23). As the sole woman descendant among the twelve men listed as Nahor's children, she is confirmed as the matriarch of the next generation.

There is a palistrophic arrangement of the whole narrative of Abraham:

A Terah's תּוֹלְדֹת , including Nahor's genealogy (11:27–32)
 B The call of Abraham: לֶךְ־לְךָ, *lek-lka*;
   threefold separation—from country, relatives, father's house (12:1–3)
    …

 B' The trial of Abraham: לֶךְ־לְךָ;
   threefold separation—from son, only son, the one loved (22:1–19)
A' Nahor's genealogy (22:20–24)

The biographical scheme is similar for all the patriarchs: there is a promise, a journey, an account of births, and a narrative of the death and burial of a wife.[2]

	Abraham	Isaac	Jacob
Promise	22:15–18	35:9–14	48:4
Journey	22:19	35:16	48:7
Birth of children	22:20–24	35:17–18	48:5–6
Death/burial of wife	23:1–20	35:18–20	48:7

As noted, Nahor had twelve sons (22:21–24), in keeping with the number of sons that Ishmael (17:20; 25:16), Jacob (35:22; 29:28), and Esau (36:2–4, 20–21) produced. In Nahor's lineage noted here, there is only a single tier, except for Rebekah who belongs to the second tier as a granddaughter. Incidentally, this makes the Israelites of double stock: the Abraham–Isaac–Jacob axis (from Abraham) and the Rebekah–

---

1. Wenham, *Genesis 16–50*, 119.
2. Ibid.

Leah–Rachel axis (from Nahor).[3] Adumbrations of the fulfillment of God's promises are thus offered to the reader in the placement of the genealogy where it is in 22:20–24.

14.2 The seeming absence of God and the non-fulfillment of God's promises do not preclude his working, nor do they stand in the way of faithful commitment to him.

Interestingly, there is no mention of God in Gen 23, except for the Hittites' labeling of Abraham as a "prince of Elohim" (נְשִׂיא אֱלֹהִים, *nsi' 'elohim*, 23:6; here the divine name might simply indicate the superlative—"*mighty* prince").

While on the surface the subject of this chapter, the purchase of a burial plot, sounds rather trivial, its mention elsewhere—in connection with Abraham's burial (25:9–10), with Jacob's will (49:29–32), and with Jacob's burial (50:13)—indicates its significance to Israelite history and to what God was doing through Abraham. Each time, the purchase and the issue of property rights are detailed.[4] It is this landing of property that is rendered more important (sixteen verses, 23:3–18, dealing with extensive negotiations and the purchase of property) than even the death, mourning for, and burial of Sarah, which occupy only three verses (23:1–2, 19). Twice the narrative mentions that Hebron, the location of Sarah's death and burial, is "in the land of Canaan" (23:2, 19). The land motif is crucial. In fact, the final note on Sarah and her burial is followed up in 23:20 with a restatement of the significance of this piece of land that the patriarch had purchased, confirming the interest of this chapter.[5] Thus the thrust of the pericope is Abraham's possession of land in Canaan; it is only secondarily about the death of Sarah. For the first time, Abraham is formally and legally a landowner in the Promised Land (though he did have some water rights in the land, 21:22–34). God's promises were beginning to be fulfilled, despite his seeming absence in the story.

Wenham considers this episode "a quite secular story" that "does not obviously relate to the promises or their fulfillment. Simple biographical interest seems to dictate its inclusion." I would disagree. Burial of the matriarch in the land indicates that a degree of permanency has been achieved. And the fact that the patriarch continued to remain in the Promised Land demonstrates his commitment to, and faith in, God's promises.

> When Abraham bought Machpelah, he was renouncing Paddan Aram (which was just brought to the reader's attention in 22:20–24). Canaan was the land his descendants would inherit. It is interesting to observe here that the only portion of the Promised Land that Abraham ever received, he bought [at an exorbitant

---

3. Mathews, *Genesis 11:27—50:26*, 309.

4. Amit, *Reading Biblical Narratives*, 53. Burials in the cave of Machpelah included those of Sarah (23:2, 19), Abraham (25:9–10), Isaac (35:27–29, in Hebron, see 23:2, 19), Rebekah (49:31), Leah (49:31), and Jacob (50:13).

5. Greidanus, *Preaching Christ from Genesis*, 214.

price]—and that was a grave. But this grave bound them to the land, for later patriarchs would die and be gathered to their ancestors—in Canaan.[6]

Jacob and Joseph, while in Egypt, insisted that their respective burials be conducted in Canaan (49:29–32 and 50:24–25). All this to say that God continues to work despite his seeming absence, and his people are called to continue in commitment to him.

14.3 Persistence in the direction of divine promise marks mature faith in God.

The bargaining for the land, 23:3–16, is set into three pairs of speeches, a common enough triadic arrangement in Hebrew narrative.

Paired Speeches	Abraham / Sons of Heth or Ephron
23:3–6 ("Abraham rose," 23:3)	"bury my dead" (23:4) "hear us, my lord"/"bury your dead" (×2) (23:6)
23:7–11 ("Abraham rose," 23:7)	"bury my dead"/"hear me" (23:8) "my lord, hear me"/"bury your dead" (23:11)
23:12–16 ("Abraham bowed," 23:12)	"bury my dead"/"hear me" (23:13) "hear me, my lord"/"bury your dead" (23:15)
23:16, Conclusion	*"hearing" of Abraham by sons of Heth* *"hearing" by Abraham of Ephron*

It appears in 23:3–6 that the Hittites are quite eager to accede to the request of Abraham. Not only do they echo his "bury my dead" (23:4) twice with their own "bury your dead" (23:6), they refute his label of himself as "stranger" and "sojourner" with their own ascription of him as "prince of God/mighty prince." They seem to want to give Abraham "the choicest of our graves," certain that "none of us will refuse you" (23:6). Indeed, their reply to Abraham's first speech is duplicated, positively and negatively.

> **A** "In the choices of our graves" (23:6b)
> **B** "bury your dead" (23:6c)
> **A'** "no man from us will withhold his grave" (23:6d)
> **B'** "to bury your dead" (23:6e)

Abraham uses the word "give" three times, once in each of his speeches (23:4, 9, 13). As if in response, Ephron also uses it thrice in 23:11. Altogether, the Hittites seem gracious. "But if so, one wonders, why does not the dialogue end right there on this cooperative note? In the circumstances, even if the characters still have arrangements to make, they are hardly of such interest as to need reporting, far less dramatizing . . . —why indeed stage it at all, instead of burying Sarah in decent silence?" Sternberg observes that all the byzantine repetitions and variants of the replies of the sons of Heth are attempts to evade the essence of Abraham's request: "Give me a אֲחֻזַּת־קֶבֶר ['akhuzat-qeber, 'burial site'; literally, 'holding of a grave'] among you" (23:4; also 23:9). אֲחֻזָּה "unequivocally refers to possession, as distinct from all other forms of occupying land."[7] The same word was used by Yahweh in his promise of the land of Canaan to

---

6. Ross, *Creation and Blessing*, 411.

7. Sternberg, "Double Cave, Double Talk," 30, 31.

Abraham and his descendants as an everlasting "possession" (אֲחֻזָּה, 17:8; also see 48:4; Deut 32:49). Essentially, the patriarch desired to inaugurate his possession of land in Canaan in a formal and acceptable way.

Moreover, he wanted this land "among you" (עִמָּכֶם, *'immakem*, Gen 23:4). No, he would not bury his wife in Canaanite land, unless it were his own—he wanted his land "among" them, rather than be a landowner who was part of them. This reflects precisely Abraham's own view of himself as a stranger and sojourner ("among you," 23:4)—he was only "among" them, but never would be part of them. In other words, the outsider was seeking to bury his family "outside" of the land owned by Canaanites, but in the land of Canaan which was his by divine promise. Abraham would bury Sarah only in his own land, only in the land given to him by Yahweh's word (12:7; 13:15, 17; 15:7; 17:8; 22:17).[8]

The Hittites are loathe to grant Abraham, the foreigner, his request; but politeness forces them to tread a fine line.

> Shorn of its trappings and considered in practical terms, what the Hittites say amounts to very little. . . . The very plural form given to the declarations, instead of multiplying their strength for extra security, actually renders them indefinite and inoperative. . . . [T]he plural ["our choicest burial grounds," 23:6] sounds impressive but jars against the humdrum fact that one usually neither dies nor rests in more than a single place. Therefore, to direct the mourner in quest of "a burial ground" to "our choicest burial grounds" is to leave him with the corpse on his hands. Further, to meet Abraham's affirmative "Give me" with the double negative "No man of us will deny thee" is to promise even less than would the sweeping engagement "Every man of us will give." A plurality or community of non-deniers does not yet make a single giver.[9]

The Hittites are careful to distribute the possessive pronouns: "our" graves and "his" grave (i.e., graves of the sons of Heth), but "your" dead (×2) (in 23:6). They seem to be asserting that, though Abraham can bury his dead in their graves, the land (and the graves) would remain theirs and theirs alone. They were not going to change the status of the patriarch from alien to resident landowner. Remarkably, in their first reply, the Hittites modify Abraham's confession of being a stranger/sojourner "among you" (עִמָּכֶם, 23:4) to his being a prince "with us" (אִתָּה, *'attah*, 23:6), likely a calculated attempt at ingratiation, or perhaps a gambit to fool the patriarch into thinking that since he was "with" them, he really did not need to execute a legal transfer of property. In other words, they would simply let Abraham use the land for burial without formally handing it over to him.[10]

---

8. A "stranger" (גֵּר, *ger*) is an alien living in a foreign land, potentially permanently, as were the Israelites in Egypt (Exod 22:21; 23:9; etc.); "sojourner" (תּוֹשָׁב, *toshab*), a rarer term than "stranger," is virtually synonymous (Lev 25:23; Ps 39:12), though sojourners seem to be on a circle further removed from strangers (Exod 12:19, 45–49 prohibits sojourners from participating in the Passover festival) (Wenham, *Genesis 16–50*, 126–27). In any case, both are landless, a fact which Abraham acknowledges.

9. Sternberg, "Double Cave, Double Talk," 31–32.

10. For "among" (עִם) as an indicator of inequality, see Lev 25:23, 25; and for "with" (אֵת, *'t*) as a mark of equality, see Exod 12:48–49; Num 35:14; etc.

But ownership of the land *was* part of Yahweh's grant. Thus far, Abraham had not taken matters into his own hands, when he could have, as, for instance, in the war to liberate Lot (Gen 14). He had until now taken no initiative to own property; he had even let Lot choose whatever portion of the terrain he wanted (Gen 13). Now, in Gen 23, an emergency forces him to take a firm step to acquire land; now he wants legal possession, not just a hospitable donation for temporary use. In fact, as Sternberg observes, Abraham's opening statement may be read as a concessive that recognizes the incongruity of his owning land: "*Although* I am a stranger and a sojourner among you, give me . . ." (23:4).[11]

That this was a formal transaction is clear: it was public (23:3, 7, 10, 11, 12, 13, 16, 18), and all relevant facts—location ("in the land of Canaan," mentioned twice: 23:2, 19), extent of property, names of buyer and seller, location of negotiations, acceptances, and witnesses—are noted.[12] The emphasis is on this first step towards the fulfillment of God's land promises to Abraham and his descendants. And Abraham persists in the trajectory of divine promises—a mark of mature faith.

14.4 A mature faith in God may be costly, encountering opposition, suffering exploitation, and experiencing little reward in the present.

Finally, though, money talks louder than principles, as Abraham offers them "full price" (23:9). He seems to concede somewhat by using "amidst you" (בְּתוֹכְכֶם, *btokkem*, 23:9; also used of Ephron sitting "amidst" the sons of Heth, 23:10), yet he does not relieve them of the pressure of giving in to his request for land.

The three layers of the Hittites' motives are politeness (there is plenty of oriental courtesy and deference shown between the two parties: Abraham rises and bows before each of his speeches; the Hittites are almost obsequious; and each side beseeches the other to give them a hearing), politics (they are unwilling to relinquish land legally to an alien), and profit (they ultimately succumb to greed and the possibility of making a quick buck by exploiting a mourner's grief).[13] Three times, Ephron promises, "I give [it] to you" (23:11). In fact, the ownership, it appears, is slowly changing hands even in Ephron's mind, even before the final consummation of the sale. What Abraham had requested—the cave "which is *his* [Ephron's]" at the edge of "*his* field" (23:9)—becomes neutral in Ephron's mouth—"*the* field" and "*the* cave" (23:11). Notice that the Hittite, likely lured by lucre, is now going so far as to offer Abraham the whole field, when the latter had only asked for the cave in the field. Clearly, this is another example of divine providence in the matter of establishing the patriarch in the land.

---

11. Sternberg, "Double Cave, Double Talk," 33.

12. "Those who enter the gate" of the city (23:10) indicates the elders who generally conducted matters civic and politic at the city gate.

13. Sternberg, "Double Cave, Double Talk," 34–35. The description of Abraham's ritual grief employs "mourning" and "weeping," suggesting traditional customs of the expression of sorrow for the loss of a loved one, such as rending garments, disheveling hair, cropping beard, fasting, etc. (Lev 21:5, 10; 2 Sam 1:11, 12; 13:31; Job 1:20; 2:12). Such rites were likely carried out in the presence of Sarah's remains, as indicated by the fact that Abraham "went in [to Sarah's tent] to mourn . . . and to weep" and that later he "rose up from before his dead" (Gen 23:2–3). See Wenham, *Genesis 16–50*, 126.

Ephron, in a clever move, now puts a tariff on his donation (23:15): four hundred shekels of silver (about 10 lbs. of the metal). That was, without a doubt, an extortion. Comparable transactions include fifty shekels for the threshing floor of Araunah purchased by David (2 Sam 24:24), seventeen shekels for the field at Anathoth purchased by Jeremiah (Jer 39:9), and six thousand shekels (two silver talents) for the entire hill of Samaria purchased by Omri (1 Kgs 16:24). "Devaluation over the centuries apart, then, the valuation at four hundred shekels must have come as a staggering blow."[14] No question, Abraham's offer of "full price" (Gen 23:9) has been mercilessly taken advantage of. That is also emphasized in the verb "and he weighed out," וַיִּשְׁקֹל (*wayyishqol*, 23:16); he literally "shekeled out" the silver, four hundred shekels of it. Abraham, the prince of Elohim (23:6), is royally duped!

Despite all of the extortion and exploitation of an old man bereaved of his wife, it is clear that Yahweh is the one who gives Abraham the land (13:15–17; 15:7, 18–19; 17:8); the Hittites were even specifically mentioned in 15:20 as mere occupants and temporary sitters. This, then, is a story of the patriarch's trust in God—a costly faith that continues to trust even when cheated, for God's plans *would* come to fruition.

Abraham could have easily avoided all these complications and especially the financial blow he had to suffer. He could simply have gone back to Ur for Sarah's burial. But his faith is mature, and his trust in God is complete: he would bury his wife in the Promised Land, even if all the acreage that he possessed was only a field with a cave. His resolution to bury her there signifies his determination to settle in, trusting God's promise. Sternberg observes the paradox. God had earlier promised him the land using terms that reappear in this narrative (in italics): "All the *land* that you see I will *give* it to you. . . . Arise, walk the length and breadth of the *land*, for I will *give* it to you" (13:15, 17). And "I am Yahweh who brought you out of Ur . . . to *give* you this *land*" (15:7), "To your descendants I *give* this *land* . . ., the land of . . . the *Hittites*" (15:18–19). Also, "I will *give* to you and to your descendants after you the *land* of your *sojournings*, all the *land* of Canaan, for an everlasting *possession*" (17:8). "[T]he echoes (down to the verbal forms) are exact, manifold, cumulative, and proportionally discordant. . . . And if men play with words to make their bargain, God does not appear to keep his at all," for all Abraham would possess at the end of this pericope is a burial cave. It would appear that this is a God who cannot keep his promises.

> It would be therefore absurd to explain the tale as a celebration of the beginning of fulfillment, Rather, the text joins forces with the context to radicalize the sense of nonfulfillment, bringing into the full view the patriarch urged for decades to regard the breadth and the length of Canaan as *his* possession yet driven to beg "the people of the land" for a cave at the edge of the field in which to bury the matriarch. Not to speak of the multiple price—emotional, spiritual, financial, inferential, all at their highest—exacted by those dealings. . . . The reader, from his vantage point in history, cannot help wondering how the hero himself inwardly

---

14. Sternberg, "Double Cave, Double Talk," 47.

squares past commitment with present straits and the question mark about the future.[15]

However, the lack of any hesitation on the part of Abraham is convincing proof that he was neither wavering nor fearing: "By faith he sojourned in the land of promise, as though foreign [i.e., the land], dwelling in tents with Isaac and Jacob, fellow heirs of the same promise; for he was looking for the city with foundations, whose architect and builder is God" (Heb 11:9–10). Yet one cannot but wonder what Abraham was feeling. All those expansive promises from God (Gen 12:7; 13:15; 15:18; 17:8; 22:17)—but, as he nears the end of his life (he has just lost his first spouse), and all he can show for those divine affirmations is a field with a cave in it, in which to bury his wife! And this purchased at an exorbitant price.

The thrust of the story not only implies that Israel's gaining of the land will be costly, it points out that the faith of *all* of God's children will be costly, demanding much; and often in this life there will not be much to show for that expensive (and expansive) exercise of trust in God, in his plans, and in his timing.

SERMON FOCUS AND OUTLINES

> **THEOLOGICAL FOCUS OF PERICOPE 14 FOR PREACHING**
>
> **14 Mature faith persists even when costly, encountering opposition, suffering exploitation, and enduring little reward in the present (22:20–23:20).**

This is quite an unusual episode, with no mention of God (except, perhaps, as a superlative, "prince of Elohim" = "mighty prince," 23:6). Not only is there no mention of deity, there is also no sign of his working. Though the first step of the fulfillment of God's promises regarding land to Abraham and his descendants is taken in this pericope, it does not appear, on the surface, that Yahweh had anything to do with it. Long negotiations fraught with setbacks, counterarguments and proposals, and exploitation and extortion are, instead, what finally lead to Abraham's first formal acquisition of land. One wonders if God could not have done better—this after a spectacular intervention and saving of Abraham who passed his final test in Gen 22. If this is the reward for passing such an incredible test—having to beg and barter to have one's spouse buried—one cannot but begin to worry about this deity. Does he care enough to do anything for his people? Or is he simply not powerful enough over circumstances?

Abraham's performance in this "test" in Genesis 23 is again stellar, and indirectly puts to rest all the doubts raised by such questions. He does not utter a word of irritation or show any tendency to mistrust his God, as would have been his wont earlier. Rather, Abraham is determined to remain in the land and bury his wife there, even at great cost. This is one committed patriarch! There would be no turning back for him now.

15. Ibid., 56.

Possible Preaching Outlines for Pericope 14

I. God: "Missing"
    > No mention of God in Gen 23:1–20
    > No sign of God's land promises coming to pass
    > Move-to-Relevance: Times when we feel God is "missing"

II. Enemies: Opposing
    > Unwillingness of the Hittites to grant Abraham's request (23:3–13)
    > Ephron, the Hittite, extorts payment, exploiting the patriarch (23:14–18)
    > Move-to-Relevance: How we are opposed, spiritually and/or otherwise in our crises

III. Abraham: Persisting
    > Abraham's resolve to remain in the land of promise (23:1–4, 13, 19–20)
    > Abraham's uncomplaining attitude; he remains polite and deferential towards his opponents (23:7, 12)
    > Abraham's faith despite his seemingly meager reward in the present: a small plot and a burial cave (23:20)
    > Move-to-Relevance: Things that keep us from persisting in our commitment to God

IV. Christian: Trusting—*Persist in faith, despite all odds!*[16]
    > How we can persist in faith, despite all odds

The following outline, focusing on the potential adversities the believer might face, is created as a variation of the outline given above. This one might be more conducive to making the situation more relevant, especially for a congregation with members in dire situations of any kind.

I. No God?
    > No mention of God in Gen 23:1–20
    > No sign of God's land promises coming to pass
    > But Abraham's faith in the land promises and resolve to remain in place (23:1–4, 13, 19–20)
    > Move-to-Relevance: Times when we feel God is "missing"

II. No mercy?
    > Unwillingness of the merciless Hittites to grant Abraham's request (23:3–13)
    > Ephron, the Hittite, extorts payment, exploiting the patriarch (23:14–18)
    > Abraham's uncomplaining attitude; he remains polite and deferential towards his opponents (23:7, 12)
    > Move-to-Relevance: How we are opposed, spiritually and/or otherwise in our crises

III. No reward?
    > Abraham's reward: a small plot and a burial cave (23:20), after all that he had been through
    > Abraham's faith despite his seemingly meager reward in the present: no sense of entitlement
    > Move-to-Relevance: How we may never see reward in our earthly days

IV. No surrender! *Persist in faith, despite all odds!*
    > How we can persist in faith, despite all odds: even when there is "no" God, no mercy, and no reward

---

16. While it is a sound practice to have a clear applicational statement in the imperative that is explicitly stated somewhere in the sermon (in outlines in this commentary, such an imperative is designated in italics), an implied imperative will work quite well, too, if specifics are provided subsequently for the congregation to respond concretely.

PERICOPE 15

Providential Guidance

Genesis 24:1–25:18

[Finding Rebekah for Isaac; Death of Abraham]

REVIEW, SUMMARY, PREVIEW

Review of Pericope 14: Genesis 22:20–23:20 sees Abraham established further in Canaan: he now owns a humble burial plot, ironic in light of the extensive land promises God had made to him and his descendants. Faith involves continued trust, even when one can see no sign of divine promises being fulfilled or divine blessings being brought about.

Summary of Pericope 15: In this pericope that describes the search for a bride for Isaac, all the protagonists—Abraham, his retainer, and Rebekah—demonstrate a firm trust in God to fulfill his purposes. God sovereignly works things out favorably for the parties involved, but in tandem with human action that is taken in faith.

Preview of Pericope 16: The next pericope (Gen 25:19–34) commences the Jacob Story with Rebekah's twin pregnancy and the sovereignly ordained prominence of the younger over the older. The subsequent strife between the twins describes the struggle for divine blessing: a failure of recognition of God's sovereignty in the matter, and a despising of one's own blessings.

15. Genesis 24:1–25:18

THEOLOGICAL FOCUS OF PERICOPE 15

15   A mature faith trusts God who works to accomplish his purposes, both through his inscrutable design as well as through human action, thus ensuring ongoing blessing (24:1–25:18).

  15.1   A mature faith trusts God who keeps his word, ensuring ongoing blessing.

  15.2   God works to accomplish his purposes, both through his inscrutable design as well as through human action.

OVERVIEW

The larger section, 22:20–25:18, the final sections of the Abraham Story, is laid out carefully, with the focus on the passing of the baton to the next generation and onward, as Isaac marries Rebekah. How this takes place under the sovereign and providential hand of God is at the heart of Pericope 15.[1]

> **A**   Genealogy of Nahor: non-chosen family (22:20–24)
> **B**   Death of Sarah (23:1–20)
> **C**   Election of Rebekah as matriarch / Isaac marries (24:1–67)
> **B'**   Death of Abraham (25:1–11)
> **A'**   Genealogy of Ishmael: non-chosen family (25:12–18)

The Abrahamic saga thus opens and closes with genealogies (11:27–31; 25:1–6; and 25:12–18).[2] It had commenced with the statement of the barrenness of the matriarch (11:30); it concludes now with a prolific family: the sons of Keturah (25:1–6), and the sons of Ishmael (25:12–18). With these out of the way, the extended history of the line of Isaac, the chosen one, is ready to be undertaken (Gen 25:19–36:43—the Jacob Story).[3]

Abraham's death is recorded in 25:7–11, adumbrating the final scenes of the lives of his son, Isaac, and his grandson, Jacob: the pattern for all three is the same[4]:

	Abraham	Isaac	Jacob
Death and burial of wife	23:1–20	35:18–20	48:7
Son's marriage	24:1–67	35:21–22	49:3–4
List of descendants	25:1–6	35:22–26	49:5–8
Death and burial of patriarch	25:7–10	35:27–29	49:29–50:14
List of descendants	25:12–17	36:1–42	
"This is the תּוֹלְדֹת (toldot) of ..."	25:19	37:2	

1. Table below from Hong, "An Exegetical Reading," 93.

2. Ishmael's genealogy, in 25:12–18, is, for the purposes of this commentary, considered with the Abraham Story.

3. This follows the model set earlier in Genesis of disposing of the lines of non-elect individuals before embarking on the narratives of the elect ones: Cain's genealogy before Seth's (4:17–24; 5:1–32), and Esau's before Jacob's (36:1–43; 46:8–27). The final section of Pericope 15, 25:1–18, including the accounts of Abraham's marriage with Keturah, his death, and the genealogy of Ishmael, will not be dealt with in further detail in the Notes than is found in this Overview.

4. From Wenham, *Genesis 16–50*, 156.

When he died at 175 (25:7), Abraham had lived for a century in Canaan (12:4), his long life fulfilling Yahweh's promise to him in 15:15; he died "satisfied" (25:8). No other patriarch goes to his fathers "in peace" (15:15—the first occurrence of שָׁלוֹם, *shalom*, in the Bible; for the demise of other patriarchs, see 35:29; 43:27; 44:20; 49:33; 50:22, 26). Even the closing statement of Abraham's age and death (25:7–8) does not follow the standard form; in line with other such notices, it should have read: "All the days of Abraham were 175 years and he died." Instead, there are considerable expansions that denote the significance of this man's life, and his death notice therefore turns out to be even longer than those of Adam (5:5) and Noah (9:29).[5]

If the chronological information in Genesis is understood correctly, Isaac was forty when he married Rebekah (25:20), when Abraham was 140 (21:5). The patriarch would die at 175 (25:7), when Isaac was seventy-five, and when Esau and Jacob were fifteen (25:26). So even though Abraham's death is noted in 25:7–11, chronologically, it occurs more than a decade after the birth of Isaac's twins that is reported in 25:19–26. All that to say, texts need not necessarily be sequenced in chronological order, for the exploitation of time in narrative is the prerogative of the narrator, based on his inspired agenda. In this case, one generation (that of Abraham) needed to be disposed of, before the story of the next commenced.[6] By the same token, it is also likely the patriarch married Keturah (25:1–6), before Isaac married Rebekah (24:61–67), but the former incident is noted after the latter for the narrative convenience of mentioning apportionment of property just prior to the notation of Abraham's death (25:7–11) and, as well, to maintain the focus of earlier chapters on Isaac (and, somewhat less, on Ishmael).

While Ishmael gets less textual space than Isaac, he does get more than that given to the children of Keturah.[7] Divine promises come to pass in his life: he becomes a nation, fulfilling 21:13, 18; his defiant stance in 25:18 fulfills 16:10, 12; and his fruitfulness in 25:13–16 fulfills 17:20. Ishmael's participation in the burial of his father in the company of Isaac (25:9), maintains his status as son of the patriarch. He was, one remembers, the first to be circumcised, and thus the first to become part of the covenanted community (17:26).[8] In other words, that he was Abraham's seed, a fact

---

5. Ibid., 160.

6. Another example of this dischronology: Jdg 1:1 shows Joshua dying, but 2:6–7 has him alive, with 2:8–9 providing another account of his demise.

7. Abraham's sons by Keturah are given gifts and "sent away from Isaac" to the east (17:6). Not only did Abraham formally leave all he had to Isaac (25:6; also 24:36), Isaac was also the son explicitly noted to have been blessed by God (25:11). While sons of wives could expect a formal division of the father's property (Num 27:1–11; Deut 21:15–17), sons of concubines were dependent upon the parent's goodwill. That was also the lot of Ishmael (21:14), sent away with provisions. In both cases, the sons of Keturah and Hagar are "sent" (שָׁלַח, *shalakh*, 21:14; 25:6). The sending of the former to the "east" also evokes memories of the expulsion of Adam and Eve, and of Cain, not to mention the travels of the Babelites (3:23–24; 4:16; 11:2).

8. Mathews, *Genesis 11:27–50:26*, 349.

mentioned twice in the same verse (25:12), enabled him to enjoy the divine blessings given to the patriarch.[9]

Besides, as had been mentioned earlier, the life of Ishmael in Genesis had the same milestones as did the life of Isaac: birth to an old father (16:16 and 21:1–7), and danger of death averted by divine intervention at the last minute (21:14–19; and 22:1–19). But Ishmael also married an Egyptian, one of his mother's race, from his "homeland" (21:21). It is only appropriate, then, that Isaac's marriage, too, be detailed; it is now due "by compositional logic." And like Ishmael, he will take a bride from the "old country."[10] Thus, Gen 24.

Genesis 24 is the longest single episode (and chapter) in Genesis, containing the longest speech in the book—that of the servant in 24:34–49. The pericope commences with Abraham and his servant, and concludes with the next patriarch, Isaac, and his wife, Rebekah.[11]

> Canaan: Abraham and his servant (24:1–9)
> Mesopotamia: the servant and Rebekah (at the well) (24:10–28)
> Mesopotamia: the servant and Laban (in the house) (24:29–61)
> Canaan: Isaac and Rebekah (and the servant) (24:62–67)

Wenham notes the many references in Gen 24 that create links both to earlier and later pericopes.[12]

	Genesis 24	Earlier Pericopes	Later Pericopes
Patriarch blessed	24:1, 35	12:2; 18:18; 22:17	
Swearing/hand under thigh	24:2, 9		47:29, 31
Wife from homeland	24:3–4, 7		28:2
Angel of God/Yahweh	24:7, 40	16:7, 9, 10, 11; 21:17; 22:11, 15	31:11; 48:16
Nahor	24:20, 15, 24	11:22–17, 29; 22:20, 23	29:5; 31:53
Betrothal type-scene	24:11–27		29:2–14
Yahweh's lovingkindness	24:12, 14, 27		32:10
Isaac given all	24:36		25:5
Patriarch walking	24:40	13:17; 17:1	
Success	24:21, 40, 42, 56		39:2, 3, 23
Lovingkindness and truth	24:27, 49		47:29
Possession of enemies' gate	24:60	22:17	
Beer-lahai-roi	24:62	16:14	
Death of Sarah	24:67	23:1–2	

Thus this concluding pericope of the Abraham narrative looks back to the many promises of God, now slowly coming to fruition; it also looks forward to the future

---

9. Strikingly, Ishmael produces twelve Aramean tribes (22:20–24), Esau twelve Edomite tribes (36:10–14), and Jacob twelve Israelite tribes (35:22; 49:28). This, too, renders Ishmael (and Esau), not entirely insignificant in the big scheme of things.

10. Sternberg, *The Poetics of Biblical Narrative*, 132.

11. Table below from Hamilton, *Genesis: Chapters 18–50*, 138.

12. Wenham, *Genesis 16–50*, 137.

stories of Abraham's seed. In all, Gen 24 serves as a fitting end to the Abraham Story, closing it, as well as signaling the things to come.

After a long and eventful life, Abraham is coming to the end of his days, and Gen 24 is an epilogue to his story; a new generation is rising. The depictions of Abraham, his servant, and Isaac in this chapter subtly hint at this changing of the guard. Abraham is still clearly the "master" (אָדוֹן, *'adon*, 24:9, 10 [×2], 12 [×2], 14, 27 [×3], 35, 36 [×2], 37, 39, 42, 48 [×2], 49, 51, 54, 56), and his "servant" is the עֶבֶד ('*ebed*, 24:2, 5, 9, 10, 17, 34, 52, 53, 59, 61, 65 [×2], 66). But this servant is also depicted as a stand-in for the patriarch—he is an important individual who bears gifts and acts wealthy, with animals and servants in his retinue—and some of the authority of the master devolves upon the servant: thus he is himself called אדון (24:18) and recognized as one who is blessed (24:31), as Abraham himself was (24:1, 35).[13] Yet, the man's anonymity keeps him in the role of Abraham's proxy, the visible manifestation of the latter to those who will never see him—his relatives in Mesopotamia. But the most significant shift is the status of Isaac, who is, for the most part, the "son" (24:3, 4, 5, 6, 7, 8, 36, 37, 38, 40, 44, 48, 51), until 24:65, when he takes on the mantle of the אדון. Now that the task of finding a spouse for the son has been accomplished, Abraham, seemingly, relinquishes his title to the son, who becomes the "master."[14] Indeed, Abraham is completely absent in the final scene of this episode (24:62–67), consummating the transition from father to son.[15]

15   *Genesis 24:1–25:18*

> **THEOLOGICAL FOCUS 15**[A]
>
> 15   A mature faith trusts God who works to accomplish his purposes, both through his inscrutable design as well as through human action, thus ensuring ongoing blessing (24:1–25:18).
>
>   15.1   *A mature faith trusts God who keeps his word, ensuring ongoing blessing.*
>
>   15.2   *God works to accomplish his purposes, both through his inscrutable design as well as through human action.*

   A. Having only one section in this pericope, the "Theological Focus 15" is identical to the "Theological Focus of Pericope 15."

NOTES 15

15.1   A mature faith trusts God who keeps his word, ensuring ongoing blessing.

The patriarch's exhortations to his servant regarding his desire that his son marry from among his own, form the last recorded words of Abraham (24:1–9). In these latter days

---

13. Though Yahweh had promised to bless Abraham (12:3; 22:17), and though Melchizedek had recognized the patriarch as being blessed (14:19), it is here, for the first time, that readers are explicitly told that Abraham was blessed (24:1; also see 24:35). See Wenham, *Genesis 16–50*, 140.

14. Teugels, "The Anonymous Matchmaker," 15–16, 21.

15. A parallel transition from Sarah to Rebekah is pictured in 24:67.

of his life, he is still confident in Yahweh's promises, resolute that he will never to return to the land he came from, and that he will never let his son, Isaac, do so either (24:7). Such a solid faith in divine promises is remarkable when one remembers that thus far, the only land Abraham has acquired was a field with a cave in it, in which his wife, Sarah, was buried (see Pericope 14). But clearly, Abraham has no doubt that Yahweh who had been faithful to him in the past would continue to be faithful to him (and to his seed) in the future (24:7, 40; see table below for his remarkable references to Yahweh that form the bases for the exhortations in his two speeches to his servant).

> Abraham's first speech (24:2–4)
>> Challenge: "Swear" (24:2)
>> Negative exhortation:
>>> "Yahweh, the God of heavens and the God of earth"; "do not take" (24:3)
>> Positive exhortation:
>>> "take" (24:4)
>
> *Servant's question (24:5)*
>
> Abraham's second speech (24:6–8)
>> Challenge: "Beware" (24:6)
>> Positive exhortation:
>>> "Yahweh, the God of heavens"; "take" (×2) (24:7)
>> Negative exhortation:
>>> "do not take" (24:8)

There is no question but that here, in the last pericope of the Abraham Story, the man who had clumsily made his way through the previous pericopes, has, literally and figuratively, come far in his faith: he has moved significantly towards divine blessing.

One might see this fairly extended pericope as being equivalent to the "deathbed" scene of Abraham, though, of course, he lived for a considerable time between the events of Gen 24 and 25. The narrator, however, intends to have readers see this final scripted scene of Abraham's life as essentially his last will and testament, as evidenced by the description of Abraham in 24:1 as "old, advanced in years," a phrase that usually accompanies the last words and deeds of a hero (Josh 13:1; 23:1; 1 Kgs 1:1; but also see Gen 18:11). The scene is similar to final cameos of Jacob (47:29–31) and Joseph (50:25), who also cause their sons take oaths, as Abraham did to his servant (24:2, 9). In fact, Abraham and Jacob make the ones swearing do so with their hand under the respective patriarch's thigh (24:2, 9; 47:29, 31).[16] In all these scenes, Jacob and Joseph want to ensure their burials in the Promised Land; Abraham wants to ensure the continuance of his seed in the same location.[17] For all the patriarchs, remaining in the land Yahweh had promised them was of paramount importance. So much so, Abraham's determination not to see Isaac return to Mesopotamia indicates his feeling

16. The act of putting one's hand under a thigh signifies touching the genitalia (Gen 46:26; Exod 1:5), indicating a solemn oath.

17. "Abraham enters history through the divine promises (12:1–3, 7); he passes out of history with this promise on his lips" (Wenham, *Genesis 16–50*, 140).

that it would be better for Isaac to stay single than to escape the Promised Land![18] His God, he was convinced, was one who could be trusted absolutely.

The bride-search episode in this pericope, with the servant's journey, arrival at destination, and rendezvous with Rebekah (24:10–28), is bounded on either side by the retainer's prayers (24:12–14 and 24:26–27; and recounted in 24:48). This attitude of deference to, and trust in, God has marked this individual: 24:12–14, 26–27, 42–44, 48, 52. In fact, "lovingkindness" (חסד, *khsd*) and "truth" (אמת, *'mt*) occur together 24:27, as the servant recollects the attributes of Yahweh that brought success to the endeavor of finding a spouse for Isaac, and thus the continued production of divinely promised seed to Abraham. The servant repeats the pair of words in 24:49 as he appeals to the family of Rebekah to demonstrate the same qualities that characterized God's favor to his master—lovingkindness and truth—as they permit her to leave with him for Canaan. "By appealing to God's 'kindness,' the servant alludes to the divine promises and their provision for Abraham; he interprets his task as an extension of the promises, making his prayer a corollary to Abraham's faith in the Lord's adequacy." To Mathews, the note about the camels kneeling (ברך, *brk*, 24:11) not only "fits the mood of repose and prayer," but by homonymity, there is an allusion to "blessing" (also ברך).[19] In any case, not only in the actions of Abraham, but in those of the servant also, we are shown a picture of one who trusts in the sovereign and providential workings of the Almighty.

In a striking turn, Abraham compares his being "taken" by God to the servant's "taking" Rebekah by the agency of God's angel (24:7). In other words, he who had left country and relatives and father's house (12:1) is now expecting Rebekah to make the same sacrifice. "Just as previously Abraham 'was taken' and himself had to go to a country which he did not know, thus the intended woman is now 'taken' and she must be willing to go to a country and a man she does not know (24:8)."[20] Rebekah's potential willingness to "go" (הלך, *hlk*) had been discussed (before the fact) by Abraham and the servant (24:5, 8); later, Rebekah herself declares her desire to "go" (24:58; also 24:61). By this expression of her willingness, "[s]he repeats in words the very response which Abraham had given more than a generation ago by wordless obedience to God's command to him to "go" (הלך, 12:1–4a)! In other words, not only is Isaac the child of Abraham's obedience, also Isaac's wife-to-be responds to the call 'to go' from her father's house to a land not known to her." In fact, Rebekah "goes forth" several times in this pericope (יצא, *yts'*, 24:13, 15, 43, 45), perhaps a hint of what she would soon do by the end of the pericope; the same word, יצא, described what Abraham is also said to

---

18. The command of Abraham to his servant is emphatic: literally, "only my son do not take back there" (24:8). While the concept of not marrying local Canaanite women for fear of religious contamination was entrenched in Israelite thinking (Exod 34:16; Num 25:1–18; Deut 7:3), not all of Abraham's relatives remained pure in their marital affiliations: Lot's incest, Abraham's palming off Sarah to an Egyptian and a Philistine, his consorting with Hagar, an Egyptian, Ishmael's marriage, Esau's marriages, Laban's polytheism, Judah's alliance with a Canaanite, Joseph's marriage to an Egyptian, etc., are all examples contrary to the principle.

19. *Genesis 11:27–50:26*, 332.

20. Van Wolde, "Telling and Retelling," 235–36, 236n17.

have done (24:5; also see 12:4, 5). Both of these protagonists leave their country, their relatives, and their fathers' houses (12:1 and 24:4, 38) and, as a result, both are blessed (12:2–3 and 24:1, 35, 60).[21]

In a sense, Rebekah is also a proxy for Isaac's move from fatherland to Promised Land; while both Abraham and Jacob make these moves themselves, Isaac himself does not, except vicariously through the emigration of Rebekah.[22] Rebekah's leaving her country and her father's house thus makes her a likeminded soul to Abraham; in fact, her name (רִבְקָה, *ribqah*), like that of her future father-in-law's (אַבְרָהָם, *'abraham*), bears two of the three consonants of the Hebrew verb "to bless"—ברך, *brk*, a word that has echoed in 24:1, 27, 31, 35, 48, 60. Indeed, "They blessed Rebekah" (וַיְבָרְכוּ אֶת־רִבְקָה, *waybaraku 'et-ribqah*, 24:60) is a play on the letters ב, ר, כ. Besides, "thousands" is רְבָבָה (*rbabah*, 24:60), which not only continues the paronomasia, but also connects with the repeated promise in Genesis regarding "multiplying" (רבה, *rbh*, 1:28; 9:1, 7; 17:2; 22:17). In other words, Rebekah is a "female Abraham," being promoted as a God-fearer with a faith akin to that of the patriarch, and with a divine blessing that is almost as propitious as Abraham's.[23] And in her decision to leave her station and go to Canaan, she, like Abraham, now becomes one who trusts Yahweh implicitly.

All the "going" and "taking" in Gen 24 further underscores divine workings. Abraham's "go" and "take" a wife for Isaac (24:4), is later reciprocated precisely by Laban and Bethuel responding to the servant with "take [Rebekah]" and "go" (24:51). God's providence is clearly manifested: "go and take," is answered by "go and take." In response, Rebekah agrees to "go" (24:58), the servant "takes" her and "goes" (61), and finally, Isaac does so too, "taking" Rebekah (24:67). The framed structure serves as a reminder that that things have fallen precisely into place—"goings" and "takings" guided, superintended, and blessed by divine providence.

> Rebecca agrees to "go" (24:58)
>> Servant "takes" her and "goes" (24:61)
> Isaac "takes" Rebekah (24:67)

Thus, the entire story seems to depend merely on the setting out and taking of people. But the individual choice of the servant and of Rebekah to go and the personal decision of the servant and of Isaac to take, only highlight the ac-

---

21. Roth, "The Wooing of Rebekah," 178–79. While Rebekah's nurse is named in 35:8 as Deborah, here this individual is anonymous, as Rebekah prepares to leave for Abraham's household (24:59); thus an anonymous nurse balances the account that has an anonymous male servant. Again, Rebekah and Abraham are being paralleled.

22. Obtaining a wife from outside Canaan emphasized the alien and foreign status of Isaac and Jacob in the Promised Land, contrasting them with their siblings, Ishmael and Esau, both of whom found wives among the Canaanites (21:21; 26:34–35).

23. Wenham, *Genesis 16–50*, 138. The verb הלך, *hlk*, also points to Gen 22 and the obedient and faithful response of Abraham to God's command to "go" (22:2, 3, 5, 6, 8, 13). Rebekah's "running" to be hospitable (24:17), shows her up again as modeling Abraham's own "running" to be gracious to his guests (18:2, 7). She complies with request of the servant "quickly" (24:18, 20, 46), again reflecting Abraham's "quick" moves to be hospitable (18:6, 7). Another striking similarity between Abraham and Rebekah is that the descendants of both are promised to "possess the gates" of their enemies (22:17; 24:60).

tive side of people in this process. In addition, a passive or receptive side, or, put differently, an active contribution on the part of Yнwн is also required. In particular the people in this story who set out, evince their awareness of the fact that they are dependent on Yhwh's contribution [24:7, 21, 40, 42, 56]. He will prosper their way.[24]

Though Abraham is presumably at the end of his days, these providential actions on the part of God, emphasized literarily in the intricacies of the narrative, confirm that divine promises will not terminate with Abraham's passing. Rather, "the Lord has made full and perfect provisions to ensure that Abraham's son will marry and continue to live in the promised land of Canaan."[25] The next generation has commenced walking with God, as demonstrated by Rebekah's attitude and actions of a mature faith, and it can expect to be duly blessed, as was the previous one.

15.2   God works to accomplish his purposes, both through his inscrutable design as well as through human action.

It is expressly noted—with a "behold!"—that as the servant completed his prayer, Rebekah came along, randomly, it would seem (24:15). But here we have human volition meeting divine purpose; or perhaps one should say, divine purpose going before human volition. Indeed, in 24:45, the servant recounts this event as having occurred "before I had finished speaking in my heart." God was working even *before* the servant had completed his *unspoken* prayer!

There is no attempt by the servant to discover beforehand the salient characteristics of Isaac's bride who needed to be single, not engaged, a virgin, and willing to leave her family for Abraham's. Purely on the basis of her attentiveness to the servant and his camels, the man proceeds to make contact with Rebekah. It must be, then, that he had asked for such a sign in a situation where nothing else would be possible—he could hardly have pressed the other issues to a woman he was meeting for the first time, not to mention that all of these exercises were being conducted by a village well, a most unlikely location for bridal negotiations. The servant was, in a sense, extending the trust of God that his master, Abraham, had had. The fact that the narrator gives us the biodata of the prospective bride, pointedly including the fact about her virginity (24:16), and that even before the servant apprehends those details, emphasizes the sovereign and providential working of God.

Upon meeting Rebekah at the well, the servant "runs" to meet her (24:17). Rebekah "runs" to water his camels (24:20), and she "runs" to her mother's household to recount what had happened.[26] Later, Laban "runs" out to meet the servant (24:29),

---

24. Van Wolde, "Telling and Retelling," 238–39.

25. Wenham, *Genesis 16–50*, 137–38.

26. Rebekah, like Abraham earlier, is "a continuous whirl of purposeful activity" (Alter, *The Art of Biblical Narrative*, 64). In the space of a few verses (Gen 24:16, 18–20), she succeeds in being the subject of eleven verbs of action and two of speech, a staccato of *wayyiqtol* verbs: she went, she filled, she came up, she said, she hastened, she lowered, she refreshed, she finished, she said, she hastened, she emptied, she ran, she drew water. This echoes the hospitality of Abraham extended to his divine visitors in 18:2–7; the same alacrity and solicitude marks Rebekah, and the narrator intends for this to be taken in a posi-

though with ulterior motives.[27] No matter: everybody is running; and consciously or not, with pure or nefarious purposes, they are hastening to accomplish the purposes of God. And everything seems to fall into place quite serendipitously. The servant arrives at the right place; Rebekah reaches the same location; she happens to be of Terah's household; she turns out to be respectful and responsible; her family appears to be amenable to letting the young woman leave home and country; etc.—all "coincidences" under the hand of God.

Later, to the family, the servant unleashes the longest speech in Genesis (24:34–49). While his address is a flood of reported direct speech and repetitiveness as he recounts transpired events to Rebekah's relatives, her own utterance is quite pithy: "I will go," 24:58, are her only words at her home. This story is about divine guidance and providence. The detailed repetition of events by the servant is hardly for the sake of information duplication. Rather, it serves the purpose of underlining the providential working of God and the corroboration of answered prayer as the servant's bride-finding enterprise proceeds and concludes with remarkable success.

There is a clear expectation throughout this pericope that while one may "go," only Yahweh can make that going successful (24:21, 40, 42, 56). Note the servant's affirmation, twice, that Yahweh "guides" (24:27, 48) providentially. It is ultimately Yahweh who determines the "success" of the entire venture (24:21, 40, 42). Yahweh's sovereign and providential working (his חֶסֶד, *khesed*, 24:12, 14, marking the beginning and end of the servant's prayer) is indirectly underscored by the narrator (24:15–16), by the servant (24:26–27), and even by Laban and Bethuel who express their agreement with the thesis that God is at work in the entire endeavor (24:50): "This matter comes from Yahweh" (24:50). Echoing Abraham's original command to the servant (24:3–4), the family of Rebekah then exhorted the servant to "take" and W"go" (24:51). Their verbless sentence could not be more clear: "Behold, Rebekah before you!" (24:51). In short, the entire chapter "affirms that the task [of finding a wife for Isaac] and its success are the result of God's providential oversight both overtly and inferentially."[28]

On the other hand one should not take this story as being *only* about divine guidance; the roles and actions of humans are not negligible in the story. Sternberg's comment about this story, "Where God has 'spoken' through the design of events, there remains little room for human speech," is puzzling.[29] Contrary to what he observes, there is considerable speech in this pericope, especially by the servant. Noting this very particularity, van Wolde asks: "Isn't this strong emphasis on providence in literature rather one sided? . . . Is it not precisely the acting as well as the speaking of

---

tive light. See Sternberg, *The Poetics of Biblical Narrative,* 138.

27. In 24:29–30, Laban's shrewd behavior towards the servant is shown to be powered by greed (he runs, as he sees the ring and bracelets given to his sister, and as he spies the camel caravan accompanying the servant), unlike the gracious and unselfish hospitality displayed earlier to the servant by his sister Rebekah. Greed, of course, is shown to be an ongoing problem for this man: see 29:25–27; 30:27–36; 31:2, 6–8, 28–29, 38–42.

28. Mathews, *Genesis 11:27–50:26,* 322.

29. Sternberg, *The Poetics of Biblical Narrative,* 152.

the people in this story that form the requirements for changes to take place? Haven't exegetes overemphasized the theological element in their interpretation of Genesis 24?"[30] There is no doubt that human responsibility and action are being emphasized in this pericope as well.

The servant is persuasive with his long speech to Rebekah's relatives (24:34–49) and, as noted earlier, Laban and Bethuel come to acknowledge that "the matter comes from Yahweh"—this is Yahweh's business and therefore, so be it (24:5). The word דבר, *dbr*, occurs twice in their reply to the servant (24:50–51): the "matter" (דבר) is Yahweh's and Yahweh has "spoken" (דבר). Thus the words of the servant are equivalent to the matter/words of God—human initiative and divine sovereignty in tandem.

> They are the two sides of the same coin: God can only make someone's way a success if that person him/herself sets out. By the embedding of speech in speech, the servant reflects the same idea. The entire pattern of narratives, speeches and embedded speeches can be interpreted as an indication of underlying correlations and of patterns of meaning, one of which is the close connection between the words and the things of people and of Yhwh, as is reflected by the functioning of the word דבר in the words of the servant.[31]

Thus this story is not only about divine guidance, but the operations of God in, through, and with, human actions. Indeed, there is a hustle and bustle of human activity: besides the planning of Abraham and his servant, and the frenetic exertions of Rebekah, there is also the resourceful and diplomatic negotiations of the servant first with Rebekah, then with her family, and the equally shrewd and artful movements of Laban. All they did, or attempted to do, was work out the sovereign design of God. "In the appearance of the messenger servant, the divine guidance has been temporarily made visible. . . . A certain transcendence is evoked in this way, which tends to enhance the reader's conviction that not merely human choice but rather divine providence is at work in the unfolding of the story."[32] Thus, divine workings and human actions are shown to be interwoven, the warp and the woof, so to speak, of real life, over which God is supremely in control. "Not only divine guidance, nor people's plain going, but the interrelated combination in particular, forms the essence of this story. In my view this pattern of mutual effort is the main theme of Genesis 24."[33]

In sum: "There are human responses that contribute to the achievement of the divine assignment. . . . Typical Hebrew narrative assumes that the true protagonist of every account is God, whether or not explicitly stated, but the human dimension is real whose decisions are authentic choices." In this pericope, through the various actors—diligent Abraham, loyal and shrewd servant, greedy Laban, and the deferential

30. Van Wolde, "Telling and Retelling," 234.
31. Ibid., 242.
32. Teugels, "The Anonymous Matchmaker," 23.
33. Van Wolde, "Telling and Retelling," 239.

but firm Rebekah—Yahweh accomplishes his sovereign purposes for the good of his people, for the furthering of his promises, for the bringing about of his blessings.[34]

SERMON FOCUS AND OUTLINES

THEOLOGICAL FOCUS OF PERICOPE 15 FOR PREACHING

15 Mature faith trusts God to accomplish his purposes through his inscrutable design and through human action (24:1–25:18).

While not as seemingly devoid of divine action as was Pericope 14, this pericope too, like the previous one, has a lot of human activity, with people planning, journeying, scheming, appraising, negotiating, recounting, etc. Yet, it is evident that the thrust of the pericope concerns God's work intertwining with human action. The Almighty God who chooses to work through his people and through his creation can be trusted to carry out his infallible purposes, even though it may involve fallible man. Rebekah is the heroine here, though the servant and his speeches take up a lot of textual space. She is the one who is the "female Abraham," being matched in all his activities by her own. Implicitly, she is being shown up as a God-fearer as was her future father-in-law. God's providential and sovereign working is also clearly depicted in the explicit attribution to that effect, and through several serendipities in the story. While the pace of human activity and speech are considerable here, the reader is assured that in, through, and with it all, divine purposes are providentially accomplished.

The sermon outline on the previous pericope (Pericope 14) focused on persistence in faith. In the outlines for Pericope 15, the focus is shifted to working hard and doing one's best, knowing that God also is working, in/through/with human action.

Possible Preaching Outlines for Pericope 15

I.   Abraham, His Servant, and His God
          Review of Abraham's trusting actions in the past (especially Gen 22)
          Resolution to remain in the land of promise no matter what (24:1–9)
          The servant's prayer, worship, and reliance upon God (24:10–49)
          God working through human actions of Abraham and his servant (see Notes)
          Move-to-Relevance: Our feeble resolutions and less than wholehearted commitment to God
II. Rebekah, Her Family, and Her God
          Her points of contact with Abraham: name, "taking" and "going," hospitality, blessings
          Her willingness to leave family, clan, and country (24:58)
          Rebekah's family's willingness to let a daughter leave (24:50–60)
          God working through human actions of Rebekah and her family (see Notes)
          Move-to-Relevance: Our unwillingness to change, to forge ahead after God
III. *Work hard, trusting God!*
          How we can do our best in all circumstances, acknowledging the sovereign work of God at the same time

Looking at the sermon from the point of view of human action and divine design, results in a slightly altered outline.

---

34. Mathews, *Genesis 11:27–50:26*, 322.

I. Human Action

        Review of Abraham's trusting actions in the past (especially Gen 22)

        Resolution to remain in the land of promise no matter what (24:1–9)

        The servant's prayer, worship, and reliance upon God (24:10–49)

        Rebekah's willingness to leave family, clan, and country (24:58)

        Move-to-Relevance: Our feeble resolutions and less than wholehearted commitment to God

II. Divine Design

        God working through human actions of Abraham and his servant (see Notes)

        God working through human actions of Rebekah and her family (see Notes)

III. *Work hard, trusting God!*

        How we can do our best in all circumstances, acknowledging the sovereign work of God at the same time

PATRIARCHAL HISTORY
Experiencing the Blessing

Genesis 25:19–36:43

(Jacob Story)

PERICOPE 16

Contention and Contempt

Genesis 25:19–34

[Esau and Jacob born; Esau disdains birthright]

REVIEW, SUMMARY, PREVIEW

Review of Pericope 15: Genesis 24:1–25:18 concluded the Abraham Story, describing the search for a bride for Isaac. All the protagonists—Abraham, his retainer, and Rebekah—demonstrate a firm trust in God to fulfill his purposes. God sovereignly works things out favorably for the parties involved, but in tandem with human action that is undertaken in faith.

Summary of Pericope 16: This pericope commences the Jacob Story with Rebekah's conception of twins and the oracle detailing the prominence of the younger over the older—a sovereignly ordained hierarchy. The subsequent strife between the twins at their birth and later on in life describes the struggle for divine blessing. In this pericope, Jacob pursues Esau out of the womb and later inveigles Esau—who was seeking instant gratification—out of his birthright. All told, the story tells of a failure to recognize God's sovereignty in the disposition of blessing, as well as of a despising of one's own blessings.

Preview of Pericope 17: The next pericope (Gen 26:1–33) details Isaac's response to God's unequivocal promise of descendants and prosperity. The patriarch, first, is shown resorting to subterfuge rather than trusting God to secure his blessings; then, in the face of opposition, he is depicted as a man of faith, believing that God will take care of him. God can be trusted to keep his promises of blessing.

16. Genesis 25:19–34

THEOLOGICAL FOCUS OF PERICOPE 16

16 Failure to recognize the sovereign distribution of God's blessing and despising one's own blessings from God, potentially lead to strife between individuals in the community (25:19–34).

16.1 Failure to recognize God's sovereign distribution of blessing creates the potential for human strife (25:19–26).

16.1.1 *God sovereignly distributes blessing.*

16.1.2 *Failure to recognize the sovereign distribution of divine blessing creates potential for human strife.*

16.2 Despising one's own blessings from God can lead to strife between individuals in the community (25:27–34).

OVERVIEW

The patriarchal saga continues with the תּוֹלְדוֹת, *toldot*, of Isaac (25:19), and with the announcement of the תּוֹלְדוֹת of Esau (36:1). These two declarations bookend the second of the patriarchal stories, that of Jacob: Gen 25–36. In 25:19, as in 11:27 (תּוֹלְדוֹת of Terah) and 37:2 (תּוֹלְדוֹת of Jacob), it is the father—here, Isaac—who heads off the subsequent section that primarily deals with the activities of the son.

The תּוֹלְדוֹת of Esau that ends the Jacob narratives (Gen 36), conforms to a pattern that the author has deliberately followed—genealogies of the chosen lines alternate with those of the non-elect ones, thus creating five patriarchal narratives to match the five family histories in Gen 1–11 (those of Cain [though not introduced as a תּוֹלְדוֹת[1]], Adam/Seth, Noah, Shem/Ham/Japheth, and Shem again).

> תּוֹלְדוֹת of Terah (Abraham Story; 11:27–25:11)
> תּוֹלְדוֹת of Ishmael (25:12–18)
> תּוֹלְדוֹת of Isaac (Jacob Story; 25:19–35:29)
> תּוֹלְדוֹת of Esau (36:1–43)
> תּוֹלְדוֹת of Jacob (Joseph Story; 37:1–50:26)

Each of the stories in the elect line begins with a word/revelation from God: Abram's call (12:1–3); Rebekah's oracle (25:23), and Joseph's dream (37:5–7, 9). Perhaps this serves to highlight the firm arm of God in the accomplishment of his purposes, despite the muddying of waters by human hands.

The Jacob and Joseph stories share themes—deception of a father (with a goat's kid involved somewhere), treachery between brothers, two decades of separation with a sibling in a faraway land, tension between Leah (and/or her sons) and Rachel (and/or her sons), silence about the life-story of the older brother(s), and eventual reunion and reconciliation between siblings. Indeed the Jacob–Joseph stories may be viewed

---

1. However, counting the תּוֹלְדוֹת of the "heavens and the earth" (2:4), there are five introductions in Gen 1:1–11:26 that employ the term: 2:4; 5:1; 6:9; 10:1; 11:10.

as a single narrative comprising two parts (Gen 25–36 and 37–50). Jacob is present actively in both, though he is not the protagonist in the Joseph story; the disharmony between Jacob and his sons at the end of the Jacob Story (see Gen 34) is resolved only at the end of the Joseph story; moreover, Jacob's birth commences the Jacob section, and his death leads to the conclusion of the Joseph section.

While the overall Pentateuchal motif of divine blessing on mankind is carried through in all of these stories, each cycle has its own thrust. In Gen 25–36, the Jacob Story answers the question: How does one experience the promised blessing? Or: How does one "help" God so that God may accomplish his purpose of blessing mankind? Jacob's incapacity to so render aid to God, and his recognition of what, instead, he must do to experience divine blessing, is the driving force of Gen 25–36. That the Jacob Story has been shaped chiastically has been oft noted.[2]

> **25:12–18:** תּוֹלְדוֹת of Ishmael
>
> **A**   **25:19–26:** Word from God regarding pregnancy; Rebekah's struggle in labor; births; Esau and Isaac together for the first time; Paddan-Aram
>
>   **B**   Jacob obtains birthright, בְּכוֹרָה, *bkorah* **(25:27–34)**
>
>   **C**   **26:1–33:** "Digression"—Jacob's father; lies, strife, pact with foreigners; "brother" (26:31); "sister" (26:7); "multiply"(26:4); "kill" (26:7); "one ... people" (26:10); "flock" (26:14 [×2]); רחב (*rkhb*, "fruitful," 26:22); "lie" (26:10); אֲחֻזַּת ('*akhuzzat*, "Ahuzzath," 26:26); בֵּינוֹתֵינוּ (*benotenu*, "between us," 26:28); "peace" (26:29, 31)
>
>   **D**   **26:34–28:9:** Jacob steals Esau's "blessing" (27:12, 35, 36, 38, 41; 28:4 flight from Canaan; "kiss" (27:26, 27); בוא (*bo'*, "bring," Hiphil, 27:10, 14); "come near" (27:21, 22, 25, 26, 27); שׂעיר (*s'ir*, "hairy," 27:23); "abundance" (27:28); "bowing" (27:29); "neck" (27:40); "times" (27:36); "wept" (27:38)
>
>   **E**   **28:10–22:** Encounter ("meet," 28:11) with angels/God; blessing promised; Jacob skeptical; "bless" (28:14); "place" (28:11, 16, 17, 19); "called the name" (28:19); "he spent [the night] there" (28:11); God of Abraham and Isaac ("your father," 28:13); "your seed" (28:13); "return" (28:15); "afraid" (28:17)
>
>   **F**   **29:1–14;** Arrival at Haran; Jacob's success with Rachel; "kiss" (29:11, 13); "roll [גלל, *gll*] ... stone" (29:3, 8, 10); "brothers" (29:14)
>
>   **G**   **29:15–30:** Deception by Laban; "service" (29:15, 18, 20, 25, 27, 30); "wages" (מַשְׂכֻּרֶת, *maskoret*, 29:15)
>
>   **H**   **29:31–30:24:** Sibling rivalry; wages (שׂכר, *skr*, 30:16, 18)

---

2. See Walsh, *Style and Structure*, 31; Fishbane, "Composition and Structure," 15–38; idem, *Text and Texture*, 40–62; Rendsburg, *The Redaction of Genesis*, 53–69; Waltke and Fredricks, *Genesis*, 352; and Wenham, *Genesis 16–50*, 169.

H   **29:31–30:24:** Sibling rivalry; wages
(שׂכר, *skr*, 30:16, 18)

30:25–31:16: Outwitting of Laban referenced (31:7)
G'   "service" (30:26 [×2], 29; 31:6);
"wages" (שׂכר, 30:28, 32, 33; 31:8 [×2])

31:17–55: Flight from Haran; Jacob's safety despite Rachel;
F'   "kiss" (31:28, 55); "heap [גל, *gl*] of stones" (31:46);
"brothers" (31:32)

32:1–32: Encounter ("meet," 32:2) with angels/God;
blessing given; Jacob submissive;
E'   "bless," (32:26, 29); "place" (32:2, 30);
"called the name" (32:2, 30); "he spent the night there" (32:13);
God of Abraham and Isaac ("my father," 32:10);
"your seed" (32:12); "return" (32:9); "afraid" (32:7)

33:1–20: Jacob returns Esau's "blessing" (33:11); return to Canaan
D'   "kiss" (33:4); בוא (Hophal, 33:11); "come near" (33:6, 7);
שׂעיר ("Seir," 33:14, 16); "abundance" (33:9); "bowing" (33:3);
"neck" (33:4); "times" (33:3); "wept" (33:4)

34:1–31: "Digression"—Jacob's children; lies, strife, pact with foreigners;
"brother" (34:11); "sister" (34:13, 14); "multiply" (34:12); "kill" (34:25–26);
C'   "one people" (34:22); "flock" (34:5, 23); רחב ("wide," 34:21);
"lie" (34:2, 7); אָחַז (*'akhaz*, "acquire property," 34:10);
בְנֹתֵינוּ (*bnotenu,* "our daughters," 34:9, 21); "peace/friendliness" (34:21)

B'   **35:1–15:** Jacob is blessed (ברכ, 35:9) again

A'   **35:16–29:** Word from midwife regarding pregnancy; Rachel's struggle in labor; birth;
Esau and Isaac together for the last time; Paddan-Aram
36:1–43: תּוֹלְדוֹת of Esau

"What occupies the Jacob narrative . . . is the metamorphosis of his character—from trickster to humbled servant—achieved against the background of serial conflicts." This transformation is also implied in the geographical shifts in the story: from Canaan to Paddan-Aram, and back to Canaan. The concentric nature of the conflicts of the Jacob Story move from outside to inside (reflecting the chiastic structure): conflicts with foreigners (Isaac with Abimelech and the Gerarites in Gen 26, and Jacob and his sons with the Shechemites in Gen 34), conflict between the brothers, Jacob and Esau (Gen 27, and 32–33), conflict with Laban (29:15–30 and 30:25–31:55), and at the center, the conflict between Jacob's wives (29:31–30:24). However, the most critical struggle is that between Jacob and God, portrayed negatively in 28:20–22 and positively in Gen 32.[3]

This first pericope, Gen 25:19–34, is rightly the entrée to the Jacob saga. Two episodes in the lives of the protagonist and his older twin prepare the reader for what is to come—"a trailer to the main story."[4] There are several parallels between these early events in Jacob's story and those in Abraham's story.

3. Mathews, *Genesis 1–11:26*, 371.

4. Wenham, *Genesis 16–50*, 172.

	Abraham Story	Jacob Story
"These are the generations of …"	11:27	25:19
Fathering of son	11:27	25:19
Marriage of son	11:29	25:20
Barrenness of the son's wife	11:30	25:21
"went" to a land/oracle	11:31	25:22
"And Yahweh said"	12:1	25:23
Divine ordaining	12:1–3	25:23
Response to divine ordaining–1	12:4	25:24–26
Age of protagonist	12:4	25:26
Response to divine ordaining–2	12:5–9	25:27–34
Wife–sister scene	12:10–20	26:1–11

Because of the deliberate similarity, Wenham urges that the words of God in 25:23 be closely examined, since it corresponds to the epochal announcement of God to Abram in 12:1–3. The oracle is "similarly programmatic," and "it announces the God-determined career of Jacob to be one of conflict culminating ultimate triumph."[5]

16.1 *Genesis 25:19–26*

THEOLOGICAL FOCUS 16.1

16.1   Failure to recognize God's sovereign distribution of blessing creates the potential for human strife (25:19–26).

16.1.1   *God sovereignly distributes blessing.*

16.1.2   *Failure to recognize the sovereign distribution of divine blessing creates potential for human strife.*

NOTES 16.1

16.1.1   God sovereignly distributes blessing.

The oracle of God, announcing the separation of two peoples and the future serving of the younger by the older, explains the conflict between Esau and Jacob—a conflict that begins in the womb, that continues as the twins come out of the womb, and that persists outside the womb for the next several decades. It must be noted, of course, that this divine word in no way necessitates that conflict. Indeed, the contention began even prior to the oracle to Rebekah. That revelation, however, interprets the struggle. This was a battle for the superiority and eminence that came through primogeniture, a clash for the blessing of the firstborn—both in birthright and in paternal patronage. The resulting antagonism, deception, and strife would plague Isaac's family for generations to come.

The story begins innocuously enough (25:19–21). One expects in 25:19, as in previous instances of the תּוֹלְדוֹת (5:1; 6:9; 10:1; 11:10, 26; 25:12), a statement that

5. Ibid., 173.

"Isaac was forty years old when he fathered Esau and Jacob." Instead we get a record of Abraham fathering Isaac. This clearly draws attention to the remarkable circumstances of the latter's birth to an until-then barren mother—an act of divine sovereignty. This mention of Isaac's birth is followed, in 25:20–26a, by a detour (the birth of Isaac's children is noted only in 25:26b) that deals mostly with Rebekah's barrenness, conception, gestation, and delivery, a narrative broken up by the odd occurrence of the twins' struggle in the womb and God's sovereign ordination of one as superior to the other. This deviation from the normal pattern draws attention to the unusual situation.

The first episode, 25:20–26, is carefully structured.

> Isaac is forty when he took Rebekah as his wife (25:20)
> *Barrenness:* Isaac "entreats" [עתר, *'tr*] Yahweh because his "wife" was barren (25:21a)
> *Conception:* Yahweh "answers" [עתר] Isaac, and Rebekah, his "wife," conceives (25:21b)
> Children struggle; Rebekah inquires of Yahweh; Yahweh sovereignly ordains (25:22–23)
> *Gestation:* Her days to give birth are fulfilled; twins in the womb (25:24)
> *Delivery:* Birth, appearance, and naming of children (25:25–26a)
> Isaac is sixty when Rebekah gave birth (25:26b)

The first and last elements provide the ages of Isaac at marriage and at the birth of his children; within the structure there is a progression from barrenness to conception to gestation to delivery, broken in the middle by the rather odd account of the children's struggle, Rebekah's inquiry, and Yahweh's sovereign declaration. This centerpiece emphasizes Yahweh's sovereign ordination of one of the children as "stronger than the other," and who will be served by the other (25:23). Indeed, it all seems to be happening by God's sovereign design: he had brought Isaac and Rebekah together (see Pericope 14 on Gen 24)[6]; and in this pericope Rebekah's conception was expressly noted to be an answer to prayer. The mention of Isaac's age is not adventitious; perhaps he interceded for his wife for two decades. It is ironic that when Rebekah left her homeland, she was blessed: "May you, our sister, become the mother of thousands of ten thousands" (24:60). But here she is, barren—"a miserable condition for any woman in ancient society, let alone one who has been promised a multitude of children."[7] And thus she remained, for two decades. All this to say, it was a sovereign work of God to open the womb of Rebekah

In fact, the structure of the final line of this episode, that again details Isaac's age, times it to the event of Rebekah giving birth (ילד, *yld*, 25:26b), not, as one might have expected, to the occasion of Isaac begetting. There is a repetition of ילד in 25:24 that emphasizes that "this pair of children is not so much begot by Isaac [whose role is downplayed] as primarily an affair between Rebekah and Yahweh, an affair of the barren woman who receives children with God's help only"—an act of divine sovereignty, almost leaving aside the role of the father.[8]

---

6. Interestingly, Isaac is the only monogamous patriarch.

7. Wenham, *Genesis 16–50*, 179.

8. Fokkelman, *Narrative Art in Genesis*, 92.

Needless to say, it is also within God's sovereign design to ordain who the first-born will be, an important privilege for the one so designated (and in line with God's sovereignty, that privilege is a divine blessing) in the ancient biblical community. In the Theological Focus, one could consider any and all of God's blessings for his children as sovereignly ordained, and differentially distributed—certain kinds of blessings to one, other kinds of blessings to another.

16.1.2 *Failure to recognize the sovereign distribution of divine blessing creates the potential for human strife.*

It all sounds routine at the beginning of the story. The barrenness of the matriarch is not a first. Neither is Yahweh's answering of prayer to open her womb. Both these were already patterned in the life of Abram and Sarai (11:30; 15:2; 20:17; 21:1–2). However the glaring difference between these initial scenes of the Jacob Story and the Abraham Story must be pointed out: "but the *sons*..." (25:22). For the first time in biblically narrated human history, there is more than one individual in the same womb at the same time![9] That there would two nations down the line was to be expected from earlier revelation (17:4–6, 16); however, that the two peoples would come from Rebekah's own body at the same time underscores the multiple births. The problem with such an exigency was the question of primogeniture: Who would be the firstborn, and who would, thus, obtain the sovereign blessing? And so the fighting begins, a struggle to be the firstborn, a drive to obtain the blessing of God, as the participants slug it out between themselves to be the first in line for divine blessing, as if they could overcome sovereign design by human vigor. The verb denoting "struggle" (רצץ, *rtsts*, 25:22) is quite a violent term ("smashing/crushing"—of skulls, Jdg 9:53; Ps 74:13; of reeds, Isa 36:6; etc.); the Hithpolel stem denotes the mutually aggressive action and reciprocity of the tussle. This is some serious intrauterine action going on within Rebekah. The children might be "separated" as peoples as God declared (25:23) but, in Rebekah's womb, they were locked together in a hostile interaction, with the younger grasping the heel of the older.

God's ordination of the final outcome—the older serving the younger who would be "stronger than the other" (25:23)—does not, of course, excuse the behaviors of the protagonists.[10] In fact, the oracle should have influenced Jacob (and Esau) otherwise: the sovereignty of God cannot be challenged—Jacob would have done well to rest in the promises and Esau to submit to the will of God. Unfortunately, the human initiative was not one of rest and submission; rather, it was one of contention. It could have been otherwise—indeed, it *should* have been otherwise—and that is the theological thrust of this pericope, and indeed of the entire Jacob narrative. Divine ordination and sovereignty in the differential distribution of blessing raises the potential of strife, when participants respond in a negative fashion. What God has set in motion always comes to pass—the one ordained to receive the blessing does get it—but from the

---

9. In fact, when "twins" are mentioned for the first time in 25:24, it is announced with an exclamation: "Behold!"

10. Fretheim, "Which Blessing?" 285.

human standpoint, this need not have been accompanied with so much distress, pain, and grief.

The naming of the children facilitates the "confusion" of the situation: Yahweh had declared, in 25:23, that the older would "serve" (יַעֲבֹד, *ya'abod*) the "younger" (צָעִיר, *tsa'ir*). The younger is named יַעֲקֹב (*ya'aqob*, "Jacob")—sharing the vowels and most of the consonants with יַעֲבֹד; and the older, Esau, comes out looking like a garment that is שֵׂעָר (*se'ar*, "hairy")—that almost sounds like צָעִיר (*tsa'ir*, "younger"). Who is who? Is יַעֲקֹב the one who will "יַעֲבֹד," and is the one who is שֵׂעָר going to be the צָעִיר?[11]

While Esau's qualities are noted as an adjective ("red") and with a circumstantial clause with nouns ("like a hairy cloak," 25:25), Jacob is described with a verb, "grasping on to Esau's heel [עָקֵב, *'qeb*]" (25:26). He is already at work, attempting to take his brother's place! The name "Jacob" (יַעֲקֹב) is a play on the word "heel," likely to indicate Jacob's prehensile tendencies as a "heel-grabber." As a noun, עקב can mean "supplanter/foe" (Ps 49:5); as a verb, "to supplant/deceive" (Jer 9:4); and as an adjective, "deceitful" (Jer 17:9). Job 18:9 indicates entrapment with the phrase "grasp the heel" (יֹאחֵז בְּעָקֵב, *yo'khez b'aqeb*) corresponding to the usage in Gen 25:26 (אֹחֶזֶת בַּעֲקֵב, *'okhezet ba'aqeb*, "holding the heel"). Altogether not a bright start for Jacob. Neither is Esau depicted in any better light. Vawter observes that "[h]airiness or shagginess seems to have been *eo ipso* a mark of incivility," a prejudice "which existed not only in the ancient Near Eastern world but well into the time of Western Christianity as well. Judas Iscariot was depicted in mediaeval art as a redhead! . . . In respect to Esau, therefore, the author's word-plays go beyond mere cleverness and insinuate a bias against him from the beginning."[12]

That Esau would serve Jacob is literally demonstrated in the ordering of words (25:23).

> and-[one]-people [Jacob]
>   than-[other]-people [Esau] *shall-be-stronger*
>   and-the-older [Esau] *shall-serve*
> the-younger [Jacob]

Esau is virtually hemmed in by Jacob. An initial reading of those lines might have assumed otherwise: after noting that one would be stronger than the other, the next line begins with "and the older"— not זָקֵן, *zaqen*, the usual word for "older," but רַב (*rab*, that also means "greater"). This might have naturally induced the reader to think that the "greater" one was the one who would be stronger. It is not until the last two words of the divine oracle, "shall-serve the-younger," that the irony is patent with the speci-

---

11. The word-plays also adumbrate later history: Esau, the firstborn, is described as "red"—אַדְמוֹנִי (*'admoni*, 25:25; red hair? skin?), an obvious play on Esau's national name, אֱדוֹם (*'edom*, Edom). His hairiness, noted above—שֵׂעָר—is also a play on Seir (שֵׂעִיר, *se'ir*), the territory of Edom (32:3; 33:14, 16). And the strife outside the womb would continue beyond the lifespans of the twins—Edom and Israel would be at loggerheads for a long time: Num 20:14–21; 2 Kgs 8:20, 22; Ps 137:7; Ezek 25:12–14; Obad 10–14, 18–21; Mal 1:4. But Edom would be submissive to Israel: Num 24:18; 2 Sam 8:14; 1 Kgs 11:15–16; Isa 11:14; Amos 9:11–12; Obad 18.

12. Vawter, *On Genesis*, 288.

fication of the younger of the twin as the superior one in this duet. The interpreter, it seems, now has to go back and reverse what seemed obvious earlier: it would *not* be elder over younger; it would be the other way round.[13]

It was normal for the older child to receive the birthright, a double portion (Deut 21:17; 2 Kgs 2:19; and see below). So if anyone is culpable in this episode, it is Jacob, seeking, ostensibly, to be in first place and obtain the divine blessing of primogeniture. Even *before* the divine announcement of reversal of primogeniture that marked Jacob as the one to be blessed, he is fighting for blessing. And what is even more surprising, *despite* the divine announcement, he, for the most of the remaining chapters of his story, continues to fight for blessing, assuming wrongly that only his belligerent attempts can accomplish that goal.

The episode of Gen 25:19–26 thus projects the theological focus of the failure to recognize the sovereign distribution of divine blessings, and the resulting potential for human strife—in this case, amongst individuals who were "equal," in the same womb, at the same time.

16.2 Genesis 25:27–34

THEOLOGICAL FOCUS 16.2

16.2 Despising one's own blessings from God can lead to strife between individuals in the community (25:27–34).

NOTES 16.2

16.2 Despising one's own blessings from God can lead to strife between individuals in the community.

The second episode is also structured with attention to detail.[14]

> **A**   Jacob cooked stew (25:29a)
> > **B**   Esau arrives hungry (25:29b)
> > > **C**   Esau asks Jacob for the "red stuff" (25:30)
> > > > **D**   Jacob demands "birthright" "today" (25:31)
> > > > > **E**   "Birthright" disdained (25:32)
> > > > **D'**   Esau sells "birthright" "today" (25:33)
> > > **C'**   Jacob gives Esau bread and stew (25:33)
> > **B'**   Esau departs after eating and drinking (25:34)
> **A'**   Esau despised birthright (25:34b)

13. Jeansonne, "Genesis 25:23," 147. The motif of the younger "usurping" the status of the older was already seen in Genesis with Isaac and Ishmael. It will reappear in the book with Zerah and Perez (also twins), and with Ephraim and Manasseh. Perhaps also with Joseph–Benjamin and the older brothers. Fraternal rivalry thus far has always favored the younger of the pair (Abel vs. Cain; Isaac vs. Ishmael).

14. Table modified from Terino, "A Text Linguistic Study," 97.

The story is framed in *A* and *A'* with three words in each element: "cooked Jacob stew" and "despised Esau birthright." The antagonists are depicted with their actions of consequence and the objects of their exchange.[15] Both the centerpiece and the editorial addendum at the end mark the thrust of this episode: the fault is squarely laid at Esau's feet for disdaining and despising what was his.

Jacob's characterization as תָּם (*tam*, 25:27) is puzzling; it is often used of blamelessness or integrity (Job 1:1, 8; 2:3; 8:20; Ps 37:37; Prov 29:10; a related word, תָּמִים, *tamim*, is used of Noah in Gen 6:9). Hamilton thinks תם may be derived from an Arabic root meaning "to be kept in subjection/enslaved." Semantic development then likely indicated one who was "domesticated" (אִישׁ תָּם, *'ish tam*) and a "tent-dweller," as opposed to Esau, a "skillful hunter, and אִישׁ שָׂדֶה, *'ish sadeh*, "man of the field."[16] However, the majority of translations adopt the sense of תם as "calm/even-tempered." Be that as it may, Esau's vocation, hunting, is shared with other another disreputable character—Nimrod (10:9; and perhaps the "archer," Ishmael, 21:20): such a characterization, by association, does not bode well for the older twin here.

The firstborn (בְּכֹר, *bkor*) had a privileged status in biblical society, perhaps based on the convention that the firstborn male was God's exclusive possession, as also was the first-fruit of the soil and the male firstlings of the flock (Gen 43:33; 49:3; Exod 13:2; 22:29; Num 8:14–18; Deut 15:19; Ps 78:51).[17] Israel, the nation itself, was God's "firstborn son" (Exod 4:22). The double portion due to the firstborn—twice as much as other siblings—upon the death of the father is noted in Deut 21:17.[18] Of course, it is not insignificant, at least in the Jacob Story, that בְּכֹרָה, *bkorah*, "birthright," is the anagram of בְּרָכָה, *brakah*, "blessing."[19] What Esau forfeits in this pericope adumbrates his far greater loss in Gen 27–28. Interestingly, God is completely absent from this episode of 25:27–34, which itself points an accusatory finger at the protagonists, one selling and the other buying. But it is in this episode that the oracle of God begins to come to pass: the heel-grabber is "stronger" than the hunter, and the older is ready to "serve" the younger (25:23).

The story focuses almost entirely on Esau, noting his histrionic outburst about his famished state: "Behold! I am going to die!" (25:32) as he dismisses the value of

---

15. Indeed, Jacob's action of "cooking" (זיד, *zid*) also sounds suspiciously like Esau's vocation of "hunting" (צַיִד, *tsayid*).

16. Hamilton, *Genesis: Chapters 18–50*, 181. While Isaac's fondness for good food (a detail that will show up again in Gen 27:4, 9, 14) propels his favoritism for Esau, Rebekah's bias towards Jacob is not given a reason (25:28). Since it is Esau's lifestyle that is noted, it might well be Jacob's lifestyle (quietness? domestication?) that put him in his mother's good books. The strife between the brothers was surely aggravated by parental partiality.

17. While often the firstborn's privilege is related to the father (Gen 49:3; Ps 78:51; 105:36), his vested status may also relate to the mother, whose womb is opened by the firstborn (Exod 13:2, 12, 15).

18. Ahroni, "Why Did Esau Spurn the Birthright?" 324–25. Similar laws are found in the Code of Hammurabi §170 and in Middle Assyrian Laws, Tablet B.1, that give the firstborn a preferential increase in parental share (*ANET* 173, 185).

19. However, these were separate inheritances as Gen 27:36 indicates; Esau sees birthright and blessing as discrete. For Joseph, it seems the two were equated (1 Chr 5:1–2).

his birthright, in favor of short-term, instant gratification. Neither does he call it "my" birthright; rather it is "a" birthright: "What use is a birthright to me?"[20] His demand for a gulp of that "red stuff" (הָאָדֹם הָאָדֹם, *ha'adom ha'adom*, literally "the red, the red," 25:30), for which he is willing to sacrifice something of immense value, has Esau the "red one" (אַדְמוֹנִי, *'admoni*, 25:25) losing out because of his lust for the "red" food. The verb לְעַט (*la'at*, "swallow/devour/gulp," 25:30) occurs only here in the OT. Jastrow adduces late Hebrew evidence pointing to its use—"to feed an animal by putting food into its mouth." This would substantiate Skinner's labeling this term as "a coarse expression suggesting bestial voracity."[21] Esau, the animal, arrives to feed; and Esau, the hunter, falls into a trap. Ross sees this as the picture of "a wild and blustery man pointing and gasping, 'Red stuff, red stuff.'"[22] In any case, Esau's attitude is one of wanton indifference to and willful negligence of the privilege of birthright highly valued in ancient Near Eastern societies. He was willing to "surrender precious long-term goods for the immediate appeasement of his hunger."[23]

Of course, that does not render Jacob wholly devoid of devious impulses. Whereas it seemed that Esau at least maintained some propriety in punctuating his request with "please" (נָא *na'*, 25:30), Jacob's reply is brusque and demanding: "Sell, today, your birthright to me" (25:31). "To me" is in the emphatic position at the end of the clause. This is clearly not a request; it is a peremptory stipulation, laid down from a position of strength; he gets to dictate the terms of this transaction. All this "suggests long premeditation and a ruthless exploitation of his brother's moment of weakness." Jacob follows up with another curt and blunt challenge: "Swear to me today" (25:33). The immediacy of the demanded transaction desired by Jacob is emphasized in his repeat of "today" (25:31, 33)—he wants to cash in right away, as instantaneously as Esau wants his food. And the deal is struck: Esau swears and sells; and Jacob gives (25:33b–34a).[24] As Hamilton observes wryly, "Esau capitulates and Jacob capitalizes."[25]

But there is no question that it is Esau and his actions that the narrator wants the reader to focus upon. The account closes with Esau's actions—*actions*, not words: he is strangely silent as he eats and departs. The cascade of five Qal *waw*-consecutive imperfects is stunning and condemning: .... וַיֹּאכַל וַיֵּשְׁתְּ וַיָּקָם וַיֵּלַךְ וַיִּבֶז (*wayyo'kal wayyosht wayyaqam wayyelak wayyivez*): "and he ate, and he drank, and he rose, and he went,

---

20. While the narrator refers to the birthright as "his" (i.e., Esau's) in 25:33, in the next verse, after the consummation of its sale, it is again an impersonal "the" birthright. Noting that eating is the transgression in this episode, just as it was in the Garden of Eden, Vrolijk observes that "this would place Jacob in the position of the deceiving snake" (*Jacob's Wealth*, 48).

21. Jastrow, *Dictionary of the Targumim*, 714; Skinner, *A Critical and Exegetical Commentary on Genesis*, 361. Speiser, *Genesis*, 195, notes that Esau is "depicted as an uncouth glutton."

22. Ross, *Creation and Blessing*, 450.

23. Wenham, *Genesis 16–50*, 179.

24. Ibid., 178. Wenham thinks there is more to the exchange: the "red, red" in 25:30 suggested a thick meaty concoction, but what passed hands was merely bread and lentil stew (25:34). Did Esau just imagine the redness in 25:30, or did Jacob cheat him, not only of the birthright, but also of the dish his brother craved, substituting beans for meat? (ibid.).

25. *Genesis: Chapters 18–50*, 186.

and he despised" (25:34b)—"the brutal simplicity of Esau's material urges."[26] The closing comment from the narrator summarizing the story and providing an editorial assessment of what happened (that Esau despised his birthright) is quite rare in OT narrative. Esau is clearly being depicted in a bad light with that pronouncement. Not that Jacob was innocent, of course; but here, the focus is upon the older one disdaining a great blessing that was his by right. And, in so disdaining the birthright/blessing, "actually Esau despises himself and also Yahweh."[27]

SERMON FOCUS AND OUTLINES

> **THEOLOGICAL FOCUS OF PERICOPE 16 FOR PREACHING**
>
> **16** Failing to recognize God's sovereign distribution of blessing, and despising one's own blessing, can lead to strife (25:19–34).

This opening pericope of the Jacob saga sets the stage for the remainder of the narrative through Gen 36. There is a clear focus on the sovereign distribution of God's blessing in the first episode, that leads to the events of the second. Divine ordination opens wombs, fixes birth order, and governs subsequent outcomes. It is appropriate to see all of this as divine blessing, of one kind or another, to one individual and/or another. Yet it becomes clear that it is the exercise of this divine prerogative to bless differentially that sets the stage for the human recipients of divine action to engage in strife. Jacob wants what Esau has (25:19–26): he begins grasping for first place. God confirms that that is what will eventually happen: the older will serve the younger (and stronger) one. Ironically, that does not keep Jacob from doing his utmost to make that oracle come to pass, as subsequent events in his story show. It is his failure to recognize the divinely ordained distribution of blessings that renders him culpable.

In the second episode, it is Esau who is clearly guilty. In almost the same fashion as Jacob, his is also a failure to recognize his own divine blessing—the magnificence thereof. He ends up despising what God has given him and wanting what another had (in his case, the instant gratification of food).

The preacher will do well to keep these thrusts (and the ones of the pericopes in this saga that follow) focused upon relationships within the community of believers. Invariably the root causes of intramural strife are those that are projected by this pericope. The recognition of God's sovereignty in differentially blessing his children, and the grateful valuing of what one has been given, will go far to minimize contention in community and maintain relationships within it that are harmonious and complementary.

Possible Preaching Outlines for Pericope 16

I.   JACOB: Failure to Recognize Sovereign Disposition of Blessing
        God's sovereignty in blessing: opening of womb, fixing of birth order, ordaining life

26. White, *Narration and Discourse*, 213.

27. Görg, "בָּזָה," *TDOT* 2:63. In Heb 12:16, Esau is characterized as immoral and godless.

outcomes (25:19–21, 23)
The struggle of the twins, instigated by the "heel-grabber," Jacob (25:22, 24–26)
Move-to-Relevance: Our struggles to obtain blessings for ourselves

II. ESAU: Failure to Value One's Own Sovereignly Distributed Blessing
Esau's need for instant gratification (25:27–32)
Esau's devaluing of his own blessing (25:32, 34)
The significant loss suffered by Esau
Move-to-Relevance: Our disdaining of what God has given us, and the resultant strife/loss

III. WE: *Recognize and respect the blessings of God!*[28]
Ways to accomplish the recognition and respecting of divine blessing upon individuals in community
The consequence of such recognition and respect: the avoidance of intramural strife and contention.

A Problem–Cause–Solution outline (a variation on Problem–Solution–Application) also works for this pericope.

I. PROBLEM: Intramural Strife Amongst Individuals in the Community of Believers
Move-to-Relevance: The strife amongst the children of God, all of whom are equally valued by God
The struggle between Jacob and Esau, occupying the same womb at the same time (25:22, 24–26)
The tussle between Jacob and Esau, seeking instant gratification "today" (25:27–32)

II. CAUSE: Failure to Recognize Sovereign Disposition of Blessing, and to Value One's Own Blessing from God
Jacob: unwilling to trust God's sovereign bestowal of blessing (25:24–26)
Esau: devaluing his own blessing (25:32, 34)

III. SOLUTION: *Recognize and respect the blessings of God!*
Ways to accomplish the recognition and respecting of divine blessing upon individuals in community
The consequence of such recognition and respect: the avoidance of intramural strife and contention

28. The specifics of "*Recognize and respect*" may well include expressions of gratitude to God for his sovereign and differential blessings upon individuals in the community. Indeed, perhaps the worship service in which this sermon is preached could create a focus upon the variegation of blessings, and the importance to the body of integrating all these blessings, for the good of God's people, and for God's glory.

PERICOPE 17

A Two-Sided Coin

Genesis 26:1–33

[Isaac Distrusts; Isaac Trusts]

REVIEW, SUMMARY, PREVIEW

Review of Pericope 16: Genesis 25:19–34 commences the Jacob Story with Rebekah's twin pregnancy and the sovereignly ordained prominence of the younger over the older. The subsequent struggle between the twins describes the struggle for divine blessing: a failure of recognition of God's sovereignty in his differential disposition of blessing, and a despising of one's own blessings.

Summary of Pericope 17: This seemingly digressive chapter details Isaac's response to God's unequivocal promise of descendants and prosperity. The first half of the pericope paints a negative picture of the patriarch who, rather than trusting God, resorts to subterfuge, passing his wife off to Abimelech as his sister. The second half, however, portrays Isaac, though besieged by opposition to his well-digging enterprises, trusting God and moving away from his opponents, with no thought of retaliation. God can be trusted to keep his promises of blessing.

Preview of Pericope 18: The next pericope (26:34–28:9) constitutes the extended account of the stealing of the blessing of the firstborn by Jacob, with all of the actants in the story guilty of trying to divert divine blessings for their own purposes. The result of this manipulation is fragmentation of family and community.

17.   *Genesis 26:1–33*

THEOLOGICAL FOCUS OF PERICOPE 17

17   God can be trusted to keep his promises of blessing, even in the face of opposition, without fearfully resorting to deception or retaliation to secure them oneself (26:1–33).

17.1   God can be trusted to secure one's blessings, without fearfully resorting to deception to secure them oneself (26:1–11).

17.2   God can be trusted to keep his promises of blessing, even in the face of opposition, without having to resort to retaliation (26:12–33).

OVERVIEW

This seemingly digressive chapter, following the birth and growth and struggles of Esau and Jacob, looks back at two episodes in the life of Jacob's father, Isaac. The reason for this detour becomes obvious when one realizes that what is pictured here is a transformation of the patriarch, a change of attitude and heart that should have marked his younger son in the rest of the Jacob narratives (and that ought to mark all of God's children).[1]

That a new unit begins in 26:1 is obvious from the new circumstance of a famine that is introduced. The pericope ends in 26:33 with a naming of a city "to this day." The two following verses, 26:34–35, belong to the next pericope, 26:34–28:9, that thereby commences and concludes with the marital exploits of Esau.

Structurally, the two episodes of this pericope are demarcated as 26:1–11 and 26:12–33. The first deals with Isaac's arrival in Gerar and the wife–sister episode (wherein Isaac claims to the locals that Rebekah, his wife, was his sister), portraying his response to the perceived threat to his life. The second concerns the envy of the surrounding peoples at Isaac's prosperity, their attempts to sabotage his wells, and the patriarch's response to this second series of threats.

This chapter looks very much like a flashback—a better fit if it had followed Gen 24 and the account of Isaac's marriage to Rebekah. For that matter, Gen 25, with its account of the birth and growth of Isaac's twin boys, would itself have worked better placed next to Gen 27, without the "interruption" of Gen 26. Needless to say, Isaac's minor role in the opening account of the Jacob Story (25:19–34)—all he does in that narrative is pray for his wife—in contrast to the major part he plays as the protagonist in Gen 26, shows that this latter chapter is out of place chronologically. However, as we will discover, the placement of this episode where it is now is a carefully thought out narrative strategy by the author/editor—what he is *doing* with what he is saying.

The events of Gen 26 likely occurred in the two decades of Rebekah's barrenness, for it is inconceivable that the men of Gerar would have accepted Isaac's lie that Rebekah was his sister, had there been two toddlers (or older children) running

---

1. This is akin to the later character change of Jacob, culminating in Gen 33, and that of one of Jacob's sons, Judah, in Gen 38.

around in the camp.[2] And Rebekah's beauty is expressly noted (26:8). As a mother she would have been in her sixties (Isaac was sixty when the twins were born, 25:26), suggesting that the current episode occurred prior to her pregnancy. "The whole passage (26:1–33) proceeds as if Isaac were unencumbered by the presence of children, had not yet received Yahweh's blessing, and possessed little personal wealth."[3] In 25:11, God is shown blessing Isaac, yet that blessing is only a promise in 26:3, which he receives in 26:12 (and it is acknowledged by others in 26:29). In similar fashion, 25:5 has Abraham giving all he had to his son Isaac—probably quite a substantial donation (12:10–20; 14:16–24; 20:1–18); yet only in 26:12–16 does Isaac come into his own, as far as wealth is concerned. "Only the suggestion that Gen. xxvi 1–33 functions as a 'flashback' does justice to the content of the narrative."[4]

If one considers the scheme of the Jacob Story (25:19–36:43; see structural layout of the whole saga in Pericope 16), another seeming digression occurs towards the end, with Gen 34. The two apparently misplaced pericopes—one dealing with Jacob's father and the other dealing with Jacob's sons—are, on second glance, not so incongruous.[5] Deception and strife followed by a pact are found in both these chapters (26:7, 26–33; 34:8–17, 13, 18–29); so also are "brother(s)" (26:31; 34:11); "sister" (26:7, 9; 34:13, 14); "multiply" (26:4; 34:12); "kill" (26:7; 34:25–26); "one" with "people" (26:10; 34:22); "flock" (26:14 [×2]; 34:5, 23); רחב (*rkhb*, "wide/enlarged," 26:22; 34:21); and illicit intercourse with an uncircumcised person/peoples (or at least a suggestion thereof). Besides, a number of key words occur in both: "lie" (26:10; 34:2, 7); אֲחֻזַּת, *'akhuzzat*, "Ahuzzath," and אָחַז, *'akhaz*, "property" (26:26; 34:10); בֵּינוֹתֵינוּ, *benotenu*, "between us," and בְּנֹתֵינוּ, *bnotenu*, "our daughters," (26:28; 34:9, 21); and "peace/friendliness" (26:29, 31; 34:21). All this to show that careful design has gone into the organizing of these pericopes and their placement in the larger Jacob Story.

The parallels between Gen 25 and part of the Abraham story (Gen 11–12) were noted in Pericope 16. The parallels continue with Gen 26, as well. Also note the connections between this pericope and Gen 20 (Abraham's second wife–sister episode).[6]

---

2. The subterfuge was discovered only after "a long time" (26:8), which itself goes to show that this was most likely a flashback.

3. Wenham, *Genesis 16–50*, 185–86.

4. Nicol, "The Narrative Structure," 344. Also see idem, "The Chronology of Genesis," 330–38. The mention of Abraham's death in 26:18 (at which point, following the chronology of the book, the twins, Esau and Jacob, would have been fifteen years old—see 21:5; 25:26; and 25:7; also see Pericope 15), does not vitiate this conclusion. There might have been a gap of several decades between the two episodes in this pericope (i.e., after 26:11) that encompassed the birth of Isaac's twins, the death of Abraham, etc.

5. Genesis 34 will be considered later. Indeed, the story of Judah in Gen 38 is another pericope that, on the surface, does not seem to fit in with the rest of the Joseph Story (37:1–50:26). But this too, I shall show, has its appointed place and role in that particular narrative.

6. From Wenham, *Genesis 16–50*, 187.

	Abraham Story	Jacob Story
Famine; wife–sister episode	12:10–20	26:1–11
Wealth and resulting strife	13:1–10	26:12–22
Separation of feuding sides	13:11–12	26:23
Yahweh's promise of seed	13:14–17	26:24
Altar built; patriarch in tent	13:18	25:22
Patriarch blessed by foreign king	14:19–20	26:29
Wife–sister episode	20:1–18	26:1–11
Ishmael and Isaac	21:1–21	
Dispute(s) about wells	21:25–30	26:15–22
Abimelech and Phicol	21:22	26:26
Divine presence acknowledged	21:22	26:28
Oaths with foreigners	21:22–24, 31–32	26:30–31
Beersheba named	21:31	26:32–33

Strikingly, what is missing in the parallel structuring of Gen 20–21 and Gen 26 is any account in the latter of children: there is no parallel with 21:1–21 that deals with the birth of Isaac and the expulsion of Ishmael, the children of Abraham (highlighted in the table above). This also substantiates the conclusion that Gen 26 is likely to be a flashback to a time before Isaac and Rebekah had children.

17.1 Genesis 26:1–11

THEOLOGICAL FOCUS 17.1

17.1 God can be trusted to secure one's blessings, without fearfully resorting to deception to secure them oneself (26:1–11).

NOTES 17.1

17.1 God can be trusted to secure one's blessings without fearfully resorting to deception to secure them oneself.[7]

The famine in which Isaac found himself (26:1) is the first instance of "famine" after 12:10. One remembers that it was in that earlier dire circumstance that Abraham decamped to Egypt, where the first wife–sister episode occurred. What would his son do? There is, however, a difference here: unlike in the case of Abraham, Yahweh instructs Isaac quite specifically that he is *not* to go to Egypt, but to a land announced later as "this land" (26:1, 3). Isaac dutifully remains where he is, at Gerar, about ten miles south of Gaza, the land of Abimelech, king of the Philistines.[8] The command is

---

7. This Theological Focus is stated in the positive; Isaac, in this episode, portrays a negative picture, one of mistrust in God.

8. It has been thought that "Philistines" is an anachronism here, since they did not populate Canaan until the early centuries of the second millennium BCE, and since their description in Genesis does not match that in Judges and Samuel. See Jost, "Abimelech," 6–7. "Abimelech" (= "my father is king") is likely to have been a titular and dynastic name for the rulers of Gerar, akin to "Pharaoh" in Egypt; likely so also was "Phicol" (besides 26:26, see 21:22, 32).

similar to what Abraham had received in 12:1 and 22:2 (both of which were followed by a promise of blessing, as also is this one in 26:2):

	Command to Go	Promise of Blessing
Abraham	12:1a [to a land] "which I will show you"	12:1b–3
Abraham	22:2 [to a mountain] "of which I will tell you"	22:16–18
Isaac	26:2a [to a land] "of which I will tell you"	26:2b

"These allusions make it clear that even if Isaac is not to walk in his father's footsteps geographically, he must follow him spiritually."[9] And the irony is obvious: "When God spoke first to Abraham, He bade him to go; when He speaks first to Isaac, God bids him to stay put."[10] But considering the similarity with Gen 22:2, Isaac's command is seen to be most similar to Abraham's final test.

Since it was God who decreed that Isaac dwell in Gerar (26:3), it would have been appropriate for Isaac to expect God to protect him in the land wherein God had directed him to remain. Especially so since God, here, promises to be with the patriarch (26:3). Not only does God promise Isaac his divine presence, later even foreigners—Abimelech and Phicol—acknowledge this fact (26:28, just as Abimelech and Phicol had recognized divine presence with Isaac's father, 21:22). Yet as this narrative progresses, one person seems to have had doubts about the presence of Yahweh—Isaac himself, and this despite the backing of a divine oath (26:3).[11]

Isaac is also promised blessing and land—"to you and to your descendants" (the recipients are in an emphatic position at the head of the sentence, 26:3). While parts of the promise had been sounded out already in 12:3; 15:5; 18:18; 22:17–18, confirming that Isaac *would* have descendants, here for the first time we are told of the promise of land specifically to *Isaac's* descendants. The promise also seems to be quite extensive, encompassing even Philistine land, an expansion hitherto unrecognized. Isaac was being promised even more than what had been promised to Abraham! There is, however, a subtle hint of contingency: not only is the declaration of blessing prefaced by "dwell in this land," it concludes with a reminder of his father Abraham's obedience to God (26:5), quite a comprehensive obedience (expanding the core "obeyed my voice," attested in 22:18): Abraham had kept Gods' "charge," his "commandments," his "statutes," and his "laws" (26:5). It was a similar (and total) obedience that Yahweh was seeking from Isaac, in order that he might bless him. As Hamilton notes, "blessing is a divine response to appropriate behavior."[12]

---

9. Wenham, *Genesis 16–50*, 189.

10. Kass, *The Beginning of Wisdom*, 385.

11. This is the only time the promise of presence is expressed to Isaac by Yahweh; Jacob would hear it later in 28:15; 31:3; and 46:4. The oath that Yahweh refers to in 26:3 is obviously that recorded in 22:16, and referred to in 24:7 and 50:24.

12. Hamilton, *Genesis: Chapters 18–50*, 194.

Commanding Isaac to "dwell" in this land (גּוּר, *gur*, 26:3), Yahweh seems to be hinting at what had happened with Abraham, his father: of the five occurrences of the verb in the Abraham Story, four of them are found in connection either with his escape to Egypt (connected with the first wife–sister episode, 12:10) or with the second wife–sister episode in Gerar (20:1; 21:23, 34). Already there is a foreshadowing of what was to come in the next few verses: a *third* wife–sister episode!

And that is exactly what transpires in 26:7–11. Isaac passes off his wife, Rebekah, as his sister, fearing for the safety of his own life. After the divine promise of presence, grounded in a divine oath, and with the assurance of abundant blessing contingent upon obedience (26:2–5), one must conclude that Isaac's fear was unjustified. Could not the God who had commanded him to remain in Gerar take care of him there?

One other literary note must be struck: the word "descendants" echoes four times in God's utterance to Isaac in 26:3–4. If Isaac's excuse was that he was afraid the amorous locals of Gerar would kill him for his beautiful bride (26:7, 9), how would that fear comport with the fourfold mention of "descendants" that God had promised him? How would Isaac die before producing those descendants (or at least one descendant to guarantee the generation of others)? It appears Isaac has forgotten Yahweh's promise to be with him; he has forgotten that it was Yahweh who had asked him to stay on at Gerar; and, above all, he has forgotten that Yahweh had, in no uncertain terms, promised him descendants. Rather than resting in the promise of God, Isaac would lie to save his own skin, regardless of what might happen to his wife.

Isaac's wife–sister deception is discovered when Abimelech, the Philistine king, spies Isaac "caressing" (מְצַחֵק, *mtsakheq*) his wife Rebekah (26:8). While the verb is itself a play on the name "Isaac" (יִצְחָק, *yitskhaq*), that it has sexual connotations seems clear from its use in 39:14, 17 (and perhaps also in Exod 32:6). "Behold! Surely . . ." (26:9), the king accuses; there was no question—this was no sister: Rebekah was Isaac's wife. Ironically, while Isaac is concerned only for himself, the foreign king is concerned about the fate of his people. As with the first Abimelech in Gen 20, this ruler too appears to have been terrified at the prospect of what might have happened had someone engaged in sexual relations with Rebekah: "You would have brought guilt upon us" (26:10). The word "guilt" (אָשָׁם, *'asham*) is often used in Lev 5:2–7, 15–19, 23–26; etc., a state incurred with egregious sins, such as adultery (Lev 19:21–22). "Isaac's behavior, [Abimelech] argues, far from bringing divine blessing on nations . . ., has actually brought him and his people into a most dangerous situation."[13] So much was his fear that Abimelech charged his people not even to touch Rebekah or Isaac, at the pain of death (26:11). Here, then, is a case of a patriarch being the potential source of a bane upon other nations, counter to the word of God in 12:3 that promised to make Abraham and his descendants a blessing to others. Abraham, himself, it will be recalled, brought about a plague upon the household of Pharaoh following his first wife–sister episode (12:17).

---

13. Wenham, *Genesis 16–50*, 190–91.

Here, Isaac, the patriarch, with whom the God of the universe had promised to be, is agonizing about his own safety, seemingly unconcerned even about his own wife! And paradoxically, in trying to save his own skin, he has put in jeopardy the status of all the townspeople in Gerar and their king, not to mention risking the purity of Rebekah, and Yahweh's promise of descendants. The same indignant demand of Abimelech—"What have you done?" (26:10)—was encountered by Abraham in the two earlier wife–sister episodes (the questions were posed by Pharaoh in 12:18, and by Abimelech in 20:9). Besides, God himself had asked that question of a couple of early felons, Adam (3:13), and Cain (4:10). All this shows that Abimelech was on the right side of God, and Isaac on the wrong.

The episode is silent about Isaac's response to his shenanigans being uncovered. No response to Abimelech's pointed charge is noted in the text. But the narrator chooses to close the scene with God's blessing, at least partially coming to pass (26:12–14): Isaac is abundantly blessed. Not only does he reap a hundredfold—an incredible harvest in any season anywhere, and this was in the patriarch's first year of sowing!—he grows rich, richer, and even more rich (גָּדֵל מְאֹד ... וְגָדֵל ... וַיִּגְדַּל, *wayyigdal ... wgadel ... gadal m'od*, 26:13)—a construction that emphasizes Isaac's steady growth in power and possessions. God's promises can be relied upon without fear of losing out (and without engaging in deceptive practices to secure promised blessings). All of Isaac's fears were unfounded; and even despite his mendacious performance that put others at risk, Yahweh protected the patriarch and kept his promise: Isaac and his household were blessed, and blessed abundantly.[14]

17.2 Genesis 26:12–33

THEOLOGICAL FOCUS 17.2

17.2 God can be trusted to keep his promises of blessing, even in the face of opposition, without resorting to retaliation (26:12–33).

NOTES 17.2

17.2 God can be trusted to keep his promises of blessing, even in the face of opposition, without having to resort to retaliation.

The fertility and abundance of the patriarchal flocks had been well documented thus far (12:16; 13:2; 24:35; 26:14), and would continue to bless future generations (Jacob, 30:43; 32:5, 15; 36:7; and Jacob's sons, 34:28–29; 47:16–18). Isaac was wealthy and prosperous. No wonder he was being envied by those around his camp (26:14). The stage is now set for the second episode of this two-sided coin of Gen 26.

---

14. This is the third time the Genesis notes the blessing of a patriarch: 24:1, 35; 25:11; and here, in 26:12.

Then a series of well-diggings and "well-fightings" commence. The first is mentioned in 26:15; the wells dug by Abraham were stopped by the Philistines. Clearly the envy of the surrounding peoples was being manifested in these inimical actions that were intended to endanger Isaac and his people: no water meant no survival in the Near East. The well-stopping seemed to be a not-so-subtle attempt to drive Isaac off the land. In fact, Abimelech explicitly confesses to wanting Isaac to leave, "for you are too powerful for us" (28:16). Isaac complies and moves to the valley of Gerar (28:17).

The second round of digging occurs in 26:18–19, apparently reworking the wells of Abraham that the Philistines had stopped up, but that endeavor is also hindered, for a quarrel arises between the herdsmen of Gerar and those of Isaac (26:20): the well is named "Esek" ("contention").

The third round of digging is noted in 26:21, followed, as before, by a struggle over water rights. Notably the name given to this well in question was Sitnah (שִׂטְנָה, *sitnah*, "accusation/hostility," see Ezra 4:6), from the root that means "to oppose/be an adversary," and from which is derived the name "Satan" (שָׂטָן, *satan*, see Job 1:6).[15]

Finally, Isaac's men commence a fourth round of well-digging (26:22), but now Isaac had moved far enough away not to raise the contentious spirits of those in the region. The patriarch exclaims, "Now Yahweh has made room for us, and we will be fruitful in the land" (26:22)—the first time "fruitful" shows up in the Jacob narratives, and juxtaposed to "multiply" in the promise of God (26:24).[16]

This is an odd account, not because of the events described, but rather because of what Isaac did *not* do. He does not so much as lift a pinky in protest.[17] Isaac and his caravan had been acknowledged as "powerful" by no other than Abimelech (26:16)[18]; the narrator had affirmed that Isaac had "a great household" (26:14). Now if Isaac was anything like his father Abraham, who had raised a homegrown army of 318 soldiers with whom he successfully waged a few wars (Gen 14), he must not have been too shabby himself. Indeed, it appears that Abimelech was actually afraid of Isaac, as 26:29 later reveals.

All of this makes the reader wonder why Isaac took no action against the aggressors. Strangely enough, the only "action" he takes is to move and dig, move and dig, move and dig. In fact, Isaac's modus operandi appears to be to evacuate "from there" (שָׁם/מִשָּׁם, *sham/misham*, occur in 26:8, 17, 19, 22, 23, 25 [×2]). Move and dig, indeed! There are no threats, no reloading of weapons, no flash of steel. Just moving and digging.

---

15. When preaching this pericope, I have drawn attention to this fact as an effective move-to-relevance: adversaries in this world, those who oppose the children of God are sometimes, if not often, empowered by the adversary-in-chief, Satan himself.

16. For "fruitful and multiply" in Genesis, see 1:22, 28; 8:17; 9:1, 7; 17:20; 28:3; 35:11.

17. Perhaps Isaac's renaming of the wells with the same names that his father had given them (26:16) is a form of protest, albeit mild, against the injustice of the Philistines in stopping up those wells.

18. The description of Israel's growth to might in Egypt has the only other use of עָצַם (*atsom*, "power/might") in the Pentateuch (Exod 1:7, 20).

What is even more surprising is that this account follows one in which the patriarch was depicted as being afraid—the wife–sister episode of 26:1–11 (see especially 26:7). What had happened in the current well-digging/fighting episode? Where was Isaac's fear now? Apparently he had learnt his lesson from the first story: God was trustworthy and could be relied upon to protect and secure Isaac's blessings even from fierce opposition. Hence, Isaac refrains from retaliation. All he does is move and dig, move and dig, move and dig.

And every single one of Isaac's moves-and-digs are successful; he strikes water everywhere he goes. This is an extension of divine blessing noted in the previous episode: Isaac's "reaping" (מָצָא, *matsa'*, 26:12), as a result of Yahweh's blessing is reflected in the patriarch's "finding" (מצא, 26:19, 32) water wherever he digs—no doubt God's work. Explicitly recognizing the hand God in his successes ("Yahweh has made room for us," 26:22), the patriarch goes to Beersheba to worship (26:23–25), as his father had done in the past (12:7–8; 13:4, 18; 4:26). Here, in Beersheba, Yahweh appears to Isaac, reaffirming the blessings earlier promised, adding "Do not fear, for I am with you" (26:24). Indeed, Isaac, unlike in the prior episode, was not going to fear. There would be no deceptive maneuvers this time, or even defensive aggression by this "powerful" man with a "great household." Instead, with faith in the great God of his who had promised to be with him, Isaac simply moves and digs. This revelation from God in 26:24 is also notable for the self-introduction of Yahweh for the first time as the "God of your father Abraham." It emphasizes, unambiguously, the presence with Isaac of a personal God, and, in its placement, almost sounds like a reward for Isaac's trust and forbearance, akin to the post-test revelation experienced by Abraham in 22:16–18.[19]

Isaac, then, not only proceeds to worship in response to his successes and the second appearance of Yahweh ("building an altar and pitching a tent"[20]), he actually digs *yet another* well (26:25). But with this dig the reader is left in limbo as to the results, for suddenly, Abimelech, Ahuzzath, and Phicol arrive on the scene (26:26). The narrator makes us wait: Did Isaac strike water in Beersheba? Had Abimelech and his gang come up to fight over this well, too?

No, they had not come to fight. They had actually come to make peace, because "we see plainly that Yahweh has been with you" (26:28), and because "You are now blessed of Yahwh" (26:29). It was "plain," obvious, and self-evident: רָאוֹ רָאִינוּ (*ra'o ra'inu*, literally, "seeing, we see," i.e., "we see clearly/plainly"). The divine word of 26:3 (promising divine presence and divine blessing) is almost precisely echoed by the pagan ruler (26:28–29). And so the visitors were viewing themselves as the weaker side in this interaction. Ironically, while the presence of Yahweh had been assured Isaac in 26:3, it was not the *first* episode in Gen 26 that proved to Abimelech that Yahweh was with the patriarch; rather, it was Isaac's actions and the divine fruit of his trust in Yahweh in the *second* episode that demonstrated to his foes the fact of God's presence

---

19. There also the personal nature of the revelation was underscored in Yahweh's striking assertion: "By Myself, I have sworn, declares Yahweh. . . ."

20. "Altar" and "tent" show up together also in 12:8; 13:18, with Abraham doing the honors there.

with Isaac and the reality of God's blessing of Isaac. Interestingly, Abimelech's recognition that Yahweh has been with Isaac is a carefully staged assertion.

26:3	Yahweh: "I will be with you"	*Future*
26:24	Yahweh: "I am with you"	*Present*
26:28	Abimelech: Yahweh has been with you"	*Past*

The patriarch is ensconced by Yahweh's presence in the past, in the present, and in the future! There can be no occasion for doubt, fear, or hesitation. Subsequently, an oath is made and a covenant struck between the feuding parties (26:28–29). If that were not enough, Isaac even wines and dines his guests, his erstwhile opponents who the next day depart in "peace" (26:30–31).[21] One is reminded of Prov 16:7: "When a man's ways are pleasing to Yahweh, He makes even his enemies to be at peace with him."[22]

And then, finally, capping off the story, the reader is told of the results of the well-digging of 26:25: Isaac strikes water *again* (26:32–33). An appropriate ending, with Isaac blessed and triumphant! In other words, there is no need for retaliation against opponents when God can be trusted to keep his promises of blessing.

> Thus this account of Isaac's dealings with the Philistines portrays Isaac as very much walking in his father's footsteps. He receives similar promises, faces similar tests, fails similarly, but eventually triumphs in like fashion. Indeed, in certain respects he is given more in the promises and achieves more. He is promised "all these lands," and by the end of the story he is securely settled in Beersheba and has a treaty with the Philistines in which they acknowledge his superiority.[23]

All in all, this two-sided coin that Gen 26 is, crystallizes, in the two episodes from Isaac's life, what Jacob should be doing and how his attitude ought to be changing—indeed, this is not just for Jacob, but for all of God's children. The rest of the Jacob narratives depict the gradual transformation of the protagonist in this direction.

SERMON FOCUS AND OUTLINES

THEOLOGICAL FOCUS OF PERICOPE 16 FOR PREACHING

17 God's certain blessings render unnecessary any attempt to secure them by retaliation against opposition (26:1–33).

The role of this pericope in the Jacob narratives is now clear. With this two-storied pericope of Gen 26—a negative picture of Isaac's mistrust of Yahweh, followed by a positive picture of his trust—the narrator summarizes for the readers how Jacob *should have* behaved. But he does not: he deceives his brother for the blessing (see

---

21. In 26:29, Abimelech claimed—falsely (see 26:15–16, 27)—to have "sent" Isaac away "in peace" after the earlier exchange. But that peace comes to pass only now, in 26:31, when *Isaac* "sends" *them* away "in peace."

22. As well, Ps 37:3, 11, 39–40.

23. Wenham, *Genesis 16–50*, 196.

Pericope 18).[24] Jacob's change of attitude would come only later in Gen 32. Thus this pericope primes readers to acknowledge that God's promised blessings are sure and that the believer will surely not lose them, even in the face of opposition. Therefore, if there is no fear of loss of divine blessings, then all deceptive and retaliatory measures, undertaken to secure blessings for oneself, are precluded.

The question of what exactly the divine blessings are, that a believer today is promised, is one the preacher must answer. Clearly blessings from the hand of God include those of his presence, his love, and his grace: God's presence is assured to the believer ("I will never leave you, nor will I ever forsake you" [Heb 13:5]); his love is inseparable from the believer (". . . neither death, nor life, nor angels, nor [demonic] rulers, nor things present, nor things to come, nor powers, nor height, nor depth, nor anything created, will be able to separate us from the love of God that is in Christ Jesus our Lord" [Rom 8:38–39]); and his grace is sufficient for the believer ("My grace is sufficient for you" [2 Cor 12:9]). The specific shape and shade these blessings take in the life of particular individuals, of course, will vary, but the truth and reality of these (and other) blessings cannot be denied. The preacher would do well to focus on and list some of these NT blessings that are valid for the Christian in this age and in this life.[25]

Possible Preaching Outlines for Pericope 17

I. NEGATIVE Picture: Isaac's Fear, Mistrusting God
     The setting of the story—a flashback
     God's promised blessing; certainty of descendants (26:1–5)
     Isaac's fearful response, betraying a lack of trust in God (26:6–11)
     God's blessing upon Isaac, despite his mistrust (26:12–14)
     Move-to-Relevance: Our fears that stem from a lack of trust in God

II. *Remember God's promises!*
     Specific promises of God valid for the believer today and how to remember them constantly

III. POSITIVE Picture: Isaac's Response to Opposition—Move and Dig
      Opposition to Isaac and his surprising lack of response (26:14–21)
      Issac's recognition of God's hand in his successes; Isaac's worship; God's reaffirmation of blessing (26:22–25)
      Consequence of Isaac's trusting actions and his refusal to retaliate: peace . . . and more blessing (26:26–33)
      Move-to-Relevance: Our retaliatory instincts when opposed

IV. *Refrain from retaliation!*
      How to keep from retaliation, and even to reconcile with grace, as Isaac did.

Another outline may be created, with an added focus on the extension of grace by Isaac to his erstwhile adversaries.

I. GOD ENSURES: *Remember the promises!*
     God's promised blessing of Isaac (26:1–6)

24. While deception is also a part of this pericope, in order to keep this one and the next pericope distinct in terms of theological thrust, it will be best to focus in this sermon on "refraining from retaliation"—the focus of the second episode.

25. See Kuruvilla, *Privilege the Text!* 252–58, for the concept of blessings this side of eternity.

Isaac's fearful response, betraying a lack of trust in God (26:6–11)

Move-to-Relevance: Specific promises of God valid for the believer today

How to remember the promises of God constantly

II. WORLD ENVIES: *Refrain from retaliation!*

God's blessing of Isaac (26:12–14)

Opposition to Isaac and his surprising lack of response (26:14–21)

Isaac's recognition of God's hand in his successes; Isaac's worship; God's reaffirmation of blessing (26:22–25)

Move-to-Relevance: Our retaliatory instincts when opposed

How to keep from retaliation in the face of opposition.

III. ISAAC ENTRUSTS: *Reconcile with grace!*

Consequence of Isaac's trusting actions and his refusal to retaliate: peace . . . and more blessing (26:26–33)

Move-to-Relevance: Our refusal to extend gracious reconciliation to our enemies

Specific steps to gracious reconciliation

PERICOPE 18

Comminuted Community

Genesis 26:34–28:9

[Isaac and Esau *v.* Rebekah and Jacob]

REVIEW, SUMMARY, PREVIEW

Review of Pericope 17: Genesis 26:1–33 details Isaac's response to God's unequivocal promise of descendants and prosperity. The patriarch is first shown resorting to subterfuge rather than trusting God; then, in the face of opposition, he is depicted as a man of faith, believing that God will provide for him. God can be trusted to keep his promises of blessing.

Summary of Pericope 18: This pericope constitutes the extended account of the passing of the blessing of the firstborn to Jacob, who obtained it by deception. In fact, the narrative clearly portrays each of the actants as culpable—Isaac, Esau, Rebekah, and Jacob himself—all trying to divert/subvert divine blessings to directions and destinations of their own choices. The result of such a frenetic chase for blessing, with deception and manipulation, is catastrophic fragmentation of family/community.

Preview of Pericope 19: In the next pericope (Gen 28:10–22), Jacob, a fugitive, encounters God in a dream. The latter reaffirms to Jacob the patriarchal promise, upon which Jacob, rather impertinently, sets conditions upon God for his trust. God's guaranteed promises should rather have impelled Jacob to worship unconditionally, even before the fulfillment of those divine promises.

18. *Genesis 26:34–28:9*

THEOLOGICAL FOCUS OF PERICOPE 18

18   **God's sovereign securing of one's blessings can be trusted, without having to resort to deception to obtain them, an enterprise that only results in catastrophic fragmentation of the community (26:34–28:9).**

    18.1   God's sovereign securing of one's divine blessings can be trusted, without having to resort to manipulation and deception to obtain them (26:34–27:40).

    18.2   The consequence of deception and guile to obtain divine blessing is catastrophic fragmentation of the community (27:41–28:9).

OVERVIEW

As was noted in Pericope 17, Gen 26:34–35 begins this pericope and 28:8–9 concludes it; thereby the pericope, 26:34–28:9, is bounded on either side by the marital exploits of Esau. The unannounced and abrupt appearance of Esau in 26:34, with the narrative beginning with וַיְהִי (*wayhi*, "and it happened"), signifies a break from what precedes. And 28:10 commences a new pericope with both a shift in characters (Esau to Jacob) and in geography (from Beersheba to Haran).[1] Within the palistrophic structure of the Jacob narratives (for which, see Pericope 16), 26:34–28:9 parallels 33:1–17 in a number of ways: one deals with the flight from Canaan, and the other the return to Canaan; the blessing is stolen in one, returned in the other (27:12, 35, 36, 38, 41; 28:4; and 33:11); "kiss" (27:26, 27; and 33:4); בּוֹא (*bo'*, "bring"; Hiphil in 27:10, 14; and Hophal in 33:11); "come near" (27:21, 22, 25, 26, 27; and 33:6, 7); שָׂעִיר (*sa'ir*, "hairy," 27:23; and, שֵׂעִיר, *se'ir*, "Seir," 33:14, 16); "multiply" (27:28; and 33:9); "bowing" and "neck" (27:29, 40; and 33:3, 4); "times" (27:36; and 33:3); "wept" (27:38; and 33:4).

This narrative is, like many others in Genesis, carefully structured, even to the extent of balancing the actants chiastically in the individual scenes. It will be immediately noted that in no scene do more than two members of this dysfunctional and disharmonious family appear together. There is community fragmentation in the very layout of the pericope![2]

---

1. Wenham notes that the Jewish lectionary begins a new reading at 28:10 (*Genesis 16–50*, 202).

2. Moreover, "Isaac and Jacob" appear in the blessing scene together *before* "Isaac and Esau"—the supplanting of the older by the younger is literarily portrayed (E and E'). The focus here on family dynamics is sustained by no less than sixty-seven references to familial relationships in this pericope (Vrolijk, *Jacob's Wealth*, 83). The table below is modified from Fokkelman, *Narrative Art in Genesis*, 98, 102; and Cotter, *Genesis*, 197. Rebekah in 27:5 (C) appears to be off the scene, but overhears Isaac. This verse begins a new scene with a disjunctive clause ("And Rebekah listened"; conjunction + subject + verb), lending it the status of a discrete scene with a newly introduced actant.

SCENES					ACTANTS
A	Esau's Hittite wives (**26:34–35**)				Esau
	B	Isaac + son of the בכרה/ברכה (*brkh/bkrh*) [Esau]; "calls" Esau, 27:1 (**27:1–4**)			Isaac and Esau
		C	Rebekah (and Isaac?) (27:5)		Rebekah (and Isaac?)
			D	Rebekah sends Jacob onstage, after hearing …, 27:6 (**27:6–17**); "Esau, her elder son," and "Jacob, her younger son," 27:15; "obey my voice," 27:8, 13	Rebekah and Jacob
				E	Jacob appears before Isaac, receives blessing (**27:18–29**); "'Who are you?'" 27:18; "Get up," "eat of game," "that your soul may bless me," 27:19	Isaac and Jacob
				E'	Esau appears before Isaac, receives "anti-blessing" (**27:30–41**); "'Who are you?'" 27:32; "Get up," "eat of game," "that your soul may bless me," 27:31	Isaac and Esau
			D'	Rebekah sends Jacob offstage, after hearing …, 27:42 (**27:41–45**); "Esau, her elder son," and "Jacob, her younger son" 27:42; "obey my voice," 27:43	Rebekah and Jacob
		C'	Rebekah and Isaac (**27:46**)		Rebekah and Isaac
	B'	Isaac + son of the בכרה/ברכה (*brkh/bkrh*) [Jacob]; "calls" Jacob, 28:1 (**28:1–5**)			Isaac and Jacob
A'	Esau's Ishmaelite wives (**28:6–9**)				Esau

The pericope is peppered with "bless/blessing"—ברך (*brk*, twenty-one times) and ברכה (*brkh*, seven times).[3] While the "birthright" concerns inheritance obtained from the father, "blessing" attends to the future situation and circumstances projected by the blessor.[4] This involves invoking and passing on the divine promises to the family mediated through Abraham (land, descendants, nationhood), as well as promises of prosperity of all kinds and in various spheres—progeny, property, politics—both personal and communal. Of course, "[t]he larger issue at stake in these divine choices is a universal one: the reclamation of the entire creation in view of sin and its deleterious effects upon life."[5] Slowly, but surely, that reclamation is taking place. Yet, strikingly, God himself is absent in this pericope as an actant. In fact, the only references to deity are in Jacob's sacrilegious attribution of his pseudo-hunting success to Yahweh (27:20) and in Isaac's blessing of Jacob (27:27–28 and 28:3–4). This is surprising, after the divine revelations in prior pericopes of Gen 25 and 26, and that in the following

3. As a verb (ברך): 27:4, 7, 10, 19, 23, 25, 27 (×2), 29 (×2), 30, 31, 33 (×2), 34, 38, 41; 28:1, 3, 6 (×2); and as a noun (ברכה): 27:12, 35, 36 (×2), 38, 41; 28:4.

4. Mathews, *Genesis 11:27–50:26*, 418.

5. Fretheim, "Which Blessing?" 281–82.

pericope, Gen 28. Nonetheless, one does sense the sovereignty and control of God amidst the humanly contrived and muddled situations.

18.1 Genesis 26:34–27:40

THEOLOGICAL FOCUS 18.1

18.1   God's sovereign securing of one's divine blessings can be trusted, without having to resort to manipulation and deception to obtain them (26:34–27:40).

NOTES 18.1

18.1   God's sovereign securing of one's divine blessings can be trusted, without having to resort to manipulation and deception to obtain them.[6]

Each of the four family members in this episode are culpable; each in his/her own way is manipulating others, engaging in machinations to direct divine blessings into the direction he/she wants.

Isaac's culpability is clear. Isaac was sixty when the twins were born (25:26), and he was hundred when Esau took Hittite wives (26:34). About that time, he claims to Esau that he is about to die (27:2). This was a man not thinking reasonably, certainly not about his own health status, for it turns out that "old" Isaac who thought he was on his deathbed (27:1–2) would survive at least another two decades, possibly more (31:41; 35:28).[7] Did he really need to undertake such a precipitous and unmindful blessing so many years before his demise? In any case, if 27:1–40 is a type scene of a death-bed blessing (as are Gen 48–49; 50:24–25; Deut 31–34; Josh 23–24; 1 Kgs 2:1–9), Isaac's summoning of only one of his two sons, Esau, is a major *faux pas*, especially since they were twins.[8] Isaac, more than likely aware of the oracle received by Rebekah in Gen 25:23, as well as of the sale of the birthright in that chapter, ought not to have sought to bless Esau; certainly not in the absence of the other son.[9] Moreover, the one Isaac had chosen to bless was one who had little concern for endogamy or monogamy (see below) and who had thereby caused his parents grief (25:34–35). The strong parallels between the divine blessing to Abraham in 12:2–3 and the blessing Isaac gives to Jacob in 27:26–29 suggests that that was Isaac's goal all along—to bestow

6. This Theological Focus is stated in the positive; all of the participants in this episode—Isaac, Rebekah, Esau, and Jacob—individually portray a negative picture, one of mistrust in God.

7. If Esau was 40 around the time of this episode (26:34), Isaac was then 100. He would die only at 180 (35:28).

8. Wenham, *Genesis 16–50*, 203.

9. Isaac's awareness of that earlier oracle is betrayed in the blessing he bestows upon Jacob in 27:27–29 that is linked to the oracle to Rebekah in 25:23: "nations/peoples" (לְאֹם, *l'om*) shows up only there and in 27:29 in the Pentateuch; "serve" also occurs in both passages; and the concept of lording over brothers (27:29) was introduced in 25:23.

the Abrahamic blessing upon Esau. Thus "Isaac has . . . failed to do what is expected of him as the patriarch."[10]

The editorial aside in 26:34 that Esau was forty years old is also telling. Abraham had gotten his son a bride when Isaac was forty (25:20 with Gen 24). Perhaps some finger-pointing at Isaac is going on here, for his shirking his responsibility to find his sons brides. Rather than send them to obtain spouses, Isaac sent Esau out into the Canaanite land to hunt for game to cook up a "savory dish such as I love," "so that my soul may bless you before I die" (27:3–4). Rebekah, in response, sent Jacob to the flock to obtain kids for food "savory dish . . . such as he loves" for the same reason—"so that he may bless you before his death" (27:9–10). There is a hint of disparagement at Isaac's culpability for Esau's endogamy, not to mention a lampooning of the patriarch's sensual appetites.[11] No doubt, that is why Isaac's eating and his blessing are juxtaposed frequently: 27:4, 7, 10, 19, 25, 31, 33. The six times "savory food" (מַטְעַמִּים, *mat'am*) is repeated—27:4, 7, 9, 14, 17, 31, its only occurrences in the Pentateuch—and its qualification three times by "such as I/he loves," 27:4, 9, 14, sounds like a pungent rebuke of the patriarch's passions. The only other instances of מַטְעַמִּים are in Prov 23:3, 6, both times with less than wholesome overtones. Everything that Isaac does in this pericope seems to be tied to his love of food. "Isaac's sensuality is more powerful than his theology," and reflects "the old man's bondage to his appetite."[12] Apparently, father and older son are very much alike, both given to indulging in their gastronomic passions. "The son despises his birthright for a good meal (25:29–34), and the father, who loves this son because he eats of his game, blesses for a good meal."[13] Both father and son put "appetite before principle, self-indulgence before justice, immediate satisfaction before long-term spiritual values."[14] And the intensity of Isaac's blessing is noted in his desire to have his "soul" bless the recipient (27:4, 25), and in the recognition by the recipients, themselves, of the blessing as coming from Isaac's "soul" (27:19, Jacob; and 27:31, Esau).[15]

10. Smith, "Reinstating Isaac," 132.

11. Kass, *The Beginning of Wisdom*, 392n15.

12. Wenham, *Genesis 16–50*, 206.

13. Sylva, "The Blessing," 270n5.

14. Wenham, *Genesis 16–50*, 215. Fishbane notes a case of "quadruple repetition," that serves to underscore the significance of Isaac's appetites. What the patriarch had instructed Isaac, regarding the serving of game so that his soul might bless the son (27:3–4) is repeated by Rebekah to Jacob (27:6–7), by Jacob to Isaac (27:19), and by Esau to Isaac (27:31); in fact it might actually be *quintuple* repetition, if one adds Isaac's echoing of a modified version of the statement in 27:33. See Fishbane, *Biblical Text and Texture*, 50.

15. Sylva, "The Blessing," 274, 275–76, 279. Isaac's blessing in 27:27–29 is an unusual blessing as far as patriarchal blessings go, for there is no mention of the common motifs of numerous progeny, gifting of land, blessing to nations, etc. (descendants and property do show up in Isaac's blessing of Jacob later in 28:3–4). God's blessing (28:10–15), following right after Isaac's (27:28–29; 28:3–4), and including items not mentioned by Isaac (land, divine presence, blessing—via Jacob and his seed—to all earthly families, and multiplication of descendants), was perhaps a hint that Isaac's words were not congruent with God's. Neither is there any mention of Yahweh in Isaac's blessing, or of the first patriarch, Abraham. Isaac's pronouncement (27:29ef) also reverses the order of blessing followed by cursing that is found in 12:3.

All of Isaac's senses in this episode are defective or untrustworthy: sight (he is noted to be blind, 27:1); touch (he grossly mistakes goatskin for human skin, 27:16, 21, 23[16]); smell (he does not recognize the difference between the smell of Esau's garments and the actual wearer thereof, 27:15, 27); taste (he is incapable of discriminating between venison, which he loves and asks Esau for [25:28; 27:3, 5, 7, 19, 25, 31, 33], and mutton which was prepared and served to him by Rebekah and Jacob [27:9, 14, 25]); and, of course, hearing (he seems to able to distinguish between the voices of his two children, but is unable to convince himself about who is who, [27:22])!

Five times the patriarchal blessing is connected to families or nations of the earth through the agency of one in the Abrahamic line (12:3; 18:18; 22:18; 26:4; 28:14). Three of those times, the blessing is mediated through a particular patriarch: twice, via Abraham (12:3; 18:18), and once through Jacob (28:14). Isaac is never explicitly seen as an agent of blessing—he is only indirectly mentioned (22:18, where the blessing is mediated by Abraham's "descendant," and in 26:4, where Isaac's descendants are the agents). Moreover, these two indirect notices of Isaac's role are lexically different from the other predictions. In 12:3; 18:18; and 28:14, the Niphal of ברך is used: people will be blessed through Abraham, Jacob, and his descendants (the passive meaning of the verb; see Pericope 7). In 22:18 and 26:4, where Isaac is indirectly mentioned as being the mediator of blessing, the Hithpael of ברך unambiguously sees this as the nations blessing themselves by Abraham's and Isaac's descendants, respectively. Though Isaac is clearly a recipient of divine blessing, "[h]e is just not one of the major instruments in passing it on."[17] That is quite an indictment! And after his various speeches in this pericope, Isaac speaks no more in Scripture.

What is also intriguing is the seemingly comprehensive listing of Isaac's "loves": Isaac loves Rebekah (24:67); Isaac loves Esau (25:28); and Isaac loves his stew (27:4, 9, 14). Conspicuously absent from the objects of his love is Jacob—about the only thing Isaac is not said to love. Not that Rebekah is any better in parental loyalty. While Esau is pointedly called "his [Isaac's] son," 27:5, Jacob is labeled "her [Rebekah's] son," 27:6, 17. Each parent seems to have had his/her favorite: Isaac always refers to Esau (or to Jacob who he thinks is Esau) as "my son"— 27:1, 18, 20, 21, 24, 25, 26, 27, 37; Jacob is never acknowledged as such by Isaac, but only "he," "your brother," or "your lord" (27:33, 35, 37). Rebekah, on the other hand, labels Jacob as "my son" (27:8, 13, 43). Of course, the reader had been warned of this partiality: 25:28 informed us that Isaac loved Esau, and that Rebekah loved Jacob. All of this has riven the family asunder.

Rebekah's culpability is no less significant than Isaac's; her injection of herself and her deceptive stratagems into matters of inheritance and marriage was a violation of cultural norms.[18] That her initiative in this episode is unique is signified by the only use of the feminine participle of צָוָה (*tsawah*, "command") in the entire OT, in

16. Even Isaac's bidding his son (Jacob) to come close and kiss him (27:21–22, 26–27)—a modality of touch—does not seem to be generated out of any obvious affection; rather it seems to serve a diagnostic purpose: Was this son really Esau?

17. Ibid., 281.

18. Smith, "Reinstating Isaac," 132.

reference to Rebekah "commanding" her son (27:8). Her charge to her son in 27:8–13 is bounded by "listen/obey" (27:8, 13; and later, in 27:43). Rebekah is doubtless the dynamo behind the deception of Isaac; she does everything (27:14–17), while Jacob gets a mere three verbs in this paragraph that describes the preparatory action: "so he went, and he got, and he brought" (27:14). Since neither curses nor blessings are transferrable (Esau could not get what was due him, which had already been passed to Jacob), Rebekah's "Your curse [be] upon me" (27:13) simply expressed the intensity of her intention, just as Isaac's blessing from his "soul" expressed the intensity of his (27:4).[19] Both father and mother are aggressively pursuing their inclinations. Besides, Rebekah does not hesitate to use "Yahweh" for her own purposes, introducing him into her report to Jacob of what Isaac had said (27:7; though there was no mention of Yahweh in Isaac's speech in 27:2–4).[20] There may have been some justification for her crafty scheming, seeing that her husband, Isaac, was not being aboveboard himself. But that was no excuse for perpetrating another fraud, and that upon an old, blind, and perhaps dying, man, even if it was to facilitate what God had decreed would happen (25:3). As the story of Abraham taught plainly, God is in no need of human help, especially not the felonious and perfidious kind!

Notwithstanding Isaac's failure to see Esau married off appropriately, Esau's own culpability remains. His decision to marry two women in the same year (26:34), suggests that he had not curbed his instinct for instant gratification. It may well also be that Esau gave scant regard to the family tradition of marrying endogamously, thus bringing about "bitterness of spirit to Isaac and Rebekah" with his illicit unions (26:35).[21] Esau's mistakes are thus multiplied: he apparently contracts the marriages on his own initiative disregarding parental opinion, he opts for exogamy, and he prefers polygamy. Rebekah confesses later that she "loathes" living, because of the "daughters of Heth"—she does not deign to call them "wives of Esau" (27:46). So after discovering that his earlier marriages had displeased his *father* (28:8–9; no mention here about the grief he brought to his mother: 26:35; 27:46), he seeks to correct matters and marries a distant relative. "In this last-minute ploy by Esau to redeem himself, to some degree at least, before his father dies, he fails. The marriage goes unnoticed by Isaac. Esau may now have three wives (two Hittite, one Ishmaelite), but he also has three family members (father, mother, brother) who have succeeded in marginalizing him."[22]

Jacob's culpability needs no expatiation. When apprised of his mother's intrigues, the morality of the transaction is not an issue for him at all. Rather, he is afraid he will be found out and labeled a deceiver, מְתַעְתֵּעַ (*mta'tea'*, 27:11–12). This rather strong word, elsewhere used only in 2 Chr 32:16 for the "mockers" of prophets, was certainly

19. And this makes Rebekah the first person to offer herself up as the subject of a curse delivered on another (Hamilton, *Genesis: Chapters 18–50*, 216–17).

20. As a chip off the old block, Jacob, too, bandies the name of Yahweh to achieve his own duplicitous ends (27:20).

21. Prohibitions against marrying Canaanites are found in: Deut 7:3–4; 1 Kgs 11:2; Ezra 9:12; Neh 13:25.

22. Hamilton, *Genesis: Chapters 18–50*, 236.

appropriate for the "mocking" of an aged and blind father by a son.[23] He acknowledges, perhaps unwittingly, that he is a "smooth" man (27:11); as in English, the adjective has connotations of deceptive speech (Pss 5:10; 12:3–4; Prov 2:16; 5:3; etc.).[24] Jacob's participation in his mother's scheme is quick and efficient (as was noted): he went, he got, he brought (referring to the animals; 27:14).

Jacob subsequently lies twice, in 27:19, 24: he is neither Esau, nor the firstborn, as he claimed to Isaac. In the process, Jacob also takes the name of Yahweh in vain: "Yahweh, your God, caused it to happen to me" (27:20), as he explains to Isaac the reason for the swift success of his "hunt"—"an appeal to deity in order to cover up duplicity."[25] And all this while embracing his father (27:26–27): "The poignancy of a parting kiss accents the despicable character of the son's treachery against his pitiable father."[26] The "deceit" (מִרְמָה, *mrmh*, 27:35) of Jacob, as accused by Isaac, indicates deliberate planning (29:25; 34:13), as the account plainly shows. This was not a spur-of-the-moment sleight of hand; this was unconscionable and inexcusable.[27] The pun on Jacob's name is also pungent: the one named "Jacob" (יַעֲקֹב, *ya'aqob*) "supplanted" (עָקַב, *'aqab*) his brother (27:36).

In 27:30, Jacob's going out and Esau's coming in are structured chiastically:

> went-out
> Jacob
> ...
> and-Esau, his-brother,
> came-in

Once it was Esau who had "come out" first, following whom Jacob "came out" (יָצָא, *yatsa'*, 25:25, 26). Now it is Jacob's turn to "come out" (יָצָא, 27:30); Esau comes in *after* Jacob. "The first round [exiting the womb, 25:25–26] Jacob had lost, but now he has won the second [obtaining the birthright, 25:19–34] and the third rounds [purloining the blessing, 27:1–29]. . . . The tables have been turned—again!"[28] Deception accomplished! The parallels between Esau's words and Jacob's depict the fraudulent reversal starkly:

---

23. See the stricture against deceiving the deaf and blind in Lev 19:14, and the curse pronounced on those who do so, Deut 27:16, 18.

24. The cover-up employing clothing is also significant. White observes that clothing motifs are "virtually never mentioned" in Genesis, except when employed "as a sign of a hidden inner state," or when "it serves to deceive"—3:7, 20; 37:3–4; 37:31–33; 38:14–15; 39:13, 15 (*Narration and Discourse*, 220).

25. Hamilton, *Genesis: Chapters 18–50*, 220. Hamilton goes on to note that Lev 6:3 describes a thief compounding his guilt by swearing falsely about his innocence upon the name of God (ibid.).

26. Mathews, *Genesis 11:27–50:26*, 431.

27. The attempt by the Targums to rehabilitate Jacob is singularly unsuccessful; they all have for 27:35: "Your brother came with wisdom (חכמתא, *khkmt'*)," rather than "deceit" (מרמה). This "deceit" would literally and literarily come back later to haunt Jacob the perpetrator. See Pericope 20 (on Gen 29:1–30).

28. Fokkelman, *Narrative Art in Genesis*, 103.

Jacob:	"I am Esau your firstborn ...;
	get up ... and eat of my game,
	so that your soul may bless me" (27:19)
Esau:	"I am your firstborn son, Esau";
	"let my father get up and eat of his son's game,
	so that your soul may bless me" (27:31–32)

Thus each of the four members of the family contributes significantly to the dysfunction that escalates, finally tearing the community apart. Rather than trust God to disburse his blessings sovereignly to his people, each one in this pericope is conspiring against and cheating others. Each one has his/her own ideas as to whom divine blessings should go, and how, and when. And the result is chaos!

However, needless to say, God's sovereign purposes do come to pass, despite the whims and fancies of man. Isaac may have been attempting to change the prediction of the oracle—his own synopsis of his first blessing to Jacob, in 27:27–29, indicates its main thrust: the recipient (presumably Esau) will rule over the other sibling who will serve (presumably Jacob; "serve," עָבַד [*'abad*], was exactly what the oracle had predicted Esau would do [25:23]). The irony, of course, is that "in this way he [Isaac] performs unconsciously the plans of Providence, which wanted to turn the relationship between older-younger upside down. By ignoring God's will he performs it . . . !"[29] God's way and will cannot be thwarted.

While the pathos of 27:30–40, when Esau returns home with his game, expecting to be blessed by his father, is poignant and powerful, the thrust of the scene is the irrevocability of the blessing: Jacob *would* remain the recipient of the blessing, no matter what (27:33—"He will indeed be blessed!"). Emphasizing this, quite unusually, the direct object precedes the verb three times, as Isaac describes to Esau the blessing he had given Jacob (27:37):

Direct object	1st person perfect verb
master	I-have-made-him (to you)
and-all-his-brothers	I-have-given (to him)
and-(with)-grain and-new-wine	I-have-sustained-him

God's plans always come to pass, no matter what.

18.2 Genesis 27:41–28:9

THEOLOGICAL FOCUS 18.2

18.2   The consequence of deception and guile to obtain divine blessing is catastrophic fragmentation of the community (27:41–28:9).

29. Ibid., 111.

NOTES 18.2

18.2 *The consequence of deception and guile to obtain divine blessing is catastrophic fragmentation of the community.*

Isaac's reaction, when he realized how he had been deceived by Jacob, is emotional and torturous (27:33). And as Esau realizes what has happened, he responds in parallel (27:34):

	Verb	Cognate noun + Superlative adjective	Prepositional phrase
27:33	"he-trembled, Isaac,	[a] tremble great,	exceedingly"
27:34	"he-cried	[a] cry great, and-bitter,	exceedingly"

There is probably no way of expressing more powerfully, in the Hebrew, the anguish of both the victims of Jacob's treachery. The consequences of deception are terrible! Esau's reaction is packed with irony: his "crying" (צָעַק, *tsa'aq*) and his "cry" (צְעָקָה, *ts'aqah*, 27:34) are wordplays on the name "Isaac" (יִצְחָק, *yitskhaq*, "he laughs"). "The son of 'He Laughs' shrieks in anguish over his father's unwitting casting him aside."[30] And the irony of the "bitterness" (27:34) of Esau's cry is that earlier, he himself was the cause of "bitterness" to his parents (26:35). Esau's complaint (27:36) is developed chiastically, with the anagrams בכרה and ברכה (*bkrh* and *brkh*, "birthright" and "blessing"), emphasizing all that he had lost.

> my birthright (בכרה)
> he took
>
> ...
>
> he took
> my blessing (ברכה)

And the negative consequences keep building up. The first line of Isaac's blessing to Esau (27:39) has a double innuendo. Superficially, it is identical to Isaac's blessing to Jacob (27:28), but in reverse order:

To Jacob (27:28a)	from the dew of the heavens and from the fatness of the earth
To Esau (27:39b)	[away] from the fatness of the earth and [away] from the dew of the heavens

Considering the context, and the subsequent stationing of the descendants of Esau in Edom, an arid terrain, Isaac's "blessing" of Esau may be considered as: "*away from* [reading the preposition מִן, *min*, in a privative sense] the fatness of the earth shall be your dwelling, and *away from* [מִן] the dew of heaven"—an "anti-blessing," if you will. The chiastic reversal of Esau's blessing also seems to substantiate the contrariness

---

30. Kass, *The Beginning of Wisdom*, 396n22.

with Jacob's blessing.[31] A tragic loss! In any case, Esau (and his descendants) would "live by the sword," militant and hostile, particularly in relationship with Jacob (and his descendants). There was acrimony and hatred between the two individuals, signified by the strong verb שָׂטַם, *satam*, the homicidal grudge borne by Esau against Jacob (27:41).[32] Not only did Esau threaten to murder Jacob after the demise of Isaac—a fratricide, after the manner of Cain—but antagonism would mark the relationship between Edom and Israel into the future (Num 20:18; 1 Sam 14:47; 1 Kgs 11:14–16; 2 Kgs 14:7, 10; Amos 1:11; Obad 1–21). The "restlessness" and "breaking off his [Jacob's] yoke from your neck" would come to pass when Edom detached itself from Israelite control (2 Kgs 8:20–22). The disastrous repercussions of the deception in this pericope would thus last many centuries.

The ramifications of the domestic chaos also affect the schemer-in-chief. Fearing for the life of "her son," Jacob, Rebekah plots to have him sent away to her brother, Laban, in Paddan-Aram (27:41–28:5). "Why should I be bereaved of both [sons] in one day?" she asks rhetorically (27:45).[33] Little did she know how true her utterance was. She had already lost Esau—who was not "her son" in this account; she would now lose Jacob as well. She thought Esau's anger would subside quickly and that he would forget Jacob's deception; she figured that she could then "send and take you from there [Paddan-Aram]" (27:45), where Jacob might stay for "a few days" (27:44). *A few days!* It would be a few *decades* (twenty years, 31:38, 41) before "her son" would return to Canaan.[34] And by then Rebekah would be dead: she would never to see "her son" again! This would be her last appearance in Genesis. "So the career of the woman whose bright start promised to make her the female equivalent of Abraham [see Pericope 15] eventually ends in shadow."[35] Deception only leads to catastrophe.

One cannot but also be struck with what Rebekah says to Jacob: ". . . until he [Esau] forgets what *you* did to him" (27:45). The blame for everything is on Jacob; Rebekah, cleverly, seems to be keeping her own machinations under cover, even as she schemes once again, this time to send Jacob away. To this second round of plotting, Jacob has nothing to say. The entire account makes Jacob a "fleer" (27:43), a recurrent theme in his life (31:20, 21, 22, 27; 35:1, 7)—all a consequence of his striving to get divine blessing his own way, in his own time, rather than trusting God to fulfill his promises.

Later on, as we find out, Jacob is himself deceived (Leah, the older daughter, is given to him as bride, instead of Rachel, the younger). Leah and her children are never Jacob's favorites and the constant state of tension between father and non-favored children casts a dark shadow over the rest of Jacob's life, spent, for the most part,

---

31. It is likely, of course, that Esau heard his father's pronouncements in a positive sense.

32. Hamilton, *Genesis: Chapters 18–50*, 229n1, notes that that root שָׂטַם is a by-form of שָׂטַן, *stn*, the root from which "Satan" is derived (the same stem is employed in 26:21).

33. This echoes her earlier cry in 25:22, again raised by the specter of her twins locked in combat.

34. In a corresponding event of irony, Jacob's twenty-year sojourn away from home, a consequence of his deception by Laban, would seem to Jacob like "a few days" (29:20).

35. Wenham, *Genesis 16–50*, 212.

grieving over the "loss" of a favored son, Joseph. Nobody wins in a back-stabbing, heel-grabbing environment. The consequences are dreadful and community is splintered, fragmented, shattered. The fact that the entire pericope is structured without having more than two family members together in any scene is evidence of what had transpired and is a warning to readers of what might happen if deception is chosen as the basic strategy of interpersonal relationships.

Despite all the dodges and deceit practiced by the actants, despite the wiles and webs spun to further individual agendas in this narrative, God's sovereign design always comes to pass, as exemplified in the second blessing that Isaac gives Jacob—it is virtually a recapitulation and recasting of the Abrahamic promises (12:2–3, 7; 13:15, 17; 15:7–8, 18; 17:1, 6, 8, 16, 20; 22:17; 24:7).[36] God's choice was Jacob, and Jacob it would be, who would inherit the "blessing of Abraham" (28:4). The certainty of this election is also phonetically sounded in the repetitive chain of second-person ך/כ (k/ka)-suffixes in 28:3–4, all pointing to Jacob: יְבָרֵךְ אֹתְךָ (ybarek 'otka, "may He bless you"), יַפְרְךָ (yafrka, "may He make you fruitful"), יַרְבֶּךָ (yarbeka, "may He multiply you"), וְיִתֶּן־לְךָ (wyitten-lka, "may He give you"), לְךָ (lka, "to you"), וּלְזַרְעֲךָ (ulzar'aka, "and to your seed"), אִתָּךְ ('ittak, "with you"), לְרִשְׁתְּךָ (lrishtka, "that you may possess"), מְגֻרֶיךָ (mgureka, "of your sojournings").[37] Thus, despite, the silence of God in this pericope (he does not speak directly), his sovereign hand is obvious as things come to pass as he had decreed in the oracle of 25:23.

SERMON FOCUS AND OUTLINES

THEOLOGICAL FOCUS OF PERICOPE 18 FOR PREACHING

18   Deception to obtain divine blessing, rather than trusting God to secure them, only results in catastrophic fragmentation of the community (26:34–28:9).

This rather lengthy pericope is best preached in one sermon. The narrative hangs together quite well. Its familiarity to churchgoers everywhere also lends itself to such a handling. Here too, as in the previous pericope, the emphasis is upon trusting God who promises blessings. But the facet on display for readers is the negative consequences that erupt when deceit and guile take over, dismembering the community, as members plot and pit themselves against each other. Not only is it dangerous to want what others have been blessed with (the thrust of Pericope 16), it is equally, if not more, disastrous when manipulation and machination become the currency of interpersonal interaction, as in the case of this dysfunctional family—Isaac, Rebekah,

---

36. The connection with the Abrahamic promises are reinforced: this is the second occurrence of "El Shaddai" (28:3); the first was in God's self-revelation to Abraham in 17:1. After 28:3, the next instance of this divine name would be a self-revelation to Jacob in 35:11. "Land of your sojournings" (28:4) also first occurred in the promise to Abraham (17:8); likewise, 28:3 has "company of peoples" (קְהַל עַמִּים, qahal 'ammim), corresponding to the "multitude of nations" (הֲמוֹן גּוֹיִם, hamon goyim) in 17:3. Incidentally, this is also the only time Isaac explicitly mentions "Abraham," and that twice; his last word in Scripture is thus his father's name.

37. Fokkelman, *Narrative Art in Genesis*, 108.

Esau, and Jacob. Each one turns out to be culpable and the net result is predictable: the community fragments. The preacher must keep the thrust of this sermon distinct from that of Pericope 20 (29:1–30) that deals with Jacob being disciplined for his duplicity. There the focus is best kept upon repentance for *past* misdeeds; here the sermon seeks to prevent *future* misdeeds. The emphasis in this pericope on the tragic consequences of deception for the community also differs from that in Pericope 20: there the consequences are more personal (one reaps what one sows).

Possible Preaching Outlines for Pericope 18

I. CONSPIRACY: Culpability of Family
    Culpability of all involved: Isaac, Rebekah, Esau, and Jacob deceiving one another
    (27:1–40)
    God's sovereignty brings about his will (25:23; 27:27–29)
    Move-to-Relevance: How, in our mistrust of God, we end up cheating one another

II. CONSEQUENCE: Fragmentation of Community
    Disaster for all involved: Isaac, Rebekah, Esau, and Jacob suffer serious consequences
    (27:41–28:9)
    God continues to be sovereign (28:3–4)
    Move-to-Relevance: The consequences for our communities, when we fail to trust God
    and instead deceive

III. *Displace duplicity!*
    Specifics on how to keep from deception, trusting God, and thus save the community
    from disintegration

One could, of course, preach this pericope character by character. For those imaginative enough, perhaps the second outline for this pericope may spark ideas about a creative display of the culpability of, and consequence to, each character sequentially. Perhaps a drama team could be organized to lay out the first four points (either discretely or by an integration of points I–IV), with the preacher taking over in point V, for the application.[38]

I. Isaac's Culpability and Consequence
    Isaac's culpability: failure to provide a bride for Esau, passions, senses, love, blessing
    Isaac's consequence: anguish, loss of son

II. Rebekah's Culpability and Consequence
    Rebekah's culpability: aggressive initiative, misplaced intent to "help" God's oracle along
    Rebekah's consequence: loss of son forever

III. Esau's Culpability and Consequence
    Esau's culpability: marriages, disregard for parents and tradition
    Esau's consequence: loss of blessing, development of homicidal tendencies

IV. Jacob's Culpability and Consequence
    Jacob's culpability: deception, invoking God in evil
    Jacob's consequence: the life of a "fleer"

---

38. There is no reason the burden of a sermon cannot be shared by more than a single individual. While a one-person sermon facilitates unity of thought, efficiency of preparation, and cohesiveness of presentation—and, no doubt, a shepherd of the flock is the one best suited to preach—on occasion, a careful division of responsibilities as suggested above can be quite effective.

V. *Displace duplicity!*

Our culpability: How, in our mistrust of God, we end up cheating one another
Our consequence: When we fail to trust God and instead deceive, community is fractured
Specifics on how to keep from deception, trusting God, and thus save the community
from disintegration

PERICOPE 19

Bargaining with God

Genesis 28:10–22

[Jacob's Fleeing; God's Promises; Jacob's Response]

REVIEW, SUMMARY, PREVIEW

Review of Pericope 18: Genesis 26:34–28:9 constitutes the extended account of the stealing of the blessing of the firstborn by Jacob, with all of the actants in the story guilty of trying to divert divine blessings for their own purposes. The result of such manipulation is fragmentation of family and community.

Summary of Pericope 19: Here Jacob, escaping from his brother and on his way to Paddan-Aram, encounters God in a dream. The latter reaffirms to Jacob the patriarchal promise, whereupon Jacob, rather impertinently, sets conditions upon God. God's guaranteed promises should, instead, have impelled him to worship unconditionally, even before the fulfillment of those promises.

Preview of Pericope 20: The next pericope (29:1–30) has Jacob arriving at his uncle's house in Paddan-Aram, and working for seven years for the hand of Rachel. Laban, his uncle, deceives him by substituting the older Leah for the younger Rachel—Jacob receives his just deserts. Discipline for misdeeds is a distinct possibility for God's people in God's economy.

19. *Genesis 28:10–22*

THEOLOGICAL FOCUS OF PERICOPE 19

19   **God's certain and guaranteed promises call for a response of trust and worship, even before their fulfillment (28:10–22).**

   19.1   God's promises are certain and guaranteed (28:10–15).

   19.2   God's promises call for a response of trust and worship, even before their fulfillment (28:16–22).

OVERVIEW

Beersheba to Haran is a distance of at least 500 miles, a journey that would have taken Jacob several days. The narrative, however, zooms in on a single night in a single place, during that long trek. The story begins with a stone pillow (28:11) and ends with a stone pillar (28:18). And the boundaries of this pericope are the commencement of a journey at one end (28:10), and a vow regarding a possible return journey at the other (28:20–22). The resumption of the journey, after the rest in 28:11–22, occurs in 29:1. This is thus a transitional pericope: "Beersheba" (28:10) harks back to 26:23–28:9, where Jacob dwelt with his parents, and "Haran" (28:10) anticipates his dwelling for the next two decades (29:1–31:54).[1]

Jacob's wanderings may be depicted thus[2]:

   A   Jacob deceives Esau—Beersheba (26:34–28:9)
      B   Angels of God and God meet Jacob—Bethel (28:10–22)
         C   Jacob in exile—Paddan Aram (29:1–31:55)
      B'   Angels of God and God meet Jacob—Mahanaim/Peniel (32:1–32)
   A'   Jacob reconciles with Esau—Canaan (likely close to Shechem, 33:1–20)

This pericope is, like many others, carefully constructed, with repetitions of some key words, as depicted below[3]:

---

1. Rebekah advised Jacob to go to her brother Laban's place in Haran (27:43), while Isaac recommended Paddan-Aram for Jacob's destination (28:2, 5, 6). That Jacob is said to have obeyed his father *and* his mother in going to Paddan-Aram (28:7), suggests some overlap between the two districts, Paddan-Aram and Haran (also see 25:20 that locates Laban at Paddan-Aram, and 11:31–12:5 that notes the presence of Abraham's clan in Haran and his departure therefrom to Canaan). The use of Haran in 28:10, Wenham suggests, may well be to link Yahweh's call of, and promises to, Abraham, with Yahweh's appearance and reiteration of his promises this time directed to Jacob (*Genesis 16–50*, 221).

2. Modified from Waltke and Fredricks, *Genesis*, 386.

3. Modified from Terino, "A Text Linguistic Study," 54–55; and Fokkelman, *Narrative Art in Genesis*, 71.

> **A**   *place* (28:11a)
>
> **B**   Jacob *took* a *stone, placed it by his head,* and lay down; ladder with *top* (28:11b–12aα)
>
> **C**   ladder to *heavens* (28:12aβ)
>
> **D**   angels of *God* (18:12b)
>
> **E**   Yahweh "by him," Jacob; "I am *Yahweh*" (28:13a)
>
> **F**   "The *land* on which you lie" (28:13b)
>
> **G**   "to *you* and to *your descendants*" (28:13c–14a)
>
> **H**   "*you* shall spread ..." (28:14b)
>
> **G'**   "in *you* and in *your descendants*" (28:14c)
>
> **F'**   "I will bring you back to this *land*" (28:15)
>
> **E'**   "Surely *Yahweh* is in this place" (28:16)
>
> **D'**   "house of *God*" (28:17b)
>
> **C'**   "gate of *heavens*" (28:17c)
>
> **B'**   Jacob rose early, *took* the *stone* he had *placed by his head;* pillar with *top* (28:18)
>
> **A'**   *place* (28:19)

As with the pericopes considered earlier, this one, too, has its parallel later in the Jacob saga (32:1–32; see chiastic structure of the Jacob Story in Pericope 16), with corresponding elements: "encounter" (28:11; and 32:2) with angels/God; blessing promised/bestowed; "bless" (28:14; and 32:26, 29); "place" (28:11, 16, 17, 19; and 32:2, 30); "called the name" (28:19; and 32:2, 30); theophoric names are given to the place by Jacob (Bethel, 28:19; and Peniel, 32:30); "he spent [the night] there" (28:11; and 32:13); "God of Abraham and Isaac, your/my father" (28:13; and 32:10); "your seed" (28:13; and 32:12); "return" (28:15; and 32:9); "afraid" (28:17; and 32:7). In this pericope, pointedly the narrator notes twice that it was dark: "night" and "sun had set" (28:11). Towards the end of the story, Jacob wakes up "early in the morning" (28:18); thus the encounter with Yahweh occurs while Jacob is asleep—that he had a dream is explicitly noted (28:12). This parallels another significant nocturnal manifestation of the divine, at Peniel, in the parallel chapter when Jacob is returning to Canaan (32:21, 24): there, too, the scene begins at night and ends at daybreak.

19.1 Genesis 28:10–15

THEOLOGICAL FOCUS 19.1

19.1   God's promises are certain and guaranteed (28:10–15).

NOTES 19.1

19.1   God's promises are certain and guaranteed.

This arrival at the "place" is apparently no accident: the verb פָּגַע, *pagats*, indicates that Jacob "encountered/struck" the place: "Whereas the narrator dismissed the journey in six words [28:10], he now considers it necessary to devote fifteen words [28:11] to introducing a place which Jacob 'happened to' reach; his listeners surmise, as good as understand, his arrival at that place cannot be entirely fortuitous!"[4] God seems to be in charge here, though behind the scenes. Interestingly enough, after "place" gets lots of notice in this account (28:11 [×3], 16, 17, 19), later it is renamed, and "Luz" becomes "Bethel." It might indicate the importance of the locus for, unwittingly, Jacob has landed at the site of one of Abraham's altars (12:8). For the first time in the text, Jacob would encounter Yahweh here: "Surely Yahweh is in this place, and I did not know it" (28:16). Not only do we find that Jacob is ignorant of the presence of God, later we will see that he is quite distrusting of the promises of God, too. Not an auspicious start to this pericope.

A staccato sequence of eight *waw*-consecutive imperfect verbs introduce the account in 28:10–12a: וַיֵּצֵא, וַיֵּלֶךְ, וַיִּפְגַּע, וַיָּלֶן, וַיִּקַּח, וַיָּשֶׂם, וַיִּשְׁכַּב, and וַיַּחֲלֹם (*wayyetse', wayyelek, wayyifga', wayyalen, wayyiqqakh, wayyasem, wayyishkav,* and *wayyakhalom;* "and he came out," "and he went," "and he encountered," "and he spent [the night]," "and he took," "and he placed," "and he lay down," "and he dreamt"). The narrator's point of view is obvious: he is recounting what happened in the past, in the accepted style. However, quite unexpectedly, this set is followed by a sequence of five participles in 28:12b–13: מֻצָּב, מַגִּיעַ, עֹלִים, וְיֹרְדִים, נִצָּב (*mutsav, maggia', 'olim, wyordim, nitsav;* "standing," "reaching," "ascending," "descending," "standing over")—"a radical change of perspective. Up till now he had been telling us all kinds of things from the superior point of the omniscient narrator, now he abandons this attitude; he withdraws behind his protagonist and in a subordinate position he records what his, Jacob's, eyes see," with a threefold repeat of "behold!" (הִנֵּה, *hinneh,* 28:12, 13, 15), escalating each time: "Behold, a ladder!" "Behold, the angels of God!" "Behold, Yahweh!"[5] All this vividly emphasizes the transcendent nature of what was observed, an awe-inspiring scene, as Jacob later confesses (28:17). But the magnificence of the vision also serves to underscore, by contrast, the rather dodgy and dubious response of Jacob to Yahweh's declarations, later in the story.

The somewhat obscure word סֻלָּם (*sullam;* a hapax) probably indicates a ramp or a stairway of some sort, rather than a ladder—likely a structure connecting earth and heaven (28:12).[6] Genesis 28:17, Jacob's own interpretation of what he saw, best explains 28:12, with the location ("place," 28:17) being the abode of God, and סֻלָּם signifying the "gate of heaven" (28:17; see below), perhaps a vertically set one between earth and heaven, *through/in* which (בוֹ, *bo*—not *on* which) angels were ascending and descending. In this scenario, Yahweh might have been standing beside/by this gate or, perhaps more accurately, beside/by "him," Jacob himself (עָלָיו, *'alayw,* "by it/him," 28:13[7])—

---

4. Fokkelman, *Narrative Art in Genesis,* 50. The unusual verb פגע occurs only twice in the Jacob narratives; its second instance is in the corresponding chapter of the Jacob Story, in 32:1; here, too, a theophany ensues. Both such "encounters" mark critical events in the patriarch's life—his escape from Canaan, and later his return thereto.

5. Fokkelman, *Narrative Art in Genesis,* 50, 51–52.

6. Arnold, *Genesis,* 252.

7. See 18:2 for the same sense of עָלָיו ("by him"). Hamilton observes that נצב, *ntsv,* in the Niphal

substantiated by Jacob confessing that Yahweh was right there, "in this place" (28:16).[8] "The wordplays then focus the reader's attention on Jacob's vision of the Lord—the standing stairway pointing to it, and the standing stone being a reminder of it."[9]

All of this adds up to form a grand spectacle—an "awesome" (from ירא, *yr'*, "to fear," 28:17) phenomenon— that provides gravitas and divine authority to what is to follow: Yahweh's promises (28:13–15). However, the significance of the angelic activity in the scene is not entirely clear. That vision and theophany might have been a numinous portrayal of the protection Jacob was being afforded as he entered a foreign land.[10] The exclamation, "behold!" to introduce the angels' ascent and descent upon the ramp (28:13) draws attention to the activity of these preternatural beings. The subsequent promise of Yahweh (28:13–15) is aptly introduced by this opening "show of strength," particularly since a key facet of the divine promise was God's presence and protection of the escaping patriarch. Thus, we have here shock and awe—intended to inspire confidence in God's assertions. Unfortunately the demonstration did not succeed with the hard-boiled agnostic that Jacob was.

God introduces himself with a unique title: "Yahweh, the God of Abraham, your father, and the God of Isaac" (28:13). The promises given to these patriarchs are immediately recalled; one can expect that these are going to be reaffirmed to the third generation here.[11] Hamilton detects a disparaging note in the divine self-introduction: "The phrase *the God of Isaac* would be particularly poignant to Jacob's ears. For Jacob now lies before the one who says in essence: I am the God of the one whom you deceived and of whom you took advantage. Jacob could supplant Esau. He could deceive Isaac. But what will he do with Yahweh?"[12] No, he cannot deceive Yahweh, but he does try bargaining to get his own way!

---

followed על, *'l*, in most cases, means "to stand by/beside" (Exod 7:15; Num 23:6, 17; 1 Sam 19:20; 22:9; etc.)—thus: "to stand in a position of authority, to preside over" (also Ruth 2:5, 6) (*Genesis: Chapters 18–50*, 240–41).

8. Oblath, "'To Sleep, Perchance to Dream,'" 117–26. Fokkelman notes that unlike the human enterprise of 11:1–9, where a vain attempt was made to scale heaven, starting on earth, here, in 28:12, the initiative is supernatural: a סלם, *slm*, is "set/stood" (נצב, *ntsv*) on earth, from above (note the directional אַרְצָה, *'artsah*, "towards earth"), successfully spanning the heaven and earth (*Narrative Art in Genesis*, 53n22). Heaven and earth are connected and that at the initiative of Yahweh, by the grace of God, and not by the hubris of man. This likely indicates the christological sense of John 3:13.

9. Ross, "Studies in the Life of Jacob Part 1," 225. It is uncertain whether the stone was being used as a pillow in 28:11. The LXX has πρὸς κεφαλῆς αὐτοῦ (*pros kephalēs autou*, "by his head," 28:11, 18).

10. Wenham, *Genesis 16–50*, 222. See Deut 32:8; Job 1:6; 2:1; Zech 1:8–17. The fact that another angel had earlier accompanied the servant of Abraham in his pursuit of a bride for Isaac (Gen 24:7, 40), seems to fit with the protective guardianship of angels. Here in 28:12 and later in 32:1 are located the only two instances of "angels of God" in Genesis.

11. Surprisingly, after all the shenanigans of Pericope 18 (26:34–28:9), the deceptions in which Jacob was the primary culprit, there is no word of rebuke from Yahweh to the malefactor, when the former speaks to the latter for the first time. But punitive action would be taken by the divine judge and Jacob would be recompensed in kind, for which, see the next pericope, Pericope 20 (29:1–30).

12. Hamilton, *Genesis: Chapters 18–50*, 241–42.

Referring back to the structure of the pericope depicted earlier, one can see how the chiastic arrangement of this episode centers around the promises of Yahweh.

<pre>
  C   "behold!"; ladder to *heavens* (28:12a)
    D   "behold!"; angels of *God* (18:12b)
      E   "behold! *Yahweh*"; "I am *Yahweh*" (28:13a)
        F–F'   Yahweh's promises (28:13b–15)
      E'   "Surely *Yahweh* is in this place" (28:16)
    D'   "house of *God*" (28:17b)
  C'   "gate of *heavens*" (28:17c)
</pre>

Of the several divine promises to Jacob's grandfather, Abraham, none parallels 28:13–14 to the extent that 13:14–16 does (other similar promises to Abraham are found in 12:7; 15:5, 18; 17:8; 22:17; 24:7): both 13:14–16 and 28:13–14 are located at Bethel (see 13:3; 28:19). Ironically, the timing of the promise to Abraham and to Jacob are starkly different: the first received it as he was entering the Promised Land (Gen 12:2–3); the latter receives it here when he is leaving the Promised Land (28:13–15).

Genesis 13:14–16	Genesis 28:13–14
"For all the land which you see"	"The land upon which you are lying"
"I will give to you and to your descendants"	"I will give to you and to your descendants"
"I will make your descendants like the dust of the earth"	"Your descendants shall be like the dust of the earth"
"Look … northward and southward and eastward and westward"	"And you will spread westward and eastward and northward and southward"
Promised when Abraham was entering the Promised Land	Promised when Jacob was leaving the Promised Land
Promised to a married patriarch	Promised to an unmarried patriarch

Other promises to the patriarchs that mention their (or their descendants') being a blessing to the nations are found in 12:3; 18:18; 22:18; and 26:4. Hamilton observes that the promise to Jacob is even more dramatic than the one to his father and grandfather: at least Abraham and Isaac were married, though childless, when these promises of numerous descendants were bestowed; Jacob, on the other hand, is not even married.[13] That, however, cannot excuse Jacob's subsequent disbelief and tendency to negotiate with God; a childless Abraham at seventy-five (and for the next quarter-century) kept on believing God's promise. That should have been Jacob's model of faith. All these emphatic connections with previous declarations of Yahweh underscore the continuity of the sovereign plan of God who had dealt similarly with Abraham and Isaac. Jacob should have taken confidence in the fact that God was inexorably bringing about his promises. That God would be with the patriarch is guaranteed; that he would keep him wherever Jacob might go is pledged; and that Jacob would return to Canaan one day is assured. "I will be with you," summarizes it all. "Massively, of jewel-like shortness, this pronouncement by God, which might serve as a title for so many passages in the O.T., expresses the unconditional, absolute support and loyalty which Jacob is to experience

13. Ibid., 242.

from God."[14] This promise to Jacob, that Yahweh would be with the patriarch, seems to have been a significant one, for it is repeated several times in Jacob's story at significant junctures: here in 28:15, as Jacob is fleeing Canaan; in 31:3, as he is preparing to return to Canaan; and in 46:4, as the patriarch and his clan are readying to move to Egypt.[15]

"You" and "your descendants" form an unusual chiasm in 28:13c–14c, intertwining the two parties as a unitary corporate personality: Jacob = his descendants.[16] Once again, this stresses the certainty of the promises coming to pass. The twice expressed "behold" (once by the narrator and once by God, 28:13, 15) further undergirds the words of God.

Behold! (28:13)
You (28:13c)   your descendants (28:13c)
        Your descendants (28:14a)   you (28:14b)
                    You (28:14c)   your descendants (28:14c)
                                  Behold! (28:15)

There is a curious sonic phenomenon in 28:14: כַּעֲפַר הָאָרֶץ (*kaʿapar haʾarets*, "like the dust of the earth") is followed by a verb with the root פרץ (*prts*, "to spread"), made up of an assimilation of the prominent consonants, פ, ר, and צ (*p, r,* and *ts*; highlighted), in כַּעֲפַר הָאָרֶץ. Not only is there a "sound fusion," the phrase explains what the verb root describes: to be "like the dust of the earth" is "to spread." "The levels of sound and meaning have become integrated: they point to each other, they explain each other, pervade each other."[17] Literally and acoustically, the promise is guaranteed, by the voice of Yahweh.[18]

A series of six phrases with Yahweh as the subject reinforces the theme of his promise: "I am," "I will keep," "I will return," "I will not leave," "I have done," "I have promised" (28:15). It is significant that the first assertion has the first-person pronoun, אָנֹכִי (*ʾanoki*, the rest employ first-person forms to indicate that the speaker, Yahweh, is the subject). The use of this free-standing pronoun emphasizes God's direct involvement in Jacob's life. In this "place," the junction of heaven and earth, Jacob is given an irrevocable promise of the presence of God. "This emphasis on Yahweh, the giver of promises, and Jacob the receiver of promises, makes it all the more clear that Jacob is the recipient of God's unconditional guarantee of involvement in, protection over, and guiding of his life."[19] How would Jacob react to this awe-inspiring event and declaration?

---

14. Fokkelman, *Narrative Art in Genesis*, 61.

15. The promise was also given to Isaac in 26:3, 24.

16. Ibid., 59; table from ibid., 58.

17. Ibid., 59.

18. Interestingly, while Abraham and Isaac were the objects of promised blessing from the hand of God in 12:2; 22:17; 26:3, Jacob, the current patriarch, is never himself promised or given such blessing until the end of his story (32:29 and 35:9). Rather than *get* the blessing, Jacob is promised in 28:14 that he will *be* the blessing.

19. Hamilton, *Genesis: Chapters 18–50*, 243.

19.2 Genesis 28:16–22

THEOLOGICAL FOCUS 19.2

19.2 God's promises call for a response of trust and worship, even before their fulfillment (28:16–22).

NOTES 19.2

19.2 God's promises call for a response of trust and worship, even before their fulfillment.[20]

Jacob's response to the stunning vision and revelation of 28:12–15 is described in two phases: 28:16–17 and 18–19. First, he awakens from his dream (28:12) with a feeling of "fear" and "awe" (both words derived from ירא, *yr'*, 28:16), as he recognizes the presence of God in that "place." While this is no doubt an appropriate response to the presence of deity (Exod 15:11; Ps 96:4), Jacob's life seems to be punctuated with fear: of his God (Gen 28:17), of his employer/father-in-law, Laban (31:31), and of his sibling, Esau (32:7, 11).[21] This is not surprising: the life of one consumed with the chase for blessing, a self-directed pursuit, can only be marked by insecurity and fear.

The two instances of "place" in Jacob's utterance in 28:16–17 are balanced in his twofold acknowledgement of the locus as "the house of God" and as "the gate of heaven" (28:17). There is also, in 28:16, Jacob's redundant first-person pronoun, אָנֹכִי, a symmetric response to God's own use of the pronoun in 28:15. Subsequently, in a series of six third-person verbs, that parallel the six first-person phrases with Yahweh as subject in 28:15, Jacob sets up a monument and renames the "place": "he rose," "he took," "he had placed," "he set," "he poured," and "he called" (28:18–19a). Then, after the narrative aside about the previous name of the "place," Jacob does one more thing: "he vows a vow" (28:20)—the second phase of his response to what he had seen and heard in 28:12–15.

Thus far, Jacob's response is, at least, appropriate: the construction of a pillar is similar to his ancestors' practices of raising altars at loci of revelation (12:7–8; 13:18; 26:25).[22] Indeed, the wordplays here are significant. The pillar is מַצֵּבָה, *matsevah*, from the root נצב (*ntsv*, "set/stand") that had already been encountered twice: "Just as the ladder ['set,' נצב, on earth, 28:12] was a prefiguration of God's appearance [as he 'stood,' נצב, 28:13], so Jacob now turns an erected stone [מַצֵּבָה, literally, "that which stands," 28:18] into a postfiguration of the theophany."[23]

---

20. This is a positive statement of a negative reaction displayed by Jacob.

21. Ibid., 244.

22. Other instances of setting up monuments in Jacob's life are found in 31:45, 51–52; 35:14 (this is the only other one directed to God), and 35:20. As far as altars go, Jacob's building enterprises are recorded in 33:20; 35:1, 3, 7.

23. Fokkelman, *Narrative Art in Genesis*, 66.

There is another curious wordplay here (28:18–19): Jacob takes the stone that he had placed "by his head" (מְרַאֲשֹׁתָיו, *mra'ashitayw*, from רֹאשׁ, *ro'sh*, "head," 28:18), pours oil on its "top" (רֹאשָׁהּ, *ro'shah*, also from רֹאשׁ), and changes the name by which the place was known by "previously" (רִאשׁוֹן, *ri'shon*, from רֹאשׁ, 28:19). One remembers that the root had already been found in 28:11 (where the stone placed "by his head" was introduced). In that earlier instance was also the ladder with its "top" (also רֹאשׁ, 28:12) reaching the heavens. Fokkelman suggests that by means of this paronomasia also—in addition to plays on נצב— the pillar symbolizes the ladder.[24] The structure (reproduced from that of the whole pericope) makes this clear:

> A   *place (28:11a)*
>
>   B   Jacob *took* a *stone, placed it by his head,* and lay down; ladder with *top* (28:11b–12aα)
>
>   C   ladder to *heavens* (28:12aβ)
>
>   …
>
>   C'   "gate of *heavens*" (28:17c)
>
>   B'   Jacob rose early, *took* the *stone* he had *placed by his head*; pillar with *top* (28:18)
>
> A'   *place (28:19)*

In all of this, there is clearly a recognition on the part of Jacob that he has witnessed something altogether significant and momentous. Will the second part of his response, his vow, reflect this cognizance? In other words, will there be cause for Yahweh, the God of Abraham and the God of Isaac (28:13), to add to his nomen the name of the patriarch *du jour*, making Yahweh now the "God of Jacob" also? That Jacob noted the omission of his own name in 28:13 seems to be clear from his subsequent response: *he* sets the conditions for Yahweh being his God (28:20–22)! Apparently, he thinks he gets to decide how Yahweh should introduce himself.[25]

This pericope contains the only instance of a patriarch making a vow (using the verb and noun from the root נדר), indeed, the only instance of that root in Genesis (excluding its use in 31:13 to refer to this same vow of Jacob. It is also the longest vow in the OT. This uniqueness gives Jacob's oath a negative tint: If no other patriarch needed to do so, why did Jacob? In fact, other patriarchs do not even raise a verbal response to divine promise, not to mention making a vow in reaction. A close examination of God's promise in 28:15 and Jacob's vow in 28:20–22, essentially a response to God's words, is revealing.

---

24. Ibid., 67. And, he comments astutely, "Key words are like buoys at sea, they mark the way which the interpreter has to go" (ibid., 67n43).

25. One also remembers how Jacob referred to God in 27:20, when speaking to Isaac: "Yahweh *your* God."

God's Promise (Genesis 28:15)	Jacob's Vow (Genesis 28:20–22)
	PROTASIS
"I am with you" (28:15a)	"If [אם] God will be [*imperfect*] with me" (28:20b)
"and I will keep you" (28:15bα)	"and [if] He will keep me [*perfect*]" (28:20cα)
"wherever you go" (28:15bβ)	
	"on this way that I am going" (28:20cβ)
	"and [if] He will give me [*perfect*] food
	... and garments" (28:20d)
"and I will return you" (28:15cα)	"and [if] I return [*perfect*]" (28:21aα)
"to this land" (28:15cβ)	
	"in peace—to my father's house" (28:21aβ)
"I shall not leave you" (28:15d)	
	"and [if] Yahweh will be [*perfect*] God to me" (28:21b)
	APODOSIS
	"then this stone will be [*imperfect*]
	God's house" (28:22a)
	"I will surely give a tenth [*infinitive + imperfect*]
	to You" (28:22b)

The sequence of mostly *waw* + perfect verbs ("he will keep," "he will give," "I return," "Yahweh will be," 28:20cα, 28:20d, 28:21aα, and 28:21b; see table above), the disjunctive opening of 28:22 (noun, "this stone," followed by the verb, "will be," unlike the previous clauses where the verb comes first), and the fact that each of the clauses in 28:20–21 has Yahweh for the subject (except for that in 28:21aα), strongly suggest that 28:21b is part of the conditional protasis (marked in the table with the addition of "if" to each of the verbs), and not part of the apodosis.[26] The elements of the protasis refer in some fashion to God's promises. Besides, after his grand vision of God and his explicit acknowledgment of the "God-ness of Yhwh"—seeing that he declares that "Yahweh is in this place" and confirms the place as the "house of God" (28:16–17)—and his initial response of setting up a pillar and anointing it, it seems very unlikely that he would displace Yahweh from being God right now in 28:21b, and relegate that status of deity for a future appropriation by putting it in the apodosis.[27]

However, even with 28:21b in the protasis, Jacob does demonstrate considerable hubris, for he is clearly not taking God at his word. Even that clause in 28:21b appears to be laying down a condition for God to fulfill: "If Yahweh will be God *to me*." He has just heard Yahweh identify himself as the "God of Abraham your father, and the God of Isaac." Jacob is now demanding that this Yahweh be the "God of Jacob," too. And, if that were not enough, while echoing, in 28:20b–c, the promises of God made in 28:15a–b, he dares to add an extra condition: the man demands food and clothing! "This pair is representative of a totality . . .; we have a merismus here that stands for 'all necessities of life, even the barest.'"[28] He is uncertain about God's intent, perhaps

26. Fokkelman, *Narrative Art in Genesis*, 75–76; also see Hamilton, *Genesis: Chapters 18–50*, 248. While 28:20b employs an imperfect verb, the conditional אם that commences that clause ensures that it is read as a condition (and part of the protasis).

27. Fokkelman, *Narrative Art in Genesis*, 76–77.

28. Ibid., 77.

even God's capacity to take care of him. So he spells it out: "It is not enough that you keep me, but you, Yahweh, also need to meet every single one of my needs." This, in response to Yahweh who promised to "give it [the land] to you and your descendants." So not only does Jacob disregard land in favor of victuals and raiment, his demand focuses on himself: "give *me*," without any thought about posterity. There is no reaction at all in Jacob's response to the part of God's promise regarding his descendants—their growth and spread—or about how he and they would be a blessing to "all the families of the earth" (28:14). Jacob's interests seem far more parochial, insular, and self-serving. "Even in this solemn moment, he still sounds like a bargain-hunter."[29]

There also seems to be a hint of doubt in Jacob's addition of "in peace" in 28:21aβ to God's promise to return him to his land. He is not too sure this God can ensure that the older brother who is now out for Jacob's blood will be kept in rein at a later date. Not to mention Jacob's preoccupation with his own personal return to his "father's house," while God's interests are more farsighted and global: Yahweh's goal was to return him to "this land," the Promised Land. Likewise, though God promised to keep him "wherever you go" (28:15b), Jacob's concern is for the here and now: he wants God to keep him "on *this way* that I am going" (28:20cβ).

All in all, in his protasis, he has doubts and so he adds conditions: he is uncertain about God's protection, he wants bread and garments, and he wants Yahweh to be his God. And he ignores a key facet of the promise of God: "I will never leave you," not recognizing that, by that assertion, Yahweh was implicitly assuring Jacob that he would be Jacob's God and would take care of *all* his needs. Thus, for Jacob, if and when Yahweh met his conditions, *then* he would make Yahweh a house and give him a tenth of his possessions. *If* God pans out, *if* God is able to fulfill his word, *if* God is as good as he claims to be—Jacob seems to be saying—*then* this stone will become a pillar, and this pillar will become a house (of God). Jacob is trading promises with God: *if* God keeps his promises, *then* I'll keep mine! There is an irony in Jacob's use of "house" in 28:21a and 28:22a: "If You return me to my *house*, I will make a *house* for You, Yahweh." "When the semi-nomad has settled down for good, his God, who went with him and who guided him through the desert, will also have his fixed abode."[30] *Until then, God, you're on your own!*

One cannot but remember the contrasting response of Abraham to the promises of God. Though he, too, was dubious about the exact nature of their fulfillment, his response was strikingly different from Jacob's. Following the promises of 12:1–3, 7, he built *two* altars to Yahweh (12:7–8)—the second in Bethel—as he called upon the name of Yahweh. After another reaffirmation of the promise in 13:14–15, Abraham repeated himself: he built another altar to Yahweh (13:18). At least twice, when Yahweh appeared to the patriarch with a promise, he responded in worship. Not so Jacob: this patriarch responds with a counteroffer, and an emphatic one at that, for both its clauses are disjunctive—subject precedes verb ("this stone . . . will be"; and "[of] all You give

---

29. Brueggemann, *Genesis*, 248.

30. Fokkelman, *Narrative Art in Genesis*, 80.

me . . . I will surely give a tenth"; 28:22)![31] "Unconditional acceptance . . . of another's generosity seems to be very hard for Jacob to accept. So deeply is it ingrained in his personality that he must carve out his life by the sweat of his own brow that he cannot countenance anything simply being given to him, gratis, by either God or man."[32]

It is also significant that until 28:22b, God/Yahweh is discussed in this pericope in the third person by Jacob. Suddenly, gone is the fear and awe, as he addresses God in the second person: "[Of] all *You* give me, I will sure give a tenth to *You*." While it may well be that Jacob is now feeling so grateful to God that he lapses into a dialogue, given the attitude he has depicted thus far, and the nuanced variations between God's promise and his, it fits the tenor of the narrative to view this direct address of Jacob to God almost as impertinence and presumption, as he tries to strike a deal, a bargain, with the Creator of the universe. "[W]hatever transformations await us in Jacob's future, Jacob is still the Trickster. For the most prominent word in his response is the qualification 'if.' . . . If all of this happens, then—and one assumes this means *only* then—will Jacob serve the God who revealed himself at Bethel."[33] Though there are other conditional vows in the OT (Num 21:2; Jdg 11:30–31; 1 Sam 1:11; 2 Sam 15:8), none of them is in direct response to a promise made by Yahweh. After all that he had seen and heard (28:12–15), there were no grounds whatsoever for Jacob's mistrust and skepticism. Rather, his response should have been, like Abraham's of yore, worship: worship, even before the fulfillment of the promises; worship, because of the certainty of God's declarations; worship, because in essence, that is the only response man can make to the words of God.[34]

Walton, too, sees Jacob's hedging as "suspiciously like another bargain. Jacob is in a 'wait-and-see' mode and wants to have his benefits up front before he delivers on anything. . . . In his vow, he presumes on the grace of God. Everything is backward here."[35] Ellen van Wolde summarizes it well: "Jacob is not talking about the land; Jacob is not talking about his offspring; Jacob is not talking about the spread of his offspring on the land; Jacob is not talking about other people being or not being blessed; Jacob

---

31. Of interest, the verb "will be" in the first clause is masculine, though the subject, "stone," is feminine. Perhaps Jacob is so consumed with his own personal role in rendering this stone/pillar into a temple that he forgets his grammar!

32. Noble, "Esau, Tamar, and Joseph," 243.

33. Cotter, *Genesis*, 217.

34. Among others, Fokkelman designates Jacob's reply to God as one of gratitude (*Narrative Art in Genesis*, 81). Wenham notes: "In making the Lord his God and offering tithes, Jacob is imitating the actions of his grandfather Abraham. . . . He is also, as father of the nation, setting a pattern for all Israel to follow" (*Genesis 16–50*, 225). As a matter of fact, he is *not*. Jacob has done nothing of the sort of actions performed by his ancestor . . . yet. He has only made some dubious pledges, essentially casting doubt upon the promises of God. One must also consider the theological trajectory of the broader narrative to arrive at a conclusion about Jacob's response, whether it is positive or negative. Seeing the saga as a whole, Jacob's change of attitude towards God does not occur until after the middle of the story, 29:31—30:25 (see chiastic structure of the whole Jacob Story in Pericope 16). Beyond the textual evidence in 28:10–22, the overall momentum of the larger story compels me to see Jacob's actions here as being not at all positive.

35. *Genesis*, 573–74.

is not talking about Yhwh as the god of his father or grandfather. However, he is very much concerned with himself; he will be concerned with Yhwh if he protects him."[36] Talk about pusillanimity! "Conditional discipleship," it appears, "is much easier than unconditional surrender."[37]

SERMON FOCUS AND OUTLINES

THEOLOGICAL FOCUS OF PERICOPE 19 FOR PREACHING

19   God's guaranteed promises call for a response of trusting worship (28:10–22).

This pericope paints a negative picture of the patriarch Jacob. Despite the grand and magnificent setting in which God gave his certain and guaranteed promises, and despite the absoluteness and comprehensiveness of those promises, Jacob remained skeptical. In fact, he bargained with God: rather than an outright acceptance of the promises and, indeed, of Yahweh himself as his God, Jacob preferred a wait-and-see approach. If God turned out to do what he claimed he would do, *then* Jacob would respond, with worship and submission (tithing). For the pragmatic agnostic that Jacob was, it was first things first: God needed to prove himself to Jacob.

It will be worthwhile to review some of the promises God has made to believers in this dispensation that are yet to be fulfilled: besides God's continuing love, presence, and grace extended to Christians (Rom 8:38–39; Heb 13:5; 2 Cor 12:9), there are also the promises for the future, both near and far, that deal with: victory over sin and Satan (1 Cor 10:13; 1 Pet 5:10), comfort in time of need (2 Cor 3–4), the blessed outcome of tribulation (Jas 1:12), the peace of God (Phil 4:7), the triumph of the church (Matt 16:18), the power of prayer (Jas 5:16), the sure completion of the work of God in us (Phil 1:6), ultimate victory in Christ, over evil (Phil 2:10–11), divine sovereignty over all matters, events, and people (Rom 8:28), every spiritual blessing in Christ (Eph 1:3), certainty of the resurrection of souls (1 Cor 15:12–58), our conformation to Christ (Rom 8:29; 1 John 3:2), the Second Advent (Titus 2:13), future rewards (1 Pet 1:3–5), eternal joy (Rev 21:3–4) and glory (2 Cor 4:17–18), the eternal reign of Christ (Rev 11:15), and a host of others.

Possible Preaching Outlines for Pericope 19

I.   GOD's Sure Promises
    The grand and magnificent setting of the giving of God's promises (28:10–12)
    Divine promises to Jacob (28:13–15)
    Move-to-Relevance: Our promises from God—their certainty and guaranteed nature

II.   JACOB's Wrong Response
    Jacob's recognition of God's presence and the momentous character of the event

36. "Cognitive Linguistics," 144. She also suspects the narrator's disdain for Jacob's explicit use of *Beth-Elohim* (בֵּית אֱלֹהִים, *bet-'elohim*, "house of God," 28:17, 22): the narrator, instead, pointedly employs *Beth-El* (בֵּית־אֵל, *bet-'el*, also "house of God," 28:19, but without the plurality implied by *Elohim*) (ibid., 145).

37. Whartenby, "Genesis 28:10–22," 404.

(28:16–19)

Jacob's presumptuous response, making his submission conditional upon promise fulfillment (28:20–22)

Move-to-Relevance: Our lack of trust in God's sure promises

III.   OUR Right Response: *Worship God even before his promises are fulfilled!*
       The right response to the certain and guaranteed promises of God is worship, even before
       their fulfillment
       Specifics on how exactly this may be accomplished

A slight tweak of the outline above yields another that oscillates between the main
characters, God and Jacob in each move.

I.   God's Presence and Jacob's Perception
     The grand and magnificent setting of the giving of God's promises (28:10–12)
     Jacob's recognition of God's presence and the momentous character of the event
     (28:16–19)
     Move-to-Relevance: The greatness of God recognized and remembered.

II. God's Declaration and Jacob's Doubt
     Divine promises to Jacob (28:13–15)
     Jacob's presumption, making his submission conditional upon promise fulfillment
     (28:20–22)

III. God's Commitment and Our Confidence: *Worship God even before his promises are fulfilled!*
     Ways to accomplish the recognition and respecting of divine blessing upon individuals in
     community
     The consequence of such recognition and respect: the avoidance of intramural strife and
     contention.

PERICOPE 20

Comeuppance

Genesis 29:1–30

[Jacob Deceived by Laban; Leah Exchanged for Rachel]

REVIEW, SUMMARY, PREVIEW

Review of Pericope 19: Genesis 28:10–22 has Jacob, a fugitive, encountering God in a dream. The latter reaffirms to Jacob the patriarchal promise, upon which Jacob, rather impertinently, sets conditions upon God. God's guaranteed promises should, instead, have impelled him to worship unconditionally, even before the fulfillment of those promises.

Summary of Pericope 20: This pericope has Jacob arriving at his uncle's house in Paddan-Aram. He works for seven years for the hand of Rachel, his uncle's daughter, but is deceived by Laban who substitutes the older Leah for the younger Rachel on the wedding night. The many parallels between the narrative here and that of the deception of Isaac earlier make it clear that Jacob is now receiving his just deserts. Discipline for misdeeds is a distinct possibility for God's people in his economy.

Preview of Pericope 21: The next pericope (29:31–30:24) depicts the struggle between Leah and Rachel. Rachel does all she can to gain a child, even engaging in deceptive practices, jealous manipulations, and obscure therapies, all in vain, until she gives up her stratagems, whereupon she conceives. The blessings of God are experienced by those who maintain a posture of openhandedness (humble dependence).

20. *Genesis 29:1–30*

THEOLOGICAL FOCUS OF PERICOPE 20

20 God's promises and blessings do not preclude the possibility of appropriate discipline for misdeeds (29:1–30).

　20.1　God keeps his promises and blesses the way of his children (29:1–14).

　20.2　God's blessings do not preclude the possibility of appropriate discipline for misdeeds (29:15–30).

OVERVIEW

As with the other pericopes in the Jacob Story, this particular pericope, too, has its parallel in a subsequent text of the broader story: 29:1–14 is paralleled by 31:1–55 with several common elements. Here we have Jacob's arrival in Haran, the other his flight from Haran; Rachel plays a significant cameo role in both; "kiss" occurs in 29:11, 13 and 31:28; there is a "rolling" (גלל, *gll*) of a stone in 29:3, 8, 10, and a "heap" (גל, *gl*) of stones in 31:46; and both deal with "brothers" (29:14 and 31:32). Likewise, the remainder of this pericope, 29:15–30, is paralleled by 30:25–43: this concerns a deception by Laban, the other an outwitting of Laban; "service" is a common theme (in this pericope in 29:15, 18, 20, 25, 27 [×2], 30; and later in 30:26 [×3], 29; 31:6, 41), as also are "wages" (מַשְׂכֹּרֶת, *maskoret*, in 29:15 and 31:7, 41; and שׂכר, *skr*, in 30:16 [×2], 18, 28, 32, 33, and 31:8 [×2]).

The part of the Jacob narratives comprising Gen 29–31 is set in Haran/Paddan-Aram, and forms the center of the structure of the entire cycle taking up two decades (31:38). Laban, and Jacob's relationship to him, governs the outer sections (*F*, *G*, *G'*, and *F'*, below[1]); the contention between Laban's daughters, Jacob's wives, for parturient productivity, priority, and preeminence, makes up the chiastic center (*H*). The two episodes, *F* and *G*, constitute Pericope 20.[2]

F	Jacob's arrival at Haran (29:1–14)			**Pericope 20**
	G	Deception by Laban (29:15–30)		**Pericope 20**
		H	Sibling rivalry: Leah and Rachel (29:31–30:24)	**Pericope 21**
	G'	Outwitting of Laban (30:25–43)		**Pericope 22**
F'	Jacob's flight from Haran (31:1–55)			**Pericope 23**

In some ways, there are similarities between Isaac's spouse-finding endeavors and those of Jacob's, and between the narratives surrounding each: both exploit a "betrothal type-scene"[3]:

1. For the chiastic patterning of the entire Jacob story in which all these parallels are reproduced, see Pericope 16.

2. To create a preachable idea that is discrete from preceding and succeeding texts, in this commentary multiple episodes are combined on occasion, as in this pericope. Of course, one could preach 29:1–14 separately from 29:15–30, but the theological thrust of each of those episodes may not be sufficiently distinct from one another. For this pragmatic reason, the two stories are combined as a single preaching unit.

3. Incidentally, the bride and groom meet for the first time in a field in both cases: Isaac meets

Elements of Betrothal Type-Scene	Isaac & Spouse	Jacob & Spouses
Offspring promised	26:4	28:14
Proscription of exogamy	24:3–4	28:1–2
Location: Haran/Paddan-Aram	24:10 (with 11:31)	27:43; 28:2
Arrival of agent/patriarch at well	24:10–11	29:1–2
Encounter with bride at well	24:15–17	29:9
Watering of flocks	24:14, 17–20	29:10
Laban and relatives	24:29–60	29:13–30
Involvement of Yahweh	24:1–4, 7, 12–14, 21, 26–27, 42–44, 48, 50, 52	

The significant difference between the two accounts—besides the fact that in the former case, an agent of the patriarch (and/or his father) was operating in this spousal search, whereas, in the latter case, the patriarch Jacob himself was involved—is the obvious and explicitly noted dependence upon Yahweh in the whole process of the Rebekah affair (highlighted above; see Pericope 15). In contrast, there is absolutely no mention of God or Yahweh in Pericope 20 (29:1–30). Of course, that does not eliminate the Chief Actant of this narrative (and of every other narrative in the Bible). It is simply a literary indication that this patriarch, at least now, does not consider God to be particularly important in his life or essential for furthering his own goals and objectives. In fact, Jacob had just gotten away with a horrible deception of his father and his brother, stealing the firstborn's blessing. And God, if he were God, did not seem to care . . . or so Jacob must have thought. No recriminations, no repercussions, no ramifications of the felonious act that Jacob had perpetrated. He must have thought this was the way to get ahead in life: cheat, connive, manipulate, backstab, and heel-grab! Little did Jacob know what was awaiting him.

20.1 Genesis 29:1–14

THEOLOGICAL FOCUS 20.1

20.1   God keeps his promises and blesses the way of his children (29:1–14).

NOTES 20.1

20.1   God keeps his promises and blesses the way of his children.

The account begins with an unusual idiom found only here: רַגְלָיו . . . וַיִּשָּׂא, *wayyisha'* . . . *raglayw*, "And he picked up . . . his feet" (29:1). Later, in 29:11, he "picks up" (also from נשׂא, *nsh'*) his voice as he weeps (with joy), upon meeting Rachel. Mathews surmises that the unique expression in 29:1 is an adumbration of his successful encounter

---

Rebekah in a "field" when she arrives in Canaan (24:63, 65); Jacob, of course, meets Rachel at the well, which was expressly located in a "field" (29:2).

with Rachel—an "auspicious beginning to his journey," implying that "the hand of God was directing Jacob's travels."[4]

The setting is detailed. The two "behold!" exclamations of the narrator also signify the momentous nature of what Jacob comes upon (29:2): a well in a field, and three flocks of sheep beside it. A disjunctive clause (beginning with *waw* + subject) provides ancillary information on the stone at the mouth of the well: it was large, emphasizing the size of the task that lay before Jacob. He would not only have to exercise his physical strength to move the stone, he would also have to demonstrate his acumen in flouting social convention—watering a flock (that of Rachel), before the rest of the flocks are gathered (29:7–8). All of this points to Jacob's successful foray, at least initially, into Haran. In sum, while Yahweh's presence is not explicitly noted, Jacob's ventures are laden with "luck." He happens to arrive at the well where shepherds from Haran congregate, which also happens to be the place where Rachel, Laban's daughter, waters her flock; the well has a large stone at its opening, that is waiting for Jacob to move it; the stone is "large" (29:2), but Jacob successfully maneuvers it off the mouth of the well (29:10). Everything is going well for the patriarch! Perhaps such an implicit divine control of events is also suggested by the motif of "stone" in this pericope, as in the previous one where a stone represented the presence of deity.[5] "Stone," therefore, achieves some prominence in this account. Fokkelman makes an astute observation about Jacob and his experience with stones: "When he received the promise of the support of the God of Abraham and the blessing of Abraham, he immortalized that theophany by means of a massebe [מַצֵּבָה, *matsevah*, "pillar," 28:18]. Now he feels that his life proceeds along the right track and he rolls the heavy stone away."[6] Indeed, this "rolling the stone from the mouth of the well" is mentioned thrice (29:3, 8, 10). That comports with the absence of any mention of Yahweh in the first half of this pericope; God may be removed from the scene without loss. Everything has been going well; surely God has forgotten Jacob's misdemeanors, and he has gotten away without so much as a slap on the wrist. Instead, Jacob has been led to the right land, to the right location, to the right relatives, and to the right bride (or so it seems). God and his righteous standards do not really seem to matter now—they may well be rolled away. Everything is coming together for the runaway patriarch and it does not seem to be an issue whether God is present or not.

Jacob's conversation with the shepherds by the well was almost an inquisition—three questions (29:4, 5, 6), an arrogant assertion about the state of events, and a series of imperatives: "water . . ., and go, pasture" (29:7).[7] Rather brash and self-confident,

---

4. *Genesis 11:27–50:26*, 460.

5. There is considerable wordplay related to the consonants ב (*b*) and נ (*n*): אֶבֶן (*'eben*, "stone," 29:2, 3 [×2], 8, 10), אָב (*'ab*, "father," 29:9, 12 [×2]), בֵּן (*ben*, "son," 29:1, 5, 12, 13), and לָבָן (*laban*, "Laban," 29:5, 10 [×3], 13).

6. Fokkelman, *Narrative Art in Genesis*, 125.

7. The question Jacob asks the shepherds about Laban and the answer he is given carry a note of irony: "Is there peace with him," asks the runaway. "Peace," comes the reply (29:6). But as it turned out, for *Jacob* there would be no peace "with him [Laban]." In fact, the word שָׁלוֹם (*shalom*) would never be used again in the Jacob story; that was something he apparently never experienced, as he would confess

and this from a foreigner completely oblivious of the customs of the land. Quite presumptuously, he breaks with convention (29:8) and moves the stone covering the well himself, as he sees Rachel approaching with her flock (29:9–10). He is in charge, or so he thinks, and things are moving according to his plan. This is further emphasized in the play of sound between שׁקה (*shqh*, "water," resounding in 29:2, 3, 7, 8, 10) and נשׁק (*nshq*, "kiss": 29:11, Jacob kisses Rachel; and 29:13, Laban kisses Jacob). All that watering has been successful, and the long-lost relatives rendezvous. Jacob kisses, lifts his voice, weeps, explains the situation; Rachel runs and tells her father; Laban runs, embraces, kisses Jacob, and brings him home.[8] All's well that begins well, one might think, for Jacob has only had good "luck" so far. It seems things are going according to plan: Rebekah had advised Jacob to stay with Laban for "a few days" (27:44); after meeting Laban, he stays with him for "a month of days" (29:14). And what Rebekah had recommended, "Stay with him" (27:44), is coming to pass: both the narrator ("he stayed with him," 29:14) and Laban himself ("stay with me," 29:19) echo that phrase. Despite what Jacob may have been thinking, the narrator clearly wants the reader to recognize the hand of God in all of these serendipities. God is keeping his word to be with Jacob (28:15), and the way of Jacob is blessed by him.

Nonetheless, there are hints of danger. Jacob was bound eastward in 29:1, and that direction has usually never boded well thus far in Genesis. East was where Cain settled when driven out of God's presence (4:16); the Babelites went eastward and engaged in a disastrous building enterprise (11:2); Lot went eastward to Sodom and Gomorrah (13:11); and Abraham's non-elect children were dispatched thereto (25:6). Thus, right at the start, there is a portent of a negative outcome.

Then the description "Laban, his mother's brother" occurs three times in 29:10, making the point rather redundantly, that Laban was the brother of *Rebekah*, the mastermind behind the deception of Isaac. The reader and, implicitly, Jacob are being put on notice: he is now dealing with "Laban, his mother's brother." Can one expect any straight dealing from the brother of Rebekah? Thrice Laban's label is mentioned, and thrice in the future Laban would attempt to cheat Jacob: the first—and only successful—attempt concerned "Rachel the daughter of Laban, his mother's brother" (29:10a; see 29:15–26 for Laban's switch of Leah for Rachel); the second concerned "the sheep of Laban, his mother's brother" (29:10b; see 30:25–31 for Laban's attempt to cheat Jacob out of his wages); and the third dealt with, again, "the sheep of Laban, his mother's brother" (29:10c; see 31:1–55 for Laban's efforts to preclude Jacob's escape with his flock).[9]

---

to Pharaoh much later (47:9, where he testified that his days were "few and painful/evil").

8. No doubt, Laban's alacrity and enthusiasm may have been impelled by thoughts of another caravan of riches arriving from his brother-in-law's place (as happened in 24:29–32, which also had Laban running). So this notation that Laban "ran" hints at his ulterior motives and foreshadows how "his mother's brother" would relate to Jacob. In fact, skeptical ancient rabbis speculated that Laban in his embrace of Jacob frisked him for any gold on his person, and in his kiss of his nephew, uncle checked out Jacob's mouth for any pearls the latter may have secreted there (*Gen. Rab.* 70.13)!

9. Moreover, Laban's subsequent acknowledgement that Jacob was "my bone and my flesh" (29:14) whispers more than it actually announces: if Jacob was a deceiver, his uncle—"his mother's brother" (i.e.,

But there is no word about marriage, for which Jacob had been sent to Paddan-Aram by his parents (28:1–5). How was God going to fulfill that part about Jacob's descendants (28:14)?

20.2 *Genesis 29:15–30*

> **THEOLOGICAL FOCUS 20.2**
>
> 20.2 God's blessings do not preclude the possibility of appropriate discipline for misdeeds (29:15–30).

NOTES 20.2

20.2 *God's blessings do not preclude the possibility of appropriate discipline for misdeeds.*

The bulk of this episode is structured chiastically around Jacob's accusation of deception and Laban's poignant defense employing the birth-order argument (see below).[10] This, in a sense, is the core of the entire pericope, for it crystallizes its thrust: appropriate discipline—comeuppance—for misdeeds.

> **A** Jacob's payment for his wife: 7 years ("love," "serve," 29:20)
> > **B** Marriage to Leah: deception by Laban ("went into," "gave maid … as maid," 29:21–24)
> > > **C** Jacob's accusation and Laban's defense (29:25–26)
> > **B'** Marriage to Rachel: negotiation by Laban ("went into," "gave maid … as maid," 29:27–30a)
> **A'** Jacob's payment for his wife: 7 years ("love," "serve,"29:30b)

As was noted earlier, "service" recurs several times in this pericope (29:15, 18, 20, 25, 27 [×2], 30), reflecting the exploitative tendencies of Uncle Laban. Jacob, though, appears to have been fair in his offer of recompense to Laban for Rachel's hand in marriage. In Old Babylonian times, a worker could expect to earn about one shekel a month.[11] The maximum dowry to be paid by the man to the family of a woman he had violated and whom he would therefore have to marry, was set at fifty shekels of silver (Deut 22:29). Thus Jacob's offer to serve seven years for Rachel (Gen 29:18) was a princely sum, in excess of the norm. One also notes that Jacob is careful to be specific as to what he is working for: "Rachel, your younger daughter" (29:18). In light of what happens later, perhaps it is no surprise that Laban's reply is quite non-specific: "It is good that I give *her* to you, than I give *her* to another man" (29:19). Who is he referring to by "her"?

---

cut from the same cloth as Rebekah)—would prove to be even more of one.

10. Modified from Ross, *Creation and Blessing,* 498.

11. Monroe, "Money and Trade," 161.

Jacob's demand of Laban, at the end of his seven-year servitude, is ominous. There is a brusqueness in his utterance, without the politeness of a "please," as he agitates for his wages: "Give my wife" (29:21). Strikingly, his reason, וְאָבוֹאָה אֵלֶיהָ, *wabo'ah 'eleha*, "that I may go in to her," turns out to carry a pun on "Leah"—לֵאָה, *le'ah*. That Laban does not reply in word to Jacob's peremptory claim is no less sinister. The uncle, "his mother's brother," had some tricks up his sleeve. He had figured out how to marry off his older daughter *and* his younger one in one fell swoop. There is no consideration of how Jacob might feel about this entrapment, neither is there any thought about Leah who, "already scorned for her plainness, is shifted off like a dummy and whose very presence will remind Jacob of his uncle's deceit every day. Laban's self-interest is more important to him."[12] He is, after all, Rebekah's brother, and Jacob ends up deceived.[13] Again, one sees wordplays on "Leah," and this even before Jacob is aware of the substitution that has been made: לֵאָה . . . אֵלָיו . . . אֵלֶיהָ (*le'ah . . . 'elayw . . . 'eleha*; "[he took] Leah . . . [brought her] to him . . . [he went] into her," 29:23).

Jacob's accusation of Laban the next day is pungent with irony: "You deceived me"—רִמִּיתָנִי (*rimmitani*, 29:25), related to the cognate noun, מִרְמָה (*mirmah*, "deceit"); that was exactly Isaac's accusation of his son in 27:35: "Your brother came with *deceit*." In fact, there is only one more occurrence of a related word in the entire Jacob story (in 34:13, to describe the "deception" of the Shechemites by Jacob's sons). Clearly the use of the word in 29:25 is to link back to 27:35.[14] Notice also the narrator's pointed assertions of time: 29:23 has וַיְהִי בָעֶרֶב (*wayhi ba'erev*, "Now it happened, in the evening"), when Laban accomplished the substitution; and 29:25 has וַיְהִי בַבֹּקֶר (*wayhi baboqer*, "Now it happened, in the morning"), when Jacob realized he had been tricked. The exact parallelism, with evening and morning, reminds us that Jacob was deceived because he could not see (in the dark). Again, this harks back to Jacob's own deception of Isaac, who was blind and could not see that it was not Esau, but Jacob, who stood

12. Fokkelman, *Narrative Art in Genesis*, 126. Leah's name may mean "cow," if derived from an Akkadian root; Rachel means "ewe" (Wenham, *Genesis 16–50*, 235). It is unclear if the characteristic of Leah's eyes—רַךְ, *rak*, "tender/weak" (29:17)—is laudatory or derogatory. The negative connotation of רַךְ is seen in Deut 20:8; 2 Sam 3:39. Considering the description of Rachel—"of beautiful form and . . . beautiful in sight" (29:17)—Leah is clearly ranked second. Even the construction of the sentence appears to emphasize that observation, contrasting the *eyes* of Leah with *Rachel* herself: "The eyes of Leah were . . ., but Rachel was. . . ." "Old, and still unmarried, 'Cow' even had unattractive eyes in comparison to the younger, stunningly beautiful, and also still available 'Lamb'" (Cotter, *Genesis*, 222).

13. Wenham, *Genesis 16–50*, 236, thinks the deception was successful because of "[t]he lateness of the hour, the veiling of the bride, and maybe a little too much drink." After all, to celebrate the wedding, Laban had prepared a "feast," מִשְׁתֶּה, *mishteh*, from שָׁתָה, *shtah*, "drink" (29:22): this was a banquet that overflowed. Josephus concurs, noting that Jacob was deceived "in drink and in the dark" (*Ant.* 1.19.7). Another reason to suspect the role of alcohol in Jacob's befuddlement is the reference to "younger" and "firstborn" (29:26); the last time the two words were found together was in 19:31, 33, 34, 35, 37, 38, in the story of Lot and his two daughters—another story of deception and intercourse . . . and inebriation. (The two descriptors בְּכִירָה, *bkirah*, "firstborn," and צְעִירָה, *tsa'irah*, "younger," occur in the feminine form only in Gen 19 and 29, in the entire Pentateuch.)

14. The verb "deceive," רמה, *rmh*, may also be a pun on Laban, for he is described as an "Aramean," אֲרַמִּי (*'arami*, 25:20; 28:5; 31:20, 24)—a more-than-appropriate match for "Jacob," יַעֲקֹב, *y'qb*, the "heel-grabber."

before him (27:1). Of course, the clinching factor that links the two deceptions is the exchange motif: older for younger. In Jacob's act of deception, he, the younger was substituted for the older, Esau. In Laban's perpetration of imposture, Leah, the older was substituted for the younger, Rachel (see below).[15] One might also recall that Jacob and Laban, both referred to each other as אָח, *'akh*, "brother" (29:12, 15); in context, each one meant "relative," of course, but the verbal links are deliberate—brother had deceived brother in Gen 27, and now "brother" had deceived "brother" in Gen 29!

It is also significant that Jacob's indignant question to Laban ("What is this you have done to me?") echoes Rebekah's warning to Jacob to watch out for Esau's murderous inclinations because of what "you [Jacob] did to him." The wording is virtually identical (עָשִׂיתָ לּוֹ, *'asita lo*, "you did to him" in 27:45; and עָשִׂיתָ לִּי, *'asita li*, "you did to me" in 29:25). The connection of one deception with the other is unmistakable. This is made all the more stinging when Laban declares, "It is not done [לֹא־יֵעָשֶׂה, *lo' ye'aseh*—Laban uses Jacob's verb, עשׂה, *'sh*] so in our place to give [in marriage] the younger before the firstborn" (29:26).[16] "Younger" and "firstborn" were the very designations of Jacob and Esau, respectively (25:23, 32; 27:19, 32). Indeed, the narrator (through Laban) suddenly springs the verbal coup of *younger-firstborn* (בְּכִיר־צָעִיר, *tsa'ir-bakir*) upon the reader, for earlier, in 29:16, the antithesis was *littler-greater* (גָּדוֹל־קָטָן, *qatan-gadol*). And in 29:18 Jacob had himself employed קָטָן rather than צָעִיר to describe his preference for Rachel.[17] But then, without warning, we have Laban's words "בְּכִיר־צָעִיר" in 29:26—a stunning blow indeed, as "Rachel-Leah" is described for the first time in terms of "Jacob-Esau," right at point of the deception. Readers are no less shocked than Jacob would have been, as he heard from Laban's mouth those terms for Rachel and Leah that had earlier described himself and Esau. Jacob *and* the readers go "Ouch!" "The meaning of this is profound. The *hybris* and highhandedness with which Jacob works at his destiny, to become ruler, have their own faultlessly measured nemesis. The crime receives its own, absolutely fitting punishment. Jacob has been unmasked, he is completely powerless."[18] In other words, what Jacob had sowed, he was now reaping. The deceiver had become the deceived. The chickens, for sure, had come home to roost. "The story of switching the daughters plainly corresponds with Jacob's own behavior in the story of the stolen blessing: hidden by his father's blindness, the younger brother (Jacob), directed by his mother, impersonates his elder brother; like-

---

15. Perhaps the assimilation of Rachel–Ewe and Leah–Cow also fits the deception redux, for Jacob's cheating of Isaac involved the skin of an animal from the flock (27:16). See Noegel, "Drinking Feasts and Deceptive Feats," 172.

16. According to Sarna, *Genesis*, 194, all three OT uses of the formula לֹא יֵעָשֶׂה, *lo' ye'aseh*, in the Bible refer to "acts of great moral turpitude"—Gen 34:7 (the rape of Dinah) and 2 Sam 13:12 (the rape of Tamar), besides Gen 29:26.

17. In a sense, "Jacob had remained true to himself . . . by preferring Rachel to the elder sister!" (Fokkelman, *Narrative Art in Genesis*, 128). Here he is again, upturning the normal orders and hierarchies.

18. Ibid., 130.

wise—but conversely—the elder sister (Leah), hidden by darkness and directed by her father (who is the brother of Jacob's mother), impersonates her younger sister."[19]

The threefold "*stay*(ed) with him/me" of Rebekah, the narrator, and Laban (27:44; 29:14, 19, respectively), now becomes, after the tables have been turned on the deceiver, a threefold "*serve*(ed) with you/me/Laban" of Jacob, Laban, and the narrator (29:25, 27, 30, respectively). Fokkelman notes that the episode that began with motif of עבד ('*bd*, "serve," 29:15) also ends, in 29:30, with עבד. "The fox is in the trap with both his hindlegs!"[20] Incidentally, עבד occurs in a deliberately patterned fashion in this pericope depicting, quite graphically, the tables being turned.[21]

29:15–20: Pre-deception	29:21–30: Post-deception
Laban's question (29:15): "Should you *serve* me for nothing?"	**Jacob's question** (29:25): "Was it not for Rachel that I *served*?"
Jacob's response (29:18): "I will *serve* you ... for Rachel."	**Laban's response** (29:27) "We will give ... for the *service* you *serve*.
Narrator's comment (29:20): "So Jacob *served* ... for Rachel."	**Narrator's comment** (29:30): "And he *served*."

The story ends on a rather sad note. On the surface, it seems things have settled down, and Jacob has married the one he wanted to in the first place. But unlike his first term of seven-year service that "became in his eyes a few days" (29:20), no such exhilaration is mentioned with his second sabbatical indenture (29:30). Instead we have a statement about spousal partiality: Jacob loved Rachel more than he did Leah. The story, then, is not over; they do *not* live happily ever after!

SERMON FOCUS AND OUTLINES

THEOLOGICAL FOCUS OF PERICOPE 20 FOR PREACHING

20 God's blessings do not preclude the possibility of appropriate discipline for misdeeds (29:1–30).

Wenham notes wisely:

> Within the narrative there is no theological comment at all, and the narrator leaves us to reflect on how these events fit in with the promises made to Jacob

19. Zakovitch, "Inner-Biblical Interpretation," 113. The sequence of events towards the end of the episode is as follows: Jacob "completed the week" for Leah (29:27–28), the bridal week of nuptial festivities; he receives Rachel as his second bride; and he serves for another seven years. Here also, Laban's bargain with Jacob employs a wordplay: "Complete [מַלֵּא, *malle'*] the week of this one [Leah] and we will give you the other [Rachel] also . . ." (29:27). "Complete" is the Piel imperative form of מלא, *ml'*, a form which verbally echoes "Leah" (לֵאָה, *le'ah*). The Piel recurs in 29:28: "He completed [וַיְמַלֵּא, *waymalle'*] this week." Noegel observes that it is only the Piel form that makes this wordplay with "Leah" possible; in fact, when the verb מלא first occurs in the Jacob–Laban contract (in 29:21, the only other occurrence of the verb in this pericope), it is in the Qal form (מָלְאוּ, *mal'u*) that does not resonate with "Leah." See Noegel, "Drinking Feasts and Deceptive Feats," 168.

20. *Narrative Art in Genesis*, 130.

21. Table below from Frisch, "'Your Brother Came with Guile,'" 284.

and the providential overruling of his career. The obvious linkages with the earlier episodes in which Jacob deceived his father . . . surely indicate that, although Jacob is chosen, he does not escape divine justice. Nowhere does Scripture allow that the elect are immune from God's discipline and punishment.[22]

The sermon on this pericope is best focused upon the comeuppance of Jacob: what he sowed, he reaped. That, of course, is not to assert that divine retribution always follows every human infraction. Thankfully, God does not operate in a contractual manner, whether for discipline or for blessing. There is mercy in discipline and grace in blessing—both divine actions being non-commensurate with human deeds. Nevertheless, the potential for appropriate discipline for misdeeds must always be borne in mind—not eternal condemnation for sin, that has been obviated by the atoning work of the Lord Jesus Christ, but the discipline of a loving Father, the consequences of malfeasance, and the divinely permitted payback in the same coin.[23] A brief reminder of the surety of the promises of God might make an appropriate opening move in the sermon, as structured below. One must keep the thrust of this sermon distinct from that of Pericope 18, which dealt with Jacob's deception of his father and brother. There the focus was upon preventing future duplicity. Here the emphasis in application is on repentance for past misdeeds.

Possible Preaching Outlines for Pericope 20

I. God's Promises: *While God's certain and guaranteed promises bless his children on the way . . .*
    Things working out well for Jacob (29:1–14)
    Despite the seeming absence of God, his presence, work, and sovereign control are indisputable (29:1–14)
    Move-to-Relevance: How we might misread the blessings of God as our own doing

II. God's Punishment: *. . . God's promises do not preclude the possibility of God's punishment, so . . .*
    Jacob receives the recompense for his earlier act of deception (29:15–30)
    Despite the seeming absence of God, his disciplinary consequences for sin may be expected (29:15–30)
    Move-to-Relevance: How we might misread the blessings of God as his forgetfulness of our wrongdoing

---

22. *Genesis 16–50*, 238. See Prov 3:12; Amos 3:2; Heb 12:5–6.

23. The Bible is clear about temporal blessings and temporal discipline. The idea that, in Christ, neither is valid is theologically unviable. God is certainly pleased by his children's obedience (John 15:10; Col 1:10; 1 John 2:5; 4:12; Jude 21) and there are consequences *now* for such obedience (Prov 3:1–10; Rom 8:6; 2 Cor 13:11; Gal 6:16; Phil 4:6–7; etc.). The number of hortatory greetings and benedictions of Paul that God may grant his readers grace, mercy, and peace, suggest that these were not automatic, at least not in this age, but contingent upon certain behaviors (see Rom 1:7; 1 Cor 1:3; 2 Cor 1:2; Gal 1:3; Eph 1:2; Phil 1:2; Col 1:2; 1 Thess 1:1; 2 Thess 3:16; 1 Tim 1:2; 2 Tim 1:2; Titus 1:4; Phlm 3; 1 Pet 1:2; 2 Pet 1:2; 2 John 3; 3 John 15; Jude 2; Rev 1:4). The corresponding negative aspect, God's discipline and chastisement of his children when they fail to walk with him, is also promised: Deut 1:31–36; 4:23–28; 5:11; 6:14–15; 7:9–10; 8:19–20; 11:16–17, 26–32; 27:12–26; 28:15–68; 30:17–18; 31:15–43; etc.; and in the NT, in 1 Cor 5:1–13; Gal 6:7; 1 Tim 6:9–10; Titus 3:9; Heb 12:5–11 (quoting Prov 3:11–12; also see Prov 15:5), 15–17; 13:17; 1 Pet 3:7; 4:17–19; Rev 2:5; 3:19; etc. For a the discussion of these issues, see Kuruvilla, *Privilege the Text!* 252–58.

III.   *. . . Recognize retribution and repent!*
The recognition of divine discipline should lead us to repent of the misdeeds that provoked it
Community repentance[24]

With a slight shift in emphasis, the sermon outline may be redone to focus upon the activity of God in blessing and disciplining, even though his hand may be indiscernible and imperceptible. Far too often, children of God tend to disregard God's blessings and misread them as the product of their own diligence, hard work, or cleverness. Not so: every blessing is of God! And, correspondingly, children of God tend to disregard God's discipline and misread it as the result of randomness, someone else's fault, or as one of life's invariable stumbles. Not so. While not every setback, injury, or wrong is divine discipline, the possibility of such discipline is real; with help from the community of God, one must be careful to recognize discipline from the hand of God and repent of the misdeeds that provoked it.

I.   God is Active in Blessing
Despite the seeming absence of God, his presence, work, and sovereign control are indisputable (29:1–14)
Move-to-Relevance: How we might misread the blessings of God as our own doing

II.   God is Active in Disciplining
Despite the seeming absence of God, his disciplinary consequences for sin are unmistakable (29:15–30)
Move-to-Relevance: How we might misread the discipline of God as merely an accidental occurrence

III.   *Recognize retribution and repent!*
The recognition of divine discipline should lead one to repent of the misdeeds that provoked it
Community repentance

24. The recognition of divine discipline for particular misdeeds is not a facile matter. Cause and effect are not always tightly linked or easily discernible. Such activities are best accomplished in community, between persons accountable to, and responsible for, one another, and they form an integral part of pastoral care and the "cure of souls." Within the worship service itself, where the sermon is ideally located, the preacher may choose to lead the congregation in corporate confession and repentance, best tied in with the celebration of the Lord's Supper. The leader must also be cognizant of the church calendar, whether it is the Lenten season, or other appropriate time, when acts of contrition and mortification are particularly appropriate.

PERICOPE 21

Openhandedness, not Highhandedness

Genesis 29:31–30:24

[Rachel and Leah Battle; Rachel Surrenders and is Blessed]

REVIEW, SUMMARY, PREVIEW

Review of Pericope 20: Genesis 29:1–30 has Jacob arriving at his uncle's house in Paddan-Aram and working for seven years for the hand of Rachel. Laban, his uncle, deceives him by substituting the older Leah for the younger Rachel, and Jacob receives his just deserts. Discipline for misdeeds is a distinct possibility for God's people in his economy.

Summary of Pericope 21: This pericope depicts the struggle between Leah and Rachel: one for her husband's love, the other for her husband's children. Rachel does all she can to gain a child, even engaging in deceptive practices, jealous manipulations, and obscure therapies, all in vain. However, the text informs us that the moment she gave up her stratagems, God opened her womb. The blessings of God are experienced not by those who maintain a posture of highhandedness, but those who adopt one of openhandedness (humble dependence).

Preview of Pericope 22: In the next pericope (30:25–31:16), Jacob decides to return to Canaan. Following upon his request for appropriate compensation from Laban, his employer, Jacob engages in some creative animal husbandry, and his flocks greatly increase in number. Later he attributes this prosperity to God's sovereign work, thus pointing to the fact that the sovereignty of God works in tandem with the faithful discharge of human responsibility.

21. *Genesis 29:31–30:24*

THEOLOGICAL FOCUS OF PERICOPE 21

21 **The proper posture for the reception of divine blessing is one of faithful submission to God, not one of highhandedness that resorts to manipulative devices to obtain blessing (29:31–30:24).**

    21.1   God's children trust in his sovereign timing for his blessings, without resorting to manipulative devices to obtain them (29:31–30:13).

    21.2   The proper posture for the reception of divine blessing is one of submission to God, not of highhandedness (30:14–34).

OVERVIEW

This pericope forms the centerpiece of the structure of the entire Jacob saga (for that structure, see Pericope 16). It recounts the rather odd struggle between the two wives of Jacob, Leah and Rachel, for reproductive priority and preeminence. On the surface, the bizarre nature of the story resists any attempt to discern the logic of its location in the center of the rest of the broader narrative. But Fokkelman is right: "At first sight this seems to be a mechanical enumeration of births, a rather perfunctory excursion. But careful listening shows otherwise."[1] Indeed! We shall find out that the pericope is a perfect fit as the turning point in the story of Jacob—a crystallization in this pericope of what the author is *doing* with what he is saying in that larger saga.

The overall time that Jacob spends in Paddan-Aram/Haran is twenty years (31:38, 41). There are two seven-year periods of service Jacob gives Laban for his two wives, Leah and Rachel—seven before the weddings, and seven after. Six more years would pass before Jacob returned to Canaan—i.e., he stayed with Laban until the birth of Joseph to Rachel, Jacob's twelfth child (30:25). Thus the events of this pericope—the conception, gestation, and delivery of twelve children (to four different women; seven to Leah alone) consume the best part of the last decade of Jacob's sojourn in Haran.

One would have thought that with his marriage to Rachel, things would settle down; after all he had run away from a dysfunctional scene at home and from a brother with murderous intent. The pretext for his escape was to achieve an endogamous marriage. And he had managed to find himself with not one, but two brides.[2] But the struggles of his life do not cease; strife seems to dog Jacob all his life; this phase is no exception.

The boundaries of this pericope are the opening of Leah's womb on one side and the opening of Rachel's on the other.

---

1. Fokkelman, *Narrative Art in Genesis*, 132.

2. While the story of Lamech (Gen 4:19) may deprecate bigamy, as also does Lev 18:18, there is no explicit condemnation of polygamy in Genesis. However, all such unions in the book only multiply problems for the concerned parties.

> **A**   Leah: Yahweh sees Leah and opens her womb (29:31–35)
>   **B**   Rachel and Jacob (30:1–3)
>   **C**   Rachel and Leah (and maids) (30:4–13)
>   **C'**   Rachel and Leah (and mandrakes) (30:14–15)
>   **B'**   Leah and Jacob (30:16–21)
> **A'**   Rachel: God remembers Rachel and opens her womb (30:22–24)

Another way to structure the pericope is by enumerating the reproductive outcomes[3]:

29:31–35	Leah: 4 children
30:1–13	Rachel and Leah, through maids: 4 children
30:14–24	Rachel and Leah: 4 children

21.1 Genesis 29:31–30:13

THEOLOGICAL FOCUS 21.1

21.1   God's children trust in his sovereign timing for his blessings, without resorting to manipulative devices to obtain them (29:31–30:13).

NOTES 21.1

21.1   *God's children trust in his sovereign timing for his blessings, without resorting to manipulative devices to obtain them.*[4]

At the start, we have the contrast between unloved Leah and beloved Rachel (29:30–31). "Unloved" (שָׂנֵא, *sn'*, 29:31, 33) is quite a strong word, almost equivalent to "hatred" (as in 24:60; 26:27; 37:4, 5, 8). Though unloved, her womb is open, and Leah proceeds to bear four sons in what is literarily rapid succession. Rather than Leah speaking to Jacob, the naming of each son is her prayer to God, hoping against hope that her husband's attitude to her will change—each child a lament to deity, ostensibly each lament-cycle lasting the duration of her nine-month gestation! With Reuben (רְאוּבֵן, *r'uben*, "look, a son," 29:32), Leah hopes that Jacob will love her because Yahweh has seen her affliction and answered her with a son; with Simeon (שִׁמְעוֹן, *shim'on*, from the root שׁמע, *shm'*, "to hear," 29:33) she is thankful for Yahweh's hearing of her unloved status; with Levi (לֵוִי, *levi*, possibly from the root לָוָה, *lavah*, "to attach," 29:34), she maintains the hope that her husband will become attached to her; and with Judah (יְהוּדָה, *yhudah*, "he will be praised," 29:35), she is certain Yahweh will be praised, perhaps because her husband's heart will be turned towards her. All of this turns out to be wishful thinking. There is no response from Jacob; in fact, the man does not even seem to play a role in the four instances of Leah's conception, let alone in the naming of his children!

---

3. From ibid., 132.

4. This is a positive restatement of Rachel's negative portrayal of the Theological Focus of this section.

What is significant at the end of round one is that Leah stopped bearing (29:35; also 30:9). We are not told why. It cannot be age, for she seems fertile enough to bear three more children later (30:17–21). It could be a divine, sovereign act of womb-closing, of course, but the text gives no hint about that. In any case, there is a "gap" in the narrative here (which will be filled later).[5]

This frenzy of baby-production by the unloved woman with the open womb— a divine act of mercy—puts the loved woman with the closed womb in desperation and in the green grip of jealousy (30:1). That sets Rachel on a course of threatening, manipulation, monopolizing, exchanging, and domineering: a highhanded attitude![6] She wants to be blessed. But her idea of how this can be accomplished is way off the mark—she appeals to Jacob in a fit of pique, demanding that he provide her with children (30:1–2). The barrenness of a matriarch was old news, having been previously encountered in 11:30 (Sarah) and 25:21 (Rebekah). The wives of all the earlier patriarchs had temporarily been through a time of barrenness, so Rachel need not have worried. Both of her ancestors had had to suffer many more years of infertility than she had to; neither one blamed her husband for the fruitlessness, as Rachel does; after all it was God who opened and closed wombs (Ps 113:9). In other words, Rachel is faithless. Her attitudes and actions, in comparison with prior Genesis history, is clearly wrong. Her peremptory demand of Jacob that he give her children "or else I die" (Gen 30:1) is not merely histrionics; she wants what she wants and when she wants it. She is manipulating to be blessed, regardless of God's sovereign action. Jacob, however, correctly diagnoses that such blessing is the exclusive work of God (30:2), and Rachel's accusation only elicits an irate rejoinder from him: "Am I in the place of God who has kept from you fruit of the womb?"[7] Or, in other words, "Am I God to bless you?" There is a stark irony in this utterance, for it came from the mouth of one who seemed to have been thinking, all along thus far, that he himself was the source of all his blessings, as he manipulated, connived, back-stabbed, and heel-grabbed his way through life. I wonder if Jacob realized, with a shock of recognition, what he had just said.[8] I wonder if he recognized in Rachel's attitude, his own. Indeed, Rachel's demand ("give," 30:1) of Jacob is as peremptory and imperious as was Jacob's demand ("give," 29:21) of Laban for his due—Rachel. In more ways than one, Rachel is a perfect match for Jacob.

---

5. Steinberg in his magisterial work, *The Poetics of Biblical Narrative,* 236, distinguishes between "gaps" and "blanks," i.e., "what was omitted for the sake of interest and what was omitted for the lack of interest," respectively. The narrator intends that the reader attend carefully to the "gaps," for what the author is *doing* with what he is (not) saying is, at least partially, discerned by following the lead of the storyteller and filling in those "gaps."

6. The first time the verb קנא (*qn'*, "to be jealous") occurs in Genesis, it is to describe the Philistines' envy of Isaac (26:14); now, the second time it is deployed it depicts not the attitude of an outsider, but that of Rachel, an insider, towards her own sister (30:1). The third and last time קנא is employed, it portrays Jacob's sons' jealousy of their sibling Joseph (37:11).

7. Wenham, *Genesis 16–50,* 244, notes that Rachel demands "sons" of Jacob; the latter refers to "fruit of the womb," acknowledging that progeny are of God (Deut 7:13; 28:4, 11, 18, 53; Ps 127:3).

8. Westermann observes wryly: "To think that after the beautiful, gentle love story of 29:1–20 this angry exchange between the two is our first and only experience of their marriage!" (*Genesis 12–36,* 474).

This struggle of Rachel to be one better than Leah—the younger attempting to upstage the older—is itself a reflection of Jacob's own machinations against Esau. It is in this sense that the narrator employs this central account of the Jacob Story to epitomize the complication/resolution phases of the Jacob story.

Even after Jacob's indignant protest, Rachel does not seek God or his intervention in her state of barrenness. Instead, she takes matters into her own hands—not unexpected, seeing how similar she was to her husband in attitude and action, initiative and intention. Rachel arranges for her maid, Bilhah, to be Jacob's concubine (30:3–4); she will do anything to get blessed, even if it means offering Jacob a surrogate; "to give birth on my knees" indicates her desire to become an adoptive mother. Another subtle—and significant—wordplay is being conducted here: "knee" is בֶּרֶךְ, *berek*, that sounds suspiciously like, and shares the same consonants as, בָּרַךְ, *barak*, "bless." Just like Jacob, the "Jacobah" (the female version of "Jacob") is gunning for blessing.[9]

The language Rachel uses to get Jacob to agree to this concubinage with Bilhah is virtually identical to that used by Sarah to persuade Abraham to have relations with her maid Hagar (16:2)—the consequences of that earlier ill-judged alliance was only disaster.

	בֹּא־נָא אֶל־שִׁפְחָתִי ... אִבָּנֶה מִמֶּנָּה
16:2	bo'-na' 'el-shifkhati ... 'ibbaneh mimmennah
	"Please *go into* my maid ... *I will be built up through her*"
	בֹּא אֵלֶיהָ ... וְאִבָּנֶה ... מִמֶּנָּה
30:3	bo' 'eleha ... w'ibbaneh ... mimmennah
	"*Go into* her ... and *I will be built up* ... *through her*"

The negative outcome of that earlier act of "unfaith" in Gen 16 colors Rachel's attempt here in Gen 30, too.

That Rachel is desperate to be like Leah, to get the blessing that her older sister possessed (which was exactly Jacob's attitude towards Esau), is sonically demonstrated as well, as Rachel offers Bilhah to Jacob as a concubine. The word אֵלֶיהָ (*'eleha*, "[go] into her," 30:3) is a pun on לֵאָה (*le'ah*, "Leah"); the word recurs in 30:4, where it is noted that Jacob went "into her" (אֵלֶיהָ). In fact, even at the end of the story, when God remembers Rachel and gives heed "to her" (אֵלֶיהָ, 30:22), "Leah" is being implicitly invoked, it seems![10]

In sum, Rachel's angst is precipitated by her infertility—a lack of blessing: She sees she is barren, and that sparks her frustrated and faithless demand of Jacob (30:1), as well as her giving her maid Bilhah to Jacob as a concubine (30:3–8).[11] The concubi-

---

9. The idea of labeling Rachel as Jacob's *doppelgänger*, a "Jacobah," was borrowed from Fokkelman, *Narrative Art in Genesis*, 135.

10. The prepositional phrase, אֵלֶיהָ is fairly common in biblical Hebrew, but Noegel shows statistically that the allusions in this pericope are significant. In Gen 29–30, "Leah" occurs eighteen times and the prepositional phrase, אֵלֶיהָ, five times. In the rest of the Jacob Story, "Leah" occurs again only five times (in Gen 33–35) and אֵלֶיהָ not at all (its next instance is in 38:2). See "Drinking Feasts and Deceptive Feats," 167 and 167–68n15.

11. Similarly, at one point, Leah sees she has stopped bearing (30:9) and proceeds to give her maid Zilpah to Jacob (30:10–13).

nage results in two sons for Rachel via Bilhah. With the arrival of the first, Rachel asserts that God has "vindicated" her—thus "Dan" (דָּן, *dan*, from דִּין, *din*, "to vindicate," 30:6). With the second, she claims that she has prevailed in her "wrestlings" against Leah—thus "Naphthali" (נַפְתּוּלִים, *naftulim*, "wrestlings," 30:8). Interestingly, "mighty wrestlings" (נַפְתּוּלֵי אֱלֹהִים, *naftule 'elohim*, the qualifier אֱלֹהִים making a superlative of the noun) could also be translated "wrestlings of (with) God." Though employing a different verb, Jacob also wrestles with God (32:24, 25); however, both Jacob and "Jacobah" are said to have "prevailed" (30:8; 32:29), further strengthening the comparison. Perhaps this is a better reading—"wrestling with God"—for she, like Jacob, is constantly struggling and striving, even with God. "In some sense, Rachel saw her struggle with Leah as a contest in which God was involved, for he had opened Leah's womb but shut hers (29:31; 30:22)."[12] Hers was a wrestling *against* the sovereign work of God in the closure of her womb; by hook or by crook, Rachel would open her own womb, even if it meant concubinage and adoption.[13] One way or another, the "Jacobah" was going to be a mother, acts of God nothwithstanding!

But this one-upmanship does not work. Leah decides two can play that game of concubinage, and so she offers her maid, Zilpah, and two more sons result: Leah is "fortunate" (thus "Gad," גָּד, *gad*, "good fortune, 30:11), and "happy" (thus "Asher," אָשֵׁר, *'asher*, "happy one," 30:13). She thinks she now has it made; she is as good as Rachel, if not better. Surely her "unloved" status would be overthrown now. The fact that through it all the narrator makes no statement about God's action in the generation of children by the maids, reserving such comments only for the conceptions and deliveries of Leah and Rachel (30:17, 22), suggests that the narrator disapproved of this womb rental that was going on.

In this flurry of baby generation throughout the pericope—twelve of them—one must note the names given to the progeny. "The names with their etymological explanations are the point at issue from paragraph to paragraph: they are the means of revealing the 'inner' meaning of the births, that the wives are engaged in keen competition for the favour of Jacob. Each name-giving serves their psychological conduct of war, which is an incessant propaganda-combat."[14] The names of the children, while serving to portray the delight and/or despair of the mother is also always a subtle jab at the other wife. Cotter labels all this action as "dueling pregnancies."[15]

However, Jacob, apparently uninvolved, does not respond to the ebullience of either wife. Throughout all this child-bearing, he seems to be merely a prop—he speaks not at all to Leah or to Rachel during their seasons of conception (beyond answering Rachel's irascible accusation in 30:2). Once he has discharged his responsibility, he is not involved in the delivery or naming of the child concerned, except for the repeated ascriptions, ". . . bore Jacob a . . . son" (30:7, 10, 12, 17, 19), and the indirect mentions

---

12. Wenham, *Genesis 16–50*, 245.

13. The verb "wrestle," פתל, *ptl*, in the Niphal elsewhere has the negative connotation of cunning and deceit (Job 5:13; Ps 18:27; Prov 8:8), an appropriate action for the "Jacobah."

14. Fokkelman, *Narrative Art in Genesis*, 133.

15. Cotter, *Genesis*, 226.

of him in the etymology of the name given to his children through Leah (29:32, 34; 30:20).

While there is no evident blessing of God being bestowed on this family, he is clearly the one who opens and closes wombs (30:2, 6, 17, 18, 20, 22, 23). It is explicitly noted that God "listened" to both Leah and Rachel (30:17, 22), resulting in pregnancies for both; not to mention the etymology of several names that adduce the help and action of God. The irony of all the frenetic activity engaged in by the women (especially Rachel with her machinations) to obtain the blessing of children is that it was all unnecessary and, indeed, counterproductive, for Yahweh sees (29:31), and Yahweh remembers (30:17, 22). And the result of his seeing and remembering is that Leah and Rachel ultimately conceive. This is God's sovereign work and, in his own time, his promised blessings (especially those of Jacob's descendants, 28:13–14, pertinent to the crises of reproduction in this pericope) come to pass. When God sees (6:5; Exod 2:25; 3:4; Deut 32:19) or remembers (Gen 8:1; 19:29; Exod 2:24), he takes decisive action, often in response to his covenant with his people. Indeed, in this pericope, God "sees," "hears," "vindicates," "gives," "gifts," "remembers," "opens (wombs)," and "takes away (reproach)"—all in relation to Jacob's wives: 29:31, 32, 33; 30:6, 17, 18, 20, 22, 23. However, there is an important condition for the reception and experience of divine blessings, as the next section details.

21.2 Genesis 30:14–24

> **THEOLOGICAL FOCUS 21.2 [WHOLE SHADED AREA IN CALIBRI PL.]**
>
> 21.2   The proper posture for the reception of divine blessing is one of submission to God, not of highhandedness (30:14–24).

NOTES 21.2

21.2   The proper posture for the reception of divine blessing is one of submission to God, not of highhandedness.

The battle for reproductive dominance rages. The crisis intensifies. And that is when Leah's oldest, Reuben, brings home mandrakes. The "mandrake" (of the genus *Mandragora,* family *Solanaceae,* subfamily *Solanoideae*—that also contains potato, pepper, tomato, eggplant, and comprises several species) is a Mediterranean perennial, known to be an aphrodisiac in ancient times. The word for mandrakes, דּוּדָאִים, *duda'im* (μῆλον μανδραγόρας, *mēlon mandragoras*) is quite similar to דֹּדִים, *dodim,* "love" (Prov 7:18; Song 1:4; 4:10; 5:1; 7:12; Ezek 16:8; 23:17; in fact, in many of these uses, eroticism and sexual activity are strongly implied).[16] Rachel clearly views this as the answer to her infertility problems and demands her share. She is "wrestling" again, attempting to overcome divine sovereignty in the closure of her womb, engaging in physiological

---

16 Harrison, "The Mandrake and the Ancient World," 87–92; Mathews, *Genesis 11:27–50:26,* 486.

manipulation with a bit of flora! And another exchange is accomplished—Jacob for mandrakes: he would be allowed by Rachel to sleep with Leah. Leah wants Jacob's love and Rachel wants Jacob's children, and a deal is struck.

This is the fourth exchange in the Jacob saga: Jacob vs. Esau (*trade:* stew for birthright), Jacob vs. Esau (*deception:* stealing of the firstborn's blessing), Rachel vs. Leah (*deception:* Leah substituted for Rachel), Rachel vs. Leah (*trade:* mandrakes for Jacob).[17]

A	Esau born first, before Jacob (25:19–26) Jacob makes an exchange with Esau (25:19–34)	
	B	Transposition of blessing: Isaac and Jacob (not Esau)
	C	Departure from Canaan: Jacob at Bethel (28:10–22) Arrival at Haran: Jacob at the well (29:1–4)
	B'	Transposition of blessing: Laban and Leah (not Rachel)
A'	Leah, a mother first, before Rachel (29:31–30:13) Rachel makes an exchange with Leah (30:14–24)	

But what is significant here is Leah's expostulation: "Is it a small thing for you take my husband? And will you take my son's mandrakes also?" (30:15). There we get the filling of the "gap" that had been created by the narrator in 29:35 and 30:9, the answer to the question of why Leah had stopped bearing. She had stopped bearing, because Rachel was not allowing Jacob to sleep with Leah! This was nothing but malevolent jealousy—if Rachel was not going to have children by Jacob, then she was not going to allow Leah that privilege either.[18] Desperate for children, Rachel would not only do whatever it took to succeed, but she would preempt others from getting ahead of her. She was looking for exclusive rights to what only God could give, and she wanted it her way, right away, as she attempted to create a monopoly on divine blessing. Truly, a "Jacobah"! The similarities between husband and wife are considerable[19]:

Jacob	Rachel
The "younger" (צָעִיר, *tsa'ir*, 25:23) ...	The "younger" (צְעִירָה, *tsa'irah*, 29:26) ...
trades his stew of lentils	trades her "right" to Jacob
(25:34, a *concrete* item),	(30:15, an *abstract* item),
making an exchange with Esau,	making an exchange with Leah,
the "firstborn"	the "firstborn"
(בְּכוֹר, *bkor*, 27:19, 32), ...	(בְּכִירָה, *bkirah*, 29:26), ...
for the birthright	for the mandrakes
(25:31–34; 27:36, an *abstract* item).	(30:15, a *concrete* item).

So Leah, in effect, hires Jacob's sexual services (30:16); and she says so explicitly to her husband. "Hire" (שָׂכַר) is a significant word in the Jacob narratives (30:16 [×2],

---

17. Table modified from Fokkelman, *Narrative Art in Genesis*, 141.

18. One might wonder why Rachel did not keep Leah's maid, Zilpah, from Jacob, as she had done with Leah. I surmise that Rachel, at that point (in 30:9–13), did not care, since her own maid was doing quite well in the labor and delivery department (30:4–8). This again only underscores her primary frustration with Leah and the latter's good fortune with pregnancies. Rachel's jealousy and highhandedness was exclusively focused upon her older sibling!

19. Table from Fokkelman, *Narrative Art in Genesis*, 140.

18, 28, 32, 33, 31:8 [×2]), occurring nowhere else in Genesis as a verb; so also is "wages" (מַשְׂכֹּרֶת, *maskoret*, 29:15; 31:7, 41), and this word does not turn up again in the Pentateuch. For Jacob, life is seemingly one of hiring and wages, contracts and pacts—self-initiated and self-attempted advancements in life, most of them marked by deception perpetrated by one party or another. Everything is commercial, including the conjugal relationship with his wives who disburse his sexual services as tariff and revenue; the spiritual does not seem to enter into the equation at all.[20]

Leah is so excited she cannot wait; she goes out meet her newly-rented husband (30:16), again lending credence to the gap-filling: Rachel had indeed kept Jacob away from Leah. But God was on the unloved Leah's side for the affliction that she had suffered at the hands of husband and sister: "And God heard Leah" (30:17), and three more children result: "Issachar" (יִשָּׂשכָר, *yissakar*, "man of reward," related to שׂכר, *skr*, 30:18), "Zebulun" (זְבֻלוּן, *zbulun*, "gifted/honored," related to זבד, *zbd*/זבל, *zbl*, "gift/honor," 30:20), and Dinah (30:21; no etymological derivation is noted). All the naming, as before, seems to be a reflection of Leah's wishful thinking that things would "finally" change with each child. Perhaps it is not insignificant that the sexual relationship between husband and older wife is always denoted by the verb שׁכב (*shkv*, "to lie," 30:15, 16) and never with ידע (*yd'*, "to know"). In fact, the last three conceptions of Leah are, like her earlier ones, seemingly disconnected from any action on Jacob's part!

On the other hand, Jacob is said to "go into" (בוא, *bo'*) Leah, thinking she was Rachel (29:21, 23); and Leah demands that that Jacob "come in" to her (also from בוא, 30:16[21]), though he only "lies" with her (30:16) as was noted. But Jacob does "go into" Rachel (בוא, 29:30)—Rachel is clearly the one preferred over Leah, albeit without fruit of children.[22] Nonetheless, as with Leah's conceptions, when Rachel subsequently becomes pregnant, her conception is not said to have been accomplished by Jacob "lying" with Rachel, or "knowing" Rachel, or "going into" Rachel; instead, it was *God* who remembered Rachel, and Rachel conceived (30:22–23).[23] We are clearly being told who is responsible!

That Jacob's sexual favor was purchased for a botanical product is filled with irony: Can דוד (*dud*, "love") be bought with דוּדָאִים (*duda'im*, "mandrakes")? Could the one who claimed that God was the source of "fruit of the womb" (30:2) himself be the fruit-provider for his wife, when she has paid for him with a plant?[24] Pointedly, it is noted that God listened to Leah, resulting in her conception (30:17): clearly mandrakes played no role in this business. Mandrakes are mentioned six times in 30:14–16: five

20. Earlier, in the previous pericope (Pericope 20 [29:1–30]), it was the sisters who were objects of trade; here that dubious distinction is granted to Jacob.

21. Again, there is a pun here on "Leah" as she requisitions Jacob's services: the preposition + pronominal suffix in אֵלַי תָּבוֹא (*'elay tabo'*, "you-must-come-into-me") sounds like לֵאָה, *le'ah*, "Leah."

22. And Bilhah, Rachel's maid, is also the recipient of Jacob's "going in" (בוא, 30:4), but not Zilpah, Leah's maid.

23. She names her firstborn "Joseph" (יוֹסֵף, *yosef*, "may he add," 30:24, from יסף, *ysf*, "to add"), in hopes of having at least one more son.

24. See Noegel, "Drinking Feasts and Deceptive Feats," 166.

times explicitly (30:14 [×2], 15 [×2], 16), and once with a particle + suffix (אֹתָם, 'otam, "them"). Remarkably, once the cycles of conception (re)commence, "God" is also mentioned six times in 30:17–23: thrice in connection with Leah (30:17, 18, 20); thrice with Rachel (30:22 [×2], 23). All in all, the narrative seems to be "dismissing the notion that such superstitions [about mandrakes] may have any validity: Leah, who gives up the mandrakes, bears three children; Rachel who possesses them, remains barren for apparently three more years."[25] Not mandrakes, but *God* is in the midst of it all!

But wait! How does Leah end up bearing *three* children, one after another, when the deal with Rachel and the mandrakes was that the older sister would get *one* night with Jacob ("He may lie with you tonight," 30:15)? Here is another "gap" that the narrator has subtly introduced. What happened? Were there more mandrakes that passed hands that bought Leah a few more nocturnal trysts with Jacob? Unlikely: mandrakes are not mentioned after 30:14–16 (instead, God is). Did Leah manage to consort with Jacob unbeknownst to Rachel? Unlikely: nothing seems to have gotten past the "Jacobah" thus far. Had Rachel forgotten the one-night deal she made? Again unlikely: with the score now Leah 5 and rolling, Rachel 0 and stuck, how could she forget? The only way Leah could have gotten at least two more nights with Jacob (to conceive Zebulun and Dinah) was with Rachel's permission (see 30:15). It appears, then, that in these final days of her crises of fertility, *Rachel has given up!* Nothing has worked for her, not jealousy, not concubinage, not obstruction, not aphrodisiacs—nothing! Did Jacob's argument finally hit her then: "Am I in the place of God who has kept from you fruit of the womb?" (30:2)? I submit that the narrator is implying that Rachel now had come to the conclusion that *God* was the only one who could render a barren womb fruitful. And the narrator wants us, the readers, to arrive at that same conclusion along with Rachel, and to realize that *that* was how Leah got her unfettered access to Jacob: because Rachel gave up! She surrendered and renounced her manipulative and conniving and deceptive tendencies and, instead, submitted to the will of Yahweh.

No wonder, then, that immediately after readers are nudged towards such a conclusion, the narrator begins the final scene of this pericope with: "*Then* God remembered Rachel" (30:22). *That's when* God remembered Rachel, *when Rachel had given up.* For, you see, the proper posture to receive the blessings of God is not one of highhandedness, grasping, exploitation, and overbearing. Not at all! If one is to obtain the blessings of God, one must adopt the posture of openhandedness, of letting go, of gracious generosity, and of humility. Rachel, the narrator suggests, has, in the end, after many days of fretting and frustration, arrived at that attitude of yieldedness.

And with that, quite abruptly, it seems that Jacob, too, has come to his senses. "It happened when Rachel gave birth to Joseph, then Jacob said to Laban, 'Send me away and let me go to my place and my country'" (30:25). It appears that, after all the frenzied conceptions, gestations, and parturitions, and after all that had transpired between wives and maids and mandrakes, and perhaps after Jacob's own unwitting exclamation that he was not God (30:2)—it appears that he has landed at the same

---

25. Sarna, *Genesis*, 197.

place of helplessness as Rachel has. Jacob realizes he has some unfinished business at home, back in Canaan, with a brother and father whom he has treated most shabbily. It looks like he, Jacob, has realized—as did Rachel, the "Jacobah"—that manipulation and conniving and deception never succeed. Rather, submission to the will of God does. And so he decides: "I have to go back home!" There are only two instances of "and God remembered" in Genesis: the first was in 8:1 towards the end of the Flood account, and the second is here in 30:22. "Both stand at the turning points in their respective stories. It was God remembering Noah that led to the flood waters declining; it was God remembering Rachel that led to her conceiving and Jacob returning to the land of promise."[26]

And with that, we readers, along with these two members of this dysfunctional family who have just comprehended what they needed to do to be blessed, come to the mid-point of the Jacob Story, the turning point. This is the chapter of crisis; the tide has now begun to turn, attitudes have begun to change, hurts have begun to heal, and Yahweh has become more real.[27] The thrust of this pericope is, in essence, that of the Jacob saga seen as a whole (Gen 25–36): How does one get blessed? The answer, given in multifaceted ways, pericope by pericope, is crystallized here in the life of the female Jacob, the "Jacobah" Rachel.

> Rachel gives up the only thing that shows her precedence, the access to Jacob, and after that God shows mercy. Now we understand that it is because of this he shows mercy. Post hoc propter hoc. As soon as the younger one gives up the high-handedness of Jacob's policy and is prepared to bend, God grants her children. Her barrenness was at the same time a symbol, envy and oppression towards Leah having condemned Rachel to sterility.[28]

SERMON FOCUS AND OUTLINES

THEOLOGICAL FOCUS OF PERICOPE 21 FOR PREACHING

21   **Highhandedness precludes God's blessing, but faithful submission to God brings it about (29:31–30:24).**

Of course, nothing can stand in God's way and his sovereign purposes, but one must never let that vitiate the role of human responsibility and receptivity to the blessings of God. There *are* certain attitudes and actions that must be adopted, in order that the child of God may be the recipient of the blessings of God—a facet of spiritual life that has shown up on multiple occasions earlier in Genesis, particularly in discus-

---

26. Wenham, *Genesis 16–50*, 248.

27. Wenham notices the curious use of "Yahweh" at the beginning and end of the pericope (29:31, 32, 33, 35; 30:24); the remaining references to deity employ "God" (30:1, 6, 17, 18, 20, 33 [×2]). He explains it this way: "After a relatively cheerful start to the marriage (cf. 29:32–35), alienation between husband and wives and between the wives and God creeps in so that they speak of him as 'God,' not the Lord ["Yahweh"]. Only in this last scene, with her prayers answered, is the more intimate covenantal name 'the Lord' invoked again by Rachel" (ibid., 249).

28. Fokkelman, *Narrative Art in Genesis*, 140–41.

sions of the conditionality of the promises to Abraham. One also remembers Jude's exhortation: "Keep yourselves in the love of God" (Jude 21). God's people have the responsibility of keeping themselves in the sphere of God's love. Unconditional though that love—or any other blessing—might be, from the point of view of a sovereign God, there is no question that the *experience* of that love is conditional. That is asserted and illustrated throughout Scripture. While the previous pericope, Pericope 20, dealt with a similar facet of the divine–human relationship (God's discipline for sin), this one deals with the positive side, God's blessings are enjoyed when one's attitudes and actions are pleasing to him.

While Leah does engage Rachel in the struggle, the focus of the pericope is upon the "Jacobah" and the consequences for her. The sermon works best if the focus remains on this lady.

Possible Preaching Outlines for Pericope 21

I.   Faithless Scheming[29]
       Leah's abundant fertility (29:31–35)
       Rachel's jealousy, and her attitude that disdains the sovereignty of God (30:1–4)
       The battle of wives (and their maids) for reproductive preeminence (30:5–13)
       Move-to-Relevance: How we want things our own way, in our own time

II. Faithful Submission
       The exchange of mandrakes (30:14–17)
       The explanation of Leah's cessation of bearing: Rachel's highhandedness (30:15)
       Rachel's giving up in desperation and its fruitful consequence (30:18–24)

III. *Let go and let God . . . bless!*
       The proper attitude for the reception of blessing: Let go (submit, surrender, yield) and let God bless
       How such an attitude may be cultivated[30]

A tweak of the above outline yields one that tackles the wrong ways and the right way to be a recipient of God's blessing.

I.   How Not to Get God's blessing
       A wrong attitude: jealousy (29:31–30:1a, the reaction to Leah's blessing)
       A wrong appeal: threatening (30:1b–2, the ultimatum to Jacob)
       A wrong action: manipulation (30:3–13, the employment of concubines)
       A wrong alternative: mandrakes (30:14–15, the recourse to aphrodisiacs)
       A wrong artifice: trickery (29:35; 30:9, 15, the stealing of Jacob)
       Move-to-Relevance: Our wrong attitudes, appeals, actions, alternatives, and artifices—all unfruitful

II. How to Get God's blessing
       The right approach: submission (30:16–24, Leah's three children; Rachel's surrender; her pregnancy)
       Move-to-Relevance: How we often come to the end of our tether before we discern the

---

29. This outline is a variation of the Problem–Solution–Application formula.

30. The concept of proper "posture" for blessing that was raised in the discussion in this pericope may be fertile ground for exploration for application. Is there something we can do each day (an actual *physical* posture to adopt, in prayer or elsewhere) to mold ourselves into the attitude of receptivity to divine blessing, instead of manipulating and scheming?

right approach

III. *Let go and let God . . . bless!*
   The proper attitude for the reception of blessing: Let go (submit, surrender, yield) and let God bless
   How such an attitude may be cultivated

PERICOPE 22

Hard Work/God's Work

Genesis 30:25–31:16

[Jacob Outwits Laban; God Prospers Jacob]

REVIEW, SUMMARY, PREVIEW

Review of Pericope 21: Genesis 29:31–30:24 depicts the struggle between Leah and Rachel. Rachel does all she can to gain a child, even engaging in deceptive practices, jealous manipulations, and obscure therapies, all in vain, until she gives up her stratagems, whereupon she conceives. The blessings of God are experienced by those who maintain a posture of openhandedness (humble dependence).

Summary of Pericope 22: In this pericope, Jacob decides to return to Canaan. His request for appropriate compensation from Laban, his employer, is countered with shady tactics on the latter's part to deprive him of his due. Jacob engages in some creative animal husbandry and his flocks greatly increase in number. Later he attributes this prosperity to God's sovereign work, thus emphasizing the fact that the sovereignty of God works in tandem with the faithful discharge of human responsibility.

Preview of Pericope 23: The next pericope (31:17–55) has Jacob returning to the Promised Land pursued by Laban who accuses Jacob of abruptly decamping with his wives and children, as well as with Laban's household gods. Rachel's theft of these idols is undetected. God's protection covers the faithful even from the dangerous consequences of sin within their own camps.

22. *Genesis 30:25–31:16*

THEOLOGICAL FOCUS OF PERICOPE 22

22   In, through, and with the diligent and honest discharge of human responsibility, God sovereignly works out his blessings for his children, despite opposition (30:25–31:16).

22.1   Despite opposition, diligent work—eschewing deception—keeps one in the will of God (30:25–43).

22.2   In tandem with the discharge of human responsibility, God sovereignly works out his blessings for his children (30:25–31:16).

OVERVIEW

The beginning of this pericope is well-marked: וַיְהִי כַּאֲשֶׁר (*wayhi ka'asher*, "And it came about when . . .," 30:25) indicates a fresh start of narrative thought. However, the ending of the pericope is not so clear. Logically it seems to end with 30:43 that summarizes the prosperity of Jacob, the result of all that happened in 30:25–42. The problem is that 31:1, without a nominal subject (the subject only shows up as a verb suffix), does not formally look like the commencement of a new section: "And-he-[Jacob]-heard . . ." (וַיִּשְׁמַע, *wayyishma'*, 31:1). This being the case, I will add on 31:1–16 as part of Pericope 22, primarily to maintain the integrity of the preaching idea—dealing with the joint work of man and of God. In 30:25–43, the focus is on the former, with the latter only implicit; in 31:1–16, the work of God is explicitly acknowledged. Moreover, 31:1–16 deals with the consequence of what happened in 30:25–43.

While blessings have been promised to outsiders by the agency of the patriarchs (12:3; 22:18; 26:4; 28:14), this pericope describes the first time an outsider (Laban) is explicitly blessed through one of them (30:27, 30).[1] This blessing is also the beginning of the fulfillment of God's promise to bless "all the families of the earth" in Jacob and his descendants (28:14). One important conclusion is that if blessing on outsiders is God's doing, then Jacob's prosperity, that led to that blessing must also be God's doing. Thus the patriarch's flourishing in the first section of this pericope, 30:25–43, is undoubtedly from the hand of God. That truth is expressly acknowledged by Jacob in the second section of this pericope, 31:1–16.[2]

---

1. Ironically, Laban's comprehension that Yahweh is blessing him comes as he employs his own deities—the *teraphim* of 31:19, 30?—for divination (30:27), a practice *verboten* in the Mosaic Law (Lev 19:26; Deut 18:10). Apparently the god of Nahor (the father of Laban) and the God of Abraham were distinct entities, as indicated by the plural, יִשְׁפְּטוּ (*yishptu*, "let them judge," Gen 31:53). However, there is some question about the translation of נִחַשְׁתִּי (*nikhashti*, "I divined," 30:27). Finkelstein, surmising that the verb may be cognate with an Akkadian word that means "to flourish/prosper," suggests it be translated as "I have grown rich." Divination, moreover, was usually conducted to ascertain the future, rather than to investigate an event in the past, such as the source of Laban's blessing, so Finkelstein may well be right ("An Old Babylonian Herding Contract," 34, 34n19).

2. Another striking detail is that while Laban is said to be blessed, Jacob, himself, is never noted to have been a recipient of divine blessing, though it is obvious that God is prospering the patriarch. There has not even been an explicit promise of blessing for Jacob thus far. Even the tremendous success of Jacob's animal breeding activities is never labeled "blessing," though it is clearly of God. In contrast, both

In the chiastic structure of the Jacob narratives, 30:25–31:16 is balanced by 29:15–30: in the first, there is the deception by Laban, and in the second, the outwitting of Laban; in both, one finds "serve/service" (29:15, 18, 20, 25, 27, 30, and 30:26 [×3], 29; 31:6) and "wages/hire" (מַשְׂכֻּרְתּ, *maskoret*, 29:15, and שׂכר, *skr*, 30:28, 32, 33; 31:7, 8 [×2]). In 31:7, Jacob explicitly refers to Laban's earlier deception (29:23–26).[3] This pericope is essentially set in three scenes, with transitions before and after each.[4]

Transition	Recap of the birth of Joseph, the prompt for Jacob's decision to return home	**30:25a**
Scene I	Jacob and Laban in negotiation for terms of Jacob's release	**30:25b–34**
Transition	Laban's response to the negotiation, removing abnormal animals	**30:35–36**
Scene II	Jacob outwits Laban and generates a myriad of abnormal animals in his flock	**30:37–42**
Transition	Outcome of the animal husbandry activities: Jacob becomes prosperous	**30:43**
Scene III	Jacob's discussion of his plans with his wives	**31:1–16**
Transition	Summary: of departure preparations	**31:17–18**

22.1 Genesis 30:25–43

> **THEOLOGICAL FOCUS 22.1**
>
> 22.1 Despite opposition, diligent work—eschewing deception—keeps one in the will of God (30:25–43).

NOTES 22.1

22.1 *Despite opposition, diligent work—eschewing deception—keeps one in the will of God.*

A change of mind for Jacob comes with the birth of Joseph (30:25); he desires to return to his homeland. As was noted in Pericope 21, it was probably the entire sequence

---

Abraham and Isaac were explicitly promised blessing (12:2; 22:17; and 26:3, 24), Abraham was blessed by Melchizedek (ostensibly an agent of Yahweh, 14:19), and Isaac was recognized, by a non-Israelite, as being blessed (26:29). Even Sarah and Ishmael were promised blessing by Yahweh (17:16 [×2], 20), and Rebekah ended up being blessed by her family (24:60). Only Jacob appears to have missed out on all of this, though he is, of course, blessed by his father, Isaac (27:27, 30)—but that turns out to be the result of mistaken identity! As we shall see, the narrator is saving the fact and event of Jacob's divine blessing for a later day (and a later pericope).

3. See Pericope 20 for details, and Pericope 16 for the chiastic structure of the whole Jacob Story. That these are key terms significant for the Jacob narrative are evidenced by their recurrence: elsewhere, "serve/service" is found in 25:23; 27:29, 40; 29:15, 18, 20, 25, 27 (×2), 30; 31:41; and "wages/hire," besides here, also turns up in 30:16 (×2), 18; 31:41.

4. The transition after 31:1–16, i.e., 31:17–18, will be considered with Pericope 23.

of events—especially the futile machinations of the "Jacobah," Rachel, until she surrendered and then was remembered by God and caused to conceive—that brought Jacob to his senses. He probably realized that what the "Jacobah" was doing, and what had happened to her as a result, was a microcosm of what had been going on in his own life. It was time to make some amends; it was time to go home. That would be the only path to divine blessing. Later, in 31:3, the reader discovers that this move was also commanded by Yahweh. Jacob is definitely aligning himself to the will of God.

Jacob's words to Laban were words Laban had heard before from Abraham's servant, when the latter desired to depart with Isaac's bride-to-be, Rebekah: "Send me away that I may go . . ." (24:56, and here, in 30:25). If the servant's action was appropriate (demonstrating his faithfulness to Abraham by discharging his responsibility to the patriarch), then so is Jacob's. And thus the Jacob narrative reaches its turning-point. Jacob wants to go back to "my place" and to "my land." The significance of "place" may be gauged from its occurrences in conjunction with God's promise of Canaan to Abraham (particularly 13:3, 4, 14). The "land" had, of course, been promised by God to Jacob (28:4, 13). And so, in his return, Jacob is planning to claim what is his by divine grant. Canaan is where he belongs and what has been promised him; that is where he will be blessed; and that is where he has some business pending—reconciliation with the brother he deceived. This return is thus clearly approved by God.

As he prepares to leave Laban, Jacob is clear about who is in his company: "*my* wives and *my* children" (30:26). Laban does not demur, but later asserts that "the daughters are *my* daughters [Leah and Rachel], and the children are *my* children [the children of Leah and Rachel]" (31:43). Laban's correction of Jacob's possession of his own wives and children makes it sound like the departure of a slave from his master; the slave, by contract, gets to take nothing with him, and has to leave behind even wife and children (Exod 21:3–6). That may well have been how Laban saw Jacob and [ab]used him—as a slave (עֶבֶד, *'ebed*). But, even though Jacob did use the related noun and verb (from עבד, Gen 30:26 [×3]) to describe his service to Laban, it appears more likely that the relationship between patriarch and father-in-law was more commercial, than one of indenture (see 29:15, and the many references to "serve" and "wages/hire," as noted earlier).[5] At any rate, Laban is not too pleased about the departure of his "slave."

Jacob's request is met by Laban's counter-request for Jacob's חֵן (*khen*, "favor") in 30:27–28 ("if I have found *favor* in your eyes"), and for Jacob to "name your wages [שׂכר]" (30:28).[6] An earlier request of Laban to Jacob that he specify his "wages" (מַשְׂכֻּרֶת, 29:15) was followed up by deception. No wonder Jacob does not trust the same request from his father-in-law this time around. The earlier offer from Laban to "give" (29:19 [×2], his promise of Rachel) turned out be fraudulent. Why should this current offer to "give" (30:28) be any less fictitious?

---

5. Wenham, *Genesis 16–50*, 254.

6. Earlier, Laban had rhetorically asked Jacob if the latter should serve him for "free" (again חֵן, "as a favor," 29:15). Ironically, the uncle who had actually gotten a month's labor gratis (from the Latin *grâtis*, "grace/favor") from his nephew, now requests "grace/favor" from the latter.

The marital contracts stipulated Jacob's service of fourteen years for his two wives (29:18, 27); that bargain (wives for labor) Laban kept, even though the second of the two seven-year periods of servitude was foisted upon an unwitting Jacob. But there are six more unaccounted years that Jacob remains with Laban (31:38, 41). Therefore, at his departure at the end of that time, he was justified in claiming more than just wives and children. And Laban, agreeing, asks Jacob to name his wages; Jacob does so, and an agreement is struck (30:28–34).

Jacob makes a reasonable request that his wages be the rarer multicolored sheep and goats in the flock (sheep are usually white; goats, black or brown) (30:32–33): no deception here. In fact, Jacob adduces his honesty (צְדָקָה, *tsdaqah*, "righteousness") explicitly, as he sets penalties on what would happen if the wrong kind of animal were found in his flock (30:33). There is no doubt that Jacob seeks to be entirely aboveboard in this transaction. Again, we see a transformed patriarch, not the deceptive one who stole his brother's blessing. This is further demonstrated in Jacob's reply to Laban's "What shall I give you?"—"You shall give nothing to me" (30:31)! This from a man who, thus far, had only sought to *get* from everybody around him; but his present declaration reminds one of Jacob's grandfather, Abraham, who refused to take anything from his captives (14:21, 23).

While it is not entirely clear, it appears that Jacob offers to go through the flock "today," to remove all the multicolored sheep and goats, so that when he later got his wages, it would be entirely the result of the breeding of a normal flock. Thus, the odds are against Jacob, for monochrome animals were less likely to generate polychrome ones. Finkelstein shows how Jacob's offer was "unmistakably" one that asked for less than the prevailing share due shepherds, usually twenty percent of the increase in the flock.[7] No wonder Laban affirmed that offer and immediately took up Jacob on it (30:34). Laban agrees to Jacob's deal, but culls the flock of the multicolored animals himself, perhaps suspecting Jacob might cheat him, and puts a distance between these animals and the normal ones in Jacob's care (30:34–36).[8] Though in doing this, Laban might not have been deceptive, he is at least incorrigibly and hardheartedly selfish, even at the expense of his own kith and kin.[9] Jacob's remonstrance is appropriate (31:6–7a):

> "With all my strength,
>   I served
>   your father.
>   And your father
>   has fooled me
> and changed my wages ten times."

7. Finkelstein, "An Old Babylonian Herding Contract," 33–35.

8. The "he" who removed the flock is possibly Laban, but could also be Jacob. The latter offered to cull the flock "today" (הַיּוֹם, *hayyom*, 30:32), and whoever was responsible did so "on that day" (בַּיּוֹם, *bayyom*, 30:35); moreover, "every/all" appears three times in each of those verses, 30:32, 35. It might well have been the same person, Jacob, offering and operating.

9. He even descends to treating his daughters like aliens, even chattel (31:15)!

Jacob gave Laban all his strength; Laban changed his wages ten times. And while Jacob "served" Laban, Laban "fooled" Jacob. Laban was a foe, indeed.

Overall, the narrative of Jacob's husbandry of the flocks is cryptic (30:37–42): Von Rad asserted that the passage was "based on the ancient and widespread belief in the magical effect of certain visual impressions."[10] Brueggemann labeled it "a series of actions which are beyond explication."[11] Mathews suspects that the reason for this opacity is twofold: firstly, it is a subtle reflection of the numerous changes made by Laban to Jacob's wages (31:41), presumably happening under cover of a rather impenetrable narrative in which there are sheep and lambs and goats, and black and white animals, and speckled and spotted and striped ones; and secondly, it emphasizes that "it was God's gracious intervention that assured Jacob's prosperity, not his bewildering schemes" (31:7).[12]

Interestingly, in the rather complicated account of breeding, even though the dark/black (חוּם, *khum*, 30:35) animals are removed from the flock, when Laban's ostensibly white animals come to drink, they are "in heat" (יֶחֱמוּ, *yakham*, 30:38, 39; this verb is related to the noun חַמָּה, *khamah*, "heat"). The similarity of the two words, both semantically ("dark/black/sunburnt" is linked to "being in heat") and phonetically, suggests that these animals are not only "in heat" but are being *made* "dark/black," i.e., made "not white." And the punning continues: Jacob exposes the white (לָבָן, *laban*) flock of Laban (לָבָן, *laban*) to the rods of poplar (לִבְנֶה, *libneh*) that Jacob peeled white (לבן) stripes in. And, in sum, in the long-term, Laban's animals become "striped" and "speckled" (עָקֹד and נָקֹד, *'aqod* and *naqod*) and end up with Jacob (יַעֲקֹב, *ya'aqob*; notice the acoustic similarity of all three words; 30:37, 39), while Laban (לבן) gets the animals that are "white" (לבן) (30:35). "The message conveyed with these puns is that Jacob is not stealing Laban's flocks but that Laban's flocks are being *transformed*

---

10. *Genesis,* 301–2. So also Westermann, who adds: "There are signs here of an earlier transition from magical to scientific thinking; it is scientific inasmuch as knowledge of animals' habits leads to calculated subjection of such to one's ends" (*Genesis 12–36,* 483). The difficulties of the passage are multiplex: not only are the various labels of animal mottling unclear (see Fokkelman, *Narrative Art in Genesis,* 145–48 for a philological analysis of the those terms), 30:40 complicates comprehension by the presence of striped animals which, one would think, had already been removed by Laban (30:35). Moreover, subsequently, with the introduction of "stronger" and "weaker" animals in 30:41–42, Jacob apparently is employing a different scheme than what he had used in 30:37–39. Mathews thinks the whole process took about six years (the six years remaining, after the fourteen served, to make up the twenty years of 31:38, 41) and that there were probably some "fluid arrangements" in the composition of herds during that time (*Genesis 11:27–50:26,* 502–3). With a nod to a scientific explanation, Hamilton concludes that "Jacob's knowledge of zoology is far from primitive. But perhaps such knowledge has been given him by God, just as his son's capacity to interpret dreams was a gift from God" (*Genesis: Chapters 18–50,* 284).

11. *Genesis,* 257.

12. *Genesis 11:27–50:26,* 500. Noegel also guesses that the perplexities of the account are deliberate, intended to "impress upon the reader a sense of deception." He advances the intriguing thesis that the "rods"—the branches of poplar, almond, and plane trees—were *faux* phalluses being employed "to alter the breeding pattern of Laban's flocks, and thus increase his [Jacob's] wages at Laban's expense" ("Sex, Sticks, and the Trickster," 12, 16).

into Jacob's."[13] Ultimately, all of this was God's work, as Jacob would subsequently acknowledge (31:6–13).

And it appears that Jacob had come to a firm acceptance of that truth. His rationale for obtaining more than just permission to leave for home (30:31–33) is grounded in the divine blessing that Laban had received through him—Laban's little had "increased" (פרץ, *prts*) to much, and Yahweh had blessed Laban "at my feet" (30:30), a reflection of the divine promise to Jacob coming true: "You shall spread [פרץ]" (28:14). Even the reference to "feet" may be Jacob's recognition that wherever he went, God had blessed him as he had promised (28:15): indeed, after that promise, the next movement of Jacob was to "lift his feet" and arrive in Haran (29:1).[14] But perhaps the key ingredient of his speech to his uncle is his employment of the verb ברך, *brk*: he recognizes Yahweh's blessing of a third party—his uncle, Laban. That he acknowledged that Yahweh was the source of blessing is, in itself, quite remarkable . . . or perhaps not. Had he not remonstrated with Rachel in 30:2 that (in effect) *God* was the source of blessing? One again comes to the conclusion that the convoluted events of Gen 29, though dealing with conception and parturition, jealousies and mandrakes, had actually led Jacob to develop this attitude of mature faith, with a perspicacioius recognition of the source of all true blessing.

There are remarkable parallels between the employment, in the previous pericope, of mandrakes as aphrodisiacs to stimulate reproduction, and the utilization of "rods" for the same purpose in this pericope: both had little scientific evidence to back up those stratagems; both attempts, one by his wives and the other by Jacob, were intended to increase fecundity; and both attempts succeed. Leah "pays wages" (or "hires," שכר, *skr*, 30:16, 18) to Jacob for sexual activity; here, Jacob's wages (שכר, 30:28, 32, 33) are the result of manipulated sexual activity. Both stories involve conception and "delivery" (from ילד, *yld*, 29:32, 33, 34, 35; 30:1, 3, 5, 7, 9, 10, 12, 17, 19, 20, 21, 23; and 30:25, 26, 39). That Leah and Rachel conceived—an abundance of children— because of God's providence (expressly noted in 30:17, 18, 20, 22, 23), and not because of the mandrakes, strongly suggests that Jacob's success in this pericope, that deals with reproduction, too—an abundance of animals—is providential, and not because of his dubious thremmatological techniques.[15]

---

13. Park, "Transformation and Demarcation," 670–71.

14. Noegel notes that if "feet" is a euphemism for genitalia, then Jacob is also reminding Laban about his role in the multiplication of both Laban's family and Laban's herds ("Drinking Feasts and Deceptive Feats," 175).

15. That there was some scientific backing for Jacob's manipulations has oft been suggested. Backon proposed that the flock's drinking water might have been contaminated by chemicals or fungi present in/ on the bark that had the potential to affect heritable changes in gene expression, as the field of epigenetics explains ("Jacob and the Spotted Sheep," 263–65). Pearson, employing Mendelian genetics, speculated that there was no reason to revert to divine intervention: "simple selective breeding would have achieved the stated result over the six years quoted," for there would have been "sufficient recessive black genes [in Jacob's flock] to produce enough black rams to undertake a selective breeding programme" ("A Mendelian Interpretation," 52, 58). There may be some ground for these scientific explanations: Laban's removal of the multicolored animals and the black sheep (30:35) suggests some knowledge of breeding techniques. Be that as it may, the thrust of the narrative is clear: Jacob employed certain tactics in his

One thing is clear here: Jacob's strategies are neither deceitful nor accomplished in stealth. "His breeding-method makes us think of magic, for a while, but the real magic is revealed by a pun simple in itself. To borrow the pun, Jacob is not guilty of black magic but uses *white* magic"—with all the play on לבן, *lbn*, noted above. While the "white" man (Laban) takes those animals with "white" on them (30:35, the striped, spotted, speckled), the other man (Jacob) takes branches of the "white" tree (and some other flora), exposes the "white" in the branches, and generates animals that are striped, spotted, and speckled—those that have "white" on them. Thus Jacob "fights Laban with Laban"—he "fights Laban with his own weapons and defeats him."[16] Whatever might have been the scientific (or pseudo-scientific) explanation for Jacob's success, in the final reckoning God was the cause of patriarch's checkmate of uncle (31:1–13). And the upshot was that Jacob became prosperous (פרץ, *prts*, 30:43); as was noted earlier, this is the fulfillment of the divine promise to Jacob (פרץ also in 28:14) that even spilled over to benefit Laban (פרץ in 30:30). It might also indicate that the tables have now been turned—it is Jacob's turn to enjoy prosperity. Poetic justice had been effected![17]

In sum: While acutely conscious of God's hand in his affairs, Jacob does not remain passive (though he seems to have given up deception altogether). He works determinedly and, even against such an obvious foe as Laban, Jacob is mindful of the working of God, and eschews any deception which, at an earlier phase of his life, would have been his *modus operandi*.

22.2 Genesis 30:25–31:16[18]

THEOLOGICAL FOCUS 22.2

22.2   In tandem with the discharge of human responsibility, God sovereignly works out his blessings for his children (30:25–31:16).

---

undertakings to produce particular kinds of progeny in his flock, but as he himself avers later, it was the hand of God that gave his endeavors success. And perhaps that is why, in his recounting to his wives the whole matter, none of his efforts—with plant rods and peeled stripes and sheep gutters and watering troughs—gain any mention (31:5–13).

16. Fokkelman, *Narrative Art in Genesis*, 150.

17. There is also the irony of Jacob being deceived in Gen 29 to take on the "cow" (Leah) as wife, instead of the "lamb" (Rachel). But here, Jacob outwits Laban to obtain the animals *he* wanted. The former substitution occurred at a "feast" (מִשְׁתֶּה, *mishteh*, 29:22, from שׁתה, *shth*, "to drink"); the latter took place when the flocks came "to drink" (לִשְׁתּוֹת, *lishtot*, 30:38, also from שׁתה). Earlier Jacob had to "serve" (עבד, *'bd*, 29:25, 27, 30) for his wives; correspondingly, here his service to Laban is referred to (also עבד, 30:26, 29). All of this wheeling and dealing, and the outwitting of Laban by Jacob, "permits the Israelites not only to laugh with the success of their hero, but to laugh at Laban" (Brueggemann, *Genesis*, 250).

18. This section, 22.2, includes the previous episode (30:25–43, the same portion of the text noted for section 22.1), in addition to the subsequent episode (31:1–16). This is because the theological focus of 22.2 is not limited to a particular episode or scene of the pericope, but is interwoven implicitly throughout the whole pericope, though explicit assertions of that focus are found only in 31:1–16.

22.2 *In tandem with the discharge of human responsibility, God sovereignly works out his blessings for his children.*

In the rather unusual first episode of this pericope, that contains no speech at all but only narration (30:37–43), we are not told what Jacob was thinking or intending, as he undertook those convoluted manipulations with his animals. But the reader spies a determined Jacob accomplishing a desired goal. "The impression, hereby created, that Jacob, from a to z the agent, now becomes the conqueror under his own steam or by his own ingenuity, is now [in Gen 31] demolished by a highly authoritative witness, . . . Jacob himself." He is not the primary agent in his success. There is no mention at all of Jacob's own activities of the previous episode. According to 31:1–16, mottled animals were apparently generated simply by the providence of God (31:7–9): he sees a dream and—*voila!*—a livestock transfer is effected.[19] But Jacob's attitude is explicitly noted in 31:7, 9, 11–13: the patriarch is aware that it is God's hand that has fructified his endeavors, and that God has steadfastly stayed true to the promises he had made to Jacob at Bethel. Not that there were no clues given to the reader before 31:1–16. The recognition of God's blessing in the earlier episode by both Laban and Jacob (30:27, 30) ensures that the reader will not misconstrue the thrust of that narrative: God *is* at work![20] As was noted, the summary of the first section, 30:43, also clinches this truth: "The man became prosperous [from פָּרַץ]"; earlier God had promised him exactly that (פָּרַץ, 28:14), and Jacob, himself, had acknowledged that, indirectly, Laban had "prospered/increased" (פָּרַץ, 30:30) because of Yahweh's blessing.[21] Moreover, רַב (*rab*, "large/multitudinous") is used to describe Jacob's prosperity (30:43), as well as Laban's (30:30). If the cause of the latter was Yahweh's blessing, as is explicitly noted, then surely the cause of the former is also divine activity.

There is another clear indication of divine working in the description of Jacob's prosperity in 30:43; this statement of his wealth is quite similar to that of the wealth of his father and grandfather—for both of whom prosperity was an explicit consequence of divine blessing (24:1, 35; 26:3, 12). Almost all of the words used to depict Jacob's wealth in 30:43 are borrowed from similar depictions of his ancestors' thriving (highlighted in the table below).

---

19. Fokkelman, *Narrative Art in Genesis*, 158–59.

20. "The scope of Jacob's speech [in 31:1–16] is the precise complement of the scope of the report in Gen. 30 [30:37–43]. That is why the two texts are corresponding descriptions of the outside and the kernel of one and the same event" (ibid., 159). God is working, whether he is visible or not, whether it is explicitly noted in the narrative or not.

21. These are the only three instances of פָּרַץ in Genesis.

Abraham (24:35)	"And Yahweh blessed	my master *greatly* and he became very rich, and he gave him *sheep* and cattle and silver and gold and *male servants* and *female servants* and *camels* and *donkeys*."
Isaac (26:13–14)	"And Yahweh blessed him	and *the man* became rich and continued to become richer until [he became] *greatly* rich *and there was to him* possessions of *sheep* and possessions of cattle and *many male servants*."
Jacob (30:43)		"… and *the man* overflowed *greatly* in prosperity and *there was to him* many *sheep* and *female servants* and *male servants* and *camels* and *donkeys*."

In other words, what had happened to Abraham and Isaac was true of Jacob, too—his wealth, just like his predecessors', was a result of divine blessing (though, as was noted, the fact that Jacob is "blessed" is not explicitly claimed, for reasons that the narrator will reveal in Gen 32, Pericope 24).[22]

The conclusion is inescapable (even without the explicit acknowledgement in 31:7, 9, 11–13): this prosperity was the result of the working of Yahweh and it was the direct fulfillment of his promises. Jacob had already alluded to God's promise to him at Bethel ("I will keep [שׁמר, *shmr*] you . . . and will return [שׁוב, *shuv*] you," 28:15) when he asserted earlier to Laban, "I will return [שׁוב] and pasture and keep [שׁמר] your flock" (30:31).[23] Obviously, after two decades, this is a changed Jacob who is speaking; he seems to have realized that God *is* able to keep, and already has—to some extent—kept, his promises. Thus, there are clear hints of God's work by the recollection in this pericope of words from Yahweh's promise in Gen 28: "keep" and "return" (28:15, 20 and 30:31), and as was noted earlier, "spread/increase/prosper" (28:14 and 30:30, 43).

The final episode of this pericope, 31:1–16, begins with dark clouds looming on the horizon. Jacob's prosperity has not gone unnoticed, especially by Laban's sons, who allege that Jacob took "all" that belonged to their father, and made "all" his wealth from what was their father's (31:1). Jacob "hears" this note of agitation, and then Jacob "sees" the negative attitude of Laban, as the parallel structures of 31:1 and 2 depict.

31:1	"And-he-heard		the-words	of-the-sons-of-Laban"
31:2	"And-he-saw,	Jacob,	the-face	of-Laban"

Laban's "face" (i.e., attitude) was not friendly "towards him" (31:2). The prepositional phrase "towards him" (עִמּוֹ, *'immo*) is perfectly balanced by "with you" (עִמָּךְ, *'immak*, 31:3)—Yahweh's attitude towards Jacob. Likewise, in 31:5, the narrator reiterates both Laban's and Yahweh's dispositions: אֵלַי, *'elay*, "unto me," of Laban; and עִמָּדִי, *'immadi*, "with me," of Yahweh (again echoing the promise made to the patriarch at Bethel,

22. Mathews, *Genesis 11:27–50:26*, 491.

23. Also see Jacob's immediate response to God's promise, echoing the same key words, שׁמר and שׁוב, in 28:20, 21.

using עִמָּך, "with you," 28:15). The foe is against him, but deity is for him. By aligning himself to the will of God, Jacob is on God's side (or perhaps, God is on Jacob's side).

Laban's sons accused Jacob of taking "all that" (כָּל־אֲשֶׁר, *kal-'asher*) was their father's, and "making" (עשה, *'sh*) his wealth of their father's property (31:1).[24] The response of the angel of God to this is appropriate: he had seen "all that" (כָּל־אֲשֶׁר) Laban had "done" (עשה) to Jacob (31:12). As if in echo, Rachel and Leah exhort Jacob to "do" (עשה) "all that" (כָּל־אֲשֶׁר) God had commanded him to do (31:16). Clearly right is on Jacob's side. Moreover, while Laban's sons assumed that Jacob had "taken away" (לקח) all that belonged to their father (31:1), Jacob claims that it was God who "rescued" (נצל, *ntsl*) Laban's livestock and gave them to him (31:9).[25] "In other words, God has not simply transferred the herds from Laban to Jacob; he has done them [the animals] a favor, giving them a much better life!"[26] God's sovereignty is on view again in 31:7b, which literally reads, "but God did not grant [נתן, *ntn*, "give"] him to do evil towards me." Instead God "gave" (נתן, 31:9) to Jacob the livestock of Laban. It was tit for tat, as the perfect parallels show[27]:

Genesis 31:8a	Genesis 31:8b
"And if he said, 'The speckled will be your wages,' then the whole flock birthed speckled."	"If he said thus, thus, 'The striped will be your wages,' then the whole flock birthed striped."

Of interest is that the mottled animals mentioned are specifically the "speckled" (נָקֹד, *naqod*) and the "striped" (עָקֹד, *'aqod*), that sound suspiciously like "Jacob" (יַעֲקֹב, *ya'aqob*); quite deliberately, then, in order to sustain the phonetic wordplay, the "spotted" ones (טָלָא, *tala'*, 30:32, 33, 35, 39) are omitted, as are the other variants, the weaker/stronger, black/white, etc. In other words, Laban's animals had Jacob's name written all over them!

The tussle here is actually not between Laban and Jacob, but between Laban and *God*. It is obvious who will be (and who actually was) the winner of that test of strength! In fact, Jacob's acknowledgement of God's working to give him success is emphasized in his recital—not once, but twice—of how the flock produced all "striped, speckled, and mottled" progeny (31:10, 12). In both tellings, a lifting up of eyes and seeing is noted, a formulaic expression often used with theophanies (13:14; 18:2). This is a significant moment and clearly marked by the presence and voice of God. That

24. Laban, in 31:43, will assert, in vain, that "all that" (כֹּל אֲשֶׁר) Jacob could see was his, Laban's. However, the narrator agrees with the evaluation made by Jacob and his wives; for instance, in 31:4, refers to "*his* [Jacob's] flock in the field." Frisch notes astutely that 31:19 has Laban going to shear *his* flock. Surely that meant that Jacob had not made off with *all* that belonged to Laban, as his sons had protested (31:1a) ("Your Brother Came with Guile," 288).

25. Jacob's wives use the same word—God's "rescue" of their father's wealth (31:16). Other uses of נצל in Genesis connote "deliverance" or "preservation": 32:12, 30; 37:21, 22; and often of the redemption of the Israelites from Egypt: Exod 3:8; 5:23; 6:6; 12:27; etc.

26. Wenham, *Genesis 16–50*, 271.

27. From Fokkelman, *Narrative Art in Genesis*, 153.

God reminds Jacob of his vow at Bethel here (31:13) is also an indication that God is keeping his part of the bargain Jacob had made with him (28:20–22).

The divine sanctioning of Jacob's desire to return to his homeland is also emphasized in the narrative (31:3), as well as in Jacob's recounting of history to his wives (31:11–13). In his call by God, Jacob is replaying the divine call of his grandfather; in fact, the structures of their respective calls (and the retellings thereof) are similar, each dealing with three similar elements:

Genesis 12:1–3 Jacob's call	Genesis 31:3 Abraham's call	Genesis 31:13–14 Jacob retelling call
"from your land"	"the land"	"from this land"
"and from your relatives"	"and to your relatives"	"to the land of your relatives"
"the house of your father"	"of your fathers"	"in our father's house"
Command, then promise (12:2–3)	Command, then promise (31:3b)	

Jacob, like his ancestor, was doing the will of God; the "return" commanded here in 31:3 was also promised earlier in 28:14 (both have שׁוּב, *shuv*, "return").

God's role in Jacob's success is not only explicitly testified to, but the similarity of the dream recounted in this section (31:10–13) and the one experienced in Gen 28, attest to divine providence. Both begin similarly: "and he saw in a dream, and behold!" (31:10), and "and he dreamt, and behold!" (28:12); both recount visions (31:10 and 28:12b), each with עלה (*'lh*, "mating" in 31:10, and "going up" in 28:12); and the visions are followed by a comment from the angel of God/God (31:11–13 and 28:13–15). Other connections with the Bethel experience of Jacob, that further provide the divine imprimatur for the outwitting of Laban, include 31:3 where God (or the angel of God speaking as God) introduces himself as "the God of Bethel, where [there] you anointed a pillar, where you vowed to me [there]" (twice the word שָׁם, *sham*, "there" [untranslated], occurs, emphasizing *that* location). The connection with the Bethel theophany is clear also in the promise of God to Jacob, "I am with you" (28:15)—echoed by Jacob, albeit as a condition, "If God will be with me" (28:20). Almost in parallel fashion, in this pericope, God repeats the promise, "And I will be with you" (31:3), and Jacob echoes it, but this time not as a condition, but as a conviction: "But the God of my father has been with me" (31:5).[28] And Jacob, of course, takes action with decisiveness and determination, in response to the divine imperatives: "Arise, leave . . ., and return . . .!" (31:13). God is in charge of Jacob's life now; he is a changed man.

In Jacob's report to his wives (31:4–16), God's work for Jacob's prosperity is unambiguously established. Not only had Yahweh protected Jacob from Laban's shenanigans, he had also guided the patriarch, by means of a dream, through his animal-breeding enterprise that eventually turned out to be a grand success (31:11–12). Thrice Jacob contrasts Laban's baleful attitude and actions towards him with God's beneficent intervention and initiatives on his behalf.[29]

---

28. Ibid., 156.

29. From Wenham, *Genesis 16–50*, 270.

31:2, 5	Laban's attitude: not "toward" Jacob	God's attitude: "with" Jacob
31:6–7	Laban's attempt to do evil to Jacob	God's intervention to protect Jacob
31:8–13	Laban's aim to cheat Jacob of wages	God's inversion of Laban's ploy

"Father" occurs several times in this final episode of the pericope: "our father" (= Laban, 31:1, 14, 16), "your fathers" (= Abraham and Isaac, 31:3), "your father" (= Laban, 31:5, 6, 7, 9), and "my father" (= Isaac, 31:5). Mathews sees this as a motif of inheritance: the sons of Laban think their father's inheritance has been stolen by Jacob; the wives of Jacob think their father has stolen the inheritance due them[30]; Jacob thinks, rightly, that his inheritance is what was promised him by Yahweh, "the God of my father," the one who is *with* him, as opposed to the other "father," Laban, who is constantly *against* him.[31]

All this goes to show that what happened, in/with/through Jacob's industry in Gen 30, was not the outcome of magic, but of divine providence. "Jacob himself has eliminated himself completely as an agent. Jacob testifies that six years had not passed without problems, but that, on the contrary, he had had to contend with Laban's full-fledged opposition which mere human cunning could not have countered. Into this Jacob weaves a grateful testimony to God in his providence, the sole agent, the creator of all his wealth, and pictures himself as innocent observer full of surprise" (31:10, 12).[32] Thus the two episodes, 30:25–43 and 31:1–16 are complementary descriptions of the same event, depicting, respectively, human responsibility and divine sovereignty/providence. God works in tandem with faithful obedience on the part of his people.

SERMON FOCUS AND OUTLINES

THEOLOGICAL FOCUS OF PERICOPE 22 FOR PREACHING

22 **God sovereignly works to bless his children, as they work responsibly and faithfully, even in adverse conditions (29:31–30:24).**

Here divine sovereignty and human responsibility works in tandem, held together in biblical tension.[33] Even though opposition arises—and Laban, one is sure, will do his utmost to deprive Jacob of his deserved wages—the nephew works diligently and conscientiously. There is no deception, no manipulation, no extortion, just the hard

---

30. Daughters did not necessarily receive a paternal inheritance that was usually divided among the sons (Num 27:3–4); but at least a dowry was expected to be given by the father to the groom. If the maids, Zilpah and Bilhah, were the dowries (29:24, 29), perhaps the indignation of Leah and Rachel in 31:14–16 may be explained in their identification with Jacob and his woes, particularly Laban's shabby treatment of him in the past decade. In recording another paronomasia, Noegel notes that the name "Laban" resounds in the daughters' reply to Jacob: "away from our father to us" is מֵאָבִינוּ לָנוּ, *me'abinu lanu*; and "and to our children" is וּלְבָנֵינוּ (*ulbanenu*, 31:16). See "Drinking Feasts and Deceptive Feats," 175.

31. Mathews, *Genesis 11:27–50:26*, 509.

32. Fokkelman, *Narrative Art in Genesis*, 158–59.

33. Such an idea was foreshadowed in Pericope 15 (Gen 24:1–25:18), but there the note of oppression was absent.

work of breeding, carefully (albeit cryptically) described in this pericope. Through it all is the undercurrent of divine sovereignty: God is working out his promises to bless. There is no avoiding the presence, agency, and operation of deity in the whole business, mostly indirectly in the first episode. But in the second episode, God's work is manifested, remembered, explicitly confessed, and celebrated with obedience. The lesson is clear: without engaging in any fraudulent behavior, without subterfuge or chicanery, the child of God must work hard, *but trusting that God is at work*, for, indeed, he is. He always is, for his children. Thus this pericope teaches the lesson of industry ("labor for God"), and faith in God's operations ("labor with God").[34]

Possible Preaching Outlines for Pericope 22

I. Foe's Work
   Jacob's decision to depart, in line with God's will ("land," "place," 30:25–26, 29–33; 31:3)
   Laban's deceptive proclivities in the past (recap Leah/Rachel substitution)
   Laban's deceptive tendencies in the present ("wages," "give," 30:28; culling flock, 30:35–36)
   Move-to-Relevance: Opposition in our lives

II. Man's Work
   Jacob makes a reasonable claim for his wage (30:29–30, 32–33)
   Jacob's determination to work for his wages, and that, honestly (30:31, 33)
   Jacob's industriousness, in an intricate account (30:25–42)
   Jacob's resolution to obey (31:3–16)
   Move-to-Relevance: How we are tempted to act in times of opposition

III. God's Work
   The parallel with the story of the mandrakes shows divine providence
   Links with divine promise in Gen 28, show God's hand at work ("return" and "keep," 30:31; "increase," 30:30, 43)
   Repeated wordplays ("dark/sunburnt," and "in heat," 30:35, 38–39)
   Comparison of statement of Jacob's wealth (30:43) with that of Abraham's and Isaac's
   Jacob's confession of God's hand upon his success (31:5, 7, 9, 11–13)
   Move-to-Relevance: God is working, even when that work may be imperceptible

IV. *Labor for God, with God!*
   How to maintain the tension between human responsibility and divine sovereignty
   Specifics on how to work hard, while trusting in God's work, especially in seasons of trouble

If the listeners are already familiar with the story, one could exposit the theology of the pericope focusing on the duality of God's sovereignty and man's responsibility, without spending too much time on the "Foe's Work."

I. God's Sovereignty
   Jacob's desire to depart; Laban's deceptive proclivities (summary of the story)
   The parallel with the story of the mandrakes shows divine providence
   Links with divine promise in Gen 28, show God's hand at work ("return" and "keep," 30:31; "increase," 30:30, 43)
   Repeated wordplays ("dark/sunburnt," and "in heat," 30:35, 38–39)
   Comparison of statement of Jacob's wealth (30:43) with that of Abraham's and Isaac's
   Jacob's confession of God's hand upon his success (31:5, 7, 9, 11–13)

34. See Kuruvilla, *Privilege the Text!* 195–209, for this concept that I call, "faith-full" obedience.

Move-to-Relevance: God is working, even when that work may be imperceptible

II.   Man's Responsibility

Jacob makes a reasonable claim for his wage (30:29–30, 32–33)
Jacob's determination to work for his wages, and that, honestly (30:31, 33)
Jacob's industriousness, in an intricate account (30:25–42)
Jacob's resolution to obey (31:3–16)
Move-to-Relevance: How we are tempted to act in times of opposition

III. *Labor for God, with God!*

How to maintain the tension between human responsibility and divine sovereignty
Specifics on how to work hard, while trusting in God's work, especially in seasons of trouble

PERICOPE 23

Protected from Peril

Genesis 31:17–55

[Laban Pursues Jacob; God Protects Jacob]

REVIEW, SUMMARY, PREVIEW

Review of Pericope 22: Genesis 30:25–31:16 depicts Jacob deciding to return to Canaan. Following his request for appropriate compensation from Laban his employer, Jacob engages in some creative animal husbandry, and his flocks greatly increase in number. Later he attributes this prosperity to God's providence, thus pointing to the fact that the sovereignty of God works in tandem with the faithful discharge of human responsibility.

Summary of Pericope 23: In this pericope, Jacob and his caravan are on their way back to the Promised Land. They are pursued by Laban who accuses Jacob of abruptly decamping with his wives and children; moreover, Laban's household gods are missing as well, stolen by Rachel, unbeknownst to others. Rachel's theft remains undetected, and Laban returns after striking a peace pact with Jacob. God's protection covers the faithful even from dangerous consequences of sin within their own camps.

Preview of Pericope 24: The next pericope (32:1–32) describes Jacob preparing to meet Esau who is approaching him with a large company. Jacob is afraid, and although he seeks protection from God, he reverts to his habit of manipulation, attempting to appease his brother with extravagant gifts. In a nocturnal wrestling match with God, Jacob recognizes deity and acknowledges that blessings come from God alone, whereupon he is finally blessed.

23   Genesis 31:17–55

THEOLOGICAL FOCUS OF PERICOPE 23

23   **Remaining in the will of God ensures protection from potential consequences of sin in one's own camp and from unscrupulous opponents—acts of divine blessing to be acknowledged with gratitude (31:17–55).**

23.1   Remaining in the will of God protects the child of God even from the potential consequences of sin in one's own camp, an act of divine blessing (31:17–35).

23.1.1   *The child of God who desires to be blessed remains in the will of God.*

23.1.2   *Remaining in the will of God protects one even from the potential consequences of sin in one's own camp, an act of divine blessing.*

23.2   Following the will of God ensures protection from unscrupulous opponents, a manifestation of divine blessing that is to be acknowledged with gratitude (31:36–55).

23.2.1   *Following the will of God ensures protection from unscrupulous opponents, another manifestation of divine blessing.*

23.2.2   *The blessing of God upon the child of God is acknowledged with gratitude.*

OVERVIEW

The previous pericope, Pericope 22 (30:25–31:16), concluded with the exhortation of Leah and Rachel to Jacob, that he do what God had told him to (31:16). The next two verses, 31:17–18, appear to be a transition that summarizes the preparation and departure phases of the journey from Haran, after which a disjunctive clause (conjunction + subject + verb) begins a new scene (31:19). At the other end of the pericope, 31:54 and 31:55 are separated by a night, but the pericope is best seen as ending at 31:55 that depicts the separation of the antagonists, Laban and Jacob, and brings a sense of resolution to the pericope. That the last verse of the chapter also closes the section with the concluding statement of Laban's departure, shows the conflict ending and the protagonists separating once and for all.[1] Needless to say, Jacob's going on his way and his encounter with the angels (32:1–2) commences a new pericope and connects with what follows: angels/messengers (32:3, 6); "company/camp" (32:7, 8, 10, 21; 33:8); and rendezvous with supernatural beings (32:22–32).

In the chiastic arrangement of the Jacob Story (for which, see Pericope 16), this pericope, that deals with the departure of Jacob and his caravan from Haran, matches Pericope 20, that details the arrival of Jacob in Haran. In the first, there is Jacob's success with Rachel at the well, and here there is Rachel's deception of Laban; both have key words: "kiss" (29:11, 13; and 31:28, 55); "roll/heap" of stone(s) (גלל, *gll*, 29:3, 8, 10;

---

1. From 31:55 through 32:32 of the English text (E), the Hebrew text (H) differs in versification: 31:55 (E) = 32:1 (H), 32:1 (E) = 32:2 (H), and so on, until 32:32 (E) = 32:33 (H). This work follows the enumeration of the English text throughout.

and גַּל, *gl*, 31:45–47; stones are prominent in both pericopes); and "brothers" occurs in both (29:14 and 31:32).

The previous pericope reiterated that God was with Jacob (31:3, 5; also a key ingredient of the divine promise to the patriarch at Bethel, 28:15). That same motif of divine presence recurs in this pericope as well (31:42). Again, divine intervention and protection was clearly manifest in the previous pericope (31:3, 7, 9, 11–13); so it is in this one, too (31:24, 29, 42, 53).

23.1 Genesis 31:17–35

> **THEOLOGICAL FOCUS 23.1**
>
> 23.1   Remaining in the will of God protects the child of God even from the potential conse-quences of sin in one's own camp, an act of divine blessing (31:17–35).
>
> 23.1.1   *The child of God who desires to be blessed remains in the will of God.*
>
> 23.1.2   *Remaining in the will of God protects one even from the potential consequences of sin in one's own camp, an act of divine blessing.*

NOTES 23.1

23.1.1   The child of God who desires to be blessed remains in the will of God.

In this pericope, Jacob is complying with divine demand: he had been asked by God to "arise," "leave," and "return" (31:13); and here he begins the long act of obedience—"he arose" and loaded up camels with his family, his livestock, and his property (31:17–18). This was a far cry from the arrival of a lone fugitive in Haran in Gen 28–29. After two decades, Jacob had accumulated not only a large family, but also great wealth. In the statement about "all the property he had gathered" (literally, "all the acquisitions he had acquired," 31:18), there is an echo of his grandfather's migration from Haran to Canaan: Abraham, too, collected "all the property he had gathered" (12:5), as he set out in compliance to divine will.[2] Jacob is following a good example; his translocation was as important as the one God called his ancestor to, and equally centered in the will of God.

The word גָּנַב, *gnb*, "to steal," occurs eight times in this pericope: 31:19, 30, 32 (of Rachel's act of theft of the teraphim), 31:20, 26, 27 (of Jacob's flight), and 31:39 (×2; of wild animals "stealing" from the flock). While the subjects of these actions vary, the victim of all of these misappropriations is Laban! It is now the turn of this wily operator to receive his payback, subtly indicated in the text by his label as the "Aramean"—אֲרַמִּי (*'arammi*, 31:20, 24).[3] The similarity of sound between this Hebrew word and רָמָה, *ramah*, "to deceive" (29:25)—Jacob's accusation of what Laban had

---

2. The phrase will show up once more in Genesis, as Jacob moves his large retinue to Egypt (46:6).

3. Laban, the "mother's brother" (29:10 [×3]), has now become a stranger, a foreigner, "the Aramean."

done to him by substituting his older daughter for the younger—indicates some deliberate composition here. Just as Jacob, who was deceitful himself (מִרְמָה, *mirmah*, from רָמָה, 27:35), was deceived by Laban, now the latter, the Aramean, gets his just deserts: all are linked by words that sound alike. And, quite likely, the indirect statement that Jacob "deceived/stole" from Laban (31:20), but using גנב, *gnb*, instead of רמה, points to Jacob's innocence in this account. The patriarch's decampment with his family and possessions was not a deception of any sort. Jacob was not playing tricks. Rather he was following the will of God. There is also a connection made here with Jacob's flight *from* Canaan with his current flight *to* Canaan: both use בָּרַח, *barakh*, "to flee" and קוּם, *qum*, "to arise" (27:43 and 31:21, 22, 27); and both fleeings are from a "brother/ relative" (27:41–45; see 29:15 for the relationship between Laban and Jacob designated similarly). The first and second phases of Jacob's life conclude in similar fashion: flight from a "brother"! However, this time, his departure is explicitly sanctioned by God (31:3, 13).

23.1.2 *Remaining in the will of God protects one even from the potential consequences of sin in one's own camp, an act of divine blessing.*

Rachel's stealing of the "teraphim" takes a good chunk of textual space in this pericope (31:19–35). "Teraphim" is a transliteration of תְּרָפִים, *trafim*, usually considered to be household gods. In 31:30, 32, both Laban and Jacob refer to these as "gods" (אֱלֹהִים, *'elohim*); elsewhere in the OT, they seem to point to idols (Jdg 17:5; 1 Sam 15:23; 19:13, 16; 2 Kgs 23:24; Ezek 21:26; Hos 3:4; Zech 10:2), presumably employed for divination (see Gen 30:27). The purpose of Rachel's absconding with these "gods" is unclear— spite? greed? security? title to inheritance? sign of patrimony?[4] In any case, Jacob is unaware of the pilfering (again גנב, *gnb*, "to steal," 31:19), and thus the "Jacobah" even "out-trumps Jacob," the deceiver, whose own act of cleverness is mentioned in the next verse (31:20; also 31:26, 27): "Jacob stole [גנב] the heart of [i.e., "deceived," in the sense of outwitted] Laban."[5] But the similarities end there: Rachel stole literally; Jacob "stole" symbolically (again portraying Jacob as having changed). As a matter of fact, he did not steal anything from Laban as he himself expostulates in defense (31:31–32, 36–42). Hers was a felonious action; his leaving surreptitiously was a defensive maneuver conducted in fear (31:31). Her closeness to Laban makes Rachel's act all the more serious, while Jacob's, on the other hand, was a lawful acquisition: 29:20–21,

4. See Hamilton, *Genesis: Chapters 18–50*, 293–95, for the various options, none of which are very convincing. *Targum Ps.-J.* on 31:19 speculates that the idols were stolen to keep them from revealing the whereabouts of the escapees. Now, if Rachel intended to "derive prosperity and 'blessing'" from these idols, her theft is most ironic, coming immediately after a striking testimony to God's providence in the life of Jacob, which was enthusiastically affirmed by his two wives (31:1–13). But when all is said and done, the text remains silent about Rachel's motives and goals, and so must we. Incidentally, Rachel was probably not the only one who took flight with dodgy idols (35:2).

5. Fishbane, "Composition and Structure," 31. There is no clue either as to why Rachel kept the whole affair a secret, not even letting her husband in on her activities. Did she figure he would not approve? The subsequent outrage of Jacob at Laban's accusation of theft (31:32), and his cursing the thief with death, indicates that Rachel had not necessarily acted on behalf of Jacob or that she was looking out for his interests (Fuchs, "'For I Have the Way of Women,'" 76–77).

27–28; 30:26–43; 31:5–12, 17–18 (*his* children, *his* wives, *his* livestock, *his* property that *he* gathered, cattle *he* acquired). There was adequate reason given for Jacob's action—31:1–13 describes all that Laban had done to him; in fact, as was noted, God himself had commanded him to depart (31:3, 13).

Laban, understandably, is not pleased by the departure of the one who was his agent of divine blessing (30:27), and who had ostensibly also swiped his favorite gods. He is not going to let Jacob get away so easily, so he (with his kinsmen, 31:23, 25—an antagonistic crowd) pursues and "overtakes" the outward bound party.[6] But Jacob's assertions to his wives that God had protected him from Laban in the past (31:5, 7, 9) is proven to be true again (31:24): God appears to Laban in a dream warning him not to "speak" (דבר, *dbr*, which also implies "do") to Jacob words of blessings or curses (or "do" to Jacob "good" or "evil": מִטּוֹב עַד־רָע, *mittov 'ad-ra'*)—i.e., Laban was not the one in charge here, God was, and God was keeping Jacob safe. Appropriately enough, Laban is rendered speechless in this oneiric encounter with God.

The subsequent scene, 31:26–32, is set as a formal dispute: Laban complains that Jacob has violated protocol as he "stole away" from his father-in-law's home (גנב, *gnb*, 31:26, 27) and that he has also "stolen" his gods (גנב, 31:30). Jacob had once accused Laban with "What is this you have done to me?" (מַה־זֹּאת עָשִׂיתָ לִּי, *mah-zo't 'asiti li*, 29:25); now Laban, after catching up with Jacob's caravan, accuses Jacob with virtually the same words, "What have you done?" (מֶה עָשִׂיתָ, *meh 'asita*, 31:26). Laban also wants to know why he "carried off" (נהג, *nhg*) his daughters (31:26); the narrator had just told us, a few verses before (31:18), that Jacob had "carried off" (נהג) his livestock and all his property that he had acquired. Obviously what was Jacob's was not for Laban to carp about, including Jacob's wives![7] Laban is annoyed that Jacob did not even give him time to kiss his sons (לְבָנַי, *lbanay*) and daughters (לִבְנֹתָי, *libnotay*) goodbye (31:28); the plays on "Laban" (לבן, *lbn*) are obvious, another attempt by the unscrupulous uncle/father-in-law to exercise (wrongly) his ownership rights![8] He even claims that "it is in my hands" to do Jacob evil, but as Laban confesses, that power was under the sovereign control of "the God of your father": Laban's hands, in fact, were tied (31:29; also see 31:7, 29). However, according to Laban, he respected Jacob's God, but that respect was not reciprocated to Laban's gods—Jacob had apparently made off with them.[9]

---

6. The word, רבק, *rbq*, "overtake," a verb in the Hiphil, often connotes hostile and ill-intentioned pursuit during battle (Jdg 18:22; 20:42, 45; 1 Sam 14:22; 31:2; 2 Sam 1:6; 1 Chr 10:2).

7. That there is no condemnation from Laban about the possessions Jacob had accumulated in his departure, once again points to the legitimacy of those acquisitions—there is no counter to the explanation Jacob made to his wives in 31:5–13 as to how he had gained his livestock.

8. Fokkelman, *Narrative Art in Genesis*, 167, notices the narrator's depiction of Laban's contradictory speech: Uncle first accuses nephew of carrying away his daughters (not "your wives"!) as if with a "sword" (חרב, *khrb*, 31:26), and then switches to calling Jacob's departure a "flight" (ברח, *brkh*, 31:27)—the consonants of the two words are reversed. "First Jacob is accused of pursuing his own ends with the sword, and then he appears to be a fugitive! The combination is absurd!" To all this, Jacob responds that his departure was because of his fear (31:31), and that he is innocent of the theft of Laban's gods (31:32).

9. Hamilton, *Genesis: Chapters 18–50*, 301.

It is unclear if such a theft as was perpetrated by Rachel would incur the death penalty, but Jacob, nonetheless, passes a terminal sentence upon the thief who, unbeknownst to him, was his favorite wife (31:31–32).[10] The hunt for the missing gods commences; after searching through Jacob's tent, Leah's tent, and the tents of the two maids, finally Laban ends up in Rachel's tent and "feels through" it (מָשַׁשׁ, *mashash*, 31:33–34, 37). Rachel, of course, was sitting on them and excused herself from rising before her father by claiming to be in her time of the month: "[s]uspense turns into malicious pleasure at the deadly fun made of the *terafim:* they are only to be 'saved' by a menstruation. This means that they are as unclean as can be, in this new position they come near functioning as . . . sanitary towels."[11] The man's search thus turns out to be in vain; and thrice we are told that "he did not find" them (31:33, 34, 35). His gods are no match for Jacob's God! Laban's "feeling through" harks back to Isaac's "feeling" (also מָשַׁשׁ) Jacob to see if he was, indeed, Esau, as he claimed to be (27:12, 22). Jacob deceives his "feeling" father of the patriarchal blessing; here the "Jacobah" deceives her "feeling" father of gods that presumably represented some kind of paternal blessing or favor.[12] Thus Rachel's deception is being equated in seriousness with Jacob's deception of his father; she is truly a "Jacobah." In any case, the thrust of the episode is to show how Jacob is protected from danger *despite* deception within his own camp.

23.2 *Genesis 31:36–55*

> **THEOLOGICAL FOCUS 23.2**
>
> 23.2   Following the will of God ensures protection from unscrupulous opponents, a manifestation of divine blessing that is to be acknowledged with gratitude (31:36–55).
>
> > 23.2.1   *Following the will of God ensures protection from unscrupulous opponents, another manifestation of divine blessing.*
> >
> > 23.2.2   *The blessing of God upon the child of God is acknowledged with gratitude.*

NOTES 23.2

23.2.1   *Following the will of God ensures protection from unscrupulous opponents, another manifestation of divine blessing.*

In the end, an aggrieved Jacob, vindicated by Laban's failure to have the accusation of thievery stick, lashes back at his father-in-law, summarizing all the mistreatment he

---

10. The Code of Hammurabi calls for the execution of one who "has stolen goods from a temple or house" (§6).

11. Fokkelman, *Narrative Art in Genesis*, 170. A woman in her menstrual cycle, and the items and furniture with which she came into contact, were declared unclean in the Mosaic Law (Lev 15:19, 25–26). Moreover, the teraphim in the camel's saddle (31:34) are probably unclean already, the animal itself being considered unclean in Israel (Lev 11:4; Deut 14:7). On the other hand, the reader cannot be sure Rachel was being truthful about her physiological status.

12. Fishbane, *Biblical Text and Texture*, 56.

had suffered the past two decades: it is almost a lawsuit that is being brought, with the technical word רִיב, *rib*, "to contend," being employed in a forensic sense, to bring a case before the "brothers" (31:36–37; Jacob's anger is also emphasized by the use of the strong verb, "to burn").

Laban is a man obsessed by chattel, emphatically made clear in Jacob's defense of himself as a shepherd; the nouns head each sentence in 31:38–39, followed by negated verbs, inverting the normal sequence of verbal priority.[13]

> Your ewes and your she-goats?—They have not miscarried!
> The rams of your flocks?—I have not eaten them!
> Animals torn by wild beasts?—I did not bring them to you.

In other words, Laban suffered absolutely no loss at the hands of Jacob, at least in his role of shepherd; things might have been a bit different in Jacob's role as breeder.[14] And all because of Yahweh! Jacob's rejoinder concludes with his declaration that had not God been with him, Laban would have "sent [him] away [שׁלח, *shlkh*] empty-handed [רֵיקָם, *reqam*]" (31:42). Jacob's sense that Laban would send him away empty-handed is at odds with Laban's stated intention to have "sent [them] away [שׁלח]" with joy and songs and timbrel and lyre (31:27); but it is very likely Jacob saw through Laban's mendacity. The phrase "send away empty-handed" immediately evokes memories of the exodus—God's promise that Pharaoh would ultimately agree to "send away" the Israelites, and that they would *not* leave "empty-handed" (also using שׁלח and רֵיקָם, Exod 3:20–21). Later, this would be reflected in the Israelites' treatment of slaves, for they, too, were forbidden to "send [the slaves] away empty-handed" (Deut 15:14). Likewise, Jacob's statement "God has seen my *affliction*" (31:42), anticipates God seeing the "affliction" of his people in Egypt (Exod 3:7; 4:31; Deut 26:7; also see Ps 31:7); in fact, God had expressly told Jacob in a dream, "I have seen . . ." (Gen 31:12).

In any case, by Jacob's confession, "the God of my father and the God of Abraham, and the fear of Isaac" had kept Jacob safe from the exploitative predilections of his employer, Laban.[15] God had seen his affliction and protected him from harm at the hands

---

13. Modified from Fokkelman, *Narrative Art in Genesis*, 175. The pun employing רְחֵלֶיךָ (*rkheleka*, "ewes," 31:38) must not be missed. For twenty years, Jacob took care of Laban's "rachels"—in more ways than one ("Rachel" is רָחֵל, *rakhel*)! As well, Jacob had not eaten Laban's "rams" (אֵילֵי, *'ele*)—note the assonance with "Leah" (לֵאָה, *le'ah*). Finkelstein notes that the unusual Piel use of חטא, *kht'* (31:40, "bore the loss," the only such use of the verb in the OT) is also found in an Old Babylonian tablet to denote the liability of a shepherd for the loss of animals placed in his care. See "An Old Babylonian Herding Contract," 30–31. So also the Code of Hammurabi (§263): "If he [the shepherd] has lost [the ox] or sheep which was committed to him, he shall make good ox for [ox], sheep for [sheep] to their owner."

14. Wenham notes that Jacob's suffering heat by day and frost by night and being sleepless while herding Laban's flock (31:40) indicates the patriarch's dramatic change of lifestyle from a homebody (25:27) (*Genesis 16–50*, 277). In fact, one might surmise that Jacob had had a lot of time on his hands to think about his life and failings as he played out his pastoral vocation; this likely knocked some sense into him.

15. "Fear of Isaac" is an unusual and unique (only here, in 31:42, 53) ascription to Yahweh, perhaps indicating the God whom Isaac feared and respected. After all, it was only the fear of God that kept Laban from doing evil to Jacob (31:24, 29). Hamilton notes that in a compound, פַּחַד, *pakhad*, "always refers to the case or source of dread, rather than the object of dread"—thus God is the one who inspires fear, "the Dreaded One of Isaac" (*Genesis: Chapters 18–50*, 310). See Exod 15:16; Deut 2:25; 11:25; 1 Sam

of Laban. This is quite surprising, since Jacob's camp (or, at least one person in Jacob's camp, the one closest to him—Rachel) was culpable. However, even though Jacob, in a sense, is guilty as a result of the misdoings of one within his household, God's presence and protection are with the patriarch.

However Laban is a sore loser; he does not want to give in so easily, "fear of Isaac" or no. In 31:43, there is a chorus of first-person suffixes: "*my* daughters" (×2), "*my* children," "*my* flocks," "*mine*"—all indicative of the man's reluctance to let go.[16] This, despite God's intervention (31:9), his daughters' assertions (31:14–16), and Jacob's protestations (31:36–42). But Laban, in the end, has no choice, and he seeks a treaty with Jacob. Other instances of non-Israelites making covenants with patriarchs place the latter in positions of superiority, as also does the transaction here (31:44–54).

Ultimately, in the extended scene, 31:25–53, that concludes this pericope, the relationship between Laban and Jacob is substantially altered. The dialogues between Laban and Jacob portray the shift: from a judicial dispute between *pater familias* who accuses and nephew who responds (31:26–42), to a strategic covenant between co-equals who mutually make a treaty (31:43–53). Jacob, one might say, is transformed. Indeed, his final remark to Laban (31:42), "is much more than the decisive climax to his speech of self-justification. It is the summary of the whole story of Jacob's life, at least in Harran. . . . Here Jacob confesses that his preservation and his wealth are all due to God's power overriding the meanness of his uncle Laban; the Lord is a God who enriches his people even in their oppression."[17] Thus the emphasis in all of this is divine protection in the past and, particularly, in the present, as even the potentially dangerous consequences of a culpable act by a member of Jacob's household are averted by God's sovereign work. Opponents who seek to overcome the one who is in the will of God are ultimately thwarted in their purposes.

23.2.2   The blessing of God upon the child of God is acknowledged with gratitude.

Interestingly, in the rest of the pericope, after his defense in 31:41–42, Jacob does not speak more than two words ("Gather stones," 31:46). As for his actions, all he does is set up a pillar and, later, swear and offer a sacrifice (31:45–46, 53–54). Laban, though, is hard at work, constructing a covenant. So the endeavors in 31:44–55 appear to be going in two different directions at the same time—Jacob's and Laban's: two stone markers (31:45–46, 51–52), two names for the pile of stones and two place names (31:47–49), two ritual meals (31:46, 54), two conditions in the pact (31:50, 52), two invocations of deity (31:49, 53), two names for God (31:49, 53, Yahweh and Elohim), and two named ancestors (31:53, Abraham and Nahor).[18] Jacob, the one who speaks not at all and acts only minimally here, is almost aloof. "For Jacob a phase of his life has come to an end, clearly rounded-off with a judgment by God. . . . As God's protégé

11:7; Esth 8:17; 9:3; Pss 36:1; 64:11; 91:5; Prov 1:33; etc.

16. And "and to my daughters" (וְלִבְנֹתַי, *wlibnotay*), and "to their sons" (לִבְנֵיהֶן, *libnehen*, 31:43) echo לָבָן (*lbn*, "Laban"). Literarily, the narrator depicts a man consumed with himself.

17. Wenham, *Genesis 16–50*, 274, 278.

18. Mathews, *Genesis 11:27–50:26*, 532.

he goes away, a victor; he is unassailable and he knows it. For him a pact is needless, he can shelter under God's wings and be safe." Jacob is clearly the superior in this interaction; Laban, the inferior, seeks to guarantee his security with a pact. It appears that the latter is rather worried, or even scared—now that his case of burglary against Jacob has fallen apart—that the God of Jacob might do him damage.[19] That "Jacob has the greater potential for belligerence," being in the stronger position is evident from the fact that he, not Laban, takes the oath (31:53).[20]

The word גַּל, *gl*, echoes seven times in 31:46–52, including its use for "heap" (31:46 [×2], 48, 51, 52 [×3]), and twice in the place "Galeed" (גַּלְעֵד, *gal'ed*, 31:47, 48). There is some serious punning going on here: גָּלַל, *gll*, "to roll," showed up earlier in 29:3, 8, 10, to describe Jacob's rolling of the "stone" off the well in Haran—an event marking divine blessing upon Jacob in his serendipitous arrival at the very well where Rachel would water her flock (אֶבֶן, *'bn*, "stone," is found in 29:2, 8, 10; and also here in 31:45, 46 [×2]). And now with more stones being rolled, divine blessing is again being emphasized. "Rolling stones" seems to be the positive motif that bookends Jacob's Haran years. When one remembers that Laban had confessed, in 30:27, that Yahweh had blessed him "on account of" (בִּגְלָלֶךָ, *biglaleka*) Jacob, this echoing set of consonants adds up to an expression of divine blessing upon the patriarch in those two decades, despite the turbulence and turmoil he had to go through. For Jacob, stones and pillars mark significant moments of recognition that Yahweh is with him: 28:11, 18, 22; and here in 31:45.[21] Jacob ostensibly looked upon these monuments as signs of the presence of Yahweh; Laban musters them as witnesses to a treaty. "To Laban it symbolizes God's patronage of the non-aggression pact; to Jacob the massebe [i.e., "pillar"] means much more, a symbolization of the God of Bethel, of the Yahweh who intervenes actively and who saves him. . . . This monument is the everlasting confession in stone of a man released from servitude." Laban's is a heart of selfishness, concerned as he is with himself and his security (31:49–53)[22]; Jacob's is a heart of gratitude, marked by a recognition of what God had done for him (31:42). The similarities between the Bethel and Haran incidents are considerable, marking as they do, significant moments of divine presence and protection in the life of the patriarch[23]:

---

19. Fokkelman, *Narrative Art in Genesis*, 188–89.

20. Hamilton, *Genesis: Chapters 18–50*, 315. This ending of the association between Jacob and Laban is fitting, for elements are found here that were also present in the first contact between the two in Gen 29: in both there is a pact between "brothers" (29:15–19 and 31:23, 25, 32, 37, 46, 54), a ceremonial meal (29:22 and 31:54; different words are used in each text), and "kisses" (29:11, 13 and 31:28). But the separation between the two protagonists is also made definite: Jacob carefully discriminates between "my brothers" and "your brothers," and between "all my goods" and "all your goods" (31:27).

21. "Jegar-sahadutha" is an Aramaism that means "a heap of witnesses," as also does "Galeed," (31:47).

22. It seems rather ironic that Laban would suddenly become concerned about his daughters (31:50), especially in light of their own indictment of their father in 31:14–16. And the promise he tries to extract from Jacob regarding multiplication of wives also sounds strange, coming from the one who had forced Jacob into bigamy. Laban also attempts to turn Jacob's accusation of oppression against him, as he warns Jacob not to "mistreat" his daughters (עָנָה, *'anah*, here in 31:50; עֳנִי, *'ani*, "affliction," in 31:42).

23. Fokkelman, *Narrative Art in Genesis*, 190, 191 (table from ibid.).

	Bethel	Haran
dream and angel(s)	28:12	31:10–12
Yahweh's manifestation	28:13	31:13
stone, pillar, vow	28:11, 18, 20–22	31:13, 45
"I am with you"	28:15	31:3, 5
"return"	28:15	31:3, 13
bread and eating	28:20	31:54
Yahweh as God "to me" (הָיָה לִי, *hayah li*)	28:21	31:42

All the naming of God towards the end of the pericope (31:53), albeit by Laban[24], raises the poignant question, especially in connection with Jacob's vow at Bethel (28:21): Will Yahweh be the God of *Jacob* as well? From all appearances, it appears that Yahweh has placed himself squarely on Jacob's side. The feeding of Jacob's kinsmen with "bread" clearly is a fulfillment of Jacob's demand in 28:20 for "bread" to eat. God has proven himself. Surely he is the "God of Jacob" now. But the explicit assertion that he is now the "God of Jacob" is delayed, just as the assertion of Jacob being blessed is. In sum, God's blessing is marked by tokens of gratefulness on the part of those so blessed.

SERMON FOCUS AND OUTLINES

THEOLOGICAL FOCUS OF PERICOPE 23 FOR PREACHING

23   Remaining in the will of God ensures protection from potential consequences of sin in one's own camp, a blessing to be gratefully acknowledged (31:17–55).

The Theological Focus for Pericope 23 includes the motif of protection from unscrupulous opponents. It might be best for the preacher to focus on the other theme, that of divine protection from the consequences of sin in one's own camp (as the Theological Focus for Preaching, above, indicates); divine protection from opposition has already been encountered in earlier pericopes of the Jacob narratives in one form or another (see Pericopes 17 and 22). One might also add the response of gratitude to divine rescue in the sermon. Indeed, this might be a good opportunity for the congregation to reflect on divine blessings in this regard, despite the presence of sin within—not the deliberate and willful tolerance of sin within the body, of course, but as in Jacob's case in this pericope, an innocent harboring of felonious action.

Possible Preaching Outlines for Pericope 23

I.   JACOB vs. RACHEL: Remaining in the Will of God
            Recap: Jacob's decision to depart, in line with God's will (31:3, 13)
            Jacob, like Abraham, and unlike the Aramaean, remains in the will of God (31:17–21)

24. Indeed, it appears that Laban's theology is also faulty: he uses the plural form of the verb when referring to the action of the "God of Abraham and the God of Nahor, the God of their father"—"may *they* judge" (יִשְׁפְּטוּ, *yishptu*, 31:53). That he had household idols (31:19) proves the man's polytheistic tendencies.

Rachel, and the sin within the camp of Jacob, without Jacob's knowledge (31:19, 22–35)
Move-to-Relevance: Human tendencies to wander from the will of God—sin within the camp

II. GOD vs. LABAN: Rescued by the Will of God
God's sovereign protection of Jacob (31:24, 29, 42)
Laban's opposition of Jacob (31:22–35, 36–42)
Jacob's grateful response to his rescue (31:43–55)
Move-to-Relevance: Potential negative consequences of sin within our circles; God's protection

III. *Relish God's rescue!*
How to make sure we remain in the will of God
Developing a heart of gratitude for divine protection

Combining the characters in the pericope differently, another option might be:

I. RACHEL and LABAN: Sin and Spite
Rachel, and the sin within the camp of Jacob (31:19, 22–35)
Laban's opposition of Jacob (31:22–35, 36–42)
Move-to-Relevance: Potential negative consequences of sin within our circles

II. JACOB and GOD: Purity and Protection
Recap: Jacob's decision to depart, in line with God's will (31:3, 13)
Jacob, like Abraham, and unlike the Aramaean, remains in the will of God (31:17–21)
God's sovereign protection of Jacob (31:24, 29, 42)
Jacob's grateful response to his rescue (31:43–55)
Move-to-Relevance: God's protection of us

III. *Relish God's rescue!*
How to make sure we remain in the will of God
Developing a heart of gratitude for divine protection

PERICOPE 24

From Chasing to Clinging

Genesis 32:1–32

[Jacob Appeasing Esau; Jacob Transformed]

REVIEW, SUMMARY, PREVIEW

Review of Pericope 23: Genesis 31:17–55 has Jacob returning to the Promised Land pursued by Laban who accuses Jacob of abruptly decamping with his wives and children, as well as with Laban's household gods. Rachel's theft of those idols is undetected, and God's protection covers the faithful Jacob (and all believers) even from the dangerous consequences of sin within his (and their) own camp(s).

Summary of Pericope 24: This pericope describes Jacob preparing to meet Esau who is approaching with a large company. Understandably, Jacob is afraid, and although he seeks protection from God, he continues his habit of manipulation, and attempts to appease his brother with extravagant gifts. In a desperate moment of his life, he encounters God in a nocturnal wrestling match, recognizes deity, and acknowledges him as the true source of blessing. With this dramatic expression of his transformation, Jacob's name is changed to "Israel"; he will not have to fight any more, for God would do the fighting for him.

Preview of Pericope 25: In Gen 33:1–20, Jacob encounters Esau. Jacob, in effect, returns the stolen blessing to Esau, the brothers are reconciled, and they go their own ways in peace. The full enjoyment of promised blessings calls for such restoration of relationships between members of God's community.

24   *Genesis 32:1–32*

THEOLOGICAL FOCUS OF PERICOPE 24

24   **The child of God remembers that God fights for him/her and lives life with confidence and fearlessness, eschewing deception and manipulation (32:1–32).**

24.1   The child of God trusts in God's promised protection and presence, rather than attempting to deceive man and manipulate God (32:1–21).

24.2   The child of God remembers that God fights for him/her and lives life with confidence and fearlessness (32:22–32).

OVERVIEW

While there remain two more pericopes to complete the Jacob narratives, this one, 32:1–32, describes the momentous event, the transformation of the protagonist of the saga. This pericope corresponds to Pericope 19 (28:10–22) in its placement in the whole scheme of the story of Jacob.[1]

	Genesis 28:10–22	Genesis 32:1–32
Nature of journey	Departure from Canaan	Arrival in Canaan
Goal of journey	Fleeing Esau	Meeting Esau
Night to dawn transition	28:11, 16–18	32:13, 21, 22, 24, 26, 31
"he spent [the night] there"	28:11	32:13
Realization/recognition in the morning	28:16–17	32:30
Plea or demand for divine favor/blessing	28:20–22	32:26, 29
"this place" and "a certain place"	28:11, 16, 17, 19	32:2, 30
"and he called the name of that place"	28:19	32:2, 30
Divine blessing promised/given	28:14	32:26, 29
"angels of God"	28:12	32:1
God of Abraham and Isaac	28:13	32:10
Jacob "went" on his "way"	28:10, 20	32:1
"encounter/meet"	28:11	32:1
"house of God/camp of God"	28:17, 19	32:2
"return"	28:15, 21	32:9
Jacob "afraid"	28:15	32:7
Innumerable descendants	28:14	32:13
Conclusion: Israelite custom	28:22 (tithing)	32:32 (diet)

1. As was noted with the previous pericope, the English (E) and Hebrew (H) versions differ in versification: 31:55 (E) = 32:1 (H), 32:1 (E) = 32:2 (H), and so on, until 32:32 (E) = 32:33 (H). The enumeration of the English text will be followed in this work. With reference to the table below, Gen 28:12 and 32:1 are the only instances of "angels of God" in the OT.

In a sense, then, the promises of God to Jacob made in Gen 28 are coming to pass here in Gen 32. Finally, what Jacob has been searching for—nay, *chasing* after—for so long, he obtains: the blessing of God. It has frequently been mentioned in previous pericopes that the narrator was reluctant to mention explicitly that Jacob had been blessed, even though it appeared that everyone around him was being blessed, and even though God had safely enabled his passage out of the sly hands of Laban, with much wealth and great possessions. That reticence of the narrator is finally explained: the explicit statement of the blessing of Jacob was being reserved for the coup at the end of this pericope.

24.1 Genesis 32:1–21

THEOLOGICAL FOCUS 24.1

24.1   The child of God trusts in God's promised protection and presence, rather than attempting to deceive man and manipulate God (32:1–21).

NOTES 24.1

24.1   The child of God trusts in God's promised protection and presence, rather than attempting to deceive man and manipulate God.

Jacob's encounter with the angels of God and the "camp of God" (32:1–2) reminds him (and the readers) of the continued presence of God and the protection of God, as Jacob and his caravan move closer to a rendezvous with Esau, who, when we last heard of him, had been harboring homicidal inclinations towards his heel-grabbing twin (27:41). Jacob, no doubt, was concerned about the danger to self and family, but instead of another explicit divine declaration of presence and protection, the patriarch is granted the vision of angels. There is a hint that this "camp of God" may have been a sight of the armies of heaven; the only other instance of "camp of God" in the OT is a military reference (1 Chr 12:22)—all the more reason for Jacob to have felt confident.[2] The pointed links between Gen 28 and this pericope emphasize in no uncertain terms that the God of promise is still with him and will keep him safe, to bring him to Canaan "in peace/safely" (28:21). Altogether, divine presence is with Jacob, every step of his way.

But unlike the Bethel theophany in Gen 28, there is no word from God here in Gen 32. God had said it all then; there was no need to say anything now. This was almost a test of Jacob's faith, even though the vision of a martial camp of God, with his angels in attendance, would have—should have!—bolstered the patriarch's assurance that he would come out of this potentially perilous situation successfully. Instead, Jacob resorts to his old tricks.

2. One, however, wonders if the reason for Jacob naming the place "*two* camps" ("Mahanaim," 32:2) was to assert his own presence there: God's camp plus *his* camp! As well, the "two camps" in 32:1 may adumbrate the division of Jacob's own holdings and caravan into "two camps" (32:7).

Jacob is constantly portrayed as striving to achieve one goal after another, in the face of a largely unsympathetic and uncooperative world. Even before he was born he wrestled with his brother, and emerged from the womb clutching Esau's heel—as though he would grab the firstborn's place for himself if he could. . . . He served Laban seven hard years for Rachel; and when he was given Leah instead he promptly served Laban another seven years to obtain the daughter he wanted, and then a further six years to acquire his own flocks. It is fundamental to Jacob's character that he must work hard for what he gets; and the narrative function of his gift to Esau, I would suggest, is to illuminate this trait from, as it were, the reverse angle. It is unthinkable to Jacob that he could simply accept Esau's goodwill for free. He *must* give in return a substantial "gift" or "blessing," which amounts to a payment in all but name.[3]

Hence his bid to bribe or buy off Esau. The rest of the first episode of this pericope describes this attempt of Jacob at mollification; he assumes that even after two decades, Esau is out to kill him (27:41). Jacob is therefore desperately seeking Esau's "grace/favor" (חֵן, *khen*, 32:5).[4] Appeasement of Esau consumes a number of verses, accompanied by a statement of the reason for these frenetic activities: great fear and distress (32:7, 11). Jacob's sending of messengers with news about gifts (32:3–6), and his division of his people into two camps (32:7–8), appear to be attempts to escape from the consequences of his deception of Esau two decades ago. The narrator multiplies the suspense in the story: "Jacob sent messengers . . . to Esau, his brother, in the land of Seir [שֵׂעִיר, *se'ir*], the region [שָׂדֶה, *sadeh*] of Edom [אֱדוֹם, *'edom*]" (32:3). "The description is ominously filled with echoes of vexed past history: Esau as the hairy [שֵׂעָר, *se'ar*] and ruddy [אַדְמוֹנִי, *'admoni*] man of the field [שָׂדֶה]); Jacob's purchase of the birthright when Esau (also known as Edom, 'Red') came from the field [שָׂדֶה] and demanded some 'red red stuff' [הָאָדֹם הָאָדֹם, *ha'adom ha'adom*]; and Jacob deceitfully gaining the blessing meant for his brother in part by faking Esau's hairiness [שֵׂעָר]."[5] Curtis thinks that Jacob, in sending מַלְאָכִים, *mal'akim*, is simply doing what God was doing— he sees מַלְאָכִים (the angels of God, 32:1), and sends מַלְאָכִים (his envoys to his brother, 32:3, 6).[6] In any case, there is no suggestion here that Jacob gained confidence from his vision, or that he was going to depend on God for help.[7]

Jacob commences with extravagant obsequiousness in his instructions to his messengers: they are to declare that Esau is his "lord," and that he is Esau's "servant" (32:4, also 32:5, 18, 20; 33:5, 14)![8] Quite in contrast, when Jacob later prays to God

---

3. Noble, "Esau, Tamar, and Joseph," 243.

4. The echo of this word and the related verb "be gracious" (חָנַן, *khanan*) becomes significant in the next pericope (33:5, 8, 10, 11, 15).

5. Kass, *The Beginning of Wisdom*, 450. On another note, one also wonders if Esau would have sent back Jacob's messengers unmolested, were he harboring malevolent intentions. No doubt, Jacob's guilty conscience was working overtime here.

6. In fact, of the seventeen uses of the word in Genesis, the two instances in 32:3 and 6 are the only ones where the word does not refer to supernatural beings, but human agents.

7. Curtis, "Structure, Style and Context," 132–33.

8. It is striking that throughout his interactions with his brother, Jacob describes himself as Esau's servant (32:4, 10, 18, 20; also 33:5, 14) when, in the blessing that he had stolen from Esau, Jacob was

about his predicament, Esau is simply "my brother" (32:11), perhaps pointing to his deceptive approach with regard to his sibling. And after Jacob had just labeled himself a "servant" of Esau (32:4), in his prayer he labels himself a "servant" of God; later he is again a "servant" of Esau (32:18, 20). One suspects that all of this is just toadying to guarantee the safety of his own skin. He is willing to be the "servant" of whoever will keep him from harm, whether it be God or Esau. Jacob is willing to manipulate man and God, if it will work out to his advantage in the end.

The reason for Jacob's endeavors at appeasement is made clear: to find favor in Esau's sight (32:5; the first instance of "favor/grace" [חן] in this pericope; also 33:8, 10, 15). However his attempts are rather devious. Jacob's description of his wealth in 32:5 is strikingly similar to that of the wealth of his ancestors and to the notation of his own prosperity earlier in 30:43. And indication of the shadiness of Jacob's exercises in appeasement is found in that the chattel listed in the cases of Abraham, Isaac, and Jacob (12:16; 26:14; 30:43) were intended for those patriarchs themselves as its recipients; but what is listed in 32:5 is earmarked for Esau.

Goods and Chattel		Recipient
12:16	*and there was to him* sheep *and* oxen *and* donkeys *and* female servants *and* male servants *and* female donkeys *and* camels	**Abraham**
26:14	*and there was to him* possessions of sheep *and* possessions of cattle *and many* male servants	**Isaac**
30:43	*and there was to him* many sheep *and* female servants *and* male servants, *and* camels *and* donkeys	**Jacob**
32:5	*and there was to him* oxen *and* donkeys, sheep *and* male servants *and* female servants	***Esau***

But flattery with the promise of cattle did not seem to have accomplished much with Esau (32:3–6). Unusually enough for the OT, the emotions of a distraught Jacob are in full view of the reader (32:7): he is "very afraid" and "distressed." Perhaps the occurrence of the consonants of חן in מחנה (*mkhnh*, "camp," 32:2) should have reminded him of God's favor upon him, despite the perilous situation he now found himself in. There had already been two explicit divine assurances of presence and protection to Jacob (28:13–15; 31:3), and several implicit ones (the very magnificence of the theophanies themselves, 28:11–12, 16–17; 32:1–2; the prosperity of Jacob's flock, 30:37–43; 31:9; the warding off of Laban the aggressor, 31:24, 29); not to mention the patriarch's own acknowledgement of providence (31:4–10, 41–42). Despite all that, Jacob is "greatly afraid and distressed" (32:7). So Jacob turns to God next (32:9–12). This is the first time he has come to God for help, and the first time he has called himself God's servant. In fact, this is the first time the text shows Jacob praying! It is one of the longest prayers in Genesis, and it commences with every major description of God: "God of Abraham," "God of Isaac," and "Yahweh"—almost exactly how Yahweh had introduced himself to Jacob in 28:13. Jacob appeals to God for his intervention and

---

tapped as the one who would be served and who would lord over his brothers (27:29). This appears to be a reversal of the divine prophecy and patriarchal blessing (see 25:23; 27:29, 40; 33:3, 6–7).

rescue, but from all appearances, his seeking God was likely to have been prompted solely by the gravity of the current crisis. Perhaps it was also intended as a reminder to God that it was his, God's, command to return to Canaan that had now gotten Jacob into this mess!

The patriarch begins and ends his prayer quoting what God himself had once said (or at least what Jacob *thinks* God had once said): "you said to me . . . I will prosper [יטב, *ytb*] you" (32:9) and "you said . . . 'I will surely prosper [יטב with the infinitive absolute] you'" (32:12). There is a manipulative tendency here that is apparent in Jacob's prayer, evident when one compares 32:9 (Jacob's appeal) with 28:15 and 31:13 (the divine promises on which he bases his appeal). Jacob's version of those promises has God promising to "prosper" (יטב, 32:10, 12) him, whereas the divine word only assured him of God's presence and protection; perhaps Jacob's was a subtle attempt to redefine God's words to his advantage.[9]

That Jacob is not at all confident about the success of his earlier ploy to divide his caravan into two companies is clear from the parallels between 32:8 and 32:11b:

32:8	"if he comes ...	and strikes it, the company which is left will escape"
32:11b	"lest he come	and strike me, [and] the mother[s] with children"

In the first case, 32:8, Jacob hopes the company left behind after Esau's attack may survive. In the second, in his prayer, 32:11b, what he really suspects will happen is made clear: *both* camps—including himself, his wives, and the children—will not survive the attack. So Jacob beseeches God for deliverance "from the hand of my brother, from the hand of Esau," emphasizing his inescapability from the firm grasp of Esau. "Only God can save him now. Jacob's ingenuity can only take him so far."[10] Interestingly enough, it was Jacob's hand that gripped Esau's heel (25:26); it was Jacob's hands that were covered with goatskin to deceive Isaac (27:16); it was into Jacob's hand that savory food and bread were given by Rebecca to satiate his father (27:17); and it was those same hands that Isaac assumed were the hands of Esau (27:22–23). Now finally, the master of the sleight of hand is now in the *hand* of his nemesis (37:11). Yes, he certainly needs God now! Not only does he appeal to divine compassion, he also makes his case for deliverance upon divine promise. In fact, he seems to be comparing his desperate situation with that of his father Isaac on Mt. Moriah: he harks back to God's promise in 22:17 that Isaac's descendants would be like the "sand on the seashore" (here in 32:12 it is "sand of the sea").

Though Jacob is desperate, there are signs of hope in his attitude: at least he recognizes, implicitly, that he has been blessed—divine lovingkindness and faithfulness (חֶסֶד, *khesed*, and אֱמֶת, *'emet*) had been "done" to him: from only a staff in his possession when he arrived in Canaan, he had now become two companies as he departed that land (32:10). "He who used to arrange his affairs himself so efficiently, preferably at the cost of his fellow-men, is now, for the first time, willing to be little"—קֹטֹן, *qtn*, "unworthy," but also means "younger" (32:10); that, of course, reminds the reader that this was the "little" brother who wanted to be big. As we arrive at the climax of this younger one's story, this is a confession by Jacob to his own littleness—i.e., he finally acknowledges his real status. And as Fokkelman notes, this is the only basis by which the God of Abraham and the God of Isaac (32:9) would become the God of Jacob (or, for that matter, the God of his people).[11]

But there is no response from Yahweh! And when all is said and done, "[i]t appears the prayer does not change Jacob's basic approach to solving his problem. This seems to be the same approach that Jacob took to get the birthright. The only difference is that the price has gone up, and he will now have to offer more than just food."[12] And he does! Following his long prayer, Jacob engages in some frenetic activity, sending three droves of animals—550 animals in all!—ahead of himself, to his brother Esau (32:13–21). With each of the three advance groups of animals, Jacob sends word that he is right behind (32:17–18, 19–20). Anderson notes that such directives, in the context of the surrounding narratives, were in actuality quite deceptive: "[A]ssuming all goes according to plan, the first dispatch responds to Esau as commanded and then summarily says Jacob is behind them. Presumably Esau will then expect Jacob to arrive next, but instead, he will be met by another installment from Jacob's camp who will summarily say Jacob is behind them, only to be followed by another group from Jacob's camp, and another."[13] Hopefully by the time brother encounters brother, Jacob hopes, Esau's heart will have been softened.

Jacob calls his gift מִנְחָה (*minkhah*, "present," 32:13, 18, 20), "'a gift that ingratiates,' 'a sweetener'" (as in Gen 43:11; Jdg 3:15); indeed, Jacob is trying to find חֵן (from two consonants of מנחה, 32:5 and 33:8, 10).[14] However, מנחה also means "sacrifice," as in Lev 2:1, 4, 5, 6, 15; not surprisingly Jacob employs quasi-sacral language as he engages in this presentation intended to "appease" Esau (כפר, *kfr*, also "atonement," as in Lev 1:4; 4:20, 26, 31, 35; etc.), so that Esau would "accept" him (רצה, *rtsh*, 33:10; also in cultic contexts: Lev 1:4; 7:18; 19:7; 22:23, 25, 27; etc.). "In the final analysis the present is self-seeking; in fact Jacob wants to buy off Esau's wrath with it. He does not yet see that this gift is no solution to the problem of a relationship broken by him."

In Jacob's instruction to his servants in 32:20, "face" occurs four times, alternating between "his" (Esau's) face and "my" (Jacob's) face.[15]

11. Fokkelman, *Narrative Art in Genesis*, 203.

12. Curtis, "Structure, Style and Context," 133. Or as Mann notes, Jacob is "at once calculating and contrite, an intextricable combination expressed by the position of Jacob's prayer in between his two precautionary manoeuvres" (*The Book of the Torah*, 60).

13. Anderson, *Jacob and the Divine Trickster*, 141.

14. The word "present" (מנחה) also shows up often in this part of the Jacob Story: 32:13, 18, 20, 21 (and also in 33:10); notably the word, מחנה (*mkhnh*, "camp/company," 31:2, 7, 8 (×2), 10, 21; also see 33:8), is an anagram of מנחה ("present").

15. "Face" shows up a number of times: 32:3, 16, 17, 20 (×4), 21 (translated as such or as "appease," "go before/in front," or "accept")—mostly dealing with the face of Esau. "Face" is also found in 32:30b (×2)—the face of God. Moreover, "Peniel," itself, means the "face of God" (32:30a). All of this likely anticipates the recurrence of "face" in 33:3, 10 (×2), 14 (×2), 18; especially in 33:10, where the face of

"I will cover his [Esau's] face"
"with the present going before my [Jacob's] face"
"I will see his [Esau's] face"
"Perhaps he will lift my [Jacob's] face"

"Jacob, hopelessly mired in the mundane, misunderstands the crucial issue before him to be 'face to face' encounter with Esau . . . when the real issue before him is 'face to face' encounter with God" (see 32:30–31).[16] Indeed, the incoherence of Jacob's stratagem is writ large in the syntax: the man intends to "cover his [Esau's] face" and thereby hopes, ironically, to "see his face." And then Esau will "lift his [Jacob's] face" (32:20)? This is a plan that is certainly not going to work out as envisioned. Especially if, all along, Jacob is doing all he can to *avoid* a tête-à-tête with his sibling. In order for reconciliation to happen, a "face-to-face" must happen, and this only *after* a "face-to-face" with God, which does take place in 32:30.

> He must face his past. He must face his brother, whom he has wronged. And in the middle of the account of his facing his brother will come the account of his most immediate contact with God in his life, his struggle after which he will say, "I've seen God face-to-face." And the two encounters, first with his God and then with his brother, will be brought together as he says to Esau "I've seen your face—like seeing God's face!" (33:10).[17]

All of Jacob's feverish activities are literarily depicted as futile, for the entire event is shrouded in darkness: the transactions begin and end at "night."

	So *he spent the night* there.
32:13a	Then he took from what he had in his hand as a *present* to Esau, his brother.
32:21	So the *present* passed over before his face and *he spent the night* in the camp.

The pericope has three units based on the time of the day; most of the action occurs at night, and Jacob remains wide awake and active throughout.

day → night: 31:55/32:1–12
night → night: 32:13–21
night → day : 32:22–32

"It is highly ironic that in 21a a whole squad of people with a great quantity of livestock should pass on to appease Esau, whereas the hero himself prefers to go . . . to sleep!"—that is, if he could sleep.[18] Apparently, he had tried to (32:13a), but it seemed that he just could not. Then, in the middle of the night, Jacob hits upon a bright idea—the appeasement of Esau with animals (32:13b–21a). After that has been organized,

---

Esau is likened to the face of God. ("Penuel" is likely a more common version of "Peniel.")

16. Snell, "Genesis 32:22–32," 279.

17. Fokkelman, *Narrative Art in Genesis*, 206.

18. Ibid., 207.

he tries again to sleep (32:21b). But now he decides he must get his family across the ford of Jabbok (for protection?[19]), and he is left alone (32:23–24), again at night, and still insomniac. In sum, Jacob strategizes in the night (32:13), sends gifts in the night (32:14–21), gets up in the night (32:22a), sends his family across at night (32:22b–23), and, for the *coup de grâce*, Jacob wrestles through the night, with none other than God (32:24–30)! Only after these nocturnal engagements does the sun finally rise on the beleaguered patriarch (32:31).

And now it appears that Jacob, the one who was always manifesting the "me-first" philosophy, is wanting to go "me-last" (32:13–21, 22–23, 24).[20] Everyone and everything is "going before" Jacob (32:16, 20, 21); and Jacob is "going after/behind" everyone and everything (32:18, 20, 21).

32:18	"to your servant Jacob …	and behold, he also	[is] behind us."
32:20	"your servant Jacob	behold, [he] also	[is] behind us."

While this all might signify that "Jacob allows himself to be passed by, for the first time willingly," it is more likely an act of cowardice, extremely fearful as he was (32:7, 11).[21]

This first act of Pericope 24, then, depicts a man who is terrified, and is willing to do anything to escape his predicament, whether it be appeasing his brother, or appealing to God—deceiving humanity and manipulating deity for his own ends.

24.2 Genesis 32:22–32

> **THEOLOGICAL FOCUS 24.2**
>
> 24.2   The child of God remembers that God fights for him/her and lives life with confidence and fearlessness (32:22–32).

NOTES 24.2

24.2   *The child of God remembers that God fights for him/her and lives life with confidence and fearlessness.*

Jacob is now at his wits' end.

> He prays for rescue, reminding God, none too subtly, of his promise to make his descendants as numerous as the sand of the sea, a process that requires mothers and children. The reader expects some divine response to the patriarch. Night comes, the time of dreams and visions. He waits, like Jacob, for a revelation and appropriate inspiriting message; something like "Fear not Jacob," . . . "I am your

---

19. The logistics of this and other crossings of the ford of Jabbok (Penuel, in 32:31?) are unclear. In any case, the words "cross over," "ford," and "Jabbok" (עָבַר, מַעֲבָר, and יַבֹּק [*'abar, ma'abar,* and *yaboq*] respectively; 32:10, 16, 21, 22, 23 [×2], 32; as well as "wrestle," אָבַק, *'abaq,* 32:24, 25) are potent wordplays with "Jacob" (יַעֲקֹב, *ya'aqob*) that literally manifest the torn conscience and heart of the erstwhile deceiver. All of this frenzied restlessness is resolved only with the "embrace" (חָבַק, *khabaq,* 33:4, yet another wordplay) of Jacob by Esau!

20. Fokkelman, *Narrative Art in Genesis,* 205.

21. Ibid., 206.

shield!" (Gen. 15:1). The "answer" is a tackle by an unintroduced man: a strange revelation indeed![22]

Strange it was, but in that wrestling match it was God himself who met Jacob. And, as a result, Jacob is changed . . . and blessed!

One may wonder why the identification of the "man" with God is not made outright. Geller is certain that the author is "playing with a known biblical convention: the inability of human actors to detect the divinity of supernatural visitors until they perform some sudden wonder." Thus the incident is "almost a 'type scene,'" accentuated by the bleak aloneness of Jacob.[23] Wessner has carefully noted the occurrences of "Jacob," "God," "Esau," "family," and "other" (i.e., all of Jacob's other possessions—animals, servants, retinue, etc.) in this wrestling section (32:22–32) and in the sections on either side, 32:1–21 and 33:1–17.[24]

Frequency of Occurrences					
	"Jacob"	"God"	"Esau"	"Family"	Goods
32:1–21	9	3	9	3	24
32:22–32	7	2	0	0	0
33:1–17	3	3	6	15	5

In other words, 32:22–32, Jacob is completely separated from everything and everyone—brother, family, chattel. Starkly, he is all alone with God, "face-to-face" (32:30). Besides Jacob, only Moses (Exod 33:11; Deut 34:10), Gideon (Jdg 6:22—with the angel of Yahweh), and eschatological Israel (Ezek 20:35) are said to have encountered God "face-to-face" in the Bible. Wessner notes that all these instances are characterized by four inherent features of such encounters: divine initiation (sudden and unexpected tussle at night), profound intimacy (in contact, name change, physical touch, giving of blessing), intentional solitude (separation from circumstances and bystanders), and supernatural verification (usually by a miracle).[25] This was deity himself, in an encounter with a human, as Jacob confesses (32:30). And it is quite clear that even as the struggle between him and the "man" continued, the patriarch recognized that he was dealing with the supernatural, for a touch from the former dislocated the hip of the latter. Realizing who it was that he was tangling with, Jacob asks to be blessed; indeed, he refuses to let go until he has been blessed (32:26). In this closing stage of his story, we see in Jacob a man who has been thoroughly chastened. All these many decades, he had been trying to secure one blessing or another by his own wheeling and dealing, by heel-grabbing and back-stabbing, by manipulating, conniving, cheating, and deceiv-

---

22. Geller, "The Struggle at the Jabbok," 44.

23. Ibid., 45. The Targums speculate that the one with whom Jacob wrestled was one of the "angels of praise" who needed to depart at daybreak to rejoin the heavenly choir that was due for a performance of praise to God (so *Tg. Ps.-J.* and *Tg. Neof.* Gen 32:27). In any case, 35:11 confirms the Namer to be Yahweh himself; so also does Hos 12:3–4.

24. "Toward a Literary Understanding of 'Face to Face,'" 173, 173n20, 173n21.

25. Ibid., 177.

ing. Now he has recognized the true source of blessing: God. And rightly, he clings on to God till he is blessed.

God responds to Jacob's request for blessing with a name-change, from "Jacob" to "Israel" (32:27–28). In response, Jacob asks the unintroduced "man" to provide his name, to which, God responds with a question: "Why?" It is almost as if Jacob is being asked: "Why do you ask my name? Don't you know me? It was me you have been chasing all your life, even though you weren't aware of it, running to and fro, hither and thither, helter and skelter" (32:29a, my version). Of course, Jacob did not need to ask God's name; he not only knew it, he had already recognized the "man" for who he was.

And finally—*finally!*—the one who has been chasing blessing all his days is blessed![26]

Introduction (32:22–24)
A   Jacob injured on the thigh (32:25)
    B   Request for release because dawn was breaking (32:26a)
      C   Blessing demanded; clinging to God (32:26b)
        D   Request for name; request answered (32:27)
          E   Renaming and explanation (32:28)
        D'   Request for name; request denied (32:29a)
      C'   Blessing given; God seen face-to-face (32:29b–30)
    B'   Jacob crosses as the sun rises (32:31a)
A'   Jacob limps on his thigh (32:31b)
Conclusion (32:32)

The thrust of the episode is on the naming, for it is by that act that Jacob's metamorphosis of character is consummated. The last time he had been asked his name, Jacob had lied (27:18–19, 24); this time he tells the truth, more so than he realizes—he is יַעֲקֹב, the "heel-grabber," who has been grabbing heels all his life. But with the divine blessing bestowed on him, the patriarch becomes "Israel." "The etymology of Israel offered by the text relates יִשְׂרָאֵל [ysr'l] 'Israel' to the verb שׂרה [srh] 'to struggle, fight.' So the word literally means 'El (God) fights'"—i.e., "God fights for you," implying that therefore, "you do not need to fight any longer for yourself."[27]

At the conclusion of the scene of tussle, we notice that Jacob's prayer for "deliverance" (32:11) is precisely answered; his life is "delivered" (32:30).[28] "In this verse Jacob moves, in his own words, from a proclamation of revelation ('I have seen God face-to-face') to a statement of testimony ('and yet my life has been preserved'), that is, he

---

26. This blessing of God upon Jacob in 32:29 (as well as 35:9 and Jacob's testimony thereof in 48:3) link this patriarch with his grandfather and his father who were themselves blessed (24:1 and 25:11 respectively). Table from Walton, *Thou Traveller Unknown*, 79n27.

27. Wenham, *Genesis 16–50*, 296. Theophoric names with an imperfect verb, such as is found here, generally make deity the subject of the verb rather than the object; hence "God fights [for you]" (See Curtis, "Structure, Style and Context," 134). שׂרה occurs only here and in Hosea's interpretation of this incident, Hos 12:3–5, where the prophet nationalizes Jacob's experience for the entire community of God's people.

28. This also goes to show that Yahweh is the unnamed wrestler here, the one who granted what was requested of him.

shifts from awe to relief."[29] And so with this name change, we can almost be certain of how Jacob's rendezvous with Esau will end. After all, it was God who was fighting `for the patriarch—things could only end well, deliverance was nigh! And a new era begins.

Jacob's opponent, Yahweh, declared that Jacob had prevailed in his strife with God and with men (32:28). But that is not to say he defeated God or man, but that he finally was victorious in his struggle-filled, strife-ridden search for blessing—"by recognizing his dependence on God he is now able to receive the promise and the blessing of God to Abraham."[30] As a result of a miraculous touch of the divine, Jacob would limp forever, a testimony to his lack of self-sufficiency and to the absolute sufficiency of Yahweh who would fight for him. No more would he need to fight; no more would the cripple be able to fight. Henceforth God was fighting for him, and for the entire nation of his descendants, betokened by their refraining from eating the hip sinew. "So this story of Jacob's struggle with God summed up for Israel their national destiny. Among all their trials and perplexities in which God seemed to be fighting against them, he was ultimately on their side; indeed, he would triumph, and in his victory, Israel would triumph too."[31]

A new day dawns. The sun did not just rise, but it "rose upon him" (32:31). "The cosmos has changed: it smiles at him, promises security and warmth after the almost sinister night, with its frightening setting. The sun symbolizes salvation, deliverance. . . . The nights of Bethel and Haran have been replaced by the glorious day of the 'Face of God,' Penuel."[32]

SERMON FOCUS AND OUTLINES

THEOLOGICAL FOCUS OF PERICOPE 23 FOR PREACHING

24   **Remembering that God fights for him/her, the child of God lives life with confidence and fearlessness (32:1–32).**

The sermon on this pericope might do well to include a recap of the past events of Jacob's life—how he has constantly been chasing for blessing and crashing in failure; he never finds blessing his own way, on his own terms, for his own ends. It is in this pericope that the realization hits him forcefully, that God alone is the source of blessing and not any other person or thing or event or exigence. Only God! This recognition is a significant part of what it means to remember that God fights for us—he is the sole source of blessing, and the child of God must necessarily cling on to this exclusive

---

29. Hamilton, *Genesis: Chapters 18–50*, 337. Jacob's exclamation, "I have seen God face to face, and I have been delivered!" (32:30), is not necessarily one of consolation that he has managed to survive after having seen God (see Exod 33:20); more likely, it is the patriarch's proleptic recognition that he will not be annihilated when he meets Esau. He is now certain of deliverance from the hand of his brother.

30. Curtis, "Structure, Style and Context," 135.

31. Wenham, *Genesis 16–50*, 303.

32. Fokkelman, *Narrative Art in Genesis*, 221–22.

fount of blessing. Only then will he or she be enabled to live a life of confidence and fearlessness, without finding it necessary to deceive or manipulate.

Possible Preaching Outlines for Pericope 24

I. Jacob the Deceiver
   Recap: Jacob's life thus far: chasing and crashing (his deception and his discipline)
   His attempts to appease Esau—his deceptive tendencies return in the crisis (32:1–8, 13–21)
   Move-to-Relevance: Our inclinations to take matters into our own hands in times of crises

II. Jacob the Desperate
   Jacob's prayer to God—his manipulative tendencies rise to the fore (32:9–12)
   Reasons for confidence in God: theophany (32:1–2), promises at Bethel (28:13–15), past experience (Gen 30–31)
   Move-to-Relevance: Our inclinations to distrust God, despite proof of his providence in the past

III. Jacob the Disabled
   Jacob's recognition that he was grappling with God, and his clinging to God for blessing (32:24–26)
   God's renaming of Jacob: "Israel" = "God fights [for you]" (32:27–29)
   Jacob will never have to fight again; he will never be able to fight again (32:30–32)

IV. *Cling to God alone!*
   How we can live in confidence, seeking only God for our blessing, remembering he fights for us

With a slightly difference focus, pitting the "self-made man" with the "re-made man," the preacher could employ this outline:

I. Jacob, the Self-made Man
   Recap: Jacob's life thus far: chasing and crashing (his deception and his discipline)
   Jacob's attempts to appease Esau—his deceptive tendencies return in the crisis (32:1–8, 13–21)
   Jacob's prayer to God—his manipulative tendencies rise to the fore (32:9–12)[33]
   Move-to-Relevance: Our inclinations to trust ourselves and our own initiatives (and what we trust in)

II. Israel, the Re-made Man
   Jacob's recognition that he was grappling with God, and his clinging to God for blessing (32:24–26)
   God's renaming of Jacob: "Israel" = "God fights [for you]" (32:27–29)
   Jacob will never have to fight again; he will never be able to fight again (32:30–32)

III. *Cling to God alone!*
   How we can live in confidence, seeking only God for our blessing, remembering he fights for us

33. It has been mentioned before, but it does not hurt to do so again: much of the material in the Notes of this commentary may not—should not!—make it into the sermon. The preacher is encouraged to use the text selectively, employing enough (and that is the key word: *enough*) exegetical detail to surface the theological thrust of the text. In other words, what is to be attempted in the public event of the sermon is a creative undertaking of theological exegesis in an inductive fashion, so that as the sermon proceeds, light is shone upon key parts of the text, to gradually unveil the theology of the pericope. Of course, the task of the preacher is only complete when some specific application is also proffered to listeners.

PERICOPE 25

From Rupture to Reconciliation

Genesis 33:1–20

[Jacob's Reconciliation with Esau]

REVIEW, SUMMARY, PREVIEW

Review of Pericope 24: Genesis 32:1–32 describes Jacob preparing to meet Esau who is approaching with a large company. Jacob is afraid, and although he seeks protection from God, he continues his habit of manipulation, and attempts to appease his brother with extravagant gifts. In a nocturnal wrestling match with deity, Jacob recognizes God and acknowledges that blessings come from him alone.

Summary of Pericope 25: The long-awaited encounter between the battling brothers, Jacob and Esau, occurs in this pericope. Beyond the lavish gifts, Jacob, in effect, returns the stolen blessing to Esau who, surprisingly, seems quite content with what God has given him and seeks no more. The brothers are reconciled and go their own ways in peace. The full enjoyment of God's promised blessings calls for restoration of broken relationships between members of God's community.

Preview of Pericope 26: The next pericope (Gen 34:1–31) describes the rape of Dinah, Jacob's daughter, by a Shechemite. Her brothers, the sons of Jacob, retaliate by deceiving the Shechemites into circumcision and, taking advantage of their incapacitation, the siblings go on a violent rampage. Jacob's silence throughout the pericope emphasizes that apathy towards evil only perpetuates more evil.

25   Genesis 33:1–20

THEOLOGICAL FOCUS OF PERICOPE 25

25   Faith in God (and the enjoyment of his blessings) involves efforts to reconcile broken relationships, resulting in forgetful forgiveness, and the restoration and maintenance of right relationships with others and with God (33:1–20).

25.1   Faith in God manifests in humble and contrite efforts to reconcile broken relationships.

25.2   The work of God manifests in forgetful forgiveness.

25.3   Restoration of broken human relationships is integral to maintaining an unbroken relationship with God, and to enjoying his blessings.

OVERVIEW

The previous pericope depicted Jacob finally receiving God's blessing. That would have been a blissful ending to the turbulent story of the patriarch. However, one more thing needed to be accomplished: reconciliation. So this pericope, where Jacob "returns" Esau's blessing, corresponds to the earlier one in 26:34–28:9, where Jacob steals it. In the earlier pericope, Jacob's brothers, it was prophesied, would bow before him (27:29); here it is Jacob who bows before his brother (33:3). The shared elements between these two pericopes also include: "blessing," 27:12, 35, 36, 38, 41; 28:4; and 33:11; "kiss," 27:26, 27, and 33:4; בוֹא, *bo'*, "bring," in the Hiphil in 27:10, 14, and in the Hophal in 33:1; "approach," 27:21, 22, 25, 26, 27, and 33:6, 7; שֵׂעִיר, *sa'ir*, "hairy/Seir," 27:23, and 33:14, 16; "abundance," 27:28 and 33:9; "bowing," 27:29 and 33:3; "neck," 27:40 and 33:4; "times," 27:36 and 33:3; and "wept," 27:38 and 33:4.[1]

Genesis 33 may be structured with narrative alternating with dialogue, the centerpiece being Dialogue 2 (the crux of the reconciliation; 33:8–11a, considered in detail below).[2]

> **A**   Narrative introduction (33:1–5a)
> **B**   **Dialogue 1** (33:5bc)
> **C**   Narrative (33:6–7)
> **D**   **Dialogue 2** (33:8–11a)
> **C'**   Narrative (33:11b)
> **B'**   **Dialogue 3** (33:12–15)
> **A'**   Narrative conclusion (33:16–20)

Pericope 25 concludes with Jacob arriving "in peace" in Shechem (in Canaan, 33:18), a literal fulfillment of the demand he had made of God in 28:21 that he be brought back "in peace" to his father's house.[3] The patriarch then builds an altar, calling upon God who is shown, for the first time, to bear Jacob's name—"El-Elohe-Israel" (33:20). The altar-building enterprise parallels the same action of Abraham upon the latter's

---

1. See Pericope 16 for the overall chiastic scheme of the Jacob Story.

2. From Vrolijk, *Jacob's Wealth*, 243.

3. No doubt, the mention of Shechem and Hamor (33:18–19) also anticipates the events of Gen 34.

own entry into Canaan (12:7–8; 13:3–4, 18); Jacob's purchase of property (33:19) also evokes his grandfather's acquisition of land (23:1–20).

25   *Genesis 33:1–20*

THEOLOGICAL FOCUS 25[A]

25   Faith in God manifests in humble and contrite efforts to reconcile broken relationships, resulting in forgetful forgiveness, and the restoration and maintenance of right relationships with others and with God (33:1–20).

    25.1   *Faith in God manifests in humble and contrite efforts to reconcile broken relationships.*

    25.2   *The work of God manifests in forgetful forgiveness.*

    25.3   *Restoration of broken human relationships is integral to maintaining an unbroken relationship with God, and to enjoying his blessings.*

    A. Having only one section in this pericope, the "Theological Focus 25" is identical to the "Theological Focus of Pericope 25."

NOTES 25

25.1   Faith in God manifests in humble and contrite efforts at reconciliation.

Once again we see the division and arrangement of Jacob's large party: maids and their children, Leah and hers, and Rachel and her son Joseph—all in front of the patriarch (33:1–2). This seems to be a return to the manipulations Jacob had performed earlier, in 32:7, 16, 22–23. The reader wonders if the Peniel experience had done anything to Jacob's attitude. Was he still the coward, hiding behind others? Had his encounter with God, his name change, and the implicit promise therein that God would fight for him not strengthened his faith? But, as Fokkelman observes wryly, "the narrator throws dust in our eyes," making it seem as if Jacob is still "Jacob" and not "Israel." For suddenly in 33:3a, we have a disjunctive clause opening with the subject, "he"—Jacob: "He himself went before their faces." "[W]e see that Jacob has accepted his personal responsibility and now goes on before them. . . . in this 'outward' action the radical change wrought at Penuel is manifested."[4] And why not? Having contended successfully with one Man in Penuel, and having been transformed into Israel, he is now ready to face four hundred men (32:6; 33:1).[5]

And so, before his brother Esau, Jacob prostrates himself seven times—a mark of great respect by vassal towards lord. The act of "bowing" (שָׁחָה, *shakhah*) was the appropriate gesture of submission to superiors (23:7, 12; 37:7, 9, 10; 42:6, 28) and, of course, to deity (18:2; 19:1; 22:5). In any case, what Isaac had prophesied in 27:29 is inverted. Whereas father had blessed the younger son with the words, "Your mother's sons will bow [שׁחה] to you," now the blessed son is himself bowing to his older sibling.

    4. Fokkelman, *Narrative Art in Genesis*, 223.

    5. Hamilton, *Genesis: Chapters 18–50*, 342.

He whom others would "serve" (עבד, *'bd*, 27:29), is now "servant" of another (עבד, 33:5, 14; also 32:18, 20), and Esau is constantly Jacob's "lord" in the account (33:8, 13, 14, 15). This is effectively Jacob's "return" to Esau of the stolen blessing. In fact, one could even see in the sevenfold bowing a reflection of the sevenfold blessing of Isaac to Jacob—the latter is specifically addressed seven times in 27:28–29: "may God give you . . ."; "may peoples serve you"; "may nations bow to you"; "may you master your brothers"; "may your mother's sons bow to you"; "may they be cursed who curse you"; "and may they be blessed who bless you." And literally, here, Jacob's face is in the ground (33:3): "Now we understand that readily and of his own free will Jacob acts counter to the blessing, which he had stolen from his brother, [and] deliberately releases his hold on the destiny he had taken from Esau. The lord makes himself a servant by complete (7×!) subjection, his face down in the dust."[6] The "pseudo-Esau" is returning the blessing to the real Esau, undoing his sins of the past by word and by deed.[7] Jacob's humble and contrite conciliatory efforts mark the patriarch's faith in God.

25.2 *The work of God manifests in forgetful forgiveness.*

The reunion is powerful beyond words: Esau runs to Jacob, embraces Jacob, falls on Jacob's neck, kisses him, . . . and *they* weep (33:4).[8] It was not one-sided. Both parties had felt the pain of a ruptured relationship and now both parties rejoice in tears at the restoration thereof.[9] "[T]he meaning of the kiss goes beyond mere high spirits on Esau's part. It calls to mind the kiss (27:27) that stole the blessing that was his by birth, and the addition of the detail that Esau fell upon Jacob's neck recalls that twenty years earlier Jacob had covered that same neck with goatskins to deceive his father [27:16]. Kissing and necks are by no means chance details in this tale."[10]

Of interest, over every Hebrew letter of וַיִּשָּׁקֵהוּ (*wayyishaqehu*, "he kissed him," 33:4) are *puncta extraordinaria*, or *nequdot* (נְקֻדוֹת, *nqudot*)—dots over letters, found fifty-three times in the Hebrew text of the OT. Such markings were known to predate the Masoretes, but their significance is uncertain. If it is true that the letters/words under the dots were considered by the scribes to be spurious[11], then, in the case of וַיִּשָּׁקֵהוּ,

---

6. Fokkelman, *Narrative Art in Genesis*, 223.

7. Ibid., 109; Wenham, *Genesis 16–50*, 298–99.

8. Five staccato *waw*-consecutive imperfects describe this stunning reunion. In Gen 25:34, five *waw*-consecutive imperfect verbs equally graphically described Esau's fall: "he ate, and he drank, and he rose, and he went, and he despised." In a sense, this was Esau's restoration, too, here in 33:4. Cotter thinks that the plural verb, וַיִּבְכּוּ (*wayyivku*, "*they* wept"), was actually a scribal error, with the suffix ו (*w*) an instance of dittography, the accidental duplication of a letter, in this case the duplication of ו that also begins the next word in the text (וַיִּשָּׂא, *wayyisa'*, "he lifted," 33:5). Such a reading that maintains "his" (Esau's) weeping (not "their" weeping) would fit the overall tone of the narrative and its trajectory in 33:4 (Cotter, *Genesis*, 250, 250n52).

9. This reminds one of the reception of the prodigal son by his father in Luke 15:20 (also see Lev 19:18; Ps 133; Matt 5:22–24).

10. Cotter, *Genesis*, 250. One notes that "come near" (33:6, 7 (×2)) and "bow" (27:29 (×3)) also hark back to the earlier incident of Jacob's deception: "come near" is also used in 27:21, 22, 25 (×2), 26, 27; and "bow" in 33:3, 6, 7 (×2).

11. See Tov, *Textual Criticism*, 55–57.

the puncta may well be an expression of the scribes' own incredulity at what had happened in this dramatic scene of reunion. But perhaps this momentous reconciliation ought not to be that surprising, for "When pleasing to Yahweh are the ways of a man, Even his enemies will be in peace with him" (Prov 16:7).

But what is truly incredible here is Esau's lack of any animosity whatsoever towards Jacob—this was the one who, when last seen, was out to murder Jacob who had stolen his most precious inheritance (27:41–42). One cannot but wonder what had happened in Esau's life in the past two decades that had wrought such a change in his attitude. Oh, the inscrutable workings of God! For all Jacob's servanthood before his brother's lordship, Esau chooses to address Jacob simply as "my brother" (33:9)—there is something poignant about that purehearted address. God *must* have been working in Esau! And in the parallelism of the wording—Esau's "I have plenty" (33:9) and Jacob's "I have plenty because of God's חֵן [*khen*]" (33:11; see below)—there is a strong hint that Esau's plenty is also the result of the same חֵן bestowed by God behind the scenes on this older brother. It is also interesting that the text specifically notes that Esau "lifted up his eyes and saw" the women and children—the products of God's חֵן (32:5)—while Jacob "lifted up his eyes and saw" and saw Esau and his four hundred (33:1). It may not be too farfetched to assume that if one was the result of God's grace, then the other (Esau's large party) was too: yes, God had worked on Esau and prospered him, as well!

Obviously Esau recognized the congeries of animals as Jacob's "gift" (מִנְחָה, *minkhah*; 32:13, 18, 20; 33:10), as Jacob had instructed his servants to explain. Yet, here in 33:8, Esau makes a pun and labels the מנחה as מַחֲנֶה (*makhaneh*), "a company." This not only shows the depth of Esau's change of heart from the murderous brother he was two decades ago, but actually shames Jacob who thought a "gift" could purchase forgiveness. Unwittingly, Esau must have touched a nerve, for the idea behind the "companies"—the division of Jacob's caravan into two groups—was an escape maneuver on the part of Jacob (32:7, 8, 10) which becomes, in retrospect, a completely unnecessary exercise. Jacob therefore wiggles away by replying that the purpose of the two companies was to find favor before Esau (33:8). In any case, this demonstration of forgetful forgiveness is a manifestation of the work of God in the lives of his people.[12]

25.3 *Restoration of broken human relationships is integral to maintaining an unbroken relationship with God, and to enjoying his blessings.*

And so for the first time, Jacob acknowledges God's "grace/favor" (חֵן, 33:5, also 33:11) upon his life, a fact obvious to readers, but only now voiced by the protagonist of these stories, Jacob.[13] The two instances of God's favor are interwoven with the three instances

---

12. I had often thought that the biblical writer was not overly interested in the astonishing shift of disposition on the part of the older brother, and so assumed that neither must readers be. But upon closer examination of the text, it is remarkable how many exegetical details the narrator is actually emphasizing, clues that portray Esau's transformation. Perhaps the preacher (and reader) *should* attend to this change and marvel, praising the Author of that remarkable reformation, and applying the divine demand in that narrative into their own lives.

13. Earlier Jacob had acknowledged God's "lovingkindness" and "faithfulness" (חסד and אמת, *khsd*

of Jacob's seeking *Esau's* favor (33:8, 10, 15; also 32:5). It was noted in Pericope 24 that the word Jacob uses to indicate Esau's favorable reception, רָצָה (*ratsah*, 33:10), was also employed in cultic contexts: Lev 1:4; 7:18; 19:7; 22:23, 25, 27; etc. As well, מִנְחָה, "present," also means "sacrifice," as used in Lev 2:1, 4, 5, 6, 15. All of this puts Jacob's relationship with Esau in equivalence with his relationship to God. In fact, it is explicitly mentioned by Jacob that "I see your face as one sees the face of God" (33:10). Fokkelman notes how "[a]lmost all the great key-words of the Story of Jacob, esp. those of Gen. 32, follow one another in a chain-reaction . . . in a concentric order," in 33:9–11, centered upon the facial equivalence![14]

> **A**   *"I have plenty"* (33:9)
> > **B**   "find *grace* [חֵן] in your eyes" (33:10a)
> > > **C**   "and *take* my **present** [מִנְחָתִי, *minkhati*] from my hand" (33:10b)
> > > > **D**   "for I *see* your *face*" (33:10c)
> > > > **D'**   "as one *sees* the *face* of God" (33:10d)
> > > **C'**   "please *take* my **gift/blessing** [בִּרְכָתִי, *birkati*]" (33:11a)
> > **B'**   "because God has been *gracious* [חָנַן, *khanan*] to me" (33:11b)
> **A'**   "and because I *have plenty*" (33:11c)

"A purified relationship to God necessarily goes with a purified relationship to his fellow-man; Jacob has spoilt and broken the relationship to God by spoiling the relationship with Esau. He had wanted to achieve the destiny assigned to him by God, but his deception of Esau had impeded this."[15] In other words, getting right with fellow-men is paralleled with getting right with God. And note the one pointed difference in the chiastic structure above (bolded): מִנְחָתִי in 33:10b (*C*) is replaced by בִּרְכָתִי in 33:11a (*C'*)—the giving of the present is now being equated to the return of the blessing! Alter notes: "In offering the tribute [ברכה], Jacob is making restitution for his primal theft, unwittingly using language [ברכה was used by Esau in 27:36] that confirms the act of restitution. No wonder Jacob insists that Esau accept it. Reconciliation was consummated with restoration."[16] Obtaining God's grace/favor is synchronized with obtaining Esau's grace/favor. The use "חן" is particularly instructive, intertwined as it is between *God's* favor and *Esau's*, along with מחנה and מנחה as shown below.[17]

> **A**   חנן, God's (33:5)
> > **B**   מחנה, Jacob's, to win Esau's favor (33:8a)
> > > **C**   חנן, Esau's (33:8b)
> > > **C'**   חנן, Esau's (33:10a)
> > **B'**   מנחה, Jacob's, to win Esau's favor (33:10b)
> **A'**   חנן, God's (33:11)

---

and '*mt*) in 32:10.

14. Fokkelman, *Narrative Art in Genesis*, 225–26; table from ibid., 226.

15. Ibid., 226–27.

16. Alter, *Genesis*, 186. The narrator uses a strong word, פצר, *ptsr*, "urged" (see 19:3, 9; 2 Kgs 2:17).

17. Table from Taschner, *Verheissung und Erfüllung*, 164.

Jacob's hope of receiving חֵן from his brother (*C, C'*) is set within and ensconced by the חֵן he had first received from God (*A, A'*).[18]

The power of this reconciliation is manifested in the way Jacob's plans are up-ended. His goal, in 32:20, was first to accomplish restoration of stolen goods ("cover his face with the present going before my face"), and then to achieve forgiveness for the felony perpetrated ("afterward I will see his face and perhaps he will lift my face"). But in Gen 33, it happens the other way around. First Jacob's face on the ground is lifted up as Esau runs, embraces, falls on his neck, and kisses him (33:4)—forgiveness. Then comes the restoration (33:9–11aβ): "*Then* he [Esau] took it [the מִנְחָה/בְּרָכָה]" (33:11b)! What Jacob had carefully planned becomes "unhinged" by God's sovereign design, and gets converted into something far more powerful, far more enduring, far more edifying: rupture had become reconciliation with forgiveness and restoration, but not the way Jacob thought it would be.[19] Forgiveness first; then restoration, not the other way round, in which case it would be a misbegotten attempt to purchase forgiveness with restoration.

The reason for Jacob's refusal of Esau's offer to go ahead of the former, and ultimately of Jacob's avoidance of Seir (33:12–17), may have had to do with Yahweh's command to him to return to Canaan, a region that did not include Seir (31:3, 13; 32:10).[20] So Jacob's statement, "until I come to my lord in Seir," is clearly a polite declining, that asserts that not everyone will go to Seir (but only Jacob—"I"); moreover it deliberately leaves Jacob's time of arrival indefinite (we do not know if Jacob even made that trip; perhaps he did). Even Esau's offer of protection is ignored: Jacob has finally learnt his lesson—*God* would be his protector (28:15; 32:30), the one who fights for him (32:28).

That they remain on peaceful terms is indicated in the collaboration of the twins in the burial of their father, Isaac (35:29). "Although the act of children burying their fathers appears to be a common literary motif in the patriarchal narratives [25:8; 35:29; 50:13], when the joint burial of their father is read against the background of their previous strained relations, it clearly highlights the quality and depth of the brothers' renewed relationship."

> [I]t is particularly significant to hear both protagonists openly renounce their greed and show themselves willing to share their time and resources with each other. Thus, it is quite revealing for Esau, who has reeled emotionally at the loss of the paternal blessing . . ., to decline the enormous gift of animals from his brother by indicating that he already has a lot. . . . In a similar manner, the man

18. Also, the fact that "embrace" (חָבַק, *khabaq*, 33:4) sounds similar to "wrestle" (אָבַק, *'abaq*, 32:24, 25) indicates again that Jacob's wrestling with one (God) is closely related to Jacob's embrace of the other (Esau).

19. Nonetheless, the value of the מִנְחָה as restoration must not be discounted, even though forgiveness comes first. Noting the cultic flavor of the account in the use of רצה, *rtsh* ("accept favorably"), חנן, *khnn*, ("be gracioius"), פנה, *pnh* ("face"), and מנחה, *mnkhh* ("present/gift"), one must remember that "[j]ust as with a sacrifice offered to God, the sacrifice does not *cause* God's acceptance, but *signifies* it." The acceptance of the gift by Esau proved the acceptance of Jacob's conciliatory efforts. See Vrolijk, *Jacob's Wealth*, 252.

20. Wenham, *Genesis 16–50*, 299.

who has spent his whole life trying to outdo everybody else is also now able to acknowledge that he has everything. . . . In short, when people no longer pose any threat to each other by what they are and what they have, reconciliation can become a real possibility even if they do not share a common physical space.[21]

In light of Jacob's promise to God to build him a house (28:22) if he, Jacob, gets to return to his father's house "in peace" (בְּשָׁלוֹם, *bshalom*), it does seem striking that Jacob first builds a dwelling for himself (33:17), the only time a patriarch is said to have done so.[22] In any case, the story concludes with Jacob's arrival in Canaan "peacefully" (שָׁלֵם, *shalom*, 28:21) and his purchase of real estate there—an appropriate end to the meanderings of this fugitive. Jacob consummates his arrival in the land of promise by building an altar, following the practice of his grandfather (33:20; for Abraham's similar actions, see 12:7, 8; 13:18; 22:8; for Isaac's, see 26:25; and for Jacob's erection of another altar later; see 35:7). In a sense, in calling the altar "El-Elohe-Israel" (33:20), not only is it being recognized that this God was now the God of Jacob, but also that Jacob had recognized that Yahweh was his God, as he had brazenly stipulated God should be (28:21). Thus the two issues of Gen 28 have been resolved: Jacob has arrived safely in his father's land and Yahweh has become his God.[23] The mending of disrupted human relationships leads to the maintenance of an unbroken relationship with God and the enjoyment of his blessings.

SERMON FOCUS AND OUTLINES

THEOLOGICAL FOCUS OF PERICOPE 25 FOR PREACHING

25   Faith in God is marked by seeking and extending forgiveness, thus restoring relationships with others, and also with God (33:1–20).

The Theological Focus for Preaching has simplified the Theological Focus of Pericope 25 by assimilating the seeking of forgiveness and the extending of forgiveness as manifestations of faith in God (and implicitly the consequence of God's work in human hearts). In turn, restored human relationships sustain a right relationship with God. For this sermon as well, a focused and brief recap of the events that rupture the relationship between Jacob and Esau (Gen 25–28) may be helpful. Both Jacob's humble efforts to reconcile (fearless [seeking for] forgiveness) and Esau's joyful willingness to reconcile (forgetful forgiveness) must be highlighted.

Possible Preaching Outlines for Pericope 25

I.   Relationship Ruptured
       Focused recap: struggle *in utero*; sale of birthright (Gen 25); stealing of blessing (Gen

21. Agyenta, "When Reconciliation Means More," 131, 132–33.

22. Later, he will therefore need to be reminded to keep his promise to God (35:1).

23. Yet there are tones ominous in this conclusion: while Abraham also had set foot in Shechem (12:6), it seems that Jacob intends to make Shechem his permanent dwelling (implied in his purchase of land, 33:19). Is there an implicit rebuke of Jacob here?

414

27–28)

Move-to-Relevance: Ruptured relationships in our lives are not uncommon

II. Relationship Restored

Jacob's humble and contrite effort to seek forgiveness, marking a faith in God (33:1–11)
Esau's remarkable extension of forgetful forgiveness, manifesting a work of God (33:1–16)
Focused recap: God is fighting for Jacob (32:28); relationships are restored with faith in such a God.
Move-to-Relevance: Why we fail to seek forgiveness humbly, and why we fail to extend it forgetfully

III. *Reconcile!*

Specifics on taking action: to seek forgiveness/to extend forgiveness, all based in a strong faith in God, the Fighter

Separating Jacob and Esau one may distinguish the two sides of relationship restoration—the seeking of forgiveness, and the extending thereof:

I. Jacob: Expecting Forgiveness

Focused recap: Jacob's culpability: struggle *in utero,* sale of birthright (Gen 25), stealing of blessing (Gen 27–28)
Jacob's humble and contrite effort to seek forgiveness, marking a faith in God (33:1–11)
Move-to-Relevance: Why we fail to seek forgiveness humbly—lack of faith in God who fights for us

II. Esau: Extending Forgiveness

Focused recap (looking at it from Esau's side): he had reason to be angry and vengeful (27:30–41)
Esau's remarkable extension of forgetful forgiveness, manifesting a work of God (33:1–16)
Move-to-Relevance: Why we fail to extend forgiveness forgetfully—lack of faith in God who fights for us

III. *Reconcile!*

Specifics on taking action: to seek forgiveness/to extend forgiveness, all based in a strong faith in God, the Fighter

PERICOPE 26

Pathetic Apathy

Genesis 34:1–31

[Rape of Dinah; Spoliation of Hivites; Apathy of Jacob]

REVIEW, SUMMARY, PREVIEW

Review of Pericope 25: In Gen 33:1–20, Jacob encounters Esau. Jacob, in effect, returns the stolen blessing to Esau, the brothers are reconciled, and they go their own ways in peace. The full enjoyment of God's promised blessings calls for such restoration of broken relationships between members of God's community.

Summary of Pericope 26: The rape of Dinah, Jacob's daughter, by a Shechemite, is described in this pericope. Her brothers, led by Simeon and Levi, retaliate. After deceiving the Shechemites into circumcision, the brothers take advantage of their incapacitation to go on a rampage, slaughtering and pillaging. Jacob's silence throughout the pericope, except for a concern for his own standing in the community, is striking. Apathy towards evil only perpetuates more evil.

Preview of Pericope 27: The next pericope (Gen 35:1–36:43) concludes the Jacob Story, with an account of Jacob keeping his earlier promise to worship after his safe return to his homeland, but only after God prompts him to do so. A genealogy of Esau's line closes out the saga. In all, the pericope moves God's people to worship him in response to his blessings, and that continues the cycle of divine blessings.

26   *Genesis 34:1–31*

OVERVIEW

This pericope—almost a digression, dealing as it does with Jacob's *children*—corresponds to Pericope 17 (Gen 26) in its placement in the Jacob Story, another seeming digression, dealing with Jacob's *father*.[1] Both concern deception and strife, and a pact with foreigners. Other common elements include: "brother" (26:31 and 34:11); "sister" (26:7 and 34:13, 14); "multiply" (26:4 and 34:12); "kill" (26:7 and 34:25–26); "one people" (26:10 and 34:22); "flock" (26:14 [×2] and 34:5, 23); רחב, *rkhb*, "make space/Rehobot" (26:22 and 34:21); "lie" (26:10 and 34:2, 7; and both times the male involved is uncircumcised); אָחַז/אֲחֻזָּת (*'akhuzzat/'akhaz*, "Ahuzzath"/"property," 26:26 and 34:10); "sister" (26:7, 9 and 34:13, 14, 27, 31); "brothers" (26:31 and 34:11, 25); בְּנֹתֵינוּ/בֵּינוֹתֵינוּ (*benotenu/bnotenu*, "between us"/"our daughters," 26:28 and 34:9, 21); and שׁלם (*shlm*, "peace"/"friendliness," 26:29, 31 and 34:21).[2] In both incidents, the patriarch in question comes off less than heroic, unwilling as each is to protect wife/daughter. The two chapters, Gen 26 and 34, are therefore balanced accounts, both dealing with deception, one for self-preservation and perpetrated by Jacob's father, the other for revenge, by Jacob's sons; and both deceptions are deprecated.

The pericope has four scenes, each containing, "went out" (34:1; 6, 24, 26)[3]:

---

1. And unusually, Gen 34 is one of the five chapters in Genesis that does not mention God (the others are Gen 23, 36, 37, and 47).

2. See Pericope 16 for details on the chiastic structure of the Jacob Story as a whole.

3. Structure from Wenham, *Genesis 16–50*, 307–8.

Jacob's daughter violated (**34:1–4**, *mostly narrative*)

A   Speech to father: "Take for me this young girl as a wife" (34:4);
      "take" (34:2, 4); "go out" (34:1)

Concludes with word from son to father (34:4)

      Hamor and Shechem propose a marital alliance

B   with Jacob's family (**34:5–19**, *dialogue*)

      Terms accepted (34:18); unit begins with "hear" (34:5); "go out" (34:6)

      Hamor and Shechem propose the marital alliance

B'   to their fellow-townsfolk (**34:20–24**, *dialogue*)

      Terms accepted (34:24); unit ends with "hear" (34:24); "go out" (34:24)

Jacob's sons violate the town (**34:25–31**, *mostly narrative*)

A'   Speech to father: "Should he treat our sister as a harlot?" (34:31);
      "take" (34:25, 26, 28); "go out" (34:26)

Concludes with word from sons to father (34:31)

As Mathews notes, "[t]here are no heroes in this episode."[4] Everyone is culpable. Shechem's violation of Dinah is reprehensible (34:2; "defiled," 34:5, 13, 27; "disgraceful," 34:7; and there is no remorse on part of the perpetrator), but he seems to show some good faith as he and his father, Hamor, enter into willing negotiations with Jacob and his family; apparently Shechem did love Dinah (34:3–4, 8). On the other hand, the Hivite father and son do not represent their discussions with Jacob fairly to their own townspeople, instead engaging in seemingly specious talk (see below). Likewise, the brothers are righteously indignant about the humiliation of their sister (34:7), yet they operate with deceit on their part (34:13, 31). Throughout, we are told later, the Hivites have been keeping Dinah in their custody, making their transactions with the Israelites quite farcical. Finally, the episode culminates in a wholesale slaughter of the Shechemite men and the raping of their city (34:25–29), a gross overreaction on the part of Jacob's sons. Jacob himself remains silent throughout most of the narrative (except for an irate protest of his sons' violent enterprises, 34:30).He seems suspiciously apathetic, demonstrating a total lack of concern for his daughter, being worried only about his status in Canaanite country.[5] This from a man who, in previous incidents, was never at a loss for words; he is named eleven times in Gen 34, but speaks only once.

All in all, the narrator performs a subtle balancing act here: both Hivites and Israelites have an admixture of commendatory and condemnatory qualities. "From beginning to end, it appears as though he [the narrator] seeks out the dangers of complexity, if not evenhandedness, as both an artistical challenge and a rhetorical policy. . . . Avoiding the crudities of polarization, he aspires to such mixed responses as leave him a narrow margin of safety and threaten him with failure if he for a moment loses control of his materials and his audience."[6] In the end, it is only Jacob who is not portrayed as having done or said anything laudatory; his lack of action, emotion, and speech (till the very end, when his only utterance is a disgruntled protest that does

4. *Genesis 11:27–50:26*, 578.

5. Ibid., 579.

6. Sternberg, *The Poetics of Biblical Narrative*, 467.

nothing to redeem him) inculpate him. Indeed, all the other characters in the story are foils for Jacob: Hamor is a better father than Jacob, Jacob's sons are more concerned about morality and ethics than he is, and even Shechem, the rapist, turns out to have at least some positive qualities. Only Jacob stands uniformly condemned by his silence, his inaction, and his last words.

26   Genesis 34:1–31

THEOLOGICAL FOCUS 26[A]

26   The enjoyment of divine blessings may be hampered by inaction and silence in the face of depradation, and such irresponsibility toward the maintenance of God's moral standards only leads to further evil (34:1–31).

  26.1   *The enjoyment of divine blessings may be hampered by inaction and silence in the face of depredation.*

  26.2   *Irresponsibility of a leader toward the maintenance of God's moral standards leads to further moral laxity on the part of those led.*

  26.3   *Apathy towards evil only generates further evil.*

A. Having only one section in this pericope, the "Theological Focus 26" is identical to the "Theological Focus of Pericope 26."

NOTES 26

26.1   The enjoyment of divine blessings may be hampered by inaction and silence in the face of depredation.

At the very outset, Shechem's act is described quite pejoratively: וַיִּשְׁכַּב אֹתָהּ, *wayyishkav 'otah*, is literally "he laid her"—a transitive construction using the direct object, as opposed to the usual "lay *with* her" (וַיִּשְׁכַּב עִמָּהּ, *wayyishkav 'immah*), employing the indirect object as in 30:16; Deut 22:29; 2 Sam 11:4; 12:24. Generally, the latter, שכב עם, *shkv 'm*, is neutral, used of both normal sexual relations and those actions that are condemned (Exod 22:19; Deut 27:20–23). On the other hand, the former, שכב את, *shkv 't*, is exclusively used of abnormal sexual acts, as the context always shows (2 Sam 13:14; but also Gen 26:10; Lev 15:24; 20:11–13; Num 5:13, 19). "The result [in Gen 34:2] is a sort of coarse and vulgar Hebrew used for instances of improper or brutal sexual encounter."[7] That Shechem's deed was a violation is explicitly noted: וַיְעַנֶּהָ, *way'anneha*, "he violated her" (34:2); Deut 22:24; Jdg 19:24; and 20:5 use ענה, *'nh*, to indicate abuse, and 2 Sam 13:14 employs both שכב את and ענה. And in the account of the three rapes in the OT, נְבָלָה (*nbalah*, "disgrace") is mentioned: Gen 34:7; Jdg 19:23, 24, 26; and 2 Sam 13:12.[8] Dinah's "defilement" (טמא, *tm'*, Gen 34:5, 13, 27) is also a gross impurity

7. Cotter, *Genesis*, 254n56. In Tamar's rape, Amnon first attempts intercourse with שִׁכְבִי עִמִּי (*shikvi 'immi*, "lie with me," 2 Sam 13:11), suggesting a consensual act. Upon her refusal, he violates her against her will, which the narrator describes as וַיִּשְׁכַּב אֹתָהּ (*wayyishkav 'otah*, "he laid her," 13:14).

8. Elsewhere "disgrace" is used often of sexual trespass, that even warranted terminal punishment

in the Mosaic Law, contaminating not only the ones involved, but even the rest of the community (Lev 18:20, 23; Num 5:3, 13–14, 20, 27–29; Deut 24:4; Ezek 18:6, 11, 15; 22:11; 23:13, 17; 33:26). Harlotry was clearly labeled טָמֵא in the prophets (Ezek 23:7; Hos 5:3; 6:10; also see Ps 106:39). Moreover, "daughters," and "saw," and "took" (Gen 34:1–2), echo the infamous episode of Gen 6:2, when the sons of God "saw" the "daughters" of men, and "took" them as wives—an act that incurred God's intense displeasure (6:3, 5–7). And besides, "saw" and "took" were the same pair of words that also described Eve's response to the fruit of the tree of the knowledge of good and evil (3:6), thus giving this incident in Gen 34 an altogether negative hue. In sum, Shechem's was a violation, a rape, of Dinah, and the narrator is clearly condemning it.[9]

The narrative's description—"he took her," "he laid her," and "he violated her"—is not only redundant, clearly pointing to predatory activity, it creates an entirely one-sided account without any dialogue.[10] Dinah is simply a sexual object, and obviously this is not a consensual act—Dinah is utterly voiceless![11] In any case, besides the obvious act of rape, Shechem had also transgressed in that he, a foreigner, had engaged in sexual relations with an Israelite, not to mention the fact that he had done so without following the protocol for betrothal and marriage.[12] Moreover, the other actants in the story recognize that Dinah has been defiled (34:5, 13, 27). And, after the fact, the perpetrator and his father show no indication of remorse or any thought of offering compensation to the shamed, dishonored, and aggrieved family, thus multiplying their own guilt.[13] All the while, one must remember, Dinah is still a hostage in Shechem's house (34:26).

Shechem's soul-bonding (וַתִּדְבַּק נַפְשׁוֹ, *wattidbaq nafsho*, "and his soul was joined," 34:3) while used of a normal relationship between man and woman (from דבק, *dbq*, "cleave/cling," 2:24), it can also be employed of illegitmate unions (as in 1 Kgs 11:2, Solomon's "bonding" to his foreign wives that resulted in his apostasy). That Shechem

---

on occasion (see, besides other references, Deut 22:21; Jdg 20:6, 10; Jer 19:23–24).

9. Noble, "A 'Balanced' Reading," 178–79. It is unclear if Dinah's "going out" in 34:1 is entirely innocent: Wenham points to a cognate Akkadian verb *waṣû* in the Code of Hammurabi (corresponding to יצא, *yts'*, "went out") that describes the improper conduct of a housewife outside her house (*Genesis 16–50*, 310). If not behaving with impropriety, Dinah may have been, at the very least, imprudent: she, the one who went "to see" (34:1), becomes the one who is "seen" (34:2).

10. And, subsequently, "his soul was bonded to Dinah," "he loved her," and "he spoke . . . to her" (34:3). Here, too, Dinah does not seem to have any say, and her feelings regarding the entire affair remain unexpressed. The paired three-part verbal description of Shechem's activity in 34:2 and 3, match the threefold portrayal of the deeds of Simeon and Levi: "they took [swords]," "they entered [the city]," and "they killed [every male]" (34:25). The narrator may be hinting that that punishment was deserved.

11. Interestingly enough, substantiating this idea of unilateral action is the narrator's refusal to name Dinah and Shechem together in 34:1–4; when one is named, the other is not, and vice versa. Moreover, Dinah is never mentioned by name in direct discourse in the entire chapter.

12. For strictures on exogamy, see Exod 34:11–16; Deut 7:1–5 (specifically mentioning the Hivites); besides Gen 24:3, 7, 37; 28:1, 6, and the negative examples in 26:34; 27:47–28:8, and Gen 38.

13. If a marriage were to be agreed upon, Shechem and his father were willing to offer a price for Dinah (34:8–12); but no indemnity or reparation was being considered for her violation. The Mosaic Law called for marriage and a fine for a sexual offence against an unengaged virgin (Exod 22:16–17; Deut 22:28–29).

loved Dinah (Gen 34:3) is also no excuse for his rape; 2 Sam 13:1–4 also has Amnon loving his victim, Tamar. Neither is Shechem's "speaking to her heart" (34:3). Though it can indicate tenderness (Hos 2:16, God's concern for Israel), it can also be entirely selfish (as in Jdg 19:3; the Levite's true feelings are portrayed in 19:25, where he gives over his concubine for gang rape, a woman to whose heart he had spoken earlier). While it might be true that in Gen 34:2 Shechem initially sees Dinah as an object, and later in 34:3 as a person, that in itself confirms the uncouthness and boorishness of the man, who thinks that "[d]efilement is just a state of mind, alterable by a change of heart."[14] In his request to his father, Shechem is blunt and curt: "Take [לְקַח, *lqh*] this child [יַלְדָּה, *yldh*] for me" (34:4), making one wonder what he actually thought of Dinah, whom he had already "taken" (לקח, 34:2). To him, she is just a kid; the narrator, however, refers to Dinah as a "young woman" (נַעֲרָה, *n'rh*, 34:3), an appellation of greater respect and worth, which, by the way, Shechem also employs when he refers to Dinah before her brothers (34:12). All this to say Shechem was guilty!

At the foundation of this shameful episode is Jacob's rather negligent and cavalier attitude to the horrible plight of Dinah, his daughter by his "unloved/hated" wife, Leah (29:31), in contrast to his constant partiality towards Joseph and Benjamin, the children of his beloved wife Rachel (29:30; 35:16–18).[15] But the narrator's introduction of Dinah as Jacob's daughter is pointed—four times the fact is mentioned in the account of the rape (34:1, 3, 5, 7). Clearly Jacob ought to have been the one responsible for her welfare. But he, of all people, is the one who does nothing and says nothing until the end of the episode.

On the other hand, Dinah is also Leah's daughter (34:1), a fact that makes prominent the initiative of two of Leah's other children, Simeon and Levi. In fact it is they who subsequently take responsibility for this daughter of Jacob and for the honor of the family. Remarkably, after Shechem and Hamor have made their marriage proposal, Dinah is never mentioned again as Jacob's daughter; instead she is "their/our sister" (34:13, 14, 31) and "our daughter" (34:17).[16] Needless to say, after this point, Jacob is never referred to as "father," either. The narrator seems to be hinting that the parent had abdicated his responsibility by virtue of neglect. Jacob shows up initially, but disappears during the negotiation phases, and reappears with a petulant question towards the end, without making any mention of his daughter or her plight, and without showing any relief at her rescue. His lack of normal paternal solicitousness prepares the stage for the brothers' overreaction to the violation. In his only utterance in Gen 34, Jacob demonstrates no moral outrage even regarding his sons' violence. Jacob is more concerned about his personal welfare and standing in the community, than any wrongdoing perpetrated upon his daughter, or any defilement incurred by/within his camp. On the other hand, on a later day, hearing of Joseph's supposed demise, this

---

14. Kass, "Regarding Daughters and Sisters," 32.

15. As far as we know, Dinah is the only daughter in the family of any of the patriarchs, Abraham, Isaac, or Jacob.

16. Dinah's siblings continue to be the "sons of Jacob" (34:5, 7, 13, 25, 27), making the shift in Dinah's label all the more emphatic.

same father would go into an agony of grief, putting on sackcloth, mourning for days, and refusing to be comforted (37:34–35). So the absence of any feeling or action on Jacob's part here in Gen 34 is striking, and must be interpreted negatively. All this points to Jacob's culpability by his silence, apathy, and inaction.[17]

In stark contrast, the brothers are gravely concerned about their sister, and her defilement grieves and angers them (34:7). Indeed, the pericope ends with their dramatic rhetorical question: "Should he treat our sister like a harlot?" (34:31). Jacob has no answer to that accusation. "He who twiddles his thumbs about the rape and deems the gifts [from Shechem and Hamor, 34:10] fair compensation is as guilty of making a whore of Dinah as the rapist and giver himself."[18]

Ironically, in Hamor you have a father who is willing to defend, speak up, and argue for his child; Shechem is called "son" six times (34:2, 8, 18, 20, 24, 26), and Hamor, "father" five times (33:19; 34:4, 6, 13, 19).[19] In 34:6, it is Hamor who has a chat with Jacob (though Shechem is present, 34:11, it is only Hamor who is mentioned initially), contrasting the two fathers: one pursues the desires of his son with alacrity, the other is mute about his daughter.[20] Hamor is quite defensive about his son, Shechem: where the narrator used דבק to denote the bonding of Shechem to Dinah (34:3), a word that might also have negative connotations, Hamor employs חשׁק, *khshq*, "be attached" (34:8) which is always positive. And the father goes on to emphasize Shechem's feelings by beginning his sentence with a noun phrase outside of the clausal construction (a *casus pendens*): "Shechem, my son—his soul is attached to your daughter." It is interesting that Hamor uses "your [plural] daughter"; and later the brothers of Dinah would call her "our daughter" (34:17). Was Hamor alluding, by means of the plural pronoun, that it was not Jacob who had ultimate responsibility of his daughter, but his sons?

Unlike their father, Jacob's sons respond immediately: their instant reactions of grief and anger (34:7) puts them in a much better light than the patriarch. The latter stirs from his stupor only much later, when he is disturbed by the action of his sons,

17. That Jacob heard the bad news of the rape even before his sons returned from the field (34:5), and before Hamor and Shechem visited him, suggests that the escapade had become the grist of the gossip mill, adding to the defilement and disgrace (34:7, 13–14, 31). It also appears, from the sequence of 34:5–7 that, after the rape, Hamor and his son Shechem arrived at Jacob's place *before* Jacob's sons came home; therefore the silence of Jacob "until his sons came in" (34:5) includes the period of time when Hamor and his son are with Jacob—the man just does not respond to them. One also observes that Hamor and Shechem had come "to speak with *him*" (34:6), though after the arrival of Jacob's sons, they "spoke to *them*" (34:8). While there may be diplomacy involved in Jacob's silence as he awaits the return of his sons, the absence of any emotion on his part to the grievous insult to his daughter —a "defilement" (34:5)—is telling.

18. Sternberg, *The Poetics of Biblical Narrative*, 475.

19. Clark, "The Silence in Dinah's Cry," 150, 150n42.

20. "Negotiations with aggrieved kinsmen, harsh conditions from political dependents, change of status quo, mass conversion—not to mention bodily pain—nothing deters this exemplary father [Hamor]" (Sternberg, *Poetics*, 451). For most of the account, Shechem is in the presence of his father, Hamor, and/or the two are mentioned together by the narrator: 34:2, 4, 6, 8, 13, 18, 20, 24. They are even murdered together, 34:26. Unfortunately, there is no corresponding unity between Jacob and his children.

and then not because of its brutality, but because of the potentially damaging effect their slaughter may have on his standing in the land (34:30).

While we are hard-pressed to explain Jacob's negligence in this pericope, perhaps the fact that he was done with all of his earlier struggles with father, brother, uncle, wives, and God, had made him look forward to an undisturbed future of tranquility. Here was a man getting ready—finally—to enjoy the blessings of God he had struggled to obtain for the last two decades. God had blessed him (32:29), and now this! Needless to say, the enjoyment of the blessings of God needs ongoing action on the believer's part: silence and apathy in the face of evil will not further one's experience of divine blessing. As a parent, it fell upon Jacob to protect the purity of his daughter. In consequence, a series of farcical, obnoxious, and ghastly enactments of otherwise noble actions come to pass, beginning with "her unjust defilement (the rape), in a horrible parody of the proper union of man and woman."

> There follow grim parodies of (1) a marriage proposal (asking for the hand of a woman already seized and violated); (2) proper fatherhood and rulership (fathers [Jacob and Hamor] serving rather than ruling the passions of their sons; a ruler [Hamor] leading his city into ruin for the sake of satisfying his son's erotic wishes); and (3) the practice of retribution by means that appear to be anything but just (the brothers' slaughter and spoiling of the entire city), involving (4) what appears to be a parody of the sacred rite of circumcision. The entire order of justice falls apart from the neglect of the purity and dignity of woman.[21]

The analysis of the situation by Dinah's brothers in 34:7, employing "Israel" anachronistically ("because he did a disgraceful thing in Israel"), indicates how different the sexual standards of Jacob's family were from that of the Canaanites: "and thus it should not be done." This makes the patriarch's inaction throughout the pericope all the more worthy of condemnation.[22] And this inaction keeps Jacob from full enjoyment of the blessings of God that he had received.

26.2 *Irresponsibility of a leader towards the maintenance of God's moral standards leads to further moral laxity on the part of those led.*

In the longest scene in this pericope, 34:5–19 (*B* in the table above), made up almost entirely of dialogue, both sides are acting duplicitously: Jacob's camp is explicitly noted to be deceptive (34:13), while Shechem (with his father) is engaging in negotiations with Jacob and his sons without any reference to his violation of Dinah, and all the while holding her hostage (34:26).

The proposal of intermarriage made by Hamor in 34:9 (using חָתַן, *khatan*, "make marriage alliances") was expressly prohibited in the Mosaic Law (Deut 7:3–4, also using חתן; and see Josh 23:12–13; Ezra 9:14). In return for this marital alliance, Hamor

---

21. Kass, *The Beginning of Wisdom,* 480.

22. Tamar pled with Amnon not to abuse her, with a similar phrase: "for such a thing is not done in Israel" (2 Sam 13:12). All three ot uses of the formula לֹא יֵעָשֶׂה, *lo' ye'aseh,* "it is not done," refer to "acts of great moral turpitude"—Gen 29:26 (Laban's rationale for the substitution of the older for the younger), 2 Sam 13:12 (the rape of Tamar), and the current text, 34:7 (Sarna, *Genesis,* 194).

promises Jacob and his family the chance to acquire "property" (אחז, *'khz*, 34:10). But, in fact, it was God who had earlier promised Abraham and his descendants that Canaan would be their everlasting "possession" (אֲחֻזָּה, *'akhuzzah*, 17:8, from the verb אחז; also see 35:12). So it seems as if Hamor is attempting to duplicate, in some fashion, God's promise. But he is in effect diminishing it for, according to God, there would be no sharing of the land—the Israelites were to have it *all*.[23]

Shechem adds his own remarks in 34:11–12, but Dinah continues to remain nameless and voiceless, chattel to be haggled over. While the son is willing to give whatever is asked in return for Dinah's hand in marriage, one must note that there is no remorse or plan for recompense for past violation, and more importantly, that Dinah is still under Shechem's control and possession, making this hardly an offer in good faith. But the deceitful counteroffer (מִרְמָה, *mirmah*, "deceit," 34:13) of Jacob's sons is also deprecated by the narrator: the only other uses of מרמה or the associated verb רמה, *rmh*, in the Jacob saga are in 27:35 (of Jacob deceiving Esau) and in 29:25 (of Laban deceiving Jacob).[24] The brothers' use of וַיַּעֲנוּ (*wayya'anu*, "they answered," 34:13) is pointed: Shechem had raped Dinah (וַיְעַנֶּהָ, *way'anneha*, 34:2) and now her siblings respond in kind, at least phonetically, employing parallel consonants (both verbs come from homonyms sharing the same stem ענה, *'nh*). This offer to accede to a marital alliance, if the Hivites were to become circumcised, was also quite meaningless in terms of its theological value. What benefit would there be to being circumcised if the one undergoing the rite did not become a Yahweh-worshiper? There is no discussion here of any attempt to convert the Hivites to Yahwism.

Again, Jacob's silence to all of this is striking: Was he willing, in principle at least, to go along with intermarriage with Hivites? His lack of response condemns him once more as a tacit partner to an exogamous undertaking that both his father and his grandfather had been unwilling to engage in (24:1–67; 27:46–28:4). Jacob, it appears, has been reduced to passivity, in a helpless (or negligent) coma.[25] It is not unlikely that the subsequent violent reaction of Dinah's brothers (led by two of Leah's children, Simeon and Levi) was, at least partially, due to parental neglect of the unfavored side of the family. Irresponsibility on the part of a leader, whether of family, church, or para-church organization (indeed, at any level of leadership), toward the maintenance of divine standards of morality and ethics, only furthers such laxity in these areas on the part of those who follow.

As was noted, the fact that Dinah was still in the hands of the Hivites (34:26) makes Hamor's offer a Hobson's choice: Jacob & Co. could either accept Hamor's proposal or leave . . . without Dinah in either case. The brothers' ultimatum that they would "take our daughter and go" if the Hivites did not accept their counterproposal

---

23. The Hivites' offer is a bit odd, seeing that Jacob had already purchased land in Shechem from the sons of Hamor (33:19). Vrolijk wonders if this offer was, therefore, a subtle threat by Hamor to strip Jacob of land he had already acquired (*Jacob's Wealth*, 268).

24. "The sons of Jacob show themselves to have learned carefully from their father [the arch deceiver], because they set out to deceive their opponent" (Cotter, *Genesis*, 255).

25. Hamilton, *Genesis: Chapters 18–50*, 363.

(34:17) is at best wishful. For how would they "take" Dinah from Shechem without a battle, and that against a foe that likely outnumbered them?

In the next phase of the dialogue (34:20–24, B' in the table above), in their presentation to their townspeople of the deal with Jacob and his sons, Hamor and Shechem subtly adjust the contents of the agreement. No mention is made of Shechem's lustful advance, or the capture of Dinah (she is not in the scene at all); rather, the advantages for their city are emphasized (34:21), and then repeated after the circumcision requirement is laid out (34:22–23). Hamor had earlier suggested that Jacob's tribe could "dwell" (ישׁב, *yshv*, [×2]) and "trade" (סחר, *skhr*) in the land, as well as "acquire property" (אחז) in it (34:10). He and his son repeat the first two verbs in their reportage to their fellowmen (ישׁב and סחר in 34:21), but carefully eliminate any mention of Jacob's party acquiring property; in the next two verses, only ישׁב is used (34:22, 23). Effectively then, a triple offer ("live/trade/possess") becomes a double offer ("live/trade"), that is finally promoted as a single offer ("live"). Moreover, the original proposal of Hamor had the Israelites giving their daughters to the Hivites, and the Israelites taking the Hivites' daughters (34:9)—ostensibly the Israelites, doing both the giving and the taking, were in control of the process. But in their address to their own people, there is a shift: the Hivites do the taking of the Israelite daughters, and they perform the giving of their own daughters (34:21); so here it is the Hivites who are in charge. As well, there is a new claim being made, that the livestock, property, and animals of Jacob's party would be appropriated by the Hivites (34:23). "Now some of these changes could be construed as merely diplomatic. . . . Nevertheless, failing to mention the land concession and claiming that the Israelite animals would be theirs verges on deceit. They are either tricking their townsmen, or if they are being frank with them, they must have been dishonest in their negotiations with Jacob and his sons."[26] To cut a long story short, the Hivites agree to the demand of Dinah's people, that they be circumcised.[27]

In sum, both parties, the sons of Jacob, and Hamor and Shechem, are being duplicitous, making this episode quite appropriate in the saga of an arch deceiver who himself got deceived! As Hamor and Shechem introduce the Israelites as "peaceful towards us" (34:21), little do they suspect how wrong they are in their assessment. They thought the Israelites' livestock, property, and animals, would soon become theirs (34:23). On the contrary, it would be the Hivites' flocks, herds, donkeys, wealth, children, and women that would soon be in the hands of the Israelites (34:28–29). Thus, negotiations on every side were marked by moral laxity; the downward slide began with Jacob's apathy.

26. Wenham, *Genesis 16–50*, 314.

27. The irony is pungent. As Sternberg put it, "Shechem's punishment started exactly where his sexual crime did" (*The Poetics of Biblical Narrative*, 466). Shechem had "bonded" with and "loved" Dinah (34:3); now the narrator notes that he was "delighted" with her (חפץ, *khfts*, 34:19, a word stronger in its emotional tone than the others; see Hamilton, *Genesis: Chapters 18–50*, 365). Infatuation or genuine affection, it appears that Shechem got himself circumcised then and there (34:19), even before ratification of the treaty by the rest of the Hivites (34:24)! This seems to be a literary way of contrasting the reasonably decent behavior of the son of Hamor and the soon-to-be-evident inexcusable actions of the sons of Jacob, as the narrator treads a fine line between condemnation and commendation.

26.3 Apathy towards evil only generates further evil.

Avenging the "taking" (34:2) of Dinah by Shechem, her two brothers, Simeon and Levi, "take" swords (34:25), "take" Dinah (34: 26), and the rest of Jacob's sons finish it off by "taking" the booty of the town (34:28). The felony has been reversed. But rape was never intended to be punished with such unmitigated and outrageous violence (see Exod 22:16–17; Deut 22:13–29). There does not seem to be any doubt that the response of Simeon and Levi and their siblings is being considered excessive by the narrator. The slaughter of the males in the city who "felt secure/were unaware" (בֶּטַח, *betakh*, 34:25) was a breach of propriety as Prov 3:29 warns: "Do not plot evil against your neighbor when he dwells *securely* [לָבֶטַח, *labetakh*] by you."

> [B]iblical law gives no warrant for such a terrible act of vengeance. A massacre of all the men of the city for one man's sin was as shocking to the narrator as it is to modern ears. Yet, he does subtly draw attention to the motives of Simeon and Levi, by noting that they are not just Jacob's sons but "brothers of Dinah." It was Jacob's failure to act that provoked them to behave in such an extreme way. He had not loved Leah, or her daughter Dinah, but they did.[28]

And with the notation that Dinah was being held in Shechem's house (Gen 34:26), the brothers' actions win some sympathy from readers: their enterprise was "a hostage rescue mission, albeit a violent one." With this trump card in hand, the Hivites offer to "give your daughters to us, and take our daughters for yourselves" takes on a more ominous and threatening tone (34:9).[29] Therefore, Sternberg sees some justification for the bloodbath.

> [The Hivites] have largely brought down that violence on themselves by seeking to impose their will on Jacob's family. With Dinah in Shechem's hands, the option of polite declining is closed to her guardians. And once the brothers refused to submit to the Hivite version of a shotgun wedding, they were left no avenue to the retrieval of their sister except force. Hence also the need for "deceit." Considering the numerical superiority of the troops behind the "prince of the land"—"two of Jacob's sons" faced a whole city—no wonder the brothers resorted to trickery to make odds more even.[30]

But even if it be granted that Simeon and Levi had a justifiable case in the perpetration of their savagery, the rest of the brothers' thuggery is inexcusable (34:27–28). These two sons of Leah seem to be focused on Dinah's rescue (34:25–26), while the rest,

---

28. Ibid., 315.

29. Earl, "Toward a Christian Hermeneutic," 33.

30. *The Poetics of Biblical Narrative*, 468. Wenham notes the similarity of the language in this account and that in Num 31, where the Israelites take revenge against the Midianites who had led them astray ("looted," Gen 34:27, 29 and Num 31:9, 32; "captured," Gen 34:29 and Num 31:9). Phinehas the Levite acts first (Num 25), followed by all Israel (Num 31), paralleling the initial action of Simeon and Levi, followed by the later deeds of their brothers in Gen 34. And all the males are killed (34:25; Num 31:7), as well as the leaders (Gen 34:26; Num 31:8) (see *Genesis 16–50*, 316). Thus there might be a hint of some approval of the action of Simeon and Levi, for the corresponding operations of Phinehas were divinely sanctioned (Num 25:11–13).

"Jacob's sons," engage an orgy of looting (34:27–29). The narrator balances the actions of Simeon/Levi and their brothers carefully: thirty-six words describe the brutality of the former (34:25–26); thirty-seven, the rapacity of the latter (34:27–29). Both sets of deeds are introduced by "they came upon" (34:25, 27), and both have, as their rationale, the "defilement" of Dinah (34:13, 27). But the true motive of "Jacob's sons" is revealed in the lingering of the narrative over the booty they had captured (34:27–29)—"a self-interested plundering of the defenceless."[31] Indeed, the narrator may have signaled that this latter violence was disproportional to the crime and unworthy to be labeled retribution: the account began in 34:1 with the first word יצא (*yts'*, "go out"); now the last word of 34:26 is again יצא. Indeed, the story had begun with Dinah "going out" (34:1) and Shechem "taking" (34:2); the concluding scene is reached with those verbs in reverse: "they [Simeon and Levi] 'took'" Dinah out, and "went out" (34:26).[32] This might well be an indication that what happens next at the hands of Jacob's sons (34:27–29) has nothing to do with righteous anger or holy recompense.[33]

In any case, there is a sharp contrast between "the brothers' fine words and their ugly deeds, between idealistic façade and materialistic reality, between deceit as sacred rage and as unholy calculation."[34] The ironic outcome is that, to avenge the taking of a woman by force, the sons of Jacob do exactly that themselves, rounding up all the town's women after killing their husbands (34:29). And, besides, after all their inveighing against marital unions with the uncircumcised, with the capture of the Hivite women it appears that intermarriage actually did take place, after all![35]

Following the action involving Simeon and Levi and the rest of "Jacob's sons," finally the patriarch reappears on the scene and, for the first time in this pericope, wakes up to utter a word. We expect some moralization, a condemnation of evil, a refocusing of eyes upon what Yahweh would want them to do. On the contrary, Jacob's overriding concern in all of this is apparently not the disaster that has befallen Dinah, or the possibility of intermarriage with Hivites, or the treachery exhibited by his sons, or even the brutality they unleashed upon Shechem—and certainly not for what Yahweh is seeking and how covenant realities may be brought about. There is not even a hint of joy at Dinah's rescue! Rather, Jacob's worry is entirely self-focused, as he fixates upon the potential of these nefarious happenings to "bring ruin" upon him by making him odious among the Canaanites. The first person pronoun echoes no less than eight times in the sixteen words that Jacob speaks, his only utterance in this pericope

31. Noble, "A 'Balanced' Reading," 193.

32. This also suggests that the next scene, that has Jacob's sons "coming upon" the slain (בוא, *bo'*, 34:27), likely does not include these two, Simeon and Levi, who had themselves "come upon" the city (בוא, 34:25), and had just "gone out" (34:26). See Sternberg, *The Poetics of Biblical Narrative*, 470. The disjunctive clause (subject + verb + object) that commences 34:27 strongly suggests that "Jacob's sons" indicates a different group of people than "Simeon + Levi" (the subjects in 34:25–26), even though "Jacob's sons" is nondescript and elsewhere (in 34:7, 13, 25) stands for the whole group.

33. Vrolijk, *Jacob's Wealth*, 276.

34. Sternberg, *The Poetics of Biblical Narrative*, 472.

35. In fact, despite all his protestations against exogamy, Simeon himself seems to have married a Canaanite, perhaps one of these very Hivite women (46:10).

(34:30): twice as the pronoun אֲנִי, *'ni*, and six times as a verb/noun/object marker suffix. So, after the successful release of Dinah, the patriarch singles out Simeon and Levi for criticism; not a word is said to his other sons for their unconscionable plundering (34:30). And much later, Simeon and Levi are the only ones among the children of Jacob to receive a curse from their father (for their barbarity; 49:5–7). All this seems rather unfair to these two sons of Leah, and bespeaks Jacob's unbalanced approach to the whole loathsome episode, merely "tactical and strategic, rather than ethical."[36] Evil and immorality have rendered Jacob's enjoyment of divine blessings uncertain and even improbable and, according to the narrator, it is all because of his own apathy towards the ungodly attitudes and actions all around him.

With almost a "Jonah-like ending," the pericope concludes with a poignant question posed by Simeon and Levi that is virtually an accusation: "Should he treat our sister as a harlot?" (34:31).[37] Their labeling Dinah as "our sister" and not "your daughter" suggests, once again, Jacob's failure as a parent.[38] "[T]hey in effect wrest her out of the father's guardianship: she may not be your daughter, but she certainly is 'our sister' and no one will treat her like a whore."[39] Indeed, "our sister" (אֲחוֹתֵנוּ, *'akhotenu*) is the last word of the pericope (34:31). And so the pericope that commenced with a kinship statement regarding Dinah ("the daughter of Leah, whom she bore to Jacob," 34:1), closes with another mark of her relational status in her family ("our sister," 34:31).

> Leadership should not allow a sister in the community to be humiliated. . . .
> Jacob is as silent as Dinah, until the end. The final discussion has Jacob speaking
> but not having he last word. The story ends with a question that is meant to pro-
> voke thought and reflection. Yet the question does not come from Jacob but his
> sons, who display leadership in a story focused around violence, manipulation,
> oppression, and fear. While vigilantism is not the answer to a leadership crisis, it
> happens when one exists.[40]

The narrator's deprecation of Jacob's dereliction of duty (and his sons' irreverent and noxious behavior) is underscored by the complete literary absence of Yahweh in this pericope (deity turns up before and after this episode, in Gen 33 and 35, respectively, but not here). While Gen 32 and 33 had showed readers a transformed Jacob/Israel, "this story shows Jacob's old nature reasserting itself, a man whose moral principles are weak, who is fearful of standing up for right when it may cost him dearly, who doubts God's power to protect, and who allows hatred to divide him from his children just as it had divided him from his brother."[41] In the final outcome, what Jacob was afraid of (34:30) does *not* come to pass; rather there was "a terror from God upon

---

36. Hamilton, *Genesis: Chapters 18–50*, 371.

37. Vrolijk, *Jacob's Wealth*, 278.

38. Indeed, both the fathers in this pericope, Jacob and Hamor, react the same way—neglecting any thought for the violation of the maiden in question.

39. Sternberg, *The Poetics of Biblical Narrative*, 474–75. In Israel, prostitution was a prohibited activity: Lev 19:29; Deut 22:21; 23:17–19; Prov 23:27–28.

40. Clark, "The Silence in Dinah's Cry," 154.

41. Wenham, *Genesis 16–50*, 318.

the cities," and it is pointedly noted that "they [those in the surrounding cities] did not pursue *the sons of Jacob*" (35:5)—obviously a rebuke to the patriarch and his fears.[42] Clearly Jacob's apprehensions were proved wrong; his lack of trust in the power of God is manifest here.

One cannot but wonder if Jacob had learnt his lesson in the previous pericopes *too well.* He had comprehended, the hard way, that the way to enjoying God's blessings was to let God bring it about. Perhaps here, in Gen 34, that idea, taken to an extreme, was what induced his apathy and lethargy. But passivity in the face of evil and wickedness is certainly not what God wishes to see in the lives of his people. Such inaction only perpetuates evil and precludes the enjoyment of divine blessing.

SERMON FOCUS AND OUTLINES

THEOLOGICAL FOCUS OF PERICOPE 26 FOR PREACHING

26   Enjoying God's blessings calls for responsible maintenance of moral standards in the face of worldly evil (34:1–31).

Throughout the Jacob narratives, the thrust has been on how one gets to enjoy God's blessings, without having to connive and manipulate, carp and cavil, back-stab and heel-grab. One does not have to fight to secure one's blessings, for no one can take away God's promised blessings. Instead, the attitude to receive divine blessings is one of putting away highhandedness and trusting in God with a posture of humility and generosity. All of these lessons were hammered home by the narrator pericope by pericope. Finally, Jacob has been blessed by God and the rift between the twins has been healed (Gen 32–33). One would have expected Jacob to have begun the full enjoyment of what God had done for him. But, alas, in a world distanced from God, evil exists and often is predatory upon the children of God. Jacob and his family are no exception. "Just as the reader expects violence but surprisingly finds peace when Jacob meets Esau, the reader expects peace at Shechem, but instead finds violence."[43]

But Jacob's response in the face of blatant evil—both from without and from within his own camp—takes us by surprise. Surely the patriarch had learnt his lesson and understood what it meant to be on God's side? Apparently he had more to learn (though as Pericope 26 closes, we are not quite sure the man has gotten it yet). His inaction and silence in response to his only daughter's rape, and his apathy towards the escalating evil perpetrated by his own sons (likely *because* he was inactive and silent to the defilement of Dinah) work together to unleash unimaginable horror, brutality, and bloodshed. No, Jacob was not going to enjoy the blessings of God—at least not yet.

Possible Preaching Outlines for Pericope 26

I.   Rise of Evil
        Focused recap: Jacob blessed (Gen 32); Jacob reconciles with his brother (Gen 33)

---

42. Sternberg, *The Poetics of Biblical Narrative*, 483.

43. Jeansonne, *The Women of Genesis*, 90.

Introduction of evil: the rape of Dinah (34:1–4)
Jacob's lack of response (34:5–19)
Move-to-Relevance: Worldly evil frequently preys on the children of God
Move-to-Relevance: Our tendency not to respond

II.   Result of Evil

Evil begets evil: the response of Jacob's sons (34:20–29)
Jacob's lack of response, and his self-concern (34:30–31)
Move-to-Relevance: Evil escalates when unchecked
Move-to-Relevance: Escalating evil prevents the enjoyment of the blessings of God

III.   *React to evil!*

How to think, speak, and act in the face of evil in our midst

One might also consider reworking the above outline, basing it upon the two son(s)–father pairs (and, as well, bringing out the contrast between one father and the other).

I.   Shechem and Hamor

Introduction of evil: the rape of Dinah (34:1–4)
Lack of remorse, and the keeping of Dinah as hostage (34:5–19)
Distorted negotiations with their own townsfolk (34:20–24)
But: Father's loyalty and concern for his son (34:5–19)
Move-to-Relevance: Worldly evil frequently preys on the children of God

II.   Sons and Jacob

Jacob's lack of response to the rape and to his sons' proposal to the Hivites (34:5–19)
The overreaction and brutality of Jacob's sons (34:20–29)
Jacob's continued lack of response, and his self-concern (34:30–31)
[*Unlike*: Hamor, who is seen to be loyal to, and concerned about, his son (34:5–19)]
Move-to-Relevance: Unchecked evil prevents the enjoyment of the blessings of God

III.   *React to evil!*

How to think, speak, and act in the face of evil in our midst

PERICOPE 27

Remembering to Worship

Genesis 35:1–36:43

[Jacob Reminded to Worship; Reaffirmation of God's Promises]

REVIEW, SUMMARY, PREVIEW

Review of Pericope 26: Genesis 34:1–34 describes the rape of Dinah, Jacob's daughter, by a Shechemite. Her brothers retaliate by deceiving the Shechemites into circumcision and, taking advantage of their incapacitation, the sons of Jacob go on a violent rampage. Jacob's silence throughout the pericope emphasizes that apathy towards evil only perpetuates more evil.

Summary of Pericope 27: This pericope concludes the Jacob Story, with an account of Jacob keeping his promise to worship after his safe return to his homeland, but only after God prompts him to do so. The patriarchal blessings are reaffirmed by God here, as well. The genealogy of Esau's line, closing out the pericope, depicts a tribe that is divinely blessed, simply because of proximity to the chosen line of Jacob. In all, the pericope moves God's people to worship for his blessings, and such an attitude of gratitude and devotion continues the cycle of divine blessings.

Preview of Pericope 28: The next pericope (Gen 37:1–36) commences the Joseph Story, with Joseph hated by his brothers for being his father's favorite. His siblings kidnap him and sell him off to slave-traders who take him to Egypt; in the process, they deceive Jacob into believing that Joseph has been killed by wild animals. Like Joseph, depicted in this saga as an agent of blessing, God's people, as agents of his blessing themselves, can expect such mistreatment.

27   *Genesis 35:1–36:43*

THEOLOGICAL FOCUS OF PERICOPE 27

27   **The blessings of God fulfilled in the past, promotes worship of God that, in turn, continues the cycle of divine blessings for the future, but in God's own time, calling for faith from recipients of his promises (35:1–36:43).**

27.1   The blessings of God promote worship of God, especially at crucial junctures of life.

27.2   Grateful worship of God, for his blessings fulfilled in the past, continues the cycle of divine blessings for the future.

27.3   The blessings of God are fulfilled in God's own time, calling for faith from recipients of his promises.

OVERVIEW

This pericope forms the formal conclusion to the Jacob Story that began in Gen 25. In the overall structure of this broader story, Gen 25 is parallel to Gen 35–36. The first has the תּוֹלְדוֹת, *toldot*, of Ishmael, a less important character (25:12–18); the other, the תּוֹלְדוֹת of Esau, another minor character (36:1–43). There is a word from God in both (25:23 and 35:1, 9–12); the wives of the patriarchs, Rebekah and Rachel, respectively, struggle in their pregnancies, and both pericopes report births; Esau and Isaac are located together for the first time in Gen 25, and for the last time in Gen 35; and Paddan-Aram first occurs in Gen 25 and finally occurs in the Jacob Story in 35:9, 26 (it is also found in 46:15, in a retrospective reference).[1]

There is, in this pericope, a collection of scattered episodes (Gen 35) along with a closing genealogy (Gen 36). Generally, in the patriarchal stories (11:27–50:26), travelogues and genealogies cluster at the beginning and end of the three sagas—those of Abraham (11:27–25:18), Jacob (25:19–36:43), and Joseph (37:1–50:26)—and Gen 35 thus is an appropriate inclusion at the end of the Jacob narrative.[2] Though Jacob also shows up in the next major section of Genesis (Gen 37–50, the Joseph Story) as a significant figure, his primary saga, the Jacob Story, concludes with Pericope 27.

Genesis 35 looks forward to the future with the report of the birth of Benjamin, Jacob's youngest son (35:18), and the atrocious behavior of Reuben, Jacob's oldest son (35:22a)—both show up as important figures in the Joseph Story, as also do the other children of Jacob; and all are given genealogical space in this chapter (35:22b–26). Wenham observes how Gen 35 contains several of the key elements of the narratives that close out the Abraham and Joseph Stories; these common elements are all placed

---

1. See under Pericope 16 for the chiastic structuring of the Jacob Story.

2. Mathews, *Genesis 11:27–50:26*, 611–12. For the itineraries and family histories see: 11:27–12:9; 25:1–11; 35:1–29; 37:2–36; and 46:1–50:14.

in the same sequence in their respective larger stories.[3] Thus Gen 35, like Gen 22 and Gen 46–49, signals a conclusion.

	Abraham Story	Jacob Story	Joseph Story
Divine call to journey	22:1–2	35:1	46:2–3
Obedience	22:3–14, 19	35:2–7, 16, 27	46:5–7; 48:5
Divine promise reaffirmed	22:16–18	35:9–15	48:3–4
Birth of sons (or mention of)	22:20–24	35:17–18, 22b–26	48:5–6
Death of wife (or mention of)	23:1–20	35:18–20	48:7
Marriage/sexual activity of son	24:1–67	35:21–22	49:3–4
List of descendants	25:1–6	35:22b–26; 36:1–43	49:3–28
Death of patriarch	25:7–10	35:27–29	49:29–50:14

One would have thought that Jacob, after the climactic events at Peniel and the reconciliation with Esau (Gen 32–33), he would "live happily ever after." Unfortunately, not only is fraternal reconciliation followed by filial rape, violence, and pillaging (Gen 34), we now have, in Gen 35, accounts of the deaths of his late mother's nurse, his beloved wife, and, finally, his father. And the bulk of the Joseph Story, the remaining portion of the book of Genesis, will only generate more anguish for the patriarch.

27   *Genesis 35:1–29*

THEOLOGICAL FOCUS 27[A]

27   The blessings of God fulfilled in the past, promotes worship of God that, in turn, continues the cycle of divine blessings for the future, but in God's own time, calling for faith from recipients of his promises (35:1–29).

27.1   *The blessings of God promote worship of God, especially at crucial junctures of life.*

27.2   *Grateful worship of God, for his blessings fulfilled in the past, continues the cycle of divine blessings for the future.*

27.3   *The blessings of God are fulfilled in God's own time, calling for faith from recipients of his promises.*

A.   Having only one section in this pericope, the "Theological Focus 27" is identical to the "Theological Focus of Pericope 27."

NOTES 27

27.1   *The blessings of God promote worship of God, especially at crucial junctures of life.*

The structure of Gen 35 makes this account a travelogue of Jacob and his camp from Shechem to Hebron, a graphic depiction of the severance of the past. Mathews notes

3. Wenham, *Genesis 16–50*, 322.

that the layout of the five locations mentioned in Gen 35 signify the end of Jacob's wanderings away from the Promised Land: Paddan-Aram (35:9) was the origin of his return trip; Shechem (35:4) was an intermediate stop where the accoutrements of idolatry were buried; Jacob and his clan subsequently move to Bethel where Deborah was buried (35:7, 8, 15), then through Bethlehem where Rachel was buried (35:19), finally arriving in Hebron where Isaac was buried (35:27). The three-part portion of this trip that takes most of Gen 35 to describe (Shechem to Bethel to Bethlehem to Hebron) is broken up by four burials (three actual burials, and one symbolic), each separated from the other by a notation of Jacob's journeying.

Burial of foreign gods at Shechem (35:4)
"Journeying" (נסע, *ns'*, 35:5)
"Burial" (קבר, *qbr*) of Deborah at Bethel (35:8)
"Journeying" (נסע, 35:16)
"Burial" (קבר) of Rachel at Bethlehem (35:19)
"Journeying" (נסע, 35:21)
"Burial" (קבר) of Isaac at Hebron (35:29)

Firstly, there is a symbolic burial in 35:2–4, that of the accumulated foreign gods and earrings that Jacob's caravan had accumulated in their departure from Paddan-Aram.[4] These false gods are undoubtedly being ridiculed: "Such gods may be stolen, sat on, stained with menstrual blood, and now *buried*."[5] Secondly, Jacob's mother Rebekah, dies. She, who had been the inciting force to send him away "for a few days" (27:44) that became twenty years, would never see her son Jacob after that departure. While there is no explicit statement as to her death, it is likely she passed away earlier, a fact implied in the death notice of Deborah, Rebekah's nurse/female attendant, who had come with Rebekah when the latter left Paddan-Aram to join Isaac as his wife (35:8; see 24:59).[6] "He [Jacob] not only does not get to see his mother, but he is forced to become undertaker for his late mother's nurse. Thus, one of Jacob's first experiences after coming back home is confronting death."[7] The third death to mark this pericope is the demise in childbirth of Jacob's favorite wife, Rachel, who had conceived while in Paddan-Aram (35:16–20). Then, towards the end of Gen 35, Isaac dies, and he is

---

4. Mathews, *Genesis 11:27–50:26*, 611. The word טמן, *tmn*, "hide," which is what Jacob did with the equipment of idol worship (35:4), can also mean "bury," as in Job 40:13.

5. Hamilton, *Genesis: Chapters 18–50*, 375, referring, of course, to Rachel's dealings with the teraphim she had filched from her father's home (31:19, 33–35).

6. Each patriarch's death and burial is carefully noted by the author: Abraham, in 25:7–11; Isaac, in 35:29; and Jacob, in 49:33–50:14. As well, the death and burial of the matriarchs: Sarah, in 23:1–20; Rachel, in 35:19. The stark exception is any mention of Rebekah's passing, except for Jacob's retrospective notation later in 49:31, that "they" buried Abraham, Sarah, Isaac, and *Rebekah* in the field of Machpelah; and he also notes that "*I* buried Leah there," suggesting Jacob's absence at the funerary rites of his mother. Deborah's passing, recorded here in such a poignant fashion with a commemoration heralded by a naming (35:8), "evidenced the deep heartache Jacob must have felt toward the passing of the nursemaid who had attended him in his childhood" (Mathews, *Genesis 11:27–50:26*, 621). I would rather think that Deborah reminded him of the loss of his mother whom he never saw again after his departure from Canaan twenty years earlier.

7. Hamilton, *Genesis: Chapters 18–50*, 378.

buried by his sons, Esau and Jacob (35:29). The formal narrative concludes with this funeral, leaving only a genealogy of Esau in Gen 36:1–43. These four passings, in a sense, sever the present from the past; the Aramean era had concluded and, henceforth, "the patriarchal story and the founding of the nation will be centered in the Canaan-Egypt orbit."[8] Thus the past was effectively done with and dismissed, and every trace of Mesopotamian influence was now eradicated/buried; a new era was beginning. And, in Gen 37, the new saga of the next generation would commence.[9]

One of the key elements of this chapter is the reappearance of God to Jacob and the reiteration of divine blessing upon him (35:9). The text has: "God appeared to Jacob again when he came from Paddan-Aram and blessed him." Both theophany and blessing had taken place once before to Jacob, in Bethel (28:13–15) and in Peniel (32:29), respectively.[10] Thus the "pinnacle events of Jacob's life" in relation to Yahweh are gathered together again for this finale: divine (re)appearance plus (re)blessing. The connection between past events is further solidified by the reduplication of the naming event of Jacob as "Israel" (evoking the Peniel encounter of Gen 32) and of the place as "Bethel" (35:7, 10, 15; evoking the episode of Gen 28).[11]

In addition, there is Jacob's own summary of how God had kept his promise to Jacob (given at Bethel): "God . . . who has been with me wherever I went" (35:3, literally, "on the way which I went"; see 28:15; 31:3; and 46:4).[12] Indeed, this realization seems to have been somewhat of a second thought, that occurred to Jacob *after* God reminded him that he had not kept his, Jacob's, promise made at Bethel, to set up God's house and to tithe (28:22). Jacob realizes, perhaps guiltily, that God had kept *his* part of the bargain, but that he had not; it was his turn now. The past was over, and the future was beginning—a crucial juncture in his life—but not before Jacob worshipped God in gratitude for all that God had done for him thus far.

In a sense, Jacob's journey is only complete after he has kept his promise to worship God. And Jacob complies; God's word is precisely followed by the patriarch, as the structuring of the first four verses indicates.[13]

---

8. Mathews, *Genesis 11:27–50:26*, 615.

9. Besides the sequencing of burials and journeys, Gen 35 can also be divided into three sections: command to, and preparations for, worship (35:1–4); the engaging in worship of God (35:5–15); and the terminus of Jacob's journey, his arrival at the side of his father (35:16–29).

10. There was also the appearance of an angel of God in Gen 31 who then proceeded to identify himself as "God" (31:11–13). And, of course, the angels of God encountered Jacob in 32:1, but God himself was not explicitly said to be present at either scene. God also speaks to Jacob in 35:1; it is unclear if that is a separate theophany, a voice, a dream, or some other means of revelation of the divine word. In all, God "appears" only six times in Genesis: thrice to Abraham, 12:7; 17:1; 18:1; twice to Isaac, 26:2, 4; and once to Jacob, 35:9.

11. Mathews, *Genesis 11:27–50:26*, 610–11.

12. The "day of distress" (35:4; also see Ps 20:1; 50:15; Nah 1:7; Zeph 1:15), in its placement in the structure of 35:1–2 and 3–4, refers to his fleeing his brother Esau (see structure below; *E* and *E'* are parallel). Jacob had earlier asked God to "be with him" on "this way that I will go" (28:20); here he acknowledges that God had "been with him" on "the way that I went" (35:3).

13. The structural layout below is modified from Terino, "A Text Linguistic Study," 59–60.

35:1–2						
A	[God:] "Arise"					
	B	"go up to Bethel"				
		C	"make an altar there to God"			
			D	"who appeared to you"		
				E	"when you fled from your brother Esau"	
					F	[Jacob:]"Put away foreign gods which are among you, purify ..., change your garments"

35:3–4						
A'	[Jacob:] "Let us arise"					
	B'	"go up to Bethel"				
		C'	"make an altar there to God"			
			D'	"who answered me"	"and has been with me"	
				E'	"in my day of distress"	"wherever I have gone"
					F'	So they gave Jacob all the foreign gods they had, and the earrings ..., and Jacob hid them.

This is the first time a patriarch is commanded by God to set up an altar (35:1); it corresponds to the command to Abraham, in the closing stages of his story, to offer a burnt sacrifice (22:2). However, in Jacob's case, this command was not a test; rather it was a pointed reminder that he had not yet done what he had promised he would do (28:20–22).[14] The worship of God, when the blessings of God have been fulfilled, is particularly important at crucial stages and in critical passages of life, as Jacob was experiencing in Gen 35: releasing the past, looking to the future. It is also the first time a patriarch is commanded by God to "dwell" in the land (35:1).[15] Both commands, to "build" an altar and to "dwell," come with the specification of locale: build *there*, dwell *there*—the importance of Bethel (signifying the Promised Land) is thereby underscored. By this, Kass notes, God expresses his displeasure with Jacob's decision to dwell with the Canaanites (Shechemites), even acquiring property among them and erecting an altar in that station (34:18–20).

> God commands Jacob to correct his plans and to change his place, physically and, by implication, spiritually. The command contains not only a reminder of God's providence but also an implicit rebuke of Jacob's previous decisions.... He must return to Beth-El and "dwell *there*," and he must "make *there* an altar" unto God. . . . In short, God instructs Jacob that there are basically two places—the right place and the wrong place—and that Jacob needs to move himself from the latter to the former, to Beth-El, the House of God.[16]

Of course, this also meant following the "right God." Yahweh had certainly been God to Jacob; the problem was that Jacob was not making Yahweh his God. This was an important act that needed to be done, a keeping of Jacob's promise to God in 28:20–22.

14. Jacob, however, is as prompt as was his grandfather, in response to this prod from God (35:2; as in 22:3).

15. Isaac had been commanded by God to "sojourn" in Gerar (26:3).

16. *The Beginning of Wisdom*, 500–501. He notes that on all three occasions when God is said to have explicitly spoken to Jacob, it has always been about relocation: 31:3, to leave Paddan-Aram and return to Canaan; 35:1, to leave Shechem and go to Bethel; and 46:3, to leave Canaan and go to Egypt (ibid., 501n33).

While that promise was tinged with arrogance (see Pericope 19), here when God reminds Jacob of his earlier pledge, Jacob responds promptly and precisely. Indeed, in 35:7 the elements of *C, D,* and *E,* and *C', D',* and *E'* (from 35:1–2 and 35:3–4, respectively; see above) recur as *C", D",* and *E"* to indicate Jacob's complete obedience:

35:7

> *C"* "And there he built an altar"
> *D"* "there God revealed himself to him"
> *E"* "when he fled from his brother"

"And there he built an altar" (35:7) is a verbatim repeat of the description of similar activities on the part of the earlier patriarchs (Abraham, 12:7, 8; 13:18; and Isaac, 26:25). And this locus where Jacob raises an altar is renamed El-Bethel (35:7). Thus what had previously been called "House of God" (Bethel) now becomes "God of the House of God" (El-Bethel), a redundancy to be sure, but intended to emphasize the patriarch's focus, no longer upon the house, but upon the *God* of the house. In a sense, this is an affirmation that God had done his part: "[if] Yahweh will be my God" (28:21), and Yahweh *had*; now Jacob was formally making Yahweh his God.

So, on his own initiative, Jacob puts away the foreign gods in his camp (35:2). That there should be no other gods before Yahweh would be enshrined in the Mosaic Law; such an act of purging, as performed by Jacob's household (35:4), would also be repeated periodically in the history of Israel (Josh 24:14, 23–24; Jdg 10:16; 1 Sam 7:3–4). If Jacob were to keep his promise to worship Yahweh, he and his company needed to divest themselves of any competing allegiance. Indeed, Jacob orders his folks to purify themselves and change their garments, an outward mark of an inward wholeness (Gen 35:2; see Exod 19:10–15; Lev 6:10–11; 2 Sam 12:20).[17]

One wonders where these foreign gods had come from. Perhaps they had been in Jacob's camp all along since Paddan-Aram, for Rachel herself had chosen to abscond with teraphim (31:19, 32). But it is more likely that all of this was a consequence of the indiscriminate looting in Gen 34, not to mention the intermarriage with Hivite women who might very well have brought with them the baggage of their foreign deities.

In sum, this section points to the importance of worshiping God, especially at critical junctures of life, in response to God's blessings in the past.

---

17. In another parallel to this incident, in Num 31:19–20, the Israelites purify themselves, following their battle with the Midianites, by making offerings of their jewelry, that included earrings (31:50). See Deut 7:25 for mention of silver and gold on idols, and the warning that the Israelites eschew those items from the spoils of war. This further suggests that the earrings in Gen 35 may have been part of the booty they captured from the Shechemites. Surprisingly, beyond the obligatory sacrifice on the altar, no mention is made in Gen 35 about Jacob fulfilling his promise to tithe of all that God gives him (28:22). Had he forgotten? On the other hand, Wenham suspects that the burial of the rings was in fact a fulfillment of the promise to tithe (*Genesis 16–50*, 329). While it all seems unclear, Jacob's obedience in constructing an altar (35:7, as instructed in 35:1) suggests that he, in all likelihood, kept his promise to tithe as well.

27.2 Grateful worship of God, for his blessings fulfilled in the past, continues the cycle of divine blessings for the future.

The alacrity with which Jacob and his tribe follow God's command, cleansing themselves and departing for Bethel, is accompanied by a divinely induced terror that falls upon the surrounding Canaanites (35:5), a phenomenon that would repeat itself later, in the days of Joshua (Josh 2:9–11). One cannot but think that this terror felt by the peoples around was not fear of *Jacob*, but rather fear of *God*, the result of Jacob's own fear of God and his submissive response to divine command. God keeps his word and protects his own.

And in response to Jacob's obedience at Bethel, God appears to Jacob and blesses him again, this time with a comprehensive blessing that covers name, seed, nation, royalty, and land (35:10–12)—appropriate enough for the closing pericope of the Jacob Story. This is the crowning declaration of God to Jacob, an affirmation he looks back to in 48:3–4.[18] And afterwards, God goes up from Jacob (35:13); no more will he "appear" to a human being in Genesis.

The renewal here of the act of blessing, already given in 32:29, is perhaps, as in the case of Abraham (22:16–18), a ratcheting up of the degree/extent of prior promises, contingent upon the obedience. In his case, Jacob had demonstrated prompt obedience in moving to Bethel and worshiping God (35:2–8). While the blessing in 32:28–29 focused on the transformation of the heel-grabber ("Jacob") into one for whom God would fight ("Israel"), here, in 35:10–12, the emphasis moves away from Jacob to his descendants and the nation that was to come through him. And for the first time, royalty is promised to Jacob's line (as also was promised to Abraham in 17:6, 16), and Israel's twelve tribal peoples are listed formally, in 35:22b–26.[19]

The "company of nations" (35:11) is puzzling, even though 17:4–5 had God promising to make Abraham the "father of nations."[20] While the kingdoms to come certainly include Israel and Judah, these two alone cannot constitute the promised "company" of nations; besides, these two become unified in the eschaton (Jer 3:18; Ezek 37:15–18). Whether in the nations' eschatological subjection to Israel's king (27:29; 49:10; Ps 72:17), or in their salvation linked to the restoration of Israel (Jer 3:6–4:4), or in their incorporation within "Israel" as "people of God" (Zech 2:11; also see Isa 19:18–25; 56:3–7), this is a fulfillment of God's promise in 12:3 and 28:14 to bless all the families of the earth through the patriarchal line (also see 1:28; 9:1).[21]

In sum, God had kept his word on his short-term promise to bring Jacob safely back to the Promised Land; now future promises are added—surely God would keep his word on those as well. Not only does "the land" form the first and last words of

---

18. This also echoes the statement of blessing upon Abraham (24:1) and upon Isaac (25:11).

19. Many of the individual promises given in 35:10–12 hark back to earlier ones from God given to the patriarchs: 12:1–3; 13:14–17; 15:5, 18–20; 17:1–6; 22:16–18; 25:23; 26:3–5, 24; 28:13–15.

20. Other parallels between 17:1–8 and 35:10–12 include the occurrence of the divine name El Shaddai, the notation of a patriarchal name change, and the mention of descendants, land, and nations. Genesis 28:3 had "company of peoples," a phrase reiterated in 48:4.

21. Lee, "גוים in Genesis 35:11," 474–79.

Gen 35:12, "give" is repeated thrice here, emphasizing the certainty of what God was going to do. And if God's first appearance and promises to Jacob at Luz led to the patriarch erecting a pillar, anointing it, and naming the location Bethel (28:18–22), God's reappearance and reaffirmation (with escalation) of promises, here in Gen 35:9–12, was surely worthy of a similar response; in fact a *greater* response is implied in the only mention of a drink offering in Genesis found here (35:14), poured out by Jacob. Moreover, in the narrator's account, the "place" where God revealed himself achieved greater significance, for thrice it is stated: "the place where he/God had spoken to him" (35:13, 14, 15). That also reflects the threefold utterances of God: "God said" (35:10a), "he called" (35:10e), and "God said"(35:11a).

And once again, in response to the (re)blessing by God, Jacob worships—this time, as he does in Gen 28, *before* said blessings are fulfilled (35:14–15). And so the cycle of promise → worship (*before* fulfillment) → promise fulfilled → worship (*after* fulfillment) → promise → worship (*before* fulfillment) . . . continues again. Grateful worship for past blessings do not obviate the need for gracious blessings for the future; that is made clear by the remaining episodes of Gen 35. The spiritual "high" with divine revelation and heartfelt worship is followed by a twofold disaster, the death of Rachel (35:16–20) and the incest of Reuben (35:21–22). God's grace is still necessary; without divine blessings, life is essentially unlivable, what with its catastrophes and disasters, many of them caused by sin.

Rachel's burial in Bethlehem is puzzling: it was only twenty-odd miles to the family burial site at Machpelah, where Abraham, Sarah, Isaac, Rebekah, and Leah were buried (49:31).[22] Indeed, if Jacob himself could have his body, and Joseph his bones, moved 200 miles from Egypt to that same burial site (Gen 50:1–14; Exod 13:19; Josh 24:32), one wonders why Rachel's remains could not have been transported a tenth of that distance to Machpelah.[23] Besides, her burial is described in the exact terms as Deborah's is, in 35:8: "And Deborah died . . . and she was buried," and "And Rachel died, and she was buried" (35:19). "But while the sort of *al fresco* burial these verses depict is appropriate for a character like Deborah, a servant who merely sojourns with Abraham's family and not a member of the Abrahamic patriline, it seems strikingly out of place for Rachel, whom we would expect to receive instead the interment in Machpelah due an honored wife, as is accorded to Sarah, Rebekah, and Leah."[24] Examining the burial practices of a variety of cultures, including that of the Israelites, Cox and Ackerman conclude that a woman in labor was considered impure (see Lev 12:2–5), and all the more so if she died in childbirth, rendering her remains a potential

---

22. The grave of Rachel was likely somewhere north of Jerusalem (1 Sam 10:2; Jer 31:15), "some distance" from Ephrath/Bethlehem (Gen 35:16). Wenham thinks "some distance," כִּבְרַת, *kibrat*, from an Akkadian cognate (the LXX, doubtful about the meaning of the word, simply transliterates it χαβραθά *chabratha*), might indicate the distance traveled in two hours—six or seven miles (*Genesis 16–50*, 326).

23. Mentions in Scripture of the transport of mortal remains, besides the two instances noted above, include those of Samson (Jdg 16:31), Asahel (2 Sam 2:32), Ahaziah (2 Kgs 9:28), and Josiah (2 Kgs 23:30). The bodies of King Saul and his sons were actually exhumed in order to be reburied in the appropriate family tomb (1 Sam 31:13; 2 Sam 21:13–14).

24. "Rachel's Tomb," 140.

source of pollution, a contagion that could spread (Num 19:11–18; 31:19). "The only acceptable response that could reasonably have been attributed to her survivors upon her death was immediately to perform an abbreviated version of the standard burial, interring her where she expired quickly and with the bare minimum of ceremony and beating a hasty retreat from the site of contagion."[25]

However, Tucker considers the intriguing possibility that Jacob was indirectly responsible for Rachel's death, referring to his oath to Laban in 31:32, that the one who had stolen Laban's gods should die. It might well be that Jacob learnt of Rachel's theft only when cleaning house and getting rid of the foreign gods (35:2–4). "There, on the outskirts of Beth-El, in the very shadow of his first *matzevah,* the stone on which he had rested his head, Jacob discovers what we, the readers, have known all along that he had unwittingly doomed his adopted Rachel. . . . [I]ndeed, in the very next scene, immediately upon leaving Beth-El, . . . Rachel goes into labor and dies in childbirth."[26] If this was the case, then her demise would be another indication of the end of the Paddan-Aram era, a tormenting conclusion, no doubt, one that respects the outcome of a terrible vow.[27] The ignominy of her death may also explain why she remained buried in Bethlehem, rather than be interred in Machpelah.

Whatever the specific reason for this odd burial, the one who had threatened, "Give me children, lest I die" (30:1), was now dead, while bearing the very child she wanted (35:19). And thus, Benjamin becomes the only one of the twelve sons of Jacob to be born in the Promised Land; he is also the only one named by his father (35:18). This one would play an important role in the Joseph Story.

Then there is the account of Reuben's incest with his father's concubine and Rachel's maid, Bilhah. "The extreme brevity with which this episode is related reflects the writer's horror at it . . .; while never glossing over wickedness, Scripture does not pander to the prurient by going into sensational detail."[28] Wenham guesses the motive behind Reuben's abhorrent act was to keep Rachel's maid from becoming his father's favorite wife; it is likely Jacob's firstborn resented his own mother's secondary status in that household. Perhaps there was also an element of usurpation of paternal status a là Absalom (2 Sam 16:21–22; also see 2 Sam 3:7; 12:8)? It is one of the sons of Leah—those who had protested about their sister's violation as being "a disgraceful thing in Israel" (34:7)—who himself now performs a disgraceful act against "Israel" (35:22). Such incest was condemned forcefully in the Mosaic Law (Lev 18:8; 20:11; 27:20). Yet once again, Jacob "hears" of an offensive deed but apparently makes no response (Gen 35:22a), just as he had "heard" of Dinah's defilement and remained apathetic (34:5). As with Simeon and Levi for their violent acts, Jacob, later on his deathbed, curses Reuben for his turpitude (49:2–3, 5–7). Incidentally, 1 Chr 5:1–2 explains that

25. Ibid., 147.

26. Tucker, "Jacob's Terrible Burden," 25–26.

27. Tucker speculates that when Jacob uttered his vow described in 31:32, Rachel would have been in her tent, with Joseph, still a baby—perhaps even pregnant with Benjamin. Such a situation would clearly explain Jacob's continued and rather obsessive protection of Rachel's boys (ibid., 27).

28. Wenham, *Genesis 16–50,* 327.

the preferred status of Joseph's sons, was a transfer of the privilege of Reuben, the firstborn, to Joseph, giving the latter a double portion; indeed the fact that the blessing of Ephraim and Manasseh (Gen 48:5–20) was followed in that narrative by the condemnation of Reuben (49:3–4) implicitly argues that the reason for this switch was Reuben's egregious behavior.[29] The presentation of Reuben in Gen 35 also foreshadows his involvement in the Joseph Story to follow.

Finally, to conclude the final narrative chapter in the Jacob Story, the patriarch arrives at his father's place in Hebron (35:27). The details of Jacob's arrival are intended to evoke memories of divine promises made in that locus in years past (13:14–18; 15:1–21; 17:1–27; 18:1–15). Moreover, it completes the fulfillment of God's promise to return Jacob to his father's house (28:15, 21). In the next verses, 35:28–29, the narrator tells of Isaac's death and his burial by his reunited twin sons, Esau and Jacob (35:28–29).[30] The description of the patriarch's interment is parallel to that of Abraham's death and burial (25:7–9): in both situations, the two estranged sons of the respective patriarch are in attendance.[31]

The listing of all the sons preceding the account of the demise of the patriarch is a repeated pattern in Genesis (Abraham, 25:1–11; Isaac, 35:22b–29; and Jacob, 49:3–27; 49:28–50:14). Also of interest is that in this list of Jacob's sons, they are grouped by their respective mothers, while other lists of the twelve, 29:32–30:24 and 49:2–27, are not that carefully organized. Perhaps this arrangement by maternal origin is paving the way for the Joseph Story, where parental partiality and sibling rivalry, based on maternal connections, plays a major role.

All in all, this section points to divine blessings being perpetuated for the future when God is gratefully worshiped for his blessings in the past.

27.3 *The blessings of God are fulfilled in God's own time, calling for faith from recipients of his promises.*

The final chapter in Pericope 27, Gen 36, is one of the longest chapters in the book and is entirely made up of genealogical details. It begins and ends similarly, with reference to Esau as the progenitor of Edom (36:1, 43). The two תֹּלְדוֹת sections for Esau in Gen 36 (36:1–8 and 9–43) are unusual: the first seems to deal with wives, children, and property, with the second concentrating on nationhood, politics, and rulership.

While it is unclear whether Esau actually received a blessing or an "anti-blessing" from his father, Isaac, in 27:39–40, there is no doubt that, as a descendant of Abraham and Isaac, he, too, is blessed (just as Ishmael was: 16:11–13; 17:20; 21:13, 18; with 25:12–18). Unlike with Ishmael, however, there has been no explicit utterance of divine blessing upon Esau. Yet, the amicable attitude he displayed towards his deceiving

---

29. Mathews, *Genesis 11:27–50:26*, 627, 627n592.

30. However the chronology seems to show a sizable lapse of time between 35:27 and 28. Jacob was 91 when Joseph was born (= 130–39; from 41:46; 45:6, 11; 47:9), and 108 when Joseph was sold at 17 (37:2). If Jacob was 120 when Isaac died (25:26; 35:28), then, chronologically, Isaac lived for 12 more years *after* the kidnapping of Joseph described in Gen 37. See ibid., 630n597.

31. That Isaac, too, was buried in Machpelah is noted in 49:29–32.

heel-grabber of a brother (Gen 33) and his acknowledgement, "I have plenty" (רב, *rb*, 33:9) with the repeated notation here, again, of his "plentifulness" (רב, 36:7), seem to be indication enough of the hand of God upon this older sibling's life (see Pericope 25 for further details on what appears to have been Esau's own transformation). Here in Gen 36, the prosperity of his lineage is confirmed: Esau is established in security (see 32:3), and a nation, Edom, is formed (36:1, 8). A number of rulers arise from Esau, centuries before there would be kings in Israel (a point specifically made in 36:31).[32] The inclusion of the king list in 36:31–39 may be seen as a fulfillment of the divine promise to Abraham (and Sarah) of kings among his descendants (17:6, 16). Jacob too had received such a promise (35:11), but it is Esau, to whom no such promise was bestowed, who is now linked with eight kings. The concluding note about "land of their [the Edomites'] *possessions*" (36:43) recalls God's promise to Abraham in 17:8, employing the same word, אֲחֻזָּה, *'akhuzzah*, perhaps a hint that the Edomites' "settlement" (מוֹשָׁב, *moshav*) was a divine allotment, or at least the consequence of patriarchal prophecy (27:39 uses the same word, מוֹשָׁב, in Isaac's blessing of Esau). This growth and prosperity of a non-Israelite nation fits with God's plan to bless all the nations through the patriarchs (12:3; 26:4; 28:14; etc.).

Thus, Esau's star seems to have risen, while Jacob and his sons continue to be mired in rape, violence, slaughter, intermarriage, and incest.[33] Jacob and his descendants would have to wait for their ascendancy. Yes, there would be kings born to this tribe (35:11; 17:6, 16; 49:10; Num 24:7), but they would have to rely, in faith, on the sovereignty and providence of God to fulfill this promise of rulership for them in God's own time.[34]

Of note is the migration of Esau and his camp to Seir, Edom (Gen 36:6), as he "goes away from the face of his brother, Jacob."[35] The one from whose "face" Jacob had once fled (35:7), is now moving from the "face" of Jacob. Esau's departing from the Promised Land depicts him abandoning familial roots, as Lot did in Gen 13. The stated reason for the separation—lack of space (36:7)—sounds rather implausible, given the Shechemites open acceptance of the Israelites in 34:10, 21 into their land and in their vicinity. In essence, here Esau and his descendants are dispossessed of Canaan that devolves to Jacob and his descendants, in keeping with the divine word: both Lot

32. Perhaps these were pre-Mosaic kings as Num 20:14 seems to indicate. "Chief" (אַלּוּף, *'alluf*, in 36:15–19, 29–30, 40–43) might have been a specific Edomite designation (Exod 15:15).

33. That is not to say all was well with Esau's line. The reiteration of the foreignness of Esau's wives (36:2–5) reminds the reader of his parents' disapproval of his exogamous tendencies (26:34–35; 27:46–28:9). "Canaan" bookends this list of wives, adding the narrator's own deprecation of Esau's marital endeavors (a similar bracketing—Isaac's prohibition of Jacob from "taking a wife of the daughters of Canaan"—is found in in 28:1, 6). However, the names of Esau's spouses in this pericope do not correspond with their names elsewhere. It is possible that some of them had more than one name each, or that they may have taken new names, or that he had more than one wife with the same name. Gordon, *The World of the Old Testament*, 126n30, noted that trying to unravel these naming vexations is "as futile as an attempt to unscramble an omelette."

34. Mathews, *Genesis 11:27–50:26*, 645.

35. The permanence of this exodus is indicated by the verb וַיֵּשֶׁב (*wayyeshev*, "and he settled," 36:8), the same description of Jacob's colonization of Canaan (37:1).

(as well as Ishmael) and Esau have thus removed themselves from the land of promise. Indeed, 36:9–43 is bounded on either side by "Esau the father of Edomites," reinforcing the contrast between the location of Esau and his clan and the location of Jacob and his, pointedly noted to be in "the land of Canaan" (37:1).[36] Jacob and his family have not seen the divine promised fulfilled completely yet; they (and all God's people) wait in faith for God to bring his blessings to them at a time of his sovereign choosing.

SERMON FOCUS AND OUTLINES

THEOLOGICAL FOCUS OF PERICOPE 27 FOR PREACHING

27   The blessings of God fulfilled in the past, promotes worship that, in turn, continues the cycle of divine blessings for the future (35:1–36:43).

It might be best for the preacher to focus on Gen 35, and stick with the idea that fulfilled blessings of God should promote worship of God. This Theological Focus is subtly different from that of Pericope 19, where the theological thrust was that God's guaranteed promises, yet unfulfilled, call for a response of trusting worship—a positive picture of Jacob's rather negative story in 28:10–22. Here, in Pericope 27, worship is called for *after* the blessings are fulfilled. The consequences of such worship is the maintenance of the cycle of blessings for the future; that, too, is well worth pointing out in the sermon.

Possible Preaching Outlines for Pericope 27

I.   Reminder
        Focused recap: Jacob's conditional promise in Gen 28:10–22 to worship if God does his part
        How God did his part (a précis of Gen 29–35: blessings of family, prosperity, protection, reconciliation, return)
        God reminds Jacob to do his part (35:1)
        How Jacob does his part (35:2–4, 6–7)
        Move-to-Relevance: Our quick forgetfulness of the blessings of God

II.   Repercussion
        Jacob continues to be blessed: protection, (re)appearance and (re)affirmation of divine word (35:5, 10–13)
        Jacob worships again (35:14–15)
        Move-to-Relevance: Consequences of grateful worship in our lives

III. Response: *Worship God when his promises are fulfilled!*
        Specifics on what does grateful worship looks like and how we may perform it

Another outline may be generated by focusing on the "cycle of worship":

I.   Promise & Worship
        God's promise (28:13–15)

36. The reason for the inclusion of a non-Abrahamic line in 36:20–30, the line of Seir the Horite, may have been the intermarriage that occurred between the Horites and the Edomites who displaced the Horites as they took over the land (Deut 2:12; see Gen 36:20, 22, 25 for names that also occur in Esau's genealogy). The Horites, too, became clan chieftains (36:29–30).

Jacob's worship *before* the fulfillment of God's promised blessing (28:18–22, howbeit conditional)

Move-to-Relevance: Not only are we called to worship even *before* God's promised blessings are fulfilled. . . .

II.   Fulfillment & Worship

Fulfillment of God's promise (Gen 29–35: blessings of family, prosperity, protection, reconciliation, return)

Jacob's worship *after* the fulfillment of God's promised blessing (35:2–4, 6–7)

Move-to-Relevance: We are also called to worship *after* God's promised blessings are fulfilled. . . .

III. Repromise & Reworship . . .

God reaffirms his promissory word with an escalation of blessing (35:10–13)

Jacob's (re)worship *before* the fulfillment of God's (re)promised blessing (35:14–15)

Move-to-Relevance: And the cycle continues—worship *before* and *after* God's promises are fulfilled

III. *Worship—before, after, and always!*

Specifics on what does grateful worship looks like and how we may perform it, before, after, whenever. . . .

PATRIARCHAL HISTORY

Being a Blessing

Genesis 37:1–50:26

(Joseph Story)

PERICOPE 28

Mistreatment of the Dreamer

Genesis 37:1–36

[Joseph Dreams; Joseph Sold; Jacob Deceived]

REVIEW, SUMMARY, PREVIEW

Review of Pericope 27: Genesis 35:1–36:43 concludes the Jacob Story, with an account of Jacob keeping his promise to worship God following his safe return to his homeland, but only after a prompt from God. A genealogy of Esau's line closes out the saga. In all, the pericope moves God's people to worship him for his past blessings, and that continues the cycle of future divine blessings upon them.

Summary of Pericope 28: This pericope commences the Joseph Story, with Joseph being hated by his brothers for being his father's favorite, a situation not helped by Joseph's dreams, misunderstood to be megalomaniacal. His siblings kidnap him and sell him off to slave-traders who take him to Egypt. In the meantime, Jacob is made to believe that Joseph has been killed by wild animals. Like Joseph, depicted in this saga as an agent of blessing, God's people, as agents of his blessing themselves, can expect such mistreatment.

Preview of Pericope 29: The next pericope (38:1–30) deals with a significant episode in the life of Judah. His two older sons' lives are taken by God for their evil acts; but Tamar, his daughter-in-law, is not given to Judah's third son in marriage as she should have been. So Tamar deceives Judah into sexual relations with her, and later, when she proves that he is the father of her twin children, Judah recognizes his own unrighteousness. As the leader of the Israelite tribes, Judah, too, is an agent of divine

447

blessing; such agents are to be characterized by concern for others and humility regarding their own weaknesses.

28   *Genesis 37:1–36*

THEOLOGICAL FOCUS OF PERICOPE 28

28   One who expects to be an agent of God's blessing to others can anticipate misunderstanding and mistreatment from them (37:1–36).

28.1   One who expects to be an agent of God's blessing to others can anticipate misunderstanding from them.

28.2   One who expects to be an agent of God's blessing to others can anticipate mistreatment from them.

OVERVIEW

The Joseph Story is the longest literary unit in the Bible, spanning fourteen chapters. It is a tumultuous story, "marked by meteoric ascents and precipitous plunges."[1] The focus of the narrative is upon Joseph as the one who brings life, the mediator of Yahweh's blessing to the rest of humanity.[2] When everyone else is in dire need and dying of famine, Egypt under Joseph is the fount of life and food to which nation "all the earth" comes (41:57; 42:2); he is the instrument of salvation (47:19, 25), a fact Joseph himself is not unaware of (42:18–20; 45:5–8; 50:19–21).[3] Thus Joseph's life is intricately tied in with his being the agent of God's blessing to the world. In fact, an underlying dynamic of the story is, therefore, how God rescues his agent of blessing, saving him from the depths of those "precipitous plunges," to experience those "meteoric ascents" where his endeavors are most effective and impactful: both Joseph's family and the nation, as well as "all the earth," are blessed by Yahweh through him.

The similarity between Exod 3:1 and Gen 37:2b, describing Moses and Joseph, respectively, both shepherding flocks, caused Levenson to explore the parallels between these two leaders:

> That the similarity in wording is not coincidence is corroborated by the remarkable parallels in the lives of the two shepherds-turned-rulers: both are separated from their families early on, both survive conspiracies to murder them, both endure exile, both marry the daughters of foreign priests, both have two sons, and the two leaders, one dead and one alive, leave Egypt together (Exod 13:19). But most important, both of them are commissioned by God to lead and provision an unruly people with a pronounced proclivity to reject their leaders. It is striking that we hear the same note at the very onset of the [Joseph] narrative

1. Levenson, *The Death and Resurrection*, 165.

2. However, both Jacob and Judah figure prominently in the narrative, as well as the collective "brothers" of Joseph.

3. Joseph as the one who "provides" is noted thrice in the story: 45:11; 47:12; 50:21. While all three times the provision is for his family, it is obvious that his status as donor and supplier signify his agency as God's instrument of life-giving to all.

that will bring Israel down to Egypt as we shall hear at the onset of the [Moses] narrative that will bring them back up to Canaan.[4]

Both Joseph (and his brothers) and Moses are agents of divine blessing, the latter primarily to the chosen nation, Israel, the former to his family, to his adopted nation, Egypt, and to "all the earth." In this sense, then, the blessing mediated by Joseph is more widespread and commences the fulfillment of the Creator's intention to bless humanity as a whole. The focus on Joseph and his turbulent life thus teaches the reader what it means to be an instrument of divine blessing to others.[5]

Just as Isaac's תלדות (*toldot*, 25:19) was preceded by that of his brother Ishmael (25:12–18), so also Jacob's תלדות (37:2) is preceded by his brother Esau's (36:1–43). And as Isaac's תלדות detailed the narrative of his son Jacob, Jacob's will now detail the story of his son Joseph.[6] The former was founded on an oracle that prophesied that the older would serve the younger; the latter gets its driving force from a dream that depicted the older brothers bowing before their younger sibling. Just as in the Jacob story, there is parental partiality in the Joseph story (37:3; see 25:28); as the older sibling intends to kill his younger brother (27:41), here the older brothers attempt to get rid of Joseph (37:20); parents in both the Jacob and Joseph stories are deceived by their children employing garments, goat body parts (blood in 37:31; skin in 27:9–16); and the oppressed son in both stories flees outside the Promised Land (37:36; see 27:42).[7]

The Joseph Story builds upon the Jacob Story, forming a "Jacob–Joseph" narrative. But in this complex, unlike the previous patriarchal narratives, the future heir is only subtly revealed—Judah, not Joseph, though the latter is the major player in the saga. As a matter of fact, all the twelve sons are blessed for the future (49:28), and these twelve progenitors of the twelve tribes of Israel seem to get almost equal billing as the first book of the Bible concludes (Gen 48–50). Perhaps the limitation of the identity of Yahweh as "the God of Abraham, Isaac, and Jacob" (50:24), excluding the subsequent seed, is an indication of the spread of divine blessing beyond particular individuals, and not necessarily through any particular person. Rather, in the future, a *people* will serve as the channel of God's blessing. And the overarching motif of the Joseph narrative itself—*being a blessing*—reflects this movement.

4. Ibid., 144.

5. No doubt, the lesson was originally for Israel—how they could be a ministerial influence to the rest of the world. However, in the canon, this has immense validity for Christian believers as well, called as they are to carry the blessing of God in Christ to "all nations," to the "end of the age" (Matt 28:19–20).

6. However, unlike the previous stories, where the parent in whose name the תלדות is introduced plays no role in the subsequent narrative, here Jacob is a significant actant all the way to the end of the saga of his son, Joseph. Indeed, only three chapters are exclusively devoted to Joseph (Gen 39–41); besides the one that deals solely with Judah (Gen 38), the remainder have a number of others in supporting roles, among them Jacob himself, as well as Judah, Reuben, Simeon, and Benjamin.

7. See Greidanus, *Preaching Christ from Genesis*, 336.

Like the Abraham Story and the Jacob Story following, the Joseph (*A–F* and *F'–A'*) chiastically organized[8]:

> Joseph and his brothers, and Jacob and Joseph part (**37:1–36**):
> Joseph alone with brothers (37:18–28);

A "land of Canaan" (37:1); Joseph's age (37:2); "evil" (37:2, 20, 33); "their father" (37:2, 4, 12, 32); "brothers saw" (37:4); "speak" (37:4); obeisance (37:7, 9, 10); "brothers went" (37:12); "mourned" (37:34, 35); Joseph travels

> > Interlude, a brother's story (**38:1–30**): Joseph absent; no Egyptian flavor;
> > שֵׁלָה (*shelah*, "Shelah," 38:5, 11, 14, 26);
> > "staff" (38:18, 25); עֵר (*'er*, "Er," 38:3, 6, 7); אוֹנָן (*'onan*, "Onan," 38:4, 8, 9);

B "remove" (38:14, 19); "come in" (38:18); "clothe" (38:19); "firstborn" (38:6); עֵז (*'ez*, "goat," 38:17, 20); נטה (*nth*, "turn," 38:1, 16); "way" (38:16); גְּדִי (*gdi*, "kid," 38:17, 20, 23); younger over older (Perez/Zerah); fall of Judah

> > > Joseph blessed in Egypt (**39:1–23**): "bless" (39:5 [×2];
> > > "he refused and said" (39:8);

C finding favor in eyes (39:4); "kindness" (39:21); "lie" (39:7, 10, 12, 14); "hand" (39:1, 3, 4, 6, 8, 12, 13, 22, 23); "food/bread" (39:6)

> > > > Joseph's plan to rescue the land (**40:1–41:57**):
> > > > "famine" (41:27, 30, 31, 36, 50, 54, 55, 56, 57); "food" (41:54, 55);

D וְתָלָה (*wtalah*, "he will hang," 40:19); "grain" (41:56, 57); קָנֶה (*qnh*, "stalk," 41:5, 22); "cities" (41:48); "fifth" (41:34); "in all the land" (41:19, 29, 44, 54)

> > > > > Journeys of the brothers to Egypt (**42:1–43:34**):
> > > > > "go down" and "Egypt" (42:1–2);

E "your servants" (42:10, 11, 13); Judah prominent (43:3–10); "send" (43:4, 5); seeing one's face (43:5); "Is your father still alive?" (43:7)

> > > > > > Joseph tests the brothers (**44:1–34**): "hasten" (44:11);
> > > > > > "mouth" of bag (44:1, 2, 8);

F Benjamin (44:12; and referred to in 44:18–34); "send" (44:3); "bring down" (44:11, 21, 23, 26, 29, 31)

---

8. Modified from Rendsburg, "Redactional Structuring," 217–25; Waltke and Fredricks, *Genesis*, 581–82; Dorsey, *The Literary Structure of the Old Testament*, 60; and Mathews, *Genesis 11:27–50:26*, 680.

F' Joseph revealed to the brothers (**45:1–28**): "hasten" (45:9);
human "mouth" (45:12, 21);
Benjamin (45:12, 14, 22); "send" (45:5, 7, 8, 23, 24, 27);
"bring down" (45:9, 13)

E' Journey of the family to Egypt (**46:1–47:12**):
"going down to Egypt" (46:3);
"your servants" (46:34; 47:3, 4 [×2]); Judah prominent (46:28);
"send" (46:28); seeing one's face (46:30);
"you are still alive" (46:30)

D' Joseph rescues the land (**47:13–27**):
"famine" (47:13 [×2], 20); "food" (47:13, 15, 17, 19);
וַתֵּלַהּ (*wattelah*, "it languished," 47:13); "grain" (47:14);
קָנָה (*qnh*, "buy," 47:19, 22, 23); "cities" (47:21); "fifth" (47:24, 26);
"in all the land" (47:13)

C' Joseph's sons blessed in Egypt (**47:28–48:22**): "bless" (48:3, 15, 16, 20 [×2]);
"he refused and said" (48:19);
finding favor in eyes (47:29); "kindness" (47:29); "lie" (47:30);
"hand" (47:29; 48:14, 17 [×2]); "house of bread" ("Bethlehem," 48:7)

B' Interlude, brothers' blessing (**49:1–28**): Joseph nominally present;
no Egyptian flavor; שִׁילֹה (*shiloh*, "Shiloh," 49:10);
scepter (49:10); עִיר (*'ir*, "donkey," 49:11);
בְּנִי אֲתֹנוֹ (*bni 'atono*, "colt," 49:11) and אוֹן (*'on*, "vigor," 49:3);
"remove" (49:10); "come in" (49:10); "clothing" (49:11);
"firstborn" (49:3); עַז (*'az*, "power," 49:3, 7); נטה (49:15); "way" (49:17);
גָּד גְּדוּד יְגוּדֶנּוּ (*gad gdud ygudenu*, "Gad: raiders will raid …," 49:19);
younger over older (Ephraim/Manasseh); rise of Judah

A' Joseph and his brothers, and Jacob and Joseph part (**49:29–50:26**):
Joseph alone with brothers (50:15–26); "land of Canaan" (50:13);
Joseph's age (50:26); "evil" (50:15, 17, 20); "their father" (50:15);
"brothers saw" (50:15); "speak" (50:4 [×2], 17, 21); obeisance (50:18);
"brothers went" (50:18); "mourned" (50:10, 11); Joseph travels

The testing of the brothers and Joseph's self-disclosure to them (*F, F'*: 44:1–45:28) form the center of the story. Famine and estrangement occur on one side (*A–E*), but after this hinge, things begin to improve with increasing prosperity and fraternal reconciliation (*E'–A'*). Joseph's extended speech, 45:5–8, in this pivotal section (*F, F'*), has a threefold repetition of "send" (45:5, 7, 8)—the subject of all three instances of the verb is God, and his sovereignty is acknowledged and emphasized unambiguously.[9] However, Arnold notes the rather different role God plays in the Joseph Story—"no theophanic appearances [as in 12:7; 17:1; 18:1; 26:2; 28:13; 35:9], revelations [as in 15:1, 13; 20:3; 25:23; 28:12–13; 31:11][10], or speeches of God [as in 12:1; 13:14; 21:12; 22:1, 11, 15; 31:3; 35:1], no *deux ex machina*, or devices of divine intervention to drive the narrative forward. Rather we have the subtleties of dialogue portraying characters

9. Brueggemann, *Genesis*, 101–102. The theological motif of divine sovereignty is further underscored towards the end of the Joseph story, 50:15–21, in the contrasts: brothers vs. Joseph; evil (50:15, 17, 20) vs. good (15:20); man's transgression (15:17) vs. God's devising (15:20); and fear vs. comfort (15:21).

10. Jacob does experience a vision in which God spoke to him, 46:1–4; the content of this visitation echoed what Isaac heard, 26:1–5, and that might explain this exception in the Joseph story: Isaac had expressly been told not to go to Egypt (26:2), but here that command is reversed.

and conflicts that build suspense to a dramatic conclusion."[11] The reader also notices a number of dreams in the Joseph saga, all of them without explicit and/or direct interpretation from God, unlike the dreams in Gen 29, 28, 31 (and also Gen 15 and 25, perhaps). God never appears to Joseph but in Gen 39 (and obliquely elsewhere), the narrator affirms divine presence with the patriarch and the blessings that ensue from such a relationship—blessings intended to be spread abroad. God's hand is clearly recognized by the protagonists: 41:16, 25, 28, 32, 39; 42:28; 43:14, 23, 29; 44:16; 45:5–9; 46:1; 47:10; 48:3–4, 9, 11 (and the remainder of Gen 48–49); 50:17, 19–20, 24–25.

Nonetheless, even with this emphasis on the sovereignty of God, there is considerable focus throughout Gen 39–50 upon Joseph and how God uses him to bring life—both physical and spiritual—to all around him. The portrait of this life-giving patriarch leads one to conclude that the Joseph Story is about "being a blessing." It sets up a pattern for the people of God, how they, through Jesus Christ, and in the power of the Spirit, can be agents of life to a dying world. The three patriarchal sections of Genesis (12–24, 25–36, and 37–50) all bear the theme of divine blessings, but in the Joseph narratives the outworking of the blessings being directed to outsiders (as in 12:3; 18:18; 22:18; 26:4; 28:14) is particularly prominent (39:1–4, 20–23; 41:56–57; 47:13; etc.).[12]

That Joseph's saga is carefully organized is also recognizable in one of its striking elements, the "doublets," the apparent duplication of events.[13]

A	Trouble between Joseph and his brothers (37:2–11)	
A'	Trouble between Joseph and brothers intensified (37:12–36)	
	B	Sexual temptation: Judah (seduction; clothing as evidence) (38:1–30)
	B	Sexual temptation: Joseph (seduction; clothing as evidence) (39:1–23)
	C	Joseph interprets two dreams (40:1–23)
	C'	Joseph interprets two more dreams (41:1–57)
	D'	Brothers come to Egypt (they bow; sacks with grain/money; Simeon serves as surety) (42:1–38)
	D'	Brothers come to Egypt (they bow; sacks with grain/money; Judah offers to be surety) (43:1–44:34)
	E	Joseph and his family (brothers; weeping; reunion) (45:1–15)
	E'	Joseph and his family again (entire clan; weeping; reunion) (45:16–47:6)
	F	Pharaoh and Egypt blessed (47:7–26)
	F'	Joseph and brothers blessed (47:27–49:32)
	G	Death of patriarch: Jacob (49:33–50:14)
	G'	Death of patriarch: Joseph (50:15–26)

11. *Genesis*, 315. Though Arnold's basic point must be granted, I, however, see divine workings scattered throughout the narrative as the commentary will indicate.

12. The Abrahamic blessing is alluded to in the Joseph narrative in 41:52; 46:1–4; 47:27; 48:15–16; 50:24. But while both Abraham and Jacob (and apparently Isaac, too) returned from their wanderings to the Promised Land, here, at the end of the Joseph narrative, this patriarch and the other progenitors of Israel's twelve tribes are all located outside, in Egypt, on their way to becoming well established in that nation. The fulfillment of the land promises thus remain in the future, an object of hope for these who are now aliens in a foreign land.

13. Structure modified from Dorsey, *The Literary Structure of the Old Testament*, 59.

One observes that all the dreams themselves occur in pairs—the two of Joseph,[14] the two of his fellow prisoners, and the two of Pharaoh. Besides, Potiphar's wife tries to seduce Joseph at least twice (37:9, 12) with "lie with me"; Joseph loses his outer garment twice, once to his brothers, once to Potiphar's wife; Joseph is confined twice, in the "pit" by his brothers (37:24), and in prison by Potiphar (considered a "pit" in 40:15); Joseph has two fellow inmates he interacts with; it takes the cupbearer two years before he remembers his erstwhile cellmate, Joseph; Joseph's brothers make two trips to Egypt, upon two commands from their father (42:2; 43:2), and have two audiences with Joseph on each occasion, not to mention their being accused of spying twice and twice finding money in their bags; Joseph comes up with two plans to have Benjamin brought to Egypt; and there are two invitations to Jacob's family to settle in Egypt (one from Joseph, another from the Pharaoh).[15] These doublets may very well be an indication of God's sovereign activity. Joseph's explanation to Pharaoh regarding the duplication of his dreams seems to substantiate this conclusion: according to Joseph, the repetition of dreams meant that "the matter has been established by God, and God will swiftly make it [happen]" (41:32).

28   Genesis 37:1–36

THEOLOGICAL FOCUS 28[A]

28   One who expects to be an agent of God's blessing to others can anticipate misunderstanding and mistreatment from them.

   28.1   One who expects to be an agent of God's blessing to others can anticipate misunderstanding from them.

   28.2   One who expects to be an agent of God's blessing to others can anticipate mistreatment from them.

A. Having only one section in this pericope, the "Theological Focus 28" is identical to the "Theological Focus of Pericope 28."

NOTES 28

28.1   One who expects to be an agent of God's blessing to others can anticipate misunderstanding from them.[16]

The last we had heard of the patriarchs, Jacob (with Esau) had buried his father, Isaac (35:27–29). The story now continues in 37:1. In fact, after 36:8 that tells us where Esau

14. After each of Joseph's two dreams, his brothers and father, respectively, respond with two rhetorical questions each (37:8, 10).

15. Notably, Joseph lives with his father for the first seventeen years of his life and then with his father again, in the last seventeen years of his father's life (37:2; 47:28). See Ackerman, "Joseph, Judah, and Jacob," 85.

16. Though Joseph, in Gen 37, is not yet an agent of blessing to others, knowing that this is the overarching theme, helps focus the theological thrust of this pericope upon what such an instrument of God can expect from others: misunderstanding and mistreatment.

dwelt, if one skips the following intervening genealogy of this older brother, the narrative moves on smoothly to 37:1 that informs us of Jacob's dwelling place. That Jacob "dwelt" (37:1) in Canaan is contrasted with the "dwellings" of the chiefs in Esau's clan (36:43). The mention of "father" (אָב, 'ab) and "sojourner" and "Canaan" echoes 17:8, that describes Abraham (אַבְרָהָם, 'abraham) as sojourning in Canaan. While "all the land of Canaan" once promised is not yet in hand in 37:1, Jacob seems to be settling in—at least for now—indicating a bit more permanence than that experienced by a sojourner.

As was noted in the previous pericope (Pericope 27, Gen 35:1–36:43), Esau appears to be thriving in the production of progeny, the possession of property, and the presence of prominent leaders in his family tree. "Unlike Esau, who is well established in a land formerly ruled by kings, Jacob dwells—perhaps prematurely—in the land of wanderings, in the place where his father was a stranger." What is going to happen to Jacob and his seed? And, to add to the suspense, the account begins rather ominously. With the תֹּלְדוֹת of Jacob announced in 37:2, rather than the expected account of the patriarch's twelve children, only one is mentioned, a lad of seventeen, Joseph. Moreover, the word-order seems to imply that Jacob had only *one* son: "These are the generations of Jacob. Joseph . . . (37:2).[17] Even more ominously, God is not mentioned in this pericope at all.

The repeated employment of "behold," in 37:7 (×3), 9 (×2), 13, 15, 19, 25, 29 tells the entire story of this pericope by literally (and literarily) manipulating the point of view of the reader: "behold" describes both of Joseph's dreams; it is used in Jacob's sending Joseph to his brothers, who "behold" him arrive after he "beholds" a man who directs him; "behold" draws attention to the arriving traders to whom Joseph is sold; and the interjection subsequently expresses Reuben's surprise that Joseph is gone from the pit.

The pericope begins with Joseph bringing to his father an "evil report" regarding his siblings (37:2). While the use of דבה, *dbh*, elsewhere indicates "slander" or "evil report" that may not necessarily be true (Num 13:32; Ps 31:4), in light of Prov 25:10 that employs the word to indicate a true (but disparaging) report, there is no reason to think that the דבה that Joseph brought back to his father about his brothers was a lie (37:2). Rather, in view of the rest of the story that shows Joseph constantly in a good light, this must have been a true report of evil doings by his brothers.[18]

As if this was not bad enough, Joseph is his father's favorite and the proud possessor of a special tunic.[19] Whatever its uniqueness, it was, no doubt, a mark of

17. Kass, *The Beginning of Wisdom*, 511–12.

18. In fact, seeing דבתם (*dbtm*, "their slander") as a subjective genitive, Peck would rather translate 37:2b as: "Joseph brought their (his brothers') slanders against him to their father." There may be grounds for this, since the LXX translates דבה as ψόγος, *psogos* ("fault/censure") here, and does so consistently when דבה is used as a subjective genitive ("Notes on Genesis 37:2," 343).

19. It is unclear what exactly כְּתֹנֶת פַּסִּים, *ktonet passim*, means (37:3); "varicolored" derives from the LXX's ποικίλος, *poikilos*, and the Vulgate's *polymitam*. The cognate Aramaic פס, *ps*, "palm/sole," might indicate that it was a long garment reaching to the wrists or ankles. Speiser speculates, from Akkadian and cuneiform evidence, that a highly ornamented robe might have been intended (*Genesis*, 290).

partiality. In fact, according to Kass, "[t]he elegant ornamented tunic that Jacob provides Joseph is not just a decorative gift to a favorite. The garb of rule, it is the sign of Joseph's elevation. Jacob anoints Joseph as his heir apparent—and he does so relatively early in Joseph's life."[20] In line with this thought, the Hertz *chumash* notes that "in the Patriarchal age, Semitic chiefs wore coats of many colours as insignia of rulership. . . . Jacob, in giving him a coat of many colours, *marked him for the chieftainship of the tribes at his father's death*."[21]

In response, his brothers come to despise Joseph—four times the negative reactions of his brothers are noted: hatred, 37:4, 5, 8; and jealousy, 37:11. Jacob surely must have been aware of the repercussions of parental favoritism; Pericope 18 (Gen 26:34–28:10) had described the fragmentation of the family that resulted from Isaac's preference for Esau, and Rebekah's for Jacob. Yet, perhaps in a carryover of his love for the favorite wife, Rachel, Jacob dotes on Joseph, her son (37:3) and later, is equally possessive about Benjamin. And, of course, one cannot forget how Abraham loved Isaac (22:2, the first time "love" enters the Bible; see Pericope 13). The result of that inordinate love was "the life-threatening ordeal that would end with the beloved son's ascent to his exalted role as second patriarch of Israel [22:1–19]. . . . The echo of this command at the onset of the Joseph story suggests that this son, too, will confront his own near-death and, like Isaac, surviving it, attain to great eminence."[22]

The escalating trend of the brothers' hatred of Joseph is depicted with each instance that Joseph is mentioned: he is loved more than all by his father, and the brothers hate him (37:4); he tells them he has had a dream and they hate him "even more" (37:5); he describes what he saw and, again, they hate him "even more" (37:8).[23] Then he has a second dream, and the brothers are jealous of him (37:11). Things were so bad between Joseph and the brothers that they could not speak to him kindly (literally, "for peace," לְשָׁלֹם, *lshalom*, 37:4). That his brothers "hated him even more" (37:5, 8) is an appropriate counter to Jacob's loving Joseph "more than all his sons" (37:3). In other words, both his father and his brothers are mistreating this son, one by favoritism, the others by disfavor.

Strikingly, while Joseph interprets everyone else's dreams with God's help (40:8; 41:16, 25, 28), he does not do so for his own; in fact, there is no mention of God at all in 37:5–11. That does not necessarily mean these dreams were non-revelatory; on the contrary, in light of the character of the other pairs of dreams in the Joseph Story, it is more than likely that Joseph's also fell into the same class—divinely ordained, to be divinely fulfilled. Of the three paired of dreams in the Joseph Story (in Gen 37, 40, and

---

20. *The Beginning of Wisdom*, 514.

21. Hertz, *The Pentateuch and Haftorahs*, 142 (emphases original).

22. Levenson, *The Death and Resurrection*, 145–46.

23. "And even more," וַיּוֹסִפוּ, *wayyosifu*, is a wordplay on יוֹסֵף (*yosef*, "Joseph"; so also is וַיְסַפֵּר, *waysapper*, "he related," 37:9, 10): the first dream account opens and closes with this expression of hatred (37:5, 8). The response of the brothers to Joseph's first dream is intense, as denoted by the infinitive absolute: "Will you *really* reign [הֲמָלֹךְ תִּמְלֹךְ, *hamalok timlok*] over us? And will you *really* have dominion [מָשׁוֹל תִּמְשֹׁל, *mashol timshol*] over us?" (37:8). Jacob's employment of the infinitive absolute, "Will we *really* come [בוֹא נָבוֹא, *bo' nabo'*] . . .?" also expresses his incredulity (37:10).

41), God is explicitly said to be responsible for the second and third (and/or for their interpretations; 40:8; 41:16). It is fair then, to assume that God is in some way responsible for the first as well. Joseph's brothers, however, seem to think that his dreams were merely a figment of his own egotistic imagination. And so, it is they who interpret the first dream (37:8), while Jacob does the honors for the second one (37:10). Joseph's dreams here are the first dreams in Genesis where God does not say a word. But since this is also the case with subsequent dreams in this narrative—dreams which come to pass, implying a divine hand in their occurrence—one cannot simply rule that these dreams were a product of Joseph's ambitious mentality. The narrator, neither explicitly nor implicitly, signals any disapproval of Joseph's words, though father and siblings seem to be considerably miffed. All of this leads one to wonder: Were the interpretations of Joseph's dream by his brothers and father accurate? Levenson is worth noting:

> Had they [the brothers], like the thirteenth-century commentator Rabbi David Qimchi, given the element of binding sheaves closer scrutiny, they might have suspected that the imagery of grain is not irrelevant to Joseph's ascent. As Qimchi puts it, it was "because of grain that he rose to greatness." Furthermore, the image of the brothers' sheaves bowing while Joseph's own remained upright (Gen 37:7) might have suggested that his supply of grain would be full when theirs had already given out. The collapsed sheaves would then have foreshadowed the brothers' empty sacks, and Joseph's upright sheaf would, by the same logic, have suggested that his sack would always be abundant when they were in dire need. Attention to detail on the part of the brothers might have led them to suspect that domination was not quite the right term to describe their eventual prostration to their younger brother.[24]

Moreover, it seems a bit odd that a shepherd (37:2) would dream of wheat sheaves. The fact is that "[t]he imagery of dream belongs to another place, to a more fertile place, where one man does indeed command obeisance from all around, namely, to Egypt."[25] Essentially, this is a prophecy, not the self-aggrandizing desires of an adolescent. Subsequent events prove Joseph right: he does become "ruler of all the land of Egypt" (45:8, 26), second only to the Pharaoh (41:38–44). And the brothers do bow down to him (42:6; 43:26, 28; 44:14; 50:18), the source of plentiful food. "When one considers that dreams were often regarded as prophetic oracles (as in the rest of the story) it becomes likely that Joseph felt under divine constraint to deliver his message." Indeed, even as he rebukes his son, Jacob "kept the saying [of the dream] in mind" (37:11); apparently he took it seriously enough, incredulous though he was at its seeming audacity.[26] But then why was Joseph rebuked by his father (37:10)? For having the dream or for relating it? He, Joseph, certainly did not interpret either of his dreams, so that could not have been what irked Jacob; in fact, it was Jacob himself who interpreted the second dream (37:10). Whatever he meant by his public denunciation

---

24. Ibid., 166–67.

25. Kass, *The Beginning of Wisdom*, 517.

26. Peck, "Notes on Genesis 37:2," 343.

of Joseph's dreams (as *he* interpreted them), Jacob seems to have made something of them in private.

The first dream has Joseph and his brothers in it. However, the *sheaves* are not these sons of Jacob. Joseph explicitly describes them as "my sheaf" and "your sheaves," and it is not the brothers who bow down to Joseph: the respective *sheaves* themselves bow down to Joseph's *sheaf*. While understandable, the brothers' interpretation of Joseph's first dream is mistaken. This is dealing with sheaves of grain, i.e., food, and Joseph's is rising and standing (37:7), while the others' are bowing. Could this not be a foreshadowing of what was to come, that when the sons of Jacob (eleven, including Benjamin) are in want of food, they would come to Joseph who would be in control of plenty? And would not such a dream perturb even Joseph—how could his family be starving and in need when he himself seemed to be neither? And when would all this happen? These questions, and the anxiety they generated, would, no doubt, have been sufficient to provoke that young man to share his dream with his family; one does not have to invoke Joseph's naïveté, egotism, or arrogance as an explanation for this.

The biggest problem with Jacob's interpretation of Joseph's second dream is the question of how Rachel, Joseph's mother, could be conceived of bowing down to him (37:10). If the eleven stars stood for Joseph's *eleven* siblings, including Benjamin, surely Rachel was dead by now, not having survived the labor and delivery of her second son (35:16–19). Wenham thinks the moon (i.e., Rachel) was included simply to complete the picture of heavenly bodies.[27] Then what of Leah—had she already died? If the eleven stars are considered to be an accurate enumeration of the children of Jacob, why would the moon not have a precise referent as well?

One thing to be borne in mind is that is not necessary to posit that the second dream was merely confirming the first (as in 41:32). The dreams in the next pair, those of Joseph's cellmates (Gen 40), are discrete and not directly related to, or confirming, each other. Neither is it necessary to assume that Jacob was right in his interpretation of his son's dream, or that he was justified in rebuking Joseph (37:10). If the patriarch was clearly not right to favor Joseph (37:3), there is no reason to think that his application of the dream and his remonstration is any more reasonable.

In light of all of these uncertainties, Pirson offers the plausible suggestion that the two dreams may not have meant the same thing. They are similar only in the presence of "bowing" (37:7, 9) and the visibility of the main character, Joseph ("my sheaf," 37:7; and "me," 37:9). The two dreams are different in length, in structure (the second has no *yiqtol* or *wayyiqtol* clauses), in vocabulary (the first is "told" [37:5], while the second is "related" [37:9, 10]), and in dynamic action (in the first, the sheaf/sheaves rise, stand erect, gather around, and bow; in the second, there is only bowing by the elements invoked). There is no separate interpretation of the first dream, but the second is given meaning by Jacob, linking astronomical bodies to family members. In fact, in his rebuke, Jacob throws in a few items of his own (those in italics were not in Joseph's second dream): "Will we *really come*—I, and your mother, and your brothers—to bow

---

27. *Genesis 16–50*, 352.

down to you *to the ground*?" (37:10): there is no mention in Joseph's dream of anyone "coming," or bowing "to the ground." Indeed, in the Joseph narrative, Jacob is never shown bowing to Joseph; in fact, it is the other way round (48:12).[28]

Pirson observes that 37:9 employs the Piel of ספר, *spr*, that not only has the sense of "relate," but also the connotation of "count."[29] Now ספר is used eight times in Genesis, six of those instances in association with dreams (24:66; 29:13; 37:9, 10; 40:8, 9; 41:8, 12). The last four (40:8, 9; 41:8, 12) have numbers that play an important role in the respective dream interpretations; they point to time intervals. Why could not this be true of the numbers in Joseph's second dream, also introduced twice with ספר (37:9, 10)? That astronomical bodies (that mark time, 1:14–18) were active in this dream inclines one towards that conclusion. Pirson suggests that the sun + moon + eleven stars = thirteen *years* (1 + 1 + 11). And thirteen years, incidentally, is the number of years Joseph would spend in Egypt before becoming its Prime Minister (see 37:2 with 41:46). As an alternative, Pirson suggests that 2 (sun + moon) × 11 (stars) = 22, the number of years before Joseph revealed his identity to his brothers, when he was thirty-nine.[30] And in this second dream, Joseph is the only identified family member ("me," 37:9): he was alone for those thirteen years, in prison (or for twenty-two years, away from his Israelite family).

Thus, while the first dream plainly adumbrates the brothers bowing before Joseph, i.e., indicating their dependence on him for food, the second likely indicates *when* that bowing would take place. Indeed, it is only twenty-two years after Joseph's dreams, at the brothers' second trip to Egypt, that *all* of them (including Benjamin) bow before him (43:26, 28; 44:14).[31] One might suspect that Joseph's second dream is distinct from the first, for the former is explicitly "another [אַחֵר, *'akher*] dream," 37:9, unlike the subsequent dreams of Pharaoh, said to be "one [אֶחָד, *'ekhad*] dream" (41:25). "In this way the pattern emerges that one person has two different dreams (which appear to be interwoven) [Joseph]; this is being followed by two people having both one dream with a common element [the baker and butler], until at last one person dreams two dreams that are one [Pharaoh]."[32]

---

28. Jacob/Israel does bow, in the presence of Joseph, in 47:31, though it is unlikely he was bowing to his son. The мт there has מִטָּה (*mittah*, "bed") to depict Jacob bowing down (or even "bent low") at the head of the bed (in worship of God? in his feebleness?). The lxx has ῥάβδος, *rhabdos*, "staff" (reading the Hebrew as מַטֶּה, *matteh*): Jacob worshiped leaning on the top of his *staff*—a reading reflected in Heb 11:21. In neither case is it necessary to postulate Jacob's bowing to Joseph.

29. See the full account in Pirson, "The Sun, the Moon and Eleven Stars," 562–67.

30. The number 22 is derived from 41:46 (thirteen years after Joseph's kidnapping at the age of seventeen; 37:2) and 45:6 (when seven years of plenty and two years of famine have elapsed): 13 + 7 + 2 = 22. Such "conjuring with figures is not uncommon in the Bible," notes Pirson, adducing several examples (ibid., 566n12).

31. See Green, *"What Profit for Us?"* 134n6, who also speculates that the numbers in the second dream dealt with time. Genesis 42:6, 9 does not vitiate this argument: what Joseph remembers there is his first dream, about the brothers' sheaves (hungry siblings) bowing to his sheaf (source of plenty).

32. Pirson, "The Sun, the Moon and Eleven Stars," 568.

Joseph, incidentally, relates the second dream first to his brothers (37:9), then to his father and brothers (37:10). The addition of his father to the list is not necessarily because Joseph assumed Jacob was referred to (the "sun"). If he actually thought so, why did he first recount it to his brothers (37:9)? It makes more sense that Joseph included his father in this second telling because he was not getting much of a response from his siblings. If this were from God, as Joseph must surely have concluded, should not something be done about this rather ominous dream? Perhaps that was what motivated him to approach his father. In any case, the serious misunderstanding of Joseph by both father and brothers is powerfully brought home.

28.2 One who expects to be an agent of God's blessing to others can anticipate mistreatment from them.

Jacob's sending Joseph to check out the welfare of his siblings is also rather dubious in its propriety. The brothers are in a place, Shechem (37:12–14), that was only recently mentioned as a locus of brutal slaughter (Gen 34). To that place, Jacob sends Joseph with an imperative from הלך (*hlk*, "come," 37:13), to which Joseph replies, הִנֵּנִי (*hinneni*, "Here I am"). Both words are eerie echoes of the *aqedah*, the aborted sacrifice of Isaac in Gen 22, where God commanded Abraham with the same verb, הלך, and to which Abraham also replied, הִנֵּנִי (22:1–2). That was a willing sacrifice of a loved son. Would this be likewise, of another loved son? "The alert reader will be horrified by what he understands Jacob to be saying to Joseph: 'Come, let me send thee unto thy brothers who hate thee, now that they are in the murderous place.'"[33] Ironically, Joseph is asked to check the "welfare" (שָׁלוֹם, *shalom*, 37:13) of those who would not speak to him in "peace" (שָׁלוֹם, 37:4). Having heard thrice that the brothers hate Joseph (37:4, 5, 8), and that they were jealous of him (37:11), one expects the worst in this encounter.

The rather odd cameo (bounded on either side by the word "found," 37:15, 17) of the "man" who encountered Joseph wandering around is puzzling; this strange person gets no introduction, his identity is mysterious, how he knows where the brothers are, or what they said, is unexplained, and he disappears from the scene and story without any further ado (37:15–17). Gellman speculates, with tongue in cheek:

> And we must ask, "Why is this incident in the Torah at all?" Who cares if Joseph found his brothers in Shechem or Dothan or Brooklyn? Why would a narrative as concise and spare as the Hebrew Bible, the Tanakh, take time to recount Joseph's false start in finding his brothers. The answer, of course, is to be found in Lewis Carroll's *Alice in Wonderland*. At the beginning of *her* journey Alice asks the Cheshire cat, "Would you tell me please, which way I ought to go from here?" The cat answers her, "That depends a good deal on where you want to get to." It's too bad Joseph did not meet the cat. He might have realized that this great short question, *ma t'vakesh* ["What are you seeking?"] was not a question about the location of his brothers, but a question about the location of his life.[34]

---

33. Kass, *The Beginning of Wisdom*, 519.

34. Gellman, "What Are You Looking For?" 20. In a delightful flight of fancy, Gellman connects his own existence to this stranger's asking Joseph *ma t'vakesh*, along the way stringing together the Exodus, Emperor Constantine, Muhammad, the Dutch East India Company, the Long Island Expressway, and

Mathews thinks the man's interception of Joseph, his knowledge of the brothers' private conversation, and his accurate direction of Joseph, all "[convey] the theological orientation of the narrative as a whole. Whether the 'man' is an angel or a human, the unseen hand of the Lord is apparent here."[35] Green agrees that at the level of the discourse, the verses are significant.

> The interlude rehearses the whole Joseph story in a moment, provides a sort of cartoon sketch of the larger canvas. While between father and brothers, apparently lost, Joseph is nonetheless directed appropriately. Joseph, temporarily marooned, will be directed by strangers and by God. A man has the crucial information and imparts it effectively; Joseph obeys. It might seem at first that the "helper" hinders, that his information pushes Joseph into the pit instead of returning him to his father, unsuccessful but safe. But in fact the pit is safety, for the whole of Jacob's family, and so the nameless and faceless man is in fact quite a significant helper.[36]

Some sort of divine presence—omnipresent and omniscient—seems to be implied here; there is divine control operating in, through, and with these minatory events. Indeed, in the end, Joseph himself acknowledges that his whole life had been directed by God: 45:5–9; 50:19–20. One remembers that just prior to this encounter with the anonymous guide, Jacob had "sent" (שלח, *shlkh*) Joseph there (37:14). But as Joseph himself will later recount, the *real* "sender" was God himself (שלח occurs in this connection in 45:5, 7, 8), further substantiating the suspicion that this stranger was more than what he seemed to be. In any case, God's sovereignty is implicitly operating here, despite the ominous clouds looming as Joseph makes his way to his hateful and jealous siblings.

The narrator informs us in 37:18 that the brothers spotted Joseph arriving from a distance. Cleverly, he does not tell us immediately how they recognized him, reserving for 37:23 the datum that he was wearing his special garb. "Behold, there is the lord of dreams coming [בוא, *bo'*]," the brothers exclaim (37:19). Later, when Joseph "came" (בוא), they seize him, strip him, and throw him into a pit (37:23). The young man is sold to a caravan of traders "coming" (בוא, 37:25) who "bring" (בוא) him to Egypt (37:28). Later, Reuben, seeing his attempts to save Joseph foiled, cries out, "Where can I go [בוא]?" (37:30). As with "behold" noted earlier, following the verb בוא through the latter part of the pericope gives one the gist of the story.

The brothers' plot to kill Joseph is expressed in no uncertain terms, employing "slay" (הרג, *harag*, 37:20, 26; a stronger word than what the narrator uses in 37:18, "kill," מות, *mut*), often employed of criminal homicide (Gen 4:8, 14; 12:12; Exod 21:14), the most recent use of which was in Esau's "plot" to exterminate his brother Jacob (Gen 27:41, 42).[37] Intent to commit fratricide is repeating itself here, though what the broth-

---

other inanities into a captivating catena of causalities—a single sentence of 859 words!

35. *Genesis 11:27–50:26*, 695.

36. *"What Profit for Us?"* 45.

37. "To plot," נכל (*nkl*, 37:18), is used only three other times in the OT, always indicating treachery (Num 25:18; Ps 105:25; Mal 1:14).

ers hope to gain by this malevolent stratagem is unclear: "We will see what becomes of his dreams" (37:20). If they believed Joseph and his dreams, they are attempting to subvert the fulfillment thereof; if they did not, they are simply (and ruthlessly) punishing him for his seeming arrogance.

In any case, what happens next is utterly reprehensible. The imprisoning of Joseph in the pit is described with the verb שׁלך (*shlk*, "throw," 37:24) which when used with a person as the object indicates the disposition of a corpse into a grave, or what will become a grave (Gen 21:15; 2 Sam 18:17; 2 Kgs 13:21; Jer 38:6; 41:9).[38] It is virtually a death sentence— a slow death by exposure (he was stripped[39]) and by thirst (he had no water, Gen 37:23–24). Reuben's objection to his siblings' action recognizes the deathly seriousness of what they were planning to do: "Let us not take his life [הכה נפשׁ, *hkh nfsh*]" (37:21). He employs "a quasi-judicial phrase often found in laws on homicide" (see Num 35:11, 15, 30; Deut 19:6, 11; 27:25).[40] Reuben's subsequent urging that they do not "lay hands on him" (Gen 37:22) also implies a lethal outcome (see 22:12). Besides, kidnapping itself was a capital crime and the sons of Jacob were already guilty of that felony (Exod 21:16; Deut 24:7).[41]

Reuben's intentions are honorable and redound to his credit: the word "rescue" surrounds Gen 37:21–22.[42] The brothers listen to him, and following Reuben's recommendation, Joseph is left in the pit (37:23–24). They then sit down for a meal in a cavalier act of brutal negligence, perhaps even enjoying the very food Joseph had transported (37:25). Ironically, the brothers ate לחם, *lkhm*, while Joseph starved. One day Joseph would feed them לחם, when *they* were starving in a time of famine (43:33–34). In another bit of narrative irony, their sitting down to "eat" (אכל, *'kl*, 37:25) happens right after they plan to tell their father that a wild beast had "eaten" Joseph (אכל, 37:20). Thus the narrative is plainly showing readers the identity of those "wild beasts."[43]

As the brothers ponder about what to do next, the statement that they "lifted up their eyes and looked, and behold . . ." (37:25) is identical to the description in 22:13, where it is noted that Abraham "lifted up his eyes and looked and behold. . . ." In both cases, a fatality was prevented—by the arrival of the Ishmaelites in one case, and by the ram caught in the thicket in the other. In both accounts there is also the proscription: against "lay[ing] hands on him" (22:12; 37:22). For Joseph, a temporary stay of execution—"a recess until after lunch"—is gained.[44]

---

38. The "pit" was probably a deep cistern cut in limestone.

39. How the motif of garment-changes is depicted through the Joseph Story will be considered in Pericope 31 (40:1–41:57).

40. Wenham, *Genesis 16–50*, 354.

41. Also see Code of Hammurabi §14: "If any one steal the minor son of another, he shall be put to death."

42. Joseph, when he later learns of Reuben's merciful intercession on his behalf, breaks down weeping (42:22–24).

43. Ross, *Creation and Blessing*, 607.

44. Kass, *The Beginning of Wisdom*, 522.

The glimpse of the Ishamelites becomes Judah's cue to speak up. Reuben's advice is now rejected (in his absence, for he has apparently left the scene, see 37:29–30), and Judah's plan to sell off Joseph (37:26–27) gains priority. This might be a failure of the firstborn to lead. Here, Reuben's brothers, and subsequently his father (42:37–38), repudiate his attempts at decision-making. And no wonder: this was a man "[f]ormerly known only for finding aphrodisiacs . . . and for incest (30:14; 35:21–22)."[45] In fact, Reuben's speech was rather anemic: he commanded action without publicly voicing reason or argument for adopting such a course (37:21–22). And the brothers' lack of response is telling, especially when compared to their response to Judah's idea: "And his brothers listened" (37:27). Kass notes that though Judah's plan sounds rather mercenary, it is actually "more prudent and even more humane than Reuben's." Judah's speech is full of first person plurals; Reuben issues second person plural imperatives. Judah, at the very least, appeals to a fraternal tie: "What profit is there to kill *our brother*?" (37:26); Reuben's public proposal, without considering his private intent to engage in a covert rescue operation, would surely lead to Joseph's death. In the end, Judah succeeds in influencing his brothers, and Reuben fails.[46] Whichever direction the plot takes, this is a horrific maneuver to get rid of a sibling. The word "brother" resounds throughout the pericope twenty-one times, a subtle deprecation by the narrator of this hideous deed, reminding the reader of the dreadfulness of what the men perpetrated upon their younger brother, Joseph.[47]

What happens next is rather unclear. Who does what to Joseph? Are the Ishamaelites and Midianites the same group with different names?[48] Or did the latter get to Joseph and abscond with him, before the brothers manage to sell him off to the Ishmaelites, and did the Midianites then pass Joseph to the Ishmaelites? The latter option is quite plausible and may explain why the Midianites are said to have sold Joseph "into" (אל, *'l*), not "in" (ב, *b*) Egypt (37:36). Moreover, the brothers, when they later repent, never confess to selling Joseph; neither do they disabuse Reuben, when he returns to the scene, of his presumption that Joseph had been killed (37:29–30; also see 42:22). The obscurity of Joseph's sale into slavery seems rather deliberate, depicting the brothers neither killing Joseph nor selling him. In 37:27, the brothers did intend to sell (מכר, *mkr*) Joseph, and Joseph does allege later that his brothers actually sold him (מכר, 45:4, 5). But 37:28 does not indicate who actually sold (מכר) Joseph to the Ishmaelites—the third person plural suffix in וַיִּמְכְּרוּ, *wayyimkru*, "and they sold him," is unclear as to its subject—and 37:36 has the Midianites "selling" (מכר) Joseph into Egypt. Ambiguities abound in terms of the human responsibility for all of these actions. And that might well have been deliberate on the part of the narrator, another hint that

---

45. Brodie, *Genesis as Dialogue*, 360.

46. Kass, *The Beginning of Wisdom*, 522–23.

47. And the narrator keeps reminding the reader of the cause of all this antagonism: the tunic figures prominently throughout (37:3, 23 [×2], 32 [×2], 33).

48. "Ishmaelites" show up in 37:27, 28; 39:1; "Midianites," in 37:28, 36. Perhaps 37:36 is equivalent to 39:1, and we should see the two designations as alternative nomenclatures for the same group (also see Jdg 8:22–24), or perhaps the Midianites were a smaller part of the larger caravan of Ishmaelites.

an unseen divine hand was accomplishing a sovereign will. As Loader notes. "Humans remain fully responsible for their plans, initiatives, deeds and the consequences arising from them. But they cannot break out of God's control. Not even the evil that humans are capable of, can bring his will into disarray. It remains a terrain where we always are in the dark." It is this tension that the ambiguities of Gen 37 heighten. "Who sold Joseph?—We do not know. Neither should we."[49] They (whoever "they" were) lifted *Joseph* (out of the pit), sold *Joseph*, and brought *Joseph* (to Egypt)—an unusual series of repeats of Joseph's name with the direct object marker (אֶת־יוֹסֵף, *ʾet-yosef*, 37:28), perhaps signifying the importance of this episode: *Joseph* arrives in Egypt! Thus, the reader is beckoned to consider God's working behind the scenes, even through an act of iniquity. Moreover, we are completely in the dark about Joseph's response to all these atrocities, (until 42:21, where we are told of his pleas for mercy). The silence from the victim once again implicitly directs readers to a divine operation.

The rest of this story is poignant. The brothers conspire to trick their father, using the very tunic given to Joseph by Jacob, soaked in the blood of a goat. This "dipping" (טָבַל, *tbl*) of the tunic in blood may subtly indicate the death of an innocent one (it is used in Exod 12:22 for the "dipping" of hyssop in the blood of the Passover lamb).[50] Jacob, a deceiver himself, who employed the skin of goats to cheat his own father (27:9), now gets cheated by his sons with the blood of goats (37:31–35). The patriarch's response is intensely emotional, in three brief statements: "The tunic is my son's. A wild animal has eaten him. He has surely been torn to pieces—Joseph!" (37:33).[51] Tormented, he ends his utterance with the name of his favorite son, "Joseph!" And Jacob's subsequent response of grief is also has three facets—the tearing of clothes, the wearing of sackcloth, and the long mourning (37:34). The patriarch is inconsolable, declaring he would go to Sheol (to his grave) mourning (37:35).[52] In God's providence, however, his separation from Joseph would be only for twenty-two years, not for life; in fact it would be *Joseph* who would weep at the demise of Jacob (50:1). Nevertheless, one cannot overstate the pathos of this scene in Gen 37.

Joseph was "sent" by his father to his brothers (שׁלח, *shlkh*, 37:13, 14); now they "send" Joseph's bloodied tunic to their father (שׁלח, 37:32). Interestingly enough, with their subterfuge here, the brothers do not lie; rather they insinuate, and let Jacob draw his own conclusions, which he does (37:33). Their request to Jacob that he "examine" the garment employs a critical verb in the Joseph Story: נכר (*nkr*, 37:32; and Jacob duly "examines" the tunic, 37:33).[53] Later on, in a twist of irony (a shift of power?), the broth-

49. "God Have or Has?" 139.

50. Mathews, *Genesis 11:27–50:26*, 700.

51. "Wild animal," חַיָּה רָעָה, *khayyah raʾah*, is also used of evil people (Lev 26:6; Ezek 34:22–25); Jacob was not very far from the truth in his assessment.

52. In the list of those who attempted to console Jacob, the mention of "daughters" is surprising (37:35), but may indicate daughters-in-law or even granddaughters.

53. The word also shows up in Tamar's request to Judah to "examine" some of his belongings (38:25); he does and "recognizes" (also נכר) them (38:26). Earlier, Isaac had failed to "recognize" (נכר) Jacob in his Esau-disguise, employing, ironically, something from a goat—its skin (27:23; see 27:15–16, 22–23).

ers fail to "recognize" (נכר) Joseph, though Joseph "recognizes" them (42:7, 8 [×2]).[54] Not only this, but every facet of the evil committed by the brothers—they ate while Joseph languished in the pit (37:28); they sold him for the price of a slave (37:28)[55]; they exchanged his blood for that of a goat (37:31); and, in a final act of utter disassociation, to Jacob they label Joseph "your son," not "our brother" (37:32)—all of this would rebound upon the brothers in various tests that Joseph puts them through: Will they sacrifice themselves for their siblings, Simeon and Judah (42:19–38; 44:1–34)? Will they be so mercenary as to decamp with unearned silver and grain (42:27–28, 35)? Do they care for family, even for one of their father's favorites (44:1–34)?

In this pericope, everyone seems to have turned against Joseph: his father, rather irresponsibly, sends him off to Shechem, to his brothers. It is unlikely he was unaware of the jealousy that his favoritism towards Joseph had provoked; besides, he had had personal experience of what such partiality could produce in a family—hatred, strife, murderous inclinations, and fragmentation. Yet, he does not seem to have a clue as to what might actually have happened to Joseph at the hands of his brothers. The brothers, of course, are merciless—even with the benefit of the doubt extended to Reuben and Judah, en masse they come across as heartless beasts, not very different in nature from the "wild animal" they claimed had devoured Joseph. But through it all, the sovereignty of God scintillates: the dreams, the strange man directing Joseph to Dothan, the utter silence of the victim, the pointed allusions to the *aqedah*, and, in retrospect, the haven that Egypt would turn out to be for the fledgling nation of Israel. At any event, this is about agents of God's blessing expecting (and suffering) misunderstanding and mistreatment.

SERMON FOCUS AND OUTLINES

THEOLOGICAL FOCUS OF PERICOPE 28 FOR PREACHING

28   Agents of God's blessing to others can expect misunderstanding and mistreatment from them (37:1–36).

As was already observed, a retrospective view (from the vantage point of Joseph's successful agency of blessing to family, "all the land of Egypt," and "all the earth" [41:55, 57]) helps put this pericope in focus and locates it within the larger narrative, as a pearl on a necklace. Thus the reader is instructed by the narrator to see Joseph as an instrument of divine blessing in the hands of God. For such a one, what can be expected is misunderstanding and mistreatment (at least initially—but, of course, there is no telling how long that time period will last; in the case of Joseph it was the first thirty-odd years of his life). As children of God, all believers in Christ are called to be agents of blessing to those around them and to the world. Thus, this pericope warns Christians

---

54. Mathews, *Genesis 11:27–50:26*, 700–701.

55. See Lev 27:5, for 20 shekels as the price of redemption of a male between five and twenty years of age; Wenham, "Leviticus 27 2–8," 264–65.

as to what can be expected when they attempt to fulfill that divine calling to be a blessing: misunderstanding and mistreatment.

Seeing that this pericope introduces the story of Joseph, it might be appropriate, particularly with the retrospective view taken here, to inaugurate the Gen 37–50 sermon series with a quick summary of the story, particularly its finale, emphasizing how Joseph becomes a blessing to all. A number of NT verses point to the Christian being a blessing in one form or another to the world: Matt 5:13–16; Luke 6:27–38; Rom 12:21; 2 Cor 5:20; Gal 6:10; Jas 1:27; 1 Pet 3:9; etc. A poem attributed to Teresa of Avila (1515–1582) puts it powerfully[56]:

> Christ has no body but yours,
> No hands, no feet on earth but yours,
> Yours are the eyes with which he looks
> Compassion on this world,
> Yours are the feet with which he walks to do good,
> Yours are the hands, with which he blesses all the world.
> Yours are the hands, yours are the feet,
> Yours are the eyes, you are his body.
> Christ has no body now but yours,
> No hands, no feet on earth but yours,
> Yours are the eyes with which he looks
> compassion on this world.
> Christ has no body now on earth but yours.

Christ-followers are the ones who "incarnate" his love and concern; they are the ones who extend God's blessings to others—truly the Body of Christ.

Possible Preaching Outlines for Pericope 28

I. Calling
    Retrospective: Joseph, the agent of divine blessing to family, nation, world
    Move-to-Relevance: The Christian's calling to be an agent of divine blessing

II. Consequences
    Joseph misunderstood (37:1–11)
    Joseph mistreated (37:12–36)
    God's implicit presence and working throughout the pericope (see Notes)
    Move-to-Relevance: The kinds of misunderstanding and mistreatment we can expect
    Move-to-Relevance: God's promises to us as we suffer enmity (Rom 8:28, 38–39; 2 Cor 12:9; Heb 13:5; etc.)

III. Conduct: *Expect and endure enmity!*
    How one can expect and endure such enmity as one goes forth to be a blessing

Focusing, instead, on the sovereign operations of God, implicit in this pericope, one might rework the outline above to generate this one:

I. Suffering
    Retrospective: Joseph, the agent of divine blessing to family, nation, world
    Move-to-Relevance: The Christian's calling to be an agent of divine blessing

56. "Christ has no Body."

        Joseph misunderstood (37:1–11)
        Joseph mistreated (37:12–36)
        Move-to-Relevance: The kinds of misunderstanding and mistreatment we can expect

II.   Sovereignty
        God's implicit presence and working throughout the pericope (see Notes)
        Move-to-Relevance: God's promises to us as we suffer enmity (Rom 8:28, 38–39; 2 Cor 12:9; Heb 13:5; etc.)

III.   Strategy: *Expect and endure enmity!*
        How one can expect and endure such enmity as one goes forth to be a blessing

PERICOPE 29

Transformation of Judah

Genesis 38:1–30

[Judah Mistreats Tamar; Judah Recognizes his Own Unrighteousness]

REVIEW, SUMMARY, PREVIEW

Review of Pericope 28: Genesis 37:1–36 commences the Joseph Story, with Joseph being hated by his brothers for being his father's favorite. His siblings kidnap him and sell him off to slave-traders who take him to Egypt, in the process deceiving Jacob into believing that Joseph had been killed by wild animals. Like Joseph, depicted in his saga as an agent of blessing, God's people, as agents of his blessing themselves, can expect such mistreatment.

Summary of Pericope 29: This pericope takes a detour to deal with a significant episode in the life of Judah. His two older sons' lives are taken by God for their evil acts, but Tamar, his daughter-in-law, is not given Judah's third son in marriage as she should have been. So she takes action to perpetuate the seed of the family by deceiving Judah into sexual relations with her. He, later, wants her killed for immorality, but when she proves that he was the father of her twin children, Judah recognizes his unrighteousness. As the leader of the Israelite tribes, Judah, too, is an agent of divine blessing; such agents are to be characterized by concern for others and humility regarding their own weaknesses.

Preview of Pericope 30: The next pericope (39:1–23) tells the well-known story of Joseph's integrity in the face of temptation. The emphasis is on divine presence and blessing in the lives of Joseph and all around

467

him, suggesting that his integrity was the reason for his finding divine favor.

29   Genesis 38:1–30

THEOLOGICAL FOCUS OF PERICOPE 29

29   **Those who will be agents of God's blessing exhibit selfless concern for others and a humble awareness of their own fallibility (38:1–30).**

29.1   Those who will be agents of God's blessing exhibit selfless concern for others.

29.2   Those who will be agents of God's blessings to others are humbly aware of their own fallibility.

OVERVIEW

Of all the stories in Genesis, this may be the most bizarre and disconcerting to the reader, not to mention to the preacher and the listening audience. Leupold declared that the exposition of Gen 38 was "[e]ntirely unsuited to homiletical use." So also Speiser, who described the narrative as one that "has no connection with the drama of Joseph, which it interrupts." Berlinerbrau labeled it "a puzzling, disorderly little yarn featuring a murderous deity, *coitus interruptus,* prostitution, deception, and near incest, among other things."[1] But these assessments are far from accurate. In *m. Meg.* 4.10, certain passages of Scripture dealing with improper sexual encounters—Gen 35:22 (Reuben's incest) and 2 Sam 11:2–17 (David's adultery)—were permitted to be read aloud, but not translated; another, 2 Sam 13:1–4 (Tamar's rape), was not even allowed to be read. Notably, Gen 38 was not included in either category. Niditch notes that whereas these three prohibited passages concerned activities that destroy the social fabric, the illicit union of Judah and Tamar, rather than ripping the cloth, repaired it. As will be seen, we do well to agree with the rabbis who wished "to set the tale of Tamar apart from the other three incidents [prohibited from being read and/or translated] and thereby acknowledge its sociologically constructive message."[2]

While Gen 38 seems oddly out of place in the smoothly moving story of Joseph (in fact, 37:36 makes a seamless connection with 39:1), there are several thematic links with the rest of the saga: "going down" (Judah in 38:1, and Joseph in 39:1), marrying foreigners (38:2; 41:45), unhappy relationships and separation of protagonists (Judah and Tamar; and Joseph and his brothers), deception (of Judah by Tamar; of Jacob by his sons led by Judah), wrongs committed (against Tamar; and against Joseph), satisfaction of need sought from the one wronged (Judah from Tamar [sex]; brothers from

---

1. Leupold, *Exposition of Genesis,* 2:990; Speiser, *Genesis,* 299; Berlinerblau, "The Bible as Literature?" 18.

2. Niditch, "The Wronged Woman Righted," 149. The odd and rather risqué nature of the story in Gen 38 is offset somewhat by the unusually high incidence of explanations as to the motivations of its characters, either offered by the actants or by the narrator. Amit finds at least eleven such accountings: 38:7, 9, 10, 11, 14, 15, 16, 23, 26, 28, 29–30. See "Narrative Analysis," 273–74.

Joseph [food]), final confrontation (between Judah and Tamar; and between brothers and Joseph), use of garments as evidence (Joseph's coat; Judah's seal, cord, and staff), wrongfulness confessed (by Judah; by Joseph's brothers), transformation of character (of Judah; of the brothers), and the generation of dual offspring with a reversal of primogeniture (Perez/Zerah; Ephraim/Manasseh).[3]

More specifically, Gen 37 and 38 share themes: both have deception and the use of evidence; goat's blood was used in 37:31–33 (and the bloodied garment was "sent," 37:32), while a goat shows up in 38:17, 20, 23 (it, too, is "sent"); and the key word "recognize," is employed in 37:32, 33 and in 38:25, 26, in precisely identical fashion and in the same Hebrew Hiphil stem that occurs only in these loci in the OT. In both, there is a request made to recognize items of clothing, and there is a response of recognition.[4]

Genesis 38:25–26	Genesis 37:32–33
"[Tamar] sent ...	"[The brothers] sent ...
and said,	and said,
'Recognize, pray ...,'	'... recognize, pray ...,'
and [Judah] recognized ...	and [Jacob] recognized it
and said, ..."	and said, ..."

Alter recognizes this wordplay as the work of "a brilliant literary artist."

> The first use of the formula [in Gen 37] was for an act of deception; the second use [in Gen 38] is for an act of unmasking. Judah with Tamar [Gen 38] after Judah with his brothers [Gen 37] is an exemplary narrative instance of the deceiver deceived, and since he was the one who proposed selling Joseph into slavery instead of killing him (Gen 37:26–27), he can easily be thought of as the leader of the brothers in the deception practiced on their father. Now he becomes their surrogate in being subject to a bizarre but peculiarly fitting principle of retaliation, taken in by a piece of attire, as his father was.[5]

---

3. See Noble, "Synchronic and Diachronic," 138–40.

4. "The Holy One, blessed be He, said to Judah, 'You deceived our father [Jacob] with a kid. By your life Tamar will deceive you with a kid'. . . . The Holy One, Praised be He, said to Judah, 'Thou didst say to the father, *Discern [know] I pray thee* . . .; as thou livest, Tamar will say to thee, *Discern, I pray thee* . . .'" (*Gen. Rab.* 85:11). These "recognitions," of course, adumbrate the "recognition" of Joseph by his brothers: 42:7–8 (×4), also using the same verb.

5. *The Art of Biblical Narrative,* 10. On goats: one immediately remembers that a generation ago, Jacob had used goatskin to cover his arms to deceive his father. In Gen 37, goats were employed by his sons (under the leadership of Judah) to deceive Jacob, and now in Gen 38, Judah, himself, is outwitted, with goats again involved in a deception, albeit indirectly. "It is as though some strange karmic force keeps this act of deception in continual ricochet, dooming the chosen family to re-experience it in succeeding generations and even within the same generation" (Levenson, *The Death and Resurrection,* 159). A simpler explanation would be divine talionic justice operating across generations with deceivers reaping what they sowed! There is also the continuing theme that employs garments: Joseph's special tunic (Gen 37), Tamar's garments of a widow and a harlot (Gen 38; we are not told that her garb was that of a harlot, but it is a fair assumption), Judah's accouterments (seal, cord, and staff—part of his gear? Gen 38), and Joseph's clothing again (Gen 39).

Many of the careful structuring tendencies noted in previous pericopes of Genesis are visible in this one as well, which moves along a narrative arc: from equilibrium, descent, and via disequilibrium, to ascent, and a re-equilibrium.[6]

A		Judah's children by his first wife (**38:1–5**): "brothers" (38:1); "name" (38:1, 2, 3, 4, 5); "give birth" (38:3, 4, 5)	EQUILIBRIUM
	B	Tamar's husbands killed for impropriety (**38:6–10**): "evil" (38: 7, 10)	
	C	Judah's promise to Tamar of groom unfulfilled (**38:11–12a**): "go," "dwell" (of Tamar, 38:11)	DESCENT
	D	Tamar seduces Judah who lies with her (**38:12b–18**)	DISEQUILIBRIUM
	C'	Judah's promise to Tamar of payment unfulfilled (**38:19–23**): "go," "dwell" (of Tamar, 38:19)	ASCENT
	B'	Tamar to be killed for impropriety (**38:24–26**): "righteous" (38:26)	
A'		Judah's children by his second "wife" (**38:27–30**): "brother" (38:29, 30); "name" (38:29, 30); "give birth"(38:27, 28)	EQUILIBRUM

The pericope may also be structured thus:

A Genealogical data (38:1–11): begins with a notice of time (38:1); "she gave birth, " 38:5
  B Tamar's act (38:12–23); begins with a notice of time (38:12)
  B' Judah's act (38:24–26); begins with a notice of time (38:24)
A' Genealogical data (38:27–30); begins with a notice of time (38:27); "she gave birth," 38:28

In either layout, the sexual alliance between Tamar and Judah take center stage—the zenith (or nadir) of disequilibrium.

In Gen 34, Simeon and Levi, because of their impetuosity and bloodthirstiness, had disqualified themselves from leadership; in Gen 35, by his incestuous relationship, Reuben—"he of the mandrakes and incest"—also had been disentitled. The next in line was Judah. (If one thought Joseph would become the appointed leader, Gen 37 summarily eliminated this early candidate, seemingly forever, by displacing him to a foreign land.) And in Gen 37, it appeared that Judah's brothers had begun to follow his lead over Reuben's.[7] But would Judah also end up disqualifying himself? It appears that in Gen 38 he does everything to keep himself out of the reckoning. And his actions prove to be a dramatic foil for Joseph who returns to the stage in the next chapter. On the one hand is Judah, characterized in Gen 38 by indiscretion and callousness: he leaves his family to marry a Canaanite, breaks a promise and violates the levirate law, he consorts with a "harlot," sires children incestuously, and finally confesses to being less than righteous. On the other hand is Joseph, unblemished and pure, integrity intact, morals shining, and constantly blessed by the presence of Yahweh with him, no

6. From Dorsey, *The Literary Structure of the Old Testament*, 63; and Lambe, "Genesis 38," 103–9.
7. Brodie, *Genesis as Dialogue*, 362; Kass, *The Beginning of Wisdom*, 527.

matter where he is, in slavery or in prison (see Pericope 30). Judah's consorting with harlots and letting his irrepressible sexual urges run amok is a glaring contrast to Joseph's integrity in Gen 39—the 17-year-old far from home exercises greater control over a potent temptation than the widowed man with three children in Gen 38. Note that both Judah (38:1) and Joseph (37:35) "went down," a subtle comparison, back to back, of these protagonists.[8] "In this way, the location of Gen 38, with its sordid and seedy details, invites comparison with Joseph's refusal to sleep with Potiphar's wife, throwing into bold relief the qualities that set Joseph apart from his brothers."[9]

JUDAH (Genesis 38)	JOSEPH (Genesis 39)
Association with foreign women (38:1–3)	Fleeing from foreign women (39:6b–12)
Sexual immorality (38:12–18)	Sexual probity (39:6b–12)
Victimizer (38:24)	Victim (39:13–20a)
Divine disapproval of Judah's actions implicit	Divine approval of Joseph's actions explicit (39:1–5, 21–23)
True accusation made by a woman (38:25)	False accusation made by a woman (39:13–20a)
Clothing as evidence (38:25)	Clothing as evidence (39:15–18)
Confession of sin (38:26)	Rejection of sin (39:10)

But there is more here than merely foil in the depiction of Judah; as the future leader, both in the continuing saga of Joseph, and among the tribes later on, the text must clarify how the rather unscrupulous and unsavory Judah of Gen 37 and most of Gen 38 becomes the exemplary Judah in Gen 43–44, displaying godly leadership qualities. Whence this transformation? One does not have to dig too far to see that Gen 38 is the turning point in the positive evolution of Judah, and therefore it occupies prime space in the Joseph Story. If the leader of the twelve tribes is to lead, then he must also be one who leads to bring divine blessing to others, for it would be through the tribes of Israel that the rest of the humankind would be blessed. What would it take for Judah to so be a leader that blesses others? These are the questions being answered in this pericope. In keeping with the overall theme of the Joseph Story, this pericope then points out that being a blessing (and retrospectively, the reader is expected to know that "Judah" becomes the prominent tribe in the south) involves the display of certain attitudes and actions as theologically propounded in this pericope: being such an agent for the disbursement of God's blessings to others involves admitting one's failures and making amends.

---

8. All of these "goings down" (ירד, *yrd*) will "take down" (also ירד) Jacob to his grave mourning (37:35; 44:29, 31).

9. Arnold, *Genesis*, 325. Table modified from Greidanus, *Preaching Christ from Genesis*, 361. One must also remember that, in Gen 38, Er was killed by Yahweh for doing "evil," and that neither was Onan spared—obviously his act was evil as well. The purity of Joseph in Gen 39 stands out even more in the light of all this palpable evil committed by Judah and his offspring.

29   Genesis 38:1–30

THEOLOGICAL FOCUS 29[A]

29   Those who will be agents of God's blessing exhibit selfless concern for others and a humble awareness of their own fallibility.

29.1   *Those who will be agents of God's blessing exhibit selfless concern for others.*

29.2   *Those who will be agents of God's blessings to others are humbly aware of their own fallibility.*

A.   Having only one section in this pericope, the "Theological Focus 29" is identical to the "Theological Focus of Pericope 29."

NOTES 29

29.1   Those who will be agents of God's blessing exhibit selfless concern for others.[10]

We are not told why, but Judah breaks off from the rest of his family and, like Esau of old (26:34–35; 27:46; 28:6–9) who engaged in this strongly deprecated practice, took a wife exogamously, the daughter of a Canaanite named Shua (38:1–2). Abraham worked hard to get Isaac a bride from within the family circle (Gen 24), and Isaac and Rebekah, likewise, sent Jacob to Laban's place to find himself a wife (27:46–28:5). On the other hand, Esau's forays into Canaanite marital alliances met with strong displeasure from his parents (26:34–35; 27:46; 28:8–9). Thus, exogamy was *not* a patriarchal value![11] Whatever Judah's reasons, his undertaking does not bode well for him. It is a declaration of independence from tradition and family, "an act of indifference and abandonment," a self-willed removal from kith and kin to congregate with the Canaanites, a tacit engagement in a fratricide of sorts.[12] In abandoning his blood loyalties, Judah does voluntarily what Joseph is forced to do: both remove (or are removed, "go down," 37:38; 38:1) from the sphere of extended family.[13] The first notation of Judah's independent activity, that he departed from his brothers (38:1), is in direct contrast to the first statement of Joseph's activity: "shepherding the flock *with his brothers*" (37:2).

While the verbs in both accounts are different, there is a similarity in the description of Judah's action and that of Shechem: both "take" a woman and have sexual relations with her (34:3; 38:2). Shechem's was, of course, a rape; but there is also a hint of deprecation at Judah's rather uncontrolled urges, which surface again, once his wife dies (38:12–18). The combination of "seeing" and "taking" (38:2) bespeaks a weak streak: elsewhere "see + take" has an illicit register, the kind of activity engaged in by Eve with

10. This, of course, is a positive statement of what Judah was not, at least not in this pericope.

11. However, it was not only Judah who was guilty of this misstep: among Jacob's sons, Simeon (46:1) and even Joseph (41:45, not that he had much choice in the matter) married outside the familial fold.

12. Kass, *The Beginning of Wisdom*, 527–28.

13. In fact, Green notes that "Judah will enact the whole Joseph story with his own sons: . . . go into exile, have sons, lose most, regain them (so to speak), return home" (referring to his reunion with his brothers as seen in the subsequent narrative). See *"What Profit for Us?"* 85n3.

regard to the fruit (3:5), the sons of God with regard to women (6:2), Pharaoh with re-gard to Sarah (12:15), and Shechem with regard to Dinah (34:2). Wenham thinks that the absence of a name for Judah's wife also points in the direction of this alliance being merely one founded on lust. In Judah's "taking" (the usual phrase for marriage is "take as wife," as in 11:29; 12:19; 21:21; 24:67; 25:1, 20; 30:9), it is implied that the daughter of Shua was simply appropriated. That the proper syntax for marriage is followed even later in this same pericope (38:6), and that the wife there is named (Tamar), makes the account of Judah's wife-seeing and wife-taking even more odious.[14] In the text, this spousal relationship is narrated in six verbs: three for Judah (he sees, he takes, he lies: 38:2) and three for the daughter of Shua (she conceives, she bares, she names [their second and third children]: 38:3, 4, 5[15]). Judah's absence around the birth of his second and third children is also rather odd and hints at parental irresponsibility on his part. In sum, Judah has not said anything yet, but his actions are loud: he has abandoned family, taken up with a Canaanite woman, and removed himself from any involvement in the births of most of his children.[16]

The narrative then speeds up rapidly. Er, married to Tamar, is killed by God for doing what was "evil in the eyes of Yahweh" (38:7). While we are not told what exactly led to Er's guilt, the similarity of the description with that of Onan's misbehavior later (38:10; both did "evil in the eyes of Yahweh"), and the identical nature of their punish-ment (both were killed by Yahweh, and the text adds "also" for Onan's death, 38:10, hinting at the similarity with Er's demise), suggests that some sexual impropriety was involved in Er's "evil" as well.[17] Judah's instruction to Onan, upon the death of Er, is telling: "Go into your brother's wife" (38:8), not "marry her" (or "take her as wife").[18] He recommends Onan do what he, himself, would later propose to Tamar and engage in, with her ("go into," 38:16 [×2], 18).[19] Incidentally, to Judah, Tamar is a faceless,

14. Wenham, *Genesis 16–50*, 366.

15. The MT has "*he* named [their first child]" (38:3) and is best retained as the more difficult reading.

16. Cotter, *Genesis*, 280–81.

17. These two, Er and Onan, are the first individuals in Scripture that Yahweh is said to have "killed" (38:7, 10), not considering the masses that died in the Flood and in the destruction of Sodom and Gomorrah. In fact, these two killings turn out to be the only actions of deity explicitly recorded in this pericope. In a neat pun that reflects the Hebrew (רַע ... עֵר, *'er ... ra'*; "Er was evil"), Wenham translates 38:7a as "Er erred" (*Genesis 16–50*, 366).

18. The giving of a brother to his widowed sister-in-law—the practice of levirate marriage (from the Latin *levir*, "brother-in-law")—was prevalent both in Israel (Deut 25:5–10; Matt 22:23–30; Mark 12:18–25; Luke 20:27–35) and among its neighbors. In fact Middle Assyrian Law A33 (and Hittite Law 193) seem to include the father in the assumption of levirate responsibility (*ANET* 182, 196). See Wenham, *Genesis 16–50*, 366. For an informative excursus on levirate marriage, see Mathews, *Genesis 11:27–50:26*, 705–10.

19. The Hebrew construction in 38:9, a "perfect frequentative," indicates that Onan's "wasting of his seed" was not a one-time event, but a repeated practice ("*whenever* he went into his brother's wife"; see GKC §159.3.A1[d]). Onan was simply using Tamar (and the levirate law!) to satisfy his sexual needs (as his father would soon do, himself, with Tamar). His refusal to procreate was probably driven by selfish reasons—not wanting to reduce his share of the family inheritance as first in line after the firstborn (Num 27:8–11). That privilege, if Onan obeyed the levirate law, would go to his son, were he to father one with his sister-in-law. As the sages remarked wryly on 38:9 (*Gen. Rab.* 85.5): "He threshed within

anonymous object: he never calls or refers to her by name. All told, Judah's concern for this widow is minimal; his interest is only in having descendants by her.

While the text tells us pointedly that it was the evil behavior of Er and Onan that got themselves killed by Yahweh (38:7–10), Judah completely misunderstands the situation—his sons' wickedness is conveniently ignored—and he blames Tamar, instead. He sends her away, essentially refusing to give his third son, Shelah, to her as he should have, and as he himself later confesses (38:26). Judah's reaction is mitigated somewhat by the fear of losing Shelah also. But he should have known that Tamar was not responsible for the earlier tragedies; moreover, one remembers that the consequences of a father's partiality towards, and over-protection of, his youngest was something Judah had personally experienced with Jacob and Joseph. Surely he should have learnt from the mistakes of his parent. And even then, Judah's fear of a "killer wife" only recalls his irresponsibility and his ignorance of why his two older sons were killed. This is a man who apparently has no idea (or interest) in what his children are doing.

In addition, when Er and Onan die, apparently in rapid succession (38:7–10), there is no statement of any grief on Judah's part. Coming right after Jacob's inconsolable mourning over the loss of his son Joseph (37:34–35), the absence of any lament by Judah is all the more striking.[20] It reinforces the impression of this son of Jacob as hard and callous, one who would sell his own brother for filthy lucre (37:26–27). Later he deceives Tamar, sending her to her back father's house with a promise to give Shelah to her, a promise he does not intend to keep (38:11). There is no doubt the narrator wants the reader to be aware of Judah's responsibility to find Tamar a husband after Er and Onan had died: it is specifically noted in 38:11 that "Judah said to his *daughter-in-law* Tamar . . .," a redundant, but pointed, description of the unfortunate widow. This responsibility to his daughter-in-law, Judah did not discharge; he had no intention of doing so, thus putting Tamar's future in jeopardy without spouse or children. He has, however, promised Shelah to Tamar (38:11): she is, in a sense, betrothed to him.[21] On that reason alone, Judah's subsequent dalliance with Tamar is adultery. He is eager to engage in sex with a prostitute, but is equally zealous in condemning Tamar as a harlot and in pronouncing sentence on her, without even bothering to hear her version of the events. Thus, in this pericope, not only does he not seem to grieve over the loss of his own sons, he has

---

and winnowed without" (דש מבפנים וזורה מבחוץ, *dsh mbpnm uzrh mbkhts*). Not only was Onan's behavior self-serving and cruel, it was a rejection of Yahweh's promise to the patriarchs that they would be fruitful and multiply (17:6, 20; 28:3; 35:11; also see 15:5; 22:17; 26:4; 32:12). The thrice repeated "descendants" (38:9) surely alludes to this divine promise. Thus "Onan's action demonstrates his opposition to the divine agenda" (Wenham, *Genesis 16–50*, 366).

20. Following the death of his wife, Judah is said to have been "consoled" (38:12), suggesting that he did mourn the loss of his spouse. But, again, Jacob was *inconsolable* (37:35).

21. One must also note that Judah had not released Tamar from *her* obligations to be free to marry another as Deut 25:5–10 later permitted widows to do: therefore her conception outside of marriage was deemed adultery. "[Tamar's] situation was impossibly ambiguous; she was not free to marry, was still under the legal responsibility of her erstwhile father-in-law, and had no way to earn a living, but had to be supported by her family. To both her and her family she must have seemed almost buried alive" (Cotter, *Genesis*, 283). But we read in 38:12 about *Judah* being free as a widower!

no thought for his twice-widowed daughter-in-law, summarily dispatching her to her father's house and later, equally peremptorily condemning her to be burnt alive.

In short, the primary failure on the part of Judah is his disinclination to do something about childlessness, a fundamental problem for those in the line of Abraham. Er dies childless, divinely disciplined, perhaps for some sexual sin; Onan has no interest in procreation or in the patriarchal promises; and Judah refuses to give their widow his third son, indicating his somewhat cavalier response to those promises. Kass observes that Judah's withholding of Shelah from Tamar is as the sin of Onan—both were withholding the possibility of seed from her. Thus, Judah "denies Tamar her marital and maternal fulfillment, he neglects the duty (Shelah's) to be one's brother's keeper, and he prefers the love of his own to the keeping of the law."[22] That put Tamar in limbo, humiliated and forgotten even "after much time" (literally, "when the days increased," 38:12). The social disgrace would have rendered her an outcast, perhaps even in her own family, to whom Judah callously shifts this "problem woman."

But, unlike Judah and his sons, blithely unconcerned about the promises of Yahweh, Tamar, a Canaanite, is concerned about bearing children for Judah's line.[23] "Such determination to propagate descendants of Abraham, especially by a Canaanite woman, is remarkable, and so despite her foreign background and irregular behavior, Tamar emerges as the heroine of this story." Here is a case where an outsider is concerned about divine promises, but insiders are not. Wenham observes that Tamar is like Melchizedek (Gen 14) and Abimelech (Gen 26), who recognize Yahweh's work in the family of Abraham and align themselves with the infant nation of Israel.[24] Remarkably, the births of Judah's children, Perez and Zerah, through Tamar, are the first recorded ones in the new generation of Jacob's grandchildren and the beginning, in this new season, of the fulfillment of Yahweh's promise to Abraham: "In you all the families of the earth will be blessed" (12:3). Ironically, it is a Canaanite woman, at great loss and cost to herself, who has to educate Judah about marriage and about what it means to be a father, a brother, a husband.[25] Only such a one, with selfless concern for others, can be an effective agent of divine blessing.

29.2 *Those who will be agents of God's blessings to others are humbly aware of their own fallibility.*

The sordid nature of Judah's story continues in the latter half of Gen 38, with Judah heading out to a sheep-shearing festival in Timnah with his friend, Hirah, the Adullamite (38:12). Such festivals, besides being well lubricated with alcohol, might

---

22. Kass, *The Beginning of Wisdom*, 529–30. "Taking seriously the commandment 'Be fruitful and multiply,' levirate marriage elevates the importance of progeny above personal gratification, and hence, the importance of lineage and community above the individual. In accepting the duty of the *levir,* a man simultaneously shows reverence for his ancestors, respect for the meaning and purpose of marriage, and devotion to the future of his family and his people" (ibid., 531).

23. While the antecedents of Tamar are not known, in view of the context and location of Judah and his family, she is likely to have been a Canaanite.

24. *Genesis 16–50,* 365.

25. Kass, *The Beginning of Wisdom,* 531.

have also been associated with ritual fornication, perhaps in a bid to increase the fertility of land and herd (Hos 4:13–14 depicts prostitution at feast times, and 9:1–2, fornication on threshing floors to increase crops).[26] The nexus between Judah and Hirah the Adullamite is suspicious in itself. Right after the first time this gentleman is mentioned, Judah breaks the principle of endogamy and marries a Canaanite (Gen 38:1–2). Immediately after Hirah shows up in the narrative the second time, Judah crosses the bounds of propriety to seek sex with a harlot (38:12–18). In the first instance, Judah "goes down" (38:1); in the second, he "goes up" (38:12).[27] Is the Adullamite the inciter of all these dodgy up-and-down enterprises that Judah has been engaging in? In any case, Judah is close enough to Hirah to employ the latter as his proxy, to pay Tamar later for her services (38:20–23).

Until this point, Tamar, in submission, has been passive, only acted upon by Judah and his two older children: all she does, thus far, is compliantly retreat ("Tamar went and lived in her father's house," 38:11). But, in the next scene, "she suddenly races into rapid, purposeful action, expressed in a detonating series of verbs: in verse 14 she quickly takes off, covers, wraps herself, sits down at the strategic location," and traps Judah in a compromising situation, negotiating with her male partner and exacting, with clinical efficiency, what is "a kind of ancient Near Eastern equivalent of all of a person's credit cards."[28] In short, Judah abandons, with his insignia, even his very heritage. Then the narrative culminates with three staccato verbs and the appropriate prepositions: he gave to her, he went into her, she conceived by him (38:18). That Tamar is taking deliberate action to redress the injustice done to her is clear from the equally deliberate narrative structuring of her actions: four verbs in each verse, before and after her sexual congress with Judah.

A	she removes (her widow's garb)			
	B	she covers (with a veil)		
		C	she wraps (herself)	**Tamar's actions in 38:14**
			D	she sits (in the gate)

Sexual liaison: Tamar and Judah (38:15–18)

			D'	she rises
		C'	she departs	
	B'	she removes (her veil)		**Tamar's actions in 38:19**
A'	she puts on (her widow's garb)			

---

26. Wenham, *Genesis 16–50*, 368.

27. Moreover, twice Judah "turns," and both times with less than chaste intentions: first he "turns" to Hirah and ends up marrying a Canaanite (38:1–2); then he "turns" to Tamar and ends up as the father of his daughter-in-law's children (38:16). The consequence of his third interaction with Hirah (38:20–23)—the failed attempt to pay his dues to Tamar and recover his identity papers—is that Judah condemns himself before her (38:24–26).

28. Wenham, *Genesis 16–50*, 367. Judah, apparently a man of prominence and property, had his own seal, likely threaded on a cord; a staff, beyond its obvious utility, would also be a symbol of prestige (see 49:10; Num 17:18; Ps 110:2; Ezek 19:11). Kruschwitz, however, thinks the staff is a phallic symbol, specifically demanded by Tamar in Gen 38:18 ("The Type-Scene Connection," 402).

While Tamar's stratagem of seduction is dubious in its propriety, one must remember that for one in Tamar's situation, discarded and distanced, there was no redress. Rather than "remaining" (ישׁב, *yshv* [×2], 38:11) as a widow in her father's house, Tamar sits (ישׁב, 38:14) at the "gateway/opening of Enaim," plying her wares. The word עֵינָיִם, *'enay-im*, is the dual form of עַיִן (*'ayin*, "spring"); thus this episode is mimicking a betrothal type-scene by a well (Gen 24:11–31; 29:1–14; Exod 2:15b–22) whence would commence the negotiations that render Tamar pregnant with Judah's children. "In Genesis 38, the type-scene functions to show that Tamar, no less than Rebekah and Rachel, is a fruitful 'wife' of an ancestor."[29] Moreover, the only other use of "veil," besides Gen 38:14, 19, is in 24:65—a veil is worn by a bride, Rebekah, as she prepares to meet Isaac. Here, Tamar, the "bride," prepares to meet Judah, the "groom." While he sees her merely as a harlot, she sees him as a husband.[30] The woman who was not "given" seed by Onan (38:9), and who was not "given" a husband (Shelah) by her father-in-law (38:14), now asks Judah what he will "give" her (38:16), and if he would "give" a pledge (38:17). Judah asks what pledge he should "give" her and, in response to Tamar's demand, "gave" her his seal, cord, and staff (38:18[×2]).[31] The ramifications of all this giving? "And he went in to her and she conceived" (38:18), which happens to be the exact sequence of events described in 38:2–3 ("and he [Judah] went in to her [daughter of Shua] and she conceived). It is almost as if Tamar was Judah's wife—or perhaps Judah is turning out to be Shelah's surrogate and acting like Tamar's husband. In any case, the pledge is agreed upon, the surety passes hands, sexual union takes place, Tamar conceives, and the two parties go their own ways . . . for now (38:18–19).

Altogether, Judah is depicted as an ignoramus: he misconstrues the cause of his sons' deaths (38:11), he does not recognize his own daughter-in-law (38:16), he is unconscious of the implications of parting with his seal, cord, and staff (38:18), he is unable to locate this "prostitute"[32] afterwards (38:20–23, "did not find her" occurs thrice), he is in danger of becoming a laughingstock (38:23), and he is mistaken in his reckoning of Tamar's guilt (38:24). Instead, he marries a Canaanite (38:2), abandons his

---

29. Cotter, *Genesis*, 284; Clifford, "Genesis 38," 529.

30. Of course עֵינָיִם could also be the dual form of עַיִן—"eye." In this case, "gateway of Enaim" might well be "opening of the eyes," thus parodying the unfortunate *closure* of Judah's eyes: Judah "saw" (38:15), but twice his eyes lead him astray—he thought Tamar was a harlot (38:15) and he did not know she was his daughter-in-law (38:16). Or, it could be that Tamar's being "seen" here at the "opening of the eyes" commences the reversal of her deplorable situation: she is finally visible to her father-in-law who has ignored her thus far (Cotter, *Genesis*, 285). This incident at Enaim later proves to be the eye-opener for Judah: When asked to "see" his paraphernalia, Judah recognizes them and acknowledges Tamar's righteousness (38:25–26). Noting that the only mention of actual eyes in this pericope is of the "eyes" of Yahweh (38:7, 10), van Wolde speculates that the "opening of the eyes" hints at Tamar's role in depicting Judah as doing what was "evil in Yahweh's eyes"—making his obnoxious behavior equivalent to the evil perpetrated by his sons. See van Wolde, "Texts in Dialogue with Texts," 25–26. In any case, whether "Enaim" indicates "eyes" or "well," the incontinent and immoral deeds of Judah are being exposed and showcased.

31. Later, Judah also confesses his guilt in not "giving" Tamar to his son Shelah as wife (38:26).

32. There is no particular reason to differentiate between the designations of a prostitute found in 38:15, 24 (זנה, *znh*) and 38:21, 22 (קדשׁ, *qdsh*); both are translated πόρνη, *pornē*, in the LXX that sees the terms as equivalent.

widowed daughter-in-law (34:11), has sex with her, fathers twins (38:18), and is finally shown to be the unrighteous person he is, by that same woman (38:26). Appropriately enough, Judah's relations with Tamar is *not* described with ידע (*yd'*, "know") in 38:18, but by בוא (*bo'*, "go in"). And later we are told, after his exposé, that he did not "know" (ידע) Tamar again (38:26). He has *never* "known" her; his estimation of her has never been accurate, and his cavalier treatment of her has only confirmed that assessment. In fact, as it turned out, she was the righteous one, not he. However strange her strategic action, Tamar, the "righteous," had aligned herself to God and his will; and Judah had not. "If ever a fool was, he was Judah in Genesis 38. Judah is his own worst enemy."[33] Later, rather ironically, Judah attempts to keep his pledge to this "harlot," by sending her the goat he had promised (38:17, 20)—he, who had not kept his paternal responsibility to his daughter-in-law by "giving" her his third son as he had promised (38:11, 14), is more honorable with a "harlot," to whom he is willing to "give" the powerful tokens of his identity and prestige. Not only has he yielded these important badges, "he has willingly surrendered his birthright and standing . . . in his refusal to uphold the rights of his son and his son's marriage."[34] On the other hand, "[Tamar] remains true to her Israelite family in spite of its glaring failures and becomes absorbed into it. Normally Canaanite women absorb Israelite men into their debased culture (Deut 7:1, 3). In that light, her deception as a Canaanite prostitute to snare her widowed father-in-law into fathering covenant seed should be evaluated as a daring act of faith."[35] Her desiring a child by Judah then brings her closer than this son of Jacob to the ideal of patriarchal endogamy. And quite impressively, only two people in Genesis are labeled "righteous"—Abraham (15:16 and, perhaps, 18:19) and Tamar (38:26)!

Judah's action of sexual intercourse with a daughter-in-law was, by the Mosaic Law, punishable by death—for both parties (Lev 18:15; 20:12). The furtive way in which Judah goes about attempting to make payment for sexual services rendered (and to repossess his pledges) points to the shamefulness of the practice of prostitution. A promiscuous daughter, according to Deut 22:21, was to be "brought out" and stoned to death, a sentence executed by the elders of the city. Here, Judah orders that Tamar be "brought out" (Gen 38:24), and he, the sole judge, declares her guilty and deserving of being burnt alive, a rare punishment in the Mosaic Law reserved for particularly egregious and disgraceful offenses (Lev 20:14; 21:19). Judah condemns Tamar in two Hebrew words (הוֹצִיאוּהָ וְתִשָּׂרֵף, *hotsi'uha wtisaref*, "Bring-her-out and-let-her-be-burned," 38:24)—no investigation, no trial, no defense, no jury. "It is highly ironic that the man who impregnated her with life . . . is the one who says so shortly: 'bring her out . . . to be killed.'"[36] He sees a "harlot," and he propositions her (38:15); he

---

33. Jackson, "Lot's Daughters and Tamar," 40. God's apparent lack of response to this gross indiscretion is conspicuous, given his violent reaction in 38:7, 10. Perhaps the conception was necessary; how it came about was not.

34. Kass, *The Beginning of Wisdom*, 534. Judah "sends" a goat to Tamar (38:17, 20, 23), but it is the "sending" done by Tamar to Judah (38:25, of his seal and cord and staff) that breaks him.

35. Waltke and Fredricks, *Genesis,* 508.

36. Andrew, "Moving from Death to Life," 266.

hears his daughter-in-law has "committed *harlotry*," and he wants her killed (38:24).[37] If he were that keen on abiding by the law (however it was known in Judah's day), he should have called for the death of *both* conspirators.

Then Tamar plays her "trump card"—the seal, cord, and staff of the one who had had relations with her. Curiously enough, Tamar's exhortation is not that Judah recognize the paraphernalia as his, but that he recognize the *person* to whom those belong (38:25). In essence, she was asking Judah to recognize himself, thus bringing him face to face not only with his sin and his deplorable treatment of her, but also—and perhaps essentially—with his own identity and responsibility, including his egregious disposal of Joseph and the equally heartless grieving of Jacob (in Gen 37).

> Now himself a father, with sons who (like Jacob's) ignore their marital and broth-
> erly obligations; now a widower (also like Jacob) who is bereaved also of (two)
> sons; now made aware, thanks to Tamar, of the consequences of putting the love
> of your son above a proper regard for the community's future and for what is
> right, Judah is able to learn what it means properly to care—as a father, as a
> brother, as a son in the house of Israel.[38]

Upon being confronted by the incontrovertible proof of his own guilt, Judah declares that Tamar is more "righteous" (צדק) than he (38:26), a word often used in forensic settings (Exod 23:7; Deut 25:1). "Judah's remark did not mean necessarily that her action was approved; rather, Judah acknowledged that her motivation was consistent with the purpose of levirate marriage, whereas Judah had attempted to circumvent the custom."[39] Later Judah would use the same root in his confession before Joseph, on behalf of his siblings (Gen 44:16): "And how can we justify [צדק] ourselves?" No doubt, the events in Gen 38 led to Judah's realization that all was not "right" with himself.

Incidentally, Judah is the first person in the Bible to acknowledge his own sin. This is a key confession and marks out Judah as one who is on the road to recovery. Henceforth, he will be portrayed only positively in the remainder of Genesis—the leader of his brothers, the instrument of reconciliation, the exemplar of selfless concern for others, the embodiment of humility: in short, he has become an agent of divine blessing to others. "Thus, Gen 38 becomes the transformative chapter in Judah's story. After his courageous acknowledgment [38:26], he rises to a level of moral behavior from which he will never deviate. Gone forever is the Judah who conspired against his brother, scorned endogamy, neglected a widow, associated with a prostitute, and recklessly condemned a family member."[40] Instead we have a transformed Judah, unselfish, self-sacrificing, deeply concerned for sibling and parent (43:8–9; 44:18–34). He is next seen back with his brothers (43:3, but presumably in Gen 42 as well, though Judah is not named there): apparently the one who had wandered off from the family

37. Judah was "told" (38:24) about Tamar's indiscretions, just as Tamar was "told" (38:13) about Judah's intentions.

38. Kass, *The Beginning of Wisdom*, 535.

39. Mathews, *Genesis 11:27–50:26*, 723.

40. Clifford, "Genesis 38," 531.

fold (38:1) had returned. Humbler and wiser, he would be the leader of the band of brothers, as the rest of the Joseph narrative shows. He becomes the one who wields influence, persuading his father to allow Benjamin to go to Egypt (43:8–10), and moving Joseph to shed his disguise and causing him to break down in tears (44:16–34; 45:1–4). Finally, Judah becomes an agent of divine blessing to others.

That "all is well that ends well" is suggested by the extra bit of information in 38:26, that Judah did not have sexual relations with Tamar again: "Judah's whoring is over. The result, in the birth of twins, is an exuberant sense of life—of breakthrough and dawn (38:27–30)."[41] Moreover, the closure of this pericope also suggests divine aproval in the depiction of a reversal of primogeniture (38:28–30), a common theme thus far in Genesis (Abel vs. Cain; Jacob vs. Esau; Joseph [the youngest born in Paddan-aram] vs. Reuben; Shelah vs. Er/Onan; Perez vs. Zerah; and later, Ephraim vs. Manasseh). In all of Scripture, only Rebekah and Tamar have twins, but Tamar does not receive the divine oracle Rebekah did (25:23). Nevertheless, her pregnancy and its aftermath appear to have been divinely approved, for the announcements of the labor and delivery of both these mothers of twins are identical: "Behold, there were twins in her womb!" (25:34; 38:27).

> [T]he absence of God in the passage at bringing about the remarkable births of the twins, unlike the births of the earlier tribal ancestors . . . [25:21; Gen 29–30], produces a disconcerting silence for the reader. This demonstrated for the author that the working out of God's purpose is not always overt but may be covert and never thwarted by the vicissitudes of life. . . . [Gen 38] implies that the hand of God is behind the events that transpire. . . . This is shown by the historic outcome of the Judah-Tamar union, producing the ancestral lineage of the royal house through Perez (Ruth 4:18–22; 2 Chr 2:5–15; Matt 1:3–6; Luke 3:31–33).[42]

The fact that such a thing occurs in Judah's line signifies that he is back in the divine good books, so to speak.[43]

41. Brodie, *Genesis as Dialogue*, 354. "Perez" = "he who breaks through" and "Zerah" = "one who shines." The story ends with two children for Judah, to replace the two that he had lost. The younger, Perez, becomes an ancestor of King David, the forerunner of Jesus Christ (Matt 1:6, 16). "Tamar, through her determination to have children, secured for Judah the honor of fathering both David and the Savior of the world" (Wenham, *Genesis 16–50*, 370).

42. Mathews, *Genesis 11:27–50:26*, 704.

43. The text implies that the events of Gen 38 commenced quite soon after the sale of Joseph into slavery (38:1, "And it happened at this time . . ."). That means most of what is described in this pericope took place in the 21–22 years between the kidnapping of Joseph and the arrival of the sons of Jacob in Egypt (Joseph's 13 years in prison [37:2; 41:46] + 7 years of plenty [41:47] + 2 years of famine [45:6] = 22 years). However, could this period of two decades include Perez begetting children? Two of his sons, Hezron and Hamul, are described in 46:12 as being part of the Jacobean party that moved to Egypt, suggesting they were born in Canaan. But unlike other similar notations of children in Gen 46 ("And the sons of *X*:" or "And these the sons of *Y*:"), 46:12 has "And the sons of Perez were. . . ." Cassuto argues that this was to indicate that Hezron and Hamul were *not* immigrants into Egypt, but that they were mentioned here only to bring the number of Judah's families to five (Hezron and Hamul [replacements for Er and Onan, in order not to let the names of the deceased be blotted out, Deut 25:6], Shelah, Zerah, and Perez [via his children after Hezron and Hamul]; Cassuto cites Num 26:19–21 in support). In other words, it is quite possible for the events of Gen 38 to have occurred in a little over twenty years.

In sum, this unfeeling and immoral brute, Judah, is in stark contrast to the tender, sensitive, compassionate, and self-sacrificing Judah we encounter in Gen 43–44, who delivers the longest speech by anyone in Gen 37–50, at the culmination of which Joseph is broken by the pathos (44:18–45:1). This dramatic change, I submit, begins in Gen 38 with his confession: "She is in the right, not I" (38:26). Without this pericope, the transformation of Judah would be inexplicable; such a conversion is in line with Abram becoming Abraham and Jacob becoming Israel, albeit without a name change for Judah.[44] He had already had shown signs of leadership in that his recommendation to sell Joseph won the brothers affirmation, over Reuben's (37:26–27). After this pericope, once again he betters Reuben by convincing Jacob to let Benjamin accompany the rest of his brothers to Egypt (43:11–14; for Reuben's failed attempt to do so, see 42:37–38). Towards the end of the narrative of Gen 37–50, Judah, in light of his changed life and character as a leader, receives Jacob's blessing that situates him as ruler over his brothers (49:8–12), apparently even over Joseph.

SERMON FOCUS AND OUTLINES

THEOLOGICAL FOCUS OF PERICOPE 28 FOR PREACHING

29 Agents of God's blessing are selflessly concerned about others and humbly aware of their own fallibility (38:1–30).

As noted earlier, a retrospective view of Judah as the one who would be the leader of his brothers and whose tribe would one day lead the nation of Israel is essential to keep this pericope in perspective. Judah, as a potential agent of divine blessing to others (through his leadership and that of his tribe) is the protagonist in this story. His characterization reveals what is expected of children of God, called to be agents of his blessing to the rest of humankind. Perhaps a brief mention of Judah's personal leadership (Gen 43–44) will be helpful, as well as a statement of the important status of the tribe of Judah. This tribe, settled south of Jerusalem, later became the most powerful and important one of the twelve (incorporating the tribe of Benjamin). From Judah came its greatest regents, David and Solomon; several of the literary prophets were Judean in their office (Isaiah, Amos, Micah, and Zechariah, among others); the exilarchs (leaders of the Jewish diaspora in exile) likely were from this this tribe as well; post-exile, Zerubbabel and Nehemiah were from Judah; and one day, from Judah would come the Messiah himself.[45]

That makes it clear why this pericope serves as the chapter of transformation of Judah (and indirectly, through his influence, of his brothers, as well). See Cassuto, "The Story of Tamar and Judah," 34–38.

44. Wenham, *Genesis 16–50*, 364.

45. The symbol of Judah, the lion, represents most Jews today, at least symbolically (see 49:9); the municipal emblem of Jerusalem has a rampant lion on its coat of arms.

Possible Preaching Outlines for Pericope 29

I.   Conceit of Judah
      Prospective: Judah's future as an agent of blessing within family, within nation (and ultimately, to the world)
      Judah's selfish enterprises: exogamy, unconcern for Tamar and his own responsibility (38:1–11)
      Move-to-Relevance: Our tendency to be selfish

II. Confession of Judah
      Judah's incontinence (38:12–23)
      Judah's exposure and confession (38:24–30)
      Move-to-Relevance: Our tendencies to downplay our own sin

III. Character of the Agent of Divine Blessing: *Be humane and humble!*
      How to develop the selfless character of one who is humane and humble

If one were to relegate the future of Judah to the consequences of his transformation, saving it as a later move in the sermon, one might employ a slightly different outline:

I.   Conceit of Judah
      Judah's selfish enterprises: exogamy, unconcern for Tamar and his own responsibility (38:1–11)
      Move-to-Relevance: Our tendency to be selfish

II. Confession of Judah
      Judah's incontinence (38:12–23)
      Judah's exposure and confession (38:24–30)
      Move-to-Relevance: Our tendencies to downplay our own sin

II. Consequences of Judah's Transformation
      Judah's future as an agent of blessing within family (43:11–14; 44:18–45:1)
      Judah's future as an agent of blessing to nation (38:27–30; 49:8–12; tribe of Judah the source of Israel's leaders)
      Judah's future as an agent of blessing to the world (38:27–30; tribe of Judah the font of the Messiah)

III. Character of the Agent of Divine Blessing: *Be humane and humble!*
      How to develop the selfless character of one who is humane and humble

PERICOPE 30

Joseph's Integrity

Genesis 39:1–23

[Joseph's Integrity Blessed]

REVIEW, SUMMARY, PREVIEW

Review of Pericope 29: Genesis 38:1–30 deals with a significant episode in the life of Judah. His two older sons' lives are taken by God for their evil acts; Tamar, his daughter-in-law, is not given Judah's third son in marriage, though she should have been. So she deceives Judah into sexual relations with her, and later, when she proves that he was the father of her twin children, Judah recognizes his own unrighteousness. Agents of divine blessing are to be characterized by concern for others and humility regarding their own weaknesses.

Summary of Pericope 30: This pericope tells the well-known story of Joseph's integrity in the face of temptation. What is striking is the powerful emphasis on divine presence and blessing in the life of Joseph, and in the lives of all around him; these assertions bracket the story of his unimpeachable probity, suggesting that Joseph's righteous character was the reason for his having found divine favor.

Preview of Pericope 31: In Gen 40:1–41:57, Joseph interprets the dreams of two of his fellow-prisoners, and they that come to pass exactly as he predicted—one is restored as butler to the Pharaoh, the other is executed. But two more years pass, and Joseph languishes in jail, until Pharaoh himself has a dream. On the recommendation of the royal butler, Joseph interprets Pharaoh's dream with divine aid. He is then freed and

483

elevated to Prime Ministership of Egypt. Agents of God's blessing trust his working and wait for his blessings that come in his sovereign timing.

30 Genesis 39:1–23

THEOLOGICAL FOCUS OF PERICOPE 30

30 One's integrity enables one to be an agent of divine blessing to others, even in one's dire circumstances (39:1–23).

30.1 God can use his people as agents of blessing even in their dire circumstances.

30.2 One's integrity enables one to be an agent of divine blessing to others.

OVERVIEW

Genesis 37:36 makes a seamless connection with 39:1; in 37:36, Joseph is sold (and Egypt is mentioned), and in 39:1, he is bought (and Egypt is mentioned again). Joseph's arrival in this new land is the beginning of the next phase of the fulfillment of Yahweh's promise to Abraham in 15:13–14. This great-grandson of Abraham would be the instrument of Abraham's descendants becoming "strangers in a land that is not theirs." The promise that this family would become a great nation (12:2) is also beginning to be realized. In a little more than a decade, the kidnapped slave, Joseph, would rise to be the Prime Minister of all Egypt, second only to the Pharaoh—divine sovereignty in action. And, in keeping with God's word to make the descendants of Abraham a blessing to all nations (12:3; 18:18; 22:18; 26:4; 28:14), Joseph becomes the primary agent of this disbursement of blessings divine—to the household to which he is attached, to the adopted land that has taken him in, to his family that reconciles with him, and to "all the earth" that comes to Egypt for sustenance in famine (41:57)—and it all begins here in Gen 39. But it is not only in Joseph's exaltation that Yahweh's presence is felt; deity is almost tangible in this pericope, even in the depths of Joseph's humiliation as a slave and a prisoner, as God blesses, prospers, makes successful, extends lovingkindness, and grants favor to the patriarch. The structuring of the account makes it clear why divine presence and prospering accompanies Joseph wherever he goes (A, A' below); with its centerpiece the purity of Joseph (B, C, B'), the pericope emphasizes the necessary character of integrity of the one who would be used by God to bless others.

A Joseph prospers in slavery (39:1–6a):
Yahweh's presence; superior's trust/favor; Joseph's prospering
   B Attempted seduction of Joseph (39:6b–7): "lie with me" (39:7)
      C Joseph's integrity (39:8–12): "lie with me" (39:12)
   B' Accusation of Joseph (39:13–19): "lie with me" (39:14)
A' Joseph prospers in prison (39:20–23):
Yahweh's presence; superior's trust/favor; Joseph's prospering

Divine sovereignty undergirds the entire Joseph Story from Gen 37–50—"God's hidden and decisive power which works in and through but also against human forms of power. A 'soft' word for that reality is *providence*. A harder word for the same reality is *predestination*. Either way—providence or predestination—the theme is that God is working out his purpose through and in spite of Egypt, through and in spite of Joseph and his brothers."[1] This motif, already on display in Gen 37 and 38, is even more clearly exhibited in Gen 39.[2]

In another sense, however, even as a sovereign God's promises are coming true, in the long-term, this movement of Joseph (and later, of his family) to Egypt is a detour that takes the chosen nation *away* from the Promised Land. Perhaps that is why God, later, had to speak to Jacob, explicitly encouraging him to move to Egypt, lock, stock, and barrel (45:3–4). And that turns out to be the only time God speaks in the Joseph Story. Towards the end of these narratives, there is a hint that a return to the Promised Land is not only expected by the patriarchs, but that it will actually take place: Jacob's remains are transported there (49:29–30), and Joseph makes his family promise to move his bones there as well (50:25).[3] Thus Egypt becomes the temporary halt for the Israelites, an incubator or nursery if you will, as they are protected during a crisis, and as their numbers expand: God's promises are beginning to be fulfilled.

30   Genesis 39:1–23

> **THEOLOGICAL FOCUS 30**[A]
>
> 30   One's integrity enables one to be an agent of divine blessing to others, even in one's dire circumstances.
>
> 30.1   *God can use his people as agents of blessing even in their dire circumstances.*
>
> 30.2   *One's integrity enables one to be an agent of divine blessing to others.*

A. Having only one section in this pericope, the "Theological Focus 30" is identical to the "Theological Focus of Pericope 30."

NOTES 30

30.1   God can use his people as agents of blessing even in their dire circumstances.

Of the three "symbolic descents" that are preludes to Joseph's ascension to the highest office in the land, two are found in Gen 39. The first was his descent into a pit (37:24–25), the second into slavery (37:36; 39:1), and the third into prison (39:20) where he remains for two years (41:1).[4] Thus Gen 39 commences the darkest period in Joseph's

1. Brueggemann, *Genesis*, 293.

2. As was noted in the previous pericope, connections between Gen 38 and 39 are obvious: both begin with the protagonist "going down" (38:1; 39:1 [×2]); and the word "hand" occurs frequently in both (38:18, 20 [×2], 28 [×2], 29, 30; and 39:1, 3, 4, 6, 8, 12, 13, 22, 23). As in Gen 38, this pericope also has at its core the story of the sexual temptation of a son of Jacob by a married, foreign woman; in the previous pericope, the tempted one falls; in this one, his integrity is maintained.

3. Wenham, *Genesis 16–50*, 358.

4. Joseph was seventeen when he was kidnapped (37:2), and thirty when he entered Pharaoh's

life: he is kidnapped and sold into slavery, and he is falsely accused of rape and cast into prison where he languishes. Nevertheless, quite unexpectedly, this pericope opens and closes with affirmations of Yahweh's presence and the prosperity with which he has blessed Joseph and all those around Joseph, particularly Potiphar and his household, and the jailer and his jail.[5]

> **A** Joseph in slavery: Joseph placed in charge;
> Yahweh's presence and prosperity (39:1–6a)
> **B** Joseph's temptation and his escape with his integrity intact (39:6b–19)
> **A'** Joseph in prison: Joseph placed in charge;
> Yahweh's presence and prosperity (39:20–23)

The parallels between the sections *A* and *A'* are striking (also see below for parallels between the sections "Joseph in Slavery" and "Joseph in Prison"). Also remarkable is that elsewhere, "Yahweh" occurs only in Gen 39 in the portions of the Joseph Story that deal explicitly with Joseph (Yahweh also shows up in 38:7 [×2], 10; and in 49:18). And strikingly, these instances of "Yahweh" are clustered in the narrative describing Joseph's time in slavery (*A*, 39:1–6 [×5]), and that detailing his life in prison (*A'*, 39:20–23 [×3]). No doubt, the presence of Yahweh is linked to all the good things happening to Joseph and those in his bleak environs. No doubt, God can use his people as agents of blessing even in their dark days, in their direst circumstances.

Divine presence with Joseph (39:2, 3, 21, 23) continues a pattern established with antecedent patriarchs (26:3, 24, 28; 28:15, 20; 31:3; and perhaps 17:3 for Abraham). "[T]he name Yahweh occurs here at what is the most uncertain moment in the life of Joseph. His future hangs in the balance. He is alone in Egypt, separated from family, vulnerable, with a cloud over his future. Or is he alone? Only the narrator, never any of the characters, uses the name Yahweh. Thus, it is the narrator who tells us . . . that in a very precarious situation, Joseph is not really alone. Yahweh is with him."[6]

Interestingly, Potiphar is labeled "master" (אָדוֹן, *'adon*, 39:2, 3, 7, 8, 16, 19, 20). If "Yawheh" was vocalized as אֲדֹנָי, *'adonay*, then the wordplay between "master" and "Lord [i.e., Yahweh]" would interlace God and Potiphar, particularly in the slavery and prison sections (39:1–6a and 39:20–23), suggesting "God's interwovenness with Joseph's daily life and fate, even when things apparently go wrong."[7] The similarities between those two sections, slavery and prison, are listed below.

---

service (41:46). This means he was in Potiphar's household as a slave and then in jail as a prisoner for thirteen years. That includes the two years he continued to be incarcerated after he had interpreted his fellow-inmates' dreams.

5. Potiphar, in its full form, Potiphera, is likely to be theophoric: "he whom Re [the sun-god] has given." "Potiphera" is also the name of Joseph's future father-in-law (41:45; 46:20); the LXX has Πετεφρης, *Petephrēs*, for both.

6. Hamilton, *Genesis: Chapters 18–50*, 459.

7. Brodie, *Genesis as Dialogue*, 367–68. Also see 24:12, 14, 27, 35–49, for a similar wordplay.

Joseph in Slavery (Genesis 39:1–6a)	Joseph in Prison (Genesis 39:20–23)
Yahweh's blessing (39:5)	Yahweh's lovingkindness (39:21)
Potiphar buys Joseph (39:1)	Potiphar takes and jails Joseph (39:20)
Yahweh's presence with Joseph:	Yahweh's presence with Joseph:
"… and Yahweh was with Joseph" (39:2)	"… and Yahweh was with Joseph" (39:21)
"Yahweh was with him" (39:3a)	"Yahweh was with him" (39:23a)
"captain" (שַׂר, *sr*, 39:1)	"chief" (שַׂר, 39:21, 22, 23)
"succeed/prosper" (39:2, 3)	"succeed/prosper" (39:23)
"Yahweh prospered	"Yahweh prospered
everything he did" (39:3b)	everything he did" (39:23b)
"he was in the house" (39:2)	"he was … in the house of roundness"
	(= jail; 39:20)
"house" (39:2, 4, 5)	"house" (39:20, 21, 22, 23)
Joseph's "hand" (39:3, 4, 6)	Joseph's "hand" (39:22, 23)
"all" (39:3, 4, 5 [×2], 6)	"all" (39:22 [×2], 23)
"give" (39:4, 8)	"give/put" (39:20, 21, 22)
"all that he did" (39:3)	"all that he did" (39:22);
	"all that was done" (39:23)
"Yahweh" (39:2, 3 [×2], 5 [×2])	"Yahweh" (39:21, 23 [×2])
"favor in his [Potiphar's] sight" (39:4)	"favor in the sight of the chief jailer" (39:21)
Oversight over "house"	Oversight over prisoners in the "house,"
and possessions (39:4, 5, 6)	and activities (39:23)
Joseph put "in charge" (39:4)	Joseph put "in charge" (40:4)
Master's unconcern about "anything" (39:6)	Jailer's unconcern about "anything" (39:23)

While we are not told how exactly Yahweh's blessing was manifest in the slavery section (39:5; blessing in Genesis frequently indicates wealth: 24:35; 26:12; 30:27, 30), it is clear that Joseph's master was impressed with his good fortune, a fact repeatedly mentioned in 39:2–6. This might well have been a foreshadowing of Joseph's future status as second in command to Pharaoh, and the efficient aid he rendered in amassing wealth for that ruler (41:40, 49; 47:15–26).[8] The use of participles to describe Joseph's success (39:2, 3, 23) and his prosperous touch (39:3, 22, 23) indicates that these blessings were typical, an ongoing pattern of prosperity, the result of Yahweh's hand upon Joseph, as explicitly noted in 39:5. Even the timing of the blessing coincides with the ascent of Joseph ("It happened from the time he made him overseer . . ., Yahweh blessed . . .; 39:5). Moreover, the scope of divine blessing is also vast, "upon all that he [Potiphar] had, in the house and in the field" (39:5).

> The whole sequence of 39:2–6 is a particularly apt and clear example of the meaning of blessing in the Old Testament. . . . Blessing embraces both people and the rest of creation. The narrator simply presupposes that the blessing can flow over from the one whom Yahweh assists to a foreign people and adherents of a foreign religion precisely because of the one whom Yahweh assists. The power inherent in the blessing is expansive; the God of the fathers is further at work in Joseph's experience of servitude in a foreign land.[9]

Thus we have in Joseph, an agent of God's blessing to others—*while in slavery*—and the beginning of the fulfillment of the Abrahamic covenant (12:3). However, while "blessing" is explicitly noted in the slavery section (39:5, "blessing" as both verb and

---

8. Mathews, *Genesis 11:27–50:26*, 732.

9. Westermann, *Genesis 37–50*, 63.

noun), Yahweh's blessing is not paralleled in the prison section. Instead, in this latter half of the pericope we have the notation of Yahweh's "lovingkindness" (חסד, *khsd*, 38:21) upon Joseph. All things considered, particularly with the parallels noted above between the slavery and prison sections, it is incontrovertible that Yahweh's blessing in the former section is being equated to the extension of his lovingkindness in the latter one. God was certainly blessing the jailer and the jail inmates and their activities (39:23), not to mention Joseph himself, blessed with success and prosperity in all that his hand undertook (39:23). The numerous instances of "all" in both sections (39:3, 4, 5 [×2], 6, 8, and 39:22 [×2], 23) indicate the magnitude and comprehensiveness of God's blessing upon Joseph no matter where he was.

While Joseph's entry into Egypt was a "descent," a "going down" (39:1 [×2]), subsequent events, in slavery and in prison, seem to be a series of "ascents." Even within the first section (39:1–6b), there appears to be a discernible upturn in Joseph's status. His master owned house and field (39:5), but after the affirmation of Yahweh's presence with Joseph, and his divinely ordained success, "he [Joseph] was in the *house* of his Egyptian master" (39:2)—perhaps a promotion from working in the field. The trifold employment of וַיְהִי, *wayhi*, in 39:2—"and Yahweh was . . .," "and he [Joseph] was . . .," "and he [Joseph] was . . ."—leads one to guess that the first actant (Yahweh) was responsible for the station of the other (Joseph). Then we have the reiteration of divine presence and Joseph's prosperity (39:3), following which another rise in Joseph's status is noted: he now becomes Potiphar's personal servant and overseer of household and chattel (39:4): שָׁרַת, *sharat*, "to serve/attend," indicates personal service, not the menial tasks of slaves (for such relationships between a superior and his inferior, see Joshua–Moses, Exod 24:13; Josh 1:1; Elijah–Elisha, 1 Kgs 19:21; Amnon–servants, 2 Sam 13:17).[10] Subsequently, yet another reaction from Yahweh is described—the Egyptian's house and all he owned is blessed (39:5); and this, in turn, results in one more corresponding elevation for the enslaved son of Jacob: Potiphar leaves everything he owned in Joseph's charge without concerning himself about anything, except his food (39:6).[11] A gradual escalation is visible, clearly the result of Yahweh's explicit and implicit blessing upon the young man.

10. Wenham, *Genesis 16–50*, 374.

11. It seems odd that Potiphar's nutrition was excepted from Joseph's charge (39:6). The parallel with 39:9 suggests that "food" may be alluding to the master's sexual needs and the source of that fulfillment—his wife (so *Gen. Rab.* 86.6; and Rashi, *Chumash*, 191—"this means his wife, but Scripture uses here a euphemism"; also see Prov 30:20). This idea is furthered in the use of "know" in the same context: "He *gives no thought* [literally, "know," ידע, *yd'*] about anything" (39:6 and repeated in 39:8)—ידע is a common biblical euphemism for sexual relations.

Yahweh's presence; Joseph's success (39:2a) →
Joseph "in the house" (39:2b)

Yahweh's presence; Joseph's actions prosper (39:3) →
Joseph becomes Potiphar's personal servant
and overseer over house and chattel (39:4)

Yahweh blesses Egyptian's house and chattel "on account of Joseph" (39:5) →
Joseph in complete charge of everything
Potiphar owned (39:6a)

Causality demonstrated by narrative structure suggests that the two strikingly parallel outer sections (39:1–6a and 39:20–23) are explained by the inner section. In other words, the reason for the rather amazing prosperity and success of Joseph (and for Yahweh's blessing and lovingkindness resting upon Joseph) in the outer sections, is to be found in the inner section. And in the outer sections, it is made plain that God uses his people as agents of his blessing even in their dire circumstances.

30.2 *One's integrity enables one to be an agent of divine blessing to others.*

The section in the middle details the temptation of Joseph and his successful eluding thereof (39:6b–19). Literary elements here, too, resonate with the other sections. Joseph rehearses the blessed situation of 39:1–6a in 39:8, employing words that showed up earlier: "did not know about [concern himself with] anything" (39:5, 8); "all that he owned . . . in hand [in charge]" (39:4, 8); the utilization of "house" (39:4, 5, 8, 9, 11, 14, 16, 20, 21, 22, 23) and "all" (39:3, 4, 5 [×2], 6, 8, 22 [×2], 23). The motif of "hand" reappears here as well: while everything in the master's house was left in Joseph's "hand" (i.e., in Joseph's charge; 39:4; also see 39:22)—except for Potiphar's wife (39:9)—he leaves his garment in the "hand" of his seducer (39:12, 13). The first "hand" and what was left in it bespoke Potiphar's confidence in Joseph (the result of divine blessing); the second "hand" and what was left in it reflected Joseph's loyalty to Potiphar (the result of Joseph's adherence to a divine standard). "Eye" shows up in 39:4, 21—Joseph finding favor in the sight of his master and his jailer; but in 39:7, it is Potiphar's wife who lifts her eyes towards Joseph: obviously he had found favor in *her* eyes, too!

A prominent motif in this middle section is Joseph's garment (בֶּגֶד, *beged*, 39:12 [×2], 13, 15, 16, 18). Sarna, noting that בָּגַד, *bagad*, indicates the unfaithfulness of adultery (Jer 3:8, 11, 20; Mal 2:10, 11, 14, 15, 16), sees the reiteration of בֶּגֶד as an emphasis on the infidelity that was being proposed in this episode.[12] What Potiphar's wife produced as evidence of attempted rape—a garment—was really corroboration of her own unfaithfulness to her husband. On this theme, there are a number of terms suggestive of sexual activity in 39:6b–19: "to lie" (39:7, 10, 12, 14), "to enter/go in" (39:11, 14, 16, 17 [×2]), not to mention "hand" which, in the current context, may be a euphemism for the male member (39:8, 12; see Isa 57:8).[13]

---

12. *Genesis*, 274.

13. Mathews, *Genesis 11:27–50:26*, 730. Ludwig Koehler and Walter Baumgartner, "יָד," *HALOT* 2:387. Also see Delcor, "Two Special Meanings," 234–40.

The sordid episode begins with an ominous statement about Joseph's physical attributes (Gen 39:6b). Incidentally, in the OT, only two people are given the compliment of being possessors of a beautiful form and face—Joseph and his mother, Rachel (29:17 and 39:6 have identical terms). Ambrose said: [A]lthough he was comely to look upon and very handsome in appearance, he did not direct the charm of his countenance toward another's wrongdoing but kept it to win grace for himself. He thought that he would be the more attractive, if he were proved more handsome not by the loss of his chastity but by the cultivation of modesty" (*On Joseph* 5.22). In any case, Potiphar's wife decided that this good-looking Hebrew slave was fair game. Alter observes that the first instance of dialogue in the entire pericope is the proposition for sex from Potiphar's wife: "Lie with me" (39:7):

> [T]he naked directness, without preliminaries or explanations, of the wife's sexual proposition, [is] presented almost as though these two words (in the Hebrew [39:7, and repeated in 39:12]) were all she ever spoke to Joseph, day after day (verse 10), until finally the plain meaning of the words is translated into the physical act of grabbing the man (verse 12). By contrast, Joseph's refusal (verses 8–9) is a voluble outpouring of language, full of repetitions which are both dramatically appropriate—as a loyal servant, he is emphatically protesting the moral scandal of the deed proposed—and thematically pointed.[14]

The account depicts her raw lust, brusquely expressed, versus his moral shock, pleadingly verbose: her "lie with me" (39:7, 12) sandwiches his expanded rebuff (39:8–9). As noted, from 39:10, the reader gets the impression that what is described in 39:7–10 was an ongoing attempt by Potiphar's wife to seduce Joseph ("day after day"), no doubt an incredibly tense and pressure-filled situation for a 17-year-old male. One cannot underestimate the potential for upward mobility that such a sexual alliance could have meant for this slave. Surely some sexual favors granted to his master's wife would propel him along to a better station in life. But Joseph, the paragon of virtue, is steadfast in his resistance. Wisely, he does not listen to her (to lie with her) and even refuses to be in her presence (39:10; 2 Tim 2:22). As he replies to the woman's advances, rather than using a pronoun to refer to the seductress, the narrator emphasizes: "And he said to *his master's wife* . . ." (Gen 39:8). That one was not Joseph's to take: he was not going to steal, neither was he going to abandon godliness. Joseph's rejoinder to the indecent proposal of Potiphar's wife "implies that there was a standard of righteousness demanded by the God of his fathers (e.g., 15:6; 17:1; 20:6, 9; 26:10; 44:16; 50:17)." Later in the Mosaic Law, adultery was strictly condemned and punishable by death (Exod 20:14; Lev 20:10).[15] Hamilton observes the irony: With God's help, Joseph succeeds in all he is "doing" (from עשׂה, '*sh*, Gen 39:3); but some things Joseph just refuses to "do" (עשׂה, 39:9: "How then can I *do* . . .?").[16] Yes, divine sovereignty operates in the blessing

---

14. *The Art of Biblical Narrative*, 108–9. "The brevity of the sexual proposition on the part of Potiphar's wife is a brilliant stylization . . . of the naked lust that impels her, and perhaps also of the peremptory tone she feels she can assume toward her Hebrew slave" (ibid., 73).

15. Mathews, *Genesis 11:27–50:26*, 726.

16. *Genesis: Chapters 18–50*, 463.

of one's life, but there are facets of human responsibility that need to be discharged in order to keep oneself in the blessing of God (see Jude 21, for instance).[17]

The reasons for Joseph's repudiation of his mistress's advances are grounded upon the relationship between himself and his master (39:8–9a), and between himself and his God (39:9b): succumbing would be a transgression against both man and God. The fact that Joseph is extensively used by God as an instrument of his blessing to others, goes to show that in order to be such an agent, one's integrity must be guarded to the utmost, in submission to divine will, not just in sexual purity, but in every facet of life. The structuring of the pericope seems to be making this point by having the two blessing sections (in slavery, 39:1–6a; and in prison, 39:20–23) bookend the middle section that glows with the brilliance of Joseph's uprightness (39:6b–19).

Potiphar's wife, though, does not make much of Joseph's protestations. She grabs him, and he flees.[18] Reinforcing the integrity of Joseph are the many iterations of "he left [his garment] and he fled" (39:12, 13, 15, 18). Thus, for the second time, Joseph is stripped of his clothing (39:12), a recurring theme in the Joseph narrative: in fact, as will be developed more fully in Pericope 31 (40:1–41:57), this donning–divesting motif reflects Joseph's "descent" and, subsequently, his "ascent" to the highest office in the land.[19]

A	Joseph clothed in a special tunic by his father (37:3)	
	B	Stripped of his clothing by his brothers; clothing used as evidence (37:23)
A¹	Joseph clothed in a garment in Potiphar's house (implied in 39:1, 4, 12)	
	B¹	Stripped of his garment by Potiphar's wife; clothing used as evidence (39:12, 13)

The shrewd predator of a woman immediately turns a disadvantageous situation to her benefit: employing the first person plural in her initial complaint, she incorporates the entire household as being collectively victimized by Joseph (". . . to make sport of *us*," 39:14)[20]; she reverses the order of events (the narrator's he left–he fled–she shouted [39:13–14] becomes her "I shouted–he left–he fled" [39:15, 18])[21]; she labels Joseph pejoratively as a "Hebrew," apparently to elicit some ethnic prejudice (39:14, 17)[22]; and she blames her husband for having introduced him into the house (39:14, 17; an echo of Adam blaming God for Eve, 3:12). All her blatant untruths are emphasized even more by another subtle twist in wording: instead of saying, as the narrator does, that "he left his garment *in her hand* and fled and went outside" (39:12), she asserts that

---

17. See Kuruvilla, *Privilege the Text!* 252–58, for the concept of divine blessing for obedience.

18. "Grab" (תפס, *tfs*, 39:12) describes an act of some violence, frequently that engaged in during wartime (Deut 9:17; 20:19; 21:19; 22:8; Josh 8:8, 23; etc.), and "flee" (נוס, *nus*, Gen 39:12, 13, 15, 18), likewise, depicts escape from a dire situation, often after a military defeat (14:10; 19:10; Exod 14:25; Lev 26:17, 36; Num 10:34; etc.).

19. Table from Nwaoru, "Change of Garment," 8. The same word for "garment" (בגד) is used in 37:29 and 39:12, 13, 15, 16, 18; indeed, the garment motif is also employed in Gen 38:14, 19—also a donning and divesting, here by Tamar.

20. Later, in her report to her husband, Joseph is "making sport of *me*" (39:17).

21. Her screaming, she guessed, would exonerate her (Deut 22:24–27).

22. Cleverly, to the other "men of the household," she labels Joseph as a Hebrew *man* (39:14); later, to her husband, Joseph is a Hebrew *slave* (39:17).

"he left his garment *beside me* and fled and went outside" (39:15, 18). That, of course, insinuates that Joseph's disrobing was voluntary, in effect making the entire episode an attempted rape of the woman.[23] All of this, declares Sternberg, "offers a signal lesson in applied rhetoric," applied by the woman that is, to her audience! And, as Hamilton observes wryly, her "[p]assion will be replaced by prevarication."[24]

Her lament to her husband, "This is what your slave did to me" (39:19), which on the surface sounds rather redundant, is actually quite exacting in the explanation of Potiphar's explosive anger: the verse describes what *he* heard. "[I]t is not the racial pressure that has done the trick (or else the text would read 'thy Hebrew slave'); nor has the social agitation (for the text fails to repeat the woman's simple definite article, '*the* slave' [39:17]). What above all infuriated Potiphar is the thought that the offender is *his* special slave, who has betrayed the position of trust to which he has been raised."[25] The irony and pathos of this reaction on the part of Potiphar is that it was precisely because Joseph *refused* to betray his high position of trust in his master's service that all this transpired against his favor (39:9).

The upshot is that Joseph ends up in prison (literally, "the round house," 39:20, 21, 22, 23). The jailing of Joseph is an unexpected punishment for, according to the Mosaic Law, execution was the rule for convicted rapists who were free citizens (Deut 22:23–27); surely a foreign slave would incur no less harsh a sentence. Wenham speculates that there may have been an unrecorded protestation of innocence on the part of Joseph that convinced Potiphar to lighten the penalty.[26] In any case, it was the sovereign hand of God that saved the life of the young man to work out his divine purpose.[27]

Joseph's prison phase begins the same way his slavery phase did, with a statement of Yahweh's presence with him (39:21), implying "quite real protection and promotion in the matters of his external life, not, to be sure, protection from distress, but rather in the midst of distress."[28] Though Potiphar had "put" (נתן, *ntn*, 39:20) Joseph in jail, Yahweh "grants" (נתן, 39:21) Joseph favor in the eyes of the jailer and, as a result, all the prisoners in the jail were "placed" (נתן, 39:22) in Joseph's charge. God is at work again! Once more we are reminded that "[t]he human figures in the large biblical landscape act as free agents out of the impulses of a memorable and often fiercely assertive individuality, but the actions they perform all ultimately fall into the symmetries and recurrences of God's comprehensive design."[29] And perhaps what is more important:

---

23. Alter, *The Art of Biblical Narrative*, 109–10.

24. Sternberg, *The Poetics of Biblical Narrative*, 426; Hamilton, *Genesis: Chapters 18–50*, 467.

25. Sternberg, *The Poetics of Biblical Narrative*, 427.

26. *Genesis 16–50*, 377. Later we are told, in 42:21, that Joseph cried to his brothers for mercy from the pit; perhaps he did so to Potiphar, too.

27. "The narrator has thus so arranged the action and setting as to bring Joseph, here at the nadir of his life, into contact with persons from the apex of Egyptian society" (White, *Narration and Discourse*, 256). I would aver that it was not the narrator, but God, who arranged matters so precisely and coincidentally.

28. Von Rad, *Genesis*, 362.

29. Alter, *The Art of Biblical Narrative*, 112–13. This sentiment is unambiguously echoed in Ps 105:17–22.

the integrity of God's people facilitates their becoming agents of divine blessing to others.[30]

As was noted, explicit blessing from Yahweh is absent from this section (unlike in the slavery phase, 39:5); however, here we have a depiction of Yahweh's lovingkindness (חסד, *khsd*, 39:21). Is this yet another ascent? Perhaps, for the blessing in the earlier section was for Potiphar's house and all that he owned, not directly upon Joseph. Here, however, the חסד of Yahweh is extended directly to him (the only such expression in the OT). Moreover, one also notices that unlike the exception to what was placed in Joseph's charge in Potiphar's house (i.e., his food, 39:6), here Joseph has comprehensive control over "whatever was done there" (39:22). A greater degree of blessing may be intended here, perhaps the direct consequence or even reward for Joseph's integrity. Such a take on the pericope would resemble the trajectory of Pericope 13 (Gen 22), where Abraham, though he had received promises of blessing earlier, becomes the beneficiary of blessing intensification after the harrowing test of the *aqedah*. "Ironically, imprisonment involves a form of promotion, greater responsibility. It also brings Joseph closer to the king, at least insofar as he is among the king's prisoners. At one level, therefore, chapter 39 portrays a descent, down to Egypt, and further down into prison. At another level, it involves positive development, greater closeness to God and greater responsibility on behalf of humans."[31] God is sovereignly and inscrutably working!

SERMON FOCUS AND OUTLINES

THEOLOGICAL FOCUS OF PERICOPE 28 FOR PREACHING

30   Integrity in every situation enables one to be an agent of divine blessing (39:1–23).

This sermon, rightly, should emphasize the integrity of God's people—agents of his blessing to a lost world. And rightly, perhaps sexual purity should be the focus, considering how much sexuality, one of the most powerful forces in human nature, is the cause of untold human suffering directly or indirectly. The amount of abuse stemming from sex makes it imperative that "each of you know how to possess his own body in holiness and honor" (1 Thess 4:4). Indeed, *Midr. Ps.* 114:9 declares that the Red Sea had parted because of the bones of Joseph borne by the Israelites departing Egypt. "The sea beheld Joseph's coffin coming down into the water. The Holy One, blessed be He, said: 'Let the sea flee from him who fled from transgression, he of whom it is said, "He . . . fled forth"' (Gen 39:13). And so the sea fled before Joseph, as it is said: 'The sea saw it, and fled.'"

---

30. Joseph's continued faithfulness to God in Egypt is expressed in later statements as well: 41:32, 38–39 (this from Pharaoh's mouth!); 42:18; 45:5–9; 50:19–20.

31. Brodie, *Genesis as Dialogue*, 368–69. But, it must be remembered that, while some immediate blessings are detected (39:20–23), the consequence of Joseph's probity was incarceration, and that for two years (41:1). Integrity of character and uprightness of behavior need not guarantee immediate rewards, or the removal of tribulation.

Yet, the sermon must not simply be a screed on sexual immorality. While there are many reasons for maintaining probity in the arena of sexuality, the thrust of the pericope (and that of the Joseph Story as a whole) must not be played down: how to become an agent of God's blessing to others. In other words, this pericope stresses the importance of integrity in all matters (including, and perhaps, especially, sexual matters) so that God's people may serve as obstruction-free conduits for the outpouring of his blessings on the world around them.

Possible Preaching Outlines for Pericope 30

I. WHAT? Prosperity through Joseph
    The blessings to/through Joseph in slavery (39:1–6a)
    The blessings to/through Joseph in prison (39:20–23)
    Move-to-Relevance: Our desire to be agents of blessing to the world around us

II. WHY? Probity of Joseph
    Joseph's probity in sexual temptation (39:6b–19)
    Move-to-Relevance: Our temptations (sexual or otherwise) and God's will that we remain pure

III. HOW? *Be pure!*
    How to be pure and thus be a blessing to the world

The outline above follows a fairly standard What?–Why?–How? schema. By addressing the prison section separately, as an indication of blessing that is more intensified than in Joseph's slavery section, one might create an outline that looks like this:

I. Commendation: Prosperity through Joseph in Enslavement
    The blessings to/through Joseph in slavery (39:1–6a)
    Move-to-Relevance: Our desire to be agents of blessing to the world around us

II. Conscientiousness: Probity of Joseph in Allurement
    Joseph's probity in sexual temptation (39:6b–19)
    Move-to-Relevance: Our temptations (sexual or otherwise) and God's will that we remain pure

II. Consequence: Prosperity through Joseph in Imprisonment
    The blessings to/through Joseph in prison (39:20–23)
    Move-to-Relevance: God's blessings and his favor upon us as we remain pure for him

III. Conduct: *Be pure and be a blessing!*
    How to be pure and thus be a blessing to the world

PERICOPE 31

Joseph Interprets Dreams

Genesis 40:1–41:57

[Dreams of Prisoners and of Pharaoh Interpreted; Joseph Exalted]

REVIEW, SUMMARY, PREVIEW

Review of Pericope 30: Genesis 39:1–23 tells the well-known story of Joseph's integrity in the face of temptation. The emphasis is on divine presence and blessing upon the life of Joseph (and upon those around him), suggesting that his integrity was the reason for his having found divine favor.

Summary of Pericope 31: Here, an episode during Joseph's years of imprisonment is recounted: he interprets the dreams of two of his fellow-prisoners and they come to pass exactly as he predicted—one is restored as butler to the Pharaoh, the other is executed. But then two more years pass, with Joseph languishing in jail, until Pharaoh himself has a dream that Joseph, on the recommendation of the royal butler, interprets with divine aid. Joseph is released, appointed to Prime Ministership, marries, and has children—a striking elevation from prison. Agents of God's blessing trust his working and wait; God's blessings come in his sovereign timing.

Preview of Pericope 32: The next pericope (Gen 42:1–43:34) deals with trips of the brothers to Egypt. There, as a result of Joseph's strategies to test them, they are convicted of their guilt in the kidnapping and enslavement of Joseph. On their second trip to Egypt, Judah, in a declaration of selflessness, persuades Jacob to allow Benjamin to go with them, as

495

Joseph had required. God's discipline of his people, and their submission to him, enable the flow of divine blessings.

31   Genesis 40:1–41:57

> **THEOLOGICAL FOCUS OF PERICOPE 31**
>
> **31   God's agents of blessing trust his working even when it is indiscernible, resulting in abundant divine blessing upon them (40:1–41:57).**
>
> 31.1   God's agents of blessings trust his workings even when they are indiscernible, and even in dire circumstances.
>
> 31.2   The blessing of God is abundantly upon the faithful agent of his blessing to others.

OVERVIEW

Joseph was thirty years old when he entered the service of Pharaoh (41:46). Taking into account the two years in prison (41:1) just prior to his elevation in Pharaoh's court, the events of Gen 40, when this pericope commences, must have occurred when he was twenty-eight.

Obvious connections exist between this pericope and the previous one. Some of the notations from the two blessing sections (in slavery and in prison) are echoed here: "jail" ("house of roundness," 39:20, 21, 22, 23 and 40:3, 5); "appoint as overseer" (39:4, 5 and 40:4; 41:34); "chief/captain" (39:1, 21, 22, 23 and 40:2, 3, 4, 9, 16, 20, 21, 22, 23; 41:9, 10, 12); "bodyguard" (39:1 and 40:3, 4, 41:10, 12); "house of master" (39:2 and 40:7); "officer(s) of Pharaoh" (39:1 and 40:7); "serve/take care" (only in 39:4 and 40:4 in Genesis); and "master" (39:2, 3, 7, 8, 16, 19, 20 and 40:1, 7). Moreover, both Gen 39 and 40 deal with offenses against superiors (concocted, of course, in Gen 39): while Joseph was unwilling to "offend/sin" (חָטָא, *khata'*) against God, and presumably, against his master (39:9), the two officials admitted to doing so against their ruler (חָטְאוּ, 40:1; 41:9). The pair of dreams of Joseph's fellow prisoners (40:8–19) clearly reflects the pair Joseph had in 37:5–10, and foreshadows the pair Pharaoh will have (41:1–32); all are inscrutable to the dreamers themselves and, in the last two episodes, Joseph turns out to be the dream-interpreter, and his interpretations come true.[1] In 40:15, Joseph himself provides a summary of the events of Gen 37 and 39, recounting his kidnapping, slavery, and his imprisonment under false pretexts. But the providential incarceration of Pharaoh's high-ranking officers with Joseph is clear indication that "[t]he crimes of those around Joseph cannot thwart the purposes of God."[2] This pericope is a story of divinely ordained transformation, indeed an ascent with the aid of God, after the descents that have marked the life of Joseph thus far:

---

1. The two dreams of the prisoners and the two of the Pharaoh are, incidentally, separated by two years (41:1).

2. Arnold, *Genesis*, 339.

favored son → kidnap victim → slave → prisoner. However, soon he will be raised to the Prime Minstership of all Egypt!

Needless to say, the ascent into Pharaoh's bureaucracy is not an easy one. It is, in fact, one more test for this 28-year-old. While the forgetfulness of the butler is reprehensible, one realizes that had Joseph been released any earlier than two years later by the good offices of Pharaoh's officials, it is unlikely he would have been around to interpret Pharaoh's dreams in Gen 41. Chrysostom agrees: "As it was, however, the wise and creative Lord, who like a fine craftsman knew how long the gold should be kept in the fire and when it ought to be taken out, allowed forgetfulness to affect the chief cupbearer for a period of two years so that the moment of Pharaoh's dreams should arrive and that by force of circumstances the good man should become known to the whole of Pharaoh's kingdom" (*Hom. Gen.* 63.11–12).[3] And the consequence of God's working, primarily through Joseph in this saga, is divine blessing to everyone around this agent (41:55–57)—a theme not new to Genesis: 12:3; 14:19–20; 18:18; 22:18; 26:4–5; 28:14; 30:27, 30.

So while Joseph's story thus far, and in this pericope, appears to be a series of setbacks—kidnapping by his brothers, a false accusation by Potiphar's wife that throws him jail, and a negligent forgetfulness by his fellow-prisoner, the cupbearer/butler, that keeps him locked up for two years—each "downturn" is actually, in God's providence, a stepping stone, an "upturn." In fact, the deliberate withholding of "Yahweh" from this pericope, and the absence of any mention of God's express action, reflects the narrator's understanding of providence and the subtlety of God's workings, even through a Pharaoh of Egypt! Joseph is "put" (נתן, *ntn*, 39:4, 8, 20, 21, 22) in various places by human agents; in this pericope he is "put" (נתן, 41:41, 43) in charge "over all the land of Egypt" by the Pharaoh. This is quite an incredible shift of status: from confinement in the house of the chief of the bodyguard (40:3), to being second only to Pharaoh in all Egypt (41:40). It cannot be aught but the work of God. For God is always at work, even if one cannot see him working. Yet, as Sherman confesses:

> [G]iven Joseph's prominent role as the patriarchal heir to Jacob and the recipient of Jacob's final favorable blessing (Gen 49:26), Joseph is unique in having no direct contact with God. Adam, Noah, the patriarchs, Moses, Aaron, and Miriam all enjoy various permutations of being addressed by, dialoguing with, or receiving direct blessings from God. Joseph, however, never has a dialogue with God. He is never spoken to or [explicitly said to have been] blessed by God, nor is he ever portrayed as having prayed or spoken to God.[4]

But this in no way minimizes the presence of God or militates against his activity. In fact, the presence and actions of God are discernible throughout the Joseph saga, as summarized by the protagonist himself in 50:24. And even here, in Pericope 31, the *literary* absence of God is not a *literal* absence of God.

---

3. *ACCS* 2:262–63.
4. Sherman, "Do Not Interpretations Belong to God?" 46.

All of the four dreams in this pericope are linked, directly or indirectly, to food. The officials are in charge of Pharaoh's food and drink, and their respective dreams deal with the appropriate victual they handle. Pharaoh's dreams concern grazing, eating, swallowing, and devouring (41:2, 4, 7, 18, 20, 21, 24), interpreted as dealing with food supply and famine (41:29–31). And finally, Joseph, placed in his lofty station, will become the manager of Egypt's food supply for the conceivable future. Thus the narrative sets in place the circumstances that will bring Joseph's family to Egypt. Yes, God is working, surely, certainly, silently, inexorably. In this pericope, he is the one who gives Pharaoh his dreams (41:25, 28, 32), he provides the interpretation (41:16), and he gives Joseph favor in the eyes of Pharaoh (41:38–44). In response, Joseph acknowledges the workings of the divine as he names his children (41:51–52). This focus on the food and staples of life, and Joseph's divinely ordained placement in an office that disburses such alimentary essentials to those in need, emphasize the provision of God through Joseph—he is the agent of divine blessing to everyone around him.

31 Genesis 40:1–41:57

THEOLOGICAL FOCUS 31[A]

31   God's agents of blessing trust his working even when it is indiscernible, resulting in abundant divine blessing upon them.

31.1   *God's agents of blessings trust his workings even when they are indiscernible, and even in dire circumstances.*

31.2   *The blessing of God is abundantly upon the faithful agent of his blessing to others.*

A. Having only one section in this pericope, the "Theological Focus 31" is identical to the "Theological Focus of Pericope 31."

NOTES 31

31.1 God's agents of blessings trust his workings even when they are indiscernible, and even in dire circumstances.

The pericope begins with "Then it happened after these things," signifying the lapse of a considerable period of time (40:1). As was noted earlier, Joseph was around twenty-eight years of age when the events of this pericope transpired. He is incarcerated, rather fortuitously with a couple of important officials from Pharaoh's court, the ruler's butler/cupbearer and his baker, those who were in charge of the ruler's food— no doubt officials of considerable influence. In light of 37:36 and 39:1, it is quite likely that the "captain of the bodyguard" (40:3, 4; 41:10, 12) was Potiphar himself. Knowing Joseph's abilities (39:4–5), it may well be that Potiphar designated the Hebrew captive for this important task of overseeing and serving these significant prisoners, officers of the Pharaoh (40:4). In any case, their placement in "the same place where Joseph was prisoner" (40:3), denotes a providential occurrence.

Both the imprisoned officials dream dreams, "coincidentally" on the same night, and both are troubled by them (40:5).[5] The dreams of the butler and the baker (40:9–19) are similar, united by the number "three" (40:10, 16), the phrase "will lift up your head" (40:13, 19), and the obvious links in both cases to the occupations of the dreamers, relating to the food and drink of Pharaoh. The imagery in the dreams resonates with triplets: three branches (40:10); branches that budded, blossomed, and ripened (40:10); and three actions taken by the butler: taking grapes, squeezing grapes, putting wine (40:11; all in the first person singular, and without conjunctions—the structure is asyndetic). The staccato series of actions without conjunctions, hardly giving the grapes any time to ferment—"a surrealistic touch," conveying "a dream aura"—may be an indication of the imminence and/or the rapid turn of the events adumbrated.[6] In Joseph's interpretation of the butler's dream (and in the subsequent fulfillment), another set of events occur similarly, in brisk succession: Pharaoh's lifting up of the butler's head, restoring him to his old office, and the butler giving the cup to Pharaoh (40:13, 20–21). The following also occur in threes: "confinement" (40:3, 4, 7); the root זכר (*zkr*, "remember/remind," 40:14 [×2], 23); and "lifting of head" (40:13, 19, 20). Moreover, "Pharaoh" and "cup" each occurs thrice in 40:11; and "Pharaoh" three more times in Joseph's interpretation (40:13–14). All of these unusual patterns of wording and event, uncannily precise, point to a divine generation (and outcome) of these dreams. Interestingly enough, dream interpretation was never an Israelite praxis.

> Despite the fact that Israel shared with its pagan neighbors a belief in the reality of dreams as a medium of divine communication, it never developed, as in Egypt and Mesopotamia, a class of professional interpreters or a dream literature. In the entire Bible, only two Israelites engage in the interpretation of dreams—Joseph and Daniel—and significantly enough, each serves a pagan monarch, the one in Egypt, the other in Mesopotamia, precisely the lands in which oneiromancy flourished. Moreover, in each case, the Israelite is careful to disclaim any innate ability, attributing all to God.[7]

Mathews observes that the word group פ-ת-ר (*p–t–r*; פָּתַר, *patar*, "to interpret," and פִּתְרוֹן, *pittaron*, "interpretation") occur only in the Joseph narrative in the OT: the verb in 40:8, 16, 22; 41:8, 12 (×2), 13, 15 (×2), and the noun in 40:5, 8, 12, 18; 41:11.[8] Whereas for the imprisoned Egyptians (and later for the Pharaoh), experts in the field seemed to be essential for the interpretation of dreams, for Joseph the source of their meaning was God (40:8, and also in 41:8, 16). "The events of the future lay in Yahweh's hand only, and only the one to whom it was revealed was empowered to interpret."[9]

---

5. The appearance of the two prisoners on the morning after their dreams is described as "depressed/ sickly." In fact, Joseph asks them in 40:7 why their faces were "sad" (רַע, *ra*, also "evil").

6. Sherman, "Do Not Interpretations Belong to God?" 41. The baker's dream also had a triplet: three baskets (40:16). Yet in the baker's dream, Pharaoh does not appear, while in the butler's there are no elements that correspond to the birds of prey that show up in the baker's vision.

7. Sarna, *Understanding Genesis*, 218–19; also see Kass, *The Beginning of Wisdom*, 550n1.

8. *Genesis 11:27–50:26*, 746–47.

9. Von Rad, *Genesis*, 371.

The rhetorical question Joseph asks his fellow-prisoners is emphatic in its placement of "God" before "interpretations"—"Are not of *God* interpretations?" (40:8). "The theme of providence emerges in two ways in Joseph's life and in his own testimony. One is Joseph's ability to interpret the happenings in his life and in that of his family as illustrative of God's control and use of otherwise inscrutable events (45:5–8; 50:20). The second is Joseph's conviction about God's control every time he interprets a dream (40:8; 41:16, 25, 28, 32)."[10] This is a man whose faith in God and God's working is undiminished by the passage of time and unhindered by the disagreeable turn of events in his life. Even in prison, he is confident of God's sovereignty and providence.

The section, 40:1–23, is structured carefully[11]:

> **A**   Joseph encounters Pharaoh's officials (40:1–4)
>   **B**   Perplexity about dreams (40:5–8)
>   **C**   Butler's dream and its interpretation (40:9–10, 11–13)
>   **D**   Joseph's request (40:14–15)
>   **C'**   Baker's dream and its interpretation (40:16–17, 18–19)
>   **B'**   Fulfillment of dreams (40:20–22)
> **A'**   Joseph forgotten by Pharaoh's official (40:23)

Joseph's request is at the center of the chiastic structure of 40:1–23 (see above): "remember/remind" (×2), "do kindness," "bring out"—all in the perfect volitional forms (40:14). Wenham observes that the wording of Joseph as he makes this entreaty is commonly used to describe divine actions in Genesis: "remember/remind" (8:1; 9:15, 16; 19:29; 30:22 and Exod 2:24), "do kindness" (Gen 24:12, 14 and Exod 20:6), and "bring out" (Gen 15:7 and Exod 6:6; 20:2).[12] While this clearly seems to foreshadow the redemption of the Israelites from Egypt centuries later, the thrust here is on the interweaving of human and divine action. In a sense, Joseph's employment of these terms in his exhortation to the butler is founded upon his understanding of God's sovereign design and ordaining. Yet, even as he is confident that God is working, Joseph does not hesitate to take the initiative and make his case.[13]

The first part of Joseph's interpretation of the baker's dream is identical to that of the butler's: three branches/three baskets = three days (Gen 40:12, 18).[14] And it

---

10. Hamilton, *Genesis: Chapters 18–50*, 476.

11. Westermann, *Genesis 37–50*, 72.

12. Wenham, *Genesis 16–50*, 383.

13. And as he does so, we finally hear Joseph's reaction (his first that is recorded) to his forlorn situations of the past decade. His kidnapping was actually a "stealing" (40:15), a crime worthy of capital punishment (Exod 21:16). Strikingly, echoing the fact that he had been put into a "cistern" (בוֹר, *bor*) by his brothers (37:20, 22, 24, 28, 29), he claims he had subsequently been thrown into a "dungeon" (also בוֹר, 40:15). "In effect he was protesting that he had been wrongly incarcerated, from dungeon to dungeon!" (Mathews, *Genesis 11:27–50:26*, 749). Joseph's inclusion of his Hebraic origins in his testimony, while autobiographical, also has the rhetorical effect of creating a sense of obligation on the butler, who has here been aided by an alien "who owes him nothing, who worships some God different from his, and who has a knowledge of mysteries far surpassing his own" (Hamilton, *Genesis: Chapters 18–50*, 481).

14. In his dream, the baker is entirely passive, while the birds, rather eerily, eat out of the basket on his head (40:16–17). The ominous nature of this dream is emphasized in the wordplay between אָפָה (*'afah*, "baker") and עוֹף (*'of*, "bird"). In the dream the עוֹף eats the מַעֲשֵׂה אֹפֶה (*ma'aseh 'ofeh*, "baked

appears that Pharaoh will "lift the head" of both dreamers (40:13, 19). However, in the first case, the lifting is metaphorical—the butler is restored to his original position (40:13, 21); in the second, the lifting up is literal—"lift up your head *from you*," and the baker is hung on a tree, impaled, and left for carrion (40:19, 22).[15] One is exonerated; the other executed. And it all happens exactly as Joseph predicted (40:22), with the interpretations paralleling their fulfillments closely. This is, no doubt, God's work (40:8), even though there is no obvious activity of God described. Moreover, that the third day was Pharaoh's birthday—the day he took action (39:20)—sounds, again, quite "coincidental." It is highly unlikely that Joseph would have known this; the narrator is thereby hinting at divine action, working through dreamers and dream-interpreter.[16]

The outcome, though, was not positive in the short-term for Joseph: despite his appeal (40:14–15), the butler "did not remember" but "forgot" both Joseph and his request (40:23).

> The process of Joseph's promotion (in 39:1–6a, 19–23; 40:1–4) now reaches a tense balance. On the one hand, he achieves a higher status than ever before [as dream-interpreter *non pareil*]. . . . He had said interpretations belong to God (40:8), yet he himself had given interpretations (40:9–10), and now (40:20–22) these interpretations prove to be true. On the other hand, this new status seems helpless. The butler did not remember him. . . . Joseph is just one more forgotten prisoner.[17]

But God, true to his character, and unlike humans, *does* remember. Joseph had earlier received lovingkindness (חֶסֶד, *khsd*) from God (39:21); here he had requested "lovingkindness" (חֶסֶד) from the cupbearer (40:14), who promptly forgot him. But the God who had shown him חֶסֶד earlier (39:21) would not forget, nor would he withhold his חֶסֶד from Joseph, even though the man is left in jail to suffer for another two years. "[N]othing is more improper, than to prescribe the time in which God shall help us; since he purposely, for a long season, keeps his own people in anxious suspense, that, by this very experiment, they may truly know what it is to trust in him" (Calvin, *Comm. Gen.* on 40:23).

31.2 The blessing of God is abundantly upon the faithful agent of his blessing to others.

This chapter, 41:1–57, may be divided into four sections: Pharaoh's dreams (41:1–13); Joseph's interpretation (41:14–36); Joseph's exaltation (41:37–45); and the fulfillment of Pharaoh's dreams (41:46–57). The two dreams of the Pharaoh (40:1–7, 14–24) are expressly considered a single dream (41:8, 15, 17, 22—"dream" is singular[18]), besides being obviously similar in theme, language, and imagery of prominent features of the

---

goods," 40:17); but in its interpretation, the עוֹף eats the אָפָה (40:19) (Sherman, "Do Not Interpretations Belong to God?" 42–43).

15. This does not necessarily have to indicate a literal decapitation.

16. "Hebrew narrative often leaves it to the reader to look beyond the human script for the divine hand that pens the events" (see 1 Sam 6:9; Esth 6:1–2; Ruth 2:3) (Mathews, *Genesis 11:27–50:26*, 752).

17. Brodie, *Genesis as Dialogue*, 370.

18. Joseph saw them as two dreams that were one (41:25, 32).

Egyptian agronomy: cows and grain, plenty and famine, not to mention the sharing of motifs between them—"seven" (41:2, 3, 4, 5, 6, 7, 18, 19, 20, 22, 23, 24), "came up" (41:2, 3, 5, 18, 19, 22), and "thin" (41:3, 4, 6, 7, 23, 24).[19] Surprisingly, Pharaoh's unsuccessful consultation with "all the diviner-priests of Egypt, and all the wise men" (41:8), which would, no doubt, have consumed considerable time, is described in one verse, while the butler's reminiscence and recommendation of the Hebrew dream-reader takes up five verses (41:9–13). The wisdom of Egypt is being eclipsed here— "[s]omething greater is at hand," and someone greater is pulling the strings.[20]

The descriptions of the cows in Pharaoh's dream are literally "beautiful in appearance and fat in flesh" and "evil in appearance and thin in flesh" (41:2–4). Pharaoh's own rehearsal of his dreams (41:17–24) varies from that of the narrator (41:1–7), with considerably more emphasis on the thin cows and thin ears: he adds to their description the adjective "poor" and "withered," respectively (41:19, 23); he admits he had never seen such "evil/ugly" cows in all of Egypt (41:19), and that, even after their cannibalizing the fat cows, the thin cows looked as "evil/ugly" as before (41:21).[21] Later, Joseph's advice also focuses on the years of famine that the evil and ugly flora and fauna represent—he employs five sentences in two verses (41:30–31); in contrast, his comment on the fat cows and ears takes only one sentence in one verse (41:29). Moreover, his interpretation of the years of abundance emphasizes the "seven" in the dream being equivalent to "seven years"; nothing is said about the appearance or stature of the animals or ears. On the other hand, regarding the famine, Joseph not only deals with the of years of its extent, but also on the appearance of the animals and ears, and he repeats himself in 41:30–31 as he stresses the seriousness of what was about to happen. Pharaoh had commented that, in spite of the cannibalism, the second set of cows were as ugly as ever, with no one "knowing" they had just eaten (יד׳, *yd'*, 41:21); likewise, in Joseph's interpretation, all the abundance would be forgotten when the famine arrived: "the abundance will not be *known*" (יד׳, 41:31). No doubt, then, the dreams were not only bizarre, but horrific and serious.[22] But, in the background, God was preparing the very individual who would be his agent of blessing amidst this horrific and serious situation. And this agent becomes divinely blessed in an incredible turn of events.

While the slavery and prison phases of Joseph's life began with emphatic assertions of divine presence with, and divine blessing upon, Joseph (39:1–6a and 39:20–23,

---

19. Mathews, *Genesis 11:27–50:26*, 743–44. The dreams are described vividly in 41:1–13, with "behold" occurring six times: 41:1, 2, 3, 5, 6, 7, and with a number of participles being employed ("dreaming," "standing," 41:1; "coming up," 41:2, 3, 5; "scorching," 41:6; "sprouting," 41:6). Wenham observes that cows were not merely domesticated animals, but that they symbolized Egypt, the primeval ocean, and even the god Isis. The number 7, too, had sacral and symbolic implications (*Genesis 16–50*, 390–91).

20. Brodie, *Genesis as Dialogue*, 374. "Diviner-priests" (חרטם, *khrtm*) is borrowed from the Egyptian *ḥyr-tp*—"a class of priests especially learned in the arcane arts" (Wenham, *Genesis 16–50*, 391).

21. While the dream itself, with its cannibalism, would have been enough to wake up Pharaoh up, another source of worry—at least for the reader in Hebrew—may well have been the wordplay between פרעה (*par'oh*, "Pharaoh") and פָּרָה (*parah*, "cow").

22. Seven-year catastrophic famines were known in period literature: *Gilgamesh Epic* 6.103–113, and *ANET*, 31–32, 2 Sam 24:13, etc. Also see Gordon, "Sabbatical Cycle or Seasonal Pattern?" 79–80.

respectively), here, with Joseph languishing in prison for two years, we spy no such optimistic introduction.[23] Yet the way the narrative has progressed so far, the storyteller intends for the reader to catch the implicit, behind-the-scenes, sovereign, and providential working of God. There is no explicit statement about God being with Joseph in Gen 41, but the "coincidences" and "fortuities" are telling. God gives Pharaoh his dreams (41:25, 28, 32); the butler just happens to remember Joseph and "mentions" him to the ruler (זכר, 41:9); God enables Joseph interpret the dreams (41:16, 25, 28); and finally, even Pharaoh credits the hand of God in Joseph's work (41:38, 39). Later, Joseph again acknowledges God's providence as he names his sons (41:51, 52). In God's sovereignty and providence, Joseph's greatest transformation—or ascent—takes place: from prisoner to Prime Minister of all Egypt, under the Pharaoh: from cell to court, exchanging prison garments for royal garb. Divine enablement of Joseph, to interpret dreams (41:16), to possess supernatural wisdom (41:33), and to exercise statesmanship (41:38), elevates Joseph from his deplorable state earlier in this pericope to his exalted standing before Pharaoh at its end.[24] Such a dramatic metamorphosis is incontrovertibly the work of God as all of the actants seem to recognize.

The narrator's notation that Joseph was brought out of the "dungeon/pit" (בור, *bor*, 41:14) to meet the Pharaoh not only points to his most recent incarceration, but also to the hole in which he had been dumped by his brothers (also בור, 37:20, 22, 24, 28, 29). The cascade of imperfects in 41:14—Pharaoh "sent," "called," they "rushed," "shaved," "changed," and Joseph "came"—mark the urgency of the situation and the remarkable rapidity with which Joseph rose in the ranks! "Joseph, so long the antagonist, is suddenly catapulted into the position of protagonist. There are no introductions, no recapitulations of Joseph's beneficence to Pharaoh's servants, no examination of Joseph's qualifications or credentials."[25] Undoubtedly, Pharaoh is convinced of Joseph's competence and suitability for the position—yet another work of God.

In response to Pharaoh's query regarding Joseph's ability as an interpreter of dreams, Joseph points away from himself to God (41:16).[26] Perhaps not surprisingly, this is his first statement recorded after his being sprung from jail: he is not at all hesitant to "confront the world with God."[27] And this was the same response he gave to the butler's inquiry earlier (40:8); he provides the same explanation when the ruler bemoans the fact that there is no one to "explain/tell" (from נגד, *ngd*, 41:24) his dreams to him: Joseph asserts that *God* has "told" (also from נגד, 41:25) it to him.[28] In other

---

23. Indeed, the account begins with a hint of desperation: "At the end of two years of days . . ." (41:1).

24. See Waltke and Fredricks, *Genesis,* 536. This pericope has the final garment change for Joseph, paralleling the stages of his life in Egypt: from special tunic (Gen 37), to slave's garment (Gen 39), to prisoner's uniform (Gen 40–41), to official garb (Gen 41)—see below for a discussion of the clothing motif in the Joseph Story.

25. Hamilton, *Genesis: Chapters 18–50,* 493.

26. Joseph declares that God would "give a response of peace" (41:16) to Pharaoh—i.e., give Pharaoh an answer that would bring him peace.

27. Ross, *Creation and Blessing,* 642.

28. Later, Joseph will again revert to God getting this primary position of honor (51:19).

words, not a whole lot of theological/spiritual change occurs with Joseph throughout his story: he is always depicted as seeking God and his glory, keenly aware of his own incapabilities, but quietly confident in God's sovereignty and providence—a God-pleasing mixture of humility and faith!

Joseph's speech before the Pharaoh has two parts: the interpretation of the dream(s) (41:25–32), and the recommended action that was to be taken as a result (41:33–36). The overall scheme of Joseph's speech is a gem of theology, interweaving as it does "providence and planning. Providence is the preface: Joseph begins by saying that what he is going to talk about is coming from God [41:5, 28]. . . . And planning is the epilogue. Without being asked, Joseph adds as part of his interpretation, a plan of practical action, beginning with the appointment of someone 'discerning and wise.' Providence does not lessen human responsibility."[29] It seems that both deity and humanity are working in tandem: "God has told Pharaoh what He is about to *do*" (from עשׂה, *'sh*, 41:25, 28; also 41:32) is balanced with "Let Pharaoh *act*" (also from עשׂה, 41:34). "What is theologically noteworthy is the way in which the strong predestination content of the speech is combined with a strong summons to action. The fact that God has determined the matter, that God hastens to bring it to pass, is precisely the reason for responsible leaders to take measures!"[30] And Joseph's trust in this great God is literarily depicted: while he does not do so in 41:16, elsewhere when speaking of God to Pharaoh, Joseph employs הָאֱלֹהִים, *ha'elohim*, with the definite article (41:25, 28, 32[×2])—*the* God, the only God. Significantly, Pharaoh's use of "God" lacks the definite article (41:38, 39)—his is a generic god.

In Joseph's quasi-prophetic declaration, "Behold, seven years are coming" (41:29), Wenham sees Joseph following the footsteps of his forbears: Abraham was described as a prophet (20:7; also see 15:1–21; 18:17–33; 20:17); Isaac took on that role (27:27–29); and Jacob will don the same mantle (48:15–49:27). No reason to think Joseph is not worthy of that calling, himself, as he proclaims the future to Pharaoh.[31] In line with Joseph's "prophetic" role, Hamilton notes that the consequence of disregarding Joseph's opinion would be the danger of the land being "cut off" (i.e., perishing; 41:36), a word common in cultic literature to describe the punishment for those who violated community standards (e.g., Lev 7:20–27; 17:4–14; 20:3–6, 17–18; etc.). In Genesis, the verb had already been used twice in this sense (9:11; 17:14). "The consequence for rejecting Joseph's counsel is judgment. This moves Joseph's words to Pharaoh out of the category of option and into the category of mandate."[32] The double mention of God in 41:32 points to the divine origin both of the dream and of its interpretation. And the "establishment" of the matter by God (41:32) shows the certainty of what has just been

---

29. Brodie, *Genesis as Dialogue*, 375.

30. Von Rad, *Genesis*, 376. Perhaps a recent analogy is Joseph's asking the butler for a favor (40:14–15), while entertaining God's sovereignty and providence at the same time (40:8).

31. *Genesis 16–50*, 393.

32. *Genesis: Chapters 18–50*, 500.

interpreted; the doubling of the dream, Joseph himself asserts, is indication of God's dispatch in bringing those events to pass.[33]

Joseph then recommends that Pharaoh look for one who is "discerning and wise" to direct famine-readiness operations (41:33); and later Pharaoh acknowledges there is "no one as discerning and wise" as Joseph (41:39).[34] To describe Joseph thus, as unparalleled in wisdom is a jab at his own counselors ("wise men," 41:8) who were unsuccessful in interpreting his dream. The ruler is perspicacious enough to realize that such discernment and wisdom as exhibited by Joseph could only be possible by the enablement of deity (41:38)—thus, "Spirit of God" is mentioned by an Egyptian![35] The emphasis here in Pharaoh's recognition is on Joseph's interpretation of the dream and his wise counsel, and how these evidenced the presence of the "Spirit of God" in him. Joseph is a man clearly blessed by God, and even unbelievers acknowledge that fact.

In Pharaoh's awestruck response, we see, once again, divine and human work go hand in hand. With Joseph's appointment as second only to Pharaoh in all of Egypt, he is now doubly credentialed: Pharaoh acknowledges his divine seal of blessing (41:39), and subsequently invests him with the human insignia of approval (41:40–45).[36] As in Potiphar's house and in the jail house (39:5, 22), so also here in Pharaoh's palace ("house," 41:40) Joseph receives complete authority; in this pericope that authority extends to "all the land of Egypt" and over "all my people" (41:40–41, 43). The exception, Pharaoh's throne, is similar to the exception made with regard to the authority exercised by Joseph in Potiphar's house—there the exception was Potiphar's food (39:6) and/or Potiphar's wife (39:9). The comprehensiveness of Pharaoh's appointment of Joseph is marked by the threefold "and Pharaoh said" (41:39, 41, 44): first, stating his intention to elevate Joseph, then bedecking him with the paraphernalia of authority, and finally reaffirming the extent of Joseph's delegated authority.[37] No one, Pharaoh declares, would "raise hand or foot" without Joseph's permission. The idiom is a merism for taking any kind of action (41:44). Ironically, Joseph had experienced his brothers lifting up their hand against him (37:21, 22, 27); he had experienced a woman lifting up her eyes against him (39:7). But no more would anybody lift up any body part against him—"hand or foot"—without his permission! And Pharaoh's "without

---

33. God's "establishment" is a frequent affirmation in the Psalms: the establishment of the righteous (Pss 7:9; 10:17; 37:23), of astronomical bodies and the earth (8:4; 24:2; 65:6; 74:16; 89:37; 93:1; 96:10; 119:90), of God's throne (9:7; 93:2; 103:19), of Jerusalem (48:8); etc.

34. The pair of words frequently describe good leaders and exemplary people elsewhere in the OT: Deut 1:13; 4:6; 1 Kgs 3:12; Prov 10:13; 14:33; 16:21; Hos 14:9; etc.

35. For another surprising declaration from an Egyptian, see 43:23.

36. The exalted role of Joseph appears to be equivalent to that of the Egyptian "vizier" as described by Breasted, *Ancient Records of Egypt*, 2: §671–672. Pharaoh announces that "at your mouth [i.e., 'command'] all my people shall kiss [i.e., "do homage"—LXX has ὑπακούω, *hypakouō*, 'obey']" (41:40). "Kissing" as paying obeisance is also found in 1 Kgs 19:18; Job 31:27; Ps 2:12; Hos 13:2.

37. Joseph's name is changed, too, and apparently, Pharaoh personally organizes Joseph's marital plans as well (41:45). Joseph's father-in-law, a priest at On (Heliopolis) was likely to have been a person of considerable social standing, involved in Egyptian sun worship (Kitchen, "On," *NBD*[3] 848). In any case, after this pericope, neither Joseph's Egyptian name nor his foreign wife are mentioned again in the Joseph Story; even Pharaoh, later, chooses to call his Prime Minister "Joseph" (49:55).

your permission" (literally, "apart from you," וּבִלְעָדֶיךָ, *ubil'adeka*, 41:44) is an echo of Joseph's refusal to accept the kudos for interpreting dreams: "It is apart from me" (i.e., "It is not in me," בִּלְעָדָי, *bil'aday*, 41:16). Rather, "but God. . . ." Perhaps Joseph's silence amidst all these plaudits is the narrator's subtle reminder that it was neither this ex-prisoner, nor that Egyptian ruler who ordained and organized these matters, but the sovereign God of the universe.[38] Indeed, the only thing Joseph seems to have done on his own initiative thus far is to stay pure!

> On the surface, Joseph is being "made" by Pharaoh. Everything he is given comes from Pharaoh's hand: his office, status, privilege, name, wife—everything. He is "reborn" as a servant of Pharaoh. The irony is that from the standpoint of Genesis, it is not the hand of Pharaoh that has remade Joseph but the hand of God. For all that Pharaoh did, God brought Joseph to the recognition of Pharaoh, and God gave Joseph wisdom and success. In the end, Joseph is not first and foremost Pharaoh's man, but God's man. He is not Pharaoh's instrument of economic survival; he is God's instrument of salvation [or, one might say, "God's instrument of *blessing*"].[39]

And that instrument of blessing is, in this pericope, being blessed himself, as God takes him from prison and puts him in a palace! That Joseph does not succumb to the awe of his incredible transformation and new station, but constantly remembers the hand of God in his exaltation, is a testimony to the steadfast faith of this agent of divine blessing.

The remainder of the narrative describes the fulfillment of the dreams, precisely as Joseph had interpreted. The abundance of the land in the years of plenty is described in no mean terms: "by handfuls" (i.e., "abundantly"), "like the sand of the sea," "immeasurable" (41:47, 49, from ספר, *sfr*). With the similar notation of the divine promise of progeny to patriarchal descendants ("sand on the seashore": 22:17; 32:17; and "immeasurable," from ספר: 15:5; 16:10; 32:12), it might well be that the narrator is indicating God's handiwork in all of this plenty—the blessing of God. Perhaps in accordance with such divine blessing, the abundance of crops and yield is juxtaposed to the generation of children for Joseph (41:50–52): both are signs of God's blessing upon individuals (Deut 28:4).

The bleakness of the following seven years of famine is described with great literary emphasis: "famine/famished" occurs six times (41:54–57), twice noted as being "severe" (41:56, 57); the extent of this crisis is depicted with numerous repeats of "all": "all" the land (41:54 [×2], 55), "all" the Egyptians (41:55), "all" the face of the earth (41:56), "all" the storehouses" (41:56), and "all" the earth (41:57 [×2]). Egypt as well as surrounding lands were affected, indeed the whole world (41:57). This, of course, anticipates the next pericope, when Joseph's brothers, also suffering the same famine, come to Egypt for food—their starved sheaves of grain bowing to his plentiful one (37:7).

---

38. Waltke and Fredricks, *Genesis,* 533.

39. Walton, *Genesis,* 691.

The narrative of Joseph is, in a sense, centered around the theme of clothing; the motif is repeated throughout the Joseph Story, with changes of garment serving as rites of passage for Joseph from one state to another. It is essentially a theological motif that recurs eight times. Nwaoru depicts it this way[40]:

A	Joseph clothed in a special tunic by his father (37:3)	
B	Stripped of his clothing by his brothers; clothing as evidence (37:23)	
A¹	Joseph clothed in a garment in Potiphar's house (implied in 39:1, 4, 12)	**Descent**
B¹	Stripped of his garment by Potiphar's wife; clothing as evidence (39:12, 13)	
A²	Joseph clothed in a prisoner's robe (implied in 41:14; see 2 Kgs 25:29)	
B²	Removal of prisoner's robe (41:14)	
A³	Joseph clothed in a new garment (41:14)	**Ascent**
A⁴	Joseph clothed in fine line by Pharaoh (41:42)	

His clothing in Gen 37 was a mark of favoritism from his father; his final change of garment in Gen 41 is another mark of favor, this time Pharaoh's. Joseph is now recognized as being a blessing to "all the earth" (41:57), as he is festively clothed by Pharaoh (in "fine linen," which occurs only here in the OT). Moreover, Joseph's first and last garments (A and A⁴) are exclusive—garments that are not shared with others and that demonstrate his privileged status. Later, Joseph himself would clothe his brothers, the ones who stripped him of his first garment (45:22).

> Perhaps the most compelling hermeneutical issue in the narrative is Joseph's indomitable spirit. Joseph does not allow the pains associated with his change of garment to dictate his future relationship with his brothers. Rather his own bitter experience taught him to reconcile and forgive his siblings who already out of fear had torn their garment (Gen 44:13). . . . The process is ratified by a joyful reversal: the brothers who stripped Joseph of his sleeved tunic are now clothed in new garments . . . by Joseph (45:22), a symbol of forgiveness (Zech 3:4). This gesture apparently brings to an end the series of instances in which garments are changed in the narrative.[41]

In sum, this pericope has God's agent of blessing being blessed abundantly himself. The names of Joseph's children reflect his recognition of divine blessing: "Manasseh"—"God has made me forget all my trouble [עָמָל, 'ml] and all my father's house" (41:51) and "Ephraim"—"God has made me fruitful in the land of my affliction [עֳנִי, 'nh]."[42] Forgetfulness and fruitfulness—the theme of Joseph's dozen years in slavery and prison: not letting himself turn sour about the past, he would concentrate

---

40. Nwaoru, "Change of Garment," 7–8.

41. Ibid., 19–20.

42. Both עָמָל and עֳנִי foreshadow what the Israelites in Egypt would go through in the centuries later: both terms are used of the "trouble" and "affliction" inflicted by the oppressors of the children of Israel (Deut 26:7).

on being fruitful in the present, trusting God, being faithful to him, maintaining his integrity.[43]

Joseph had been kidnapped when he was seventeen (37:2); at the end of this pericope he is thirty (41:46). Thirteen years of near-death, slavery, injustice, imprisonment, and waiting had concluded and Joseph, the kidnapped slave-prisoner, had now been transformed into the highest officer in Egypt, a standing of considerable dignity and authority in the land. He had been blessed with a wife and two children, and God had blessed him with a portfolio of incredible influence in a nation in time of dire need: the blessed Joseph becomes, even more than before, an agent of divine blessing to others.[44]

SERMON FOCUS AND OUTLINES

> **THEOLOGICAL FOCUS OF PERICOPE 31 FOR PREACHING**
>
> **31   Trusting in God's working, even when it is indiscernible, results in abundant divine blessing (40:1–41:57).**

The previous pericope focused upon the integrity of the agent of God's blessing, demonstrated even in dire circumstances, resulting in blessing upon others. The Theological Focus of this pericope retains the same context—dire circumstances—but the thrust is not so much on the integrity of the agents of blessing but on their faithfulness in these situations of crisis, when God's working is not discernible. While the aspect of faithfulness in the previous pericope was one's integrity (sexual and/or otherwise), here the faithfulness is best focused upon solid trust in God's perfect timetable for action. And as a result, in, through, and despite desperate situations, God works to bless his people abundantly, as he did Joseph. It must be remembered that one can never stipulate or predict *how* God blesses, or *when* he blesses. It was in one fashion for Joseph; it will likely be in other ways for the rest of us. While the manner of God's blessings or its timing cannot be anticipated, the fact that he does bless his faithful children must not be forgotten. That is the lesson of this pericope.[45]

Possible Preaching Outlines for Pericope 31

I.   DESPERATION: Dangers to Joseph
      The dire circumstances of Joseph's incarceration (recap: Gen 37, 39)
      Joseph's time in jail—the first eleven years of suffering (passed over in silence in the text)
      Joseph's next two years in jail—forgotten and abandoned by even the one he had helped (40:5–15, 23)

---

43. Ross notes the connection between "fruit" and Joseph's line: in 30:2, God had withheld the "fruit" of Rachel's womb—the fruit that eventually was Joseph; in 49:22, Jacob calls Joseph a "fruitful bough"; in Hos 13:15, Ephraim is described as being "fruitful"; of course the name "Ephraim" itself derives from פְּרִי, *pri*, "fruit" (Ross, *Creation and Blessing,* 644). This was a man marked by faithfulness.

44. Hamilton, *Genesis: Chapters 18–50,* 508.

45. See Kuruvilla, *Privilege the Text!* 252–58, for a discussion of the concept of divine blessing, especially as it relates to preaching.

Move-to-Relevance: Dire situations in our lives, and the indiscernible working of God

II.   DEVOTION: Faithfulness of Joseph
           Joseph's loyalty to God throughout (40:8; 41:16, 25, 28, 32–33)
           Pharaoh's recognition of Joseph's God (41:38–39)
           Move-to-Relevance: Our loyalty to God, even in our dire circumstances (or why we are *not* loyal)

III.   DECORATION: Blessing upon Joseph
           Joseph exalted by Pharaoh (41:40–45)
           God's inscrutable workings throughout the pericope (see Notes)
           Joseph's abundant blessings and his recognition thereof in the names of his children (41:45, 50–52)

IV.   *Endure to enjoy!*
           How we can endure through the tough times to enjoy abundant divine blessing in our lives

A simpler outline deals with what is visible (dire circumstances) and what is not so visible (divine causation), concluding with an application of how the children of God (the agents of blessing) should conduct themselves in such phases of life.

I.   Dire Circumstances (and Joseph's Devotion)
           Joseph's time in jail—the first eleven years of suffering (passed over in silence in the text)
           Joseph's next two years in jail—forgotten and abandoned by even the one he had helped (40:5–15, 23)
           Joseph's loyalty to God throughout (40:8; 41:16, 25, 28, 32–33)
           Pharaoh's recognition of Joseph's God (41:38–39)
           Move-to-Relevance: Dire situations in our lives and in the indiscernible working of God
           Move-to-Relevance: Our loyalty to God, even in our dire circumstances (or why we are *not* loyal)

II.   Divine Causation (and Joseph's Decoration)
           God's inscrutable workings throughout the pericope (see Notes)
           Joseph exalted by Pharaoh (41:40–45)
           Joseph's abundant blessings and his recognition thereof in the names of his children (41:45, 50–52)

III. *Endure to enjoy!*
           How we can endure through the tough times to enjoy abundant divine blessing in our lives

PERICOPE 32

The Guilt of the Brothers

Genesis 42:1–43:34

[Trips to Egypt; Guilty Brothers Tested]

REVIEW, SUMMARY, PREVIEW

Review of Pericope 31: Genesis 40:1–41:57 has Joseph interpreting the dreams of two of his fellow-prisoners and they come to pass exactly as he predicted—one is restored as butler to the Pharaoh, the other is executed. But two more years pass, and Joseph languishes in jail, until Pharaoh himself has a dream that Joseph, on the recommendation of the royal butler, interprets with divine aid. Joseph is freed and appointed to Prime Ministership. Agents of God's blessing trust his working and wait; God's blessings come in his sovereign timing.

Summary of Pericope 32: This pericope deals entirely with trips of Joseph's brothers to Egypt, in search of food. There, as a result of Joseph's strategies to test them, they are convicted of their own guilt in the kidnapping and enslavement of Joseph. On their second trip to Egypt, Judah, in a declaration of selflessness, leads the way in persuading Jacob to allow Benjamin to go with them, as Joseph had required. God's discipline of his people, and their submission to him, enable resolution of past sins and permit the flow of divine blessings.

Preview of Pericope 33: In Gen 44:1–45:28, Benjamin is found with the missing goblet of the Prime Minister and is in danger of being enslaved. Judah intervenes, sacrificing himself for the sake of his younger brother and his aging father, upon which Joseph breaks down and reveals his identity; he attributes to God's providence all that had happened. Agents of divine blessing are faithful to those suffering, they are selfless, and they acknowledge God's sovereignty in all events.

32   *Genesis 42:1–43:34*

THEOLOGICAL FOCUS OF PERICOPE 32

32   The discipline of God and their own selflessness and submission to him, lead agents of divine blessings to resolve past sins against others (42:1–43:34).

32.1   The discipline of God prompts agents of divine blessing to resolve issues of their past sins against others.

32.2   Selflessness and submission to God, demonstrated by the agents of divine blessing, are critical to resolving sins of the past.

OVERVIEW

Unlike the previous pericope that dealt with dreams of the future, this one deals with issues of the past, primarily concerning Joseph's brothers who had, more than two decades ago, kidnapped and sold him into slavery.[1] This pericope begins the process of their repentance for those misdeeds. Brodie sees it as "the kernel of a conversion account," like the one that occurred in the life of Judah (Gen 38).

> [B]ut this chapter goes further: it gives not only a conversion's kernel, but, as it were, its basic anatomy. The process of conversion is seen most clearly in chapter 42, in the contrast between diverse stages (42:1, 28). At the beginning there is no communication between the brothers. All they do is look at each other with un-spoken guilt (42:1). In fact, in the biblical narrative they have not spoken to one another since the day they sold Joseph. But later, after they have gone through a process of learning to communicate, remember, and reflect, they open not only their mouths but their hearts ("Their hearts went out, and they trembled each toward his brother . . .," 42:28).[2]

There have been, as noted, three "ascents" in the life of Joseph: a rise to become the head of Potiphar's household (39:1–6), an elevation to manager of royal prisoners (39:21–40:4), and the exaltation as Prime Minister in Pharaoh's court (41:40–44). Likewise, there are three trips to Egypt made by members of Joseph's family: by his older brothers (42:1–38), by his brothers, including Benjamin (43:1–45:28), and by his brothers, his father, and the extended family (46:1–47:12), "each one more momentous and emotional [and taking more members in its caravan] than the previous one."[3]

---

1. Joseph was seventeen when he was enslaved (37:2), and thirty when he was exalted in Pharaoh's court (41:46). Adding the seven years of plenty (41:53) and two years of famine (45:6), about twenty-two years have elapsed since his kidnapping.

2. *Genesis as Dialogue*, 371.

3. Wenham, *Genesis 16–50*, 403.

The first trip, 42:1–38, is structured thus[4]:

A		Jacob and his sons; reluctance to part with Benjamin ("if harm befall him," 42:4); Canaan (**42:1–4**)
	B	Brothers journey to Egypt (**42:5**) Brothers and Joseph (**42:6–16**)
		C interrogation; "honest men," 42:11; "confine," 42:16; "younger comes" (בוא, *bo'*), 42:15
		D Brothers in prison (**42:17**) Brothers and Joseph (**42:18–24**)
		C' interrogation; "honest men," 42:19; "confine," 42:19; "bring younger" (בוא), 42:20
	B'	Brothers journey to Egypt (**42:25–28**)
A'		Jacob and his sons; reluctance to part with Benjamin ("if harm befall him," 42:38); Canaan (**42:29–38**)

Joseph's determination to have the younger brother "brought" (42:15, 20, in *C* and *C'*), is countered by Jacob's equally determined refusal to part with him, lest "harm befall him" (42:4, 38, in *A* and *A'*). And in a striking tussle between hostage held in Egypt (Simeon) vs. parental favorite held in Canaan (Benjamin), the latter wins—at least for now—as Jacob allows Simeon to remain the prisoner of Joseph, rather than let Benjamin be put at risk.

The second trip to Egypt (43:1–45:28) parallels the first. Both trips are primarily intended for obtaining food during the famine (42:1–3 and 43:1–2); both deal with Jacob's reluctance to send Benjamin along (42:4 and 42:36–38; 43:3–7); and both involve rather hostile encounters with Joseph, the Prime Minister of Egypt, including the subterfuge of hiding money (and a chalice in the second trip) in the bags of the brothers (42:25 and 44:1–2). The similarities are shown in the table below.[5]

	First Trip Genesis 42:1–38	Second Trip Genesis 43:1–45:28
Plans	**42:1–5**	**43:1–14**
Issue: food	42:1–3	43:1–2
Sent by Jacob	42:1–2	43:1–2, 11–12
Reluctance to send Benjamin	42:4	42:36–43:2
Journey	**42:5–8**	**43:15–45:24**
Arrival in Egypt	42:5	43:15
First audience with Joseph	42:6–16	43:15–16
Interlude	42:17	43:17–25
Second audience with Joseph	42:18–22	43:26–34
Joseph's private reaction	42:23–24	43:30–31
Interlude: money in sacks	42:25–28 (return)	44:1–13 (return aborted)
Third audience with Joseph		44:14–34
Reconciliation		45:1–24
Report	**42:29–38**	**45:25–28**

4. Table from ibid., 404.

5. Modified from Green, "What Profit for Us?" 137; and Humphreys, *Joseph and His Family*, 97. The highlighted boxes show the critical differences between the two trips: the brothers' third audience with Joseph and the reconciliation between them.

This pericope and the next form the high point of the Joseph Story, with the plot finding its resolution in the reconciliation and reunion of Jacob and his family with Joseph. Most of these two pericopes, therefore, is made up of dialogue.[6]

While, as noted, the main reason for the brothers' second trip to Egypt was food, there seems to be an abundance being distributed among the protagonists: Jacob is unusually generous as he sends food *to* Egypt in this time of scarcity (43:11); Joseph prepares and hosts a grand meal for his brothers (43:16, 24, 32–34) and, later, he sends them back loaded with food (44:1; also see 45:23). All of this betokens the reconciliation that is going to take place in the next pericope. But though this pericope looks forward to what is ahead, there are also several connections made here with what happened earlier, particularly at the commencement of the Joseph saga: references to dreams, parental favoritism, deception, Joseph's knowledge beyond that of his siblings, a lost brother, a report to the father, etc., indicating that the family dynamics in this dysfunctional clan are still as distorted as they ever were.[7] Nothing apparently has changed, except for Joseph's exalted situation and elevated status. But in this pericope, with their two trips to Egypt, things *are* changing for Joseph's brothers: guilt for their previous misdeeds overwhelms them, and they are more cognizant of the workings of God amidst all the crises.[8] Indeed, the next pericope will demonstrate that the brothers have metamorphosed from hardhearted, callous, and murderous brutes into sympathetic, sensitive, and concerned siblings and sons.

Genesis 42 begins and ends with Jacob and his sons and the father's reluctance to let Benjamin out of his sight (42:1–4, 35–38). Genesis 43:1–14 continues the same theme, again dealing with "famine" (43:1; see 42:5), "grain" (43:2, 4; see 42:1,2, 3, 5, 6, 7), and "Egypt" (43:2; see 42:1, 2, 3), but this time Jacob's resistance is broken by the dire need of the hour for food. So he permits Benjamin to accompany his brothers to

6. While Gen 42:1–43:34 is a sizable chunk of text, the "pericope" is a continuous story, as evidenced by the facile use of the pronouns "they" and "their father" in 43:2, taking off where Gen 42 had left. Though the boundary of the second trip of the brothers to Egypt extends to 45:28 when they return home, I have chosen to conclude the preaching unit ("pericope" in the non-technical sense, as a term for a unit of Scripture chosen for preaching—i.e., a preaching text, regardless of size) at 43:34 for the simple reason that it unifies the section (42:1–43:34) that deals with aspects of the brothers' past sins and their resulting guilt, while separating the pivot or the turning point of the story—the final test, Judah's speech, and the fraternal reconciliation (44:1–45:28), which is the centerpiece of the whole saga (see chiastic structure in Pericope 28). Thus a preachable idea distinct from that of the pericope preceding and following may be isolated. Such a pragmatic consideration is an integral part of the preacher's decision-making and pastoral discernment. That also means that there is sufficient freedom for the preacher to alter the delimitation of pericopes as found here or elsewhere in this commentary: the primary criterion for such a determination ought to be what distinct theological thrust of the text can be preached from a given pericope, a thrust that is discrete from those of its textual environs, and that serves to change the lives of the people of God in a specific manner, for the glory of God.

7. Shared motifs between this pericope and the one previous include: "buy" (41:56, 57; and 42:1, 2, 3, 5, 6, 7, 10, 19, 26; 43:2, 4, 20, 22); "grain" (41:35, 49; and 42:3, 25); "food" (41:35 [×2], 36, 48 [×3]; and 42:7, 10; 43:2, 4, 20, 22); both pericopes mention the famine (41:27, 30, 31, 36, 50, 54, 55, 56, 57; and 42:5; 43:1). Incidentally, a famine seems to have been the *de rigueur* experience of all the patriarchs: see 12:10 for Abraham's, and 26:1 for Isaac's.

8. Even Jacob acknowledges the hand of God in these proceedings, as he releases his favorite child, Benjamin, into the mercies of the Almighty (43:14).

Egypt. This sense of doubling is reinforced by the two trips the brothers make to Egypt. Moreover, Joseph is twice said to have "recognized" his brothers (42:8); he makes two explicit accusations against them of espionage (42:9, 14); and there are two discoveries of money in sacks (42:27, 35).[9] There is also Joseph's double testing of his brothers on their first trip—first this way (nine stay, while one returns to pick up Benjamin; 42:16), then that (one stays, while nine return to pick up Benjamin; 42:18–19). And in both Egypt trips featured in this pericope, the fate of the favorite son is front and central. That parental favoritism is again brought to the fore (42:4), suggests the test may also have implicitly included Jacob as its subject, for it was his favoritism of a sibling that had triggered much of the antipathy of the brothers. Has the father now learnt his lesson? Will the brothers resort to fratricide again, letting Benjamin be enslaved after the events of the next pericope (Pericope 33: 44:1–45:28)? There are hints that all of this is what Joseph is testing—"whether there is אֱמֶת [*ʾemet*, 'truth/faithfulness'] in you" (42:16).

At any rate, there is clear indication in this pericope that things are going to end well: what begins with famine, ends with a feast (43:31–34). Even though there is yet more suspense for the reader (in Gen 44), the bounteous ending of this pericope, in the midst of a famine, adumbrates a resolution to the intrafamily dysfunction.[10]

32   Genesis 42:1–43:34

THEOLOGICAL FOCUS 32[A]

32   The discipline of God and their own selflessness and submission to him, lead agents of divine blessings to resolve past sins against others.

32.1   *The discipline of God prompts agents of divine blessing to resolve issues of their past sins against others.*

32.2   *Selflessness and submission to God, demonstrated by the agents of divine blessing, are critical to resolving sins of the past.*

A. Having only one section in this pericope, the "Theological Focus 32" is identical to the "Theological Focus of Pericope 32."

NOTES 32

32.1   The discipline of God prompts agents of divine blessing to resolve issues of their own past sins against others.

The pericope begins with the famine of 41:57 being assumed as the background of Jacob's rather irate questioning of his sons who are seemingly just sitting around

---

9. Mathews, *Genesis 11:27–50:26*, 770. There are, however, differences in the two journeys of this pericope: paternal instruction in the first case was a response of indignation and frustration (42:1–2), while in the second, Jacob is resigned and submissive to the will of God (43:1–14); earlier Jacob had refused to let Benjamin part with him (42:2), while in the later episode, he finally concedes, albeit reluctantly, to Benjamin's departure (43:1–14).

10. See ibid., 771–72.

"looking at each other" (42:1). Jacob is still demonstrating favoritism, now to the one he believes is the only surviving son of Rachel—Benjamin; the sons of Leah are of less concern to the patriarch. He wants to ensure no "harm" (42:4) befalls this lastborn. The word occurs thrice in the Joseph story (42:4, 38; 44:29). Elsewhere in the OT, it occurs only twice, in Exod 21:22–23, describing injury to an unborn child *in utero*. Likely, Jacob is protective of his youngest child, as vulnerable as one in a womb. Though the patriarch seems to be blaming the other children for Joseph's loss in 42:36, it is unlikely that he suspects the truth. The brothers are only being held responsible for Joseph's "bereavement" to the same extent that they are for Simeon's: after all, siblings were expected to look after their own.

When the brothers arrive in Egypt, one cannot but wonder how their path intersected with that of Joseph. Surely he was not looking for them; in fact, as the name of one of his children indicates, he wanted to *forget* them (41:51).[11] That a tiny group of people, among the many hungry foreigners flocking to Egypt for food (not to mention natives of Egypt), just happened to meet the Prime Minister of the land would be an astounding coincidence, were it not for our knowledge of the sovereignty and providence of God, who has been, and continues to be, at work all through the Joseph Story.

The brothers' first action is to bow before their sibling Joseph (42:6). And in doing so Joseph's dreams are fulfilled (37:7, 9, both in the action of his brothers and in the timing of the event); it is noted twice in 42:6 that Joseph is in a position to provide for his brothers' need: he is the "ruler of the land" and the "one who sold grain to all in the land."[12] Joseph "recognized" (נכר, *nkr*) his brothers, but "pretended-to-be-a-stranger" (also נכר) to them (42:7). The word echoes its other significant occurrences earlier: in 37:32–33, Jacob "recognized" his son's special tunic and was deceived; in 38:25–26, Judah "recognized" his own belongings and realized he had been deceived/outwitted; here Joseph "recognizes" his brothers and decides to—in a sense—deceive them as he assesses their good faith and intentions. The word נכר recurs twice in 42:8 as well, underscoring Joseph's recognition and his brothers' failure to reciprocate.[13] Whatever his motives, one thing is clear: Joseph does not trust his brothers. But these stratagems do not appear to be the design of one inclined to exact revenge; if that were Joseph's goal, he would have revealed himself to them immediately, confronting them and brutally

---

11. What Joseph had tried to "forget" (41:51), however, comes flooding back now as he "remembers" (42:9).

12. See Pericope 28 on why I hold that Joseph's second dream had nothing to do with who would bow to whom; rather it demarcated the years before such obeisance would occur. The brothers bow again in 43:26, 28 and 44:14; Benjamin is most likely included in these latter instances, which makes only this first instance action of bowing (42:6) a perfect fulfillment of 37:7: Joseph had addressed his dream to his ten brothers, whose sheaves bowed to him (and this only indicated the dependence of the brothers upon Joseph as the source of food, not submission to authority).

13. That the brothers did not recognize Joseph is hardly surprising (42:7–8). Not only was Joseph's reappearance as Prime Minister of Egypt utterly unimaginable, his foreign name and appearance (likely clean shaven, wearing Egyptian clothing, and speaking another tongue while employing an interpreter with them [42:23]), made it virtually impossible for him to be recognized.

crushing their hopes as their "nemesis" was revealed. Rather as he himself declares, the brothers are being tested (42:15, 16).

It may well be that התנכר (*htnkr*, "he pretended to be a stranger," 42:7) is a word-play on התנכל (*htnkl*, "they plotted," 37:18). "The rich pun . . . draws together the starting points of criminal action and punitive counteraction . . . to encapsulate the reversal of fortune and shape the two conspiracies [Joseph's brothers' and his own tests of them] into a causal chain of sin and retribution."[14] There is a tit-for-tat going on, not in the sense of payback or recompense, but as a "test" (42:15, 16) of whether the brothers' attitudes of the past had changed or not. The intention to test his siblings may also explain Joseph's speaking "harshly" to them (42:7) with an accusation of espionage (42:9).[15] In 37:4, we had been told that Joseph's brothers could not speak "peacefully" to him—another tit-for-tat: they are getting what they first meted out—roles are being reversed as victimizers now become victims themselves.[16]

And so the test proceeds. The accusations and defenses—"spies" vs. "honest men"—are traded back and forth precisely, both in the occurrence and the recounting thereof later to Jacob, and mostly in a sequence of verbless statements:

EVENT AS IT OCCURRED	EVENT AS IT WAS RECOUNTED
Accusation and defense	**Accusation and defense**
Joseph: "spies [are] you" (42:9)	*Brothers*: "he took us for spies" (42:30)
Brothers: "honest [are] we" (42:11)	*Brothers*: "honest [are] we" (42:31)
Brothers: "your servants are not spies" (42:11)	*Brothers*: "we are not spies" (42:31)
Proof demanded	**Proof demanded**
Joseph: "spies [are] you" (42:14)	*Joseph*: "... honest [are] you" (42:33)
Joseph: "spies [are] you" (42:16)	*Joseph*: "... not spies [are] you" (42:34)
Joseph: "if honest [are] you ..." (42:19)	*Joseph*: "... but honest [are] you" (42:34)

The brothers frequenty assert their good intentions, employing כן (*kn*, "honest"; also echoed by Joseph; 42:11, 19, 31, 33, 34); but thus far, these men have not demonstrated any integrity, or given Joseph any reason to believe them. A test is surely called for. Hamilton observes that the word בָּחַן, *bakhan*, "test" (42:15, 16), has a metallurgical connotation (as in Jer 6:27; Job 23:10; Ps 66:10)—"to test in the sense of determining or finding out the value of something."[17]

14. Sternberg, *The Poetics of Biblical Narrative*, 288.

15. Literally, Joseph accuses his brothers of wanting to see the "nakedness [i.e., vulnerability] of the land" (42:9, 12). The accusation of espionage was not entirely a concoction of Joseph's imagination. Egypt's traditional enemies, the Hittites and the Assyrians, were likely to have engaged in such cloak-and-dagger operations.

16. It might also be that Joseph, not noticing Benjamin with the ten, is suspecting some sort of foul play perpetrated against that son of Rachel as well.

17. Hamilton, *Genesis: Chapters 18–50*, 522. One wonders why Joseph did not ask about, or for, his father. Later as Judah makes his case to Joseph, he recounts what he and his brothers had said to Joseph (a statement not recorded in this pericope), that Benjamin could not leave his father (44:22). Perhaps Joseph assumed then, that if they were inseparable, asking for Benjamin to be brought would result in the arrival of both father and youngest son to Egypt. This seems to be a reasonable assumption, for upon their second visit to Egypt (with Benjamin), Joseph's first recorded words deal with his father, whether Jacob was alive (43:27): he had probably expected to see the patriarch, too, along with Benjamin, but

All of this is likely to have brought home powerfully to the brothers the impact of a false accusation and imprisonment. It surely must have gotten them thinking about what they had done once to an innocent brother, Joseph; that they are so reminded is evident in their subsequent utterances (Gen 42:21–22). Sternberg sees the whole charge of spying as carefully nuanced to reproduce Joseph's own suffering in their experience:

> [I]t reenacts the final phase of Joseph's own suffering: vilification, by Potiphar's wife, leading to imprisonment. . . . [The charge] imposes on the brothers an ignoble and dangerous role that comes as close as possible to the one he himself was reduced to by the woman's slander: hence his appositional exegesis of "spying" in terms of "seeing the nakedness of the land" [42:9, 12]. By figurative analogy, the ten are thus branded as the would-be Hebrew rapists of Egypt.[18]

Talionic justice indeed. Not only was "confinement/prison" (42:17, 19) used in connection with Joseph's detention (40:3, 4, 7), the act of "putting" them in there, וַיֶּאֱסֹף (wayye'esof, 42:17), sounds suspiciously like וְיוֹסֵף (wyosef, "and Joseph"). Joseph's own imprisonment was being mirrored here in the punishment/test of his brothers, though for far shorter than his thirteen years of suffering. But then Joseph permits the brothers to return, except for one who would remain hostage (42:18–20). Whatever happened in prison in those three days—or perhaps in the last two decades since the "disappearance" of Joseph—one thing is clear: this is a changed group of characters. They confess among themselves, and appear to be truly remorseful of what they had done to their brother Joseph many years ago: the words "guilty" and "sin," and even mention of "blood" and a "reckoning" thereof (דָּרַשׁ, darash, or "offering," 42:21–22; see Lev 10:16) have clear connotations of grievous culpability: indeed, in Gen 9:5, God had declared thrice that he would "require" (דרשׁ) the blood of the one who shed his brother's blood (also see Ps 9:12). What is quite amazing is how the brothers connect their present "distress" with the "distress" (both צָרָה, tsarah, Gen 42:21) they had themselves inflicted on another innocent twenty years ago.

Incidentally, this is the first we hear of Joseph having begged for mercy (חָנַן, khanan, in the Hithpael stem = "beseech for *mercy* [חֵן, khen]") when he was callously thrown into the pit (42:21), making their crime all the more heinous.[19] And the wordplay is poignant: their "We did not listen [שָׁמַע, shm']" (42:21) is balanced by Reuben's "You did not listen [שָׁמַע]" (42:22), and countered by "Joseph listened/understood [שָׁמַע]" (42:23). And not only do they relive the loss of one brother in conversation,

---

his ploy had not succeeded. So, at that juncture, to get Jacob also to Egypt, Joseph would try yet another scheme and attempt to imprison Benjamin (44:1–15). Of course, thereupon, Judah makes his passionate plea that breaks the heart of Joseph—without Benjamin, Jacob would surely die (44:30–31)—and the story quickly rolls to its *finis* without any further plotting, as Joseph reveals his identity (44:16–45:2). See Turner, *Announcements of Plot*, 161–62.

18. Sternberg, *The Poetics of Biblical Narrative*, 288.

19. Ironically, the one who begged for חֵן, is the one who extends חֵן (43:29). Later, the test will be whether the other son of Rachel, Benjamin, will obtain חֵן from his brothers.

they are then made to watch as Simeon is bound (42:24)—they actually observe another fraternal loss.

In other words, there is a rationing out of punishment in kind—what Joseph experienced, the brothers were being put through, albeit in much lesser intensity ("role-reversal"). They get a taste of Joseph's own suffering in precise sequence: helplessness as they are bullied, false charges with serious repercussions, imprisonment, and abrupt commutation of sentence. In addition, there is also a rehearsal of those events that led to Joseph's abandonment ("role-duplication")—a replay, so to speak, with an implicit question: How would the brothers react this time?[20]

The two alternative strategies Joseph proposes (42:16, 19–20; confine all, but send one vs. send all, but confine one) parallels the dual plan of the brothers to dispose of Joseph in Gen 37 (first by imprisoning him in a pit, and then by selling him off to the Ishmaelites). And Joseph's second plan, to let everyone but the hostage return, would recreate a potential situation of fraternal neglect: the nine would have enough food (at least for a while), and quite a bit of money (42:25), so they could theoretically (and heartlessly) let their hostage sibling remain in prison, just as they had done to Joseph. Not only were they being asked to bring back Benjamin, they were also being tested as to whether they would care enough about the one left behind.[21] Sternberg sees Joseph's train of thought as proceeding on this route:

> "To reproduce the past, I will put the life of one of them into the hands of the rest and plant temptation in their bags to equal or exceed the profit they hoped to make by selling me into slavery ['silver,' in this pericope, occurs in 42:25, 27, 28, 35, besides 43:12, 15, 18, 21, 22, 23; the last time it showed up before this pericope was in 37:28]. Will they now opt for the brother or for the money? Will they return at once to redeem the hostage or play a waiting game till hunger forces them back, in which case undue delay may become as revealing as outright desertion. True, Simeon cannot be hated by them as I was; but then to keep this money they do not have to dirty their hands—they can simply abandon him to his fate at mine."[22]

Thus, one sees in the various phases of this dramatic text, not only *role-reversal*, but also *role-duplication*—with the money in their bags, they are being tested to see if they will now make the same egregious choice as they did before, to abandon a brother.[23] As Maimonides said, "What is complete repentance? When a person has the opportunity to commit the original sin again, and is physically able to sin again, but one doesn't

---

20. These terms, "role-reversal" and "role-duplication," are from ibid., 294 (also see below).

21. Sternberg speculates that the choice of Simeon was strategic: Joseph held this second son of Leah as hostage, so that the brothers would return with Benjamin, the second son of Rachel (ibid., 291). Did Joseph decide upon Simeon after eavesdropping on the brothers' discussion and being convinced of Reuben's good intentions in Gen 37? Also, perhaps, Simeon's imprisonment would likely have resulted in less perturbation of the fragile Jacob, since the son had already given his father cause for angst (34:30; see 49:5–7).

22. Ibid., 293.

23. Ibid., 294.

sin because of his repentance" (*Hilchos Teshuva* 2.1). This, then, was a test of their repentance.

Interestingly in Joseph's first attempt at testing his siblings, he swears "by the life of the Pharaoh" twice (42:15, 16). But then he switches to "God, I fear" (42:18). "Fearing God" puts him in the same posture as was his great-grandfather Abraham (22:12—the last occurrence of the fear of God before this one); this is a fundamental response of God's people to him (also see Exod 1:17; Lev 19:14, 32; Deut 6:2, 13; Prov 1:7; Eccl 12:13; etc.). Joseph is apparently claiming to be a person of integrity, hinting, of course, that the ones he was addressing were not. Appropriately enough, the brothers immediately begin confessing their evil (42:21–23), recognizing the deeper truth of the "Egyptian's" accusation: even the Egyptian was God-fearing, while they were not, at least not in their obnoxious treatment of a family member.

Joseph is so moved by this first demonstration of his brothers' repentance (in their guilt-ridden discussions amongst themselves, 42:21–22) that he is brought to tears (42:24); he will weep several more times before the end of his story: when he sees Benjamin (43:30), after Judah's powerful plea and the revelation of his identity (45:2), as he reconciles with Benjamin and the others (45:14–15), when he is reunited with his father (46:29), upon his father's demise (50:1), and again in the final reconciliation with his brothers (50:17).[24] "For all his apparent harshness toward his brothers, this action proves that he still loves them and that if they continue to show a change of heart, reconciliation will be possible ultimately."[25] But not just yet; the bridge of trust has not yet been repaired fully and so the test must go on. So the brothers are allowed to leave for Canaan.

On their journey back, they discover money in the sack of one of the brothers (42:27–28), and the siblings are thrown into consternation. Once again they see the hand of God operating against them in judgment for past misdeeds (42:27–28). Of course, they are unaware that it is the hand of Joseph—or rather the hand of God through the hand of Joseph—that has created this problem (42:25). In other words, the narrator appears to be acknowledging a "double system of causation, human and divine."[26] In fact, Joseph himself would confess as much to his brothers in 45:5–9. Ross observes the irony in the brothers' question, "What is this God has done to us?" (42:28). Thus far in Genesis, such a question—"What is this you have done?"—has only been asked in interrogations of the sinful about their guilt (3:13; 4:10; 12:18; 20:9; 26:10; 29:25; 31:26).[27] Here it is almost as if God is questioning them—the sinful ones—about their guilt.

When the brothers return home, they spin the episode to their father without any of the dangerous overtones, perhaps to keep from over-burdening their father now hit hard by the loss of another son. They omit any mention of accusations of espio-

---

24. "If Jeremiah is the so-called 'weeping prophet,' Joseph is the 'weeping patriarch'" (Mathews, *Genesis 11:27–50:26*, 791).

25. Wenham, *Genesis 16–50*, 409.

26. Alter, *The Five Books of Moses*, 243–44n28.

27. *Creation and Blessing*, 653.

nage (42:9–15), their incarceration (42:16–17), Simeon being held as hostage (42:19), Joseph's veiled threat to execute them (42:20), their own sense of guilt (42:21–22), and of the discovery of money in one of their sacks (42:27–28). Instead, they invent Joseph's promise to let them trade freely if Benjamin accompanies them back (42:34). But despite their best efforts, Jacob remains unconvinced. To him, it is the same song again, verse two: he had lost one son earlier; now he has lost another, and does not plan to lose a third. "Everything is against me," he laments (42:36), as he exercises a parental veto on his sons' plan to return to Egypt with Benjamin (42:37–38).

After the brothers arrive home (a time lapse between 42:34 and 42:35 is implied by the וַיְהִי (*wayhi*) + a participial clause, 42:35), they are shocked to discover money in *all* of their sacks (42:35; as opposed to finding it in just one brother's sack, 42:27–28). For them, it is simply another divine indictment of their abandonment of Joseph many years ago. For Jacob, however, his dismay may have had another reason: Simeon has disappeared, and money has appeared—perhaps Simeon has been sold into slavery by his brothers?[28] In the narrative, Jacob's sons leave home twice (Gen 37 and 42), and return home both times minus brother, but plus extra silver. Hardly a coincidence, Jacob may have surmised. That would explain his intransigence in 42:36; he is not about to let Benjamin out of his sight now, what with the possibility of his siblings plotting another abduction. His statement that harm might befall Benjamin "on the journey you take"—rather than "at the hands of the Egyptian ruler" (42:38)—hints again at where Jacob's suspicions lie. And if Jacob, the father, is so suspicious of his children, it is no wonder Joseph has not yet come around to trust them.

Of course, that accusation impassions Reuben who, in desperation, agrees to have his two sons executed if he does not return from Egypt with Benjamin; that only makes things worse (42:37). He could hardly tell his father that, indeed, they had sold off his favorite son, Joseph, but that in Simeon's case they were innocent! "Caught in this grotesque visitation of the past, Reuben tries the indirect father-to-father approach: 'My two sons thou mayest kill if I do not bring him to thee.'"[29] In fact, Reuben, we discover in 46:9, had *four* sons. Perhaps the reason for his offering up two of them, is to satisfy justice; his guilt is clear, for he seems to be asserting, "I'll sacrifice two of my sons, for the two sons I've cost you—Joseph and Benjamin." Guilt is a terrible thing! But for Jacob who had already lost two sons, the potential loss of another, accompanied by the loss of two grandchildren, is certainly not an appealing vision. Jacob now declares Joseph "dead," and labels Benjamin as "*his* [Joseph's] brother" (42:38)—effectively severing any relationship between the sons of Rachel and those of Leah, Bilhah, and Zilpah. Jacob might even have been cutting off his other boys from himself as he asserts: "He [Benjamin] alone is left," as if he had no other sons. So Jacob, as expected, refuses to let Benjamin go with his brothers (42:38). If he were to "go down"

---

28. Sternberg, *The Poetics of Biblical Narrative*, 298. *Targum Ps.-J, Gen. Rab.* 91.9, and Calvin (*Comm. Gen.* on 42:36) agree that Jacob may have begun to entertain suspicions about his sons' perfidious activities.

29. Sternberg, *The Poetics of Biblical Narrative*, 298–99.

(יָרַד, *yrd*), Jacob's gray hair would be "brought down" (also יָרַד) to Sheol in grief, sentiments similar to what Jacob had expressed at Joseph's loss (37:35).

31.2 Selflessness and submission to God, demonstrated by the agents of divine blessing, are critical to resolving sins of the past.

In this section (43:1–34), the second trip to Egypt is commenced by the brothers, *sans* Simeon still in custody in Egypt, but with Benjamin. Judah successfully persuades Jacob to send Benjamin with them on this journey (43:3–10). Reuben's earlier, and rather bizarre, attempt to convince Jacob to do so (42:37–39) had been in vain, not helped at all by his having been in disfavor with Jacob (35:22; see 49:4); Levi perhaps kept silent because of his already poor standing with his father (34:30; and see 49:5–7); of course, Simeon was not around. Judah, then, is the next oldest, in line to take charge of the family, and henceforth he will be the spokesman for the family until they are reconciled with Joseph. His argument begins and ends with the threat delivered by Joseph (43:3, 5; see 42:15, 20). With three infinitive absolutes, Judah and his siblings emphasize the importance of taking Benjamin with them this time around ("solemnly warned," 43:3; "thoroughly questioned," 43:7; and "really know," 43:7).

Judah's reference to Benjamin as "*our* brother" (43:4) counters Jacob's label ("my son") and the exclusivity ("he alone is left") with which he talks of Benjamin (42:38). Moreover, there is no resentment expressed or exhibited with regard to the aspersions cast by Jacob on Judah and his brothers, that they had done away with Simeon (42:36). There is no insolent countercharge of the kind made by Simeon and Levi in an earlier case of paternal neglect of another child of Leah (34:31; after all, Jacob's refusal to send Benjamin along was, in effect, to abandon Simeon to continued confinement in Egypt). And there is no hint of thoughtlessness in Judah's address, as there was in Reuben's (42:37). Instead, Judah points out that it is actually a double bind, and no choice at all: death from starvation on one hand, and potential risk to Benjamin (and the rest) on the other. So he offers himself as a surety, offering to take the blame forever (43:9), should Benjamin not return: interestingly, "send . . . with us" in 43:4 becomes "send . . . with me" (43:8). A doublet within another doublet (almost a chiastic structure) is seen in 43:3–5, where Judah makes a case for Benjamin to accompany them back to Egypt.[30]

> **A** Joseph's warning recounted:
> "You shall not see my face, unless your brother is with you" (43:3)
>> **B** Positive option offered:
>> If Jacob will send Benjamin, they will go down and buy food (43:4)
>> **B'** Negative option offered:
>> If Jacob will not send Benjamin, they will not go down (43:5a)
> **A'** Joseph's warning recounted:
> "You shall not see my face, unless your brother is with you" (43:5b)

30. Hyman, "The Transition to the Second Trip," 77. This is also followed by a "doublet" of rhetorical questions, one from Jacob, and the other from his sons (43:6, 7). Indeed, Judah himself speaks twice (43:3–5 and 43:8–10), echoing "send" in each case. As well, words for "double/twice" show up in 43:10 (פַּעַם, *pa'am*) and 43:15 (מִשְׁנֶה, *mishneh*). Doublets in the Joseph saga have been noted earlier.

Judah, in arguing for Benjamin's going with them, quotes Jacob verbatim, as he says, ". . . that we may live and not die" (43:8, citing 42:2). Reuben pledges his children, but Judah pledges himself.[31] The last time Judah pledged something in the Joseph Story, it was a foolish undertaking as he bequeathed his paraphernalia to a prostitute (38:18). Clearly, the man has been transformed as he now offers himself as security: it is a noble deed that he performs here, powerful enough to convince his skeptical father of his good intentions and sincerity.[32] His selflessness and submissiveness here for the sake of the larger family unit/tribe is remarkable (more on that in Pericope 33).

Thus Jacob is finally persuaded to release Benjamin into the hands of the brothers traveling back to Egypt (43:13).[33] In Jacob's instruction (and presumably in the brothers' response), there are parallels between this second trip to Egypt that takes Benjamin, and the Ishmaelite caravan that took the kidnapped Joseph there (43:11 and 37:25). Both carried at least some identical products: balm, spices, and myrrh, and a son of Rachel.[34] In the first case, the brothers received "money" (37:28); here, they took "money" to Egypt (43:12, 15). In describing the brothers' preparations, the sequence of items listed as taken by them is painfully telling: "The men took this present, they took double the money in their hand, and Benjamin" (43:15). Benjamin is mentioned last, a delayed notice. "The 'and Benjamin' hangs like the resigned sigh of a father trapped between the need to live and the possibility of a life made utterly empty through another loss."[35]

The wheel seems to have come full circle. The plot movement that started with a brother leaving home in all innocence to join his brothers, only to find himself the property of a trading caravan bound for Egypt, now moves towards closure as the same brothers leave home in a caravan to rescue the same sibling in Egypt.[36] Indeed, this is almost a recapitulation of Joseph's journey—role-duplication—which also meant

31. And it appears that, unlike Reuben, Judah is also concerned about the next generation as he pleads with his father for "our children" (43:8).

32. Indeed, the word "surety" (from עָרַב, *'arab*, 43:9) is a clear, albeit unwitting, allusion to his "pledge" (עֵרָבוֹן, *'erabon*) to Tamar in 38:17–18, 20. But what such surety might entail is unclear. It surely could not mean that Jacob could take Judah's life if Benjamin did not return. Perhaps Judah is offering to relinquish his paternal blessing on account of the guilt that he might incur, not to mention the burden of shame he would bear the rest of his life.

33. Benjamin is reduced to a foil or a prop throughout the story. He never utters a word. One wonders what he was thinking about this business of his being used as a bargaining chip. But the narrator is not interested in that aspect of the episode, so neither should we.

34. While this gift is not as extravagant as the one Jacob gave his brother in Gen 32, there are similarities: both are labeled מִנְחָה (*minkhah*, 43:11, 15, 25, 26 and 32:13, 18, 20, 21; 33:10; after Jacob's "gift" in Gen 32–33, the word is found only in Gen 43 for the remainder of Genesis); and in both situations, God's help is invoked (43:14 and 32:9–12).

35. Humphreys, *Joseph and His Family*, 45.

36. Sternberg, *The Poetics of Biblical Narrative*, 300–301. The cascade of eight imperatives with which Jacob responds in 43:11–13 likely indicates his heartfelt acceptance of Judah's efforts at persuasion: "do," "take," "go down," "take," "return," "take," "arise," "return." Moreover, the switch from Jacob's earlier "my son" (42:38) to "your brother" (43:13), may also point to a softening on the patriarch's part towards his other children, especially after Judah's reference to Benjamin as "our brother" (43:4). Jacob seems to be convinced of Judah's good faith.

subjecting a father to intense agony over the potential loss of a favorite son.[37] In any case, Jacob's prayer is one of resignation and submission to the mercies of God (43:14); indeed, this is the first instance of "mercies" (רַחֲמִים, *rakhamim*) in the Bible—it occurs only twice in Genesis, both times in this pericope. The second instance, in 43:30, is an answer to Jacob's prayer: there, Joseph is "powerfully moved" (also רחמים, 43:30). Thus, Jacob's trust in divine sovereignty seems total: a good outcome will not be the work of man, but of "El Shaddai." Even if it means being bereaved of his children, Jacob is willing to accept it as an act of God (43:14).

After the brothers reach Egypt for the second time, it is rather remarkable that upon being received well by Joseph (43:16–17), they are immediately fearful, assuming the worst: "He wants to capture us [literally, "to roll himself upon us and to fall upon us"] and enslave us" (43:18), which was precisely what they had done to Joseph—again, a role-reversal. No wonder they are afraid! As Humphreys noted, "For the guilty, even hospitality can seem ominous."[38]

All of this testing—with role-reversals and role-duplications—is having a remarkable effect on the brothers: there are clear indications in this episode that the attitude of the brothers is being seen by the narrator as appropriately contrite. God is at work, and divine providence is at the forefront again, this time explicitly confessed by a foreigner—the steward's reassurance that God had given them the money in their sacks (43:23). Incidentally, this is another instance, besides 41:38–39, of an Egyptian making an acknowledgement of the workings of God.[39] Later Joseph himself will acknowledge the working of God in all of these events (45:5–9; 50:20). He is, here, the instrument of God: he wishes God's "grace" (חֵן, 43:29) upon Benjamin, in effect dispensing grace to his brothers. Another sign of the brothers' correct attitude is that as they are brought into Joseph's house, the narrator mentions that they wash their "feet" (רַגְלֵיהֶם, *raglehem*, 43:24). One is reminded of Joseph's charge against them earlier, that they were "spies" (מְרַגְּלִים, *mragglim*, literally, "those who go about on foot [to scope out the land]," 42:9, 11, 14, 16). The foot-traveling snoops are now washing their feet, cleansing themselves.[40] But that is not all. The brothers bow again: 43:26, 28 (also 42:6; 44:14). In the second of these instances, in 43:28, they bow *and prostrate* themselves, going way beyond what Joseph had dreamt would happen (37:7; again confirming that Joseph's first dream had less to do with submission and subjugation than with dependence upon a food-provider). With every turn of the story, the broth-

---

37. The brothers' having to return to Canaan after their first Egypt trip with the news of the loss of another brother (this time, Simeon), would have been role-duplication in itself.

38. *Joseph and His Family*, 83.

39. That the steward says, "Your money came to me" (i.e., "I had your money," 43:23) is not entirely inaccurate: he *did* have their money; only, he put it back in their sacks right away, before the brothers left Egypt after their first visit.

40. Curiously, the scene, 43:24–34, begins with the brothers washing their feet and giving their donkeys food (43:24), and ends with Joseph washing his face and giving his brothers food (43:30–34). One can also see a progression in the brothers' "seeing Joseph's face": from the threat that they will not (43:3, 5), to the hope that they might (43:14–15, "before Joseph's face"), and to the reality that they do (43:31, after Joseph washes his face).

ers are demonstrating their guilt and repentance. Humphreys remarks on the fact that earlier the brothers could not speak in "peace" (שָׁלוֹם, *shalom*, 37:4), but now there is a "veritable burst of *šālôms*" as both Joseph and his brothers trade the word to each other (43:27, 28).[41]

In this poignant scene, Joseph is deeply stirred as he sees Benjamin, "his brother" and "his mother's son"—an unusual constellation of relational terms in an episode where the other brothers are simply "the men" and Joseph, "the man" (43:29–30).[42] Joseph's displays of emotion in this second visit of his brothers to Egypt sequentially intensify: first he weeps silently, turning away to conceal his tears (42:24); then he retires in private to weep (43:30); finally he weeps loudly, in their presence, as he reveals himself to his brothers (45:2, 14–15). The emotional impact gradually escalates as the story moves along.

Calling Benjamin "my son" must have sounded rather unusual to the rest of the brothers. But Joseph will exercise this partiality towards his closest sibling again, in seeing that he gets five times as much food as the others (43:34; later Benjamin will get five changes of clothing, too, 45:22). That itself would be another test of the brothers— and perhaps it was deliberate on the part of Joseph: role-duplication. Would they fret and fume over one more exhibition of favoritism? As it turns out, their responsive is far from malicious. Neither did the surprise of orderly age-based seating arrangements spoil their fun with the feasting and imbibing (43:33–34)—"they drank and they were intoxicated."[43] "The point of Joseph's trial is that repentance is only complete when one knows that if he were placed in the same position he would not act in the same way he had acted before."[44] Although one more test in the form of a role-duplication is on its way (see Pericope 33: Gen 44:1–45:28), Jacob's sons, in this pericope, seem to have passed the tests set by Joseph. Children of God must selflessly submit to God and resolve past sin, if they want to be instruments of divine blessing in God's hands.

SERMON FOCUS AND OUTLINES

> **THEOLOGICAL FOCUS OF PERICOPE 32 FOR PREACHING**
>
> 32   God's discipline and their selflessness and submission to God, lead agents of divine blessings to resolve past sin. (42:1–43:34).

In this pericope, the focus is upon Joseph's brothers. Forming the twelve tribes of the nation of Israel, all the brothers (Joseph and Benjamin) ought to be viewed as agents of future divine blessing upon the rest of humankind. The three patriarchal sections of Genesis (12–24, 25–36, and 37–50, dealing respectively with Abraham, Jacob, and Joseph) all emphasize how the chosen family, tribe, and nation are agents of divine

41. Ibid., 95.

42. Wenham, *Genesis 16–50*, 423.

43. "Joseph hosts a meal for his brothers [43:31–34], who years before had callously sat down to eat while he languished in the pit [37:25] . . .—a piquant note" (Sarna, *Genesis*, 302).

44. Sacks, "The Lion and the Ass," 141.

blessing to those outside this perimeter: 12:3; 18:18; 22:18; 26:4; 28:14; 39:1–4, 20–23; 41:56–57; 47:13; etc. Therefore the lessons to be learnt from the lives of Joseph's brothers are also valid for God's people, all of whom are agents of divine blessing in this dispensation, to a world outside.[45]

Possible Preaching Outlines for Pericope 32

I.   God's Recompense: CHASTISEMENT—Discipline of God
   Role-reversal and role-duplication (42:9–15, 16–20, 25–28, 35; 43:11–12, 18; and see Notes)
   Acknowledgement of God's working and their own guilt (42:6, 18, 21–22, 28; 43:14, 23, 29)
   Move-to-Relevance: Unresolved sin in our lives; our indifference to God's prompting through discipline

II. Brothers' Reaction: COMPLIANCE—Submission to God
   Judah's willingness to submit himself as surety (43:3–10)
   Absence of any envy on part of the brothers to favoritism of Benjamin (by Jacob and Joseph; see Notes)
   Narrator's approval of their submissive attitude (see Notes)

III. Our Response: *Be sensitive and selfless!*
   How to develop appropriate attitudes, prompted by divine discipline, to resolve past sin
   How such resolutions make for effective agency of divine blessing to others

Another way of organizing the sermon, making a brief recap of the brothers' sin against Joseph:

I.   Execution of Past Sins
   Recap: the brothers egregious offense against Joseph (Gen 37; 42:21)
   Move-to-Relevance: Our past sinful deeds, particularly those against others

II. Experience of Present Guilt
   Role-reversal and role-duplication (42:9–15, 16–20, 25–28, 35; 43:11–12, 18; and see Notes)
   Acknowledgement of God's working and their own guilt (42:6, 18, 21–22, 28; 43:14, 23, 29)
   Move-to-Relevance: Unresolved sin in our lives; our indifference to God's prompting through discipline

III. Expectation of Future Resolution
   Judah's willingness to submit himself as surety (43:3–10)
   Absence of any envy on part of the brothers to favoritism of Benjamin (by Jacob and Joseph; see Notes)
   Narrator's approval of their submissive attitude (see Notes)

IV. *Be sensitive and selfless!*
   How to develop appropriate attitudes, prompted by divine discipline, to resolve past sin
   How such resolutions make for effective agency of divine blessing to others

---

45. See Matt 5:13–16; Luke 6:27–38; Rom 12:21; 2 Cor 5:20; Gal 6:10; Jas 1:27; 1 Pet 3:9; etc.

PERICOPE 33

Reconciliation

Genesis 44:1–45:28

[Brothers' Final Test; Judah's Speech; Reconciliation]

REVIEW, SUMMARY, PREVIEW

Review of Pericope 32: Genesis 42:1–43:34 describe the two trips of the brothers to Egypt. There, as a result of Joseph's strategies to test them, they are convicted of their own guilt in the kidnapping and enslavement of Joseph. On their second trip to Egypt, Judah, in a declaration of selflessness, persuades Jacob to allow Benjamin to go with them, as Joseph had required. God's discipline of his people, and their submission to him, enable the flow of divine blessings.

Summary of Pericope 33: This pericope continues the account of the brothers' second trip to Egypt. Benjamin has been found with the missing goblet of the Prime Minister and is in danger of being enslaved. Judah intervenes, sacrificing himself for the sake of his younger brother and his aging father, upon which Joseph breaks down and reveals his identity. He attributes to God's providence all that had happened. Agents of divine blessing are faithful to those suffering, are selfless, and acknowledge God's sovereignty in all events.

Preview of Pericope 34: The next pericope (Gen 46:1–47:31) shows Jacob and the extended family, at the behest of Joseph, moving *en masse* to Egypt. There, Jacob, the patriarch, blesses Pharoah, the ruler of Egypt, and immediately we have an account of the result of divine blessing mediated through Jacob's family: Joseph's wise policies saved Egypt and its people from sure death in a time of famine. God's people serve as agents of his blessing to others.

33 *Genesis 44:1–45:28*

THEOLOGICAL FOCUS OF PERICOPE 33

33 Agents of divine blessing demonstrate faithful solidarity with those suffering, sacrificially put others before themselves, and recognize God's overriding sovereignty (44:1–45:28).

33.1 Agents of divine blessing, conscious of their own failings, demonstrate faithful solidarity with those suffering.

33.2 Agents of blessing sacrificially put others before themselves, thus opening the doors to abundant divine blessing.

33.3 The recognition of God's overriding sovereignty enables reconciliation and the uninterrupted flow of divine blessing.

OVERVIEW

This pericope describes the remainder of the events on that fateful second trip to Egypt made by Joseph's brothers. The story continues where it left off in the previous pericope: the brothers had arrived in Egypt for the second time, Benjamin had been brought along, and Simeon's release had been accomplished (though not explicitly mentioned). Joseph, still incognito to his brothers, invites them to a grand feast and everything appears to be fine and dandy, at least till they get ready to return to Canaan. Then comes another test!

Genesis 44 has elements that correspond to those in Gen 43: both have Joseph's directives to his steward (43:16–17 and 44:1–2, 4–6); in both, the brothers appeal to the steward (43:18–23 and 44:7–13); and they bow before Joseph in both (43:26, 28 and 44:14).[1]

As was noted in the previous pericope, there were indications that the brothers had undergone a transformation of attitude. In this pericope, however, there is no doubt about their change of heart. The striking elements here are the incredible solidarity of the brothers with their accused (and supposedly guilty) sibling, and Judah's moving and powerful speech that causes Joseph to weep—unassailable evidence of the brothers' reformation.

There are many instances of "death" in this pericope: 43:8 (death by famine); 44:9 (death as penalty); 44:20, (death by wild animals); 44:22, 31 (death by grief). "[T]he reader realizes just how far the forces of death have infiltrated this family. Joseph's absence has left an open sore that nothing has been able to heal."[2] Here, Judah seeks to put an end to all that trauma by his self-sacrifice, an offer that he had successfully made once before (43:9). At that time, Jacob had released his "only" son. In this pericope, in Gen 44, when Judah makes that offer again, Joseph releases that same

---

1. Ross, *Creation and Blessing*, 664. For more details that unite the entire second trip, 43:1–45:28, see Pericope 32.

2. Harris, "Genesis 44:18–34," 179.

son of Jacob from potential enslavement. And with Judah's self-sacrifice, bonds are broken, reconciliation is achieved, and relationships are restored—the blessing of God is experienced by one and all. The abundance of divine blessing is unprecedented: the entire family is reunited, all seventy of them relocate to Egypt where they live in comfort, and "the death force of the famine [and interpersonal rivalry] is pushed back. . . . Judah's self-denial for the good of the family breaks the grief-death cycle, and enables abundant life for all," by sacrificing himself for a brother more loved than himself![3]

"All the episodes in the Joseph story contribute to demonstrating how God's purposes are ultimately fulfilled through and in spite of human deeds, whether or not those deeds are morally right. The apparent secularity of much of the story, which has led some commentators to see wisdom influence, is rather witness to the invisibility of God's actions in human affairs: only in retrospect can man see what God has been doing."[4] But I submit that divine sovereignty is front and center in this pericope and, indeed, throughout the Joseph saga: God sends dreams and people, watches dungeons and jailhouses, superintends famines and journeys, controls masters and rulers, times events and actions, and governs attitudes and desires. But while divine sovereignty is prominent in the story and even overrides human failures, sin is not excused, condoned, or overlooked: the brothers suffer for their wrongdoing, and they repent (42:21; 44:16; etc.). And sin takes its toll on the innocent as well, as Joseph's own life-experiences have detailed in the earlier chapters of his saga. Nevertheless, Joseph chooses to see the hand of God through all that, and he—and his brothers—become agents of divine blessing to the families they are part of, to the society to which they belong, and to the nation in which they sojourn.

33   Genesis 44:1–45:28

THEOLOGICAL FOCUS 33[A]

33   Agents of divine blessing demonstrate faithful solidarity with those suffering, sacrificially put others before themselves, and recognize God's overriding sovereignty.

    33.1   *Agents of divine blessing, conscious of their own failings, demonstrate faithful solidarity with those suffering.*

    33.2   *Agents of blessing sacrificially put others before themselves, thus opening the doors to abundant divine blessing.*

    33.3   *The recognition of God's overriding sovereignty enables reconciliation and the uninterrupted flow of divine blessing.*

A. Having only one section in this pericope, the "Theological Focus 33" is identical to the "Theological Focus of Pericope 33."

3. Ibid., 181.

4. Wenham, *Genesis 16–50*, 432.

NOTES 33

33.1 *Agents of divine blessing, conscious of their own failings, demonstrate faithful solidarity with those suffering.*

Initially, in 44:3, all seems to be well that ends well; mission had been accomplished—both brothers' lives (Simeon's and Benjamin's) were intact, and the food they had come for had been procured. But one more test remained. This final test consisted in "turning back the wheel of time to the original crime against himself [Joseph], with the circumstances reproduced and the ten [potentially] ranged against Benjamin," another paternal favorite—another test of role-duplication (see Pericope 32).[5] "Joseph's motivation for this additional ruse becomes clear only when read in the context of the larger narrative complex. . . . Has anything really changed? Have they come to terms with their father's favoritism? Or now with Simeon released, will they take the food and the extra money, and run, abandoning Benjamin forever [when he is accused of theft]? . . . Joseph has devised this test to determine their character."[6] The earlier test in the preceding pericope commenced with an "order" from Joseph (42:25)—as it also does here, in 44:1—to "fill" the men's sacks with grain/food and to put money in their loads. However, there is a difference: this time Joseph's goblet—"my cup, the silver cup" is at the head of the sentence for emphasis—is hidden in Benjamin's sack.[7] Mathews sees the repeated references to "silver" in 44:1–2, 8 (×5) as a hint to the reader to recall the silver obtained by the brothers' sale of Joseph (37:28).[8] "[T]his emphasis on the silver is understandable. On the one hand the silver is the symbol of the still-unresolved betrayal (Joseph had been sold for twenty silver pieces, 37:28). Ever since, the silver seems to stick to them. Like Lady Macbeth, unable to get the blood of the murdered king off her hands, they cannot get away from the bloody silver."[9] It bespeaks their terrible guilt.

The brothers are quite sure they had nothing to do with the missing goblet: they deny the charge (44:7a), they swear their ignorance (44:7b), they appeal to their past upright behavior (44:8), and they promise that the thief will be executed (44:9). While it is the certainty of their innocence that prompts them to sentence the guilty to death,

---

5. Sternberg, *The Poetics of Biblical Narrative*, 303.

6. Arnold, *Genesis*, 358–59. Needless to say, the test also examines their love and concern for their father, Jacob, as will be evident in Judah's later response to Joseph.

7. Joseph's cup, according to his steward, was employed for divination, perhaps with liquids—lecanomancy or hydromancy (44:5). It is doubtful if Joseph actually engaged in that practice, later forbidden in the Mosaic Law (Lev 19:26; Deut 18:10); there has never been a hint in all of the Joseph narrative that he adopted Egyptian rituals. In all likelihood the postulated utility of the vessel, as asserted by the steward, simply served to increase its value and the gravity of its theft, as the infinitive absolute ("he indeed practices divination") indicates. Later, Joseph, questioning the brothers about the purloining of the goblet, also employs the same infinitive absolute—"A man like me can indeed practice divination" (44:15). Both statements, of lord and of steward, might well have been intended to intensify the psychological pressure on the accused, and need not necessarily be evidence of Joseph's pagan practices.

8. *Genesis 11:27–50:26*, 797–98. In fact, there are twenty references to silver in 42:25–45:22.

9. Brodie, *Genesis as Dialogue*, 387.

the brothers are simultaneously making an unwitting admission that rebounds on themselves: they, the ones who stole Joseph, should die for the crime—an appropriate sentence.[10] And to the brothers' "far be it" (חָלִילָה, *khalilah*, 44:7), protesting their innocence regarding theft, Joseph later responds with his own "far be it" (חָלִילָה, 44:17), as he adopts a posture of fairness in wanting to enslave the thief (חלילה is a substantive meaning "desecration," thus the utterance becomes an oath: "May it be a desecration if . . ."). He is giving it back to them in their own coin—role-reversal.[11]

A deliberate and meticulous search for the missing goblet commences, beginning with the bags of the oldest and moving to the youngest, escalating the tension (44:11–12). And rather than the steward finding the cup, the narrator dramatizes the discovery by utilizing a passive verb to emphasize the object found: "and the cup was found in Benjamin's sack" (44:12).

How would the brothers deal with Benjamin now, when he is accused of a crime and is seemingly guilty? Would they abandon him, as they did Joseph, thus ridding themselves of the one remaining object of parental favoritism? Indeed, unlike in Joseph's case, no deception would be necessary here; they could simply return to Jacob complaining about the harsh ruler in Egypt who had imprisoned Benjamin—the father himself had envisioned this possibility (43:14). The brothers would have to do nothing to achieve this end; on the other hand, to undo this calamity they would have to work hard. Which option would they choose—dispose of Benjamin or defend him? In effect, then, this test is a return to the situation of Gen 37—role-duplication. Simeon's incarceration succeeded in drawing Benjamin to Egypt. Now Joseph was going intensify the pressure on his siblings. But in the brothers' mind, all of this is recompense for their evil deeds towards Joseph—God had found them out![12] The word "find" echoes in this pericope (also "find/overtake," in 44:34). Money and the goblet are the objects of the finding in 44:8, 9, 10, 12, 16b, 17. But that is not all: *God* has been doing some finding, too, and he it is who has "found out the evil" of the brothers (44:16a).

For a reader attending to the text, there are signs in this pericope that events are moving towards a happy ending. In particular, the response of the brothers to

---

10. That the brothers are confident in each other to make such strong claims of innocence regarding the missing goblet also goes far to show them as a united group. Interestingly enough, it appears that history is repeating itself. Their father, Jacob, was once accused of theft, whereupon he, too, promised death for the pilferer (31:32). Rachel, the culprit then, got away undetected. Her son would not be so fortunate now.

11. The same phrase was used by Abraham of God to appeal to the justice of deity (18:25). These are the only three occurrences of the word in Genesis. For "role-duplication" and "role-reversal," borrowed from Sternberg, *The Poetics of Biblical Narrative*, 294, see Pericope 32.

12. Later, Judah does not argue the case of the missing goblet. He does not bring in the suspicious circumstances of odd objects (silver) being found in mouths of their sacks in times past. In fact, he does not even protest the way the brothers did when first accused by the steward (44:7–9), adducing their past probity and promising capital punishment for the one found guilty. Rather, he acknowledges that "God has found out the guilt of your servants" (44:16). That guilt is obviously not the theft of the goblet, of which at least ten of the eleven siblings were innocent. The nagging culpability that Judah (and his siblings) are burdened by is that of their wickedness towards another brother decades ago, a guilt that had already been brought to the fore in their first Egypt trip (42:21–23).

Benjamin's accusation is striking. Together, they rend their clothes in a sign of powerful fraternity, and return to Joseph's house without a moment's hesitation, and without a single (recorded) word (44:13), this even after having been told firmly that the innocent would be released and only the guilty would be detained (44:10). They only act, and their actions are louder than words. Tearing of clothing last occurred in Genesis when Jacob came to believe that Joseph had died (37:34). Indeed, the narrator may be subtly indicating the brothers perfect repentance by using the same words to describe these rendings of clothes, too.[13] This time it is the brothers who demonstrate this sign of great grief, when another parental favorite's life is jeopardized. It is likely that the brothers had no choice but to believe that Benjamin had made off with the cup; that makes their solidarity even more impressive: the innocent were willing to suffer with one ostensibly guilty, all for the sake of family. The collective responsibility assumed by the siblings is remarkable—they act as one! They had left Joseph's house as "men" (44:3); now they return as "Judah and his brothers" (44:14)[14], "a shift in designation that augurs well both as a reminder of the newly dominant figure and as a hint of solidarity" with the one now in deep trouble.[15]

Unlike their earlier obeisance to the Egyptian lord (42:6), they now "fall before his face to the ground" (44:14), struck dumb. The brothers' posture here is far more submissive than their earlier bowing and prostration (42:6; 43:26, 28; also see 37:7, 9). Of course, this time the situation is also far more dangerous, and they recognize they are totally at the mercy of this Egyptian ruler. Key words are repeated: "servant(s)" (44:18 [×2], 19, 21, 23, 24, 27, 30, 31, 32, 33 [×2]) and "lord" (44:18 [×2], 19, 20, 22, 24, 33). They are desperate! But it is quite ironic: once they were guilty up to their necks and showed no grief, no remorse. Now they are innocent[16], and demonstrate anguish.[17] "[N]one of them even thinks of deserting Benjamin. At last, they clearly show

13. Navon, "*Beged or Simlah*," 268. He argues that the use of שִׂמְלָה, *simlah*, rather than בֶּגֶד, *beged*, for "garment" in 37:34 and 44:13 is deliberate, especially given that בָּגַד, *bagad*, is a homonym meaning "to deceive." In fact, it is constantly used in Genesis in the context of deception: 37:29; 38:14, 19; 39:12, 13, 15, 18. So while בגד may have been more natural in this situation, the narrator's use of שמלה throws the earlier instance of Jacob's robe-rending into moral juxtaposition with the brothers'. Jacob's act underscored the sin committed against him, a sin that would be atoned for only by a tearing of the שמלה by the same guilty sinners on a future day—i.e., in this pericope (ibid., 268–69).

14. For the first time, the text has "Judah and his brothers," signifying the leadership role he will soon be playing. Indeed, the verb used is singular (וַיָּבֹא, *wayyabo'*, "come"): "And-he-came Judah and-his-brothers." Judah is rightly the focus for the remainder of the chapter.

15. Sternberg, *The Poetics of Biblical Narrative*, 305. In a sense, Judah's subsequent speech is rendered redundant, for there is enough in this section to show that the brothers were transformed persons, completely unwilling to act as they had done before with Joseph—they had aced the role-duplication test! Thus, while Judah is a hero for his magnificent words in 44:18–34, the rest of the brothers are equally creditworthy in their honorable, self-sacrificial response to a sibling in danger.

16. At least most of them are innocent: Benjamin's guilt was probably debatable in the brothers' minds, for the appearance of the money in sacks this second time—even though it is not mentioned (but is implied in 44:1–2)—must have given them grounds to suspect some hanky-panky on the part of the ruler and his steward.

17. Mathews, *Genesis 11:27–50:26*, 800. One cannot but wonder about what was going through Benjamin's mind in all this. At least, unlike the unfortunate case of Joseph in Gen 37, he was not aban-

themselves to be their brother's keepers. They will try to stand or fall together. They do not ask—as did Abraham of God regarding Sodom [18:23]—why the righteous must suffer with the guilty. For one thing, they know that they are not righteous. For another, they are at last affirming the principle of the unity of the whole tribe."[18] But the brothers' guilt, and even their joint rending of clothing and their return to Joseph's house, has not proven to Joseph a change in their attitude. Neither has anything been said or done thus far that has shown their concern for an aging father. For all that to be discovered the brothers would need to be put through the wringer: hence Joseph's order that they return home to Canaan without Benjamin who will remain enslaved in Egypt (44:17). What will they do now?

33.2 *Agents of blessing sacrificially put others before themselves, thus opening the doors to abundant divine blessing.*

Benjamin is clearly in big trouble. The Prime Minister's goblet has been found in his sack and Joseph, at least in façade, is indignant (43:14–15). To this exigency, Judah is rendered almost speechless at first, being only able to blurt out some penitential rhetorical questions: "What can we say . . . ?" and "What can we speak?" and "How can we justify ourselves?" (44:16). But the confession is explicit: *God* had found them out (44:16).

While the brothers, earlier, with their confidence that the cup would not be found among them, had promised death for the thief (43:9), they are now put in a delicate situation. Obviously exacting his life was not an appropriate course of action against Benjamin. Judah quietly deletes that offer, retaining only the assertion of their willingness to be the Egyptian's slaves, along with Benjamin (43:9, 16), more than what Joseph had wanted (43:10, 17). The guilty one will be detained, and the rest of them, he says, can "go up *in peace* to your father." In peace, without Benjamin? Obviously, Joseph's ploy is intended to provoke the brothers for "a response to an old-new scenario that leads them back to Jacob . . . to report his last favorite gone for life."[19] Another instance of role-duplication, as they are forced to return to an old man with the news that another of his sons has gone missing.[20]

This was Joseph's second test. How would the brothers respond to Benjamin's enslavement—and his alone? Would they facilely get rid of another favorite brother and return home? There was really no reason for the brothers to return to Joseph's house and for Judah to engage him with such an impassioned plea: they would only have stood to gain by getting rid of the last of Jacob's favorites (or so they might have assumed), and that without sullying their own hands.[21] Again there is both role-re-

---

doned by his siblings.

18. Kass, *The Beginning of Wisdom*, 592.

19. Sternberg, *The Poetics of Biblical Narrative*, 306–307.

20. Benjamin's "not [being] with us" (אֵינֶנּוּ, *ʾenennu*, 44:30) employs the same Hebrew word that described the death of Joseph: "He is no more" (אֵינֶנּוּ, 42:13, 32, 36).

21. When Joseph asks, "What is this deed you have done?" (44:15), one option available to the brothers was to deny any knowledge of theft and point collective fingers at Benjamin—"He is the guilty one."

versal, "(divine) tit for (human) tat and theft revealed [of the cup] for theft concealed [the kidnapping of Joseph]," and role-duplication, "to tempt them to desert Benjamin and betray their fraternal bond once again."[22] A critical juncture in the story has been reached: the brothers can either stick with their brother or abandon him.

But by their return to Joseph's house in solidarity with Benjamin (44:13–14), one gets the sense that abandoning this sibling is not what they are going to do. To the increased pressure of this second test—and, indeed, a second chance to succeed in a similar situation where once they had failed—Judah responds, on behalf of his siblings . . . and passes the test with flying colors (44:18–34)![23] Judah's is a most persuasive and influential discourse that falls into three parts: a review of the past (44:18–29, including the first encounter with Joseph and the brothers' report of the trip to Jacob), a fearful anticipation of the near future (44:30–32, detailing the lethal consequences to Jacob of Benjamin not returning), and a resolution for the present (44:33–34, Judah's offering of himself as a substitute for Benjamin).[24] Again, as he had promised his father in 43:9, he places his own life on the line here (44:32–34). What is striking is that his act of sacrifice is not being performed for Benjamin, though that aspect is present of course, but primarily for the sake of an already wounded and deeply hurting father who was advancing in age: Judah uses "father" fourteen times in his speech to Joseph (44:16, 18–34), beginning and ending with references to Jacob (44:19, 34). The gist of Judah's speech is that his father has lost one of his favorite sons already and they— Judah and his brothers—are not willing to put their parent through another similar loss, the shock of which might well kill him.[25] Judah concludes by addressing Joseph's plan to keep the guilty one as a slave and let the others go: he, Judah, will take the place of Benjamin (44:33–34).[26] He is willing to forsake his very life, rather than put

---

Indeed, they would have been in the right to have done exactly that and could then have returned home, guiltless . . . and without Benjamin.

22. Sternberg, *The Poetics of Biblical Narrative*, 306.

23. Judah's address has been rightly called "a speech of singular pathos and beauty, remarkable not less for grace and persuasive eloquence than for frankness and generosity" (Driver, *Genesis*, 359), and "the finest specimen of dignified and persuasive eloquence in the OT" (Skinner, *Genesis*, 485). "No more moving example of true contrition and repentance is to be found in Scripture, unless it be the parable of the prodigal son (Luke 15)" (Wenham, *Genesis 16–50*, 431). "[Judah's] magnanimous and self-sacrificing offer to remain as Joseph's slave in Benjamin's stead is unparalleled in the book of Genesis; in the Torah, it is surpassed only by Moses' plea to God to forgive Israel for the golden calf, asking to be erased from God's book should He refuse to forgive his people for their sin" (Kass, *The Beginning of Wisdom*, 602).

24. From Wenham, *Genesis 16–50*, 426.

25. In describing Jacob's response to the loss of Joseph, Judah uses the same words Jacob did, when he grieved uncontrollably: "torn to pieces" occurs in both 37:33 and here, in 44:28. This, by the way, was probably the first time Joseph had heard of his father's reaction to that event. Elsewhere, it was asserted by his family only that Joseph had died (37:33; 42:13, 22, 32, 36, 38; 44:20).

26. "Once before Judah witnessed how the crushing news of Joseph's loss indelibly altered his father's spirit (37:34–35). Now he would rather suffer the remainder of his days as a slave than bear the blame of his father's dying grief" (Mathews, *Genesis 11:27–50:26*, 806). A key word that shows up at the beginning of Gen 44 is echoed in Judah's speech: "for/instead of" (תַּחַת, *takhat*, 44:4—"evil *for* good"; and 44:33—Judah *for* Benjamin). This substitution is intriguing: earlier the brothers had done evil to a good man; by the end of Gen 45, an innocent man (Judah) is willing to substitute for an ostensibly guilty one

his father through the agony of another "bereavement" (42:36). This, despite the fact that this father loves him and his brothers *less* than he does the two favorite children of his (37:3; 42:4, 36, 38). Such a selfless attitude could only be the result of a drastic transformation! Incidentally the use of "love" here is the only other use of the verb in the Joseph Story; its first instance was in 37:3 stating the love of the same father for another son of the same wife. In addition, one must note that Judah's putting his father's partiality into words is incredibly self-deprecating: "'You know that my wife bore me two sons'" (44:27). Judah virtually excludes himself and the others from the circle of Jacob's children! Yet, despite such agonizing loss of face, Judah is willing to be substituted for the favored one (and he suggests, in 44:16, that his brothers would be equally willing to serve as stand-ins as well). "That Judah should adduce the father's favoritism as the ground for self-sacrifice is such an irresistible proof of filial devotion that it breaks down Joseph's last defenses."[27]

> [T]his remarkable speech is a point-for-point undoing, morally and psychologically, of the brothers' earlier violation of fraternal and filial bonds. . . . Twenty-two years earlier, Judah engineered the selling of Joseph into slavery; now he is prepared to offer himself as a slave so that the other son of Rachel can be set free. Twenty-two years earlier, he stood with his brothers and silently watched when the bloodied tunic they had brought to Jacob sent their father into a fit of anguish; now he is willing to do anything in order not to have to see his father suffer that way again. Judah, then, as spokesman for the brothers, has admirably completed the painful process of learning to which Joseph and circumstances have made him submit. . . .[28]

It is impossible not to see the remarkable contrast between the Judah of Gen 37 and the Judah of the later chapters of the Joseph narrative, especially Gen 44. Once Judah sold a parental favorite; now Judah tries to save another parental favorite: "In the context of Judah's whole development, such an offer may be interpreted as an atonement for past evil committed against Jacob and Joseph in Genesis 37."[29] This is a broken man, Judah, well aware of his own guilt and his own burdens of responsibility. In fact, even Joseph did not have to go through these particular emotional upheavals. In that sense Judah is a strong competitor with Joseph to be the hero of this saga and the leader of his siblings.

(Benjamin), showing that the brothers' rehabilitation is complete. Other words that show up in Judah's petition from the earlier part of Gen 44 are "evil" (44:4, 5 and 44:34) and "die" (44:9 and 44:20, 22, 31).

27. Sternberg, *The Poetics of Biblical Narrative*, 308. Moreover, Benjamin is also referred to by Judah as "our youngest brother" (44:26 [×2]) and "lad" (44:22, 30, 31, 32, 33 [×2], 34), evidence, once again, of the bond of fraternity. "So intimate is the speech [of Judah] . . . that not a word is said about the presence of an interpreter. One would assume that an interpreter would be formally required, in keeping with Joseph's charade not to understand the Hebrew tongue [and see 42:23 for an interpreter who was used], but as the story is presented, it is almost as if Judah's speech moves Joseph without being translated" (Kass, *The Beginning of Wisdom*, 597).

28. Alter, *The Art of Biblical Narrative*, 174–75.

29. Lambe, "Judah's Development," 64.

In more ways than one, Gen 38 is clearly the transformative event of Judah's life: not only did he there understand his own guilt (38:26) and his failure to support, protect, and care for his family, but in having lost two children of his own in that chapter, he can now empathize perfectly with his father who, apparently, is in danger of losing two of his children. In Gen 38, unwittingly Judah was made a substitute for a family member—Judah, instead of Shelah, would raise children through Tamar; here in Gen 44:32–34 (and in 43:9), he willingly offers himself as a substitute for his brother Benjamin. "Judah's self-pledging alludes to his penitent attitude: whereas Judah earlier had selfishly neglected to fulfill his pledge to a prostitute . . ., he now selflessly offers up himself as a pledge."[30]

The verb "justify" (צדק, *tsdq*) occurs only twice in Genesis: in 38:26 and in 44:16. Both times Judah is the one employing the word. He had learnt his lesson there, and he applies that lesson here. He, with his brothers ("we . . . ourselves," 44:16), are not guiltless, innocent though they may be of the particular crimes they have been accused of in Gen 42 (spying) and Gen 44 (stealing). "Rather he has in mind the crime against their long-lost brother. For Judah this mistaken charge against them [in this pericope] is recompense for the crime they had not atoned for. There was no human explanation for the peculiar circumstances of the cup."[31] Indeed, it was God who "found" their guilt (44:16). "This is God's way, says Judah, of visiting their past misdeeds upon them. They withheld mercy from Joseph (42:21). Now God will withhold mercy from them. They deserve what is happening to them even if they are not guilty of this particular crime. Here is a graphic illustration of the Bible's emphasis on God's justice. The wrongs one does will be repaid, someway, somehow, somewhere."[32]

Bechtold remarks on the motif of sight in the timeline of Judah's story in Gen 37, 38, and 42–44: Judah "saw" Joseph treated specially by his father and responded with hatred (37:4); he "saw" his brother coming and responded with murderous intent (37:18), to "see" what would become of his dreams (37:20); he "saw" the caravan of Ishmaelites and responded by selling Joseph to them (37:25–28); he "saw" a Canaanite and took her as wife (38:2); he "saw" and had relations with his daughter-in-law (38:15)—all in all, a disreputable performance of this son of Jacob in response to his sight. Later, however, Judah "sees" the returned silver and fears (42:27, 35); he remembers "seeing" the distress of Joseph (42:21); and in his final speech before Joseph he tells of Jacob's anguish at not having "seen" Joseph's face since the fateful day of his kidnapping (44:27–28), and of Jacob's certain heartbrokenness when Jacob "sees" that Benjamin has not returned (44:31). How, Judah asks, will he be able to return to his father without Benjamin and "see" the evil that will befall the old man (44:34)—an

---

30. Kruschwitz, "The Type-Scene Connection," 408–9. "Pledge," עֵרָבוֹן, *'erabon*, in 38:17, 18, 20, is closely related to the verb used of Judah—"to be surety," עָרַב (*'arab*, 43:9; 44:32).

31. Mathews, *Genesis 11:27–50:26*, 802.

32. Hamilton, *Genesis: Chapters 18–50*, 566. That, of course, is not to deny God's overwhelming and amazing grace.

unbearable situation for Judah, now clearly a changed man! Yes, indeed, his eyes had been opened.[33]

Judah's magnificent address concludes with a rhetorical question that itself ends with the word אָבִי (ʾavi, "my father," 44:34); in fact אָבִי is heard four times in 44:30–34. Judah ends with the pathos of "my father" echoing on his tongue and, needless to say, in the ears of Joseph. Joseph's total breakdown (45:1–2) after this lengthy and passionate plea from Judah (44:18–34) reveals the potency of Judah's address. Perhaps the connection between address and response is also revealed in the employment of "approach": Judah "approaches" Joseph (44:18), and after he is done speaking, Joseph bids his brothers "approach" him (45:4 [×2]).[34]

33.3 *The recognition of God's overriding sovereignty enables reconciliation and the uninterrupted flow of divine blessing.*

The reconciliation between Joseph and his brothers takes place in Gen 45. Restoration of relationships occurs as the "men" (44:1, 3, 4, 11; nine times in Gen 43–44) now become Joseph's "brothers" (45:1, 3 [×2], 4 [×2], 12, 14, 15, 16, 17, 24). That the brothers are noted to be talking with Joseph (45:15) when, in an earlier day, they could not speak peaceably with him (37:4), indicates the repair of alienation and the bridging of schisms. Joseph, of course, is *indirectly* responsible for the outcome, having set up the various tests and forcing the brothers' hands. But the *direct* and immediate responsibility for this blessed result lies with Judah and his speech of 44:18–34, an unparalleled example of persuasive discourse that perfectly met the exigencies of the situation. Judah is the hero in this pericope overall. But here in Gen 45, Joseph stands out. He might have orchestrated the events and Judah may have precipitated the reconciliation. But it was the hand of God working providentially and sovereignly throughout Joseph's life and that of his family that had accomplished this glorious end. Five times Joseph points to divine intention (45:5, 7, 8, 9—three times God is one who sent Joseph to Egypt, and twice God is the one who made Joseph great there), working in, and with, and through human activity.[35] "Joseph's speech is a luminous illustration of the Bible's double system of causation, human and divine."[36] Thus Joseph's self-disclosure is simultaneously a revelation of God. "From a worm's-eye view, [Joseph's] narrative reads like a nightmare, a cacophony of outrageous excesses unjustly inflicted upon him. A rational conclusion that it is all absurd from this perspective could have made him an existentialist, a cynic, or a nihilist. But he chooses the heavenly perspective that God is working through him to bring about what is good. . . . This enables him to forgive and encourage his brothers to do the same."[37] Joseph's recognition of God's overriding sovereignty is the key concept here.

---

33. See Bechtold, "Sight Elements."

34. Mathews, *Genesis 11:27–50:26*, 793–94.

35. Also see 39:9; 40:8; 41:16, 25, 28, 32, 51, 52; 42:18; 43:29; 50:19–20 for Joseph's keen awareness of God's workings in his life.

36. Alter, *The Five Books of Moses*, 261.

37. Waltke and Fredricks, *Genesis*, 565.

The impact of Joseph speaking to them in their own tongue[38], and revealing himself as their long-lost, and presumed-dead, brother is so powerful, the brothers are rendered speechless and even terrified (45:3). After all that they had been through at the hands of this anonymous Egyptian ruler, what would a powerful Joseph—whom they had once sold into slavery—do to them? They do not answer Joseph's question about their father (45:3), and he has to repeat himself (45:4—"I am Joseph"). In fact, they say nothing at all in this episode (that is reported in direct speech) until they arrive back in Canaan (45:26)! Their fear of reprisal may have only been magnified when Joseph adds, "I am your brother Joseph, *whom you sold into Egypt*" (45:4; see 37:27, 28, 36). He, therefore, is quick to recount God's overriding control of the events of the past two decades (45:5–9), and to reassure his siblings about the future (45:10–11).

Joseph's account of ending up in Egypt as a high-ranking official is noted seven times in 45:4–9: "you sold me" (×2), "God sent me" (×3), "He made me father"[39] . . ., lord . . ., ruler[40] . . .," and "God made me lord." All this emphsizes that Joseph was/is indeed an agent of divine blessing. The infinitives in 45:7, "to secure for you a remnant on the earth and to sustain life for you by a great deliverance," may have either God or Joseph as its subject. Perhaps the subject is *both* God and Joseph—God through Joseph as his agent of blessing.[41] Another indication of this human instrumentality in divine hands is in Joseph's instruction to tell Jacob about his, Joseph's, "honor"—כָּבוֹד, *kabod*, often used of God's "honor/glory" (45:13). Joseph seems to be looking "like" God.

At the same time it becomes clear that the recognition of the sovereignty of God is also the first step of forgiveness and reconciliation. This, of course, is not a condoning or minimizing of sin—in this case, the sin of Joseph's brothers. But because of God's work through his human agents, Joseph and Judah, reconciliation occurs. Joseph had already wept twice before his brothers, unbeknownst to them (42:24; 43:30); this time he is unable to keep his emotions private: 45:1–2 and 45:14–15 describe his breaking down, and brackets his self-disclosure on either side. His response to his brothers after all these years is one that bears no ill-will, grudge, or plans for revenge. He simply rejoices in the restoration, points to God as the author of it all, and begs that his father be brought to Egypt quickly ("hurry," bookends Joseph's final instructions, 45:9, 13)—

38. Subtly, the narrator had noted that Joseph had everyone else leave the room at this time (45:1)—presumably, he is now speaking to his brothers without an interpreter. That seems also to be implied in 45:12.

39. By "father" to Pharaoh, Joseph means chief advisor or one in acting as a father figure. See Jdg 17:10; 18:19; 2 Kgs 6:21; 13:14; etc.

40. There is an ironic touch in Joseph's description of himself as one who was sent by God to be a "ruler" (from מָשַׁל, *mshl*, 45:8; also see 45:26); מֹשֵׁל was used indignantly by the brothers in response to Joseph's dream in 37:8.

41. This is also seen in 50:19–20. The infinitive, "to sustain life," in 45:5 is less ambiguous, though in light of 45:7, it, too, may be considered to have a dual subject. One wonders when Joseph came to this conclusion. "Nothing thus far in the narrative has prepared us for this eloquent and magnificent theologizing on his pilgrimage. We must assume that Joseph perceived bit by bit the hand of God in this nightmare" (Hamilton, *Genesis: Chapters 18–50*, 575).

and all this even before the normal gestures of an emotional meeting are conducted (45:14–15). "Then the scene breaks into mutual hugs and tears, for the joy at seeing a long lost brother and the sheer relief of no longer bearing the guilt of twenty years. In a very real sense they are now all set free from slavery."[42] As was noted, Judah's "approaching" (44:18) the Egyptian ruler results, ultimately, in all of them "approaching" (45:4 [×2]) one another.[43] The breach between them is being obliterated. Indeed, Joseph's speech, unlike Judah's, focuses on life (45:3, 28). Joseph's question, הַעוֹד ... חָי (*ha'od . . . khay*, "Is [my father] still alive?" 45:3) is matched by Jacob's exclamation at the end of the chapter, עוֹד ... חָי (*'od . . . khay*, "[My son Joseph] is still alive!" 45:28).[44]

That Pharaoh readily initiates the invitation to Jacob and his family to move to Egypt (45:17–20; though Joseph had already suggested it to his brothers, 45:9–11, 13), implies the esteem held by Joseph in Pharaoh's eyes. Again, God is working to grant Joseph favor before others.[45] And while a famine is ongoing, plenty is promised to Joseph and his relatives (45:11, 18, 20, 23)—God's blessing in action. Indeed, Pharaoh's open arms seem to be wider than Joseph's: the latter formally invited "you [the brothers], your sons, and your sons' sons" (45:10), while the former expanded this to include "your little ones and your wives" (45:19), as well as assuring them of "the best of all the land of Egypt" and "the fat of the land" (45:18, 20; also see 47:6, 11), not to mention wagons to transport the infirm and incapacitated (45:19). Twice the Pharaoh exhorts the brothers, "This do," emphasizing his earnestness and sincerity (45:17, 19).

Once again, in 45:22, we see Benjamin showered with far more gifts than were given to his siblings (as in 43:34). There was no danger of jealousy now, since such issues had been dealt with conclusively. It is interesting that the two haunting motifs of clothing (37:3, 31–33; 38:14, 19; 39:12–18; 41:14, 42) and silver (37:28; 42:25, 27, 28, 35; 43:12, 15, 18, 21, 22, 23; 44:1, 2, 8) show up here in 45:22 as well, and that together. He who was stripped of his clothes now himself clothes the ones who did the stripping.[46] The "garments" given to the brothers (שִׂמְלָה, *smlh*, 45:22) correspond to what the father and brothers were wearing before they were rent (37:34 and 44:13; also

---

42. Cotter, *Genesis*, 317.

43. According to *Gen. Rab.* 93.10, the reason for Joseph's drawing his brothers close (45:4) was to expose himself to them and provide them with proof of his circumcision. Rather unlikely, in my opinion, that the Egyptian lord would send everyone out of the room and disrobe.

44. Judah's repetition of "my father" eight times in 44:18–34 is matched by Joseph's frequent mention of the same individual—"my father" (45:3, 9, 13 [×2]). It is only after the father's fate and future is ascertained that Joseph turns to Benjamin in an embrace (45:14–15).

45. One notes that Pharaoh *and* his servants were delighted with the arrival of Joseph's relatives (the news was "good in the eyes of Pharaoh and his servants," 45:16)—he must have been quite a popular guy! And no wonder, he was saving countless lives in those dark days of widespread famine in Egypt. When Joseph had first stated his plans for those years of suffering, a similar response had been reported—his advice was "good in the eyes of Pharaoh and in the eyes of all his servants" (41:37).

46. See Pericope 31, for details of the garment changes undergone by Joseph through his story.

שׁמלה). By this newness of שׁמלה, the period of mourning is declared to be over![47] And to the ones who sold him for silver, he gives silver—the circle of kindness is complete.[48]

Joseph's parting exhortation to his brothers, that they not be "overcome with fear" (רגז, *rgz*, as used in Exod 15:14; literally, "to stir up") might have been to reassure them of the future—a major move to life in a new place, and in proximity of a brother who, at least in their minds, might revisit their old felonies upon them (see 50:15–19). Perhaps Joseph was also concerned about whether his siblings would be bold enough to confess that earlier crime to their father, a necessity given the circumstances of Joseph's "resurrection." Whatever else Jacob might think when he hears the news, one thing is clear: he was going to learn of what really happened to Joseph. The brothers cannot conceivably tell him they had found Joseph, without revealing how they had gotten rid of him in the first place. "Transformed they may be, but there is a great deal of truth telling that must yet take place," and that would be essential for complete healing to occur.[49]

Jacob, when he hears the news of Joseph being alive, is stunned (literally, "his heart became numb," 45:26), but his spirit revives as he assimilates the details and sees proof in the goods from Egypt (45:27). The old patriarch's incredulity is emphasized in the careful structuring of 45:25–28.[50]

A	Joseph's brothers go from Egypt and enter Canaan (45:25)			
	B	"Joseph is still alive" (45:26a)		
		C	Jacob's "heart became numb" (45:26b)	
			D	"Words of Joseph" told to Jacob (45:27a)
			D'	"Wagons of Joseph" seen by Jacob (45:27b)
		C'	Jacob's "spirit revived" (45:27c)	
	B'	"Joseph is still alive" (45:28a)		
A'	Jacob resolves to go (from Canaan) and see Joseph (in Egypt) (45:28b)			

"This closing scene [45:25–28] offers a marvelous contrast to the two previous occasions when the brothers returned to Jacob. Then he said, 'Joseph has been torn to bits . . . I shall go down to Sheol in mourning' (37:33, 35). 'There is no Joseph,' 'he is dead,' 'you will bring me down in my old age to Sheol with sorrow' (42:36, 38). Now he says, 'Joseph my son is still alive. I will go down to see him before I die' (45:28)."[51] "Enough," he says (using the single Hebrew word, רב, 45:28): the man is not interested in the silver, grain, donkeys, wagons, or even Benjamin now! He just wants to see his long-lost son, twenty-two years after he had presumed him dead! Jacob's "I have not seen [ראה, *r'h*] him since" (44:28, recounted by Judah), becomes, "I will go and see [ראה] him before I die" (45:28).

---

47. Mathews, *Genesis 11:27–50:26*, 818.

48. Hamilton, *Genesis: Chapters 18–50*, 586. As well indicating generosity, forgiveness, and kindness, the "ten" donkeys, particularly those loaded with "grain" (45:23), might reflect the original journey of the "ten" brothers to Egypt for "grain" (42:3, 25).

49. Cotter, *Genesis*, 317.

50. Table below modified from Longacre, *Joseph*, 37.

51. Wenham, *Genesis 16–50*, 430. "Go down" is ירד, *yrd*, in 37:35 and 42:38, but עלה, *'lh*, in 45:28.

In the last verse of the pericope, "Jacob" suddenly is labeled "Israel." "Israel is Jacob's new name, a name that speaks of a new destiny and a new future. Here is Israel with a new hope and a new expectation."[52] A new era was beginning for the nascent nation. Only such a recognition of God's sovereignty as seen in this pericope, and as demonstrated by the protagonists therein, enables the continued flow of his blessings to his people.

SERMON FOCUS AND OUTLINES

THEOLOGICAL FOCUS OF PERICOPE 33 FOR PREACHING

33   Self-sacrificial solidarity with the suffering, recognizing God's overriding sovereignty, promotes divine blessing (44:1–45:28).

The brothers' solidarity with Benjamin, Judah's self-sacrificial attitude, and Joseph's recognition of providence form the three major thrusts of this pericope. In the Theological Focus for Preaching, and as visible in the Sermon Outlines, I have chosen to conflate some of these emphases: "self-sacrificial solidarity with the suffering" is intended to include the brothers' support of Benjamin, Judah's giving of himself for the sake of his father and brother, and Joseph's willingness to forgive. The ground for such selflessness is a recognition of God's overriding sovereignty. It is God's providential dealings with humanity that enable one to forget self and live for others.

The selflessness demonstrated by Judah here is a stronger echo of what was found in Pericope 32 (in Gen 43, where Judah offered himself as a surety for Benjamin's return). While the thrust in that particular section was on self-sacrifice to undo the sins of the past, here it is primarily self-sacrifice for the sake of others: Judah sacrifices himself for his father, Jacob, by offering to be a substitute for his brother, Benjamin—a self-sacrifice that unleashes a flood of divine blessing.

The divine blessing in this pericope is the restoration of broken relationships and the outflow of blessings therefrom. A number of homiletical imperatives are possible here, derived from self-sacrifice, solidarity, trust in providence, forgiveness and reconciliation, etc.

Possible Preaching Outlines for Pericope 33

I.   WHAT? *Stand with the suffering of others . . .*
      The brothers' solidarity with Benjamin (44:1–13)
      Judah's self-sacrificial stance, for his father, and for his brother (44:14–34)
      Joseph's forgiveness of his brothers (45:1–8)
      Specifics on suffering with others, sacrificing oneself, and forgiving[53]

II. HOW? *Recognizing the sovereignty of God, . . .*
      The brothers' and Judah's acknowledgement of the working of God (44:16)
      Joseph's recognition of divine sovereignty (45:1–8)

52. Hamilton, *Genesis: Chapters 18–50*, 587.

53. The preacher may be better off focusing on one of these three facets—suffering, sacrificing, or forgiving.

Move-to-Relevance: The sovereign working of God frees us to live for others

III.   WHY? *So that divine blessing may overflow!*
       The consequences of the actions of the brothers, Judah, and Joseph (45:9–28)
       Move-to-Relevance: The divine blessing that is an outcome of standing with the suffering
       of others

The first outline thus has an extended homiletical imperative: *Stand with the suffering of others, recognizing the sovereignty of God, so that divine blessing may overflow!* If one desires, this What?–How?–Why? may be modified for another similar scheme, but one that avoids having the specifics of application show up in the first major move of the sermon. The outline below results not in a direct imperative, but in an implied one: *Divine blessing overflows as we stand with the suffering of others, recognizing the sovereignty of God.*

I.   WHAT? *Divine blessing overflows . . .*
      The consequences of the actions of the brothers, Judah, and Joseph (45:9–28)
      Move-to-Relevance: The divine blessing that is an outcome of standing with the suffering
      of others

II.   HOW? *. . . as we stand with the suffering of others, . . .*
      The brothers' solidarity with Benjamin (44:1–13)
      Judah's self-sacrificial stance, for his father, and for his brother (44:14–34)
      Joseph's forgiveness of his brothers (45:1–8)
      Specifics on suffering with others, sacrificing oneself, and forgiving

III. WHY?[54] *. . . recognizing the sovereignty of God.*
      The brothers' and Judah's acknowledgement of the working of God (44:16)
      Joseph's recognition of divine sovereignty (45:1–8)
      Move-to-Relevance: The sovereign working of God frees us to live for others

---

54. The "Why?" in this case explains the basis for one's being able to stand in suffering with others—because one recognizes the sovereignty of God and his providential workings in life.

PERICOPE 34

Blessing Received and Extended

Genesis 46:1–47:31

[Jacob and Family in Egypt; Jacob blesses Pharaoh; Egypt Saved]

REVIEW, SUMMARY, PREVIEW

Review of Pericope 33: Genesis 44:1–45:28 finds Benjamin with the missing goblet of the Prime Minister, and in danger of being enslaved. Judah intervenes, sacrificing himself for the sake of his younger brother and his aging father, upon which Joseph breaks down and reveals his identity. He attributes to God's providence all that had happened in the past decades. Agents of divine blessing are faithful to those suffering, they are selfless, and they acknowledge God's sovereignty in all events.

Summary of Pericope 34: In this pericope, Jacob and his extended family, at the behest of Joseph, move *en masse* to Egypt. There, Jacob, the patriarch, blesses Pharoah, the ruler of Egypt, and immediately following, we have an account of that blessing coming to pass: Joseph's wise policies saves Egypt and its people from sure death in a time of famine. God's people serve as agents of his blessing to others.

Preview of Pericope 35: The next pericope (48:1–50:26) concludes the Joseph Story and the book of Genesis. Jacob utters an extended blessing of his children and gives his last instructions for the disposal of his remains in Canaan. After Jacob's death and burial, Joseph's brothers seek a final reconciliation with him, which he graciously offers, again attributing to God's providence all the events of the past. Later, Joseph himself directs

542

that his bones be returned to the Promised Land one day. Thus, agents of divine blessing pass blessings on to others, as they look to the future for the consummation of God's promises.

34 *Genesis 46:1–47:31*

THEOLOGICAL FOCUS OF PERICOPE 34

34   **Agents of divine blessing, obediently trusting God to bring about his blessing in their own lives, take the initiative to extend God's blessing to others (46:1–47:31).**

34.1   Agents of divine blessing trust the sovereignty of God in obedience, to bring about his blessing in their own lives.

34.2   Agents of divine blessing take the initiative to extend God's blessing to others.

OVERVIEW

Towards the conclusion of his saga, Abraham was asked to undertake a journey to offer his son whom he loved (22:2); towards the end of another saga, Jacob is asked to undertake a journey to meet his son whom he loves (37:3, 4). Indeed, Jacob's journey to Egypt to join Joseph is quite similar in wording to that of Abraham in his testing in Gen 22. Both accounts have Beersheba (22:19 [×2] and 46:1, 5), "arise" (22:3, 19 and 46:5), departing and returning (22:5, 19 and 46:3–4), and offering of sacrifice(s) (22:2, 3, 7, 8, 13 and 46:1—though not using the same words); the patriarchs are called twice by name and each answers with הִנֵּנִי (*hinneni*, "Here I am," 22:11 and 46:2; in both cases this is the last recorded word of the respective patriarch to God), there is stretching out/putting a hand (22:10, 12 and 46:4—"Joseph will put his hand over your eyes"), divine blessing for the future (22:16–18 and 46:3–4), and a concluding genealogy (2:20–24 and 46:8–27). In a sense, then, this pericope describes Jacob's "test."[1]

On the other hand, this trip to Egypt was totally unlike that made by Jacob's grandfather to the same land in Gen 12.

> Both seek out the safety of Egypt because of famine. To save himself Abraham engages in deceit. To save his family Jacob engages in blessing. The Pharaoh at Abraham's visit was only too happy to see Abraham return to his own country. The Pharaoh at Jacob's visit insists that Jacob stay and settle on some choice land. Abraham retreats from Egypt. For Jacob Egypt is his new home. Abraham leaves Egypt alive (and happy to be so!). Jacob will leave Egypt dead.[2]

The pattern of descents and ascents in the Joseph narrative is also telling: Jacob had said he would "go down" (ירד, *yrd)* to Sheol (37:35); Joseph was "brought down" (ירד) to Egypt (39:1); Judah offered to remain as a slave in Egypt so that Benjamin might "go up [עלה, *'lh*]" with his brothers and Jacob might not "go down [ירד]" to

---

1. Brodie, *Genesis as Dialogue*, 391. Incidentally, the lives of both Abraham and Jacob are bracketed by promises of God: 12:1–3/22:15–18 and 28:13–16/46:2–4, respectively.

2. Hamilton, *Genesis: Chapters 18–50*, 613.

Sheol (44:31, 33). Instead, Jacob is exhorted by God to "go down [ירד]" to Egypt with the promise that he would one day be "brought up [עלה]" (46:3–4). All of this seems to emphasize the operation of divine sovereignty, already acknowledged in 45:4–9.

This pericope details the third and final journey of Jacob's family to Egypt. Like the earlier two (in Gen 42 and 43), this one also is undertaken at Jacob's initiative (42:1–2; 43:1–14; 45:28–46:7); in each of the trips, Joseph meets members of the family (42:6–24; 43:26–45:15; 46:28–47:12); and at the end of each, Jacob talks about his death (42:38; 45:28; 46:30; 47:29–31). But unlike the previous journeys, this one in Gen 46 is preceded by a theophanic nocturnal vision (46:2); moreover, the entire family relocates without immediate plans of returning.[3] Links here with Gen 45 (part of the previous pericope) include: "dwell in the land of Goshen" (45:10 and 47:6); "sons and sons' sons" (45:10 and 46:7); "flocks and herds" (45:10 and 46:32; 47:1); "falling upon his neck: (45:14 and 46:29); and Joseph, the "provider" of the "household" (45:11 and 47:12).

In the vision of God that Jacob sees (46:2–4), the divine utterances hark back to patriarchal promises given earlier: "I am God, the God of your father" (46:3; see 26:24; 28:13; 32:10); "Do not be afraid" (46:3; see 15:1; 21:17; 26:24; 35:17); "I will make you into a great nation there" (46:3; see 12:2; 17:6, 20; 18:18; 21:13, 18); "I will go down with you" (46:4; see 28:15, 20; 31:3); and "I will surely also bring you up" (46:4; see 15:14; 12:1, 7; 13:15). Likewise also in the final scene of this pericope (47:27–31): "fruitful and very numerous" (47:27; see 35:11; 17:6, 20; 28:3); and "lie down with my fathers" (47:29: see 23:1–20; 25:8–10; 35:29).

Waltke and Fredricks note that, beginning with the account of the reconciliation in Gen 45, the story appears to be laid out in an alternating structure, in terms of the characters involved.[4]

> **A** Joseph's family reunited (45:1–15): hugging "on neck" and weeping, 45:14–15
> **B** Pharaoh and those in Egypt (45:16–28)
> **A'** Joseph's family reunited (46:1–30): hugging "on neck" and weeping, 46:29
> **B'** Pharaoh and those in Egypt (46:31–47:10)
> **A''** Joseph's family settled (47:11–12)
> **B''** Pharaoh and those in Egypt (47:13–26)
> **A'''** Joseph's family settled (47:27)

Such a layout is deliberately adopted to show how reconciliation between the brothers had repercussions upon all around them, particularly with regard to the divine blessings that come to pass.

---

3. Wenham, *Genesis 16–50*, 437. The description of Jacob's trip also has parallels with Esau's movements; together they explain how Isaac's two sons fared and where they ended up; in both, one finds fraternal reconciliation (33:15 and 45:1–15), genealogy (36:2–5 and 46:8–27), a move to Seir or to Egypt (33:16; 36:6–8 and 46:28–47:27), and a final "settling/living" (ישׁב, *yshv*, 36:8 and 47:27) (see ibid., 438).

4. Waltke and Fredricks, *Genesis*, 570–71.

34   *Genesis 46:1–47:31*

> **THEOLOGICAL FOCUS 34**[A]
>
> 34   Agents of divine blessing obediently trusting God to bring about his blessing in their own lives, take the initiative to extend God's blessing to others.
>
> 34.1   *Agents of divine blessing trust the sovereignty of God in obedience, to bring about his blessing in their own lives.*
>
> 34.2   *Agents of divine blessing take the initiative to extend God's blessing to others.*

A. Having only one section in this pericope, the "Theological Focus 34" is identical to the "Theological Focus of Pericope 34."

NOTES 34

34.1   Agents of divine blessing trust the sovereignty of God in obedience, to bring about his blessing in their own lives.

At the southern border of the Promised Land, at Beersheba, comes the critical vision from God, encouraging Jacob to go to Egypt. His move was as momentous, if not more so, than the expedition of Abraham from Ur to Canaan (12:1–3), and the escape of Jacob, himself, from Canaan to Paddan-Aram (28:1–22). Theophanic visions accompanied all of these major relocations (28:15; 31:13; 35:12).[5]

The exhortation to Jacob in 46:2–4 is the last time God is noted to have spoken to the patriarchs, and the last divine speech in Genesis. In fact, as Kass observes, this will be the last reported address of God for the next four centuries! When his voice is next heard, he is calling Moses, repeating his name, "Moses, Moses" (as Jacob was called in 46:2—"Jacob, Jacob"), to which Moses responds as Jacob does here, with הִנֵּנִי (*hinneni*, "Here I am," Exod 3:4).

Jacob's sacrifice precedes the vision and speech of Yahweh. Only of Jacob is the verb זָבַח (*zavakh*, "offer sacrifice") used in Genesis—here in Gen 46:1 and earlier in 31:53–54.[6] Jacob had once before departed the Promised Land from Beersheba and a theophanic dream had sustained him, as was noted (28:10–22); it was happening again, this time as Jacob prepared to leave once more from Beersheba. It is almost as if he is asking for permission to leave Canaan, while at the same time promising to return. Moving to Egypt had either been expressly forbidden in the past (26:2), or had had negative repercussions (12:10–13:1). Jacob's likely awareness of God's prophetic word regarding the enslavement and oppression of his people in "a strange land that is not theirs" (15:13) would not have helped his state of mind, either. Jacob certainly needed God's affirmation in this move, and he gets it. Divine promises of presence, of

5. A word from God also came to Jacob as he planned to return to Canaan from Paddan-Aram, 31:3–4. However, "visions" (מַרְאָה, *mar'ah*) is used only here in Genesis (46:2); 15:1 employs a different word for Abraham's vision, מַחֲזֶה, *makhazeh*.

6. Here, at Beersheba, God had once appeared to Isaac as the "God of his father Abraham" and, in response, Isaac had built an altar (26:23–25). Abraham, too, had called upon Yahweh at Beersheba (21:33).

return, of greatness of nation, and to be unafraid[7]—all encourage the patriarch in his decision, and he arrives in Egypt with his entourage (46:3–4).

What is new in God's word of exhortation is that he promises to make Jacob "a great nation *there*," in Egypt, in a foreign land. That would also remind Jacob that this move was not a brief, temporary excursion, but a long-term transfer, and Egypt would be "the womb" for this nascent nation.[8] But it would also be the tomb for Jacob, albeit temporary, for he would die there; God's promise to "bring him up" (עלה, *'lh*, 46:4) would be fulfilled only upon Jacob's mortal remains.[9] The personal pronoun, "I," that God employs is emphatic, as is the infinitive absolute that declares that God, himself, would "*surely* bring you up" (46:4): a return to Canaan, therefore, remained the final end of all these relocations.[10] It seems clear that Jacob recognized this ultimate goal, an indication of which is that he refuses to heed Pharaoh's instruction in 45:20 to leave all his goods behind in Canaan; instead, Jacob brings with him all he has (46:1, 6). He was not going to be assimilated into Egypt with the paraphernalia and accouterments of that foreign land. Later, to Pharaoh, Jacob would emphasize his alien status (47:9)—life, for Jacob, was entirely a sojourn, and indeed, that classification would mark his descendants for the next four centuries, until the exodus from Egypt, when they would to return to their rightful land. As if to hammer this point home, the narrator mentions Jacob's death and burial *thrice*, as instruction to Joseph (47:29–30), as exhortation to his sons (49:29–31), and as the actual event of interment (50:5–14). In faith, sojourners look to the ultimate realization of their promises after their return "home."[11]

The movement of Jacob's family with "property they had acquired" (46:6; also see 46:1) is reminiscent of the en masse transfer conducted by Abraham (12:5), and earlier by Jacob himself (31:18), as well as by Esau (36:6). The double mention of "seed/descendants" (46:6, 7) harks back to God's covenantal promises of the past regarding multiplicity of progeny (13:17; 15:5; 16:10; 22:17; 24:60; 26:4, 24; 28:14; 32:12), and his promise in the present to make "a great nation" of Jacob (46:4).[12]

---

7. The exhortation not to fear was extended by God to all the patriarchs, to Abraham (15:1; 21:17), Isaac (26:24), and now, to Jacob (46:3).

8. Hamilton, *Genesis: Chapters 18–50*, 591.

9. This, of course, was unlike God's earlier promise to Jacob, 28:15, that was fulfilled in Jacob's personal (and live) return to the Promised Land. However, centuries later, Israel, the nation, would also be "brought up" (עלה, also used of the exodus, Exod 3:8, 17).

10. "God, who has been working so hard to get the family relocated, writes out the return ticket before the last of the group has left the land. Going is crucial; so is return" (Green, *"What Profit for Us?"* 178–79). The promise that Joseph would close Jacob's eyes (46:4) would have served as confirmation that Joseph was indeed alive, and that there would be no more separation of father and son.

11. Mathews, *Genesis 11:27–50:26*, 849.

12. Also note earlier references to "great nation" and to the fruitfulness of the patriarchs: 12:2; 17:6; 18:8; 35:11; and later, 48:4, 19. Interestingly enough, the phrase that begins the genealogy/census ("and these [are the] names," 46:8) is the exact one that begins the count of the Hebrews in Egypt in Exod 1:1; of course, by then, the seventy (Gen 46:27) had become over a half million males, twenty or more years old (see Num 1; perhaps two million total, including women and children).

The whole relocation enterprise takes on a celebratory and processional flavor: Jacob and others in wagons, followed by property and livestock, and a list of seventy names "spelled out in rhythmic solemnity, add to the impression of a serene parade," which is met, on the other side, by Joseph in a chariot (46:28–29).[13] Thus 46:1–4 (God's promise and assurance) deals with the *divine* company that will escort Jacob to Egypt (and back); 46:5–27 deals with the *human* company that goes with him. The family of Jacob that relocated to Egypt is noted to have seventy members (46:27; Exod 1:5; Deut 10:22). The same figure, incidentally, is also used as a round number for large groups: elders under Moses (Exod 24:1, 9; Num 11:16, 24, 25); number of kings killed by Adoni-bezek (Jdg 1:7); sons of Gideon (Jdg 8:30); sons of Jerubbaal (Jdg 9:2); sons and donkeys of Abdon (Jdg 12:14); etc. Thus, there is a sense of unnaturalness about the total.[14] The genealogical scheme has several instances of the number 7 and its multiples: the total number of children of Leah and her maid Zilpah is forty-nine (33 + 16; Gen 46:15, 18); the seventh son is Gad, the consonants of whose name, ג (= 3) and ד (= 4), make 7; and Gad has seven sons (47:16); Rachel has fourteen children (47:22); Bilhah has seven (47:25); and the sum of of Jacob's descendants is noted to be seventy (47:27). "The count leaves us with the impression that the generation of Jacob's grandsons is pleasingly full and there are even scions of the next generation on the scene."[15] Surprisingly, Laban shows up in the census as having given Zilpah and Bilhah to Leah and Rachel, respectively (46:18, 25). Perhaps it is a reminder of Jacob's season of affliction (mostly created by his own foibles and failures), and of the days when his

---

13. Brodie, *Genesis as Dialogue*, 395–96.

14. The seventy may have originally been composed of thirty-three descendants from Leah, sixteen from Zilpah, fourteen from Rachel, and seven from Bilhah (46:15, 18, 22, 25). But Er and Onan died in Canaan (38:7, 9; 46:12), and Joseph's sons were, of course, born in Egypt (41:52; 46:27). The narrator does note specifically that sixty-six came with to Egypt with Jacob (46:26), though how the summation, to obtain the totals of sixty-six and seventy (47:26, 27), is achieved is unclear. Oddities in the list include the inclusions of Serah, the sister of the sons of Asher (46:17), and the sons of Beriah as if they were sons of Jacob (46:17). The notation of Joseph's sons are different from that of others of that generation: whereas "and the sons of X" introduces the children of Jacob's sons (46:9, 10, 11, 12[×2], 13, 14, 16, 17, 21, 23, 24), the sons of Joseph are listed with "To Joseph . . . were born . . ." (46:20), perhaps to emphasize their birth outside the Promised Land. Moreover, only one of Jacob's daughters-in-law is named: Joseph's wife, Asenath (along with her antecedents), perhaps to underscore Joseph's foreign connections (46:20). The question of whether Benjamin, when he entered Egypt, was old enough to have had ten sons, as 46:21 indicates, is unanswerable, and is complicated by variations in parallel Benjamite genealogies in Num 26:38–40 and 1 Chr 7:6–12; 8:1–5, that show alterations in spelling, numerical differences, and missing names. Earlier, in Gen 35:22b–26, the list of those "born to him [Jacob] in Paddan Aram" (35:26) included Benjamin, who was actually born in Canaan (35:16–18)—an accounting made, no doubt, for convenience and expediency, as was likely also to be the case here in Gen 46. "The narrator is more concerned with ideology than with historical precision" (Waltke and Fredricks, *Genesis*, 569). There is diversity as well among the ancient versions; for instance, in 46:27, the LXX gives a total of seventy-five. "All of this suggests that there is a bit of artificiality in Gen 46:8–27, and that the genealogy need not be pressed for historical exactness" (Hamilton, *Genesis: Chapters 18–50*, 599). In sum, the catalog presents a tribe of twelve that has grown to seventy, and that is directed by God to enter the Egyptian incubator to further multiply into "a great nation" (46:3)—God's sovereign blessing in operation!

15. Green, *"What Profit for Us?"* 179.

kin barely ran into two digits. Now he has over three score in his tribe.[16] This is clearly the consequence of divine blessing and the fulfillment of divine promise.

Familial bonds are quite prominent in the next section, 46:28–47:12, as the story continues—and the blessings of reconciliation echo in this section: "his father" (46:29, 31; 47:7, 11, 12 [×2]); "my father" (46:31; 47:1); "his brothers" (46:31; 47:2, 3, 11, 12): "my brothers" (46:31); "your father and your brothers" (47:5, 6).[17] The cascade of *waw* imperfects as the long-separated father meets long-lost son is impressive: "and they came . . ., and [Joseph] harnessed . . ., and he went up . . ., and he appeared . . ., and he wept . . ., and [Israel] said . . ." (46:28–30). In God's amazing grace, all the earlier negative experiences have now been overridden by this positive one. And, in response, Jacob's earlier lament that he would die mourning (37:35; 42:38) is converted into a joyful anticipation of passing away in peace (46:30).[18]

In sum, God's faithfulness to Jacob and his family, indeed to all the patriarchs, is demonstrated in his blessing of the tribe as they move and settle and multiply in Egypt as "sojourners" (47:4)—Israel's historic confession and hymnody expressly celebrate this fact (Deut 26:5; Ps 105:23–24). Thus, this move by Jacob & Co. was a new beginning, that would create a "great nation" out of this chosen family, through whom the age-old patriarchal promises would come to pass, blessing the rest of humankind. So rather than a hiatus or a parenthesis in God's scheme for mankind, this movement to Egypt advances his program to bless both Israel and the rest of the world.

34.2 Agents of divine blessing take the initiative to extend God's blessing to others.

Emphasizing the role of humans as agents of divine blessing is the remarkable "appearance" of Joseph before his father (46:29). Elsewhere in the patriarchal accounts such "appearances" are always predicated of deity (12:7; 17:1; 18:1; 22:14; 26:2, 24; 35:9; 48:3); this is the only instance of "appearance" being used of an encounter between of two humans. Its application to Joseph indicates the hand of God in the reunion of father and son, with Joseph as God's agent of blessing to all.

However, in the next section, we see that it is not only Joseph who is the agent of God's blessing, but Jacob, too, who conveys God's blessing upon Pharaoh, not once, but twice (47:7, 10). In the audience between Jacob's sons and Pharaoh (47:1–4), the former are recipients of the latter's favor; but in the audience between Jacob and

---

16. Also of note, Rachel is labeled "Jacob's wife" (46:19), while Leah is not.

17. Mathews, *Genesis 11:27–50:26*, 840. Judah continues his role as leader—he was the instigator in the separation of father and son (37:26–27), he led the impetus for a reconciliation (43:3–10; 44:14–34), and now he takes the initiative in the reunion of father and son (46:28). Both in the forward position of his name in the sentence and in his function, he is prominent. Jacob "sends" Judah to meet Joseph (שׁלח, *shlkh*, 46:28), a reversal of the original situation where Jacob "sent" Joseph to the brothers to commence this fateful saga (שׁלח, 37:13–14). This will be Judah's final active appearance in the Joseph story and in Genesis.

18. Jacob declares he is ready to die (46:30), but he lives for another seventeen years (47:28). Joseph, one will remember, was seventeen when he was kidnapped and enslaved (37:2). Is Jacob now getting a second chance to undo the seventeen years of damaging parental favoritism and live in relative peace, father with brothers and reunited son?

Pharaoh (47:7–10), Pharaoh is at the receiving end! It is therefore no surprise that this ruler is blessed at the hand of God's agent, Jacob.

> **A**   Jacob stands "before the face of Pharaoh" (47:7a)
>   **B**   Jacob blesses Pharaoh (47:7b)
>   **C**   Jacob's age (47:8–9)
>   **B'**   Jacob blesses Pharaoh (47:10a)
> **A'**   Jacob departs "from the face of Pharaoh" (47:10b)

The emphasis of the structure is upon Jacob's own blessing from God (his age, C), and upon God's blessing of Pharaoh at Jacob's hands (mentioned twice, B and B'). Perhaps Jacob's initial blessing was for Pharaoh's long life (as in 2 Sam 16:16; 1 Kgs 1:31; Dan 2:4; 5:10; 6:6); that might explain Pharaoh's questioning Jacob about his age.[19] In any case, this section demonstrates that divine blessing falls not only upon the agent of such blessing, but also upon all those associated with that agent.[20] This is the only instance of a foreigner explicitly receiving a blessing at the hands of a patriarch, although there are implicit indications of such felicities in the Genesis narratives (14:18–24; 18:22–33; 20:17–18; 26:26–33; 39:1–23; not to mention the blessings upon Ishmael and Esau). Incidentally, there is no mention of any obeisance of Jacob before this ruler of Egypt; after all Jacob is the blessor! There are similarities between this critical encounter and that of Abraham with Melchizedek: in both there is no introduction, prologue, or preface. Here, Joseph brings, Joseph presents, Jacob blesses, Pharaoh asks, Jacob answers, Jacob blesses (again), and Jacob exits.

Then comes the seeming interpolation of the effect of the famine upon the citizens of Egypt. Why interrupt the story of the relocation of Israel with this bit of administrative trivia (47:13–26), not to mention the ethical perplexity that it seems to portray? Without it, 47:12 leads smoothly into 47:27. This final part of the pericope serves to detail the effect of the famine upon the Egyptians themselves (47:13–26), in contrast to Jacob's family that is protected and living in reasonable comfort (47:11–12, 27).[21] Right after Joseph provided "food" (47:12) for his family, we are told that there was no "food" in all the land because of the severe famine (47:13, 15, 19). Jacob's family keep their money (42:25; 44:1), and there is no indication that they had to pay for the grain they

---

19. However, despite his long life that seems to have impressed Pharaoh, Jacob summarizes his own feelings about his longevity as years that were "short and evil" (47:9)—"a poignant comment on Jacob's life, his flight to Mesopotamia, the rape of his daughter, his favorite wife's death, and his favorite son's apparent death," not a few of which agonies were brought about by Jacob's own doings or negligence: deceiving his brother, cheating his father, hating a wife, neglecting his daughter, and favoring certain sons (Wenham, *Genesis 16–50*, 446–47).

20. From McKenzie, "Jacob's Blessing of Pharaoh," 391 (see 394n28, for indications of a linkage between advanced age and divine favor in Egyptian thought).

21. Tact and diplomacy mark Joseph's plans for his family: not only is he sensitive to Egyptian idiosyncrasies regarding the pastoral vocation, he wants to assure Pharaoh that they will not be a burden on an already famine-beleaguered state (46:31–34). There does not appear to be any indication in contemporaneous literature of Egyptian antipathy towards shepherding, as Joseph indicates in 46:34. The thrust of that statement is therefore unclear. But see Exod 8:21–22 that seems to suggest that sheep were an abomination to the Egyptians.

received; instead Joseph provides for them (45:11; 47:12). The Egyptians, on the other hand, give all their money for grain and food (47:14–15). Jacob's family bring all their livestock with them to Egypt, and ostensibly keep them all (45:10; 46:6; 47:1), even taking care of Pharaoh's own stables (47:6). But the Egyptians lose all their animals, and eventually become slaves to Pharaoh (47:16–17). Jacob's tribe settles in the best part of the land (47:6). The Egyptians surrender all their land as tenants in a feudal system.[22] Though Jacob's family came to "sojourn" (47:4), Joseph gives them "property" (אֲחֻזָּה, 'akhuzzah, 47:11, 27), perhaps a move towards the fulfillment of God's promise to Jacob that they would become "a great nation" (47:3). The word here "refers to the inalienable property received from a sovereign, or at least from one who has the power to release or retain land."[23] No wonder "property" has echoed throughout the patriarchal stories as a promissory note in the chord of divine grants to Abraham and his descendants: 17:8; 23:4, 9, 20; 36:43; 48:4; 49:30; 50:13. In other words, for the family of Jacob, the consequences of Joseph's treatment of them was that "they were fruitful and they multiplied" (47:27; and this during a famine!), fulfilling a divine mandate and a patriarchal promise: God's blessing was upon them.

The contrast with the situation of the Egyptians is clearly a hint as to what might have occurred to the nascent nation of Israel, had not the providence and sovereignty of God intervened through Jacob, Joseph, and Judah, a possibility that was considered by Joseph (45:11). Sigmon speculates with a series of counterfactuals—"what ifs."[24]

> What if Joseph's brothers had gone along with their initial plan of killing Joseph instead of selling him? What if another Egyptian had bought Joseph instead of Potiphar, or what if the official's wife had succeeded in persuading Joseph to sleep with her? How might things have been different if Pharaoh's cupbearer had never remembered Joseph, or if Joseph had not recognized his brothers, or if, having recognized them, in the end had decided to repay evil for evil? What if Yhwh had not been with Joseph, even in servitude and in prison? The famine was world-wide, and reached into Canaan as well (Gen 47:13). Even without Joseph's invitation to join him, Jacob could have had to journey to Egypt, for the famine was severe in Canaan. If anything had gone differently, Jacob could have paid all his silver in exchange for grain, as the Egyptians had. Like them, he could have been forced to sell all his livestock the following year, and all that he had acquired through Yhwh's blessing in Paddan-Aram (Gen 30:43) would have perished. He also could have finally lost his land and become a slave to Pharaoh. By showing how the Egyptians fared under the famine, Gen 47:13–26 acts as a sideshadow and 'conjures the ghostly presence' of these countless might-have-beens, any of which could have resulted in Jacob and his family journeying into Egypt in such a way that they too would have been dispossessed, and the patriarchal promises and blessings would have dissipated.

In sum, the contrast emphasizes the blessing of God upon Jacob's family, amidst the dire situation of the famine that sorely affected the Egyptians (47:13–26). But blessing

---

22. See Sigmon, "Shadowing Jacob's Journey," 465–67, for further details.
23. Hamilton, *Genesis: Chapters 18–50*, 613.
24. Sigmon, "Shadowing Jacob's Journey," 468–69.

by the agency of Joseph also comes to these afflicted ones: ultimately it is Joseph who feeds not only his family (47:12), but also the Egyptians (47:17). The latter explicitly acknowledge that Joseph has saved their lives (47:25).

The section 47:13–26 carefully alternates narration with dialogue.[25]

Introduction	Severity of famine (47:13)	
Narrative	Joseph receives money for food (47:14)	
	Dialogue	People request food/Joseph replies (47:15–16)
Narrative	Joseph receives livestock for food (47:17)	
	Dialogue	People request food and seed (47:18–19)
Narrative	Joseph accepts land and enslavement (47:20–22)	
	Dialogue	People agree to enslavement (47:23–25)
Conclusion	Precedent for a new law (47:26)	

First the Egyptians (and Canaanites) give their money and livestock for food (47:14–17); then in a more ruinous situation, they yield their land and their freedom (47:18–21). Over the years of the famine, in exchange for grain, food, and seed (47:14, 17, 19, 23), Pharaoh gains possession of all the money, livestock, and land in Egypt (with the exception of priestly possessions), and even of the populace of the country in bondage (47:15, 17, 20, 21). With this centralization of assets, both material and human, the people are relocated into urban centers where, apparently, the grain stores were (47:21). While it appears that Joseph "bought" the people and their land (47:23), what is created is "an informal agrarian pact, not treatment of the people as chattel." Planning for the future, a law calling for a fifth of the produce to be given to the Pharaoh is promulgated (excepting the priestly class and their lands), a law that set precedent for the future (47:24, 26). A system of "land tenure" was thus established: the state provided seed and the tenants returned a fifth of their yield (41:34; 47:20–26).[26] In fact, Joseph's reforms outlived him, perhaps a recognition of their fairness and utility (47:26). To

---

25. From Mathews, *Genesis 11:27–50:26*, 855.

26. Mathews, *Genesis 11:27–50:26*, 850–51. He notes that the 20% return to the lender is "generous compared to what is known elsewhere in the ancient Near East" (ibid., 851). First Maccabeus 10:30 mentions a tax of "the third of the grain and the half of the fruit of the trees." Von Rad, *Genesis*, 406, notes that interest rates for purchase of seed corn in the ancient days was as high as 40–60%. The Torah specified a fifth as appropriate in connection with laws of restitution: Lev 5:16, 24; 27:13–31. Note also the exception that was made with regard to the land in cultic use and the support of religious functionaries (47:22, 26), making it far from a heartless and wholesale land grab. Thus Joseph is not made out to be a harsh taskmaster but a concerned overlord, who sets in place a system whereby the people could survive in the years of the famine and beyond. Indeed, it appears that the takeover of the land towards the end of the seven-year famine was to ensure the land did not remain desolate into the future (47:19, 23). On slavery, Wenham, *Genesis 16–50*, 449, observes: "[I]n ancient society slavery was the accepted way of bailing out the destitute, and under a benevolent master could be quite a comfortable status. . . . Indeed, the law envisages some temporary slaves electing to become permanent slaves rather than take the freedom to which they were entitled after six years of service. Ancient slavery at its best was like tenured employment, whereas the free man was more like someone who is self-employed. The latter may be free, but he faces more risk" (see Exod 21:5–6; Deut 15:12–17). In other words: "In Exod 1:8–11 the Pharaoh makes slaves of the Hebrew, and the Hebrews groan under the misery. In Gen 47:21, a Hebrew makes slaves of the Egyptians, and the Egyptians praise Joseph for saving them. The double contrast implies the ingratitude and cruelty of the Pharaoh of the Exodus. It also implies Joseph's wise administration" (Waltke and Fredricks, *Genesis*, 589).

all this, the response of the Egyptians is gratitude, even looking upon Joseph in terms usually reserved for deity: "May we find favor in the eyes of my lord and we will be slaves to Pharaoh" (47:25).[27]

The interposing of this section with the closing stages of the reunion story must therefore be understood as the fulfillment of Jacob's two-fold blessing on Pharaoh (47:7, 10). Following right after Jacob's blessing of Pharaoh, the powerful impact of Joseph's famine-related program is described (47:13–26)—the manifestation of divine blessing upon Pharaoh and his nation. McKenzie spells out the reasons for such a reading:

> There is no reason why the pattern [of explicit blessing of those around Joseph] established in Gen 39:1–6 to illustrate Gen 12:3a should fail when Joseph is elevated to the highest authority by Pharaoh (41:39–45). If this consideration is valid, the blessing upon Pharaoh in 47:13–26 is anticipated by three events in the Joseph cycle, namely Pharaoh's elevation of Joseph, Pharaoh's favour to Jacob and his other eleven sons, and Jacob's verbal blessing of Pharaoh. . . . [T]here is no other adequate explanation for the inclusion of an extensive account of Joseph's land reforms.[28]

In other words, 47:13–26, is both a contrast to the blessing of Joseph's family, *and* an expression of divine blessing upon the Egyptians themselves, at the hands of Joseph (and Jacob).

It must be emphasized that this is not necessarily a demeaning of the Egyptians nor does it lead to a negative evaluation of Joseph's policies towards them. After all, it was the Egyptians themselves who came up with the idea of giving up their land, and later themselves into bondage (47:19). And, with the success of the program, the Egyptian beneficiaries are quite grateful (47:25). Where death was the only alternative, Joseph's wise approach saved lives (47:25). In any case, there is no suggestion of hoarding by Pharaoh or that this was an attempt to enrich his coffers. On the contrary, Joseph is always clear that he was simply fulfilling God's purpose (45:5; 50:20).

Of course, the relative prosperity and freedom of the children of Israel raises the risk of their gradual assimilation into Egypt and its society (and its mores). Indeed, Jacob addresses that very issue at the end of the current pericope (47:28–31). He makes Joseph promise to have him buried not in Egypt, but in the Promised Land with his fathers—Jacob's "death right."[29] "Jacob knows that there is to be no permanent residence in Egypt for his people. Egypt is to Jacob and his family what the ark was to Noah—a temporary shelter from the disaster on the outside." This is the second time Jacob demands an oath of someone; the first was his making Esau swear to yield his birthright to him (25:33)—a clear act of *mistrust* in God's sovereignty, in light of the

---

27. Kass, *The Beginning of Wisdom*, 631.

28. McKenzie, "Jacob's Blessing of Pharaoh," 396.

29. Kass, *The Beginning of Wisdom*, 637. It is likely that the placement of a promiser's hand "under the thigh" euphemistically means to touch the genitalia. It thus was a way of effecting long-term validity for whatever was promised (see Falk, "Gestures Expressing Affirmation," 269; Malul, "More on *Paḥad Yiṣḥāq*," 192–200; and idem, "Touching the Sexual Organs," 491–92).

birth oracle to Rebekah (25:23). Now, nearing death, he makes his son take an oath, but this time it is an equally clear act of *trust* in God's sovereignty.[30] He had no doubts at all about God's word that he would "surely bring you up" (46:4). "Jacob, in life too often the cunning schemer who trusted his own wiliness to achieve his ends, now in the face of death shows that the ultimate hope is the promise of God."[31]

SERMON FOCUS AND OUTLINES

THEOLOGICAL FOCUS OF PERICOPE 34 FOR PREACHING

34   Agents of divine blessing, obediently trusting God for blessing in their own lives, extend God's blessing to others (46:1–47:31).

The thrust of this pericope deals with the "faith-full" obedience of Jacob (and his family) to God's exhortation to move boldly to Egypt. The result of such obedience is two-fold: Jacob and his family are blessed (increase in number and fruitfulness; provision during a season of dire famine), and Pharaoh and his nation are blessed, by the agency of Jacob and Joseph (sustenance and survival despite the devastation of the famine). Thus agents of divine blessing obey God, trusting him to bring about blessing in their own lives, and they take the initiative to bring divine blessing into the lives of those around them.

Possible Preaching Outlines for Pericope 34

I. Blessing for Oneself: *"Faith-fully" obey God!*
        Jacob's trust in God's sovereignty and his obedience (46:1–7)
        Jacob's confidence in God for the return to Canaan (46:1; 6; 47:28–31)
        Result: Blessing upon Jacob and his family (46:8–27; 46:28–47:6; 47:11–12, 27)
        Specifics on obedience to God and his word

II. Blessing for Others: *Freely oblige others!*
        Jacob's blessing of Pharaoh (47:7–10)
        Recap: Joseph's blessing of Pharaoh and Egypt by his sagacity (42:28–41)
        Result: Blessing upon Pharaoh and his nation (47:13–26)
        Specifics on serving and obliging others[32]

---

30. Hamilton, *Genesis: Chapters 18–50*, 625. The rather curious action of Jacob ostensibly bowing to Joseph (47:31) deserves comment. While Israel's "bowing" (47:31) may recall Joseph's dream in 37:9, 10 with the sun, moon, and stars "bowing" before him, it is unlikely that this is the fulfillment of that dream, or even its right interpretation: see Pericope 28. In Jacob's interpretation of that dream, the sun and moon stood for Jacob and Rachel; Rachel, of course, long gone, does not bow to her son. Jacob's action here may be one of respect, already indicated by his request to find favor in Joseph's eyes (47:29), or his bowing (or bending low) at the head of his bed in worship of God (or simply a result of his feebleness). The LXX vocalizes the MT מִטָּה (*mittah*, "bed, couch") as מַטֶּה, *matteh*, translating it as ῥάβδος (*rhabdos*, "staff," which is followed in Heb 11:21): perhaps Jacob worshiped God leaning on the top of his *staff*. In any case is it not necessary to postulate Jacob's bowing to Joseph.

31. Wenham, *Genesis 16–50*, 452.

32. This, too, is broad. Perhaps as a congregation, one or more activities may be engaged in, that are a blessing to the community/society around: serving the homeless/refugees, refurbishing public places, helping shut-ins, widows, disabled, etc.

This first outline has, thus, only two moves; there is nothing magical about a particular number thereof, of course. The ultimate consideration is how the theological thrust of the pericope may be conveyed to the listeners expediently, efficiently, and effectively, so that lives may be changed for the glory of God through the instrumentality of this particular pericope. In the second outline, separating God's exhortation, the actions of the agents of blessing, and the results thereof, yields a slightly different structure, with the homiletical imperative appearing as a move in the middle (making it an "inductive–deductive" outline).

I.   REASON: God's Promises

    God's exhortation, promises, and the expression of his sovereignty and providence (46:2–4)

    Recap: God's sovereignty and providence throughout the Joseph saga thus far

    Move-to-Relevance: The assurance of God's care, control, and provision for his children

II.   RESPONSE: *"Faith-fully" obey God! Freely oblige others!*

    Jacob's trust in God's sovereignty and his obedience (46:1–7, 28–31)

    Specifics on obedience to God and his word

    Jacob's blessing of Pharaoh (47:7–10)

    Specifics on serving and obliging others

III.   RESULT: God's Blessing

    Result: Blessing upon Jacob and his family (46:8–27; 46:28–47:6; 47:11–12, 27)

    Result: Blessing upon Pharaoh and his nation (47:13–26)

    Move-to-Relevance: Blessings in our lives and in the lives of those around us

PERICOPE 35

Blessing for the Future

Genesis 48:1–50:26

[Jacob's Blessing, Death, and Burial; Final Reconciliation of Brothers; Joseph's Death]

REVIEW, SUMMARY[1]

Review of Pericope 34: Genesis 46:1–47:31 showed Jacob and the extended family, at the behest of Joseph, moving *en masse* to Egypt. There, Jacob, the patriarch, blesses Pharoah, the ruler of Egypt, and immediately we have an account of Jacob's family being a source of blessing to Egypt: Joseph's wise policies saved Egypt and its people from sure death in a time of famine. God's people serve as agents of his blessing to others.

Summary of Pericope 35: This pericope concludes the Joseph Story and the book of Genesis. Jacob utters an extended blessing of his children and gives his last instructions for the disposal of his remains—back in Canaan. Upon his death, a grand cortege takes his body back to the Promised Land. After Jacob's burial, Joseph's brothers seek a final reconciliation with him, which he graciously offers, again attributing to God's providence all the events that had transpired. Later, Joseph himself gives directions that his bones be taken back to the Promised Land one day. Thus, agents of divine blessing pass blessings on to others, even as they look to the future for the consummation of God's promises.

---

1. This chapter, dealing with the last pericope of the book of Genesis, will, of course, have no Preview of an upcoming pericope.

35 Genesis 48:1–50:26

THEOLOGICAL FOCUS OF PERICOPE 35

35 Agents of divine blessing remember the blessings they have experienced, pass on the blessings to others, and expect consummation of blessings in the future (48:1–50:26).

    35.1   Agents of divine blessing, constantly remembering the blessings they have experienced, pass them on to generations to come (48:1–49:28).

        35.1.1   Agents of divine blessing constantly remember the blessings they have experienced, even as they pass them on to others.

        35.1.2   God's blessings, bestowed through the agency of his people, have manifold repercussions across generations.

    35.2   The people of God, trusting God's sovereignty and providence, look to the future for the consummation of his promises of blessing (49:29–50:26).

OVERVIEW

This pericope deals with the closing sections of Genesis, from 48:1–50:26, involving the blessings bestowed by Jacob on his deathbed (48:1–49:28), the account of his deathbed wishes and burial (49:29–50:13), the final reconciliation between his sons (50:14–21), and the instruction of Joseph regarding the disposal of his own remains (50:22–26). All of these are united by the theme of blessing: ברך (*brk*, 48:3, 9, 15, 16, 20; 49:25, 28 [×2]) and בְּרָכָה (*brakah,* 49:25 [×3], 26 [×2], 28), together, occur fourteen times in this pericope; as well, the implicit notions of "blessing" in Gen 50 (described below).

The first section, 48:1–49:28, describing Jacob's blessings upon his sons and grandchildren, along with 47:27–31 and 49:29–33, make a chiastic structure, centered upon the patriarchal blessings bestowed (*C, D,* and *C',* below). As would-be progenitors of the twelve tribes of Israel, they are (or will be), in effect, sources of blessing for all mankind; it is therefore appropriate that considerable space be devoted to the patriarchal blessing of these individuals.[2]

> **A**   Summary of Jacob's life; announcement of death (47:27–29a)
>   **B**   Jacob's charge to Joseph to bury him with his fathers (47:29b–31)
>   **C**   Jacob's blessing of Joseph's sons (48:1–20)
>   **D**   Jacob's blessing of Joseph (48:21–22)
>   **C'**   Jacob's blessing of his sons (49:1–28)
>   **B'**   Jacob's charge to his sons to bury him with his fathers (49:29–32)
> **A'**   Summary of Jacob's death; description of death (49:33)

Wenham notes the similarities between this two-stage blessing of Jacob (of grandchildren, 48:1–22; and of children, 49:1–28) and that of Isaac of his two sons.[3]

---

2. Structure below from Dorsey, *The Literary Structure of the Old Testament,* 62.

3. Wenham, *Genesis 16–50,* 460.

	Isaac's Blessings	Jacob's Blessings
Patriarchal blindness	27:1	48:10
Patriarch kisses recipient	27:26–27	48:10
Blessing of the younger son	27:27–28	48:14–16
Protestation of inversion	27:34–36	48:17–18
Reaffirmation of inversion	27:37–40	48:19–20
Second blessing	28:1–6	49:1–27

Jacob, himself, seems to link the current blessing of his grandchildren with his own blessing by his father: he cites the utterance of Isaac (28:3) as he prepares to make his bestowal upon his grandsons (48:4): fruitfulness, multiplication of seed, and becoming a "company of peoples" occur in both (as also in 35:11).

The section, 48:1–49:28, essentially forms a type-scene—a deathbed blessing scene, one that has occurred before in Genesis: Abraham's charge to his servant in 24:1–9 is presumably that patriarch's closing scene, as is 27:1–28:9 for Isaac.[4] In Jacob's case, the scene is split into two: in the first, 48:1–22, Joseph's two sons are blessed; in the second, 49:1–28, Jacob's twelve sons receive his blessing. One might even consider Jacob's death and burial, 49:29–50:14, as another third part of the larger scene related to his demise.

The Joseph saga ends with two shorter scenes summarizing, in effect, the thrust of the entire narrative that commenced in Gen 37. Genesis 50:15–21 gives the narrator yet another opportunity to affirm divine sovereignty and providence in a dialogue between guilt-ridden brothers and a magnanimous and gracious Joseph. Here, the theme of blessing to all is reiterated: God's sovereign design was "to keep many people alive" (50:20), and so it continues to be, as the Abrahamic blessing echoes across generations (12:3; 18:18; 22:18; 26:4; 28:14). The theme of blessing is also implicit in the final reconciliation between Joseph and his brothers, with the recognition of God's sovereign design to bless that family and the world, as well as in Joseph's own resolution to be returned to the Promised Land.

Joseph was elevated in Pharaoh's court when he was thirty (41:46), and he died at 110 (50:26). In the eight decades of his service in Egypt, we are permitted a glimpse of only three of his audiences with Pharaoh: upon his ascent to Prime Ministership (41:41–46), at the relocation of his family to Egypt (46:31–47:10), and here when his father's remains are returning to Canaan (50:4–6). These episodes are not randomly chosen; they point to the major phases in the life of Joseph and his brothers as divinely ordained, yet coming to pass through the intermediate agency of a foreign king, no less! The book of Genesis closes with Joseph reiterating the sovereignty of God and his providential workings in the lives of mankind (50:14–21), highlighted in his deathbed scene where he insists that his bones be returned to Canaan (50:22–26), following the similar sentiments of his father (47:29–31; 48:21; 49:29–32).

---

4. Understandably, Abraham with only one son by Sarah, did not pronounce a formal blessing upon Isaac, though undertaking the responsibility of finding him a wife effectively constituted that act.

35.1 Genesis 48:1–49:28

> **THEOLOGICAL FOCUS 35.1**
>
> 35.1 Agents of divine blessing, constantly remembering the blessings they have experienced, pass them on to generations to come (48:1–49:28).
>
> > 35.1.1 *Agents of divine blessing constantly remember the blessings they have experienced, even as they pass them on to others.*
> >
> > 35.1.2 *God's blessings, bestowed through the agency of his people, have manifold repercussions across generations.*

NOTES 35.1

35.1.1 *Agents of divine blessing constantly remember the blessings they have experienced, even as they pass them on to others.*

The announcement of Jacob's terminal illness (חָלָה, *khalah*, "sick," as in 1 Kgs 14:1, 5; 2 Kgs 8:7; all of Jacob's last three appearances occur on his deathbed—47:31; 48:2; and 49:33) prompts Joseph's visit to his father, with his two sons. Jacob engages in a summarization of his life, focusing once again upon divine promises and their fulfillment. He echoes the promises made to him at Luz/Bethel upon his return to Canaan from Paddan-Aram (35:9–13)[5]; he is convinced his own words of blessings will come to pass as his children and their families return to Canaan one day. Whereas at Bethel the similar utterance from God that *Jacob* be fruitful and that *he* multiply are exhortations patterned after the creation blessings (1:22, 28; 9:1, 7 in 28:3–4), here the divine initiative is more in view: "*I [God] will make you* fruitful and to multiply" (as recited by Jacob in 48:4).

And, for the third time, Jacob makes the point that his remains *must* be returned to the Promised Land for burial with his ancestors (47:29–31; 48:21; and here, 49:29–32).[6] This was in accordance with the divine promise made to Jacob that God would

---

5. Jacob also conflates 28:3–4 and 17:8, utilizing "everlasting possession" (אֲחֻזַּת עוֹלָם, *'akhuzzat 'olam*), thus including his ancestors in the stream of divine blessings. This "everlasting possession" clearly contrasts with the *temporary* possessions granted in Goshen by Pharaoh/Joseph to the family of Jacob (אֲחֻזָּה, *'akhuzzah*, 47:6, 11; אָחַז, *'akhaz*, 47:27). That may well have been a subtle reminder to Joseph about the permanence of God's promises that could be fulfilled only in the Promised Land.

6. In these three exhortations of Jacob regarding the return to Canaan, the narrator always makes "Israel" the one requesting to be buried in the Promised Land. In a subtle hint that the nation is perhaps slowly becoming Egyptianized, "Israel" is also the one who is embalmed by the physicians of Egypt (40:3), while in the rest of the burial narrative (50:1–14), Jacob is always referred to in relation to Joseph, as "his/my/your father" (50:1, 2, 5 [×2], 6, 7, 8, 10, 14). *Jacob* dies; and Joseph commands that *his father* be embalmed; but the physicians of Egypt embalm *Israel* (49:33; 50:2). "Here is 'Israel,' who longed to merit the same ancestral burial as his forebears, now laid out upon the mortuary table of the Egyptian physicians with his innards subjected to Egyptian ritual day after day for forty days, 'for such was the custom'" (50:3). There may be an adumbration here of assimilation of the Jacobean family to Egyptian ways and the adoption of their customs and mores. See Berman, "Identity Politics," 24. The embalming and the mummification of Jacob and Joseph (50:2–3, 26) are the only examples of such in the Bible. King Asa's body underwent some kind of treatment, though not embalming, to prevent decomposition

return him to Canaan (46:4). His exhortation to Joseph is therefore a stubborn "act of resistance," as he rejects his land of exile as his final resting place and Egypt as the future of his descendants.[7] His was an "unyielding faith in God's promise for the future prosperity [blessing] of the family."[8] Thus, in the end, after many tumultuous years ("few and evil," 47:9), his faith has only become stronger, and Jacob expresses his great confidence in the promises of his God (48:21–22). He is grateful to God for having allowed him to see Joseph and even Joseph's children (48:10–11), and he anticipates that his descendants will become a great nation as God had promised him and his forefathers, even bearing royalty in their ranks (12:2; 17:4, 6, 16; 18:18; 28:3; 35:11; 49:10).[9] Beyond his wildest dreams, Jacob had been blessed by God: not only did he see his son Joseph again, he lived to see Joseph's descendants as well (48:11; see 37:33–35; 42:36; 45:28; later Joseph, himself, would see his own great-grandchildren, 50:23). Jacob's attribution of this blessing to God parallels Joseph's own statement of divine blessing in his having had sons in Egypt (48:9; also 41:51–52).[10]

Jacob proceeds to adopt Joseph's children as his own (48:5), equating them with his two older sons, Reuben and Simeon (48:5).[11] Hamilton thinks that Jacob's action is actually a further elevation of Joseph, another ascent in this one's life: from kidnapped, to slave, to Prime Minister, and now to patriarch—for, in equating Joseph's sons as his own, Jacob was equating Joseph with himself.[12] Jacob, well aware that God is the true source of blessing (32:26; see Pericope 24), now seeks to be an agent of that blessing to his grandsons (48:9, 14–20), and later to his sons (49:1–27).

As they arrived to see Jacob (48:1), Joseph's two sons were listed in proper order of birth, Manasseh followed by Ephraim. However, that order is inverted by their grandfather as he gives the younger a special blessing (48:5; 14). Joseph, though, is careful about protocol, placing his two sons such that the elder is aligned with Jacob's right hand, and the younger with Jacob's left, thus enabling the former to receive the greater blessing; apparently he did not catch Jacob's inversion of their name order in 48:5, even though Jacob had listed his own sons, Reuben and Simeon, accurately by

---

(2 Chr 16:14). Transport of bones without embalmment occurs for other regents, Ahaziah (2 Kgs 9:28), Amaziah (2 Kgs 14:20), and Josiah (1 Kgs 23:30).

7. Ibid., 20.

8. Mathews, *Genesis 11:27–50:26*, 914.

9. The introduction of Rachel in 48:7 is puzzling. Perhaps the best sense that can be made of Jacob's reminiscence is that his adoption of Joseph's sons works out to be a posthumous increase of the number of Rachel's children from two to four. See Hamilton, *Genesis: Chapters 18–50*, 630.

10. Though their lives may have overlapped, none of the other patriarchs before Jacob are shown having any interaction with their grandchildren.

11. Such adoptions were not unusual in the ancient Near East; see, for e.g., Code of Hammurabi §170. The "twelve tribes" therefore become somewhat fluid in composition in the OT. Simeon is deleted and Joseph's two sons are added in Deut 33:17; later, in Ezek 47:13–14, Simeon is present, as also are the sons of Joseph, but Levi does not receive an allotment (44:28); Levi alone is omitted in Num 1, and Dan alone in Rev 7:5–8.

12. *Genesis: Chapters 18–50*, 630. Kass thinks that this is a preplanned action on Jacob's part, as he announces his intentions even before knowing that his grandsons are present at his bedside (49:2, 8–9) (*The Beginning of Wisdom*, 640).

birth order. The reason for Jacob's switch is not something the narrator speculates on, though the pattern of the younger having precedence over the older had already been established in Genesis: Abel over Cain, 4:1–8; Isaac over Ishmael, 21:12–13; Jacob over Esau, 25:23; 27:1–45; and Perez over Zerah, 38:27–30. Kass may well be right:

> When a society is well established and running smoothly, preferences are usually given to the firstborn, for the firstborn is the one who, naturally, guarantees a next generation; in arranging for perpetuation, custom follows and ratifies the natural order of succession. . . . [Joseph] sees himself as the last of the founding fathers and wants that way to be conserved through primogeniture. Jacob corrects Joseph's tacit belief that everything is now fully established and ripe for perpetuation in Egypt. And looking ahead, Jacob prophesies that the nation of Israel shall bless by Ephraim and Manasseh, memorializing in such a blessing Jacob's inversion of the birth order, a deed that symbolizes Israel's rejection of . . . [Joseph's] complacent belief that the new way was finally secure.[13]

Such an interpretation harmonizes with the focus in this section on divine promises/blessings, to be fulfilled and experienced *only* as the children of Israel return to Canaan.[14]

Jacob designates God as the one before whom his forefathers walked (48:15). Abraham and Isaac are said to have walked *before* God, as God had called them to do (17:1; 24:40; 48:15); this is likely to be equivalent to walking *with* God, as Enoch and Noah did (5:22, 24; 6:9; also see 2 Kgs 20:3 = Isa 38:3). Jacob's own life was marked by divine presence (Gen 28:15, 20; 31:3; 35:3), as was Joseph's (39:2, 3, 21, 23; 48:21)—theirs were lives lived in the presence of God (Lev 26:12; Ps 56:13; Zech 10:12). Appropriately enough, Jacob employs the imagery of the divine "shepherd" (Gen 48:15), a portrayal of God that is carried through the rest of Scripture (49:24; Pss 23:1; 28:9; 80:1; Eccl 12:11; Isa 40:11; Ezek 34:12; Micah 5:3; 7:14; John 10:11, 14; Heb 13:20; 1 Pet 2:25; 5:4; Rev 7:17). "Walking" with or before God is thus equated here with God's shepherding activities. In a sense, Jacob seems to assert that while Abraham and Isaac walked before God and were blessed, *God* walked before him, blessing him.[15]

What Jacob actually blesses Joseph with (שְׁכֶם, *shkem*, Gen 48:22) is rather ambiguous: the word could mean "portion," or "mountain slope," or even the proper name "Shechem"—Joseph would later be buried in Shechem (Josh 24:32). The context indicates that the donation is likely to have been a parcel of ground; in other words, Jacob is so sure of gaining Canaan that he can, even now, dispose of it as he chooses (Gen 48:22). This is a man whose trust in God is absolute. Throughout this section,

---

13. Ibid., 643–44.

14. In any case, the blessing of Jacob is a single one to both his grandsons; besides, it is equated with a blessing on Joseph (48:15–16), though some subtle (and unclear) distinctions appear in 48:19 between the blessings to the two grandchildren—perhaps the difference is only one of degree: "greater" (48:19), and "multitude" vs. "fullness of nations" (48:16, 19). One also notices the tripartite invocation of deity as "God," "God," and "the angel" (48:15–16a; the "angel" is likely to have been God himself, as in 16:11, 13; 21:17, 19; 22:15–18; 31:11, 13; also see 32:28 with Hos 12:5).

15. Hamilton, *Genesis: Chapters 18–50,* 637.

what God has done for him (and what God will do for the ones Jacob is passing the blessing to) is uppermost in the patriarch's mind (48:3–4, 11, 15–16, 20, 21).

35.1.2 *God's blessings, bestowed through the agency of his people, have manifold repercussions across generations.*

Thus far Jacob, blessed by God (32:29; 35:9), has blessed Pharaoh (47:7, 10), and he has blessed Joseph and his sons (48:15, 17–20); to finalize matters, he now proceeds to bless all his sons (49:28). For one whose life began with an oracle (25:23), it is appropriate that Jacob's last words are also prophetic blessings. Thus, this section, 49:1–28, is an extended account of Jacob's deathbed utterances to his sons.

Not everyone addressed here obtains a blessing; there are curses as well (for Reuben and Simeon/Levi, and perhaps for Issachar: 49:3–4, 5–7, 14–15, respectively), and therefore, 49:1–28 is best labeled "Testament of Jacob," rather than "Blessing of Jacob."[16] "What follows is part blessing, part prophecy, part settling of scores, and part redirection of future family and tribal relations. The remarks are sometimes about the sons themselves, sometimes about the tribes in Israel to which they give their names," and once an interjection directed to Yahweh himself (49:18; see below).[17] An underlying theme of the dispensation of Jacob's blessings (*God's* blessings through Jacob's agency) is that the faithfulness (or lack thereof) of the sons of Jacob would be consequential for the experience (or not) of divine blessings. This, of course, is not a new theme in Genesis. All throughout the book, the lives of the various protagonists have demonstrated what it means to partake of (or miss out on) divine blessings as the result of their faithfulness (or faithlessness): the salvation of Noah and the destruction of the Flood, the blessings on the patriarchs and their descendants, the destruction of Sodom and Gomorrah, etc.

Longacre notes that ten of the twenty-five verses of Jacob's testament deal with Judah and Joseph (49:8–12, 22–26), commensurate with their importance as protagonists in the Joseph Story. Another five verses concern brothers who are mentioned in the saga by name: Reuben and Simeon (49:3–7).[18] The remainder of the siblings are relegated to eight verses (49:13–17, 19–21). Incidentally, the four major recipients in Gen 49, Reuben, Simeon, Judah, and Joseph, are the four whose births are also annotated by their respective mothers in connection with the divine name "Yahweh" (39:32, 35; 30:24)—perhaps an adumbration of their key roles later in the narrative.[19]

---

16. Wenham, *Genesis 16–50*, 468.

17. Kass, *The Beginning of Wisdom*, 645. This is also the longest poem in the book.

18. In the Joseph story, Judah is a major player in 37:26–27; 38:1–26; 43:3–10; 44:14–34; 46:28; moreover, he is promised rulership over the nation, what with the three older sons being disqualified due to their infamous conduct; Reuben and Simeon (though not Levi) are mentioned in 37:21–22, 29–30; 42:22, 37; 48:5; 42:24, 36; 43:23.

19. Wenham, *Genesis 16–50*, 469. Other than the observation that every son of Jacob seems to be linked with an animal of some sort in this chapter of blessings, the precise nuances of the literary detail (and the historical reality they ostensibly refer to) are hard to pinpoint. Therefore, for the most part, this commentary will not address the various interpretive options of the perplexing prophetic details regarding individual sons of Jacob, especially when the choices do not particularly affect the theological

The account in Gen 49 is bookended by "gather/assemble" (49:1 and 49:29, 33), and "Israel your/their father" (49:1, 2 and 49:28). This depiction of Jacob, as well as the double exhortation to listen to him (49:2), and the poetic parallelisms, make for a discourse that resembles wisdom literature, with the speaker as a sage (see Prov 1:8; 41:1). Jacob's address is carefully arranged by the narrator.[20]

> **A**   Sons of Leah (49:3–15a)
>   **B**   Son of a handmaid (49:16–17; in six lines)
>   **C**   Jacob's prayer (49:18)
>   **B'**   Sons of handmaids (49:19–21; in six lines)
> **A'**   Sons of Rachel (49:22–27)

At the center lies Jacob's prayer: "For your salvation, I wait, Yahweh!" (Gen 49:18). This first-person interlude is addressed to Yahweh—the only time he shows up in this chapter, and the last occurrence of his name in the book of Genesis. It returns to the theme of human dependency upon God and divine sufficiency for man. As Jacob contemplates the future of his children and their descendants, he realizes, once and for all, that only God, in his grace, can make something out of the motley crew of vulnerable humanity, in particular of Jacob's flesh and blood, both now and in future generations.

Reuben was disqualified from leadership because of his incest with Jacob's concubine (35:22; 49:3–4): his turpitude is noted thrice—"you went up to your father's bed," "you defiled it," and "he went up to my couch." Simeon and Levi lost their privileges because of their egregious acts of violence against the Shechemites: 34:25–26; 49:5–7. Instead of these three, it is the fourth son, Judah, who is promised supremacy over his brothers (49:8). Judah gets the most words from his father (Joseph gets the next longest section). Judah's superiority is noted in 49:8 with his leadership being praised—his hand is on the neck of his enemies, and his siblings are bowing to him and "praising" (ידה, *ydh*) him. Pröbstle observes that only deity is the appropriate object of "praise" (ידה) in the OT (see Job 40:10–14).[21] Thus it stands to reason that the use of the verb ידה in 49:8 may carry divine connotations for Judah or a descendant of his.[22] That his naming at his birth was connected with the praise of Yahweh adds substance to this conclusion (29:35). No doubt, much of the praise to this fourth son of Jacob comes from his exemplary performance in the latter half of the Joseph Story that saw a dramatically transformed Judah, unlike the one pictured in Gen 37–38 (see 43:8–10; 44:14–34; 46:28).[23]

---

thrust of the pericope.

20. Lunn, "The Last Words of Jacob," 168n24.

21. "'Lion of Judah,'" 32. Whereas Ps 45:17 praises the king, it is in deific terms and the ruler is clearly messianic (see 45:6–7); and Ps 49:19 has the wrongful praise of a wicked man.

22. The wordplays on Judah's name are worth noting: "Judah [יְהוּדָה, *yhudah*], your brothers—they praise you [יוֹדוּךָ, *yoduka*]; your hand [יָדְךָ, *yadka*] shall be on the neck of your enemies" (49:8).

23. That Jacob mentions a "scepter" (שֵׁבֶט, *shevet*) that will not depart from Judah, and a ruler's "staff" (חָקַק, *khaqaq*, 49:10), reminds the reader of the earlier irresponsible actions of Judah in 38:16–18, that included the giving away of his "staff" (חקק) and seal (later returned). Judges 5:14 employs both חקק and שבט as parallels. Other subtleties of wording in Gen 49:9–11 also suggest allusions to past events in

Genesis 49:10, particularly the word שִׁילֹה, *shiloh*, is a major crux of this chapter, made even more complicated by the fact that שִׁילֹה is feminine, but is the subject of a masculine verb ("*he*-comes"). A number of options have been suggested for the interpretation of this verse.[24] 1) "Shiloh" has been seen as a geographical location where the ark rested (Jdg 18:31)—thus: "until he [Judah] comes to Shiloh." But when a place is indicated, it is usually spelt שִׁלֹה (*shiloh*, as in some manuscripts); moreover, in the days of the monarchy, Shiloh was politically insignificant. 2) שִׁילֹה may be considered a corruption of מֹשְׁלֹה, *mshlh* = "his ruler" (מֹשֵׁל, *mshl*, "ruler")—thus: "until his ruler comes." 3) Others divide the שִׁילֹה into שַׁי (*shay*) + לֹה (*loh*) = "tribute to him"—thus reading "until tribute to him comes," making a reasonable parallel with "obedience of the peoples/nations" in the next line (49:10d). 4) Some ancient versions (LXX, some Samaritan Pentateuch manuscripts, Symmachus, Theodotion, etc.) consider the emended שְׁלֹה (*shlh*) as שֶׁ (*she*) + לֹה /לֹו (*lo/loh*) = "which is to him/whose it is"—thus attempting to read "until he comes whose it [the scepter] is," or "until that which is his [the scepter] comes"— i.e., the coming of the Davidic king and/or his scepter. A messianic allusion is thus likely; the only other use of "scepter" (שֵׁבֶט, *shbt*) in the Pentateuch, in Num 24:17, has it "rising from Israel." There, the LXX translates שבט as ἄνθρωπος (*anthrōpos*, "man"), and the Peshitta has ܪܝܫܐ (*rsh'*, "prince/leader"), while *Tg. Ps.-J* reads it as מְשִׁיחָא, *mshykh'* ("messiah"). Ezekiel 19:11, 14 employs שבט ("scepter") for Judah's blessing, along with images of lions (19:2, 6), cubs (19:2, 3, 5), prey (19:3), couching (19:2), going up (19:3), and vines (19:10)—all related to kingship in Israel.[25] The mixed imagery creates an awe-inspiring status for שִׁילֹה: a lion, its prey, and its crouching (Gen 49:9); kingship elements including scepter, ruler's staff, and obedience of people (49:10); and prosperity and beauty (vine, foal, donkey's colt, wine, darkness of eyes, whiteness of teeth (49:11–12).[26] Another reason to consider this impenetrable text as messianic is the close parallel with Zech 9:9 (except for an inversion of the subject–verb order; see below).

Gen 49:10–11	"he comes … שִׁילֹה … foal … donkey's colt"
Zech 9:9	"your king … he comes … foal … donkey's colt"

Judah's life: שִׁילֹה with שֵׁלָה (*shelah*, Shelah); עַיִר (*'ayir*, "foal") with עֵר (*'er*, "Er"); and בְּנִי אָתוֹן (*bni 'aton*, "donkey's colt") with אוֹנָן (*'onan*, "Onan"), not to mention the ass imagery associated with Canaanites (one of whom Judah married, 38:2; see 49:5–6, 14). The statement about עֵינָיִם (*'enayim*, "eyes," 49:12) suggests עֵינָיִם (*'enayim*, "Enaim," the place where Judah met Tamar for his tryst, 38:14, 21). Also of interest is the soaking of garment in the *blood* of grapes" (49:11)—perhaps an allusion to Joseph's garment, so stained to deceive his father (37:31) (Carmichael, "Some Sayings in Genesis 49, 440–43). And while the lion in 49:9 is likely a symbolic of royalty, perhaps there is some connection here with Jacob's "wild beast" in 37:33; the father's exclamation there regarding his son's supposed fate—"surely torn to pieces [טָרֹף טֹרָף, *tarof toraf*]"—echoes the mention of "prey," טֶרֶף, *teref*, in 49:9.

24. See Wenham, *Genesis 16–50*, 476–78; and Pröbstle, "Lion of Judah," 39–42.

25. Ibid., 37n17. Judah and staff (חקק, *khqq*) are also linked in Pss 60:7; 108:8; and Isa 33:22, all dealing with rulership.

26. From ibid., 29.

All of this lends credence to a messianic interpretation of שִׁילֹה, whatever the precise nuance of the clause might be. It is the Lion of Judah who would be prominent not only among the twelve tribes in the history of nation, but also in the future, in the world, as Rev 5:5–6 announces—the Agent *par excellence* of blessing to mankind.

The blessing on Joseph is no less obscure than the ones it follows. "Text-critical issues . . . intertwine with multiple problems in the MT Hebrew to make this an exegete's nightmare."[27] The word בֵּן, *ben*, "son," and בַּת, *bat*, "daughter" in 49:22 (usually translated "bough" and "branches," respectively), are rarely, if ever, used to indicate plants. And all of the other sons of Jacob have animal comparisons, leading one to reconsider the standard translations in Joseph's case. It is possible that פֹּרָת (*porat*, usually translated "be fruitful") is the feminine of פֶּרֶא, *pere'*, "wild ass" (16:12), and that בְּנֹות צָעֲדָה (*banot tsa'adah*, usually translated "branches running") is equivalent to an Arabic expression that means "wild asses/colts."[28] That makes Joseph "like a wild ass—a wild ass by a spring, his wild colts by a wall" (49:22). In any case, Joseph's is a blessed tribe: the root בָרַךְ, *brk*, occurs six times in the blessing to this son of Jacob (49:25–26). Even when he was persecuted (by "archers," 49:23–24), he was sustained by "the Mighty One of Jacob," "the Shepherd," "the Stone of Israel," "the God of your fathers who helps you," and "the Almighty who blesses you"—an unusual co-location of epithets for Yahweh, found in this fashion nowhere else in the OT. God surely is the hero of Joseph's saga (and, indeed, of all of Genesis). The "attack"/"opposition" (שָׂטַם, *satam*, 49:23) that Joseph faced was probably intended to refer to the fraternal violence he suffered, for the word reappears in 50:15 as the "grudge" (שָׂטַם) his brothers thought he might be bearing against them (also used of Esau's "grudge" against Jacob, 27:41—another fraternal dispute). Divine sovereignty overcame all of Joseph's horrible experiences, and divine providence blessed him exceedingly (49:25–26)—not only him, but also his immediate family, his extended family, his adoptive nation, and "all the world" (41:57). In fact, Joseph is here blessed illimitably—"up to the utmost ends of the age-old hills" (49:26). And he becomes the "prince" (49:26, or "superior/distinguished one") among his brothers, though royalty per se is reserved for Judah and his tribe (49:9–10). The oracle about Joseph commenced with him being the prey; it concludes with him being the prince—a sovereign blessing from God, indeed!

In short, "[b]lessing is one of the key words of Genesis . . ., occurring some eighty-eight times in the book. Here in two verses, like the finale of a fireworks display, the root occurs six times . . . making a brilliant climax to the last words of Jacob" (49:25–26). The wordplays make this an artistic construction: "heaven," שָׁמַיִם, *shamayim*, with "breast," שָׁדַיִם (*shadayim*, also similar in sound is "Almighty," שַׁדַּי, *shadday*), and "deep," תְּהוֹם, *thom*, with "womb," רֶחֶם, *rekhem*. "This deliberate balancing of divine blessing on male and female spheres of interest suggests the completeness of God's promises to all Joseph's descendants, both men and women."[29] The final occurrence of the root בָרַךְ

---

27. Wenham, *Genesis 16–50*, 484.

28. Caquot, "Ben Porat," 43–56; Hamilton, *Genesis: Chapters 18–50*, 678. See Hos 8:9; 13:15, that compare Joseph's son, Ephraim, to a wild ass.

29. Wenham, *Genesis 16–50*, 486–87.

in Genesis is in 49:28, where it echoes thrice as the progenitors of the twelve tribes of Israel are blessed.

35.2 Genesis 49:29–50:26

THEOLOGICAL FOCUS 35.2

35.2   The people of God, trusting God's sovereignty and providence, look to the future for the consummation of his promises of blessing (49:29–50:26).

NOTES 35.2

35.2   *The people of God, trusting God's sovereignty and providence, look to the future for the consummation of his promises of blessing.*

Death predominates in this last section, 49:29–50:26. The root קבר, *qbr*, occurs fourteen times: as a verb ("bury") in 49:29, 31 (×3); 50:5 (×2), 6, 7, 13, 14 (×2), and as a noun ("grave") in 49:30; 50:5, 13. That the death and interment is of a loved one is clear: "father" occurs fifteen times in 49:29; 50:1, 2, 5 (×2), 6, 7, 8, 10, 14 (×2), 15, 16, 17, 22. Another key verb that repeats itself is עלה, *'lh*, "go up" (50:6, 7, 9, 14, 24, 25); the word achieves significance in Exodus as it indicates the return of the children of Israel to their Promised Land, the fulfillment of Jacob's dream and God's promise to the patriarchs (Exod 1:10: 3:8, 17; 12:38; 13:19; 17:3; etc.).

This section is carefully laid out[30]:

A   Last words and death of Jacob (**49:29–50:3**)—*monologue*
       "He said to …" (49:29); no explicit response from listeners, but wishes granted; statement of approaching death, instructions regarding remains (49:29); patriarchs and Promised Land named (49:30); death and embalmment (50:2)

B   Joseph's appeal to Pharaoh (**50:4–6**)—*dialogue*
       request and positive response (50:4–6);
       "father made me swear, saying …" (50:5); "therefore … please …" (50:6)

C   Funeral of Jacob (**50:7–14**)—*narrative*
       Bookended by: "Joseph" as subject (50:7, 14);
       infinitival clause "to bury his father" (50:7, 14);
       "all … went up with him" (50:7, 14); "and his brothers" (50:8, 14)

B'   Brothers' appeal to Joseph (**50:15–21**)—*dialogue*
       request and positive response (50:16–21);
       "father charged … saying, …" (50:16); "therefore … please …" (50:17)

A'   Last words and death of Joseph (**50:22–26**)—*monologue*
       "He said to …" (50:24); no explicit response from listeners, but wishes granted; statement of approaching death, instructions regarding remains (50:24–25); patriarchs and Promised Land named (49:30); death and embalmment (50:26)

---

30. From Lunn, "The Last Words of Jacob," 164–66.

The recounting of Jacob's death and burial (Gen 49:29–50:14; *A*, *B*, and *C*) consumes most of this section, and is the longest of its kind in Genesis, perhaps in all of the OT.[31] Not only is this appropriate for the patriarch, Israel, who would be the father of the nation, Israel, it also emphasizes Jacob's constant demand that his remains be returned to the "homeland," in anticipation of the fulfillment of God's promises to him and to his descendants (48:7, 21–22; 49:29–32; 50:5–14). That Jacob is not expressly said to have "died," but only retracted his feet and breathed his last, perhaps focuses on Jacob's faith in the future God had promised for him—both Abraham and Isaac are said to have "breathed [their] last and died" (25:8, 17; 35:29). In other words, "[Jacob] is not dead but asleep, waiting for the realization of the promises"; clearly the emphasis in the text is not on his departure, but on his arrival, as he is "gathered to his people" (49:29).[32]

The last words of the patriarchs are also patterned.[33] Jacob's (49:29–33) can be visualized as shown (for Joseph's words, similarly organized, see below):

> **A**   "charged"; "gathered to my people" (49:29a)
>   **B**   "cave"; "field" (×3); "Hittite" (×2); "bought" (49:29b–30)
>   **C**   Burial of Abraham and Sarah, Isaac and Rebekah, and Leah (49:31)
>   **B'**   "cave"; "field"; "sons of Heth"; "bought" (49:32)
> **A'**   "charged"; "gathered to his people" (49:33)

The centerpiece (*C*) of Jacob's last words is in 49:31, a listing of his ancestors and their spouses buried in the first acquisition of land in Canaan of this divinely chosen family—at least those members of the family in the line of the Messiah: Abraham, Sarah (not Hagar), Isaac (not Ishmael), Leah (but not Zilpah, Bilhah, or Rachel, or even Joseph—see Josh 24:32), and, later, Jacob himself (but not Esau). Speaking to his sons who know all this information, Jacob's purpose must surely have been rhetorical. Lunn makes a perceptive observation about the listing of the five individuals in 49:31, a highly stylized notation that is semi-poetic[34]:

---

31. "The grandest state funeral recorded in the Bible was given to Jacob" and, for one whose story covers half the chapters of Genesis and who is the progenitor of the nation of Israel, this is probably appropriate (Wenham, *Genesis 16–50*, 488). The massive cortege was made up of "all the servants of Pharaoh," "all the elders of the land of Egypt," and "all the household of Joseph and his brothers and his father's household"—"a very great/glorious company" (50:7–9). Brodie (*Genesis as Dialogue*, 415) notes that since the death of Jacob happened after the events of 47:13–26, virtually the entire populace of Egypt would have been indentured servants to Pharaoh at that time. Thus "all the servants of Pharaoh" could indicate, in hyperbole, all of the citizenry of Egypt! In contrast, the burials of Jacob's father and grandfather were conducted with minimal fuss (25:9; 35:29). Moses' demise gets only three verses, Deut 34:6–8; and David's, only a mention, 1 Kgs 2:10. Perhaps there is also an eschatological allusion involved here, as Sailhamer suggests. A recurring image in the prophets was a future return of Israel to the land accompanied by many from foreign nations, all streaming to Jerusalem (Isa 2:2–3; 66:20; Zech 8:23; Ps 87; etc.). A type of that ultimate regathering might be this vast caravan heading to the Promised Land, foreigners and all. See "Genesis," 282.

32. Mathews, *Genesis 11:27–50:26*, 915; Hamilton, *Genesis: Chapters 18–50*, 689.

33. From Lunn, "The Last Words of Jacob," 166–67.

34. Ibid., 170–72; also 170–71n33.

"*There* they buried Abraham,
and Sarah, his wife;
there they buried Isaac,
and Rebekah, his wife;
and *there* I buried Leah."

The location is given undue prominence: "there" is mentioned thrice (italics above)—
"the cave that is in the field of Machpelah, which is before Mamre, in the land of Canaan,
which Abraham bought" (49:30). This was the small parcel of land that Abraham
had purchased from the Hittites, the family possession (אֲחֻזַּת־קֶבֶר, 'akhuzzath-qeber,
"burial *possession*/site," 23:4, 9, 20); it represented the "down payment" on the "eternal
possession" (אֲחֻזַּת עוֹלָם, 'akhuzzath 'olam, 17:8; 48:4) that God had promised the patriarch and his descendants. It is in this location that Jacob wants to be buried with his
ancestors (אֲחֻזָּה קֶבֶר, 49:30; 50:13). There is a striking detail in 49:31 that must not be
missed: the first letters of the named people, in the order in which they appear are א, שׂ,
י, ר, and ל (', *s*, *y*, *r*, and *l*). It is immediately obvious that the rearranged letters of that
artistic anagram spell יִשְׂרָאֵל, "Israel."

> This fact might be conceived as merely coincidental, especially since the order in
> which the letters occur seems arbitrary. Yet it is contended here that the sequence
> is significant and itself is indicative of deliberate design. In considering these
> consonants, the prevalence of inverted structures in Genesis must be borne in
> mind. . . . Inverted symmetrical patterns have been found employed at all levels.[35]

Indeed, Lunn shows that if those initial consonants of the five listed names are read
working outwards (concentrically) from the center (Isaac → Sarah → Rebekah →
Abraham → Leah), the letters are in the correct order, making up יִשְׂרָאֵל.

א (אַבְרָהָם, 'abraham, Abraham)

שׂ (שָׂרָה, sarah, Sarah)

י (יִצְחָק, yitskhaq, Isaac)

ר (רִבְקָה, ribqah, Rebekah)

ל (לֵאָה, le'ah, Leah)

"Jacob is there requesting his sons to bury him in the cave in Canaan, not simply because
his forefathers rest there, but because in cryptic fashion 'Israel' lies there. Jacob, who is
called Israel, must needs be laid to rest in the promised land with this other 'Israel.'"[36]
As has been noted before, this is a striking emphasis, both from the mouth of the dying patriarch, as well as from the hands of an astute narrator, upon the faithfulness of
God and the veracity of his promises. Canaan was where the blessings were promised;
Canaan was where the children of Israel belonged; Canaan was where they would return.

Likewise playing on the same theme, Joseph's last words (50:24–26) are arranged
as shown:

35. Ibid., 172; for examples of such intricate wordplays in Scripture, see ibid., 172–73.
36. Ibid., 174.

> **A**   "die" (50:24a)
>   **B**   "God will surely visit you"; "take you up"; "from this land" (50:24b)
>   **C**   "oath" (50:24c): by God, to Abraham, Isaac, and Jacob
>   **C'** "oath" (50:25a): by sons of Israel, to Joseph
>   **B'** "God will surely visit you"; "you will take up"; "from here" (50:25b)
> **A'** "died" (50:26)

The centerpiece of Joseph's final utterance deals with oaths (50:24c, 25a; *C* and *C'*): the first oath is one made by God regarding the Promised Land; the second is the oath being sworn by Joseph's siblings regarding taking his remains back to that same land. The latter oath, it appears, is dependent upon the former one—the sovereign promise of God. The past oath of deity becomes ground for the present oath of humanity.[37] The thrust of this oath is that Joseph's remains be returned to Canaan.

All of this—the final statements of both patriarchs, Jacob and Joseph—is thoroughly based upon God's sovereign word and reflects an utmost trust in the ability of deity to bring about what he had promised (the land promises in Genesis are found in 12:7; 13:15; 15:7; 17:8; 24:7; 26:3; 28:13; 35:12; 48:4). Such an attitude, on the part of Jacob was adumbrated in the central placement of his attribution of salvation from Yahweh alone, in the blessing oracle he uttered to his sons (49:18, at the center of 49:1–27). As for Joseph, just prior to the narrative of his deathbed wishes, he has unambiguously declared his trust in the sovereignty of God that had controlled the tumultuous events of his life (50:19–21); to further underscore his faith, he is shown as having declared *twice* that God would bring his descendants back to Canaan (50:24–25; both times with an infinitive absolute).[38]

Berman notes that the fulfillment phrase "and he/they did as told/commanded" occurs twenty-four times in the OT as specific injunctions are obeyed by those so commanded. In all of those cases, but one, the fulfillment phrase immediately follows upon the commandment. Only in this pericope is the command (of Jacob, 49:29–32) separated by a number of verses, and by a lengthy period of time, from the fulfillment phrase—in 50:12–13, and this after forty days of embalmment, followed by thirty days of mourning, and the time for a journey to Canaan, plus another seven more days of mourning (50:1–12).[39] Lunn speculates that this relative prominence given to the burial of Jacob (50:1–14), as opposed to the single verse describing Joseph's death (only eleven words in the Hebrew) might be to underscore the fact that 50:7–14 serves as a type of the exodus, another movement from Egypt to Canaan. Several key words are repeated in this move and the one four centuries later: "go up" (עלה, *'lh*, 50:7 [×2]; see Exod 13:18; 17:3; 32:1, 7; etc.)[40]; כָּבֵד מְאֹד (*kabed mo'd*, "very great," Gen 50:9; see Exod 12:38); presence of Canaanites in the Promised Land (Gen 50:11; see Exod

---

37. Ibid., 169–70.

38. Ibid., 168.

39. Berman, "Identity Politics," 21.

40. It might well also be that Joseph's request to the Pharaoh to let him "go up" (עלה, 50:5; and Pharaoh's assent that he "go up," עלה, 50:6) is a foreshadowing of the "going up" of the children of Israel at the exodus.

3:8, 17; 13:5, 11); אֲחֻזָּה (*'akhuzzah*, "possession," Gen 50:13; Lev 14:34; 25:24; Deut 32:49; etc.); "sheep and cattle," and "livestock: (Gen 50:8; see Exod 10:26; 12:32, 38); "chariots and horsemen" (Gen 50:9; see Exod 14:9, 17, 18, 23, 26, 28; 15:19); "infants" (Gen 50:8; Exod 10:24; 12:37); "company," i.e., the Egyptian army (Gen 50:9; see Exod 14:20); "servants of Pharaoh" (Gen 50:7; see Exod 9:20; 10:7; 11:3; etc.); "Pharaoh's house" (Gen 50:7; see Exod 8:24).[41] All of this takes on the appearance of a "rehearsal for the Exodus," here in Gen 50.[42] Kass also comments on the strangeness of the route taken by the burial party, not a straight shot northeast from Egypt to Hebron, up the Mediterranean coast and crossing the Negev desert. Instead, "we are told (twice) that the procession entered Canaan from 'beyond the Jordan,' an expression that means 'from the *east* of the river,' that is, from trans-Jordan. It seems as if Joseph directed the procession to take a circuitous route across the Sinai and around the Dead Sea (a route, as it happens, not unlike the one the Israelites will take after the exodus)." In fact, that might have been the point of the mention of the itinerary, another adumbration of the exodus.[43]

It appears that this closing chapter of the book is underscoring the certainty of Israel's return to the Promised Land, both in explicit utterances of the dying patriarchs and their burial wishes, and in the implicit parallels between the journey from Egypt—albeit temporary—to bury Jacob and the exodus four centuries later. Again, God's sovereign will is shown to come to pass, and his people are blessed!

Before Joseph plans the disposal of his own remains (50:22–26), a final reconciliation between this son of Jacob and his brothers remains to be accomplished. Just as Joseph's earliest recorded utterances are directed to his brothers (37:5, 9), so his final recorded utterance, too, is directed to the same company (50:24).[44] While Joseph's intent to forgive had already been made evident in Gen 45 (especially in 45:5, as he exhorted them not to be grieved or angry), the brothers had until now never asked for forgiveness. Perhaps they suspected that Joseph's magnanimity was merely a nod to their aging father's feelings. They now fear that the sibling they so mistreated "bears a grudge" against them (50:15). Thus, ironically, the Joseph narrative that commenced with the brothers' *real* hatred of Joseph (37:4, 5, 8), ends with an *imaginary* grudge (in their minds) that Joseph bore against them (50:15).[45] Still feeling guilty and afraid (50:19, 21), they send an emissary to Joseph and ask for his forgiveness (50:16), confessing their "transgression," their "sin," and their "wrong": "please forgive" occurs twice in 50:17.[46] They appeal for his forgiveness as they name "the God of your father"

---

41. Lunn, "The Last Words of Jacob," 175–78.

42. Brodie, *Genesis as Dialogue*, 415.

43. *The Beginning of Wisdom*, 654n18. About the actual reason for the circumambulation, we are not told.

44. This, however, does not necessitate that he preceded them in death; "brothers" might simply be an inclusive term for the extended family Joseph belonged to.

45. Hamilton, *Genesis: Chapters 18–50*, 702.

46. Though these are the quoted words of Jacob, it is likely that in citing them, the brothers were actually making those words their own, thus confessing their wrongdoings. They themselves employ

whose slaves they are—an implicit entreaty that Joseph act like that God, "who forgives iniquity, transgression, and sin" (Exod 34:7; Pss 32:1, 5; 103:3; 130:3–4; Mic 7:18).[47]

Joseph's first reaction is to break down in tears (50:17).[48] The text notes that he wept when the brothers "spoke" (דבר, *dbr*) to him, i.e., when the message they sent was passed on to him. But דבר also recalls the situation of Gen 37 when these same siblings could *not* "speak" (דבר) to him peaceably (37:4); indeed, a few moments later, Joseph would "speak" (דבר) kindly to them (50:21). In this literary fashion, the account books are being closed, relationships are being restored, reconciliation is being accomplished. When the brothers subsequently come to Joseph, they "fall before his face" and acknowledge that they, servants of God (50:17), deserve only to be the servants of Joseph (50:18; Judah had already confessed that status before Joseph in 44:16, 33—the brothers "fell before [Joseph's] face" at that time as well, 44:14). Ephrem the Syrian (*Commentary on Genesis* 44.2) observed that "Joseph wept and said, 'Do not be afraid of me, for although your father has died, the God of your father, on account of whom I will never strike you, is still alive."[49] With this encounter, the sorry episode of many decades ago is finally laid to rest—brothers united, family restored.

Once again the sovereignty of God that operated in/through/with what the brothers had done is emphasized; Joseph had already made that clear once before in 45:5–9. What they meant for evil (חשב רעה, *khshv r'h*), God meant for good (חשב לטבה, *khshv ltvh*). "[W]hatever poison Satan produces, God turns it into medicine for his elect" (Calvin, *Comm. Gen.* on 50:20). While both divine sovereignty and human responsibility act in tandem, Joseph makes it obvious which one has veto power, overriding the other (see Prov 19:21). Joseph's response to his brothers (Gen 50:19–21) captures in a nutshell not only the theology of the Joseph narrative, but that of the book of Genesis as well—the good–evil polarity, and God's working out good from evil, began with the events of creation and those in the Garden of Eden.[50] Man is not in the place of God ("Am I in the place of God?," 50:19); rather, he must acquiesce to the divine will, trusting that God knows what he is about ("Do not be afraid," 50:19). Indeed, God does, for in/with/through the evils perpetrated and sins committed by mankind, God inscrutably and ineluctably works out his sovereign purposes ("You

---

"evil" and "transgression" (50:15, 17). In fact, three of the four major OT terms for wickedness are found here; the only one missing is עון, *'on*, "iniquity/guilt."

47. Wenham, *Genesis 16–50*, 490.

48. No one person in the Bible is recorded to have wept as often as did Joseph (42:24; 43:30; 45:1–2, 14–15; 46:29; 50:1; and here, 50:17)! Benno Jacob eloquently says of the lachrymose situation of 50:17: "[Joseph] weeps because they believe a go-between necessary, because they are afraid of him, because they think him capable of such attitude, because he hears the father's voice. His youth which had been poisoned by their hatred rises up before him, and it is they who in their self-humiliation remind him of it. These his last tears are really their tears" (*The First Book of the Bible*, 341).

49. *ACCS* 2.350–51.

50. One might conceive of the primeval events this way: first God meant it for good (as the refrain in the account of creation establishes, 1:4, 10, 12, 18, 21, 25, 31), but then man meant it for evil (2:9, 17; 3:5, 22; and especially 6:5 and 8:21). With the entry of sin, however, God has another go: what man meant for evil, God meant for good—he works good even from evil, for his sovereignty is illimitable and his power incontestable.

meant it for evil, but God meant it for good," 50:20). And a key purpose of God is the blessing of mankind ("to preserve alive many people," which included Egyptians, 50:20), a blessing that is extended to others by God's agent(s) thereof ("I will provide for you and your little ones," 50:21).

The last section of the pericope, of the Joseph Story, and of the Book of Genesis, 50:22–26, begins with Joseph "living" (50:22), along with a notation of his age; it ends with Joseph "dying" (50:26), with another notation of his age.[51] In between, in 50:24, 25, Joseph twice asserts God's "visitation" (i.e., divine intervention, פָּקַד, *pqd*) of his brothers and the extended family, a promise fulfilled in the exodus as God "visits" his people to rescue them (also פָּקַד; Exod 3:16; 4:31). Like his father, Joseph, too, makes his family swear to take his remains back to the Promised Land (Gen 50:24–25; see Exod 13:19). Joseph's trust in God is as complete as was Jacob's, even though Joseph was not personally granted a divine promise regarding his descendants and their return to the land of promise (unlike the experience of his ancestors). Rather, he trusts the God who testified to his forefathers to that effect. Moreover, one remembers that Joseph lived in Promised Land for a mere seventeen years, dwelling for the remaining ninety-three years in a foreign land. Therefore, his attachment to the land of his fathers is even more remarkable and makes his faith in God even more exemplary! This was a man looking to God and to a future promised by God. "Genesis ends with a haunting picture. . . . The story of Genesis that began with God creating a beautiful Paradise on earth for his creatures ends with Joseph in a coffin in Egypt—waiting, waiting for God to bring his people back to the Promised Land."[52] In that sense, the story still remains incomplete. That the last Hebrew word of the book of Genesis is "Egypt" indicates where the incidents of the next installment of the serial will take place.[53]

---

51. Gevirtz suggests that Joseph's age is symbolic, since the ages of the patriarchs preceding him and that of his own form a distinct pattern. Abraham's age—$175 = 7 \times 5^2$; Isaac's age—$180 = 5 \times 6^2$; Jacob's age—$147 = 3 \times 7^2$; these form as multiples of square numbers in succession: 5^2, 6^2, and 7^2. Perhaps it is only a coincidence, but Joseph's age—$110 = 5^2 + 6^2 + 7^2$, the sum of his predecessors, in a sense. Or, if one looks at this equation as $110 = 1 \times (5^2 + 6^2 + 7^2)$, Joseph becomes the successor of his predecessors, in the pattern of $7 \to 5 \to 3 \to 1$. Not only does this integrally link the Joseph story with the preceding ones of his ancestors, it also serves to close out, with some degree of finality, the entire saga of Patriarchal History. The first mention in Scripture of the grand old patriarchs together—"Abraham, Isaac, and Jacob" (50:24)—also makes for a fitting conclusion. See Gevirtz, "The Life Spans of Joseph," 570–71, and also Labuschagne, "The Lifespan of the Patriarchs," 121–27. The note about the "third generation" of Ephraim's sons and the sons of Machir, Joseph's grandson, are also likely deliberate (50:23); that would make this generation the "fourth generation" in the divine promise to Abraham in 15:16. It might well be that Joseph saw with his own eyes the very generation of the exodus—his great-grandchildren (Ausloos, "The Deuteronomist," 389).

52. Greidanus, *Preaching Christ from Genesis*, 471.

53. Incidentally, 50:26 has the only mention of "coffin" (אָרוֹן, *ʾaron*) in Genesis; the Hebrew word also means "ark," in which was placed the two tables of the Ten Commandments (Deut 10:5). Both one and the other אָרוֹן were carried about by the children of Israel until the coffin of Joseph was interred by Joshua (Josh 24:29). "All this time in the desert Israel carried two shrines with them, the one the coffin containing the bones of the dead man Joseph, the other the Ark containing the covenant of the Living God. The wayfarers who saw the two receptacles wondered, and they would ask, 'How doth the ark of the dead come next to the ark of the Ever-living?' The answer was, 'The dead man enshrined in the one fulfilled the commandments enshrined in the other'" (Ginzberg and Cohen, *Legends of the Jews*, 183).

Thus, throughout the book, the narrator of Genesis has managed to keep the focus squarely upon divine blessing. The book began with God's intention to bless humanity, a plan thwarted by the sinfulness of mankind. God then chose the family of Abraham to be the vehicle of his universal blessing, the fullness of which could only be experienced by faith of the kind exercised by Abraham, the one who feared God. Jacob's life was characterized by a series of missteps in his vain attempt to secure divine blessing by his own stratagems, and with his own resources. He finally obtains the blessing in a posture of surrender. Joseph's story then continues the drama, narratively depicting what it takes for God's children to be the agents of his blessing, both for their own families, as well as for those around them.

SERMON FOCUS AND OUTLINES

> **THEOLOGICAL FOCUS OF PERICOPE 35 FOR PREACHING**
>
> **35   Agents of divine blessing remember the blessings of the past, pass on the blessings in the present, and expect the consummation of blessings in the future (48:1–50:26).**

The two protagonists of the Joseph saga, Joseph himself, and his father, Jacob, are the agents of blessing to be emulated. Jacob, in Gen 48, remembers God's promises and blessings of the past; in Gen 48–49, he passes on blessings to his children and grandchildren; in Gen 50, Joseph (as Jacob did in previous chapters), trusts God's sovereignty and expects the consummation of blessings in the future.

Possible Preaching Outlines for Pericope 35

I.   PAST: *Recall the blessings!*
      Jacob's recollection of divine promises and blessings (48:3–7, 11, 15–16)
      Joseph's attribution of blessings to God's sovereign working (50:19–20)
      How we can remember God's blessings of the past

II. PRESENT: *Release the blessings!*
      Jacob's blessing of his grandchildren and his sons (48:9, 12–14, 19–20; 49:1–27)
      Joseph's blessing of his brothers in his forgiveness and his provision (50:15–21)
      Joseph's blessings of his children and grandchildren (50:22–23)
      How we can be a blessing to those around us

III. FUTURE: *Realize the blessings!*
      Jacob's confidence in God for the return to Canaan (48:21–22; 49:28–33)
      Jacob's mortal remains returned to Canaan (50:1–14)
      Joseph's confidence in God for the return to Canaan (50:24–26)
      How we can solidify the hope of our future blessings

By separating out the main characters, Jacob and Joseph, in the main moves, another outline may be created.

I.   JACOB as God's Agent of Blessing
      Past: Jacob's recollection of divine promises and blessings (48:3–7, 11, 15–16)
      Present: Jacob's blessing of his grandchildren and his sons (48:9, 12–14, 19–20; 49:1–27)
      Future: Jacob's confidence in God for the return to Canaan; the return (48:21–22; 49:28–33; 50:1–14)

II. JOSEPH as God's Agent of Blessing
   Past: Joseph's attribution of blessings to God's sovereign working (50:19–20)
   Present Joseph's blessing of his brothers, children, and grandchildren (50:15–21, 22–23)
   Future: Joseph's confidence in God for the return to Canaan (50:24–26)

III. BELIEVERS as God's Agents of Blessing: *Recall, Release, Realize God's blessings!*
   Past: How we can remember God's blessings of the past
   Present: How we can be a blessing to those around us
   Future: How we can solidify the hope of our future blessings

CONCLUSION

"'I will not let you go unless you bless me.'
Then God blessed him there."

Genesis 32:26, 29

Those who labor in pulpits on a weekly basis deal with the "the astonishing supposition that texts which are between possibly 3,000 and almost 2,000 years old can offer orientation for the discovery of truth in the third millennium."[1] It is, indeed, a remarkable predication that from these ancient texts may be discerned and preached, not just truth that informs, but truth that transforms—that is applicable, and that changes lives for the glory of God. Yet the lot of the homiletician is not easy, neither is the responsibility of such a one minimal: each week, the preacher has to negotiate that formidable passage from ancient text to modern audience to expound, with authority and relevance, a specific biblical pericope for the faithful. Thus this intrepid soul, aided by the Holy Spirit, becomes the pastoral communicative agent of the life-transforming truths of Scripture. *Genesis: A Theological Commentary for Preachers* is one small attempt in a larger endeavor to help the preacher move safely, accurately, and effectively across the gulf between text and application.

Karl Barth's indictment must be carefully heeded:

> My complaint is that recent commentators confine themselves to an interpretation of the text which seems to me to be no commentary at all, but merely the first step toward a commentary. Recent [NT] commentaries contain no more than a reconstruction of the text, a rendering of the Greek words and phrases by their precise equivalents, a number of additional notes in which archaeological and philological material is gathered together, and a more or less plausible arrangement of the subject matter in such a manner that it may be made historically and psychologically intelligible from the standpoint of pure pragmatism.[2]

This author has attended to Barth's concerns, and attempted to go beyond the "first step toward a commentary," to deliver in comprehensible fashion not only what the

---

1. Schwöbel, "The Preacher's Art," 7.
2. Barth, *The Epistle to the Romans*, 6.

author was saying, but also what the author was *doing* with what he was saying. This commentary agrees that "[t]he storyteller is not merely conveying the contents of a story but is trying to do something to the audience in the process of telling the story." Genesis, like any other book of the Bible, is designed to "seduce" its readers to change their lives in thought, in feeling, and in action, to comply with the precepts, priorities, and practices of God's world (i.e., the theology of the pericope) that is displayed in, with, and through the inspired writing. To that end, the book of Genesis (and, for that matter, *every* biblical book) "works predominantly along the rhetorical axis of language to affect the reader rather than predominantly along the referential axis of language to convey information."[3] All this to move God's people to dwell in God's ideal world, aligned to God's demand. Or, to put it another way, so that pericope by pericope, God's people would move towards Christlikeness—a *christiconic* mode of interpreting Scripture.[4]

In other words, the author of Genesis is *doing* something with what he is saying. The theological agenda of the writer mandates that interpreters, particularly those who interpret for preaching purposes, attend not only to what is being said, but also to what is being *done* with what is being said. In aiding the preacher, this commentary has approached Genesis in a unique fashion, undertaking a form of exegesis geared towards discerning the theology of the pericope—the theological focus of each pericope of the book, the *doing-with-its-saying*.[5]

It is a foundational conviction of this work that valid application of a pericope of Scripture may be arrived at only via this critical intermediary between text and praxis, pericopal theology.[6] The hermeneutical philosophy behind this commentary also holds that such valid application to change lives for the glory of God is the appropriate goal of every sermon. Interpretation of the text is, after all, ultimately a "rewriting the text of the work within the text of our lives."[7] And the task of the preacher with a pastoral heart ought to include the proffering of specific ways in which the theological focus of the pericope, with all its narrated potency, may be translated into the real life of real people.

Overall, in Genesis, the theme of blessing predominates. God's *creating for blessing* (Gen 1–11, Primeval History) explains his plans and purposes for the world, and particularly for the acme of his creation, mankind. The section also describes how man has constantly failed God, bringing to naught God's desire to bless him. Abraham's *moving to blessing* (Gen 11–25, the Abraham Story), not only details God's choice of one man (and one nation through that man) to be the agency of divine blessing to

---

3. Fowler, *Let the Reader Understand*, 10, 222.

4. See Kuruvilla, *Privilege the Text!* 238–69.

5. See Introduction, and Kuruvilla, *Privilege the Text!* 33–65; idem, *Text to Praxis*, 142–190; and idem, "Pericopal Theology," 265–283, for details on this hermeneutical entity, pericopal theology, and its value for the homiletical process.

6. In the commentary, this is called the "Theological Focus." Such a theological thrust, I have proposed elsewhere (see references above), is what the author was *doing* with what he was saying.

7. Barthes, "Day by Day," 101.

mankind, but also—and perhaps more importantly from a preaching point of view—points out what it means to appropriate that blessing of God by faithful commitment to him (fear of God). Jacob's *experiencing the blessing* (Gen 25–36, the Jacob Story), extends the theme of the prior section, emphasizing the divine initiative in the blessing of man, in contrast to the inutility of human initiative in appropriating such blessings—God alone is the source of blessing. Joseph's *being a blessing* (Gen 37–50, the Joseph Story), carries God's purpose further and portrays how God's people become agents of blessing for those around them—for their families, their communities, their nations, and indeed, for the whole world. In sum, the theological thrust of Genesis exhorts that: *The people of God, intended to be blessed by God who created for blessing, move towards blessing in faith, experience God's blessing by recognizing him alone as the source of blessing, and become a blessing to others as they live lives of integrity.*

In every broad section of Genesis, each pericope therein contributes a slice or a quantum of theology to the larger theological focus of its section and to the plenary theme of blessing of the whole book. The goal of this theological commentary has been primarily to explicate that quantum of theology for each pericope. In preaching the book of Genesis, then, week by week and pericope by pericope, preachers are called to fulfill the august responsibility, with divine aid from the Holy Spirit, to move themselves and their listeners closer to God's blessing—understanding it, experiencing it, moving towards it, and becoming agents of it. Inasmuch as the application propounded by homileticians in sermons is faithfully assimilated into listeners' lives, creating Christian dispositions and forming Christlike character, the people of God will have aligned themselves to the will of God for the glory of God—the goal of preaching.[8] Then text will have become praxis, the people of God will have experienced and enjoyed divine blessings, and Christlikeness will have been inculcated in God's children, as each pericope of Genesis depicts (and directs). Then one can say, not that the kingdom of God is near, but that it, with its manifold blessings, is *here*!

---

8. It bears repeating that this commentary is only a "theological" commentary, not a "preaching" commentary. It takes the preacher only part of the way to a sermon, from text to theology (the hermeneutical step). It remains the preacher's burden to complete the crossing by moving from theology to application, i.e., making concrete application from the theology of the passage—application that is specific for the particular audience—and presenting all of that in a sermon that is powerful and persuasive (the rhetorical step).

BIBLIOGRAPHY

Abusch, Tzvi. "An Early Form of the Witchcraft Ritual *Maqlû* and the Origin of a Babylonian Magical Ceremony." Pages 1–58 in *Lingering over Words: Studies in Ancient Near Eastern Literature in Honor of William L. Moran.* Edited by Tzvi Abusch, John Huehnergard, and Piotr Steinkeller. Atlanta: Scholars Press, 1990.

Ackerman, James. "Joseph, Judah, and Jacob." Pages 85–113 in *Literary Interpretations of Biblical Narratives, Volume 2.* Edited by Kenneth R. R. Gros Louis. Nashville: Abingdon, 1982.

Agyenta, Alfred. "When Reconciliation Means More than the 'Re-Membering' of Former Enemies: The Problem of the Conclusion to the Jacob–Esau Story from a Narrative Perspective (Gen 33,1–17)." *ETL* 83 (2007): 123–34.

Ahroni, Reuben. "Why Did Esau Spurn the Birthright?: A Study in Biblical Interpretation." *Jud* 29 (1980): 323–31.

Alexander, T. D. "Abraham Reassessed Theologically." Pages 7–28 in *He Swore an Oath: Biblical Themes from Genesis 12–50.* Edited by R. S. Hess, P. E. Sattherthwaite, and G. J. Wenham. Carlisle, U.K.: Paternoster, 1994.

Allis, Oswald T. *God Spake By Moses.* Philadelphia: Presbyterian and Reformed, 1951.

Alter, Robert. *The Art of Biblical Narrative.* New York: Basic Books, 1981.

———. *The Five Books of Moses: A Translation with Commentary.* New York: W. W. Norton, 2004.

———. *Genesis.* New York: Norton, 1996.

———. "Sodom as Nexus: The Web of Design in Biblical Narrative." Pages 146–60 in *The Book and the Text: The Bible and Literary Theory.* Edited by Regina M. Schwartz. Cambridge, Mass.: Blackwell, 1990.

Amit, Yairah. "Narrative Analysis: Meaning, Context, and Origins of Genesis 38." Pages 271–91 in *Method Matters: Essays on the Interpretation of the Hebrew Bible in Honor of David L. Petersen.* Edited by Joel M. LeMon and Kent Harold Richards. Atlanta: SBL, 2009.

———. *Reading Biblical Narratives: Literary Criticism and the Hebrew Bible.* Translated by Yael Lotan. Minneapolis: Augsburg Fortress, 2001.

Anderson, John E. *Jacob and the Divine Trickster: A Theology of Deception and Yhwh's Fidelity to the Ancestral Promise in the Jacob Cycle.* Siphrut 5. Winona Lake: Eisenbrauns, 2011.

Andrew, M. E. "Moving from Death to Life: Verbs of Motion in the Story of Judah and Tamar in Gen 38." *ZAW* 105 (1993): 262–69.

Arbez, Edward P., and John P. Weisengoff. "Exegetical Notes on Genesis 1:1–2." *CBQ* 10 (1948): 140–50.

Arnold, Bill T. *Genesis.* NCBC. Cambridge: Cambridge University Press, 2009.

Auld, Graeme. "*Imago dei* in Genesis: Speaking in the Image of God." *ExpTim* 116 (2005): 259–62.

Ausloos, Hans. "The Deuteronomist and the Account of Joseph's Death (Gen 50,22–26)." Pages 381–95 in *Studies in the Book of Genesis: Literature, Redaction and History.* BETL 155. Edited by A. Wénin. Leuven: Leuven University Press, 2001.

Averbeck, R. E. "Sumer, the Bible, and Comparative Method: Historiography and Temple Building." Pages 88–125 in *Mesopotamia and the Bible.* Edited by M. W. Chavalas and K. L. Younger, Jr. Grand Rapids: Baker, 2002.

Awabdy, Mark A. "Babel, Suspense, and the Introduction to the Terah–Abram Narrative." *JSOT* 35 (2010): 3–29.

Backon, Joshua. "Jacob and the Spotted Sheep: The Role of Prenatal Nutrition on Epigenetics of Fur Color." *JBQ* 36 (2008): 263–65.

Bibliography

Baden, Joel S. "The Tower of Babel: A Case Study in the Competing Methods of Historical and Modern Literary Criticism." *JBL* 128 (2009): 209–24.

Bahrani, Zainab. *The Graven Image: Representation in Babylonia and Assyria.* Philadelphia: University of Pennsylvania Press, 2003.

Balserak, Jon. "Luther, Calvin and Musculus on Abraham's Trial: Exegetical History and the Transformation of Genesis 22." *RRR* 6 (2004): 361–73.

Bar-Efrat, Shimon. *Narrative Art in the Bible.* JSOTSup 70. Sheffield: Almond Press, 1989.

———. "Some Observations on the Analysis of Structure in Biblical Narrative." *VT* 30 (1980): 154–73.

Barr, James. "Was Everything that God Created Really Good: A Question in the First Verse of the Bible." Pages 55–65 in *God in the Fray: A Tribute to Walter Brueggemann.* Edited by Tod Linafelt and Timothy K. Beal. Minneapolis: Fortress, 1998.

Barth, Karl. *Church Dogmatics, Volume III, Part 1: The Creation of God.* Translated by G. W. Bromiley. Edited by G. W. Bromiley and T. F. Torrance. London: T. & T. Clark, 1958.

———. *The Epistle to the Romans.* Second edition. Translated by Edwyn C. Hoskyns. London: Oxford University Press, 1968.

Barthes, Roland. "Day by Day with Roland Barthes." Pages 98–117 in *On Signs.* By Roland Barthes. Edited by Marshall Blonsky. Baltimore: Johns Hopkins University Press, 1985.

Bassett, Frederick W. "Noah's Nakedness and the Curse of Canaan a Case of Incest?" *VT* 21 (1971): 232–37.

Bavinck, Herman. *In the Beginning.* Edited by John Bolt. Grand Rapids: Baker, 1999.

Beauchamp, Paul. *Création et séparation: Etude exégétique du premier chapitre de la Genèse.* Paris: Desclée de Brouwer, 1969.

Bechtold, William K. "Sight Elements in the Characterization of Judah (Gen 37–50)." Pages 1–21. Cited 22 Feb 2013. Online: http://www.ibr-bbr.org/files/pdf/2012/Bechtold_Sight_Elements_IBR_Emerging_OT_2012.pdf.

Beck, Peter. "The Fall of Man and the Failure of Jonathan Edwards." *EQ* 79 (2007): 209–25.

Bergen, Robert D. "The Role of Genesis 22:1–19 in the Abraham Cycle: A Computer-Assisted Textual Interpretation." *CTR* 4 (1990): 313–26.

Bergsma, John Sietze, and Scott Walker Hahn. "Noah's Nakedness and the Curse on Canaan (Genesis 9:20–27)." *JBL* 124 (2005): 25–40.

Berlin, Adele. *Poetics and Interpretation of Biblical Narrative.* Bible and Literature Series 9. Sheffield: Almond Press, 1983.

Berlinerblau, Jacques. "The Bible as Literature?" *HS* 45 (2004): 9–26.

Berman, Joshua. "Identity Politics and the Burial of Jacob (Genesis 50:1–14)." *CBQ* 68 (2006): 11–31.

Berry, R. J. "This Cursed Earth: Is 'the Fall' Credible?" *Science & Christian Belief* 11 (1999): 29–49.

Best, Ernest. "The Reading and Writing of Commentaries." *ExpTim* 107 (1996): 358–62.

Bird, Phyllis A. "'Male and Female He Created Them': Gen 1:27b in the Context of the Priestly Account of Creation." *HTR* 74 (1981): 129–59.

Black, C. Clifton. "Rhetorical Criticism." Pages 256–277 in *Hearing the New Testament: Strategies for Interpretation.* Edited by Joel B. Green. Grand Rapids: Eerdmans, 1995.

Blocher, Henri. *In the Beginning: The Opening Chapters of Genesis.* Translated by David G. Preston. Downers Grove: InterVarsity, 1984.

Booth, Wayne C. *The Company We Keep: An Ethics of Fiction.* Berkeley, Calif.: University of California Press, 1988.

Breasted, James Henry. *Ancient Records of Egypt.* 5 volumes. Chicago: University of Chicago Press, 1906–1907.

Brodie, Thomas L. *Genesis as Dialogue: A Literary, Historical, and Theological Commentary.* New York: Oxford University Press, 2001.

Brueggemann, Walter. *Genesis.* Atlanta: John Knox, 1982.

———. "Of the Same Flesh and Bone (Gn 2,23a)." *CBQ* 32 (1970): 532–42.

———. "Remember, You are Dust." *Journal for Preachers* 14 (1991): 3–10.

C. H. Gordon, "Sabbatical Cycle or Seasonal Pattern? Reflections on a New Book." *Or* 22 (1953): 79–81.

Callender, Dexter E. *Adam in Myth and History: Ancient Israelite Perspectives on the Primal Human.* Harvard Semitic Studies. Winona Lake: Eisenbrauns, 2000.

Campbell, George Van Pelt. "Refusing God's Blessing: An Exposition of Genesis 11:27–32." *BSac* 165 (2008): 268–82.

———. "Rushing Ahead of God: An Exposition of Genesis 16:1–16." *BSac* 163 (2006): 276–91.

Caquot, André. "Ben Porat (Genìse, 49, 22)." *Sem* 39 (1980): 43–56.

Carmichael, Calum M. "Some Sayings in Genesis 49." *JBL* 88 (1969): 435–44.

Cassuto, Umberto. *A Commentary on the Book of Genesis: Part I From Adam to Noah: Genesis I–VI 8.* Translated by Israel Abrahams. Jerusalem: Magnes, 1961.

———. "The Story of Tamar and Judah." Pages 29–40 in *Biblical and Oriental Studies, Vol. 1: The Bible.* By Umberto Cassuto. Translated by Israel Abrahams. Jerusalem: Magnes, 1973.

Charles, J. Daryl, ed. *Reading Genesis 1–2: An Evangelical Conversation.* Peabody, Mass.: Hendrickson, 2013.

Chisholm, Robert B. "Anatomy of an Anthropomorphism: Does God Discover Facts?" *BSac* 164 (2007): 3–20.

Clark, Ron. "The Silence in Dinah's Cry." *ResQ* 49 (2007): 143–58.

Clark, W. Malcolm. "A Legal Background to the Yahwist's Use of 'Good and Evil' in Genesis 2–3." *JBL* 88 (1969): 266–78.

Clendenen, E. Ray. "Religious Background of the Old Testament." Pages 277–90 in *Foundations for Biblical Interpretation.* Edited by David S. Dockery, Kenneth S. Matthews, and Robert B. Sloan. Nashville: Broadman and Holman, 1994.

Clifford, Richard J. *Creation Accounts in the Ancient Near East and in the Bible.* CBQMS 26. Washington, D.C.: Catholic Bible Association of America, 1994.

———. "Genesis 38: Its Contribution to the Jacob Story." *CBQ* 66 (2004): 519–32.

———. "The Hebrew Scriptures and the Theology of Creation." *TS* 46 (1985): 507–23.

Clines, David J. A. "The Image of God in Man." *TynBul* 19 (1968): 53–103.

———. *The Theme of the Pentateuch.* Sheffield: Sheffield University Press, 1978.

Coats, George W. "The Curse in God's Blessing: Gen 12,1–4a in the Structure and Theology of the Yahwist." Pages 31–41 in *Die Botschaft und die Boten: Festschrif für Hans Walter Wolff zum 70. Geburtsag.* Edited by Jörg Jeremias and Lothar Perlitt. Neukirchen-Vluyn, Germany: Neukirchener Verlag, 1981.

———. *Genesis: With an Introduction to Narrative Literature.* FOTL 1. Grand Rapids: Eerdmans, 1983.

———. "Lot a Foil in the Abraham Saga." Pages 113–32 in *Understanding the Word: Essays in Honor of Bernhard W. Anderson.* JSOTSup 37. Edited by James T. Butler, Edgar W. Conrad, and Ben C. Ollenburger. Sheffield: The JSOT Press, 1985.

Cohen, Mark E. *The Cultic Calendars of the Ancient Near East.* Bethesda, Md.: CDL Press, 1993.

Cole, Timothy J. "Enoch, a Man who Walked with God." *BSac* 148 (1991): 288–97.

Colet, John. "Second Letter of Colet to Radulphus." Pages 7–13, 269–73 in *Letters to Radulphus on the Mosaic Account of the Creation Together with Other Treatises.* By John Colet. Translated by J. H. Lupton. London: George Bell and Sons, 1876.

Collins, C. John. "Reading Genesis 1–2 with the Grain: Analogical Days." Pages 72–92 in *Reading Genesis 1–2: An Evangelical Conversation.* Edited by J. Daryl Charles. Peabody, Mass.: Hendrickson, 2013.

———. "What Happened to Adam and Eve? A Literary-Theological Approach to Genesis 3." *Presbyterion* 27 (2001): 12–44.

Collins, Jack. "A Syntactical Note (Genesis 3:15): Is the Woman's Seed Singular or Plural?" *TynBul* 48 (1997): 139–48.

Cotter, David W. *Genesis.* Berit Olam: Studies in Hebrew Narrative and Poetry. Collegeville, Minn.: Liturgical Press, 2003.

Cox, Benjamin D., and Susan Ackerman. "Rachel's Tomb." *JBL* 128 (2009): 135–48.

Craig, Kenneth M. "Misspeaking in Eden, or, Fielding Questions in the Garden (Genesis 2:16–3:13)." *PRSt* 27 (2000): 235–47.

Curtis, Edward M. "Structure, Style and Context as a Key to Interpreting Jacob's Encounter at Peniel." *JETS* 30 (1987): 129–37.

Dahood, Mitchell. "Eblaite *i-du* and Hebrew *ēd*, 'Rain Cloud.'" *CBQ* 43 (1981): 534–38.

Dalley, Stephanie, ed. *Myths From Mesopotamia: Creation, the Flood, Gilgamesh, and Others.* Revised edition. Oxford: Oxford University Press, 2000.

Davies, P. R., and B. D. Chilton. "The Aqedah: A Revised Tradition History." *CBQ* 40 (1978): 514–46.

Derouchie, Jason S. "Circumcision in the Hebrew Bible and Targums: Theology, Rhetoric, and the Handling of Metaphor." *BBR* 14 (2004): 175–203.

Dodd, C. H. *The Interpretation of the Fourth Gospel.* Cambridge: Cambridge University Press, 1955.

Dorsey, David A. *The Literary Structure of the Old Testament: A Commentary on Genesis–Malachi.* Grand Rapids: Baker, 1999.

Drey, Philip R. "The Role of Hagar in Genesis 16," *AUSS* 40 (2002): 179–95.

Driver, S. R. *The Book of Genesis.* Sixth edition. London: Methuen, 1907.

Dumbrell, William J. "Genesis 2:1–17: A Foreshadowing of the New Creation." Pages 53–65 in *Biblical Theology: Retrospect and Prospect.* Edited by Scott J. Hafemann. Downers Grove: InterVarsity, 2002.

Earl, Douglas S. "Toward a Christian Hermeneutic of Old Testament Narrative: Why Genesis 34 Fails to Find Christian Significance." *CBQ* 73 (2011): 30–49.

Edwards, Jonathan. "Miscellany: No. 534." Page 78 in *The Works of Jonathan Edwards, Vol. 18: The "Miscellanies" 501–832.* By Jonathan Edwards. Edited by Ava Chamberlain. New Haven: Yale University Press, 2000.

———. "Miscellany: No. 1010." Page 342 in *The Works of Jonathan Edwards, Vol. 20: The "Miscellanies" 833–1152.* By Jonathan Edwards. Edited by Amy Plantinga Pauw. New Haven: Yale University Press, 2002.

Eichrodt, Walter. "Covenant and Law: Thoughts on Recent Discussion." *Int* 20 (1966): 302–21.

Elgavish, David. "The Encounter of Abram and Melchizedek King of Salem: A Covenant Establishing Ceremony." Pages 495–508 in *Studies in the Book of Genesis: Literature, Redaction and History.* BETL 155. Edited by A. Wénin. Leiden: Leuven University Press, 2001.

Ellul, Jacques. *The Meaning of the City.* Grand Rapids: Eerdmans, 1970.

Emmrich, Martin. "The Temptation Narrative of Genesis 3:1–67: A Prelude to the Pentateuch and the History of Israel." *EQ* 73 (2001): 3–20.

Eslinger, Lyle. "A Contextual Identification of the *bene haʾelohim* and *benoth haʾadam* in Genesis 6:1–4." *JSOT* 13 (1979): 65–73.

———. "Prehistory in the Call to Abraham." *BibInt* 14 (2006): 189–208.

Exum, J. Cheryl. "Who's Afraid of 'The Endangered Ancestress'?" Pages 91–113 in *The New Literary Criticism and the Hebrew Bible.* Edited by J. Cheryl Exum and David J. A. Clines. JSOTSup 143. Sheffield: Sheffield Academic Press, 1993.

Falk, Ze'ev W. "Gestures Expressing Affirmation." *JSS* 4 (1959): 268–69.

Finkelstein, J. J. "An Old Babylonian Herding Contract and Genesis 31:38f." *JAOS* 88 (1968): 30–36.

Fishbane, Michael. "Composition and Structure in the Jacob Cycle (Gen. 25:19–35:22)." *JJS* 26 (1975): 15–38.

———. *Text and Texture: Close Readings of Selected Biblical Texts.* New York: Schocken, 1979.

Fleishman, Joseph. "On the Significance of a Name Change and Circumcision in Genesis 17." *JANES* 28 (2011): 19–32.

Fockner, Steve. "Reopening the Discussion: Another Contextual Look at the Sons of God." *JSOT* 32 (2008): 435–56.

Foh, Susan T. "What is the Woman's Desire?" *WTJ* 37 (1975): 376–83.

Fokkelman, J. P. *Narrative Art in Genesis: Specimens of Stylistic and Structural Analysis.* Amsterdam: Van Gorcum, 1975.

Fowler, Robert M. *Let the Reader Understand: Reader-Response Criticism and the Gospel of Mark.* Minneapolis: Fortress, 1991.

Fox, Michael V. "The Sign of the Covenant: Circumcision in the Light of the Priestly *ʾōt* Etiologies." *RB* 81 (1974): 551–96.

Freeman, Travis R. "A New Look at the Genesis 5 and 11 Fluidity Problem." *AUSS* 42 (2004): 259–86.

Fretheim, Terence E. "Is Genesis 3 a Fall Story?" *Word & World* 14 (1994): 144–53.

———. "Which Blessing Does Isaac Give Jacob?" Pages 279–91 in *Jews, Christians, and the Theology of the Hebrew Scriptures.* Symposium Series 8. Edited by Alice Ogden Bellis and Joel S. Kaminsky. Atlanta: Society of Biblical Literature, 2000.

Frisch, Amos. "'Your Brother Came with Guile': Responses to an Explicit Moral Evaluation in Biblical Narrative." *Prooftexts* 23 (2003): 271–96.

Frye, Northrop. *The Great Code: The Bible and Literature*. New York: Harcourt Brace & Company, 1982.

Fuchs, Esther. "'For I Have the Way of Women': Deception, Gender, and Ideology in Biblical Narrative." *Semeia* 42 (1988): 68–83.

Futato, Mark D. "Because it had Rained: A Study of Gen 2:5–7 with Implications for Gen 2:4–25 and Gen 1:1–2:3." *WTJ* 60 (1998): 1–21.

Galilei, Galileo. "Letter to Castelli." Pages 195–201 in *Galileo, Bellarmine, and the Bible*. By Richard J. Blackwell. Notre Dame, Ind.: University of Notre Dame Press, 1991.

Garr, W. Randall. "'Image' and 'Likeness' in the Inscription from Tell Fakhariyeh." *IEJ* 50 (2000): 227–34.

Garrett, Duane A. *Rethinking Genesis: The Sources and Authorship of the First Book of the Pentateuch*. Grand Rapids: Baker, 1991.

Geller, Stephen A. "The Struggle at the Jabbok: The Uses of Enigma in a Biblical Narrative." *JANES* 14 (1982): 37–60.

Gellman, Marc. "What Are You Looking For?" *First Things* 71 (1997): 20–23.

George, Andrew. "The Tower of Babel: Archaeology, History and Cuneiform Texts." *AfO* 51 (2005/2006): 75–95.

Gevirtz, Stanley. "The Life Spans of Joseph and Enoch and the Parallelism *šibʿātayim—šibʿîm wěšibāh*." *JBL* 96 (1977): 570–71.

Ginzberg, Louis, and Boaz Cohen. *Legends of the Jews: Bible Times and Characters From Joseph to the Exodus*. Translated by Henrietta Szold. Philadelphia: Jewish Publication Society, 1910.

Gnuse, Robert. "The Tale of Babel: Parable of Divine Judgment or Human Cultural Diversification?" *BZ* 54 (2010): 229–44.

Gordis, Daniel H. "Lies, Wives and Sisters: The Wife-Sister Motif Revisited." *Judaism* 34 (1985): 344–59.

Gordon, Cynthia. "Hagar: A Throw-Away Character among the Matriarchs?" Pages 271–77 in *Society of Biblical Literature 1985 Seminar Papers*. SBL Seminar Papers 24. Edited by Kent Harold Richards. Atlanta: Scholars Press, 1985.

Gordon, Cyrus H. *The World of the Old Testament*. Garden City, N.Y.: Doubleday, 1958.

Görg, M. "בָּזָה." Page 63 in *Theological Dictionary of the Old Testament, Volume 2*. Edited by G. J. Botterweck and H. Ringgren. Translated by J. T. Willis, G. W. Bromiley, and D. E. Green. 15 volumes. Grand Rapids, 1974–2006.

Green, Barbara. *"What Profit for Us?" Remembering the Story of Joseph*. Lanham, Md.: University Press of America, 1996.

Greidanus, Sidney. *Preaching Christ from Genesis: Foundations for Expository Sermons*. Grand Rapids: Eerdmans, 2007.

———. *Preaching Christ from the Old Testament: A Contemporary Hermeneutical Method*. Grand Rapids: Eerdmans, 1999.

Gunkel, Hermann. *Genesis*. Third edition. Translated by Mark E. Biddle. Macon, Ga.: Mercer University Press, 1997.

Hamilton, Victor P. *The Book of Genesis Chapters 1–17*. NICOT. Grand Rapids: Eerdmans, 1990.

———. *The Book of Genesis Chapters 18–50*. NICOT. Grand Rapids: Eerdmans, 1995.

Harris, J. S. Randolph. "Genesis 44:18–34." *Int* 52 (1998): 178–81.

Harrison, R. K. "The Mandrake and the Ancient World." *EvQ* 28 (1956): 87–92.

Hart, Ian. "Genesis 1:1–2:3 as a Prologue to the Book of Genesis." *TynBul* 46 (1995): 315–36.

Hartman, T. C. "Some Thoughts on the Sumerian King List and Genesis 5 and 11b." *JBL* 91 (1972): 25–32.

Hasel, Gerhard F. "The Genealogies of Genesis 5 and 11 and Their Alleged Babylonian Background." *AUSS* 16 (1978): 361–74.

———. "The Meaning of the Animal Rite in Genesis 15." *JSOT* 19 (1981): 61–78.

———. "The Polemic Nature of the Genesis Cosmology." *EvQ* 46 (1974): 81–102.

———. "The Significance of the Cosmology in Genesis 1 in Relation to Ancient Near Eastern Parallels." *AUSS* 10 (1972): 1–20.

Hauser, Alan J. "Genesis 2–3: The Theme of Intimacy and Alienation." Pages 20–36 in *Art and Meaning: Rhetoric in Biblical Literature*. JSOTSup 19. Edited by David J. A. Clines, David M. Gunn, and Alan J. Hauser. Sheffield: Sheffield Academic Press, 1982.

———. "Linguistic and Thematic Links between Genesis 4:1–16 and Genesis 2–3." *JETS* 23 (1980): 297–305.

Heidel, Alexander. *The Babylonian Genesis*. Revised edition. Chicago: University of Chicago Press, 1963.

Helyer, Larry R. "The Separation of Abram and Lot: Its Significance in the Patriarchal Narratives." *JSOT* 26 (1983): 77–88.

Henry, Matthew. *An Exposition of the Old and New Testament: Volume 1*. Philadelphia: Haswell, Barrington & Haswell, 1838.

Hepner, Gershon. "The Sacrifices in the Covenant between the Pieces Allude to the Laws of Leviticus and the Covenant of the Flesh." *BN* 112 (2002): 38–73.

Hertz, J. H., ed. *The Pentateuch and Haftorahs: Hebrew Text, English Translation, and Commentary*. Second edition. London: Soncino, 1960.

Hess, Richard S. "The Book of Joshua as a Land Grant." *Bib* 83 (2002): 493–506.

———. "Genesis 1–2 in its Literary Context." *TynBul* 41 (1990): 143–53.

———. "The Slaughter of the Animals in Genesis 15: Genesis 15:8–21 and its Ancient Near Eastern Context." Pages 55–65 in *He Swore an Oath: Biblical Themes from Genesis 12–50*. Edited by Richard S. Hess, Gordon J. Wenham, and Philip E. Satterthwaite. Grand Rapids: Baker, 1994.

Hoffmeier, J. K. "Some Thoughts on Genesis 1 and 2 and Egyptian Cosmology." *JANES* 15 (1983): 39–49.

Hoffner, H. A. "Paškuwatti's Ritual against Male Impotence." *AuOr* 5 (1987): 271–87.

Hom, Mary Katherine Y. H. "'. . . A Mighty Hunter before YHWH': Genesis 10:9 and the Moral-Theological Evaluation of Nimrod." *VT* 60 (2010): 63–68.

Hong, Kyu Sik. "An Exegetical Reading of the Abraham Narrative in Genesis: Semantic, Textuality and Theology." Ph.D. dissertation. University of Pretoria, 2007.

Hummel, Charles E. "Interpreting Genesis One." *JASA* 38 (1986): 175–85.

Humphreys, W. Lee. *Joseph and His Family: A Literary Study*. Columbia, S.C.: University of South Carolina Press, 1988.

Hurowitz, Victor. "The Genesis of Genesis: Is the Creation Story Babylonian?" *BR* 21 (2005): 36–48, 52–54.

———. *I Have Built You an Exalted House: Temple Building in the Bible in Light of Mesopotamian and Northwest Semitic Writings*. JSOTSup 115. Sheffield: Sheffield Academic Press, 1992.

Hutter, Manfred. "Aspects of Luwian Religion." Pages 211–78 in *The Luwians*. HO 68. Edited by H. Craig Melchert. Leiden: Brill, 2003.

Hyman, Ronald T. "The Transition to the Second Trip to Egypt: Narrative Devices in Genesis 43:1–14." *JBQ* 38 (2010): 73–84.

Iverson, Kelly R. *Gentiles in the Gospel of Mark: 'Even the Dogs Under the Table Eat the Children's Crumbs.'* LNTS 339. London: T. & T. Clark, 2007.

Jackson, Melissa. "Lot's Daughters and Tamar as Tricksters and the Patriarchal Narratives as Feminist Theology." *JSOT* 98 (2002): 29–46.

Jacob, Benno. *The First Book of the Bible: Genesis*. Edited and translated by Ernest I. Jacob and Walter Jacob. New York: Ktav, 1974.

Jacobsen, Thorkild. "The Eridu Genesis." *JBL* 100 (1981): 529–39.

Jastrow, Marcus. *Dictionary of the Targumim, the Talmud Babli and Yerushalmi, and the Midrashic Literature*. Peabody, Mass.: Hendrickson, 2006.

Jeansonne, Sharon P. "Genesis 25:23—The Use of Poetry in the Rebekah Narrative." Pages 145–52 in *The Psalms and Other Studies on the Old Testament*. Edited by Jacob Knight and Lawrence A. Sinclair. Nashotah, Wisc.: Forward Movement, 1990.

———. *The Women of Genesis: From Sarah to Potiphar's Wife*. Minneapolis: Fortress, 1990.

Johnston, Gordon. "A Critical Evaluation of Moshe Weinfeld's Approach to the Davidic Covenant in the Light of Ancient Near Eastern Royal Grants: What Did He Get Right and What Did He Get Wrong?" Paper presented at the annual meeting of the Evangelical Theological Society, San Francisco, Calif., 18 October 2011.

———. "Genesis 1 and Ancient Egyptian Creation Myths." *BSac* 165 (2008): 178–94.

———. "The Smoking Brazier and Flaming Torch in Genesis 15:17 in the Light of Ancient Near Eastern Literature and Ritual." Paper presented at the national meeting of the Society of Biblical Literature, Boston, Mass., 24 November 2008.

Jost, F. L. "Abimelech." Pages 6–7 in *Dictionary of the Old Testament: Pentateuch*. Edited by T. Desmond Alexander and David W. Baker. Downers Grove: Intervarsity, 2003.

Kahl, Brigitte. "And She Called His Name Seth . . . (Gen 4:25): The Birth of Critical Knowledge and the Unread End of Eve's Story." *USQR* 53 (1999): 19–28.

Kalimi, Isaac. "'Go, I Beg You, Take Your Beloved Son and Slay Him!' The Binding of Isaac in Rabbinic Literature and Thought." *Review of Rabbinic Judaism* 13 (2010): 1–29.

Kass, Leon R. *The Beginning of Wisdom: Reading Genesis.* New York: Free Press, 2003.

———. "The Humanist Dream: Babel Then and Now." *Greg* 81 (2000): 633–57.

———. "Regarding Daughters and Sisters: The Rape of Dinah." *Commentary* 93 (1992): 29–38.

Kearney, Peter J. "Creation and Liturgy: The P Redaction of Ex 25–40." *ZAW* 89 (1977): 375–87.

Keiser, Thomas A. "Genesis 1–11: Its Literary Coherence and Theological Message." Ph.D. dissertation. Dallas Theological Seminary, 2007.

Kelsey, David H. "The Bible and Christian Theology." *JAAR* 48 (1980): 385–402.

Kessler, Edward. *Bound by the Bible: Jews, Christians and the Sacrifice of Isaac.* Cambridge: Cambridge University Press, 2004.

Kidner, Derek. *Genesis: An Introduction and Commentary.* TOTC. Downers Grove: InterVarsity, 1967.

Kierkegaard, Søren. *Fear and Trembling.* Translated by H. Honig and E. Honig. Princeton: Princeton University Press, 1983.

Kikawada, Isaac M. "The Double Creation of Mankind in *Enki and Ninmah, Atrahasis* I 1–351, and *Genesis 1–2.*" *Iraq* 45 (1982): 43–45.

Kikawada, Isaac M., and Arthur Quinn. *Before Abraham Was: The Unity of Genesis 1–11.* Nashville: Abingdon, 1985.

Kitchen, K. A. *Ancient Orient and Old Testament.* Downers Grove: InterVarsity, 1966.

———. "On." Pages 847–48 in *New Bible Dictionary.* Third edition. Edited by I. Howard Marshall, A. R. Millard, J. I. Packer, and D. J. Wiseman. Downers Grove: InterVarsity, 1996.

Kline, Meredith G. "'Because It Had Not Rained.'" *WTJ* 20 (1958): 146–57.

———. "Divine Kingship and Genesis 6:1–4." *WTJ* 24 (1962): 187–204.

Knoppers, Gary. "Ancient Near Eastern Royal Grants and the Davidic Covenant: A Parallel?" *JAOS* 116 (1996): 670–97.

Koehler, Ludwig and Walter Baumgartner. "דִּי." Page 387 in vol. 2 of *The Hebrew and Aramaic Lexicon of the Old Testament.* By Ludwig Koehler, Walter Baumgartner, and J. J. Stamm. Translated and edited by M. E. J. Richardson. 4 volumes. Leiden: Brill, 1994–1999.

Kramer, Samuel Noah. "The 'Babel of Tongues': A Sumerian Version." *JAOS* 88 (1968): 108–11.

Krašovec, Jože. "Punishment and Mercy in the Primeval History (Gen 1–11)." *ETL* 70 (1994): 5–33.

Kraus, Christina Shuttleworth. "Introduction: Reading Commentaries/Commentaries as Reading." Pages 1–27 in *The Classical Commentary: History, Practices, Theory.* Mnemosyne Sup 232. Edited by Roy K. Gibson and Christina Shuttleworth Kraus. Leiden: Brill, 2002.

Kruschwitz, Jonathan. "The Type-Scene Connection between Genesis 38 and the Joseph Story." *JSOT* 36 (2012): 383–410.

Kugel, James L. *Traditions of the Bible: A Guide to the Bible as it Was at the Start of the Common Era.* Cambridge: Harvard University Press, 1998.

Kuruvilla, Abraham. "The *Aqedah*: What the Author is *Doing* with What He is *Saying.*" *JETS* 55 (2012): 489–508.

———. *Mark: A Theological Commentary for Preachers.* Eugene, Oreg.: Cascade, 2012.

———. "Pericopal Theology: An Intermediary between Text and Application." *TrinJ* 31NS (2010): 265–83.

———. *Privilege the Text! A Theological Hermeneutic for Preaching.* Chicago: Moody, 2013.

———. *Text to Praxis: Hermeneutics and Homiletics in Dialogue.* LNTS 393. London: T. & T. Clark, 2009.

Kuyper, Lester J. "'To know Good and Evil.'" *Int* 1 (1947): 490–92.

Laansma, Jon. *'I Will Give You Rest': The Rest Motif in the New Testament with Special Reference to Mt 11 and Heb 3–4.* WUNT Reihe 2.98. Tübingen: Mohr Siebeck, 1997.

Labuschagne, C. J. "The Lifespan of the Patriarchs." Pages 121–27 in *New Avenues in the Study of the Old Testament.* OtSt 25. Edited by A. S van der Woude. Leiden: Brill, 1989.

LaCocque, André. "Whatever Happened in the Valley of Shinar? A Response to Theodore Hiebert." *JBL* 128 (2009): 29–41.

Lambe, Anthony J. "Genesis 38: Structure and Literary Design." Pages 102–20 in *The World of Genesis: Persons, Places, Perspectives*. JSOTSup 257. Edited by Philip R. Davies and David J. A. Clines. Sheffield: Sheffield Academic Press, 1998.

———. "Judah's Development: The Pattern of Departure–Transition–Return." *JSOT* 83 (1999): 53–68.

Lambert, W. G., and A. R. Millard. *Atrahasis: the Babylonian Story of the Flood*. Oxford: Clarendon, 1969.

Lang, Bernhard. "Non-Semitic Deluge Stories and the Book of Genesis: A Bibliographical and Critical Survey." *Anthropos* 80 (1985): 605–16.

Lee, Chee-Chiew. "נוים in Genesis 35:11 and the Abrahamic Promise of Blessings for the Nations." *JETS* 52 (2009): 467–82.

———. "Once Again: The Niphal and the Hithpael of ברך in the Abrahamic Blessing for the Nations." *JSOT* 36 (2012): 279–96.

Lennox, John C. *Seven Days that Divide the World*. Grand Rapids: Zondervan, 2011.

Letellier, Robert Ignatius. *Day in Mamre, Night in Sodom: Abraham and Lot in Genesis 18 and 19*. Leiden: Brill, 1995.

Leupold, H. C. *Exposition of Genesis*. 2 volumes. Grand Rapids: Baker, 1942.

Levenson, Jon D. *The Death and Resurrection of the Beloved Son: The Transformation of Child Sacrifice in Judaism and Christianity*. New Haven: Yale University Press, 1993.

———. "The Paronomasia of Solomon's Seventh Petition." *HAR* 6 (1982): 135–38.

———. *Sinai and Zion: An Entry into the Jewish Bible*. Minneapolis, Minn.: Winston, 1985.

———. "The Temple and the World." *JR* 64 (1984): 275–98.

Leviant, Curt. "Parallel Lives: The Trials and Traumas of Isaac and Ishmael." *BR* 15.2 (1990): 20–25, 47.

Lewis, C. S. *The Voyage of the Dawn Treader*. New York: HarperCollins, 1952.

Lewis, Jack P. "The Woman's Seed (Gen 3:15)." *JETS* 34 (1991): 299–319.

Loader, Jimmy A. "God Have or Has? Unclarity and Insight." *JNSL* 24 (1998): 129–40.

Lohr, Joel N. "'So YHWH Established a Sign for Cain': Rethinking Genesis 4,15." *ZAW* 121 (2009): 101–3.

Longacre, Robert E. *Joseph: A Story of Divine Providence: A Text Theoretical and Textlinguistic Analysis of Genesis 37 and 39–48*. Winona Lake: Eisenbrauns, 2003.

———. "*Weqatal* Forms in Biblical Hebrew Prose." Pages 50–98 in *Biblical Hebrew and Discourse Linguistics*. Edited by Robert D. Bergen. Winona Lake: Eisenbrauns, 1994.

Lowenstamm, Samuel E. "Anat's Victory Over the Tunnanu." *JSS* 20 (1975): 22–27.

Lundquist, John M. "What is a Temple? A Preliminary Typology." Pages 205–19 in *The Quest for the Kingdom of God: Studies in Honor of George E. Mendenhall*. Edited by H. B. Huffmon, F. A. Spina, and A. R. W. Green. Winona Lake: Eisenbrauns, 1983.

Lunn, Nicholas P. "The Last Words of Jacob and Joseph: A Rhetorico-Structural Analysis of Genesis 49:29–33 and 50:24–26." *TynBul* 59 (2008): 161–79.

Luther, Martin. *Lectures on Genesis Chapter 6–14, Luther's Works Vol. 2*. Translated by George V. Schick. St. Louis: Concordia, 1960.

Lyke, Larry L. "Where Does 'the Boy' Belong? Compositional Strategy in Genesis 21:14." *CBQ* 56 (1994): 637–48.

MacDonald, Nathan. "Listening to Abraham—Listening to Yhwh: Divine Justice and Mercy in Genesis 18:16–33." *CBQ* 66 (2004): 25–43.

Macrae, A. A. "עלם." Pages 672–73 in *Theological Wordbook of the Old Testament*. Edited by R. L. Harris, G. L. Archer, Jr. and B. K. Waltke;. Chicago: Moody Press, 1999.

Malamat, Abraham. "King Lists of the Old Babylonian Period and Biblical Genealogies." *JAOS* 88 (1968): 163–73.

Malul, Meir. "More on *Paḥad Yiṣḥāq* (Genesis XXXI 42, 53) and the Oath by the Thigh." *VT* 35 (1985): 192–200.

———. "Touching the Sexual Organs as an Oath Ceremony in an Akkadian Letter." *VT* 37 (1987): 491–92.

Mann, Thomas. *The Magic Mountain*. New York: Alfred A. Knopf, 1995.

Mann, Thomas. W. *The Book of the Torah: The Narrative Integrity of the Pentateuch*. Atlanta: John Knox, 1988.

Martin, R. A. "The Earliest Messianic Interpretation of Genesis 3 15." *JBL* 84 (1965): 425–27.

Martin, Troy W. "The Covenant of Circumcision (Genesis 17:9–14) and the Situational Antitheses in Galatians 3:28." *JBL* 122 (2003): 111–25.

Mason, Steven D. "Another Flood? Genesis 9 and Isaiah's Broken Eternal Covenant." *JSOT* 32 (2007): 177–98.

Mathews, Kenneth A. *Genesis 1–11:26*. NAC 1A. Nashville: Broadman and Holman, 1996.

———. *Genesis 11:27–50:26*. NAC 1B. Nashville: Broadman and Holman, 2005.

McBride, S. Dean, Jr. "Divine Protocol: Genesis 1:1–2:3 as Prologue to the Pentateuch." Pages 3–41 in *God Who Creates: Essays in Honor of W. Sibley Towner*. Edited by William P. Brown and S. Dean McBride Jr. Grand Rapids: Eerdmans, 2000.

McConville, J. Gordon. "Abraham and Melchizedek: Horizons in Genesis 14." Pages 93–118 in *He Swore an Oath: Biblical Themes from Genesis 12–50*. Second edition. Edited by Richard S. Hess, Gordon J. Wenham, and Philip E. Satterthwaite. Grand Rapids: Baker, 1994.

McEntire, Mark. "Being Seen and Not Heard: The Interpretation of Genesis 4.8." Pages 4–13 in *Of Scribes and Sages: Early Jewish Interpretation and Transmission of Scripture, Volume 1: Ancient Versions and Traditions*. Studies in Scripture in Early Judaism and Christianity 9. Library of Second Temple Studies 50. Edited by Craig A. Evans. London: T. & T. Clark, 2004.

McEvenue, Sean. "Reading Genesis with Faith and Reason." *Word & World* 14 (1994): 136–43.

McKenzie, Brian Alexander. "Jacob's Blessing of Pharaoh: An Interpretation of Gen 46:31–47:26." *WTJ* 45 (1983): 386–99.

McKenzie, Steven. "The Typology of the Davidic Covnenant." Pages 152–78 in *The Land that I Will Show You: Essays on the History and Archaeology of the Ancient Near East in Honor of J. Maxwell Miller*. Edited by J. Andrew Dearman and M. Patrick Graham. London: Continuum, 2001.

Meyers, Carol L. *The Tabernacle Menorah: A Synthetic Study of a Symbol from the Biblical Cult*. ASOR Dissertation Series 2. Missoula, Mont.: Scholars Press, 1976.

Michalowski, Piotr. "The Torch and the Censer." Pages 152–62 in *The Tablet and the Scroll: Near Eastern Studies in Honor of William W. Hallo*. Edited by Mark E. Cohen, Daniel C. Snell, and David B. Weisberg. Bethesda, Md.: CDL Press, 1993.

Middleton, Richard. *The Liberating Image: The* Imago Dei *in Genesis 1*. Grand Rapids: Brazos, 2005.

Milgrom, Jacob. "The Alleged 'Hidden Light.'" Pages 41–44 in *The Idea of Biblical Interpretation: Essays in Honor of James L. Kugel*. Supplements to the Journal for the Study of Judaism 83. Edited by Hindy Najman and Judith H. Newman. Leiden: Brill, 2004.

Millard A. R., and P. Bordreuil. "A Statue from Syria with Assyrian and Aramaic Inscriptions." *BA* (1982): 135–41.

Moberly, R. W. L. "Abraham's Righteousness (Genesis XV 6)." Pages 103–30 in *Studies in the Pentateuch*. Supplements to Vetus Testamentum 41. Edited by J. A. Emerton. Leiden: Brill, 1990.

———. *The Bible, Theology, and Faith: A Study of Abraham and Jesus*. Cambridge: Cambridge University Press, 2000.

———. "The Earliest Commentary on the Aqedah." *VT* 37 (1988): 302–23.

———. "The Mark of Cain—Revealed at Last?" *HTR* 100 (2007): 11–28.

———. "What is Theological Interpretation of Scripture?" *JTI* 3 (2009): 161–78.

Monroe, Christopher M. "Money and Trade." Pages 155–68 in *A Companion to the Ancient Near East*. Edited by Daniel C. Snell. Malden, Mass.: Blackwell, 2005.

Morales, L. Michael. *The Tabernacle Pre-figured: Cosmic Mountain Ideology in Genesis and Exodus*. Biblical Tools and Studies 15. Leuven: Peeters, 2012.

Moran, William L. "Atrahasis: The Babylonian Story of the Flood." *Bib* 52 (1971): 51–61.

Mulzac, Kenneth. "Genesis 9:1–7: Its Theological Connections with the Creation Motif." *JATS* 12 (2001): 65–77.

Muraoka, T. "On the So-called *dativus ethicus*." *JTS* 29 (1978): 495–98.

Murgia, Charles E. "Review of Francis R. D. Goodyear, *The Annals of Tacitus, Books 1–6, Volume 2: Annals 1.55–81 and Annals 2*." *Classical Philology* 79 (1984): 314–26.

Murray, John. "Covenant." Pages 265–66 in *New Bible Dictionary*. Edited by J. D. Douglas. Grand Rapids: Eerdmans, 1962.

———. *Principles of Conduct: Aspects of Biblical Ethics*. Grand Rapids: Eerdmans, 1957.

Nachmanides. *Commentary on the Torah: Genesis.* Translated by Charles B. Chavel. New York: Shilo, 1971.

Navon, Mois A. "*Beged* or *Simlah*—Is There a Difference?" *JBQ* 32 (2004): 265–69.

Nelson, Harold H. "The Significance of the Temple in the Ancient Near East: I. The Egyptian Temple." *BA* 7 (1944): 44–53.

Nicol, George G. "The Chronology of Genesis: Genesis XXVI 1–33 as 'Flashback.'" *VT* 46 (1996): 330–38.

———. "The Narrative Structure and Interpretation of Genesis XXVI 1–33." *VT* 46 (1996): 339–60.

Niditch, Susan. "The Wronged Woman Righted: An Analysis of Genesis 38." *HTR* 72 (1979): 143–49.

Noble, Paul. "A 'Balanced' Reading of the Rape of Dinah: Some Exegetical and Methodological Observations." *BibInt* 4 (1996): 173–204.

———. "Esau, Tamar, and Joseph: Criteria for Identifying Inner-Biblical Allusions." *VT* 52 (2002): 219–52.

———. "Synchronic and Diachronic Approaches to Biblical Interpretation." *Journal of Literature & Theology* 7 (1993): 136–48.

Noegel, Scott B. "Drinking Feasts and Deceptive Feats: Jacob and Laban's Double Talk." Pages 163–79 in *Puns and Pundits: Word Play in the Hebrew Bible and Ancient Near Eastern Literature.* Edited by Scott B. Noegel. Bethesda, Md.: CDL Press, 2000.

———. "Sex, Sticks, and the Trickster in Gen. 30:31–43." *JANES* 25 (1997): 7–17.

Noort, Ed. "The Stories of the Great Flood: Notes on Gen 6:5–9:17 in its Context of the Ancient Near East." Pages 1–38 in *Interpretation of the Flood.* Themes in Biblical Narrative: Jewish and Christian Traditions 1. Edited by Florentino García Martínez and Gerard P. Luttikhuizen. Leiden: Brill, 1999.

Nwaoru, Emmanuel O. "Change of Garment: A Symbolic 'Rite of Passage' in Joseph Narrative (Gen 37; 39; 41)." *BN* 143 (2009): 5–22.

Oblath, Michael. "'To Sleep, Perchance to Dream . . .': What Jacob Saw at Bethel (Genesis 28.10–22)." *JSOT* 95 (2001): 117–26.

Olley, John. "Mixed Blessings for Animals: The Contrasts of Genesis 9." Pages 130–39 in *The Earth Story in Genesis.* The Earth Bible 2. Edited by Norman C. Habel and Shirley Wurst. Sheffield: Sheffield Academic Press, 2000.

Ouro, Roberto. "The Earth of Genesis 1:2: Abiotic or Chaotic? Part I." *AUSS* 35 (1998): 259–76.

———. "Linguistic and Thematic Parallels Between Genesis 1 and 3." *JATS* 13 (2002): 44–54.

Park, Song-Mi Suzie. "Transformation and Demarcation of Jacob's 'Flocks' in Genesis 30:25–43: Identity, Election, and the Role of the Divine." *CBQ* 72 (2010): 667–77.

Patai, Raphael. *Man and Temple in Ancient Jewish Myth and Ritual.* New York: Ktav, 1967.

Pearson, J. D. "A Mendelian Interpretation of Jacob's Sheep." *Science and Christian Belief* 13 (2001): 51–58.

Peck, John. "Notes on Genesis 37:2 and Joseph's Character." *ExpTim* 82 (1970/71): 342–43.

Peels, Eric. "The World's First Murder: Violence and Justice in Genesis 4:1–16." Pages 19–39 in *Animosity, the Bible, and Us: Some European, North American, and South African Perspectives.* SBL Global Perspectives on Biblical Scholarship 12. Edited by John T. Fitzgerald, Fika J. van Rensburg, and Herrie F. van Rooy. Atlanta: Society of Biblical Literature, 2009.

Peleg, Yitzhak (Itzik). "Was the Ancestress of Israel in Danger? Did Pharaoh touch (נגע) Sarai?" *ZAW* 118 (2006): 197–208.

Penley, Paul T. "A Historical Reading of Genesis 11:1–9: The Sumerian Demise and Dispersion under the Ur III Dynasty." *JETS* 50 (2007): 693–714.

Pink, A. W. *The Divine Covenants.* Grand Rapids: Baker, 1973.

Pirson, Ron. "The Sun, the Moon and Eleven Stars: An Interpretation of Joseph's Second Dream." Pages 561–68 in *Studies in the Book of Genesis: Literature, Redaction and History.* BETL 155. Edited by A. Wénin. Leuven: Leuven University Press, 2001.

Polak, Frank H. "Poetic Structure and Parallelism in the Creation Account (Genesis 1.1–2.3)." Pages 2–31 in *Creation in Jewish and Christian Tradition.* JSOTSup 319. Edited by Henning Graf Reventlow and Yair Hoffman. London: Sheffield Academic Press, 2002.

Pröbstle, Martin. "'Lion of Judah': The Blessing on Judah in Genesis 49:8–12." Pages 23–49 in *"For You Have Strengthened Me": Biblical and Theological Studies in Honor of Gerhard Pfandl in Celebration of his Sixty-fifth Birthday.* Edited by Martin Pröbstle. St Peter am Hart, Austria: Seminar Schloss Bogenhoffen, 2007.

Reis, Pamela Tamarkin. "Hagar Requited." *JSOT* 87 (2000): 75–109.

———. "What Cain Said: A Note on Genesis 4.8." *JSOT* 27 (2002): 107–13.

Rendsburg, Gary A. *The Redaction of Genesis.* Winona Lake: Eisenbrauns, 1986.

———. "Redactional Structuring in the Joseph Story: Genesis 37–50." Pages 215–32 in *Mappings of the Biblical Terrain: The Bible as Text.* Edited by Vincent L. Tollers and John Maier. Lewisburg, Penna.: Bucknell University Press, 1990.

Rickett, Dan. "Rethinking the Place and Purpose of Genesis 13." *JSOT* 36 (2011): 31–53.

Riemann, Paul A. "Am I My Brother's Keeper?" *Int* 24 (1970): 482–91.

Roberts, J. J. M. "Davidic Covenant." Pages 206–11 in *Dictionary of the Old Testament: Historical Books.* Edited by Bill T. Arnold and H. G. M. Williamson. Downers Grove: InterVarsity, 2005.

Robinson, Robert B. "Literary Functions of the Genealogies of Genesis." *CBQ* 48 (1986): 595–608.

Rogland, Max. "Interpreting אד in Genesis 2.5–6: Neglected Rabbinic and Intertextual Evidence," *JSOT* 34 (2010): 379–93.

Ronning, John. "The Naming of Isaac: The Role of the Wife/Sister Episodes in the Redaction of Genesis." *WTJ* 53 (1991): 1–27.

Rosenstock, Bruce. "Inner-Biblical Exegesis in the Book of the Covenant." *Conservative Judaism* 44 (1993): 37–49.

Ross, Allen P. *Creation and Blessing: A Guide to the Study and Exposition of Genesis.* Grand Rapids: Baker, 1998.

———. "The Dispersion of the Nations in Genesis 11:1–9." *BSac* 138 (1981): 119–38.

———. "Studies in the Life of Jacob Part 1: Jacob's Vision: The Founding of Bethel." *BSac* 142 (1985): 224–37.

Roth, Wolfgang M. W. "The Wooing of Rebekah: A Tradition-Critical Study of Genesis 24." *CBQ* 34 (1972): 177–87.

Sacks, Robert. "The Lion and the Ass: A Commentary on the Book of Genesis (Chapters 44–50)." *Int* 12 (1984): 141–92.

Sailhamer, John H. "Genesis." Pages 21–332 in *The Expositor's Bible Commentary, Volume 1.* Revised edition. Edited by Tremper Longman and David E. Garland. Grand Rapids: Zondervan, 2008.

———. *Genesis Unbound: A Provocative New Look at the Creation Account.* Portland, Oreg.: Multnomah, 1996.

———. *The Pentateuch as Narrative: A Biblical-Theological Commentary.* Grand Rapids: Zondervan, 1992.

Sarna, Nahum M. *Genesis.* JPSTC. Philadelphia: Jewish Publication Society, 1989.

Sasson, Jack M. "Circumcision in the Ancient Near East." *JBL* 85 (1966): 473–76.

———. "A Genealogical 'Convention' in Biblical Chronography?" *ZAW* 90 (1978): 171–85.

Schwöbel, Christoph. "The Preacher's Art: Preaching Theologically." Pages 1–20 in *Theology Through Preaching.* By Colin Gunton. Edinburgh: T. & T. Clark, 2001.

Sherman, Miriam. "Do Not Interpretations Belong to God? A Narrative Assessment of Genesis 40 as it Elucidates the Persona of Joseph." Pages 37–49 in *Milk and Honey: Essays on Ancient Israel and the Bible in Appreciation of the Judaic Studies Program at the University of California, San Diego.* Edited by Sarah Malena and David Miano. Winona Lake: Eisenbrauns, 2007.

Sigmon, Brian O. "Shadowing Jacob's Journey: Gen 47:13–26 as a Sideshow." *BibInt* 19 (2011): 454–70.

Skinner, John. *A Critical and Exegetical Commentary on Genesis.* Second edition. Edinburgh: T. & T. Clark, 1930.

Smith, Craig A. "Reinstating Isaac: The Centrality of Abraham's Son in the 'Jacob–Esau' Narrative of Genesis 27." *BTB* 31 (2001): 130–34.

Snell, Robert T. "Genesis 32:22–32." *Int* 50 (1996): 277–80.

Speiser, E. A. *Genesis.* AB 1. New York: Doubleday, 1964.

———. "Word Plays on the Creation Epic's Version of the Founding of Babylon." *Or* 25 (1955/56): 317–23.

Steinmann, Andrew E. "אחד as an Ordinal Number and the Meaning of Genesis 1:5." *JETS* 45 (2002): 577–84.

Steinmetz, Devora. "Vineyard, Farm, and Garden: The Drunkenness of Noah in the Context of Primeval History." *JBL* 113 (1994): 193–207.

Stek, John H. "What Says the Scripture?" Pages 203–65 in *Portraits of Creation: Biblical and Scientific Perspectives on the World's Formation*. By Howard J. Van Till, Robert Snow, John H. Stek, and Davis A. Young. Grand Rapids: Eerdmans, 1990.

Sterchi, David A. "Does Genesis 1 Provide a Chronological Sequence?" *JETS* 39 (1996): 529–36.

Sternberg, Meir. "Biblical Poetics and Sexual Politics: From Reading to Counterreading." *JBL* 111 (1992): 463–88.

———. "Double Cave, Double Talk: The Indirections of Biblical Dialogue." Pages 28–57 in *"Not in Heaven": Coherence and Complexity in Biblical Narrative*. Indiana Studies in Biblical Literature. Edited by Jason P. Rosenblatt and Joseph C. Sitterson. Bloomington, Ind.: Indiana University Press, 1991.

———. *The Poetics of Biblical Narrative: Ideological Literature and the Drama of Reading*. Indiana Studies in Biblical Literature. Bloomington, Ind.: Indiana University Press, 1985.

Strong, John T. "Shattering the Image of God: A Response to Theodore Hiebert's Interpretation of the Story of the Tower of Babel." *JBL* 127 (2008): 625–34.

Sturtevant, Edgar H. and George Bechtel. *A Hittite Chrestomathy*. Philadelphia: University of Pennsylvania Press, 1935.

Sylva, Dennis. "The Blessing of a Wounded Patriarch: Genesis 27.1–40." *JSOT* 32 (2008): 267–86.

Taschner, J. *Verheissung und Erfüllung in der Jakoberzählung (Gen 25, 19–33, 17): Eine Analyse Ihres Spunnungsbogens*. Herders Biblische Studien 27. Freiburg, Germany: Herder, 2000.

Teresa of Avila. "Christ has no Body." No pages. Cited April 27, 2013. Online: http://www.journeywithjesus.net/PoemsAndPrayers/Teresa_Of_Avila_Christ_Has_No_Body.shtml.

Terino, Jonathan. "A Text Linguistic Study of the Jacob Narrative." *VE* 18 (1988): 45–62.

Teugels, Lieve. "The Anonymous Matchmaker: An Enquiry into the Characterization of the Servant of Abraham in Genesis 24." *JSOT* 65 (1995): 13–23.

Todorov, Tzvetan. *The Poetics of Prose. Translated by* Richard Howard. Ithaca, N.Y.: Cornell University Press, 1977.

Tov, Emanuel. *Textual Criticism of the Hebrew Bible*. Revised edition. Minneapolis: Augsburg Fortress, 2001.

Trible, Phyllis. "The Other Woman: A Literary and Theological Study of the Hagar Narratives." Pages 221–46 in *Understanding the Word: Essays in Honor of Bernhard W. Anderson*. JSOTSup 37. Edited by James T. Butler, Edgar W. Conrad, and Ben C. Ollenburger. Sheffield: JSOT Press, 1985.

———. "The Test." Pages 219–48 in *Genesis: A Living Conversation*. Edited by Bill Moyers. New York: Doubleday, 1996.

Tsevat, Matitiahu. *The Meaning of the Book of Job and Other Biblical Studies: Essays on the Literature and Religion of the Hebrew Bible*. New York: Ktav, 1980.

Tsumura, David Toshio. *The Earth and the Waters in Genesis 1 and 2: A Linguistic Investigation*. JSOTSup 83. Sheffield: JSOT Press, 1989.

Tucker, Gordon. "Jacob's Terrible Burden: In the Shadow of the Text." *BR* 10.3 (1994): 21–28, 54.

Turner, Laurence A. *Announcements of Plot in Genesis*. JSOTSup 96. Sheffield: JSOT Press, 1990.

———. "The Rainbow as the Sign of the Covenant in Genesis IX 11–13," *VT* 43 (1993): 119–24.

Van Ruiten, Jacques. "Eve's Pain in Childbearing? Interpretations of Gen 3:16a in Biblical and Early Jewish Texts." Pages 3–26 in *Eve's Children: The Biblical Stories Retold and Interpreted in Jewish and Christian Traditions*. Themes in Biblical Narrative: Jewish and Christian Traditions 5. Edited by Gerard P. Luttikhuizen. Leiden: Brill, 2003.

Van Wolde, Ellen. "Cognitive Linguistics and Its Application to Genesis 28:10–22." Pages 125–48 in *One Text, A Thousand Methods: Studies in Memory of Sjef van Tilborg*. Biblical Interpretation Series 71. Edited by Patrick Chatelion Counet and Ulrich Berges. Leiden: Brill, 2005.

———. "Telling and Retelling: The Words of the Servant in Genesis 24." Pages 227–44 in *Synchronic or Diachronic? A Debate on Method in Old Testament Exegesis*. OtSt 34. Edited by Johannes C. de Moor. Leiden: Brill, 1995.

———. "The Text as an Eloquent Guide: Rhetorical, Linguistic and Literary Features in Genesis 1." Pages 134–51 in *Literary Structure and Rhetorical Strategies in the Hebrew Bible*. Edited by L. J. de Regt, J. de Waard, and J. P. Fokkelman. Assen, Netherlands: Van Gorcum, 1996.

———. "Texts in Dialogue with Texts: Intertextuality in the Ruth and Tamar Narratives." *BibInt* 5 (1997): 1–28.

VanDrunen, David. "Natural Law in Noahic Accent: A Covenantal Conception of Natural Law Drawn from Genesis 9." *Journal of the Society of Christian Ethics* 30 (2010): 131–49.

Vanhoozer, Kevin J. "Lost in Interpretation? Truth, Scripture, and Hermeneutics." *JETS* 48 (2005): 89–114.

Vawter, Bruce. *On Genesis: A New Reading.* Garden City, N.Y.: Doubleday, 1977.

Vervenne, Marc. "What Shall We Do with the Drunken Sailor? A Critical Re-examination of Genesis 9.20–27." *JSOT* 68 (1995): 33–55.

Vogels, Walter. "Enoch Walked with God and God Took Enoch (Genesis 5:21–24)." *Theoforum* 34 (2003): 283–303.

———. "The Power Struggle between Man and Woman (Gen 2,16b)." *Bib* 77 (1996): 197–209.

Von Rad, Gerhard. *Das Opfer des Abraham.* Kaiser Traktate 6. Munich: Kaiser, 1971.

———. *Genesis.* Translated by John H Marks. Revised edition. Philadelphia: Westminster, 1972.

Vrolijk, Paul D. *Jacob's Wealth: An Examination into the Nature and Role of Material Possessions in the Jacob-Cycle (Gen 25:19–35:29).* Supplements to Vetus Testamentum 146. Leiden: Brill, 2011.

Wallace, Howard N. "The Toledot of Adam." Pages 17–33 in *Studies in the Pentateuch.* Supplements to Vetus Testamentum 41. Edited by J. A. Emerton. Leiden: Brill, 1990.

Walsh, Jerome T. "Genesis 2:4b–3:24: A Synchronic Approach." *JBL* 96 (1977): 161–77.

———. *Style and Structure in Biblical Hebrew Narrative.* Collegeville, Minn.: Liturgical Press, 2001.

Walters, Stanley D. "Wood, Sand and Stars: Structure and Theology in Gn 22:1–19." *TJT* 3 (1987): 301–30.

Waltke, Bruce K. "Cain and His Offering." *WTJ* 48 (1986): 363–72.

———. "The Creation Account in Genesis 1:1–3: Part III: The Initial Chaos Theory and the Precreation Chaos Theory." *BSac* 132 (1975): 216–28.

———. "The Creation Account in Genesis 1:1–3: Part IV: The Theology of Genesis 1." *BSac* 132 (1975): 327–42.

Waltke, Bruce K., and Cathi J. Fredricks. *Genesis: A Commentary.* Grand Rapids: Zondervan, 2001.

Walton, John H. "Creation in Genesis 1:1–2:3 and the Ancient Near East: Order out of Disorder after *Chaoskampf.*" *CTJ* 43 (2008): 48–63.

———. *Genesis.* NIVAC. Grand Rapids: Zondervan, 2001.

———. *Genesis 1 as Ancient Cosmology.* Winona Lake: Eisenbrauns, 2011.

———. *The Lost World of Genesis One: Ancient Cosmology and the Origins Debate.* Downers Grove: InterVarsity, 2009.

———. "Reading Genesis 1 as Ancient Cosmology." Pages 141–69 in *Reading Genesis 1–2: An Evangelical Conversation.* Edited by J. Daryl Charles. Peabody, Mass.: Hendrickson, 2013.

Walton, Kevin. *Thou Traveller Unknown: The Presence and Absence of God in the Jacob Narrative.* Paternoster Biblical and Theological Monographs. Carlisle, U.K.: Paternoster, 2003.

Warfield, B. B. "Evolution or Development." Pages 114–31 in *Evolution, Scripture, and Science: Selected Writings.* By B. B. Warfield. Edited by Mark A. Noll and David N. Livingstone. Grand Rapids: Baker, 2000.

Weinfeld, Moshe. "Sabbath, Temple and the Enthronement of the Lord—the Problem of the *Sitz im Leben* of Genesis 1:1–2:3." Pages 505–12 in *Mélanges bibliques et orientaux en l'honneur de M. Henri Cazelles.* Alter Orient und Altes Testament 212. Edited by André Caquot and Mathias Delcor. Kevelaer, Germany: Butzon & Bercker, 1981.

Weis, Richard D. "Lessons on Wrestling with the Unseen: Jacob at the Jabbok." *Reformed Review* 42 (1989): 96–112.

Wenham, Gordon J. "The Aqedah: A Paradigm of Sacrifice." Pages 93–102 in *Pomegranates and Golden Bells: Studies in Biblical, Jewish, and Near Eastern Ritual, Law, and Literature in Honor of Jacob Milgrom.* Edited by David P. Wright, David Noel Freedman, and Avi Hurvitz. Winona Lake: Eisenbrauns, 1995.

———. "The Coherence of the Flood Narrative." *VT* 28 (1978): 336–48.

———. *Genesis 1–15.* WBC. Nashville: Thomas Nelson, 1987.

———. *Genesis 16–50.* WBC. Nashville: Thomas Nelson, 1994.

———. "Sanctuary Symbolism in the Garden of Eden Story." Pages 399–404 in *"I Studied Inscriptions from before the Flood": Ancient Near Eastern, Literary, and Linguistic Approaches to Genesis 1–11.*

Sources for Biblical and Theological Study 4. Edited by Richard S. Hess and David Toshio Tsumura. Winona Lake: Eisenbrauns, 1994.

Wessner, Mark D. "Toward a Literary Understanding of 'Face to Face' (פָּנִים אֶל־פָּנִים) in Genesis 32:23–32." *ResQ* 42 (2000): 169–77.

Westermann, Claus. *Genesis 1–11: A Commentary.* Translated by John J. Scullion. Minneapolis: Augsburg, 1984.

Whartenby, Thomas J. "Genesis 28:10–22." *Int* 45 (1991): 402–5.

White, Hugh C. *Narration and Discourse in the Book of Genesis.* Cambridge: Cambridge University Press, 1991.

Wilder, Amos. "Norman Perrin, *What is Redaction Criticism?*" Pages 91–96 in *Christology and a Modern Pilgrimage: A Discussion with Norman Perrin.* Revised edition. Edited by Hans Dieter Betz. Missoula, Mont.: Scholars Press, 1974.

Williamson, Paul R. *Abraham, Israel and the Nations: The Patriarchal Promise and its Covenantal Development in Genesis.* JSOTSup 315. Sheffield: Sheffield Academic Press, 2000.

Wilson, Robert R. *Genealogy and History in the Biblical World.* Yale Near Eastern Researches 7. New Haven: Yale University Press, 1977.

———. "The Old Testament Genealogies in Recent Research." *JBL* 94 (1975): 169–89.

Wolff, Hans Walter. "The Elohistic Fragments in the Pentateuch." Translated by Keith R. Crim. *Int* 26 (1972): 158–73.

Worthington, Jonathan D. *Creation in Paul and Philo: The Beginning and Before.* WUNT 317. Tübingen: Mohr Siebeck, 2011.

Wright, G. Ernest. "The Significance of the Temple in the Ancient Near East: III. The Temple in Palestine-Syria." *BA* 7 (1944): 66–77.

Wright, J. Edward. "Whither Elijah? The Ascension of Elijah in Biblical and Extrabiblical Traditions." Pages 595–608 in *Things Revealed: Studies in Early Jewish and Christian Literature in Honor of Michael E. Stone.* JSJSup 89. Edited by Esther G. Chazon, David Satran, and Ruth A. Clements. Leiden: Brill, 2004.

Young, Davis A. "Scripture in the Hands of Geologists (Part Two)." *WTJ* 49 (1987): 257–304.

Youngblood, Ronald. "The Abrahamic Covenant: Conditional or Unconditional?" Pages 31–46 in *The Living and Active Word of God: Studies in Honor of Samuel J. Schultz.* Edited by Morris Inch and Ronald Youngblood. Winona Lake: Eisenbrauns, 1983.

Zakovitch, Yair. "Inner-Biblical Interpretation." Pages 92–118 in *Reading Genesis: Ten Methods.* Edited by Ronald Hendel. New York: Cambridge University Press, 2010.

INDEX OF ANCIENT SOURCES

OTHER ANCIENT WRITINGS

INDEX OF MODERN AUTHORS

INDEX OF SCRIPTURE

OLD TESTAMENT

Genesis
(Also see within the appropriate chapter for particular verses of a pericope.)

1–11	85, 110, 575, 150, 157, 292
1:1–11:26	7, 292n1
1–8	121n36
1–2	8, 10, 13, 14, 15
1:1–2:3	11, 11n33, 19n56, 20, 21, 52, 53, 54, 55, 58, 77, 92
1	10n32, 13, 22
1:1–2:3	23, 24
1:1–3	16
1:1	10, 11, 16, 17, 17n49, 18, 20, 31, 54
1:2–31	17, 31
1:2–5	11, 11n33
1:2	10, 12n34, 16, 17, 119
1:3–13	12
1:3–4	21
1:3	16, 19, 19n56, 21, 55
1:4	18, 24n70, 570n50
1:5	9, 11, 18n51, 21, 22, 119n30
1:6–13	11
1:6–8	11n33, 16
1:6–7	124n55
1:6	10, 18, 19, 19n56, 55
1:7–8	119
1:7	17, 18, 19n56, 55, 171
1:8	10n32, 11, 21, 119n30
1:9–10	16
1:9	12, 19, 19n56, 55, 119
1:10	11, 12, 24n70, 55, 570n50
1:11–12	119n30
1:11	10n32, 12, 19, 19n56, 55, 80
1:12	10n32, 12, 19, 24n70, 55, 80, 570n50
1:13	18, 21, 119n30

1:14–15	10n31
1:14–18	458
1:14	9, 19, 19n56, 55, 119n30
1:16	119n30
1:14–31	12
1:14–19	11, 11n33, 34
1:14a	34
1:15	19n56, 34, 55
1:16	9, 17, 34
1:17	34, 278
1:18	9, 18, 19, 24n70, 119n30, 150, 570n50
1:18a	34
1:18b	34
1:19	21, 119n30
1:20–31	11
1:20–23	11n33
1:20–22	119n30
1:20	10n31, 19, 19n56, 55, 57, 106, 119, 119n30
1:21	10, 10n32, 17, 19, 24n70, 64, 114, 119n30, 570n50
1:22–25	122
1:22	10, 19, 55, 67, 114, 119n30, 159, 213, 311n16, 558
1:23	21
1:24	10n32
1:24–31	11n33
1:24–30	106
1:24–25	119n30
1:24	12, 19, 19n56, 55, 57, 119, 119n30
1:25	10n32, 12, 17, 19, 24n70, 55, 119n30, 570n50
1:26–30	118
1:26–27	20, 60
1:26	119n30
1:26	10n32, 12, 19, 19n56, 55, 60, 119, 119n30, 141
1:27–28	96

603

34:25	123
34:28	123
36:2	212n14
37	36n29
37:1	139
37:5	122n42
37:12	122n42
37:15–18	438
37:19	122n42
37:21	122n42
38:22	224n5
39:1	122n42
39:4–6	123
39:7	122n42
40:1	218n32
42:7	18n51
43:25–26	43
44:12	84n27
44:15	211n7
44:22	242
44:28	559n11
47:1–12	58n18
47:1–2	59
47:13–14	559n11

Daniel

1:2	135, 140
2:4	549
2:22	18n51
3:25	103n45
5:10	549
6:6	549
9:14	190

Hosea

1:10	103
2:16	421
2:18	123
3:4	386
4:3	10n32
4:10	61
4:13–14	476
5:3	420
6:5	18n51
6:10	420
8:9	203n70, 564n28
9:1–2	476
10:11–13	218n35
11:1	103
12:3–5	404n27
12:5	560n14
13:2	505n36

13:15	508n43, 564n28
14:9	505n34

Joel

3:18	59, 59n18
4:16	16n46

Amos

1:11	326
3:2	353n22
4:2	262n35
4:11	229
4:13	15, 17, 20
5:21	121
6:8	262n35
8:5	323
9:6	19n55, 20
9:11–12	298n11

Obadiah

1–21	326
10–14	298n11
18–21	298n11
18	298n11

Jonah

3:3	135
3:4	106
3:7–8	125n58

Micah

5:3	560
6:8	97
7:14	212n14, 560
7:18	570

Nahum

1:7	24n70, 435n12

Habakkuk

1:14	10n32
3:4	18n51
3:11	18n51

Zephaniah

1:3	10n32
1:15	435n12

NEW TESTAMENT

Lightning Source UK Ltd.
Milton Keynes UK
UKOW05f2208210816

281151UK00003B/23/P